2 dos

McDOUGAL LITTELL

# ¡En español!

## Teacher's Edition

AUTHORS

Estella Gahala

Patricia Hamilton Carlin

Audrey L. Heining-Boynton

Ricardo Otheguy

Barbara J. Rupert

CULTURE CONSULTANT

Jorge A. Capetillo-Ponce

McDougal Littell

A HOUGHTON MIFFLIN COMPANY

Evanston, Illinois • Boston • Dallas

**Cover Photography**

Center: Large image taken in Costa Rica by Martha Granger/EDGE Productions.

Bottom, from left to right: Painted wooden cactus sculpture, Oaxaca, Mexico, RMIP/Richard Haynes; El Morro Fort in San Juan, Puerto Rico, Mark Harris/Tony Stone Images (also on back cover); Painted dog figure from Guatemala, Superstock; Plaza Mayor, Madrid, Spain, Martha Granger/EDGE Productions.

**Photography**

T1 RMIP/Richard Haynes (b); T4 David Fritts/Tony Stone Images/PNI (br); T15 H. Rogers/Monkmeyer Press (c); T19 School Division, Houghton Mifflin Company (l, r); E. R. Degginger/Photo Researchers, Inc. (c); T23 Degas-Parra/Ask Images/Viesti Associates, Inc. (l); Suzanne Murphy-Larronde/FPG International (c); Fernando Botero, *Los Músicos*, 1979. Courtesy Marlborough Gallery, New York (r); T48 N. Frank/Viesti Associates, Inc. (tc); Tanya Braganti/Tom Keller & Associates (b); T49 San Francisco Museum of Modern Art/Albert M. Bender Collection/Gift of Albert M. Bender (tcl); Suzanne Murphy-Larronde (tcr); School Division, Houghton Mifflin Company (tr); T50 Jose L. Pelaez/The Stock Market (tcl); Tim Hunt (tcr); Superstock (b); T51 Victor Ramos/ International Stock Photo (tl); Courtesy of Puerto Rico Industrial Development Company (tc); 27A School Division, Houghton Mifflin Company; 99A Bob Daemmrich/Stock Boston (b); 99F RMIP/Richard Haynes; 243B Superstock (c); 315A Kirk Condyles/Impact Visuals/ PNI (tc); Jose Azel/Aurora & Quanta Productions/PNI (tr); 315B Stephen J. Kraseman/DRK Photo (tl); Roy Fontaine/Photo Researchers, Inc. (tc); Tom Boyden (c); Michael Fogden/ Animals Animals (b).

All other photography: Martha Granger/EDGE Productions



ISBN: 0-395-91084-6 4 5 6 7 8 9 - VMI - 05 04 03 02

Internet: www.mcdougallittell.com

# About the Authors

**Estella Gahala** holds a Ph.D. in Educational Administration and Curriculum from Northwestern University. A career teacher of Spanish and French, she has worked with a wide range of students at the secondary level. She has also served as foreign language department chair and district director of curriculum and instruction.

**Patricia Hamilton Carlin** completed her M.A. in Spanish at the University of California, Davis and a Master of Secondary Education with specialization in foreign languages from the University of Arkansas. She currently teaches Spanish and methodology at the University of Central Arkansas.

**Audrey L. Heining-Boynton** received her Ph.D. in Curriculum and Instruction from Michigan State University. She is a Professor of Education and Romance Languages at The University of North Carolina at Chapel Hill, where she is a second language teacher educator and Professor of Spanish. She has also taught Spanish, French, and ESL at the K–12 level.

**Ricardo Otheguy** received his Ph.D. in Linguistics from the City University of New York, where he is currently Professor of Linguistics at the Graduate School and University Center. He has written extensively on topics related to Spanish grammar as well as on bilingual education and the Spanish of the United States.

**Barbara J. Rupert** has taught Level 1 through A.P. Spanish during her many years of high school teaching. She is a graduate of Western Washington University and serves as the World Languages Department Chair, District Trainer and Chair of her school's Site Council.

**Jorge A. Capetillo-Ponce**
**Culture Consultant**
is presently a Ph.D. candidate in Sociology at the New School for Social Research, where he is also Special Consultant to the Dean of The Graduate Faculty. His graduate studies at the New School and El Colegio de México include international relations, socio-political analysis, cultural theory, and sociology.

For further information about the authors see page xxii.

## Contributing Writers

**Mary Lemiere Campion**
Westwood, MA

**Mary Ann Dellinger**
University of Phoenix; Pueblo High School
Tucson, AZ

**Marisa Garman**
Scituate, MA

**Jane M. Govoni**
Eckerd College; Shorecrest Preparatory School
St. Petersburg, FL

**Willard A. Heller, Jr.**
Perry Junior-Senior High School; Perry, NY

**Cynthia Prieto**
Mount Vernon High School
Fairfax, VA

**Ann Tollefson**
Natrona County School District
Casper, WY

## Consulting Authors

**Dan Battisti**

**Dr. Teresa Carrera-Hanley**

**Bill Lionetti**

**Patty Murguía Bohannan**

**Lorena Richins Layser**

## Reviewers

**Sue Arandjelovic**
Dobson High School
Mesa, AZ

**Lavonne Berry**
Oak Grove High School
North Little Rock, AR

**Rebecca Carr**
William G. Enloe High School
Raleigh, NC

**Kathleen Gliewe**
Helena Middle School
Helena, MT

**Joan Horwitt**
Yorktown High School
Arlington, VA

**Sharon Larracoechea**
South Junior High School
Boise, ID

**Dr. Carolyn O'Keefe**
Northshore School District
Bothell, WA

**Carol Rechel Espinoza**
Boulder High School
Boulder, CO

**Maureen Rehusch**
Palatine High School
Hoffman Estates, IL

**T. Jeffrey Richards**
Roosevelt High School
Sioux Falls, SD

**Pamela Ross**
North Allegheny Intermediate High School
Pittsburgh, PA

# CONTENTS



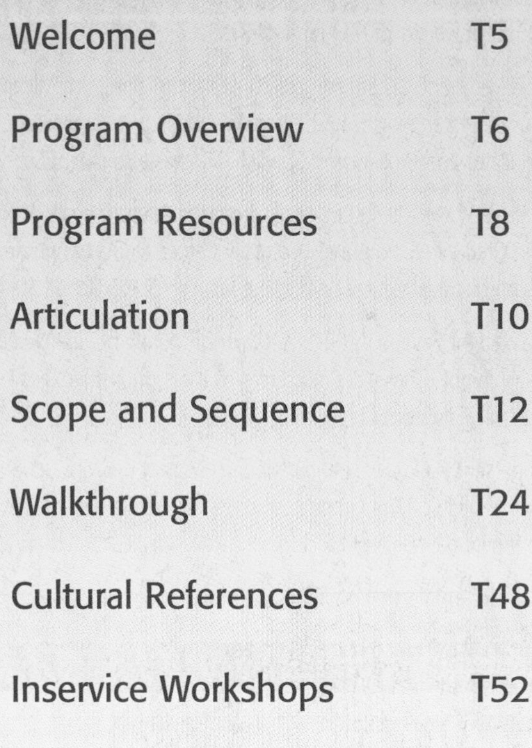

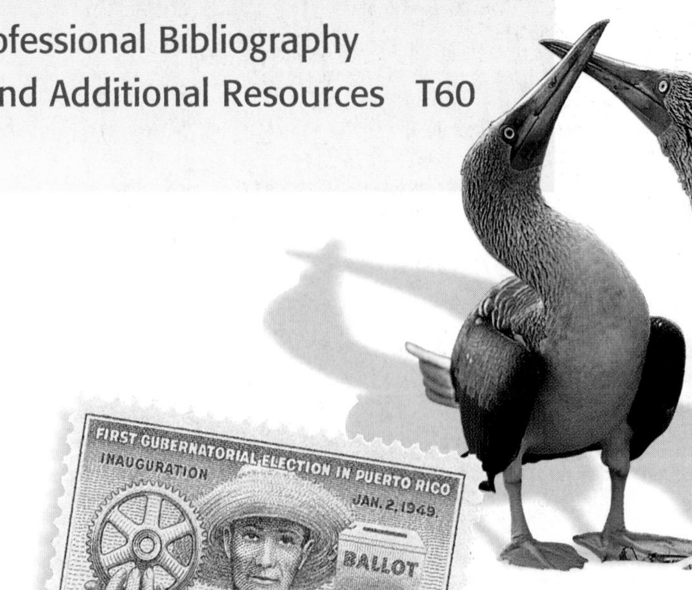

FIRST GUBERNATORIAL ELECTION IN PUERTO RICO
INAUGURATION
JAN. 2, 1949.
BALLOT
3¢
U.S. POSTAGE
3¢

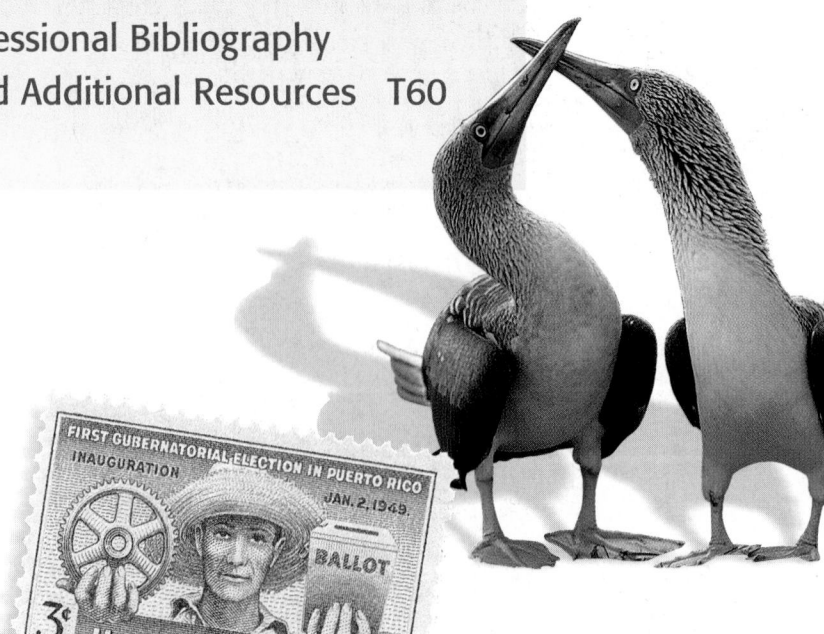

## Welcome back...

**WHERE:** ¡En español!

*A new kind of Spanish program*

**WHAT:** *A program that...*

- *Boosts student confidence and retention and motivates language learning.*
- *Balances teaching for communication and accuracy, offering a balance of proficiency and grammar.*
- *Adapts to the varied learning styles and ability levels of today's students.*
- *Integrates technology to immerse stude in authentic language and culture.*

# ¡En español!

## Building Confidence for Communication

### Balances proficiency and grammar

- Activity sequences lead students through controlled, transitional, and open-ended activities to assure development of communication skills.
- Grammar is presented with multiple examples, graphics, and visuals to illustrate concepts clearly.

### Boosts student confidence and retention

- Strategies for developing listening, speaking, reading, and writing skills as well as for comparing cultures are included in each *etapa* of the pupil edition.
- Special student study hints are included in each unit. These hints help students learn how to approach learning a language more effectively.

## Adapts to varied learning styles and abilities

- Classroom Community notes in the Teacher's Edition provide guidance for managing pair and group work right at point-of-use.
- Teaching All Students notes in the Teacher's Edition offer extra help and more challenging activities, activities suited to the various intelligences as well as material for the native speaker.

## Integrates technology to immerse students in authentic language and culture

- Fully-integrated video provides input for presenting vocabulary and grammar in their cultural context.
- CD-ROM provides leveled practice and review of core vocabulary and grammar in a motivating game format.
- Electronic Teacher Tools with Test Generator offers the flexibility of having all ancillaries on CD-ROM.
- ClassZone, a dynamic Internet connection, is available to all users of ***¡En español!***

# Program Resources

## Extensive resources tailored to the needs of today's students!

**TEACHER'S EDITION**

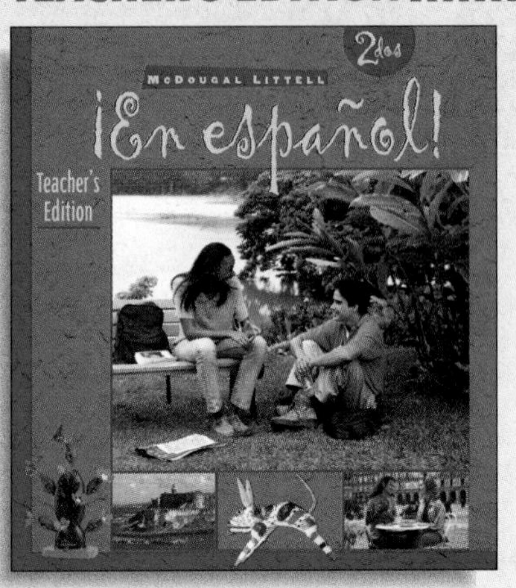


**TEACHER'S RESOURCE PACKAGE**

- **Unit Resource Books**

***Includes resources for each unit:***
*Más práctica (cuaderno)* TE
*Cuaderno para hispanohablantes* TE
Information Gap Activities
Family Involvement
Video Activities
Videoscript
Audioscript

***Assessment Program***
Cooperative Quizzes
Etapa Exams, Forms A & B
*Exámenes para hispanohablantes*
Unit Comprehensive Tests
*ruebas comprensivas para*
*ispanohablantes*
ple Choice Test Questions
Assessment

- **Block Scheduling Copymasters**

- **Electronic Teacher Tools/Test Generator CD-ROM**

## ADDITIONAL RESOURCES

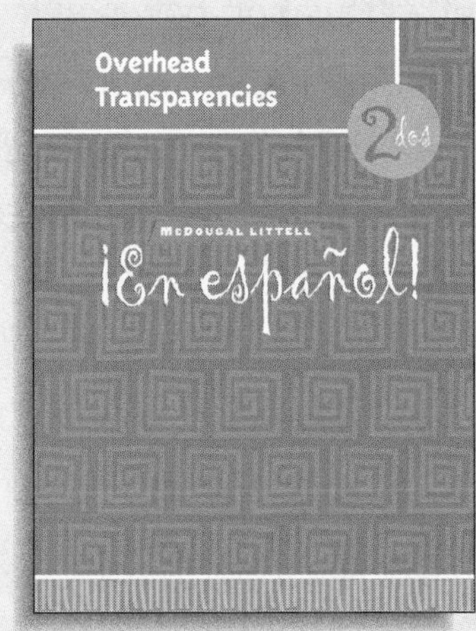


- **Overhead Transparencies**

**STUDENT WORKBOOKS**

- ***Más práctica (cuaderno)* PE**
- ***Cuaderno para hispanohablantes* PE**

## INTERNET RESOURCES

Visit the World Languages curriculum area at **www.mcdougallittell.com** for a wide range of resources.

## TECHNOLOGY

**Audio Program**
- Completely integrated with the text and ancillaries
- Available on cassette and audio CD

**Canciones**
- Audiocassette or audio CD

**Video Program**
- Completely integrated video program provides comprehensible input and cultural information
- Available on videocassette and videodisc

***Intrigas y aventuras* CD-ROM**
- For levels 1 and 2

# Easy Articulation

***¡En español!*** addresses the challenges of articulation between levels by providing a unique instructional overlap. All the grammar and vocabulary taught in Units 5 and 6 are covered again in the following level, so teachers can choose how far into the grammatical and functional sequence they wish to go. Students' study of Spanish can continue seamlessly!

## GRAMMAR ACROSS LEVELS

### LEVEL 2

#### Unit 1

**Etapa 1**
- Regular preterite verbs (p. 36)
- Preterite with *-car, -gar,* and *-zar* spelling changes (p. 38)
- Preterite of *ir, ser, hacer, dar, ver* (p. 40)

**Etapa 2**
- Irregular preterite verbs (p. 61)

**Etapa 3**
- Demonstrative adjectives and pronouns (p. 82)
- Stem-changing preterite verbs (p. 84)
- Preterite verbs with *i* to *y* spelling change (p. 85)

#### Unit 2

**Etapa 1**
- Reflexive pronouns and verbs (p. 110)

**Etapa 2**
- Progressive tenses (p. 130)
- Ordinals (p. 132)

#### Unit 3

**Etapa 1**
- Pronoun placement with commands (p. 180)

**Etapa 2**
- Affirmative *tú* commands, regular and irregular (p. 202)
- Negative *tú* commands (p. 204)
- Adverbs ending in *-mente* (p. 206)

### LEVEL 1

#### Unit 5

**Etapa 1**
- Reflexive verbs (p. 320)
- Irregular affirmative *tú* commands (p. 322)
- Negative *tú* commands (p. 324)
- Pronoun placement with commands (p. 325)

**Etapa 2**
- Pronoun placement with the present progressive tense (p. 342)
- *Deber* (p. 345)
- Adverbs ending in *-mente* (p. 347)

**Etapa 3**
- Superlatives (p. 364)
- egular *-ar* preterite verbs (p. 366)
- *-gar, -zar* preterite verbs (p. 368)

#### Unit 6

**Etapa 1**
- Regular *-er, -ir* preterite verbs (p. 392)
- Preterite verbs with *i* to *y* spelling change (p. 394)
- Preterite forms of *ir, hacer, ser* (p. 395)

**Etapa 2**
- Location words (p. 414)
- Demonstrative adjectives and pronouns (p. 416)
- Ordinals (p. 418)
- Irregular preterite verbs (p. 419)

**Etapa 3**
- All review

| | Unit 4 | Unit 5 | Unit 6 |
|---|---|---|---|
| | **Etapa 2**<br>• Location words (p. 227)<br>**Etapa 3**<br>• Comparisons and superlatives (p. 296)<br>• *Deber* (p. 292) | **Etapa 1**<br>• Future tense (p. 324)<br>• Using *por* (p. 326)<br>• *Nosotros* commands (p. 328)<br>**Etapa 2**<br>• Irregular future tense (p. 346)<br>• Using *para* (p. 350)<br>**Etapa 3**<br>• *Por* vs. *para* (p. 368)<br>• Conditional tense (p. 370) | **Etapa 1**<br>• Impersonal *se* (p. 399)<br>• Past participles as adjectives (p. 401)<br>**Etapa 2**<br>• Using the preterite and imperfect tenses (p. 418)<br>• Present perfect tense (p. 420)<br>• Irregular verbs in the present perfect tense (p. 423)<br>**Etapa 3**<br>• Reported speech (p. 444) |

| LEVEL 3 | Unit 1 | Unit 2 | Unit 4 | Unit 6 |
|---|---|---|---|---|
| | **Etapa 1**<br>• Preterite/imperfect tenses contrasted (p. 41)<br>• Present/past perfect tenses, regular/irregular, including past participles (p. 44)<br>**Etapa 2**<br>• *Por* vs. *para* (p. 61)<br>• Future tense, regular and irregular (p. 63)<br>• Impersonal *se* (p. 87) | **Etapa 1**<br>• *Nosotros* commands (p. 112)<br>• Conditional tense (p. 115) | **Etapa 1**<br>• Present progressive, regular and irregular (p. 256) | **Etapa 1**<br>• Reported speech (p. 405) |

# ¡En español!

## Level 1 Scope & Sequence

| | | Communication | Grammar | Culture | Recycling | Strategies |
|---|---|---|---|---|---|---|
| **PRELIMINAR** | **Etapa preliminar** p. 1<br>*¡Hola, bienvenidos!* | • Greet people<br>• Introduce yourself<br>• Say where you are from<br>• Exchange phone numbers<br>• Say which day it is | **Grammar is presented lexically here**<br>• *Me llamo, te llamas*<br>• *Soy, eres, es* + *de*<br>Notas<br>*encantado / encantada; sí* and *no* | Notas Culturales<br>• Greetings<br>• Variations on good-bye<br>• Articles before country names | | |
| **UNIDAD 1 Mi mundo • Estados Unidos** | **Etapa 1** p. 24<br>**Miami**<br>*¡Bienvenido a Miami!*<br>Unit Opener Culture Notes<br>• *Fajitas*<br>• Murals<br>• El Álamo<br>• *Cascarones*<br>• *Sándwich cubano*<br>• Jon Secada | • Greet others<br>• Introduce others<br>• Say where people are from<br>• Express likes | • Familiar and formal greetings<br>• Subject pronouns and *ser*<br>• *Ser* + *de*<br>• *Gustar* + infinitive: *me, te, le*<br>Notas<br>plurals; *le presento a / te presento a; vivo en* | En voces<br>*Los latinos de Estados Unidos*<br>Conexiones<br>*Los estudios sociales:* compare communities<br>Notas culturales<br>• Miami: international city<br>• Architectural influences<br>• Last names | Vocabulary from *Etapa preliminar* | Listening: Listen to intonation<br>Speaking: Practice; Understand, then speak<br>Reading: Preview graphics |
| | **Etapa 2** p. 46<br>**San Antonio**<br>*Mis buenos amigos* | • Describe others<br>• Give others' likes and dislikes<br>• Describe clothing | • Definite articles<br>• Indefinite articles<br>• Noun-adjective agreement: gender<br>• Noun-adjective agreement: number<br>Notas<br>*¿Qué lleva?; llevo;* shortened forms of adjectives; *cómo* + *ser; tiene* | En colores<br>*El conjunto tejano* (video)<br>Conexiones<br>*La música:* music styles<br>Notas culturales<br>• *la charreada* | **Activity 3:** *gustar* + infinitive<br>**Activity 6:** professions | Listening: Listen to stress<br>Speaking: Trust your first impulse; Think, plan, then speak<br>Culture: Recognize regional music |
| | **Etapa 3** p. 68<br>**Los Ángeles**<br>*Te presento a mi familia* | • Describe family<br>• Ask and tell ages<br>• Talk about birthdays<br>• Give dates<br>• Express possession | • *Tener*<br>• Possession using *de*<br>• Possessive adjectives<br>• Giving dates<br>Notas<br>*¿De quién es…?, Es de…; ¿Quién es?, ¿Quiénes son?; hay* | En voces<br>*Las celebraciones del año*<br>En colores<br>*La quinceañera*<br>Tú en la comunidad<br>Notas culturales<br>• The oldest house in L.A.<br>• Street names<br>• Writing the date | **Activity 4:** physical descriptions<br>**Activity 6:** personal characteristics<br>**Activity 10:** clothing<br>**Activity 13:** clothing<br>**Activity 14:** *ser*<br>**Activity 15:** clothing | Listening: Visualize; Get the main idea<br>Speaking: Rehearse; Practice speaking smoothly<br>Reading: Look for cognates<br>Writing: Use different kinds of descriptive words<br>Culture: Compare rites of passage |

| | | Communication | Grammar | Culture | Recycling | Strategies |
|---|---|---|---|---|---|---|
| **UNIDAD 2 Una semana típica • Ciudad de México** | **Etapa 1** p. 96<br>*Un día de clases*<br>UNIT OPENER<br>CULTURE NOTES<br>• *Tortillas*<br>• Diego Rivera<br>• *El Palacio de Bellas Artes*<br>• *El Ballet Folklórico*<br>• *El metro*<br>• Lázaro Cárdenas | • Describe classes and classroom objects<br>• Say how often you do something<br>• Discuss obligations | • Present tense of regular *-ar* verbs<br>• Adverbs of frequency<br>• *Tener que, hay que*<br>NOTA<br>Use of articles with titles | EN VOCES<br>*Una encuesta escolar*<br>CONEXIONES<br>*Las matemáticas:* take a survey<br>NOTAS CULTURALES<br>• *Universidad Autónoma de México*<br>• The origin of *pluma* | **Activity 3:** *hay,* colors<br>**Activity 4:** *hay,* numbers | LISTENING: Listen for feelings<br>SPEAKING: Develop more than one way of expressing an idea; Expand the conversation<br>READING: Use context clues |
| | **Etapa 2** p. 118<br>*¡Un horario difícil!* | • Talk about schedules<br>• Ask and tell time<br>• Ask questions<br>• Say where you are going<br>• Request food | • *Ir*<br>• Telling time<br>• *Estar* + location<br>• Interrogative words<br>NOTAS<br>*¿Quieres comer…?* and *¿Quieres beber…?; al;* "on" + days of the week | EN COLORES: *¿Quieres comer una merienda mexicana?*<br>CONEXIONES<br>*La salud*: nutrition<br>NOTAS CULTURALES<br>• Mexican school schedules<br>• *torta, bocadillo, pastel*<br>• Olympic Stadium | **Activity 3:** *-ar* verbs, school terms<br>**Activity 7:** days of the week | LISTENING: Listen for the main idea<br>SPEAKING: Take risks; Help your partner<br>CULTURE: Compare snack foods |
| | **Etapa 3** p. 140<br>*Mis actividades* | • Discuss plans<br>• Sequence events<br>• Talk about places and people you know | • *Ir a* + infinitive<br>• Present tense: regular *-er* and *-ir* verbs<br>• Irregular *yo* forms: *hacer, conocer;* personal *a*<br>• *Oír*<br>NOTA<br>*tener sed, tener hambre* | EN VOCES<br>*México y sus jóvenes*<br>EN COLORES<br>*El Zócalo: centro de México* (video)<br>TÚ EN LA COMUNIDAD<br>NOTAS CULTURALES<br>• *Museo Nacional de Antropología*<br>• Mexican mealtimes | **Activity 3:** *estar* + location, places<br>**Activity 6:** snacks<br>**Activity 7:** telling time<br>**Activity 11:** *gustar* + infinitive, *tener que*<br>**Activity 13:** adverbs of frequency<br>**Activity 17:** friends and family<br>**Activity 19:** places | LISTENING: Listen and observe<br>SPEAKING: Use all you know; Ask for clarification<br>READING: Skim<br>WRITING: Organize information chronologically and by category<br>CULTURE: Compare places |

| | | Communication | Grammar | Culture | Recycling | Strategies |
|---|---|---|---|---|---|---|
| **UNIDAD 3 El fin de semana • San Juan, Puerto Rico** | **Etapa 1** p. 168<br>*¡Me gusta el tiempo libre!*<br>UNIT OPENER<br>CULTURE NOTES<br>• Gigi Fernández<br>• *Pasta de guayaba*<br>• *El Morro*<br>• Luis Muñoz Marín<br>• *Taínos*<br>• *El loro puertorriqueño* | • Extend invitations<br>• Talk on the phone<br>• Express feelings<br>• Say where you are coming from<br>• Say what just happened | • *Estar* + adjectives<br>• *Acabar de* + infinitive<br>• *Venir*<br>• *Gustar* + infinitive: *nos, os, les*<br>NOTAS<br>*cuando; del; conmigo, contigo* | EN VOCES<br>*Bomba y plena*<br>CONEXIONES<br>*La música:* songs<br>NOTAS CULTURALES<br>• The name *Puerto Rico*<br>• Ricky Martin | **Activity 3:** *gustar* + infinitive<br>**Activity 4:** activities, sequencing<br>**Activity 9:** activities<br>**Activity 13:** *ir a…*<br>**Activity 14:** places<br>**Activity 17:** activities<br>**Activity 19:** interrogatives | LISTENING: Listen for a purpose<br>SPEAKING: Personalize; Use your tone to convey meaning<br>READING: Scan |
| | **Etapa 2** p. 190<br>*¡Deportes para todos!* | • Talk about sports<br>• Express preferences<br>• Say what you know<br>• Make comparisons | • *Jugar*<br>• Stem-changing verbs: *e*→*ie*<br>• *Saber*<br>• Comparatives | EN COLORES<br>*Béisbol: el pasatiempo nacional*<br>TÚ EN LA COMUNIDAD<br>NOTAS CULTURALES<br>• *La Fortaleza*<br>• Puerto Rico and the U.S.<br>• Roberto Clemente | **Activity 12:** activities<br>**Activity 16:** descriptions<br>**Activity 19:** interrogatives | LISTENING: Listen for "turn-taking" tactics<br>SPEAKING: Monitor yourself; Give reasons for your preferences<br>CULTURE: Reflect on sports traditions |
| | **Etapa 3** p. 212<br>*El tiempo en El Yunque* | • Describe the weather<br>• Discuss clothing and accessories<br>• State an opinion<br>• Describe how you feel<br>• Say what is happening | • *Tener* expressions<br>• Weather expressions<br>• Direct object pronouns<br>• Present progressive<br>NOTAS<br>*llevar; creer* | EN VOCES: *El coquí*<br>EN COLORES<br>*Una excursión por la isla* (video)<br>CONEXIONES<br>*Las ciencias:* temperature<br>NOTAS CULTURALES<br>• *El Yunque* | **Activity 3:** colors, clothing<br>**Activity 8:** stem-changing verbs: *e*→*ie*<br>**Activity 9:** *ir a…, llevar*<br>**Activity 11:** *tener,* activities<br>**Activity 14:** sports<br>**Activity 19:** activities | LISTENING: Sort and categorize details<br>SPEAKING: Say how often; Get specific information<br>READING: Distinguish details<br>WRITING: Appeal to the senses<br>CULTURE: Define travel and tourism |

## UNIDAD 4 ¡De visita! • Oaxaca, México

| | Communication | Grammar | Culture | Recycling | Strategies |
|---|---|---|---|---|---|
| **Etapa 1** p. 240<br>*¡A visitar a mi prima!*<br>Unit Opener Culture Notes<br>• *Animalitos*<br>• *Pesos*<br>• *Mole negro*<br>• Rufino Tamayo<br>• Benito Juárez<br>• *Monte Albán* | • Identify places<br>• Give addresses<br>• Choose transportation<br>• Request directions<br>• Give instructions | • *Decir*<br>• Prepositions of location<br>• Regular affirmative *tú* commands<br>Notas<br>*por; salir;* numbers in addresses | En voces<br>*¡Visita Oaxaca! Un paseo a pie*<br>Conexiones<br>*La educación física:* Mexican folk dances<br>Notas culturales<br>• *Guelaguetza*<br>• The name *Oaxaca* | **Activity 3:** *hay*<br>**Activity 5:** seasons<br>**Activity 13:** activities<br>**Activity 14:** direct object pronouns<br>**Activity 15:** sequencing<br>**Activity 16:** direct object pronouns | **Listening:** Listen and follow directions<br>**Speaking:** Recognize and use set phrases; Use variety to give directions<br>**Reading:** Combine strategies |
| **Etapa 2** p. 262<br>*En el mercado* | • Talk about shopping<br>• Make purchases<br>• Talk about giving gifts<br>• Bargain | • Stem-changing verbs: *o*→*ue*<br>• Indirect object pronouns<br>• Indirect object pronoun placement<br>Notas<br>*para; ¿Cuánto cuesta(n)?; dar* | En colores<br>*El Mercado Benito Juárez*<br>Conexiones: *Las matemáticas: un mercado*<br>Notas culturales<br>• Monte Albán jewelry<br>• Benito Juárez | **Activity 5:** numbers<br>**Activity 7:** places<br>**Activity 8:** time<br>**Activity 9:** places, time<br>**Activity 10:** transportation | **Listening:** Observe as you listen<br>**Speaking:** Express emotion; Disagree politely<br>**Culture:** Compare bargaining customs |
| **Etapa 3** p. 284<br>*¿Qué hacer en Oaxaca?* | • Order food<br>• Request the check<br>• Talk about food<br>• Express extremes<br>• Say where you went | • *Gustar* + nouns<br>• Affirmative and negative words<br>• Stem-changing verbs: *e*→*i*<br>Notas<br>*fui/fuiste; ningunos(as); traer;* superlatives; *poner; desayunar* | En voces<br>*Andrés, joven aprendiz de alfarero* (video)<br>En colores<br>*Monte Albán: ruinas, misteriosas*<br>Tú en la comunidad<br>Notas culturales<br>• Oaxaca's cuisine<br>• Oaxaca's artistic heritage<br>• Zapotec traditions | **Activity 5:** prepositions of location<br>**Activity 6:** stores<br>**Activity 9:** clothing<br>**Activity 19:** direct object pronouns | **Listening:** Integrate your skills<br>**Speaking:** Vary ways to express preferences; Borrow useful expressions<br>**Reading:** Gather and sort information as you read<br>**Writing:** Tell who, what, where, when, why, and how<br>**Culture:** Analyze and recommend |

## UNIDAD 5 Preparaciones especiales • Barcelona, España

| | Communication | Grammar | Culture | Recycling | Strategies |
|---|---|---|---|---|---|
| **Etapa 1** p. 312<br>*¿Cómo es tu rutina?*<br>Unit Opener Culture Notes<br>• *Las Ramblas*<br>• Joan Miró<br>• Cristóbal Colón<br>• *Aceitunas*<br>• Cervantes<br>• *La Sagrada Familia* | • Describe daily routine<br>• Talk about grooming<br>• Tell others to do something<br>• Discuss daily chores | • Reflexive verbs<br>• Irregular affirmative *tú* commands<br>• Negative *tú* commands<br>• Pronoun placement with commands | En voces<br>*Una exhibición especial de Picasso*<br>Conexiones<br>*El arte:* paintings<br>Notas culturales<br>• *Catalán*<br>• *Rock con raíces*<br>• Pablo Picasso | **Activity 3:** time<br>**Activity 16:** restaurant phrases | **Listening:** Listen for a mood or a feeling<br>**Speaking:** Sequence events; Use gestures<br>**Reading:** Scan for crucial details |
| **Etapa 2** p. 334<br>*¿Qué debo hacer?* | • Say what people are doing<br>• Persuade others<br>• Describe a house<br>• Negotiate responsibilities | • Pronoun placement with present progressive<br>• *Deber*<br>• Adverbs with *-mente*<br>Notas<br>*si;* reflexive pronouns | En colores<br>*Las tapas: una experiencia muy española*<br>Tú en la comunidad<br>Notas culturales<br>• *Tortilla* | **Activity 3:** *poner*<br>**Activity 8:** reflexive verbs<br>**Activity 13:** irregular affirmative *tú* commands<br>**Activity 17:** restaurant phrases<br>**Activity 19:** interrogatives | **Listening:** Note and compare<br>**Speaking:** Negotiate; Detect misunderstandings<br>**Culture:** Predict reactions about restaurants |
| **Etapa 3** p. 356<br>*¡Qué buena celebración!* | • Plan a party<br>• Describe past activities<br>• Express extremes<br>• Purchase food | • Superlatives<br>• Regular *-ar* preterite verbs<br>• *-car, -gar, -zar* preterite<br>Notas<br>*¿A cuánto está(n)…?* | En voces<br>*Los favoritos de la cocina española*<br>En colores<br>*Barcelona, joya de arquitectura* (video)<br>Conexiones<br>*La salud:* favorite foods<br>Notas culturales:<br>• *Pesetas*<br>• *Paella*<br>• Gothic Quarter | **Activity 7:** furniture; adjective agreement<br>**Activity 10:** chores | **Listening:** Listen and take notes<br>**Speaking:** Say what is the best and worst; Maintain conversational flow<br>**Reading:** Reorganize information to check understanding<br>**Writing:** Engage the reader by addressing him or her personally<br>**Culture:** Make a historical time line |

**UNIDAD 6 La ciudad y el campo • Quito, Ecuador**

| | Communication | Grammar | Culture | Recycling | Strategies |
|---|---|---|---|---|---|
| **Etapa 1** p. 384<br>*La vida de la ciudad*<br>Unit Opener<br>Culture Notes<br>• *La casa de Sucre*<br>• *Papas*<br>• *La Mitad del Mundo*<br>• Atahualpa<br>• *Tapices*<br>• *Rondador* | • Tell what happened<br>• Make suggestions to a group<br>• Describe city buildings<br>• Talk about professions | • Regular *-er, -ir* preterites<br>• Preterite verbs with *i* → *y* spelling change<br>• Preterite of *ir, hacer, ser*<br>Notas<br>*Vamos a* + infinitive; *estar de acuerdo; ver* | En voces<br>*Saludos desde Quito*<br>Tú en la comunidad<br>Notas culturales<br>• Quito<br>• *Sucre;* currency<br>• *Colonia/colonial* | **Activity 7:** superlatives<br>**Activity 10:** time words | **Listening:** Distinguish what is said and not said<br>**Speaking:** Exaggerate and react to exaggerations; Relate details<br>**Reading:** Recognize place names |
| **Etapa 2** p. 406<br>*A conocer el campo* | • Point out specific people and things<br>• Tell where things are located<br>• Talk about the past | • Location words<br>• Demonstrative adjectives and pronouns<br>• Ordinals<br>• Irregular preterite<br>Notas<br>*darle(s) de comer* | En colores<br>*Los otavaleños* (video)<br>Conexiones<br>*Las ciencias:* regional animals<br>Notas culturales<br>• *Quichua* | **Activity 5:** professions<br>**Activity 7:** prepositions of location<br>**Activity 10:** clothing, sports equipment<br>**Activity 11:** school objects, comparisons<br>**Activity 17:** places | **Listening:** Listen for implied statements<br>**Speaking:** Recall what you know; Use words that direct others' attention<br>**Culture:** Research cultural groups |
| **Etapa 3** p. 428<br>*¡A ganar el concurso!* | • Talk about the present and future<br>• Give instructions to someone<br>• Discuss the past | • Review: present progressive, *ir a…*<br>• Review: affirmative *tú* commands<br>• Review: regular preterite<br>• Review: irregular preterite | En voces<br>*Un paseo por Ecuador*<br>En colores<br>*Cómo las Américas cambiaron la comida europea*<br>Conexiones<br>*La salud:* typical food<br>Notas culturales<br>• Galápagos<br>• Ecuador's diverse regions | This *etapa* recycles grammar and vocabulary from throughout the book. | **Listening:** Listen and take notes<br>**Speaking:** Use storytelling techniques; Rely on the basics<br>**Reading:** Reflect on journal writing<br>**Writing:** Support a general statement with informative details<br>**Culture:** Identify international foods |

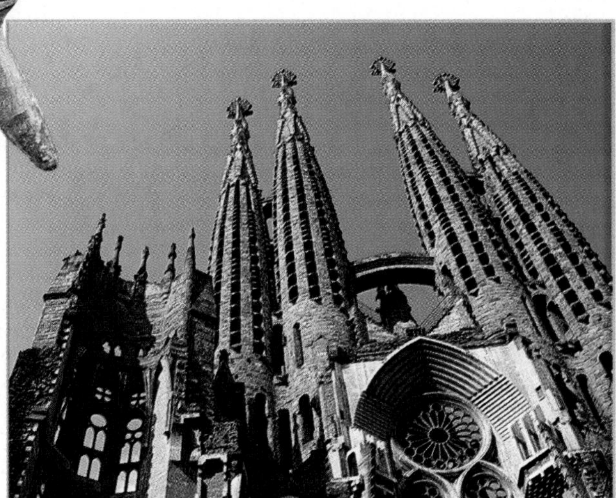

# ¡En español!

## Level 2 Scope & Sequence

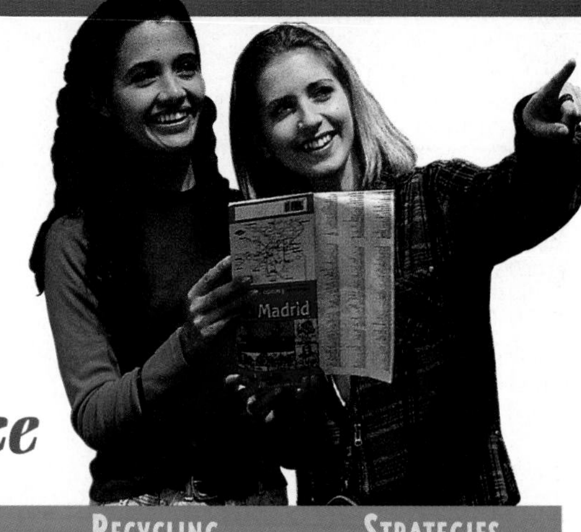


| PRELIMINAR | | Communication | Grammar | Culture | Recycling | Strategies |
|---|---|---|---|---|---|---|
| PRELIMINAR | **Etapa preliminar** p. 1<br>**Northeastern U.S.**<br>*Día a día* | • Exchange greetings<br>• Discuss likes and dislikes<br>• Describe people and places<br>• Ask for and give information<br>• Talk about school life<br>• Talk about the new school year | NOTA<br>*Gustar* and indirect object pronouns; *preguntar;* expressions of frequency; *venir, decir* | NOTAS CULTURALES<br>• *En Nueva York y New Jersey*<br>• *La población latina*<br>• *De Connecticut*<br>• City Year | • Use adjectives to describe<br>• The verb *tener*<br>• *ser* vs. *estar*<br>• Interrogative words<br>• Tell time<br>• Regular present tense verbs<br>• The verb *ir*<br>• Stem-changing verbs: *e → ie, o → ue*<br>• Irregular *yo* verbs | SPEAKING: Give and get personal information |

| UNIDAD 1 ¿Qué pasa? • Estados Unidos | | Communication | Grammar | Culture | Recycling | Strategies |
|---|---|---|---|---|---|---|
| UNIDAD 1 ¿Qué pasa? • Estados Unidos | **Etapa 1** p. 28<br>**Los Ángeles**<br>*Pasatiempos*<br>UNIT OPENER<br>CULTURE NOTES<br>• *La misión San Fernando Rey de España*<br>• *Hispaños en Hollywood*<br>• *Tostones*<br>• *Artistas y la comunidad*<br>• *Televisión*<br>• Gloria Estefan<br>• Jorge Ramos y María Elena Salinas | • Talk about where you went and what you did<br>• Discuss leisure time<br>• Comment on airplane travel | All grammar presented in this *etapa* is listed in the recycling category. | EN VOCES<br>*¿Cuánto sabes?*<br>TÚ EN LA COMUNIDAD<br>NOTAS CULTURALES<br>• *La calle Olvera*<br>• *Los murales* | • Regular preterite<br>• Preterite with *-car, -gar,* and *-zar* spelling changes<br>• Irregular preterite: *ir, ser, hacer, dar, ver*<br>**Ya sabes:** Preterite with *-car, -gar,* and *-zar* | LISTENING: Identify key words<br>SPEAKING: Encourage others; get more information<br>READING: Read, don't translate; use visuals and titles to predict the general idea; scan for cognates |
| | **Etapa 2** p. 50<br>**Chicago**<br>*¿Qué prefieres?* | • Comment on food<br>• Talk about the past<br>• Express activity preferences<br>• Discuss fine art | • Irregular preterite verbs<br>NOTA<br>*estar de acuerdo* | EN COLORES: *El arte latino de Chicago:* murals (video)<br>CONEXIONES<br>*El arte:* artists' inspirations<br>NOTAS CULTURALES<br>• *El Centro Museo de Bellas Artes*<br>• *La cena* | • Stem-changing verbs: *e → i, u → ue*<br>**Activity 3:** *¡A viajar!* (travel)<br>**Activity 14:** *¿Cuántas veces?* (expressions of frequency)<br>**Ya sabes:** *jugar, pedir, servir* | LISTENING: Identify the main idea<br>SPEAKING: Use all you know; give reasons why<br>CULTURE: Learn about other cultures; describe the nature of murals |
| | **Etapa 3** p. 72<br>**Miami**<br>*¿Viste las noticias?* | • Discuss ways to communicate<br>• React to news<br>• Ask for and give information<br>• Talk about things and people you know | • Demonstrative adjectives and pronouns<br>• Stem-changing preterite<br>NOTAS<br>*estar bien informado;* adjectives of nationality; *saber* vs. *conocer; hubo; i → y* with preterite | EN VOCES<br>*¿Leíste el periódico hoy?*<br>EN COLORES<br>*Miami: Puerta de las Américas*<br>CONEXIONES<br>*Las matemáticas:* calculate percentages of television viewing<br>NOTAS CULTURALES<br>• *A la fiesta*<br>• *Periódicos por computadora* | **Activity 3:** *¡Qué reunión!* (irregular preterite)<br>**Ya sabes:** stem-changing verbs; *saber, conocer* | LISTENING: Listen with a purpose<br>SPEAKING: Present findings; provide additional information<br>READING: Skim for the general idea; scan for specific information<br>WRITING: Bring your event to life<br>CULTURE: Identify characteristics of neighborhoods |

## UNIDAD 2 Ayer y hoy • Ciudad de México

| | Communication | Grammar | Culture | Recycling | Strategies |
|---|---|---|---|---|---|
| **Etapa 1** p. 100<br>*De pequeño*<br>Unit Opener<br>Culture Notes<br>• *Los tamales*<br>• *La piñata*<br>• *Hoy no circula*<br>• *El Popocatépetl*<br>• Cristian Castro<br>• Frida Kahlo<br>• Padre Miguel Hidalgo y Costilla | • Describe childhood experiences<br>• Express personal reactions<br>• Discuss family relationships | • Possessive adjectives and pronouns<br>• Imperfect tense<br>Notas<br>*dentro de, fuera de;* expressions with *tener (tener hambre, tener sed,* etc.); *había* | En voces<br>*El monte de nuestro alimento:* legend<br>Conexiones<br>*Los estudios sociales:* Aztec calendar<br>Notas culturales<br>• *Las marionetas*<br>• *El Bosque de Chapultepec* | • Reflexive pronouns and verbs<br>**Activity 3:** *¡Los conozco!* (nationalities) | Listening: Listen for related details<br>Speaking: Tell when you were always or never (im)perfect; add variety to your conversation<br>Reading: Analyze folkloric traditions |
| **Etapa 2** p. 122<br>*Había una vez...* | • Narrate in the past<br>• Discuss family celebrations<br>• Talk about activities in progress | • Progressive tenses<br>• Preterite vs. imperfect | En colores:<br>*¡Temblor!:* the earthquake of 1985<br>Conexiones: *El arte:*<br>*El muralista Diego Rivera*<br>Notas culturales<br>• *La piñata*<br>• *El Museo Nacional de Antropología* | **Activity 4:** *Una reunión escolar* (imperfect)<br>**Activity 5:** *Reacciones* (reflexives) | Listening: Listen for a series of events<br>Speaking: Brainstorm to get ideas; interact by expressing approval, disapproval, or astonishment<br>Culture: Observe and generalize |
| **Etapa 3** p. 144<br>*Hoy en la ciudad* | • Order in a restaurant<br>• Ask for and pay a restaurant bill<br>• Talk about things to do in the city | • Double object pronouns<br>Notas<br>indirect object pronouns with verbs like *gustar; dar una vuelta* | En voces: *Teotihuacán: Ciudad misteriosa* (video)<br>En colores<br>*¡Buen provecho!: La comida mexicana*<br>Tú en la comunidad<br>Notas culturales<br>• *El baile folklórico*<br>• *El Palacio de Bellas Artes*<br>• *Las telenovelas* | • Direct object pronouns<br>• Indirect object pronouns<br>**Activity 3:** *¡A divertirse en la ciudad!* (preterite vs. imperfect) | Listening: Listen for useful expressions<br>Speaking: Personalize responses; resolve misconceptions<br>Reading: Identify gaps in knowledge<br>Writing: Develop your story<br>Culture: Compare meals and mealtimes |

## UNIDAD 3 Sol y sombra • Puerto Rico

| | Communication | Grammar | Culture | Recycling | Strategies |
|---|---|---|---|---|---|
| **Etapa 1** p. 172<br>*¿Estás en forma?*<br>Unit Opener<br>Culture Notes<br>• *El observatorio de Arecibo*<br>• *Los pasteles*<br>• *Piratas*<br>• *La ceiba de Ponce*<br>• *El Yunque*<br>• Marc Anthony | • Discuss ways to stay fit and healthy<br>• Make suggestions<br>• Talk about daily routine and personal care | • *Usted/ustedes* commands<br>• Commands and pronoun placement | En voces<br>*Puerto Rico: Lugar maravilloso*<br>Conexiones<br>*Las ciencias:* phosphorescence<br>Notas culturales<br>• *El béisbol*<br>• *El Viejo San Juan* | • Pronoun placement<br>**Activity 4:** *¿Siempre o nunca?* (expressions of frequency, double object pronouns)<br>**Ya sabes:** *las preparaciones* | Listening: Listen and sort details<br>Speaking: Use gestures to convey meaning; react to daily routines<br>Reading: Observe organization of ideas |
| **Etapa 2** p. 194<br>*Preparaciones* | • Discuss beach activities<br>• Tell someone what to do<br>• Talk about chores<br>• Say if something has already been done | Nota<br>*acabar de* + infinitive | En colores<br>*El Yunque: Bosque Nacional* (video)<br>Tú en la comunidad<br>Notas culturales<br>• *Después de las clases*<br>• *El manatí* | • Affirmative *tú* commands<br>• Negative *tú* commands<br>• Adverbs ending in *-mente*<br>**Activity 3:** *Por la mañana* (daily routine)<br>**Ya sabes:** *los quehaceres* | Listening: Listen and categorize information<br>Speaking: Improvise; encourage or discourage certain behaviors<br>Culture: Recognize unique natural wonders |
| **Etapa 3** p. 216<br>*¿Cómo te sientes?* | • Describe time periods<br>• Talk about health and illness<br>• Give advice | • *Hacer* with expressions of time<br>• Subjunctive with impersonal expressions<br>Nota<br>*doler* with indirect object pronouns; subjunctive after impersonal expressions | En voces<br>*El estatus político de Puerto Rico*<br>En colores<br>*Una voz de la tierra*<br>Conexiones<br>*La historia:* pirates<br>Notas culturales<br>• *Los huracanes*<br>• *La celebración de Carnaval*<br>• *La cultura de los jíbaros* | **Activity 3:** *Los quehaceres en tu casa* (chores) | Listening: Listen sympathetically<br>Speaking: Give feedback; use language for problem-solving<br>Reading: Activate associated knowledge<br>Writing: Compare and contrast to make strong descriptions<br>Culture: Discover many cultures inside one country |

| | | Communication | Grammar | Culture | Recycling | Strategies |
|---|---|---|---|---|---|---|
| **UNIDAD 4 Un viaje • Madrid, España** | **Etapa 1** p. 244<br>*En la pensión*<br>Unit Opener<br>Culture Notes<br>• *El Prado*<br>• *La guitarra*<br>• *Paella*<br>• *El rey y la reina de España*<br>• Antonio Banderas<br>• El Greco | • Talk about travel plans<br>• Persuade others<br>• Describe rooms, furniture, and appliances | • Subjunctive to express hopes and wishes<br>• Irregular subjunctive forms | En voces<br>*Felices sueños:* hotel descriptions<br>Conexiones<br>*El arte:* Spanish artists<br>Notas culturales<br>• *La Plaza de la Cibeles*<br>• *Alojamiento* | **Activity 4:** *Es mejor que…* (subjunctive)<br>**Activity 15:** *El metro de Madrid* (giving directions)<br>**Ya sabes:** expressing hopes and wishes | Listening: Listen and check details<br>Speaking: Persuade; make and express decisions<br>Reading: Compare related details |
| | **Etapa 2** p. 266<br>*Conoce la ciudad* | • Describe your city or town<br>• Make suggestions<br>• Ask for and give directions | • Subjunctive stem-changes: *-ar, -er* verbs<br>• Stem-changing *-ir* verbs in the subjunctive<br>• Subjunctive vs. infinitive<br>Notas: *ni;* question words such as *cuando* and *donde* as bridges mid-sentence | En colores<br>*Vamos a bailar:* Gipsy Kings<br>Conexiones: *La tecnología:* creating a webpage<br>Notas culturales<br>• *La Plaza Mayor*<br>• *El paseo*<br>• *Los gitanos y el flamenco* | **Activity 3:** *Una lección* (giving advice using the subjunctive) | Listening: Listen and distinguish<br>Speaking: Ask for and give directions; work cooperatively<br>Culture: Identify characteristics of successful musical groups |
| | **Etapa 3** p. 288<br>*Vamos de compras* | • Talk about shopping for clothes<br>• Ask for and give opinions<br>• Make comparisons<br>• Discuss ways to save and spend money | • Subjunctive with expressions of doubt<br>• Subjunctive with expressions of emotion<br>Nota<br>Subjunctive vs. indicative | En voces<br>*Nos vemos en Madrid:* highlights of the city<br>En colores: *¿En qué te puedo atender?:* shopping (video)<br>Tú en la comunidad<br>Notas culturales<br>• *Miguel de Cervantes*<br>• *¿Qué talla usas?* | • Comparisons and superlatives<br>**Activity 4:** *¿Qué me sugieres?* (making suggestions using the subjunctive)<br>**Ya sabes:** equal/unequal comparisons, expressions of doubt, expressions of emotion | Listening: Listen and infer<br>Speaking: Interpret the feelings or values of others; observe courtesies and exchange information<br>Reading: Categorize details<br>Writing: Persuade your reader<br>Culture: Analyze and draw conclusions about shopping as a cultural activity |

| | | Communication | Grammar | Culture | Recycling | Strategies |
|---|---|---|---|---|---|---|
| **UNIDAD 5 La naturaleza • San José, Costa Rica** | **Etapa 1** p. 316<br>*En el bosque tropical*<br>Unit Opener<br>Culture Notes<br>• José Figueres<br>• *Gallo pinto*<br>• Francisco Zúñiga<br>• *El quetzal*<br>• *La cerámica de Nicoya*<br>• *El fútbol* | • Describe geographic characteristics<br>• Make future plans<br>• Talk about nature and the environment | • Future tense<br>• Expressions with *por*<br>• *Nosotros* commands | En voces<br>*El Parque Nacional de Volcán Poás*<br>Conexiones<br>*La geografía:* tropical forest locations<br>Notas culturales<br>• *El 8 de septiembre de 1502*<br>• *Los saludos* | **Activity 3:** *Predicciones* (making predictions) | Listening: Organize and summarize environmental information<br>Speaking: Share personal plans and feelings; anticipate future plans<br>Reading: Confirm or deny hearsay with reliable information |
| | **Etapa 2** p. 338<br>*Nuestro medio ambiente* | • Discuss outdoor activities<br>• Describe the weather<br>• Make predictions<br>• Talk about ecology | • Irregular future<br>• Expressions with *para* | En colores<br>*Costa Rica, ¡la pura vida!* (video)<br>Tú en la comunidad<br>Notas culturales<br>• *Los parques nacionales*<br>• *Navegar los rápidos* | • Weather expressions with *hacer*<br>**Activity 5:** *¿Qué vas a hacer este verano?* (future tense) | Listening: Observe relationships between actions and motives<br>Speaking: Find alternate ways to communicate; make recommendations<br>Culture: Predict appeal to ecotourists |
| | **Etapa 3** p. 360<br>*¿Cómo será el futuro?* | • Comment on conservation and the environment<br>• Talk about how you would solve problems | • *Por* or *para*<br>• Conditional tense<br>Nota<br>*Si estuviera…*<br>*o Si pudieras…* | En voces: *La cascada de la novia:* legend<br>En colores: *Cumbre ecológica centroamericana: Se reúnen jóvenes en San José*<br>Conexiones: *Los estudios sociales:* advertising about the environment<br>Notas culturales<br>• *Los campamentos* • *La economía* • *Las leyendas* | **Activity 5:** *¿Cómo será?* (future tense)<br>**Activity 6:** *¿Por o para?* (*por* vs. *para*) | Listening: Propose solutions<br>Speaking: Identify problems and your commitment to solving them; hypothesize about the future<br>Reading: Recognize characteristics of legends<br>Writing: Present a thorough and balanced review<br>Culture: Prioritize |

**UNIDAD 6 El mundo del trabajo • Quito, Ecuador**

| | Communication | Grammar | Culture | Recycling | Strategies |
|---|---|---|---|---|---|
| **Etapa 1** p. 388<br>*Se busca trabajo*<br><br>Unit Opener<br>Culture Notes<br>• *Llapingachos*<br>• *Las Islas Galápagos*<br>• *La música andina*<br>• *Andar en bicicleta de montaña*<br>• *La toquilla*<br>• Antonio José de Sucre | • Discuss jobs and professions<br>• Describe people, places, and things<br>• Complete an application | • Impersonal *se*<br>• Past participles used as adjectives | En voces<br>*Bienvenidos a la isla Santa Cruz:* Galapagos Islands (video)<br>Conexiones<br>*La geografía:* equatorial regions<br>Notas culturales<br>• *Quito*<br>• *La ocarina* | • Present and present progressive<br>**Activity 5:** *Una cápsula de tiempo* (conditional) | Listening: Evaluate a plan<br>Speaking: Participate in an interview; check comprehension<br>Reading: Use context to find meaning |
| **Etapa 2** p. 410<br>*La entrevista* | • Prepare for an interview<br>• Interview for a job<br>• Evaluate situations and people | • Present perfect<br>• Irregular present perfect | En colores<br>*Ciberespacio en Quito*<br>Conexiones<br>*La música:* pan flute<br>Notas culturales<br>• *Los grupos indígenas*<br>• *Las empresas del mundo hispano* | • Preterite and imperfect<br>**Activity 3:** *¿Qué está dibujado?* (past participle) | Listening: Evaluate behavior<br>Speaking: Give advice; refine interview skills<br>Culture: Assess use of e-mail |
| **Etapa 3** p. 432<br>*¡A trabajar!* | • Talk on the telephone<br>• Report on past, present, and future events<br>• Describe duties, people, and surroundings | • Reported speech | En voces:<br>Jorge Carrera Andrade–*Pasajero del planeta*<br>En colores<br>*Música de las montañas:* Andean music<br>Tú en la comunidad<br>Notas culturales<br>• *Guayaquil*<br>• *Los festivales* | • Future tense<br>• Conditional tense | Listening: Report what others said<br>Speaking: Persuade or convince others; report on events<br>Reading: Observe characteristics of poems<br>Writing: State your message using a positive tone<br>Culture: Reflect on music |

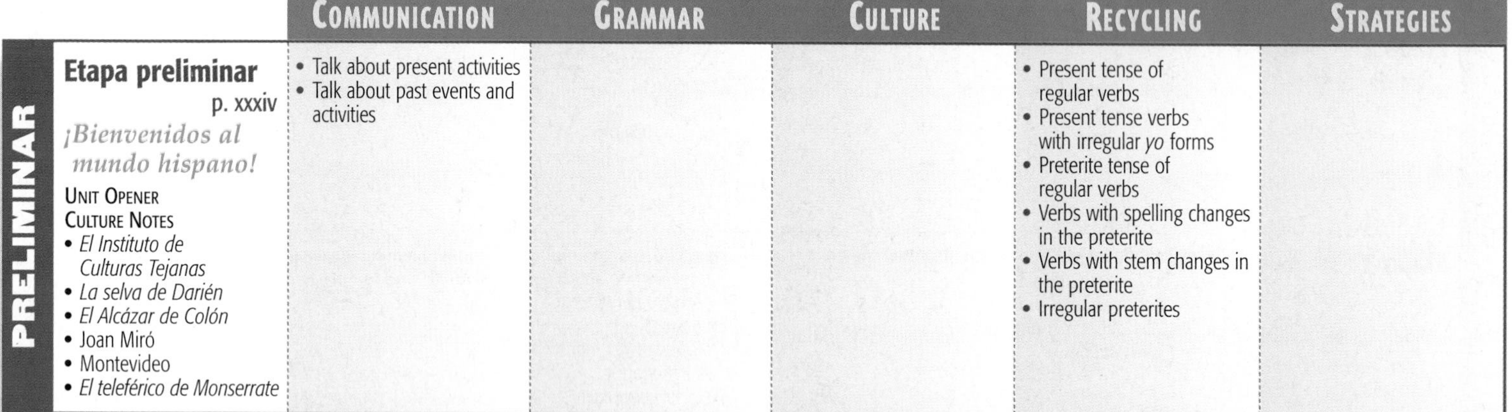


# Level 3 Scope & Sequence

| | Communication | Grammar | Culture | Recycling | Strategies |
|---|---|---|---|---|---|
| **PRELIMINAR** — **Etapa preliminar** p. xxxiv<br>*¡Bienvenidos al mundo hispano!*<br>Unit Opener<br>Culture Notes<br>• *El Instituto de Culturas Tejanas*<br>• *La selva de Darién*<br>• *El Alcázar de Colón*<br>• Joan Miró<br>• Montevideo<br>• *El teleférico de Monserrate* | • Talk about present activities<br>• Talk about past events and activities | | | • Present tense of regular verbs<br>• Present tense verbs with irregular *yo* forms<br>• Preterite tense of regular verbs<br>• Verbs with spelling changes in the preterite<br>• Verbs with stem changes in the preterite<br>• Irregular preterites | |
| **UNIDAD 1 Así somos • Estados Unidos** — **Etapa 1** p. 30<br>*¿Cómo soy?*<br>Unit Opener<br>Culture Notes<br>• Oscar de la Hoya<br>• *Comida mexicana*<br>• *Repertorio Español*<br>• Ellen Ochoa<br>• *La Prensa* | • Describe people<br>• Talk about experiences<br>• List accomplishments | • Present and past perfect | En voces<br>Cristina García–*Soñar en cubano*<br>Conexiones<br>*El arte:* self portrait<br>Notas culturales<br>• Concept of *barrio*<br>• *Los apodos*<br>• Spanish-speaking immigrants and identity | • *Ser* vs. *estar*<br>• Imperfect tense<br>• Preterite vs. imperfect<br>**Ya sabes:** *Características* | **Listening:** Recognize descriptions<br>**Speaking:** Add details to descriptions; describe personal characteristics and actions<br>**Reading:** Observe how verb tenses reveal time |
| **Etapa 2** p. 52<br>*¿Cómo me veo?* | • Describe fashions<br>• Talk about pastimes<br>• Talk about the future<br>• Predict actions | • Future tense<br>• Future of probability | En colores<br>*Un gran diseñador:* Oscar de la Renta<br>Conexiones<br>*Las matemáticas:* create an annual budget<br>Notas culturales<br>• Araceli Segarra, climber of Mt. Everest<br>• Pet sounds and names | • Verbs like *gustar*<br>• *Por* and *para*<br>**Activity 4:** *De compras* (clothing)<br>**Activity 15:** *¿Dónde estarán?* (wondering about location)<br>**Ya sabes:** *¿De qué es?* | **Listening:** Distinguish admiring and critical remarks<br>**Speaking:** Use familiar vocabulary in a new setting; brainstorm to get lots of ideas<br>**Culture:** Examine the cultural role of fashion |
| **Etapa 3** p. 74<br>*¡Hay tanto que hacer!* | • Talk about household chores<br>• Say what friends do<br>• Express feelings | • Reflexives used reciprocally<br>Nota<br>*saber/conocer* | En voces<br>Sandra Cisneros–*La casa en Mango Street*<br>En colores<br>*El legendario rey del mambo:* Tito Puente<br>Tú en la comunidad<br>Notas culturales<br>• *El compadrazgo*<br>• Sammy Sosa<br>• Greater Eastside, LA | • Reflexive verbs<br>• Impersonal constructions with *se*<br>**Activity 2:** *¡Hazlo!* (say what you have to do)<br>**Activity 5:** *Un día desastroso* (reflexive verbs)<br>**Activity 9:** *Mi padrino* (imperfect) | **Listening:** Make an argument for and against hiring others to maintain a home<br>**Speaking:** Identify feelings important in a friendship<br>**Reading:** Chart contrasts between dreams and reality<br>**Writing:** Use details to enrich a description<br>**Culture:** Interview, report, and value musical influences |

| | Communication | Grammar | Culture | Recycling | Strategies |
|---|---|---|---|---|---|
| **UNIDAD 2 ¡El mundo es nuestro! • México y América Central** | | | | | |
| **Etapa 1** p. 102<br>*Pensemos en los demás*<br>UNIT OPENER CULTURE NOTES:<br>• María Izquierdo • *¡Protege la selva tropical!* • *Tejidos Guatemaltecos* • *Ruinas de Copán* • *Cebiche mixto*<br>• Oscar Arias | • Say what you want to do<br>• Make requests<br>• Make suggestions | NOTA<br>pronoun placement with commands | EN VOCES<br>Elizabeth Burgos– *Me llamo Rigoberta Menchú*<br>TÚ EN LA COMUNIDAD<br>NOTAS CULTURALES<br>• Youth groups in Mexico and C.A.<br>• Young people addressing adults<br>• *Castellano* | • Command forms<br>• *Nosotros* commands<br>• Speculating with the conditional<br>**Activity 2:** *¿Qué vas a hacer?* (say what you are going to do) • **Activity 5:** *La clase de ejercicio (tú, usted o ustedes)* • **Activity 12:** *Costa Rica* (conditional) | LISTENING: Anticipate, compare and contrast<br>SPEAKING: Name social problems then propose solutions; identify the general ideas, then delegate responsibilities<br>READING: Comprehend complex sentences |
| **Etapa 2** p. 124<br>*Un planeta en peligro* | • Say what should be done<br>• React to the ecology<br>• React to others' actions | • Present perfect subjunctive<br>NOTA<br>*-uir* verbs add a *y* in subjunctive form | EN COLORES: *Unidos podemos hacerlo:* literacy in Nicaragua<br>CONEXIONES<br>*Las ciencias:* recycling<br>NOTAS CULTURALES<br>• Currencies in C.A. and Mexico<br>• *Grupo de los Cien/* international conservation | • Present subjunctives<br>**Activity 2:** *El horario de Ángela* (describe schedules)<br>**Activity 5:** *La ecóloga* (subjunctive)<br>**Ya sabes:** *Es bueno que…* etc. | LISTENING: Inventory efforts to save the environment<br>SPEAKING: Consider the effect of words and tone of voice; express support (or lack of)<br>CULTURE: Gather and analyze information about literacy |
| **Etapa 3** p. 146<br>*La riqueza natural* | • React to nature<br>• Express doubt<br>• Relate events in time | • Subjunctive with *cuando* and other conjunctions of time<br>NOTA<br>*-cer* verbs add a *z* in the subjunctive | EN VOCES<br>Juan José Arreola– *Baby H.P.*<br>EN COLORES<br>*Un país de encanto:* Costa Rican rainforests<br>CONEXIONES<br>*Las ciencias:* the products of a rainforest<br>NOTAS CULTURALES<br>• *Isla de Ometepe/Lago Nicaragua*<br>• *Reservas naturales en Centroamérica* | • Subjunctive with expressions of emotion<br>• Subjunctive to express doubt and uncertainty<br>**Activity 3:** *¿Has visto…?* (animals) • **Activity 7:** *El mundo de hoy* (expressing emotion) • **Activity 9:** *No te creo* (expressing doubt)<br>• **Activity 12:** *Tan pronto como*<br>• **Activity 13:** *Los quehaceres* (conjunctions of time)<br>**Ya sabes:** Expressions of emotion and doubt | LISTENING: Determine your purpose for listening<br>SPEAKING: Gain thinking time before speaking; reassure others<br>READING: Recognize uses of satire, parody, and irony<br>WRITING: Persuade by presenting solutions to problems<br>CULTURE: Analyze advantages and disadvantages of ecotourism |

| | Communication | Grammar | Culture | Recycling | Strategies |
|---|---|---|---|---|---|
| **UNIDAD 3 Celebración de mi mundo • Caribe** | | | | | |
| **Etapa 1** p. 174<br>*¡Al fin la graduación!*<br>UNIT OPENER CULTURE NOTES:<br>• *Los Muñequitos de Matanzas* • Maracas • *Frutas tropicales* • Rosario Ferré • Juan Luis Guerra • *Parque ceremonial Taíno, Utuado* | • Describe personal celebrations<br>• Say what people want<br>• Link events and ideas | • Subjunctive with conjunctions<br>• Imperfect subjunctive<br>NOTA<br>*-ger* verbs change *g* to *j* in subjunctive | EN VOCES<br>Nicolás Guillén– *Ébano Real*<br>TÚ EN LA COMUNIDAD<br>NOTAS CULTURALES<br>• Graduation ceremony in the Dominican Republic<br>• *Fiesta de graduación* | • Subjunctive for expressing wishes<br>**Activity 5:** *Pedro* (subjunctive with impersonal expressions)<br>**Activity 13:** *Los chismes* (expressions of doubt)<br>**Activity 14:** *Permiso* (recreation)<br>**Ya sabes:** *otros verbos, conjunciones, el futuro* | LISTENING: Recognize major transitions<br>SPEAKING: Accept or reject advice; give advice and best wishes<br>READING: Interpret metaphors |
| **Etapa 2** p. 196<br>*¡Próspero Año Nuevo!* | • Talk about holidays<br>• Hypothesize<br>• Express doubt and disagree<br>• Describe ideals | • Subjunctive with nonexistent and indefinite antecedents<br>• Conditional sentences<br>NOTA<br>*sembrar, recoger, educar* spelling changes in subjunctive | EN COLORES: *Una tradición de Puerto Rico:* masks<br>CONEXIONES: *El arte:* art of the Caribbean<br>NOTAS CULTURALES<br>• *salsa*<br>• *Chayanne*<br>• Holidays in Puerto Rico | • Subjunctive for disagreement and denial<br>**Activity 5:** *En la comunidad* (nonexistent and indefinite)<br>**Activity 14:** *Las profesiones* (subj/profession)<br>**Ya sabes:** *dar las gracias, dudar que…,* etc. | LISTENING: Observe interview techniques<br>SPEAKING: Socialize as host or guest; encourage participation<br>CULTURE: Recognize and describe uses of disguise |
| **Etapa 3** p. 218<br>*Celebraciones de patria* | • Describe historic events<br>• Make suggestions and wishes<br>• Express emotion and doubt<br>• State cause and effect | • Subjunctive vs. indicative<br>NOTA<br>*-cer* verbs change to *z* in subjunctive, *-gar* verbs change to *gu* in the subjunctive | EN VOCES: José Martí– *de Versos sencillos: I.*<br>EN COLORES: *Una historia única:* celebrations in the D.R.<br>CONEXIONES: *Los estudios sociales*– independence days<br>NOTAS CULTURALES<br>• *El naufragio de la Santa María*<br>• *El Himno Nacional de la R.D.*<br>• *Guantanamera* | • Summary of the subjunctive<br>**Activity 4:** *Los costumbres* (holidays)<br>**Activity 7:** *¡Santo Domingo!* (subjunctive)<br>**Activity 9:** *La comunidad* (subjunctive)<br>**Ya sabes:** *dudar/creer, etc.* | LISTENING: Listen and take notes<br>SPEAKING: Describe celebrations; express yourself<br>READING: Observe what makes poetry<br>WRITING: Use transitions to make text flow smoothly<br>CULTURE: Analyze national celebrations |

| | Communication | Grammar | Culture | Recycling | Strategies |
|---|---|---|---|---|---|
| **UNIDAD 4 Un futuro brillante • Cono Sur** | | | | | |
| **Etapa 1** p. 246 *El próximo paso* UNIT OPENER CULTURE NOTES • Antonio Berni • Rafael Guarga • *El arpa andina* • *Mate* • *La bolsa* • *La Universidad de Chile* | • Describe your studies • Ask questions • Say what you are doing • Say what you were doing | • Progressive with *ir, andar,* and *seguir* • Past progressive | EN VOCES Jorge Luis Borges–*Borges y yo* TÚ EN LA COMUNIDAD NOTAS CULTURALES • Hand gestures • Professional titles • First name usage • Borges' blindness | • Interrogative words • Present progressive **Activity 8:** *Las llamadas* (present progressive, reflexives) **Activity 9:** *La limpieza* (present progressive, household chores) **Ya sabes:** question words | LISTENING: Evaluate recommendations SPEAKING: Establish closer relationships; extend a conversation READING: Analyze the role of identity and fantasy |
| **Etapa 2** p. 268 *¿Cuál será tu profesión?* | • Talk about careers • Confirm and deny • Express emotions • Hypothesize | • Past perfect subjunctive • Conditional perfect NOTA placement of object pronouns | EN COLORES: *Los jóvenes y el futuro:* career choices CONEXIONES *Los estudios sociales:* what professions interest you NOTAS CULTURALES • Getting into a university • Popular professions in the Spanish-speaking world | • Affirmative and negative expressions **Activity 6:** *Necesitas saber* (affirmative/negative) **Activity 8:** *La celebración* (past perfect subjunctive) **Ya sabes:** negatives/ affirmatives | LISTENING: Identify key information for careers SPEAKING: Anticipate what others want to know; conduct an interview CULTURE: Formulate plans for the future |
| **Etapa 3** p. 290 *Un mundo de posibilidades* | • Learn about Latin American economics • Clarify possession • Express possession • Express past probability | • Future perfect | EN VOCES Isabel Allende–*Paula* EN COLORES: *Se hablan… ¡muchos idiomas!:* Spanish language origins CONEXIONES *Los estudios sociales:* ONU/OEA NOTAS CULTURALES • Job-hunting process in South America • Saving money | • Subject and stressed object pronouns • Possessive pronouns **Activity 3:** *Internet* (numbers) **Activity 5:** *¿Quién?* (subject/ stressed object pronouns) **Activity 9:** *¿De Argentina o Chile?* (possessive pronouns) **Ya sabes:** *comparaciones numéricas,* possessive pronouns, subject/object pronouns | LISTENING: Use statistics to evaluate predictions SPEAKING: Guess cognates; speculate about the past READING: Speculate about the author WRITING: Use cause and effect to demonstrate ability CULTURE: Observe how language reflects culture |
| **UNIDAD 5 Artes en España y las Américas • España** | | | | | |
| **Etapa 1** p. 318 *Tradiciones españolas* UNIT OPENER CULTURE NOTES • Fernando Botero • *Chocolate y churros* • *La reina Isabel* • *Los cantos gregorianos* • Salvador Dalí • *Teatro Colón* | • Identify and specify • Request clarification • Express relationships • Discuss art forms | • *¿qué? vs. ¿cuál?* • Relative pronouns | EN VOCES Miguel de Unamuno and Ana María Matute CONEXIONES *Los estudios sociales:* create a timeline of the Spanish Civil War NOTAS CULTURALES • *El Museo del Prado* | • Demonstrative adjectives and pronouns **Activity 7:** *Las respuestas* (¿qué? vs. ¿cuál?) **Activity 14:** *Los artistas* (relative pronouns, literature) **Ya sabes:** *La pintura, La literatura* | LISTENING: Use advance knowledge of the topic SPEAKING: Discuss a painting; organize ideas for research READING: Compare famous authors |
| **Etapa 2** p. 340 *El Nuevo Mundo* | • Refer to people and objects • Express relationships • Make generalizations • Describe arts and crafts | • Relative pronouns • *Lo que* | EN COLORES *Un arquitecto y sus obras:* Mexican architect CONEXIONES: *Las matemáticas:* Mayan numerals NOTAS CULTURALES • *Bailes típicos* • *El inca Garcilaso de la Vega* • *Las ruinas de Tikal* | • Direct object pronouns • Indirect object pronouns **Activity 4:** *¿Lo conoces?* (direct object pronouns) **Activity 7:** *Después de la entrevista* (indirect object pronouns, work) **Activity 8:** *El viaje* (indirect object pronouns) | LISTENING: Improve your auditory memory SPEAKING: Maintain a discussion; discuss Latin American dance CULTURE: Use architecture as a cultural text |
| **Etapa 3** p. 362 *Lo mejor de dos mundos* | • Talk about literature • Talk about film • Avoid redundancy | • Nominalization [box 1] • Nominalization [box 2] | EN VOCES: Federico García Lorca–*La casa de Bernarda Alba* EN COLORES *Tres directores:* Spanish-speaking film directors TÚ EN LA COMUNIDAD NOTAS CULTURALES • Movie titles in Spanish and English • Rosario Ferré | • Double object pronouns **Activity 5:** *El (La) presidente* (double object pronouns) **Activity 12:** *Clarificaciones* (nominalization) | LISTENING: Evaluate discussions SPEAKING: Discuss a novel; critique a film READING: Interpret a drama WRITING: Support an opinion with facts and examples CULTURE: Reflect on the international appeal of movies |

**UNIDAD 6 ¡Ya llegó el futuro! • Bolivia, Colombia, Ecuador, Perú, Venezuela**

| | Communication | Grammar | Culture | Recycling | Strategies |
|---|---|---|---|---|---|
| **Etapa 1** p. 390<br>*¿Qué quieres ver?*<br>UNIT OPENER<br>CULTURE NOTES<br>• *Parque de Ciencia y Tecnología Maloka*<br>• Machu Picchu<br>• Simón Bolívar<br>• Armando Reverón<br>• *El teléfono celular*<br>• Plátanos fritos | • Narrate in the past<br>• Express doubt and certainty<br>• Report what others say<br>• Talk about television | • Sequence of tenses | EN VOCES<br>*Brillo afuera, oscuridad en casa:* Spanish language soap operas<br>TÚ EN LA COMUNIDAD<br>NOTAS CULTURALES<br>• *Telenovelas*<br>• Invitation implies inviter pays | • Preterite vs. imperfect<br>• Indicative vs. subjunctive<br>• Reported speech<br>**Activity 1:** *¿Por qué no…?* (movies)<br>**Activity 9:** *¡Es dudoso!* (subjunctive with doubt)<br>**Activity 14:** *Abuelo* (reported speech) | LISTENING: Keep up with what is said and agreed<br>SPEAKING: Negotiate; retell memories<br>READING: Distinguish facts from interpretations |
| **Etapa 2** p. 412<br>*Aquí tienes mi número…* | • Talk about technology<br>• State locations<br>• Make contrasts<br>• Describe unplanned events | • *Pero* vs. *sino*<br>• *Se* for unplanned occurrences | EN COLORES<br>*¿Un aparato democrático?:* cell phones in Latin America<br>CONEXIONES<br>*El arte:* make an ad for electronics<br>NOTAS CULTURALES<br>• Game shows in Spanish | • Conjunctions<br>• Prepositions and adverbs of location<br>**Activity 2:** *¡Voy a ElectroMundo!* (electronics)<br>**Ya sabes:** Prepositions/ adverbs of location; conjunctions with subjunctive | LISTENING: Analyze the appeal in radio ads<br>SPEAKING: Make excuses; consider the factors for and against an electronic purchase<br>CULTURE: Survey technology in daily life |
| **Etapa 3** p. 434<br>*¡Un viaje al ciberespacio!* | • Compare and evaluate<br>• Express precise relationships<br>• Navigate cyberspace | • Verbs with prepositions | EN VOCES<br>Gabriel García Márquez<br>EN COLORES<br>*Bolivia en la red:* Bolivian web page<br>CONEXIONES<br>*La tecnología:* evaluate computer configurations for your classroom<br>NOTAS CULTURALES<br>• Spread of computer technology in Latin America<br>• Searching for Spanish websites<br>• *Macondo* in works by Márquez | • Summary of prepositions<br>• Comparatives and superlatives<br>**Activity 4:** *Comparaciones* (comparatives)<br>**Activity 5:** *Marcos* (comparatives, computers)<br>**Ya sabes:** verbs with prepositions | LISTENING: Identify important computer vocabulary<br>SPEAKING: Compare and evaluate films; compare and evaluate computer configurations<br>READING: Monitor comprehension<br>WRITING: Prioritize information in order of importance<br>CULTURE: Evaluate the Internet as a means of developing cultural knowledge and understanding |

# Starting the Year Off Right

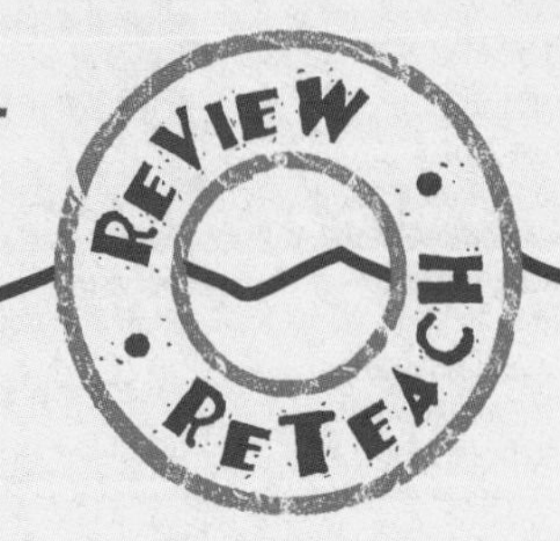


The extensive preliminary review etapa refreshes students' memory of the vocabulary and grammar concepts from the previous year to better prepare them to be successful in Level 2.

**Etapa preliminar** helps students recall and practice Level 1 concepts.

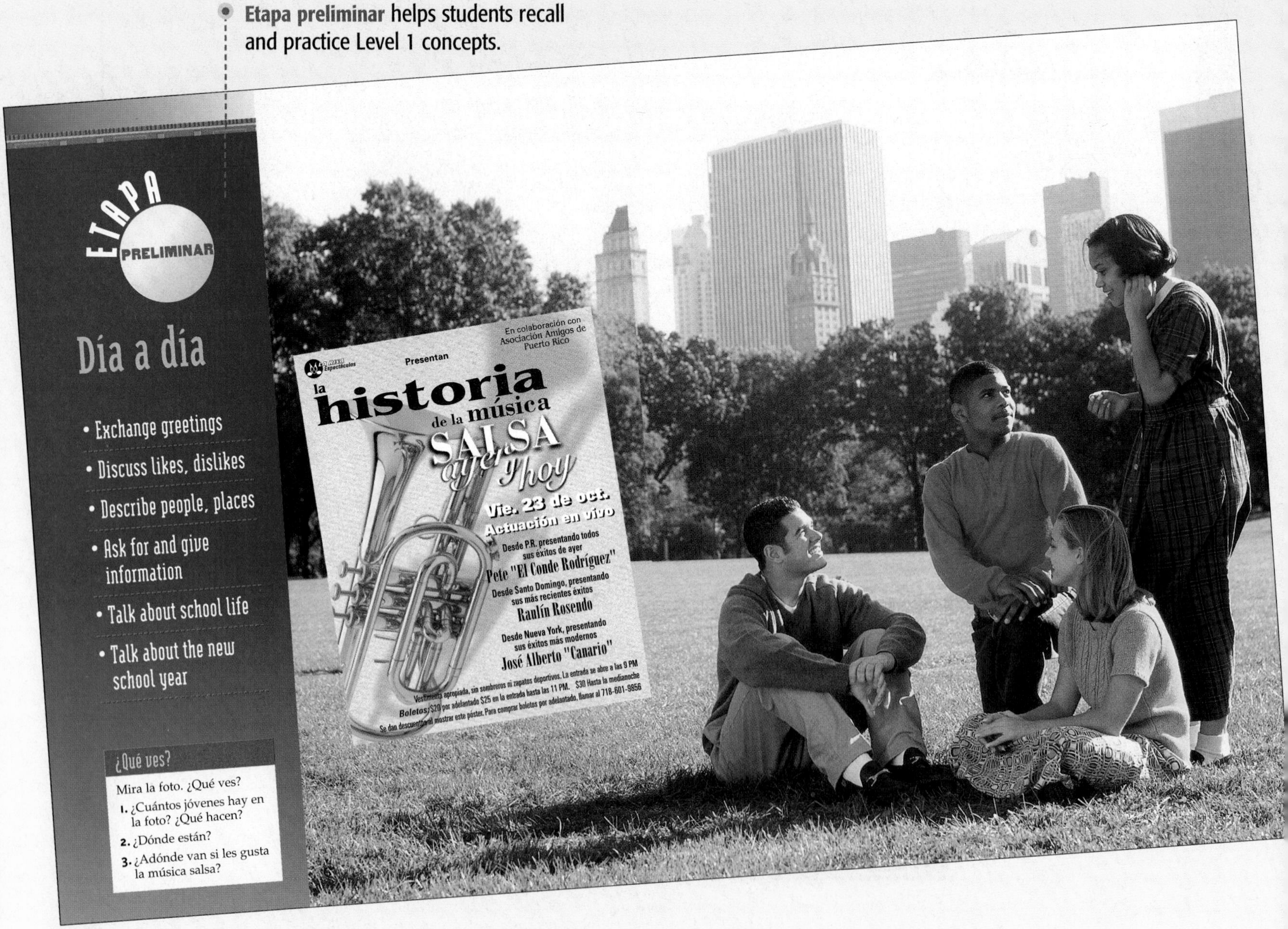

## Día a día

- Exchange greetings
- Discuss likes, dislikes
- Describe people, places
- Ask for and give information
- Talk about school life
- Talk about the new school year

En colaboración con Asociación Amigos de Puerto Rico

Presentan

la historia de la música SALSA ayer y hoy

Vie. 23 de oct.

Actuación en vivo

Desde P.R. presentando todos sus éxitos de ayer

Pete "El Conde Rodríguez"

Desde Santo Domingo, presentando sus más recientes éxitos

Raulín Rosendo

Desde Nueva York, presentando sus éxitos más modernos

José Alberto "Canario"

**¿Qué ves?**

Mira la foto. ¿Qué ves?

1. ¿Cuántos jóvenes hay en la foto? ¿Qué hacen?
2. ¿Dónde están?
3. ¿Adónde van si les gusta la música salsa?

"I could do so much with this in my classroom... it's a fantastic tool and all wonderfully integrated with grammar and vocabulary."

Marco García
Lincoln Park High School
Chicago, IL

**Practice activities** give students a chance to figure out what they remember as well as find out if they need more help.

# En la escuela

## VOCABULARIO Y GRAMÁTICA

**OBJECTIVES**
- Talk about school life
- Review: Use regular present tense verbs
- Review: Use *ir*

**Boston, Massachusetts** Look at the photos and read about what these students do in Boston.

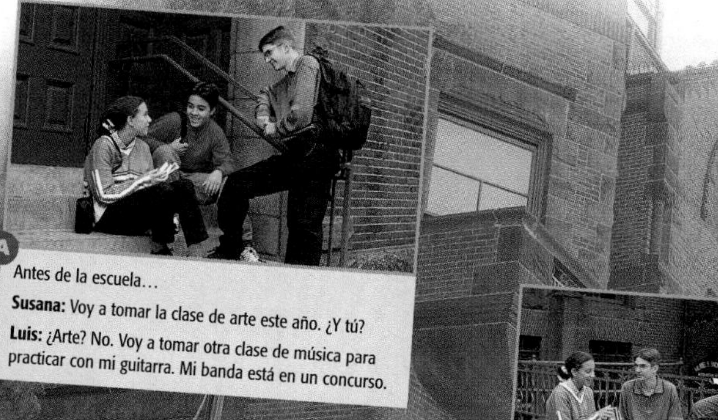

**A** Antes de la escuela…

**Susana:** Voy a tomar la clase de arte este año. ¿Y tú?

**Luis:** ¿Arte? No. Voy a tomar otra clase de música para practicar con mi guitarra. Mi banda está en un concurso.

**B** Luego, Luis y Susana van a la clase de español. Le preguntan a la señora Rivera si van a hablar español todo el tiempo. La señora Rivera contesta que sólo van a usar español.

**C** Todos los estudiantes descansan durante el día. Estos jóvenes comen su almuerzo.

**D** Después de la escuela, David corre con un equipo.

**Entrenador Santiago:** ¿Corres en tu tiempo libre, David?

**David:** Sí, un poco. Pero, como no vivo cerca de aquí, corro en mi barrio.

**Entrenador Santiago:** Está bien.

**E** Susana y Luis caminan a la biblioteca después de la escuela. Tienen mucha tarea y van a estudiar. ¿Tienes mucha tarea?

16 dieciséis
Etapa preliminar

ACTIVIDAD **20** **Durante el día**

**Leer/Escribir** Contesta las preguntas sobre lo que hacen los jóvenes durante el día escolar.
*(Hint: Answer questions about the school day.)*

1. ¿Qué clase va a tomar Susana? ¿y Luis?
2. ¿Van a hablar español e inglés en la clase de español?
3. ¿Qué clase da la señora Rivera?
4. ¿Qué hace David después de la escuela? ¿y Susana y Luis?

**REPASO**

**Regular Present Tense Verbs**

To talk about things you do, you use the present tense. To form the present tense of a regular verb, drop the **-ar**, **-er**, or **-ir** and add the appropriate ending.

**Regular Verbs**

| | -ar hablar | -er comer | -ir vivir |
|---|---|---|---|
| yo | hablo | como | vivo |
| tú | hablas | comes | vives |
| usted, él, ella | habla | come | vive |
| nosotros | hablamos | comemos | vivimos |
| vosotros | habláis | coméis | vivís |
| ustedes, ellos, ellas | hablan | comen | viven |

diecisiete 17
Etapa preliminar

**Vocabulary in context** reintroduces students to the vocabulary they already know.

**Repaso grammar boxes** remind students of Level 1 grammar concepts so they can successfully progress through Level 2.

# *Setting the Stage for Communication*

Each unit is set in a different Spanish-speaking country to excite students about the new places and new things they're going to learn.

- **Unit Objectives** preview for the students what they will be able to do at the end of the unit.

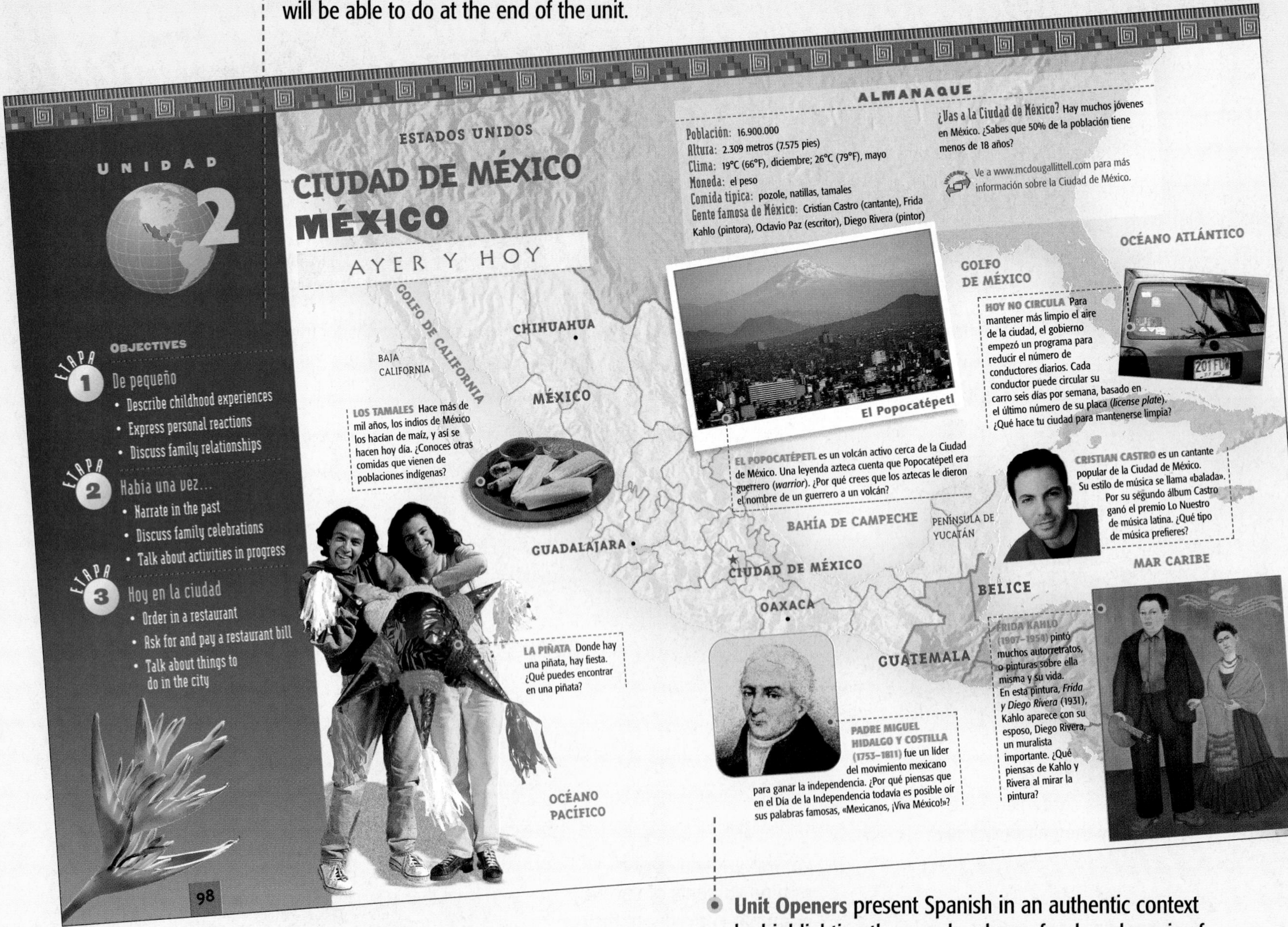

UNIDAD 2

ESTADOS UNIDOS

## CIUDAD DE MÉXICO MÉXICO

AYER Y HOY

**OBJECTIVES**

**ETAPA 1 De pequeño**

- Describe childhood experiences
- Express personal reactions
- Discuss family relationships

**ETAPA 2 Había una vez...**

- Narrate in the past
- Discuss family celebrations
- Talk about activities in progress

**ETAPA 3 Hoy en la ciudad**

- Order in a restaurant
- Ask for and pay a restaurant bill
- Talk about things to do in the city

**ALMANAQUE**

**Población:** 16.900.000
**Altura:** 2.309 metros (7.575 pies)
**Clima:** 19°C (66°F), diciembre; 26°C (79°F), mayo
**Moneda:** el peso
**Comida típica:** pozole, natillas, tamales
**Gente famosa de México:** Cristian Castro (cantante), Frida Kahlo (pintora), Octavio Paz (escritor), Diego Rivera (pintor)

**¿Vas a la Ciudad de México?** Hay muchos jóvenes en México. ¿Sabes que 50% de la población tiene menos de 18 años?

Ve a www.mcdougallittell.com para más información sobre la Ciudad de México.

GOLFO DE CALIFORNIA · BAJA CALIFORNIA · CHIHUAHUA · MÉXICO · GUADALAJARA · GOLFO DE MÉXICO · OCÉANO ATLÁNTICO · BAHÍA DE CAMPECHE · PENÍNSULA DE YUCATÁN · CIUDAD DE MÉXICO · OAXACA · BELICE · GUATEMALA · MAR CARIBE · OCÉANO PACÍFICO

**LOS TAMALES** Hace más de mil años, los indios de México los hacían de maíz, y así se hacen hoy día. ¿Conoces otras comidas que vienen de poblaciones indígenas?

El Popocatépetl

**EL POPOCATÉPETL** es un volcán activo cerca de la Ciudad de México. Una leyenda azteca cuenta que Popocatépetl era guerrero (*warrior*). ¿Por qué crees que los aztecas le dieron el nombre de un guerrero a un volcán?

**HOY NO CIRCULA** Para mantener más limpio el aire de la ciudad, el gobierno empezó un programa para reducir el número de conductores diarios. Cada conductor puede circular su carro seis días por semana, basado en el último número de su placa (*license plate*). ¿Qué hace tu ciudad para mantenerse limpia?

**CRISTIAN CASTRO** es un cantante popular de la Ciudad de México. Su estilo de música se llama «balada». Por su segundo álbum Castro ganó el premio Lo Nuestro de música latina. ¿Qué tipo de música prefieres?

**LA PIÑATA** Donde hay una piñata, hay fiesta. ¿Qué puedes encontrar en una piñata?

**PADRE MIGUEL HIDALGO Y COSTILLA (1753–1811)** fue un líder del movimiento mexicano para ganar la independencia. ¿Por qué piensas que en el Día de la Independencia todavía es posible oír sus palabras famosas, «Mexicanos, ¡Viva México!»?

**FRIDA KAHLO (1907–1954)** pintó muchos autorretratos, o pinturas sobre ella misma y su vida. En esta pintura, *Frida y Diego Rivera* (1931), Kahlo aparece con su esposo, Diego Rivera, un muralista importante. ¿Qué piensas de Kahlo y Rivera al mirar la pintura?

98

- **Unit Openers** present Spanish in an authentic context by highlighting the people, places, food, and music of the featured culture.

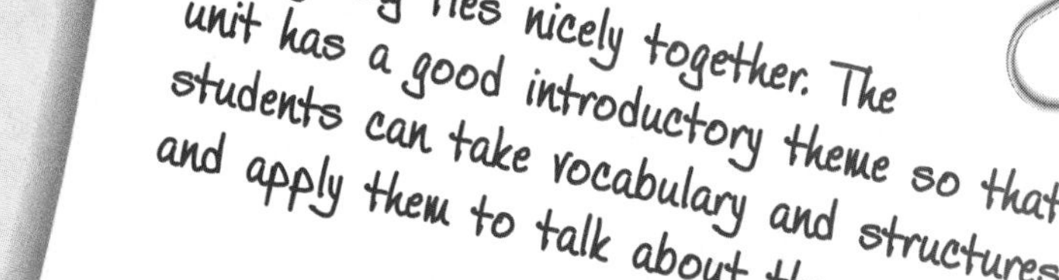

"Everything ties nicely together. The unit has a good introductory theme so that students can take vocabulary and structures and apply them to talk about themselves."

Elizabeth Torosian
Dokerty Middle School
Andover, MA

**Etapa Openers** remind students of the communicative objectives.

UNIDAD 2

# Hoy en la ciudad

- Order in a restaurant
- Ask for and pay a restaurant bill
- Talk about things to do in the city

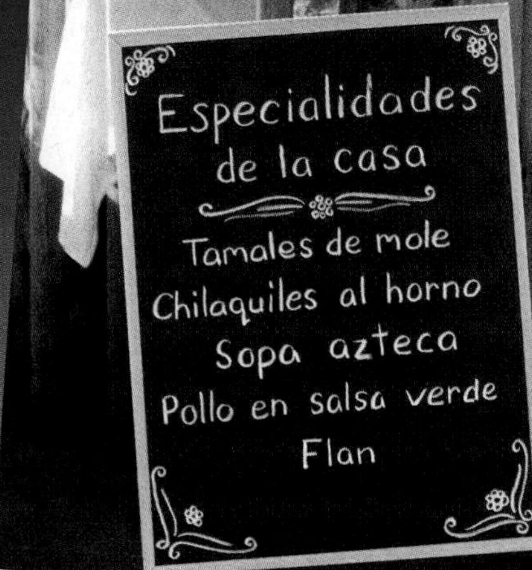

Especialidades
de la casa
Tamales de mole
Chilaquiles al horno
Sopa azteca
Pollo en salsa verde
Flan


¿Qué ves?

Mira la foto y contesta las preguntas.

1. ¿Dónde están Isabel y Laura?
2. ¿Qué cosas están en la mesa?
3. ¿Qué trae el mesero?
4. ¿Te gustaría alguna de las especialidades de la casa?

144

**¿Qué ves?** reviews language for application in the new cultural context.

MOTIVATE TO COMMUNICATE ¡En español!

# Strengthen proficiency through meaningful communicative contexts

IMPROVE • COMPREHENSION

Two stages of vocabulary introduction better prepare students for recognition and comprehension.

**En contexto** visually preteaches active vocabulary in a relevant context.

En contexto
VOCABULARIO
Mira las ilustraciones de Laura e Isabel en la Ciudad de México.
A Fui a cenar con Laura, de la revista Onda Internacional. Al entrar al restaurante, el mesero nos preguntó: —¿Qué desean comer?
Contestamos: —¿Qué nos recomienda?
B El mesero nos dijo: —Aquí sirven unos sándwiches o tortas de pollo y frijoles. Para comer la torta no necesitas cubiertos, pero para comer los frijoles sí. También se necesita una servilleta. ¡No hay que ensuciar el mantel!
el mantel
la torta
la servilleta
los frijoles
los cubiertos
C Aquí brindamos con los vasos: —¡Salud!
la cuenta
D Después de comer, el mesero nos preguntó: —¿Se les ofrece algo más? Ya queríamos ir. Entonces pedimos la cuenta y dejamos la propina.
PERDER LA CABEZA
Teatro El Galeon
RESTAURANTE EL BUEN COMER
TEATRO DE LAS ARTES
TAQUERÍA MEXICANA
E Luego queríamos ir a una obra de teatro que no era muy seria. Decidimos ir a un musical romántico para escuchar a una cantante famosa.
TAQUERÍA
F Pero… ¡todavía teníamos hambre! Fuimos a una taquería a comer tacos… Ay, ¡qué sabrosos!
Preguntas personales
1. ¿Te gusta salir a comer en restaurantes?
2. Cuando sales a comer, ¿qué comida te gusta?
3. ¿Alguna vez comiste tacos? ¿Te gustan?
4. ¿Vas al cine o al teatro? ¿Te gusta?
5. ¿Qué obras de teatro conoces?
6. ¿Qué cantantes famosos conoces?
146 ciento cuarenta y seis Unidad 2
ciento cuarenta y siete Etapa 3 147


**Preguntas personales** encourage students to recognize the active vocabulary and make it meaningful to them.

"Early success in Spanish is motivating for students. The combination of En contexto and En vivo provides the perfect means to boost student confidence and desire to learn Spanish."

Sharon Larracoechea
South Junior High School
Boise, ID

**Listening strategies** help comprehension by providing a starting point and focus for the dialog.

# En vivo
## DIÁLOGO

Laura

Isabel

Mesero

**PARA ESCUCHAR • STRATEGY: LISTENING**

**Listen for useful expressions** When traveling in another country, observe the local customs of politeness. What expressions can you borrow from Isabel and Laura when you are in a restaurant?

### En un restaurante…

1 ▸ **Laura:** Me encanta la comida mexicana, pero hay algunos platillos en el menú que no conozco.
**Isabel:** ¿Como qué? Yo te explico.
**Laura:** ¿Qué son los chilaquiles?

2 ▸ **Isabel:** Los chilaquiles… aquí los preparan con tortillas, salsa verde, queso, pollo…
**Laura:** No tengo mucha hambre. Prefiero una torta o unos tacos.

3 ▸ **Isabel:** Si quieres tacos, vamos mañana a una taquería.
**Mesero:** ¿Qué desean comer?
**Laura:** Para mí, una torta de pollo con guacamole. Y también me trae frijoles. Gracias.

4 ▸ **Isabel:** ¿Qué me recomienda hoy?
**Mesero:** Los tamales de mole están deliciosos. Se los recomiendo.
**Isabel:** Muy bien, entonces, ¿me los trae, por favor?

5 ▸ **Mesero:** ¿Qué les traigo de tomar?
**Laura:** Un agua de sandía, por favor.
**Isabel:** Una botella de agua, gracias. Y señor, me faltan unos cubiertos y una servilleta.

6 ▸ **Laura:** Sentí mucho no estar contigo para la entrevista con don Miguel. ¿Cómo estuvo?
**Isabel:** Todo salió muy bien. Creo que vas a estar muy contenta.

7 ▸ *(después de comer)*
**Mesero:** ¿Se les ofrece algo más?
**Isabel:** No, gracias, nada más. Nos trae la cuenta, por favor.
**Mesero:** Sí, cómo no. Se la traigo en seguida.

8 ▸ **Isabel:** ¿Qué te interesa hacer?
**Laura:** Podemos ir a una obra de teatro.
**Isabel:** Hay una nueva obra musical. La cantante que tiene el papel principal es extraordinaria.

9 ▸ **Mesero:** Aquí tienen la cuenta. Muchas gracias.
**Laura:** Yo voy a pagarla.
**Isabel:** Muchísimas gracias, Laura.
**Laura:** De nada. Gracias a ti por hacer la entrevista ayer.

10 ▸ **Laura:** Oye, quiero dejarle una buena propina. El mesero fue muy amable. ¿Cuánto dejo?
**Isabel:** A ver… ¿cuánto fue?

148 ciento cuarenta y ocho
**Unidad 2**

ciento cuarenta y nueve
**Etapa 3** 149

**Motivating dialogs** with embedded vocabulary and structures depict real-life situations.

MOTIVATE TO COMMUNICATE ¡En español!

# Build vocabulary for success from recognition to production

VISUALIZE SUCCESS

The carefully crafted vocabulary supports the students' learning to insure confidence and success.

**The systematic overlap of grammar concepts** provides a seamless connection between Levels 1 and 2. The grammar taught in the latter part of Level 1 is comprehensively reviewed in Level 2. See pp. T10–T11 for details.

## En acción
### VOCABULARIO Y GRAMÁTICA

**OBJECTIVES**
- Order in a restaurant
- Ask for and pay a restaurant bill
- Talk about things to do in the city
- *Review: Use direct object pronouns*
- *Review: Use indirect object pronouns*
- *Use double object pronouns*

ACTIVIDAD 1

**¿Quién?**

**Escuchar** ¿A quién se refiere cada frase: a Isabel, a Laura o al mesero? *(Hint: Whom are these sentences about?)*

1. Hay platos en el menú que no conoce.
2. Prefiere una torta.
3. Recomienda los tamales.
4. Quiere tomar una botella de agua.
5. Le faltan cubiertos.
6. Sintió mucho no estar en la entrevista.
7. Le gustaría ver el nuevo musical.
8. Les trae la cuenta en seguida.
9. Paga la cuenta.
10. Quiere dejar una buena propina.

ACTIVIDAD 2

**Palabras perdidas**

**Escuchar/Escribir** Usa estas palabras para completar la descripción del diálogo. *(Hint: Complete each description.)*

una taquería | hambre | la cuenta | una obra de teatro | unos cubiertos | propina

1. Laura no tiene mucha _____.
2. Mañana Isabel y Laura van a ir a _____ para comer.
3. No había ni una servilleta ni _____ en la mesa.
4. Isabel y Laura sólo querían _____.
5. Ellas pensaron ir a _____ para divertirse.
6. Laura quería dejar una buena _____ porque el mesero era amable.

ACTIVIDAD 3

**¡A divertirse en la ciudad!**

**Escribir** Laura cuenta de su primer día en la Ciudad de México. Termina su historia con el pretérito o el imperfecto. *(Hint: Complete the story with the preterite or the imperfect.)*

El primer día que __1__ (estar) en México, __2__ (ir) al Bosque de Chapultepec. __3__ (Hacer) mucho sol. __4__ (Haber) mucha gente en el parque. Los niños __5__ (estar) trepando a los árboles. Mientras __6__ (caminar) por el parque, __7__ (ver) el Árbol de Moctezuma y el Castillo de Chapultepec. __8__ (Llegar) al Museo Nacional de Antropología y __9__ (entrar). __10__ (Andar) de salón a salón. Luego __11__ (ir) a ver unos bailarines folklóricos. ¡ __12__ (Pasar) un día maravilloso!

ACTIVIDAD 4

**¿A qué corresponde?**

**Hablar/Leer** ¿A qué corresponde cada oración: el restaurante o el teatro? *(Hint: Say which: the restaurant or the theater?)*

1. Leí que la cantante es extraordinaria.
2. Vamos a cenar a las nueve.
3. ¿Qué desea beber?
4. ¿Qué me recomienda para tomar?
5. ¿Se les ofrece algo más?
6. Dicen que la obra es muy romántica.
7. El musical abre mañana.
8. Cuando hay buen servicio, siempre dejo una buena propina.

El restaurante

El teatro

**NOTA CULTURAL**

**El baile folklórico** de México varía mucho entre las regiones del país. Una persona puede ver los bailarines en los centros culturales de los diferentes estados. Pero una cosa es cierta —los trajes de los bailarines siempre son elegantes y de muchos colores.

**Repaso grammar boxes** reteach Level 1 grammar concepts so students are whole-heartedly prepared to approach Level 2 concepts.

"I find it very cohesive. I could follow the progression without difficulty. The unit theme is well represented throughout."

Jim Rudy
Glen Este High School
Cincinnati, OH

## Adivínala

**Hablar** Escoge una palabra o frase de la lista. Luego ayuda a un(a) compañero(a) a adivinar tu palabra. *(Hint: Give clues to help your partner guess each word.)*

**modelo**

*una obra de teatro*

**Tú:** *Es algo con actores y actrices que ves en el teatro.*

**Compañero(a):** *Es una obra de teatro.*

- una obra de teatro
- una taquería
- una servilleta
- una torta
- un(a) cantante
- unos cubiertos
- un musical

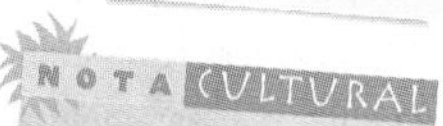

En el magnífico Palacio de Bellas Artes se presentan obras de teatro y obras musicales de todo tipo. El telón (*stage curtain*) es un mosaico de casi un millón de pedazos de cristal que representa dos volcanes mexicanos.

REPASO

## Direct Object Pronouns

Remember that you use **direct object pronouns** when you don't want to keep repeating the **direct object nouns.**

Comemos **tamales.** *We eat tamales.* —becomes→ **Los** comemos. *We eat them.*

Llamamos al **mesero.** *We called the waiter.* —becomes→ **Lo** llamamos. *We called him.*

Note that **mesero** is the **direct object** even though it takes a personal **a**.

**Direct Object Pronouns**

| | |
|---|---|
| me | nos |
| te | os |
| lo/la | los/las |

Direct object pronouns are usually placed before **conjugated verbs**. They may follow **infinitives** and **-ndo forms**.

**Lo llamamos.** *We called him.*

When you put the pronoun after the **infinitive** or **-ndo** form, it attaches to the verb.

**Lo vamos** a llamar. *We're going to call him.* ↔ Vamos a **llamarlo**.

**Lo estamos** llamando. *We're calling him.* ↔ Estamos **llamándolo**.

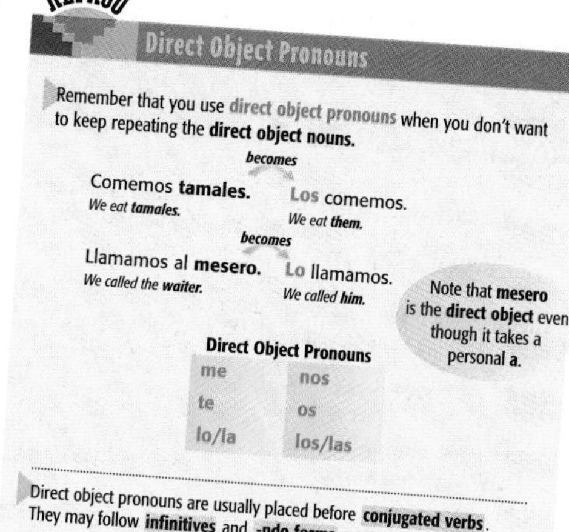

La mesera puso la **mesa** con cubiertos. *The waitress set the table with silverware.* —becomes→ **La puso** con cubiertos. *She set it with silverware.*



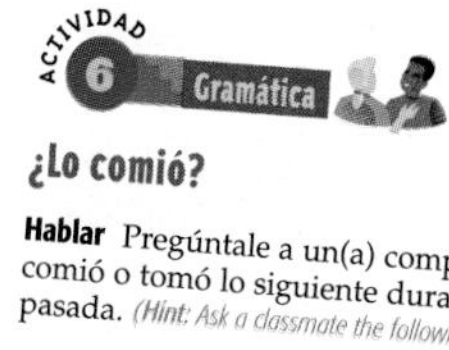

## ¿Lo comió?

**Hablar** Pregúntale a un(a) compañero(a) si comió o tomó lo siguiente durante la semana pasada. *(Hint: Ask a classmate the following.)*

**modelo**

*comer frijoles*

**Tú:** *¿Comiste frijoles?*

**Compañero(a):** *Sí, (No, no) los comí.*

1. tomar un batido de chocolate
2. comer una zanahoria
3. comer arroz
4. comer unas salchichas
5. tomar jugo de manzana
6. comer pan con mantequilla

**MÁS PRÁCTICA** *cuaderno* p. 61

**PARA HISPANOHABLANTES** *cuaderno* p. 59

## La sopa del día

**Hablar** Imagínate que preparas una sopa riquísima. Pregúntale a un(a) compañero(a) si quiere poner estos ingredientes en la sopa. *(Hint: Does your friend like these ingredients?)*

**modelo**

*el queso*

**Tú:** *¿Quieres poner el queso en la sopa?*

**Compañero(a):** *Sí, (No, no) lo quiero poner en la sopa. (Sí, [No, no] quiero ponerlo en la sopa.)*

1. las papas
2. el aceite
3. las verduras
4. la carne de res
5. el azúcar
6. la sal y la pimienta
7. las cerezas
8. los tomates
9. las cebollas
10. la pasta
11. la harina
12. el pescado

### Vocabulario Unas comidas

¿Cuál es tu comida preferida?



MOTIVATE TO COMMUNICATE ¡En español!

# Present grammar concepts visually to improve comprehension & retention

PRACTICE MAKES PERFECT

Illustrated grammar makes it easier for students to understand, remember, and apply new concepts.

- **Visual grammar concepts** help students see how the language works.

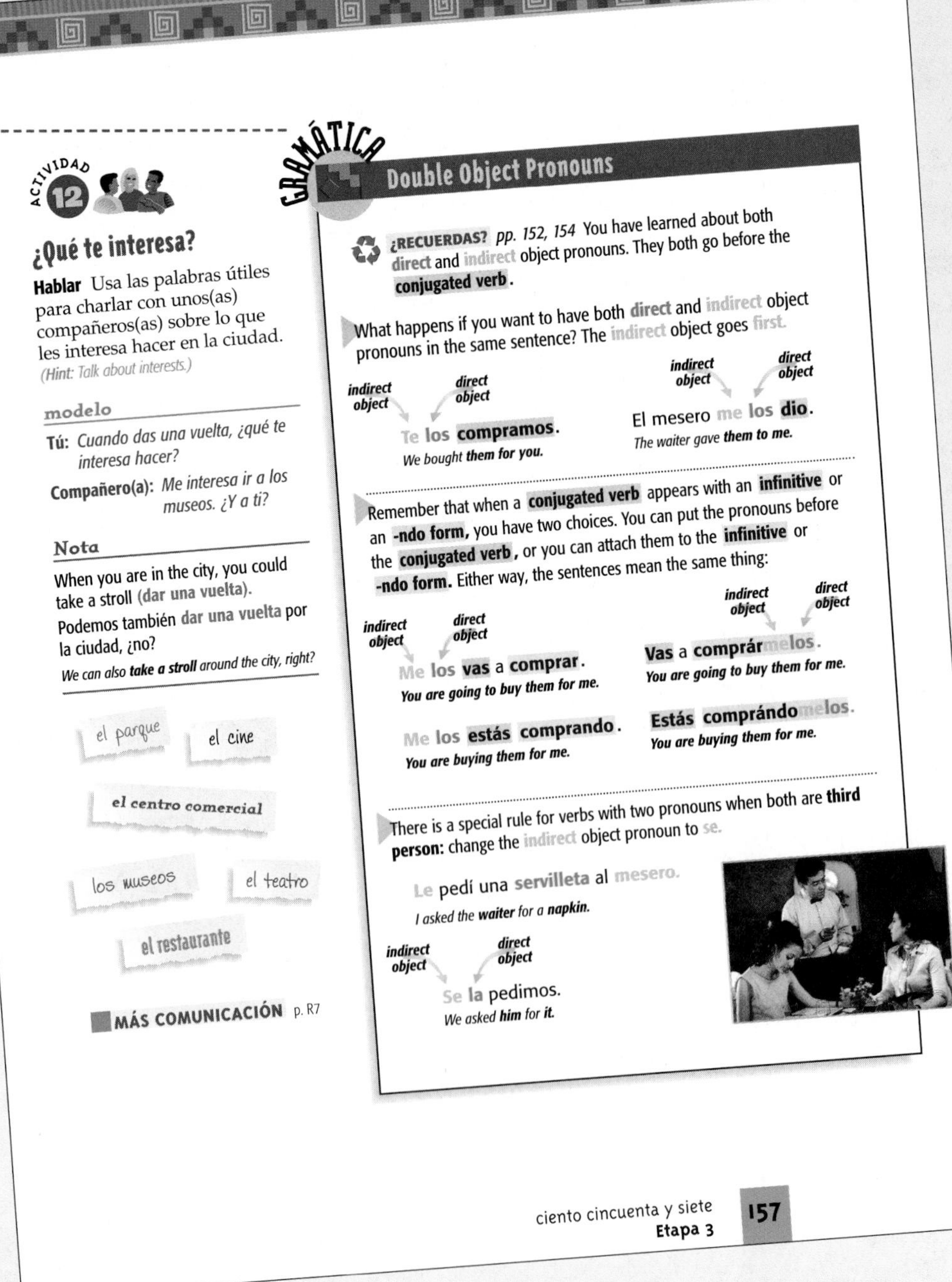

ACTIVIDAD 12

**¿Qué te interesa?**

**Hablar** Usa las palabras útiles para charlar con unos(as) compañeros(as) sobre lo que les interesa hacer en la ciudad. *(Hint: Talk about interests.)*

**modelo**

**Tú:** *Cuando das una vuelta, ¿qué te interesa hacer?*

**Compañero(a):** *Me interesa ir a los museos. ¿Y a ti?*

**Nota**

When you are in the city, you could take a stroll (**dar una vuelta**). Podemos también **dar una vuelta** por la ciudad, ¿no? *We can also* ***take a stroll*** *around the city, right?*

el parque · el cine · el centro comercial · los museos · el teatro · el restaurante

**MÁS COMUNICACIÓN** p. R7

GRAMÁTICA

## Double Object Pronouns

**¿RECUERDAS?** *pp. 152, 154* You have learned about both **direct** and **indirect** object pronouns. They both go before the **conjugated verb**.

What happens if you want to have both **direct** and **indirect** object pronouns in the same sentence? The **indirect** object goes **first**.

indirect object · direct object
**Te los compramos.** *We bought* ***them for you.***

indirect object · direct object
El mesero **me los dio.** *The waiter gave* ***them to me.***

Remember that when a **conjugated verb** appears with an **infinitive** or an **-ndo form**, you have two choices. You can put the pronouns before the **conjugated verb**, or you can attach them to the **infinitive** or **-ndo form.** Either way, the sentences mean the same thing:

indirect object · direct object
**Me los vas a comprar.** *You are going to buy them for me.*

indirect object · direct object
**Vas a comprármelos.** *You are going to buy them for me.*

**Me los estás comprando.** *You are buying them for me.*

**Estás comprándomelos.** *You are buying them for me.*

There is a special rule for verbs with two pronouns when both are **third person:** change the **indirect** object pronoun to **se.**

**Le** pedí una **servilleta** al **mesero.** *I asked the* ***waiter*** *for a* ***napkin.***

indirect object · direct object
**Se la** pedimos. *We asked* ***him*** *for* ***it.***

ciento cincuenta y siete **Etapa 3** **157**

**The activity sequence,** from controlled to open-ended activities, guides students through a solid progression that builds vocabulary and grammar skills.

**Clear models** make it easier for students to understand what they are supposed to do.

"I love it!! It is very practical and students are able to learn the material because of the variety of activities."

Lucy García
Pueblo East High School
Pueblo, CO

**Actividad 13 Gramática**

### A dar una vuelta

**Escribir** Isabel da una vuelta por la ciudad. Mira lo que dicen varias personas. Condensa las oraciones usando doble pronombres. *(Hint: Use double object pronouns to condense the sentences.)*

**modelo**

*La mesera les sirve los tacos a las señoras.*
*La mesera se los sirve.*

1. Tú les das dinero a los pobres.
2. ¿Me vas a escribir muchas cartas?
3. Mis nietos me dan muchos abrazos a mí.
4. Siempre me dicen la verdad.
5. Le estoy explicando la información a la señora.
6. Compramos boletos para nuestros amigos.
7. Ese chavo compra una bolsa para su novia.
8. El cine vende boletos más baratos para estudiantes.

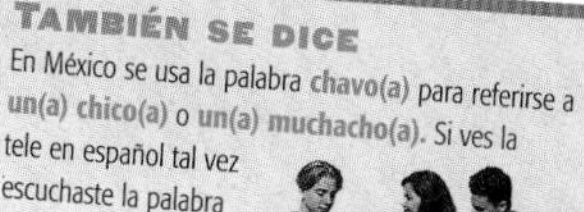

**TAMBIÉN SE DICE**

En México se usa la palabra **chavo(a)** para referirse a **un(a) chico(a)** o **un(a) muchacho(a)**. Si ves la tele en español tal vez escuchaste la palabra antes porque hay un programa famoso para niños que se llama «El chavo del ocho».

**Actividad 14 Gramática**

### Muchos favores

**Leer/Escribir** Hoy todo el mundo te pide favores. ¿Qué te pide? *(Hint: What favors does everyone want from you? Match the columns.)*

**modelo**

*Nosotros queremos más postre.*
*¿Nos lo pasas, por favor?*

**Nota**

The verb **ofrecer** *to offer* is often used with an indirect object pronoun.

**Me ofrecieron** un trabajo. *They **offered** me a job.*

1. No entiendo el tema de la obra de teatro.
2. Me gustaría unas enchiladas.
3. Tu hermanito necesita zapatos nuevos.
4. Tu amigo perdió los boletos para el concierto.
5. Tu mamá quiere otra taza de café.
6. No recordamos el nombre de una nueva comediante.

a. ¿Se los buscas?
b. ¿Me lo explicas?
c. ¿Me las preparas?
d. ¿Nos lo dices?
e. ¿Se la ofreces?
f. ¿Se los compras?

**MÁS PRÁCTICA** *cuaderno* pp. 63–64
**PARA HISPANOHABLANTES** *cuaderno* pp. 61–62

**Actividad 15**

### ¿Un estreno fenomenal?

**Escribir** Con tus compañeros(as), mira el anuncio. Luego prepara una crítica de la película, usando las palabras de la lista. *(Hint: Write a movie review.)*

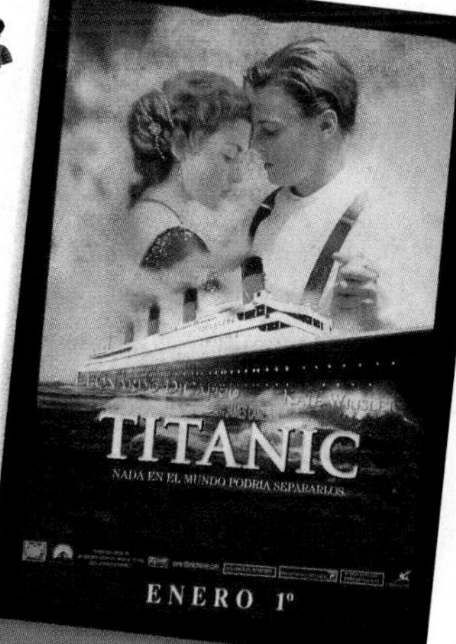

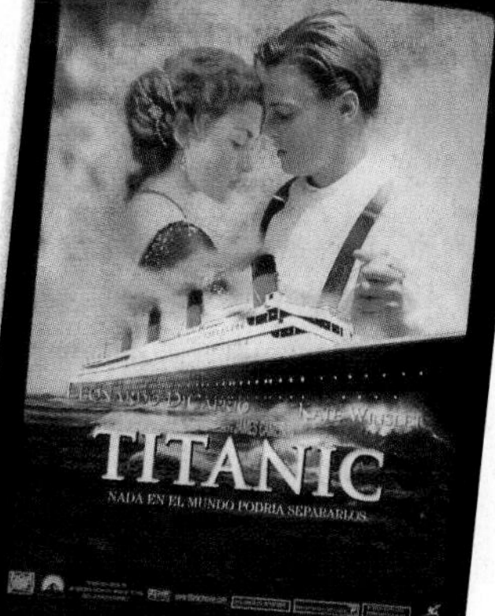
TITANIC
NADA EN EL MUNDO PODRÍA SEPARARLOS
ENERO 1º

**Vocabulario**

Para tu crítica...

| | |
|---|---|
| **bastante** *enough* | **mojado(a)** *wet* |
| **demasiado(a)** *too much* | **seco(a)** *dry* |
| **llenar** *to fill* | **vacío(a)** *empty* |
| **lleno(a)** *full* | |

¿Qué palabras pertenecen a esta película?

**Actividad 16**

### Las recomendaciones

**Escuchar/Escribir** Escucha las siguientes descripciones de varios programas y decide si las personas que hablan se los recomiendan a sus amigos(as) o no. *(Hint: Do the speakers recommend the performances?)*

**modelo**

*el tema*
*No se lo recomienda.*

1. el estreno
2. las aventuras
3. la obra de teatro
4. los comediantes
5. el drama

**Actividad 17**

### En un restaurante elegante

**Hablar** Con dos compañeros(as), presenta una escena en un restaurante elegante. Sé creativo(a). *(Hint: Present a creative restaurant scene.)*

**MÁS COMUNICACIÓN** p. R7

**Refrán**

**Se me hace la boca agua.**

Este refrán quiere decir que unas comidas son tan deliciosas que tenemos hambre cuando las vemos. Con un(a) compañero(a), hagan una lista de las comidas que «se les hace la boca agua».

158 ciento cincuenta y ocho
Unidad 2

ciento cincuenta y nueve
Etapa 3 159

**Refranes** make learning Spanish and its embedded cultural beliefs both memorable and fun.

MOTIVATE TO COMMUNICATE ¡En español!

# Improve students' reading skills with a variety of high-interest selections

VARIETY OF READINGS

Engaging reading selections, that are read and summarized on audio, provide students with a tremendous advantage to increase their literacy in Spanish.

- **Reading strategies** develop students' skills by emphasizing different ways to approach a variety of readings and genres.

En voces

LECTURA

**PARA LEER** • **STRATEGY: READING**

**Analyze folkloric traditions** Among the oral traditions of ancient people are mythic legends about important origins in their culture. In these stories gods or semidivine heroes bring important gifts to the people through supernatural means. What aspects of **«El monte de nuestro alimento** *(nourishment)***»** reflect these characteristics?

- **Personajes sobrenaturales**
- **Sucesos sobrenaturales**
- **El regalo a la gente**

What other stories like this do you know?

## El monte de nuestro alimento

### *Una leyenda náhuatl de México*

*Antes de la llegada de Colón ya había poblaciones indígenas que tenían sus propias culturas, idiomas y religiones. Entre ellas estaban los aztecas, los mayas y los incas. Esta leyenda viene del náhuatl, el idioma de los aztecas.*

Un día, Quetzalcóatl[1] vio una hormiga[2] en la ciudad de Teotihuacán. La hormiga tenía un grano de maíz.

—Señora hormiga, ¿dónde encontró ese maíz? —preguntó Quetzalcóatl.

—En el monte de nuestro alimento —respondió la hormiga y lo invitó a seguirla.

[1] an Aztec god [2] ant

Quetzalcóatl siguió a la hormiga hasta el monte pero el dios era demasiado grande para entrar con las hormigas. Entonces se transformó en hormiga y así entró.

Al entrar Quetzalcóatl vio muchísimo maíz. —Toma —dijo la hormiga. Y le dio suficiente para compartir con los otros dioses. Quetzalcóatl le dijo «gracias» a la hormiga y se despidieron. Llevó su maíz y se lo dio a los otros dioses. Luego ellos le dieron de comer a la humanidad.

Algún tiempo después los dioses necesitaron más maíz. Pero era muy difícil para Quetzalcóatl transformarse en hormiga y sacar los granos poco a poco. Entonces trató de llevar el monte entero pero no pudo.

Los dioses le pidieron ayuda al sabio[3] Oxomo. —Con un rayo de Nanáhuatl, el dios del sol, el monte se puede abrir —les dijo.

[3] sage, wise man

Al otro día pidieron la ayuda del dios del sol. Cuando Nanáhuatl lanzaba[4] su rayo, el monte se abrió y cayeron los granos de nuestro alimento, el maíz y el frijol. Los dioses tomaron los granos para la humanidad.

*Todavía hoy en México, el maíz y los frijoles son alimentos básicos de la dieta mexicana.*

[4] cast

**¿Comprendiste?**

1. ¿De qué grupo indígena es el cuento?
2. ¿Qué llevaba la hormiga?
3. ¿Qué hizo Quetzalcóatl con el maíz?
4. ¿Por qué pidieron ayuda los dioses?
5. ¿Qué pasó cuando Nanáhuatl lanzó su rayo?

**¿Qué piensas?**

¿Conoces otros cuentos parecidos a esta leyenda que expliquen algún suceso u objeto en la naturaleza? ¿Cómo crees que pasaron de una generación a otra? ¿Es importante conservarlos para generaciones futuras?

116 ciento dieciséis Unidad 2

ciento diecisiete Etapa 1 117

- **¿Comprendiste?** checks students' basic understanding of what they've read.

"The strategy boxes will be useful. I'm a true believer in the metacognitive focus of teaching strategies."

Bill Heller
Perry Jr./Sr. High School
Perry, NY

# En voces
LECTURA

**PARA LEER** • STRATEGY: READING
**Identify gaps in knowledge** Careful writing is clear about what is known and what is speculation or a guess. As you read about Teotihuacán, jot down what is known and not known about this **ciudad misteriosa.** Make a chart like the one started here.

| Teotihuacán | |
|---|---|
| conocido | desconocido |
| el plan maestro | origen |

## Teotihuacán: Ciudad misteriosa

En el siglo XIV los aztecas descubrieron una ciudad gigante pero abandonada en un valle. La llamaron Teotihuacán o la Ciudad de los Dioses. Hay un misterio sobre el origen de la gente que construyó las pirámides y templos de esta ciudad. Por las esculturas y cerámicas que dejaron parece que ellos fueron una gente pacífica[1].

Parece que Teotihuacán fue diseñada por un plan maestro[2]. Tiene una avenida central, la Avenida de los Muertos. Aquí están las pirámides principales. Desde la avenida las calles secundarias salen en forma cuadriculada[3]. Alrededor de la avenida central hay ruinas de casas lujosas y en los sectores exteriores, casas más sencillas.

En un lado de la Avenida de los Muertos hay un sector grande que probablemente fue un mercado. Los arqueólogos piensan que aquí llegaron negociantes de otras partes de México a comprar la obsidiana[4] y la cerámica fabricada en Teotihuacán, y a vender sus propios productos.

Teotihuacán fue el centro urbano más grande e importante en el Valle Central de México durante la época precolombina. Llegó a tener una población de más de 150.000 personas alrededor del siglo III o IV[5]. Pero aproximadamente en el año 750, por razones desconocidas hasta hoy, la ciudad fue quemada o destruida[6] y, al final, abandonada.

Los artefactos de Teotihuacán incluyen joyas, máscaras, ollas y estatuas.

*Avenida de los Muertos, Teotihuacán*

Si vas al Museo Nacional de Antropología, puedes ver esta máscara de jade y coral de Teotihuacán.

[1] peaceful [2] master plan [3] square

[4] hard, black, volcanic rock
[5] third or fourth century
[6] burned or destroyed

### ¿Comprendiste?

1. ¿De dónde viene el nombre Teotihuacán?
2. ¿Por qué parece que Teotihuacán fue diseñada por un plan maestro?
3. ¿Qué productos estaban de venta en el mercado?
4. ¿Sabemos exactamente por qué la civilización desapareció? Explica tu respuesta.

### ¿Qué piensas?

1. ¿Puedes hacer unas comparaciones entre Teotihuacán y tu ciudad?
2. ¿Tienen las calles de tu ciudad un plano regular o irregular? ¿Qué son los edificios importantes? ¿Cómo son las casas? ¿Dónde están con relación al centro?

160 ciento sesenta Unidad 2

ciento sesenta y uno Etapa 3 161

**¿Qué piensas?** asks students to think critically about the reading selection.

# Encourage students to experience different cultures

EXPAND VIEWPOINTS

Focused cultural strategies improve students' ability to understand and appreciate the target culture.

**Cultural strategies** help students understand their own culture and other cultures to broaden their world view.

En colores
CULTURA Y COMPARACIONES

## ¡Temblor!

Después del temblor, el gobierno de México cambió las reglas de construcción.

En el rescate los vecinos se ayudaron entre sí.

**PARA CONOCERNOS**
**STRATEGY: CONNECTING CULTURES**
**Observe and generalize** Think of a disaster that you have seen or heard about. How do you think people generally behave at such a time? Make a chart like the one below to show what you have personally observed or what you have read about the actions of people in a particular disaster.

| Desastre | Buenas acciones | Malas acciones |
|---|---|---|
| Temblor de 1985 | La gente se ayuda. | |
| | solidaridad | |

El 19 de septiembre de 1985, a las 7:19 de la mañana el suelo tembló por un minuto y medio en la Ciudad de México. Así fue que en ese instante mientras unos se levantaban y otros dormían, los edificios de la Ciudad de México cayeron encima de sus habitantes. En el sector más afectado, el centro de la ciudad, más del cincuenta por ciento (50%) de los edificios destruidos fueron casas y apartamentos.

Al día siguiente hubo otro temblor casi intenso. Más de 9.500 personas se murieron en el primer temblor y el segundo.

Al principio todo el mundo estaba paralizado. Pero poco a poco la gente se dio cuenta de la magnitud de la destrucción, y se organizaron brigadas de auxilio. El pánico y el horror del primer momento fueron reemplazados por la solidaridad de la gente que sobrevivió.

Algunos se dedicaron a recolectar ropa, comida y dinero para la gente que sufría de la destrucción. Esta ayuda entre vecinos (de lejos y cerca) continuó por varias semanas.

**¿Comprendiste?**

1. ¿Cuándo ocurrió el temblor en la Ciudad de México?
2. ¿Qué hacían los habitantes cuando empezó el temblor?
3. ¿Cómo reaccionó la gente al temblor y a los efectos?

**¿Qué piensas?**

1. ¿Sentiste los efectos de un temblor alguna vez? ¿Fueron suaves o fuertes los movimientos del terreno?
2. ¿Hubo algún desastre causado por la naturaleza en tu comunidad? ¿Qué pasó? ¿Cómo reaccionó la gente?

**Hazlo tú** 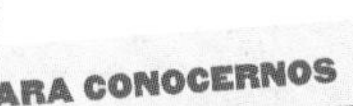

Muchas personas necesitaban ayuda durante el temblor de 1985. En grupos pequeños, presenten una situación en que unas personas necesitan la ayuda de otras personas que no conocen. ¿Qué pasó? ¿Qué van a hacer?

138 ciento treinta y ocho Unidad 2

ciento treinta y nueve Etapa 2 139

**¿Comprendiste?** asks students to recall the information in the selection.

"Teaching culture is a real challenge but so important. You have done more with culture than any other series that I have seen."

Deborah Hagen
Ionia High School
Ionia, MI

# En colores

## CULTURA Y COMPARACIONES

### PARA CONOCERNOS

**STRATEGY: CONNECTING CULTURES**

**Compare meals and mealtimes** Interview three people of different ages or backgrounds to find out at what time of day they eat their main meal and the name for that meal. Make a chart like the one here and then compare your answers.

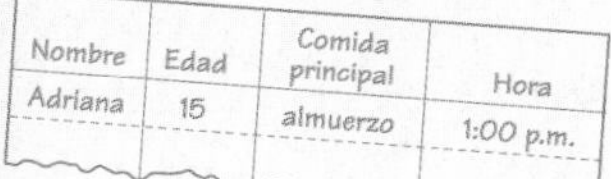

| Nombre | Edad | Comida principal | Hora |
|---|---|---|---|
| Adriana | 15 | almuerzo | 1:00 p.m. |

***La cochinita pibil,*** *puerco asado en una hoja de plátano y servido en tacos o tamales, es típico del sur de México.*

***Los chiles rellenos*** *de este tipo se vende mucho en Veracruz, una ciudad en el centro de México.*

***El mole negro*** *Puedes pedir mole negro, un platillo que incluye una salsa con más de 20 ingredientes, cuando visitas Oaxaca, una ciudad en el sur del país.*

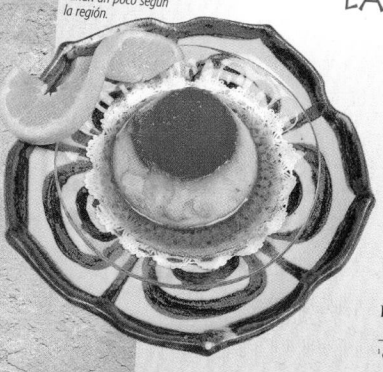

***El flan*** *es un postre que se ve por todo el país. Los ingredientes varían un poco según la región.*

# ¡BUEN PROVECHO!

## LA COMIDA MEXICANA

La cocina[1] mexicana es una de las más variadas del mundo. La mayor parte de platos mexicanos tienen su origen en el mundo precolombino, pero hay otros que son variantes de platos españoles. En Estados Unidos se comen algunos platos mexicanos típicos como los tacos, las enchiladas, el guacamole y la salsa picante.

La cocina mexicana es a base de maíz[2]. De la harina de maíz se hacen las tortillas, el equivalente mexicano del pan. Las tortillas son un elemento importante en muchas recetas. Otros alimentos importantes en México son el arroz, los frijoles, el chocolate, los chiles y los tomates.

En cuanto a[3] las costumbres de comida, lo que es tradicional en México es un desayuno y, generalmente alrededor de las dos de la tarde, un almuerzo fuerte (la comida principal del día) que se llama *la comida*. Típicamente, la cena es ligera[4], como un yogur o un sándwich.

[1] cuisine [2] corn

[3] as for [4] light

### ¿Comprendiste?

1. ¿Qué orígenes tiene la comida mexicana?
2. ¿Qué platos mexicanos se comen en Estados Unidos?
3. ¿Cuál es el alimento básico en México?
4. Describe las tres comidas del día en México.

### ¿Qué piensas?

1. ¿Cuáles son los alimentos que se usan en más de un plato?
2. ¿Por qué crees que algunos platos mexicanos son de origen precolombino y otros de origen español?

### Hazlo tú

Con unos(as) compañeros(as), busquen unas recetas mexicanas. Estúdienlas para ver cuáles pueden hacer en Estados Unidos. Escojan una, háganla y preséntensela a la clase. Sírvanles el plato a sus compañeros(as), contándoles de qué región viene y cómo se hace. ¡Buen provecho!

162 ciento sesenta y dos
Unidad 2

ciento sesenta y tres
Etapa 3 163

- **¿Qué piensas?** helps students to think critically about the target culture as well as their own culture.
- **Hazlo tú** offers an expansion activity for students to try out the new cultural concepts.

MOTIVATE TO COMMUNICATE
¡En español!

# Follow up with diagnostic review

The comprehensive review, correlated to the etapa objectives, thoroughly reviews and prepares the students to be successful for assessment.

**The side column learning channel** helps students self-diagnose and review what they can do and where they can go to get help.

## En uso

### REPASO Y MÁS COMUNICACIÓN

**OBJECTIVES**
- Order in a restaurant
- Ask for and pay a restaurant bill
- Talk about things to do in the city

*Now you can...*
- order in a restaurant.

*To review*
- direct object pronouns, see p. 152.

**ACTIVIDAD 1 ¿Me ayudas?**

Estás comiendo en un restaurante con un niño pequeño. Explícale cómo comer las siguientes cosas. *(Hint: Tell a child how to eat the different foods.)*

**modelo**
*¿Cerezas o tomate?*
*¿Los tacos? Puedes comerlos con tomate.*

1. ¿El cuchillo o la cuchara?
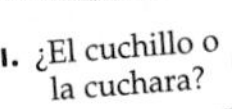
2. ¿Sal o azúcar?

3. ¿La cuchara o las manos?

4. ¿Las manos o el tenedor?

5. ¿Mantequilla o mantequilla de cacahuate?

6. ¿Aceite o harina?

*Now you can...*
- talk about things to do in the city.

*To review*
- indirect object pronouns, see p. 154.
- verbs similar to **gustar,** see p. 155.

**ACTIVIDAD 2 ¡Vamos al centro!**

Todos están hablando de actividades en la ciudad. ¿Qué dicen? *(Hint: Tell people's opinions of city activities.)*

**modelo**
*Juan y yo (interesar) visitar los museos*
*A Juan y a mí nos interesa visitar los museos.*

1. mis padres (encantar) las galerías de arte
2. yo (gustar) los actores mexicanos
3. tú (importar) ver los estrenos
4. nosotros (molestar) pagar los precios de los boletos
5. Tomás y Berta (fascinar) las obras de teatro
6. ustedes (faltar) dinero para salir



*Now you can...*
- order in a restaurant.

*To review*
- indirect object pronouns, see p. 154.
- double object pronouns, see p. 157.

**ACTIVIDAD 3 ¿Qué nos recomienda?**

Raúl y sus amigos piden la comida en un restaurante mexicano. ¿Qué les recomiendan los meseros? ¿Cómo se lo van a servir? *(Hint: Tell what the waiters recommend and how it will be served.)*

**modelo**
*María: la sopa (una torta)*
*Le recomiendan la sopa. Van a servírsela con una torta.*

1. nosotros: los tacos (salsa picante)
2. yo: el pescado (cebolla)
3. Gabriel: las verduras (sal y pimienta)
4. Salvador y yo: el melón (azúcar)
5. tú: el pollo (tortillas)
6. ustedes: la carne de res (frijoles)
7. yo: las papas asadas (mantequilla)
8. Alex y Sandra: la pasta (queso)

*Now you can...*
- order in a restaurant.
- ask for and pay a restaurant bill.

*To review*
- double object pronouns, see p. 157.

**ACTIVIDAD 4 ¿Qué desean?**

Imagínate que trabajas en un restaurante como mesero(a). Contesta que sí a las preguntas de los clientes. *(Hint: You are a waiter or waitress at a restaurant. Answer yes to the customers' questions.)*

**modelo**
*¿Me trae unos cubiertos, por favor?*
*Sí, se los traigo.*

1. ¿Me trae el menú, por favor?
2. ¿Nos recomienda las enchiladas?
3. ¿Le sirve un café a mi esposa, por favor?
4. ¿Nos trae más pan, por favor?
5. ¿Les sirve más limonada a mis hijos, por favor?
6. ¿Me trae la cuenta, por favor?
7. ¿Le doy la tarjeta de crédito a usted?
8. ¿Le dejo la propina en la mesa?

**Speaking strategies** help students become better communicators by expanding their repertoire of expressions through tone of voice, personalization, gestures, etc.

**En tu propia voz** prompts students with a short writing assignment to sharpen their language skills.

"I like the fact that there seems to be a good balance between activities that practice new structures and then progress to activities that require more creative uses of language in communicative situations."

Vickie Mike
Horseheads High School
Horseheads, NY

ACTIVIDAD 5 **¿Me pasas...?**

**PARA CONVERSAR**

STRATEGY: SPEAKING

**Resolve misconceptions** Your partner may ask for something you don't have. To resolve the misunderstanding, offer what you do have: **No tengo X, pero puedo pasarte Y.**

Estás comiendo en un restaurante con tu amigo(a). Dibuja cuatro cosas, comidas o cubiertos, en papeles separados. Entonces, pídeselas a tu amigo(a). *(Hint: You and a partner draw restaurant items and ask each other for them.)*

modelo

**Tú:** *Las cerezas... ¿me las pasas, por favor?*

**Amigo(a):** *¡Cómo no! Te las paso en seguida.*

ACTIVIDAD 6 **¡Problemas!**

Tú y dos compañeros(as) están en un restaurante. Una persona hace el papel del (de la) mesero(a) y las otras hacen el papel de los clientes. El (La) pobre mesero(a) tiene problemas porque un cliente lo critica todo y el otro le hace muchas preguntas. *(Hint: A server is trying to please two difficult customers. Act out the scene.)*

ACTIVIDAD 7 **En tu propia voz**

**ESCRITURA** Imagínate que estás de vacaciones con tu familia. Escríbele una tarjeta postal a un(a) amigo(a). Incluye las reacciones de varios miembros de la familia a cinco actividades que hicieron durante el viaje. *(Hint: Write a postcard describing a vacation.)*

México
XOCHIMILCO
Querida Sonia:
Me gusta mucho México. Me fascinan los museos pero a mamá no le gusta visitarlos. Prefiere ir al teatro. Le encantan las obras musicales. Los cantantes mexicanos son muy buenos.
¡Saludos!
—Catarina
Sonia Díaz
2 Main St.
Rye, NY 01580
U.S.A.

**TÚ EN LA COMUNIDAD**

**Sharon** es una estudiante de Massachusetts. Cuando estaba trabajando de consejera (*counselor*) en un campamento, hablaba español con algunos niños que no podían expresarse en inglés. También habla español con parientes, amigos y gente de la comunidad. ¿Con quién practicas el español?

# En resumen

## REPASO DE VOCABULARIO

### ORDER IN A RESTAURANT

**At the Restaurant**

| | |
|---|---|
| el aceite | *oil* |
| la carne de res | *beef* |
| las cebollas | *onions* |
| las cerezas | *cherries* |
| los cubiertos | *silverware* |
| los frijoles | *beans* |
| la harina | *flour* |
| el mantel | *tablecloth* |
| las manzanas | *apples* |
| el pan | *bread* |
| las papas | *potatoes* |
| la pasta | *pasta* |
| las peras | *pears* |
| el pescado | *fish* |
| la pimienta | *pepper* |
| la sal | *salt* |
| las salchichas | *hot dogs, sausages* |
| la servilleta | *napkin* |
| el taco | *taco* |
| la taquería | *taco restaurant* |
| los tomates | *tomatoes* |
| la torta | *sandwich* |
| las verduras | *vegetables* |
| las zanahorias | *carrots* |

**Common Expressions**

| | |
|---|---|
| ¿Qué desea(n)? | *What would you like?* |
| ¿Qué me (nos) recomienda? | *What do you recommend?* |
| ¡Salud! | *Cheers!* |
| ¿Se le(s) ofrece algo más? | *May I offer you anything more?* |

### ASK FOR/PAY A RESTAURANT BILL

| | |
|---|---|
| la cuenta | *bill* |
| dejar la propina | *to leave the tip* |

### THINGS TO DO IN THE CITY

**People**

| | |
|---|---|
| el actor | *actor* |
| la actriz | *actress* |
| el (la) cantante | *singer* |
| el (la) comediante | *comedian* |

**Activities and Events**

| | |
|---|---|
| las aventuras | *adventures* |
| la ciencia ficción | *science fiction* |
| la comedia | *comedy* |
| dar una vuelta | *to take a walk, stroll, or ride* |
| la escena | *scene* |
| el estreno | *new release* |
| el horror | *horror* |
| el musical | *musical* |
| la obra de teatro | *theatrical production* |
| romántico(a) | *romantic* |
| la serie | *series* |
| la telenovela | *soap opera* |
| el tema | *theme, subject* |

### OTHER WORDS AND PHRASES

| | |
|---|---|
| bastante | *enough* |
| cenar | *to eat dinner* |
| demasiado(a) | *too much* |
| llenar | *to fill* |
| lleno(a) | *full* |
| mojado(a) | *wet* |
| ofrecer | *to offer* |
| el papel | *role* |
| seco(a) | *dry* |
| vacío(a) | *empty* |

**Verbs Similar to *gustar***

| | |
|---|---|
| encantar | *to delight* |
| faltar | *to lack* |
| fascinar | *to fascinate, to love (sports, food, etc.)* |
| importar | *to be important to, to matter* |
| interesar | *to interest* |
| molestar | *to bother* |

**Juego**

**¿Qué soy yo?**

Puedo ser feliz o triste, y tal vez romántica. Te puedo llevar a muchos lugares. Alguien me escribió y otros me presentan. Necesito personas que se ven, personas que no se ven y personas que ven para salir bien. Tal vez necesitas boletos para verme. ¿Qué soy yo?



**Tú en la comunidad,** which occurs once in every unit, features real students using Spanish in their own community.

# Cultivate better writers through the writing process

The writing process at the end of each unit works as a tutor-in-the-book to teach students how to improve their writing step by step.

**Writing strategies** offer students new methods for improving writing skills.

**Student models** show students what to watch out for and how the assignment is supposed to look.

UNIDAD 2

## En tu propia voz

ESCRITURA

### Escribe un cuento

The Spanish classes at your school were invited to write and illustrate children's picture books in Spanish for local elementary schools. Write a short story that would appeal to young children.

**Purpose:** Provide books in Spanish for local children
**Audience:** Elementary schoolchildren
**Subject:** Story writing
**Structure:** Picture book

**PARA ESCRIBIR • STRATEGY: WRITING**

**Develop your story** An interesting, well-planned story will hold your reader's attention. Remember to thoroughly develop your ideas for characters and plot.

### Modelo del estudiante

Había una vez una granja pequeña en México. En la granja vivía un cerdito pequeño, Quique. Quique era muy amable: obediente, sociable y animado. Le gustaba contar chistes y jugar con los otros animales.

The writer tells where the story takes place.

The writer describes the main character of the story.

El día de su cumpleaños empezó muy mal para Quique. Se levantó tarde por la mañana y no había más desayuno. –No hay problema –dijo Quique–. Voy a celebrar con mis amigos.

Entonces, salió del corral en busca de los otros animales, pero no había nadie por ninguna parte. El pobre cerdito estaba muy triste.

The story contains a series of events that make up the plot.

Quique regresó al corral, solito. De repente, todos sus amigos saltaron de los rincones del corral y gritaron: –¡Feliz cumpleaños, Quiquito!

–¡Qué sorpresa! –exclamó Quique alegremente. Luego todos los animales celebraron con una fiesta magnífica y Quique rompió la piñata.

The story has a happy ending.

168 ciento sesenta y ocho
**Unidad 2**

"All the pieces are there for a good text that will bring us to the 21st century."

Janet Wohlers
Weston Middle School
Weston, MA

## …ategias para escribir

**…es de escribir…**
…ood children's story contains a …ing (time, place), a few characters, … a basic plot (series of events). … action of the story moves along …ckly, usually toward a happy …ding. Before you write, create a story …p like this one to plan and organize …ur ideas.

| | |
|---|---|
| Personaje central: | un pato tímido |
| Lugar: | un río de Nueva York |
| Situación: | El pato no sabía nadar. No podía ir de vacaciones con la familia. |
| Lo que pasa: | 1. Consultó con otros.<br>2. Miraba a sus hermanos.<br>3. Practicaba cada mañana.<br>4.<br>5. |
| Fin: | Aprendió a nadar. |

**…evisiones**
…hare your draft with a partner. …hen ask

- *Do the characters' words and actions make sense?*
- *Is there a real problem or situation that moves the story along?*
- *Does the story come to a natural or interesting stopping point?*

…Revise your draft based on your partner's answers.

**La versión final**
Before you create the final draft of your story, check your writing and use proofreading symbols (p. 97) to correct any errors you find. Look over your work with the following questions in mind:

- *Did I use the preterite in the right places?*

**Try this:** Find each preterite form and make sure it refers to a completed action in the past. If not, change to the imperfect.

- *Did I use the imperfect correctly?*

**Try this:** Locate each imperfect form. Does each refer to an ongoing action or description in the past? If not, change to the preterite.

Cerca de un río de Nueva York vivía un pato tímido con su familia. Todos los días el pato Danilo miraba las nubes o corrió de un lugar a otro. Sus hermanos siempre jugaron en el río, pero Danilo no. Un día los padres llamó a sus hijos y les dicieron sus planes para ir de vacaciones.

Share your writing on www.mcdougallittell.com

ciento sesenta y nueve **Unidad 2** 169

The Internet connection will offer more writing support. The best written submissions will be posted on the McDougal Littell website.

# Implement ideas and lesson plans easily and effectively

CREATIVE AND PRACTICAL

The Ampliación and Etapa Overview in the Teacher's Edition offer outstanding support to make teaching Spanish adaptable to every situation.

**Ampliación** features multi-modal activities that spark students' excitement with new ways to learn language and culture.

UNIDAD 2
**Projects, Games, Crafts**

Planning Ahead...

## Ampliación

These activities may be used at various points in the Unit 2 sequence.

For Block Schedule, you may find that these projects will provide a welcome change of pace while reviewing and reinforcing the material presented in the unit. See the Block Schedule Copymasters.

### PROJECTS

**Create birthday greeting cards** in Spanish. Have students decorate the card's cover and write a birthday greeting inside in Spanish. You can display the birthday cards on a bulletin board or sell them to raise money to benefit the Spanish Club or for a class **fiesta**.

PACING SUGGESTION: Upon completion of Etapa 2.

**Film or record an audiovisual guide** for eating in a Mexican restaurant. Divide the class into groups and assign each group a dialog topic which illustrates special dining tips (e.g., how to read a menu, how to order, how to eat a taco, how to pay the bill, etc.). Encourage creativity and humor.

PACING SUGGESTION: Upon completion of Etapa 3.

### STORYTELLING

**El cumpleaños de la abuela** After reviewing the vocabulary on family and holiday celebrations, model a mini-story (using student actors or pictures from the text) that students will revise, retell, and expand:

> La semana pasada celebraron el cumpleaños de la abuela de Isabel. Isabel le contó a Ricardo los detalles de la fiesta. Ricardo preguntó, «¿Cuántos años tiene su abuela?» Isabel respondió, «Cumplió setenta años». Ricardo preguntó, «¿Cuántas personas estaban en la fiesta?» e Isabel contestó, «Más de 25 personas: todos mis primos, mis tíos, mi abuelo, mis hermanos y mis padres. Somos una familia grande». Y luego Isabel le contó qué hicieron en la fiesta...

As you give your model, be sure to pause as the story is being told so that students may fill in words and act out gestures. Students should then write, narrate, and read aloud a longer main story. This new version should include vocabulary from **Unidad 2**. Students can write, illustrate, and act out additional new stories based on this storytelling experience.

**Vamos a dar una fiesta** Ask students to tell a story about planning their own celebration (birthday, graduation, etc.). They may plan the activities, the refreshments, and the guest list.

PACING SUGGESTION: Upon completion of Etapa 2.

### BULLETIN BOARDS / POSTERS

**Bulletin board Plan ahead:** Have students bring in photos of their family members or friends (or an imaginary family) and write a short description in Spanish. Display the captioned photos on the bulletin board.

**Posters Have students create • Family trees** on a poster • **Menu** for a Mexican restaurant • **Mexican restaurant** advertisement poster • **Calendar** with months' illustrations and important dates pertaining to Mexico • **Recipe calendar** with a different illustration and recipe for each month

99A Projects, Games, Crafts • UNIDAD 2

UNIDAD 2
**Projects, Games, Crafts**

### GAMES

**Había una vez...**
Have students form a circle. Taking turns, each student will contribute a part of an ongoing story in the past tense. The teacher can start with **"Había una vez dos muchachos...,"** the next student might add **"que fueron a una fiesta,"** and so on. Encourage students to be as creative and humorous as possible. You may want to stick close to the chapter vocabulary and practice using verbs in the preterite and imperfect tenses.

PACING SUGGESTION: Upon completion of Etapa 2.

### HANDS-ON CRAFTS

Work with the art department to create a **piñata** out of *papier maché*. Prepare ahead: Newspapers torn in strips, flour and water to make a paste, a balloon to make a mold for the **piñata**, and paints or colored paper to decorate it. Have students dip the newspaper strips in the flour paste and wrap them around the balloon in criss-cross layers to make the desired shape. After the shape is completely dry, students can decorate the **piñata** with paints or colored paper and streamers. You may also find **piñatas** already made at a local party store. Have students bring in small toys or candies to help fill the **piñata** and bring it to a class **fiesta**.

Como Hecha en Casa
COMIDA MEXICANA
Mariachis de Jueves a Domingo

### MUSIC

**Mariachi** music is native to Mexico. A **mariachi** band consists of strolling musicians who play guitars, violins, and trumpets, and sing. Some believe that the origin of the word **mariachi** came from the French word for "marriage" since Mexican folk bands used to play at parties during the days of Maximillian, a Frenchman who was emperor of Mexico in the 19th century. Others believe "mariachi" comes from a pre-Hispanic word.

*Canciones de mi padre* is a collection of some typical mariachi music by Linda Ronstadt. (Linda Ronstadt, *Canciones de mi padre* © 1987 Elektra/Asylum Records.) Have students learn the words to a song, such as "Las mañanitas" (Song 9). Other songs from Mexico are available on the the *Canciones* Cassette/CD.

### RECIPE

**Tacos** You can create a "Make-your-own-taco" feast for your class. To make it easier to prepare and serve these tacos in class, use a black bean and salsa mixture for the main ingredient, instead of spiced chicken or meat. Use taco shells or flour tortillas for soft tacos.

Although this is an easy recipe, this will be the first time that students actually learn the Spanish words for the ingredients. As an ongoing project students can prepare bilingual recipe cards with the Spanish version on the front and the English translation on the back.

## Receta

**Tacos**
*1 lata de frijoles*
*2 tazas de salsa picante*
*1 cebolla picada*
*2 tomates cortados en pedazos pequeños*
*lechuga cortada en pedazos pequeños*
*1 taza de queso rallado (Cheddar o Monterey Jack)*
*tortillas*
*Opcional: guacamole, pollo (o carne) picado y sazonado*

*Mezcle los frijoles con 1/2 taza de salsa picante (o más, a su gusto). Ponga la mezcla en un plato hondo. Prepare los otros ingredientes (la cebolla, los tomates, la lechuga, el queso rallado y el resto de la salsa), póngalos en distintos platos hondos y colóquelos en una mesa. Cada persona puede crear su propio taco con los ingredientes que hay en la mesa.*

Projects, Games, Crafts • UNIDAD 2 99B

**Easy-to-prepare recipes** give students a delicious opportunity to experience new cultural cuisines.

"WOW! ¡En español! has it all. I'd love to teach from this book."

Kathleen Gliewe
Helena Middle School
Helena, MT

**At-a-glance overview** outlines the objectives, strategies, and program resources for time-saving support.

UNIDAD 2 ETAPA 3 HOY EN LA CIUDAD

pages 144–167

# *Planning Guide* CLASSROOM MANAGEMENT

## OBJECTIVES

**Communication**
- Order in a restaurant *pp. 146–147, 148–149*
- Ask for and pay a restaurant bill *pp. 147, 148–149*
- Talk about things to do in the city *pp. 146–147*

**Grammar**
- Verbs similar to **gustar** *p. 155*
- Double object pronouns *p. 157*

**Culture**
- **El baile folklórico** *p. 151*
- **El Palacio de Bellas Artes** *p. 152*
- **Las telenovelas** *p. 156*
- **Teotihuacán** *pp. 160–161*
- **La comida mexicana** *pp. 162–163*

**Recycling**
- Direct object pronouns *p. 152*
- Indirect object pronouns *p. 154*
- Preterite and imperfect *p. 151*
- The verb **gustar** *p. 155*
- Double object pronouns *p. 157*

## STRATEGIES

**Listening Strategies**
- Listen for useful expressions *p. 148*

**Speaking Strategies**
- Personalize responses *p. 156*
- Resolve misconceptions *p. 166*

**Reading Strategies**
- Identify gaps in knowledge *p. 160*
- Summarize important information *TE p. 163*

**Writing Strategies**
- Organize information chronologically and by category *Actividad 7, TE p. 167*
- Develop your story *pp. 168–169*

**Connecting Cultures Strategies**
- Compare meals and mealtimes *p. 162*
- Learn about dance traditions in Mexico *TE pp. 151–152*
- Compare **Teotihuacán** and early settlements in the U.S. *TE p. 161*

## PROGRAM RESOURCES

### Print
- *Más práctica* Workbook PE *pp. 57–64*
- Block Scheduling Copymasters *pp. 49–56*
- Unit 2 Resource Book
  - *Más práctica* Workbook TE *pp. 103–110*
  - *Cuaderno para hispanohablantes* TE *pp. 111–118*
  - Information Gap Activities *pp. 119–122*
  - Family Involvement *pp. 123–124*
  - Video Activities *pp. 125–127*
  - Videoscript *pp. 128–129*
  - Audioscript *pp. 130–134*
  - Assessment Program Unit 2 Etapa 3 *pp. 135–153; 154–169; 170–178*
  - Answer Keys *pp. 179–183*

### Audiovisual
- Audio Program Cassette 6A, 6B / CD 6
- *Canciones* Cassette/CD
- Video Program Videotape 2 / Videodisc 2A
- Overhead Transparencies M1, M2; GO1–GO5; 59–68

### Technology
- Electronic Teacher Tools/Test Generator
- *Intrigas y aventuras* CD-ROM, Disc 1
- www.mcdougallittell.com

### Assessment Program Options
- Cooperative Quizzes (Unit 2 Resource Book)
- Etapa Exam Forms A and B (Unit 2 Resource Book)
- *Examen para hispanohablantes* (Unit 2 Resource Book)
- Portfolio Assessment (Unit 2 Resource Book)
- Unit 2 Comprehensive Test (Unit 2 Resource Book)
- *Prueba comprensiva para hispanohablantes,* **Unit 2** (Unit 2 Resource Book)
- Multiple Choice Test Questions (Unit 2 Resource Book)
- Audio Program Cassette 19A, 19B / CD 19
- Electronic Teacher Tools/Test Generator

### Native Speakers
- *Cuaderno para hispanohablantes* PE *pp. 57–64*
- *Cuaderno para hispanohablantes* TE (Unit 2 Resource Book)
- *Examen para hispanohablantes* (Unit 2 Resource Book)
- *Prueba comprensiva para hispanohablantes,* **Unit 2** (Unit 2 Resource Book)
- Audio Program *(Para hispanohablantes)* Cassettes 6B, 19 / CD 6, CD 19
- Audioscript (Unit 2 Resource Book)

143A Planning Guide • UNIDAD 2 Etapa 3

# *Student Text Listening Activity Scripts*

Laura | Isabel | Mesero

### Videoscript: Diálogo *pages 148–149*

- Videotape 2, 25:37 • Videodisc 2A
  Search Chapter 2, Play to 3. U2E3, En vivo (Dialog)
- Use the videoscript with **Actividades 1, 2** *page 150*

Isabel: Éste es mi restaurante favorito, Laura. Sirven la mejor comida mexicana de toda la ciudad.
Laura: A mí me encanta la comida mexicana... pero hay algunos platillos en el menú que no conozco.
Isabel: ¿Cómo qué? Yo te explico.
Laura: ¿Qué son los chilaquiles?
Isabel: Bueno, los chilaquiles... aquí los preparan con tortillas fritas, salsa verde, queso blanco, pollo... Te los recomiendo. Son riquísimos.
Laura: Es que no tengo mucha hambre. Prefiero algo ligero, tal vez una torta o unos tacos al carbón.
Isabel: Si quieres tacos, vamos mañana a una taquería que está cerca de mi casa. Sirven los mejores tacos del mundo.
Mesero: ¿Qué desean comer?
Laura: Para mí, una torta de pollo con guacamole. Y también me trae frijoles. Gracias.
Isabel: ¿Qué me recomienda hoy, las enchiladas o los tamales de mole?
Mesero: Los tamales de mole están deliciosos hoy. Se los recomiendo.
Isabel: Muy bien, entonces, ¿me los trae, por favor?
Mesero: Sí, cómo no. ¿Y qué les traigo de tomar?
Laura: Para mí, un agua de fruta ¿Qué aguas tiene?
Mesero: Hoy tenemos agua de melón, de papaya, y de sandía.
Laura: Un agua de sandía, por favor.
Mesero: ¿Y para Ud., señorita?
Isabel: Para mí, una botella de agua, gracias.
Mesero: Sí, cómo no.
Isabel: Ah, y señor, a mí me faltan unos cubiertos y una servilleta.
Mesero: En un momento.
Isabel: Así que por fin pasó la lluvia en Atlanta y pudiste salir. ¿Cuánto tiempo esperaste en el aeropuerto?
Laura: Ay, fue horrible. Esperé cuatro horas. Y después cancelaron el vuelo y fui a un hotel. Por eso no pude salir anoche. Tuve que esperar hasta esta mañana.
Isabel: Bueno, ahora estás aquí. Más vale tarde que nunca, ¿verdad?
Laura: Sí, pero sentí mucho no estar contigo para la entrevista con don Miguel. ¿Cómo estuvo?
Isabel: Ay, todo salió muy bien. Creo que vas a estar muy contenta.
Mesero: ¿Se les ofrece algo más?
Isabel: No, gracias, nada más. Nos trae la cuenta, por favor.
Mesero: Sí, cómo no. Se la traigo en seguida.
Isabel: Bueno, Laura, ¿qué te interesa hacer aquí en la Ciudad de México? Debemos hacer algo divertido mañana.
Laura: A ver... sabes, me fascina el teatro. Podemos ir a una obra de teatro. ¿Qué te parece?
Isabel: ¡Sí! Hay una nueva obra musical. Me gustaría mucho verla. La cantante que tiene el papel principal es extraordinaria.
Laura: Pues, me parece excelente. Podemos ir a comprar los boletos esta tarde. Y podemos también dar una vuelta por la ciudad, ¿no? Me interesa ver más de la Ciudad de México.
Mesero: Aquí tienen la cuenta. Muchas gracias.
Laura: A usted. No, Isa. Yo voy a pagarla.
Isabel: ¿Seguro? Bueno, muchísimas gracias, Laura.
Laura: De nada, Isabel. Gracias a ti por hacer la entrevista ayer. Oye, quiero dejarle una buena propina. El mesero fue muy amable. ¿Cuánto dejo?
Isabel: A ver... ¿cuánto fue?

### Actividad 8 ¡A comer! *page 154*

Isabel: ¿Qué vas a pedir tú, Laura?
Laura: Yo quiero una torta de pollo y unos frijoles.
Isabel: Yo creo que voy a pedir los tamales de mole.
Mesero: Buenas tardes, señoritas. Para empezar, les traigo unas tortillas con guacamole.
Laura: Gracias.
Mesero: ¿Desean algo de tomar?
Isabel: Por favor, sólo agua para mí. ¿Y tú, Laura?
Laura: Agua de sandía, por favor.
Mesero: ¿Y qué desean comer?
Laura: Primero tú, Isabel.
Isabel: Bueno. Los tamales de mole, por favor.
Laura: Y para mí, la torta de pollo y unos frijoles, por favor.
Mesero: Muy bien.

### Actividad 16 Las recomendaciones *page 159*

1. El estreno que vi es horrible. Me molesta la violencia y los actores no me convencen.
2. Siempre me fascinan las aventuras. La acción es muy emocionante, por eso las aventuras me interesan mucho.
3. Es la mejor obra de teatro del año. Me encantan los musicales. Los cantantes me parecen fenomenales. Ustedes deben verla.
4. Los comediantes son cómicos... sí, muy cómicos. No me importa el precio del boleto porque vale el dinero. Nos reímos toda la noche. ¡Qué divertido!
5. El drama me pareció aburrido. No me interesó. Es que le faltaba un buen tema.

### Quick Start Review Answers

**p. 148** Ordinal numbers
Primero, tienes que poner los cubiertos y las... Segundo, ...traer el menú. Tercero, debes preguntar, «¿Qué desean comer?» Cuarto, recomiendas la especialidad... Quinto, debes servir la comida. Sexto, debes preguntar, «¿Se les ofrece...» Séptimo, ... traer la cuenta.

**p. 152** Direct objects
1. el menú
2. los chilaquiles con pollo y salsa verde
3. las servilletas
4. la cuenta
5. una propina

**p. 154** Direct object pronouns
1. Sí, (No, no) la traje.
2. Sí, (No, no) la hice.
3. Sí, (No, no) lo tengo.
4. Sí, (No, no) lo puedes usar.
5. Sí, (No, no) lo comí.

**p. 156** Indirect object pronouns
1. Le compré los casetes.
2. Le compré la torta.
3. Te compré el boleto.
4. Les compré la pintura.
5. Me compré una rosa.

**p. 158** Present progressive
1. Sí, estoy poniéndolos.
2. Sí, estoy sacándolos.
3. Sí, estoy lavándolos.
4. Sí, estoy abriéndola.

**p. 160** Countries
Stonehenge/Inglaterra
Machu Picchu/Perú
Chichén-Itzá/México
Pompeya/Italia

**p. 164** Direct object pronouns
1. Sí, la compré.
2. Sí, lo compré.
3. Sí, las compré.
4. Sí, lo compré.
5. Sí, la compré.
6. Sí, las compré.

Listening Scripts • UNIDAD 2 Etapa 3 143B

**Listening scripts** in the Teacher's Edition provide practical information needed for easier lesson preparation.

# Suggests practical teaching ideas for lesson planning

FLEXIBLE · AND · EXCEPTIONAL ·

The comprehensive Teacher's Edition and resource materials provide the support you need to introduce, explain, and expand your lessons.

- **Time-saving lesson plans** present sequenced teaching suggestions and ideas.

UNIDAD 2 ETAPA 3 **Pacing Guide**

## Sample Lesson Plan - 50 Minute Schedule

**DAY 1**

***Etapa* Opener**
- Quick Start Review (TE, p. 144). 5 MIN.
- Have students look at the *Etapa* opener and answer questions. 5 MIN.

**En contexto: Vocabulario**
- Quick Start Review (TE, p. 146). 5 MIN.
- Discuss picture, have students use context and pictures to learn *Etapa* vocabulary. Answer questions, TE p. 147. 10 MIN.

**En vivo: Diálogo**
- Quick Start Review (TE, p. 148). 5 MIN.
- Review Listening Strategy, p. 148. Play audio or show video for the dialog shown on pp. 148–149. 5 MIN.
- Replay twice. Read aloud, students taking on roles of characters. 10 MIN.
- Students role-play in groups while looking at the photos in their texts. Encourage them to come up with logical dialog using familiar vocabulary. 5 MIN.

**Homework Option**
- Video Activities, Unit 2 Resource Book, pp. 125–127.

**DAY 2**

**En acción: Vocabulario y gramática**
- Check homework. 5 MIN.
- Quick Start Review (TE, p. 150). 5 MIN.
- Ask students for a summary of *En vivo* dialog to check recall. 5 MIN.
- Replay the *En vivo* dialog using the audiovisual resources and have students do *Actividades* 1 and 2 orally. 10 MIN.
- Have students complete *Actividades* 3 and 4, then *Actividad* 5 in pairs. 10 MIN.
- Use a game or expansion activity (TE, pp. 150–151) to reinforce retention of vocabulary and dialog structures. 10 MIN.
- Review *Nota cultural,* p. 152. 5 MIN.

**Homework Option**
- *Más práctica* Workbook, pp. 57–60 as needed. *Cuaderno para hispanohablantes*, pp. 57–59 as needed.

**DAY 3**

**En acción (cont.)**
- Check homework. 5 MIN.
- Quick Start Review (TE, p. 152). 5 MIN.
- Present *Gramática:* Direct Object Pronouns, p. 152. 10 MIN.
- Review the vocabulary in the box on p. 153. 5 MIN.
- Have students do *Actividades* 6 and 7 in pairs. 15 MIN.
- Play the audio and do *Actividad* 8 orally. Students can also write their summary. 10 MIN.

**Homework Option**
- Have students complete *Actividades* 6 and 7 in writing. *Más práctica* Workbook, p. 161.

**DAY 4**

**En acción (cont.)**
- Check homework. 5 MIN.
- Quick Start Review (TE, p. 154). 5 MIN.
- Present *Gramática*: Indirect Object Pronouns and *Vocabulario* on p. 154–155. 10 MIN.
- Have students do *Actividades* 9 and 10. 10 MIN.
- Present *Vocabulario* and Speaking Strategy, p. 156. Have students complete *Actividad* 11 in pairs. 10 MIN.
- Have students do *Actividad* 12 in class by interviewing 5 classmates. 10 MIN.

**Homework Option**
- Have students do *Actividad* 15 in writing. *Más práctica* Workbook, p. 62. *Cuaderno para hispanohablantes*, p. 60.

**DAY 5**

**En acción (cont.)**
- Check homework. 5 MIN.
- Quick Start Review (TE, p. 156). 5 MIN.
- Present *Gramática:* Double Object Pronouns. 10 MIN.
- Have students complete *Actividades* 13 and 14 orally. 10 MIN.
- Play audio for students and do *Actividad* 16 orally with the whole class. 10 MIN.
- Have students complete *Actividad* 17 in small groups. 10 MIN.

**Homework Option**
- Have students do *Actividad* 15, p. 159.
- *Más práctica* Workbook, pp. 63–64. *Cuaderno para hispanohablantes*, pp. 61–62.

**DAY 6**

**En voces: Lectura**
- Check homework. 5 MIN.
- Quick Start Review (TE, p. 160). 5 MIN.
- Review Reading Strategy, p. 160, and have students read silently. 5 MIN.
- Have students read *Teotihuacán: Ciudad misteriosa* aloud taking turns. 10 MIN.
- Call on volunteers to answer *¿Comprendiste?* questions and start answering *¿Qué piensas?* questions. 10 MIN.

**En uso: Repaso y más comunicación**
- Quick Start Review (TE, p. 164). 5 MIN.
- Complete *Actividades* 1–4 in writing, pp. 164–165. 10 MIN.

**Homework Option**
- Finish answering *¿Qué piensas?* questions, p. 161.
- Review for *Etapa* 3 exam.

**DAY 7**

**En uso: Repaso y más comunicación**
- Check homework and review grammar questions as necessary. 10 MIN.
- Review Speaking Strategy, p. 166. Then do *Actividad* 5 in pairs and *Actividad* 6 in groups. 10 MIN.
- Complete *Etapa 3* Exam 20 MIN.
- Begin *Actividad* 7 writing activity. 10 MIN.

**Homework Option**
- Finish *Actividad* 7. Review for Unit 2 Exam.

**DAY 8**

**En colores: Cultura y comparaciones**
- Review Connecting Cultures Strategy, p. 162. 3 MIN.
- Read *¡Buen provecho! La comida mexicana* aloud with students. 7 MIN.
- Answer *¿Comprendiste?* and *¿Qué piensas?* questions orally. 5 MIN.
- Review grammar questions as needed for Unit 2. 5 MIN.
- Complete Unit 2 Exam. 30 MIN.

**Homework Option**
- Complete *En tu propia voz,* pp. 168–16

143C Pacing Guide • UNIDAD 2 Etapa 3

"There is a step-by-step sequence. The whole unit is structured around a topic and each etapa contributes meaningful elements to the whole."

M. Mercedes Stephenson
Hazelwood Central High School
Florissant, MO

**Block Scheduling Lesson Plans** offer options for pacing and variety.

## ample Lesson Plan - Block Schedule (90 mi

**DAY 1**

***tapa Opener***
Quick Start Review (TE, p. 144). 5 MIN.
Have students look at the *Etapa* Opener and answer questions. 10 MIN.

***En contexto: Vocabulario***
- Quick Start Review (TE, p. 146). 5 MIN.
- Discuss photos, have students use context and photos to learn *Etapa* vocabulary. Answer questions, p. 147. 10 MIN.

***En vivo: Diálogo***
- Quick Start Review (TE, p. 148). 5 MIN.
- Review Listening Strategy, p. 148. Play audio or show video for the dialog shown on pp. 148–149. 5 MIN.
- Ask Comprehension Questions (TE, p. 149). 5 MIN.
- Replay twice. Read aloud. Students take roles of characters. 10 MIN.
- Students role-play in groups while looking at the photos in their texts. 5 MIN.
- Use Block Scheduling Copymasters for variety. 5 MIN.

***En acción: Vocabulario y gramática***
- Quick Start Review (TE, p. 150). 5 MIN.
- Have students do *Actividades* 1 and 2 orally. 10 MIN.
- Have students complete *Actividades* 3, 4, and 5 in pairs. 10 MIN.

***Homework Option***
- Video Activities, Unit 2 Resource Book, pp. 125–127.

**DAY 2**

***En acción (cont.)***
- Check homework. 10 MIN.
- Quick Start Review (TE, p. 152). 5 MIN.
- Present *Gramática:* Direct Object Pronouns, p. 152. 10 MIN.
- Review the vocabulary in the box on p. 153. 5 MIN.
- Have students do *Actividades* 6 and 7 orally. 10 MIN.
- Play the audio and do *Actividad* 8 orally. 10 MIN.
- Present *Gramática:* Indirect Object Pronouns, p. 154. 10 MIN.
- Have students do *Actividades* 9 and 10 in writing. 10 MIN.
- Present Speaking Strategy, p. 156 and have students do *Actividad* 11 in pairs and *Actividad* 12 in small groups. 15 MIN.
- Use *Más comunicación* activity, p. R7, for variety. 5 MIN.

***Homework Option***
- *Más práctica* Workbook, pp. 57–62 as needed. *Cuaderno para hispanohablantes*, pp. 57–60 as needed.

**DAY 3**

***En acción (cont.)***
- Quick Start Review (TE, p. 156). 5 MIN.
- Present *Gramática:* Double Object Pronouns, p. 157. 10 MIN.
- Quick Start Review (TE, p. 158). 5 MIN.
- Have students complete *Actividades* 13 and 14 orally. 10 MIN.
- Present *Vocabulario*, p. 159, then have students complete *Actividad* 15 in writing. 10 MIN.
- Play audio for students and do *Actividades* 16 and 17 orally with the whole class. 10 MIN.

***En voces: Lectura***
- Quick Start Review (TE, p. 160). 5 MIN.
- Review Reading Strategy, p. 160. 5 MIN.
- Have students read *Teotihuacán: Ciudad misteriosa* silently, then have students read it aloud in turns. 10 MIN.
- Call on volunteers to answer *¿Comprendiste?* questions. Refer back to the reading if students give the incorrect answer. 10 MIN.
- Have students begin *Actividad* 7. 10 MIN.

***Homework Option***
- Have students finish *Actividad* 7. *Más práctica* Workbook, pp. 63–64. *Cuaderno para hispanohablantes*, pp. 61–62.
- Prepare for *Etapa* 3 Exam.

**DAY 4**

***En colores: Cultura y comparaciones***
- Check homework. 10 MIN.
- Quick Start Review (TE, p. 162). 5 MIN.
- Present Connecting Cultures Strategy, p. 162. 10 MIN.
- Read *¡Buen provecho! La comida mexicana* aloud with students. 10 MIN.
- Have students answer the *¿Comprendiste?* questions orally. 10 MIN.

***En uso: Repaso y más comunicación***
- Quick Start Review (TE, p. 164). 5 MIN.
- Review Now You Can… and do *Actividades* 1–4 orally. 15 MIN.
- Present Speaking Strategy, p. 166, then have students do *Actividad* 5 and 6 in groups of four. 10 MIN.
- Complete *Etapa* 3 Exam. 20 MIN.

***Homework Option***
- Write answers to *¿Qué piensas?* questions. Read *Tu en la comunidad*, p. 166. Prepare for Unit 2 Exam.

**DAY 5**

***En uso: Repaso y más comunicación***
- Check homework. 10 MIN.
- Quick Start Review (TE, p. 166). 5 MIN.
- Review grammar from the unit as necessary. 10 MIN.
- Complete Unit 2 Exam. 30 MIN.

***En tu propia voz: Escritura***
- Begin writing activity, pp. 168–169. 15 MIN.

***Ampliación***
- Use a suggested project, game, or activity (TE pp. 99A–99B). 20 MIN.

***Homework Option***
- Finish writing activity and preview *Unidad* 3 Opener, pp. 168–169.

▼ Isabel y Laura comen en un restaurante.

Pacing Guide • UNIDAD 2 Etapa 3 133D

MOTIVATE TO COMMUNICATE ¡En español!

# Support students' varied learning styles & ability levels

The Teacher's Edition and ancillaries offer strategies that address multiple intelligences, different ability levels, and native-speaker needs.

**Quick Start Reviews** set up short student-directed activities that review and reinforce previously learned vocabulary and grammar concepts.

**Classroom Community** provides paired, group, and cooperative learning activities to help build your classroom community of Spanish speakers.

UNIDAD 2 Etapa 3
**Vocabulary/Grammar**

**Teaching Resource Options**

**Print**
*Más práctica* Workbook PE, pp. 63–64
*Cuaderno para hispanohablantes* PE, pp. 61–62
Block Scheduling Copymasters
Unit 2 Resource Book
*Más práctica* Workbook TE, pp. 109–110
*Cuaderno para hispanohablantes* TE, pp. 115–116
Information Gap Activities, p. 119

**Audiovisual**
OHT 67 (Quick Start)

**Technology**
*Intrigas y aventuras* CD-ROM, Disc 1

**Quick Start Review**
Indirect object pronouns
Use OHT 67 or write on board: Answer the questions following the cue given. In your answer substitute an indirect object pronoun for the indirect object.
¿Qué compraste para Vivián? (un libro) Le compré un libro.
1. ¿Qué compraste para Luis? (los casetes)
2. ¿Qué compraste para Carmen? (la torta)
3. ¿Qué compraste para mí? (el boleto)
4. ¿Qué compraste para mis padres? (la pintura)
5. ¿Qué compraste para ti? (una rosa)

**Answers**, see p. 143B.

**Teaching Suggestion**
Before doing **Actividad 11**, have students brainstorm their favorite actors/actresses, comedians, movies, and/or television shows.

ACTIVIDAD 11 **Objective:** Open-ended practice
Expressing opinions
Indirect object pronouns/family vocabulary
*Answers will vary. Sentences should include indirect object pronouns.*



ACTIVIDAD 11 **¡Opiniones!**

**PARA CONVERSAR** • STRATEGY: SPEAKING
**Personalize responses** Perhaps you see a great many films and even some plays. You've probably also read or seen reviews of these productions. Do you usually agree with the critics? Here's a chance for you to express your own personal preferences and feelings about show business.

**Hablar** Habla con un(a) compañero(a) de las opiniones de las siguientes personas sobre el mundo del espectáculo. *(Hint: Talk with a classmate about opinions related to show business.)*

**modelo**
**Tú:** *¿A tus amigos les fascinan las series de ciencia ficción?*
**Compañero(a):** *No, no (Sí,) les fascinan.*

a ti
a tu mejor amigo(a)
a tu madre/padre
a tu profesor(a) de [clase]
a tus amigos(as)
a tu hermano(a)
a ti y tus amigos(as)
¿?

me
te
le
nos
os
les

encantar
fascinar
gustar
importar
interesar
molestar

el actor/la actriz (*nombre*)
las películas de aventuras
las series de ciencia ficción
el (la) comediante (*nombre*)
las escenas de horror y violencia
el estreno (*nombre de la película*)
las telenovelas
la obra de teatro *Les Misérables*

**NOTA CULTURAL**
**Las telenovelas** ¿Te gusta ver la tele? Entonces debes saber que en el mundo hispano a mucha gente le gusta ver las telenovelas. Son diferentes porque sólo duran unos meses en contraste con las de Estados Unidos, que duran décadas.

**Vocabulario**

**El mundo del espectáculo**
**el actor/la actriz** *actor, actress*
**las aventuras** *adventures*
**la ciencia ficción** *science fiction*
**la comedia** *comedy*
**el (la) comediante** *comedian*
**la escena** *scene*
**el estreno** *new release*
**el horror** *horror*
**el papel** *role*
**la serie** *series*
**la telenovela** *soap opera*
**el tema** *theme, subject*

¿Cuáles te encantan?



**Classroom Community**

**Group Activity** Have students describe one of the words in the vocabulary box on p. 156 and ask other students to identify it.

**Pair Work** Divide the class into pairs. Student 1 (S1) makes a list of 3 direct object pronouns. S2 makes a list of 3 indirect object pronouns. S1 and S2 then forms sentences that use both a direct and indirect object pronoun. S1 proofreads the sentences and S2 reads them to the class.

**Portfolio** Have students write in their journal about their favorite actor/actress and the role he/she plays.

**Rubric: Writing**

| Criteria | Scale |
|---|---|
| Vocabulary use | 1 2 3 4 5 |
| Accuracy | 1 2 3 4 5 |
| Creativity | 1 2 3 4 5 |

A = 13–15 pts.
B = 10–12 pts.
C = 7–9 pts.
D = 4–6 pts.
F = < 4 pts.

"This incorporates many positive features: relevant context, much exposure to culture, strategy development, recycling, and meaningful practice."

Pam Urdal Silva
East Lake High School
Tarpon Springs, FL

GRAMÁTICA

## Double Object Pronouns

¿RECUERDAS? pp. 152, 154 You have learned about both **direct** and **indirect** object pronouns. They both go before the **conjugated verb**.

What happens if you want to have both **direct** and **indirect** object pronouns in the same sentence? The **indirect** object goes **first**.

indirect object / direct object
Te los compramos.
*We bought them for you.*

indirect object / direct object
El mesero me los dio.
*The waiter gave them to me.*

Remember that when a **conjugated verb** appears with an **infinitive** or an **-ndo form**, you have two choices. You can put the pronouns before the **conjugated verb**, or you can attach them to the **infinitive** or **-ndo form**. Either way, the sentences mean the same thing:

indirect object / direct object
Me los vas a comprar.
*You are going to buy them for me.*

indirect object / direct object
Vas a comprármelos.
*You are going to buy them for me.*

Me los estás comprando.
*You are buying them for me.*

Estás comprándomelos.
*You are buying them for me.*

There is a special rule for verbs with two pronouns when both are **third person**: change the **indirect** object pronoun to **se**.

Le pedí una servilleta al mesero.
*I asked the waiter for a napkin.*

indirect object / direct object
Se la pedimos.
*We asked him for it.*

ciento cincuenta y siete
Etapa 3 157

### UNIDAD 2 Etapa 3
### Vocabulary/Grammar

**Teaching Suggestions**
**Presenting Double Object Pronouns**
- Remind students about the substitution and placement rules they already know for direct and indirect object pronouns. Practice substitution of pronouns for objects.
- Remind students that **se** is used when there are two third person object pronouns, and it is also the third person reflexive pronoun, as in **Ellos se levantan a las ocho.**
- Remind students to add accents with double object pronouns when attaching them to an infinitive or **-ndo** form.

**Actividad 12 Objective:** Open-ended practice
Indirect object pronouns
**Things to do in the city**
*Answers will vary. They may include:*
**Me interesa ir de compras. Me interesa ir a la Alameda. Me interesa comer helado. Me interesa ir al cine.**

**Culture Highlights**
- **SHOPPING IN MEXICO CITY** The more elegant shops are found in the Polanco area or in La Zona Rosa in the West End of Mexico City. Outdoor markets are scattered around the city, the more popular ones being Mercado San Juan, Plaza Ciudadela, and Mercado San Ángel.
- **PARQUE ALAMEDA** is a park with gardens, fountains, and walking paths. It was once the site of the Aztec market.

**Community Connection**
Spanish-speaking actors have become more popular in the U.S. recently. Have students try to make a list of those they know. Point out Antonio Banderas (**español**), Edward James Olmos (**chicano**), Rosie Pérez (**puertorriqueña**), Jennifer López (**puertorriqueña**), Andy García (**cubanoamericano**), etc.

**Block Schedule**
**Retention** Divide students into pairs. Have them use the verbs **gustar, molestar, encantar,** and **interesar** to discuss television show preferences. (For additional activities, see **Block Scheduling Copymasters.**)

**...ching All Students**
**...a Help** Have students write 5 more sentences ...d on the expressions given in **Actividad 11**.
**...ve Speakers** Have Spanish speakers describe ...plays or movies they have seen in Spanish using ...ocabulary on p. 156.

**Multiple Intelligences**
**Interpersonal** Have students brainstorm a list of recent movies that fit the categories **aventura, comedia, ciencia ficción,** and **horror**. Then have students work in pairs to determine if they like or dislike the movies listed (e.g., **Me gusta/No me gusta, Me encanta,** etc.).

Vocabulary/Grammar • UNIDAD 2 Etapa 3 157

**Block Scheduling Suggestions** at point-of-use help teachers vary and streamline their lessons.

**Teaching All Students** features numerous creative ideas to address different types of students.

MOTIVATE TO COMMUNICATE ¡En español!

# Cultural References

**Note:** *Page numbers in bold type refer to the Teacher's Edition.*

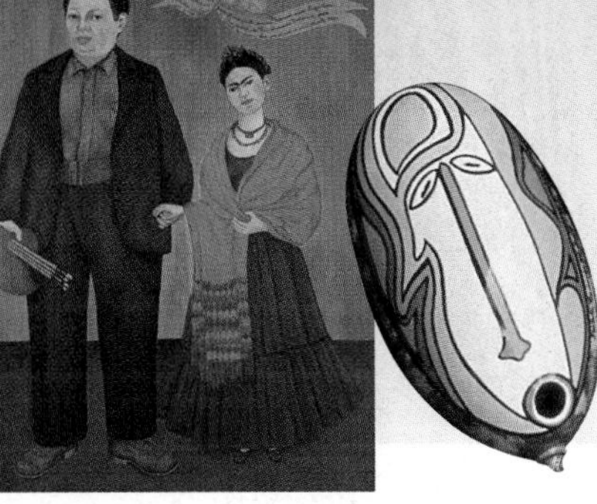

# CULTURAL REFERENCES

## People



## Puerto Rico



## Shopping



## Spain



## United States

¡En español!

# INSERVICE WORKSHOPS

This section of your Teacher's Edition contains professional development materials for reference throughout the school year. You may also access www.mcdougallittell.com for additional information.



# Managing Your Classroom


**Barbara J. Rupert**
Franklin Pierce High School
Tacoma, WA


## Techniques for Keeping Students in the Target Language

Keeping students in the target language will build their confidence, motivate them and enhance their language skills. However, most students naturally seek the easiest path to communication, their native tongue, so the following tips can help.

- Teach them all the necessary language skills for following directions and classroom routines first. Also, create bulletin board posters with their most common requests. Grant only those requests asked in the target language and watch their motivation increase.
- Avoid direct error correction. Students, fearful of making mistakes, may be afraid to speak Spanish. When they do take a linguistic risk, teachers, eager to help, can unintentionally inhibit language production by openly correcting them. To prevent embarrassment, gently model the correct Spanish without pointing out their error. They will learn from your skillful modeling. Boost confidence by reminding students that in informal classroom situations, it is how much Spanish they speak, not how perfectly, that matters. Studies show that the students who are willing to speak the target language early on, even if perhaps not as gracefully, are the ones to become most fluent in the long run. When they realize that your classroom is a safe place to take risks, they will speak more Spanish and their confidence will grow. ***¡En español!*** gives students speaking and learning strategies in every lesson to boost confidence and retention.
- Create "Spanish only" situations early on. Before students can operate entirely in the target language, strictly enforce the *"¡No inglés!"* rule during all partner and structured group activities. Remind the students that they have the skills and resources necessary to communicate in Spanish.
- Make a game of it. The game *"El Banco"* motivates and creates accountability. Give the students a predetermined number of extra credit coupons per semester (pretend *pesetas,* or other monetary units work well). When the teacher says, *"El banco está abierto,"* only Spanish is allowed. Anyone who speaks English must give up a *peseta*. Students love the next part of this game. If the teacher speaks English while the bank is open, he or she must pay each student in the class a peseta. The game is over when the teacher says, *"El banco está cerrado."*

## Tips for Enhancing On-Task Behavior

The satisfying hum of engaged and focused students brings energy to teachers and students alike. Consider these suggesting for boosting on-task behavior.

- Minimize direct instruction. Research on the brain has indicated that students can absorb from two to ten minutes of information (direct instruction) into their short-term memories. Then, they need to use that information in some way to transfer it into their long term memories. Therefore, keep direct instruction to a minimum and make sure your students have plenty of opportunities to apply what you've taught, moving that information into their long term memories.
- Involve movement in classroom activities. Once again, researchers studying the brain have provided useful teaching information. Studies show that students' brains are more receptive to learning when physical activity is integrated into the lesson. Games that involve movement and Total Physical Response activities actually help prepare students to be successful in subsequent activities as well. Try to involve some type of movement, even stretching, every half hour.
- Balance proficiency and grammar to maximize communication. If you ask your students why they are studying Spanish, the majority will give you one of two answers: either they want to be able to speak it, or they need it for college. Rarely does a student say, "I like to study grammar." ***¡En español!*** balances proficiency and grammar to maximize communication. Take advantage of their motivation and show them how their capacity to speak the language is enhanced by learning grammar. Students can memorize a basic conversation, but if they understand the grammar behind it, they can extend their ability to communicate into novel situations. Grammar is not the **point** of instruction; it is a **tool** to expand their skills.
- Vary classroom activities. Boredom is the cause of many classroom management problems. Good lesson planning involves balancing listening, speaking, reading, writing, and culture activities throughout a class period. Teachers can move from direct instruction to partner activities to guided individual practice to small and large group activities focusing on a single or many instructional objectives.

Technology provides yet another opportunity to engage students in new ways. Working on a CD-ROM seems more like playing to most students. Internet connections create a sense of adventure, videos entertain as they teach, and listening activities demand focused attention while they build skills.

With all the resources at hand, planning a minimum of five different combinations of activities for a traditional period and doubling that number on a block schedule is manageable.

This chart illustrates a way to present and practice a single function, EXPRESSING LIKES AND DISLIKES, in a variety of ways during a 50-minute class period.

**FUNCTION: EXPRESSING LIKES AND DISLIKES**

| Presentation Practice | Skill(s) | Direct Instruction | Individual Activity | Paired Activity | Group Activity | Tech |
|---|---|---|---|---|---|---|
| Video / Audio Presentation | Listening / Culture | ✔ | | | | ✔ |
| Presentation of **gustar** | Listening | | | | | |
| Note-taking | Writing | ✔ | ✔ | | | |
| Basic yes / no, one-word responses | Speaking / Writing | | | | ✔ | |
| Extend to classroom discussion | Speaking | | | | ✔ | |
| Controlled Activity | Speaking / Reading / Writing | | ✔ | ✔ | | |
| Transitional Activity | Speaking / Reading / Writing | | ✔ | ✔ | ✔ | |
| Open-ended Activity | Speaking / Reading / Writing | | ✔ | ✔ | ✔ | |

### Quick Start Review

♻ Preterite/**En contexto** vocabulary

Use OHT 45 or write on board: List three activities you did with children on your last baby-sitting job. If you don't baby-sit, tell about any time you played with a child. You may invent details. Use the preterite and any subject you wish. For example: **Anduvimos en bicicleta.**

*Answers will vary.*

### Quick Start Review

♻ Identifying the direct object

Use OHT 66 or write on board: Underline the direct object in each sentence. Remember the direct object answers the question "what?" in relation to the verb.

1. Tengo el menú.
2. Preparan los chilaquiles con pollo y salsa verde.
3. ¿Pusiste las servilletas en la mesa?
4. El mesero trajo la cuenta en seguida.
5. Le dejaron una propina al mesero.

**Answers**, see p. 143B.

### Quick Wrap-up

In small groups or pairs have students ask each other: **Cuando tienes tiempo libre, ¿qué haces?** Tell students to use as many reflexive verbs as possible. This could also be done as a whole class activity if you wish to pose the question to several students.

By including vocabulary activities, review, games, projects and music, the possibilities for creating varied lessons are endless. Besides keeping students engaged, variety provides the important added benefit of engaging many different learning styles.

- Reinforce positive behavior: confidence builds success. When a student's behavior pleases you, the best way to insure that it will continue is to reinforce it. The key to successful reinforcement is to acknowledge the behavior while it is in progress and in a very specific context. A positive comment, smile, extra credit coupon or other treat can be very motivating. Surprisingly, even most seniors like to get stickers! Keeping a stack of *"talones"* or extra credit coupons in your pocket makes it quick and easy to acknowledge a student's participation. Don't feel you need to reinforce every student at the same time; that would render the praise ineffective. Rather, students will see that over time when you "catch" them speaking Spanish spontaneously, working hard or helping a classmate, their positive behavior will be recognized.

## Routines that Maximize Learning Time

Teaching students how to handle everyday classroom routines in an efficient manner will provide more time for the "fun stuff." Teach students what to do upon entering the classroom: how to pass in papers, how to form pairs and small groups, and what your expectations are for the close of the class period.

- Build entry activities into the routine. Entry and exit activities engage students at the beginning and end of the period when off-task behavior is most likely to occur. The ***¡En español! Teacher's Edition*** provides Quick Start Reviews to make this easy. Students can keep the week's activities on a single sheet of paper to be turned in on Friday. Teach the students to begin the Quick Start activity immediately (and reinforce those who do!) so you can take role and assist students who were absent without losing instruction time. One way to build in accountability is to call on several students randomly to share their answers each day. You can write students' names

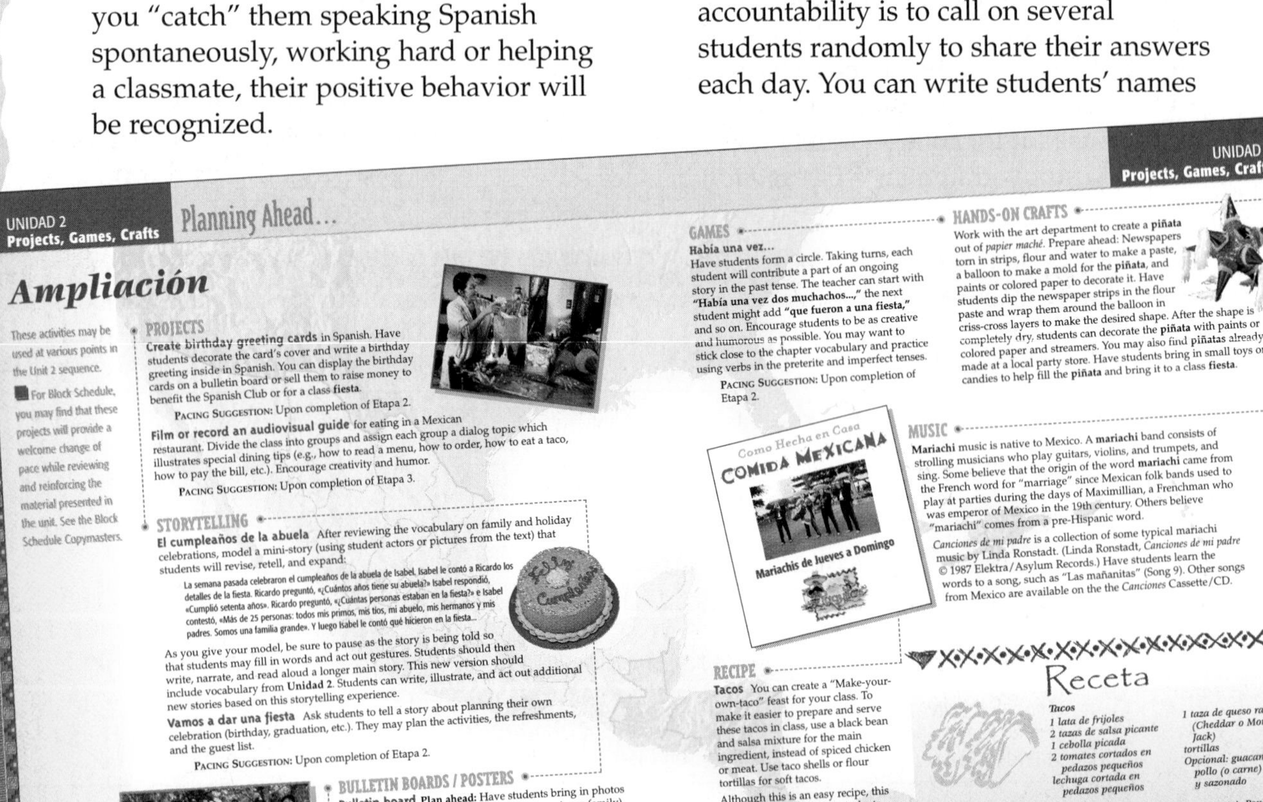

UNIDAD 2
**Projects, Games, Crafts**

Planning Ahead...

# Ampliación

These activities may be used at various points in the Unit 2 sequence.

For Block Schedule, you may find that these projects will provide a welcome change of pace while reviewing and reinforcing the material presented in the unit. See the Block Schedule Copymasters.

PROJECTS

**Create birthday greeting cards** in Spanish. Have students decorate the card's cover and write a birthday greeting inside in Spanish. You can display the birthday cards on a bulletin board or sell them to raise money to benefit the Spanish Club or for a class **fiesta**.

PACING SUGGESTION: Upon completion of Etapa 2.

**Film or record an audiovisual guide** for eating in a Mexican restaurant. Divide the class into groups and assign each group a dialog topic which illustrates special dining tips (e.g., how to read a menu, how to order, how to eat a taco, how to pay the bill, etc.). Encourage creativity and humor.

PACING SUGGESTION: Upon completion of Etapa 3.

STORYTELLING

**El cumpleaños de la abuela** After reviewing the vocabulary on family and holiday celebrations, model a mini-story (using student actors or pictures from the text) that students will revise, retell, and expand:

La semana pasada celebraron el cumpleaños de la abuela de Isabel. Isabel le contó a Ricardo los detalles de la fiesta. Ricardo preguntó, «¿Cuántos años tiene su abuela?» Isabel respondió, «Cumplió setenta años». Ricardo preguntó, «¿Cuántas personas estaban en la fiesta?» e Isabel contestó, «Más de 25 personas: todos mis primos, mis tíos, mi abuelo, mis hermanos y mis padres. Somos una familia grande». Y luego Isabel le contó qué hicieron en la fiesta...

As you give your model, be sure to pause as the story is being told so that students may fill in words and act out gestures. Students should then write, narrate, and read aloud a longer main story. This new version should include vocabulary from **Unidad 2**. Students can write, illustrate, and act out additional new stories based on this storytelling experience.

**Vamos a dar una fiesta** Ask students to tell a story about planning their own celebration (birthday, graduation, etc.). They may plan the activities, the refreshments, and the guest list.

PACING SUGGESTION: Upon completion of Etapa 2.

BULLETIN BOARDS / POSTERS

**Bulletin board Plan ahead:** Have students bring in photos of their family members or friends (or an imaginary family) and write a short description in Spanish. Display the captioned photos on the bulletin board.

**Posters Have students create • Family trees** on a poster • **Menu** for a Mexican restaurant • **Mexican restaurant** advertisement poster • **Calendar** with months' illustrations and important dates pertaining to Mexico • **Recipe calendar** with a different illustration and recipe for each month

99A Projects, Games, Crafts • UNIDAD 2

UNIDAD 2
**Projects, Games, Crafts**

GAMES

**Había una vez...**
Have students form a circle. Taking turns, each student will contribute a part of an ongoing story in the past tense. The teacher can start with **"Había una vez dos muchachos...,"** the next student might add **"que fueron a una fiesta,"** and so on. Encourage students to be as creative and humorous as possible. You may want to stick close to the chapter vocabulary and practice using verbs in the preterite and imperfect tenses.

PACING SUGGESTION: Upon completion of Etapa 2.

HANDS-ON CRAFTS

Work with the art department to create a **piñata** out of *papier maché*. Prepare ahead: Newspapers torn in strips, flour and water to make a paste, a balloon to make a mold for the **piñata**, and paints or colored paper to decorate it. Have students dip the newspaper strips in the flour paste and wrap them around the balloon in criss-cross layers to make the desired shape. After the shape is completely dry, students can decorate the **piñata** with paints or colored paper and streamers. You may also find **piñatas** already made at a local party store. Have students bring in small toys or candies to help fill the **piñata** and bring it to a class **fiesta**.



MUSIC

**Mariachi** music is native to Mexico. A **mariachi** band consists of strolling musicians who play guitars, violins, and trumpets, and sing. Some believe that the origin of the word **mariachi** came from the French word for "marriage" since Mexican folk bands used to play at parties during the days of Maximillian, a Frenchman who was emperor of Mexico in the 19th century. Others believe "mariachi" comes from a pre-Hispanic word.

*Canciones de mi padre* is a collection of some typical mariachi music by Linda Ronstadt. (Linda Ronstadt, *Canciones de mi padre* © 1987 Elektra/Asylum Records.) Have students learn the words to a song, such as "Las mañanitas" (Song 9). Other songs from Mexico are available on the the *Canciones* Cassette/CD.

RECIPE

**Tacos** You can create a "Make-your-own-taco" feast for your class. To make it easier to prepare and serve these tacos in class, use a black bean and salsa mixture for the main ingredient, instead of spiced chicken or meat. Use taco shells or flour tortillas for soft tacos.

Although this is an easy recipe, this will be the first time that students actually learn the Spanish words for the ingredients. As an ongoing project students can prepare bilingual recipe cards with the Spanish version on the front and the English translation on the back.

Receta

**Tacos**
*1 lata de frijoles*
*2 tazas de salsa picante*
*1 cebolla picada*
*2 tomates cortados en pedazos pequeños*
*lechuga cortada en pedazos pequeños*
*1 taza de queso rallado (Cheddar o Monterey Jack)*
*tortillas*
*Opcional: guacamole, pollo (o carne) pica[do] y sazonado*

*Mezcle los frijoles con 1/2 taza de salsa picante (o más, a su gusto). Ponga la mezcla en un plato hondo. Prepare los otros ingredientes (la cebolla, los tom[ates], la lechuga, el queso rallado y el resto de la salsa), póngalos en distintos plato[s] hondos y colóquelos en una mesa. Cada persona puede crear su propio taco [con] los ingredientes que hay en la mesa.*

Projects, Games, Crafts • UNIDAD 2

on index cards to keep track of who has answered and even grade their responses if desired.

- Provide closure for the day with an exit activity. ***¡En español!*** has Quick Wrap-up activities at many points in the lesson sequence, found in the Teacher's Edition. Exit activities can even be as simple as having students say good-bye to you in a culturally appropriate way. The Quick Wrap-up can be a daily or weekly activity.

## Design Your Classroom to Facilitate Pair and Group Work

Pair and group work provide wonderful practice for students while allowing the teacher to be off centerstage. Creating a community of learners gives students peer support, offers opportunities for peer teaching, and increases confidence. While students may prefer to work with close friends, varying partners allows them to get to know other classmates and combines students of different learning styles and abilities. Creating seating arrangements conducive to group and pair work and changing the seating chart on a regular basis (every two to four weeks) will accomplish several goals: reduce transition time, assure that all students are included, and easily facilitate new combinations of groups and pairs. Many computerized gradebook programs can scramble student seats with the push of a button. When you post each seating chart, use a highlighter to indicate how groups and pairs will be formed.

Whatever seating arrangement you prefer, it is important that no one has his or her back to the board or overhead. Here are some examples of seating charts that facilitate group and pair work:

Another way to randomly group students, borrowed from cooperative learning specialists, uses a deck of cards. As the students enter the classroom, they choose a card from the stack and sit in the seat assigned to that card (all the aces would form one group, the twos would form another and so on). It is a good idea to record the card drawn by each student to eliminate swapping. Teachers can quickly create different pairs by combining suits. For example, for one activity the hearts would work with the diamonds and the clubs would work with the spades. For the next activity the hearts would work with the clubs and so forth. For group activities, all four group members work together.

## Creating a Community of Learners

When lots of learning is taking place, the classroom can be a wonderfully messy place! A view of your classroom would include students moving around, interacting with each other, working in groups, using technology, and taking risks with their new skills. With ***¡En español!*** your students will thrive on being actively involved in the learning process — and it will show.

### Classroom Community

**Cooperative Learning** Divide the class into 4 groups. Have students research aspects of Teotihuacán mentioned in this reading. Group 1 researches temples and pyramids. Group 2 researches the people who lived there. Group 3 researches artifacts. Group 4 researches the mysterious abandonment of the temples and pyramids. Cue students to use the Internet or library resources. Groups then share their findings with the class.

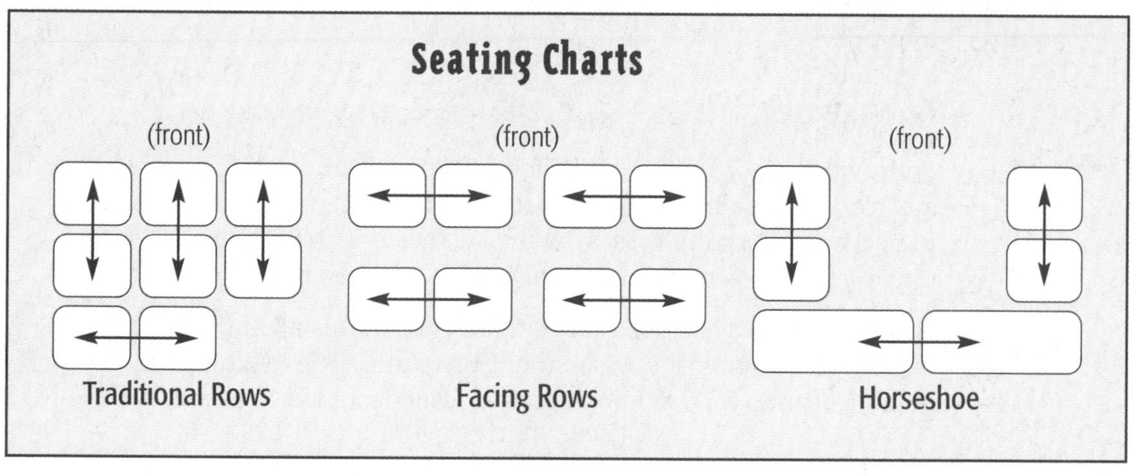

# Uniting Teaching, Learning, and Assessment

**Patricia Hamilton Carlin**
University of Central Arkansas
Conway, AR

Assessment is an essential component of the teaching/learning process. Assessment helps teachers, students, parents, and administrators measure the progress that is being made toward reaching course objectives and instructional goals. Planning for assessment involves a consideration of national, state, and local guidelines, as well as parental expectations. Also, the teacher must decide how to design appropriate assessment instruments for students with varying interests, abilities, and learning styles. Teachers must also decide how to assign an appropriate "weight" to the various components of the student's grade.

There are several different ways to handle assessment. Here are some basic tips which can help both veteran and novice teachers design a balanced assessment plan for their classes.

## PROGRAM RESOURCES

### Assessment Options

- **Cooperative Quizzes** (Unit 2 Resource Book)
- **Etapa Exam** Forms A and B (Unit 2 Resource Book)
- ***Examen para hispanohablantes*** (Unit 2 Resource Book)
- **Portfolio Assessment** (Unit 2 Resource Book)
- **Multiple Choice Test Questions** (Unit 2 Resource Book)
- **Audio Program** Cassette 19A / CD 19
- **Electronic Teacher Tools/Test Generator**

## Include Formative and Summative Assessments

Include both formative and summative assessments as components of the student's grade. Formative assessments are the stepping stones that help students build their skills, while summative assessments provide a summation of what has been learned to that point.

Quizzes, a common type of formative assessment, can provide helpful feedback to both teacher and students. Giving quizzes cooperatively in pairs or small groups can be particularly effective and fun. The ***¡En español!*** Cooperative Quizzes lower students' anxiety level, help students think critically about linguistic structures, and increase retention of the material. (Also, the teacher has fewer papers to grade!)

## Include Traditional and Alternative Assessments

Provide opportunities for different types of students to excel in their areas of strength by including both traditional assessments (pencil and paper) and alternative assessments such as portfolios, journals, video/class presentations, visual/audio projects, interviews, etc.

***¡En español!*** provides excellent support in this area. (See pages T8–T9 for a description of the Assessment Program.) The testing program includes contextualized quizzes and tests designed to assess both discrete and global skills in listening, speaking, reading, writing, and culture at both the Etapa and Unit level, as well as mid-year and final exams. An easy-to-use Test Generator and additional printed Multiple Choice Questions make individualizing assessment convenient. Rubrics for grading projects, writing assignments, and oral activities are provided at point-of-use in the Teacher's Edition as general guidelines. As always, the classroom teacher may expand and specify these rubrics for individual needs.

## View Assessment as a Process

Remember that assessment is an ongoing process, and that *you,* the classroom teacher, are in charge. Continually monitor the progress that your students are making, and don't be afraid to make adjustments to your assessment plans, as needed, to enhance the teaching-learning process. For example, assessing the progress of native speakers of Spanish in your classes may begin with the Diagnostic exams, and continue with the *Para hispanohablantes* testing materials. Once you have established a level of performance for students, assessment may expand to include special research projects, reports, and presentations.

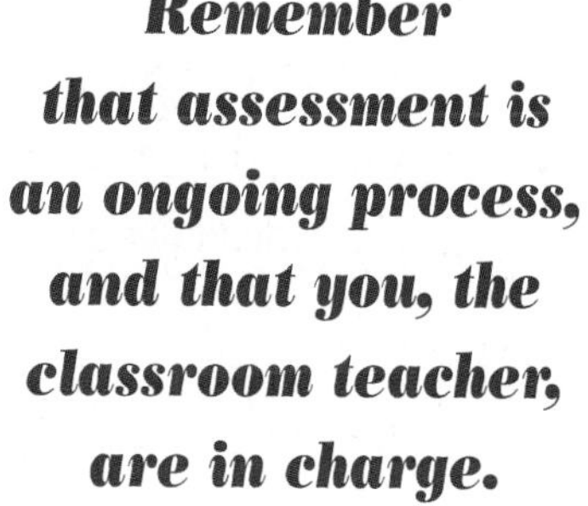
Remember
that assessment is
an ongoing process,
and that you, the
classroom teacher,
are in charge.

## Develop a Sense of Community

Finally, look for ways to make assessment more enjoyable for both you and your students. If you are using the *¡En español!* Cooperative Quizzes, you may find that they can provide a non-threatening culmination activity that synthesizes material for students at the end of the class period. As the sense of collaborative learning is reinforced, the classroom can truly become a community of learners. Develop projects that allow students to collaborate and extend the sense of community within the classroom. When assigning grades for these projects, reward students for creativity and effort, as well as for linguistic accuracy. The *¡En español!* program provides Portfolio Assessment materials, as well as suggestions for portfolio projects in the Teacher's Edition.

Assessing a second language involves the careful balance between formative and evaluative instruments, between traditional and alternative formats, and the appropriate assessment of all skills. The *¡En español!* Assessment Program provides a wide range of support materials to allow teachers to choose the most effective tools to manage class time efficiently to reach their course objectives and instructional goals. Designing a balanced assessment plan helps to create a program that *encourages* students to build the skills they need to communicate and interact in the community of Spanish speakers.

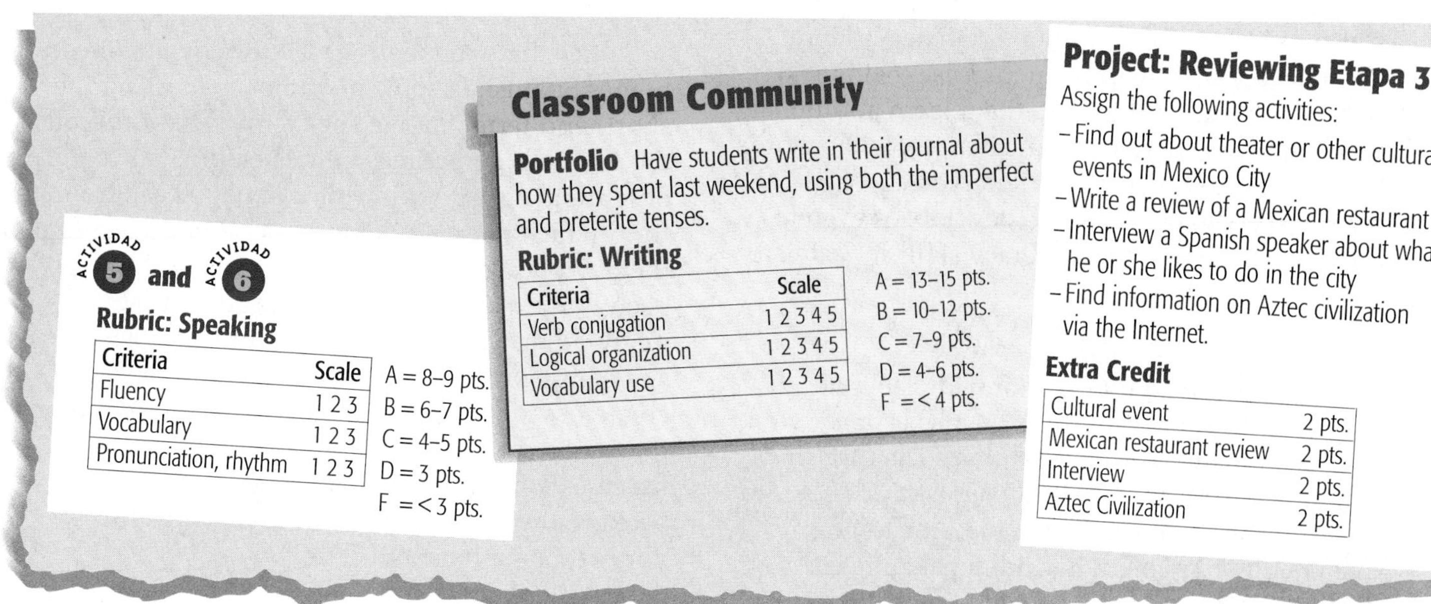

Actividad 5 and Actividad 6

**Rubric: Speaking**

| Criteria | Scale |
|---|---|
| Fluency | 1 2 3 |
| Vocabulary | 1 2 3 |
| Pronunciation, rhythm | 1 2 3 |

A = 8–9 pts.
B = 6–7 pts.
C = 4–5 pts.
D = 3 pts.
F = <3 pts.

**Classroom Community**

**Portfolio** Have students write in their journal about how they spent last weekend, using both the imperfect and preterite tenses.

**Rubric: Writing**

| Criteria | Scale |
|---|---|
| Verb conjugation | 1 2 3 4 5 |
| Logical organization | 1 2 3 4 5 |
| Vocabulary use | 1 2 3 4 5 |

A = 13–15 pts.
B = 10–12 pts.
C = 7–9 pts.
D = 4–6 pts.
F = <4 pts.

**Project: Reviewing Etapa 3**

Assign the following activities:

- Find out about theater or other cultural events in Mexico City
- Write a review of a Mexican restaurant
- Interview a Spanish speaker about what he or she likes to do in the city
- Find information on Aztec civilization via the Internet.

**Extra Credit**

| | |
|---|---|
| Cultural event | 2 pts. |
| Mexican restaurant review | 2 pts. |
| Interview | 2 pts. |
| Aztec Civilization | 2 pts. |

# Encouraging Native Speakers

**Ricardo Otheguy**
City University of New York
New York, NY

## PROGRAM RESOURCES

**Native Speakers**

- *Cuaderno para hispanohablantes* PE *pp. 41–48*
- *Cuaderno para hispanohablantes* TE (Unit 2 Resource Book)
- *Examen para hispanohablantes* (Unit 2 Resource Book)
- Audio Program *(Para hispanohablantes)* Cassette 4A, 4B, 19A / CD 4, 19
- Audioscript (Unit 2 Resource Book)

Like many other teachers of Spanish, you may discover at the beginning of the year that in one or several of your classes there are students in whose homes Spanish is spoken. If you do, consider yourself fortunate! These students will help enhance the quality of your teaching even as you enhance their knowledge of Spanish. They are a great resource and offer a great opportunity for your teaching.

## A Wide Variety of Language Experiences

Keep in mind the enormous variety of students, and the wide variety of educational and language experiences that are covered under the term "native speaker." Get to know each of your students personally: each one of them needs you as a teacher. How? They need you to celebrate and reaffirm their knowledge of Spanish, however much or little they have, and of whatever kind. They need you to help them increase their spoken Spanish fluency and to help them learn additional words and additional pronunciations for the words they know. And most important, you as their teacher have to help them to develop, or even to acquire for the first time, literacy skills in Spanish.

## How *¡En español!* Can Help

The ***¡En español!*** program provides specialized resources to help you address the needs of native speaker students in your classroom. The *Cuaderno para hispanohablantes,* the *Para hispanohablantes* audio materials, and the *Para hispanohablantes* testing materials all bring you the additional targeted components for successful integration of Spanish speakers into your classes. Classroom Management suggestions, Peer Teaching, and Native Speaker teaching hints are available in the Teacher's Edition as part of the point-of-use teaching materials. Note that if your school has separate classes for Spanish-speaking students, we also have a special program (that includes ***Tu mundo*** and ***Nuestro mundo****)* for these classes. ***¡En español!*** provides the support that makes both you and your native speaker students confident, comfortable, and highly motivated.

## Individual Variation

Notice that we mentioned "students in whose homes Spanish is spoken" rather than using the shorthand term "native speakers." That is because the term can sometimes be misleading, since it can obscure the great variety of language backgrounds from which these students come. Remember, first, the obvious: Many of these students will have been born in Spanish-speaking countries, but many others will come to you from Spanish-speaking homes in the U.S. These differences create obvious consequences for your expectations regarding their Spanish. Be sure to find out as much as you can about the individual language background of your students in order to focus your teaching most effectively.

## A Continuum of Language and Literacy

Because families come to the U.S. with children of all ages, each one of your students who was born in Latin America will have had a specific and unique level of exposure to Spanish language and literacy. Some Latin American-born students come to the U.S. with a lot of experience in Spanish-language schools and some with only a year or two of education in Spanish, while others immigrated too young to have gone to school there at all. Also bear in mind that, in some cases, there will be students who, for a variety of reasons, never attended school, even though they came to the U.S. well past the age when it would have been expected.

Many of your native speakers, perhaps most, will have been born in Spanish-speaking homes in the U.S., in which case their exposure to Spanish, and to literacy in Spanish, will again be very diverse.

- Some of these U.S.-born Spanish-speakers may have grown up in families where Spanish is spoken by both parents all the time.
- Others will come from homes where one parent is Hispanic but the other is not.
- Most will come from homes where both Spanish and English are spoken with different levels of fluency and with different amounts of time, interest, and intensity.
- Some of these students will be spoken to and themselves speak Spanish at home.
- Many will live in homes where they are spoken to in Spanish but where they themselves mostly speak in English.
- Some will have attended Spanish-language classes in bilingual programs in the U.S.; most will not.
- Some will come from families where literacy in Spanish is encouraged.
- Many will not have any familiarity with Spanish in printed form at all.

## Levels of Language

Your native speakers can be a great resource on matters of pronunciation. Make them part of your teaching. Encourage them to speak up, to serve as models of pronunciation for you and for the class. Also encourage them to teach you and the class words that they may know that are not necessarily presented in *¡En español!*. But remember that many of your native speakers will be insecure about their pronunciation and about the words they use. Your role is to be supportive and to help them overcome the insecurity. Tell them that you and their classmates want to learn from them. Explain to them that there are many different levels of Spanish just like there are many levels of English. Teach them new pronunciations, and new words, for the words they already know.

## Celebrate, Support, and Affirm

Take a positive, additive attitude. Tell them that what they know is great and is interesting (which it is!) and then tell them that you're teaching them additional ways of saying things. Be accurate. Think of their ways as local or regional, and of what you're adding as more general. Don't think that they are wrong and that you're going to teach them the only right or correct way to speak and write Spanish. Literacy in Spanish is an important goal that you should have for these students. But don't forget that in many cases their literacy, and their knowledge of rules of grammar, is no greater than that of your English-speaking students. The main thing to remember is that these students are in class to learn Spanish from you, just like everybody else. So first find out what they know. Then celebrate, support and affirm their Spanish. And then, most important, teach them more!

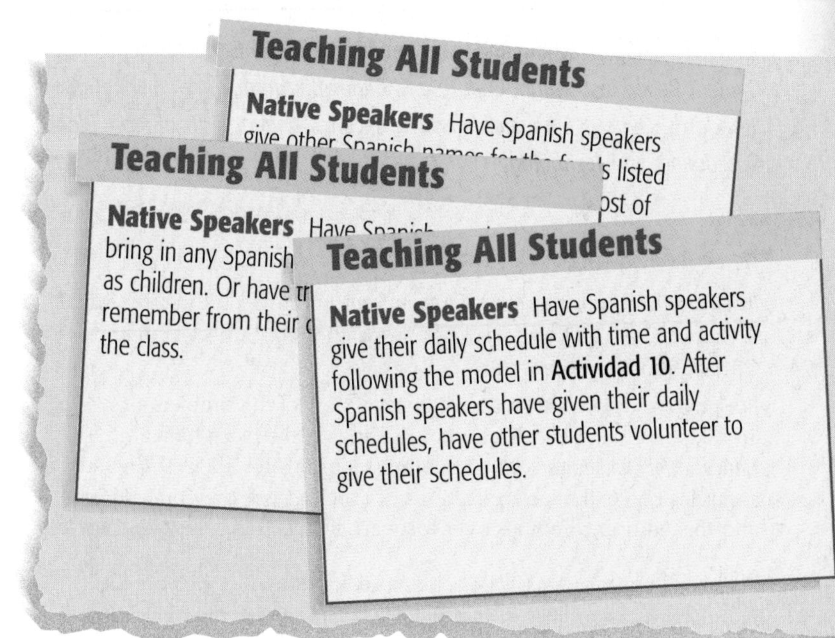

Teaching All Students
Native Speakers Have Spanish speakers
Teaching All Students
Native Speakers
bring in any Spanish
as children. Or have
remember from their
the class.
Teaching All Students
Native Speakers Have Spanish speakers give their daily schedule with time and activity following the model in Actividad 10. After Spanish speakers have given their daily schedules, have other students volunteer to give their schedules.

# Professional Bibliography and Additional Resources

**Audrey L. Heining-Boynton**
University of North Carolina
Chapel Hill, NC

Part of being a dedicated teacher is committing to life long learning, keeping abreast of the latest trends and issues. It is helpful to have a synthesis of types and genres of sources and resources where you can find further information on a given topic. What follows is a synthesis of a variety of texts and articles that will provide you with a starting point to explore pertinent issues and "hot topics." If you have other favorite sources that are not listed here, contact the ***¡En español!*** website to share your suggestions.

There are several journals or yearly reports that will provide you with an excellent choice of articles. They are *Modern Language Journal, Foreign Language Annals, The ACTFL Foreign Language Education Series, Dimensions, Hispania,* the *TESOL Quarterly, Educational Leadership, The Phi Delta Kappan*, and publications from regional and local educational groups, including *Central States Reports* and *Northeast Conference Reports* and publications from SWCOLT, SCOLT, and PacNW.

What follows are selected articles or texts that deal with eight areas of foreign language teaching and learning: *At-Risk Students, Assessment, Content-Based Instruction, Culture and Multiculturalism, Foreign Language Standards, General Educational Issues, Second Language Acquisition, Block Scheduling,* and *Technology*.

## At-risk Students

- *Readings from Educational Leadership: Students at Risk.* Edited by Ronald S. Brandt (1990). Alexandria, VA: Association for Supervision and Curriculum Development.

  For anyone who wants a thorough overview of the problem of at-risk students, this collection of readings is the place to begin. *Educational Leadership,* one of the finest journals for all K-12 teachers, compiles books that are collections of articles from previous editions, and this edition combines over forty articles on this compelling topic.

- Heining-Boynton, A. (1994). "The At-Risk Student in the Foreign Language Classroom." In *Meeting New Challenges in the Foreign Language Classroom.* Edited by Gale K. Crouse. Lincolnwood, IL: National Textbook Company.

  This article provides a review of the literature regarding at-risk students, and then provides teaching techniques on how best to meet the needs of these special students. Also listed at the end of the volume is an annotated bibliography with other references dealing with the at-risk learner.

## Assessment

- Herman, J.L., Aschbacher, P.R. and Winters, L. (1992). *A Practical Guide to Alternative Assessment.* Alexandria, VA: Association for Supervision and Curriculum Development.

  This text is useful because it provides teachers with ways to determine the purpose of assessment, select the tasks and set the criteria, ensure reliable scoring, and incorporate interdisciplinary factors in the equation.

- Marzano, R.J., Pickering, D. and McTighe, J. (1993). *Assessing Student Outcomes: Performance Assessment Using the Dimensions of Learning Model.* Alexandria, VA: Association for Supervision and Curriculum Development.

  Beginning with a definition of how assessment standards are linked to the five dimensions of learning, the text offers suggestions on how teachers can assess and keep track of student performance. The authors share an extensive rubric to be used in the process.

- Moeller, A. (1994). "Portfolio Assessment: A Showcase for Growth and Learning in the Foreign Language Classroom." In *Meeting New Challenges in the Foreign Language Classroom.* Edited by Gale K. Crouse. Lincolnwood, IL: National Textbook Company.

  This article offers a rationale for the process of portfolio assessment and provides a step-by-step method for foreign language teachers to include this as a holistic component to their instruction and assessment.

- *Teaching, Testing, and Assessment: Making the Connection.* (1994). Northeast Conference Reports. Editor, Charles Hancock. Lincolnwood, IL: National Textbook Company.

  Besides an overview of conceptualization that connects teaching, testing, and assessment, the chapters offer ideas for assessing all language skills in a variety of ways.

## Content-based Instruction

- Anderson, Karen C. (1993). *Kid's Giant Book of Games*. New York, NY: Times Books, Inc.

  Karen Anderson has published a series of game books. Her ideas lend themselves to adaptation to include higher-order thinking in a content-based context.

- Anderson, Karen C., and Cumbaa, Stephen. (1993). *The Bones and Skeleton Game Book.* New York, NY: Workman Publishing Company.

  Particularly appealing for second language teachers/students are the critical thinking activities/puzzles in this book. The activities practice basis concepts such as genetics in an engaging way that help students learn language in context while employing higher-order thinking.

- Cantoni-Harvey, Gina. (1987). *Content-Area Language Instruction: Approaches and Strategies.* New York, NY: Addison-Wesley Publishing Company.

  This text gives an overview of what content-based instruction is and how to incorporate it in a curriculum.

- Heining-Boynton, Audrey L. & Sonia Torres-Quiñones. (1996). *¡Anímate! Focus on Science and Math. Introductory Spanish.* Addison-Wesley Publishing Company, 1996: White Plains, NY.

  This text and teacher's guide provide Spanish teachers with necessary vocabulary on the environment, endangered species, and other science terms that can be used to make connections with other content areas. Also available are activities that can be age-adjusted.

- Kenda, Margaret, and Williams, Phyllis S. (1992). *Science Wizardry for Kids.* Hauppage, NY: Barron's Educational Series, Inc.

  This series has activity after activity that foreign language teachers can adapt for their classrooms. This and the other books in the series are also non-threatening to the non-science individual.

- Kenda, Margaret, and Williams, Phyllis S. (1995). *Math Wizardry for Kids.* Hauppage, NY: Barron's Educational Series, Inc.

  This text affords a multitude of activities that teachers can adapt for the foreign language classroom. These activities reinforce mathematics in fun, "magic" ways.

- Petreshene, Susan S. (1994) *Brain Teasers!* The Center for Applied Research in Education, Inc.

  Over 180 quick higher order thinking activities are available in this book that can easily be adapted for the foreign language classroom.

- Petreshene, Susan S. *Mind Joggers!* (1985) The Center for Applied Research in Education, Inc.

  As with *Brain Teasers!*, this book offers a multitude of activities that take from five to fifteen minutes.

- Ruiz, José Curbelo; Hernandez, María Teresa; and Zuazo, Prudencio. *La Ciencia 1, 2, 3 y 4.* SM Ediciones. (1985).

  This series from Puerto Rico helps teachers with needed vocabulary and concepts to incorporate science in the language classroom.

- Short, Deborah J. *How to Integrate Language and Content Instruction: A Training Manual.* Center for Applied Linguistics, Washington DC. (1991).

  This practical, how-to manual gives step-by-step instructions on how to incorporate content-based, content-related instruction in the foreign language instruction.

## Culture and Multiculturalism

- Noble, J. and Lacasa, J. (1995). *The Hispanic Way.* Lincolnwood, IL: Passport Books.

  This small book provides cultural/sociological information on a variety of topics that encompass the attitudes, behavior, and customs of the Spanish-speaking world.

- Richard-Amato, P. and Snow, M. (1992). *The Multicultural Classroom.* White Plains, NY: Longman.

  Although it is important for foreign language teachers to share target-culture specific information with their students, it is also important for teachers to see the big picture in terms of why we are teaching culture. This text provides that overview.

- *Newsweek en español, People en español, etc.*

  A number of weekly and monthly publications exist to help Spanish teachers maintain a current knowledge of what is happening throughout the Spanish-speaking world. Publications like *Newsweek en español, People en español*, and daily newspapers from the countries that can be accessed on the Internet are filled with news from Spanish-speaking countries. Another excellent resource is *National Geographic.*

- *Teaching Tolerance*

  This free quarterly publication available from the Southern Poverty Law Center is an outstanding resource for teachers. Activities abound that can be adapted for the foreign language classroom to help students learn about other cultures and at the same time appreciate, understand and respect students and community members at home. Write to: Teaching Tolerance, 400 Washington Ave., Montgomery, AL 36014.

## Foreign Language Standards

- *National Standards: A Catalyst for Reform.* Edited by Robert C. Lafayette. (1996). Lincolnwood, IL: National Textbook Company.

  This compendium looks at the foreign language standards and how they impact all aspects of foreign language teaching. This volume is a good overview of where the profession is headed, from teacher training to classroom implications for the standards.

- *Standards for Foreign Language Learning: Preparing for the 21st Century.* (1996). American Council on the Teaching of Foreign Languages, 6 Executive Plaza, Yonkers, NY.

  Foreign language teaching and learning is now organized by five principles known as the five C's of foreign language education: communication, cultures, connections, comparisons, and communities.

## General Educational Issues

### Block Scheduling

- Canady, R.L. & Rettig, M.D. (1995). *Block Scheduling: A Catalyst for Change in High Schools.* Larchmont, NY: Eye on Education.
- Canady, R.L. & Rettig, M.D. (1996). *Teaching in the Block: Strategies for Engaging Active Learners.* Larchmont, NY: Eye on Education.
- Cunningham, R. David. Jr. & Nogle, Sue Ann. (December 1996). "Six Keys to Block Scheduling." *The High School Magazine,* 29-32.
- Elkins, G. (Spring 1996). "Making Longer Better: Staff Development for Block Scheduling." Arlington, VA: ASCD Professional Development Newsletter.
- Gerking, Janet L. (April 1995). "Building Block Schedules: A Firsthand Assessment of Restructuring the School Day." *The Science Teacher,* 23–27.
- Hottenstein, D.S. (Winter 1996). "Supporting Block Scheduling: A Response to Critics." *Alliance* 1(2), 11. Reston, VA: The National Alliance of High Schools, a division of the National Association of Secondary School Principals.
- Wisconsin Association of Foreign Language Teachers. (1995). *Redesigning High School Schedules: A Report of the Task Force on Block Scheduling by the Wisconsin Association of Foreign Language Teachers.* Madison, WI: WAFLT (can be found on ERIC on the Internet).

### Classroom Management

- Johnson, D. and Johnson, R. (1995). *Reducing School Violence Through Conflict Resolution.* Alexandria VA: Association for Supervision and Curriculum Development.

  This text offers guidance to teachers on how to teach conflict resolution and actually create an environment that prevents conflict and violence.

- Jones, F. (1987). *Positive Classroom Discipline.* New York, NY: McGraw Hill.

  Dr. Jones spoke at the Central States Conference several years ago, and was a hit. Why? Because everyone could relate to what he was saying! Jones has foolproof ways to have the discipline and classroom management we all want and deserve.

- Kohn, A. (1996). *Beyond Discipline: From Compliance to Community.* Alexandria, VA: Association for Supervision and Curriculum Development.

  This text takes a new approach to classroom management/discipline.

### Multiple Intelligences

- Armstrong, Thomas. (1991). *Awakening Your Child's Natural Genius.* Los Angeles, CA: Jeremy P. Tarcher, Inc.
- Armstrong, Thomas. (1987). *Discovering and Encouraging Your Child's Personal Learning Style.* Los Angeles, CA: Jeremy P. Tarcher, Inc., Distributed by St. Martin's Press.
- Armstrong, Thomas. (1994). *Multiple Intelligences in the Classroom.* Alexandria, VA: Association for Supervision and Curriculum Development.
- Gardner, Howard. (1983). F*rames of Mind: The Theory of Multiple Intelligences.* New York, NY: Basic Books.
- Kline, Peter. (1988). *The Everyday Genius: Restoring Children's Natural Joy of Learning, and Yours Too.* Arlington, VA: Great Ocean Puublishers.
- Lazear, David. (1994) *Seven Pathways of Learning: Teaching Students and Parents about Multiple Intelligences.* Tucson, AZ: Zephyr Press.

  This text gives a good overview of multiple intelligences and provides suggested activity types to include in any kind of classroom.

## Second Language Acquisition

- Krashen, S.D. and Terrell, T.D. (1983) *The Natural Approach: Language Acquisition in the Classroom.* Englewood Cliffs, NJ: Prentice-Hall.

  This text provides the philosophy and approach to teaching second language based on research in linguistics, psychology, and psycholinguistics. Its major concepts are the Input Hypothesis and the Affective Filter Hypothesis.

- Larsen-Freeman, D. and Long, M.H. (1992). *An Introduction to Second Language Acquisition Research.* New York, NY: Longman.

  A complete overview of second language theories, this is a sophisticated text that provides a lengthy bibliography and set of references for further investigation.

- *Research in Language Learning: Principles, Processes, and Prospects.* (1993) Editor, Alice Omaggio Hadley. Lincolnwood, IL: National Textbook Company.

  This text, one of the series of ACTFL Foreign Language Education Series, is dedicated to research in language learning. Articles such as "Second Language Production: SLA Research in Speaking and Writing" by Susan Gass and Sally Sieloff Magnan offer a variety of perspectives on language acquisition research and how it applies to the classroom.

- *TESOL Quarterly*

  This journal provides research articles on second language acquisition. Foreign language educators have gained much from the research conducted by second language acquisition researchers whose primary function is working with the English to Speakers of Other Languages (ESOL) student population. We continue to benefit from their research.

- Omaggio Hadley, A. (1993) *Teaching Language in Context.* Boston, MA: Heinle and Heinle.

  Omaggio Hadley's text sets the standard for a thorough exploration of the teaching of the four skills. At the end of each chapter she offers an extensive list of sources for additional consultation.

## Technology

- Blyth, C.S. (1998). *Untangling the Web.* New York, NY: St. Martin's Press.

  This no-nonsense, easy to read text demystifies using the World Wide Web. Easy illustrations that show how the computer screen should appear at each step walk beginners and intermediate Internet users through the jungle of terms to achieve positive results when surfing the web.

- Bush, M.D. & Terry, R.M. (Eds.). (1997). *Technology-Enhanced Language Learning.* Illinois: National Textbook Company.

  This ACTFL Foreign Language Education Series volume explores multiple uses of technology in the foreign language classroom. Chapter titles include "Hypermedia Technology for Teaching Reading," "Teaching Listening: How Technology Can Help," and "Learning Language and Culture with Internet Technologies."

- *Educational Leadership* Volume 54, No. 3, November 1996.

  This volume, entitled "Networking", begins, as usual, with a point/counterpoint regarding technology and in particular, the use of the Internet. Articles such as "How Schools Can Create Their Own Web Pages" and "Online Mentors: Experimenting in Science Class" offer excellent ideas for second/foreign language teachers to incorporate in their instruction.

- *Educational Leadership* Volume 53, No. 2, October 1995.

  This issue entitled "How Technology is Transforming Teaching" explores global issues of technology such as "Selling a School Technology Budget" and "How to Fund Technology Projects." And, as in all issues of this journal, there exists an international section that looks at what is occurring outside the United States. One such article from New Zealand, "Computers Empower Students with Special Needs", reports on successful practices with at-risk students.

- *PC Computing*

  This general magazine on microcomputers provides interesting information for both the novice and the computer devoté and expert. Periodic issues list, for example, the editors' picks on the 1,000 best free WWW downloads. Also provided are evaluations and comparisons of technology products and gadgets.

- *Technological Horizons in Education Journal.* 150 El Camino Real, Suite 112, Tustin CA 92680-8670

  THE Journal reports school-based research projects and lists successful ideas that incorporate technology in the classroom. For example, in the December 1995 issue there appeared an article entitled "Maya Mythology & Multimedia: Using Each to Teach the Other."

## Additional Resources

There are many organizations that can provide a wealth of additional information and support for Spanish teachers. The list below will help you to expand your classroom resources and contact other teachers. Remember, however, that addresses and telephone numbers often change; it is advisable to verify them before sending inquiries.

### Professional Organizations

The American Council on the Teaching of Foreign Languages (ACTFL)
6 Executive Plaza
Yonkers, NY 10701
(914) 963-8830
http://www.actfl.org

American Association of Teachers of Spanish and Portuguese (AATSP)
Gunter Hall, Room 106
University of Northern Colorado
Greely, CO 80639
(303) 351-1090
http://www.aatsp.org

### Cultural Offices/Embassies/Consulates/Tourist Offices

Consult the telephone listings in most major cities for a listing of the embassies and consulates of Spanish-speaking countries closest to you.

Tourist Office of Spain
665 Fifth Avenue
New York, NY 10022
(212) 759-8822
http://www.okspain.org

Mexican Government Tourist Office
2707 N. Loop West, Suite 450
Houston, TX 77008
(713) 880-5153
http://www.mexico-travel.com

### Penpal Exchanges

Student Letter Exchange (League of Friendship)
630 Third Avenue
New York, NY 10017
(212) 557-3312

World Pen Pals
1694 Como Avenue
St. Paul, MN 55108
(612) 647-0191

### Travel/Cultural Exchange

CIEE Student Travel Services
205 East 42nd St.
New York, NY 10017
(212) 661-1414
http://www.counciltravel.com

American Field Service
220 East 42nd St., 3rd Floor
New York, NY 10017
(212) 949-4242
http://www.afs.org/usa

### Periodicals/Films

Subscriptions may be purchased for the school through the companies listed below, or through others in your local area:

EBSCO Subscription Services
P.O. Box 1943
Birmingham, AL 35201-1943

Gessler Publishing Company
55 West 13th St.
New York, NY 10011
(212) 627-0099

Continental Book Company
8000 Cooper Avenue Bldg. 29
Glendale, NY 11385
(718) 326-0572

The International Film Bureau
332 South Michigan Avenue
Chicago, IL 60604-4382
(312) 427-4545

### Online Contacts

Many organizations now maintain websites. Since, again, these are subject to change, it is advisable to check before contacting. We encourage you to visit the McDougal Littell website for materials specific to the ***¡En español!*** program. In addition, FLTEACH provides a discussion forum for teacher exchange of ideas and information:

www.mcdougallittell.com

FLTEACH
To subscribe or obtain information:
LISTSERV@listserv.acsu.buffalo.edu

In your message, put the following:
SUBSCRIBE FLTEACH, first name, last name
(to unsubscribe, send UNSUB FLTEACH, first name, last name)

To send messages to all FLTEACH subscribers:
FLTEACH@listserv.acsu.buffalo.edu

2 dos

McDOUGAL LITTELL

# ¡En español!

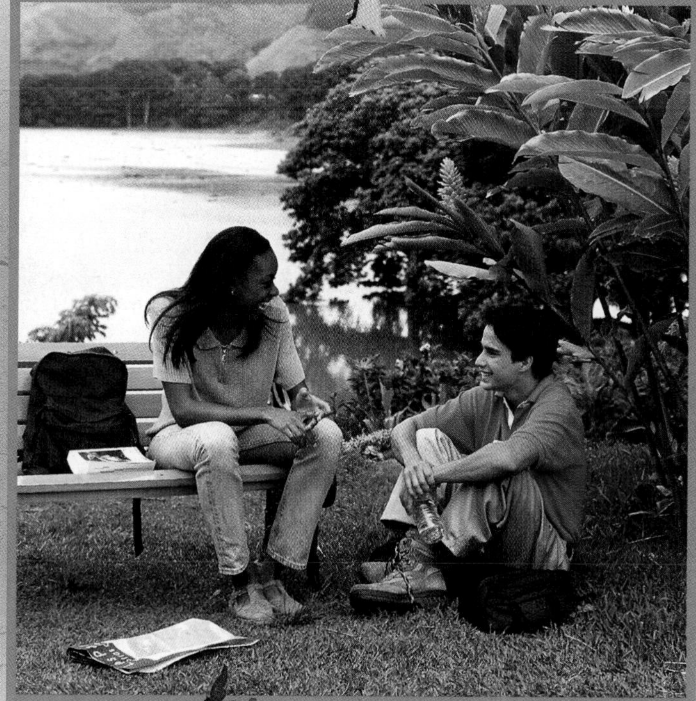

AUTHORS

Estella Gahala

Patricia Hamilton Carlin

Audrey L. Heining-Boynton

Ricardo Otheguy

Barbara J. Rupert

CULTURE CONSULTANT

Jorge A. Capetillo-Ponce

McDougal Littell

A HOUGHTON MIFFLIN COMPANY

Evanston, Illinois • Boston • Dallas

**Cover Photography**

Center: Large image taken in Costa Rica by Martha Granger/EDGE Productions.

Bottom, from left to right: Painted wooden cactus sculpture, Oaxaca, Mexico, RMIP/Richard Haynes; El Morro Fort in San Juan, Puerto Rico, Mark Harris/Tony Stone Images (also on back cover); Painted dog figure from Guatemala, Superstock; Plaza Mayor, Madrid, Spain, Martha Granger/EDGE Productions.



Acknowledgments for copyrighted material are on page R82 and constitute an extension of this page.



ISBN: 0-395-91083-8

4 5 6 7 8 9--WVK--05 04 03 02

Internet: www.mcdougallittell.com

# CONTENIDO

## OBJECTIVES

- Exchange greetings
- Discuss likes and dislikes
- Describe people and places
- Ask for and give information
- Talk about school life
- Talk about the new school year

## Etapa preliminar: Día a día 1

iii

UNIDAD
ETAPA 1
OBJECTIVES
• Talk about where you went and what you did
• Discuss leisure time
• Comment on airplane travel

# ESTADOS UNIDOS

## ¿QUÉ PASA?

***Visit Los Angeles, Chicago, and Miami with Francisco, his family, and friends.***

EL PUEBLO DE LOS ANGELES HISTORIC MONUMENT
¡VIVA EL PUEBLO!

UNIDAD 1

ETAPA 2

## Chicago - ¿Qué prefieres? 50

**OBJECTIVES**

- Comment on food
- Talk about the past
- Express activity preferences
- Discuss fine art

***Gitana***, *por Arturo Gordon Vargas*

UNIDAD 1

OBJECTIVES

- Discuss ways to communicate
- React to news
- Ask for and give information
- Talk about things and people you know

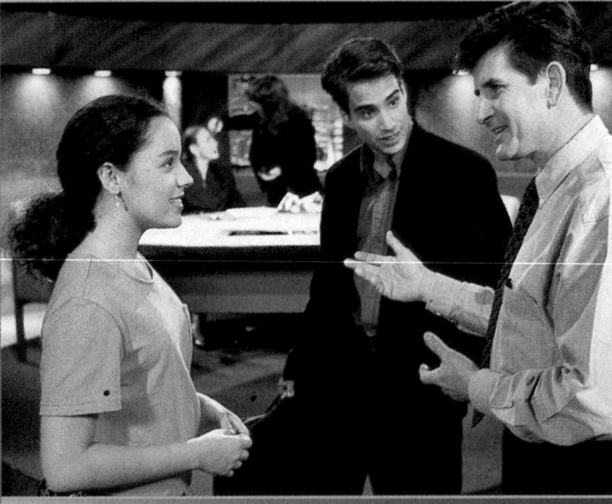

5B Noticias internacionales
1D Anuncios clasificados
6A Crítica
8B Noticias locales
1C Diversiones

El Universo

Robo en el museo, ladrón atrapado

¡Rescate dramático! Héroe local rescata a niño

## Miami - ¿Viste las noticias? 72

vi

# CIUDAD DE MÉXICO
## MÉXICO

AYER Y HOY

***Explore Mexico City with Isabel.***

### OBJECTIVES

- Describe childhood experiences
- Express personal reactions
- Discuss family relationships

UNIDAD 2

ETAPA 2

OBJECTIVES

- Narrate in the past
- Discuss family celebrations
- Talk about activities in progress

## Había una vez... 122

viii

UNIDAD 2

## OBJECTIVES

- Order in a restaurant
- Ask for and pay a restaurant bill
- Talk about things to do in the city

# Hoy en la ciudad 144





ix

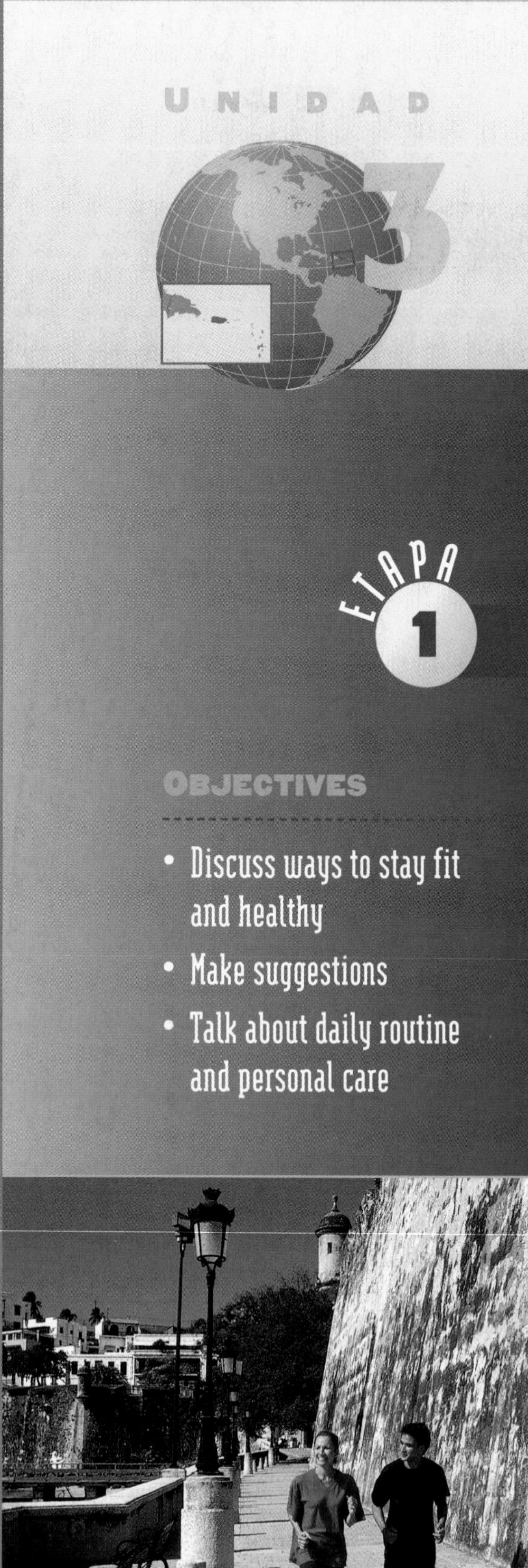


**OBJECTIVES**

- Discuss ways to stay fit and healthy
- Make suggestions
- Talk about daily routine and personal care

# SAN JUAN PUERTO RICO

## SOL Y SOMBRA

***Discover Puerto Rico while you stay fit with Francisco and his relatives.***





x

UNIDAD 3

## Preparaciones 194

OBJECTIVES

- Discuss beach activities
- Tell someone what to do
- Talk about chores
- Say if something has already been done

UNIDAD 3

ETAPA 3

OBJECTIVES

- Describe time periods
- Talk about health and illness
- Give advice

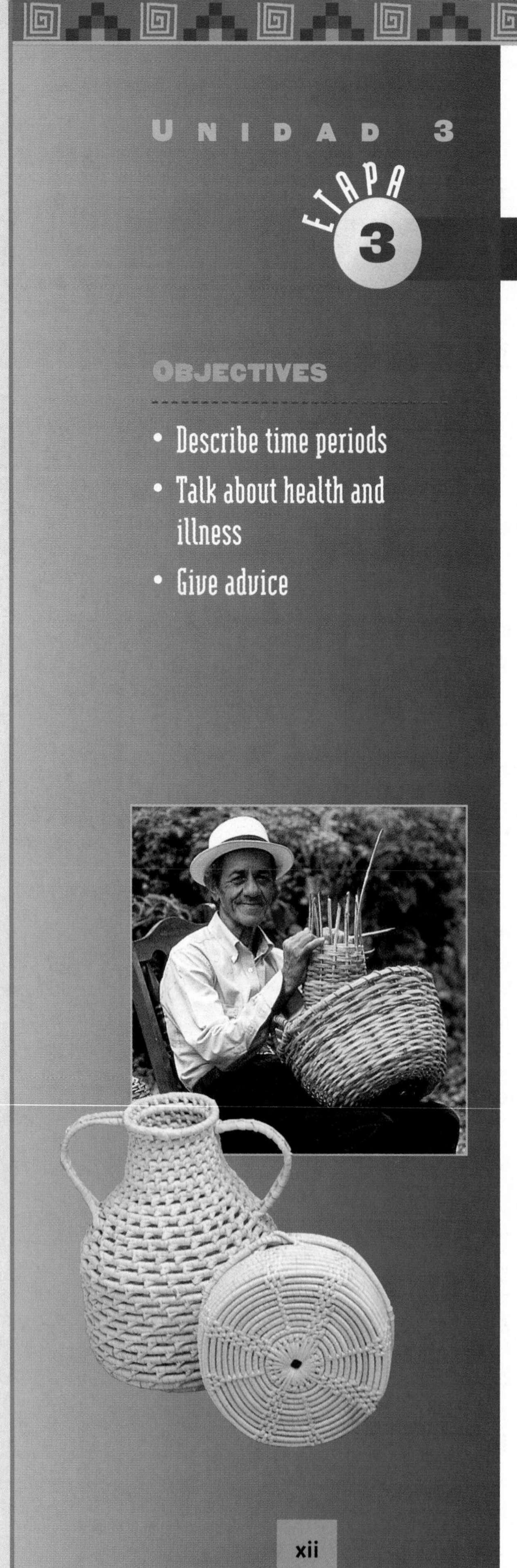

## ¿Cómo te sientes? 216





xii

# MADRID
## ESPAÑA

### UN VIAJE

***Explore Madrid and do some shopping with Isabel and Andrea.***

ETAPA 1

**OBJECTIVES**

- Talk about travel plans
- Persuade others
- Describe rooms, furniture, and appliances

xiii

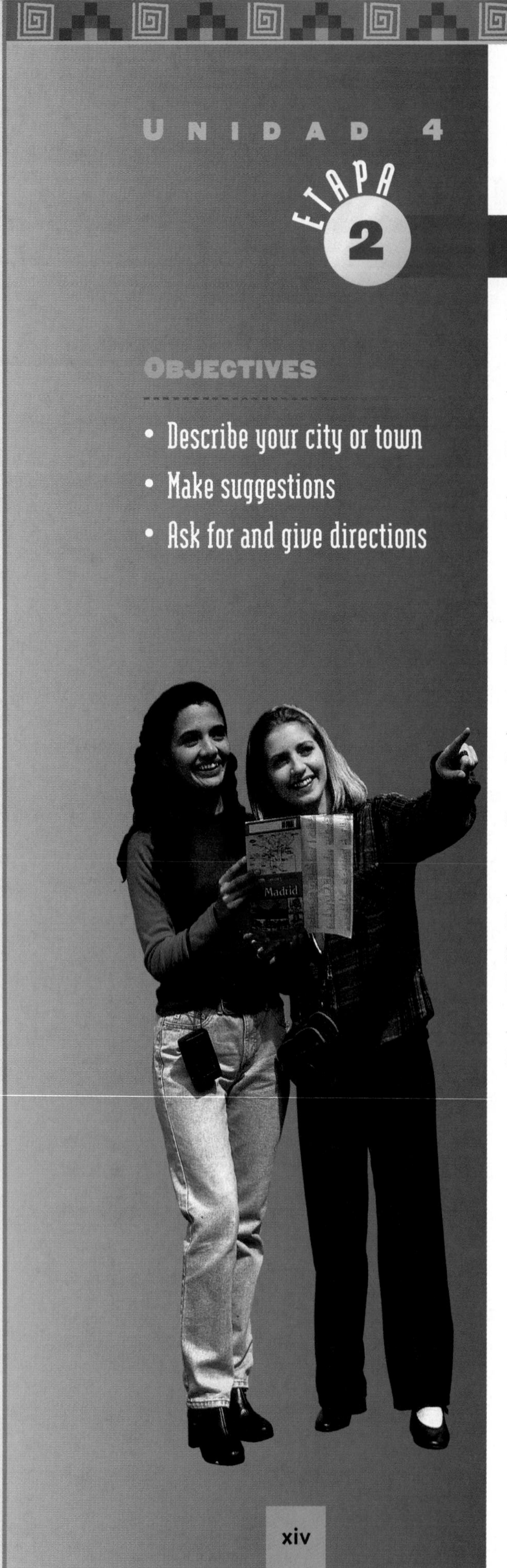
UNIDAD 4
ETAPA 2
OBJECTIVES
• Describe your city or town
• Make suggestions
• Ask for and give directions

## Conoce la ciudad 266

EL PAIS

xiv

UNIDAD 4

OBJECTIVES

- Talk about shopping for clothes
- Ask for and give opinions
- Make comparisons
- Discuss ways to save and spend money

## Vamos de compras 288



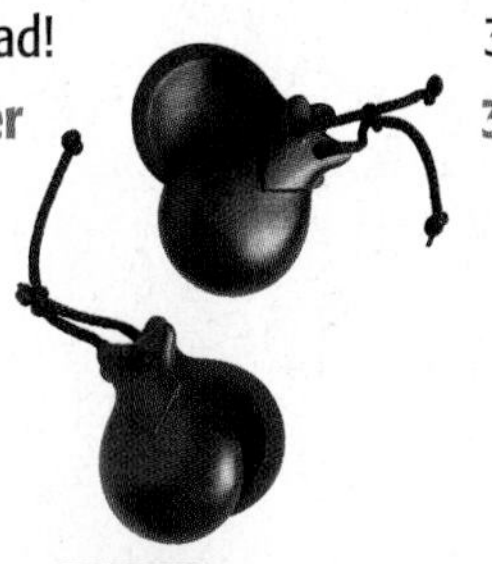



xv

UNIDAD 5

# SAN JOSÉ COSTA RICA

## LA NATURALEZA

***Learn about the environment and see Costa Rica with Francisco and his new friends.***

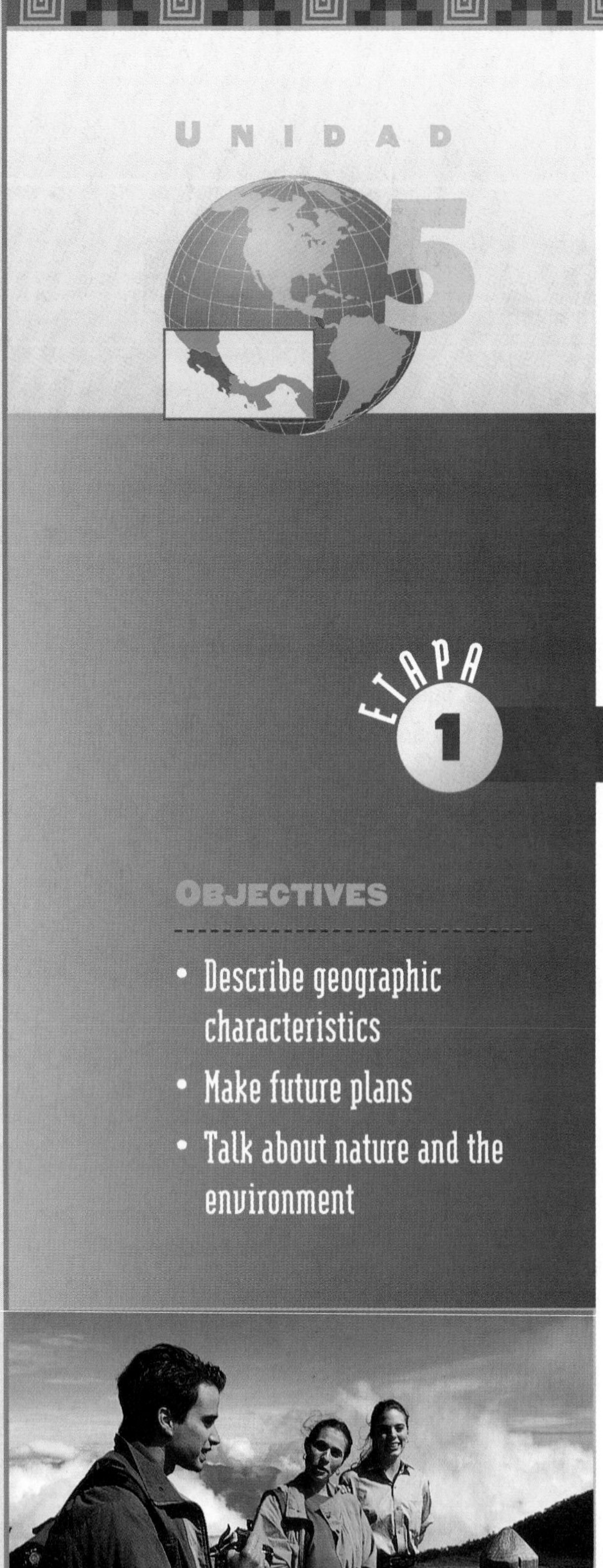

**OBJECTIVES**

- Describe geographic characteristics
- Make future plans
- Talk about nature and the environment

ETAPA 1





xvi

**OBJECTIVES**

- Discuss outdoor activities
- Describe the weather
- Make predictions
- Talk about ecology

## Nuestro medio ambiente 338

xvii

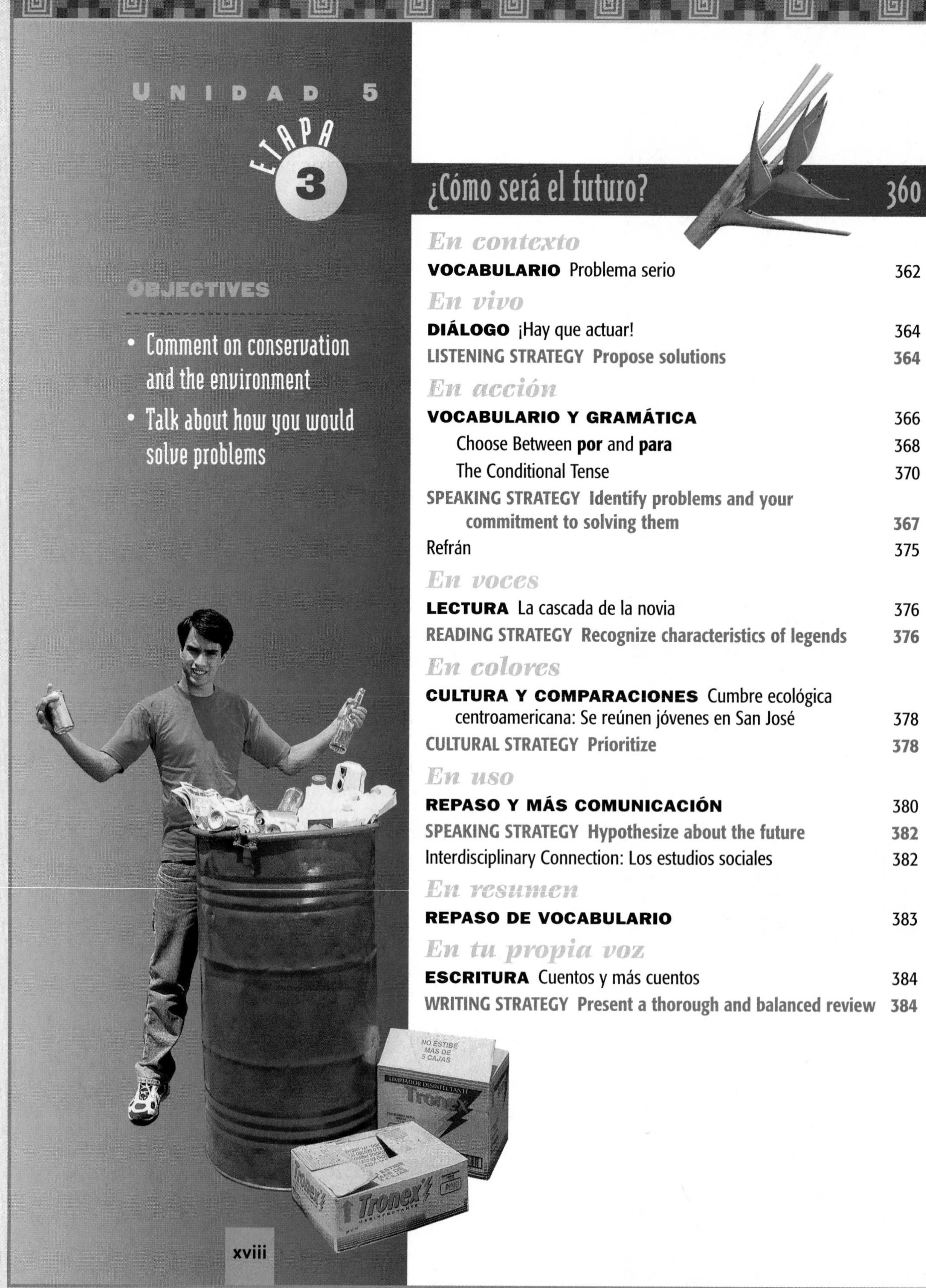

UNIDAD 5

ETAPA 3

OBJECTIVES

- Comment on conservation and the environment
- Talk about how you would solve problems

## ¿Cómo será el futuro? 360





xviii

UNIDAD 6

# QUITO
# ECUADOR

## EL MUNDO DEL TRABAJO

***Find out about the world of work as you travel to Ecuador with Isabel.***

ETAPA 1

### OBJECTIVES

- Discuss jobs and professions
- Describe people, places, and things
- Complete an application

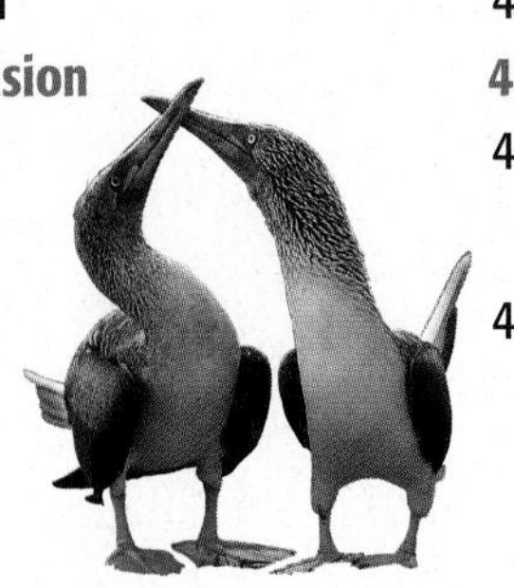



xix

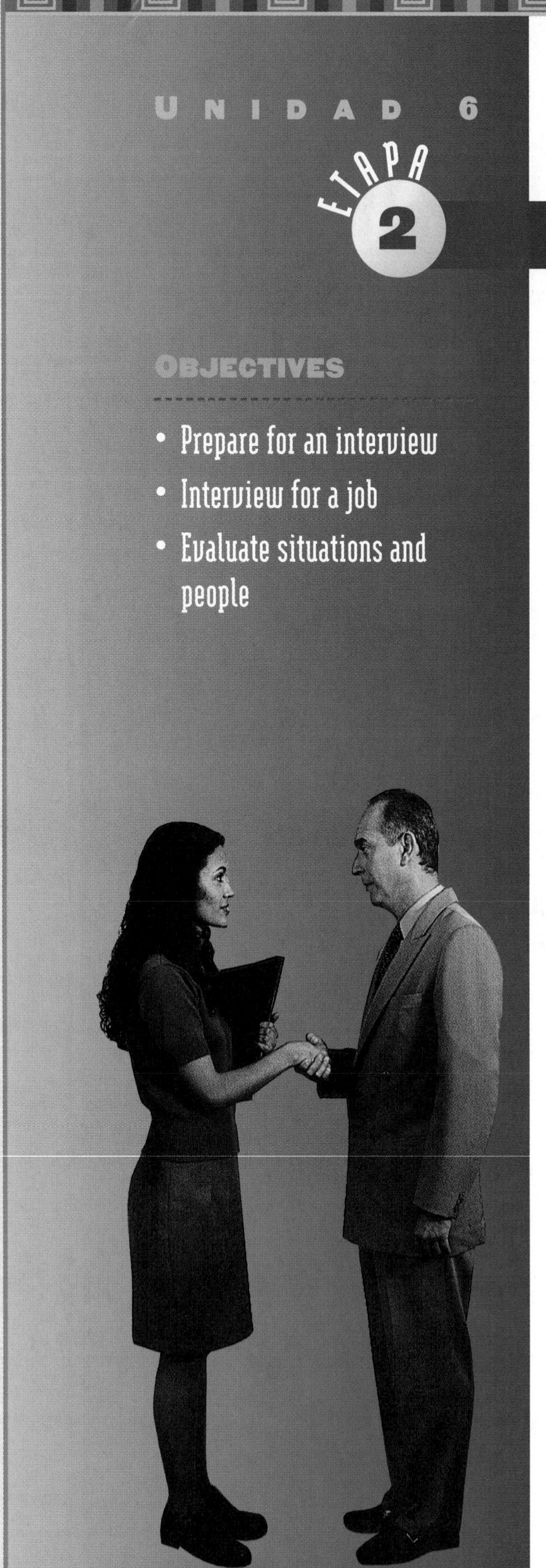

UNIDAD 6

ETAPA 2

OBJECTIVES

- Prepare for an interview
- Interview for a job
- Evaluate situations and people

## La entrevista 410

UNIDAD 6

## ¡A trabajar! 432

OBJECTIVES

- Talk on the telephone
- Report on past, present, and future events
- Describe duties, people, and surroundings

xxi

# About the Authors

**Estella Gahala** holds a Ph.D. in Educational Administration and Curriculum from Northwestern University. A career teacher of Spanish and French, she has worked with a wide range of students at the secondary level. She has also served as foreign language department chair and district director of curriculum and instruction. Her workshops at national, regional, and state conferences as well as numerous published articles draw upon the current research in language learning, learning strategies, articulation of foreign language sequences, and implications of the national Standards for Foreign Language Learning upon curriculum, instruction, and assessment. She has coauthored six basal textbooks.

**Patricia Hamilton Carlin** completed her M.A. in Spanish at the University of California, Davis, where she also taught as a lecturer. She also holds a Master of Secondary Education with specialization in foreign languages from the University of Arkansas. She has taught preschool through college, and her secondary programs in Arkansas have received national recognition. A coauthor of the *¡DIME! UNO* and *¡DIME! DOS* secondary textbooks, she currently teaches Spanish and methodology at the University of Central Arkansas, where she also supervises student teachers. She is a frequent presenter at local, regional, and national foreign language conferences.

**Audrey L. Heining-Boynton** received her Ph.D. in Curriculum and Instruction from Michigan State University. She is a Professor of Education and Romance Languages at The University of North Carolina at Chapel Hill, where she is a second language teacher educator and Professor of Spanish. She has also taught Spanish, French, and ESL at the K–12 level. Dr. Heining-Boynton was the president of the National Network for Early Language Learning, has been on the Executive Council of ACTFL, and involved with AATSP, Phi Delta Kappa, and state foreign language associations. She has presented both nationally and internationally, and has published over forty books, articles, and curricula.

**Ricardo Otheguy** received his Ph.D. in Linguistics from the City University of New York, where he is currently Professor of Linguistics at the Graduate School and University Center. He has written extensively on topics related to Spanish grammar as well as on bilingual education and the Spanish of the United States. He is coauthor of *Tu mundo: Curso para hispanohablantes,* a Spanish high school textbook for Spanish speakers, and of *Prueba de ubicación para hispanohablantes,* a high school Spanish placement test.

**Barbara J. Rupert** has taught Level 1 through A.P. Spanish during her many years of high school teaching. She is a graduate of Western Washington University, and has broadened her knowledge and skills base with numerous graduate level courses emphasizing language acquisition, authentic assessment, and educational leadership and reform. She serves as the World Languages Department Chair, District Trainer and Chair of her school's Site Council. Barbara is the author of CD-ROM activities for the *¡Bravo!* series and presents at a variety of foreign language conferences. In 1996, Barbara received the Christa McAuliffe Award for Excellence in Education.

## Culture Consultant

**Jorge A. Capetillo-Ponce** is presently a Ph.D. candidate in Sociology at the New School for Social Research, where he is also Special Consultant to the Dean of The Graduate Faculty. His graduate studies at the New School and El Colegio de México include a diversity of fields such as international relations, sociopolitical analysis, cultural theory, and sociology. He has published a wide range of essays on art, politics, religion, international relations, and society in Latin America, the United States, and the Middle East; as well as being an advisor to a number of politicians and public figures, a researcher and editor, and a college professor and television producer in Mexico, Nicaragua, and the United States.

## Consulting Authors

Dan Battisti
Dr. Teresa Carrera-Hanley
Bill Lionetti
Patty Murguía Bohannan
Lorena Richins Layser

## Regional Language Reviewers

Dolores Acosta (Mexico)
Jaime M. Fatás Cabeza (Spain)
Grisel Lozano-Garcini (Puerto Rico)
Isabel Picado (Costa Rica)
Juan Pablo Rovayo (Ecuador)

## Contributing Writers

Ronni L. Gordon
Christa Harris
Debra Lowry
Sylvia Madrigal Velasco
Sandra Rosenstiel
David M. Stillman
Jill K. Welch

## Ad hoc Representatives

Vicki Armstrong
Jane Asano
Kathy Cavers
Dan Griffith
Rita McGuire
Gretchen Toole

## Senior Reviewers

O. Lynn Bolton
Dr. Jane Govoni
Elías G. Rodríguez
Ann Tollefson

## Teacher Reviewers

**Susan Arbuckle**
Mahomet-Seymour High School
Mahomet, IL

**Silvia Armstrong**
Mills High School
Little Rock, AR

**Sandra Martín Arnold**
Palisades Charter High School
Pacific Palisades, CA

**Warren Bender**
Duluth East High School
Duluth, MN

**Adrienne Chamberlain-Parris**
Mariner High School
Everett, WA

**Norma Coto**
Bishop Moore High School
Orlando, FL

**Roberto del Valle**
Shorecrest High School
Shoreline, WA

**Rubén D. Elías**
Roosevelt High School
Fresno, CA

**José Esparza**
Curie Metroplitan High School
Chicago, IL

**Lorraine A. Estrada**
Cabarrus County Schools
Concord, NC

**Alberto Ferreiro**
Harrisburg High School
Harrisburg, PA

**Judith C. Floyd**
Henry Foss High School
Tacoma, WA

**Lucy H. García**
Pueblo East High School
Pueblo, CO

**Marco García**
Lincoln Park High School
Chicago, IL

**Raquel R. González**
Odessa High School
Odessa, TX

**Linda Grau**
Shorecrest Preparatory School
St. Petersburg, FL

**Deborah Hagen**
Ionia High School
Ionia, MI

**Sandra Hammond**
St. Petersburg High School
St. Petersburg, FL

**Bill Heller**
Perry Junior/Senior High School
Perry, NY

**Jody Klopp**
Oklahoma State Department of Education
Edmond, OK

**Richard Ladd**
Ipswich High School
Ipswich, MA

**Carol Leach**
Francis Scott Key High School
Union Bridge, MD

**Laura McCormick**
East Seneca Senior High School
West Seneca, NY

**Rafaela McLeod**
Southeast Raleigh High School
Raleigh, NC

**Kathleen L. Michaels**
Palm Harbor University High School
Palm Harbor, FL

**Vickie A. Mike**
Horseheads High School
Horseheads, NY

**Terri Nies**
Mannford High School
Mannford, OK

**María Emma Nunn**
John Tyler High School
Tyler, TX

**Lewis Olvera**
Hiram Johnson West Campus High School
Sacramento, CA

**Anne-Marie Quihuis**
Paradise Valley High School
Phoenix, AZ

**Rita Risco**
Palm Harbor University High School
Palm Harbor, FL

**James J. Rudy, Jr.**
Glen Este High School
Cincinnati, OH

**Pamela Urdal Silva**
East Lake High School
Tarpon Springs, FL

**Kathleen Solórzano**
Homestead High School
Mequon, WI

**Sarah Spiesman**
Whitmer High School
Toledo, OH

**M. Mercedes Stephenson**
Hazelwood Central High School
Florissant, MO

**Carol Thorp**
East Mecklenburg High School
Charlotte, NC

**Elizabeth Torosian**
Doherty Middle School
Andover, MA

**Wendy Villanueva**
Lakeville High School
Lakeville, MN

**Helen Webb**
Arkadelphia High School
Arkadelphia, AR

**Jena Williams**
Jonesboro High School
Jonesboro, AR

**Janet Wohlers**
Weston Middle School
Weston, MA

## Teacher Panel

**Linda Amour**
Highland High School
Bakersfield, CA

**Dena Bachman**
Lafayette Senior High School
St. Joseph, MO

**Sharon Barnes**
J. C. Harmon High School
Kansas City, KS

**Ben Barrientos**
Calvin Simmons Junior High School
Oakland, CA

**Paula Biggar**
Sumner Academy of Arts & Science
Kansas City, KS

**Edda Cardenas**
Blue Valley North High School
Leawood, KS

**Joyce Chow**
Crespi Junior High School
Richmond , CA

**Mike Cooperider**
Truman High School
Independence, MO

**Judy Dozier**
Shawnee Mission South High School
Shawnee Mission, KS

**Maggie Elliott**
Bell Junior High School
San Diego, CA

**Dana Galloway-Grey**
Ontario High School
Ontario, CA

**Nieves Gerber**
Chatsworth Senior High School
Chatsworth, CA

**Susanne Kissane**
Shawnee Mission Northwest High School
Shawnee Mission, KS

**Ann Lopez**
Pala Middle School
San Jose, CA

**Beatrice Marino**
Palos Verdes Peninsula High School
Rolling Hills Estates, CA

**Barbara Mortanian**
Tenaya Middle School
Fresno, CA

**Vickie Musni**
Pioneer High School
San Jose, CA

**Rodolfo Orihuela**
C. K. McClatchy High School
Sacramento, CA

**Terrie Rynard**
Olathe South High School
Olathe, KS

**Beth Slinkard**
Lee's Summit High School
Lee's Summit, MO

**Rosa Stein**
Park Hill High School
Kansas City, MO

## Urban Panel

**Rebecca Carr**
William G. Enloe High School
Raleigh, NC

**Norha Franco**
East Side High School
Newark, NJ

**Kathryn Gardner**
Riverside University High School
Milwaukee, WI

**Eula Glenn**
Remtec Center
Detroit, MI

**Jeana Harper**
Detroit Fine Arts High School
Detroit, MI

**Guillermina Jauregui**
Los Angeles Senior High School
Los Angeles, CA

**Lula Lewis**
Hyde Park Career Academy High School
Chicago, IL

**Florence Meyers**
Overbrook High School
Philadelphia, PA

**Vivian Selenikas**
Long Island City High School
Long Island City, NY

**Sadia White**
Spingarn Stay Senior High School
Washington, DC

## Block Scheduling Panel

**Barbara Baker**
Wichita Northwest High School
Wichita, KS

**Patty Banker**
Lexington High School
Lexington, NC

**Beverly Blackburn**
Reynoldsburg Senior High School
Reynoldsburg, OH

**Henry Foust**
Northwood High School
Pittsboro, NC

**Gloria Hawks**
A. L. Brown High School
Kannapolis, NC

**Lois Hillman**
North Kitsap High School
Poulsbo, WA

**Nick Patterson**
Central High School
Davenport, IA

**Sharyn Petkus**
Grafton Memorial High School
Grafton, MA

**Cynthia Prieto**
Mount Vernon High School
Alexandria, VA

**Julie Sanchez**
Western High School
Fort Lauderdale, FL

**Marilyn Settlemyer**
Freedom High School
Morganton, NC

## Student Review Board

**Andrea Avila**
Fannin Middle School
Amarillo, TX

**Maya Beynishes**
Edward R. Murrow High School
Brooklyn, NY

**James Dock**
Guilford High School
Rockford, IL

**Richard Elkins**
Nevin Platt Middle School
Boulder, CO

**Kathryn Finn**
Charles S. Pierce Middle School
Milton, MA

**Robert Foulis**
Stratford High School
Houston, TX

**Lorrain Garcia**
Luther Burbank High School
Sacramento, CA

**Katie Hagen**
Ionia High School
Ionia, MI

**Steven Hailey**
Davis Drive School
Apex, NC

**Eli Harel**
Thomas Edison Intermediate School
Westfield, NJ

**Cheryl Kim**
Dr. Leo Cigarroa High School
Laredo, TX

**Jennifer Kim**
Kellogg Middle School
Seattle, WA

**Jordan Leitner**
Scripps Ranch High School
San Diego, CA

**Courtney McPherson**
Miramar High School
Miramar, FL

**Zachary Nelson**
Warsaw Community High School
Warsaw, IN

**Diana Parrish**
Oak Crest Junior High School
Encinitas, CA

**Kimberly Robinson**
Perryville Senior High School
Perryville, AR

**John Roland**
Mountain Pointe High School
Phoenix, AZ

**Nichole Ryan**
Bermudian Springs High School
York Springs, PA

**Ryan Shore**
West Miami Middle School
Miami, FL

**Tiffany Stadler**
Titusville High School
Titusville, FL

**Michael Szymanski**
West Seneca East High School
West Seneca, NY

**Anela Talic**
Soldan International Studies High School
St. Louis, MO

**Gary Thompson**
Fort Dorchester High School
Charleston, SC

**Bethany Traynor**
Glen Este High School
Cincinnati, OH

**Gerard White**
Paramount High School
Paramount, CA

**Nichols Wilson**
Waubonsie Valley High School
Aurora, IL

**Amy Wyron**
Robert Frost Intermediate School
Rockville, MD

**Karina Zepeda**
West Mecklenburg High School
Charlotte, NC


Acknowledgments xxv

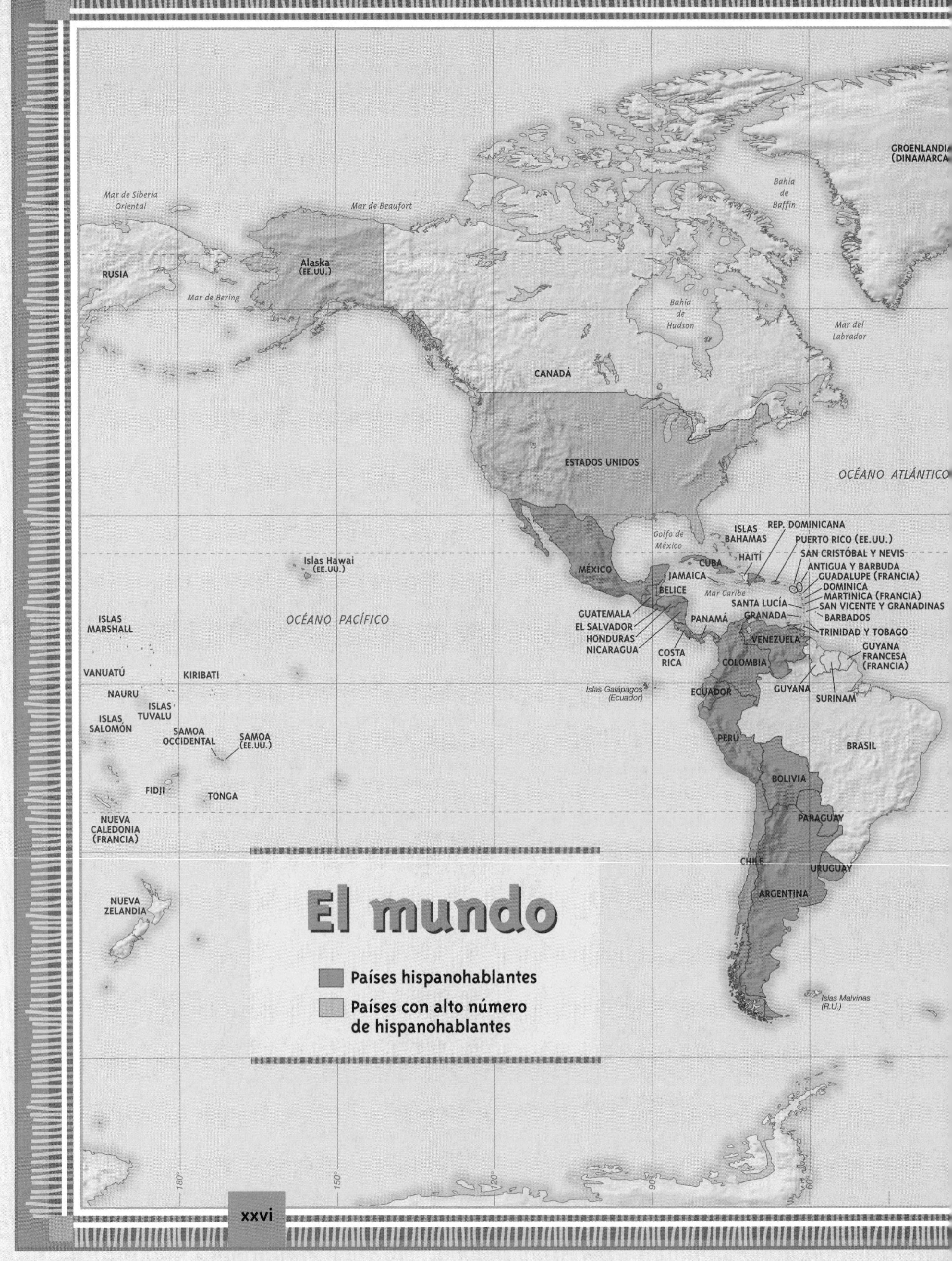

El mundo
Países hispanohablantes
Países con alto número de hispanohablantes
Mar de Siberia Oriental
Mar de Beaufort
RUSIA
Alaska (EE.UU.)
Mar de Bering
CANADÁ
Bahía de Baffin
GROENLANDIA (DINAMARCA)
Bahía de Hudson
Mar del Labrador
ESTADOS UNIDOS
OCÉANO ATLÁNTICO
Golfo de México
MÉXICO
Islas Hawai (EE.UU.)
OCÉANO PACÍFICO
ISLAS BAHAMAS
REP. DOMINICANA
PUERTO RICO (EE.UU.)
HAITÍ
CUBA
SAN CRISTÓBAL Y NEVIS
ANTIGUA Y BARBUDA
GUADALUPE (FRANCIA)
DOMINICA
MARTINICA (FRANCIA)
SAN VICENTE Y GRANADINAS
BARBADOS
JAMAICA
BELICE
Mar Caribe
SANTA LUCÍA
GRANADA
TRINIDAD Y TOBAGO
GUATEMALA
EL SALVADOR
HONDURAS
NICARAGUA
COSTA RICA
PANAMÁ
VENEZUELA
GUYANA FRANCESA (FRANCIA)
COLOMBIA
GUYANA
SURINAM
Islas Galápagos (Ecuador)
ECUADOR
PERÚ
BRASIL
BOLIVIA
PARAGUAY
CHILE
URUGUAY
ARGENTINA
Islas Malvinas (R.U.)
ISLAS MARSHALL
VANUATÚ
KIRIBATI
NAURU
ISLAS TUVALU
ISLAS SALOMÓN
SAMOA OCCIDENTAL
SAMOA (EE.UU.)
FIDJI
TONGA
NUEVA CALEDONIA (FRANCIA)
NUEVA ZELANDIA
180°
150°
120°
90°
60°
xxvi

OCÉANO ÁRTICO
Mar de Laptev
Mar de Kara
Mar de Barents
Mar de Noruega
ISLANDIA
SUECIA
FINLANDIA
NORUEGA
RUSIA
ESTONIA
LETONIA
LITUANIA
REINO UNIDO
Mar del Norte
Mar Báltico
IRLANDA
ALEMANIA
POLONIA
BIELORRUSIA
UCRANIA
MOLDAVIA
FRANCIA
AUSTRIA
RUMANIA
ANDORRA
ESPAÑA
PORTUGAL
ITALIA
GRECIA
Mar Negro
GEORGIA
TURQUÍA
ARMENIA
AZERBAIYÁN
Mar Caspio
Mar de Aral
KAZAKSTÁN
UZBEKISTÁN
TURKMENISTÁN
KIRGUISTÁN
TADJIKISTÁN
MONGOLIA
Lago Baikal
Mar de Ojotsk
COREA DEL NORTE
COREA DEL SUR
Mar de Japón
JAPÓN
CHINA
GIBRALTAR (R.U.)
Mar Mediterráneo
CHIPRE
LÍBANO
SIRIA
IRAQ
IRÁN
AFGANISTÁN
Islas Canarias (Esp.)
MARRUECOS
ISRAEL
JORDANIA
KUWAIT
QATAR
BAHREIN
E.A.U.
PAQUISTÁN
NEPAL
BHUTÁN
SAHARA OCCIDENTAL
ARGELIA
LIBIA
EGIPTO
ARABIA SAUDITA
OMÁN
INDIA
MYANMAR
LAOS
Trópico de Cáncer
TAIWÁN
GUAM (EE.UU.)
MAURITANIA
MALÍ
NÍGER
CHAD
SUDÁN
ERITREA
YEMEN
Mar Rojo
BANGLADESH
TAILANDIA
VIETNAM
Mar de China
SENEGAL
BURKINA FASO
BENIN
NIGERIA
GUINEA
COSTA DE MARFIL
TOGO
GHANA
LIBERIA
SIERRA LEONA
YIBUTI
Mar Arábigo
Golfo de Bengala
CAMBOYA
FILIPINAS
REP. CENTRO-AFRICANA
ETIOPÍA
SOMALIA
CAMERÚN
BRUNEI
PALAU
MICRONESIA
GUINEA ECUATORIAL
CONGO
GABÓN
REP. DEL CONGO
UGANDA
KENIA
RUANDA
ISLAS MALDIVAS
SRI LANKA
MALAYSIA
Ecuador
SINGAPUR
BURUNDI
TANZANÍA
INDONESIA
PAPUASIA NUEVA GUINEA
CABINDA (ANGOLA)
SEYCHELLES
MALAWI
ANGOLA
ZAMBIA
COMORES
MOZAMBIQUE
MAURICIO
OCÉANO ÍNDICO
NAMIBIA
ZIMBABWE
BOTSWANA
MADAGASCAR
Trópico de Capricornio
AUSTRALIA
SUAZILANDIA
SUDÁFRICA
LESOTHO
1 DINAMARCA
2 HOLANDA
3 BÉLGICA
4 LUXEMBURGO
5 SUIZA
6 REPÚBLICA CHECA
7 ESLOVAQUIA
8 HUNGRÍA
9 ESLOVENIA
10 CROACIA
11 BOSNIA Y HERZEGOVINA
12 YUGOSLAVIA
13 ALBANIA
14 MACEDONIA
15 BULGARIA
16 MALTA
N
0 1000 2000 kilómetros
0 1000 2000 millas
ANTÁRTIDA
0°
30°
60°
90°
120°
xxvii

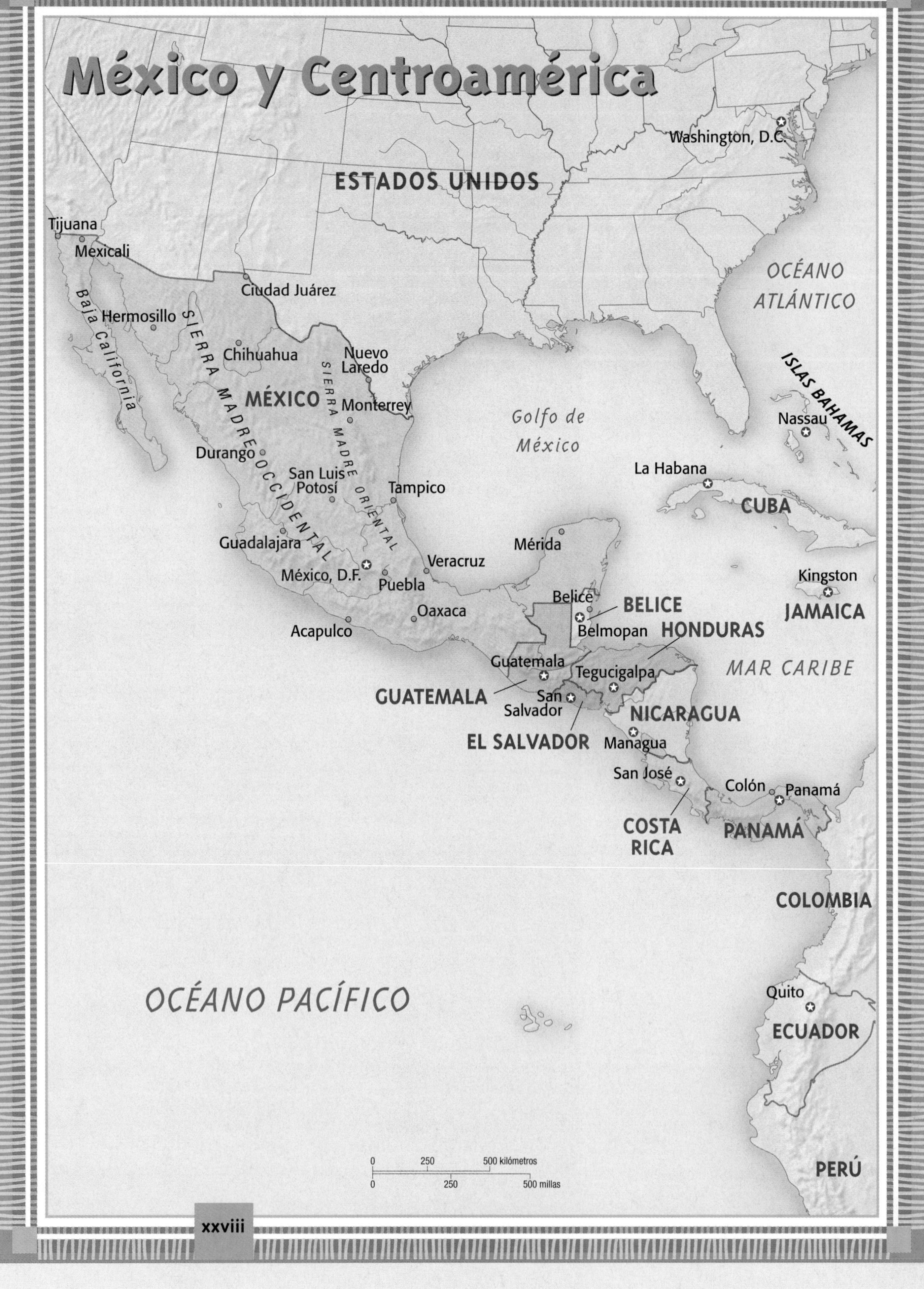
México y Centroamérica
ESTADOS UNIDOS
Washington, D.C.
OCÉANO ATLÁNTICO
Tijuana
Mexicali
Ciudad Juárez
Baja California
Hermosillo
SIERRA MADRE OCCIDENTAL
Chihuahua
Nuevo Laredo
SIERRA MADRE ORIENTAL
MÉXICO
Monterrey
Golfo de México
ISLAS BAHAMAS
Nassau
Durango
San Luis Potosí
Tampico
La Habana
CUBA
Guadalajara
Mérida
Veracruz
México, D.F.
Puebla
Kingston
JAMAICA
Belice
BELICE
Oaxaca
Acapulco
Belmopan
HONDURAS
MAR CARIBE
Guatemala
Tegucigalpa
GUATEMALA
San Salvador
NICARAGUA
EL SALVADOR
Managua
San José
Colón
Panamá
COSTA RICA
PANAMÁ
COLOMBIA
OCÉANO PACÍFICO
Quito
ECUADOR
PERÚ
0 250 500 kilómetros
0 250 500 millas
xxviii

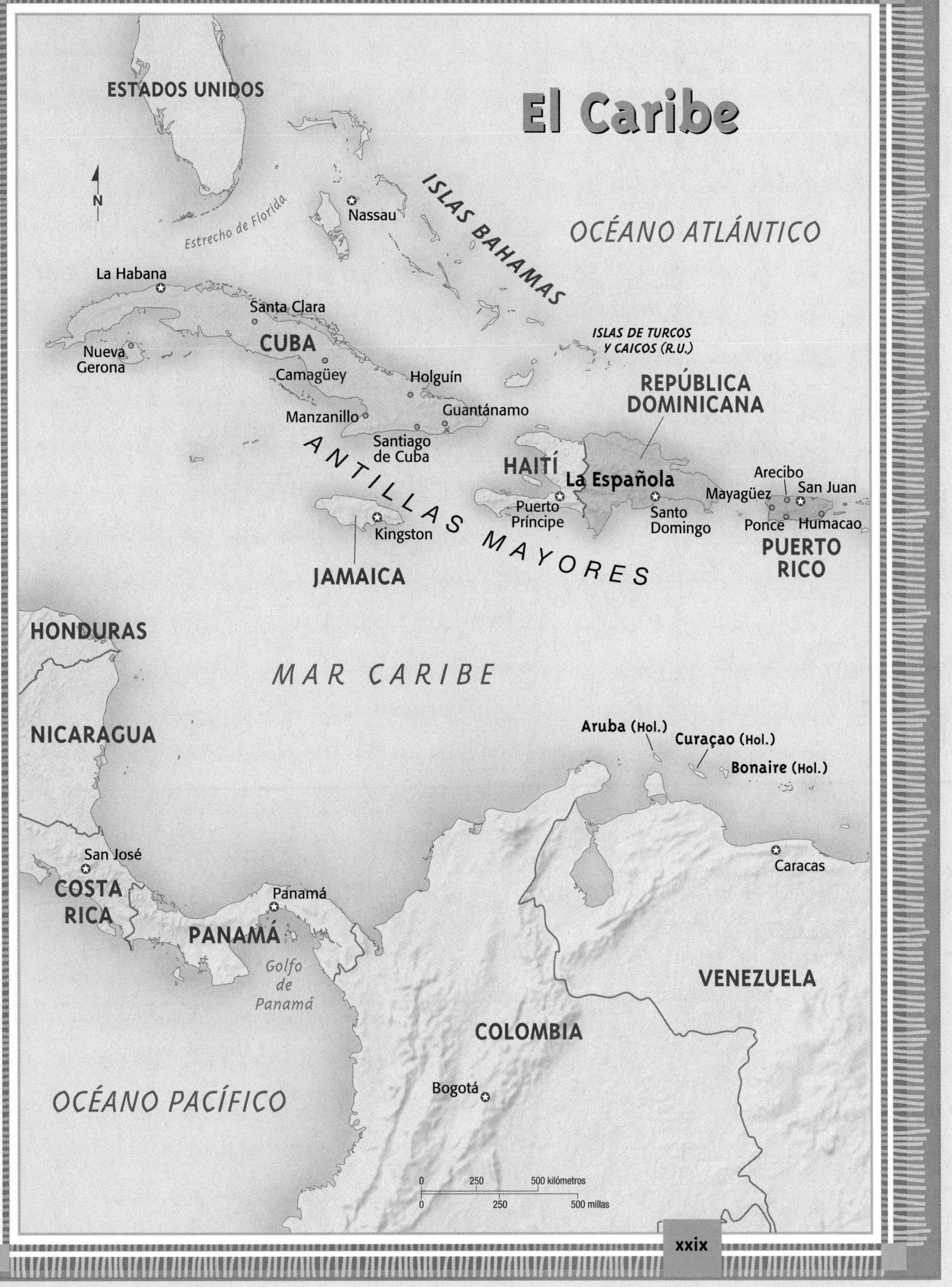

El Caribe
ESTADOS UNIDOS
N
Estrecho de Florida
Nassau
ISLAS BAHAMAS
OCÉANO ATLÁNTICO
La Habana
Santa Clara
CUBA
Nueva Gerona
Camagüey
Holguín
ISLAS DE TURCOS Y CAICOS (R.U.)
REPÚBLICA DOMINICANA
Manzanillo
Guantánamo
Santiago de Cuba
ANTILLAS MAYORES
HAITÍ
La Española
Arecibo
San Juan
Mayagüez
Puerto Príncipe
Santo Domingo
Ponce
Humacao
Kingston
PUERTO RICO
JAMAICA
HONDURAS
MAR CARIBE
NICARAGUA
Aruba (Hol.)
Curaçao (Hol.)
Bonaire (Hol.)
San José
COSTA RICA
Panamá
PANAMÁ
Caracas
Golfo de Panamá
VENEZUELA
COLOMBIA
OCÉANO PACÍFICO
Bogotá
0 250 500 kilómetros
0 250 500 millas


xxix

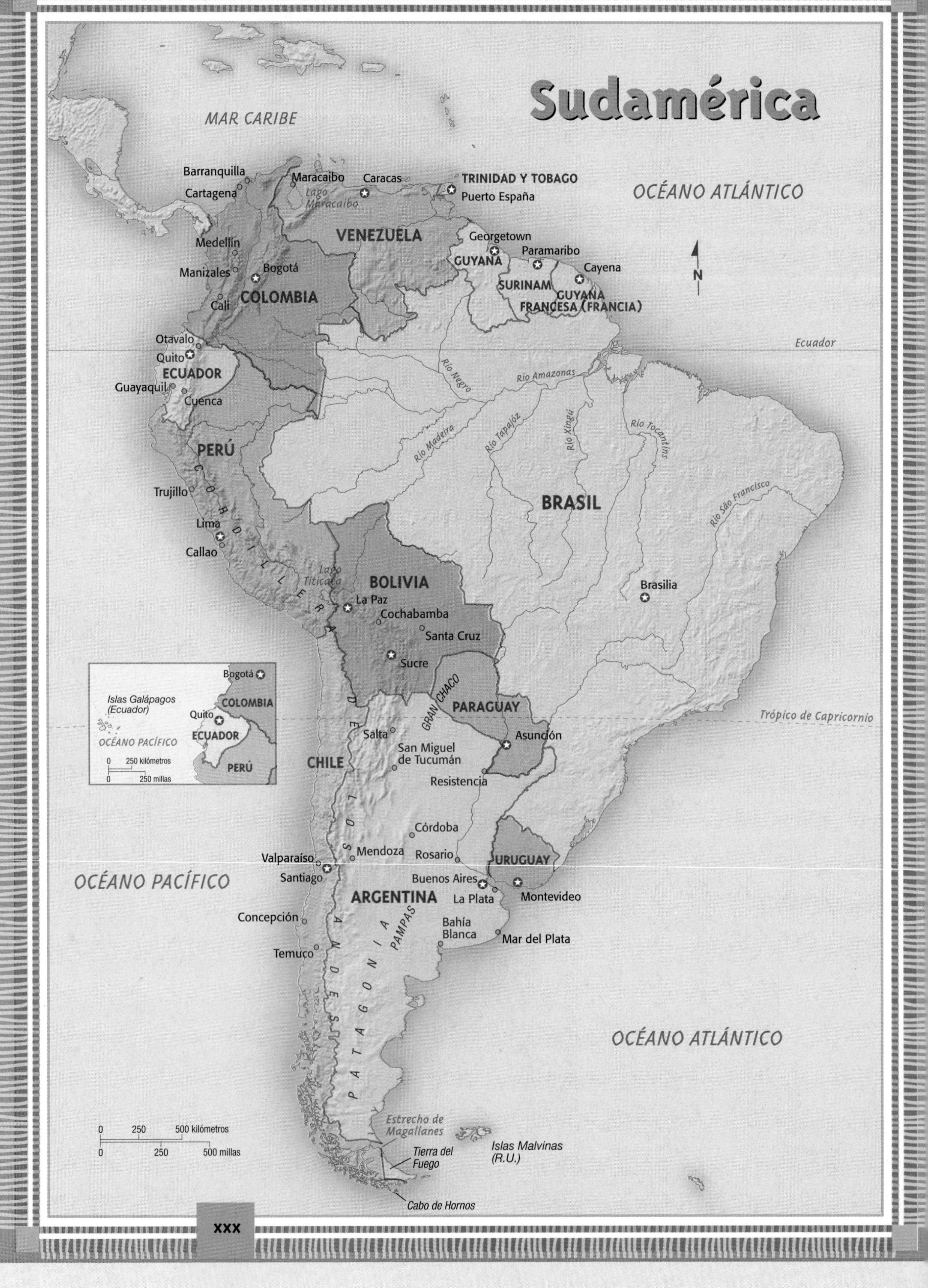
Sudamérica
MAR CARIBE
OCÉANO ATLÁNTICO
OCÉANO PACÍFICO
OCÉANO ATLÁNTICO
N
Barranquilla
Cartagena
Maracaibo
Lago Maracaibo
Caracas
TRINIDAD Y TOBAGO
Puerto España
VENEZUELA
Georgetown
GUYANA
Paramaribo
SURINAM
Cayena
GUYANA FRANCESA (FRANCIA)
Medellín
Manizales
Bogotá
Cali
COLOMBIA
Otavalo
Quito
ECUADOR
Guayaquil
Cuenca
Ecuador
Río Negro
Río Amazonas
Río Madeira
Río Tapajóz
Río Xingu
Río Tocantins
Río São Francisco
PERÚ
CORDILLERA DE LOS ANDES
Trujillo
Lima
Callao
BRASIL
Lago Titicaca
BOLIVIA
La Paz
Cochabamba
Santa Cruz
Sucre
Brasilia
GRAN CHACO
PARAGUAY
Trópico de Capricornio
Asunción
Salta
San Miguel de Tucumán
Resistencia
CHILE
Córdoba
Mendoza
Rosario
URUGUAY
Valparaíso
Santiago
Buenos Aires
La Plata
Montevideo
ARGENTINA
PAMPAS
Concepción
Bahía Blanca
Mar del Plata
Temuco
PATAGONIA
Estrecho de Magallanes
Tierra del Fuego
Islas Malvinas (R.U.)
Cabo de Hornos
0 250 500 kilómetros
0 250 500 millas
Bogotá
Islas Galápagos (Ecuador)
COLOMBIA
Quito
ECUADOR
OCÉANO PACÍFICO
PERÚ
0 250 kilómetros
0 250 millas
xxx

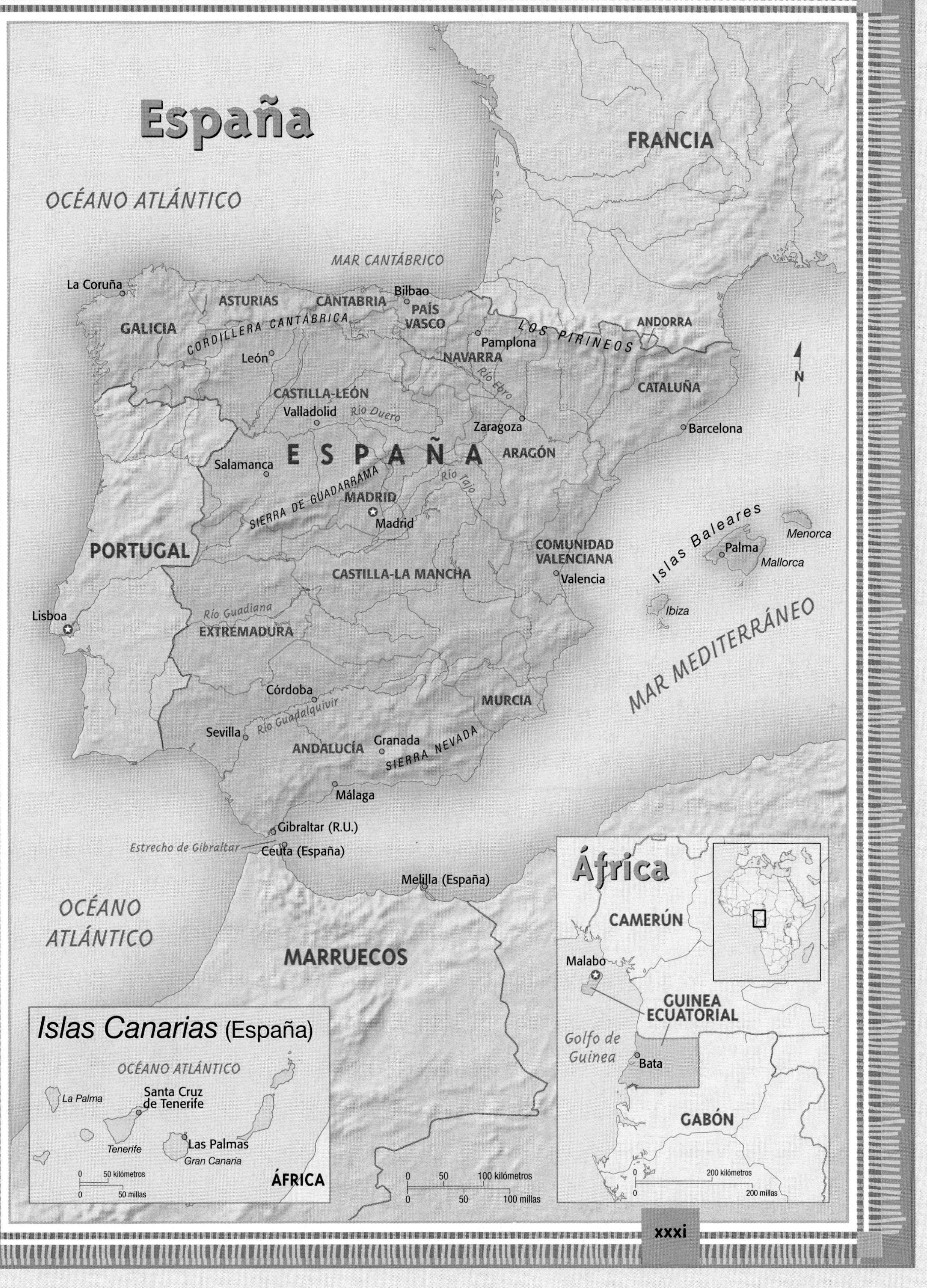

España
OCÉANO ATLÁNTICO
FRANCIA
MAR CANTÁBRICO
La Coruña
ASTURIAS
CANTABRIA
Bilbao
PAÍS VASCO
GALICIA
CORDILLERA CANTÁBRICA
LOS PIRINEOS
ANDORRA
Pamplona
León
NAVARRA
Río Ebro
CATALUÑA
CASTILLA-LEÓN
Valladolid
Río Duero
Zaragoza
Barcelona
Salamanca
E S P A Ñ A
ARAGÓN
SIERRA DE GUADARRAMA
Río Tajo
MADRID
Madrid
Islas Baleares
Menorca
Palma
Mallorca
PORTUGAL
COMUNIDAD VALENCIANA
Valencia
CASTILLA-LA MANCHA
Lisboa
Río Guadiana
EXTREMADURA
Ibiza
MAR MEDITERRÁNEO
Córdoba
MURCIA
Río Guadalquivir
Sevilla
ANDALUCÍA
Granada
SIERRA NEVADA
Málaga
Gibraltar (R.U.)
Estrecho de Gibraltar
Ceuta (España)
Melilla (España)
OCÉANO ATLÁNTICO
MARRUECOS
Islas Canarias (España)
OCÉANO ATLÁNTICO
La Palma
Santa Cruz de Tenerife
Tenerife
Las Palmas
Gran Canaria
0 50 kilómetros
0 50 millas
ÁFRICA
0 50 100 kilómetros
0 50 100 millas
África
CAMERÚN
Malabo
GUINEA ECUATORIAL
Golfo de Guinea
Bata
GABÓN
0 200 kilómetros
0 200 millas
N

# How to Study Spanish

## Use Strategies

**Listening strategies** provide a starting point to help you understand.

**Speaking strategies** will help you express yourself in Spanish.

**Reading strategies** will show you different ways to approach reading.

**Writing strategies** help you out with your writing skills.

**Cultural strategies** help you compare Spanish-speaking cultures of the world to your own culture.

**PARA CONVERSAR**

**STRATEGY: SPEAKING**

**Use all you know** The models in exercises are a guide to help you get started. It is better to say more than what is shown in the model. Take risks! Recombine what you have learned in fresh new ways. That is how you become a good speaker of Spanish.

## Use Study Hints

The **Apoyo para estudiar** feature provides study hints that will help you learn Spanish.

**Pronoun placement**

Remember that when you attach any object pronoun (direct, indirect, or reflexive) to an affirmative command of two or more syllables, you need to add a written accent to the stressed syllable of the verb. Examples: **Escríbalo. Tráigame. Siéntese. Póngase la gorra. Acuéstese.** But… **Hazlo. Ponlos.**

## Build Your Confidence

Everyone learns differently, and there are different ways to achieve a goal. Find out what works for you. Grammar boxes are set up with an explanation, a visual representation, and examples from real-life contexts. Use this combination of words and graphics to help you learn Spanish. Focus on whatever helps you most.

### Hacer with Expressions of Time

In Spanish, if someone asks, "How long has this been going on?" or "How long has it been?" you answer with the verb **hacer:**

**hace** + **the period of time** + **que** + **the present tense**

Ay, Elena, **hace quince años que quiero** venir a tu programa.
*Oh, Elena, **I've been wanting** to come to your program **for fifteen years.***

Ay, doctor, **hace una hora que** lo **espero.**
*Oh, doctor, **I've been waiting** for you **for an hour.***

xxxii How to Study Spanish

## Have Fun

Taking a foreign language does not have to be all serious work. The dialogs in this book present the Spanish language in **entertaining, real-life contexts.**

- Pair and group activities give you a chance to **interact with your classmates.**
- Vocabulary and grammar puzzles will test your knowledge, but will also be **fun to do.**

## Listen to Spanish Inside and Outside of Class

Hearing Spanish will help you understand it. Pay attention to the **dialogs** and the **listening activities** in class.

Take advantage of opportunities to **hear Spanish outside of class** as well.

- Do you know someone who speaks Spanish?
- Are there any Spanish-language radio and/or television stations in your area?
- Does your video store have any Spanish-language movies?

## Take Risks

The goal of studying a foreign language like Spanish is to **communicate.**

Don't be afraid to **speak.**

Everyone makes mistakes, so don't worry if you make a few. When you do make a mistake, **pause and then try again.**

*pages xxxiv–25*

# Planning Guide CLASSROOM MANAGEMENT

## OBJECTIVES

**Communication**
- Exchange greetings *pp. 2–3*
- Discuss likes, dislikes *pp. 4–5*
- Describe people, places *pp. 6–7*
- Ask for and give information *pp. 12–13*
- Talk about school life *pp. 16–17*
- Talk about the new school year *pp. 20–21*

**Grammar Review**
- The verb **gustar** *p. 5*
- Use adjectives to describe *p. 7*
- The verb **tener** *p. 9*
- Describe people and things: **ser** vs. **estar** *p. 10*
- Interrogative words *p. 13*
- Tell time *p. 15*
- Regular present tense verbs *p. 17*
- The verb **preguntar** *p. 18*
- The verb **ir** *p. 19*
- Stem-changing verbs: **e→ie, o→ue** *p. 21*
- Expressions of frequency *p. 22*
- Irregular **yo** verbs *p. 23*
- The verbs **decir**, **venir** *p. 23*

**Culture**
- Latinos en Nueva York y New Jersey *p. 9*
- La población latina *p. 11*
- Los latinos de Connecticut *p. 14*
- «City Year» en Massachusetts *p. 22*

**♻ Recycling**
- Use adjectives to describe *p. 7*
- The verb **tener** *p. 9*
- Describe people and things: **ser** vs. **estar** *p. 10*
- Interrogative words *p. 13*
- Tell time *p. 15*
- Regular present tense verbs *p. 17*
- The verb **ir** *p. 19*
- Stem-changing verbs *p. 21*
- Irregular **yo** verbs *p. 23*

## STRATEGIES

**Speaking Strategies**
- Give and get personal information *p. 24*

## PROGRAM RESOURCES

### Print

- *Más práctica* Workbook PE *pp. 1–10*
- Block Scheduling Copymasters *pp. 1–8*
- Preliminary/Unit 1 Resource Book
  - Diagnostic Placement Test *pp. 1–8*
  - *Más práctica* Workbook TE *pp. 9–18*
  - *Cuaderno para hispanohablantes* TE *pp. 19–28*
  - Information Gap Activities *pp. 29–32*
  - Family Involvement *pp. 33–34*
  - Audioscript *pp. 35–38*
  - Assessment Program, Etapa preliminar *pp. 39–57; 240–242*
  - Answer Keys *pp. 252–253*

### Audiovisual

- Audio Program Cassette 1A, 1B / CD 1
- *Canciones* Cassette/CD
- Overhead Transparencies M1; P1–P10

### Technology

- Electronic Teacher Tools / Test Generator
- 

www.mcdougallittell.com

### Assessment Program Options

- Diagnostic Placement Test (Preliminary/Unit 1 Resource Book)
- Cooperative Quizzes (Preliminary/Unit 1 Resource Book)
- Etapa Exam Forms A and B (Preliminary/Unit 1 Resource Book)
- *Examen para hispanohablantes* (Preliminary/Unit 1 Resource Book)
- Portfolio Assessment (Preliminary/Unit 1 Resource Book)
- Multiple Choice Test Questions (Preliminary/Unit 1 Resource Book)
- Audio Program Cassette 19A / CD 19
- Electronic Teacher Tools / Test Generator

### Native Speakers

- *Cuaderno para hispanohablantes* PE *pp. 1–10*
- *Cuaderno para hispanohablantes* TE (Preliminary/Unit 1 Resource Book)
- *Examen para hispanohablantes* (Preliminary/Unit 1 Resource Book)
- Audio Program *(Para hispanohablantes)* Cassettes 1B, 19A / CD 1, CD 19
- Audioscript (Preliminary/Unit 1 Resource Book)

# Student Text Listening Activity Scripts

The following presentations are recorded in the Audio Program:

**¡Saludos!** *pages 2–3*

**¿Qué te gusta?** *pages 4–5*

**¡A describir!** *pages 6–7*

**¡A preguntar!** *pages 12–13*

**En la escuela** *pages 16–17*

**¿Qué haces?** *pages 20–21*

## Actividad 13 Un retrato *page 11*

**Raúl:** Ella se llama Linda y tiene quince años. Es de Los Ángeles. Está visitando a la familia de Sofía aquí en Nueva York. Lleva un suéter amarillo y una falda de muchos colores. Es delgada y baja. Su pelo es rubio, largo y muy bonito. Es buena amiga de Sofía y muy simpática.

## Actividad 29 Después de la escuela *page 22*

Después de clases siempre salgo con mi amigo Luis. Muchas veces vamos al centro a tomar un helado. También nos gusta mirar a la gente que pasea por las calles. Luego caminamos por el parque. Hay jardines con flores y un lago muy bonito. De vez en cuando nos sentamos al lado del lago y miramos los botes. Cuando queremos cenar regresamos a casa. Rara vez lo pasamos mal.

▼ Se saludan en la Ciudad de Nueva York.

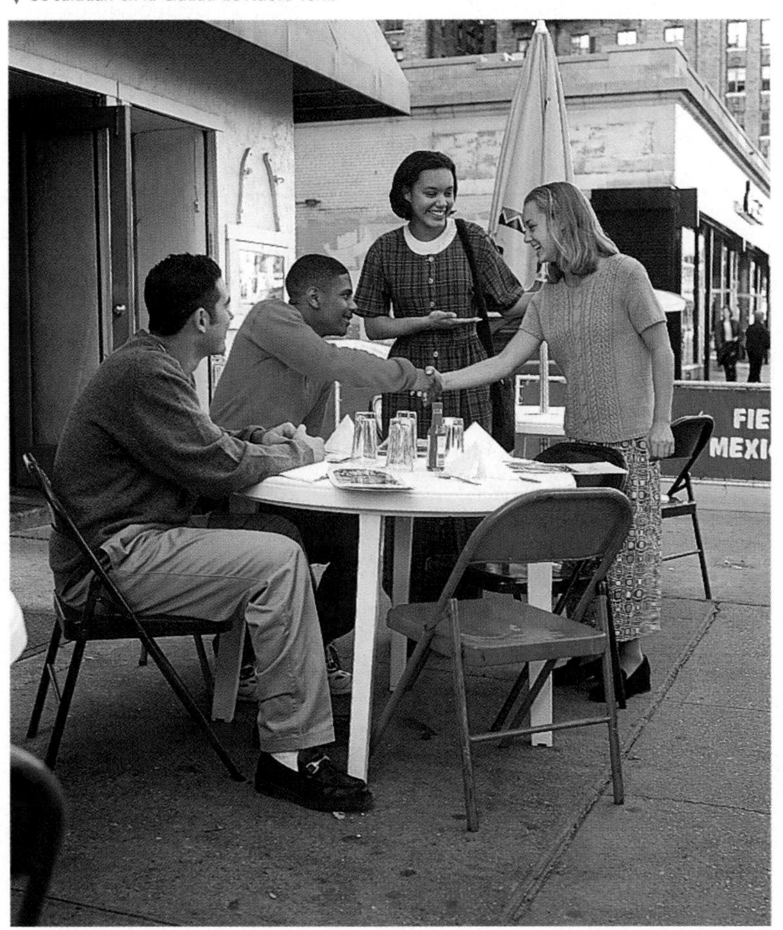

▼ Se saludan en Hartford, Connecticut.

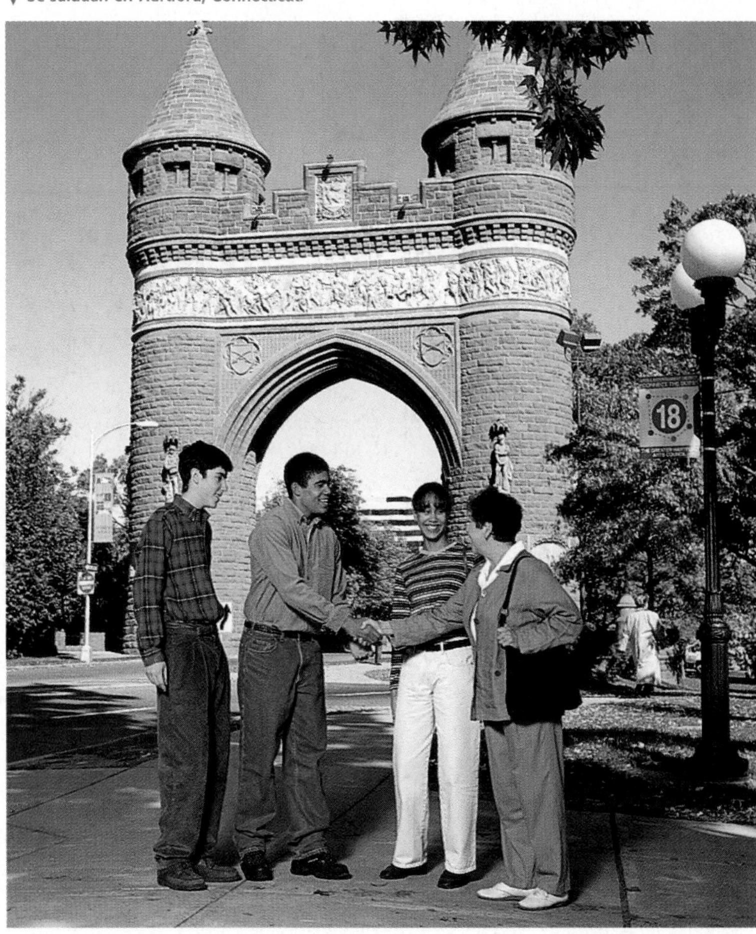

## Sample Lesson Plan - 50 Minute Schedule

### DAY 1

- Greet students / take care of school business. 10 MIN.
- Have students explore books as you check out texts. 7 MIN.

***Etapa Opener***

- Have students look at photo and respond to the *¿Qué ves?* questions on p. xxxiv. 5 MIN.

***Vocabulario y Gramática***

- Quick Start Review (TE, p. 2). 5 MIN.
- Present *¡Saludos!*, pp. 2–3. Have students work in small groups to role-play the 4 scenes. 10 MIN.
- Have small groups complete *Actividad* 2. 10 MIN.
- Quick Wrap-up (TE, p. 3). 3 MIN.

***Homework Option:***

- Have students complete *Actividad* 1 at home.

### DAY 2

***Vocabulario y gramática (cont.)***

- Check homework. 5 MIN.
- Quick Start Review (TE, p. 4). 5 MIN.
- Review greetings and presentations. Have students circulate and introduce themselves and/or other classmates to each other. 5 MIN.
- Present *¿Qué te gusta?*, pp. 4–5. 10 MIN.
- Have students do *Actividades* 3 and 4 orally. 10 MIN.
- Present *¡A describir!* pp. 6–7. 5 MIN.
- Review the *Repaso* box on adjectives, p. 7. 5 MIN.
- Have students complete *Actividad* 5 orally. 5 MIN.

***Homework Option:***

- *Más práctica* Workbook, p. 2. *Cuaderno para hispanohablantes*, p. 2.

### DAY 3

***Vocabulario y gramática (cont.)***

- Check homework. 5 MIN.
- Quick Start Review (TE, p. 6). 5 MIN.
- Review *Repaso:* Use adjectives to describe, p. 7. 5 MIN.
- Have students complete *Actividad* 6. 5 MIN.
- Have students work in small groups to complete *Actividad* 7. 10 MIN.
- Have different groups do *Actividad* 8. 10 MIN.
- Review *Repaso* box on *tener*, p. 9, and have students complete *Actividad* 9. 10 MIN.

***Homework Options***

- *Más práctica* Workbook, p. 3. *Cuaderno para hispanohablantes*, p. 3.
- Have students prepare *Actividad 10*.

### DAY 4

***Vocabulario y gramática (cont.)***

- Check homework. 5 MIN.
- Quick Start Review (TE, p. 10). 5 MIN.
- Have students review *Actividad* 10 orally. 5 MIN.
- Review *Repaso* box on *ser* and *estar*, p. 10. 5 MIN.
- Have students complete *Actividades* 11 and 12. 5 MIN.
- Play the audio and have students complete *Actividad* 13. 5 MIN.
- Quick Start Review (TE, p. 12). 3 MIN.
- Present *¡A preguntar!* on pp. 12–13. 7 MIN.
- Review *Repaso:* Interrogative Words, p. 13. 5 MIN.
- Have students complete *Actividad* 14 individually. 5 MIN.

***Homework Option:***

- *Más práctica* Workbook, pp. 4–5. *Cuaderno para hispanohablantes*, pp. 4–5.

### DAY 5

***Vocabulario y gramática (cont.)***

- Check homework. 5 MIN.
- Have students work in pairs to complete *Actividad* 15 on p. 14. 5 MIN.
- Have students work in small groups to complete *Actividades* 16 and 17. 10 MIN.
- Quick Start Review (TE, p. 14). 5 MIN.
- Review *Repaso:* Telling Time, p. 15, and have students complete *Actividad* 18. 10 MIN.
- Have groups do *Actividad* 19. 5 MIN.
- Present *En la escuela* on pp. 16–17 and have students answer *Actividad* 20 questions orally. 10 MIN.

***Homework Option:***

- *Más práctica* Workbook, p. 6. *Cuaderno para hispanohablantes*, p. 6.

### DAY 6

***Vocabulario y gramática (cont.)***

- Check homework. 5 MIN.
- Quick Start Review (TE, p. 16). 5 MIN.
- Review *Repaso* box on present tense verbs, p. 17. 5 MIN.
- Have students complete *Actividades* 21 and 22. 10 MIN.
- Have students work in small groups to complete *Actividad* 23. 5 MIN.
- Review *Repaso* box on *ir*, p. 19. Have students work in pairs to complete *Actividades* 24 and 25. 10 MIN.
- Present *¿Qué haces?* on pp. 20–21, and do *Actividad* 26 questions orally. 10 MIN.

***Homework Option:***

- *Más práctica* Workbook, pp. 7–8. *Cuaderno para hispanohablantes*, pp. 7–8.

### DAY 7

***Vocabulario y gramática (cont.)***

- Check homework. 5 MIN.
- Quick Start Review (TE, p. 20). 5 MIN.
- Review *Repaso:* Stem-Changing Verbs, p. 21. Have students complete *Actividades* 27 and 28. 10 MIN.
- Play audio and have students complete *Actividad* 29. 5 MIN.
- Review *Repaso:* Irregular *yo* Verbs, p. 23, and have students do *Actividad* 30. 10 MIN.
- Have students complete *Actividad* 31 in pairs. 5 MIN.
- Have students complete *Actividades* 32 and 33 in small groups. 10 MIN.

***Homework Option***

- *Más práctica* Workbook, pp. 9–10. *Cuaderno para hispanohablantes*, pp. 9–10.
- Review for *Etapa preliminar* Exam.

### DAY 8

***Vocabulario y Gramática (cont.)***

- Check homework. 5 MIN.
- Quick Start Review (TE, p. 24). 5 MIN.
- Have students complete *Actividad* 34 in pairs. 5 MIN.
- Review *Etapa* content and questions as necessary. 10 MIN.
- Administer *Etapa preliminar* Exam. 20 MIN.
- Quick Wrap-up (TE, p. 25). 5 MIN.

***Homework Option***

- Have students preview Unit 1 Cultural Opener on pp. 26–27.

# Sample Lesson Plan - Block Schedule (90 minutes)

## DAY 1

- Greet students / take care of school business. 10 MIN.
- Have students explore books as you check out texts. 10 MIN.

***Etapa* Opener**

- Have students look at photo and respond to the *¿Qué ves?* questions on p. xxxiv. 10 MIN.
- Talk about the poster and activate Spanish words. 10 MIN.
- Use Block Scheduling Copymasters. 5 MIN.

**Vocabulario y gramática**

- Quick Start Review (TE, p. 2). 5 MIN.
- Present *¡Saludos!*, pp. 2–3. Have students work in small groups to role–play the 4 scenes. 10 MIN.
- Have students complete *Actividad* 1 orally. 5 MIN.
- Have students work in groups to role-play *Actividad* 2 situations. 10 MIN.
- Present *¿Qué te gusta?*, pp. 4–5. 5 MIN.
- Have students complete *Actividades* 3 and 4 orally. 10 MIN.

**Homework Option:**

- Have students write original scenes based on *Actividad* 2.
- *Más práctica* Workbook, p. 1. *Cuaderno para hispanohablantes*, p. 1

## DAY 2

**Vocabulario y gramática (cont.)**

- Check homework. 5 MIN.
- Quick Start Review (TE, p. 4). 5 MIN.
- Have students circulate to introduce themselves and / or a classmate to each other. Have volunteers role-play the scenes they prepared for homework. 5 MIN.
- Present *¡A describir!* pp. 6–7. 5 MIN.
- Review the *Repaso* box on adjectives, p. 7. 5 MIN.
- Have students complete *Actividad* 5 orally. 5 MIN.
- Do *Actividad* 6 on p. 8. 5 MIN.
- Have students work in small groups to complete *Actividad* 7. 10 MIN.
- Have students prepare *Actividad* 8 in writing, then play the guessing game. 10 MIN.
- Review *Repaso* box on *tener,* p. 9. 5 MIN.
- Have students prepare for *Actividad* 9 in writing, then work in pairs to check them. 10 MIN.
- Have students complete *Actividad* 10 orally. 5 MIN.
- Review *Repaso* box on **ser** and **estar**. 5 MIN.
- Have students complete *Actividades* 11 and 12 in writing, then check orally. 10 MIN.

**Homework Options**

- *Más práctica* Workbook, pp. 2–3. *Cuaderno para hispanohablantes*, pp. 2–3.

## DAY 3

**Vocabulario y gramática (cont.)**

- Check homework. 5 MIN.
- Quick Start Review (TE, p. 10). 5 MIN.
- Play audio and have students complete *Actividad* 13, p. 11. 5 MIN.
- Quick Wrap-up (TE, p. 11). 2 MIN.
- Quick Start Review (TE, p. 12). 3 MIN.
- Describe or have volunteers describe famous people for the class to identify. 7 MIN.
- Present *¡A preguntar!* on pp. 12–13. 5 MIN.
- Review *Repaso:* Interrogative Words, p. 13. 5 MIN.
- Have students complete *Actividad* 14 orally. 5 MIN.
- Have students work in pairs to complete *Actividad* 15. 5 MIN.
- Have students complete *Actividad* 16. 5 MIN.
- Have students complete *Actividad* 17 in groups. 5 MIN.
- Review *Repaso:* Telling Time, p. 15. 5 MIN.
- Have students complete *Actividad* 18. 5 MIN.
- Have students complete *Actividad* 19 in pairs. 5 MIN.
- Present *En la escuela* on pp. 16–17 and have students answer *Actividad 20* questions orally. 8 MIN.
- Review *Repaso* box on present tense verbs and have students complete *Actividades* 21 and 22. 10 MIN.

**Homework Option:**

- *Más práctica* Workbook, pp. 4–6. *Cuaderno para hispanohablantes*, pp. 4–6.

## DAY 4

**Vocabulario y gramática (cont.)**

- Check homework. 5 MIN.
- Quick Start Review (TE, p. 18). 5 MIN.
- Have students do *Actividad* 23 in groups, p. 18. 10 MIN.
- Review *Repaso* box on *ir,* p. 19, and have students do *Actividades* 24 and 25. 10 MIN.
- Present *¿Qué haces?,* pp. 20–21, and have students answer *Actividad 26* orally. 10 MIN.
- Quick Start Review (TE, p. 20). 5 MIN.
- Review *Repaso:* Stem-Changing Verbs, p. 21. 5 MIN.
- Have students complete *Actividades* 27 and 28. 10 MIN.
- Play audio and have students complete *Actividad* 29. 5 MIN.
- Review *Repaso:* Irregular *yo* Verbs, p. 23. Have students do *Actividades* 30 and 31. 10 MIN.
- Do *Actividades* 32 and 33. 10 MIN.
- Do Classroom Community activity (TE, p. 22). 5 MIN.

**Homework Option:**

- *Más práctica* Workbook, pp. 7–10. *Cuaderno para hispanohablantes*, pp. 7–10.
- Review for *Etapa preliminar* Exam.

## DAY 5

**Vocabulario y Gramática (cont.)**

- Check homework. 5 MIN.
- Quick Start Review (TE, p. 24). 5 MIN.
- Have students complete *Actividad* 34 in pairs. 10 MIN.
- Use **Block Scheduling Copymasters** as needed. 10 MIN.
- Review *Etapa* content and questions as necessary. 20 MIN.
- Quick Wrap-up (TE, p. 25). 5 MIN.
- Administer *Etapa preliminar* Exam. 20 MIN.
- Portfolio Assessment (TE, p. 24). Then peer edit work. 15 MIN.

**Homework Option:**

- Have students answer *¿Qué ves?* questions on pp. 28–29.

▼ Unos amigos están en un parque en Union City, New Jersey.

# Etapa preliminar
# **Opener**

## Etapa Theme

**Exchanging greetings and introductions, describing people and places, exchanging personal information, discussing school.**

## Grammar Objectives

- **Gustar** with indirect object pronouns
- Using adjectives
- **Tener**
- **Ser** and **estar**
- Interrogatives
- Telling time
- Regular present tense verbs
- **Ir**
- Stem-changing verbs (**e→ie, o→ue**)
- Verbs with irregular **yo** forms

### Teaching Resource Options

**Print**

**Block Scheduling Copymasters**
Preliminary/Unit 1 Resource Book
Diagnostic Placement Test, pp. 1–8

**Audiovisual**

**OHT** P1 (Quick Start)
**Audio Program** Cassette 19A / CD 19
***Canciones*** Cassette/CD Songs 1, 6, 8, 13

### Quick Start Review

Greetings

Use OHT P1 or write on the board: How many greetings do you remember? Fill in the missing letters from these greetings.

¡__ __ l __ !
B __ __ __ __ __ t __ __ __ __ __ .
B __ __ __ __ __ d __ __ __ .
¿Q __ __ t __ __ ?
¿C __ __ __ e __ __ __ s?

**Answers**
¡Hola!; Buenas tardes.; Buenos días.; ¿Qué tal?; ¿Cómo estás?

### Teaching Suggestions
**Diagnostic Placement Test**

The diagnostic placement test that appears at the beginning of the Preliminary/Unit 1 Resource Book can be given either at the beginning or the end of the **Etapa preliminar**.

# Día a día

- Exchange greetings
- Discuss likes, dislikes
- Describe people, places
- Ask for and give information
- Talk about school life
- Talk about the new school year

### ¿Qué ves?

Mira la foto. ¿Qué ves?

1. ¿Cuántos jóvenes hay en la foto? ¿Qué hacen?
2. ¿Dónde están?
3. ¿Adónde van si les gusta la música salsa?

## Classroom Management

**Peer Review** Ask students to review the objectives and brainstorm a list of topics they anticipate exploring in the **Etapa**, e.g., greetings, likes and dislikes, etc.

**Organizing Paired/Group Work** Assign students to pairs/groups and arrange classroom locations for group work early on the first day. Post these group/location assignments to facilitate students' work in the first few classes. Monitor pairs and groups to encourage on-task interactions and good habits. See p. T52 for additional information.

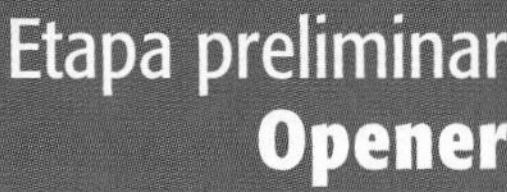

## Teaching Suggestions
### Previewing the Etapa

- Have students complete the Peer review activity on p. xxxiv. Then, bring the whole class together to share ideas. Write lists of topics students expect to cover on the board.
- Use **¿Qué ves?** questions to talk about the photo and **Etapa preliminar**.

## Culture Highlights

- **LA CIUDAD DE NUEVA YORK** This photo was taken in Central Park with the New York cityscape in the background.
- **SALSA** Point out that **salsa** originated in **El Barrio** (Spanish Harlem) in New York City. Tito Puente, who still performs, was involved in **salsa** from the early days (50s and 60s).
- **EL BARRIO** Point out that **El Barrio** is on Manhattan Island, just north of Central Park. **El Museo del Barrio**, murals by Hispanic artists, and many other Hispanic attractions can be found there. **El Barrio** has its own website on the Internet with photos, descriptions, and "letters to home."

## Cross Cultural Connections

Have students list music they associate with the Spanish-speaking world. Then have them list other music types that they associate with specific countries or geographic areas. Have them describe and compare the music.

## Supplementary Vocabulary

| | |
|---|---|
| **deportivo(a)** | athletic |
| **el descuento** | discount |
| **los éxitos** | hits, successes |
| **por adelantado** | in advance |
| **el vestimento** | attire |

## Teaching All Students

**Extra Help** Ask students to note what they see in the photo. Have students compare notes within small groups or as part of a whole class discussion.

**Native Speakers** Have native speakers discuss **salsa** music and dance. Have them bring in examples of **salsa** and possibly demonstrate dance steps to the class.

**Multiple Intelligences**

**Visual** Ask students to study the photo for 2–3 minutes. Have them close their books and list what they remember.

**Musical/Rhythmic** Ask students to share their favorite music. Bring in samples of **salsa** music. Have students compare their favorite music to **salsa**.

## Block Schedule

**Peer Teaching** Have students work with partners to preview the **Etapa preliminar**. Encourage them to leaf through the **Etapa** and pick out items they remember from previous study.

## Teaching Resource Options

**Print** 

Block Scheduling Copymasters
Preliminary/Unit 1 Resource Book
Audioscript, p. 35

**Audiovisual** 

**OHT** P1 (Quick Start), P2
**Audio Program** Cassette 1A / CD 1

## Quick Start Review

Greeting people

Use OHT P1 or write on the board: Write four ways you might greet four people of different ages in Spanish. Indicate the person you are greeting.

*Answers will vary.*

## Teaching Suggestions

### Introducing Vocabulary

- Ask students what they know about the four places on pp. 2–3.
- Read, then have volunteers role-play the conversations on pp. 2–3.
- List the phrases from **Actividad 2** on the board. Have students close their texts, and take turns role-playing a scene for the class.
- It might be helpful for students to review excerpts of the Level 1 video to refamiliarize themselves with Isabel and the other characters from the Video Program.

## Gestures

Review gestures students learned in Level 1. Two women or a man and a woman normally kiss each other on one cheek when greeting. In Spain, people kiss on each cheek.

# ¡Saludos!

## VOCABULARIO Y GRAMÁTICA

**OBJECTIVE**

- Exchange greetings and introductions

Look at the pictures and read the captions to see how Spanish speakers in the United States greet one another.

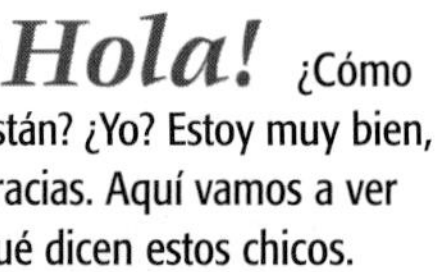

**¡Hola!** ¿Cómo están? ¿Yo? Estoy muy bien, gracias. Aquí vamos a ver qué dicen estos chicos.

### Ciudad de Nueva York

A

**Sofía:** Buenas tardes, Raúl y Carlos. Les presento a mi amiga, Linda.

**Raúl:** Mucho gusto.

**Linda:** Encantada.

### Union City, New Jersey

B

**Marcos:** Hola. ¿Qué pasa? Les presento a mi prima, Luisa. Ella es de California.

**Arturo:** Mi nombre es Arturo Alcázar. Mucho gusto.

**Luisa:** El gusto es mío.



## Classroom Community

**Portfolio** Ask students to write a short paragraph that introduces them and tells three interesting things about their lives.

**Rubric: Writing**

| Criteria | Scale |
|---|---|
| Accuracy | 1 2 3 4 5 |
| Logical organization | 1 2 3 4 5 |
| Vocabulary use | 1 2 3 4 5 |

A = 13–15 pts.
B = 10–12 pts.
C = 7–9 pts.
D = 4–6 pts.
F = < 4 pts.

**Group Activity** Have students brainstorm and list different places where they meet people. Next to each place list a person, e.g., **un(a) amigo(a)**, **el/la maestro(a)**, etc. Have students work in groups of three to role-play an encounter at each place where one member of the group is the person listed and is being introduced by the second member to the third member. Remind students to use formal language when appropriate.

Boston, Massachusetts

C

**Estudiantes:** Hola, señora Rivera. ¿Cómo está usted?

**Señora Rivera:** Bien. Vamos a clase, ¿no?

Hartford, Connecticut

D

**Miguel:** ¿Qué tal, Patricia? Hola, señora. Me llamo Miguel.

**Señora:** Mucho gusto. Soy la abuela de Patricia. ¿Cómo están?

**Miguel y Lalo:** Regular. ¿Y ustedes?

## Actividad 1 ¿Qué pasa?

**Leer/Escribir** Escoge la respuesta correcta según la lectura. *(Hint: Choose the correct answer.)*

1. Sofía les presenta a su amiga a…
   - **a.** unos chicos
   - **b.** un restaurante
   - **c.** Linda y otra chica
2. Marcos…
   - **a.** es el hermano de Raúl
   - **b.** dice que su prima es de Texas
   - **c.** le presenta a su prima a Arturo
3. La señora Rivera va…
   - **a.** a clase
   - **b.** de compras
   - **c.** a comer
4. La abuela de Patricia…
   - **a.** se llama Lalo
   - **b.** está regular
   - **c.** habla con Miguel y Lalo

## Actividad 2 Te presento a...

**Hablar** En grupos pequeños, hagan presentaciones informales y formales. Usen estas expresiones. *(Hint: Practice introductions.)*

| | |
|---|---|
| Hola. | ¿Qué pasa? |
| Bien. | Mucho gusto. |
| Buenos días. | ¿Cómo estás? |
| Te/Le presento a… | Regular. |
| Buenas tardes. | ¿Cómo está usted? |
| Mi nombre es… | Terrible. |
| ¿Qué tal? | Soy… |
| Me llamo… | |



### Teaching Suggestions

Encourage students to brainstorm and list other greetings and introduction words they know and use them in **Actividad 2**.

### Actividad 1 Answers

1. a. unos chicos
2. c. le presenta a su prima a Arturo
3. a. a clase
4. c. habla con Miguel y Lalo

### Actividad 2 Answers

*Answers will vary. Sample answer:*
- Buenas tardes. Mi nombre es Ricardo.
- Mucho gusto, Ricardo. Me llamo Isabel. ¿Cómo estás?
- Regular.

### Quick Wrap-up

Have students introduce the student next to them. Have them mirror the language in the dialog. For example:

S1: **Buenos días. Me llamo ___. Le presento a mi amigo(a) ___.**
Maestro(a): **Mucho gusto.**
S2: **Encantado(a)./El gusto es mío.**

Use culturally correct body language such as shaking hands on the introduction.

### Teaching All Students

**Extra Help** Ask students to role-play the dialogs on pp. 2–3 using their own names.

**Native Speakers** Have Spanish speakers expand on the greetings in **Actividad 2**, adding appropriate expressions for *good-bye*.

**Multiple Intelligences**

**Interpersonal** In small groups, students should introduce themselves and share two or three hobbies.

### Block Schedule

**Retention** Have students work in groups to think of as many responses as they can to the questions **¿Qué pasa?** and **¿Qué tal?** Share the lists with the entire class. (For additional activities, see **Block Scheduling Copymasters**.)

## Teaching Resource Options

**Print** 

*Más práctica* Workbook PE, p. 1
*Cuaderno para hispanohablantes* PE, p. 1
Block Scheduling Copymasters
Preliminary/Unit 1 Resource Book
*Más práctica* Workbook TE, p. 9
*Cuaderno para hispanohablantes* TE, p. 19
Audioscript, p. 35

**Audiovisual** 

OHT P1 (Quick Start), P3
Audio Program Cassette 1A / CD 1

## Quick Start Review

Stating names

Use OHT P1 or write on the board: Tell the names of the following people in Spanish.

For example: **mi maestra de matemáticas**

**Mi maestra de matemáticas se llama señorita Blanco.**

**mi amigo(a)**
**mi hermano(a)**
**mi maestro(a) de inglés**
**mi primo(a)**
**mi tío(a)**

*Answers will vary.*

## Culture Highlights

● **UNION CITY, N.J.** The background photo was taken on Bergenline Avenue in Union City, New Jersey. Encourage students to point out the Spanish signs in this photo.

# ¿Qué te gusta?

## VOCABULARIO Y GRAMÁTICA

**OBJECTIVES**

- Discuss likes and dislikes

**Union City, New Jersey** Look at the pictures and read about what young people from New Jersey like to do in their free time.

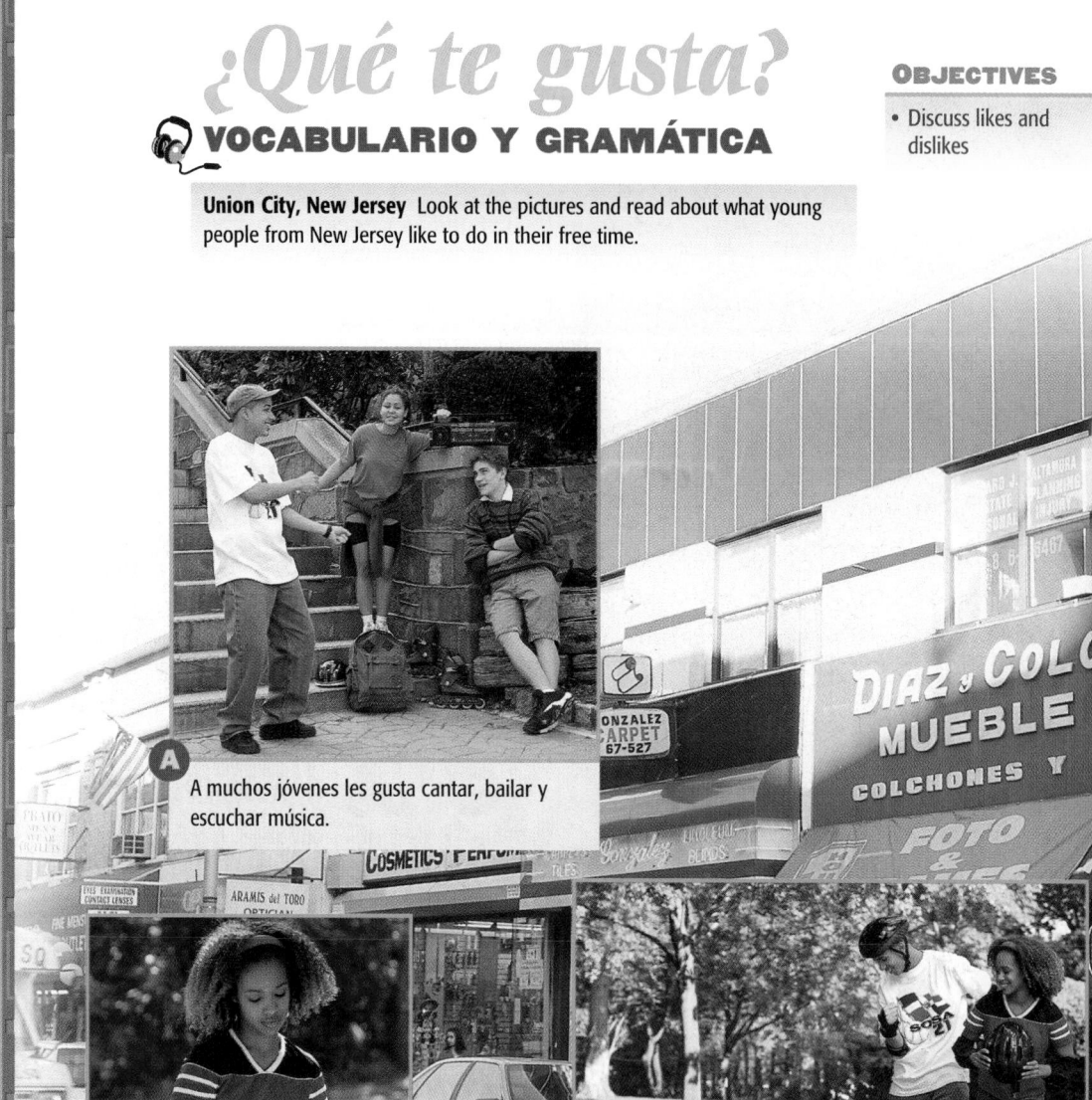

A — A muchos jóvenes les gusta cantar, bailar y escuchar música.

B — Me gusta escribir en mi diario en mi tiempo libre.

C — Nos gusta patinar con patines en línea.



## Classroom Community

**Storytelling** Have students tell a chain story by taking turns contributing to an ongoing list of activities that their Spanish teacher likes to do during free time.

**Paired Activity** Have students ask each other what they like by using the verb **gustar**, e.g., **¿Te gusta esquiar? ¿Te gustan los videos?**

**Game** Divide the class into 2 teams. Have each team choose a famous person and describe the things he/she likes to do. Have the other team guess the person's identity. For example, **Le gusta jugar al baloncesto. Le gusta ganar todos los juegos. Le gusta vivir en Chicago.** Answer: **Michael Jordan.**

• Review: Use **gustar**

Y claro, como todos los chicos, a nosotros nos gusta comer. ¡Uuuuffff!

## ACTIVIDAD 3 ¿Qué les gusta más?

**Hablar/Escribir** Describe lo que a las siguientes personas les gusta hacer. *(Hint: Which activities do these people prefer?)*

**modelo**

*mi hermano(a): bailar / nadar*

*A mi hermano le gusta nadar. (A mi hermano no le gusta bailar.)*

**Nota**

Remember that when you talk about what you or someone else likes to do, you use the verb **gustar** + an infinitive. **Gustar** always takes an indirect object pronoun (**me, te, le, os, nos, les**).

**Me gusta cantar.** *I like to sing.*

**¿Te gusta cantar?** *Do you like to sing?*

1. yo: cantar / escuchar música
2. tú, (nombre) : ir de compras / practicar deportes
3. mis padres: comer en la casa / comer en un restaurante
4. mis amigos y yo: ir a fiestas / ir al cine
5. los estudiantes: escribir / leer

## ACTIVIDAD 4 ¿A quién le gusta...?

**Hablar/Escribir** ¿Qué les gusta hacer a ti y a tus amigos? Haz oraciones afirmativas o negativas usando estas expresiones. *(Hint: What do you like to do?)*

bailar cantar escribir escuchar
comer alquilar un video leer
visitar a amigos

**MÁS PRÁCTICA** *cuaderno* p. 1

**PARA HISPANOHABLANTES** *cuaderno* p. 1



## Teaching Suggestions

- Present the sentences on pp. 4–5.
- Have volunteers read the captions under the photos, then tell if they feel the same way. Write the word **también** (*also*) on the board.
- Write prepositional phrases **a mí, a ti, a él,** on the board and have students match the correct indirect object pronoun (**me, te, le[s], nos, os**).
- Give additional **gustar** sentences about yourself, and ask students **¿Y a ti?** For example, **A mí me gusta caminar en el parque. ¿Y a ti?**
- Complete the presentation by asking questions like **¿Qué te gusta hacer después de las clases?**

### ACTIVIDAD 3 Answers

*Answers will vary. Sample answers:*

1. A mí (no) me gusta cantar. A mí (no) me gusta escuchar música.
2. A ti (no) te gusta ir de compras. A ti (no) te gusta practicar deportes.
3. A mis padres (no) les gusta comer en la casa. A mis padres (no) les gusta comer en un restaurante.
4. A mis amigos y yo (no) nos gusta ir a fiestas. A mis amigos y yo (no) nos gusta ir al cine.
5. A los estudiantes (no) les gusta escribir. A los estudiantes (no) les gusta leer.

### ACTIVIDAD 4 Answers

*Answers will vary.*

## Language Note

Tell students they can use **encantar** to express that they love to do something: **Me encanta patinar. Nos encanta cantar y bailar.** If they absolutely don't like something, they can use the phrase **en absoluto** or **para nada: No me gusta patinar en absoluto. No nos gusta cantar ni bailar en absoluto.**

## Teaching All Students

**Extra Help** Write several examples using **gustar** + infinitive on the board. **Me gusta comer en un restaurante. A mi hermano le gusta comer en casa. A nadie le gusta comer en la escuela.** Have students write additional sentences on the board that follow the models.

**Challenge** Ask students to state what they like or dislike by choosing a word beginning with each letter of the alphabet, e.g., **Me gustan mis amigos, me gusta beber refrescos, no me gusta cocinar,** etc.

### Multiple Intelligences

**Verbal** Have students brainstorm activities that they like or dislike. Write them on a transparency or on the board. Ask students to classify the activities into two groups. (Be creative with group headings.)

## Block Schedule

**Change of Pace** Scramble a short paragraph about likes and dislikes on a transparency or on the board. Ask students to rewrite the sentences in a logical order.

## Teaching Resource Options

**Print** 

Block Scheduling Copymasters
Preliminary/Unit 1 Resource Book
Audioscript, p. 35

**Audiovisual**

OHT P4 (Quick Start), P5
Audio Program Cassette 1A / CD 1

## Quick Start Review

Discussing preferences

Use OHT P4 or write on the board: What do you like to do? Write as many sentences as you can that describe activities you like to do. Then write two sentences about what you do not like to do. Use the following activities or add some of your own.

**Me gusta...**
**bailar, cantar, correr, leer, escuchar música, nadar, hablar por teléfono, estudiar, descansar, usar la computadora, mirar la televisión, tocar el piano, ir al parque, ir al museo, ir de compras, practicar deportes**

*Answers will vary.*

## Teaching Suggestions

- Have students cover the descriptions on p. 6, and brainstorm and list words (adjectives) in Spanish that might describe the subjects of the photo.
- Read the descriptions together. Check off the words on the board that appear in the descriptions. List separately any additional words from the descriptions.
- Describe students in the classroom and have the class identify the person you describe. Include yourself in one description.
- Have students turn to pp. 2 and 3 to describe the other characters in this **Etapa**.

# ¡A describir!

## VOCABULARIO Y GRAMÁTICA

**OBJECTIVES**
- Describe people and places

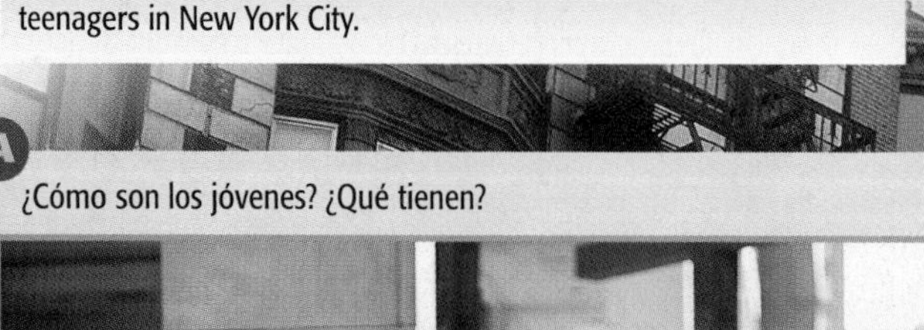

**Ciudad de Nueva York** Look at the pictures and read about these teenagers in New York City.

**A** ¿Cómo son los jóvenes? ¿Qué tienen?

**Carlos** es alto, de pelo castaño. Tiene un suéter verde.

**Linda** es baja y delgada. Tiene pelo rubio y largo. Su suéter es amarillo y su falda es de muchos colores.

**Raúl** tiene una camisa anaranjada y jeans. Es muy guapo.

**Sofía** tiene pelo corto. Usa un vestido azul y una bolsa morada.

**Panza, el perro,** no es delgado. Es gordo. También es feo.

6 seis
**Etapa preliminar**

## Classroom Community

**Portfolio** Ask students to write a short paragraph describing themselves, using the adjectives on p. 7.

**Rubric: Writing**

| Criteria | Scale |
|---|---|
| Accuracy of information | 1 2 3 4 5 |
| Logical organization | 1 2 3 4 5 |
| Vocabulary use | 1 2 3 4 5 |

A = 13–15 pts.
B = 10–12 pts.
C = 7–9 pts.
D = 4–6 pts.
F = < 4 pts.

**TPR** Ask students to take turns acting out an adjective listed in **Actividad 5** for others to guess.

**Storytelling** Have students work in small groups to make sketches of 2–3 characters. Then have volunteers present their characters to the class, telling who they are, where they are from, what they like to do, what they look like, what they are like to be around, and what they have.

- *Review: Use adjectives to describe*
- *Review: Use* ***tener***
- *Review: Use* ***ser*** *and* ***estar***

## ACTIVIDAD 5 Unas descripciones

**Hablar/Escribir** Tú conoces a Linda, Raúl, Sofía, Carlos y el perro de Carlos en Nueva York. Haz oraciones para explicar cómo son, cómo están y qué tienen. Usa estas expresiones. *(Hint: You meet Linda, Raúl, Sofía, Carlos, and Carlos's dog in New York City. Describe them, using these expressions.)*

| | | |
|---|---|---|
| alegre | cómico(a) | serio(a) |
| alto(a) | delgado(a) | un suéter |
| amarillo(a) | una falda | triste |
| azul | pelo castaño | verde |
| bajo(a) | pelo rubio | un vestido |

## REPASO Use Adjectives to Describe

Remember that **adjectives** describe nouns. They match the gender and number of the nouns they describe. In Spanish, **adjectives** usually follow the noun.

| Masculine adjectives often end in -o. | Feminine adjectives often end in -a. |
|---|---|
| el chico **guapo** *the good-looking boy* | la chica **guapa** *the good-looking girl* |

Most adjectives that end with **-e** or a **consonant** refer to both genders.

*same word*

el chico **paciente** la chica **paciente**

To make an adjective **plural**, add **-s** if it ends with a vowel, **-es** if it ends with a consonant.

los chicos **guapos**
los chicos **trabajadores**

When an adjective describes a group containing both genders, the **masculine** form of the adjective is used.



## Culture Highlights

● **LA CIUDAD DE NUEVA YORK** The background photo was taken on 141st Street and Broadway in New York City. Encourage students to hunt for interesting signs in the photo.

### ACTIVIDAD 5 Answers

*Answers will vary but will include information from captions.*

## Dictation

Read each sentence twice. Have volunteers draw the description on the board.

**Julio es alto y delgado. Tiene pelo castaño y corto. Lleva una camiseta, jeans y una chaqueta. No lleva zapatos. Tiene un perro bajo y gordo con mucho pelo.**

## Quick Wrap-up

Write on the board and have students complete the following sentences with the correct form of the word. Collect papers or review answers in class.

1. Mi amiga Ángela es (alto) y (bonito). Tiene pelo (corto) y (rizado).
2. Tus amigos son (cómico) y (divertido), pero llevan ropa muy (feo).
3. Bernardo es (inteligente) y (serio), y tiene clases muy (difícil).

**Answers**
1. alta, bonita, corto, rizado; 2. cómicos, divertidos, fea; 3. inteligente, serio, difíciles

## Teaching All Students

**Extra Help** Ask students to rewrite the captions on p. 6, replacing the names in the text with the names of their friends.

**Multiple Intelligences**

**Visual** Have students bring magazine clippings of people or family photos. Organize 4–5 workstations where the clippings and photos are organized. Divide class into 4–5 groups and have them rotate from station to station. At each station, they take turns describing someone in one of the photos so the other members of the group can identify the person being described. Ask students to provide additional (personality) information about people in their own family photos.

## Block Schedule

**Change of Pace** Have the class start a journal for the year. Topics might include new friends, the first day of school, new school subjects, etc. Make sure the topics are broad enough so they can write regardless of how much Spanish they remember.

## Teaching Resource Options

**Print**

*Más práctica* Workbook PE, pp. 2–3
*Cuaderno para hispanohablantes* PE, pp. 2–3
Block Scheduling Copymasters
Preliminary/Unit 1 Resource Book
*Más práctica* Workbook TE, pp. 10–11
*Cuaderno para hispanohablantes* TE, pp. 20–21
Audioscript, p. 37

**Audiovisual**

OHT P4 (Quick Start)
Audio Program Cassette 1B / CD 1

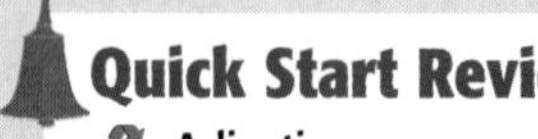

## Quick Start Review

Adjectives

Use OHT P4 or write on the board: Describe the President of the United States or the principal of your school. What does he/she look like? What other adjectives could you use to describe him/her?

*Answers will vary.*

## Teaching Suggestions

- Practice colors by describing the colors of clothing and things in the classroom. After modeling 1 or 2 sentences, elicit responses from students beginning with yes/no questions (**¿El pizarrón es verde?**), then either/or questions (**¿Es verde o negro el pizarrón?**), and finally information questions (**¿De qué color es el pizarrón?**).
- Use TPR activity to reinforce colors.

### Actividad 6 Answers

1. baja
2. corto, castaño
3. gorda
4. grandes, verdes
5. amarillas
6. azules
7. simpática
8. bonito

### Actividad 7 Answers

*Answers will vary but should include the following descriptions.*

1. unos zapatos rojos
2. una blusa marrón
3. un suéter anaranjado
4. un vestido amarillo
5. unos pantalones azules
6. una camisa roja

## Actividad 6 ¿Cómo es?

**Escribir** ¿Cómo es la tía de Isabel? Completa la descripción. Luego dibújala con esas características. *(Hint: Complete the description of Isabel's aunt. Then draw her.)*

1. Mi tía es (alto, altos, baja, bajas).
2. Tiene pelo (larga, largas, corto, cortos) y (rubia, rubias, castaño, castaños).
3. Ella es un poco (gorda, gordas, delgado, delgados).
4. Tiene ojos (grande, grandes, pequeña, pequeñas) y (azul, verdes).
5. Sus blusas favoritas son (rojo, rojos, amarilla, amarillas).
6. Le gusta llevarlas con sus pantalones (negro, negra, azul, azules).
7. Ella es muy (simpática, simpáticas, perezoso, perezosos).
8. Mi tía tiene un nombre (bonito, bonitos, cómica, cómicas). Se llama Gloria.

### También se dice

Si caminas por la calle y alguien te dice «¡Oye, flaco!», no te enojes (*don't get mad*). Es una forma cariñosa que usan en los países hispanos. **Viejo(a)** es otra de estas palabras cariñosas que puedes oír.

## Actividad 7 ¿De qué color?

**Hablar** Pregúntales a tus compañeros(as) sobre la ropa que llevan hoy. Usa estos colores en tu conversación. *(Hint: Ask what people are wearing today.)*

**modelo**

**Tú:** *¿Quién lleva una chaqueta roja?*

**Compañero(a):** *Teresa lleva una chaqueta roja.*

## Classroom Community

**Portfolio** Ask students to write a short paragraph describing a member of their family and the things that he/she likes to do. Use the vocabulary given on p. 9.

**Rubric: Writing**

| Criteria | Scale |
|---|---|
| Accuracy | 1 2 3 4 5 |
| Logical organization | 1 2 3 4 5 |
| Vocabulary use | 1 2 3 4 5 |

A = 13–15 pts.
B = 10–12 pts.
C = 7–9 pts.
D = 4–6 pts.
F = < 4 pts.

**TPR** Review the colors in Spanish by asking students to stand if they are wearing the color you call out, e.g., **Levántense si llevan azul.** Alternately, you can use questions to have students stand: **¿Quién lleva una camisa blanca?**

## ¡Adivina!

**Leer/Escribir** Escribe tres descripciones: una sobre un(a) estudiante de tu clase, otra sobre un(a) profesor(a) y otra sobre alguien famoso (real o imaginario). Léeles cada descripción a tus compañeros(as). Ellos van a adivinar quién es. *(Hint: Write three descriptions of people for classmates to guess.)*

| | |
|---|---|
| alto(a) | joven |
| bajo(a) | largo(a) |
| bonito(a) | mayor |
| castaño(a) | menor |
| corto(a) | moreno(a) |
| delgado(a) | pelirrojo(a) |
| fuerte | pequeño(a) |
| gordo(a) | rubio(a) |
| guapo(a) | viejo(a) |

**MÁS PRÁCTICA** *cuaderno* p. 2

**PARA HISPANOHABLANTES** *cuaderno* p. 2

En Nueva York y New Jersey encontramos grupos latinos de todos los países de habla hispana, incluyendo México, España, América Central, el Caribe y América del Sur. Pero la gran mayoría vienen de tres islas del Caribe: Puerto Rico, República Dominicana y Cuba.

## REPASO: The Verb tener

When you want to talk about what you have, use the verb **tener**.

| | |
|---|---|
| tengo | tenemos |
| tienes | tenéis |
| tiene | tienen |

La chica **tiene** pelo rubio.
*The girl **has** blond hair.*

**Tener** is also used to talk about how old a person is.

El chico **tiene** quince **años.**
*The boy **is** fifteen **years old**.*

## La edad

**Hablar/Escribir** ¿Cuántos años tienen las siguientes personas? Si no sabes la edad exacta, adivina. Escribe tus respuestas y luego habla con un(a) compañero(a). *(Hint: Tell the ages of these people.)*

**modelo**

*mi tía*
*Mi tía tiene treinta y ocho años.*

1. mi amigo *(nombre)*
2. mis amigas *(nombre)* y *(nombre)*
3. yo
4. mi hermano(a)
5. mi madre/padre
6. mi primo(a)
7. mi perro/gato/pez/pájaro/¿?
8. *(una persona famosa)*

**Objective:** Open-ended practice
Describing people

*Answers will vary but should reflect correct subject/adjective agreement.*

**Objective:** Transitional practice
Expressing age with **tener**

### Answers

*Answers will vary but should include the correct conjugation of **tener**.*

1. tiene
2. tienen
3. tengo
4. tiene
5. tiene
6. tiene
7. tiene
8. tiene

### Expansion

Have students include physical descriptions in Actividad 9.

### Teaching Suggestions

Review the nationalities associated with each Spanish-speaking region mentioned in the **Nota cultural** on p. 9: **mexicano(a), español(a), centroamericano(a), caribeño(a), sudamericano(a), puertorriqueño(a), dominicano(a),** and **cubano(a).**

### Interdisciplinary Connection

**Science** Have students give color formulas in Spanish: **Azul y amarillo son verde.**

### Teaching All Students

**Extra Help** Ask students to describe a famous person using the adjectives in **Actividad 8**.

**Native Speakers** Have Spanish speakers provide additional color words in Spanish. For example, there are many different shades of blue with specific names. Have students jot down these colors in their notebooks for future reference.

**Multiple Intelligences**

**Visual** Refer to the **Etapa** Opener on pp. xxiv–1 and ask students to describe the people in the photo using words from **Actividad 8**.

**Kinesthetic** Ask students to make gestures that best describe the words given in **Actividad 8**.

### Block Schedule

**Variety** Draw 7 arcs on the board. Have students fill in the names of the colors of the rainbow. Then have them brainstorm as many things as possible that they associate with each color. Write the Spanish word for each thing they name inside the corresponding arc. Alternately, you can divide the class into teams. Which team can name the most things in Spanish for each color?

## Teaching Resource Options

**Print** 

*Más práctica* Workbook PE, pp. 3–4
*Cuaderno para hispanohablantes* PE, pp. 3–4
Block Scheduling Copymasters
Preliminary/Unit 1 Resource Book
*Más práctica* Workbook TE, pp. 11–12
*Cuaderno para hispanohablantes* TE, pp. 21–22
Audioscript, pp. 35, 37, 38

**Audiovisual**

OHT P4 (Quick Start)
Audio Program Cassette 1A, 1B / CD 1;
(*Para hispanohablantes* Cassette 1B / CD 1)

## Quick Start Review

**Tener**

Use OHT P4 or write on the board: Tell how many people are in your family.

**Yo (tener) ___ hermanos(as).**
**¿primos(as)?**
**¿tíos(as)?**

Now choose one person and describe him or her. Tell something he or she likes to do. For example: **Mi primo Antonio es inteligente. Le gusta leer libros.**

*Answers will vary.*

## Teaching Suggestions

To contrast origin and location (**ser vs. estar**), write 8–10 names on the board (include sketches or stick figures if you like). Above each name write the place of origin and below each name write where he or she is. You can include pairs of people. Begin by modeling sentences, e.g., **Julio es de España. Está en Nueva York.** Then elicit sentences from students by asking yes/no, either/or, and information questions.

**Answers**

*Answers will vary. Sample answer provided:*
Mi madre tiene ojos azules.

## ¿Se parecen?

**Hablar/Escribir** ¿Tú y tu familia se parecen? ¿Y tus amigos(as)? Describe el pelo y los ojos de tu familia y de tus amigos(as), combinando elementos de cada columna. ¡Ojo! Cuidado con las formas de los adjetivos.
*(Hint: Describe your family and friends.)*

**modelo**

*Mi amiga Lupita y yo tenemos pelo largo.*

| | | | |
|---|---|---|---|
| mi madre<br>mi hermano(a) y yo<br>yo<br>tú, (*nombre*)<br>mi amigo(a) y yo<br>mis hermanos(as)<br>mi amiga, (*nombre*)<br>mi madre/padre y yo | tengo<br>tienes<br>tiene<br>tenemos<br>tienen | pelo<br>ojos | largo(s)<br>rubio(s)<br>azul(es)<br>corto(s)<br>verde(s)<br>castaño(s)<br>negro(s)<br>marrón(es) |

**MÁS PRÁCTICA** *cuaderno* p. 3
**PARA HISPANOHABLANTES** *cuaderno* p. 3

REPASO

### Describe People and Things: ser vs. estar

Remember that even though **ser** and **estar** both correspond to the English verb *to be*, their uses are very different.

| | |
|---|---|
| soy | somos |
| eres | sois |
| es | son |

**Ser** is used
- to tell who the subject is or what the subject is like.
- to describe origin, profession, and basic characteristics.

Ella **es** alta. **Es** de Nueva York.
*She **is** tall. She **is** from New York.*

| | |
|---|---|
| estoy | estamos |
| estás | estáis |
| está | están |

**Estar** is used
- to tell where the subject is or how the subject feels.
- to describe location and feelings that may change.

El chico **está** bien. **Está** en Nueva York.
*The boy **is** O.K. He **is** in New York.*



## Classroom Community

**Paired Activity** Ask students to work with a partner to carry on several short conversations about a trip, including descriptions of people they met.

**Peer Teaching** Ask one group of students to teach the differences between **ser** and **estar** to another small group of students.

**Learning Scenario** Have students work in small groups to create scenarios where S1 is looking for someone. To help find the person, S1 asks for information about the person, including place of origin. S2, S3, S4 respond. The rest of the class tries to identify the person being described. Groups can use people from the class, from the school or community, or famous people students would know.

## Actividad 11 ¡Saludos desde Nueva York!

**Escribir** Linda está visitando Nueva York con su amiga y le escribe esta carta a su familia. Complétala con la forma correcta de **ser** o **estar**. *(Hint: Complete the postcard with the correct forms of **ser** and **estar**.)*

Querida familia:

¿Saben dónde __1__? Hoy __2__ en la Estatua de la Libertad con Sofía y su amigo. Su amigo se llama Raúl. __3__ de Nueva York también. __4__ muy simpático. También __5__ muy guapo. ¡__6__ muy bien y muy contenta!

Un abrazo,

Linda

### NOTA CULTURAL

**La población latina** El censo (*census*) de 1845 menciona «508 personas de México y Sudamérica» en Nueva York. La población latina de esta ciudad ha crecido (*has grown*) mucho. Se estima (*it is estimated*) que en el año 2000, cerca de tres millones de habitantes de Nueva York serán (*will be*) de origen latino.

## Actividad 12 ¡A describir!

**Hablar/Escribir** Usa las expresiones entre paréntesis y la forma apropiada de **ser** o **estar** para describir a las siguientes personas. Luego, describe a dos personas de tu clase. *(Hint: Describe these people using **ser** and **estar**.)*

**modelo**

*Mary (rubia / alta / de New Hampshire)*

*Mary es rubia. Es alta. Es de New Hampshire.*

1. Carlos (de Buenos Aires / en Nueva York / alegre)
2. Melisa (en casa / de Santo Domingo / triste)
3. Miguel (preocupado / maestro / de San Francisco)
4. Ana (de México / simpática / en Italia)
5. ¿?
6. ¿?

## Actividad 13 Un retrato

**Escuchar/Escribir** Unos chicos le piden a Raúl que describa a Linda. Escucha su descripción. Luego, contesta las preguntas. *(Hint: Listen to the tape and answer the questions.)*

1. ¿Cuántos años tiene Linda?
2. ¿De dónde es ella?
3. ¿Dónde está ahora?
4. ¿Qué ropa tiene ella?
5. ¿Cómo es?

**MÁS PRÁCTICA** *cuaderno* p. 4

**PARA HISPANOHABLANTES** *cuaderno* p. 4



### Actividad 11 Answers

1. estoy
2. estoy
3. Es
4. Es
5. es
6. Estoy

### Actividad 12 Answers

1. Carlos es de Buenos Aires. Está en Nueva York. Está alegre.
2. Melisa está en casa. Es de Santo Domingo. Está triste.
3. Miguel está preocupado. Es maestro. Es de San Francisco.
4. Ana es de México. Es simpática. Está en Italia.
5. *Answers will vary.*
6. *Answers will vary.*

### Actividad 13 Answers

(See script, TE p. xxxiiiB.)

1. Linda tiene quince años.
2. Es de Los Ángeles.
3. Ahora está en Nueva York.
4. Tiene un suéter amarillo y una falda de muchos colores.
5. Es delgada y baja. Tiene pelo rubio y bonito. Es muy simpática.

### Quick Wrap-up

Write on board and have students write sentences with **gustar**. Collect papers to identify problem areas, and/or review the answers in class.

1. Mi abuela es ___ y tiene los ojos ___.
   a. vieja, blanco b. viejo, verdes c. vieja, azules
2. La muchacha ___ que tiene ___ rojo es mi prima.
   a. alto, los pantalones b. alta, el vestido c. alta, la blusa
3. ¿Cuántos años ___ tú?
   a. tienes b. eres c. estás
4. La maestra ___ en la oficina ahora.
   a. está b. es c. están

**Answers**
1. c, 2. b, 3. a, 4. a

## Teaching All Students

**Extra Help** Ask students to mind map (make a visual representation of) **ser** and **estar**, comparing and contrasting their uses, then write a short paragraph about a friend's visit.

**Challenge** Have students look up Hispanic capitals and well-known cities. Have them invent pretend birthplaces and circulate to discuss origin, e.g., **¿De dónde eres? Soy de Quito.** The student asking should try to follow up with a question about nationality: **¿Eres de Ecuador?/¿Eres ecuatoriano(a)?**

### Multiple Intelligences

**Logical/Mathematical** Have students research the figure changes in population of Spanish-speakers in the U.S. (or in their area). Prepare a graph showing changes from 1979, 1989, 1999. Are there current predictions for future changes?

### Block Schedule

**Variety** Divide the class into two teams. Play the audio for **Actividad 13** and have students listen for the general idea. Play the audio a second time and have one team raise their hands when they hear the verb **ser** and the other team raise their hands when they hear **estar**. (For additional activities, see **Block Scheduling Copymasters**.)

### Teaching Resource Options

**Print**

Block Scheduling Copymasters
Preliminary/Unit 1 Resource Book
Audioscript, p. 36

**Audiovisual**

OHT P6 (Quick Start), P7
Audio Program Cassette 1A / CD 1

### Quick Start Review

Numbers

Use OHT P6 or write on the board: Write the numbers in Spanish from 1–20.

**Answers**

uno, dos, tres, cuatro, cinco, seis, siete, ocho, nueve, diez, once, doce, trece, catorce, quince, dieciséis, diecisiete, dieciocho, diecinueve, veinte

### Teaching Suggestions

- Model the conversations on pp. 12–13. Then have students take turns role-playing these conversations.
- Use **Actividad 14** to check comprehension.
- Have students skim the conversations for question words.
- Ask and model answers to questions from the conversations, e.g., **¿Qué hora es? –Son las nueve y cuarto.** Then ask 3–4 students questions. Finally have volunteers ask you information questions.

# ¡A preguntar!

## VOCABULARIO Y GRAMÁTICA

**OBJECTIVES**

- Ask for and give information

**Hartford, Connecticut** Look at the pictures and read about Patricia's plans for a Saturday afternoon in Hartford.

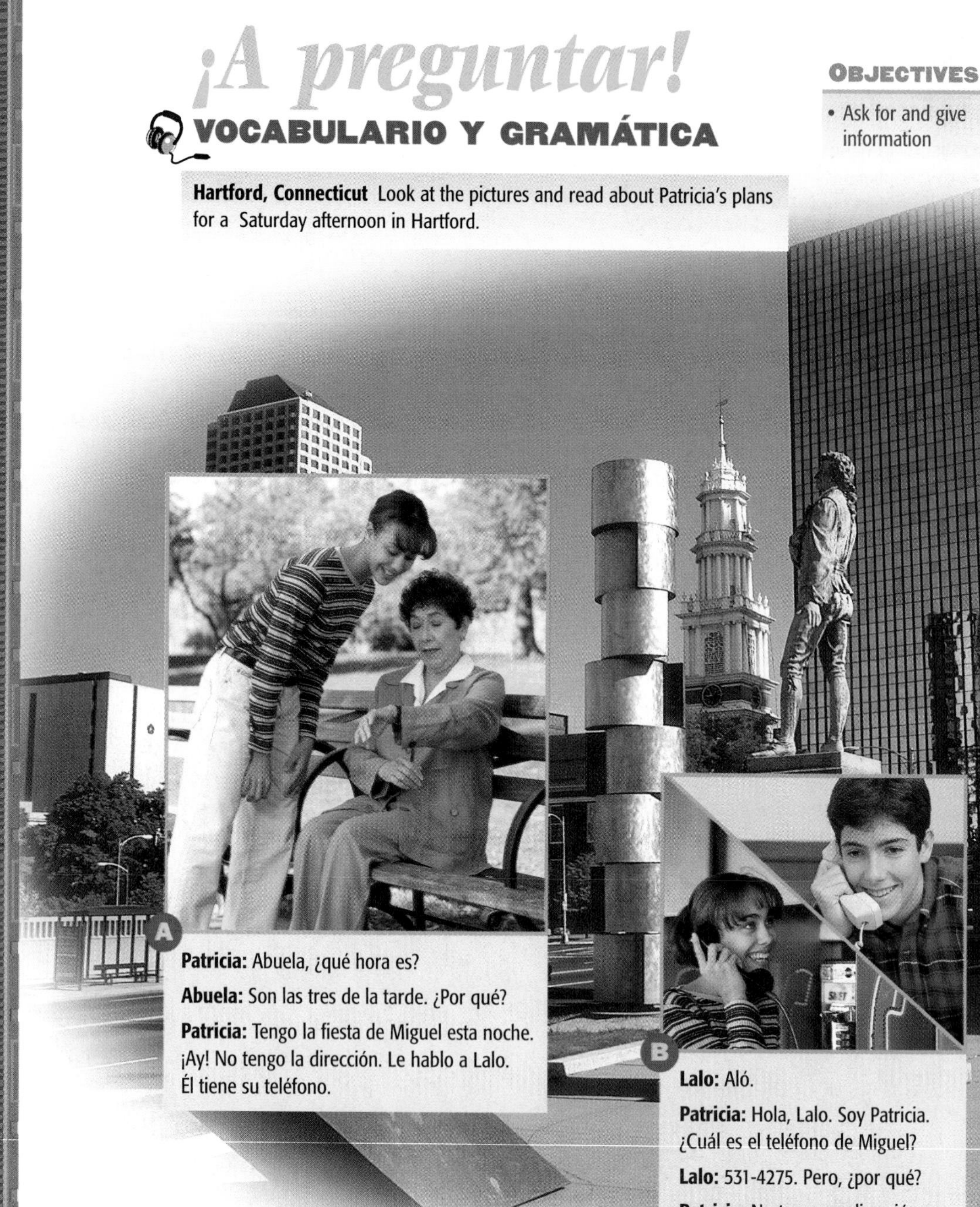

**A**

**Patricia:** Abuela, ¿qué hora es?

**Abuela:** Son las tres de la tarde. ¿Por qué?

**Patricia:** Tengo la fiesta de Miguel esta noche. ¡Ay! No tengo la dirección. Le hablo a Lalo. Él tiene su teléfono.

**B**

**Lalo:** Aló.

**Patricia:** Hola, Lalo. Soy Patricia. ¿Cuál es el teléfono de Miguel?

**Lalo:** 531-4275. Pero, ¿por qué?

**Patricia:** No tengo su dirección.

**Lalo:** ¿Por qué no vas conmigo a la fiesta?

**Patricia:** Muy bien. Chao.



### Classroom Community

**Paired Activity** Ask students to list at least 10 activities that they do on Saturday afternoons.

**Group Activity** Write the sentence **Yolanda tiene tres años**, and underline the word **tres**. Write the question **¿Cuántos años tiene Yolanda?** under the sentence. Then erase the underscore under **tres** and underscore **Yolanda**. Write the question **¿Quién tiene tres años?** under the 1st question. Then have groups work together to come up with a logical sentence. The challenge is to write a sentence that answers as many questions as possible. Groups should demonstrate their sentences on the board, underscoring different pieces of information, then writing the appropriate questions.

- *Review: Use interrogatives*
- *Review: Tell time*

C **Lalo:** Sí. Aquí está el apartamento. Está en esta calle.
**Patricia:** ¡Ay, qué bien!

D **Miguel:** Hola. Bienvenidos.
**Patricia:** ¿Qué tal?
**Lalo:** ¿Cómo estás, hombre?

## Actividad 14 En Hartford...

**Leer/Escribir** Contesta las preguntas sobre lo que Patricia, su abuela y sus amigos hacen en la ciudad. *(Hint: Answer questions about Patricia's plans.)*

1. Según la abuela, ¿qué hora es?
2. ¿Por qué quiere saber Patricia la hora?
3. ¿Cuál es el teléfono de Miguel?
4. ¿Vive Miguel en un apartamento o una casa?
5. ¿Por qué van Lalo y Patricia a la casa de Miguel?

## Repaso

### Interrogative Words

Remember that Spanish has many words that introduce a question. These words are called **interrogatives.** Some questions are formed by putting a **conjugated verb** after the **question word.**

***Each interrogative word has an accent on the appropriate vowel.***

***All questions are preceded by an inverted question mark and followed by a question mark.***

| | |
|---|---|
| **adónde** *(to) where* | ¿**Adónde vas** con Ana? |
| **cómo** *how* | ¿**Cómo está** el chico? |
| **cuál(es)** *which (ones)* | ¿**Cuál es** el libro? |
| **cuándo** *when* | ¿**Cuándo estudias**? |
| **cuánto** *how much* | ¿**Cuánto cuesta**? |
| **cuántos(as)** *how many* | ¿**Cuántos** años **tienes**? |
| **dónde** *where* | ¿**Dónde está** el carro? |
| **por qué** *why* | ¿**Por qué vas** a casa? |
| **qué** *what* | ¿**Qué es**? |
| **quién(es)** *who* | ¿**Quién(es) habla(n)**? |



## Culture Highlights

**HARTFORD** The Hispanic presence is getting stronger in central Connecticut. As of 1992, almost 32% of Hartford's population was Hispanic. The background photo was taken in downtown Hartford, Connecticut.

### Actividad 14 Answers

1. Según la abuela, son las tres de la tarde.
2. Patricia quiere saber la hora porque tiene la fiesta de Miguel esta noche.
3. El teléfono de Miguel es 531-4275.
4. Miguel vive en un apartamento.
5. Lalo y Patricia van a la casa de Miguel porque hay una fiesta.

## Teaching All Students

**Extra Help** Have students look at the photos and read the captions. Have them split into groups of 4 and compile a list of vocabulary words they remember that match the topics of the dialogs.

**Native Speakers** Have Spanish speakers read the dialogs aloud, modeling pronunciation and intonation for the rest of the class.

**Multiple Intelligences**

**Visual** Have students create a collage of magazine or newspaper photos they have gathered and label the photos with questions using the interrogatives they have learned.

## Block Schedule

**FunBreak** Bring a stuffed animal to class. Carry it around with you as class starts. The students will ask what it is. Have them ask as many questions as they can in Spanish about the stuffed animal: **¿Cómo se llama? ¿Cuántos años tiene?** etc. (For additional activities, see **Block Scheduling Copymasters.**)

## Teaching Resource Options

**Print** 

*Más práctica* Workbook PE, pp. 5–6
*Cuaderno para hispanohablantes* PE, pp. 5–6
Block Scheduling Copymasters
Preliminary/Unit 1 Resource Book
*Más práctica* Workbook TE, pp. 13–14
*Cuaderno para hispanohablantes* TE, pp. 23–24
Audioscript, p. 37

**Audiovisual**

OHT P6 (Quick Start)
Audio Program Cassette 1B / CD 1

## Quick Start Review

**Numbers**

Use OHT P6 or write on the board: Write out your telephone number spelling out the numbers in Spanish.

*Answers will vary.*

## Teaching Suggestions

- Before assigning **Actividades 15–17**, review numbers 0–1,000,000 with students.
- After students complete **Actividad 15**, have them use the questions to circulate and interview each other.

### Actividad 15 Answers

1. Cómo
2. De dónde
3. Cómo/Quién
4. Dónde
5. Cuál
6. Cuántos
7. Cuál
8. Por qué
9. Quién
10. Quién

### Actividad 16 Answers

*Answers will vary.*

### Actividad 17 Answers

*Answers will vary.*

## Actividad 15 Una conversación

**Hablar/Escribir** Completa las preguntas y las respuestas. Luego practícalas con un(a) compañero(a). *(Hint: Complete the questions. Practice them with a classmate.)*

**adónde** **cómo** **cuál(es)** **cuándo** **dónde** **por qué** **qué** **cuántos(as)** **de dónde** **quién(es)**

1. ¿ _____ te llamas? — Me llamo...
2. ¿ _____ eres? — Soy de...
3. ¿ _____ eres? — Soy...
4. ¿ _____ vives? — Vivo en...
5. ¿ _____ es tu dirección? — Mi dirección es...
6. ¿ _____ años tienes? — Tengo...
7. ¿ _____ es tu clase favorita? — Me gusta más la clase de...
8. ¿ _____ te gusta esa clase? — Es mi favorita porque...
9. ¿ _____ es tu mejor profesor(a)? — Mi mejor profesor(a) es...
10. ¿ _____ es tu mejor amigo(a)? — Mi mejor amigo(a) es...

## Actividad 16 ¿Cuál es...?

**Hablar/Escribir** Tu maestro(a) te va a dar tres minutos para preguntarles a tus amigos(as) su número de teléfono y dirección. Escribe la información en un papel. La persona que tenga la lista más larga y correcta gana. ¡Ojo! Sólo puedes hablar español. *(Hint: Race to see how many phone numbers and addresses you can collect in three minutes. You are only allowed to give information when asked in Spanish!)*

¿Cuál es tu teléfono? ¿Cuál es tu dirección?

## Actividad 17 Escríbelas

**Hablar/Escribir** Escribe las direcciones en español de tres lugares de tu pueblo o ciudad. Usa la guía telefónica si es necesario. Luego dile las direcciones a un grupo de compañeros(as). ¿Conocen el lugar? *(Hint: Write addresses of three places in your city or town. Tell a group. Can they name the place?)*

**MÁS PRÁCTICA** *cuaderno* p. 5
**PARA HISPANOHABLANTES** *cuaderno* p. 5

**De Connecticut** La gente de habla hispana de Connecticut es reconocida (*recognized*) por ser políticamente fuerte, creando asociaciones latinas y eventos culturales por todo el estado.

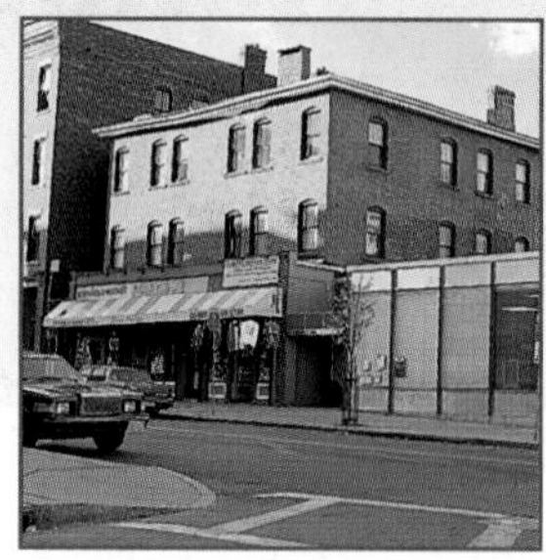



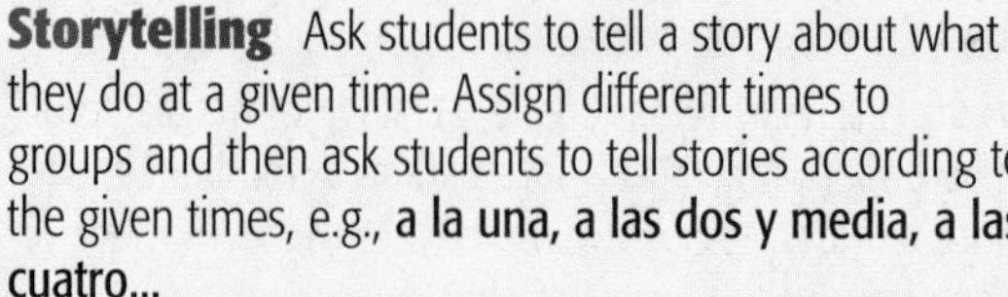

## Classroom Community

**Storytelling** Ask students to tell a story about what they do at a given time. Assign different times to groups and then ask students to tell stories according to the given times, e.g., **a la una, a las dos y media, a las cuatro...**

**Paired Activity** Ask pairs of students to exchange information about their daily schedule based on the times you give them. For example, 7:00 A.M.: **Yo estoy en la cama. Es muy temprano.** Challenge students to use **ser/estar** correctly and review if they are having difficulty at first.

## REPASO
## Tell Time

To talk about what time it is, use:

**¿Qué hora es?**
*What time is it?*

Son las doce y *minutes*

Use y + *minutes* for the number of minutes **after** the hour.

Son las doce. (12:00)
Son las doce y diez. (12:10)
Son las doce y media. (12:30)

Use **cuarto** for a quarter of an hour and **media** for half an hour.

Es la una menos *minutes*

Use menos + *minutes* for the number of minutes **before** the hour.

Es la una. (1:00)
Es la una menos cuarto. (12:45)

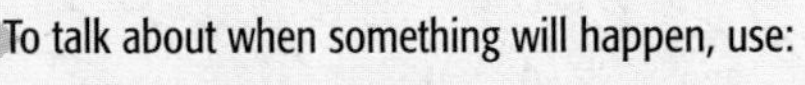

To talk about when something will happen, use:

**¿A qué hora es la clase?** *What time is the class?*
**A las (dos, tres).** *At (two o'clock, three o'clock).*
**A la una.** *At one o'clock.*

### ACTIVIDAD 18 ¿Qué hora es?

**Leer/Escribir** Isabel llama a casa durante el día para decirles a sus padres dónde está. Según su calendario, ¿qué hora es cada vez que llama? *(Hint: Tell what time it is.)*

| 5 | septiembre |
|---|---|
| 9:10 | caminar con el perro |
| 10:30 | comprar fruta para la fiesta |
| 11:15 | gimnasio |
| 12:00 | tomar algo con Patricia |
| 12:45 | sacar un libro |
| 1:00 | buscar zapatos nuevos |
| 1:20 | ir a la tienda de videos |
| 2:00 | comer con mi familia |

1. «Hola, estoy en el mercado.»
2. «Bueno, mis amigas y yo vamos a jugar al baloncesto.»
3. «Acabo de llegar al café.»
4. «Oye, estoy en la biblioteca.»
5. «Voy a alquilar un video. ¿Quieres uno también?»

### ACTIVIDAD 19 ¿A qué hora?

**Hablar/Escribir** ¿A qué hora es cada uno de estas actividades? Habla con un grupo de compañeros(as). *(Hint: Tell at what time these activities begin.)*

tu programa favorito de televisión
la clase de español
el almuerzo
la escuela
las películas baratas en el cine
la práctica de deportes escolares

**MÁS PRÁCTICA** *cuaderno* p. 6
**PARA HISPANOHABLANTES** *cuaderno* p. 6



## Culture Highlights

**PHONE NUMBERS** Point out that in Spanish-speaking countries, phone numbers are usually recited in tens, not ones (e.g., 98-23-46, *not* 9-8-2-3-4-6).

### ACTIVIDAD 18 Answers

1. Son las diez y media.
2. Son las once y cuarto.
3. Son las doce.
4. Es la una menos cuarto.
5. Es la una y veinte.

### ACTIVIDAD 19 Answers

*Answers will vary.*

## Project

Divide the class into groups. Have each group imagine that they are seeking funding for a study of Hispanic communities in U.S. cities. Part of the presentation to receive the funding includes submitting the interview preparations for different people and organizations they would approach. Have students choose a city, decide how to divide the interview tasks, and organize interview questions–what kinds of organizations would they consult, who would they talk to within the communities, etc. After deciding which city and approach, students should compile a list of questions that corresponds to their assignment. Each group should write a general statement of purpose.

**Extra Credit**

| | |
|---|---|
| Organization of information | 2 pts. |
| Interview questions | 2 pts. |
| Purpose statement | 2 pts. |

## Teaching All Students

**Extra Help** Give students a set of sentences, and ask them to write corresponding questions, e.g., **Ella es profesora de historia – ¿Quién es?; Ellos viven lejos de la escuela – ¿Dónde viven?; Es una manzana roja – ¿Qué es?**, etc.

**Multiple Intelligences**

**Intrapersonal** Ask students to write their daily activities in diary format, e.g., **A las ocho de la mañana, yo salgo de casa. A las nueve estoy en la clase de español**, etc.

**Logical/Mathematical** Ask students to list as many activities as they can. Write them on a transparency or on the board. Ask students to rewrite the list in the order things would logically be done and give the time of the day they would do them.

## Block Schedule

**Variety** Have students ask you questions about objects you've placed around the room. The more unusual and unexpected the object, the more they will be willing to question. Hints in Spanish may sometimes be necessary. (For additional activities, see **Block Scheduling Copymasters**.)

### Teaching Resource Options

**Print** 

Block Scheduling Copymasters
Preliminary/Unit 1 Resource Book
Audioscript, p. 36

**Audiovisual** 

OHT P6 (Quick Start), P8
Audio Program Cassette 1A / CD 1

### Quick Start Review

Telling time

Use OHT P6 or write on the board: Match the time with an appropriate activity and form complete sentences.

| | |
|---|---|
| a las ocho de la mañana | juego al béisbol |
| a la una y cuarto | voy a la escuela |
| a las tres | estudio para un examen |
| a las siete y media | voy a la clase de arte |

**Answers**

A las ocho de la mañana voy a la escuela.
A la una y cuarto voy a la clase de arte.
A las tres juego al béisbol.
A las siete y media estudio para un examen.
*Answers will vary.*

### Culture Highlights

**BOSTON** The background photo was taken outside Snowden International Academy in Boston, Massachusetts. The students in section E are standing in front of the Boston Public Library.

### Supplementary Vocabulary

- You may want to review the days of the week. School days include: **lunes, martes, miércoles, jueves, viernes,** and the weekend consists of **sábado, domingo.**
- Also review the expressions:

| | |
|---|---|
| **por la mañana** | in the morning |
| **por la tarde** | in the afternoon |
| **por la noche** | in the evening/at night |

# En la escuela

## VOCABULARIO Y GRAMÁTICA

**OBJECTIVES**

- Talk about school life

**Boston, Massachusetts** Look at the photos and read about what these students do in Boston.

A

Antes de la escuela...

**Susana:** Voy a tomar la clase de arte este año. ¿Y tú?

**Luis:** ¿Arte? No. Voy a tomar otra clase de música para practicar con mi guitarra. Mi banda está en un concurso.

B

Luego, Luis y Susana van a la clase de español. Le preguntan a la señora Rivera si van a hablar español todo el tiempo. La señora Rivera contesta que sólo van a usar español.

C

Todos los estudiantes descansan durante el día. Estos jóvenes comen su almuerzo.



### Classroom Community

**Paired Activity** Have students ask additional questions to find out about their partner's school day based on the **En la escuela** scenario.

**Portfolio** Have students write a short paragraph about a typical school day.

**Rubric: Writing**

| Criteria | Scale |
|---|---|
| Accuracy | 1 2 3 4 5 |
| Logical organization | 1 2 3 4 5 |
| Vocabulary use | 1 2 3 4 5 |

A = 13–15 pts.
B = 10–12 pts.
C = 7–9 pts.
D = 4–6 pts.
F = < 4 pts.

- *Review: Use regular present tense verbs*
- *Review: Use **ir***

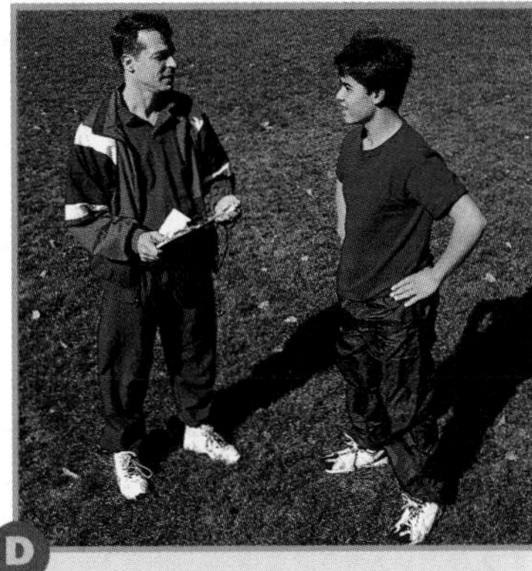

**D** Después de la escuela, David corre con un equipo.

**Entrenador Santiago:** ¿Corres en tu tiempo libre, David?

**David:** Sí, un poco. Pero, como no vivo cerca de aquí, corro en mi barrio.

**Entrenador Santiago:** Está bien.

**E** Susana y Luis caminan a la biblioteca después de la escuela. Tienen mucha tarea y van a estudiar. ¿Tienes mucha tarea?

## Actividad 20 Durante el día

**Leer/Escribir** Contesta las preguntas sobre lo que hacen los jóvenes durante el día escolar.
*(Hint: Answer questions about the school day.)*

1. ¿Qué clase va a tomar Susana? ¿y Luis?
2. ¿Van a hablar español e inglés en la clase de español?
3. ¿Qué clase da la señora Rivera?
4. ¿Qué hace David después de la escuela? ¿y Susana y Luis?

## REPASO Regular Present Tense Verbs

To talk about things you do, you use the present tense. To form the present tense of a regular verb, drop the **-ar**, **-er**, or **-ir** and add the appropriate **ending.**

**Regular Verbs**

| | -ar hablar | -er comer | -ir vivir |
|---|---|---|---|
| yo | hablo | como | vivo |
| tú | hablas | comes | vives |
| usted, él, ella | habla | come | vive |
| nosotros | hablamos | comemos | vivimos |
| vosotros | habláis | coméis | vivís |
| ustedes, ellos, ellas | hablan | comen | viven |

## Actividad 20 Answers

1. Susana va a tomar la clase de arte. Luis va a tomar la clase de música.
2. No, sólo van a hablar español en la clase de español.
3. La señora Rivera da la clase de español.
4. Después de la escuela David corre con un equipo. Susana y Luis van a la biblioteca. Hacen la tarea y estudian.

## Supplementary Vocabulary

You might find it useful to review some of the classroom vocabulary. Additional useful phrases include:

Cooperative/small group work

| | |
|---|---|
| **Ayúdense.** | Encourage each other. |
| **Concéntrense.** | Concentrate. |
| **Hablen en voz baja.** | Speak softly. |
| **Trabajen en equipo.** | Work together. |
| **Túrnense.** | Take turns. |

Pairs or small groups (student to student)

| | |
|---|---|
| **Es tu turno.** | It's your turn. |
| **Intenta de nuevo.** | Try again. |
| **No, estás equivocado.** | No, you are wrong. |
| **¿Qué tenemos que hacer?** | What are we supposed to do? |
| **Sí, tienes razón.** | Yes, you are right. |

Permission (student to teacher)

| | |
|---|---|
| **¿Puedo hablar en inglés?** | May I speak in English? |
| **¿Puedo ir al baño?** | May I go to the bathroom? |
| **¿Puedo ir a mi armario?** | May I go to my locker? |
| **¿Puedo ir a tomar agua?** | May I get a drink of water? |
| **¿Puedo sacarle punta al lápiz?** | May I sharpen my pencil? |

Confusion (student to teacher or other students)

| | |
|---|---|
| **Estoy confundido.** | I'm confused. |
| **No comprendo.** | I don't understand. |
| **No sé.** | I don't know. |

## Teaching All Students

**Extra Help** Have students designate a section of their notebooks for verb charts. They should copy conjugations of all verbs they learn here for reference. Have them copy the conjugations of **hablar, comer,** and **vivir,** plus at least 3 more regular present tense verbs of their choice (e.g., **caminar, comprar, estudiar, correr, escribir,** etc.).

**Multiple Intelligences**

**Intrapersonal** Have students write a list of verbs in the infinitive that describe what they do during the school day. Then have them write a short paragraph about a typical school day.

## Block Schedule

**Variety** Write different activities on slips of paper. Hand them out to students and have them ask at least 3 other students at what time of day they do the activity listed on their slip of paper.

## Teaching Resource Options

**Print** 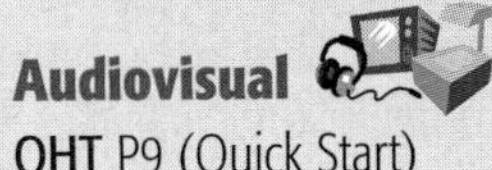

*Más práctica* Workbook PE, pp. 7–8
*Cuaderno para hispanohablantes* PE, pp. 7–8
Block Scheduling Copymasters
Preliminary/Unit 1 Resource Book
*Más práctica* Workbook TE, pp. 15–16
*Cuaderno para hispanohablantes* TE, pp. 25–26

**Audiovisual** 

OHT P9 (Quick Start)

## Quick Start Review

Present Tense

Use OHT P9 or write on the board: Fill in the endings to complete these sentences in the present tense.

1. Yo estudi__ español.
2. Tú beb__ un refresco.
3. Nosotros viv__ en Miami.
4. Tú camin__ con el perro.
5. Ellos descans__ después de la escuela.
6. Luís com__ con su amigo.

**Answers**
1. o, 2. es, 3. imos, 4. as, 5. an, 6. e

## Teaching Suggestions

Before completing **Actividad 21**, conduct a review of school-related vocabulary if you haven't already done so.

### Actividad 21 Answers

1. comemos, la cafetería
2. nadan, la piscina
3. lees, la biblioteca
4. hablo, la clase de español
5. corren, el gimnasio (la cancha, el estadio)

## Critical Thinking

Have students brainstorm a list of professions, then list or make word maps of activities associated with each, e.g. **maestro(a)/enseña, escribe, lee,** etc.

## Actividad 21 ¿Dónde?

**Escribir** Tú describes las actividades de varias personas en la escuela. Completa las oraciones e indica dónde tienen lugar las actividades. *(Hint: Complete the sentences and tell where the activity takes place.)*

**la biblioteca** · **la cafetería** · **el auditorio** · **el gimnasio** · **el campo** · **la cancha** · **la clase de ¿?** · **el estadio** · **la piscina**

1. Nosotros (comer) el almuerzo en _____.
2. Mis amigos (nadar) en _____.
3. Tú (leer) literatura en _____.
4. Yo (hablar) en español en _____.
5. En la clase de educación física, ustedes (correr) en _____.

## Actividad 22 En nuestra escuela

**Hablar/Escribir** Completa las oraciones y explica si estas actividades pasan en tu escuela. Si la actividad no pasa en tu escuela, cambia la oración para describir una actividad que sí pasa. *(Hint: Complete the sentences. Change any that do not apply.)*

**modelo**

*Los estudiantes / preparar / jugo / en la cafetería*

*Los estudiantes preparan jugo en la cafetería. (Los estudiantes no preparan jugo en la cafetería. Beben jugo en la cafetería.)*

**Nota**

Remember that using the right verb ending is important. Sometimes an incorrect ending changes a word's meaning, even with regular verbs like **preguntar**.

**Pregunto** a la maestra. ***I ask*** *the teacher.*

**Pregunta** a la maestra. ***He asks*** *the teacher.*

1. Yo / llegar / a clase a tiempo
2. Mis amigos / vender / la tarea
3. El (La) director(a) / caminar / a la escuela
4. Tú  (nombre) / visitar / durante las clases
5. Mis amigos y yo / beber / refrescos en clase

## Actividad 23 Las clases

**Hablar/Escribir** Habla sobre las clases con un grupo de compañeros(as). Describe lo que haces en cada clase, cómo es y dónde tiene lugar *(takes place)*. *(Hint: Talk about classes with a group.)*

**modelo**

**Tú:** *¿Qué hacen ustedes en la clase de francés?*

**Compañero(a) 1:** *Hablamos mucho francés y aprendemos mucho.*

**Tú:** *¿Cómo es?*

**Compañero(a) 2:** *Es interesante y divertida.*

**Tú:** *¿Dónde tiene lugar?*

**Compañero(a) 3:** *Es en el salón número mil trescientos cuatro.*

**el arte**
**la biología**
**las ciencias**
**la computación**
**la educación física**
**los estudios sociales**
**la física**
**la historia**
**la literatura**
**las matemáticas**
**la música**

**MÁS PRÁCTICA** *cuaderno* p. 7

**PARA HISPANOHABLANTES** *cuaderno* p. 7



## Classroom Community

**Paired Activity** Expand on **Actividad 22** by having students work in pairs to write additional sentences that describe activities in their school. Then have them take turns asking questions using the interrogative words that correspond to each sentence.

**Portfolio** Based on the list given in **Actividad 23**, ask students to write about the class they like most (**me gusta[n] más**) and explain why.

**Rubric: Writing**

| Criteria | Scale |
|---|---|
| Accuracy | 1 2 3 4 5 |
| Logical organization | 1 2 3 4 5 |
| Vocabulary use | 1 2 3 4 5 |

A = 13–15 pts.
B = 10–12 pts.
C = 7–9 pts.
D = 4–6 pts.
F = < 4 pts.

REPASO

## The Verb ir

Remember that when you talk about where someone is going, you use the verb **ir**, *to go.*

| voy | vamos |
|---|---|
| vas | vais |
| va | van |

Remember that forms of **ir** are usually followed by the preposition *a.*

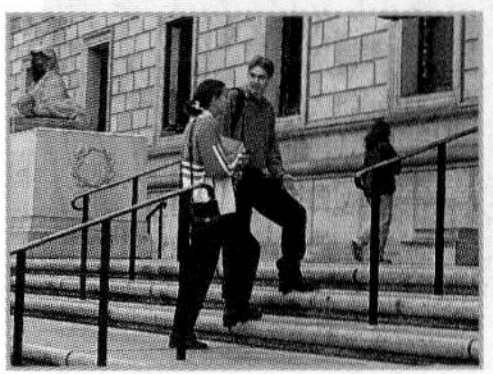

Susana y Luis **van** a la biblioteca.
*Susana and Luis **go** to the library.*

### Actividad 24 ¿Adónde van?

**Hablar/Escribir** ¿Adónde van estas personas en la escuela? *(Hint: Tell where these people are going.)*

**modelo**

*Jorge necesita tomar una prueba de computadoras.*
*Va a la clase de computación.*

1. Comemos el almuerzo.
2. Buscas información sobre Puerto Rico.
3. Practico deportes en mi próxima clase.
4. Juegan al tenis.
5. Nadamos hoy en la clase de educación física.
6. Tomo una prueba de plantas y animales.

### Actividad 25  ¿Qué haces allí?

**Hablar** Imagínate que vas a los siguientes lugares. Habla con un(a) compañero(a) sobre adónde vas y qué vas a hacer allí. *(Hint: Tell where you are going and what you will do there.)*

la oficina · la biblioteca · el español · la cafetería · el gimnasio · las ciencias

**modelo**

**Compañero(a):** *¿Adónde vas?*
**Tú:** *Voy al auditorio.*
**Compañero(a):** *¿Qué vas a hacer allí?*
**Tú:** ...

1.

2.

3.

4.

**MÁS PRÁCTICA** *cuaderno* p. 8
**PARA HISPANOHABLANTES** *cuaderno* p. 8

**TAMBIÉN SE DICE**

Muchas palabras en inglés vienen del español u otros idiomas romanos. ¿Crees que la palabra **cafetería** tiene sus orígenes en el inglés o el español? ¿Qué tal estas palabras: **el rodeo, la plaza, el récord, la televisión**? Si no sabes, ¿dónde puedes buscar esta información?



## Quick Start Review

Time/Classes

Use OHT P9 or write on the board: Describe your schedule today. Include all of your classes and the time.

A las ____, voy a la clase de _____.

*Answers will vary.*

## Teaching Suggestions

Have students refer to a Spanish-English dictionary or to an English dictionary to research the origins of the words listed in the **También se dice** sections.

### Actividad 22 Answers

*Answers may vary.*
1. Yo (no) llego a clase a tiempo.
2. Mis amigos no venden la tarea. Mis amigos hacen la tarea.
3. El (La) director(a) (no) camina a la escuela. (Corre a la escuela.)
4. Tú (no) visitas durante las clases.
5. Mis amigos y yo (no) bebemos refrescos en clase.

### Actividad 23 Answers

*Answers will vary.*

### Actividad 24 Answers

1. Vamos a la cafetería.
2. Vas a la biblioteca.
3. Voy al gimnasio.
4. Van a la cancha de tenis.
5. Vamos a la piscina.
6. Voy a la clase de biología (ciencias).

### Actividad 25 Answers

*Answers will vary but should include the following:*
1. Voy a la biblioteca.
2. Voy a clase (a la oficina).
3. Voy a la cancha de baloncesto.
4. Voy a la cafetería.

## Teaching All Students

**Extra Help** Ask students to talk about three places they like to go, e.g., **Me gusta ir ...**

**Native Speakers** Have Spanish speakers create longer dialogs in which students talk about the new school year and their future plans. Record or videotape them as models for additional practice.

**Challenge** Ask students to develop a crossword puzzle using the list of classes in **Actividad 23**.

**Multiple Intelligences**

**Intrapersonal** Have students write about things they like to do using the following pattern: state what they like to do; when they do it; where they go to do it. Write the following model on the board: **Me gusta comer enchiladas. Como enchiladas después de clase los viernes. Voy a un restaurante para comer enchiladas.** Encourage students to be creative. Have volunteers read their sentences to the class.

## Block Schedule

**Change of Pace** Movement in the classroom can provide a welcome change of pace. For **Actividad 25**, designate a different part of the classroom for each location listed: **la oficina, la biblioteca,** etc. Have pairs of students move to each location when doing each item.

## Teaching Resource Options

**Print** 

Block Scheduling Copymasters
Preliminary/Unit 1 Resource Book
Audioscript, p. 36

**Audiovisual** 

**OHT** P9 (Quick Start), P10
**Audio Program** Cassette 1A / CD 1

## Quick Start Review

Present Tense

Use OHT P9 or write on the board: Describe what Rosa does on Saturdays. Use the present tense.

1. Rosa / hablar / con su abuela por teléfono
2. ella / leer / una revista
3. andar / en bicicleta
4. comer / en un café con sus amigas
5. alquilar / un video

**Answers**
1. habla, 2. lee, 3. anda, 4. come, 5. alquila

## Teaching Suggestions

- Present photos and captions on pp. 20–21.
- Have volunteers role-play the conversation in photo A.
- Ask questions to check comprehension.
- Present Stem-Changing Verbs **Repaso** box and have students skim the photo captions for stem-changing verbs.

## Culture Highlights

**BOSTON** The background photo was taken in Copley Square with Trinity Church in the background. The mirrored building that appears in the background on p. 21 is the John Hancock Tower—the tallest building in Boston.

# ¿Qué haces?

## VOCABULARIO Y GRAMÁTICA

**OBJECTIVES**
- Talk about the new school year

**Boston, Massachusetts** Look at the pictures and read about these students' goals for the upcoming school year.

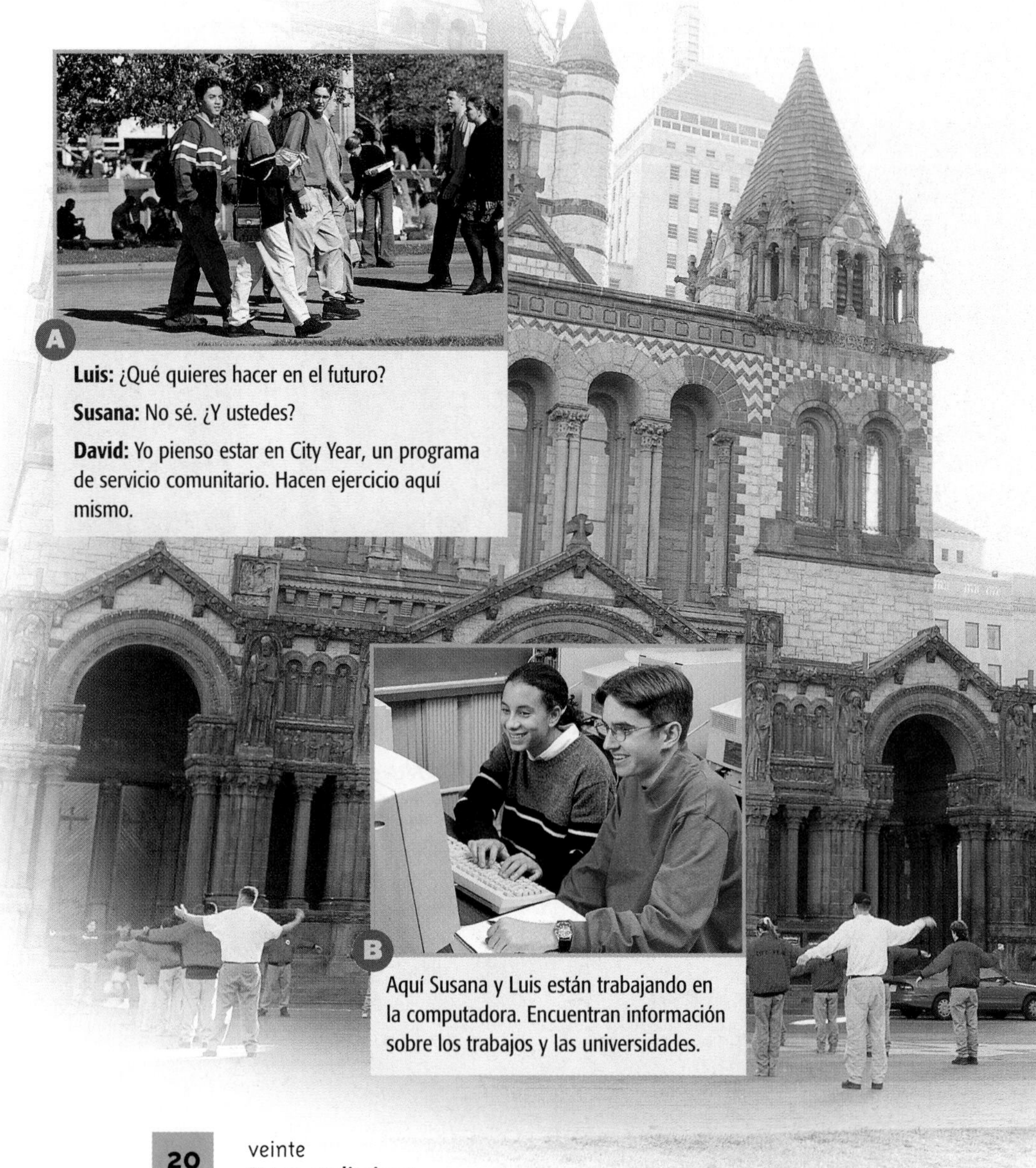

**A**

**Luis:** ¿Qué quieres hacer en el futuro?

**Susana:** No sé. ¿Y ustedes?

**David:** Yo pienso estar en City Year, un programa de servicio comunitario. Hacen ejercicio aquí mismo.

**B**

Aquí Susana y Luis están trabajando en la computadora. Encuentran información sobre los trabajos y las universidades.



## Classroom Community 

**Cooperative Learning** Divide the class into three groups and assign each an objective. Allow each group to review the objective and make a presentation to the entire class. S1 gives vocabulary and a sample sentence about the new school year, S2 gives examples of stem-changing verbs, S3 uses verbs with irregular **yo** forms in sentences.

**Game** Have students brainstorm a list of stem-changing verbs. Who can list the most?

- *Review: Use stem-changing verbs (e → ie, o → ue)*
- *Review: Use verbs with irregular **yo** forms*

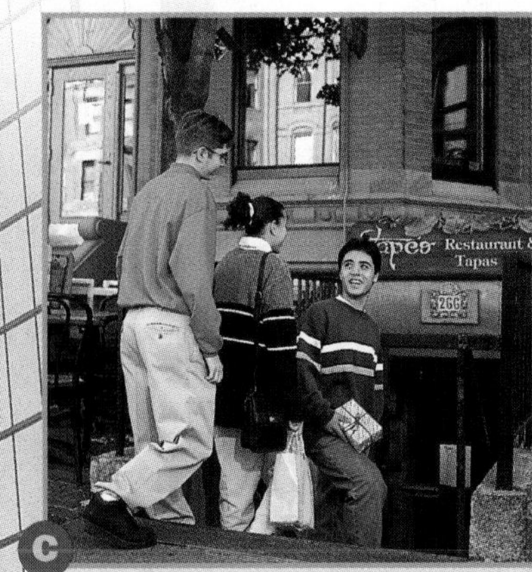


C Durante el año escolar, puedes comer con los amigos.

D También puedes entrar en la universidad. ¡Hay muchas universidades aquí en Boston!

## ACTIVIDAD 26 Unas preguntas personales

**Hablar/Escribir** Ya sabes lo que hacen Luis, Susana y David. Luego contesta las preguntas sobre lo que haces tú. *(Hint: Answer the questions.)*

1. ¿Qué quieres hacer este año?
2. ¿Encuentras información por computadora? ¿Qué tipo?
3. ¿Dónde almuerzas?
4. ¿Qué piensas hacer este fin de semana?
5. ¿Vuelves a la misma escuela el año que viene?
6. ¿Prefieres salir con tus amigos(as) o hacer la tarea?

## REPASO Stem-Changing Verbs

As you know, Spanish has many stem-changing verbs. Review the ones that follow.

**pensar** *to think*
**e → ie**

| | |
|---|---|
| **pienso** | **pensamos** |
| **piensas** | **pensáis** |
| **piensa** | **piensan** |

The stem doesn't change for the **nosotros** (*we*) or **vosotros** (*you*) form.

**almorzar** *to eat lunch*
**o → ue**

| | |
|---|---|
| **almuerzo** | **almorzamos** |
| **almuerzas** | **almorzáis** |
| **almuerza** | **almuerzan** |

For a complete list of stem-changing verbs, refer to pp. R30–R31.



### Teaching Suggestions

Other stem-changing verbs (**u→ue** and **e→i**) are reviewed in Unit 1.

### ACTIVIDAD 26 Answers

*Answers will vary.*

**More Practice**
Have students use these questions to interview each other.

## Teaching All Students

**Extra Help** Ask students to bring in 2–3 facts in Spanish about the Boston area. Encourage them to use the Internet.

**Extra Help** Point out that the structures **ir a** + infinitive, **querer** + infinitive, **poder** + infinitive, and **pensar** + infinitive can be used to talk about the future. Have them practice talking about what they want, plan, could, and are going to do in the near future.

**Multiple Intelligences**

**Intrapersonal** Ask students to discuss their goals for the school year. List them on a transparency and use as an opener for the following day.

**Verbal** Ask students to write a short paragraph describing their personal goals for the school year.

**Interpersonal** Have students analyze and discuss similarities and differences in their goals.

### Block Schedule

**Process Time** Have students write down any questions, concerns, or study tips they have about the material they are studying and place them in a "Suggestion Box." The teacher should regularly check the box and address the students' questions or concerns with the class. (For additional activities, see **Block Scheduling Copymasters.**)

## Teaching Resource Options

### Print

*Más práctica* Workbook PE, pp. 9–10
*Cuaderno para hispanohablantes* PE, pp. 9–10
Block Scheduling Copymasters
Preliminary/Unit 1 Resource Book
*Más práctica* Workbook TE, pp. 17–18
*Cuaderno para hispanohablantes* TE, pp. 27–28
Audioscript, pp. 36–37, 38

### Audiovisual

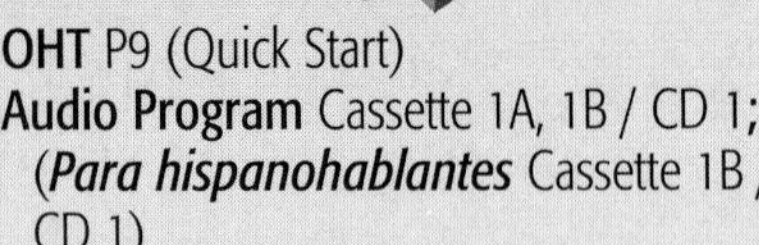

OHT P9 (Quick Start)
Audio Program Cassette 1A, 1B / CD 1; (*Para hispanohablantes* Cassette 1B / CD 1)

## Quick Start Review

Adjectives

Use OHT P9 or write on the board: Describe yourself in Spanish. Use at least three adjectives.

*Answers will vary.*

### Actividad 27 Answers

1. cuenta
2. cuestan
3. pueden
4. podemos
5. encuentro
6. vuelvo
7. encuentro
8. Duermes

### Actividad 28 Answers

*Answers will vary. Sample answers:*

1. Siempre cuento mi dinero.
2. Nunca duermo en clase.
3. De vez en cuando almuerzo con mis padres.
4. Rara vez pierdo un partido.
5. Pienso en el pasado mucho.
6. Nunca entiendo las matemáticas.
7. Siempre cierro la casa con llave.
8. De vez en cuando vuelvo a casa después de las once.

### More Practice

Have students expand on **Actividad 28** by telling how often they do these activities:
**bailar, comer en un restaurante, escuchar música, escribir una carta, caminar a la escuela, mirar la televisión.**

## Actividad 27 ¿Qué pasa?

**Leer/Escribir** Meche participa en un concurso en su escuela. Completa su descripción. *(Hint: Complete Meche's description of a contest at her school.)*

Mi amiga me __1__ (contar) de un concurso en nuestra escuela para ganar dinero para nuevos uniformes. Los uniformes __2__ (costar) mucho. El concurso es un maratón de tenis y los estudiantes __3__ (poder) participar por doce horas. Nosotros __4__ (poder) ganar un premio. Pero yo no __5__ (encontrar) mi raqueta. Entonces __6__ (volver) a casa y la __7__ (encontrar) en mi cuarto. Terminamos y... ¡qué cansada estoy! Ahora voy a dormir mucho. ¿ __8__ (Dormir) tú mucho después de jugar tanto?

**City Year** es un programa nacional para jóvenes que tienen de 17 a 23 años. Los participantes ofrecen un año de servicio para los habitantes de una comunidad estadounidense. En la página 20 los jóvenes de **City Year** hacen ejercicio. ¿Por qué crees que lo hacen?

## Actividad 28 ¿Cuántas veces?

**Hablar/Escribir** ¿Cuántas veces haces las siguientes actividades? Usa expresiones como **nunca, rara vez, de vez en cuando, mucho** y **siempre** en tus respuestas. *(Hint: How often do you do these things?)*

**modelo**

*dormir en casa de un(a) amigo(a)*
*De vez en cuando duermo en casa de un amigo.*

**Nota**

*nunca* — *rara vez* — *de vez en cuando* — *mucho* — *siempre*

To say how often you do something, you can use **nunca** (*never*), **rara vez** (*rarely*), **de vez en cuando** (*sometimes*), and **mucho** (*often*) or **siempre** (*always*). In negative sentences, you can use a negative word and the word **no.**

No, no como en restaurantes **nunca.** *No, I **never** eat in restaurants.*

1. contar tu dinero
2. dormir en clase
3. almorzar con tus padres
4. perder un partido
5. pensar en el pasado
6. entender las matemáticas
7. cerrar la casa con llave
8. volver a casa después de las once

## Actividad 29 Después de la escuela

**Escuchar/Hablar** ¿Qué hacen los chicos después de clases? Escucha la descripción y ordena las fotos según lo que escuchaste. *(Hint: Listen to the description. Then put photos in chronological order.)*

a.

b.

c.

**MÁS PRÁCTICA** *cuaderno* pp. 8–9
**PARA HISPANOHABLANTES** *cuaderno* pp. 8–9



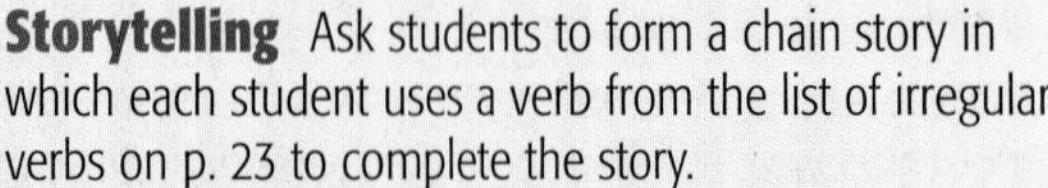

## Classroom Community

**Storytelling** Ask students to form a chain story in which each student uses a verb from the list of irregular verbs on p. 23 to complete the story.

**Paired Activity** Have students work in pairs to develop a scene between two people. The relationship between the two people should not be stated in the conversation, but should become obvious through the questions and answers. For example, the scene can be about an overanxious parent making sure his or her son or daughter has done everything he or she needs to do for school. Have volunteers present their scene to the class. The class should try to guess what the relationship is between the two.

## REPASO

### Irregular yo Verbs

Remember that some verbs are only irregular in the first person singular (yo) form. Compare the yo and **tú** forms of these verbs.

- These take the ending -go.

| | **caer** *to fall* | **hacer** *to make, to do* | **poner** *to put* | **salir** *to go out, to leave* | **traer** *to bring* |
|---|---|---|---|---|---|
| yo | **caigo** | **hago** | **pongo** | **salgo** | **traigo** |
| tú | **caes** | **haces** | **pones** | **sales** | **traes** |

- Other verbs that are irregular in the yo form only are **conocer, dar, saber,** and **ver.**

| | **conocer** *to know, to meet* | **dar** *to give* | **saber** *to know* | **ver** *to see* |
|---|---|---|---|---|
| yo | **conozco** | **doy** | **sé** | **veo** |
| tú | **conoces** | **das** | **sabes** | **ves** |

### ACTIVIDAD 30 Unas actividades

**Hablar/Escribir** ¿Haces estas cosas? Completa las oraciones para explicar si haces las siguientes actividades. *(Hint: Do you do these things?)*

**modelo**

*hacer la tarea por la mañana*

*Yo no hago la tarea por la mañana.*

1. traer el cuaderno a clase
2. hacer la cama todos los días
3. poner la ropa en su lugar todos los días
4. dar fiestas para tus padres
5. siempre saber las respuestas de la tarea
6. ver la televisión hasta la medianoche
7. conocer a una persona famosa
8. salir de la casa a las cinco de la mañana

### ACTIVIDAD 31 ¿Y tú?

**Hablar/Leer** Lee sobre David, un estudiante de Boston. Dile a un(a) compañero(a) si las situaciones también te pasan a ti. *(Hint: Read the descriptions and tell a classmate if they are true for you.)*

**modelo**

*David ve pájaros de su ventana por la mañana.*

*Sí, (No, no) veo pájaros de mi ventana por la mañana.*

**Nota**

Remember that the verbs **decir** *to say, to tell* and **venir** *to come* are irregular. Like the irregular **yo** verbs, they have first person singular forms ending in **-go** (**digo**, **vengo**).

**Vengo** del mercado. ***I come** from the market.*

1. Generalmente hace la tarea por la mañana.
2. Él ve todas las películas que salen.
3. Él les dice sus problemas a sus amigos.
4. Sale para la escuela muy temprano.
5. David trae sus libros en una mochila.
6. Él les da papel a sus amigos en clase.
7. David sabe hablar español bien.
8. Viene a la escuela en moto.

**MÁS PRÁCTICA** *cuaderno* p. 10

**PARA HISPANOHABLANTES** *cuaderno* p. 10



### Teaching Suggestions

- Have students use the cues in **Actividad 28** to ask each other questions. They should use yes/no questions, e.g., **¿Duermes en casa de un(a) amigo(a) mucho?** Encourage them to add other activities to the list.
- Ask random questions about how often students do different activities. Include the irregular **yo** verbs. (Remind students: **yo tengo.**)
- Most of the spell-change verbs have been reviewed at the beginning of Level 2. However, you might also want to review the verbs **conocer** (**c→zc**), and **oír**.

### ACTIVIDAD 29 Answers

(See script, TE p. xxxiiiB.)
Correct order: c, a, b

### ACTIVIDAD 30 Answers

1. Yo (no) traigo el cuaderno a clase.
2. Yo (no) hago la cama todos los días.
3. Yo (no) pongo la ropa en su lugar todos los días.
4. Yo (no) doy fiestas para mis padres.
5. Yo siempre sé las respuestas de la tarea. (Yo no sé las respuestas de la tarea.)
6. Yo (no) veo la televisión hasta la medianoche.
7. Yo (no) conozco a una persona famosa.
8. Yo (no) salgo de la casa a las cinco de la mañana.

### ACTIVIDAD 31 Answers

1. Generalmente (no) hago la tarea por la mañana.
2. Sí, (No, no) veo todas las películas que salen.
3. Sí, (No, no) les digo mis problemas a mis amigos.
4. Sí, (No, no) salgo para la escuela muy temprano.
5. Sí, (No, no) traigo mis libros en una mochila.
6. Sí, (No, no) les doy papel a mis amigos en clase.
7. Sí, (No, no) sé hablar español bien.
8. Sí, (No, no) vengo a la escuela en moto.

### Block Schedule

**FunBreak** Have students create simple crossword puzzles with present tense verbs. The cues should be sentences with missing verbs. For example, the cue for **traigo** might be: **Yo siempre ____ la tarea a clase.** Have students exchange and solve each other's puzzles. (For additional activities, see **Block Scheduling Copymasters.**)

## Teaching All Students

**Extra Help** Ask students to conjugate the present tense verb forms of **caer, hacer, poner, salir, traer, conocer, dar, saber,** and **ver** in their notebooks. They can also make flashcards for quick reference.

**Multiple Intelligences**

**Verbal** List verbs on a transparency or on the board. Ask students to form sentences using the verbs.

**Logical/Mathematical** Ask students to brainstorm a list of Spanish verbs. They may refer to the **En resumen** vocabulary list on p. 25. Then have them classify the verbs as regular **ar/er/ir**, irregular, or irregular **yo**. How many verbs do they have of each kind?

## Teaching Resource Options

**Print**

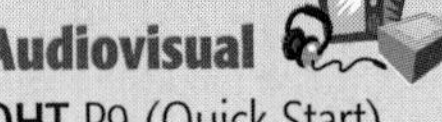

Block Scheduling Copymasters
Preliminary/Unit 1 Resource Book
- **Information Gap Activities**, pp. 29–32
- **Family Involvement**, pp. 33–34
- **Cooperative Quizzes**, pp. 39–40
- **Etapa Exam**, Forms A and B, pp. 41–50
- *Examen para hispanohablantes* pp. 51–55
- **Portfolio Assessment**, pp. 56–57
- **Multiple Choice Test Questions**, pp. 240–242

**Audiovisual**

**OHT** P9 (Quick Start)
**Audio Program** Cassette 19A / CD 19; (*Para hispanohablantes* Cassette 19A / CD 19)

## Quick Start Review

Verbs

Use OHT P9 or write on the board: Give the **yo** forms of each verb, then write 5 sentences about yourself using verbs from the list.

| | | |
|---|---|---|
| 1. caer | 5. tener | 9. ir |
| 2. saber | 6. ver | 10. dar |
| 3. estar | 7. ser | |
| 4. decir | 8. salir | |

**Answers**
*Sentences will vary.*
1. caigo, 2. sé, 3. estoy, 4. digo, 5. tengo, 6. veo, 7. soy, 8. salgo, 9. voy, 10. doy

**Answers**

*Answers will vary.*

**Answers**

*Answers will vary.*

**Answers**

*Answers will vary.*

**Rubric: Speaking**

| Criteria | Scale |
|---|---|
| Fluency | 1 2 3 4 5 |
| Vocabulary use | 1 2 3 4 5 |
| Pronunciation | 1 2 3 4 5 |

A = 13–15 pts.
B = 10–12 pts.
C = 7–9 pts.
D = 4–6 pts.
F = < 4 pts.

## Actividad 32 Unas preguntas

**Hablar/Escribir** Contesta estas preguntas con un grupo de compañeros(as). Luego escribe un resumen de las respuestas. *(Hint: Answer these questions with a group of classmates.)*

1. ¿Qué traes a clase todos los días?
2. ¿Prefieres ir a la escuela o trabajar? Explica.
3. ¿Sabes hacer algo bien? ¿Puedes enseñarles la actividad a otros?
4. ¿Le das dinero a alguien o a una institución? ¿Por qué?
5. ¿Qué quieres aprender este año?
6. ¿Qué cosa nueva quieres hacer este año?

## Actividad 33 ¿Quién soy yo?

**Hablar/Escribir** Completa las oraciones y presenta la información en una forma artística que simbolice lo que escribes. *(Hint: Make a poster that represents you. Present the information in a symbolic manner.)*

1. Me llamo (nombre).
2. Soy (dos descripciones físicas).
3. También soy (dos descripciones de tu personalidad).
4. Mi familia es (dos descripciones).
5. Mis amigos son (dos descripciones).
6. Me gusta (tres actividades).

## Actividad 34 Las presentaciones

### PARA CONVERSAR

**STRATEGY: SPEAKING**

**Give and get personal information** Getting acquainted involves sharing information about yourself as well as getting information about others.

For example, tell something about yourself and then ask your new classmate a related question: **—A mí me gusta estudiar después de la cena. Y tú, ¿cuándo prefieres estudiar?**

Or after asking the question, react to the answer: **—Prefiero estudiar antes de la cena cuando no estoy cansado.**
**—¡Qué buena idea!**

**Hablar/Escribir** Haz una entrevista con un(a) compañero(a) de clase que no conozcas bien. Primero, escribe una lista de preguntas e incluye todos los elementos de la lista. Luego preséntale la persona a la clase y comparte cinco cosas nuevas que ya sabes. *(Hint: Interview a classmate and then introduce him or her to the class.)*

| | | |
|---|---|---|
| nombre | gustos | clases |
| origen | dirección | actividades |
| edad | teléfono | metas *(goals)* |

**MÁS COMUNICACIÓN** p. R1



## Classroom Community

**Portfolios** Ask students to write a paragraph about themselves using the **Etapa** vocabulary.

**Rubric: Writing**

| Criteria | Scale |
|---|---|
| Accuracy | 1 2 3 4 5 |
| Logical organization | 1 2 3 4 5 |
| Vocabulary use | 1 2 3 4 5 |

A = 13–15 pts.
B = 10–12 pts.
C = 7–9 pts.
D = 4–6 pts.
F = < 4 pts.

**TPR** Ask students to act out a given vocabulary word for classmates to guess. For verbs, students should act out the actions. For adjectives of emotion, have them use facial expressions. For descriptive adjectives about physical appearance, have them stand only if the adjective applies to them.

# En resumen

## YA SABES

### DISCUSS LIKES AND DISLIKES

| | |
|---|---|
| **gustar** | *to like* |

**Activities**

| | |
|---|---|
| **bailar** | *to dance* |
| **cantar** | *to sing* |
| **comer** | *to eat* |
| **escribir** | *to write* |
| **escuchar música** | *to listen to music* |
| **patinar** | *to skate* |

### DESCRIBE PEOPLE AND PLACES

| | |
|---|---|
| **estar** | *to be* |
| **ser** | *to be* |
| **tener** | *to have* |

**Appearance and Personality**

| | |
|---|---|
| **alegre** | *happy* |
| **alto(a)** | *tall* |
| **bajo(a)** | *short (height)* |
| **castaño(a)** | *brown (hair)* |
| **cómico(a)** | *funny, comical* |
| **corto(a)** | *short (length)* |
| **delgado(a)** | *thin* |
| **guapo(a)** | *good-looking* |
| **largo(a)** | *long* |
| **moreno(a)** | *dark (hair and skin)* |
| **nervioso(a)** | *nervous* |
| **rubio(a)** | *blond* |
| **serio(a)** | *serious* |
| **tranquilo(a)** | *calm* |
| **triste** | *sad* |

### EXCHANGE GREETINGS

| | |
|---|---|
| **Buenas tardes.** | *Good afternoon.* |
| **¿Cómo estás?** | *How are you?* |
| **¿Cómo te llamas?** | *What is your name?* |
| **¿De dónde eres?** | *Where are you from?* |
| **El gusto es mío.** | *The pleasure is mine.* |
| **Encantado(a).** | *Delighted.* |
| **Les presento a…** | *I'd like to introduce you to…* |
| **Me llamo…** | *My name is…* |
| **Se llama…** | *His/Her name is…* |
| **Soy de…** | *I am from…* |

### THE NEW SCHOOL YEAR

**Stem-Changing Verbs**

| | |
|---|---|
| **almorzar (o →ue)** | *to eat lunch* |
| **cerrar (e →ie)** | *to close* |
| **costar (o →ue)** | *to cost* |
| **dormir (o →ue)** | *to sleep* |
| **encontrar (o →ue)** | *to find, to meet* |
| **entender (e →ie)** | *to understand* |
| **pensar (e →ie)** | *to think, to plan* |
| **poder (o →ue)** | *to be able, can* |
| **preferir (e →ie)** | *to prefer* |
| **querer (e →ie)** | *to want* |
| **recordar (o →ue)** | *to remember* |
| **volver (o →ue)** | *to return, to come back* |

### TALK ABOUT SCHOOL LIFE

| | |
|---|---|
| **caminar** | *to walk* |
| **contestar** | *to answer* |
| **correr** | *to run* |
| **descansar** | *to rest* |
| **estudiar** | *to study* |
| **hablar** | *to talk, to speak* |
| **ir** | *to go* |
| **preguntar** | *to ask* |
| **terminar** | *to finish* |
| **tomar** | *to take, to eat or drink* |
| **vivir** | *to live* |

### ASK FOR/GIVE INFORMATION

| | |
|---|---|
| **adónde** | *(to) where* |
| **cómo** | *how* |
| **cuál(es)** | *which (ones), what* |
| **cuándo** | *when* |
| **¿Cuántos años tiene…?** | *How old is …?* |
| **dónde** | *where* |
| **por qué** | *why* |
| **qué** | *what* |
| **quién(es)** | *who* |

### Juego

Adriana y Paula se encuentran por la calle.

**Adriana:** ¿Cómo están tus hijas? ¿Cuántos años tienen?

**Paula:** El producto de las tres edades es 36 y la suma es el mismo que el número de tu casa.

**Adriana:** Sé que vivo en el 13. Pero todavía necesito más información.

**Paula:** Sí. Es cierto. Mi hija mayor toca el piano.

¿Cuántos años tiene cada hija?

## Teaching Suggestions

- This **En resumen** word list includes a selected number of crucial words that are reviewed in the **Etapa preliminar**, but because of space constraints, it does not include all the words that were reviewed. Use this list as a springboard for additional vocabulary review.

## Community Connections

Have students look in the TV guide to see what channels in the area (if any) broadcast in Spanish. Have students choose one program to watch, then have them briefly summarize it for the class.

## Juego

### Answers

2, 2, 9

Note: Remind students that **producto** (product) is the total of multiplied numbers and that **suma** (sum) is the total when numbers are added. This should help them figure out the answer to the **juego**.

## Quick Wrap-up

To review objectives and vocabulary, ask quick, random questions. Students can use 1-word answers, but should respond quickly to keep the questions at a lively pace. Sample questions:

**¿Cómo te llamas?**
**¿De dónde eres?**
**¿Cuántas clases tienes?**
**¿Qué prefieres estudiar?**
**¿Cómo es tu pelo?**
**¿De qué color es tu camisa?**
**¿Cómo estás?** etc.

## Teaching All Students

**Extra Help** Ask students to greet each other using the given vocabulary. Then have students role play in pairs to review conversational exchange.

**Multiple Intelligences**

**Interpersonal** Ask students to choose a vocabulary grouping and re-teach the meanings to another student.

**Visual** Ask students to bring in pictures to practice a given set of vocabulary (you may even want to divide vocabulary among the entire class). As an alternate, have students in groups write and illustrate comic strips that ask/give information, describe people and places, etc.

## Block Schedule

**Retention** As a review of the unit, have students create questions that they think would make a good unit test. Then have students find the answers to the questions. Share with the class. (For additional activities, see **Block Scheduling Copymasters**.)

## Unit Theme

**Discussing leisure activities, expressing preferences, and talking about things, people.**

**Communication**
- Talking about where you went and what you did in the past
- Discussing leisure time activities
- Expressing activity preferences
- Commenting on travel, food, art
- Reacting to news
- Asking for and giving information
- Talking about things/people you know

**Cultures**
- Learning about food and fine art from the Hispanic communities in the U.S.
- Learning about Hispanic communities in Los Angeles, Chicago, Miami

**Connections**
- Connecting to Art: Comparing art forms and artists in the Spanish-speaking world and the U.S.
- Connecting to Journalism: Comparing news in Spanish and English
- Connecting to Mathematics: Creating graphs based on surveys in Spanish

**Comparisons**
- Comparing travel in the U.S. and abroad
- Comparing foods
- Comparing media and communication

**Communities**
- Using Spanish to help others
- Using Spanish in the workplace

## Teaching Resource Options

**Print**

Block Scheduling Copymasters

**Audiovisual**

OHT 1–4; M1–M2

*Canciones* Audiocassette / CD Songs 1, 3, 8, 13

Video Program Videotape 1, 0:00 / Videodisc 1A

Search Chapter 1, Play to 2
U1 Cultural Introduction

Videotape 1, 1:24 / Videodisc 1A

Search Chapter 2, Play to 3
Prologue

UNIDAD 1

# ESTADOS UNIDOS

## ¿QUÉ PASA?

**OBJECTIVES**

**ETAPA 1 Pasatiempos**
- Talk about where you went and what you did
- Discuss leisure time
- Comment on airplane travel

**ETAPA 2 ¿Qué prefieres?**
- Comment on food
- Talk about the past
- Express activity preferences
- Discuss fine art

**ETAPA 3 ¿Viste las noticias?**
- Discuss ways to communicate
- React to news
- Ask for and give information
- Talk about things and people you know

**LA MISIÓN SAN FERNANDO REY DE ESPAÑA,** fundada por el Padre Fermín Lasuén en 1797, está cerca de Los Ángeles. Puedes ver la misión en las películas y en la televisión. ¿Conoces otras misiones en California?

SAN JOSÉ

LOS ÁNGELES

SAN DIEGO

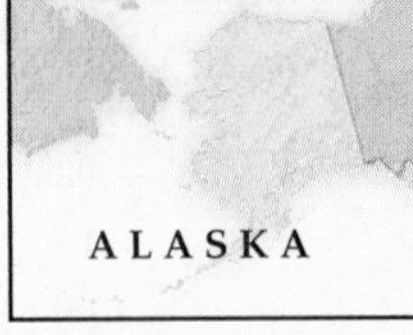

**HISPANOS EN HOLLYWOOD** Edward James Olmos, Jennifer López y Jimmy Smits están entre los actores latinos más famosos de Hollywood. Todos salen en esta película, *Mi familia,* que cuenta de una familia que llegó a California en 1920.

ALASKA

ISLAS HAWAI

26

## Classroom Community

**Paired Activity** Have students work in pairs for 2 minutes to brainstorm and list in one column as many Hispanic foods as possible. In a second column have students categorize the foods into breakfast (**desayuno**), lunch (**almuerzo**), or dinner (**cena**) items.

**Learning Scenario** After reviewing the Hispanic personalities, ask the students if they know other famous Hispanics in writing, music, television, or movies. Then ask students to tell a story about meeting one of the Spanish-speaking actors or musicians. They can write a short dialog or write a list of questions they would like to ask this person.

## ALMANAQUE

**Población total:** 265,557,000
**Población de descendencia hispana:** 28,269,000
**Ciudad con más latinos:** Nueva York
**Ciudad con mayor porcentaje (%):** El Paso

**En Estados Unidos...** ¿Qué tienen en común todas las ciudades que ves en el mapa? Son las 10 ciudades con el mayor número de gente de descendencia hispana. Los Ángeles, Chicago y Miami son las ciudades que vas a conocer en esta unidad. ¡Vamos!

INTERNET Ve a www.mcdougallittell.com para más información sobre Estados Unidos.

**TOSTONES** Se puede encontrar esta comida típica de Puerto Rico y otros países del área caribeña en los restaurantes de Chicago. Tostones son plátanos verdes fritos. ¿Conoces algún plato como éste?

**ARTISTAS Y LA COMUNIDAD** Alejandro Romero es un artista de México que celebra la comunidad latina en Chicago. ¿Qué otros artistas conoces?

**TELEVISIÓN** Hay muchos canales de televisión en español. Los dos más populares son Univisión y Telemundo, que tienen oficinas en Miami y en Los Ángeles. ¿Ves la tele en español?

**GLORIA ESTEFAN** es una cantante famosa que vive en Florida. ¿Conoces sus canciones?

**JORGE RAMOS Y MARÍA ELENA SALINAS** son reporteros famosos que trabajan desde Miami.

## Teaching All Students

**Native Speakers** If any of your students have connections to Los Angeles, Miami, or Chicago, have them discuss the Spanish-speaking communities there, as well as leisure activities and food. Ask them to name other famous Hispanics. You may also wish to show films dealing with cultural depictions of Spanish-speaking communities in the U.S.

**Multiple Intelligences**

**Logical/Mathematical** Have students figure out the percentage of the Hispanic population in the U.S. Have them find out the size of the Hispanic population in their own community. (Population figures in the **Almanaque** are from 1996.)

**Musical/Rhythmic** Have students bring in a cassette or CD by Gloria Estefan or other Spanish-speaking singers to share with the class.



## Teaching Suggestions
### Previewing the Unit

Point out that this unit centers on some Spanish-speaking communities in the U.S. Ask students to scan the pages for 25 seconds, then close their books. Then ask what they remember.

## Culture Highlights

- **MISIONES DE CALIFORNIA** Mission San Fernando Rey de España is one of 21 historical missions in California. Others include San Juan Capistrano, San Luis Obispo, Santa Cruz, Santa Inés, and San Juan Bautista, among others.
- **HISPANOS IN HOLLYWOOD** Edward James Olmos is a Chicano television and movie actor from East Los Angeles. He is known for his television role in **Miami Vice** and the movies **Stand and Deliver**, **Blade Runner**, and **The Ballad of Gregorio Cortez**. Jennifer López, a Puerto Rican raised in New York, is a popular model and rising actress, with movie roles in **Selena** and **Out of Sight**. Jimmy Smits, another New York Puerto Rican, is known for his television roles on **NYPD Blue** and **L.A. Law** and is now taking on more movie roles.
- **ARTISTAS EN LA COMUNIDAD** Alejandro and Oscar Romero are 2 brothers from Chicago who are Hispanic artists. They are featured in the **En colores** reading in **Etapa 2**, pp. 66–67.
- **GLORIA ESTEFAN** is a bilingual Cuban-American singer from Miami. Her Grammy award-winning album, **Mi tierra** (1993), was dedicated to Cuba, the island she left with her family when she was a baby.

## Block Schedule

**Retention** Divide class into groups of 3 or 4 students and have them brainstorm a list of places in the U.S. where they may encounter Spanish, either spoken or written.

# Ampliación

These activities may be used at various points in the Unit 1 sequence.

For Block Schedule, you may find that these projects will provide a welcome change of pace while reviewing and reinforcing the material presented in the unit. See the **Block Scheduling Copymasters**.

## PROJECTS

**Create a television morning show.** Include news, weather, sports, food, and a celebrity interview. Divide the class into "news teams," with "reporters" in Miami, Chicago, and Los Angeles. Videotape the project to share with other classes. If time permits, you may wish to add several short commercials to the show.

PACING SUGGESTION: Upon completion of Etapa 3.

**Create a guide for leisure time activities** to do in your area. First, brainstorm a list of possible activities with the whole class. Then, divide the class into groups and assign each group one activity to describe in more detail. Each group is responsible for writing and illustrating its section of the guide. Groups should include information on where and when this activity takes place, and what equipment may be needed. The completed project may be displayed or duplicated to share with other Spanish students.

PACING SUGGESTION: Upon completion of Etapa 1.

## STORYTELLING

**Francisco y sus deportes favoritos** After reviewing the vocabulary for sports and the formation of the preterite, model a mini-story (using student actors or photos, sports equipment, or pictures from the text or magazines) that students will revise, expand, and retell.

A Francisco le gustan mucho los deportes. En Chicago, fue a un partido de fútbol. También anduvo en bicicleta en el parque. En Miami nadó en el mar. Pero su deporte favorito es el béisbol. Le gusta mucho jugar al béisbol. El verano pasado su equipo ganó el campeonato de la ciudad.

As you give your model, be sure to pause as the story is being told so that students may fill in words and act out gestures. Students should then write, narrate, and read aloud a longer main story. This new version should include vocabulary from **Unidad 1**.

**Tus deportes favoritos** Ask students to tell a story about a busy week or weekend they had. They can talk about the different sports or activities they participated in. As a variation/time-saver, you may wish to have students write and illustrate their stories instead of acting them out.

PACING SUGGESTION: Upon completion of Etapa 2.

## BULLETIN BOARDS / POSTERS

**Bulletin board** **Plan ahead:** Collect newspaper or magazine photos and have students create new Spanish captions. The school newspaper can also be used. Decorate a bulletin board with their news clippings titled **"Noticias de hoy."**

**Posters** **Have students create:** • **Event** posters for local exhibits or events that would interest Spanish speakers in your community • **Menus** for restaurants that serve Hispanic food • **Museum** or artisan posters • **Sporting event** posters • **Safe driver** posters for teens.

## GAMES

### ¿Qué hicieron durante las vacaciones?

**Prepare ahead:** Write 10–15 infinitive verbs on index cards. Write 5–10 pastimes or sports on another set of index cards. Write 5–10 cities and countries on another set of index cards.

Divide the class into teams and have each team choose 5 cards from each pile. Give each team 10 minutes to create a story about a recent vacation according to the cards they chose. They must use all the verbs in the preterite form to tell the story. The stories should be written down, then presented to the class. When they are presented, have the class vote on the most creative or most fun vacation. Return the cards to the two piles and draw again to tell another set of fun stories.

PACING SUGGESTION: Upon completion of Etapa 1.

## HANDS-ON CRAFTS

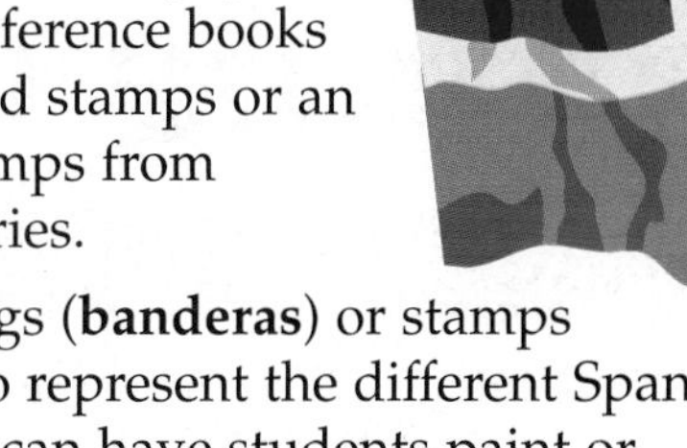

**Preparation materials:** colored paper or fabric, art supplies, reference books on international flags and stamps or an encyclopedia; actual stamps from Spanish-speaking countries.

Have students create flags (**banderas**) or stamps (**timbres**, **estampillas**) to represent the different Spanish-speaking countries. You can have students paint or draw the flags or stamps for the countries that have the greatest number of Spanish-speakers in the U.S., such as Mexico, Puerto Rico, Cuba, and the Dominican Republic. To practice using nationalities, you can label each flag or stamp with the country and nationality and use them to decorate a bulletin board.

## MUSIC

Latin music is very popular in the United States. You can get cassettes or CDs with the lyrics to play for your class from most music stores. The lyrics can be used for cloze activities. In the southwest and California you will hear Tejano and Mariachi. (Try Tish Hinojosa with her bilingual collection, *Cada niño / Every Child,* or music by Luis Miguel or Mariachi Vargas.) In the northeast, Chicago, and Florida you will hear music from the Caribbean, such as salsa, merengue, or Latino jazz. (Try Rubén Blades, Celia Cruz, Tito Puente, Willie Colón, Juan Luis Guerra and 440, and Gloria Estefan.) You can also have students interview native speakers in your community to find out their favorite Latin musicians. Play the *Canciones* Cassette/CD in class for a sampling of the music styles mentioned above.

## RECIPE

**Tostones** are served with many Puerto Rican and Cuban meals just as potatoes are served with many North American meals. **Tostones** are made from green plantains or **plátanos**. They can be made ahead of time and warmed up for the class. You may also be able to find bags of **platanutre**, or plaintain chips (similar to potato chips), a popular snack food in the Caribbean.

## Receta

***Tostones de plátano***

*3 plátanos verdes*
*4 tazas de agua con 2 ajos*
*4 tazas de agua con 2 cucharadas de sal*
*2 tazas de aceite vegetal o de manteca*

*Corte los plátanos diagonalmente en tajadas de 1" de ancho. Remójelas durante 15 minutos en el agua con los ajos. Caliente el aceite a fuego alto. Escurra las tajadas y fríalas a fuego moderado durante 5 minutos. Sáquelas y aplástelas. Échelas en el agua con la sal y sáquelas inmediatemente. Escúrralas. Fríalas nuevamente con la grasa un poco más caliente alrededor de 5 minutos, hasta que se pongan doradas. Sáquelas y póngalas sobre papel absorbente. Ponga más sal a su gusto y sírvalas. ¡Buen provecho!*

# Planning Guide CLASSROOM MANAGEMENT

## OBJECTIVES

**Communication**
- Talk about where you went and what you did *pp. 32-33*
- Discuss leisure time *pp. 32-33*
- Comment on airline travel *pp. 30-31*

**Grammar**
- Regular preterite verbs *pp. 36-37*
- Preterite of verbs ending in **-car**, **-gar**, and **-zar** *pp. 38-39*
- Preterite of **ir**, **ser**, **hacer**, **dar**, **ver** *pp. 40-41*

**Culture**
- Olvera Street in Los Angeles *p. 37*
- Murals in Los Angeles *p. 42*
- Hispanics in the United States *pp. 44-45*

**Recycling**
- Greetings
- Talk about plans
- People, places, activities
- Present tense of regular and irregular verbs
- Interrogatives

## STRATEGIES

**Listening Strategies**
- Identify key words *pp. 32-33*
- Summarize what you hear *Actividad 8, p. 38*

**Speaking Strategies**
- Encourage others *p. 43*
- Get more information *p. 48*

**Reading Strategies**
- Read—don't translate *pp. 44-45*
- Use visuals and titles to predict the general idea *pp. 44-45*
- Scan for cognates *pp. 44-45*

**Writing Strategies**
- Answer questions to organize your ideas before you write *Actividad 7, TE p. 48*

**Connecting Cultures Strategies**
- Use Spanish in volunteer work and in the workplace *p. 48*
- Connect and compare what you know about your own culture to help you learn about a new culture *pp. 26-27, 42, 44-45*
- Identify interesting facts *TE p. 44*

## PROGRAM RESOURCES

### Print
- *Más práctica* Workbook PE *pp. 11-20*
- Block Scheduling Copymasters *pp. 9-16*
- Unit 1 Resource Book
  - *Más práctica* Workbook TE *pp. 59-68*
  - *Cuaderno para hispanohablantes* TE *pp. 69-78*
  - Information Gap Activities *pp. 79-82*
  - Family Involvement *pp. 83-84*
  - Video Activities *pp. 85-87*
  - Videoscript *pp. 89-90*
  - Audioscript *pp. 91-94*
  - Assessment Program, Unit 1 Etapa 1 *pp. 95-113; 243-245*
  - Answer Keys *pp. 253-254; 258*

### Audiovisual
- Audio Program Cassette 1A, 1B / CD 1
- *Canciones* Cassette/CD
- Video Program Videotape 1 / Videodisc 1A
- Overhead Transparencies M1–M5; 1–14

### Technology
- Electronic Teacher Tools/Test Generator
- *Intrigas y aventuras* CD-ROM, Disc 1
-  www.mcdougallittell.com

### Assessment Program Options
- Cooperative Quizzes (Unit 1 Resource Book)
- Etapa Exam Forms A and B (Unit 1 Resource Book)
- *Examen para hispanohablantes* (Unit 1 Resource Book)
- Portfolio Assessment (Unit 1 Resource Book)
- Multiple Choice Test Questions (Unit 1 Resource Book)
- Audio Program Cassette 19A / CD 19
- Electronic Teacher Tools/Test Generator

### Native Speakers
- *Cuaderno para hispanohablantes* PE, *pp. 11-20*
- *Cuaderno para hispanohablantes* TE (Unit 1 Resource Book)
- *Examen para hispanohablantes* (Unit 1 Resource Book)
- Audio Program *(Para hispanohablantes)* Cassettes 1B, 19A / CD 1, CD 19
- Audioscript (Unit 1 Resource Book)

# Student Text Listening Activity Scripts

##  Videoscript: Diálogo *pages 32–33*

• Videotape 1, 5:40 • Videodisc 1A

Search Chapter 4, Play to 5. U1E1, En vivo (Dialog)

• Use the videoscript with **Actividades 1, 2** *page 34*

Verónica: Ay, ¿cómo fue que ganaste el concurso?
Francisco: Mandé mi material a la revista, y no lo pensé más. Seis semanas después, me llamaron. ¡Gané! Todavía no lo puedo creer.
Verónica: Debes de estar muy emocionado, Paco. Qué bien, viajar a Chicago, Puerto Rico, y Costa Rica.
Abuela: Pues, yo viajé a Costa Rica el verano pasado. Fui con unas amigas. Me gustó muchísimo. Fuimos al bosque tropical, acampamos en un parque y caminamos por San José.
Verónica: Dicen que Costa Rica es un país hermoso.
Abuela: Sí, es muy hermoso. Fue un viaje inolvidable.
Francisco: ¿Qué más hiciste, abuela?
Abuela: Pues, hicimos mucho. Fuimos a la playa. Nadamos, tomamos el sol. Mi amiga Rocío esquió en el agua.
Verónica: Abuela, ¿y esquiaste tú?
Abuela: Ay, no, yo no esquié. No me interesa.
Tío Javier: ¡Hola, Paco! Así que te vas mañana.
Francisco: Sí, tío Javier. El avión sale para Chicago a las cuatro. Ya tengo todo listo. Tengo mis boletos de avión y tengo mi equipaje listo.
Tío Javier: Sabes que toda la familia está muy orgullosa de ti.
Francisco: Muchas gracias, tío.
Abuela: Mira, tu abuelo está quemando la carne. ¡Héctor! ¿Qué haces? Vamos, jóvenes, vamos a ayudarle a su abuelo. ¡Héctor! ¿Qué haces?
Verónica: Ay, me gustaría ir contigo. Me encanta viajar. Sabes, me gustaría ser auxiliar de vuelo algún día... o mejor, piloto.
Francisco: No sé. No es un trabajo fácil. Tantos pasajeros todos los días, llegadas y salidas a cada hora...
Verónica: Sí, pero qué bien viajar por el mundo.
Francisco: Sabes, ya es hora. Mi vuelo a Chicago sale a las cuatro. ¿A qué hora viene tu padre?
Verónica: Debe llegar pronto. Fue al banco primero, y después, a hacer unas compras.
Francisco: Todavía tengo que presentarme en el mostrador y registrar mi equipaje. Y quiero cambiar mi asiento. Tengo asiento de pasillo, y quiero asiento de ventanilla. Y después tengo que pasar por seguridad.
Verónica: Está bien, vas a llegar con tiempo. Tienes todo, ¿no? ¿Los boletos? ¿La identificación?
Francisco: Sí, claro. Aquí está la identificación... y los boletos... ¡Ay, no! ¿Qué hice con los boletos?
Verónica: Es mi padre... Francisco, cálmate. ¿Dónde los dejaste?
Francisco: No sé... No sé...
Verónica: Ay, Francisco.
Francisco: No tengo tiempo para hablar. Tengo que encontrar mis boletos.
Verónica: ¡Francisco! ¡Bobo! Los boletos están en tu bolsillo.
Francisco: En mi... uf. Bueno, vamos.
Verónica: ¿Qué tienes en esta maleta? ¿Rocas? Paquito, me parece que vas a tener exceso de equipaje.

## Actividad 8 Ay, ¡qué verano! *page 38*

Lo pasé muy bien durante mis vacaciones. Viajé a Los Ángeles con mi tía y mis primas. El primer día comimos en el "Farmer's Market", donde hay varios restaurantes. Allí venden comida de todo tipo. ¡Hasta puedes comprar frutas y verduras en el mercado! Luego, al otro día tomamos un tren desde la estación "Union Station" hasta San Diego, donde fuimos al parque zoológico. El viaje fue magnífico. Quiero regresar algún día.

## Actividad 16 ¡Puro juego en Los Ángeles! *page 43*

Hice muchas cosas cuando estuve en Los Ángeles con mi familia. Un día fuimos a la playa a tomar el sol. Después, en la noche, fuimos al "pier" de Santa Mónica para comer y disfrutar de los juegos que tienen allí. Al otro día mi tío nos llevó a Hollywood por la mañana para conocer dónde trabajan todos los actores de cine y de televisión. Luego, fuimos al Parque Griffith para tener un picnic con mis abuelos. Al día siguiente fui con mi primo Andrés a dos sitios. Por la mañana, fuimos al observatorio. Por la tarde, fuimos al parque zoológico. Llegamos a casa muy cansados. En mi último día, fui al este de Los Ángeles donde venden muchos productos hispanos. Compré un regalo que voy a llevarle al señor que trabaja para la revista *Onda Internacional.* Como puedes ver, lo pasé chévere en Los Ángeles.

### Quick Start Review Answers

**p. 30** Transportation
*Answers will vary. Answers could include:*

| | |
|---|---|
| el tren | el avión |
| el coche | el bote |

**p. 32** Ordinal numbers
Primero, tengo que ir al aeropuerto.
Segundo, tengo que registrar mi equipaje.
Tercero, tengo que pasar por seguridad.
Cuarto, tengo que abordar el avión.

**p. 42** Preterite: irregular verbs
1. Yo hice un viaje.
2. Mi hermana fue también.
3. Fuimos a México.
4. Vimos muchas cosas interesantes.
5. Le di una jarra de cerámica a mi madre de regalo.

**p. 46** Preterite

**caminar**

| | |
|---|---|
| yo | caminé |
| tú | caminaste |
| usted, él, ella | caminó |
| nosotros(as) | caminamos |
| vosotros(as) | caminasteis |
| ustedes, ellos, ellas | caminaron |

**beber**

| | |
|---|---|
| yo | bebí |
| tú | bebiste |
| usted, él, ella | bebió |
| nosotros(as) | bebimos |
| vosotros(as) | bebisteis |
| ustedes, ellos, ellas | bebieron |

**ir**

| | |
|---|---|
| yo | fui |
| tú | fuiste |
| usted, él, ella | fue |
| nosotros(as) | fuimos |
| vosotros(as) | fuisteis |
| ustedes, ellos, ellas | fueron |

**ver**

| | |
|---|---|
| yo | vi |
| tú | viste |
| usted, él, ella | vio |
| nosotros(as) | vimos |
| vosotros(as) | visteis |
| ustedes, ellos, ellas | vieron |

**p. 48** Interrogatives
*Answers will vary. Answers could include:*
1. ¿Adónde fuiste?
2. ¿Qué compró?
3. ¿Cuándo comió?

# Pacing Guide

## Sample Lesson Plan - 50 Minute Schedule

### DAY 1

**Unit Opener**
- Anticipate/Activate prior knowledge: Present the *Almanaque* and the cultural notes. Use Map OHTs as needed. 10 MIN.

**Etapa Opener**
- Quick Start Review (TE, p. 28) 5 MIN.
- Have students look at the *Etapa* Opener and answer questions. 5 MIN.

**En contexto: Vocabulario**
- Quick Start Review (TE, p. 30) 5 MIN.
- Have students use context and pictures to learn *Etapa* vocabulary. Answer questions p. 31. 10 MIN.

**En vivo: Diálogo**
- Quick Start Review (TE, p. 32) 5 MIN.
- Review Listening Strategy, p. 32. Play audio or show video for the dialog shown on pp. 32–33. 5 MIN.
- Replay and have students take on roles of characters. 5 MIN.

**Homework Option:**
- Video Activities, Unit 1 Resource Book, pp. 85–87.

### DAY 2

**En acción: Vocabulario y gramática**
- Check homework. 5 MIN.
- Quick Start Review (TE, p. 34) 5 MIN.
- Ask students for a summary of *En vivo* dialog to check recall. 5 MIN.
- Have students answer Comprehension Questions (TE, p. 33) 5 MIN.
- Replay the *En vivo* dialog using the audiovisual resources and have students do *Actividades* 1 and 2 orally. 10 MIN.
- Have students complete *Actividades* 3 and 4 in pairs. 10 MIN.
- Do some activities from Teaching All Students (TE, p. 35). 10 MIN.

**Homework Option:**
- *Más práctica* Workbook, pp. 13–14. *Cuaderno para hispanohablantes*, pp. 11–12.

### DAY 3

**En acción (cont.)**
- Check homework. 5 MIN.
- Quick Start Review (TE, p. 36) 5 MIN.
- Present *Gramática:* Regular preterite verbs, p. 36. 10 MIN.
- Review the vocabulary in the box on p. 37. 5 MIN.
- Have students do *Actividades* 5 and 6. Check orally. Students can write *Actividad* 6 as a postcard. 10 MIN.
- Have students do *Actividad* 7 in pairs. 5 MIN.
- Play the audio and do *Actividad* 8 orally. Students can also write their summary. 10 MIN.

**Homework Option:**
- *Más práctica* Workbook, pp. 15–16. *Cuaderno para hispanohablantes*, pp. 13–14.

### DAY 4

**En acción (cont.)**
- Check homework. 5 MIN.
- Quick Start Review (TE, p. 38) 5 MIN.
- Present *Gramática:* Preterite of *-car, -gar,* and *-zar* verbs on p. 38 and *Vocabulario* on p. 39. 10 MIN.
- Have students do *Actividad* 9 in writing and *Actividad* 10 orally by filling in the chart. 12 MIN.
- Have students do *Actividad* 11 in pairs. 8 MIN.
- Present Irregular Preterite verbs: *ir, ser, hacer, dar* on p. 40. 5 MIN.
- Have students complete *Actividad* 12 in writing. Check orally. 5 MIN.

**Homework Option:**
- Have students do *Actividades* 12 and 14 in writing. *Más práctica* Workbook, pp. 17–18. *Cuaderno para hispanohablantes*, pp. 15–16.

### DAY 5

**En acción (cont.)**
- Check homework. 5 MIN.
- Quick Start Review (TE, p. 42). 5 MIN.
- Present *Apoyo para estudiar,* p. 41. 5 MIN.
- Review irregular preterites, p. 40. Have students do *Actividad* 13 in pairs. 10 MIN.
- Have students write *Actividad* 14, check orally. 10 MIN.
- Present *Nota,* p. 42. Have students complete *Actividad* 15 orally. 10 MIN.
- Play audio; do *Actividad* 16. 5 MIN.

**Homework Option:**
- *Más práctica* Workbook, pp. 19–20. *Cuaderno para hispanohablantes*, pp. 17–18.

### DAY 6

**En voces: Lectura**
- Check homework. 5 MIN.
- Present Speaking Strategy, p. 43. Have students complete *Actividad* 17. 8 MIN.
- Expand with *Más comunicación,* p. R2. 7 MIN.
- Quick Start Review (TE, p. 44) 5 MIN.
- Review Reading Strategy, p. 44. 5 MIN.
- Have students read *Lectura* silently. Then have various students read the *Lectura* aloud. 10 MIN.
- Call on volunteers to answer *¿Comprendiste?* questions. 5 MIN.
- Begin discussion of *¿Qué piensas?* questions. 5 MIN.

**Homework Option:**
- Have students finish answering *¿Comprendiste?* questions and answer the *¿Qué piensas?* in writing, p. 45. *Cuaderno para hispanohablantes*, pp. 19–20.

### DAY 7

**En uso: Repaso y más comunicación**
- Check homework. 5 MIN.
- Quick Start Review (TE, p. 46) 5 MIN.
- Do *Actividades* 1 and 2 orally. 10 MIN.
- Do *Actividades* 3 and 4 orally. 10 MIN.
- Review Speaking Strategy, p. 48. Then do *Actividad* 5 orally in pairs and *Actividad* 6 in groups of four. 10 MIN.

**En tu propia voz: Escritura**
- Begin *Actividad* 7. 10 MIN.

**Homework Option:**
- Have students finish *Actividad* 7 at home. Review for *Etapa* 1 Exam.

### DAY 8

**En resumen: Repaso de vocabulario**
- Check homework. 5 MIN.
- Present *Tú en la comunidad,* p. 48. 5 MIN.
- Quick Start Review (TE, p. 48) 5 MIN.
- Review grammar questions, etc. as necessary. 5 MIN.
- Complete *Etapa 1* Exam 20 MIN.

**Ampliación**
- Use a suggested project, game, or activity. (TE pp. 27A–27B) 10 MIN.

**Homework Option:**
- Preview *Etapa 2* Opener, pp. 50–51.

# Sample Lesson Plan - Block Schedule (90 minutes)

## DAY 1

### Unit Opener
- Anticipate/Activate prior knowledge: Present the *Almanaque* and the cultural notes. Use Map OHTs as needed. 10 MIN.

### Etapa Opener
- Quick Start Review (TE, p. 28) 5 MIN.
- Have students look at the *Etapa* Opener and answer questions. 5 MIN.
- Use Block Scheduling Copymasters. 5 MIN.

### En contexto: Vocabulario
- Quick Start Review (TE, p. 30) 5 MIN.
- Have students use context and pictures to learn *Etapa* vocabulary. Answer questions, p. 31. Use the Situational OHTs for additional practice. 10 MIN.

### En vivo: Diálogo
- Quick Start Review (TE, p. 32) 5 MIN.
- Review Listening Strategy, p. 32. Play audio or show video for the dialog shown on pp. 32–33. 10 MIN.
- Ask Comprehension Questions (TE, p. 33) 5 MIN.
- Read aloud, students taking roles of characters. 5 MIN.

### En acción: Vocabulario y gramática
- Quick Start Review (TE, p. 34) 5 MIN.
- Have students do *Actividades* 1 and 2 orally. 10 MIN.
- Have students complete *Actividades* 3 and 4 in pairs. 10 MIN.

### Homework Option:
- Have students prepare two T/F or yes/no questions about the dialog. Video Activities, Unit 1 Resource Book, pp. 85–87.

## DAY 2

### En acción (cont.)
- Check homework. 5 MIN.
- Quick Start Review (TE, p. 36) 5 MIN.
- Present *Gramática:* Regular preterite verbs, p. 36. 10 MIN.
- Review the vocabulary in the box on p. 37. 5 MIN.
- Have students do *Actividades* 5 and 6 in writing. Check orally. 10 MIN.
- Have students do *Actividad* 7 in pairs. 5 MIN.
- Play the audio and do *Actividad* 8 orally. Students can also write their summary. 10 MIN.
- Quick Start Review (TE, p. 32) 5 MIN.
- Present *Gramática:* Preterite of *-car, -gar,* and *-zar* verbs and *Vocabulario* on pp. 38 and 39. 10 MIN.
- Have students do *Actividad* 9 in writing and *Actividad* 10 orally by filling in the chart. 10 MIN.
- Have students do *Actividad* 11 in pairs. 10 MIN.
- Use Block Scheduling Copymasters for a change of pace as needed. 5 MIN.

### Homework Option:
- *Más práctica* Workbook, pp. 13–16 as needed. *Cuaderno para hispanohablantes*, pp. 12–14 as needed.

## DAY 3

### En acción (cont.)
- Check homework. 10 MIN.
- Quick Start Review (TE, p. 40) 5 MIN.
- Present *Gramática:* Irregular Preterite verbs: *ir, ser, hacer, dar* on p. 40. 10 MIN.
- Have students complete *Actividad* 12 in writing and *Actividad* 13 in pairs. 10 MIN.
- Have students write *Actividad* 14, then check. Expand with *Más comunicación,* p. R2. 15 MIN.
- Quick Start Review (TE, p. 41) 5 MIN.
- Have students complete *Actividad* 15 in pairs. 5 MIN.
- Play the audio for students and do *Actividad* 16 orally with the whole class. 5 MIN.
- Discuss Speaking Strategy, p. 43. Have students do *Actividad* 17 in pairs. 10 MIN.

### Ampliación
- Use 1 or 2 suggested projects, games, or activities. (TE pp. 26A–27B) 15 MIN.

### Homework Option:
- *Más práctica* Workbook, pp. 17–20. *Cuaderno para hispanohablantes*, pp. 15–20.

## DAY 4

### En voces: Lectura
- Check homework. 10 MIN.
- Quick Start Review (TE, p. 44) 5 MIN.
- Review Reading Strategy, p. 44. 5 MIN.
- Have students read *Lectura* silently, then have students read *Lectura* aloud in turns. 10 MIN.
- Call on volunteers to answer *¿Comprendiste?* questions. 10 MIN.
- Have students do the *¿Qué piensas?* activity in writing, then discuss orally. 10 MIN.

### En uso: Repaso y más comunicación
- Quick Start Review (TE, p. 46) 5 MIN.
- Have students write *Actividades* 1 and 2, then check answers with the whole class. 10 MIN.
- Do *Actividades* 3 and 4 orally. 10 MIN.
- Present the Speaking Strategy, p. 48, and have students do *Actividad* 5 in pairs. 5 MIN.
- Have students do *Actividad* 6 in groups. Have volunteers perform their dialog for the class. 10 MIN.

### Homework Option:
- Review for *Etapa* 1 Exam.

## DAY 5

### En tu propia voz: Escritura
- Check homework. 10 MIN.
- Quick Start Review (TE, p. 48) 5 MIN.
- Do *Actividad* 7 in writing. Ask volunteers to present their paragraphs to the class. 15 MIN.

### Tú en la comunidad
- Read and discuss. 10 MIN.

### En resumen: Repaso de vocabulario
- Review grammar questions, etc., as necessary. 10 MIN.
- Complete *Etapa* 1 Exam. 20 MIN.

### Ampliación
- Use another suggested project, game, or activity. (TE, pp. 27A–27B) 20 MIN.

### Homework Options:
- Preview *Etapa* 2 Opener, pp. 50–51.

▼ Francisco, Verónica y su abuela hablan y comen en el parque.

## Etapa Theme

**Talking about where you went and what you did, discussing leisure activities, traveling by airplane**

## Grammar Objectives

- Regular preterite, including **-car**, **-gar**, and **-zar** spelling changes
- Preterite of **ir**, **ser**, **hacer**, **dar**, **ver**

### Teaching Resource Options

**Print**

Block Scheduling Copymasters

**Audiovisual**

**OHT** 11 (Quick Start)

### Quick Start Review

Family members

Use OHT 11 or write on board: Write four sentences about members of your family. Use four of the following words: **abuelo(a), tío(a), primo(a), hermano(a).** Follow the model.

**Mi tío se llama Javier y vive en Los Ángeles. Mi abuela nos invita a comer en el parque. Mi prima tiene pelo largo y es bonita. Mi hermano está nervioso porque va de viaje.**

Now write an original sentence speculating about one of the family members in the photo.

*Answers will vary.*

### Teaching Suggestions
**Previewing the Etapa**

- Ask students to study the photo on pp. 28–29 (1 min.).
- Close books; ask students to share at least 3 items that they noticed.
- Reopen books and look at the picture again (1 min.); close books and share 3 more details.
- Use the **¿Qué ves?** questions to focus discussion.

UNIDAD 1

# Pasatiempos

- Talk about where you went and what you did
- Discuss leisure time
- Comment on airplane travel

### ¿Qué ves?

Mira la foto y contesta las preguntas.

1. ¿Dónde están las personas de la foto?
2. ¿Qué hacen?
3. ¿Qué relación crees que hay entre ellos?
4. ¿Puedes nombrar un monumento histórico de Los Ángeles?

28

### Classroom Management

**Planning Ahead** Gather photographs or drawings of different leisure time activities or ask students to bring their own. You may wish to use the game **¿Qué hicieron durante las vacaciones?** in the **Ampliación** section on page 27B as a wrap-up activity for this Etapa.

**Peer Teaching** Have partners work together to write additional **¿Qué ves?** questions to ask another set of partners.

EL PUEBLO DE LOS ÁNGELES HISTORIC MONUMENT
¡VIVA EL PUEBLO!


## Supplementary Vocabulary

You might want to review family vocabulary:

| | |
|---|---|
| **el padre** | father |
| **la madre** | mother |
| **el abuelo** | grandfather |
| **la abuela** | grandmother |
| **los tíos** | uncles, uncle(s) and aunt(s) |
| **las tías** | aunts |
| **los primos** | cousins |
| **los hijos** | sons |
| **las hijas** | daughters |
| **los hermanos** | brothers, brother(s) and sister(s) |
| **las hermanas** | sisters |
| **los hermanastros** | stepbrothers |
| **las hermanastras** | stepsisters |
| **la madrastra** | stepmother |
| **el padrastro** | stepfather |
| **el (la) ahijado(a)** | goddaughter, godson |
| **la comadre, madrina** | godmother |
| **el compadre, padrino** | godfather |

## Culture Highlights

- **GRIFFITH PARK** The photo on pp. 28–29 was taken in Griffith Park, Los Angeles, CA, the largest municipal park and urban wilderness area in the U.S. It is located on 4,107 acres of the eastern Santa Monica mountain range. The park offers hiking, horseback riding, and all kinds of educational/cultural institutions including museums, a Greek theater, a zoo, an observatory, and other attractions.
- **EL PUEBLO DE LOS ÁNGELES** This part of Los Angeles dates back to 1781 when 44 settlers established a farming community there. In 1953 it was designated a state historical park since it was the oldest and most historical section of Los Angeles. El Pueblo now consists of more than 30 historic buildings, 4 museums, and a Mexican marketplace full of food and craft stalls. It is located near Olvera Street, one of the oldest streets in the city. For more information, see the **Nota cultural** on p. 37.

## Block Schedule

**FunBreak** Plan a class "picnic." Have students be responsible for assigning tasks (tablecloths, coolers, music, games) and bringing in healthy snacks–all labeled in Spanish for the day of the event.

## Teaching All Students

**Extra Help** Ask students to describe the people on pp. 28–29 using the following questions as a guide: **¿Cuántas personas hay en la foto? ¿Es una familia o una clase? ¿Cuántos hombres y cuántas mujeres hay? ¿Comen en un restaurante o en un parque? ¿Qué llevan?**

**Multiple Intelligences**

**Interpersonal** Ask students to find each other's similarities and differences by describing a typical get-together on the weekend. Do they go on picnics or to a restaurant? Do they eat at home, or do they go out with family members or friends?

**Naturalist** Have students research Griffith Park and bring in information on the zoo and geographical facts on the nature of the urban wilderness area.

## Teaching Resource Options

**Print** 

Unit 1 Resource Book
- *Video Activities*, p. 85
- *Videoscript*, p. 88
- *Audioscript*, p. 90

**Audiovisual** 

OHT 5, 6, 7, 7A, 8, 8A, 11 (Quick Start)
Audio Program Cassette 1A / CD 1
Video Program Videotape 1, 3:20 / Videodisc 1A

Search Chapter 3, Play to 4
U1E1, En contexto (Vocabulary)

**Technology**

*Intrigas y aventuras* CD-ROM, Disc 1

## Quick Start Review

**Transportation**

Use OHT 11 or write on board: List in Spanish four or more different types of transportation people use when taking a trip.

**Answers**, see p. 27D.

## Teaching Suggestions

### Introducing Vocabulary

- Have students look at pp. 30–31. Use OHT 5-6 and Audiocassette 1A/CD 1 to present the vocabulary.
- Ask the Comprehension Questions in order of yes/no (questions 1–4), either/or (questions 5–7), and simple word or phrase (questions 8–10). Expand by adding similar questions.
- Use the video vocabulary presentation for review and reinforcement.

# En contexto

## VOCABULARIO

Francisco va a viajar. Mira las ilustraciones de sus preparaciones. Te ayudan a comprender las palabras en azul y a responder a las preguntas personales.

**¡Hola!** Como ya saben, voy de **viaje**. Soy **el pasajero**. Tengo todo listo. Tengo **la identificación**, **el pasaporte** y **el boleto**.

Mira mi **equipaje**. Va a ser un problema. Tengo muchísimas **maletas**. ¡Voy a tener **un exceso de equipaje**!

**A** En **el mostrador** de **la aerolínea**, me van a dar un pase de **abordar**. **La agente de viajes** me va a indicar dónde esperar. **Los letreros** me ayudan a ver adónde ir. Tengo que pasar por **seguridad**.

**B** Antes de entrar al aeropuerto, todas las personas que vienen de otros países tienen que pasar por **la aduana**.



## Classroom Community

**Paired Activity** Have students work with a partner to write out questions on strips of paper based on pictures on pp. 30–31. Then, collect papers and have students choose them from a box or hat to ask the entire class.

**TPR** Create a mock airplane in the classroom by setting up chairs in several rows with an aisle down the middle and 2 seats up front for the cockpit. Assign students the roles of **pilotos**, **auxiliares de vuelo** and **pasajeros**. Have students act out your instructions in Spanish: **Los pasajeros abordan el avión con sus maletas. Los pasajeros pasan por el pasillo para abordar el avión. Unos tienen asientos de pasillo y otros asientos de ventanilla. El piloto se prepara para la salida del avión**, etc. To extend and practice the preterite, have students take turns re-telling the events in the past tense.

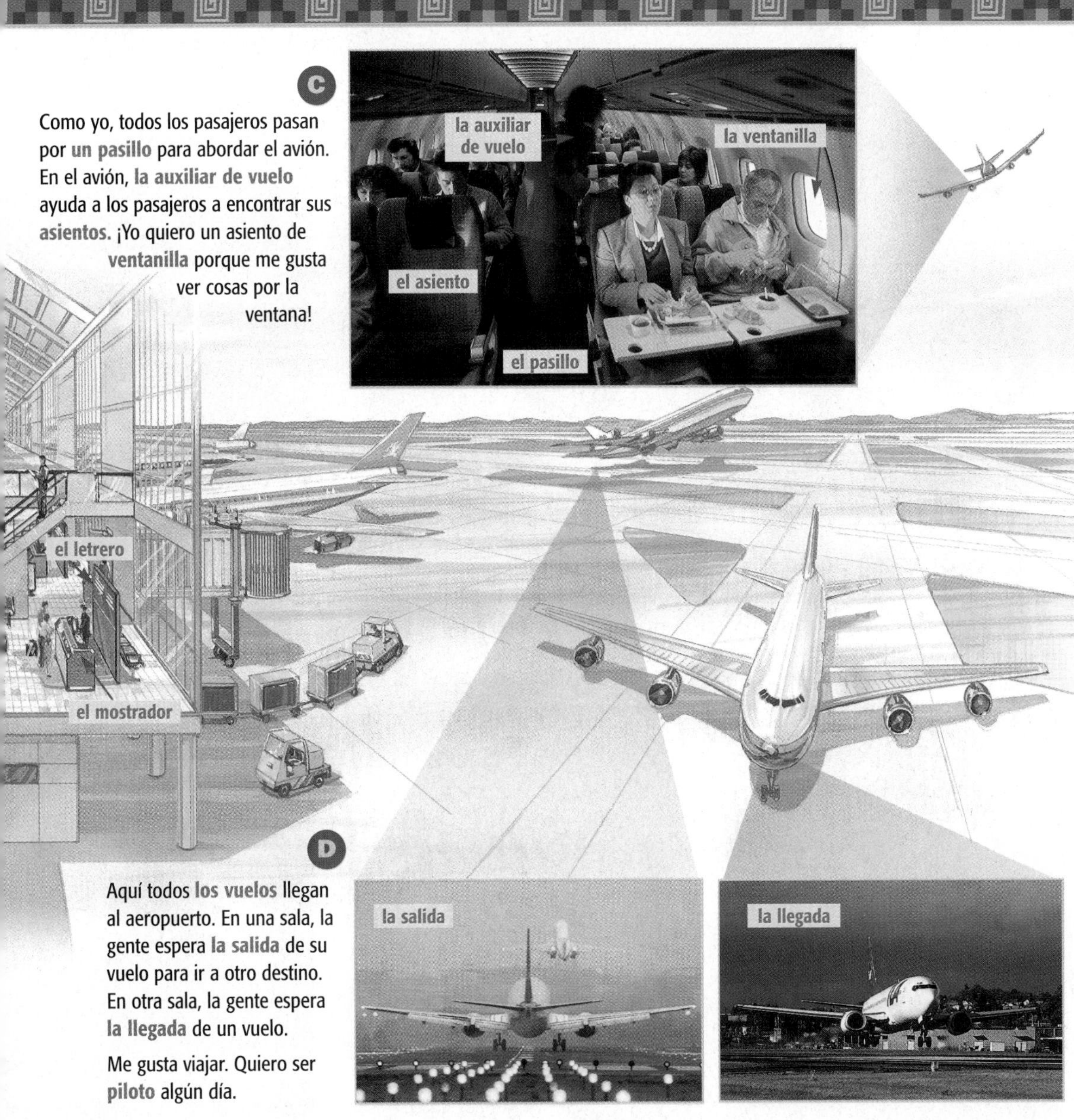


**C**

Como yo, todos los pasajeros pasan por **un pasillo** para abordar el avión. En el avión, **la auxiliar de vuelo** ayuda a los pasajeros a encontrar sus **asientos**. ¡Yo quiero un asiento de **ventanilla** porque me gusta ver cosas por la ventana!

**D**

Aquí todos **los vuelos** llegan al aeropuerto. En una sala, la gente espera **la salida** de su vuelo para ir a otro destino. En otra sala, la gente espera **la llegada** de un vuelo.

Me gusta viajar. Quiero ser **piloto** algún día.

la salida

la llegada

## Preguntas personales

1. ¿Te gusta viajar o te gusta estar en tu casa?
2. ¿Adónde te gustaría ir de viaje?
3. ¿Prefieres llevar mucho o poco equipaje?
4. ¿Prefieres un asiento de ventanilla o de pasillo? ¿Por qué?
5. ¿Qué debes llevar para ser un(a) pasajero(a) preparado(a)?





## Comprehension Questions

1. ¿Va Francisco de viaje? **(Sí)**
2. ¿Tiene pocas maletas? **(No)**
3. ¿Necesita el pasaporte para un vuelo internacional? **(Sí)**
4. ¿Necesita un pase de abordar? **(Sí)**
5. ¿Es Francisco el pasajero o el piloto? **(el pasajero)**
6. ¿Antes de abordar el avión, pasa por seguridad o por la aduana? **(por seguridad)**
7. ¿Espera Francisco la salida de su vuelo o la llegada? **(la salida)**
8. ¿Quiénes tienen que pasar por la aduana? **(los pasajeros de vuelos internacionales)**
9. ¿Quién ayuda a los pasajeros en el avión? **(el auxiliar de vuelo)**
10. ¿Qué asiento quiere Francisco? **(un asiento de ventanilla)**

## Language Note

Many U.S. airlines now give their safety information announcements in English and Spanish on domestic and international flights. Ask students when and where they have heard bilingual announcements. Have them bring in airline realia in Spanish.

## Supplementary Vocabulary

**en el centro** in the middle/center
**en medio de** between

## Teaching All Students

**Extra Help** Divide the class into partners and have one student say a vocabulary word; the other writes it down, then spells it aloud. Have students take turns dictating and writing.

**Challenge** Ask students to write a description of the new vocabulary items. Then students read the description and the class tries to guess the correct vocabulary item (**¿Quién soy yo?**).

**Native Speakers** You may ask Spanish speakers if they can suggest additional words for **boletos** or **auxiliar de vuelo**.

### Multiple Intelligences

**Intrapersonal** Ask students to record personal travel/transportation experience in Spanish, giving good (and bad) points and explaining why they liked or disliked the travel.

## Block Schedule

**FunBreak** Have students form groups of 3–4. Each group either brings in a model airplane or draws an illustration of one. Give groups about 10–15 minutes to find the Spanish words for as many parts and areas of the airplane (internal and external) as possible. Groups present the vocabulary they have found and make a list on the board. The group with the longest, most accurate list wins.

## Teaching Resource Options

**Print**

Block Scheduling Copymasters
Unit 1 Resource Book
Video Activities, pp. 86–87
Videoscript, p. 89
Audioscript, p. 90

**Audiovisual**

OHT 9–10, 11 (Quick Start)
Audio Program Cassette 1A / CD 1
Video Program Videotape 1, 5:40 / Videodisc 1A

Search Chapter 4, Play to 5
U1E1, En vivo (Dialog)

**Technology**

*Intrigas y aventuras* CD-ROM, Disc 1

## Quick Start Review

Ordinal numbers

Use OHT 11 or write on board: Put the following sentences in order. Begin each sentence with: **primero**, **segundo**, **tercero**, or **cuarto**.

Tengo que pasar por seguridad.
Tengo que ir al aeropuerto.
Tengo que abordar el avión.
Tengo que registrar mi equipaje.

**Answers**, see p. 27D.

## Cross Cultural Connections

Point out that **Paco**, **Paquito**, **Pancho**, and **Panchito** are Spanish nicknames for **Francisco.** Have students list nicknames they know for English names. Other common **apodos** are: **Chela**, **Chabela (Isabel)**, **Lola (Dolores)**, **Nacho (Ignacio)**, **Chuy**, **Chucho**, **Chuchito (Jesús)**, **Pepe (José)**.

# En vivo

## DIÁLOGO

Verónica

Francisco

Abuela

Tío Javier

**PARA ESCUCHAR • STRATEGY: LISTENING**

**Identify key words** In these scenes, some events have already happened; others are happening now. Verb tenses **(fue, viajé)** and key expressions of time **(el verano pasado)** give valuable clues about when things take place. What events happened in the past? Can you hear other clues to past events?

### En Los Ángeles…

1 ▸ Verónica: ¿Cómo fue que ganaste?
Francisco: Mandé mi material a la revista, y me llamaron. ¡Gané!
Verónica: Qué bien, viajar a Chicago, Puerto Rico y Costa Rica.

5 ▸ Verónica: Sabes, me gustaría ser auxiliar de vuelo algún día… o mejor, piloto.
Francisco: No sé… tantos pasajeros todos los días, llegadas y salidas a cada hora…

6 ▸ Francisco: Ya es hora. Mi vuelo sale a las cuatro. ¿A qué hora viene tu padre?
Verónica: Debe llegar pronto. Fue al banco primero, y después, a hacer unas compras.

7 ▸ Francisco: Tengo que presentarme en el mostrador, registrar mi equipaje y cambiar mi asiento. Tengo asiento de pasillo, y quiero asiento de ventanilla. Y tengo que pasar por seguridad.

## Classroom Community

**Paired Activity** Have students work in pairs to write a 3 frame sequel to the dialog.

**TPR** Divide the class into 4 groups and assign each group one of the characters in the **Diálogo: Verónica**, **Francisco**, **Abuela**, and **Tío Javier**. Play the audio only for the class and have those students who represent each character stand up when their character is speaking and sit down when another character is speaking. This will make students listen for a specific purpose and help them to distinguish between changes in speakers.

**Storytelling** After watching the video, divide the class into groups. Have each group retell a part of the dialog in their own words using gestures as much as possible.

2 ► Abuela: Yo viajé a Costa Rica el verano pasado. Fui con unas amigas. Fuimos al bosque tropical, acampamos en un parque y caminamos por San José. Fue un viaje inolvidable.

3 ► Francisco: ¿Qué más hiciste, abuela?
Abuela: Pues, hicimos mucho. Fuimos a la playa. Nadamos, tomamos el sol… Mi amiga Rocío esquió en el agua.
Verónica: Abuela, ¿y esquiaste tú?
Abuela: Ay, no. No me interesa.

4 ► Tío Javier: ¡Hola, Paco! Así que te vas mañana.
Francisco: Sí, tío Javier. El avión sale para Chicago a las cuatro.
Abuela: Mira, tu abuelo está quemando la carne. ¡Héctor!

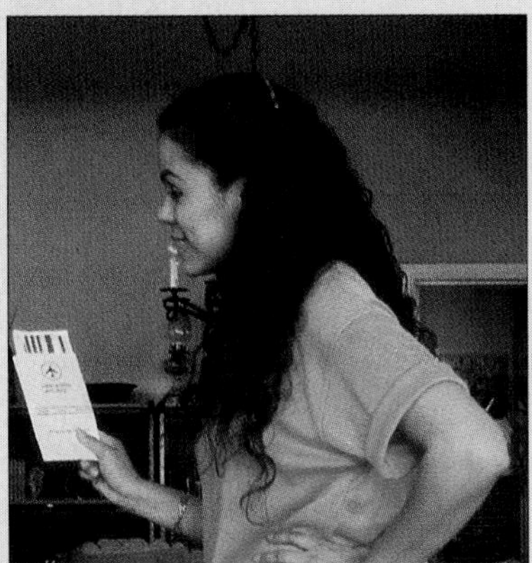

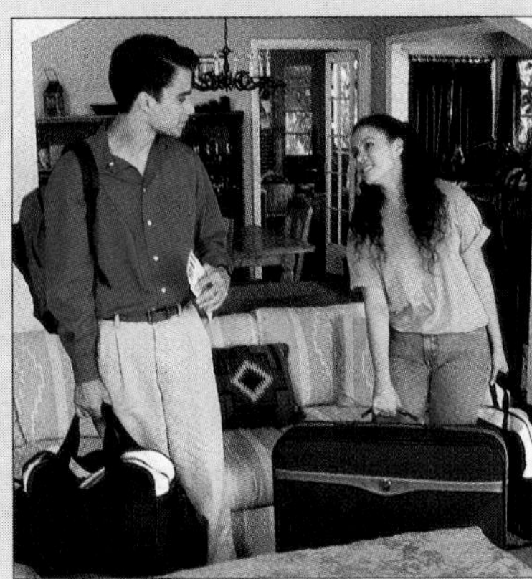

8 ► Francisco: Aquí está la identificación… ¡Ay, no! ¿Qué hice con los boletos?
Verónica: ¿Dónde los dejaste?
Francisco: No sé… No sé.

9 ► Verónica: ¡Francisco! ¡Bobo! Los boletos están en tu bolsillo.
Francisco: En mi… ah. Bueno, vamos.

10 ► Verónica: ¿Qué tienes en esta maleta? ¿Rocas? Paquito, vas a tener exceso de equipaje.



## Teaching Suggestions
### Presenting the Dialog

- Prepare students for listening by focusing on the dialog context using yes/no or either/or questions.
- Point out that **facturar equipaje** is often used, although Spanish speakers from the U.S. use **registrar**. **Tarjeta de embarque** is also used for **pase de abordar**.
- Use the video, audiocassette, or CD to present the dialog. The video version shows expanded dialog for additional comprehension practice.

### Video Synopsis

- Francisco tells some family members about his upcoming trip to Chicago, Puerto Rico, and Costa Rica. For a complete transcript of the video dialog, see p. 27D.
- The video shows scenes in Griffith Park.

## Comprehension Questions

1. ¿Ganó el concurso Francisco? **(Sí)**
2. ¿Fue la abuela a Costa Rica con su familia? **(No)**
3. ¿Fue al bosque tropical? **(Sí)**
4. ¿Fue aburrido o divertido el viaje de la abuela? **(divertido)**
5. ¿Va Francisco primero a Chicago o a Puerto Rico? **(Chicago)**
6. ¿Sale el vuelo a las cuatro o a las ocho? **(a las cuatro)**
7. ¿Dónde registra Francisco su equipaje? **(en el mostrador)**
8. ¿Dónde están sus boletos? **(en su bolsillo)**

## Gestures

Have students identify any gestures they recognize in the photographs, looking at frames 6–8 to identify Francisco's gestures that show concern.

## Teaching All Students

**Extra Help** Have students listen to the dialog several times for different purposes. Have them listen once for "the big picture." Then have them listen a second time for specific verbs in the past tense or present tense. Have them listen with their books open to match dialog with pictures, and with their books closed for retention.

### Multiple Intelligences

**Logical/Mathematical** Think about a time when you lost something of importance. List the steps you took to look for the item(s), e.g., **Yo perdí mi cartera en la calle en Nueva York. Primero, la busqué en las calles y...**

**Musical/Rhythmic** Have students choose background music to accompany the two scenes in the dialog—the picnic scene and the trip preparation scene. Then play the music during role-plays.

## Block Schedule

**Brain-based Learning** With students' books closed, read aloud 1 or 2 sentences a character says in the dialogue. Using the clues from the sentences, students raise their hands and guess which character is speaking. Student must explain what information allowed him/her to identify the speaker.

## Teaching Resource Options

**Print**

**Unit 1 Resource Book**
**Video Activities,** pp. 86–87
**Videoscript,** p. 89
**Audioscript,** p. 90

**Audiovisual**

**OHT** 12 (Quick Start)
**Audio Program** Cassette 1A / CD 1
**Video Program** Videotape 1, 5:40 / Videodisc 1A

## Quick Start Review

Expressing likes and dislikes

Use OHT 12 or write on board: Imagine you are **Abuela** talking to a friend about your vacation trip to Costa Rica.

**Cuando voy de viaje a Costa Rica me gusta... ir al bosque tropical.**

Add four more activities **Abuela** likes to do when on vacation.

*Answers will vary. Answers could include:*
**Cuando voy de viaje a Costa Rica me gusta acampar en un parque/caminar por San José/ir a la playa/nadar/ tomar el sol.**

## Teaching Suggestions
### Comprehension Check

- Use **Actividades 1** and **2** to assess retention after the dialog.
- Review family vocabulary by discussing the relationships between Francisco, Verónica, Tío Javier, and Abuela. For example, **Tío Javier es el hijo de Abuela. Francisco y Verónica son los nietos de Abuela. Francisco es el sobrino de Tío Javier. Francisco y Verónica son primos.**

# En acción
## VOCABULARIO Y GRAMÁTICA

**OBJECTIVES**
- Talk about where you went and what you did
- Discuss leisure time
- Comment on airplane travel

### ¿Qué pasa?

**Escuchar** Escoge la(s) respuesta(s) correcta(s), según el diálogo. ¡Ojo! Algunas oraciones tienen más de una respuesta correcta.
*(Hint: Choose the correct answers.)*

1. Francisco gana un premio. Él va...
   a. a Chicago
   b. al parque
   c. a Costa Rica
2. El verano pasado en Costa Rica, la abuela de Francisco...
   a. fue al bosque tropical
   b. caminó por San José
   c. esquió en el agua
3. El abuelo de Francisco...
   a. se va a Costa Rica
   b. quema la carne
   c. es auxiliar de vuelo
4. La persona que quiere ser piloto es...
   a. Francisco
   b. Abuela
   c. Verónica
5. En el aeropuerto, Francisco tiene que...
   a. comprar el boleto de avión
   b. registrar su equipaje
   c. pedir un asiento de ventanilla
6. Francisco deja los boletos de avión en...
   a. el equipaje
   b. el banco
   c. el bolsillo

### ¿Quién habla?

**Escuchar** ¿Quién habla: Francisco, Verónica, el tío Javier o la abuela? *(Hint: Who speaks?)*

1. «Mandé mi material a la revista, y... ¡Gané!»
2. «Fuimos a la playa. Nadamos, tomamos el sol...»
3. «Así que te vas mañana.»
4. «Sabes, me gustaría ser auxiliar de vuelo algún día...»
5. «Y tengo que pasar por seguridad.»
6. «¿Qué tienes en esta maleta?»

**TAMBIÉN SE DICE** Se usa **maleta** en todo el mundo hispano. En algunas regiones puedes oír
**valija** (Argentina) **petaca** (México)
Pero si vas a hacer un viaje corto, llevas una **mochila** (*backpack*) o un **bolso** (*duffel bag*).



## Classroom Management

**TPR** Using the drawing on pp. 30-31, ask the questions in **Actividad 3** and have students point to the appropriate area in the airport for the answer. You can also put a large photo or drawing of an airport in the front of the room and have students go up and touch the appropriate area.

**Portfolio** Short speeches: Have students present an imaginary trip to the class, being sure to include items such as those mentioned in **Actividad 3**. You can record the speeches on audio or video for students to hear their own presentations.

**Rubric: Speaking**

| Speaking Criteria | Scale |
|---|---|
| Vocabulary use | 1 2 3 |
| Fluency, intonation | 1 2 3 |
| Pronunciation | 1 2 3 |
| Accuracy | 1 2 3 |

A = 11–12 pts.
B = 8–10 pts.
C = 6–7 pts.
D = 4–5 pts.
F = < 4 pts.

- *Review: Use regular preterite verbs*
- *Review: Use irregular preterite verbs: **ir, ser, hacer, dar, ver***

## Un viaje en avión

**Hablar** Tu compañero(a) va a hacer su primer viaje en avión. Dile dónde debe hacer estas cosas. *(Hint: Tell where the following things are done.)*

modelo

**Compañero(a):** *¿Dónde paso por la aduana?*

**Tú:** *En el aeropuerto.*

la agencia de viajes

la casa

el mostrador

el aeropuerto

1. ¿Dónde hago las maletas *(pack)*?
2. ¿Dónde compro los boletos?
3. ¿Dónde miran mi pasaporte?
4. ¿Dónde registro mi equipaje?
5. ¿Dónde pido un asiento de ventanilla?
6. ¿Dónde hablo con un agente de viajes?
7. ¿Dónde miran mis documentos de identificación?
8. ¿Dónde me dan un pase de abordar?
9. ¿Dónde paso por seguridad?
10. ¿Dónde tienen información turística?

## ¿Estás listo?

**Hablar** Mañana tu amigo(a) viaja a San José, Costa Rica. Pregúntale si tiene todo lo necesario. *(Hint: Is your friend ready to go to San José?)*

modelo

**Tú:** *¿Tienes la identificación?*

**Tu amigo(a):** *Sí, (No, no) tengo la identificación.*

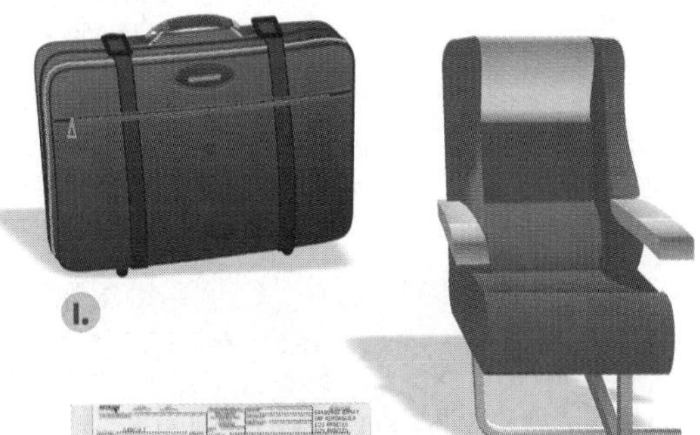
1.
2.

3.
4.
5.

treinta y cinco
**Etapa 1**

35

## Teaching All Students

**Extra Help** Working in groups of 4, have students read aloud the dialog on pp. 32–33 and then respond orally to the questions in **Actividad 1**.

### Multiple Intelligences

**Visual** Have students create a floor plan of the ideal airport for the 21st century. Then have students label their drawings in Spanish.

**Logical/Mathematical** **Plan ahead:** Obtain itineraries from airline flight schedules to Mexico, Spain, Costa Rica, etc. Working in groups, give each group an itinerary and ask them to pretend to "book a flight" based on their present schedule. Have them check on flight times, distance, time spent in flight, etc. After the group has confirmed the information, have each group try to "sell" their trip to the class!

**Objective:** Transitional practice
Listening comprehension/vocabulary

**Answers**

| | |
|---|---|
| 1. a, c | 4. c |
| 2. a, b | 5. b, c |
| 3. b | 6. c |

**Objective:** Transitional practice
Listening comprehension/vocabulary

**Answers**

1. Francisco 2. Abuela 3. Tío Javier
4. Verónica 5. Francisco 6. Verónica

### Extra Practice

**Paired Activity** Have students choose one of the characters (Francisco, Tío Javier, Verónica, Abuela) and act out the roles. The partner should try to guess the character being role-played.

**Objective:** Transitional practice
Speaking/travel vocabulary

**Answers**

1. En la casa.
2. En la agencia de viajes / el mostrador.
3. En el aeropuerto / el mostrador.
4. En el aeropuerto / el mostrador.
5. En el aeropuerto / el mostrador.
6. En la agencia de viajes.
7. En el aeropuerto / el mostrador.
8. En el aeropuerto / el mostrador.
9. En el aeropuerto.
10. En la agencia de viajes.

**Objective:** Transitional practice
**En contexto** vocabulary

**Tener**

**Answers**

*Answers should follow model in Pupil Edition and incorporate vocabulary based on the illustration.*

| | |
|---|---|
| 1. la maleta | 4. el pasaporte |
| 2. el asiento | 5. un exceso de equipaje (las maletas) |
| 3. el boleto | |

**Note:** Extend this activity by having students use classroom objects.

### Block Schedule

**Change of Pace** Do an oral "chain story" with the whole class focusing on the steps one takes when going on a trip and getting on the plane. The first student starts: **Hago las maletas.** The next student adds the next detail: **Voy al aeropuerto.** Continue with as many students as possible.

## Teaching Resource Options

**Print**

*Más práctica* Workbook PE, pp. 15–16
*Cuaderno para hispanohablantes* PE, pp. 13–14
Block Scheduling Copymasters
Unit 1 Resource Book
*Más práctica* Workbook TE, pp. 63–64
*Cuaderno para hispanohablantes* TE, pp. 71–72

**Audiovisual**

OHT 12 (Quick Start)

**Technology**

*Intrigas y aventuras* CD-ROM, Disc 1

## Quick Start Review

Regular verbs

Use OHT 12 or write on board: Divide your paper into three columns with the headings **AR, ER,** and **IR** verbs. Write in as many verbs as you can in each category. Keep it in your notebook for future reference and continue to add to the list as you learn new verbs.

*Answers will vary.*

## Teaching Suggestions
### Presenting Regular Preterite Verbs

- Conjugate other regular verbs students know, such as **caminar, comprar, estudiar,** and **escribir.** First model the conjugation of one verb, then ask students to conjugate the others.
- Model the **yo** form, then ask students to talk about what they did last night: **Anoche, yo hablé por teléfono, no estudié**, etc.
- Then model the **tú** form and ask students to continue. Complete contextualized practice for the rest of the paradigm.

## Talk About the Past Using Regular Preterite Verbs

The preterite tense tells what happened or what you did. It is used when the action described has already been completed. Regular preterite verbs, like present tense verbs, are formed by adding tense endings to the stem.

| | -ar hablar | -er comer | -ir vivir |
|---|---|---|---|
| yo | hablé | comí | viví |
| tú | hablaste | comiste | viviste |
| usted, él, ella | habló | comió | vivió |
| nosotros(as) | hablamos | comimos | vivimos |
| vosotros(as) | hablasteis | comisteis | vivisteis |
| ustedes, ellos, ellas | hablaron | comieron | vivieron |

Regular **-er** and **-ir** verbs take the same endings.

The **nosotros** forms of **-ar** and **-ir** verbs are the same in the preterite and present tense.

Look at the chart above. The nosotros forms of **-ar** and **-ir** verbs are the same in the preterite and in the present tense. But we can usually tell if someone is referring to the past or present from the context.

Abuela says:

—Yo **viajé** a Costa Rica el verano pasado. Acampamos en un parque y caminamos por San José.

*I **traveled** to Costa Rica last summer. We **camped** in a park and **walked** through San José.*

Even though Abuela uses the words acampamos and caminamos, we know that she is talking about an event that happened in the past because she used the word **viajé** in the previous sentence.

36 treinta y seis
**Unidad 1**

## Classroom Community

**Paired Activity** Ask students to bring in a picture of a "place" they have visited (or make a drawing) and tell their partner what they did there. Have students use the preterite as they discuss the picture.

**Game: "Burbujas"** **Plan ahead:** You will need bubble liquid and flash cards with infinitive verbs clearly written on each card. Call on a student, then blow **burbujas** and show the student a verb. The student needs to conjugate the verb in the preterite tense before all of the **burbujas** have popped!

## El verano pasado

**Hablar/Escribir** Explica lo que pasó el verano pasado. *(Hint: Tell what they did.)*

**modelo**

*mi hermana / caminar con el perro*
*Mi hermana (no) caminó con el perro.*

1. yo / alquilar un video
2. mi primo / bajar un río en canoa
3. los estudiantes / cantar en el coro
4. yo / comprar un juego de ajedrez
5. mis padres / disfrutar con los amigos
6. yo / tomar un curso de natación
7. mi mejor amigo(a) / estudiar las artes marciales
8. tú / acampar en las montañas

**MÁS PRÁCTICA** *cuaderno* pp. 15–16
**PARA HISPANOHABLANTES** *cuaderno* pp. 13–14

### Vocabulario

**El tiempo libre**

**acampar en las montañas** *to camp in the mountains*
**bajar un río en canoa** *to go down a river by canoe*
**cantar en el coro** *to sing in the chorus*
**disfrutar con los amigos** *to enjoy time with friends*
**estudiar las artes marciales** *to study martial arts*
**jugar (u→ue) al ajedrez** *to play chess*
**tomar un curso de natación** *to take a swimming class*

¿Qué te gusta hacer?

ACTIVIDAD 6

## Saliendo de Los Ángeles

**Escribir** Antes de salir de Los Ángeles, Francisco le escribió esta tarjeta postal a su familia. Ayúdalo a completarla con el pretérito.
*(Hint: Complete the postcard.)*

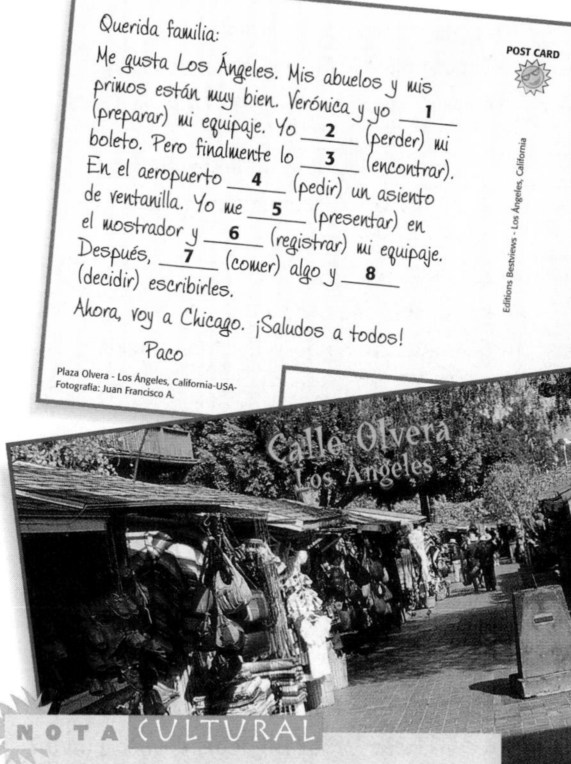

Querida familia:
Me gusta Los Ángeles. Mis abuelos y mis primos están muy bien. Verónica y yo __1__ (preparar) mi equipaje. Yo __2__ (perder) mi boleto. Pero finalmente lo __3__ (encontrar). En el aeropuerto __4__ (pedir) un asiento de ventanilla. Yo me __5__ (presentar) en el mostrador y __6__ (registrar) mi equipaje. Después, __7__ (comer) algo y __8__ (decidir) escribirles.
Ahora, voy a Chicago. ¡Saludos a todos!
Paco



**NOTA CULTURAL**

**La calle Olvera** es parte de un parque histórico que se llama El Pueblo de Los Ángeles. Muchas personas de México vivieron en El Pueblo hace más de cien años. Hoy en la calle Olvera hay muchos restaurantes mexicanos y tiendas que venden artesanías de Latinoamérica.



### Teaching Suggestion

Use the activating question (**¿Qué te gusta hacer?**) to present the new vocabulary words, asking students to point to an answer from the list. Then, have students do **Actividad 5**.

**Objective:** Controlled practice
Regular preterites, leisure vocabulary

**Answers**

1. Yo (no) alquilé un video.
2. Mi primo (no) bajó un río en canoa.
3. Los estudiantes (no) cantaron en el coro.
4. Yo (no) compré un juego de ajedrez.
5. Mis padres (no) disfrutaron con los amigos.
6. Yo (no) tomé un curso de natación.
7. Mi mejor amigo(a) (no) estudió las artes marciales.
8. Tú (no) acampaste en las montañas.

**Objective:** Transitional practice
Regular preterites, travel vocabulary

**Answers**

1. preparamos
2. perdí
3. encontré
4. pedí
5. presenté
6. registré
7. comí
8. decidí

### Supplementary Vocabulary

Other leisure time activities that students may remember from Level 1 include:

**andar en bicicleta** to ride a bicycle
**caminar con el perro** to walk the dog
**hacer ejercicio** to exercise
**leer** to read
**ver la televisión** to watch TV
**tocar el piano/la guitarra** to play the piano/guitar

### Block Schedule

**FunBreak** **Postcards:** Give each student a strip of paper with a name of a classmate clearly written on it. Have students write a postcard (use index cards) to the student named and put them in a class mailbox. You can distribute the "mail" later in the class or the next day. (Decide if students should sign postcards or write anonymously.) (For additional activities, see **Block Scheduling Copymasters**.)

## Teaching All Students

**Extra Help** On index cards, write out several verbs in the infinitive form that are regular in the preterite (e.g., **caminar**, **preparar**, **comer**, **decidir**, etc.). Show a verb card to students and ask them to a) conjugate it, b) form a sentence with the verb, c) form a question for another student with the verb.

**Multiple Intelligences**
**Verbal** Ask students to tape-record themselves reading **Actividad 6**. Allow time for students to hear recordings of others in small groups.

**Rubric: Speaking**

| Speaking Criteria | Scale | |
|---|---|---|
| Fluency, intonation | 1 2 3 | A = 8–9 pts. |
| Pronunciation | 1 2 3 | B = 6–7 pts. |
| Accuracy | 1 2 3 | C = 4–5 pts. |
| | | D = 2–3 pts. |
| | | F = < 2 pts. |

## Teaching Resource Options

**Print**

*Más práctica* Workbook PE, pp. 17–18
*Cuaderno para hispanohablantes* PE, pp. 15–16
Unit 1 Resource Book
*Más práctica* Workbook TE, pp. 65–66
*Cuaderno para hispanohablantes* TE, pp. 73–74
Audioscript, p. 88

**Audiovisual**

OHT 12 (Quick Start)
Audio Program Cassette 1A / CD 1

**Technology**

*Intrigas y aventuras* CD-ROM, Disc 1

## Quick Start Review

Preterite

Use OHT 12 or write on board: Change the verbs in the following sentences to the preterite tense.

En el aeropuerto me presento en el mostrador.
Registro mi equipaje.
Cambio mi asiento.
Paso por seguridad.

**Answers**

En el aeropuerto me presenté en el mostrador.
Registré mi equipaje.
Cambié mi asiento.
Pasé por seguridad.

## Teaching Suggestions
### Presenting the Preterite of -car, -gar, and -zar Verbs

Have students conjugate the verbs in the **Repaso** and **Vocabulario** boxes on pp. 38 and 39 on the board for extra practice.

ACTIVIDAD 7

### Las vacaciones

**Hablar** Pregúntales a tus compañeros(as) sobre sus actividades durante las vacaciones pasadas.
*(Hint: Ask classmates about activities.)*

**modelo**

*acampar en las montañas*
**Tú:** *¿Acampaste en las montañas?*
**Compañero(a) 1:** *Sí, acampé en las montañas.*
**Compañero(a) 2:** *No, no acampé en las montañas.*

1. comer en casa de un amigo
2. hablar con tus amigos por teléfono
3. caminar con el perro
4. tomar un curso
5. escribir una carta
6. volver a casa después de las once

ACTIVIDAD 8

### Ay, ¡qué verano!

**Escuchar/Hablar** Mariana disfrutó mucho las vacaciones de verano. Escucha lo que dice sobre las fotos. Luego, haz un resumen de lo que hizo.
*(Hint: Listen to the audiotape and look at the pictures. Then summarize what happened.)*

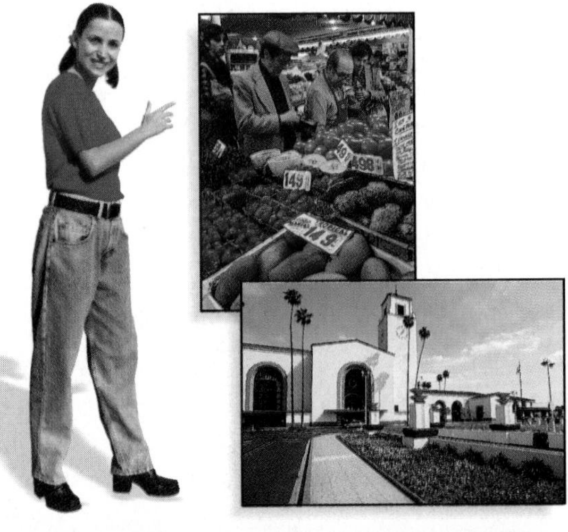

## REPASO
### Talk About the Past Using the Preterite: -car, -gar, and -zar

In the preterite, verbs that end in **-car, -gar,** and **-zar** are spelled differently in the **yo** form. The spelling changes in order to keep the pronunciation the same.

Compare the **yo** form with the **tú** form of these verbs:

| | Tú Form | | becomes | | Yo Form |
|---|---|---|---|---|---|
| **sacar** | ¿**Sac**aste fotos del aeropuerto?<br>***Did you take*** *photos of the airport?* | **sac** | becomes | **saqu** | Sí, **saqu**é fotos del aeropuerto.<br>*Yes,* ***I took*** *photos of the airport.* |
| **jugar** | ¿Con quién **jug**aste al fútbol?<br>*With whom* ***did you play*** *soccer?* | **jug** | becomes | **jugu** | **Jugu**é con mi primo.<br>***I played*** *with my cousin.* |
| **almorzar** | ¿Dónde **almorz**aste ayer?<br>*Where* ***did you eat lunch*** *yesterday?* | **almorz** | becomes | **almorc** | **Almorc**é con mi familia en Griffith Park.<br>***I ate lunch*** *with my family in Griffith Park.* |



## Classroom Community

**Group Activity** List on board students' favorite places to visit. Then divide class by favorite places—all those who enjoy the zoo will form a group, etc. Have groups write a short summary of their experiences at the given place, using the preterite tense as much as possible. This may also be assigned as individual homework.

**Learning Scenario** Mind Map: Using regular verbs in the preterite tense, have students design a mind map of verb endings. (A mind map is a visual representation of one's personal understanding of how the verbs are conjugated.) For example, arrange the preterite endings for **-ar** verbs (**-é, -aste, -ó, -amos, -asteis, -aron**) in 2 columns on the board and circle the **-é** and **-ó** that require accents.

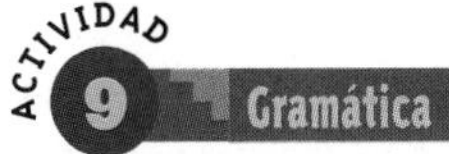


## El viaje de Francisco

**Escribir** Francisco pasó el verano en Los Ángeles con su familia. Según Francisco, ¿qué hicieron? *(Hint: Tell what they did last summer.)*

**modelo**

*Yo / buscar unas maletas*

*Yo busqué unas maletas.*

1. Verónica y yo / almorzar temprano
2. Mi tío / pagar mi boleto de avión
3. Yo / explicarle mis planes a mi tío
4. Tú / sacar libros de la biblioteca
5. Mi primo / jugar al baloncesto
6. Yo / practicar deportes
7. Mis abuelos / comenzar a hacer ejercicio
8. Yo / llegar tarde del cine

**MÁS PRÁCTICA** *cuaderno* pp. 17–18

**PARA HISPANOHABLANTES** *cuaderno* pp. 15–16

### Vocabulario

**Verbs with -car, -gar, and -zar Spelling Changes**

*c → qu* **explicar** *to explain*

*z → c* **comenzar (e→ie)** *to start*

*c → qu* **buscar** *to look for*

**practicar** *to practice*

**tocar** *to touch, to play (a musical instrument)*

*g → gu* **llegar** *to arrive*

**pagar** *to pay*

*z → c* **empezar (e→ie)** *to begin*

¿Qué vas a hacer, buscar a tus amigos o practicar un deporte?

## Unas actividades

**Hablar/Escribir** Pregúntales a cinco compañeros(as) de clase si participaron en estas actividades el verano pasado. Completa una tabla como la siguiente. *(Hint: Ask about activities and complete a chart.)*

**modelo**

| Nombre | Actividad |
|---|---|
| 1. René | tocó el piano |
| 2. | |
| 3. | |
| 4. | |
| 5. | |

**Tú:** *¿Tocaste el piano?*

**René:** *Sí, toqué el piano.*

1. acampar en las montañas
2. recibir correspondencia
3. comer en un restaurante mexicano
4. pasar un rato con los amigos
5. practicar deportes
6. jugar al ajedrez
7. tomar un curso de artes marciales
8. escribir una carta
9. bajar un río en canoa
10. beber muchos refrescos
11. disfrutar de la playa
12. viajar a otro estado o país



### Teaching All Students

**Extra Help** Have students create flashcards with infinitives on one side and complete conjugations in the preterite on the other. Pairs can exchange cards and quiz each other.

**Native Speakers** Verbs with spelling changes are often difficult for both native speakers and non-native speakers to master. Have Spanish speakers practice all forms of the verbs by writing them out.

**Multiple Intelligences**

**Verbal Brainstorm activity:** Have students list as many **-car, -zar, -gar** verbs in the Spanish language as they can find. Use outside sources! Then divide the class into groups and have each group conjugate a verb on large poster board. Display the charts in class.

**Objective:** Transitional practice
Regular preterites, leisure vocabulary

**Answers**

*Answers should reflect comprehension of preterite tense: the first response conjugated in the second person (**tú**) form and the second response in the first person (**yo**) form.*

1. comiste / comí
2. hablaste / hablé
3. caminaste / caminé
4. tomaste / tomé
5. escribiste / escribí
6. volviste / volví

**Objective:** Open-ended practice
Describing a vacation

**Answers** (See script, p. TE 27D.)
*Answers will vary.*

**Objective:** Controlled practice
Preterites in **-car, -gar, -zar**

**Answers**

1. Verónica y yo almorzamos temprano.
2. Mi tío pagó mi boleto de avión.
3. Yo le expliqué mis planes a mi tío.
4. Tú sacaste libros de la biblioteca.
5. Mi primo jugó al baloncesto.
6. Yo practiqué deportes.
7. Mis abuelos comenzaron a hacer ejercicio.
8. Yo llegué tarde al cine.

**Objective:** Transitional practice
Preterite, leisure vocabulary

**Note:** Extend this activity by having students make a graph and/or report to the class.
*Answers will vary.*

### More Practice

As a follow-up to **Actividad 10**, ask students to describe their own summer vacation in five sentences similar to the ones they use here.

### Quick Wrap-up

**Role play** Divide students into pairs. Have them role-play an interview on the TV show **"La vida de los ricos."** One student chooses a celebrity identity and the interviewer asks one question about what he/she did on a recent grand vacation.

### Block Schedule

**Process Time** Have students listen again to the audio for **Actividad 8** and choose which place sounds the most/least fascinating to them. Have them write a short reflection in their portfolio.

## Teaching Resource Options

**Print** 

*Más práctica* Workbook PE, pp. 19–20
*Cuaderno para hispanohablantes* PE, pp. 17–18
Block Scheduling Copymasters
Unit 1 Resource Book
*Más práctica* Workbook TE, pp. 67–68
*Cuaderno para hispanohablantes* TE, pp. 75–76
Information Gap Activities, p. 79

**Audiovisual** 

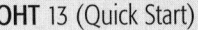

OHT 13 (Quick Start)

**Technology**

*Intrigas y aventuras* CD-ROM, Disc 1

## Quick Start Review

Preterite: regular verbs

Use OHT 13 or write on board: In 3 minutes, write as many sentences as you can telling about what you did yesterday. The person with the longest list containing the highest number of accurate verbs in the preterite gets a break on homework or extra credit.

*Answers will vary.*

## Teaching Suggestions

### Presenting irregular preterite verbs: ir, ser, hacer, dar, ver

To reinforce the use of context to differentiate between **ir** and **ser** in the preterite, give students the following examples: **Ayer fue el cumpleaños de mi abuela y fui a su fiesta con mi familia. Todos mis primos fueron también. Fue un día muy especial para todos.**

**Objective:** Open-ended practice
Talking about past activities

Interrogatives

*Answers will vary.*

**Note:** This activity can be expanded by asking students to personalize: **El fin de semana pasado (lo que hice...)**

ACTIVIDAD 11

## El fin de semana pasado

**Hablar** Pregúntales a tus compañeros(as) qué hicieron durante el fin de semana.
*(Hint: Ask your friends what they did.)*

**modelo**

*hablar (¿con quién?)*

**Tú:** *¿Con quién hablaste durante el fin de semana?*

**Compañero(a):** *Hablé con un chico de mi clase de matemáticas.*

1. llamar por teléfono (¿a quiénes?)
2. visitar (¿a quiénes?)
3. encontrar (¿qué?)
4. jugar (¿a qué?)
5. almorzar (¿dónde?)
6. comprar (¿qué?)
7. bailar (¿dónde?)
8. buscar (¿qué?)

**MÁS COMUNICACIÓN** p. R2

## Irregular Preterite: ir, ser, hacer, dar, ver

**¿RECUERDAS?** *p. 36* You learned that the preterite is used to tell what happened or what you did. You also learned that regular preterite verbs attach specific preterite tense endings to the stem.

The verbs **ir, ser,** and **hacer,** which are all frequently used, are irregular in the preterite.

**ir** and **ser** have the same irregular forms

| ir | ser | hacer |
|---|---|---|
| fui | fui | hice |
| fuiste | fuiste | hiciste |
| fue | fue | hizo |
| fuimos | fuimos | hicimos |
| fuisteis | fuisteis | hicisteis |
| fueron | fueron | hicieron |

Abuela says:

—Yo **viajé** a Costa Rica el verano pasado. **Fui** con unas amigas.
***I traveled** to Costa Rica last summer. **I went** with some friends.*

The context makes it clear that **fui** means ***I went.***

The verbs **dar** and **ver** take regular **-er/-ir** past tense endings in the preterite but have no written accent marks.

| dar | ver |
|---|---|
| di | vi |
| diste | viste |
| dio | vio |
| dimos | vimos |
| disteis | visteis |
| dieron | vieron |



## Classroom Community

**Group Activity** Poster Contest: Have students create a verb chart for the regular **-ar, -er,** and **-ir** verbs and 5 irregular verbs in the preterite. Judge posters.

**Cooperative Learning** Chain Links: Use **ir, ser, hacer, dar,** and **ver** plus regular verbs to tell a story. Form small groups; each person will add to the story, using only the preterite, for a total of two rounds, e.g, S1: **Yo fui a la biblioteca.** S2: **Mi hermano no caminó con nosotros a la biblioteca,** etc. You may assign a recorder to jot down the story and a reader to read aloud the completed story to the class.

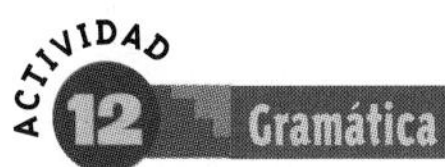

## ¡Una fiesta!

**Escribir** Verónica celebró su cumpleaños el domingo. Para saber lo que pasó, completa el párrafo con la forma apropiada de **ir, ser, hacer, dar** o **ver.** *(Hint: Complete the paragraph.)*

Ayer yo fui (ir) a la fiesta de Verónica. Yo __1__ (ver) a todos nuestros amigos. ¡La fiesta __2__ (ser) inolvidable! Nosotros __3__ (hacer) muchas cosas interesantes: bailar, escuchar música y comer. Los padres de Verónica le regalaron una computadora. El novio de Verónica __4__ (hacer) algo muy especial al final de la fiesta: le cantó una canción original. Después, él le __5__ (dar) unas flores muy bonitas. ¡Qué romántico! ¿Por qué no __6__ (ir) tú?

**MÁS PRÁCTICA** *cuaderno* pp. 19–20

**PARA HISPANOHABLANTES** *cuaderno* pp. 17–18

## Unos viajes

**Hablar** Imagínate que tú, tu familia y tus amigos viajaron por todo el mundo. Habla con tu compañero(a) sobre el viaje. Usa el pretérito de **ir** y **hacer** y escoge una actividad. *(Hint: Tell where you went and what you did.)*

**modelo**

*mi amigo: España → tomar un curso de español*

**Tú:** *Mi amigo fue a España.*

**Compañero(a):** *¿Qué hizo allí?*

**Tú:** *Tomó un curso de español.*

1. mis padres: México
2. mis hermanos y yo: Inglaterra
3. mi abuelo: Chicago
4. mi mamá: Ecuador
5. mis primos: Miami
6. yo: Nueva York

a. dar un paseo por la ciudad
b. ir a un concierto de la orquesta
c. acampar en las montañas
d. almorzar en un restaurante mexicano
e. buscar regalos para sus amigos
f. ver una película

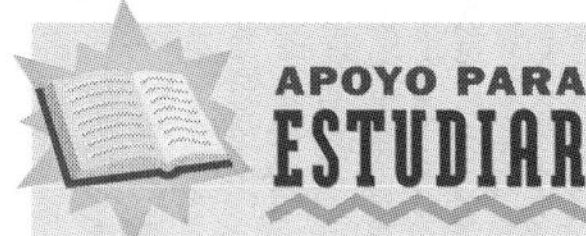

### The Preterite

A good way to learn new verbs is to practice them with other students in a question-and-answer exercise. Replace the words in parentheses to create your own meaning.

¿Adónde fuiste? Fui (a la agencia de viajes).
¿Qué hiciste? Compré (un boleto de avión).
¿Qué / A quién viste? Vi (a la agente de viajes).
¿Adónde fueron ustedes? Fuimos (a Los Ángeles).
¿Qué hicieron? Visitamos (el parque).

**Objective:** Controlled practice
Irregular preterites

### Answers
1. vi
2. fue
3. hicimos
4. hizo
5. dio
6. fuiste

**Objective:** Transitional practice
Preterite of **ir**, **hacer**, **dar**, and **ver**
Regular preterites

*Answers will vary.*

### More Practice

Make logical and illogical sentences about what students did yesterday, e.g., **Ayer fueron con sus amigos. Anoche llamaron por teléfono. Ayer viajaron a México.** Students respond **Sí, es posible** or **No, no es posible.**

### Project

**Essay Contest** Pretend that your school is having an essay contest open to all students. Choose a topic.

**Rubric: Writing**

| Criteria | Scale |
|---|---|
| Correct sentence structure | 1 2 3 4 5 |
| Vocabulary use | 1 2 3 4 5 |
| Creativity | 1 2 3 4 5 |
| Logical organization | 1 2 3 4 5 |

A = 17–20 pts.
B = 13–16 pts.
C = 9–12 pts.
D = 5–8 pts.
F = < 5 pts.

## Teaching All Students

**Extra Help** Have students expand on the **Apoyo para estudiar** activity by creating more questions and answers to do in pairs.

### Multiple Intelligences

**Kinesthetic** Have students create "puzzle" pieces for the preterite verbs to highlight stems and spelling changes. Have them work in pairs to create new verb forms from the "puzzle" pieces.

**Logical/Mathematical** Decide on a theme, e.g., **El sábado pasado.** Each student forms a logical sentence to develop a story, e.g., S1: **Ayer fuimos al restaurante.** S2: **Comimos tostados y...** S3: **Vimos una película de intriga a la una y...**

## Block Schedule

**Retention** Write some preterite verb forms on cards and have students create sentences. (For additional activities, see **Block Scheduling Copymasters.**)

## Teaching Resource Options

**Print** 

*Más práctica* Workbook PE, pp. 11–14
*Cuaderno para hispanohablantes* PE, pp. 11–12
Block Scheduling Copymasters
Unit 1 Resource Book
*Más práctica* Workbook TE, pp. 59–63
*Cuaderno para hispanohablantes* TE, pp. 69–70
Information Gap Activities, pp. 80–81
Audioscript, pp. 92–94

**Audiovisual**

OHT 13 (Quick Start)
Audio Program Cassette 1A, 1B / CD 1; (*Para hispanohablantes* Cassette 1B / CD 1)

**Technology**

*Intrigas y aventuras* CD-ROM, Disc 1

## Quick Start Review

Preterite: irregular verbs

Use OHT 13 or write on board:

Rewrite the following sentences in the preterite.

1. Yo hago un viaje.
2. Mi hermana va también.
3. Vamos a México.
4. Vemos muchas cosas interesantes.
5. Le doy una jarra de cerámica a mi madre de regalo.

**Answers**, see p. 27D.

Actividad 14 **Objective:** Transitional practice
Preterite/travel vocabulary

### Answers

1. b, fuimos
2. f, hizo
3. e, hice
4. d, fuimos
5. g, llegué
6. c, fui, vi, conocí
7. a, hicimos, vimos

Actividad 15 **Objective:** Transitional practice
Preterite/leisure activities

*Answers will vary.*

## Cross Cultural Connections

Ask students to describe what they see in the mural on p. 42. What do they think is the message of the mural? Are there any murals in their community that also have a message?

Actividad 14

## Un viaje estupendo

**Leer/Escribir** Imagínate que hiciste un viaje a Los Ángeles. Pon las oraciones en orden cronológico y escribe el pretérito de cada verbo entre paréntesis. *(Hint: Order sentences and conjugate verbs in the preterite.)*

a. En Los Ángeles mis nuevos amigos y yo (hacer) y (ver) muchas cosas interesantes.
b. Antes de salir, mi madre y yo (ir) a la agencia de viajes.
c. Yo (ir) a Hollywood, (ver) unos murales y (conocer) a unos nuevos amigos.
d. Todos nosotros (ir) al aeropuerto.
e. Yo (hacer) las maletas.
f. El agente de viajes (hacer) las reservaciones.
g. Yo (llegar) a Los Ángeles por la tarde.

Actividad 15

## ¿Cómo pasaron el verano?

**Hablar/Escribir** Pregúntales a unos(as) compañeros(as) con qué frecuencia hicieron estas actividades en el verano. *(Hint: How frequently were these activities done?)*

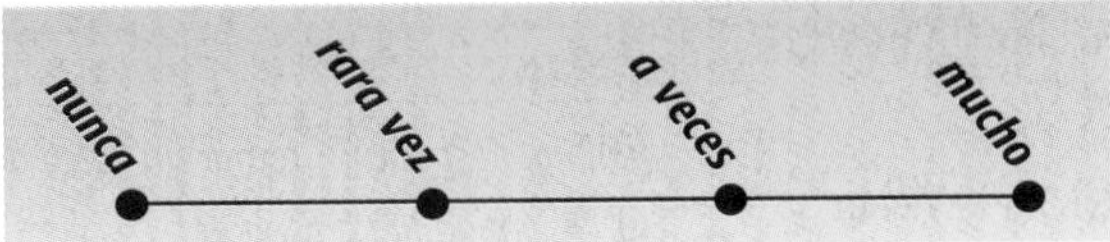


**modelo**

*descansar durante el verano*
**Tú:** *¿Descansaste durante el verano?*
**Compañero(a) 1:** *Sí, descansé mucho.*
**Compañero(a) 2:** *No, no descansé.*

1. ir de compras
2. tomar un curso
3. practicar artes marciales
4. ir a fiestas con tus amigos
5. ver conciertos
6. hacer ejercicio
7. descansar
8. trabajar

**NOTA CULTURAL**

**Los murales** Se puede aprender mucho de la historia y de la cultura de Los Ángeles a través de los murales que están pintados por toda la ciudad. Este mural que se encuentra en el este de la ciudad se llama *Tree of Knowledge* porque muestra la importancia de la lectura.

## Classroom Community 

**TPR Plan ahead:** Have students list 10 or more activities that a "typical" student does. Copy and distribute. One student will act out his/her daily routine, while the rest of the class sequences events, e.g., **Salí de la casa a las siete y media. Llegué a la escuela a las ocho. Asistí a la clase de español...**

**Paired Activity** Have students share with their partner **"Lo que hice anoche/ayer."**

**Portfolios** Ask students to write about something they did last week that was interesting, e.g., **Yo fui a la clase de artes marciales...**

**Rubric: Writing**

| Criteria | Scale |
|---|---|
| Correct sentence structure | 1 2 3 4 5 |
| Vocabulary use | 1 2 3 4 5 |
| Creativity | 1 2 3 4 5 |
| Logical organization | 1 2 3 4 5 |

A = 17–20 pts.
B = 13–16 pts.
C = 9–12 pts.
D = 5–8 pts.
F = < 5 pts.

## ¡Puro juego en Los Ángeles!

**Escuchar** Escucha lo que hizo Francisco en Los Ángeles. Luego ordena las fotos según lo que escuchaste. *(Hint: Put photos in chronological order.)*

a.

b.

c.

d.

## Para conocerte mejor

**PARA CONVERSAR**

**STRATEGY: SPEAKING**

**Encourage others** It is easier to converse with someone who seems interested in what you say. Try these phrases to make positive, encouraging responses to your partner's answers:

- **¡Qué interesante / difícil / chévere!**
- **¡Cómo no!**
- **¡No me digas!**

**Hablar** Usa estas preguntas para charlar con un(a) compañero(a). Luego preséntale las respuestas a la clase. *(Hint: Ask these questions. Then share answers.)*

1. ¿Cómo te fue el verano pasado? ¿Por qué?
2. ¿Qué actividades interesantes hiciste? ¿Con quién?
3. ¿Trabajaste? ¿Dónde?
4. ¿Fuiste al cine? ¿Qué película te gustó más?
5. ¿Adónde fuiste para pasarlo bien? ¿Con quién?

**MÁS COMUNICACIÓN** p. R2

### Refrán

**En la tierra a que fuiste, haz lo que viste.**

Este refrán quiere decir que debes hacer las cosas como la gente del lugar donde estás. Por ejemplo, en Los Ángeles casi nadie camina por la ciudad; siempre van en carro. En grupos, presenten situaciones en que una persona tiene que adaptarse y hacer algo como los demás.

## Teaching All Students

**Extra Help** Give students a list of interrogative words (**qué, por qué, quién...**) and ask them to practice writing questions in the preterite. A chart of interrogatives could be posted for reference.

**Native Speakers** Ask Spanish speakers to analyze the **refrán** on p. 43. Ask them to write other **refranes** they know on the board and explain them to the class.

**Multiple Intelligences**

**Musical/Rhythmic** Have students present a short chant to the class based on the preterite–it could be as simple as spelling the regular vs. irregular endings. For example, **-ar** verbs: **yo -é, tú -aste, él/ella/Ud. -ó, nosotros -amos, ellos/ellas/Uds. -aron.** The chant should also include samples of the forms in sentences.



## Teaching Suggestions

- **Practicing dialogs** Have students make positive, encouraging responses to each other as they do **Actividad 17**. You can model a dialog with another student, then ask for volunteers to share their dialogs with the class.
- Expand on the Speaking Strategy in **Actividad 17** by listing on the board other positive responses students can use when speaking with their partners.

**Objective:** Transitional practice
Listening comprehension practice/ discussing past activities

**Answers** (See script, p. TE 27D.)

1. b
2. a
3. d
4. c

**Objective:** Open-ended practice
Discussing leisure activities

Interrogatives

**Rubric: Speaking**

| Criteria | Scale |
|---|---|
| Use of encouragement | 1 2 3 |
| Fluency | 1 2 3 |
| Pronunciation, rhythm | 1 2 3 |

A = 8–9 pts.; B = 6–7 pts.; C = 4–5 pts.; D = 2–3 pts.; F = < 2 pts.

## Dictation

Have students silently reread the **Nota cultural** then close their books. Dictate the **Nota cultural** and have students check their work.

## Block Schedule

**Variety** **Plan ahead:** Have students write out names of vacation spots on individual strips of paper. Ask each student to choose a "Vacation Strip" and list the items needed at the airport in order to reach the destination, e.g., **"Yo voy de viaje a Puerto Rico. Tengo identificación, y no necesito un pasaporte. Tengo un boleto y muchas maletas. Tengo exceso de equipaje...."**

### Teaching Resource Options

**Print**

*Cuaderno para hispanohablantes* PE, pp. 19–20

Unit 1 Resource Book

*Cuaderno para hispanohablantes* TE, pp. 77–78

Audioscript, pp. 91–92

**Audiovisual**

OHT 13 (Quick Start)

Audio Program Cassette 1A / CD 1

*Canciones* Cassette / CD Songs 3, 8

### Quick Start Review

Handicrafts/shopping

Use OHT 13 or write on board: Name as many items as you can in the photograph of places in Los Angeles.

*Answers will vary.*

### Teaching Suggestions

- **Strategy: Use visuals and titles to predict the general idea** With a partner, have students describe the photos on pp. 44–45. What does the format tell about the title **"¿Cuánto sabes?"**
- **Strategy: Scan for cognates** Ask students to identify the cognate words in the reading. List them on the board.
- **Reading Suggestion** Read answers first to target question reading. Then read questions and answers as if taking a test.
- **Post-Reading** Tally how many answers students knew. Which questions did everyone get correct? Which were most frequently missed?

### Cross Cultural Connections

**Strategy** Identify interesting facts. Create a board or card game to tell interesting facts about people, places, and things in your town or a major city you know.

# En voces

**LECTURA**

## ¿CUÁNTO SABES?

**PARA LEER**

**STRATEGIES: READING**

**Read; don't translate** Your goal is to read Spanish; it is not to turn Spanish into English. You have learned many reading strategies to help you attain that goal. Let's review some of them.

**Use visuals and titles to predict the general idea** After reading, decide whether you need to revise your prediction.

**Scan for cognates** Glance quickly to identify words you already know because of their similarity to English.

**A** ¿Cuál queda más cerca de Los Ángeles?
a. el mar Caribe
b. el océano Pacífico
c. el río Grande

**B** ¿Qué porcentaje de la población de Los Ángeles es de descendencia hispana?
a. 21%
b. 38%
c. 43%

**C** La ciudad de Los Ángeles tiene todo tipo de arte. Pero el arte que puedes encontrar en paredes de edificios y en carreteras tiene el nombre de
a. murales.
b. cerámica.
c. estatuas.

**D** Sepulveda, Ventura, La Cienega y Santa Monica son
a. nombres de ciudades de España.
b. nombres de los primeros exploradores.
c. calles o avenidas de Los Ángeles.

44

### Classroom Community

**Paired Activity** Have students work in pairs to describe the photos on pp. 44–45. Then have them form additional quiz show questions based on the same pictures.

**Game** Have students use the questions and answers on pp. 44–45 in a mock game show. Have one student be the host, two students are the guests, another student can be the judge of correct answers, and the rest of the class is the audience. Ask students to come up with additional questions/answers based on the chapter material as a homework assignment.

HOLLYWOOD
E
¿Cuáles de estos tipos de música puedes escuchar en los clubes de Los Ángeles?
a. reggae
b. salsa
c. rock en español
F
En Hollywood hay muchas personas que quieren ser estrellas. De las siguientes actrices, ¿cuáles son latinas?
a. Jennifer López
b. Salma Hayek
c. Rosie Pérez
G
La casa más vieja de Los Ángeles se llama Ávila Adobe. El ranchero mexicano Francisco Ávila vivió allí en los años 1800. Esta casa está en
a. Olvera Street.
b. Rodeo Drive.
c. Sunset Boulevard.
H
¿Cuáles de estas comidas puedes comprar en Los Ángeles?
a. chiles rellenos
b. una hamburguesa y papas fritas
c. un sándwich cubano
2 PUNTOS
5 PUNTOS
2 PUNTOS
REGRESA 3


Respuestas:

A. b
B. b
C. a
D. c
E. a, b, c
F. a, b, c
G. a
H. a, b, c

## ¿Comprendiste?

1. ¿Dónde queda Los Ángeles?
2. ¿Qué tipo de comida encuentras en Los Ángeles?
3. ¿Qué tipo de música se escucha allí?

## ¿Qué piensas?

Los Ángeles es una ciudad que tiene gente de varios países. ¿Cuáles crees que son las ventajas y desventajas (*advantages and disadvantages*) de vivir en una ciudad con gente de todas partes?



## Community Connection

Ask students to identify city or street names in their area that may come from the Spanish language. Then ask them to identify city names in other parts of the U.S. that come from Spanish, such as San Francisco, El Paso, Santa Fe, and Los Angeles.

## Culture Highlights

- **ACTRICES LATINAS** Jennifer López is a Puerto Rican model and actress who has been in the films **Selena** and **Out of Sight**. She was born and raised in the Bronx section of New York. Salma Hayek is of Arab and Mexican descent. She started her acting career in Mexican soap operas and has been in the films **Desperado**, **From Dusk Till Dawn**, **Fools Rush In**, and **Breaking Up**. Rosie Pérez, a Puerto Rican actress and dancer from Brooklyn, New York, was an Oscar nominee for her supporting role in **Do the Right Thing.** She has also been in **White Men Can't Jump** and **Fearless**.

## ¿Comprendiste?

### Answers

1. En el sur de California, en la costa del océano Pacífico.
2. Encuentras muchos tipos de comida en Los Ángeles: chiles rellenos, hamburguesas con papas fritas y sándwiches cubanos.
3. Se escucha muchos tipos de música: reggae, salsa y rock en español.

## Critical Thinking

Have students compare the Hispanic influences in Los Angeles with the Hispanic influences in another American city they have either studied or know something about (Miami, for example). How do the populations compare? How are food, art, games, traditions, etc. influenced?

## Teaching All Students

**Extra Help** Have students re-read the **¿Cuánto sabes?** reading and summarize the main points.

**Native Speakers** Ask Spanish speakers to create additional questions and possible answers about their Hispanic community. They can write them on index cards with a multiple-choice format and share them with the class.

**Multiple Intelligences**

**Verbal** Have students list other Latin American movie stars, musicians, athletes, or writers they know.

**Visual** Have students draw a mural to reflect the important places and historical events of their area.

## Block Schedule

**Process Time** Suggest that students read the **¿Comprendiste?** and **¿Qué piensas?** questions before the beginning of the reading. Allow 10 minutes for students to read quietly before beginning whole class work.

## Teaching Resource Options

**Print** 

Unit 1 Resource Book
Information Gap Activities, p. 82
Family Involvement, pp. 83–84
Multiple Choice Test Questions, pp. 229–237

**Audiovisual** 

OHT 14 (Quick Start)

**Technology** 

Electronic Teacher Tools/Test Generator
*Intrigas y aventuras* CD-ROM, Disc 1

## Quick Start Review

Preterite

Use OHT 14 or write on board: Conjugate these verbs in the preterite:
**caminar, beber, ir, ver**

**Answers**, see p. 27D.

### Actividad 1 Answers

1. Manuel disfrutó con los amigos.
2. La profesora escribió poemas.
3. Nosotros tomamos un curso de arte.
4. Yo comí mucha pizza.
5. Mis hermanas cantaron en el coro.
6. Mis amigos y yo asistimos a conciertos.
7. Tú viajaste a México.
8. Sarita y Homero vendieron libros.
9. Yo trabajé en un restaurante.
10. Tú recibiste muchas cartas.

### Actividad 2 Answers

1. Mi mejor amiga y yo patinamos.
2. Tú corriste.
3. Jorge escribió.
4. Yo estudié. (Yo leí.)
5. Ustedes bailaron.
6. Lilia caminó.

Etapa 1

# En uso

## REPASO Y MÁS COMUNICACIÓN

**OBJECTIVES**
- Talk about where you went and what you did
- Discuss leisure time
- Comment on airplane travel

*Now you can...*
- talk about where you went and what you did.

*To review*
- regular preterite verbs, see p. 36.

### Actividad 1 Muchas actividades

Todos hablan del verano pasado. ¿Qué hicieron? *(Hint: Tell what they did.)*

**modelo**

*Ana y Roberto / jugar al ajedrez*
*Ana y Roberto jugaron al ajedrez.*

1. Manuel / disfrutar con los amigos
2. la profesora / escribir poemas
3. nosotros / tomar un curso de arte
4. yo / comer mucha pizza
5. mis hermanas / cantar en el coro
6. mis amigos y yo / asistir a conciertos
7. tú / viajar a México
8. Sarita y Homero / vender libros
9. yo / trabajar en un restaurante
10. tú / recibir muchas cartas

*Now you can...*
- discuss leisure time.

*To review*
- regular preterite verbs, see p. 36.

### Actividad 2 En el parque

Explica lo que hicieron estas personas en el parque el sábado pasado.
*(Hint: Tell what people did.)*

**modelo**

*yo*
*Yo descansé.*

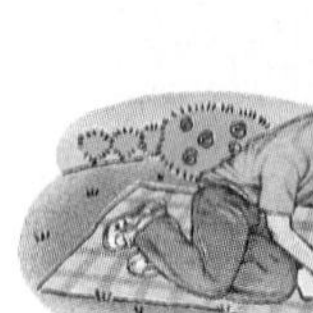

1. mi mejor amiga y yo
2. tú 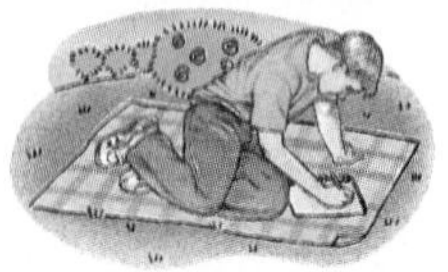
3. Jorge

4. yo
5. ustedes
6. Lilia



## Classroom Community

**Cooperative Learning** Divide the class into groups of four students. Have each group write a review sheet for one of the objectives listed at the top of p. 46. Within each group, S1 is the recorder, S2, S3, and S4 are the researchers who find the examples. Each review sheet must have numerous examples of each objective. Compile the lists and copy and distribute them as a special review of the **Etapa**.

**Game: Concentration** **Plan ahead:** Write on index cards 15 different forms of regular preterite verbs and 15 random subjects. Mix them up and place face down and have students play Concentration by matching subjects with verbs. For example, students match **almuerzo** with the subject **yo** and **vamos** with **mi mejor amigo y yo**.

*Now you can...*
- comment on airplane travel.

*To review*
- regular preterite verbs, see pp. 36, 38.

## ACTIVIDAD 3 ¡Qué viaje!

Ramón salió de viaje el viernes pasado. Para saber lo que pasó, completa el párrafo con la forma apropiada de los verbos indicados. *(Hint: Complete the paragraph.)*

> El viernes pasado yo __1__ (jugar) al tenis hasta las once y __2__ (llegar) tarde al aeropuerto. Me __3__ (presentar) en el mostrador con mis cinco maletas y __4__ (empezar) a buscar mi boleto. Yo __5__ (buscar) en mi mochila y mi madre __6__ (buscar) en las maletas. Por fin, yo __7__ (sacar) mi identificación del bolsillo y __8__ (encontrar) el boleto. Entonces, __9__ (pagar) el exceso de equipaje y __10__ (correr) a abordar el avión. Esa tarde mis padres __11__ (almorzar) bistec en el restaurante del aeropuerto y yo __12__ (almorzar) un sándwich en el avión.

*Now you can...*
- talk about where you went and what you did.

*To review*
- some irregular preterite verbs, see p. 40.

## ACTIVIDAD 4 ¿Qúe hicieron?

Di lo que hicieron o no hicieron estas personas ayer. *(Hint: Tell what these people did or did not do.)*

**modelo**

*Estela / ver a su mejor amiga (sí)*
*Estela vio a su mejor amiga.*

1. ustedes / dar una fiesta (no)
2. Mariano / hacer unas enchiladas (sí)
3. Ernesto y yo / ver una película (sí)
4. él / ir a la escuela (no)
5. nosotros/ hacer la tarea (sí)
6. Soledad y Raúl / hacer la tarea (no)
7. yo / dar un paseo (sí)
8. tú / ir de compras (no)
9. Mónica / hacer la cena (no)
10. mi hermano(a) / ver la televisión (no)
11. Jorge / viajar en moto (sí)
12. mis abuelos(as) / jugar al ajedrez (sí)



## Teaching All Students

**Extra Help** Have students make a list of what they did last summer modeled on **Actividad 1**.

**Challenge** Have students write an ending to the narration in **Actividad 3** using additional preterite verbs.

**Multiple Intelligences**

**Visual** Have students create a new story based on the pictures in **Actividad 2**. They can create additional pictures to tie the story together.

**Kinesthetic** Have students act out the narration in **Actividad 3** in small groups.

## Teaching Suggestions

### What Have Students Learned?

Ask students to look at the activities on pp. 46–48 and write down all the objectives covered in each activity.

Talk about where you went and what you did – **Act. 1, 4, 5**; Discuss leisure time activities – **Act. 1, 2, 6**; Comment on airline travel – **Act. 3, 7**; Use regular preterite verbs – **Act. 1, 2, 3, 5, 6, 7**; Use some irregular preterite verbs – **Act. 4, 5, 7**

Point out that if students feel they need to review material before doing the activities, they should consult the "To review" notes.

### ACTIVIDAD 3 Answers

1. jugué
2. llegué
3. presenté
4. empecé
5. busqué
6. buscó
7. saqué
8. encontré
9. pagué
10. corrí
11. almorzaron
12. almorcé

### ACTIVIDAD 4 Answers

1. Ustedes no dieron una fiesta.
2. Mariano hizo unas enchiladas.
3. Ernesto y yo vimos una película.
4. Él no fue a la escuela.
5. Nosotros hicimos la tarea.
6. Soledad y Raúl no hicieron la tarea.
7. Yo di un paseo.
8. Tú no fuiste de compras.
9. Mónica no hizo la cena.
10. Mi hermano(a) no vio la televisión.
11. Jorge viajó en moto.
12. Mis abuelos(as) jugaron al ajedrez.

## Block Schedule

**Skit—La clase como aeropuerto**

Ask students to bring in vocabulary items (**boletos, maletas, pasaportes, documentos de identificación, pases de abordar,** etc.). Designate specific roles for students, e.g., **los auxiliares de vuelo, los agentes de viaje, los pasajeros, los agentes de aduana,** etc. Ask small groups to develop and present a skit.

## Teaching Resource Options

### Print

Unit 1 Resource Book
Audioscript, p. 94
Cooperative Quizzes, pp. 95–96
Etapa Exam, Forms A and B, pp. 97–106
*Examen para hispanohablantes,* pp. 107–111
Portfolio Assessment, pp. 112–113
Multiple Choice Test Questions, pp. 243–245

### Audiovisual

OHT 5–6, 14 (Quick Start)
Audio Program Cassette 19 / CD 19; (*Para hispanohablantes* Cassette 19A / CD 19)

### Technology

Electronic Teacher Tools/Test Generator
www.mcdougallittell.com

## Quick Start Review

Interrogatives

Use OHT 14 or write on board: Use a word from each column to create as many questions as you can. Verbs should be in the preterite.

| | | |
|---|---|---|
| ¿Dónde | ir | tú? |
| ¿Cuándo | comprar | ella? |
| ¿Por qué | tomar un curso | Ud.? |
| ¿Qué | comer | |
| | acampar | |

**Answers**, see p. 27D.

### Actividad 5 and Actividad 6

**Rubric: Speaking**

| Criteria | Scale | |
|---|---|---|
| Fluency | 1 2 3 | A = 8–9 pts. |
| Vocabulary | 1 2 3 | B = 6–7 pts. |
| Pronunciation, rhythm | 1 2 3 | C = 4–5 pts. |
| | | D = 2–3 pts. |
| | | F = < 2 pts. |

### Actividad 7 En tu propia voz

**Rubric: Writing**

| Criteria | Scale | |
|---|---|---|
| Vocabulary use | 1 2 3 4 5 | A = 14–15 pts. |
| Accuracy | 1 2 3 4 5 | B = 12–13 pts. |
| Creativity, appearance | 1 2 3 4 5 | C = 10–11 pts. |
| | | D = 8–9 pts. |
| | | F = < 8 pts. |

## Actividad 5 ¿Y tú?

**PARA CONVERSAR**

**STRATEGY: SPEAKING**

**Get more information** How do you keep a conversation going? One way is to ask questions that cannot be answered with **sí** or **no.** Find out more from your partner by asking an additional question that uses **qué, cómo, cuándo, quién, cuál, dónde,** or **por qué.**

Pregúntale a tu compañero(a) de clase si participó en varias actividades el verano pasado. Completa una tabla como la siguiente. *(Hint: Ask your partner about activities and complete a chart.)*

**modelo**

**Tú:** *¿Trabajaste?*
**Compañero(a):** *Sí, trabajé en un restaurante.*
**Tú:** *¿Qué hiciste? ¿Estudiaste?*
**Compañero(a):** *No, no estudié. Fui a Florida.*

| Sí | No | Más información |
|---|---|---|
| 1. Trabajó en un restaurante. | 1. No estudió. | 1. Fue a Florida. |
| 2. | 2. | 2. |
| 3. | 3. | 3. |

## Actividad 6 El verano

Usando la información de la Actividad 5, conversen en grupos de cuatro sobre las actividades de los compañeros. Después, completen las oraciones con las actividades más interesantes del grupo. *(Hint: Discuss your partners' summer activities, and complete the sentences.)*

1. Una persona trabajó en un restaurante.
2. Otra persona _____.
3. Dos personas _____.
4. Todos nosotros _____, _____ y _____.

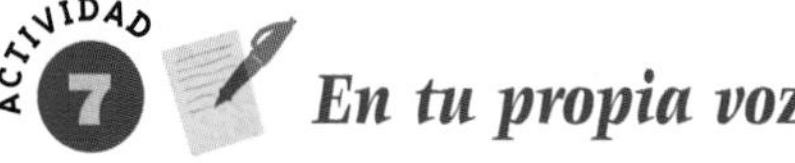

## Actividad 7 *En tu propia voz*

**ESCRITURA** Imagínate que fuiste de viaje a otro país. Describe el viaje, contestando las preguntas. Luego escribe un párrafo. *(Hint: Describe an imaginary trip. Write a paragraph using your answers to the questions.)*

1. ¿Adónde fuiste?
2. ¿Qué hiciste en preparación para el viaje? ¿Hablaste con un agente de viajes?
3. ¿Qué pasó en el aeropuerto?
4. ¿Qué hiciste en el otro país?

### TÚ EN LA COMUNIDAD

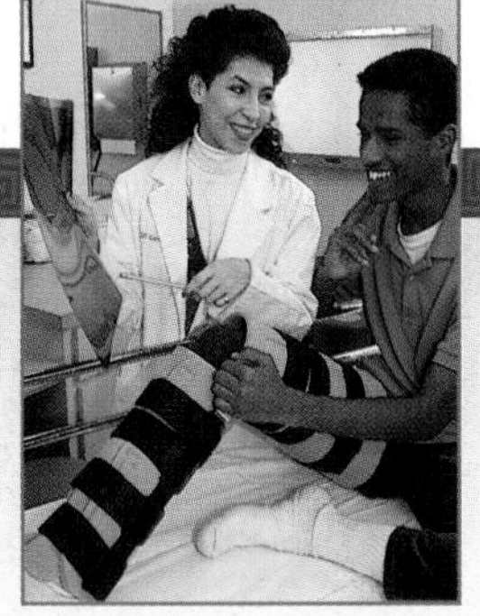

**Francisco** nació en la República Dominicana y ahora es estudiante en New Jersey. Él trabaja después de las clases y frecuentemente usa el español cuando tiene que ayudar a su jefe a conversar con clientes. También, en su trabajo de voluntario en un hospital, usó su español para ayudar a un paciente a comunicarse con los doctores. ¿Usas tu español para ayudar a los demás?



## Classroom Community

**Group Activity** **Chain Links:** Go around the class and have students contribute to a chain story using the preterite verbs listed on p. 49. Each student should repeat what the previous student(s) said and add another sentence.

**Learning Scenario** **Mini-skit:** In small groups have students create a mini-skit using as much of the lesson's vocabulary as possible. Have them solve one of the following air travel problems: The traveler missed his/her flight. The baggage was too heavy. The traveler can't find his/her ticket. The problems could be put on cards so students can choose one and work quickly with a group to develop a dialog.

# En resumen

## REPASO DE VOCABULARIO

### TALK ABOUT WHERE YOU WENT AND WHAT YOU DID

**Ya sabes: Regular Preterite Verbs**

| | |
|---|---|
| **comer** | *to eat* |
| **hablar** | *to speak, to talk* |
| **vivir** | *to live* |

**The Preterite: -car, -gar, and -zar**

| | |
|---|---|
| **comenzar (e→ie)** | *to start* |
| **explicar** | *to explain* |

**Ya sabes**

| | |
|---|---|
| **almorzar (o→ue)** | *to eat lunch* |
| **buscar** | *to look for* |
| **empezar (e→ie)** | *to begin* |
| **jugar (u→ue)** | *to play* |
| **llegar** | *to arrive* |
| **pagar** | *to pay* |
| **practicar** | *to practice* |
| **sacar** | *to take* |
| **tocar** | *to touch, to play (a musical instrument)* |

**Ya sabes: Irregular Preterite Verbs**

| | |
|---|---|
| **dar** | *to give* |
| **hacer** | *to make, to do* |
| **ir** | *to go* |
| **ser** | *to be* |
| **ver** | *to see* |

### DISCUSS LEISURE TIME

| | |
|---|---|
| **acampar en las montañas** | *to camp in the mountains* |
| **bajar un río en canoa** | *to go down a river by canoe* |
| **cantar en el coro** | *to sing in the chorus* |
| **disfrutar con los amigos** | *to enjoy time with friends* |
| **estudiar las artes marciales** | *to study martial arts* |
| **jugar (u→ue) al ajedrez** | *to play chess* |
| **tomar un curso de natación** | *to take a swimming class* |

### COMMENT ON AIRPLANE TRAVEL

| | |
|---|---|
| **abordar** | *to board* |
| **la aduana** | *customs* |
| **la aerolínea** | *airline* |
| **el (la) agente de viajes** | *travel agent* |
| **el asiento** | *seat* |
| **el (la) auxiliar de vuelo** | *flight attendant* |
| **el boleto** | *ticket* |
| **el equipaje** | *luggage* |
| **el exceso de equipaje** | *excess luggage* |
| **la identificación** | *identification* |
| **el letrero** | *sign* |
| **la llegada** | *arrival* |
| **la maleta** | *suitcase* |
| **el mostrador** | *counter* |
| **el (la) pasajero(a)** | *passenger* |
| **el pasaporte** | *passport* |
| **el pasillo** | *aisle* |
| **el piloto** | *pilot* |
| **la salida** | *departure* |
| **la seguridad** | *security* |
| **la ventanilla** | *window* |
| **el viaje** | *trip* |
| **el vuelo** | *flight* |

### Juego

Pablo, Tania, Luis y Josefa hacen actividades diferentes. Usa las frases y la tabla para decidir a quién le gusta cantar en el coro, a quién le gusta jugar al ajedrez, a quién le gusta acampar y a quién le gusta practicar las artes marciales.

1. A Pablo no le gusta el ajedrez.
2. Luis tiene que cuidar su voz.
3. Josefa ganó un cinturón negro.
4. Una chica juega al ajedrez.

| | coro | ajedrez | artes marciales | acampar |
|---|---|---|---|---|
| Pablo | | | | |
| Tania | | | | |
| Luis | | | | |
| Josefa | | | | |



## Teaching Note: En tu propia voz

**Writing Strategy** After reading the questions in **Actividad 7**, have students brainstorm additional questions they might ask. The more questions they have to answer, the more details they will have for their paragraphs.

## Teaching Suggestion

**Vocabulary Review**
Have students look at the "Now you can..." notes listed in the left margin of pp. 46–47. Point out that if they feel they need to review material before doing the activities or taking the test, they should consult the "To review" notes.

## Juego

**Answers**
A Pablo le gusta acampar, a Tania le gusta jugar al ajedrez, a Luis le gusta cantar en el coro, y a Josefa le gusta practicar las artes marciales.

## Community Connection

Have students list the places where they might be able to use Spanish in their own community and discuss which Spanish expressions would be most useful in each place they list.

## Project: Reviewing Etapa 1

- Find out about a current event in a Spanish-speaking community in the U.S. (via Internet, etc.)
- Have students scan the headlines of a Spanish publication and write a short summary of it.

**Extra Credit**

| | |
|---|---|
| Current event | 4 pts. |
| Spanish publication | 4 pts. |

## Block Schedule

**Peer Teaching** In pairs, have students exchange their review notes and quiz each other.

## Teaching All Students

**Extra Help** Have students start a verb chart in their notebooks in which they conjugate new verbs they learn in the preterite. Students can start the chart with the verbs listed on p. 49.

**Native Speakers** Have Spanish speakers create additional **Juegos** similar to the one on p. 49 for the class to analyze.

### Multiple Intelligences

**Intrapersonal** Have students copy 10 vocabulary words for a personal list in their notebooks. Have students expand the list by adding other words or phrases associated with these words, which will help them remember them. You can then have students share their annotated lists with their classmates.

# Planning Guide CLASSROOM MANAGEMENT

## OBJECTIVES

**Communication**
- Discuss fine art *pp. 52, 54–55, 64, 66–67*
- Comment on food *pp. 53, 55, 57, 60*
- Talk about the past *pp. 61–63*
- Express activity preferences *pp. 55, 59*

**Grammar**
- The present tense of **e→ie** and **u→ue** verbs *p. 58*
- Irregular preterite verbs *p. 61*

**Culture**
- **El Centro Museo de Bellas Artes Mexicanas de Chicago** *p. 62*
- **La hora de la cena en muchos países hispanos** *p. 65*
- Chicago Latino artists *pp. 66–67*

**Recycling**
- Present tense stem-changing verbs, **i→ie** and **o→ue**
- The irregular preterite verbs **ir**, **ser**, **hacer**, **ver**, **dar**
- Food vocabulary
- Talking about leisure time activities
- Telling time
- Travel vocabulary
- Expressions of frequency

## STRATEGIES

**Listening Strategies**
- Identify the main idea *p. 54*

**Speaking Strategies**
- Use all you know *p. 59*
- Give reasons why *p. 70*

**Reading Strategies**
- Scan for proper names *TE p. 66*

**Writing Strategies**
- Use interrogatives to organize details, *Actividad* 8, *TE p. 70*

**Connecting Cultures Strategies**
- Describe the nature of murals *p. 66*
- Become aware of murals in your community *p. 66*

## PROGRAM RESOURCES

### Print

- *Más práctica* Workbook PE *pp. 21–30*
- Block Scheduling Copymasters *pp. 17–24*
- Unit 1 Resource Book
  - *Más práctica* Workbook TE *pp. 114–123*
  - *Cuaderno para hispanohablantes* TE *pp. 124–133*
  - Information Gap Activities *pp. 134–137*
  - Family Involvement *pp. 138–139*
  - Video Activities *pp. 140–142*
  - Videoscript *pp. 143–144*
  - Audioscript *pp. 145–149*
  - Assessment Program Unit 1 Etapa 2 *pp. 151–168; 246–248*
  - Answer Keys *pp. 254–255; 258*

### Audiovisual

- Audio Program Cassette 2A, 2B / CD 2
- Video Program Videotape 1 / Videodisc 1A
- Overheard Transparencies M1–M5; 15–24

### Technology

- Electronic Teacher Tools/Test Generator
- *Intrigas y aventuras* CD-ROM, Disc 1
- 

www.mcdougallittell.com

### Assessment Program Options

- Cooperative Quizzes (Unit 1 Resource Book)
- Etapa Exam Forms A and B (Unit 1 Resource Book)
- *Examen para hispanohablantes* (Unit 1 Resource Book)
- Multiple Choice Test Questions (Unit 1 Resource Book)
- Portfolio Assessment (Unit 1 Resource Book)
- Audio Program Cassette 19A / CD 19
- Electronic Teacher Tools/Test Generator

### Native Speakers

- *Cuaderno para hispanohablantes* PE *pp. 21–30*
- *Cuaderno para hispanohablantes* TE (Unit 1 Resource Book)
- *Examen para hispanohablantes* (Unit 1 Resource Book)
- Audio Program *(Para hispanohablantes)* Cassettes 2B, 19A / CD 2, CD 19
- Audioscript (Unit 1 Resource Book)

Pedro | Francisco | Señora Álvarez

# Student Text Listening Activity Scripts

##  Videoscript: Diálogo *pages 54–55*

• Videotape 1, 13:27 • Videodisc 1A

Search Chapter 6, Play to 7
U1E2, En vivo (Dialog)

• Use the videoscript with **Actividades 1, 2** *page 56*

Pedro: Bienvenido a Chicago, Francisco. Mi esposa me preguntó si te gusta el cuarto que te preparamos.

Francisco: Sí, muchas gracias. Me gusta mucho. Tu esposa es muy simpática, Pedro. Y tu hija es preciosa. ¿Cuántos años tiene?

Pedro: La semana pasada cumplió siete años. Oye, viniste directamente de Los Ángeles, ¿no?

Francisco: Sí, estuve la semana pasada con mi familia en Los Ángeles. Lo pasé muy bien. Vi a mis abuelos y mis tíos, y salí con mi prima Verónica.

Pedro: ¿Estás listo para tu primer trabajo?

Francisco: Sí, pero estoy un poco nervioso. ¿Cúando empezamos?

Pedro: Tranquilo, Paco. Hay tiempo. Tenemos una cita esta tarde con la señora Álvarez en la galería de arte. Ahora, vamos a comer algo. ¿No tienes hambre?

Francisco: Me muero de hambre.

Pedro: ¿Qué deseas comer, comida puertorriqueña o comida china? No muy lejos de aquí encuentras las dos.

Francisco: Pues, prefiero el restaurante puertorriqueño.

Pedro: Perfecto. La última vez que estuve allí, me sirvieron un postre de uvas y melón delicioso. Y la especialidad de la casa es pollo asado con tostones, arroz, y habichuelas coloradas. Lo recomiendo.

Francisco: ¡Qué buena exposición! Tienen de todo. Hay pinturas, retratos, esculturas. Mira esa escultura. ¡Qué bella!

Pedro: Sí, es excelente. Pero, no conozco al escultor.

Francisco: Chicago es una ciudad con mucho arte, ¿verdad?

Pedro: Sí, por eso decidimos preparar un artículo sobre las bellas artes en Chicago, y en particular sobre los artistas latinos. ¿Qué más te gusta hacer, Francisco?

Francisco: Pues, me encantan los deportes, sobre todo el béisbol. ¿Y a ti te gustan los deportes?

Pedro: Sí, bastante, pero no participo mucho en deportes de equipo. Prefiero los deportes que se hacen a solas. Me encanta la natación.

Sra. Álvarez: Buenas tardes, Sr. Camacho.

Pedro: Buenas tardes, Sra. Álvarez. Gracias por su tiempo.

Sra. Álvarez: Es un placer. ¿Así que tú eres Francisco García, y vas a entrevistar a Alejandro Romero?

Francisco: Sí, mucho gusto en conocerla, Sra. Álvarez.

Sra. Álvarez: Igualmente. Bueno, vamos, y les cuento algo del pintor.

Pedro: ¿Trajiste tu cuaderno? Debes tomar apuntes.

Francisco: Sí, lo traje. Aquí está.

Sra. Álvarez: Alejandro Romero es uno de nuestros artistas más famosos. Él nació en México pero ahora vive en Chicago. Esta pintura es de él. Es una de mis favoritas.

Francisco: Me encanta... Quiero escribir un buen artículo pero estoy un poco nervioso. ¿Qué debo preguntarle a Alejandro Romero en la entrevista? ¡No sé! ¡No sé!

Pedro: Cálmate, Francisco. Pronto estamos en mi casa. ¿No quieres decansar un ratito?

Francisco: Sí, tienes razón. No dormí mucho anoche.

Pedro: Pues, ¿por qué no duermes un hora? Después, tú y yo podemos hablar de las preguntas para la entrevista.

Francisco: Sí, perfecto. A ver... Le puedo preguntar cuándo vino a Chicago, o le puedo preguntar si prefiere colores brillantes o colores suaves...

##  Actividad 9 En Chicago *page 60*

En el museo, Francisco ve muchas pinturas, retratos y esculturas. En las tiendas turísticas del museo, él compra fotografías de esculturas de artistas latinoamericanos. En general, Francisco prefiere las esculturas porque piensa que son la forma de arte más difícil. Después de ver el arte en la galería, Francisco y Pedro van a almorzar a un restaurante puertorriqueño. Ellos deciden ir allí porque a Francisco le gusta mucho el pollo asado, los tostones y las habichuelas coloradas.

## Actividad 16 Una semana internacional *page 65*

¡Muy buenas! Soy Tina y quiero decirles lo que hicimos en nuestro colegio para celebrar *La semana internacional de lenguas extranjeras.* Todos los estudiantes participaron. Les cuento ejemplos de sus actividades. La señorita Martín ayudó a pensar en actividades culturales. En mi clase, Sara trajo su guitarra y tocó música española. Los estudiantes de francés trajeron comida sabrosa a la escuela y la clase de español hizo una piñata. ¡Qué divertido! El viernes, Rocío y Emilio bailaron un baile tradicional de México. Fue muy bonito. El director de la escuela también participó; cada día saludó en varias lenguas. Y, ¿qué hice yo? Pues, esta presentación, ¡claro!

### Quick Start Review Answers

**p. 54** En contexto vocabulary
1. a. retrato; 2. c. pintor; 3. b. galería de arte

**p. 56** Preterite
1. Pedro y Francisco fueron a un restaurante puertorriqueño.
2. Ellos comieron pollo asado.
3. Ellos visitaron una galería de arte.
4. Francisco vio una escultura muy bella.
5. La señora Álvarez habló de la vida de Alejandro Romero.

**p. 61** Irregular preterite
1. Nosotros hicimos un viaje a Los Ángeles.
2. Yo fui de compras.
3. Luis y Ana fueron a un partido de béisbol.
4. Nosotros vimos unos murales bellísimos.

**p. 64** Adjectives
*Answers will vary. Answers could include:*
1. Las esculturas son bellas.
2. La galería de arte es pequeña.
3. Pedro es simpático.
4. Los museos de Chicago son interesantes.

# Pacing Guide

## Sample Lesson Plan - 50 Minute Schedule

### DAY 1

**Etapa Opener**
- Quick Start Review (TE, p. 50) 5 MIN.
- Anticipate/Activate prior knowledge: Have students look at the *Etapa* Opener and answer *¿Qué ves?* questions. 10 MIN.

**En contexto: Vocabulario**
- Quick Start Review (TE, p. 52) 3 MIN.
- Discuss pictures, have students use context and pictures to learn *Etapa* vocabulary. Answer questions, p. 53. 10 MIN.

**En vivo: Diálogo**
- Quick Start Review (TE, p. 54) 2 MIN.
- Review Listening strategy, p. 54. Play audio or show video for the dialog on pp. 54–55. 7 MIN.
- Replay dialog. Read aloud, students taking roles of characters. 8 MIN.
- Students role-play in groups while looking at the photos in their texts. Encourage them to come up with logical dialog using familiar vocabulary. 5 MIN.

**Homework Option:**
- Video Activities, Unit 1 Resource Book, pp. 140–142.

### DAY 2

**En acción: Vocabulario y gramática**
- Check homework. 5 MIN.
- Quick Start Review (TE, p. 56) 5 MIN.
- Ask students for a summary of *En vivo* dialog to check recall. 5 MIN.
- Replay the *En vivo* dialog using the audiovisual resources and have students do *Actividades* 1 and 2 orally. 10 MIN.
- Have students complete *Actividad* 3 orally. 5 MIN.
- Present *Nota,* p. 57, and have students do *Actividad* 4 in pairs. 7 MIN.
- Use a scenario game or expansion activity (TE, pp. 56–57) to reinforce retention of vocabulary and dialog structures. 13 MIN.

**Homework Option:**
- *Más práctica* Workbook, pp. 23–24 as needed. *Cuaderno para hispanohablantes*, p. 22.

### DAY 3

**En acción (cont.)**
- Check homework. 5 MIN.
- Quick Start Review (TE, p. 58). 5 MIN.
- Present *Gramática:* Present Tense of i→ie and u→ue Verbs, p. 58. 10 MIN.
- Have students do *Actividad* 5 in writing. Check orally. 5 MIN.
- Discuss Speaking Strategy, p. 59. Have students do *Actividades* 6 and 7 in pairs. 10 MIN.
- Present vocabulary and do *Actividad* 8 in groups. 5 MIN.
- Play audio and do *Actividad* 9 orally. 10 MIN.

**Homework Option:**
- Have students do *Actividad* 9 in writing. *Más práctica* Workbook, pp. 25–26. *Cuaderno para hispanohablantes*, pp. 23–24.

### DAY 4

**En acción (cont.)**
- Check homework. 5 MIN.
- Quick Start Review (TE, p. 61). 5 MIN.
- Present *Gramática:* Irregular Preterite Verbs, p. 61. 10 MIN.
- Have students do *Actividad* 10 in writing. Check orally. 5 MIN.
- Have students do *Actividades* 11, 12, and 13 in pairs. 15 MIN.
- Review vocabulary on p. 63 and have students complete *Actividad* 14 orally or in writing. 10 MIN.

**Homework Option:**
- *Más práctica* Workbook, pp. 27–30. *Cuaderno para hispanohablantes*, pp. 25–28.

### DAY 5

**En acción (cont.)**
- Check homework. 5 MIN.
- Quick Start Review (TE, p. 64) 5 MIN.
- Present vocabulary on p. 64 and have students complete *Actividad* 15 orally. Have volunteers present their opinions. 10 MIN.
- Play audio for students and do *Actividad* 16 in writing. You can also review orally with the whole class. 10 MIN.
- Have students do *Actividad* 17 in pairs. Expand with *Más comunicación,* p. R3. 8 MIN.
- Discuss *Nota cultural* on p. 62 and p. 65. 7 MIN.
- Quick Wrap-Up (TE, p. 65) 5 MIN.

**Homework Option:**
- Have students do *Actividad* 17 in writing.

### DAY 6

- Check homework. 5 MIN.
- Review the *Refrán* on page 65. 5 MIN.
- Quick Start Review (TE, p. 66) 5 MIN.

**En colores: Cultura y comparaciones**
- Review Connecting Cultures Strategy, p. 66. 5 MIN.
- Read *El arte latino de Chicago* aloud with students. 10 MIN.
- Have students answer the *¿Comprendiste?* and *¿Qué piensas?* activities orally. 7 MIN.
- Divide class into small groups and have them begin the *Hazlo tú* activity on p. 67. 13 MIN.

**Homework Option:**
- Have students do *En uso, Actividades* 1–5, pp. 68–69. *Cuaderno para hispanohablantes*, pp. 29-30.

### DAY 7

**En uso: Repaso**
- Quick Start Review (TE, p. 68) 5 MIN.
- Have students peer-check *Actividades* 1–5 (homework), then check orally with class. Discuss problem areas. 20 MIN.

**En uso: Más comunicación y conexiones**
- Review Speaking Strategy, p. 70. Then do *Actividad* 6 orally in pairs and *Actividad* 7 in groups. 15 MIN.
- Begin *Actividad* 8. 10 MIN.

**Homework Option:**
- Have students review for the *Etapa* 2 Exam. Finish *Actividad* 8.

### DAY 8

**En tu propia voz: Escritura**
- Peer-edit *Actividad* 8. Have students share descriptions with class. 10 MIN.

**Conexiones**
- Read and discuss. 5 MIN.
- Review grammar questions, etc. as necessary. 5 MIN.
- Complete *Etapa* 2 Exam. 20 MIN.

**Ampliación**
- Use a suggested project, game, or activity. (TE pp. 27A–27B) 10 MIN.

**Homework Option:**
- Preview *Etapa* 3 Opener, pp. 72–73.

# Sample Lesson Plan - Block Schedule (90 minutes)

## DAY 1

***Etapa* Opener**
- Quick Start Review (TE, p. 50) 5 MIN.
- Anticipate/Activate prior knowledge: Have students look at the *Etapa* Opener and answer *¿Qué ves?* questions. 10 MIN.

**En contexto: Vocabulario**
- Quick Start Review (TE, p. 52) 5 MIN.
- Discuss pictures, have students use context and pictures to learn *Etapa* vocabulary. Answer questions, p. 53. 10 MIN.

**En vivo: Diálogo**
- Review Listening Strategy, p. 54. Play audio or show video for the dialog on pp. 54–55. 10 MIN.
- Ask Comprehension Questions (TE, p. 55). 5 MIN.
- Replay dialog. Read aloud, students taking roles of characters. 10 MIN.
- Students role-play in groups while looking at the photos in their texts. Encourage them to come up with logical dialog using familiar vocabulary. 10 MIN.

**En acción: Vocabulario y gramática**
- Quick Start Review (TE, p. 56) 5 MIN.
- Ask students for a summary of the *En vivo* dialog. Have students do *Actividades* 1 and 2 orally. 10 MIN.
- Do *Actividad* 3 orally. 5 MIN.
- Present *Nota,* p. 57. Have students do *Actividad* 4 in pairs. 5 MIN.

**Homework Option:**
- Have students prepare two T/F or yes/no questions about the dialog. Video Activities, Unit 1 Resource Book, pp. 140–142.

## DAY 2

**En acción (cont.)**
- Check homework. 5 MIN.
- Quick Start Review (TE, p. 58) 5 MIN.
- Present *Gramática:* Present Tense of i→ie and u→ue Verbs, p. 58. 10 MIN.
- Have students write *Actividad* 5. Check on the board. 5 MIN.
- Discuss Strategy, p. 59. Have students do *Actividades* 6 and 7 in pairs. 10 MIN.
- Present *Vocabulario,* p. 60, and do *Actividad* 8 in groups. 10 MIN.
- Play audio and do *Actividad* 9 orally. 5 MIN.
- Present *Gramática*: Irregular Preterite Verbs on p. 61. 10 MIN.
- Have students do *Actividad* 10 in writing. 5 MIN.
- Have students do *Actividades* 11, 12, and 13 in pairs. 15 MIN.
- Review vocabulary on p. 63 and have students complete *Actividad* 14 in writing. 10 MIN.

**Homework Option:**
- *Más práctica* Workbook, pp. 23–30 as needed. *Cuaderno para hispanohablantes*, pp. 22–28 as needed.

## DAY 3

- Check homework. 5 MIN.
- Quick Start Review (TE, p. 64) 5 MIN.

**En acción (cont.)**
- Present vocabulary on p. 64 and have students complete *Actividad* 15 orally. Have volunteers present their opinions. 10 MIN.
- Play audio for students and do *Actividad* 16 in writing. Review answers orally with the whole class. 10 MIN.
- Have students do *Actividad* 17 in pairs. Expand with *Más comunicación,* p. R3. 10 MIN.
- Discuss *Nota cultural* on p. 62 and p. 65. 10 MIN.
- Review the *Refrán* on p. 65. 5 MIN.
- Use Block Scheduling Copymasters. 10 MIN.
- Quick Wrap-Up (TE, p. 65) 5 MIN.

**Ampliación**
- Use a suggested project, game, or activity. (TE pp. 27A–27B) 20 MIN.

**Homework Option:**
- Have students complete *Actividad* 17 in writing. *Cuaderno para hispanohablantes*, pp. 29–30.

## DAY 4

**En colores: Cultura y comparaciones**
- Quick Start Review (TE, p. 66) 5 MIN.
- Review Connecting Cultures Strategy, p. 66. 5 MIN.
- Read *El Arte latino de Chicago* aloud with students. 15 MIN.
- Have students answer the *¿Comprendiste?* and *¿Qué piensas?* activities in writing. Check orally. 15 MIN.
- Divide class into small groups and have them begin the *Hazlo tú* activity on p. 67. 15 MIN.
- Quick Wrap-Up (TE, p. 65) 5 MIN.

**Ampliación**
- Use a suggested project, game, or activity. (TE pp. 27A– 27B) 20 MIN.
- Discuss and begin *En uso* Activities, pp. 68–69. 10 MIN.

**Homework Option:**
- Have students complete *En uso* Activities 1–4, pp. 68–69. *Cuaderno para hispanohablantes*, pp. 29–30.

## DAY 5

**En uso: Repaso**
- Quick Start Review (TE, p. 68) 5 MIN.
- Have students peer-check *Actividades* 1–4 (homework), then check orally with class. Discuss problem areas. 25 MIN.

**En uso: Más comunicación y conexiones**
- Review Speaking Strategy, p. 70. Then do *Actividad* 6 orally in pairs and *Actividad* 7 in groups. 15 MIN.

**Conexiones**
- Read and discuss. 5 MIN.
- Review grammar questions, etc. as necessary. 10 MIN.
- Complete *Etapa* 2 Exam. 20 MIN.

**En tu propia voz: Escritura**
- Start *Actividad* 8. 10 MIN.

**Homework Option:**
- Finish *Actividad* 8 and preview *Etapa* 3 Opener, pp. 72–73.

▼ Francisco y Pedro escuchan a la señora Álvarez en la galería.

## Etapa Theme

**Expressing activity preferences, commenting on food and fine art, talking about the past**

## Grammar Objectives

- Irregular preterite verbs
- Present-tense stem-changing verbs e→ie, u→ue

### Teaching Resource Options

**Print** 

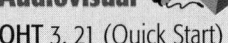

Block Scheduling Copymasters

**Audiovisual**

OHT 3, 21 (Quick Start)

### Quick Start Review

Food

Use OHT 21 or write on board: Copy the list of words and circle the food items you see in the painting on p. 50.

| | |
|---|---|
| el melón | la cebolla |
| el queso | el helado |
| la salchicha | el pimiento |

*Items that should be circled:*
el melón, la cebolla, el pimiento

### Teaching Suggestions
**Previewing the Etapa**

- Ask students to study the people and the setting of the photo on pp. 50–51.
- Ask students to comment on the artwork they see in the photo.
- Ask students to predict what the 3 people in the photo may be discussing. Have them create a short dialog.

## Critical Thinking

Ask students to discuss various art forms they have already studied. How does art contribute to their lives?

UNIDAD 1

# ¿Qué prefieres?

- Comment on food
- Talk about the past
- Express activity preferences
- Discuss fine art

# EL ARTE LATINO

### ¿Qué ves?

Mira la foto de la galería. ¿Qué ves?

1. Haz una lista de todo lo que ves en la foto.
2. ¿Dónde crees que están Francisco y las otras personas?
3. ¿Qué hacen allí?

50

## Classroom Management

**Planning Ahead** Prepare to introduce students to discussing art in Spanish by gathering photographs or prints from a variety of Hispanic artists. You may also wish to gather pictures of food or menus from restaurants in your area that serve food from Spanish-speaking countries to use when commenting on food in this Etapa.

**Peer Teaching** After you have reviewed the **¿Qué ves?** questions with the class, have students work with a partner to create 2 additional **¿Qué ves?** questions. Then have each set of partners ask another set of partners their new questions.

DE CHICAGO

## Cross Cultural Connections

Ask students what kinds of influences they might find in artwork done by Spanish-speaking artists who live in the U.S. Can they think of any Spanish-speaking artists in their community?

## Culture Highlights

- **SPANISH SPEAKERS IN CHICAGO** Almost 20% of the population of Chicago is Hispanic with the majority being from Mexico and Puerto Rico.
- **ALEJANDRO ROMERO** Both paintings on pp. 50–51 are by the Mexican-American artist Alejandro Romero. The painting on p. 50 is *Untitled,* and the one on p. 51 is called *Minotauro #2.* Students will learn more about Alejandro Romero in the **En colores** reading in this Etapa (pp. 66–67).

## Teaching Suggestions

### Photo

- The art gallery shown is located in Chicago's **Barrio Pilsen**.
- Have students try to guess the identity of the people in the photograph. (Francisco meets with his friend Pedro and Señora Álvarez, the gallery director.) Ask students the following questions: **¿Dónde están? ¿De qué hablan las tres personas? ¿Qué piensas del arte en la foto?**

## Teaching All Students

**Extra Help** Post a list of adjectives that could describe art. Have students choose an example of artwork from the textbook and say why they like or dislike it, using **(No) Me gusta porque...**

**Native Speakers** Ask Spanish speakers to discuss any Hispanic artists they may know from their community. Ask them to bring in examples of their artwork and describe it to the class.

### Multiple Intelligences

**Visual** Ask students to describe the artwork on pp. 50–51 using these questions as a guide: **¿Qué colores ven en las pinturas? ¿Qué comida ven en las pinturas?**

## Block Schedule

**Change of Pace** Have students list all the artists they know on the board. Then have them identify if they work on **pintura, escultura, retrato,** or **otra cosa** (another medium). (For additional activities, see **Block Scheduling Copymasters.**)

## Teaching Resource Options

**Print** 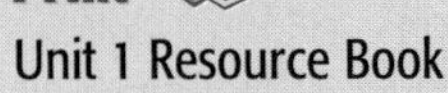

**Unit 1 Resource Book**
- Video Activities, p. 140
- Videoscript, p. 143
- Audioscript, p. 145

**Audiovisual** 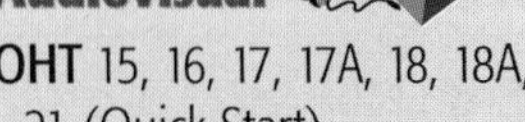

**OHT** 15, 16, 17, 17A, 18, 18A, 21 (Quick Start)

**Audio Program** Cassette 2A / CD 2

**Video Program** Videotape 1, 11:12 / Videodisc 1A

Search Chapter 5, Play to 6
U1E2, En contexto (Vocabulary)

**Technology** 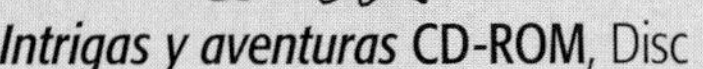

*Intrigas y aventuras* **CD-ROM**, Disc 1

## Quick Start Review

**Snacks**

Use **OHT** 21 or write on board: Answer the following with a complete sentence in Spanish.

1. ¿Cuando vas a un café, pides un vaso de agua o un refresco?
2. ¿Prefieres comer las papas fritas o una ensalada?
3. ¿Para una merienda comes fruta o helado?
4. ¿Prefieres las papas fritas o la pizza?

*Answers will vary.*
1. Pido un...
2. Prefiero comer...
3. Para una merienda como...
4. Prefiero...

# En contexto

## VOCABULARIO

Francisco está en Chicago. Las ilustraciones y las palabras en **azul** te ayudan a comprender lo que dice y a responder a las preguntas personales.

***En Chicago*** hay lugares muy modernos. Hay muchas cosas que ver y hacer. Y claro, ¡hay comida sabrosa!

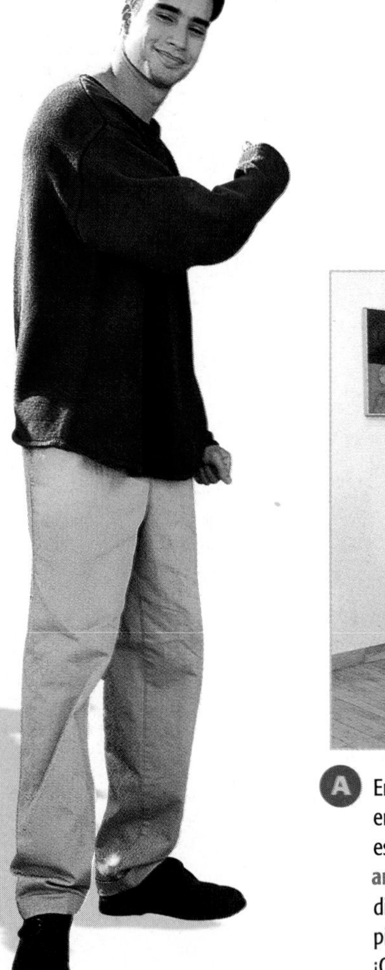

**A** En la galería de arte, puedes encontrar arte tradicional y arte que es un poco raro. **Los escultores, artistas** que hacen **esculturas,** son diferentes de **los pintores.** Los pintores hacen **retratos** y **pinturas.** ¡Qué talento!

el retrato



## Classroom Community

**TPR Prepare Ahead:** Bring in 3 examples of artwork: **pintura**, **escultura**, and **retrato**, and put each one in a different part of the classroom. Have selected groups of students take turns standing up and following your directions. When you say **pintura** students go to the painting; when you say **escultura** students go to the sculpture, etc. You can also say the verb forms for them to follow your direction: **pintar**, **esculpir**, **retratar**.

**Paired Activity** Have students choose one of the new vocabulary words and describe it in Spanish or act it out to a partner. The partner should be able to guess the word.

**B** Hay muchos restaurantes en Chicago. En los restaurantes puedes hablar con algunos artistas mientras tomas un café. Los meseros son muy simpáticos y te pueden **recomendar** algo rico.

¡Bienvenidos!
Especialidades del día
Habichuelas coloradas
red beans
Tostones
fried plantains
Pollo asado
barbecued chicken
Batido de plátano
banana milk shake
¡Sabroso!

las uvas

el melón

**C** Si **deseas** comer, aquí vas a encontrar **las especialidades de la casa:** arroz con **habichuelas coloradas, tostones** de **plátano verde** y **pollo asado.** Si tienes sed, tal vez te gustaría un **batido.** También puedes comer frutas como **melón** o **uvas.**

¡Me encanta Chicago! Lo debes visitar algún día.

### Preguntas personales

1. A mucha gente le gustan los museos. ¿Hay un museo cerca de tu comunidad?
2. ¿Fuiste a un museo con tu escuela? ¿A cuál fuiste?
3. ¿Prefieres la escultura o la pintura? ¿Por qué?
4. A Francisco le gusta la comida de Puerto Rico. ¿A ti te gusta la comida puertorriqueña o la comida china?
5. ¿Cuál es tu comida favorita? ¿Qué postres te gustan?



## Teaching Suggestions

### Introducing Vocabulary

- Have students look at pp. 52–53. Use OHT 15–16 and Audiocassette 2A / CD 2 to present the vocabulary.
- Ask the Comprehension Questions in order of yes/no (questions 1–3), either/or (questions 4–6), and simple word or phrase (questions 7–10). You may expand by adding similar questions.
- Use the video vocabulary presentation for review and reinforcement.

## Comprehension Questions

1. ¿Está Francisco en California? (**No**)
2. ¿Está en una galería de arte? (**Sí**)
3. ¿Hacen retratos los pintores? (**Sí**)
4. ¿Los escultores hacen pinturas o esculturas? (**esculturas**)
5. ¿Hay batidos o refrescos en el menú? (**batidos**)
6. ¿Es el menú de un restaurante chino, puertorriqueño o italiano? (**puertorriqueño**)
7. ¿Hay uvas o naranjas en el menú? (**uvas**)
8. ¿Qué beben las dos personas de la foto? (**café**)
9. ¿Con quién consulta el señor de la izquierda? (**el mesero**)
10. ¿Qué pueden recomendar los meseros? (**algo rico, una especialidad de la casa**)

## Cross Cultural Connection

Many restaurants that serve food from Spanish-speaking countries or have Spanish-speaking customers may have their menus in English and Spanish. Ask students if they have been to any restaurants with menus in Spanish. Then ask them to describe the foods, menu, and Spanish words they recognized.

## Teaching All Students

**Extra Help** Explain the relationship between the following words: **el (la) artista** (artist) and **el arte** (art). Have students discuss the relationship between **pintor/pintura** and **escultor/escultura.** Then see if students can think of other examples.

**Challenge** Ask the following questions:
**¿Dónde se puede encontrar arte tradicional?**
**Explica lo que hace un escultor. ¿Y un pintor?**

**Native Speakers** You may ask Spanish speakers if they can suggest additional words for **mesero(a).**

### Multiple Intelligences

**Kinesthetic** Role-play in groups of 3 students. One student is the tour guide of the art gallery featured on pp. 52–53 and the other 2 students are tourists. Have them create a short dialog of their guided visit, including gestures.

## Block Schedule

**FunBreak** Plan ahead and bring in a blender or mixer and the ingredients needed to prepare **batidos** in class. You will need fresh fruits, milk, and ice.

## Teaching Resource Options

**Print**

Block Scheduling Copymasters
Unit 1 Resource Book
Video Activities, pp. 141–142
Videoscript, pp. 143–144
Audioscript, p. 145

**Audiovisual**

**OHT** 19, 20, 21 (Quick Start)
**Audio Program** Cassette 2A / CD 2
**Video Program** Videotape 1, 13:27 / Videodisc 1A

Search Chapter 6, Play to 7
U1E2, En vivo (Dialog)

**Technology**

*Intrigas y aventuras* **CD-ROM**, Disc 1

## Quick Start Review

**En contexto** vocabulary

Use OHT 21 or write on board: Match each of the following with an appropriate word in the second column.

1. pintura de una persona
2. Picasso
3. puedes ver o comprar arte allí

a. retrato
b. galería de arte
c. pintor

**Answers**, see p. 49B.

## Teaching Suggestions
### Presenting the Dialog

Focus on the dialog context using yes/no or either/or questions. Reintroduce the characters and the setting: ¿Está Francisco en una galería de arte? ¿Visita Francisco a Pedro o a su familia? ¿Va a trabajar Francisco durante su visita?

### Gestures

Have students note any gestures they see in the video for **Actividades 1** and **2**. Do the gestures assist them in understanding?

# En vivo
## DIÁLOGO

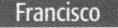

Pedro

Francisco

Señora Álvarez

**PARA ESCUCHAR • STRATEGY: LISTENING**

**Identify the main idea** Listening for the gist of a conversation is like skimming a reading to see what it's about. Try not to let the details distract you from the main idea. Listen for nouns and verbs as they carry the meaning. What task is Francisco getting ready for?

## En Chicago…

1► **Pedro:** Bienvenido a Chicago, Francisco. Viniste directamente de Los Ángeles, ¿no?
**Francisco:** Sí, estuve con mi familia. Vi a mis abuelos y mis tíos, y salí con mi prima Verónica.

5► **Francisco:** ¡Qué buena exposición! Hay pinturas, retratos, esculturas. Mira esta escultura. ¡Qué bella!
**Pedro:** Sí, es excelente. Pero no conozco al escultor.

6► **Señora Álvarez:** Buenas tardes.
**Pedro:** Gracias por su tiempo.
**Señora Álvarez:** Es un placer. ¿Así que tú eres Francisco García, y vas a entrevistar a Alejandro Romero? Vamos, y les cuento algo del pintor.

7► **Pedro:** ¿Trajiste tu cuaderno? Debes tomar apuntes.
**Francisco:** Sí, lo traje. Aquí está.



## Classroom Community

**Paired Activity** Have students choose a frame and describe it to their partner without referring to captions. The partner should be able to guess the appropriate frame.

**TPR** Create an art gallery in the classroom with several examples of artwork (posters, statues, etc.) around the room. Have students walk around and give their reactions to the artwork with comments and corresponding gestures. You can give them some sample comments, such as **¡Qué bonito!, Es excelente, (No) me gusta, ¡Qué feo!**, etc.

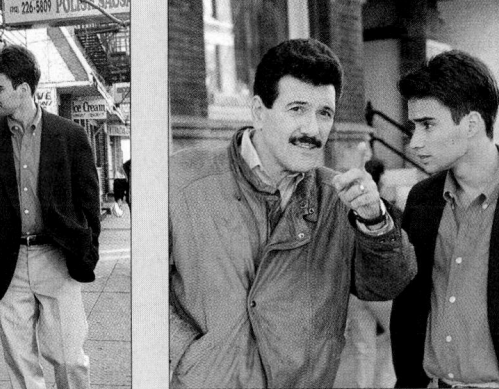

2 ▶ Pedro: ¿Estás listo para tu trabajo?
Francisco: Estoy un poco nervioso. ¿Cuándo empezamos?
Pedro: Esta tarde, en la galería de arte. Ahora, vamos a comer.

3 ▶ Pedro: ¿Qué deseas –comida puertorriqueña o comida china? No muy lejos de aquí encuentras las dos.
Francisco: Pues, prefiero el restaurante puertorriqueño.

4 ▶ Pedro: Perfecto. La última vez que estuve allí, me sirvieron un postre de uvas y melón delicioso. Y la especialidad de la casa es pollo asado con tostones, arroz y habichuelas coloradas. Lo recomiendo.

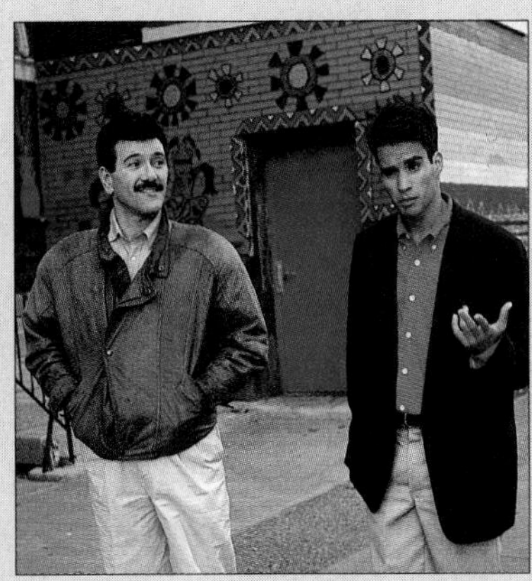

8 ▶ Señora Álvarez: Alejandro Romero es uno de nuestros artistas más famosos. Nació en México pero ahora vive en Chicago. Esta pintura es de él. Es una de mis favoritas.

9 ▶ Francisco: ¿Qué debo preguntarle a Alejandro Romero? ¡No sé! ¡No sé!
Pedro: Cálmate, Francisco. Pronto estamos en mi casa. ¿Por qué no duermes una hora? Después, podemos hablar de la entrevista.

10 ▶ Francisco: Sí, perfecto. A ver… Le puedo preguntar cuándo vino a Chicago, o le puedo preguntar si prefiere colores brillantes o colores suaves…



## Teaching All Students

**Extra Help** Have students work in groups of 3 to role-play portions of the dialog on pp. 54–55.

**Native Speakers** If there are Spanish speakers from Puerto Rico, ask them to discuss other Puerto Rican foods they like. Ask them to describe their favorite food and when they eat it. If possible, have them bring in the recipe or actual food to class.

**Challenge** Have students write the script for the interview between Francisco and artist Alejandro Romero.

### Multiple Intelligences

**Logical/Mathematical** Have students map out the places that Francisco visited upon his arrival in Chicago: **(el restaurante, la galería, la casa de Pedro...).**

## Video Synopsis

Use the video, audiocassette, or CD to present the dialog. The video version offers expanded language opportunities. Francisco arrives in Chicago, he goes to eat with Pedro and prepares to interview the artist Alejandro Romero. For a complete transcript of the video dialog, see p. 49B.

## Comprehension Questions

1. ¿Es de Chicago Pedro? **(Sí)**
2. ¿Está Francisco nervioso? **(Sí)**
3. ¿Van al cine por la tarde? **(No)**
4. ¿Prefiere Francisco la comida puertorriqueña o la comida china? **(puertorriqueña)**
5. ¿Es la especialidad de la casa pollo asado con tostones o bistec con papas fritas? **(pollo asado con tostones)**
6. ¿Va Francisco a la galería solamente para mirar el arte o va a hacer un trabajo? **(va a hacer un trabajo)**
7. ¿Va Francisco a entrevistar a Alejandro Romero o a Carmen Lomas Garza? **(a Alejandro Romero)**
8. ¿Quién es Alejandro Romero? **(es artista)**
9. ¿Dónde nació Romero? **(en México)**
10. ¿Adónde van Francisco y Pedro antes de la entrevista? **(a la casa de Pedro)**

## Culture Highlights

- **POLLO ASADO** is roast chicken with spices.
- **TOSTONES** are fried slices of green plantains or **plátanos**. They are a popular side dish in many Puerto Rican and Cuban meals. (See recipe, p. 27B.)
- **ARROZ CON HABICHUELAS COLORADAS** is a common meal in Puerto Rico. The rice can be white or flavored and is served with **habichuelas**, which are like small kidney beans, in a tomato-based sauce with native spices.

## Block Schedule

**Process Time** Have students listen to the audio again and follow along in the text. (For additional activities, see **Block Scheduling Copymasters.**)

## Teaching Resource Options

**Print** 

Unit 1 Resource Book
Video Activities, pp. 141–142
Videoscript, pp. 143–144
Audioscript, p. 145

**Audiovisual**

OHT 22 (Quick Start)
Audio Program Cassette 2A / CD 2
Video Program Videotape 1, 13:27 / Videodisc 1A

**Technology** 

*Intrigas y aventuras* CD-ROM, Disc 1

## Quick Start Review

**Preterite**

Use OHT 22 or write on board: Conjugate the verbs in the preterite to complete each sentence.

1. Pedro y Francisco (ir) a un restaurante puertorriqueño.
2. Ellos (comer) pollo asado.
3. Ellos (visitar) una galería de arte.
4. Francisco (ver) una escultura muy bella.
5. La Sra. Álvarez (hablar) de la vida de Alejandro Romero.

**Answers**, see p. 49B.

## Teaching Suggestions

**Comprehension Check** Use **Actividades 1** and **2** to assess retention after the dialog. If a sentence in **Actividad 1** is false, have students rewrite it so it will be true.

## Supplementary Vocabulary

Other expressions to use when discussing food include:

| | |
|---|---|
| **Me gusta/No me gusta...** | I like/I don't like |
| **caliente/frío(a)** | hot/cold |
| **picante** | spicy |

# En acción

## VOCABULARIO Y GRAMÁTICA

**OBJECTIVES**
- Comment on food
- Talk about the past
- Express activity preferences
- Discuss fine art

ACTIVIDAD 1

### ¿Es cierto?

**Escuchar** Según el diálogo, ¿son las oraciones **ciertas** o **falsas**? *(Hint: Are these sentences true or false?)*

1. Antes de llegar a Chicago, Francisco visitó a su familia en Los Ángeles.
2. A Francisco le gusta la comida puertorriqueña.
3. A Francisco no le gusta la exposición.
4. La exposición sólo tiene retratos.
5. Francisco va a entrevistar a un artista que se llama Alejandro Romero.
6. La señora Álvarez no sabe nada sobre el artista.
7. Antes de la entrevista, Francisco está nervioso.
8. Francisco va a la casa de Pedro.

**TAMBIÉN SE DICE**

En el diálogo, tal vez notaste que Pedro y la señora Álvarez usan la segunda persona, **tú**. Aparte de **tú**, **usted** y **ustedes**, en otros países puedes escuchar

- **vos,** una forma de la segunda persona singular que se usa en Costa Rica, Argentina, Nicaragua, Uruguay y Paraguay
- **vosotros,** una forma de la segunda persona plural, que se usa en España

ACTIVIDAD 2

### ¿Quién habla?

**Escuchar** ¿Quién habla: Pedro, Francisco o la señora Álvarez? *(Hint: Say who speaks.)*

1. «Bienvenido a Chicago.»
2. «¿Estás listo para tu trabajo?»
3. «Estoy un poco nervioso.»
4. «Y la especialidad de la casa es pollo asado con tostones…»
5. «¿Así que tú eres Francisco García…?»
6. «Vamos, y les cuento algo del pintor.»
7. «¿Trajiste tu cuaderno? Debes tomar apuntes.»
8. «Después, podemos hablar de la entrevista.»



## Classroom Management

**Time Saver** Start with a quick whole-class review of the dialog. Begin by saying, **Francisco llega a Chicago e inmediatamente visita una exposición de arte para entrevistar al artista, Alejandro Romero.** Ask students to continue telling the story in their own words. Then do **Actividades 1** and **2** orally.

**Streamlining** Ask students to scan the questions in **Actividades 1** and **2** before replaying the video. Have students prepare **Actividades 3** and **4** in writing before class to pinpoint areas that need additional practice or reteaching.

- *Review: Use present-tense stem-changing verbs (e → i, u → ue)*
- *Use irregular preterite verbs*

## ¡A viajar!

**Hablar/Escribir** Describe el viaje en avión que Francisco hizo a Chicago, usando estas palabras y las ilustraciones. *(Hint: Describe Francisco's trip to Chicago.)*

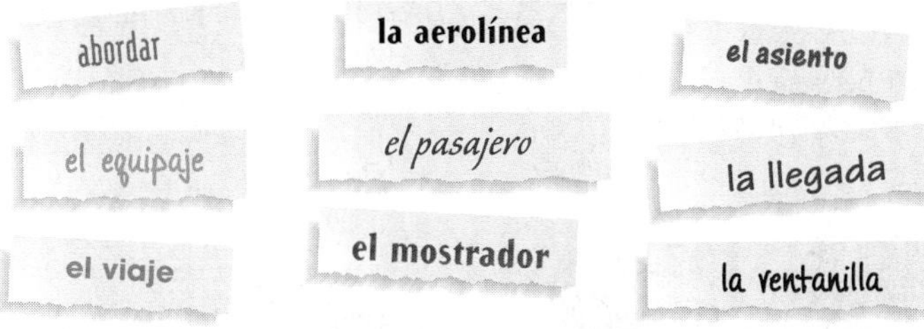

## En la cafetería

**Hablar** ¿Qué piensas de la cafetería de tu escuela? Habla con un(a) compañero(a) para ver si están de acuerdo. *(Hint: Do you and your partner agree?)*

**modelo**

*En la cafetería venden comida buena.*

**Tú:** *En la cafetería venden comida buena. ¿Estás de acuerdo?*

**Compañero(a):** *No, no (Sí,) estoy de acuerdo.*

**Nota**

To explain whether or not you agree with someone or something, use **estar de acuerdo**.

La comida está buena. **¿Estás de acuerdo?**
*The food is good.* ***Do you agree?***

Sí, **estoy de acuerdo** contigo.
*Yes,* ***I agree*** *with you.*

1. Traigo mi almuerzo. Es mejor que comprarlo.
2. Tienen batidos deliciosos.
3. Generalmente, la especialidad de la casa es riquísima.
4. Por la mañana, deseo comprar el desayuno caliente en la cafetería.
5. A mí me gusta el pollo asado con fruta. Es sabroso.



### Teaching All Students

**Extra Help** **Plan ahead:** Prepare a list of foods (or bring in pictures of foods) and ask students to determine if they are **bueno**, **delicioso**, **dulce**, **picante**, **rico**, or **sabroso**. Remind students that the adjectives must match the gender and number of the food items.

**Challenge** Have students interview a partner on one of the following topics: a trip he/she took recently, his/her favorite restaurant(s) and foods, or the school cafeteria. Have them report back to the class.

**Multiple Intelligences**

**Logical/Mathematical** **Plan ahead:** Have students write each word from any of the sentences in **Actividad 2** on a separate index card. Mix up cards and give out one card per student. Students stand up holding the cards, and the class rearranges the words to form a logical sentence.



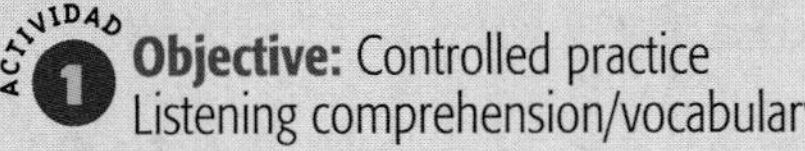

**Objective:** Controlled practice
Listening comprehension/vocabulary

**Answers**

| | |
|---|---|
| 1. cierto | 5. cierto |
| 2. cierto | 6. falso |
| 3. falso | 7. cierto |
| 4. falso | 8. cierto |

**Objective:** Controlled practice
Listening comprehension/vocabulary

**Answers**

| | |
|---|---|
| 1. Pedro | 5. Sra. Álvarez |
| 2. Pedro | 6. Sra. Álvarez |
| 3. Francisco | 7. Pedro |
| 4. Pedro | 8. Pedro |

**Objective:** Open-ended practice
Discussing air travel

Travel vocabulary (*Etapa* 1)

*Answers will vary but should include vocabulary words and verbs conjugated in the preterite.*

a. Francisco llevó su equipaje al mostrador.
b. Abordó el avión con una maleta pequeña.
c. Se sentó en un asiento de pasillo.
d. El avión salió tarde.
e. Celebró la llegada del avión con los otros pasajeros.

**Objective:** Open-ended practice
Discussing food

**Estar** / food vocabulary

*Answers will vary but should reflect correct usage of the phrase* ***estar de acuerdo****.*

### More Practice

After doing **Actividad 4**, have student pairs create reviews of the food in their school cafeteria. Model: **La comida de la cafetería siempre está fría. No me gusta mucho. Pero los viernes cuando sirven pizza yo como en la cafetería.**

### Block Schedule

**Retention** Have students write about an experience they had in the school cafeteria. Have them use the preterite to develop the situation. Possible verbs: **comer, pedir, pasar, entrar, salir, recomendar**, etc.

## Teaching Resource Options

**Print**

*Más práctica* Workbook PE, pp. 25–26
*Cuaderno para hispanohablantes* PE, pp. 23–24
Block Scheduling Copymasters
Unit 1 Resource Book
*Más práctica* Workbook TE, pp. 118–119
*Cuaderno para hispanohablantes* TE, pp. 126–127

**Audiovisual**

OHT 22 (Quick Start)

**Technology**

*Intrigas y aventuras* CD-ROM, Disc 1

## Quick Start Review

Sports

Use OHT 22 or write on board: Finish the phrase **"Me gusta jugar al…"** by combining words from each column. Create four sentences.

Me gusta jugar al...

| | |
|---|---|
| baloncesto | con mis amigos |
| béisbol | en el otoño |
| fútbol | en la primavera |
| fútbol americano | en el verano |
| voleibol | después de clase |
| golf | |
| tenis | |

*Answers will vary. Sample answer:*
Me gusta jugar al tenis en la primavera.

## Teaching Suggestions

### Presenting the Present Tense of e→i and u→ue Verbs

- Review other stem-changing verbs, such as **querer**, **pensar**, **preferir** (**e→ie**) and **volver**, **almorzar**, and **dormir** (**o→ue**). First model the conjugation of one verb, then ask students to conjugate the others.
- Present all stem-changing verbs as "boot verbs" to enhance recall. Remind students to double-check infinitive endings when conjugating the verb.

## REPASO

### Stem-Changing Verbs: e → i, u → ue

**¿RECUERDAS?** *p. 21* You've seen several stem-changing verbs in which the stem changes or alternates between **e** and **ie**, **o** and **ue** in the present tense.

**recomendar** *to recommend*

| | |
|---|---|
| **recomiendo** | **recomendamos** |
| **recomiendas** | **recomendáis** |
| **recomienda** | **recomiendan** |

**mostrar** *to show*

| | |
|---|---|
| **muestro** | **mostramos** |
| **muestras** | **mostráis** |
| **muestra** | **muestran** |

Other Spanish verbs have stems that alternate between **e** and **i**, such as **competir** *to compete*, **pedir** *to ask for*, **repetir** *to repeat*, and **servir** *to serve*.

**servir** *to serve*

| | |
|---|---|
| **sirvo** | **servimos** |
| **sirves** | **servís** |
| **sirve** | **sirven** |

Pedro says:

—**Sirven** un delicioso postre de uvas y melón.
*They serve a delicious grape and melon dessert.*

**Jugar** *to play* has the stem change **u** → **ue** in the present tense.

**jugar** *to play*

| | |
|---|---|
| **juego** | **jugamos** |
| **juegas** | **jugáis** |
| **juega** | **juegan** |

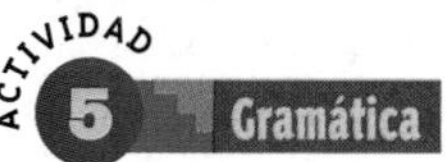


### ¡A pasarlo bien!

**Escribir** ¿Qué hacen Francisco, Pedro y la familia de Pedro en Chicago? ¿Qué haces tú? *(Hint: What do they do?)*

**modelo**

*la esposa de Pedro / pedir ropa por correo*
*La esposa de Pedro pide ropa por correo.*

1. Francisco y Pedro / jugar al tenis con unos vecinos
2. yo / pedir direcciones para ir a un restaurante
3. Francisco / pedir ayuda con su entrevista
4. mi amigo(a) y yo / competir en un concurso de arte
5. Pedro y su esposa / mostrarle unas fotos a Francisco
6. Pedro y su hija / repetir las canciones del radio
7. tú / jugar al baloncesto con unos amigos
8. la esposa de Pedro / servir una cena deliciosa

**MÁS PRÁCTICA** *cuaderno* pp. 25–26

**PARA HISPANOHABLANTES** *cuaderno* pp. 23–24



## Classroom Community

**Paired Activity** For **Actividad 6**, have students work in pairs to ask each other questions based on the verbs in the first column and the information from the second column. e.g., S1: **¿Tú siempre pides ayuda con la tarea?** S2: **Sí, siempre pido ayuda con la tarea.**

**Portfolio** Have students choose a favorite sport or game they like to play and write about it for their portfolio. They can discuss where they play, when they play, and with whom they play this sport/game.

**Rubric: Writing**

| Criteria | Scale | |
|---|---|---|
| Correct sentence structure | 1 2 3 4 5 | A = 17–20 pts. |
| Vocabulary use | 1 2 3 4 5 | B = 13–16 pts. |
| Creativity | 1 2 3 4 5 | C = 9–12 pts. |
| Logical organization | 1 2 3 4 5 | D = 5–8 pts. |
| | | F = < 5 pts. |

## ¿Lo hacen o no?

**PARA CONVERSAR**

**STRATEGY: SPEAKING**

**Use all you know** The models in exercises are a guide to help you get started. It is better to say more than what is shown in the model. Take risks! Recombine what you have learned in fresh new ways. That is how you become a good speaker of Spanish.

**Hablar** Di lo que hacen y no hacen tú y varias personas que conoces, combinando frases de cada columna. *(Hint: Tell what you and others do.)*

**modelo**

*yo: dormir tarde → los sábados*

*Yo (no) duermo tarde los sábados.*

1. tú siempre: pedir
2. ellos: repetir
3. yo: competir
4. mis amigos y yo: practicar deportes
5. mi amiga: perder
6. mi tía: servir
7. ustedes: recomendar
8. mi hermano(a): entender

a. las clases de arte
b. mis problemas
c. las llaves del carro
d. al aire libre
e. las instrucciones del maestro
f. comidas deliciosas
g. en un partido el sábado
h. ayuda con la tarea

## Las diversiones

**Hablar** Pregúntales a tus amigos(as) si juegan a los siguientes deportes y con quién. *(Hint: Do your friends play these sports?)*

**modelo**

**Tú:** *¿Juegas al voleibol?*

**Tu amigo(a):** *Sí, (No, no) juego al voleibol.*

**Tú:** *¿Con quién juegas?*

**Tu amigo(a):** *Juego con…*

## Teaching All Students

**Extra Help** Remind students that there is a conjugation chart in the back of their book for easy reference.

**Native Speakers** Have Spanish speakers create a "rap" to practice stem-changing **e→i** and **u→ue** verbs. For example, **"Yo recuerdo la información cuando duermo en mi habitación, ..."**

**Challenge** Have students create a story using as many stem-changing verbs as possible.

**Multiple Intelligences**

**Visual** Have students draw a logo for each of the sports/games listed in **Actividad 7**. Then have them draw additional logos for other sports they know in Spanish. Logos should include the Spanish word. Bonus points may be given for the most successful logo.

**Objective:** Controlled practice
e→i, u→ue verbs

Leisure activities

**Answers**

1. Francisco y Pedro juegan al tenis con unos vecinos.
2. Yo pido direcciones para ir a un restaurante.
3. Francisco pide ayuda con su entrevista.
4. Mi amigo(a) y yo competimos en un concurso de arte.
5. Pedro y su esposa le muestran unas fotos a Francisco.
6. Pedro y su hija repiten las canciones del radio.
7. Tú juegas al baloncesto con unos amigos.
8. La esposa de Pedro sirve una cena deliciosa.

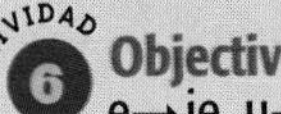

**Objective:** Transitional practice
e→ie, u→ue verbs

**Answers**

*Answers will vary but all should reflect correct conjugation of verbs.*

1. pides
2. repiten
3. compito
4. practicamos deportes
5. pierde
6. sirve
7. recomiendan
8. entiende

**Objective:** Open-ended practice
Discussing sports activities

Sports

**Answers**

*Answers will vary but all should reflect correct conjugation of verbs and incorporate the following sports:*

1. tenis
2. fútbol
3. béisbol
4. fútbol americano
5. baloncesto

### Teaching Suggestions

- **Present Tense of e→i and u→ue Verbs** Ask students for 5 sample sentences using the new verbs they have learned and write them on the board.
- **Variation** Write the following verbs on the board and ask students to create sample sentences using them: **competir, pedir, repetir, servir, jugar.**

### Block Schedule

**Dictation** Have students write down the following radio announcement.

**Chicago compite con Houston esta noche en el campeonato de baloncesto. Los Bulls juegan bien pero los Rockets muestran mucho talento. El partido empieza a las ocho en el canal siete.**

To extend the activity, divide students into pairs and have them write an announcement for their school team. (For additional activities, see **Block Scheduling Copymasters**.)

## Teaching Resource Options

**Print**

Block Scheduling Copymasters
Unit 1 Resource Book
Audioscript, p. 140
Information Gap Activities, pp. 134–135

**Audiovisual**

OHT 22 (Quick Start)
Audio Program Cassette 2A / CD 2

**Technology**

*Intrigas y aventuras* CD-ROM, Disc 1

## Teaching Suggestions

### Presenting Vocabulario

Have students try to guess what all the food items are in the **Vocabulario** box. They were presented in Level 1 so most will be review.

## Culture Highlights

There are many **supermercados** or supermarkets in Spanish-speaking countries now. But many shoppers continue to shop for their daily groceries in smaller markets called the **colmado** in Puerto Rico, the **bodega** in Ecuador, and the **almacén** in Argentina.

**Actividad 8 Objective:** Transitional practice
Preferir

Answers will vary but should contain **prefieres** and **prefiero**.

**Actividad 9 Objective:** Open-ended practice
Listening comprehension

**Answers** (See script, TE p. 49B)
*Answers may vary.*
1. Ve muchas pinturas, retratos y esculturas.
2. Compra fotografías de esculturas de artistas latinoamericanos.
3. Francisco prefiere la escultura porque piensa que es la forma de arte más difícil.
4. Va a un restaurante puertorriqueño con Pedro.
5. Almuerzan.
6. A Francisco le gusta comer pollo asado, tostones y habichuelas coloradas.

Actividad 8

## A cada uno, su gusto

**Hablar** Pregúntales a tus compañeros(as) qué prefieren comprar en el supermercado. *(Hint: Ask classmates what they prefer to buy.)*

**modelo**

*¿un sándwich de jamón o de atún?*
**Tú:** *¿Prefieres un sándwich de jamón o de atún?*
**Compañero(a):** *Prefiero un sándwich de jamón (atún).*

1. ¿yogur con sabor a fresa o helado?
2. ¿cereal o huevos?
3. ¿atún o jamón?
4. ¿jugo o leche?
5. ¿galletas con sabor a chocolate o un sabroso pastel de crema?
6. ¿mantequilla de cacahuate o mantequilla?

Actividad 9

## En Chicago

**Escuchar/Escribir** Escucha la descripción de lo que hace Francisco en Chicago. Luego, contesta las preguntas. *(Hint: Listen to the description. Then answer the questions.)*

1. ¿Qué ve Francisco en el museo?
2. ¿Qué compra en las tiendas?
3. ¿Prefiere Francisco esculturas, retratos o pinturas? ¿Por qué?
4. ¿Adónde va después de ver el arte en la galería? ¿Con quién?
5. ¿Qué hacen allí?
6. ¿A Francisco qué le gusta comer?

MÁS COMUNICACIÓN p. R3

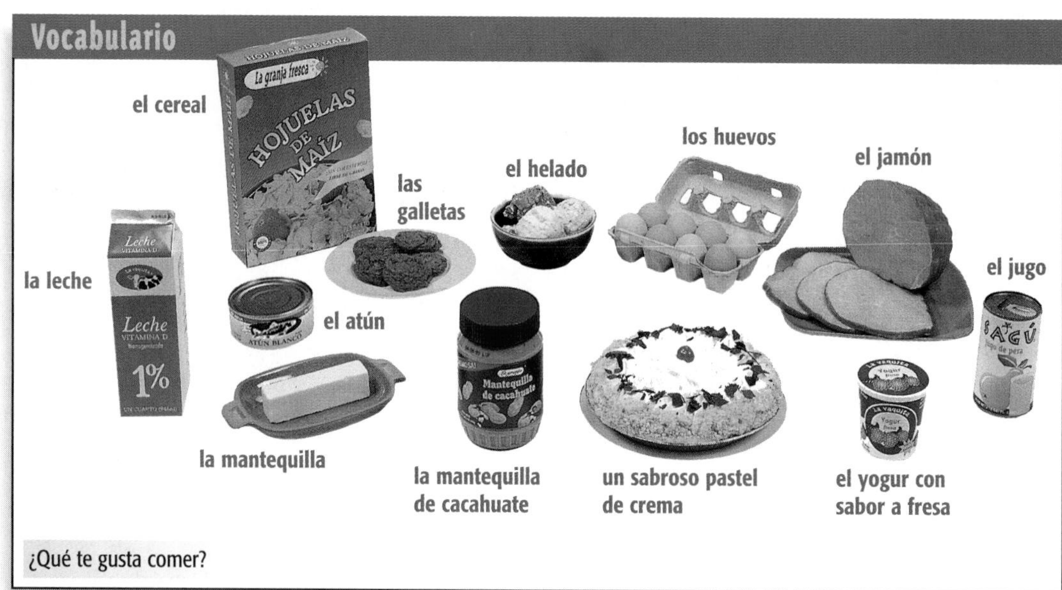




## Classroom Community

**TPR** Have students act out the various infinitive verbs from p. 61. Other students will state what the student just did using the preterite tense.

S1: (Acts out **conducir**)
S2: **Jaime condujo un carro.**

**Cooperative Learning** Divide the class into 4 groups and assign each group one of the following food categories: **bebidas** (drinks), **comidas** (meals), **meriendas** (snacks), and **postres** (desserts). Have each group brainstorm other food items they already know in Spanish in their category (S1=recorder, S2=presenter). Then have each group share their list with the whole class for a master food list.

## Talk About the Past Using Irregular Preterite Verbs

**¿RECUERDAS?** *p. 40* In Etapa 1, you reviewed five irregular verbs in the preterite: **ir, ser, dar, ver,** and **hacer.**

Like the verb **hacer**, the following verbs have irregular stems in the **preterite.** They take these **irregular preterite verb endings**.

There are other verbs that end in **-cir** that follow the same pattern as **decir.** These include

**conducir** *to drive*
**producir** *to produce*
**traducir** *to translate*

| verb | stem | preterite endings |
|---|---|---|
| **andar** *to walk* | anduv- | -e |
| **decir** *to say, to tell* | dij- | |
| **estar** *to be* | estuv- | -iste |
| **poder** *to be able* | pud- | |
| **poner** *to put* | pus- | -o |
| **querer** *to want, to love* | quis- | -imos |
| **saber** *to know* | sup- | |
| **tener** *to have* | tuv- | -isteis |
| **traer** *to bring* | traj- | -ieron/-eron |
| **venir** *to come* | vin- | |

Verbs with stems that end in j drop the **i** and add **-eron** to the **ustedes/ellos/ellas** ending.

For example,

**decir** → **dij** + **ieron** → **dijeron**

**traer** → **trajeron**

**Trajeron** un cuaderno para tomar apuntes.
***They brought** a notebook to take notes.*



### Quick Start Review

Irregular preterite

Use OHT 22 or write on board: Write out the following sentences, conjugating the verb in the preterite.

1. nosotros / hacer / un viaje a Los Ángeles
2. yo / ir / de compras.
3. Luis y Ana / ir / a un partido de béisbol
4. nosotros / ver / unos murales bellísimos

**Answers**, p. 49B.

### Teaching Suggestions
#### Presenting the Irregular Preterite Verbs

- Remind students that they have already learned the conjugation of 5 irregular verbs: **ir**, **ser**, **ver**, **dar**, and **hacer**. Write the conjugations on the board for review.
- Have students write out the conjugations of the new verbs on p. 61 in their notebooks after you model a few on the board. Remind students that although the verbs have irregular stems, all the verb endings have the same forms in the preterite.
- Point out that some preterites have other meanings, e.g., **poder** (to manage to), **no querer** (to refuse), and **saber** (to find out), among others.

### Supplementary Vocabulary

Other food vocabulary items that students may remember from Level 1 include:

| | |
|---|---|
| **el agua** *(f.)* | water |
| **la fruta** | fruit |
| **la hamburguesa** | hamburger |
| **el refresco** | soft drink |
| **el sándwich** | sandwich |
| **la merienda** | snack |

### Block Schedule

**Variety** Plan ahead: Write "stems" on overhead and ask students to form a sentence based on given stem, e.g., **anduv-, Yo anduve por el mercado para comprar melones.** (For additional activities, see **Block Scheduling Copymasters.**)

### Teaching All Students

**Extra Help** Have students restate a sentence in the past tense using irregular preterite forms, e.g., **Francisco trae su cuaderno para la entrevista. Francisco trajo su cuaderno para la entrevista.**

**Native Speakers** For additional practice, have Spanish speakers write a story using as many verbs with spelling changes as possible.

**Multiple Intelligences**

**Interpersonal** Have students work with a partner to find out about each other's favorite foods from the vocabulary list on p. 60.

**Visual** Have students design and illustrate a simple menu for breakfast or lunch using the vocabulary list on p. 60. Encourage them to add more items.

## Teaching Resource Options

**Print** 

*Más práctica* Workbook PE, pp. 27–30
*Cuaderno para hispanohablantes* PE, pp. 25–28
Block Scheduling Copymasters
Unit 1 Resource Book
*Más práctica* Workbook TE, pp. 120–123
*Cuaderno para hispanohablantes* TE, pp. 128–131

**Audiovisual**

OHT 23 (Quick Start)

## Quick Start Review

**Leisure time activities**

Use OHT 23 or write on board: You will be hosting a student from Mexico. Jot down a list of four activities you could do in your town. Use the infinitive as you list the verbs. For example: **caminar en el parque**. Hint: Think about sports, restaurants, movies, concerts, etc.

*Answers will vary.*

## Culture Highlight

● **BARRIO PILSEN** is a neighborhood of Chicago with a large Hispanic population from Mexico and Latin America. Barrio Pilsen is known for its active community of Hispanic artists, including sculptors, painters, and muralists who work with Mexican themes.

**Objective:** Controlled practice
Irregular preterites

**Answers**

1. Fernando no vino porque tuvo que ayudar a su tía.
2. Yo no vine porque no pude encontrar la casa.
3. Inés no vino porque no supo de la fiesta.
4. Enrique y Luis no vinieron porque estuvieron en el hospital.
5. Susana y yo no vinimos porque estuvimos en México.

**Objective:** Transitional practice
Irregular preterites

**Answers**

*Answers will vary but all should reflect correct conjugation of verbs.*

1. anduviste / anduve
2. hiciste / hice
3. estuviste / estuve
4. trajiste / traje

## Excusas, excusas

**Escribir** La señora Álvarez organizó una fiesta para sus empleados, pero no vinieron. Haz una oración dando la excusa de cada uno. *(Hint: Explain why each person didn't come.)*

**modelo**

*Carmen: tiene un accidente*
*Carmen no vino porque tuvo un accidente.*

1. Fernando: tiene que ayudar a su tía
2. yo: no puedo encontrar la casa
3. Inés: no sabe de la fiesta
4. Enrique y Luis: están en el hospital
5. Susana y yo: estamos en México

**MÁS PRÁCTICA** *cuaderno* pp. 27–30
**PARA HISPANOHABLANTES** *cuaderno* pp. 25–28

## ¿Qué pasó?

**Hablar** Pregúntales a tus compañeros(as) si hicieron las siguientes cosas la semana pasada. *(Hint: Ask classmates if they did these things.)*

**modelo**

*estar en la escuela a tiempo*
**Tú:** *¿Estuviste en la escuela a tiempo?*
**Compañero(a):** *Sí, (No, no) estuve en la escuela a tiempo.*

1. andar por las calles con tus amigos
2. hacer una fiesta
3. estar en casa de tus amigos
4. traer la ropa de la lavandería

## Un buen día

**Hablar/Escribir** Recibiste una carta de un(a) amigo(a) y quieres contarle a tu mamá lo que te dijo. Cambia los verbos y otras palabras según se necesite. *(Hint: Tell what your friend said.)*

**modelo**

*Tuve un día maravilloso ayer.*
*Tuvo un día maravilloso ayer.*

Tuve un día maravilloso ayer. Fui (1) a la cancha con mi raqueta y vi (2) al campeón de tenis de mi ciudad. Luego, mi mejor amigo y yo estuvimos (3) en un museo del barrio Pilsen y conocimos (4) a una escultora magnífica. Vimos (5) muchas pinturas muy bonitas. Después, fuimos (6) a comer en un restaurante de la ciudad. ¡Qué buen día!

**NOTA CULTURAL**

El Centro Museo de Bellas Artes Mexicanas de Chicago tiene las obras de muchos artistas. También ofrece clases y programas sobre la cultura mexicana. En el otoño el museo organiza excursiones a las panaderías mexicanas del barrio Pilsen.

## Classroom Community

**TPR** In groups of 3, have the first student act out a verb from p. 61; the second tries to guess the verb; and the third creates a sentence using the verb in the preterite tense. e.g., S1 (Acts out **conducir**); S2: **conducir**; S3: **Mi hermano condujo el carro con cuidado.**

**Learning Scenario** Ask students to give an excuse for why they missed Spanish class one day or why they did not bring their homework. **Yo no pude venir a la clase de español/Yo no traje mi tarea porque...**

**Paired Activity** Have students create index cards with the verbs from p. 61 on one side and the corresponding preterite stem on the other side. With a partner, have students take turns showing either side of the card and ask the partner to give the corresponding stem or infinitive and then create a sentence using the verb in the preterite.

## El viernes pasado

**Leer/Escribir** Lee la agenda de Pedro del viernes pasado. Luego mira la lista de cosas que hizo. ¿Cuándo crees que las hizo? *(Hint: Say when Pedro did these things.)*

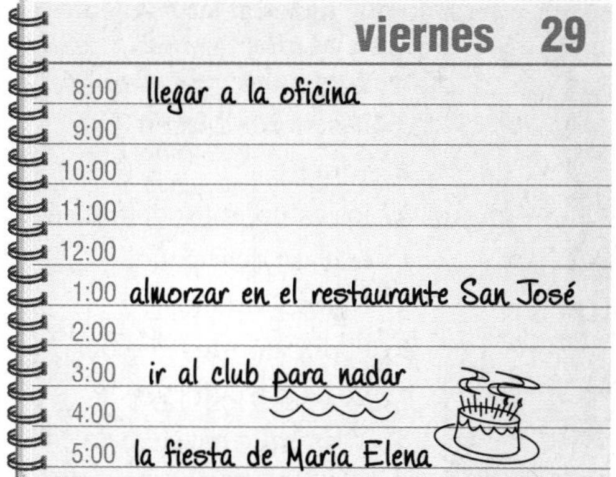


**modelo**

*hacer un reporte en la computadora*

*Pedro probablemente hizo un reporte en la computadora después de las ocho.*

1. estar en el restaurante San José
2. tomar un curso de natación
3. salir de la oficina
4. poner dinero en la mesa
5. traer un regalo a la fiesta
6. comer un pastel de chocolate
7. manejar su carro a la oficina
8. decirle «buenas noches» a su hija

## ¿Cuántas veces?

**Hablar/Escribir** ¿Haces las siguientes actividades? Usa expresiones como **nunca, rara vez, de vez en cuando, casi siempre** o **siempre** en tus respuestas. *(Hint: Do you do these activities? Use expressions of frequency in your answers.)*

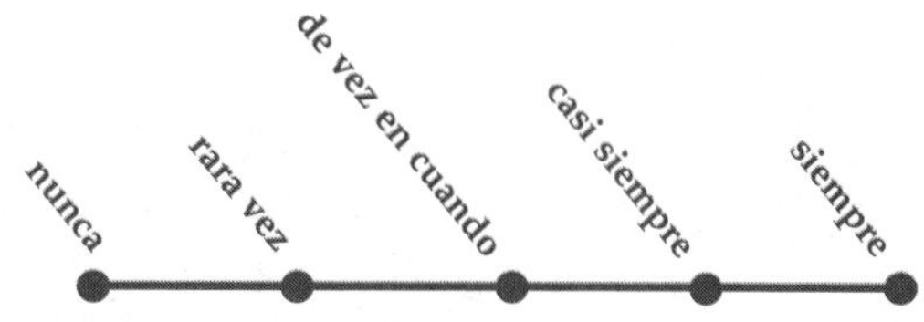


**modelo**

*visitar a los abuelos*

*De vez en cuando, visito a mis abuelos.*

1. tomar clases de natación
2. devolver los libros a la biblioteca
3. ser ganador(a) de un premio
4. dormir una siesta
5. competir en un partido de fútbol
6. jugar al dominó
7. ir al cine
8. participar en un concurso
9. ver la televisión
10. hablar por teléfono

**Objective:** Controlled practice
Irregular preterites

**Answers**

1. Fue
2. vio
3. estuvieron
4. conocieron
5. Vieron
6. fueron

**Objective:** Open-ended practice
Talking about the past
Telling time

**Answers**

*Answers will vary but should reflect correct conjugation of the preterite verbs.*

1. Pedro probablemente estuvo en el restaurante San José después de la una.
2. ... tomó un curso de natación después de las tres.
3. ... quiso salir de la oficina después de las doce.
4. ... puso dinero en la mesa después de la una.
5. ... trajo un regalo a la fiesta después de las cinco.
6. ... comió un pastel de chocolate después de las cinco.
7. ... manejó su carro a la oficina después de las siete.
8. ... le dijo «buenas noches» a su hija después de las nueve.

**Objective:** Open-ended practice
Preterite
Expressions of frequency

*Answers will vary but should reflect knowledge of expressions of frequency.*

### Quick Wrap-up

Divide the students into pairs to interview each other about what they did last Saturday. Then have students report one activity their partner did. Keep a tally on the board to determine the activity most people did. You might have students express their opinions on which activity was the most fun.

## Teaching All Students

**Extra Help** Ask students to list 3–5 activities they did yesterday. Refer them to the list of verbs on pp. 58 and 61.

**Native Speakers** Have Spanish speakers discuss the most popular sports or games in their community. Ask them to discuss the sports or games they participate in and which sports or sporting events they like to watch live or on television.

**Multiple Intelligences**

**Logical/Mathematical** Have students form questions from the information in Actividad 14, e.g., **¿Tomaste clases de natación?** Write the 10 questions on the board and poll the entire class to see how many students have done each activity. Write the number of students next to each question. Then have students form sentences that give the class results, e.g., **Siete estudiantes tomaron clases de natación.**

### Block Schedule

**Change of Pace** Plan ahead: Have students write a list of activities that were done yesterday. Cut out each activity and ask students to put them in sequential order. (For additional activities, see **Block Scheduling Copymasters.**)

## Teaching Resource Options

**Print** 

*Más práctica* Workbook PE, pp. 21–24
*Cuaderno para hispanohablantes* PE, pp. 21–22
Block Scheduling Copymasters
Unit 1 Resource Book
*Más práctica* Workbook TE, pp. 114–117
*Cuaderno para hispanohablantes* TE, pp. 124–125
Information Gap Activities, pp. 136–137
Audioscript, pp. 146–148

**Audiovisual** 

OHT 23 (Quick Start)
Audio Program Cassette 2A, 2B / CD 2; (*Para hispanohablantes* Cassette 2B / CD 2)

**Technology**

*Intrigas y aventuras* CD-ROM, Disc 1

## Quick Start Review

Adjectives

Use OHT 23 or write on board: Complete the sentences with one of the adjectives listed. More than one adjective could be used. Make sure the adjective agrees with the noun. For example: **retratos antiguos.**

**bello** **interesante** **pequeño** **simpático** **sabroso**

1. Las esculturas son…
2. La galería de arte es…
3. Pedro es…
4. Los museos de Chicago son…

**Answers**, see p. 49B.

## Language Note

Point out to students that many of the words in the vocabulary list on p. 64 are cognates. Remind students that cognates are Spanish words that look or sound similar to their English counterparts (e.g., **artista, exposición, galería, moderno, tradicional**).

**Objective:** Transitional practice
Discussing fine art/adjectives

*Answers will vary.*

## Tus opiniones

**Hablar/Escribir** Expresa lo que piensas de *Blue Chicago*, usando los elementos de las tres columnas y tus propias palabras también.
*(**Hint:** Say what you think of the painting, using elements from all three columns.)*

**modelo**

*La pintura es muy moderna y rara.*

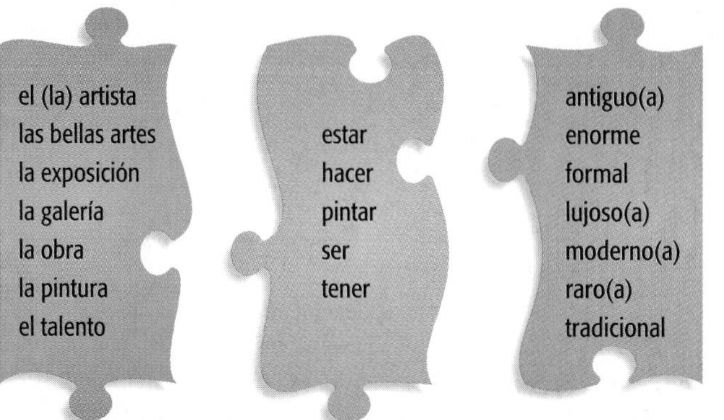

el (la) artista
las bellas artes
la exposición
la galería
la obra
la pintura
el talento
estar
hacer
pintar
ser
tener
antiguo(a)
enorme
formal
lujoso(a)
moderno(a)
raro(a)
tradicional

## Una semana internacional

**Escuchar/Escribir** Para celebrar *La semana internacional de lenguas extranjeras*, muchos estudiantes hicieron cosas especiales. Escucha la descripción. Luego, escribe lo que hicieron las siguientes personas. *(**Hint:** Listen to the description. Then write down what each person did.)*

1. la señorita Martín
2. Sara
3. los estudiantes de francés
4. la clase de español
5. Rocío y Emilio
6. el director de la escuela
7. yo, la narradora
8. Y tú, ¿qué hiciste para celebrar?

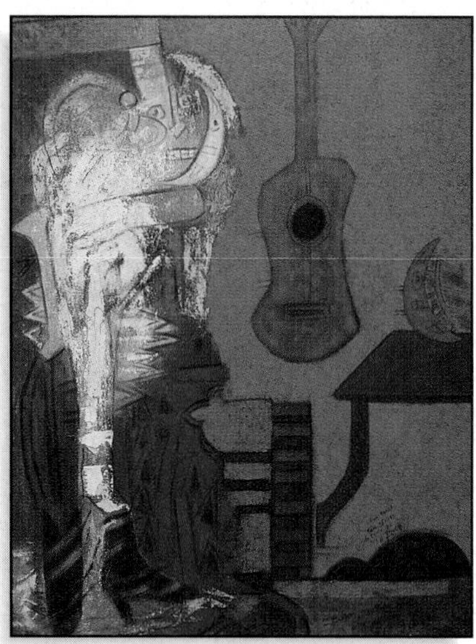

***Blue Chicago**, por Alejandro Nava*

### Vocabulario

| El arte | Unas descripciones |
|---|---|
| **las bellas artes** *fine arts* | **antiguo(a)** *old* |
| **la exposición** *exhibit* | **enorme** *enormous* |
| **la galería** *gallery* | **formal** *formal* |
| **la obra** *work of art* | **lujoso(a)** *luxurious* |
| **el talento** *talent* | **moderno(a)** *modern* |
| | **raro(a)** *rare, strange* |
| | **tradicional** *traditional* |

Cuando piensas en arte, ¿qué prefieres?



## Classroom Community

**Paired Activity** Have students work in pairs to describe the artwork and illustrations they see on pp. 64–65, using the new vocabulary they have learned. After they have described the artwork, have them give an opinion.

**Storytelling** **Prepare Ahead:** Have students compile pictures from magazines that deal with the Etapa themes of favorite activities, art, or food. The pictures can be unrelated and should be placed face down. Divide the class into small groups. Each group selects at least 3 pictures and writes a story about them in the past tense. A member of each group reads the story then asks the class comprehension questions. Then have volunteers retell the story in their own words.

## ¿Cuál es el problema?

**Hablar/Escribir** Mira el dibujo del restaurante. Trabaja con un(a) compañero(a) para anotar qué está mal. *(Hint: What's wrong with the drawing?)*

**MÁS COMUNICACIÓN** p. R3

### NOTA CULTURAL

**La cena** En Estados Unidos, la mayoría de la gente cena alrededor de las seis de la tarde. Pero en muchos países hispanos, la gente cena más tarde –cerca de las diez de la noche. ¿La razón? Toman un descanso o **una siesta** durante el día y no terminan de trabajar hasta las siete u ocho de la noche.

### Refrán

**Muchas manos en un plato siempre causan arrebato.**

Este refrán quiere decir que si muchas personas desean participar en una cosa al mismo tiempo, todo se puede echar a perder (*get ruined*). Con un(a) compañero(a), presenta una situación en que pase algo así.

**Objective:** Open-ended practice
Listening comprehension

**Answers** (See script, p. 48B.)
*Answers will vary but should express the following ideas.*
1. La señorita Martín les ayudó a los estudiantes a pensar en actividades culturales.
2. Sara trajo su guitarra a clase y tocó música española.
3. Los estudiantes de francés trajeron comida sabrosa a la escuela.
4. La clase de español hizo una piñata.
5. Rocío y Emilio bailaron un baile tradicional de México.
6. El director de la escuela también participó; cada día saludó en varias lenguas.
7. Yo, la narradora, hice esta presentación.
8. Answers will vary.

**Objective:** Open-ended practice
Discussing food

**Answers**
*Answers will vary and may include the following.*
El mesero tiene un radio, una pelota de baloncesto y unos libros.
Una niña patina en el restaurante.
Un cocodrilo entra al restaurante.
La cocinera come en el restaurante.
Una gallina y un pato están en el restaurante.

### More Practice

For an expansion on **Actividad 17**, have students work in pairs to write about a bad restaurant/cafeteria experience they may have had.

### Quick Wrap-up

Ask students to list as many activities as they can to describe what they did last weekend. Assign a prize to the student with the longest list of activities that correctly uses different preterite verbs.

## Teaching All Students

**Extra Help** Using the **Vocabulario** box on p. 64, have students describe a piece of art found in their school.

**Native Speakers** Ask native speakers to research additional **refranes** to share with the class. The new **refranes** may be illustrated to aid comprehension.

**Multiple Intelligences**

**Intrapersonal Plan ahead:** Bring in an art piece (painting, sculpture, etc.). Have students compare your art piece to the picture in **Actividad 15** and discuss their personal reactions.

**Musical/Rhythmic** Have students connect a musical piece to the artwork featured in **Actividad 15** or any artwork in the Etapa. Show CD covers (Hispanic music), then listen to music and have students compare the musical style with a particular piece of artwork.

### Block Schedule

**Time Out for Art** Bring in other examples of artwork and have students describe what they see and express their opinions about each example using the new vocabulary. (For additional activities, see **Block Scheduling Copymasters**.)

## Teaching Resource Options

**Print** 

*Cuaderno para hispanohablantes* PE, pp. 30–31
Unit 1 Resource Book
*Cuaderno para hispanohablantes* TE, pp. 132–133
Video Activities, p. 142
Videoscript, p. 144

**Audiovisual** 

OHT 23 (Quick Start)
Video Program Videotape 1, 18:33 / Videodisc 1A

Search Chapter 7, Play to 8
U1E2, En colores (Culture), Spanish

Search Chapter 7, Play to 8
U1E2, En colores (Culture), English

## Quick Start Review

**Describing fine art**

Use OHT 23 or write on board: Look at the mural on p. 67. Write down three phrases in Spanish to describe it. You could focus on color, content, or your opinion of the mural.

*Answers will vary.*

## Teaching Suggestions

- **Prereading** Have students look at the pictures on pp. 66–67 and quickly scan the cultural reading. Have them write down 3 guesses as to what the reading will be about.
- Have students scan for 3 words they don't know and discuss context clues.
- Brainstorm with students the common qualities of a mural.
- **Video** Use the video to expand and enrich the cultural information.

## Reading Strategies

Have students scan the reading for proper names. Ask them if they know the artists mentioned in the reading. Discuss how quotes might be important in this personal interview. Remind students to review the **¿Comprendiste?** questions before reading.

# En colores

## CULTURA Y COMPARACIONES

# El arte latino de Chicago

### PARA CONOCERNOS

**STRATEGIES: CONNECTING CULTURES**

**Learn about other cultures as well as your own** Learning about other people who share a language, a way of life, traditions, and world contributions helps you understand your own culture.

**Describe the nature of murals** What is a mural? Are there murals in your town? How do people feel about them? Use a Venn diagram to chart the similarities between a mural and graffiti.

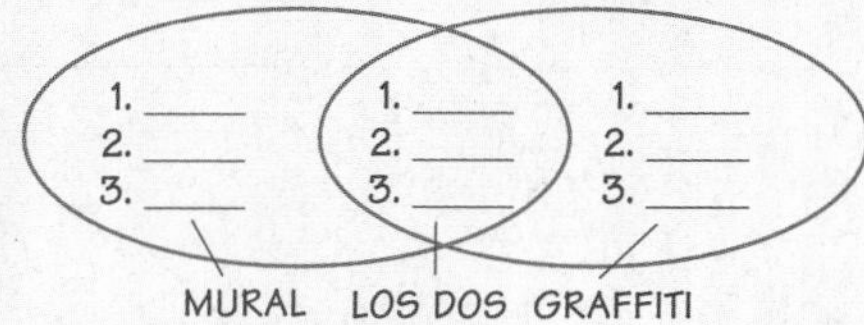


Después de su visita a Chicago y su entrevista con Alejandro Romero y su hermano Oscar, Francisco escribe un artículo para *Onda Internacional*.

Unas estudiantes de Madonna High School pintan un mural.

¡Me encantó Chicago —por su arte e historia! Tiene una gran diversidad de cultura que se ve cuando caminas por sus calles. Venden todo tipo de comida y tienen arte que representa muchas culturas distintas.

Entrevisté a dos artistas latinos, Alejandro y Oscar Romero. Son hermanos y desde niños pintaron y dibujaron juntos. Ellos llevan el estilo del arte mexicano a la comunidad.

A los dos les gusta pintar murales porque «puedes pintar un mural en tu casa, o en una pared del campo».

66

## Classroom Community

**Group Activity** Have students work in small groups to brainstorm what they might encounter when reading a personal interview in a newspaper or magazine. Compile a list with the whole class as a prereading activity for Francisco's *Onda Internacional* article on Alejandro and Oscar Romero.

**Cooperative Learning** Divide the class into groups and have each group plan and draw a mural based on a chosen theme or message. (S1 = recorder; S2, S3 = theme planners; all students contribute as artists.) Use large paper and allow students to draw or paint on their own section of the paper, or make a collage of photographs from magazines. Display the final results.

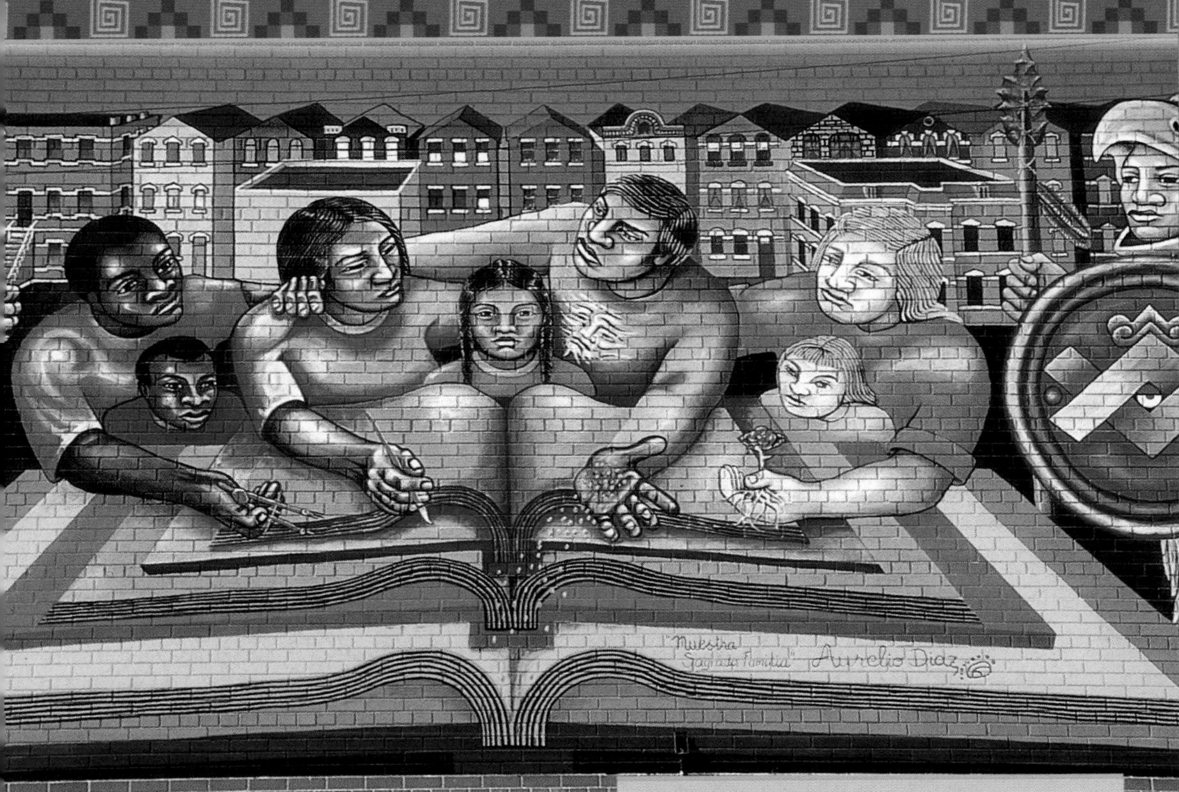


A Oscar y Alejandro les encanta trabajar con gente joven. Alejandro y unos jóvenes de Chicago pintaron un mural muy grande. Oscar ayudó a las estudiantes de Madonna High School a pintar un mural. Según él, para decidir el tema uno tiene que imaginar que está «poniendo un mensaje en una botella y lanzándola al mar».

Alejandro y Oscar enseñan a los jóvenes a expresarse por medio del arte. «Todos tienen acceso a la pintura», dice Oscar. «Nadie te detiene las manos.»

## ¿Comprendiste?

1. ¿Cuándo empezaron los hermanos Romero a pintar?
2. ¿Por qué les gusta pintar murales?
3. ¿Qué hicieron Alejandro y Oscar para ayudar a los jóvenes de Chicago?

## ¿Qué piensas?

1. Ya sabes más sobre los murales. Repasa tu diagrama de Venn. ¿Quieres añadir algo? ¿Quieres cambiar algo?
2. ¿Por qué crees que Oscar piensa que el tema de un mural es como «un mensaje en una botella»? ¿Qué tienen en común una botella en el mar y un mural?

## Hazlo tú 

Con unos(as) compañeros(as) escojan un tema para un mural. Luego hagan un dibujo de lo que quieren expresar. Después pinten el mural y pónganlo en una pared de la escuela.



## Culture Highlights

- **MEXICAN MURALISTS** were commissioned by the Mexican government to decorate public buildings with murals that glorify the Mexican revolution and the pre-Columbian history of Mexico. The three most prominent muralists were Diego Rivera, David Alfaro Siqueiros, and José Clemente Orozco. From 1927 to 1934, Orozco lived in the United States, where he also painted several murals.
- **NUESTRA SAGRADA FAMILIA** The large mural from Chicago shown in the photograph is *Nuestra Sagrada Familia* by Aurelio Díaz.

## Community Connection

Ask students if they have seen any murals in their community. What themes do they see in the murals? What do they know about the painter? Who is the target audience for the murals?

## ¿Comprendiste?

### Answers

1. Desde niños, los hermanos Romero pintaron.
2. Les gusta pintar murales porque es posible pintarlos en cualquier parte.
3. Les enseñaron a los jóvenes a expresarse por medio de la pintura.

## Teaching All Students

**Extra Help** Have students review Francisco's article on pp. 66–67 and make a list of all the preterite verbs they find in one column. Then identify the corresponding infinitive verb in a second column.

**Challenge** If possible, plan a field trip to a local art museum near your school and ask for a Spanish-speaking tour guide. If the whole class can't go, assign this task as extra credit and have students write a summary of their visit. Some museums also offer books, video and audiotape guides by mail.

### Multiple Intelligences

**Verbal** Have students write a brief description of Alejandro and Oscar Romero including nationality, occupation, and at least 3 things they learned.

**Musical/Rhythmic** Play the **Canciones** Cassette/CD for the class. As students listen to one of the musical selections, have them note images that come to mind.

## Block Schedule

**Peer Teaching** Divide the class into groups and assign each a different artist to research. They might choose **Alejandro** and **Oscar Romero** (Mexican artists in Chicago), or the 20th-century Mexican muralists **David Alfaro Siqueiros, Diego Rivera,** and **José Clemente Orozco.** Each group can prepare a short presentation for the class or create a poster to show their research findings.

## Teaching Resource Options

**Print** 

Unit 1 Resource Book
Family Involvement, pp. 138–139
Multiple Choice Test Questions, pp. 246–248

**Audiovisual** 

OHT 24 (Quick Start)

**Technology**

Electronic Teacher Tools/Test Generator
*Intrigas y aventuras* CD-ROM, Disc 1

## Quick Start Review

Describing food

Use OHT 24 or write on board: You are a restaurant reviewer for a radio show. Write a quick review. Name the restaurant, three foods you ate, and an adjective to describe each.

*Answers will vary.*

## Teaching Suggestions
### What Have Students Learned?

- Have students look at the "Now you can..." notes listed on the left side of pp. 68–69. Point out that if they feel they need to review material before doing the activities, they should consult the "To review" notes.
- Use the video to review vocabulary and structures.

# En uso
## REPASO Y MÁS COMUNICACIÓN

**OBJECTIVES**
- Comment on food
- Talk about the past
- Express activity preferences
- Discuss fine art

*Now you can...*
- comment on food.

*To review*
- present-tense stem-changing verbs, see p. 58.

### ACTIVIDAD 1 Un nuevo café

Gabriel describe un nuevo café que le gusta mucho. ¿Qué dice? *(Hint: Complete the paragraph.)*

Yo __1__ (recomendar) el Café Caribeño. Ellos __2__ (servir) comida excelente. Yo casi siempre __3__ (pedir) la especialidad de la casa: el arroz con pollo. Mis padres __4__ (preferir) el jamón. Mi hermana Mariela siempre __5__ (pedir) un plato nuevo. Ella nunca __6__ (repetir). Mariela __7__ (decir) que todos los platos son muy sabrosos. ¿Y tú? ¿Dónde __8__ (preferir) comer? ¿Cuál es tu restaurante favorito?

*Now you can...*
- express activity preferences.

*To review*
- present-tense stem-changing verbs, see p. 58.

### ACTIVIDAD 2 ¡A jugar!

Describe los pasatiempos favoritos de estas personas. *(Hint: Tell people's hobbies.)*

**modelo**
*Sancho*
*Sancho juega al ajedrez.*

1. Soledad 
2. Tú 
3. Rubén y Leticia 
4. Yo 
5. Ustedes 
6. Mis amigos y yo 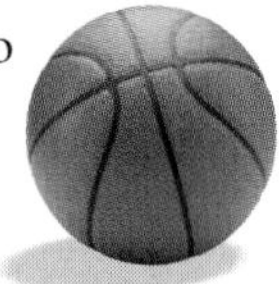



## Classroom Community

**Group Activity** Divide the class into small groups. Have students take a poll of their group on their activity preferences based on the pictures in **Actividad 2**. Then compile the results of all the groups on the board to find the activity preferences of the whole class.

**Portfolio** Ask students to write a brief answer to the question **¿Cuál es tu restaurante favorito y por qué?** and add it to their Portfolio.

**Rubric: Writing**

| Criteria | Scale |
|---|---|
| Correct sentence structure | 1 2 3 4 5 |
| Vocabulary use | 1 2 3 4 5 |
| Creativity | 1 2 3 4 5 |
| Logical organization | 1 2 3 4 5 |

A = 17–20 pts.
B = 13–16 pts.
C = 9–12 pts.
D = 5–8 pts.
F = < 5 pts.

*Now you can...*
- express activity preferences.

*To review*
- present-tense stem-changing verbs, see p. 58.

## ACTIVIDAD 3 Un fin de semana típico

Di si estas cosas pasan o no pasan durante un fin de semana típico. *(Hint: Tell whether these things happen.)*

**modelo**

*yo / servir comida en un restaurante*

*Yo (no) sirvo comida en un restaurante.*

1. la profesora / servir una cena
2. yo / dormir mucho
3. yo / competir en un concurso
4. mis amigos y yo / pedir una pizza
5. mi familia y yo / jugar al ajedrez
6. los estudiantes / querer estudiar

*Now you can...*
- discuss fine art.

*To review*
- irregular preterite verbs, see p. 61.

## ACTIVIDAD 4 Un día terrible

Ayer fue un día terrible para Horacio. Para saber por qué, cambia los verbos al pretérito. *(Hint: Change the underlined verbs to the preterite.)*

La galería de arte de la ciudad pone (1) nuevas pinturas de una famosa artista hoy. Horacio quiere (2) ir a las tres de la tarde. Él va (3) caminando. Anda (4) lentamente y no está (5) cuando abre (6) la galería. Cuando llega (7), no puede (8) abrir la puerta. Horacio no dice (9) nada; sólo vuelve (10) a casa.

*Now you can...*
- talk about the past.

*To review*
- irregular preterite verbs, see p. 61.

## ACTIVIDAD 5 ¡Una gran fiesta!

Adela hizo una fiesta el viernes pasado y todos participaron. ¿Qué hicieron? *(Hint: Tell how people participated in Adela's party.)*

1. Rigo y yo / venir muy temprano para ayudar
2. Adela / poner la mesa
3. tú / traer los platos a la mesa
4. Andrea / querer tocar la guitarra
5. nosotros / estar presentes a las seis
6. tú / hacer los sándwiches de atún



### ACTIVIDAD 1 Answers

1. recomiendo
2. sirven
3. pido
4. prefieren
5. pide
6. repite
7. dice
8. prefieres

### ACTIVIDAD 2 Answers

1. Soledad juega al béisbol.
2. Tú juegas al fútbol.
3. Rubén y Leticia juegan al fútbol americano.
4. Yo juego al golf.
5. Ustedes juegan al dominó.
6. Mis amigos y yo jugamos al baloncesto.

### ACTIVIDAD 3 Answers

1. La profesora (no) sirve una cena.
2. Yo (no) duermo mucho.
3. Yo (no) compito en un concurso.
4. Mis amigos y yo (no) pedimos una pizza.
5. Mi familia y yo (no) jugamos al ajedrez.
6. Los estudiantes (no) quieren estudiar.

### ACTIVIDAD 4 Answers

1. puso
2. quiso
3. fue
4. anduvo
5. estuvo
6. abrió
7. llegó
8. pudo
9. dijo
10. volvió

### ACTIVIDAD 5 Answers

1. Rigo y yo vinimos muy temprano para ayudar.
2. Adela puso la mesa.
3. Tú trajiste los platos a la mesa.
4. Andrea quiso tocar la guitarra.
5. Nosotros estuvimos presentes a las seis.
6. Tú hiciste los sándwiches de atún.

### Dictation

After students have completed **Actividad 4**, use it as a dictation exercise. Students close their books and write down what they hear as you read the letter aloud. You may use either the present or the preterite.

### Teaching All Students

**Extra Help** Using **Actividad 5** as a model, have students describe a party or special event they attended recently. Be sure they use verbs in the preterite to narrate the events in the past.

**Native Speakers** Ask Spanish speakers to describe a recent party they attended in their cultural community. Ask them about the refreshments served, the activities, and who attended. If possible, have them bring a sample of the refreshments served.

**Challenge** Ask students to write a short paragraph on what they did over the weekend. Then collect papers and divide the class into small groups. Give each group several papers and have them form questions based on the activities, e.g., **¿Quién miró la película? ¿Quiénes fueron a la playa?** Other members of the group can answer the questions using the information from the students' papers.

### Block Schedule

**FunBreak** Plan a snack for the class—include **batidos, tostones de plátano verde**, or **arroz con habichuelas.** Have a sign-up sheet and ask students to bring in other foods as well!

# UNIDAD 1 Etapa 2
# Review

## Teaching Resource Options

**Print** 

Unit 1 Resource Book
- Audioscript, p. 149
- Cooperative Quizzes, pp. 150–151
- Etapa Exam, Forms A and B, pp. 152–161
- *Examen para hispanohablantes*, pp. 162–166
- Portfolio Assessment, pp. 167–168
- Multiple Choice Test Questions, pp. 246–248

**Audiovisual** 

OHT 15–16 (Quick Start)
Audio Program Cassette 19A / CD 19;
(*Para hispanohablantes* Cassette 19A / CD 19)
*Canciones* Cassette / CD

**Technology** 

Electronic Teacher Tools/Test Generator
www.mcdougallittell.com

## Quick Start Review

**En contexto** vocabulary

Use OHT 24 or write on board: Name three things you might find at an international festival. Jot down your ideas in Spanish and be specific. What dishes might you find? Music? Decorations? Handicrafts? Art?

*Answers will vary.*

**Actividad 6 and Actividad 7**

Answers will vary but should reflect correct conjugation of verbs in preterite.

**Rubric: Speaking**

| Criteria | Scale |
|---|---|
| Fluency | 1 2 3 |
| Vocabulary | 1 2 3 |
| Pronunciation, rhythm | 1 2 3 |

A = 8–9 pts.
B = 6–7 pts.
C = 4–5 pts.
D = 2–3 pts.
F = < 2 pts.

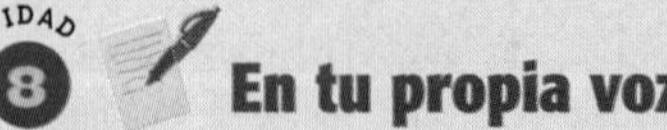

**Actividad 8 En tu propia voz**

**Rubric: Writing**

| Criteria | Scale |
|---|---|
| Vocabulary use | 1 2 3 4 5 |
| Accuracy | 1 2 3 4 5 |
| Creativity, appearance | 1 2 3 4 5 |

A = 13–15 pts.
B = 10–12 pts.
C = 7–9 pts.
D = 4–6 pts.
F = < 4 pts.

## Actividad 6 Preferencias

**PARA CONVERSAR**

**STRATEGY: SPEAKING**

**Give reasons why** When presented with a choice, give more than just a brief answer. Be inventive when explaining your choices in this activity. Perhaps there is a certain quality, a personal liking, or a personal skill that you can use in your response. Scan the previous activities to get ideas for reasons.

Habla con tu compañero(a) sobre sus preferencias. ¿Por qué prefieren estas cosas? *(Hint: Find out what your partner prefers and why.)*

el pollo asado
el pollo frito
una ensalada
un sándwich
las pinturas antiguas
las pinturas modernas
el voleibol
el ajedrez
la comida china
la comida italiana

**modelo**

**Tú:** *¿Prefieres la comida china o la comida italiana?*
**Compañero(a):** *Prefiero la comida china porque es más sabrosa y porque me encanta el arroz.*

## Actividad 7 ¿Cierto o falso?

Conversando en grupos, adivinen cuáles de los otros estudiantes participaron en estas actividades la semana pasada. Escriban cinco oraciones. *(Hint: Discuss who in your class might have done these activities. Write five sentences with your guesses.)*

**modelo**

*ir a un partido*
*José y Elena fueron a un partido.*

1. comer una pizza
2. hablar español en casa
3. venir a la escuela el sábado
4. manejar un coche nuevo
5. ganar un premio
6. participar en un concurso

## Actividad 8 En tu propia voz

**ESCRITURA** Describe un festival internacional (real o imaginario) que tuvo lugar en tu escuela. Incluye la siguiente información. *(Hint: Describe a real or imaginary international festival.)*

- cuándo y dónde celebraron el festival
- quiénes participaron
- qué cosas trajeron
- qué hicieron todos

## CONEXIONES

**El arte** ¿De dónde viene la inspiración de los artistas? Algunos dicen que viene de la naturaleza. Otros dicen que viene de personas o lugares. Hay muchos artistas estadounidenses y cada uno tiene su propio estilo. Selecciona un artista que te guste y haz una investigación sobre sus inspiraciones. Explícales a tus compañeros(as) de clase qué inspira a este artista y muéstrales ejemplos de su arte.

## Classroom Community

**Game: Matamoscas (Flyswatter) Prepare ahead:** Gather pictures that represent items in the vocabulary list on p. 71. Divide the class into 2 teams. Have them line up and give the first player from each team a flyswatter. As you put 2 pictures face up in front of the two players, say only one of them aloud in Spanish. The first player to hit the corresponding picture with the flyswatter gets a point for his/her team. This is a fun way to review vocabulary.

**Paired Activity** Have students work in pairs to choose a "non-traditional" art object in the classroom or in their school, e.g., a clock, an old car, a desk chair. Have them describe the "object" as if it were precious artwork using the vocabulary for discussing fine art. Have students share their descriptions with the class.

# En resumen

## REPASO DE VOCABULARIO

### COMMENT ON FOOD

**Types of Foods**

| | |
|---|---|
| **el atún** | *tuna* |
| **el batido** | *milk shake* |
| **el cereal** | *cereal* |
| **la crema** | *cream* |
| **la fresa** | *strawberry* |
| **las galletas** | *cookies* |
| **las habichuelas coloradas** | *red beans* |
| **el helado** | *ice cream* |
| **los huevos** | *eggs* |
| **el jamón** | *ham* |
| **el jugo** | *juice* |
| **la leche** | *milk* |
| **la mantequilla** | *butter* |
| **la mantequilla de cacahuate** | *peanut butter* |
| **el melón** | *melon* |
| **el plátano verde** | *plantain* |
| **el pollo asado** | *barbecued chicken* |
| **los tostones** | *fried plantains* |
| **las uvas** | *grapes* |
| **el yogur** | *yogurt* |

**Talk About Food**

| | |
|---|---|
| **desear** | *to desire* |
| **la especialidad de la casa** | *specialty of the house* |
| **estar de acuerdo** | *to be in agreement* |
| **el sabor** | *taste, flavor* |
| **sabroso(a)** | *tasty* |

### DISCUSS FINE ART

**Art**

| | |
|---|---|
| **el (la) artista** | *artist* |
| **las bellas artes** | *fine arts* |
| **el (la) escultor(a)** | *sculptor* |
| **la escultura** | *sculpture* |
| **la exposición** | *exhibit* |
| **la galería** | *gallery* |
| **la obra** | *work of art* |
| **el (la) pintor(a)** | *painter* |
| **la pintura** | *painting* |
| **el retrato** | *portrait* |
| **el talento** | *talent* |

**Describing Art**

| | |
|---|---|
| **antiguo(a)** | *old* |
| **enorme** | *enormous* |
| **formal** | *formal* |
| **lujoso(a)** | *luxurious* |
| **moderno(a)** | *modern* |
| **raro(a)** | *rare, strange* |
| **tradicional** | *traditional* |

### TALK ABOUT THE PAST

**Irregular Preterite Verbs**

| | |
|---|---|
| **andar** | *to walk* |

 **Ya sabes**

| | |
|---|---|
| **decir** | *to say, to tell* |
| **estar** | *to be* |
| **poder (o→ue)** | *to be able* |
| **poner** | *to put* |
| **querer (e→ie)** | *to want, to love* |
| **saber** | *to know* |
| **tener** | *to have* |
| **traer** | *to bring* |
| **venir** | *to come* |

### EXPRESS ACTIVITY PREFERENCES

**Present Tense Stem-Changing Verbs**

| | |
|---|---|
| **competir (e→i)** | *to compete* |
| **mostrar (o→ue)** | *to show* |
| **recomendar (e→ie)** | *to recommend* |
| **repetir (e→i)** | *to repeat* |

**Ya sabes**

| | |
|---|---|
| **jugar (u→ue)** | *to play* |
| **pedir (e→i)** | *to ask for, to order* |
| **servir (e→i)** | *to serve* |

### Juego

El pato pintó un retrato del gato.
O, ¿el gato pintó un retrato del pato?

## Teaching All Students

**Extra Help** Have students make 3 columns on a piece of paper with the headings: **el desayuno**, **el almuerzo**, and **la cena**. Have them categorize the food vocabulary listed above under these 3 meals depending on their personal diets, then compare lists with a partner.

**Multiple Intelligences**

**Musical/Rhythmic** Have students work in small groups to choose appropriate music for these situations: in an art gallery showing work of Hispanic artists, in a Mexican restaurant, and in the kitchen when preparing a snack for Spanish class. You may play the **Canciones** Cassette/CD or bring in your own sample of Hispanic music.



### Teaching Note: En tu propia voz

**Writing Strategy** A well-written description uses many details. To cover all the details, have students answer these interrogatives: **¿Quién? ¿Qué? ¿Dónde? ¿Cuándo? ¿Por qué? ¿Cómo?**

### Teaching Suggestions

**Vocabulary Review**

Give students 2 minutes to study the first vocabulary list (*Comment on Food*). Ask them to close their books and write down as many vocabulary words as they can, then check their list with the book. Working with a partner, have them continue through the vocabulary list.

### Interdisciplinary Connections

**Art** Work with the art department at your school to prepare a comparative display of the student research reports (see **Conexiones**, p. 70).

### Language Note

**Conexiones** is related to **conexionar**, not **conectar** (the incorrect form **"conección"** is sometimes seen).

### Juego

**Answer**

El pato pintó un retrato del gato.

### Project: Reviewing Etapa 2

- Bring in a menu for a restaurant that serves food from a Spanish-speaking country.
- Research an art exhibit that highlights artists from a Spanish-speaking community in the U.S.
- Research a Mexican muralist and say what you like/dislike about his/her work.

**Extra Credit**

| | |
|---|---|
| Menu | 2 pts. |
| Art Exhibit | 2 pts. |
| Mexican Muralist | 2 pts. |

### Block Schedule

**Personalizing** Ask students to think about how they learn best, and plan a study strategy for the **Etapa** Exam.

# Planning Guide CLASSROOM MANAGEMENT

## OBJECTIVES

**Communication**
- Discuss ways to communicate *pp. 74–77*
- React to news *pp. 76–77, 87, 88–89*
- Ask for and give information *pp. 80, 84, 86*
- Talk about things and people you know *pp. 79, 81*

**Grammar**
- Demonstrative adjectives and pronouns *pp. 82–83*
- **Saber** and **conocer** *p. 81*
- **Hubo** *p. 84*
- Stem-changing preterite verbs (**e→i, o→u**) *pp. 84–85*
- Spelling change preterite verbs (**i→y**) *p. 85*

**Culture**
- **Los periódicos en español dentro de los EE.UU.** *pp. 88–89*
- **Cuándo llegar a una fiesta** *p. 79*
- **Periódicos españoles en Internet** *p. 87*
- **Miami– Puerta de las Américas** *pp. 90–91*

**Recycling**
- Irregular preterite forms

## STRATEGIES

**Listening Strategies**
- Listen with a purpose *p. 76*

**Speaking Strategies**
- Present your findings *p. 86*
- Provide additional information *p. 94*

**Reading Strategies**
- Skim for the general idea *pp. 88–89*
- Scan for specific information *pp. 88–89*

**Writing Strategies**
- Use connectors in a description *Actividad* 8, *p. 94*

**Connecting Cultures Strategies**
- Identify characteristics of neighborhoods *pp. 90–91*
- Learn about other cultures to understand one's own *TE p. 89*
- Learn about concepts of social time *p. 79*

## PROGRAM RESOURCES

### Print
- *Más práctica* Workbook PE *pp. 31–40*
- Block Scheduling Copymasters *pp. 25–32*
- Unit 1 Resource Book
  - *Más práctica* Workbook TE *pp. 169–178*
  - *Cuaderno para hispanohablantes* TE *pp. 178–188*
  - Information Gap Activities *pp. 189–192*
  - Family Involvement *pp. 193–194*
  - Video Activities *pp. 195–197*
  - Videoscript *pp. 198–199*
  - Audioscript *pp. 200–204*
  - Assessment Program, Unit 1 Etapa 3 *pp. 205–239; 249–251*
  - Answer Keys *pp. 256–258*

### Audiovisual
- Audio Program Cassette 3A, 3B / CD 3
- Video Program Videotape 1 / Videodisc 1A
- Overhead Transparencies M1–M5; GO1–GO5; 4; 25–34

### Technology
- Electronic Teacher Tools/Test Generator
- *Intrigas y aventuras* CD-ROM, Disc 1
-   www.mcdougallittell.com

### Assessment Program Options
- Cooperative Quizzes (Unit 1 Resource Book)
- Etapa Exam Forms A and B (Unit 1 Resource Book)
- *Examen para hispanohablantes* (Unit 1 Resource Book)
- Portfolio Assessment (Unit 1 Resource Book)
- Unit 1 Comprehensive Test (Unit 1 Resource Book)
- *Prueba comprensiva para hispanohablantes* Unit 1 (Unit 1 Resource Book)
- Multiple Choice Test Questions (Unit 1 Resource Book)
- Audio Program Cassette 19A / CD 19
- Electronic Teacher Tools/Test Generator

### Native Speakers
- *Cuaderno para hispanohablantes* PE *pp. 31–40*
- *Cuaderno para hispanohablantes* TE (Unit 1 Resource Book)
- *Examen para hispanohablantes* (Unit 1 Resource Book)
- *Prueba comprensiva para hispanohablantes* Unit 1 (Unit 1 Resource Book)
- Audio Program (*Para hispanohablantes*) Cassettes 2B, 19A / CD 2, CD 19
- Audioscript (Unit 1 Resource Book)

# Student Text Listening Activity Scripts

## Videoscript: Diálogo *pages 76–77*

- Videotape 1, 22:30 • Videodisc 1A
  Search Chapter 9, Play to end. U1E3, En vivo (Dialog)
- Use the videoscript with **Actividades 1, 2** page 78

Francisco: ¿Aló?
Alma: Hola, Francisco. Soy yo.
Francisco: ¿Alma? Qué bien. ¿Qué haces?
Alma: Estoy leyendo el periódico. ¿Lo leíste?
Francisco: No, no pude. Estoy trabajando en mi artículo. ¿Por qué?
Alma: Hay un titular que dice "Hubo un rescate dramático en Miami ayer. Francisco García es el héroe de toda la ciudad porque rescató un gato."
Francisco: ¡Alma!
Alma: No es verdad. ¿Y cómo va tu artículo?
Francisco: Bien. Pidieron un artículo sobre un canal de televisión en Miami. Mañana voy a ir al estudio donde transmiten un noticiero.
Alma: ¡Ay, qué interesante! ¿Puedo ir contigo?
Francisco: Sí, claro. Ven aquí, y salimos a las tres.
Alma: ¡Perfecto! Bueno, te veo mañana a las tres. ¡Bye!
Francisco: Hasta luego.
Francisco: (escribiendo su artículo) Hay varios canales de televisión en español que transmiten desde Miami. Y las transmisiones llegan a toda Latinoamérica, no sólo a los Estados Unidos. Todos los países reciben los canales de televisión de Miami a través de los satélites y el cable...
Sr. Campos: Aquí preparamos los noticieros; trabajamos en estas computadoras, escribiendo el texto del noticiero.
Francisco: ¿Usan el Internet también?
Sr. Campos: Sí, a veces usamos el Internet en el proceso de investigar los reportajes. Mucha de la información de nuestro noticiero anoche vino del Internet. Éste es uno de nuestros estudios. Es aquí donde filmamos las noticias. Nuestra programación incluye noticias internacionales y locales. Los televidentes están bien informados, y saben lo que está pasando en el mundo.
Alma: Vi su noticiero anoche. Dieron un reportaje sobre los cubanoamericanos en Miami. Fue muy interesante.
Sr. Campos: Sí, quisimos presentarles un reportaje muy informativo y objetivo. ¿Saben quién es esa señora?
Alma: ¿Ésa? Sí, ella es la reportera que dio el reportaje anoche. Es muy famosa.
Sr. Campos: ¿Les gustaría conocerla?
Francisco: Sí, nos encantaría conocerla. ¡Muchísimas gracias!
Sr. Campos: Pues, vamos.
Alma: ¿Dijiste algo sobre la reportera que conocimos?
Francisco: Sí. Sabes, creo que este artículo está listo.
Alma: Francisco, ¿escribiste tú este poema?
Francisco: ¡Alma! Dame ese cuaderno. Eso es personal.
Alma: ¿Qué cuaderno? ¿Éste? Vamos, Paco. Somos amigos. Nos conocemos muy bien. Léeme el poema.
Francisco: No sé.
Alma: Por favor.
Francisco: Bueno, por qué no.
Nos conocimos esa tarde tranquila
Yo, una puerta cerrada, la llave perdida.
Llamaste, tocaste...y fue tu sonrisa
Qué abrió lo cerrado... y entró una amiga.
Alma:: ¡Qué bonito! ¿Y quién es la amiga?
Francisco: ¿Quién es? ¡Boba! Eres tú.
Alma: ¿Yo?
Francisco: Sí, tú.
Alma: Gracias, Paco. Es la primera vez que alguien me escribe un poema.

## Actividad 11 ¿Dónde hubo... ? *page 84*

Buenas tardes. Bienvenidos a nuestra edición de la tarde. Y ahora, las noticias: Hoy, hubo un huracán y dos estadounidenses quedaron atrapados. En un rescate dramático, unos empleados españoles rescataron a un niño de un árbol cerca de su oficina. El policía paraguayo investigó a un señor que de repente tuvo millones en el banco. Esta mañana un oficial cubano anunció que el precio de los plátanos va a bajar. Para estar bien informados, escuchen nuestro programa todos los días.

## Actividad 14 ¿Es cierto? *page 85*

Ana: Hola, Víctor, gracias por la entrevista. ¿Cuándo viniste de Paraguay a Miami?
Víctor: Vine aquí el primero de septiembre, Ana.
Ana: Ah, viniste en septiembre, cuando empezó la escuela. Bueno. ¿A quiénes conociste al llegar?
Víctor: Pues, conocí a mi familia norteamericana en el aeropuerto – el señor y la señora Trelevean y sus tres hijos.
Ana: Muy bien. ¿Qué le pediste de comer a tu mamá norteamericana la primera vez?
Víctor: Le pedí una hamburguesa con queso y papas fritas, claro.
Ana: Yo como muchas hamburguesas también. ¿Qué hiciste con tu familia estadounidense durante las vacaciones?
Víctor: Nosotros fuimos a la playa y a un estudio de televisión para niños.
Ana: ¿Cómo fue ese viaje?
Víctor: Muy bien. Nos divertimos muchísimo.
Ana: ¿Qué puedes decir de tu primer mes aquí en Estados Unidos?
Víctor: Estoy muy contento aquí. Durante mi primer mes conocí a muchos amigos nuevos y me reí mucho.
Ana: Gracias, Víctor. El artículo con esta entrevista va a estar en la próxima edición del periódico escolar. Nos vemos.
Víctor: Bueno. Hasta luego.

### Quick Start Review Answers

**p. 72** Describing others
1. **Alma tiene pelo castaño.**
2. **Alma es joven.**
3. **La señora de la izquierda tiene pelo largo.**
4. **Francisco lleva una camisa.**
5. **Francisco es trabajador.**

**p. 80** Countries/origins
*Answers will vary. Answers could include:*
**Argentina, Bolivia, Chile, España, Guatemala, Honduras, México, Paraguay, Uruguay**

**p. 84** e→i stem-changing verbs: present
1. **Luis pide pollo asado.**
2. **Yo pido jamón.**
3. **Ellos piden la especialidad de la casa.**
4. **Los niños piden unas hamburguesas.**
5. **Nosotros pedimos bistec.**

**p. 92** Nationalities
1. **José es puertorriqueño.**
2. **Pierre es canadiense.**
3. **Lupe es nicaragüense.**
4. **Teresa es ecuatoriana.**
5. **Helen es inglesa.**

# Pacing Guide

## Sample Lesson Plan - 50 Minute Schedule

### DAY 1

***Etapa* Opener**
- Quick Start Review (TE, p. 72) 5 MIN.
- Anticipate/Activate prior knowledge: Have students look at the *Etapa* Opener and answer questions. 10 MIN.

**En contexto: Vocabulario**
- Quick Start Review (TE, p. 74) 3 MIN.
- Discuss pictures, have students use context and pictures to learn *Etapa* vocabulary. Answer questions p. 75. 10 MIN.

**En vivo: Diálogo**
- Quick Start Review (TE, p. 76) 2 MIN.
- Review Listening Strategy, p. 76. Play audio or show video for the dialog shown on pp. 76–77. 8 MIN.
- Read aloud, students taking roles of characters. 7 MIN.
- Groups role-play while looking at the photos in their texts. Encourage logical dialog with familiar vocabulary. 5 MIN.

**Homework Option:**
- Video Activities, Unit 1 Resource Book, pp. 195–197.

### DAY 2

**En acción: Vocabulario y gramática**
- Quick Start Review (TE, p. 78) 5 MIN.
- Ask students for a summary of *En vivo* dialog to check recall. 5 MIN.
- Check homework. 5 MIN.
- Replay the *En vivo* dialog using the audiovisual resources and have students do *Actividades* 1 and 2 orally. 10 MIN.
- Have students complete *Actividad* 3 orally and *Actividad* 4 in pairs. 10 MIN.
- Use a map to review countries and introduce nationalities, p. 80. 10 MIN.
- Have students begin writing *Actividad* 5. 5 MIN.

**Homework Option:**
- Finish *Actividad* 5. *Más práctica* Workbook, p. 35. *Cuaderno para hispanohablantes*, p. 33.

### DAY 3

**En acción (cont.)**
- Quick Start Review (TE, p. 80) 5 MIN.
- Check homework. 5 MIN.
- Have students do *Actividades* 6 and 7 in pairs, then go over them orally. 10 MIN.
- Present *Nota: Saber* and *conocer,* p. 81, and complete *Actividad* 8. 10 MIN.
- Present *Gramática:* Demonstrative Adjectives and Pronouns, p. 82. 10 MIN.
- Present *Vocabulario,* p. 83. Have students begin writing *Actividad* 9. 10 MIN.

**Homework Option:**
- Finish *Actividades* 9 and 10, p. 83. *Más práctica* Workbook, pp. 36–38, as needed. *Cuaderno para hispanohablantes*, pp. 34–36 as needed.

### DAY 4

**En acción (cont.)**
- Check homework. 5 MIN.
- Quick Start Review (TE, p. 84) 5 MIN.
- Play the audio and do *Actividad* 11 orally. 7 MIN.
- Present *Gramática*: Stem-Changing Verbs in the Preterite and *Vocabulario,* p. 84. 8 MIN.
- Have students do *Actividad* 12 in writing. 5 MIN.
- Do *Actividad* 13 orally with the class. 5 MIN.
- Play the audio, then do *Actividad* 14 orally. 5 MIN.
- Have students do *Actividad* 15 in pairs. 5 MIN.
- Present Speaking Strategy on p. 86 and have students complete *Actividad* 16 orally in a group. 5 MIN.

**Homework Option:**
- Have students do *Actividad* 17 in writing. *Más práctica* Workbook, pp. 39–40, *Cuaderno para hispanohablantes*, pp. 37–38.

### DAY 5

**En acción (cont.)**
- Check homework. 5 MIN.
- Quick Start Review (TE, p. 86) 5 MIN.
- Do *Más comunicación* activity, p. R4. 5 MIN.
- Read and discuss *Nota cultural* and *Refrán,* p. 87. 5 MIN.

**En voces: Lectura**
- Quick Start Review (TE, p. 88). 5 MIN.
- Review Reading Strategy on p. 88 and have students read *Lectura* silently. 10 MIN.
- Have students read *Lectura* aloud taking turns. 10 MIN.
- Have students answer *¿Comprendiste?* questions orally. 5 MIN.

**Homework Option:**
- Have students finish *¿Comprendiste?* and *¿Qué piensas?* questions in writing.
- *Más práctica* Workbook, pp. 31–34. *Cuaderno para hispanohablantes*, pp. 31–32.

### DAY 6

**En voces: Lectura**
- Review answers to *¿Comprendiste?* and *¿Qué piensas?* 5 MIN.

**En colores: Cultura y comparaciones**
- Quick Start Review (TE, p. 90) 5 MIN.
- Review Connecting Cultures Strategy, p. 90. 5 MIN.
- Read *Miami: Puerta de las Américas* aloud with students. 5 MIN.
- Students answer *¿Comprendiste?* and *¿Qué piensas?* 10 MIN.
- Have small groups role-play *Hazlo tú* on p. 91. 10 MIN.

**En uso: Repaso y Más comunicación**
- Do *Actividades* 1, 2, and 3 orally. 10 MIN.

**Homework Option:**
- Have students write *Actividades* 3, 4, and 5.

### DAY 7

**En uso (cont.)**
- Check homework. 5 MIN.
- Quick Start Review (TE, p. 92) 5 MIN.
- Review Speaking Strategy, p. 94. Then do *Actividad* 6 orally in pairs and *Actividad* 7 in groups. 10 MIN.
- Present Strategy, TE p. 94. Have students do *Actividad* 8. 5 MIN.

**En resumen: Repaso de vocabulario**
- Complete *Etapa* 3 Exam. 20 MIN.

**Conexiones**
- Read and discuss. 5 MIN.

**Homework Option:**
- Review for Unit 3 Comprehensive Test.

### DAY 8

- Review grammar questions, etc., as necessary. 5 MIN.
- Complete Unit 3 Comprehensive Test. 30 MIN.

**En tu propia voz: Escritura**
- Start writing activity and assign the rest for homework. 5 MIN.

**Ampliación**
- Use a suggested project, game, or activity. (TE pp. 27A–27B) 10 MIN.

**Homework Option:**
- Finish *Ampliación* project.
- Preview *Unidad* 2 Opener, pp. 96–97.

# Sample Lesson Plan – Block Schedule (90 minutes)

## DAY 1

***Etapa* Opener**
- Quick Start Review (TE, p. 72) 5 MIN.
- Anticipate/Activate prior knowledge: Have students look at the *Etapa* Opener and answer questions. 10 MIN.

**En contexto: Vocabulario**
- Quick Start Review (TE, p. 74) 3 MIN.
- Discuss pictures, have students use context and pictures to learn *Etapa* vocabulary. Answer questions p. 75. 10 MIN.

**En vivo: Diálogo**
- Quick Start Review (TE, p. 76) 2 MIN.
- Review Listening Strategy, p. 76. Play audio or show video for the dialog shown on pp. 76–77. 5 MIN.
- Ask Comprehension Questions (TE, p. 77) 10 MIN.
- Read aloud, students taking roles of characters. 10 MIN.
- Groups role-play while looking at the photos in their texts. Encourage logical dialog with familiar vocabulary. 5 MIN.

**En acción: Vocabulario y gramática**
- Quick Start Review (TE, p. 78) 5 MIN.
- Have students do *Actividades* 1 and 2 orally. 15 MIN.
- Have students complete *Actividad* 3 orally and *Actividad* 4 in pairs. 10 MIN.

**Homework Option:**
- Have students prepare two T/F or yes/no questions about the dialog.
- Video Activities, Unit 1 Resource Book, pp. 195–197.

## DAY 2

**En acción (cont.)**
- Check homework. 5 MIN.
- Quick Start Review (TE, p. 80) 5 MIN.
- Use a map to review countries and introduce nationalities, p. 80. 5 MIN.
- Have students write *Actividad* 5. Check orally. 5 MIN.
- Have students do *Actividades* 6 and 7 in pairs. 10 MIN.
- Present *Nota* on *saber* and *conocer,* p. 81, and complete *Actividad* 8 orally. 10 MIN.
- Present *Gramática:* Demonstrative Adjectives and Pronouns, p. 82. 10 MIN.
- Present *Vocabulario,* p. 83. Have students write *Actividad* 9, then do *Actividad* 10 in pairs. 10 MIN.
- Use Block Scheduling Copymasters.
- Play the audio and do *Actividad* 11 orally. Students can also write their summary. 10 MIN.
- Present *Gramática*: Stem-changing Verbs in the Preterite, p. 84. 10 MIN.
- Have students do *Actividad* 12 in writing. 5 MIN.
- Present Nota on *leer, creer,* and *oir,* p 85. Then do *Actividad* 13 orally with the class. 5 MIN.

**Homework Option:**
- *Más práctica* Workbook, pp. 33–40 as needed. *Cuaderno para hispanohablantes*, pp. 33–38, as needed.

## DAY 3

**En acción (cont.)**
- Check homework. 5 MIN.
- Quick Start Review (TE, p. 86) 5 MIN.
- Review Stem-changing Verbs in the preterite. 10 MIN.
- Play audio for students and do *Actividad* 14 orally with the whole class. 10 MIN.
- Present vocabulary on p. 86 and have students complete *Actividad* 15 in pairs. 10 MIN.
- Review Speaking Strategy, p. 86, then have students do *Actividades* 16 and 17 in pairs. 10 MIN.
- Discuss *Nota cultural* and *Refrán* with class. 5 MIN.
- Use Block Scheduling Copymasters.

**En voces: Lectura**
- Quick Start Review (TE, p. 88). 5 MIN.
- Review Reading Strategy on p. 88 and have students read *Lectura* silently. 10 MIN.
- Have students read *Lectura* aloud taking turns. 5 MIN.
- Have students answer *¿Comprendiste?* questions on p. 89. Refer back to *Lectura* if students get incorrect answers. 5 MIN.
- Do the *¿Qué piensas?* activity in writing. 10 MIN.

**Homework Option:**
- Have students finish *¿Qué piensas?* activity as written homework.
- *Más práctica* Workbook, pp. 31–34. *Cuaderno para hispanohablantes*, pp. 31–32, 39–40.
- Review for *Etapa 3* Exam.

## DAY 4

**En colores: Cultura y comparaciones**
- Check homework. 5 MIN.
- Quick Start Review (TE, p. 90) 5 MIN.
- Review Connecting Cultures Strategy, p. 90. 5 MIN.
- Read *Miami: Puerta de las Américas* aloud with students. 10 MIN.
- Have students answer the *¿Comprendiste?* questions orally. 5 MIN.
- Have students start the *¿Qué piensas?* activities in writing. 10 MIN.
- Have small groups discuss *Hazlo tú* on p. 91. 10 MIN.

**En uso: Repaso y Más comunicación**
- Do *En uso Actividades* 1, 2, and 3 orally. 10 MIN.
- Do *Actividades* 4 and 5 orally or in writing. 10 MIN.

**En resumen: Repaso de vocabulario**
- Complete *Etapa* 3 Exam. 20 MIN.

**Homework Option:**
- Block Scheduling Copymasters.
- Review for Unit 1 Comprehensive Test.

## DAY 5

**En uso (cont.)**
- Quick Start Review (TE, p. 94) 5 MIN.
- Review Speaking Strategy, p. 94. Then do *Actividad* 6 orally in pairs and *Actividad* 7 in groups. 10 MIN.

**Conexiones**
- Assign this activity for students to do outside of class and bring in the results to discuss. 5 MIN.

**En resumen: Repaso de vocabulario**
- Review grammar questions, etc. as necessary. 10 MIN.
- Complete Unit 1 Comprehensive Test. 30 MIN.

**En tu propia voz: Escritura**
- Start writing activity. 10 MIN.

**Ampliación**
- Use a suggested project, game, or activity. (TE pp. 27A–27B) 20 MIN.

**Homework Option:**
- Finish *En tu propia voz* writing activity.
- Preview *Unidad* 2 Opener, pp. 96–97.

▼ El señor Campos les enseña la estación de televisión a Francisco y a Alma.

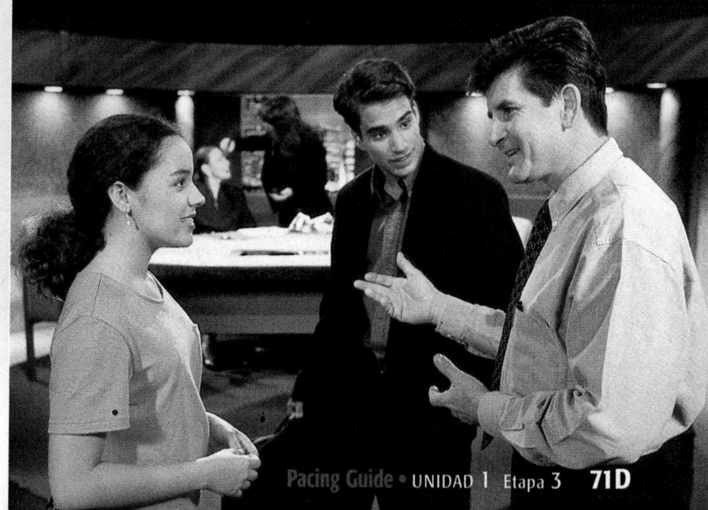

## Etapa Theme

**Touring a television station in Miami**
**Discussing ways to communicate**

## Grammar Objectives

- Demonstrative adjectives and pronouns
- Stem-changing preterites (e→i, o→u)
- **Saber** and **conocer**
- Spelling change preterites
- Preterite of **hay**

### Teaching Resource Options

**Print** 

Block Scheduling Copymasters

**Audiovisual**

**OHT** 4, 31 (Quick Start)

### Quick Start Review

Describing others

Use **OHT** 31 or write on board: Study the picture of Francisco and his friend Alma as they interview a television reporter on pp. 72–73. Then answer the following questions.

1. ¿Tiene Alma pelo rubio o castaño?
2. ¿Es joven o vieja Alma?
3. ¿Tiene pelo corto o largo la señora de la izquierda?
4. ¿Lleva Francisco una camisa o una camiseta?
5. ¿Es Francisco perezoso o trabajador?

**Answers**, see p. 71B.

### Teaching Suggestions
**Previewing the Etapa**

- Ask students to study the picture on pp. 72–73 and focus on the setting.
- Ask students to guess the location of the picture and what is happening. Ask them to provide the clues they used to guess.
- Use the **¿Qué ves?** questions to further analyze the picture.

UNIDAD 1

# ¿Viste las noticias?

- Discuss ways to communicate
- React to news
- Ask for and give information
- Talk about things and people you know

### ¿Qué ves?

Mira la foto del canal y contesta las preguntas.

1. ¿Cuántas personas hay en la foto? ¿Qué hacen?
2. ¿Conoces a algunas personas de la foto? ¿Quiénes son?
3. ¿Qué programa quieres ver?

### Classroom Management

**Planning Ahead** Prepare to introduce students to the media in Spanish by collecting Spanish-language newspapers or magazines from the U.S. or other countries. You may also wish to videotape a news program in Spanish from a Spanish cable station, such as **Univisión** or **Telemundo**.

**Time Saver** At the end of the first unit, students should be able to take on more responsibility in starting the new Etapa. They should be able to answer the **¿Qué ves?** questions in pairs/groups by themselves. They should also be able to review for the first time at home the **En contexto** vocabulary input on pp. 74–75.

PROGRAMACIÓN DE 7 A.M. A MEDIANOCHE

LO MEJOR PARA HOY

7:00 p.m. GALA **La Tocada** Emmanuel es el invitado en el programa de entrevistas y música conducido por Verónica Castro.

Emmanuel

9:00 p.m. 17 **Swellegant Elegance** Harvey Fierstein y la leyenda del jazz Diane Schuur se unen al Seattle's Men's Choir en un homenaje al compositor Cole Porter.

17 The Big Comfy Couch (cc)
51 CINE
FSA Noticias
GALA ECO Noticiero
GEMS El Rosa y el Azul
HBO MOVIE *Once Upon a Forest* ★★ G (1:15) ESP
OLETV El Cuerpo Humano
SHO The Busy World of Richard Scarry (cc)
SHO (8:25) The Busy World of Richard Scarry

**8:30 AM**

2 Arthur (cc)
17 Zoobilee Zoo (cc)
CINE (8:45) MOVIE *Meatballs* ★ PG (1:45)
OLETV El Cerebro: Un Cosmo Misterioso

4 The Price Is Right (cc)
6 News (cc)
7 Hawaii Five-0
10 Sally Jessy Raphael
17 HealthWeek (cc)
23 Agujetas de Color de Rosa
40 Videos, Videos
51 Las Juanas
FSA Noticias
GALA Home Shopping Network: En Español
GEMS Menú del Día
HBO MOVIE *Dominick and Eugene* ★★★ PG-13 (2:00)
OLETV Reporte Medicinal
SHO (11:20) The Busy World of Richard Scarry
SUR El Noticiero Venezuela- 2da Edición

**11:30 AM**

2 Reading Rainbow (cc)
13 40 Programa pagado
17 Breakthrough: Television's Journal of Science and Medicine
GEMS La Otra Familia
OLETV El Cerebro: Un Cosmo Misterioso
SHO (11:45) MOVIE *The Mugger* ★ (1:15)

**Mediodía**

2 America's Historic Trails With Tom Bodett
4 News (cc)
6 Another World (cc)
7 10 News (cc)
13 En una Hora
17 Jenkins' Art Workshop
40 Espejo Público
51 CINE *Carrera Contra la Muerte*
CINE (12:15) MOVIE *The Evening Star* ★★ PG-13 (2:15) ESP
FSA Programa pagado
GEMS Sabor Latino
OLETV Caminos Hacia el Arte
SUR Noticiero P.A.T. Bolivia

**12:30 PM**



## Cross Cultural Connections

Ask students if they notice any differences between the television studio in the photograph on pp. 72–73 and television studios from their local news in English. Ask them to identify the people in the photograph and what they might do. The photograph was taken at a television station in Miami, FL.

## Culture Highlights

● **SPANISH TELEVISION IN THE U.S.** The largest Spanish language network in the U.S. is **Univisión** with 20 owned/operated stations, 27 affiliates, and over 800 cable stations all over the country. The cable network of **Univisión** is called **Galavisión**, which is the leading Hispanic cable network in the U.S. Both networks broadcast a variety of programs including sports, movies, music, news, variety shows, and soap operas.

## Critical Thinking

Divide the class into groups. Have each group formulate a question about the people in the photo based on the functions on p. 72 and hypothesize an answer. Review the questions and answers at the end of the Etapa.

## Teaching All Students

**Extra Help** Review the TV listings with students and have them pick out programs they recognize.

**Native Speakers** Ask Spanish speakers to list the Spanish TV or radio stations they know, either in their community or in other cities. Have them describe programs they have seen in Spanish and explain any similarities or differences from the English TV or radio stations that are familiar to the class.

**Challenge** Have students write additional **¿Qué ves?** questions to ask each other about the Spanish TV listing on p. 73. Then give a section of a Spanish-language newspaper to different groups of students and have them write more **¿Qué ves?** questions to ask each other.

## Block Schedule

**Retention** Ask students to work in groups of 3 to write a short dialog between the 3 people in the picture on p. 73. Then have each member of the group take on one of the roles and act out the dialog. (For additional activities, see **Block Scheduling Copymasters**.)

## Teaching Resource Options

**Print** 

Unit 1 Resource Book
- Video Activities, p. 195
- Videoscript, p. 198
- Audioscript, p. 200

**Audiovisual** 

**OHT** 25, 26, 27, 27A, 28, 28A, 31 (Quick Start)
**Audio Program** Cassette 3A / CD 3
**Video Program** Videotape 1, 19:52 / Videodisc 1A

Search Chapter 8, Play to 9
U1E3, En contexto (Vocabulary)

**Technology** 

*Intrigas y aventuras* CD-ROM, Disc 1

## Quick Start Review

**Stating preferences**

Use OHT 31 or write on board: Use the following words to create three sentences about what you and your family prefer.

En la televisión esta noche…

yo / mis padres / mi hermano(a) (preferir) mirar…
- el campeonato de béisbol
- un partido de fútbol
- una película cómica
- un concierto

*Answers will vary. Answers could include:*

En la televisión esta noche yo prefiero mirar un concierto.
... mis padres prefieren mirar una película cómica.
... mi hermano prefiere mirar un partido de fútbol.

# En contexto

## VOCABULARIO

Mira las ilustraciones de periódico y de la estación de televisión en Miami. Te ayudan a comprender las palabras en **azul** y a responder a las preguntas personales.

¿Por qué lees el periódico? Lees el periódico para saber lo que pasa en la ciudad y en el mundo. Muchos periódicos publican **críticas** de **las noticias** en diferentes **ediciones.** Algunos tienen una edición por la mañana y otra por la tarde. **El titular** de este periódico reporta sobre **un ladrón** que **robó** pinturas y esculturas. **El robo** es una noticia importante de la primera página.

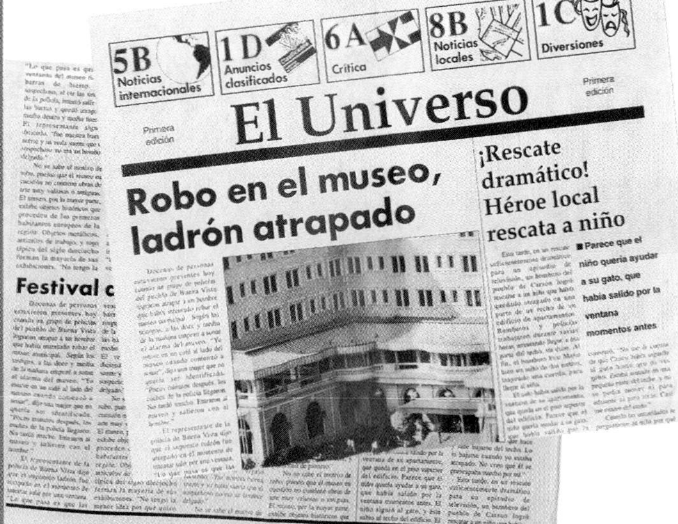

5B Noticias internacionales | 1D Anuncios clasificados | 6A Crítica | 8B Noticias locales | 1C Diversiones

Primera edición

**El Universo**

Primera edición

**Robo en el museo, ladrón atrapado**

**¡Rescate dramático! Héroe local rescata a niño**

**Festival c**

■ Parece que el niño quería ayudar a su gato, que había salido por la ventana momentos antes

También los periódicos reportan de personas que son **héroes** o **heroínas** porque **rescatan** a otras. Si **de repente** una persona necesita ayuda, el héroe está preparado. En este **rescate,** los señores ayudan a otras personas.

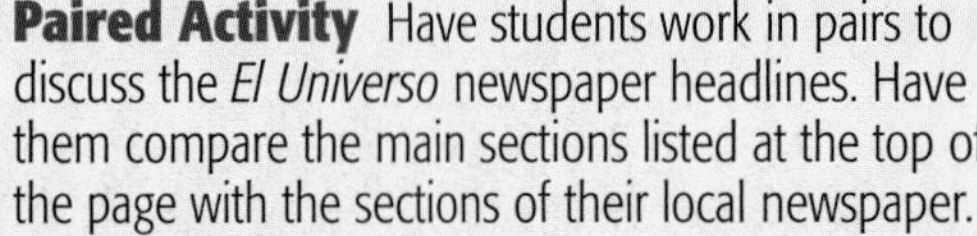

## Classroom Community

**Paired Activity** Have students work in pairs to discuss the *El Universo* newspaper headlines. Have them compare the main sections listed at the top of the page with the sections of their local newspaper.

**TPR** **Prepare ahead:** Photocopy a page from a Spanish TV listing. As you call out a type of television program, students should locate it in the listing they are holding and stand up when they find it. Students can also call out the title of the program so others can follow along. You can call out **las noticias, un programa de deportes, un programa histórico, los anuncios, un programa cómico.**

**Storytelling** Based on photos B–E above, have students create their own story about the media. Students can work in pairs or small groups and they should write, narrate, and read the story aloud to the class.

**C** Las noticias **locales** te dicen lo que pasa en tu ciudad. Por ejemplo, te dicen los resultados de juegos locales. Las noticias **internacionales** tienen **reportajes** sobre otros países, incluyendo noticias de deportes de todo el mundo.

**D** **Los canales** de televisión transmiten diferentes tipos de programas. Hay programas históricos y cómicos. Hay programas de deportes y programas de noticias, como **los noticieros.** En este noticiero, **el reportero** cuenta las noticias más importantes del día. Muchos **televidentes** miran el noticiero todos los días.

**E** Los canales también tienen muchos **anuncios.** Los anuncios te hablan de cosas para comprar, lugares adonde ir, comida, otros programas... ¡todo lo que ves en la vida diaria!

### Preguntas personales

1. ¿Cuál es tu programa de televisión favorito?
2. Nombra una noticia importante del noticiero de esta semana.
3. ¿Cuál es la noticia en la primera página del periódico de hoy?
4. Nombra dos productos que ves en los anuncios de la televisión.
5. ¿Qué anuncios te gustan más? ¿Por qué?



## Teaching Suggestions
### Introducing Vocabulary

- Have students look at pp. 74–75. Use OHT 25–26 and Audiocassette 3A / CD 3 to present the vocabulary.
- Ask the Comprehension Questions in order of yes/no (questions 1–3), either/or (questions 4–5), and simple word or phrase (questions 6–8). You may expand by adding similar questions.
- Point out that the newspaper on this page is the same one that is shown in the video.

## Comprehension Questions

1. ¿Leemos qué pasa en el periódico? **(Sí)**
2. ¿Están en la primera página las noticias insignificantes? **(No)**
3. ¿Roban cosas los ladrones? **(Sí)**
4. ¿Es el programa de la foto de las páginas 72 y 73 un programa histórico o un programa de noticias? **(de noticias)**
5. ¿Hacen los héroes cosas extraordinarias u ordinarias? **(extraordinarias)**
6. ¿Cuál es otra palabra para un programa de noticias? **(el noticiero)**
7. ¿De qué hablan los anuncios? **(productos, comida)**
8. ¿De qué habla el anuncio de la foto? **(de un jugo de fruta)**

## Language Note

Point out that many advertisements use the command forms when addressing the public. Have students guess why commands are used.

## Teaching All Students

**Extra Help** Randomly call out the active vocabulary words from pp. 74–75 and have students point to the photos in their textbooks. Then use an actual newspaper to illustrate **noticias locales**, **noticias internacionales**, etc.

**Native Speakers** Ask Spanish speakers to bring in any newspapers or magazines in Spanish. Have them describe the publication by answering the following questions: Who reads the publication? What kind of news/information is found in it? Which section(s) do they like the best?

## Block Schedule

**Oral Presentation** Elaborate on the **Preguntas personales** by having students record parts of their favorite shows or a newscast. They are to introduce the part to the class and then play it for them and explain why they chose it. The class can use a variety of shows, or a theme can be established, e.g., commercials.

### Teaching Resource Options

**Print** 

Block Scheduling Copymasters
Unit 1 Resource Book
Video Activities, pp. 196–197
Videoscript, pp. 198–199
Audioscript, p. 200

**Audiovisual** 

**OHT** 29, 30, 31 (Quick Start)
**Audio Program** Cassette 3A / CD 3
**Video Program** Videotape 1, 19:52 / Videodisc 1A

Search Chapter 9, Play to end
U1E3, En vivo (Dialog)

**Technology** 

*Intrigas y aventuras* CD-ROM, Disc 1

### Quick Start Review

Stating agreement

Use OHT 31 or write on board: Indicate if you agree with these statements by stating **Estoy de acuerdo** or **No estoy de acuerdo**. Support your opinion.

1. Hay mucha violencia en la televisión.
2. Yo aprendo mucho de la televisión.
3. Muchos programas de televisión son ridículos.
4. Los jóvenes deben mirar menos programas de televisión.

*Answers will vary.*

### Gestures

Show the video without sound and have students note how gestures and facial expression communicate meaning.

# En vivo

## DIÁLOGO

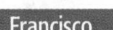

Francisco

Alma

Señor Campos

**PARA ESCUCHAR** • **STRATEGY: LISTENING**

**Listen with a purpose** Listening for a specific piece of information is like scanning a reading. Try listening for one idea: how does Alma get Francisco's attention? Do you think she is **seria** or **cómica**? Explain.

## En Miami...

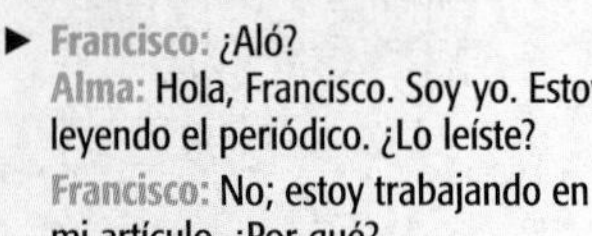

1 ▶ Francisco: ¿Aló?
Alma: Hola, Francisco. Soy yo. Estoy leyendo el periódico. ¿Lo leíste?
Francisco: No; estoy trabajando en mi artículo. ¿Por qué?

5 ▶ Señor Campos: Aquí preparamos los noticieros; trabajamos en estas computadoras. A veces usamos Internet en el proceso de investigar los reportajes.

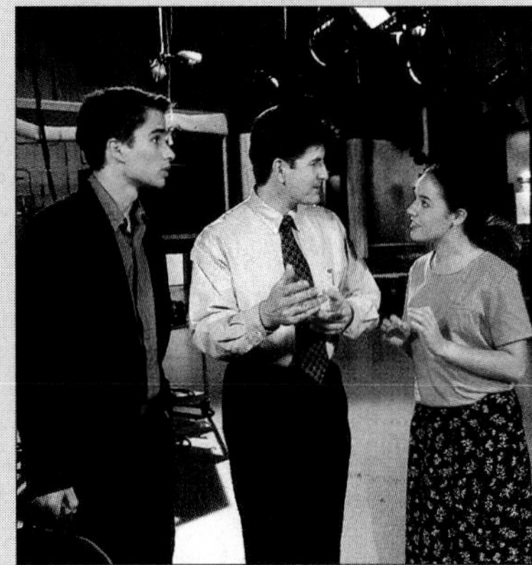

6 ▶ Señor Campos: Nuestra programación incluye noticias internacionales y locales. Los televidentes saben lo que está pasando en el mundo.
Alma: Vi su noticiero sobre los cubanoamericanos. Fue interesante.

7 ▶ Alma: Ésa es la reportera que dio el reportaje anoche. Es famosa.
Señor Campos: ¿Les gustaría conocerla?
Francisco: Sí, nos encantaría. Muchísimas gracias.



### Classroom Community

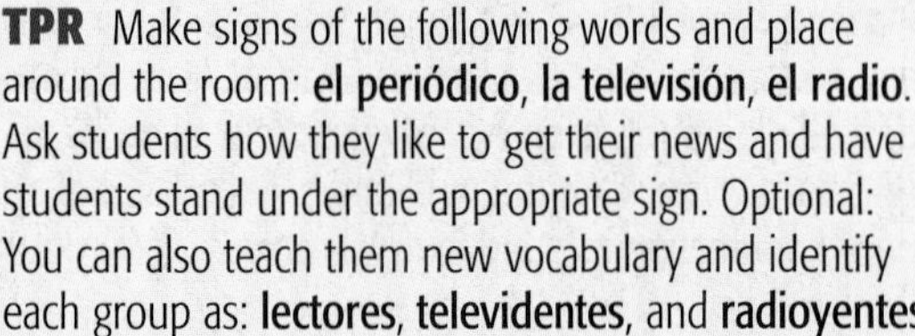

**TPR** Make signs of the following words and place around the room: **el periódico**, **la televisión**, **el radio**. Ask students how they like to get their news and have students stand under the appropriate sign. Optional: You can also teach them new vocabulary and identify each group as: **lectores**, **televidentes**, and **radioyentes**.

**Group Activity** Working in groups of 4, have students take on the roles of Alma, señor Campos, Francisco, and a reporter. Have them role-play the dialog as they visit the sports desk at the television station.

2 ▶ Alma: Hay un titular que dice «Hubo rescate ayer. Francisco García es héroe porque rescató un gato.»
Francisco: ¡Alma!
Alma: No es verdad.

3 ▶ Alma: ¿Cómo va tu artículo?
Francisco: Bien. Pidieron un artículo sobre un canal de televisión en Miami. Mañana voy a ir al estudio.
Alma: ¿Puedo ir contigo?
Francisco: Sí, claro. Salimos a las tres.

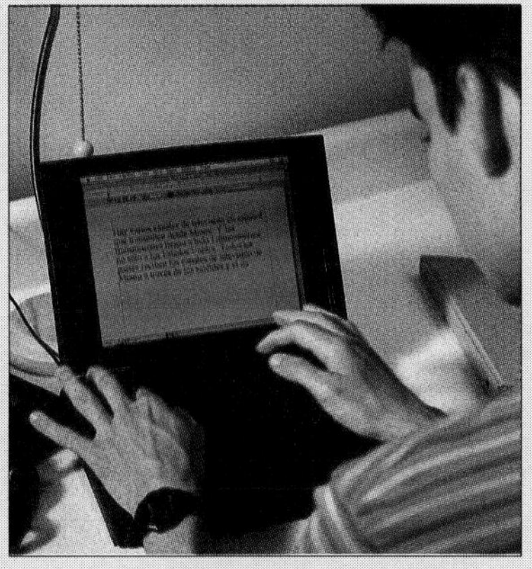

4 ▶ Francisco: (*escribiendo su artículo*) Hay varios canales de televisión en español que transmiten desde Miami. Las transmisiones llegan a toda Latinoamérica. Los países reciben los canales a través de los satélites y el cable.

8 ▶ Alma: Francisco, ¿escribiste tú este poema?
Francisco: ¡Alma! Dame ese cuaderno. Eso es personal.
Alma: ¿Qué cuaderno? ¿Éste? ¡Vamos! Léeme el poema.

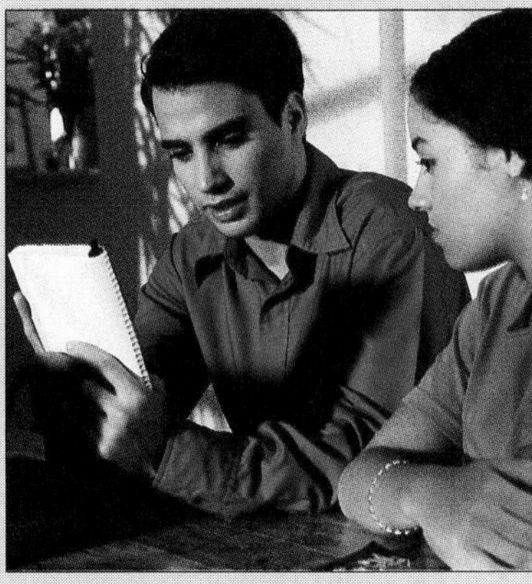

9 ▶ Francisco: Bueno, ¿por qué no?
«Nos conocimos esa tarde tranquila
Yo, una puerta cerrada, la llave perdida.
Llamaste, tocaste y fue tu sonrisa
Que abrió lo cerrado y entró una amiga.»

10 ▶ Alma: ¡Qué bonito! ¿Y quién es la amiga?
Francisco: ¿Quién es? ¡Boba! Eres tú.
Alma: ¿Yo? Gracias, Paco. Es la primera vez que alguien me escribe un poema.



## Teaching All Students

**Extra Help** Have students write a list of the cognates they recognize in frames 2–7 of the dialog. In a second column have them write the corresponding English word for comparison.

**Native Speakers** Ask Spanish speakers to describe any news programs they may watch on television and to recommend a Spanish cable station or favorite program for the class to watch.

**Multiple Intelligences**

**Verbal** Working in small groups, have one student act as **un(a) reportero(a)** who investigates a topic of interest with the group, (school event, sports, cafeteria, etc.) Switch roles.

## Teaching Suggestions

### Presenting the Dialog

- Focus on the dialog context using the following questions. **¿Con quién habla por teléfono Francisco? ¿Es Alma una prima o una amiga de Francisco? ¿Qué hace Francisco durante su visita? ¿Cuáles son las dos cosas que escribe Francisco?**
- Use the video, audiocassette, or CD to present the dialog.

### Video Synopsis

- When Francisco arrives in Miami, he calls his friend Alma and they make plans to go to a television station the next day. Alma learns that Francisco also writes poetry. For a transcript of the video dialog, see p. 71B.

## Comprehension Questions

1. ¿Llama la madre de Francisco por teléfono? **(No)**
2. ¿Lee Alma el periódico? **(Sí)**
3. ¿Rescató Francisco un gato? **(No)**
4. ¿Es cómica o seria Alma? **(cómica)**
5. ¿Escribe Francisco un artículo sobre unas estrellas de cine o un canal de televisión? **(un canal de televisión)**
6. ¿Es un canal que transmite en español o en inglés? **(en español)**
7. ¿Llega la transmisión sólo a Estados Unidos o también a toda Latinoamérica? **(a toda Latinoamérica)**
8. ¿Qué usan los reporteros para investigar los reportajes? **(Internet)**
9. ¿Qué escribió Francisco en su cuaderno? **(un poema)**
10. ¿Para quién lo escribió? **(para Alma)**

## Block Schedule

**Peer Teaching** Have the class list the names of famous people on the board. Working in pairs, one person takes on the role of a famous person and the other person interviews this person about his/her lifestyle, works, accomplishments, and fame. (For additional activities, see **Block Scheduling Copymasters**.)

## Teaching Resource Options

**Print** 

Unit 1 Resource Book
- **Video Activities**, pp. 196–197
- **Videoscript**, p. 198–199
- **Audioscript**, p. 200

**Audiovisual** 

**OHT** 32 (Quick Start)
**Audio Program** Cassette 3A / CD 3
**Video Program** Videotape 1, 19:52 / Videodisc 1A

**Technology** 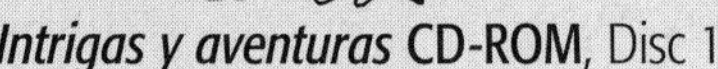

*Intrigas y aventuras* CD-ROM, Disc 1

## Quick Start Review

**En contexto** vocabulary

Use **OHT** 32 or write on board: Unscramble these sentences about the dialog.

1. a un canal de televisión / Francisco y Alma / en Miami / van
2. usan computadoras / los noticieros / para preparar
3. incluyen / las noticias / internacionales y locales / reportajes

**Answers**
1. Francisco y Alma van a un canal de televisión en Miami.
2. Los noticieros usan computadoras para preparar.
3. Las noticias incluyen reportajes internacionales y locales.

## Teaching Suggestions

- **Comprehension Check** Use **Actividades 1** and **2** to assess retention after the dialog. Have students identify the frame that helped them get each answer.
- Have students practice phone etiquette by calling each other on the phone. Model a short dialog with a student first.
- Have volunteers model their phone calls for the whole class.

# En acción
## VOCABULARIO Y GRAMÁTICA

**OBJECTIVES**
- Discuss ways to communicate
- React to news
- Ask for and give information
- Talk about things and people you know

ACTIVIDAD 1

### Todo parejo

**Escuchar** Empareja las dos columnas de acuerdo con el diálogo. *(Hint: Match columns.)*

1. «Hay varios canales de televisión en español
2. «Los televidentes saben
3. «Francisco García es héroe
4. «Es la primera vez que
5. «¿Y quién es la amiga?
6. «Los países reciben los canales

a. ¿Quién es? ¡Boba! Eres tú.»
b. porque rescató un gato.»
c. lo que está pasando en el mundo.»
d. alguien me escribe un poema.»
e. a través de los satélites y el cable.»
f. que transmiten desde Miami.»

**TAMBIÉN SE DICE** Cuando el señor Campos habla de las telecomunicaciones, él usa la palabra **Internet.** En los países hispanos, también se usa **la red** para referirse al ciberespacio.

ACTIVIDAD 2

### ¿Quién lo hizo?

**Escuchar** ¿Quién hizo las siguientes actividades: Alma, Francisco o el señor Campos? *(Hint: Who did these things?)*

Alma

Francisco

Señor Campos

1. Llamó a Francisco por teléfono.
2. Inventó un titular de un rescate espectacular.
3. Fue con Alma al estudio donde transmiten noticieros.
4. Dijo que el estudio usa Internet para preparar reportajes.
5. Les presentó una reportera a los jóvenes.
6. Escribió un poema romántico.



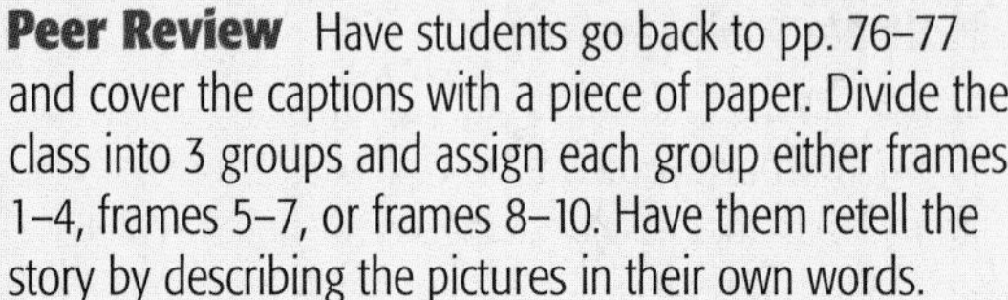

## Classroom Management 

**Peer Review** Have students go back to pp. 76–77 and cover the captions with a piece of paper. Divide the class into 3 groups and assign each group either frames 1–4, frames 5–7, or frames 8–10. Have them retell the story by describing the pictures in their own words.

**Paired/Group Work** After students work in pairs to combine the phrases in **Actividad 1**, review the answers with the whole class. Call on 6 volunteers to read aloud the answers. Have the class direct those 6 students to stand in the proper order and read the sentences to match the dialog.

- *Use demonstrative adjectives and pronouns*
- *Use stem-changing preterite verbs (e→i, o→u)*

## ¡Qué reunión!

**Hablar/Escribir** La familia de Francisco hizo una reunión de bienvenida para él. ¿Por qué salió mal? *(Hint: Why did the party turn out badly?)*

**modelo**

*Alma / no traer los refrescos*

*Alma no trajo los refrescos.*

1. La mamá de Francisco / no saber de la fiesta
2. La comida / estar malísima
3. Los amigos de Francisco / venir tarde
4. Alma / no poner la música
5. Los invitados / no querer bailar
6. El papá de Francisco / no poder encontrar la casa

**A la fiesta** Cuando te invitan a una fiesta en los Estados Unidos, es muy común ver en las invitaciones la hora que empieza y la hora que termina la fiesta. Pero, en muchos países hispanos, la misma invitación solamente te dice a qué hora empieza la diversión.

## ¿Están bien informados?

**Hablar** En pares, decidan si las siguientes personas están bien informadas. *(Hint: Are they well informed?)*

**Nota**

When you want to talk about knowing something well, use **estar bien informado(a).**

Francisco **está bien informado** sobre Internet.
*Francisco **is well informed** about the Internet.*

**modelo**

*los televidentes (los rescates)*

**Tú:** *¿Están bien informados los televidentes sobre los rescates?*

**Compañero(a):** *Sí, (No, no) están bien informados.*

1. los reporteros (los eventos de la escuela)
2. los profesores (las noticias internacionales)
3. tu vecino(a) (la música popular)
4. el (la) crítico(a) de películas (los gustos de los jóvenes)
5. tú y tus amigos (Internet)
6. tú (las noticias locales)
7. tus amigos (la ropa popular)
8. tus padres (los eventos de la comunidad)



## Teaching All Students

**Extra Help** Rewrite the sentences in **Actividad 2**, using the **yo** form instead of the **él/ella** forms.

**Native Speakers** Ask Spanish speakers to share the way they answer the phone in Spanish. Also ask them to comment on the **Nota cultural** and suggest a reason for not giving an end time for a party.

**Multiple Intelligences**

**Verbal** Have students work in pairs to create a short dialog about a phone conversation in one of the following situations: Alma and Francisco talk about their day at the television station, Francisco calls Sr. Campos to thank him for the interview, or Francisco calls home to tell his family about his visit to Miami.



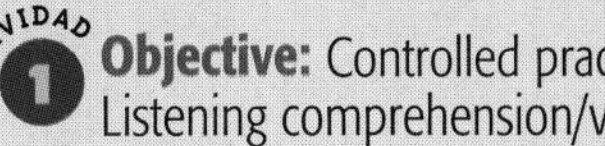

**Objective:** Controlled practice
Listening comprehension/vocabulary

**Answers**

| | |
|---|---|
| 1. f | 4. d |
| 2. c | 5. a |
| 3. b | 6. e |

**Objective:** Controlled practice
Listening comprehension/vocabulary

**Answers**

| | |
|---|---|
| 1. Alma | 4. el señor Campos |
| 2. Alma | 5. el señor Campos |
| 3. Francisco | 6. Francisco |

**Objective:** Controlled practice
Describing past activities
Irregular preterite verbs

**Answers**

1. La mamá de Francisco no supo de la fiesta.
2. La comida estuvo malísima.
3. Los amigos de Francisco vinieron tarde.
4. Alma no puso la música.
5. Los invitados no quisieron bailar.
6. El papá de Francisco no pudo encontrar la casa.

**Objective:** Transitional practice
Estar bien informado(a)

**Answers**

*Answers will vary but should demonstrate correct usage of **estar bien informado(a)**.*

1. Sí, (No, no) están bien informados.
2. Sí, (No, no) están bien informados.
3. Sí, (No, no) está bien informado(a).
4. Sí, (No, no) está bien informado(a).
5. Sí, (No, no) estamos bien informados.
6. Sí, (No, no) estoy bien informado(a).
7. Sí, (No, no) están bien informados.
8. Sí, (No, no) están bien informados.

### Quick Wrap-up

Have students do this wrap-up orally or in writing. Ask students to name four people they know who are **bien informados(as)** and give the reasons why. For example, **Mi padre está muy bien informado porque lee el periódico todos los días.**

### Block Schedule

**Variety** Have students write at least 5 sentences using the preterite to describe a party they attended recently.

## Teaching Resource Options

**Print**

*Más práctica* Workbook PE, pp. 35–36
*Cuaderno para hispanohablantes* PE, pp. 33–34
Block Scheduling Copymasters
Unit 1 Resource Book
*Más práctica* Workbook TE, pp. 173–174
*Cuaderno para hispanohablantes* TE, pp. 181–182

**Audiovisual**

OHT 32 (Quick Start)

**Technology**

*Intrigas y aventuras* CD-ROM, Disc 1

## Quick Start Review

Countries/origins

Use OHT 32 or write on board: List as many countries as you can that have Spanish as the official language. Extra credit if you can write a sentence in Spanish about a famous person from that country. **Diego Maradona es de Argentina.**

*Answers will vary.*

## More Practice

Give students 2 minutes to choose and jot down a "pretend" nationality and family background. Then go around and ask students' nationalities. Remind students that the nationality must match in gender and number. For example, **Yo soy japonesa y puertorriqueña porque mi mamá es japonesa y mi papá es puertorriqueño.**

**Objective:** Controlled practice
Adjectives of nationality

### Answers

1. Gerardo es mexicano.
2. Yanitzia es cubana.
3. Rick es chino.
4. Teresa es ecuatoriana.
5. Los hermanos Vázquez son bolivianos.
6. José es español.

## ¿De dónde?

**Hablar/Escribir** Francisco tiene amigos de todas partes. ¿Cuál es la nacionalidad de cada uno? *(Hint: What are their nationalities?)*

**modelo**

*Bob: Estados Unidos* — *Bob es estadounidense.*

**Nota**

Adjectives of nationality agree in gender and number with the noun they modify.

Juan es **peruano.** *Juan is* ***Peruvian.***

María y Ana son **peruanas.** *María and Ana are* ***Peruvian.***

1. Gerardo: México
2. Yanitzia: Cuba
3. Rick: China
4. Teresa: Ecuador
5. los hermanos Vázquez: Bolivia
6. José: España

## ¿De qué país?

**Hablar** Tu amigo(a) no sabe las nacionalidades de sus compañeros(as) en español. Explícale de qué país son. *(Hint: Where are they from?)*

**modelo**

*Carlos: Buenos Aires*

**Amigo(a):** *Carlos es de Buenos Aires, ¿no?*

**Tú:** *Sí. Carlos es argentino.*

1. Jane: Londres
2. Rubén: Lima
3. Pablo: Barcelona
4. Tomoko: Tokio
5. Peter: Nueva York

## Classroom Community

**TPR** Have students point to countries on a world map as you give them nationalities. For example, **¿Dónde viven los franceses?** Students point to France.

**Portfolio** Have students pretend that they are Spanish-speaking foreign exchange students and ask them to write a letter to a friend from home telling him/her what it is like to live in their town. Add to students' portfolio.

**Rubric: Writing**

| Criteria | Scale |
|---|---|
| Correct sentence structure | 1 2 3 |
| Vocabulary use | 1 2 3 |
| Creativity | 1 2 3 |
| Logical organization | 1 2 3 |

A = 11–12 pts.
B = 8–10 pts.
C = 6–7 pts.
D = 4–5 pts.
F = < 3 pts.

## ¿De dónde vino tu familia?

**Hablar/Escribir** ¿De qué país es tu familia? ¿De qué países son las familias de tus compañeros(as)? Habla con tus compañeros(as) y haz una tabla con los resultados. *(Hint: Talk about nationalities. Then make a chart.)*

**modelo**

**Tú:** *Mi familia es de España. Es española.*

**Compañero(a):** *Mi familia es de Italia. Es italiana.*

| Nombre | País | Nacionalidad |
|---|---|---|
| María | España | española |
| Javier | México | mexicana |
| Collette | Francia | francesa |

### Juego

Un inglés, un francés y un mexicano fueron a un restaurante internacional y pidieron pan francés, arroz mexicano y un sándwich cubano. El que vive en Francia no comió nada de Europa. Y alguien comió algo de su propio país. ¿Qué comió cada persona?

## ¡Socorro!

**Leer/Escribir** Francisco recibió esta postal, pero su hermanito borró (*erased*) algunas palabras. Ayuda a Francisco a leerla. Pon el presente o el pretérito de **saber** o **conocer** en los espacios en blanco. *(Hint: Complete the postcard.)*

**Nota**

**Saber** and **conocer** both mean ***to know.*** Use **saber** with facts, information, and when telling how to do something. Use **conocer** to express being familiar or acquainted with a person, place, or thing.

¿**Saben** quién es esa reportera? *Do **you know** who that reporter is?*

Yo la **conozco.** ¿Les gustaría **conocerla**? ***I know** her. Would you like **to meet her**?*

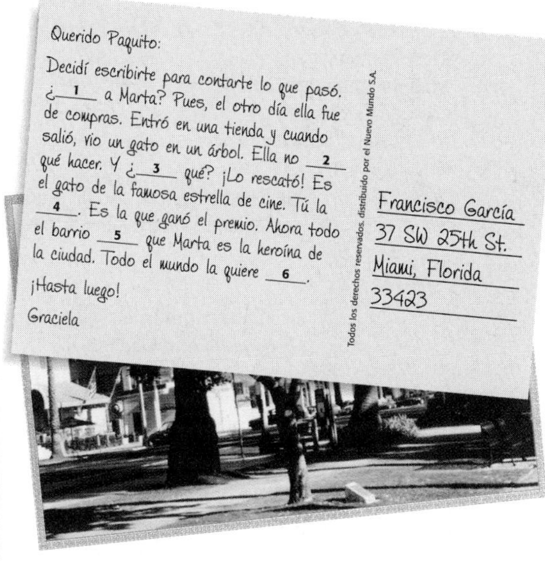

Querido Paquito:

Decidí escribirte para contarte lo que pasó. ¿__1__ a Marta? Pues, el otro día ella fue de compras. Entró en una tienda y cuando salió, vio un gato en un árbol. Ella no __2__ qué hacer. Y ¿__3__ qué? ¡Lo rescató! Es el gato de la famosa estrella de cine. Tú la __4__. Es la que ganó el premio. Ahora todo el barrio __5__ que Marta es la heroína de la ciudad. Todo el mundo la quiere __6__.

¡Hasta luego!

Graciela

Francisco García
37 SW 25th St.
Miami, Florida
33423



MÁS COMUNICACIÓN p. R4

**Objective:** Transitional practice
Adjectives of nationality

**Partial Answers**

1. Sí, Jane es inglesa.
2. Sí, Rubén es peruano.
3. Sí, Pablo es español.
4. Sí, Tomoko es japonesa.
5. Sí, Peter es estadounidense.

**Objective:** Open-ended practice
Exchanging information

*Answers will vary but should follow the model and reflect knowledge of nationality vocabulary.*

**Note:** Have students make a class map of nationalities.

**Objective:** Transitional practice
Saber and conocer

*The focus of Actividad 8 is on the different uses of the two verbs. (Both present and preterite are used.)*

**Answers**

1. Conoces
2. supo
3. sabes
4. conoces
5. sabe
6. conocer

**Note:** The irregular **yo** forms of **saber** and **conocer** were reviewed in the *Etapa preliminar.*

### Supplementary Vocabulary

Other nationalities:

| | |
|---|---|
| **irlandés/irlandesa** | Irish |
| **australiano(a)** | Australian |
| **sueco(a)** | Swedish |
| **noruego(a)** | Norwegian |

More nationalities are in the index at the back of the book. Note that students will not be tested on nationalities.

### Juego

**Answer**

El inglés comió pan francés; el francés comió el sándwich cubano; el mexicano comió el arroz mexicano.



## Teaching All Students

**Extra Help** Give each student a small index card that says **saber** on one side and **conocer** on the other. Read aloud the sentences from **Actividad 8** and ask students to show the appropriate verb.

**Native Speakers** Ask Spanish speakers to describe the region or cities their families came from.

**Multiple Intelligences**

**Naturalist** Have students choose one of the Spanish-speaking countries shown on the map on p. 80 and research the climate and geography. Have them prepare a short weather forecast and videotape it if possible.

## Block Schedule

**Change of Pace** Have students place flags or labels in Spanish on the countries of a world map that correspond to the nationalities represented in the class. (For additional activities, see **Block Scheduling Copymasters**.)

## Teaching Resource Options

**Print** 

*Más práctica* Workbook PE, pp. 37–38
*Cuaderno para hispanohablantes* PE, p. 35–36
Block Scheduling Copymasters
Unit 1 Resource Book
*Más práctica* Workbook TE, pp. 175–176
*Cuaderno para hispanohablantes* TE, pp. 183–184
Information Gap Activities, pp. 189–190

**Audiovisual** 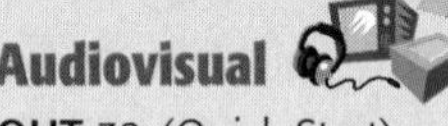

OHT 32 (Quick Start)

**Technology** 

*Intrigas y aventuras* CD-ROM, Disc 1

## Quick Start Review

Gender of nouns

Use OHT 32 or write on board: Write **el** or **la** before each of these nouns.

| | |
|---|---|
| anuncio | galería |
| televisión | retrato |
| titular | edición |
| reportaje | programa |

**Answers**
el anuncio; la televisión; el titular; el reportaje; la galería; el retrato; la edición; el programa

## Teaching Suggestions

### Presenting Demonstrative Adjectives and Pronouns

Place some objects around the room and go around and identify them using demonstrative adjectives. For example, **Este libro verde está aquí. Ese libro rojo está allí. Aquellos libros azules están muy lejos.** You can then use the demonstrative pronouns in the same way. **Éste está aquí. Ése está allá. Aquéllos están muy lejos.**

## Language Note

Demonstrative pronouns frequently include written accents. However, those accent marks are only required in ambiguous situations.

## GRAMÁTICA: Express Position Using Demonstrative Adjectives and Pronouns

As you know, there are three kinds of demonstratives in Spanish:

- one that points out someone or something **near** the speaker
- one that points out someone or something **farther away**
- one that points out someone or something **at a great distance**

**Demonstrative Adjectives**

| | near | | farther away | | at a great distance | |
|---|---|---|---|---|---|---|
| | **m.** | **f.** | **m.** | **f.** | **m.** | **f.** |
| **Singular** | este | esta | ese | esa | aquel | aquella |
| **Plural** | estos | estas | esos | esas | aquellos | aquellas |

Francisco, ¿escribiste tú **este** poema?
*Francisco, did you write* ***this*** *poem?*

¡Dame **ese** cuaderno!
*Give me* ***that*** *notebook!*

**Aquella** reportera es del canal dos.
***That*** *reporter is from Channel 2.*

Demonstrative adjectives agree in number and gender with the **noun** they modify, and they usually go before the noun.

Demonstratives can also be **pronouns** that take the place of **nouns.** They have the same number and gender as the **noun** they replace and have a written accent.

¿Saben quién es **ese señor**?
*Do you know who* ***that*** *man is?*
*becomes*
¿**Ése**? Sí, es el reportero.
***That one?*** *Yes, he's the reporter.*

**Aquella reportera** es del canal dos.
***That*** *reporter is from Channel 2.*
*becomes*
**Aquélla** es del canal cinco.
***That one*** *is from Channel 5.*



## Classroom Community

**TPR** Assign different gestures to represent **este** (point to area directly in front), **ese** (point to an area a few feet away), and **aquel** (gesture across the room). Read the model phrases on pp. 82–83 and have students make corresponding gestures.

**Paired Activity** Have students work in pairs to combine a demonstrative adjective with new vocabulary words to tell a story, e.g., **este artículo es de... porque esta fotógrafa sacó aquellas fotos....** Students may also prepare a chart of demonstrative pronouns for reference.

## Problemas del periódico

**Escribir** Cambia el artículo definido a la forma correcta del adjetivo demostrativo para hablar de los problemas del periódico. Escribe cada oración de tres maneras. *(Hint: Write sentences with demonstratives.)*

**modelo**

*El artículo sobre los ladrones está mal escrito.*
*Este artículo sobre los ladrones está mal escrito.*
*Ese artículo sobre los ladrones está mal escrito.*
*Aquel artículo sobre los ladrones está mal escrito.*

1. La cámara no sirve.
2. Las tiras cómicas no tienen color.
3. El escritor no investigó los detalles.
4. Los hechos del artículo no son correctos.
5. Las noticias no son muy interesantes.
6. El autor no estudió periodismo.
7. No funciona el programa en la computadora.
8. La editora duerme durante el día de trabajo.

**MÁS PRÁCTICA**
*cuaderno* pp. 35–38

**PARA HISPANOHABLANTES**
*cuaderno* pp. 33–36

## La oficina de periodismo

**Hablar/Escribir** Tú trabajas en una oficina de periodismo. Explícales a unos amigos lo que hacen el periodista, la editora y la fotógrafa. Usa **éste(a), ése(a)** o **aquél(la)** en tus respuestas. *(Hint: Tell what each person does.)*

el periodista — la editora — la fotógrafa

**modelo**

*investiga los hechos y las causas y escribe detalles*
*Éste es el periodista. Él investiga los hechos y las causas y escribe detalles.*

1. habla por teléfono
2. busca errores en los artículos
3. tiene una cámara
4. tiene un periódico y una computadora
5. lee las tiras cómicas

### Vocabulario

**Las telecomunicaciones**

**el artículo** *article*
**el (la) autor(a)** *author*
**la cámara** *camera*
**la causa** *cause*
**el detalle** *detail*
**el (la) editor(a)** *editor*
**el (la) escritor(a)** *writer*
**el (la) fotógrafo(a)** *photographer*
**el hecho** *fact*
**el periodismo** *journalism*
**el (la) periodista** *journalist*
**el programa** *program*
**la tira cómica** *comic strip*

Cuando piensas en las telecomunicaciones, ¿en qué piensas?



### Teaching Suggestion

Before doing **Actividades 9** and **10**, be sure to review the vocabulary in the box at the bottom of p. 83.

**Objective:** Controlled practice
Demonstrative adjectives/ telecommunications vocabulary

**Answers**

*Answers will use the demonstrative adjectives shown.*

1. Esta / Esa / Aquella
2. Estas / Esas / Aquellas
3. estos / esos / aquellos
4. de este / de ese / de aquel
5. Estas / Esas / Aquellas
6. Este / Ese / Aquel
7. esta / esa / aquella
8. Esta / Esa / Aquella

**Objective:** Transitional practice
Demonstrative pronouns

**Answers**

*Answers will vary but should reflect comprehension of demonstrative pronouns.*

1. Éste es el periodista. Él habla por teléfono.
2. Ésa es la editora. Ella busca errores en los artículos.
3. Aquélla es la fotógrafa. Ella tiene una cámara.
4. Ésa es la editora. Ella tiene un periódico y una computadora.
5. Ésa es la editora. Ella lee las tiras cómicas.

### Language Note

Tell students about the demonstrative pronouns **esto**, **eso**, and **aquello** (no accents, ending in **-o**), used to refer to ideas, concepts, and situations. An example can be found in the *En vivo* dialog on p. 77: **Eso es personal.**

### Teaching All Students

**Extra Help** Have students take turns describing 3 students near them by using **éste**, **ése**, and **aquél** while the other classmates try to guess who is being described.

**Multiple Intelligences**

**Musical/Rhythmic** Have students develop a chant or poem to demonstrate the differences between **este**, **ese**, and **aquel**. (e.g., **Este, esta, estos llevan T, ese, esa, esos la T se fue.**)

**Verbal** Using vocabulary words, ask students to work together to form a short story using a demonstrative adjective and one vocabulary word. The first student stands and begins the story, e.g., **Este artículo es interesante.** The next student stands and continues the story, e.g., **Esta escritora escribió sobre...**, etc.

### Block Schedule

**Variety** Gather photos from newspapers or magazines and have students describe what they see in them using **este**, **ese**, and **aquel**. (For additional activities, see **Block Scheduling Copymasters**.)

## Teaching Resource Options

**Print** 

*Más práctica* Workbook PE, pp. 39–40
*Cuaderno para hispanohablantes* PE, pp. 37–38
Block Scheduling Copymasters
Unit 1 Resource Book
*Más práctica* Workbook TE, pp. 177–178
*Cuaderno para hispanohablantes* TE, pp. 185–186
Audioscript, pp. 200–201

**Audiovisual** 

OHT 33 (Quick Start)
Audio Program Cassette 3A / CD 3

**Technology**

*Intrigas y aventuras* CD-ROM, Disc 1

## Quick Start Review

e→i stem-changing verbs: present

Use OHT 33 or write on board: Say what each person orders when going out to eat. Use the present tense of **pedir**. For example: **Ana pide helado**.

1. Luis / pollo asado
2. yo / jamón
3. ellos / la especialidad de la casa
4. los niños / unas hamburguesas
5. nosotros / bistec

**Answers**, see p. 71B.

## Teaching Suggestions
### Presenting the Stem-Changing Verbs in the Preterite

- Remind students that they have already learned the conjugation of stem-changing "boot verbs" in the present tense. Write the conjugations on the board for review.
- Have students write out the conjugations in their notebooks after you model a few on the board. Remind students that although the verbs have stem changes, they all have the same endings in the preterite.

ACTIVIDAD 11

## ¿Dónde hubo...?

**Escuchar/Hablar** Escucha este noticiero internacional. Usa la lista de países para ayudarte a contestar las preguntas. Luego haz un resumen de lo que escuchaste. *(Hint: Answer the questions and summarize the tape.)*

**Nota**

To express "there was" or "there were," you may use **hubo,** the preterite of **hay.**

**Hubo** dos personas que ganaron.
***There were** two people who won.*

1. ¿Dónde hubo un huracán?
2. ¿Dónde hubo un rescate?
3. ¿Dónde hubo un señor que tuvo millones?
4. ¿Dónde hubo un anuncio sobre el precio de los plátanos?

## GRAMÁTICA: Stem-Changing Verbs in the Preterite

 **¿RECUERDAS?** *pp. 21, 58* Remember that many Spanish verbs have stem changes in the present tense. These changes take place in the **singular** and in the **ellos/ellas/ustedes** forms.

For example, the verb **pedir** *to ask for* alternates between **e** and **i** in the present tense.

**pedir** *to ask for*

| | |
|---|---|
| pido | pedimos |
| pides | pedís |
| pide | piden |

Stem-changing **-ir** verbs change vowels in the **preterite** too. However, the change only occurs in the **él/ella/usted** and the **ellos/ellas/ustedes** forms.

**e → i**

**pedir** *to ask for*

| | |
|---|---|
| pedí | pedimos |
| pediste | pedisteis |
| pidió | pidieron |

**o → u**

**dormir** *to sleep*

| | |
|---|---|
| dormí | dormimos |
| dormiste | dormisteis |
| durmió | durmieron |

—¿Qué **pidió** *Onda Internacional*?
*What **did** Onda Internacional **ask for**?*

—**Pidieron** un artículo sobre un canal de televisión.
***They asked for** an article about a television station.*

### Vocabulario

**Preterite Stem-Changing Verbs**

Ya Sabes e→i

**competir** *to compete*
**preferir** *to prefer*
**repetir** *to repeat*
**servir** *to serve*

o→u

**morir** *to die*

Additional stem-changing verbs are listed on pp. R30–R31.



## Classroom Community

**Cooperative Learning** Divide the class into groups. Have each group prepare a short scenario to present to the class using the preterite of the stem-changing verbs on p. 84. As each group presents its scenario, the rest of the class identifies that they have heard one of the verb forms by raising hands.

**Paired Activity** Divide the class into pairs. After pointing out the **Nota** on p. 84, have each pair practice writing new sentences using **leer**, **creer**, and **oír** in the preterite.

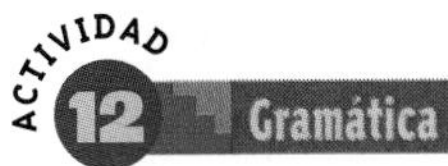

## ¿Qué hicieron?

**Escribir** ¿Qué hicieron las personas en las siguientes situaciones? Completa las oraciones con el pretérito del verbo indicado. *(Hint: Complete the sentences.)*

1. La editora les _____ (pedir) muchos más detalles a los escritores.
2. Los escritores no _____ (repetir) el titular en la segunda edición.
3. Yo _____ (preferir) el artículo sobre el héroe que rescató al niño.
4. Los amigos de la reportera _____ (competir) en un concurso de baile.
5. Los televidentes escucharon que el presidente _____ (morir).
6. Los fotógrafos _____ (pedir) unas cámaras nuevas.
7. La reportera mexicana _____ (preferir) escribir en español.
8. La periodista guatemalteca escribió un artículo sobre unas plantas que _____ (morir).

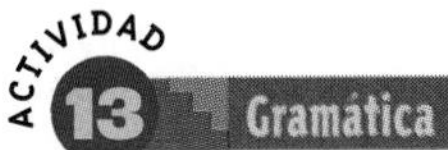

## En clase

**Hablar/Escribir** Describe lo que hicieron o no hicieron estas personas en la clase de español ayer. *(Hint: Tell what these people did.)*

**modelo**

*(La profesora / Yo) / (no) escribir en el pizarrón*

*La profesora escribió en el pizarrón. / Yo no escribí en el pizarrón.*

**Nota**

Verbs such as **leer** *to read,* **creer** *to believe,* and **oír** *to hear* change the **i** to **y** in the **él/ella/usted** and in the **ellos/ellas/ustedes** forms of the preterite.

Alma **leyó** el poema. *Alma **read** the poem.*

Mis hermanos **no creyeron** las noticias. *My brothers **didn't believe** the news.*

1. (Mi amigo(a)/Yo) / (no) oír las palabras
2. (La profesora/Los estudiantes) / (no) leer el artículo
3. (Mi hermano/Tu hermana) / (no) pedir ayuda
4. (Tú/Yo) / (no) preferir escribir poemas
5. (María y yo/Ana) / (no) servir los helados

**MÁS PRÁCTICA** *cuaderno* pp. 39–40

**PARA HISPANOHABLANTES** *cuaderno* pp. 37–38

## ¿Es cierto?

**Escuchar/Escribir** Escucha lo que dice Víctor, un estudiante de Paraguay. Luego, contesta **cierto** o **falso** a las preguntas. Si son falsas, explica por qué. *(Hint: Answer true or false. Then correct false answers.)*

1. Vino a Miami en diciembre.
2. Víctor le pidió a su mamá norteamericana una hamburguesa con queso y papas fritas.
3. No hizo nada durante las vacaciones.
4. Víctor no está muy contento.
5. El artículo sobre Víctor va a salir en el periódico escolar.



### Teaching Suggestions

It might be helpful to write the complete conjugation of one of the verbs (**leer, creer, oír**) on the board so students can see the spelling change in the **él/ella/usted** and **ellos/ellas/ustedes** forms of the preterite.

**Objective:** Open-ended practice
Listening comprehension
Preterite of **haber**

**Answers** (See script, p. 71B.)

1. Hubo un huracán en Estados Unidos.
2. Hubo un rescate en España.
3. Hubo un señor que tuvo millones en Paraguay.
4. Hubo un anuncio sobre el precio de los plátanos en Cuba.

**Objective:** Controlled practice
Stem-changing preterites

**Answers**

1. pidió
2. repitieron
3. preferí
4. compitieron
5. murió
6. pidieron
7. prefirió
8. murieron

**Objective:** Controlled practice
Stem-changing preterites

**Answers**

*Answers will vary. All answers should show correct conjugation.*

1. oyó / (no) oí las palabras
2. leyó / (no) leyeron el artículo
3. pidió / (no) pidió ayuda
4. preferiste / (no) preferí escribir poemas
5. servimos / (no) sirvió los helados

**Objective:** Transitional practice
Listening comprehension

**Answers** (See script, p. 71B.)

1. falso / Vino a Miami en septiembre.
2. cierto
3. falso / Fue a la playa y a un estudio de televisión.
4. falso / Está muy contento.
5. cierto

### Teaching All Students

**Extra Help** As a follow-up to **Actividad 14**, have students tell the story about Víctor, the exchange student, in their own words.

**Native Speakers** Ask Spanish speakers to share their tips on how to remember conjugations of stem-changing verbs in the preterite or any other general verb conjugating tips they may know.

**Multiple Intelligences**

**Logical/Mathematical** Have students form a mind map of stem-changing verbs in the present and preterite tenses.

### Block Schedule

**Process Time** Using the vocabulary on nationalities, have students write 5 sentences using a nationality and a stem-changing verb. Ask some students to write their sentences on the board. (For additional activities, see **Block Scheduling Copymasters.**)

## Teaching Resource Options

**Print**

*Más práctica* Workbook PE, pp. 31–34
*Cuaderno para hispanohablantes* PE, pp. 31–32
Unit 1 Resource Book
*Más práctica* Workbook TE, pp. 169–172
*Cuaderno para hispanohablantes* TE, pp. 179–180
Audioscript, pp. 202–203
Information Gap Activities, pp. 191–192

**Audiovisual**

OHT 33 (Quick Start)

**Technology**

*Intrigas y aventuras* CD-ROM, Disc 1

## Quick Start Review

e→i stem-changing verbs: preterite

Use OHT 33 or write on the board: You are writing for the sports page of a newspaper. Follow the model and write three more sentences using the verb **competir** in the preterite. Use your favorite professional teams, local teams, or your own high school team in any sport you wish.

Los Red Sox y los Yanquis compitieron anoche en Fenway Park. Los Red Sox ganaron 3 a 0.

*Answers will vary.*

## Teaching Suggestions

To complete *Actividad* 15 students will need to review the vocabulary in the box at the bottom of p. 86. Other possible responses include: **¡No! ¡Imposible!** or **No lo creo.**

**Objective:** Transitional practice Stem-changing preterites

**Answers**

*Student reactions to* **compañero(a)** *sentences will vary.*

1. Sí, Geraldo leyó.
2. Graciela y Alegra no escribieron.
3. Sí, nosotros dormimos.
4. Sí, le pediste más tarea al maestro.
5. La profesora no creyó las noticias.
6. Sí, Vicente prefirió estudiar.

ACTIVIDAD 15

## ¿Qué hacen?

**Hablar** Margarita durmió en la casa de una amiga. Habla con un(a) compañero(a) y di qué hicieron o no hicieron otras personas. Luego, responde a tu compañero(a). *(Hint: Talk about what others did.)*

**modelo**

*Margarita: dormir en la casa de una amiga (sí)*
**Tú:** *¿Durmió Margarita en la casa de una amiga?*
**Compañero(a):** *Sí, Margarita durmió en la casa de una amiga.*
**Tú:** *Yo dormí en la casa de una amiga también.*
**Compañero(a):** *¡No me digas!*

1. Geraldo: leer un libro (sí)
2. Graciela y Alegra: escribir una carta (no)
3. Nosotros: dormir en clase (sí)
4. Yo: pedirle más tarea al maestro (sí)
5. La profesora: creer las noticias (no)
6. Vicente: preferir estudiar a bailar (sí)

**Vocabulario**

Cuando hablas...

**¿De veras?** *Really?*
**¡No me digas!** *Don't tell me!*
**¿Tú crees?** *Do you think so?*
**¡Ya lo sé!** *I already know!*

¿Con qué palabras te gusta responder?

ACTIVIDAD 16

## Ay, ¡qué cansados!

**PARA CONVERSAR**
**STRATEGY: SPEAKING**

**Present findings** When reporting information that is summarized on a chart, reading aloud may not be an effective way of reporting. You may want to report general information **(en general, por lo general).** You can compare two groups **(los adultos durmieron más/menos que los jóvenes).** You can report exceptional behavior **(lo más/menos que durmió una persona fue...).** Finally you can summarize whether people got enough sleep **(en resumen).**

**Hablar/Escribir** A veces hay personas que no duermen lo suficiente. Habla con tus compañeros(as) para ver cuántas horas ellos(as) y sus familias durmieron anoche. Luego haz una tabla con las respuestas y preséntale los resultados a la clase. *(Hint: Make a chart.)*

| ¿Quién? | ¿Cuánto? | ¿Fue suficiente? |
|---|---|---|
| Yo dormí | ocho horas | Fue suficiente. |
| Mi hermano durmió | seis horas | No fue suficiente. |
| Mis padres... | | |
| Susana... | | |



## Classroom Community

**Group Activity** After students have collected information for **Actividad 16**, have them figure out who slept the most/least (**que más /menos durmió**).

**TPR** Have students make up gestures using physical reactions to the vocabulary expressions on p. 86.

**Portfolio** Using the vocabulary expressions in the box, write a short dialog to include all 4 expressions.

**Rubric: Writing**

| Criteria | Scale | |
|---|---|---|
| Correct sentence structure | 1 2 3 4 5 | A = 17–20 pts. |
| Vocabulary use | 1 2 3 4 5 | B = 13–16 pts. |
| Creativity | 1 2 3 4 5 | C = 9–12 pts. |
| Logical organization | 1 2 3 4 5 | D = 5–8 pts. |
| | | F = < 5 pts. |

## Las noticias

**Hablar/Leer** El periódico siempre tiene noticias de todo tipo. En pares, lean estos titulares y reaccionen a cada uno. *(Hint: Read and react to headlines.)*

**Presidente quiere 11 meses de escuela**

Anoche en el noticier...

EL INFORMANTE MATUTINO

**Chicos rescatan a un bebé**

Rigoberto Centeno, Daniel Araiza y Melissa Rojas, tres estudiantes del Colegio Santa Rosa, escucharon ... Resulta que el bebé, ... contra viento y m... lo cierto es que si siempre sucede co...

**Señora con 20 gatos busca casa**

¿Vives en ... tiene que ... los gatos ... número de ... al final de ...

**NOTA CULTURAL**

**Periódicos por computadora** Hay una gran variedad de periódicos en español en Internet. *ABC* y *El País,* de España, *El Diario Clarín,* de Argentina, y muchos otros tienen ediciones digitales.

**MÁS COMUNICACIÓN** p. R4

### Refrán

**Antes de hablar es bueno pensar.**

Lo que quiere decir este refrán es muy claro: debes pensar en lo que vas a decir antes de decirlo, o puedes tener problemas. En pares, hablen de situaciones en que hablaron sin pensar. ¿Es cierto lo que dice el refrán?

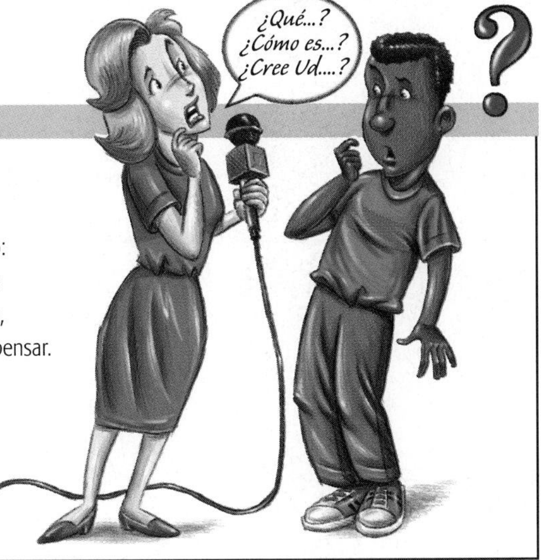






## Teaching Suggestions

### Las noticias

Gather additional Spanish newspapers and have students react to the headlines they see, using expressions like those in the box on p. 86.

**Objective:** Open-ended practice
Preterite of **dormir**
Family vocabulary

**Rubric: Speaking**

| Criteria | Scale | |
|---|---|---|
| Use of Generalizing Structures | 1 2 3 | A = 11–12 pts. |
| | | B = 8–10 pts. |
| Variety, creativity | 1 2 3 | C = 6–7 pts. |
| Summarizing | 1 2 3 | D = 4–5 pts. |
| Pronunciation, Fluency | 1 2 3 | F = < 3 pts. |

**Objective:** Open-ended practice
Reading/reacting to news

*Answers will vary.*

### Project

Have students use the Internet to search for titles of Spanish newspapers, locate a newspaper, and choose an article to summarize.

### Interdisciplinary Connection

**Social Studies** Have students investigate a Spanish-language newspaper, magazine, or news program and report similarities and differences between U.S. publications in English and those in Spanish to the class.

## Teaching All Students

**Extra Help** Have students form complete sentences using the following expressions for summarizing or reporting: **por lo general, más/menos que, en resumen.**

**Native Speakers** Ask Spanish speakers to make a list of common expressions similar to those on p. 86. Then have them demonstrate the use of the expressions with the proper gestures and intonation.

**Multiple Intelligences**

**Kinesthetic** Have the class work together to match the vocabulary expressions (**¿De veras? ¡No me digas!, ¿Tú crees?,** and **¡Ya lo sé!**) with appropriate hand motions or gestures. As you say each expression, have students respond with the matching gesture. Then read sentences aloud and ask students to respond with the matching expression and gestures.

## Block Schedule

**Process Time** Give students 5 minutes to list at least five situations when they would use expressions such as those in the vocabulary box on p. 86. Discuss the situations with the whole class to be sure students are using the vocabulary correctly.

### Teaching Resource Options

**Print** 

*Cuaderno para hispanohablantes* PE, p. 39
Block Scheduling Copymasters
Unit 1 Resource Book
*Cuaderno para hispanohablantes* TE, p. 187
Audioscript, pp. 201–202

**Audiovisual**

OHT 33 (Quick Start)
Audio Program Cassette 3A / CD 3

### Quick Start Review

School subjects/activities

Use OHT 33 or write on board: If you were the publisher of a town newspaper for teens only, what topics would you include? What would be the title of each section of the paper? Write down two or three ideas in Spanish.

*Answers will vary.*

### Teaching Suggestions

- **Prereading** Ask students to identify the cognate in the reading. Then invite students to look at pages 88–89, quickly scan the title and subtitle of the reading, and write down 3 guesses as to what the reading will be about. Have them share their ideas with the class.
- **Reading Strategy: Scan for specific information** Have students jot down their notes as they scan the reading, looking for answers to the ¿Comprendiste? questions.
- **Post-Reading** Encourage students to make 2 or 3 comparisons of the two newspapers in this reading to improve retention.
- **Strategy: Skim for the general idea** Have students practice skimming other readings in their textbook to get the gist.

# En voces

LECTURA

# ¿Leíste el periódico hoy?

**PARA LEER • STRATEGIES: READING**

**Skim for the general idea** Let your eyes run quickly over the text of this article. What seems to be the gist?

**Scan for specific information** Look quickly for the names of the newspapers mentioned. What are their names? Where are they located?

¿Qué sección del periódico te gusta más? ¿Los deportes? ¿Los editoriales? Si visitas Miami, puedes leer tu sección favorita del periódico en español. *El Nuevo Herald*, una edición del *Miami Herald*, es el periódico en español más grande de Estados Unidos.

Además de las secciones que tienen todos los periódicos, *El Nuevo Herald* ofrece secciones especiales sobre lo que pasa en diversos países latinoamericanos. También publica artículos sobre las noticias locales de interés para las personas de origen hispano que viven en Miami.

¿Qué pasa si quieres leer *El Nuevo Herald* y no estás en Miami? Con una computadora puedes leerlo sin levantarte[1] de tu silla, porque *El Nuevo Herald* está en Internet todos los días.

[1] getting out



### Classroom Community

**Paired/Group Activity** Have students cut out various headlines of interest from the local newspaper and bring them to class. Then have them categorize the headlines into the main newspaper sections and/or determine which belong on the front page.

**Cooperative Learning** Have students develop a Spanish newspaper for your school. Ask for volunteers to be the editor, photographer, sportswriter, etc. Working in small groups, have them first plan out an edition. Then have them write, edit, and illustrate articles for the newspaper. You may distribute the finished product to the other Spanish classes or perhaps to Spanish classes at a school close by.

# «La Voz» de los estudiantes

¿Te gustaría saber tu horóscopo, leer las noticias y practicar tu español al mismo tiempo? *La Voz Mundial*, una publicación de los estudiantes de Miami Springs Senior High School, te da esta oportunidad. El periódico es completamente en español y contiene noticias del mundo, poesía estudiantil y mucho más.

Volumen 4 La Voz Mundial

Miami Springs Senior High 751 Dove Avenue Miami Springs, FL 33166

**Mejoras Salariales Relacionadas al Conocimiento de Idiomas**

Por: Rodney Castillo
Editor

Muchas personas no conocen cuan importante es saber diferentes idiomas. Esta importancia se puede muy bien expresar en una sola oración: El tener dominio sobre los idiomas es poseer la habilidad de comunicarse en más de una lengua con cualquier persona en el mundo.

No importa que carrera el estudiante piense estudiar. El ser poligiota le da ventajas sobre los otros jóvenes en todos los sentidos. Tomemos por ejemplo cualquier carrera en el campo de las ciencias como la física o la química. [...]

[...] de trabajo.

Tener dominio sobre múltiples idiomas nos enseña más sobre nosotros mismos y aprendemos a comprender a las personas que nos rodean. Otra ventaja es que nos enseña a tener una postura más positiva ante otras culturas. También los idiomas son importantes cuando se habla de sentimientos ya que puedes expresar lo que sientes a cualquier persona en el mundo sin importar su nacionalidad. También cuando aprendemos un idioma, este nos facilita el aprendizaje de [...]

problemas de la vida cotidiana, el aprender a pensar analíticamente y con mayor creatividad y para obtener mayores calificaciones en exámenes como el HSCT o el SAT ya que aunque son en inglés todos los idiomas están relacionados entre sí. También es sabido que a todos los estudiantes se les exije que tomen dos clases de un mismo idioma para poder graduarse de High School.

El departamento de idiomas extranjeros de M.S.S.H. ofrece una amplia selección de lenguas tales como español, [...]

Editoriales Pg. 2

Locales Pg. 3

Deportes Pg. 5

Es popular no sólo[2] entre hispanohablantes[3] sino también[4] entre los que aprenden el español y los que tienen interés en las lenguas y culturas del mundo.

[2] not only [3] speakers of Spanish [4] but also

## ¿Comprendiste?

1. ¿Qué es *El Nuevo Herald*?
2. ¿Una persona que no vive en Miami puede leer este periódico? ¿Cómo?
3. ¿Quién publica *La Voz Mundial*?
4. ¿En qué es diferente *La Voz Mundial* de otros periódicos escolares?

## ¿Qué piensas?

¿Son los periódicos, la televisión y la radio partes importantes de nuestra sociedad? ¿Por qué? Habla con tus compañeros(as) de clase y compartan sus ideas.



## Teaching All Students

**Extra Help** Have students first focus only on getting the gist of the headlines.

**Native Speakers** Ask Spanish speakers to make 5 comparisons or contrasts between a Spanish newspaper from their cultural community and the local English newspaper. They can compare the different sections, the target audience, the layout or photos, and the advertisements.

**Multiple Intelligences**

**Interpersonal** Have students set up correspondence via e-mail with a school nearby to share the weekly weather report, sports announcements, school happenings, etc.

**Intrapersonal** Have students write a short description of themselves for a newspaper spotlight article.



## Culture Highlights

● **EL NUEVO HERALD** You can access *El Nuevo Herald/The Miami Herald* on the Internet in Spanish or English. If students have access to the Internet, have them review the front page headlines (**primera plana**) or choose their favorite section to view.

www.mcdougallittell.com

## Cross Cultural Connections

**Strategy** Remind students that learning about other cultures helps them to better understand their own. Ask students if reading a Spanish newspaper from Miami might give them a different perspective on the news.

## Community Connection

Ask students if there are any local newspapers in your community that are in another language or are targeted to a certain group of people. If so, ask them what sections it has. Who is the target audience? How often is it published? Ask students to bring examples to class.

## Language Note

Have students look closely at the language in the newspaper headlines on this page. The purpose of a headline is to attract attention so the reader will read the article. Headlines must be brief, full of information, and intriguing.

## ¿Comprendiste?

**Answers**

1. un periódico en español de Miami
2. Sí, por Internet
3. los estudiantes de Miami Springs Senior High School
4. Es completamente en español, tiene noticias del mundo y poesías de los estudiantes.

## Block Schedule

**Variety** If your school has a newspaper, have students compare the front page to *La Voz Mundial*. (For additional activities, see **Block Scheduling Copymasters**.)

### Teaching Resource Options

**Print** 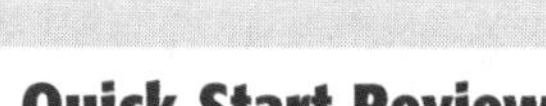

*Cuaderno para hispanohablantes* PE, p. 40

Unit 1 Resource Book
*Cuaderno para hispanohablantes* TE, p. 188

**Audiovisual**

OHT 34 (Quick Start)

### Quick Start Review

Leisure time activities

Use OHT 34 or write on board: You are planning a trip to Miami, Florida. Jot down a list of activities you can do there. For example: **En Miami puedo ir a la playa y tomar el sol.** Think about sports, restaurants, museums, etc.

*Answers will vary.*

### Teaching Suggestions

- **Presenting En colores** Begin by asking students to guess the topic of the culture section. Write the list of possibilities on the board.
- **Strategy: Identify characteristics of neighborhoods** Have students map out their town on the board. Have them identify the names of different neighborhoods. You can also have students write their names on the neighborhood where they live. Have students from the same neighborhood describe where they live. Choose two groups to compare/contrast their neighborhoods. What do the neighborhoods have in common? How are they different?

### Reading Strategy

Remind students to skim for the general idea and scan for specific information. Ask them to give a few specific facts and list on the board.

### Dictation

After students have read the text, have them close their books. Dictate the opening paragraph (**Miami es…**) while students write it in their notebooks.

# En colores

## CULTURA Y COMPARACIONES

### PARA CONOCERNOS

**STRATEGY: CONNECTING CULTURES**

**Identify characteristics of neighborhoods** Neighborhoods contribute to the unique flavor of a town. Does your town have different neighborhoods? How can you identify them? By name? By the people? Choose two neighborhoods and use a chart to compare them.

# Miami

## Puerta de las Américas

***Sin título,*** *Carolina Zuniga*

Miami es un imán[1] para viajeros[2] de todas partes del mundo. Vienen para tomar el sol en las playas blancas, nadar en el océano azul y visitar los hoteles lujosos. Pero muchas otras personas vienen a Miami para vivir.

[1] magnet [2] travelers



### Classroom Community

**Cooperative Learning** Miami is one major area for international tourists in Florida. Have students research the Internet to discover other areas with large Hispanic populations in Florida (e.g., Tampa, Orlando, St. Augustine, St. Petersburg).

**Portfolio** Choose an area in Florida where there is a large Spanish-speaking population and have students research pertinent information about the area. Ask students to summarize what they found and add this information to their portfolio.

**Rubric: Writing**

| Criteria | Scale | |
|---|---|---|
| Correct sentence structure | 1 2 3 4 5 | A = 17–20 pts. |
| Vocabulary use | 1 2 3 4 5 | B = 13–16 pts. |
| Content/Accuracy | 1 2 3 4 5 | C = 9–12 pts. |
| Logical organization | 1 2 3 4 5 | D = 5–8 pts. |
| | | F = < 5 pts. |

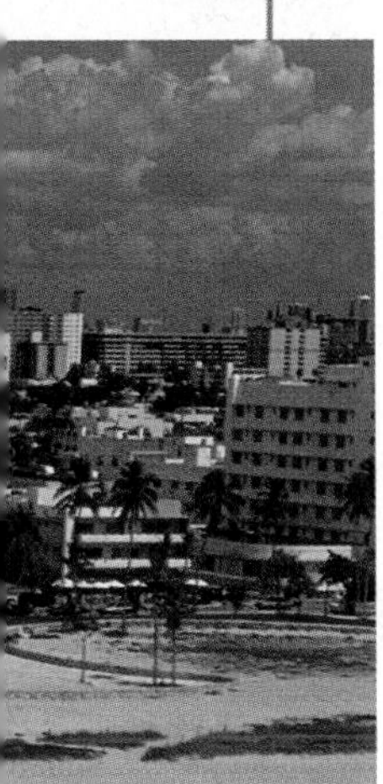

Florida está cerca de la isla[3] de Cuba —solamente a 90 millas— y tiene un clima parecido[4].

En los años 60 muchos cubanos emigraron a la ciudad de Miami. Después de los cubanos vinieron personas de Colombia, Nicaragua y otros países hispanoamericanos.

Estos emigrantes convirtieron a Miami en una ciudad bilingüe y un lugar donde se unen[5] culturas diferentes. En la Pequeña Habana, el barrio cubano más grande de Miami, se puede comprar helado de guayaba y bailar la música salsa al aire libre en la Calle Ocho.

Miami también es un lugar de comercio internacional y un gran centro financiero. Muchos barcos extranjeros, sobre todo barcos de Latinoamérica, paran[6] en Miami porque esta ciudad tiene conexiones con todos los países de las Américas.

[3]island [4]similar [5]unite

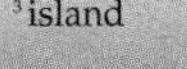
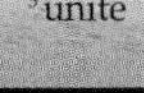

[6]stop

El cantante y compositor Jon Secada nació en Cuba y vino a Miami con su familia cuando era niño. Estudió la música vocal de jazz y participó en el grupo Miami Sound Machine.

## ¿Comprendiste?

1. ¿Para qué vienen los turistas a Miami?
2. ¿Cómo ayudaron los hispanoamericanos a transformar la ciudad de Miami?
3. ¿Qué es la Pequeña Habana?
4. ¿En qué aspectos de la vida comercial tiene Miami una importancia internacional?

## ¿Qué piensas?

1. ¿Es importante saber español en Miami? ¿Por qué?
2. ¿Hay gente de tu comunidad que viene de otros países? ¿Qué sabes de sus culturas?

## Hazlo tú 

En grupos pequeños, hablen de los diferentes vecindarios de tu comunidad. ¿Qué tienen en común? Luego, compartan tus resultados.



## Culture Highlights

● **MIAMI,** being close to the Caribbean, Central and South America, and having a good seaport and airport system, serves as an important international trade center. Miami also continues to be a popular tourist destination. Over 2 million people live in Greater Miami, with Hispanics representing 50% of the population.

## ¿Comprendiste?

**Answers**

1. Vienen para tomar el sol, nadar y visitar los hoteles lujosos.
2. Convirtieron a Miami en una ciudad bilingüe y un lugar donde se unen culturas diferentes.
3. Es el barrio cubano más grande de Miami.
4. Es un lugar de comercio internacional y un gran centro financiero para todos los países latinoamericanos.

## Hazlo tú

Have students use the article about Miami as a model for their own article, or bring in other model articles from travel magazines or brochures.

## Cross Cultural Connections

Ask students to research and discuss other cities where it is important to know both English and Spanish. Locate them on a map.

## Critical Thinking

Have students think about the advantages of being part of a bilingual community. Have they ever visited a bilingual city? Which one? Would they like to live in such a community? Why or why not?

## Teaching All Students

**Extra Help** Using a map of Florida and Latin America, have students locate the following places: Miami, Cuba, Havana, Colombia, and Nicaragua.

**Native Speakers** Ask native speakers to expand on the answers to the **¿Qué piensas?** and **Hazlo tú** questions.

**Multiple Intelligences**

**Interpersonal** Have students interview a neighbor/friend/relative who came from another country. Ask them to summarize the information.

**Verbal** Have students develop a story based on their interview for the class newspaper.

**Visual** Have students gather photos or draw a picture to illustrate the interview for the class newspaper.

## Block Schedule

**FunBreak** Plan a 10-minute music break, using music by Jon Secada or another Miami-based musician. If possible, ask a local dance instructor to demonstrate some appropriate dance steps.

## Teaching Resource Options

**Print** 

Block Scheduling Copymasters
Unit 1 Resource Book
Family Involvement, pp. 193–194
Multiple Choice Test Questions, pp. 249–251

**Audiovisual**

OHT 34 (Quick Start)

**Technology** 

Electronic Teacher Tools/Test Generator
*Intrigas y aventuras* CD-ROM, Disc 1

## Quick Start Review

Nationalities

Use **OHT** 34 or write on board: Write a sentence giving the nationality of each person.

1. José: Puerto Rico
2. Pierre: Canadá
3. Lupe: Nicaragua
4. Teresa: Ecuador
5. Helen: Inglaterra

**Answers**, see p. 71B.

## Teaching Suggestions
### What Have Students Learned?

Have students look at the "Now you can..." notes listed on the left side of pp. 92–93. To review material before doing the activities or taking the test, have them consult the "To review" notes.

# En uso
## REPASO Y MÁS COMUNICACIÓN

**OBJECTIVES**
- Discuss ways to communicate
- React to news
- Ask for and give information
- Talk about things and people you know

*Now you can...*
- talk about things and people you know.

*To review*
- demonstrative adjectives, see p. 82.

### ACTIVIDAD 1 ¿De dónde son?

Di las personas que conoces y de dónde son. *(Hint: Tell the people you know.)*

Japón | Alemania | Nicaragua | Argentina | Francia | Puerto Rico | México | Italia

**modelo**

*(aquel) señoras* → **Perú**

*Conozco a aquellas señoras peruanas.*

1. (este) señores
2. (ese) chica
3. (aquel) muchacho
4. (este) niñas
5. (ese) hombres
6. (aquel) señora
7. (este) niño
8. (aquel) chicos

*Now you can...*
- talk about things and people you know.

*To review*
- demonstrative pronouns, see p. 82.

### ACTIVIDAD 2 En la tienda

Tú y un(a) amigo(a) están en una tienda. Ustedes hablan de sus preferencias. ¿Qué dicen? *(Hint: Discuss preferences.)*

**modelo**

*un libro*
**Tú:** *¿Prefieres este libro o éste?*
**Amigo(a):** *Prefiero aquél.*

1. la pluma
2. un sándwich
3. una bebida
4. una revista
5. una computadora
6. un juego
7. un sombrero
8. una videograbadora



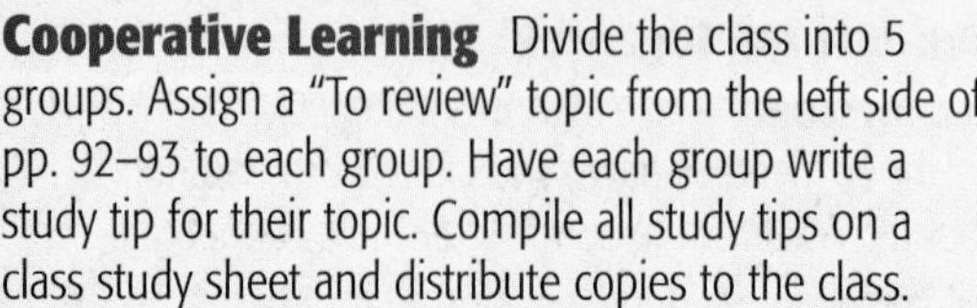

## Classroom Community

**Cooperative Learning** Divide the class into 5 groups. Assign a "To review" topic from the left side of pp. 92–93 to each group. Have each group write a study tip for their topic. Compile all study tips on a class study sheet and distribute copies to the class.

**Paired Activity** As an expansion of **Actividad 6**, have students work with a partner to find out what foods their partner prefers and why. For example, S1: **¿Prefieres la comida italiana o la comida japonesa?** S2: **Prefiero la comida italiana porque me gusta mucho la pasta.**

## Actividad 3 Un sabelotodo

*Now you can...*
- talk about things and people you know.

*To review*
- **saber** and **conocer**, see p. 81.

¿Eres un «sabelotodo»? Para saberlo, escribe oraciones con **sé** o **conozco.** *(Hint: Complete the sentences.)*

**modelo**

*el presidente*

*Sí, (No, no) conozco al presidente.*

1. qué hora es
2. los compañeros de clase
3. hablar italiano
4. la Casa Blanca
5. nadar bien
6. un buen restaurante francés

## Actividad 4 ¿Crees en las noticias?

*Now you can...*
- discuss ways to communicate.
- react to news.

*To review*
- verbs with preterite spelling changes (i → y), see p. 85.

Todos leyeron el periódico esta mañana pero no creyeron nada. Explica lo que leyeron. *(Hint: Tell who read what in the newspaper.)*

**modelo**

*María: los anuncios*

*María leyó los anuncios pero no creyó nada.*

1. yo: los editoriales
2. Samuel: los anuncios clasificados
3. mis padres: las noticias locales
4. tú: las noticias internacionales
5. nosotros: los titulares
6. ustedes: todo el periódico

## ¿Y tú?

*Now you can...*
- ask for and give information.

*To review*
- stem-changing preterite verbs, see p. 84.

¿Qué hicieron tú, tus amigos y tu familia? Habla con un(a) compañero(a) sobre lo que hicieron. *(Hint: What did you do?)*

1. tus amigos: pedir comida china
2. tu hermano: dormir en casa de un amigo
3. tu tío: preferir ver la televisión en el sofá
4. tu vecino(a): competir en un concurso
5. mis amigos y yo: servir una comida deliciosa





### Actividad 1 Answers

1. Conozco a estos señores japoneses.
2. Conozco a esa chica francesa.
3. Conozco a aquel muchacho alemán.
4. Conozco a estas niñas puertorriqueñas.
5. Conozco a esos hombres nicaragüenses.
6. Conozco a aquella señora mexicana.
7. Conozco a este niño argentino.
8. Conozco a aquellos chicos italianos.

*Answers to questions will vary.*

### Actividad 2 Answers

1. ¿Prefieres esta pluma o ésa? Prefiero aquélla.
2. ¿Prefieres este sándwich o ése? Prefiero aquél.
3. ¿Prefieres esta bebida o ésa? Prefiero aquélla.
4. ¿Prefieres esta revista o ésa? Prefiero aquélla.
5. ¿Prefieres esta computadora o ésa? Prefiero aquélla.
6. ¿Prefieres este juego o ése? Prefiero aquél.
7. ¿Prefieres este sombrero o ése? Prefiero aquél.
8. ¿Prefieres esta videograbadora o ésa? Prefiero aquélla.

### Answers

1. Sí, (No, no) sé qué hora es.
2. Sí, (No, no) conozco a los compañeros de clase.
3. Sí, (No, no) sé hablar italiano.
4. Sí, (No, no) conozco la Casa Blanca.
5. Sí, (No, no) sé nadar bien.
6. Sí, (No, no) conozco un buen restaurante francés.

### Answers

1. Yo leí los editoriales pero no creí nada.
2. Samuel leyó los anuncios clasificados pero no creyó nada.
3. Mis padres leyeron las noticias locales pero no creyeron nada.
4. Tú leíste las noticias internacionales pero no creíste nada.
5. Nosotros leímos los titulares pero no creímos nada.
6. Ustedes leyeron todo el periódico pero no creyeron nada.

### Answers

1. ¿Pidieron comida china tus amigos?
2. ¿Durmió en casa de un amigo tu hermano?
3. ¿Prefirió ver la televisión en el sofá tu tío?
4. ¿Compitió en un concurso tu vecino(a)?
5. ¿Servimos una comida deliciosa mis amigos y yo?

*Answers to questions will vary.*

## Teaching All Students

**Extra Help** Have students review the newspaper vocabulary by labeling the different sections of a newspaper on sticky notes labels and posting them on the actual newspaper.

**Challenge** Have students work in small groups to make a list of 5 reasons to have a Spanish school newspaper at their school or a Spanish-language newspaper in their community.

**Multiple Intelligences**

**Verbal** Have students work in small groups to write the script for a radio/TV commercial that advertises one of the local newspapers.

**Logical/Mathematical** Have students research the Internet to find out how many Spanish-language newspapers there are in the U.S. Have them determine which regions have the most and which have the least offerings for Spanish readers.

## Block Schedule

**Peer Teaching** Divide the class into groups. Have each group prepare a review sheet for one of the **En uso** activities. Then have groups exchange sheets.

## Teaching Resource Options

**Print** 

Unit 1 Resource Book
Audioscript, pp. 203–204
Cooperative Quizzes, pp. 205–206
Etapa Exam, Forms A and B, pp. 207–216
*Examen para hispanohablantes*, pp. 217–221
Portfolio Assessment, pp. 222–223
Unit 1 Comprehensive Test, pp. 224–231
*Prueba comprensiva para hispanohablantes,* Unit 1, pp. 232–239
Multiple Choice Test Questions, pp. 249–251

**Audiovisual** 

OHT 34 (Quick Start)
Audio Program Cassette 19A / CD 19; (*Para hispanohablantes* Cassette 19A / CD 19)

**Technology**

Electronic Teacher Tools/Test Generator
www.mcdougallittell.com

## Teaching Suggestion

**Preparation** Students can review the dialogs on pp. 32–33, 54–55, 76–77 before they start the assignment.

### Actividad 6 and Actividad 7

**Rubric: Speaking**

| Criteria | Scale | |
|---|---|---|
| Fluency | 1 2 3 | A = 8–9 pts. |
| Vocabulary | 1 2 3 | B = 6–7 pts. |
| Pronunciation, rhythm | 1 2 3 | C = 4–5 pts. |
| | | D = 3 pts. |
| | | F = < 3 pts. |

### Actividad 8 En tu propia voz

**Rubric: Writing**

| Criteria | Scale | |
|---|---|---|
| Vocabulary use | 1 2 3 4 5 | A = 13–15 pts. |
| Accuracy | 1 2 3 4 5 | B = 10–12 pts. |
| Creativity, appearance | 1 2 3 4 5 | C = 7–9 pts. |
| | | D = 4–6 pts. |
| | | F = < 4 pts. |

## Teaching Note: En tu propia voz

**Writing Strategy** Have students use the connectors given in *Actividad* 8 to clarify the sequence of events when telling the story.

## Actividad 6 ¿Cuál prefieres?

**PARA CONVERSAR**

**STRATEGY: SPEAKING**

**Provide additional information** Sometimes you have certain preferences because something is missing: **Prefiero ... porque no es aburrido / porque no me gusta(n) / porque no tengo / porque no puedo...** Try using these phrases in your response.

Habla con tu compañero(a) sobre las cosas que ven en la clase. ¿Qué ven? ¿Qué cosas prefieren? ¿Por qué? *(Hint: What does your partner prefer?)*

**modelo**

**Tú:** *¿Prefieres este libro o ése?*
**Compañero(a):** *Prefiero éste porque no es aburrido.*
**Tú:** *¿Prefieres esa falda o aquélla?*
**Compañero(a):** *Prefiero ésa porque no es de cuadros.*

## Actividad 7 Un tour

Hagan un tour imaginario de un estudio de televisión y expliquen lo que ven. Una persona va a servir de guía y las otras van a hacerle preguntas. *(Hint: Conduct an imaginary tour.)*

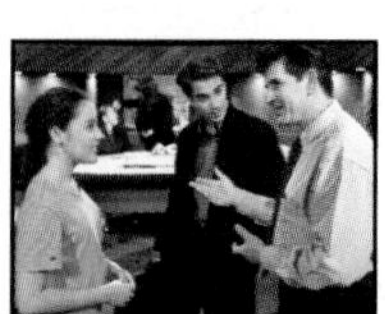

**modelo**

**Estudiante:** *¿Quién es esa señora?*
**Guía:** *Ella es una reportera muy famosa.*

## Actividad 8 En tu propia voz

**ESCRITURA** Combina las siguientes frases para describir las experiencias de Francisco. Usa palabras como **por eso** *(that's why)*, **y, entonces, luego, después** y **finalmente.** Puedes añadir otros detalles. *(Hint: Describe Francisco's experiences.)*

- ganar el concurso de una revista
- viajar a Chicago
- regresar a Miami
- visitar un estudio de televisión con su amiga Alma
- conocer a una reportera famosa
- leerle un poema a Alma

## CONEXIONES

**Las matemáticas** Háblales a tus amigos para saber lo siguiente sobre las telecomunicaciones. Luego, haz un gráfico de las respuestas, calculando los porcentajes de la gente que tiene respuestas en común.

- ¿Cuál es tu anuncio favorito?
- ¿Qué canal ves más?
- ¿Qué noticiero ves más?
- ¿Qué tipo de programación no te gusta?

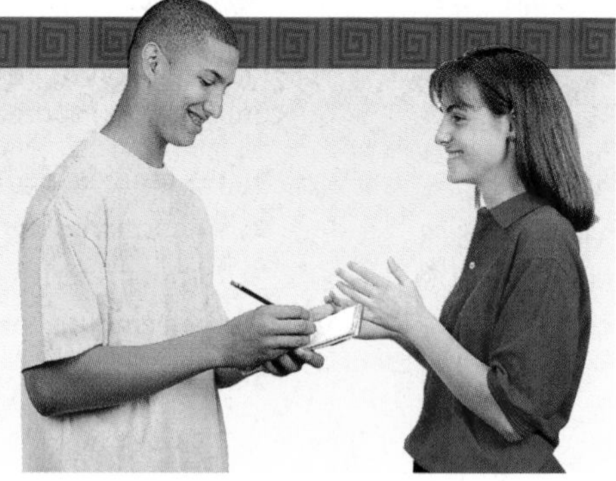



## Classroom Community

**Games** Have the class form pairs and ask each person to take on the role of a famous person or character. They should interview each other from the point of view of their person, e.g., S1: Hank Aaron and S2: Babe Ruth. Their questions and answers are *always* from the point of view of their character. Thus both students *must* know both characters well enough to carry on an interview. It is sometimes easier if you give them a list of compatible people. Some possible partners include Batman and Robin, the president of the U.S. and the president of Mexico, the mayor of your town and the principal of your school, etc.

# En resumen

## REPASO DE VOCABULARIO

### TALK ABOUT THINGS AND PEOPLE YOU KNOW

**Stem-Changing Preterite Verbs**

| | |
|---|---|
| **morir (o→ue, u)** | *to die* |

**Ya sabes**

| | |
|---|---|
| **competir (e→i, i)** | *to compete* |
| **dormir (o→ue, u)** | *to sleep* |
| **pedir (e→i, i)** | *to ask for, to order* |
| **preferir (e→ie, i)** | *to prefer* |
| **repetir (e→i, i)** | *to repeat* |
| **servir (e→i, i)** | *to serve* |

**Spelling Changes in the Preterite (i → y)**

| | |
|---|---|
| **creer** | *to believe* |
| **leer** | *to read* |
| **oír** | *to hear* |

**Ya sabes**

| | |
|---|---|
| **conocer** | *to know, to meet* |
| **saber** | *to know* |

### DISCUSS WAYS TO COMMUNICATE

**Newspapers**

| | |
|---|---|
| **el artículo** | *article* |
| **el (la) autor(a)** | *author* |
| **la crítica** | *criticism, review* |
| **la edición** | *edition* |
| **el (la) editor(a)** | *editor* |
| **el (la) escritor(a)** | *writer* |
| **el (la) fotógrafo(a)** | *photographer* |
| **el periodismo** | *journalism* |
| **el (la) periodista** | *journalist* |
| **la tira cómica** | *comic strip* |
| **el titular** | *headline* |

**Television**

| | |
|---|---|
| **el anuncio** | *commercial* |
| **la cámara** | *camera* |
| **el canal** | *channel, station* |
| **el noticiero** | *news program* |
| **el programa** | *program* |
| **el reportaje** | *report* |
| **el (la) reportero(a)** | *reporter* |
| **el (la) televidente** | *viewer* |

### REACT TO NEWS

| | |
|---|---|
| **¿De veras?** | *Really?* |
| **¡No me digas!** | *Don't tell me!* |
| **¿Tú crees?** | *Do you think so?* |
| **¡Ya lo sé!** | *I already know!* |

### ASK FOR AND GIVE INFORMATION

| | |
|---|---|
| **la causa** | *cause* |
| **de repente** | *suddenly* |
| **el detalle** | *detail* |
| **estar bien informado(a)** | *to be well informed* |
| **el hecho** | *fact* |
| **el héroe** | *hero* |
| **la heroína** | *heroine* |
| **hubo** | *there was, there were* |
| **internacional** | *international* |
| **el (la) ladrón(ona)** | *thief* |
| **local** | *local* |
| **las noticias** | *news* |
| **rescatar** | *to rescue* |
| **el rescate** | *rescue* |
| **robar** | *to steal* |
| **el robo** | *robbery* |

### Juego

Yo no soy un editor,
ni un televidente.
Tampoco soy un escritor;
si me ves, es evidente.

Siempre te cuento las
noticias con mucho coraje[1].
¿Sabes quién soy, quizás?
¡Te doy el reportaje!

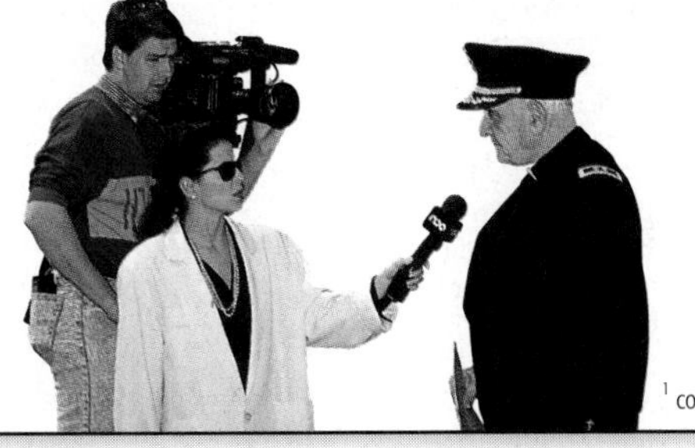

[1] courage



## Teaching All Students

**Extra Help** Have students demonstrate that they know the different uses of **saber** and **conocer** by having them write 3 sentences using each verb.

### Multiple Intelligences

**Logical/Mathematical** Have students find out how many radio and television programs are broadcast in Spanish in your area. They can consult the local listings, call a local cable company or radio/television station. Have students create a comparative graph to show the number of English programs vs. Spanish programs.

**Verbal** Have students write a newspaper article about what is happening at your school this month.

**Visual** Have students design a display (poster/visual) of the Spanish TV shows and Spanish radio stations that are broadcast in your area.

## Interdisciplinary Connection

**Mathematics** Have students ask 5 additional people outside of the class the questions in the **Conexiones** box. Compile the findings on the board and have students work in small groups to analyze the results.

## Teaching Suggestions

### Vocabulary Review

Have students make flashcards of the words in the **Repaso de vocabulario** on p. 95. Break students into groups of 3 or 4. Deal 5 cards per group. See how many sentences students can make using the vocabulary cards. The team with the most grammatically correct sentences wins. Bonus points for anyone who puts all 5 vocabulary words in the same sentence.

## Project

Have students prepare a Spanish TV commercial: Ask the class to brainstorm products to advertise and list them on the board. Divide into small groups and ask each group to choose a product to advertise. Have them design a slogan, make a visual aid (e.g., poster) to represent the product, and be prepared to present their commercial to the entire class.

**Rubric: Project**

| Criteria | Scale |
|---|---|
| Oral Presentation | 1 2 3 |
| Clarity of Expression | 1 2 3 |
| Grammar | 1 2 3 |
| Use of vocabulary | 1 2 3 |
| Visual and Slogan Creativity | 1 2 3 |

A = 13–15 pts.
B = 10–12 pts.
C = 7–9 pts.
D = 4–6 pts.
F = < 4 pts.

## Juego

**Answer**
el (la) reportero(a)

## Block Schedule

**Change of Pace** Ask students to write down three things they did yesterday using the preterite. Then have them order the sentences using the words: **primero**, **luego**, **finalmente**.

### Teaching Resource Options

**Print** 
Block Scheduling Copymasters

**Audiovisual**
OHT GO1–GO5; 34 (Quick Start)

**Technology**
*Intrigas y aventuras* CD-ROM, Disc 1

 www.mcdougallittell.com

### Quick Start Review

Noun/adjective agreement

Use OHT 34 or write on the board: Choose adjectives to describe these nouns. Be sure they agree!

un viaje — unos lugares
unas vacaciones — una amiga

*Answers will vary.*

### Teaching Strategies

**Prewriting**

- Bring in magazine pictures or photos of young people doing different activities. Have students use these illustrations to help them brainstorm ideas for their own descriptive paragraphs.
- Have students review the **diálogos** on pp. 32–33, 54–55, 76–77 to see models of some descriptions of past experiences.
- Point out the PASS list at the beginning of the page: Purpose, Audience, Subject, Structure. This will be their PASS key to a well-structured writing assignment in every unit.

**Post-writing**

- Have students exchange paragraphs and organization charts with a partner to review the development of the main idea and supporting details. Have them make suggestions to better organize the paragraph.

UNIDAD 1

# En tu propia voz

## ESCRITURA

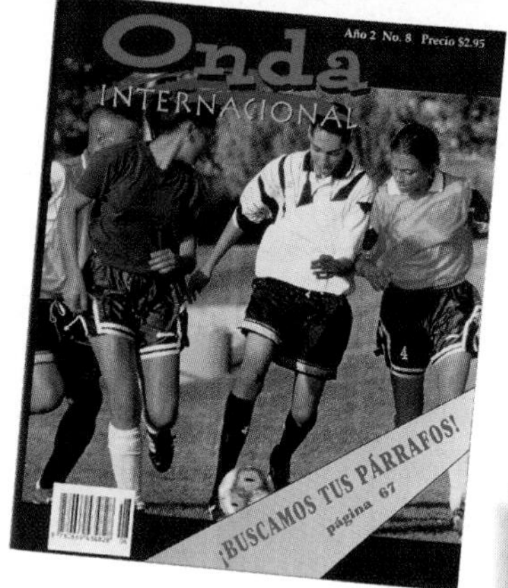


## ¿Qué hicieron?

Next month's *Onda Internacional* will feature Spanish students from around the world. One segment will highlight school break activities. Write a one-paragraph description of an event that took place during a recent school break to submit to the magazine.

**Purpose:** Describe an event that took place during school break
**Audience:** Magazine readers
**Subject:** School break event
**Structure:** Descriptive paragraph

**PARA ESCRIBIR • STRATEGY: WRITING**

**Bring your event to life** Describing an event or personal experience means more than giving out a few facts. Share how you feel about what is happening—about the people, places, and objects that make the event memorable. Bring your subject to life by using sensory details in your writing.

### Modelo del estudiante

*Una fiesta sensacional*

Dimos una fiesta muy buena durante el verano pasado. Mi hermana y yo invitamos a unos amigos. Pero llegó mucha gente, ¡como cincuenta personas! La comida quedó muy rica. Mi hermana y yo hicimos nachos y papas fritas y pedimos unas pizzas. Mucha gente trajo comida, como pasteles y sándwiches, y bebidas. Una chica hizo un pastel de vainilla con piezas de chocolate. Quedó delicioso. También bailamos. Pusimos la música muy fuerte. Después no oí nada. Sé bailar pero aprendí algunas cosas nuevas también. Dormí muchas horas después de la fiesta. Lo pasé muy bien. ¡Todos dijeron que fue una fiesta sensacional!

The writer introduces the main idea of her paragraph.

The writer adds sensory details, including **taste**, to bring the event to life.

The writer uses references to the **sounds** of the party to make readers feel as if they were there.

The writer concludes by describing her feelings about the event.



### Classroom Community

**Paired Activity** Have students work with a partner to fill in the chart to organize their ideas. Have students ask each other questions to better develop their ideas.

**Group Activity** After students have created their organizational chart, divide the class into groups with similar topics, i.e. travel, sports, etc. Have members of each group compare the information in their charts and share ideas before they start developing their paragraphs.

**Portfolio** Have students save this paragraph for their portfolios. Subsequent writing projects will show their progress in Spanish.

## Estrategias para escribir

MI FIESTA

mucha gente
decoraciones
vista (sight)

música fuerte
salsa
rock
oído (sound)

nachos
papas fritas
pasteles
gusto/olfato (taste/smell)

bailar
poco espacio
tacto (touch)

nuevos amigos
cansada
contenta
sentimientos (feelings)

### Antes de escribir…

Begin by freewriting about your recent school break experience. Remember that when freewriting, you write down everything you can think of, and select from it later. Be sure to include people you met, things you saw and did, details about actions and events, and why it was a meaningful experience.

After selecting an event, create an idea tree like this one to organize the sensory details of your experience.

### Revisiones

Share your draft with a partner. Then ask

- *How does the first sentence attract your attention?*
- *What else would you like to know?*
- *Did the paragraph hold your attention? What could be added to better hold your attention?*

You may want to make revisions based on your partner's answers to these questions.

**PROOFREADING SYMBOLS**

- ^ Add letters, words, or punctuation marks.
- ~ Switch the position of letters or words.
- ≡ Capitalize a letter.
- —ℓ Take out letters or words.
- / Make a capital letter lowercase.

### La versión final

Before you create the final draft of your paragraph, use proofreading symbols to mark any errors in grammar, usage, spelling, and punctuation. As you check your work, keep the following question in mind:

- *Did I use correct preterite verb forms?*

**Try this:** Circle every past-tense verb and identify its subject. Have the correct preterite forms been used?

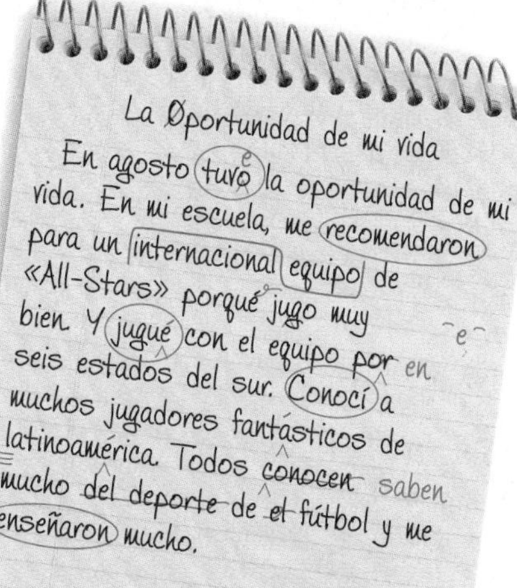

La Oportunidad de mi vida
En agosto tuvo la oportunidad de mi vida. En mi escuela, me recomendaron para un internacional equipo de «All-Stars» porque jugo muy bien. Y jugué con el equipo por en seis estados del sur. Conocí a muchos jugadores fantásticos de latinoamérica. Todos conocen saben mucho del deporte de el fútbol y me enseñaron mucho.

Share your writing on www.mcdougallittell.com



## Supplementary Vocabulary

| | |
|---|---|
| el trabajo | work |
| el viaje | trip |
| el deporte | sport |
| las experiencias | experiences |

## Rubric: Writing

Let students know ahead of time which elements of their writing you will be evaluating. A global evaluation is more helpful to students than a correction of every mistake made. Consider the following in scoring compositions.

| | Sentences |
|---|---|
| 1 | Most not logical |
| 2 | In logical order |
| 3 | Flow purposefully |
| | **Details** |
| 1 | Few details |
| 2 | Sufficient basic details |
| 3 | Clear and vivid details |
| | **Organization** |
| 1 | Not well organized |
| 2 | Some organization |
| 3 | Strong organization |
| | **Accuracy** |
| 1 | Errors prevent comprehension |
| 2 | Some spelling and agreement errors throughout |
| 3 | Very few errors |

| Criteria | Scale |
|---|---|
| Logical sentence order | 1 2 3 |
| Clear and vivid detail | 1 2 3 |
| Organization | 1 2 3 |
| Accuracy | 1 2 3 |

A = 10–12 pts.
B = 7–9 pts.
C = 5–6 pts.
D = 4 pts.
F = < 4 pts.

## Teaching All Students

**Extra Help** Review structures with students before writing:

- Use of adjectives that agree in gender and number with the subject
- Use of preterite: regular and irregular verbs
- Use of **saber** and **conocer**
- Use of demonstrative adjectives and pronouns

**Challenge** Have students gather all the students' descriptions to create a special edition of *Onda Internacional* for publication. Assign students the roles of editors, designers, and production staff. Make the publication available to other Spanish classes.

**Native Speakers** Have Spanish speakers present their descriptions to the class as a model for other students.

## Block Schedule

**FunBreak** Have students bring in photos or brochures that illustrate their descriptive paragraphs. You can post some of the completed illustrated descriptions on the board for all to see. (For additional activities, see **Block Scheduling Copymasters**.)

## UNIDAD 2
## Cultural Opener

### Unit Theme

**Discussing childhood memories and family, relating a series of events in the past, eating in a restaurant, and talking about things to do in the city.**

**Communication**
- Describing childhood experiences
- Expressing personal reactions
- Discussing family relationships and celebrations
- Narrating in the past
- Talking about activities in progress
- Ordering and paying in a restaurant
- Talking about things to do in the city

**Cultures**
- Learning about the history of Mexico City and its surroundings
- Learning about the ancient Aztec civilization in Mexico
- Learning about traditional Mexican foods and eating customs
- Learning about city life in Mexico City

**Connections**
- Connecting to Social Studies: Learning about family relationships and eating customs in Mexico
- Connecting to Art: Murals in Mexico and artifacts from Teotihuacán

**Comparisons**
- Comparing children's activities in Mexico and the U.S.
- Comparing family relationships
- Comparing holidays/celebrations
- Comparing restaurants and eating customs

**Communities**
- Using Spanish for personal interest in restaurants and theaters
- Using Spanish in the workplace

### Teaching Resource Options

**Print** 

Block Scheduling Copymasters

**Audiovisual** 

OHT 35–38

*Canciones* Cassette / CD Songs 4, 7, 9, 11, 14

Video Program Videotape 2, 0:00 / Videodisc 1B

Search Chapter 1, Play to 2; U2 Cultural Introduction

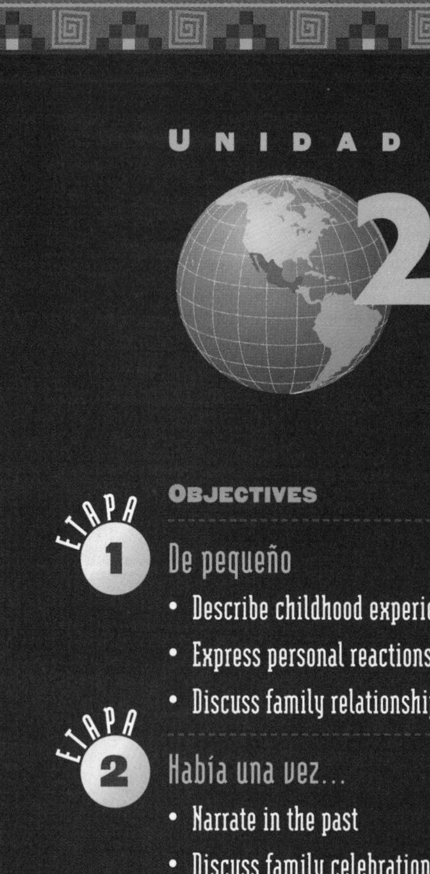


# CIUDAD DE MÉXICO
# MÉXICO
## AYER Y HOY

**OBJECTIVES**

**ETAPA 1 De pequeño**
- Describe childhood experiences
- Express personal reactions
- Discuss family relationships

**ETAPA 2 Había una vez...**
- Narrate in the past
- Discuss family celebrations
- Talk about activities in progress

**ETAPA 3 Hoy en la ciudad**
- Order in a restaurant
- Ask for and pay a restaurant bill
- Talk about things to do in the city

**LOS TAMALES** Hace más de mil años, los indios de México los hacían de maíz, y así se hacen hoy día. ¿Conoces otras comidas que vienen de poblaciones indígenas?

**LA PIÑATA** Donde hay una piñata, hay fiesta. ¿Qué puedes encontrar en una piñata?

98

### Classroom Community

**Paired Activity** Have students work in pairs to brainstorm all the Mexican cities or towns they know and try to locate them on the map on pp. 98–99. Have students brainstorm names of U.S. cities that reflect a Spanish influence.

**Group Activity** Ask students to locate a local newspaper or news magazine and find any articles that may deal with Mexico or Mexican culture and bring them to class. Assign groups to each article and have them prepare a summary for the class. Indicate on a map where the article took place.

## ALMANAQUE

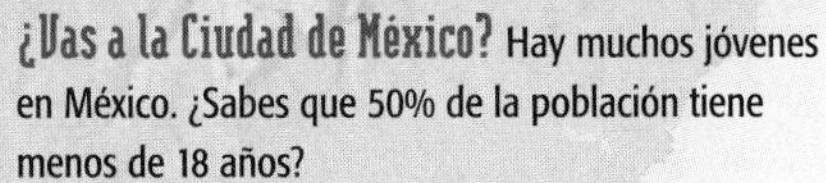

**Población:** 16.900.000
**Altura:** 2.309 metros (7.575 pies)
**Clima:** 19°C (66°F), diciembre; 26°C (79°F), mayo
**Moneda:** el peso
**Comida típica:** pozole, natillas, tamales
**Gente famosa de México:** Cristian Castro (cantante), Frida Kahlo (pintora), Octavio Paz (escritor), Diego Rivera (pintor)

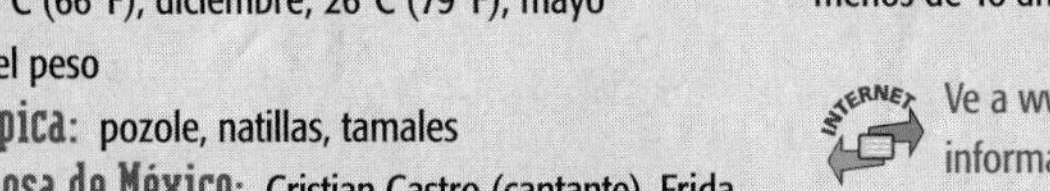

**¿Vas a la Ciudad de México?** Hay muchos jóvenes en México. ¿Sabes que 50% de la población tiene menos de 18 años?

INTERNET Ve a www.mcdougallittell.com para más información sobre la Ciudad de México.

OCÉANO ATLÁNTICO
GOLFO DE MÉXICO
BAHÍA DE CAMPECHE
PENÍNSULA DE YUCATÁN
CIUDAD DE MÉXICO
OAXACA
BELICE
MAR CARIBE
GUATEMALA

El Popocatépetl

**EL POPOCATÉPETL** es un volcán activo cerca de la Ciudad de México. Una leyenda azteca cuenta que Popocatépetl era guerrero (*warrior*). ¿Por qué crees que los aztecas le dieron el nombre de un guerrero a un volcán?

**HOY NO CIRCULA** Para mantener más limpio el aire de la ciudad, el gobierno empezó un programa para reducir el número de conductores diarios. Cada conductor puede circular su carro seis días por semana, basado en el último número de su placa (*license plate*). ¿Qué hace tu ciudad para mantenerse limpia?

**CRISTIAN CASTRO** es un cantante popular de la Ciudad de México. Su estilo de música se llama «balada». Por su segundo álbum Castro ganó el premio Lo Nuestro de música latina. ¿Qué tipo de música prefieres?

**PADRE MIGUEL HIDALGO Y COSTILLA (1753–1811)** fue un líder del movimiento mexicano para ganar la independencia. ¿Por qué piensas que en el Día de la Independencia todavía es posible oír sus palabras famosas, «Mexicanos, ¡Viva México!»?

**FRIDA KAHLO (1907–1954)** pintó muchos autorretratos, o pinturas sobre ella misma y su vida. En esta pintura, *Frida y Diego Rivera* (1931), Kahlo aparece con su esposo, Diego Rivera, un muralista importante. ¿Qué piensas de Kahlo y Rivera al mirar la pintura?

## Teaching Suggestions

### Previewing the Unit

- Use the video to preview the unit. Tell students that this unit centers around Mexico. Ask students to brainstorm what they know about Mexico and Mexican culture.
- In the **Almanaque**, point out the use of decimal points instead of commas to show place value.

## Culture Highlights

- **TAMALES** are made of cornmeal dough with spiced fillings then wrapped in cornhusks (sometimes plantain leaves) to be steamed. They are sometimes eaten with rice and beans.
- **POPOCATÉPETL** (nicknamed "Popo") is an active volcano just 60 kilometers from Mexico City. It last erupted in 1998, throwing ash on the Mexico City area.
- **CRISTIAN CASTRO** is a young singer from Mexico who is popular with the Spanish-speaking population in the U.S. and Latin America.
- **FRIDA KAHLO** The wife of the great Mexican muralist, Diego Rivera, Kahlo was also an accomplished artist in her own right. Her greatest works include a series of self-portrait paintings. Rivera (1886–1957) created many murals depicting life in Mexico.
- **PADRE MIGUEL HIDALGO Y COSTILLA** was a priest of the Dolores parish who became an important patriot for Mexican independence. His battlecry, known as the **Grito de Dolores**, triggered the fight for Mexican Independence (September 16, 1810). He is known as **"el padre de la independencia mexicana."**

## Teaching All Students

**Extra Help** With books closed, have students locate Mexico and Mexico City on a globe or world map.

**Native Speakers** If you have any students with family from Mexico, ask them to discuss the region they are from. Have them bring in any photos, artifacts, or handicrafts from that region. Locate the region on a map.

**Multiple Intelligences**

**Visual** Show other examples of works by Frida Kahlo and Diego Rivera. Students react and discuss.

**Musical/Rhythmic** Find music by Cristian Castro and play it for students with the lyrics, if possible. Ask students to review, listing comments on the board.

## Block Schedule

**FunBreak** Give student groups 5 min. to make 3 game cards based on the Unit Opener, drawing a picture on one side and a descriptive sentence on the other. Collect all the cards and use them to "quiz" the class. (For additional activities, see **Block Scheduling Copymasters**.)

# Ampliación

These activities may be used at various points in the Unit 2 sequence.

For Block Schedule, you may find that these projects will provide a welcome change of pace while reviewing and reinforcing the material presented in the unit. See the Block Schedule Copymasters.

## PROJECTS

**Create birthday greeting cards** in Spanish. Have students decorate the card's cover and write a birthday greeting inside in Spanish. You can display the birthday cards on a bulletin board or sell them to raise money to benefit the Spanish Club or for a class **fiesta**.

PACING SUGGESTION: Upon completion of Etapa 2.

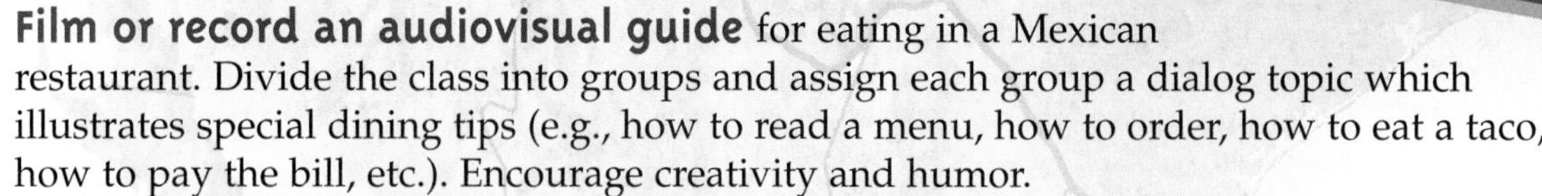

**Film or record an audiovisual guide** for eating in a Mexican restaurant. Divide the class into groups and assign each group a dialog topic which illustrates special dining tips (e.g., how to read a menu, how to order, how to eat a taco, how to pay the bill, etc.). Encourage creativity and humor.

PACING SUGGESTION: Upon completion of Etapa 3.

## STORYTELLING

**El cumpleaños de la abuela** After reviewing the vocabulary on family and holiday celebrations, model a mini-story (using student actors or pictures from the text) that students will revise, retell, and expand:

> La semana pasada celebraron el cumpleaños de la abuela de Isabel. Isabel le contó a Ricardo los detalles de la fiesta. Ricardo preguntó, «¿Cuántos años tiene su abuela?» Isabel respondió, «Cumplió setenta años». Ricardo preguntó, «¿Cuántas personas estaban en la fiesta?» e Isabel contestó, «Más de 25 personas: todos mis primos, mis tíos, mi abuelo, mis hermanos y mis padres. Somos una familia grande». Y luego Isabel le contó qué hicieron en la fiesta...

As you give your model, be sure to pause as the story is being told so that students may fill in words and act out gestures. Students should then write, narrate, and read aloud a longer main story. This new version should include vocabulary from **Unidad 2**. Students can write, illustrate, and act out additional new stories based on this storytelling experience.

**Vamos a dar una fiesta** Ask students to tell a story about planning their own celebration (birthday, graduation, etc.). They may plan the activities, the refreshments, and the guest list.

PACING SUGGESTION: Upon completion of Etapa 2.

## BULLETIN BOARDS / POSTERS

**Bulletin board Plan ahead:** Have students bring in photos of their family members or friends (or an imaginary family) and write a short description in Spanish. Display the captioned photos on the bulletin board.

**Posters Have students create** • **Family trees** on a poster • **Menu** for a Mexican restaurant • **Mexican restaurant** advertisement poster • **Calendar** with months' illustrations and important dates pertaining to Mexico • **Recipe calendar** with a different illustration and recipe for each month

## GAMES

**Había una vez...**
Have students form a circle. Taking turns, each student will contribute a part of an ongoing story in the past tense. The teacher can start with **"Había una vez dos muchachos...,"** the next student might add **"que fueron a una fiesta,"** and so on. Encourage students to be as creative and humorous as possible. You may want to stick close to the chapter vocabulary and practice using verbs in the preterite and imperfect tenses.

PACING SUGGESTION: Upon completion of Etapa 2.

## HANDS-ON CRAFTS

Work with the art department to create a **piñata** out of *papier maché.* Prepare ahead: Newspapers torn in strips, flour and water to make a paste, a balloon to make a mold for the **piñata**, and paints or colored paper to decorate it. Have students dip the newspaper strips in the flour paste and wrap them around the balloon in criss-cross layers to make the desired shape. After the shape is completely dry, students can decorate the **piñata** with paints or colored paper and streamers. You may also find **piñatas** already made at a local party store. Have students bring in small toys or candies to help fill the **piñata** and bring it to a class **fiesta**.

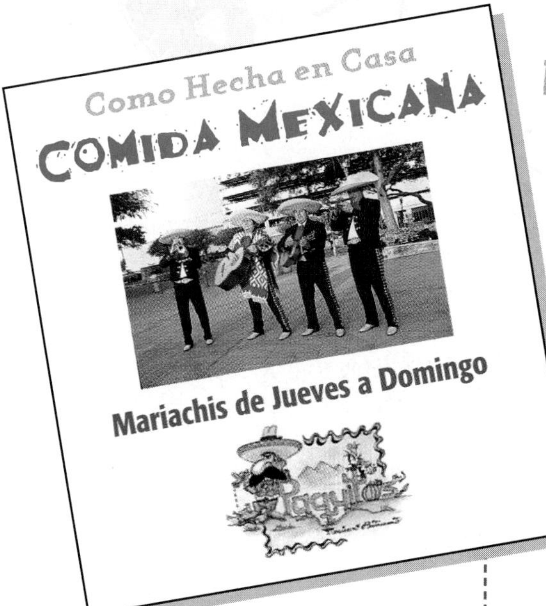

Como Hecha en Casa
COMIDA MEXICANA
Mariachis de Jueves a Domingo


## MUSIC

**Mariachi** music is native to Mexico. A **mariachi** band consists of strolling musicians who play guitars, violins, and trumpets, and sing. Some believe that the origin of the word **mariachi** came from the French word for "marriage" since Mexican folk bands used to play at parties during the days of Maximillian, a Frenchman who was emperor of Mexico in the 19th century. Others believe "mariachi" comes from a pre-Hispanic word.

*Canciones de mi padre* is a collection of some typical mariachi music by Linda Ronstadt. (Linda Ronstadt, *Canciones de mi padre* © 1987 Elektra/Asylum Records.) Have students learn the words to a song, such as "Las mañanitas" (Song 9). Other songs from Mexico are available on the the *Canciones* Cassette/CD.

## RECIPE

**Tacos** You can create a "Make-your-own-taco" feast for your class. To make it easier to prepare and serve these tacos in class, use a black bean and salsa mixture for the main ingredient, instead of spiced chicken or meat. Use taco shells or flour tortillas for soft tacos.

Although this is an easy recipe, this will be the first time that students actually learn the Spanish words for the ingredients. As an ongoing project students can prepare bilingual recipe cards with the Spanish version on the front and the English translation on the back.

### Receta

***Tacos***

*1 lata de frijoles*
*2 tazas de salsa picante*
*1 cebolla picada*
*2 tomates cortados en pedazos pequeños*
*lechuga cortada en pedazos pequeños*
*1 taza de queso rallado (Cheddar o Monterey Jack)*
*tortillas*
*Opcional: guacamole, pollo (o carne) picado y sazonado*

*Mezcle los frijoles con 1/2 taza de salsa picante (o más, a su gusto). Ponga la mezcla en un plato hondo. Prepare los otros ingredientes (la cebolla, los tomates, la lechuga, el queso rallado y el resto de la salsa), póngalos en distintos platos hondos y colóquelos en una mesa. Cada persona puede crear su propio taco con los ingredientes que hay en la mesa.*

# *Planning Guide* CLASSROOM MANAGEMENT

## OBJECTIVES

**Communication**
- Describe childhood experiences *pp. 102–103, 104–105*
- Express personal reactions *pp. 110–111, 114*
- Discuss family relationships *pp. 109, 114*

**Grammar**
- Possessive adjectives and pronouns *p. 108*
- Imperfect (including irregulars) *p. 112*
- Expressions with **tener** *p. 114*
- **Había** *p. 115*

**Culture**
- Aspects of Mexico City *pp. 98–99*
- **Las marionetas** *p. 108*
- **El Bosque de Chapultepec** *p. 113*
- ***El monte de nuestro alimento* (leyenda)** *pp. 116–117*

**Recycling**
- Nationalities *p. 107*
- Reflexive pronouns and verbs *p. 110*
- Preterite tense *p. 112*
- Adjective agreement *p. 118*

## STRATEGIES

**Listening Strategies**
- Listen for related details *p. 104*

**Speaking Strategies**
- Tell when you were always or never (im)perfect *p. 114*
- Add variety to your conversation *p. 120*

**Reading Strategies**
- Analyze folkloric traditions *p. 116*

**Writing Strategies**
- Use details to enrich a description *Actividad 7, TE p. 120*

**Connecting Cultures Strategies**
- Compare & contrast folklore and legends, *TE p. 117*
- Find information on the Aztec and Mayan calendar *TE p. 120*

## PROGRAM RESOURCES

### Print

- *Más práctica* Workbook PE *pp. 41–48*
- Block Scheduling Copymasters, *pp. 33–40*
- Unit 2 Resource Book
  - *Más práctica* Workbook TE *pp. 1–8*
  - *Cuaderno para hispanohablantes* TE *pp. 9–16*
  - Information Gap Activities *pp. 17–20*
  - Family Involvement *pp. 21–22*
  - Video Activities *pp. 23–25*
  - Videoscript *pp. 26–27*
  - Audioscript *pp. 28–32*
  - Assessment Program, Unit 2 Etapa 1 *pp. 33–51; 170–172*
  - Answer Keys *pp. 179–183*

### Audiovisual

- Audio Program Cassette 4A, 4B / CD 4
- *Canciones* Cassette/CD
- Video Program Videotape 2 / Videodisc 1B
- Overhead Transparencies M1, M2; 35–48

### Technology

- Electronic Teacher Tools/Test Generator
- *Intrigas y aventuras* CD-ROM, Disc 1
-  www.mcdougallittell.com

### Assessment Program Options

- Cooperative Quizzes (Unit 2 Resource Book)
- Etapa Exam Forms A and B (Unit 2 Resource Book)
- *Examen para hispanohablantes* (Unit 2 Resource Book)
- Portfolio Assessment (Unit 2 Resource Book)
- Multiple Choice Test Questions (Unit 2 Resource Book)
- Audio Program Cassette 19A / CD 19
- Electronic Teacher Tools/Test Generator

### Native Speakers

- *Cuaderno para hispanohablantes* PE *pp. 41–48*
- *Cuaderno para hispanohablantes* TE (Unit 2 Resource Book)
- *Examen para hispanohablantes* (Unit 2 Resource Book)
- Audio Program *(Para hispanohablantes)* Cassettes 4B, 19A / CD 4, CD 19
- Audioscript (Unit 2 Resource Book)

# Student Text Listening Activity Scripts

Isabel

Ricardo

Laura

Don Miguel

## Videoscript: Diálogo *pages 104–105*

• Videotape 2, 3:58 • Videodisc 1B
Search Chapter 3, Play to 4. U2E1, En vivo (Dialog)
• Use the videoscript with **Actividades 1, 2** *page 106*

**Ricardo:** Gracias.
**Isabel:** Me llamaron por teléfono y me dieron las buenas noticias. ¡Gané! Estoy tan contenta.
**Ricardo:** Ay, qué suerte. También ganó un muchacho de los Estados Unidos, ¿no ?
**Isabel:** Sí, creo que es de Miami. No estoy segura. Sus viajes son a diferentes lugares.
**Ricardo:** Y los tuyos, ¿a dónde son?
**Isabel:** Los míos son a Madrid y a Quito. Pero mi primer proyecto es aquí en la Ciudad de México.
**Ricardo:** ¡Ecuador! Tengo envidia. ¿Me llevas contigo? ¿Ándale, sí?
**Isabel:** ¿Bueno?
**Laura:** ¿Isabel? Soy Laura Maldonado, de la revista *Onda Internacional.*
**Isabel:** Hola, Laura.
**Laura:** Tengo malas noticias. Estoy en un hotel cerca del aeropuerto de Atlanta. Cerraron el aeropuerto después de que llegó mi vuelo. Hace muy mal tiempo aquí. No voy a llegar a México hoy.
**Isabel:** ¿No llegas hoy? ¿Cómo voy a preparar mi artículo? Necesito tu ayuda. ¡Y tenemos una entrevista con don Miguel esta tarde!
**Laura:** Sí, ya lo sé. Lo siento mucho. Pero Isabel, estoy segura que tú lo puedes hacer sin mí. No te preocupes. Nos vemos mañana. Hasta luego.
**Isabel:** Bueno, adiós.
**Laura:** Adiós.
**Ricardo:** ¿Qué pasa?
**Isabel:** Gracias por venir conmigo, Ricardo. Estoy un poco nerviosa.
**Ricardo:** No te preocupes, todo va a salir muy bien.
**Don Miguel:** Y después de ese día, todo cambió. Antes los dos amigos se portaban mal y se peleaban mucho. Ahora se portan bien. Bueno, niños, es todo por hoy. ¡Hasta mañana!
**Isabel:** ¿Don Miguel? Soy Isabel Palacios.
**Niño:** ¡Adiós, don Miguel, adiós!
**Don Miguel:** Adiós, Ramón, ¡Hasta mañana!
**Isabel:** Los niños lo quieren mucho, ¿no?
**Don Miguel:** Sí, y yo los quiero mucho también. Cuando yo era niño, siempre iba al parque con mi madre y escuchaba a un señor viejo que contaba chistes y cuentos. Ahora yo soy el viejo que lo hace.
**Isabel:** ¿Y viene Ud. todos los días al parque con sus marionetas?
**Don Miguel:** No, no todos los días. Antes, cuando trabajaba en el banco, venía solamente los sábados. Ahora, estoy aquí cuatro días por semana. Me siento bien cuando los niños se sonríen y cuando escucho sus risas.
**Isabel:** ¿Y su familia es grande?
**Don Miguel:** No muy grande, pero ¡soy bisabuelo!
**Isabel:** ¿Bisabuelo?
**Don Miguel:** Mi nieta–la hija de mi hijo Felipe– tiene ahora un bebé. Así que soy bisabuelo.
**Ricardo:** ¿Es Ud. de la Ciudad de México?
**Don Miguel:** Sí, soy de aquí. Todos mis parientes son de aquí también.
**Isabel:** ¿Cómo era la Ciudad de México cuando Ud. era niño? ¿Es muy diferente hoy en día?
**Don Miguel:** ¡Claro que sí! La ciudad es muy diferente, y en aquellos tiempos hacíamos cosas diferentes.
**Isabel:** ¿Cómo qué?
**Don Miguel:** Por ejemplo, los niños ahora ven mucha televisión, o juegan con videojuegos. Tienen tantos juguetes electrónicos hoy. Cuando yo era niño, no veíamos televisión porque no había. Y no había videojuegos. Pasábamos más tiempo afuera.
**Isabel:** ¿Qué hacían?
**Don Miguel:** Uy, hacíamos tantas cosas. Jugábamos en los parques. A veces trepábamos a los árboles o nos escondíamos. Mis amigas saltaban a la cuerda como esas niñas de allí.
**Isabel:** Yo también saltaba a la cuerda cuando era niña. Y jugaba mucho con mis muñecos de peluche.
**Don Miguel:** Y además yo dibujaba mucho. Y mi hermano siempre construía edificios con bloques de madera.
**Ricardo:** Sí, yo todavía construyo casas con bloques.
**Isabel:** Pero los tuyos son bloques especiales, ¿no?
**Ricardo:** Sí, los míos son para arquitectos. Son de mi padre.
**Don Miguel:** ¿Tu papá es arquitecto?
**Ricardo:** Sí. Y yo también quiero ser arquitecto. Don Miguel, ¿qué más hacían ustedes en aquellos días?
**Don Miguel:** Hablábamos mucho, y mi bisabuelo siempre contaba chistes muy divertidos. Me acuerdo que me reía mucho, mucho. ¡Ahora yo soy el bisabuelo! Qué rápido pasa el tiempo. Bueno, hijos, pronto estamos en mi casa. Allí van a conocer a mi querida esposa.

## Actividad 10 ¿Bien o mal? *page 112*

**Rubén:** Soy Rubén y tengo dos hermanas. Generalmente no me enojo con ellas porque son menores. Quiero ser un buen hermano. Cuando ellas saltan la cuerda o trepan a los árboles, a veces se caen. Me asusto cuando se caen y no me río. Nunca me gusta pelear con mis hermanas.
**Girl's voice:** Cuando mi hermana y yo jugamos, a veces tomamos los juguetes de nuestro hermano y los perdemos... o a veces el perro se los come cuando los dejamos en el piso. Cuando nuestra mamá nos llama, nos escondemos y no venimos. Ella se enoja mucho. Todos los días nos reímos mucho pero Rubén no se ríe. Nos divertimos cuando le causamos problemas a Rubén. Creemos que es nuestro trabajo.

## Actividad 13 En el Bosque de Chapultepec *page 113*

De niña, yo siempre iba con mi mamá y unas vecinas al Bosque de Chapultepec. Allí hay mucho que hacer. Cuando era muy chica, nos llevaban de picnic en el bosque. Pero, cuando ya era mayor, íbamos a los juguetes mecánicos. ¡Era como un carnaval!

Me acuerdo que muchas veces nos subimos a los botes que tienen en el lago del parque. Me pasé muy bien.

Pero, lo que me gustaba más que todo era lo que comíamos allí: refrescos, dulces, palomitas y mi cosa favorita –jícama con chile piquín.

### Quick Start Review Answers

**p. 102** Likes and dislikes
*Answers will vary.*
1. A mí no me gusta trabajar.
2. A los niños les gusta esquiar.
3. A nosotros nos gusta jugar al baloncesto.
4. A mis padres les gusta ir al cine.
5. A mi amigo le gusta hacer ejercicio.

**p. 108** Nationalities
Pablo es español.
Suzanne es francesa.
Bill es estadounidense.

**p. 112** Preterite
*Answers will vary.*
Comí...; Bebí...; Salí a las...; Llegué a las...; Fui primero a...

**p. 118** Reflexive verbs

| | |
|---|---|
| yo | me asusto |
| tú | te asustas |
| usted, él, ella | se asusta |
| nosotros | nos asustamos |
| vosotros | os asustáis |
| ustedes, ellos, ellas | se asustan |
| yo | me asustaba |
| tú | te asustabas |
| usted, él, ella | se asustaba |
| nosotros | nos asustábamos |
| vosotros | os asustabais |
| ustedes, ellos, ellas | se asustaban |
| yo | me siento |
| tú | te sientes |
| usted, él, ella | se siente |
| nosotros | nos sentimos |
| vosotros | os sentís |
| ustedes, ellos, ellas | se sienten |
| yo | me sentía |
| tú | te sentías |
| usted, él, ella | se sentía |
| nosotros | nos sentíamos |
| vosotros | os sentíais |
| ustedes, ellos, ellas | se sentían |

# Pacing Guide

## Sample Lesson Plan - 50 Minute Schedule

### DAY 1

**Unit Opener**
- Anticipate/Activate prior knowledge: Present the *Almanaque* and the cultural notes. Use Map OHTs as needed. 5 MIN.

**Etapa Opener**
- Quick Start Review (TE, p. 100). 5 MIN.
- Have students look at *Etapa* Opener and answer questions. 5 MIN.

**En contexto: Vocabulario**
- Quick Start Review (TE, p. 102). 5 MIN.
- Have students use context and pictures to learn *Etapa* vocabulary. Answer questions, p. 103. 10 MIN.

**En vivo: Diálogo**
- Quick Start Review (TE, p. 104). 5 MIN.
- Review Listening Strategy, p. 104. Play audio or show video for the dialog shown on pp. 104–105. 5 MIN.
- Replay and have students take on roles of characters. 10 MIN.

**Homework Option**
- Video Activities, Unit 2 Resource Book, pp. 23–24.

### DAY 2

**En acción: Vocabulario y Gramática**
- Check homework. 5 MIN.
- Quick Start Review (TE, p. 106). 5 MIN.
- Ask students for a summary of *En vivo* dialog to check recall. 5 MIN.
- Have students answer Comprehension Questions (TE, p. 105). 5 MIN.
- Replay the *En vivo* dialog using the audiovisual resources and have students do *Actividades* 1 and 2 orally. 10 MIN.
- Have students complete *Actividades* 3 and 4 in pairs. 10 MIN.
- Use a scenario game or expansion activity (TE, pp. 104–107) to reinforce retention of vocabulary and dialog structures. 10 MIN.

**Homework Option**
- *Más práctica* Workbook, pp. 41–44. *Cuaderno para hispanohablantes*, pp. 41–42.

### DAY 3

**En acción (cont.)**
- Check homework. 5 MIN.
- Quick Start Review (TE, p. 108). 5 MIN.
- Present *Gramática*: Possessive Adjectives and Pronouns, p. 108. 10 MIN.
- Review the vocabulary in the box on p. 109. 5 MIN.
- Have students do *Actividades* 5 and 6 orally. 15 MIN.
- Have students do *Actividad* 7 in pairs. 10 MIN.

**Homework Option**
- Have students complete *Actividades* 5 and 6 in writing. *Más práctica* Workbook, p. 45. *Cuaderno para hispanohablantes*, p. 43.

### DAY 4

**En acción (cont.)**
- Check homework. 5 MIN.
- Quick Start Review (TE, p. 110). 5 MIN.
- Present *Gramática*: Reflexive Pronouns and Verbs and *Vocabulario* on p. 110. 10 MIN.
- Have students do *Actividad* 8 orally and 9 in writing. 10 MIN.
- Play the audio and have students complete *Actividad* 10. 5 MIN.
- Present *Gramática*: Using the Imperfect Tense on p. 112. 10 MIN.
- Have students complete *Actividades* 11 and 12 orally in pairs. 5 MIN.

**Homework Option**
- Have students do *Actividad* 11 in writing. *Más práctica* Workbook, p. 46. *Cuaderno para hispanohablantes*, p. 44.

### DAY 5

**En acción (cont.)**
- Check homework. 5 MIN.
- Play the audio and do *Actividad* 13 orally with the whole class. 10 MIN.
- Quick Start Review (TE, p. 114). 5 MIN.
- Present Speaking Strategy and *Nota,* p. 114, then have students complete *Actividad* 14. 10 MIN.
- Have students complete *Actividades* 15 and/or 17 with the whole class. 10 MIN.
- *Actividad* 16 can be started in class, then finished as homework. 5 MIN.
- Read and discuss *Refrán*, p. 115. 5 MIN.

**Homework Option:**
- Have students finish *Actividad* 16 in writing. *Más práctica* Workbook, pp. 47–48. *Cuaderno para hispanohablantes*, pp. 45–46.

### DAY 6

**En voces: Lectura**
- Check homework. 5 MIN.
- Quick Start Review (TE, p. 116). 5 MIN.
- Review Reading Strategy, p. 116. 5 MIN.
- Review the Prereading, Reading, and Post-reading strategies, TE p. 116. 10 MIN.
- Have students read *Lectura* silently, then have various students read aloud, taking turns. 10 MIN.
- Call on volunteers to answer *¿Comprendiste?* questions. 10 MIN.
- Begin discussion of *¿Qué piensas?* questions. 5 MIN.

**Homework Option**
- Have students finish the *¿Qué piensas?* questions in writing, p. 117.

### DAY 7

**En uso: Repaso y más comunicación**
- Check homework. 5 MIN.
- Quick Start Review (TE, p. 118). 5 MIN.
- Do *Actividades* 1, 2, 3, and 4 orally. 15 MIN.
- Review Speaking Strategy, p. 120. Then do *Actividad* 5 orally in pairs and *Actividad* 6 in groups of four. 15 MIN.

**En tu propia voz: Escritura**
- Begin *Actividad* 7. 10 MIN.

**Homework Option**
- Complete *Actividad* 7. Review for *Etapa* 1 Exam. *Cuaderno para hispanohablantes*, pp. 47–48.

### DAY 8

**En resumen: Repaso de vocabulario**
- Check homework. 5 MIN.
- Quick Start Review (TE, p. 120). 5 MIN.
- Review grammar questions, etc. as necessary. 5 MIN.
- Complete *Etapa* 1 Exam. 20 MIN.

**Conexiones**
- Read and discuss, p. 120. 5 MIN.

**Ampliación**
- Use a suggested project, game, or activity (TE pp. 99A–99B). 10 MIN.

**Homework Option**
- Preview next *Etapa* Opener, pp. 122–123.

# Sample Lesson Plan - Block Schedule (90 minutes)

## DAY 1

**Unit Opener**
- Anticipate/Activate prior knowledge: Present the *Almanaque* and the cultural notes. Use Map OHTs as needed. 5 MIN.

**Etapa Opener**
- Quick Start Review (TE, p. 100). 5 MIN.
- Have students look at the *Etapa* Opener and answer questions. 5 MIN.
- Use Block Scheduling Copymasters. 5 MIN.

**En contexto: Vocabulario**
- Quick Start Review (TE, p. 102). 5 MIN.
- Have students use context and pictures to learn *Etapa* vocabulary. Answer questions, p. 103. Use the Situational OHTs for additional practice. 15 MIN.

**En vivo: Diálogo**
- Quick Start Review (TE, p. 104). 5 MIN.
- Review Listening Strategy, p. 104. Play audio or show video for the dialog shown on pp. 104–105. 10 MIN.
- Ask Comprehension Questions (TE, p. 105). 5 MIN.
- Replay twice. Read aloud, students taking roles of characters. 10 MIN.

**En acción: Vocabulario y gramática**
- Quick Start Review (TE, p. 106). 5 MIN.
- Have students do *Actividades* 1 and 2 orally. 5 MIN.
- Have students complete *Actividades* 3 and 4 in pairs. 10 MIN.

**Homework Option**
- Have students prepare two true/false or yes/no questions about the dialog.

## DAY 2

**En acción (cont.)**
- Check homework. 10 MIN.
- Quick Start Review (TE, p. 108). 5 MIN.
- Present *Gramática*: Possessive Adjectives and Pronouns, p. 108. 10 MIN.
- Review the vocabulary in the box on p. 109. Have students do *Actividades* 5 and 6 orally. 10 MIN.
- Have students do *Actividad* 7 in pairs. 10 MIN.
- Quick Start Review (TE, p. 110). 5 MIN.
- Present *Gramática*: Reflexive Pronouns and Verbs and *Vocabulario* on p. 110. 10 MIN.
- Have students do *Actividades* 8 and 9 orally. 10 MIN.
- Play the audio and have students complete *Actividad* 10. Students can also write their responses to *Actividad* 10 as homework. 10 MIN.
- Use Block Scheduling Copymasters for a change of pace as needed. 10 MIN.

**Homework Option**
- Have students complete *Actividad* 10 in writing. *Más práctica* Workbook, pp. 41–46 as needed. *Cuaderno para hispanohablantes*, pp. 41–44 as needed.

## DAY 3

**En acción (cont.)**
- Check homework. 10 MIN.
- Quick Start Review (TE, p. 112). 5 MIN.
- Present *Gramática*: Using the Imperfect Tense on p. 112. 10 MIN.
- Have students complete *Actividad* 11 in writing and 12 orally in pairs. 10 MIN.
- Play the audio and do *Actividad* 13 orally with the whole class. 10 MIN.
- Present Speaking Strategy and *Nota,* p. 114, then have students complete *Actividad* 14. 10 MIN.
- Present *Vocabulario,* p. 114. 5 MIN.
- Have students complete *Actividad* 15 or 17 in small groups. *Actividad* 16 can be started in class and finished as homework. 15 MIN.

**Ampliación**
- Use a suggested project, game, or activity (TE pp. 99A–99B). 15 MIN.

**Homework Option**
- *Más práctica* Workbook, pp. 47–48. *Cuaderno para hispanohablantes*, pp. 45–46.

## DAY 4

**En voces: Lectura**
- Check homework. 5 MIN.
- Read and discuss *Refrán,* p. 115. 5 MIN.
- Quick Start Review (TE, p. 116). 5 MIN.
- Review Reading Strategy, p. 116. 5 MIN.
- Review the strategies, TE p. 116. 10 MIN.
- Have students read *Lectura.* 10 MIN.
- Call on volunteers to answer *¿Comprendiste?* questions. 5 MIN.
- Begin discussion of *¿Qué piensas?* questions, then assign as homework. 5 MIN.

**En uso: Repaso y más comunicación**
- Quick Start Review (TE, p. 118). 5 MIN.
- Do *Actividades* 1, 2, 3, and 4 orally. 15 MIN.
- Quick Start Review (TE, p. 120). 5 MIN.
- Review Speaking Strategy, p. 120. Then do *Actividad* 5 in pairs, *Actividad* 6 in groups. 15 MIN.

**Homework Option**
- Have students finish the *¿Qué piensas?* questions in writing.
- Review for *Etapa* 1 exam.

## DAY 5

**En tu propia voz: Escritura**
- Check homework. 5 MIN.
- Quick Start Review (TE, p. 120). 5 MIN.
- Do *Actividad* 7 in writing. Ask volunteers to present their paragraphs to the class. 15 MIN.

**Conexiones**
- Read and discuss. 5 MIN.
- Review other culture notes in *Etapa,* pp. 108, 113. 10 MIN.

**En resumen: Repaso de vocabulario**
- Review grammar questions, etc. as necessary. 10 MIN.
- Complete *Etapa* 1 Exam. 20 MIN.

**Ampliación**
- Use a suggested project, game, or activity (TE pp. 99A–99B). 20 MIN.

**Homework Option**
- Finish writing activity and preview next *Etapa* Opener, pp. 122–123.

▼ Los niños se sientan y se ríen al oír cuentos que dan risa.

## Etapa Theme

**Visiting a park in Mexico City and discussing childhood experiences**

## Grammar Objectives

- Possessive adjectives and pronouns
- Review: Reflexive pronouns and verbs
- Introduction to the imperfect

### Teaching Resource Options

**Print**

Block Scheduling Copymasters

**Audiovisual**

**OHT** 45 (Quick Start)
*Canciones* Cassette / CD Songs 4, 7

### Quick Start Review

Discussing art

Use OHT 45 or write on board: Describe the sculpture you see in the photo on p. 100. Write at least 3 sentences. If you need help recalling adjectives you may refer to page 64.

*Answers will vary. Answers could include:*
La escultura está en el parque. Tiene dos caras misteriosas. Es muy antigua.

### Teaching Suggestions
**Previewing the Etapa**

- Ask students to study the picture on pp. 100–101 (1 min.).
- Have them name similar parks in their community.
- Have them list who might go to this park and what activities might go on there.
- Use the **¿Qué ves?** questions to focus discussion on the photo.

### Critical Thinking

Ask students to look at the list of functions on the Etapa Opener and discuss how the photo and realia illustrates what they will be learning.

UNIDAD 2

ETAPA 1

# De pequeño

- Describe childhood experiences
- Express personal reactions
- Discuss family relationships

## ¿Qué ves?

Mira la foto y contesta las preguntas.

1. ¿Cuántas personas hay en la foto?
2. ¿Qué hacen?
3. ¿Dónde crees que están?
4. Mira el folleto. ¿Qué hora es?



### Classroom Management

**Planning Ahead** Prepare students to discuss their family and childhood experiences. Ask volunteers to bring in old family photos and display them on a bulletin board. You may wish to have students create a family tree as suggested in the **Ampliación** section on page 99A as a warm-up activity for this **Etapa**.

**Time Saver** If time is short, have students prepare the answers to the **¿Qué ves?** questions as homework, then review the answers in class.

## Culture Highlights

- **PARQUE HUNDIDO** is a small neighborhood park with gardens and trees. It is located on Avenida Insurgentes in Mexico City.

## Cross Cultural Connection

Ask students to describe a family outing from their childhood. What did they do? Where did they go?

## Supplementary Vocabulary

You might want to review the family vocabulary from Level 1:

| | |
|---|---|
| **el padre** | father |
| **la madre** | mother |
| **el abuelo** | grandfather |
| **la abuela** | grandmother |
| **los hijos** | sons, children |
| **las hijas** | daughters |
| **los hermanos** | brothers, brothers and sisters |
| **las hermanas** | sisters |
| **los tíos** | uncles, aunts and uncles |
| **las tías** | aunts |
| **los primos** | cousins |

You may wish to have students review additional extended family vocabulary from **Unidad 1 Etapa 1**, p. 29 TE either on a transparency or on the board.

## Teaching All Students

**Extra Help** Help students identify the objects and people in the photo by pointing to each item as you say the word and having students point to it too.

**Challenge** Have students try to guess the relationships among the people in the photo. Encourage them to use their imaginations.

**Multiple Intelligences**

**Intrapersonal** Ask students to look at the photo and list as many adjectives as they can to describe how they react to the photo. They may also describe any puppet or marionette shows they have seen.

## Block Schedule

**Process Time** Have students preview this **Etapa** by preparing the questions for homework. Encourage them to leaf through the **Etapa** as well. What do they expect to learn? (For additional activities, see **Block Scheduling Copymasters**.)

## Teaching Resource Options

**Print** 

Unit 2 Resource Book
Video Activities, p. 23
Videoscript, p. 26
Audioscript, p. 28

**Audiovisual** 

OHT 39, 40, 45 (Quick Start)
Audio Program Cassette 4A / CD 4
Video Program Videotape 2, 1:11 / Videodisc 1B

Search Chapter 2, Play to 3
U2E1, En contexto (Vocabulary)

**Technology**

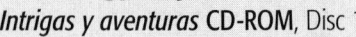

*Intrigas y aventuras* CD-ROM, Disc 1

## Quick Start Review

Expressing likes and dislikes

Use OHT 45 or write on board: Use the following cues to create sentences expressing what people like (or don't like) to do. For example: **No me gusta bailar.** Write at least 5 sentences.

| | (no) gustar |
|---|---|
| a mí | trabajar |
| a los niños | hacer ejercicio |
| a nosotros | jugar al baloncesto |
| a mis padres | esquiar |
| a mi amigo(a) | ir al cine |

**Answers**, p. 99D.

## Teaching Suggestions
### Introducing Vocabulary

Have students look at pp. 102–103 and identify the people or things they might already know in Spanish. Then use OHT 39–40 and Audiocassette 4A/CD 4 to present the new vocabulary.

# En contexto

## VOCABULARIO

Mira las fotos y las ilustraciones de lo que hacía Isabel cuando era niña.

**A** A los niños les gusta jugar con **juguetes** como **muñecas, marionetas** y **muñecos de peluche.** A muchas niñas les gusta jugar a la casita con las muñecas como **bebés.**

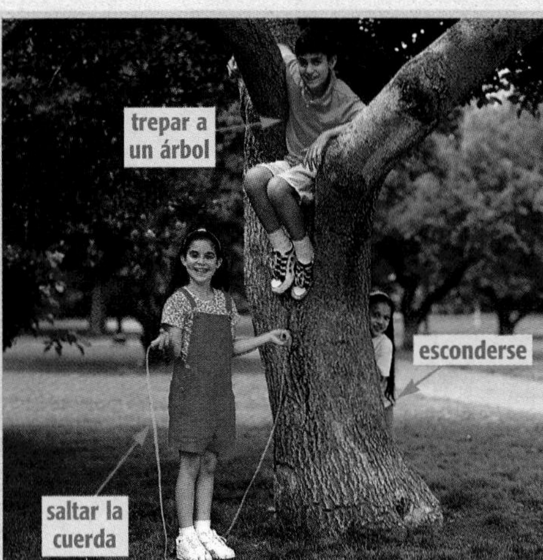

**B** Los niños **se esconden** en los árboles cuando juegan a las escondidas. También suben o **trepan a los árboles.** Muchos niños **saltan la cuerda. A veces** cuando no están contentos… **se pelean.**



## Classroom Community

**Paired Activity** Have students work in pairs to describe pictures and then read aloud scenarios.

**TPR** Ask students to recall activities they used to do as children and act them out in front of other students to guess.

**Storytelling** After studying new vocabulary, have students work in small groups to draw something comical and ask a group member to tell a funny story about it. They can write a short story or a list of questions they would like to ask the artist.

Pero es mejor **contar chistes** y **sonreírse** que pelearse. Por eso, los niños **se sientan** y **se ríen** al oír cuentos que dan **risa**.

**D** **Cuando era niña,** me gustaba **dibujar** igual que a mi **bisabuelo,** el papá de mi abuelo, **un pariente** que no conocí. Todavía me gusta dibujar. Algún día quiero **construir** edificios. ¿Qué quieres hacer tú?

el bisabuelo

### Preguntas personales

1. De niño(a), ¿te gustaba jugar con muñecas, marionetas o muñecos de peluche?
2. ¿Te gustaba saltar la cuerda o trepar a los árboles?
3. ¿Cuál era tu juguete favorito?
4. ¿Qué hacen los niños?
5. ¿Qué te gusta hacer ahora?



## Teaching Strategy
### Introducing Vocabulary

- Ask the Comprehension Questions in order of yes/no (questions 1–3), either/or (question 4–7), and simple word or phrase (questions 8–10). You may expand by adding similar questions.
- Use the video vocabulary presentation for review and reinforcement.

## Comprehension Questions

1. ¿Reciben los niños juguetes en algunos restaurantes populares? **(Sí)**
2. ¿Juegan los niños y las niñas con muñecos de peluche? **(Sí)**
3. ¿A las niñas les gusta jugar a la casita? **(Sí)**
4. Cuando llueve, ¿juegan los niños con bloques o trepan a los árboles? **(Juegan con bloques.)**
5. ¿Juegan los niños a las escondidas con una persona o con muchas personas? **(Con muchas personas.)**
6. ¿Te ríes con tus hermanos o peleas con ellos? **(Answers will vary.)**
7. ¿Tienes un bisabuelo o una bisabuela? **(Answers will vary.)**
8. ¿Qué hacen los niños cuando oyen un cuento cómico? **(Se ríen./Se sonríen.)**
9. ¿Qué hace Isabel en la foto D? **(Dibuja.)**
10. ¿Quién cuenta chistes que dan risa? **(Answers will vary.)**

## Language Note

- Have students look at pp. 102–103 and point out the uses of the verb **gustar**. You may want to review the formation and uses of this verb both in the present tense and the imperfect tense.
- Discuss the relationship between nouns and verbs as in the examples: **jugar** and **juguete**, **sonreír** and **sonrisa**, **reír** and **risa**, and **dibujar** and **dibujo**.

## Teaching All Students

**Extra Help** Plan ahead: Write the new vocabulary words on the board or show OHT 39–40. After reviewing, ask students to form a short story using as many words as possible.

**Native Speakers** Have Spanish speakers describe their favorite childhood activities or their favorite toys. If they know any jokes or riddles in Spanish, have them tell the class. Remind them to explain any cultural differences.

### Multiple Intelligences

**Visual** Have students bring in a picture of children playing and share what happens in the picture.

**Interpersonal** Have students interview a friend or relative about what he/she used to do as a child and ask them to share the information with class in Spanish.

## Block Schedule

**Change of Pace** Give students 30 seconds to draw their favorite childhood toy or **muñeco de peluche**. Have them share the **dibujos** with classmates.

## Teaching Resource Options

### Print 

Block Scheduling Copymasters
Unit 2 Resource Book
Video Activities, pp. 24–25
Videoscript, p. 27
Audioscript, p. 28

### Audiovisual 

**OHT** 43–44, 45 (Quick Start)
**Audio Program** Cassette 4A/CD 4
**Video Program** Videotape 2, 3:58 / Videodisc 1B

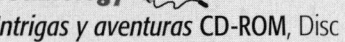

Search Chapter 3, Play to 4
U2E1, En vivo (Dialog)

### Technology

*Intrigas y aventuras* CD-ROM, Disc 1

## Quick Start Review

Preterite/**En contexto** vocabulary

Use OHT 45 or write on board: List three activities you did with children on your last baby-sitting job. If you don't baby-sit, tell about any time you played with a child. You may invent details. Use the preterite and any subject you wish. For example: **Anduvimos en bicicleta.**

*Answers will vary.*

## Teaching Suggestions
### Presenting the Dialog

Introduce the characters' names and the setting: ¿La chica se llama Isabel? ¿El chico se llama Ricardo? ¿Quién es el hombre mayor que está en el parque? ¿Para qué hace la entrevista Isabel? ¿Adónde van Isabel, Ricardo y don Miguel?

# En vivo

## DIÁLOGO

Isabel

Ricardo

Laura

Don Miguel

**PARA ESCUCHAR • STRATEGY: LISTENING**

**Listen for related details** First get the general idea about a conversation. Then listen for details that explain that idea. Here Isabel asks Don Miguel about his childhood. After he says, **"Cuando yo era niño,"** he relates many details. He includes childhood activities that you have just learned. How many can you name? If the action words (verbs) sound different, that is because he is talking about the past.

## Buenas noticias

1► Isabel: Me llamaron por teléfono. ¡Gané!
Ricardo: ¡Qué suerte!
Isabel: Mi primer proyecto es aquí en la Ciudad de México.
*(Suena el teléfono.)*

5► Isabel: ¿Y su familia es grande?
Don Miguel: No, pero mi nieta tiene un bebé, así que soy bisabuelo.
Ricardo: ¿Es usted de la Ciudad de México?

6► Don Miguel: Sí. Todos mis parientes son de aquí también.
Isabel: ¿Cómo era la Ciudad de México cuando usted era niño?
Don Miguel: Diferente, y en aquellos tiempos hacíamos cosas diferentes.

7► Don Miguel: Los niños tienen tantos juguetes electrónicos hoy. Cuando yo era niño, no había videojuegos. Pasábamos más tiempo afuera. A veces trepábamos a los árboles o nos escondíamos.



## Classroom Community

**TPR** Using Vocabulary OHTs 39 and 40, have students take turns touching or pointing to new items they recognize as the dialog audio plays in segments. Then have students take turns acting out a childhood activity, asking the class to guess what it is.

**Game** Make copies of the dialog script from the Unit 2 Resource Book and cut up each of the characters' lines. Mix up the lines and give each group of students a cluster of lines and ask them to piece the dialog together. You may want to limit it to only 3–4 frames.

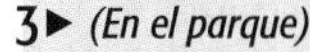

2► Laura: Tengo malas noticias. No voy a llegar a México hoy.
Isabel: ¡Tenemos una entrevista con don Miguel esta tarde!
Laura: Estoy segura que tú lo puedes hacer sin mí.

3► *(En el parque)*
Don Miguel: Y después de ese día, todo cambió. Antes los dos amigos se portaban mal y se peleaban mucho. Ahora se portan bien. Bueno, niños, es todo por hoy. ¡Hasta mañana!

4► Isabel: ¿Viene todos los días al parque con sus marionetas?
Don Miguel: No, estoy aquí cuatro días por semana. Me siento bien cuando los niños se sonríen y cuando escucho sus risas.

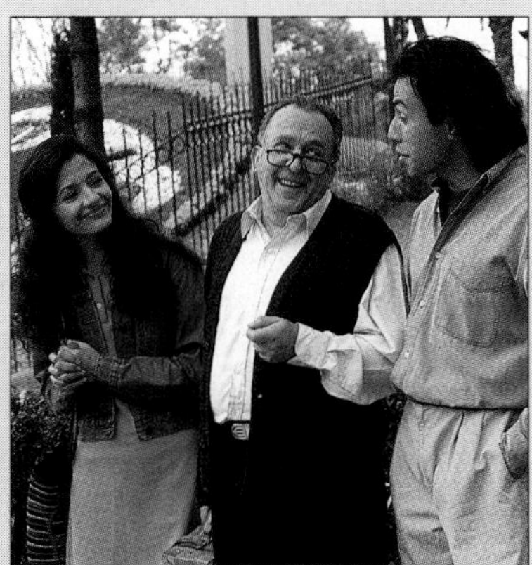

8► Isabel: Yo saltaba la cuerda cuando era niña. Y jugaba con mis muñecos de peluche.
Don Miguel: Además yo dibujaba. Y mi hermano construía edificios con bloques.

9► Ricardo: Yo todavía construyo casas con bloques.
Isabel: Pero los tuyos son bloques especiales, ¿no?
Ricardo: Sí, los míos son para arquitectos. Son de mi padre.

10► Ricardo: Don Miguel, ¿qué más hacían ustedes en aquellos días?
Don Miguel: Hablábamos mucho… y mi bisabuelo contaba chistes. Me acuerdo que me reía mucho. Bueno, hijos, pronto estamos en mi casa.



## Teaching All Students

**Extra Help** Have students listen to the dialog again. Ask them to recall as much as they can about what just happened and write down a list of events. (e.g., **Isabel recibió buenas noticias, Laura tuvo malas noticias, Don Miguel...**)

**Challenge** Play the video again. Have students write 5 True/False statements and then exchange papers with another student (or small group). Each person/group marks the statements as T/F, then returns papers to original person/group to be scored.

### Multiple Intelligences

**Intrapersonal** Ask students to quickly sketch or write about their personal assessment of what happened after each major scene. This activity may be called **"En la radio"** and done using audiocassettes.

## Video Synopsis

Isabel and Ricardo set out to interview the puppeteer don Miguel for *Onda Internacional* magazine in Mexico City. For a complete transcript of the video dialog, see p. 99D.

## Language Note

Point out how Isabel and Ricardo use **don Miguel** to address an older man with respect. It is like saying "Mister Jones" but using the first name instead. The female counterpart of **don** is **doña**.

## Comprehension Questions

1. ¿Tiene Isabel una entrevista en la Ciudad de México? **(Sí)**
2. ¿Llega Laura a México a tiempo para la entrevista? **(No)**
3. ¿A los niños les gustan las marionetas de don Miguel? **(Sí)**
4. ¿Va don Miguel al parque todos los días o solamente cuatro días por semana? **(cuatro días)**
5. ¿Es la familia de don Miguel grande o pequeña? **(pequeña)**
6. ¿Son sus parientes de la Ciudad de Panamá o de la Ciudad de México? **(Ciudad de México)**
7. Cuando don Miguel era niño, ¿trepaba a los árboles o jugaba a los videojuegos? **(Trepaba a los árboles.)**
8. ¿Qué hacía Isabel cuando era niña? **(Saltaba la cuerda, jugaba con muñecos de peluche.)**
9. ¿Qué tipo de bloques usa Ricardo? **(bloques para arquitectos)**
10. ¿Qué contaba el bisabuelo de don Miguel? **(chistes)**

## Gestures

Ask students to look for and imitate a gesture that shows happiness, a gesture used as a greeting, a gesture used when telling a story, and a gesture for giving information.

## Block Schedule

**Process Time** Give students 5 min. to re-read the dialog and make a personal vocabulary list for their notebooks.

## Teaching Resource Options

**Print** 

Block Scheduling Copymasters
Unit 2 Resource Book
Video Activities, p. 25
Videoscript, pp. 26–27
Audioscript, p. 29

**Audiovisual** 

OHT 46 (Quick Start)
Audio Program Cassette 4A / CD 4
Video Program Videotape 2, 3:58 / Videodisc 1B

**Technology**

*Intrigas y aventuras* CD-ROM, Disc 1

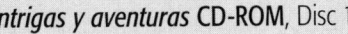

## Quick Start Review

Reacting to information

Use OHT 46 or write on board: React to the following statements using one of these expressions.

¿De veras? ¡Ya lo sé!
¡No me digas! ¿Tú crees?

1. Isabel ganó el concurso.
2. Isabel tiene que hacer la entrevista sin Laura.
3. Don Miguel va al parque con sus marionetas y nadie le paga.
4. Don Miguel es bisabuelo.

*Answers will vary.*

Actividad 1 **Objective:** Controlled practice Listening comprehension/vocabulary

**Answers**
1. Isabel
2. la Ciudad de México
3. Ricardo
4. marionetas
5. de la Ciudad de México
6. trepaba a los árboles
7. saltaba la cuerda
8. Ricardo

# En acción
## VOCABULARIO Y GRAMÁTICA

**OBJECTIVES**
- Describe childhood experiences
- Express personal reactions
- Discuss family relationships

Actividad 1

### ¿Qué pasó?

**Escuchar/Escribir** Completa las oraciones según el diálogo. *(Hint: Complete the sentences.)*

1. _____ (Isabel / Ricardo) ganó el concurso de la revista *Onda Internacional.*
2. Su primer proyecto tiene lugar en _____ (Madrid / la Ciudad de México).
3. _____ (Ricardo / Laura) va a la entrevista con Isabel.
4. Don Miguel usa _____ (marionetas / muñecos de peluche).
5. Los parientes de don Miguel son _____ (de la Ciudad de México / de Quito).
6. Cuando don Miguel era jóven, _____ (veía mucha televisión / trepaba a los árboles).
7. Cuando era niña, Isabel _____ (contaba chistes / saltaba la cuerda).
8. _____ (Ricardo / El nieto de don Miguel) todavía construye casas con bloques.

Actividad 2

### ¿Lo sabes?

**Escuchar/Escribir** Indica si las oraciones son **ciertas** o **falsas.** Si son falsas, explica por qué. *(Hint: True or false? If false, explain why.)*

1. Laura tiene buenas noticias.
2. Laura puede ayudar con la entrevista.
3. Don Miguel va al parque todos los días.
4. La nieta de don Miguel tiene un bebé.
5. A veces don Miguel y sus hermanos se peleaban.
6. Cuando era niña, Isabel trepaba a los árboles.
7. Ricardo jugaba con muñecos de peluche.
8. Cuando era niño, don Miguel no se reía mucho.

**TAMBIÉN SE DICE**

Muchos mexicanos dicen **D.F.** o **México** en vez de **la Ciudad de México.** Estas expresiones se refieren a la ciudad capital. Se usan las letras **D.F.** para hablar del Distrito Federal de la ciudad. Desde el piso cuarenta y dos de la Torre Latino Americana hay una vista panorámica de la ciudad entera.

## Classroom Management

**Time Saver** Have students review the content of the dialog by retelling the story in their own words. You can start, **Isabel ganó un concurso y va a...** Then do **Actividades 1** and **2** orally.

**Peer Review** Have students work in pairs to do **Actividad 4**. The first student can describe the drawings in the present tense, then the second student can describe the scenes in the past tense.

- Use possessive adjectives and pronouns
- Review: Use reflexives
- Use the imperfect tense

## ¡Los conozco!

**Hablar** Tu compañero(a) quiere saber si conoces a gente de otros países. ¿Qué le dices?
*(Hint: Tell nationalities.)*

**modelo**

*Margarita: México*

**Compañero(a):** *¿Conoces a alguien de México?*

**Tú:** *Sí, conozco a una chica que se llama Margarita. Ella es mexicana.*

1. Lupita: Guatemala
2. Pablo: El Salvador
3. Carlota y Marta: Honduras
4. Enrique: Nicaragua
5. Luz María: Costa Rica
6. Tomás y Andrés: Panamá
7. Carina: Cuba
8. Ana Paula y Manuel: la República Dominicana
9. Michel: Francia
10. Andrew y Brian: Estados Unidos
11. María y Érica: Venezuela
12. Sue: China

## De niño

**Hablar/Escribir** ¿Qué hacen los niños? Usando estas expresiones y tus propias ideas, haz varias oraciones sobre cada dibujo.
*(Hint: Write sentences about the illustrations.)*

los muñecos de peluche · saltar la cuerda · construir con bloques · los juguetes · trepar a los árboles · las muñecas · disfrutar con los amigos · jugar al béisbol

## Teaching All Students

**Extra Help** Ask students to raise their hands if they do any of the activities in **Actividad 4** as you call them out. **¿Cuántas personas juegan al béisbol?**

**Native Speakers** Ask students if they have ever traveled to or lived in any of the places mentioned in **Actividad 3**. If so, ask them to share their experiences with the class.

**Multiple Intelligences**

**Visual** As a follow-up to **Actividad 4**, ask students to draw pictures or cartoons of at least 3 more childhood activities.

**Verbal** Have students write Spanish captions for the pictures drawn above.

**Objective:** Controlled practice
Listening comprehension/vocabulary

**Answers**

1. Falso. Laura tiene mala noticias.
2. Falso. Laura no puede ir a la entrevista.
3. Falso. Don Miguel va al parque cuatro días por semana.
4. Cierto.
5. Falso. El diálogo no menciona esto.
6. Falso. Saltaba la cuerda y jugaba con muñecos de peluche.
7. Falso. Isabel jugaba con muñecos de peluche.
8. Falso. Don Miguel reía mucho.

**Objective:** Transitional practice
**Conocer**/nationalities

**Answers**

1. ¿Conoces a alguien de Guatemala?
   Sí, conozco a Lupita. Es guatemalteca.
2. ¿Conoces a alguien de El Salvador?
   Sí, conozco a Pablo. Es salvadoreño.
3. ¿Conoces a alguien de Honduras?
   Sí, conozco a Carlota y a Marta. Son hondureñas.
4. ¿Conoces a alguien de Nicaragua?
   Sí, conozco a Enrique. Es nicaragüense.
5. ¿Conoces a alguien de Costa Rica?
   Sí, conozco a Luz María. Es costarricense.
6. ¿Conoces a alguien de Panamá?
   Sí, conozco a Tomás y a Andrés. Son panameños.
7. ¿Conoces a alguien de Cuba?
   Sí, conozco a Carina. Es cubana.
8. ¿Conoces a alguien de la República Dominicana?
   Sí, conozco a Ana Paula y a Manuel. Son dominicanos.
9. ¿Conoces a alguien de Francia?
   Sí, conozco a Michel. Es francés.
10. ¿Conoces a alguien de Estados Unidos?
    Sí, conozco a Andrew y Brian. Son estadounidenses.
11. ¿Conoces a alguien de Venezuela?
    Sí, conozco a María y a Érica. Son venezolanas.
12. ¿Conoces a alguien de China?
    Sí, conozco a Sue. Es china.

**Objective:** Open-ended practice
Describing childhood activities

**Answers**

1. La niña construye con bloques.
2. Los niños saltan la cuerda.
3. Las niñas juegan con muñecos de peluche.
4. La niña trepa a los árboles.
5. El niño juega al béisbol.

## Block Schedule

**Variety** Show students photographs of famous people from other countries and play a guessing game about their nationalities. (e.g., **¿Quién es un actor de España? Antonio Banderas es un actor español.**) (For additional activities, see **Block Scheduling Copymasters.**)

## Teaching Resource Options

**Print** 

*Más práctica* Workbook PE, p. 45
*Cuaderno para hispanohablantes* PE, p. 43
Block Scheduling Copymasters
Unit 2 Resource Book
*Más práctica* Workbook TE, p. 5
*Cuaderno para hispanohablantes* TE, p. 11

**Audiovisual** 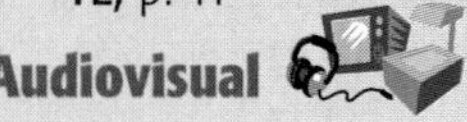

OHT 46 (Quick Start)

**Technology**

*Intrigas y aventuras* CD-ROM, Disc 1

## Quick Start Review

Nationalities

Use OHT 46 or write on board: Fill in the adjective of nationality for each person.

Pablo es de España.
Pablo es _______.
Suzanne es de Francia.
Suzanne es _______.
Bill es de los Estados Unidos.
Bill es _______.

**Answers**, see p. 99D.

## Teaching Suggestions
### Presenting Possessive Adjectives and Pronouns

- Review the short form of possessive adjectives by choosing certain objects in the classroom that may belong to different students. For example, **Ésta es mi pluma. Ésa es tu pluma. Ésa es la pluma de Carlos. Es su pluma.**
- Remind students that possessive adjectives always agree in gender and number with the possessed object, not the person who possesses the object.

**Objective:** Controlled practice Possessive adjectives

Preterite of **traer**

**Answers**
1. Yo traje mi video de "Plaza Sésamo".
2. Ustedes trajeron sus fotos.
3. Alex trajo sus marionetas.
4. Tú trajiste tus libros de chistes.
5. Tavo e Irene trajeron su marioneta.
6. María y yo trajimos nuestras muñecas.

## Possessive Adjectives and Pronouns

As you know, **possessive adjectives** show personal relationships or possession. All **possessive adjectives**—including **mi(s), tu(s), su(s), nuestro(a/os/as),** and **vuestro(a/os/as)**—agree in gender and number with the nouns they describe.

Possessive adjectives also have a **long form.** It is more expressive. You use it, for example, when talking of a special friend.

un **amigo mío**
*a friend **of mine***

Unlike the regular (or short) form, the **long form** follows the **noun.**

Comemos con unos **amigos nuestros.**
*We are eating with some friends **of ours.***

| Possessives Long Form – Singular | | Possessives Long Form – Plural | |
|---|---|---|---|
| mío(a) | nuestro(a) | míos(as) | nuestros(as) |
| tuyo(a) | vuestro(a) | tuyos(as) | vuestros(as) |
| suyo(a) | suyo(a) | suyos(as) | suyos(as) |

**Possessive pronouns** also show personal relationships. To form a possessive pronoun,

1. Use the **long form** of the possessive adjective.
2. Add **el, la, los, las** according to the gender and number of the **noun** it replaces.

—Sus **viajes** son a diferentes lugares.
*His **trips** are to different places.*

—Y **los tuyos,** ¿adónde son?
*And **yours,** where are they to?*

### Actividad 5 Gramática

## ¿Qué trajiste?

**Hablar/Escribir** Todos trajeron objetos de su niñez para una presentación en la escuela. ¿Qué trajeron? Haz oraciones con **mi(s), tu(s), su(s), nuestro(a/os/as).** *(Hint: Tell what people brought.)*

**modelo**

*Silvia trajo una cuerda.*
*Silvia trajo su cuerda.*

1. Yo traje un video de «Plaza Sésamo».
2. Ustedes trajeron unas fotos.
3. Alex trajo unas marionetas.
4. Tú trajiste libros de chistes.
5. Tavo e Irene trajeron una marioneta.
6. María y yo trajimos muñecas.

**MÁS PRÁCTICA** *cuaderno* p. 45

**PARA HISPANOHABLANTES** *cuaderno* p. 43

**NOTA CULTURAL**

Las marionetas, como las de don Miguel, son juguetes muy comunes en México. Se manipulan con cuerdas.

## Classroom Community

**Paired Activity** Given a list of 10–12 objects, one student forms a sentence and another restates the sentence using a possessive pronoun and changing the color, e.g., **la camisa**—S1: **Yo llevo una camisa blanca.** S2: **La suya es roja.**

**Game** Have students bring in a small item and put all items in a box. Taking turns, have students pick out an item and try to guess who owns it using possessive adjectives. **Juan, ¿es tu pluma? Sí, es mi pluma.** or **No, no es mi pluma, es su pluma.**

**Cooperative Learning** Have students make their own **marioneta** or **títere.** Have students work in pairs with their marionettes. Student 1 (S1) should place several classroom objects near his/her marionette. Student 2 (S2) needs to find out which objects belong to S1's marionette by asking questions. Switch roles.

## Durante las vacaciones

**Hablar/Escribir** Estas personas van a visitar a varios amigos y parientes durante las vacaciones. Sigue el modelo para decir a quiénes van a visitar. *(Hint: Say whom they're visiting.)*

**modelo**

*Don Miguel (una nieta)*
*Don Miguel va a visitar a una nieta suya.*

1. nosotros (el padrastro)
2. tú (la madrastra)
3. Ricardo (una novia)
4. el tío (un sobrino)
5. usted (una hermanastra)
6. Isabel (una compañera)
7. mi tía (unos amigos)
8. ustedes (un cuñado)

### Vocabulario

**Familia, amigos, amigas**

**la amistad** *friendship, acquaintance*
**el (la) compañero(a)** *classmate, companion*
**el (la) cuñado(a)** *brother-in-law, sister-in-law*
**los (las) gemelos(as)** *twins*
**el (la) hermanastro(a)** *stepbrother, stepsister*
**la madrastra** *stepmother*
**el (la) novio(a)** *boyfriend, girlfriend; groom, bride*
**el padrastro** *stepfather*
**el (la) sobrino(a)** *nephew, niece*

¿Quién eres tú?

## ¿Puedo...?

**Hablar** No tienes estas cosas. Pregúntale a tu compañero(a) si puedes usar las suyas. *(Hint: Ask for items.)*

**modelo**

**Tú:** *No tengo calculadora. ¿Puedo usar la tuya?*
**Compañero(a):** *Claro, (No, no) puedes usar la mía.*

1.

2.

3.

4.

5.



### Language Note

Point out to students that **va a visitar** in **Actividad 6** is the form **ir + a +** *infinitive verb* and is used to express something that will happen in the future. **Don Miguel va a visitar a una nieta suya** means *Don Miguel is going to visit his granddaughter.*

### Teaching Suggestions

- Be sure to review the vocabulary in the box at the bottom of p. 109 before doing **Actividad 6**.
- Note that family relationships may be a sensitive issue for some students so instead of referring to students' families, you can use well-known families from television or movies when practicing the family vocabulary.

**Objective:** Controlled practice
Possessive adjectives/family members

**Answers**

1. Nosotros vamos a visitar al padrastro nuestro.
2. Tú vas a visitar a la madrastra tuya.
3. Ricardo va a visitar a una novia suya.
4. El tío va a visitar a un sobrino suyo.
5. Usted va a visitar a una hermanastra suya.
6. Isabel va a visitar a una compañera suya.
7. Mi tía va a visitar a unos amigos suyos.
8. Ustedes van a visitar a un cuñado suyo.

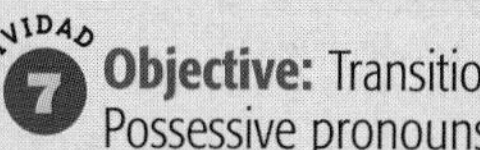

**Objective:** Transitional practice
Possessive pronouns

**Answers**

*Answers will vary.*

1. No tengo pelota (de fútbol). ¿Puedo usar la tuya? ¡Claro! (No, no) Puedes usar la mía.
2. No tengo marioneta. ¿Puedo usar la tuya? ... Puedes usar la mía.
3. No tengo periódico. ¿Puedo usar el tuyo? ... Puedes usar el mío.
4. No tengo patines. ¿Puedo usar los tuyos? ... Puedes usar los míos.
5. No tengo reloj. ¿Puedo usar el tuyo? ... Puedes usar el mío.

### Teaching All Students

**Extra Help** Have students create an imaginary family tree for a famous person of their choice using the vocabulary from the box on p. 109 and other family vocabulary.

**Multiple Intelligences**

**Verbal** Ask students if they have certain items with them today, then have them describe the items using possessive pronouns. **¿Quién tiene un cuaderno hoy? ¿Cómo es? El mío es azul.**

**Interpersonal** Have students interview each other to find one item they both own that has different characteristics.

**Logical/Mathematical** Have students go back to the dialog on pp. 104–105 and count how many times possessive adjectives and pronouns are used.

### Block Schedule

**Retention** Have students ask to borrow items from their classmates. Use the same format as **Actividad 7**. Possible cues:

| | |
|---|---|
| libro | diccionario |
| cuaderno | lápiz |
| calculadora | pluma |

## Teaching Resource Options

**Print**

*Más práctica* Workbook PE, p. 46
*Cuaderno para hispanohablantes* PE, p. 44
Block Scheduling Copymasters
Unit 2 Resource Book
*Más práctica* Workbook TE, p. 6
*Cuaderno para hispanohablantes* TE, p. 12

**Audiovisual**

OHT 46 (Quick Start)

**Technology**

*Intrigas y aventuras* CD-ROM, Disc 1

## Quick Start Review

Present tense

Use OHT 46 or write on board: Write sentences, conjugating the verb in the present tense.

1. Ella / los casetes (comprar)
2. Nosotros / la comida (traer)
3. Yo / el dinero (tener)
4. Tú / una bolsa (¿necesitar?)
5. Nosotros / a los gemelos (ver)

**Answers**

1. Ella compra los casetes.
2. Nosotros traemos la comida.
3. Yo tengo el dinero.
4. ¿Necesitas tú una bolsa?
5. Nosotros vemos a los gemelos.

## Teaching Suggestions
### Presenting the Reflexive Pronouns and Verbs

- Have students go through the list of reflexive verbs and choose 3 verbs to describe actions that they do themselves. For example, **Me asusto cuando veo películas de horror.**
- You can have students conjugate these reflexive verbs in the present tense or the past tense in their notebooks.
- Remind students that the placement of the reflexive pronoun is before a conjugated verb or attached to the end of an infinitive verb.

## Reflexive Pronouns and Verbs

You've already learned that you can use **direct object pronouns (me, te, lo, la, nos, os, los, las)** with verbs. For example, in this photograph the girl is hiding a doll behind a tree. She says,

*different*

**La** escond**o.**
***I'm** hiding **it.***

Notice that the subject (yo) and the direct object pronoun (la) are **different.**

**Reflexive verbs** take a special direct object pronoun called a **reflexive pronoun.** While the usual direct object is different from the subject, a reflexive pronoun is the **same** person, place, or thing as the **subject.**

*same*

**Me** escond**o.**
***I'm** hiding (myself).*

The subject (yo) and the direct object pronoun (me) are the **same** person; you call this object **reflexive.**

**Reflexive Pronouns**

| *same* | *same* |
|---|---|
| **me** escond**o** | **nos** escond**emos** |
| **te** escond**es** | **os** escond**éis** |
| **se** escond**e** | **se** escond**en** |

A verb used reflexively tells you that *only* the subject of the verb is involved in the action. When using a reflexive verb in the infinitive form, attach the **pronoun** to the **infinitive.**

Vamos a **pelearnos** por el cuaderno.
***We** are going **to fight** over the notebook.*

### Vocabulario

**Reflexive Verbs**

**aburrirse** *to get bored*
**asustarse de** *to be scared of*
**caerse** *to fall down*
**cansarse** *to get tired*
**darse cuenta de** *to realize*
**despedirse (e→i, i) de** *to say good-bye to*
**disculparse** *to apologize*
**divertirse (e→ie, i)** *to enjoy oneself*
**enojarse con** *to get angry with*
**portarse bien/mal** *to behave well/badly*
**preocuparse por** *to be worried about*
**reunirse** *to get together*
**sentirse (e→ie, i)** *to feel*



## Classroom Community

**Paired Activity** Using the reflexive verb list, have students work in pairs to form sentences describing typical actions performed by their family members. For example, **Mi hermano se sonríe cuando oye chistes.**

**TPR** Go around the room: the 1st student acts out a reflexive verb. The 2nd student guesses the correct verb. The 3rd student must then give a complete sentence using this verb. Then the next person starts again and acts out another reflexive verb and the process continues around the room.

**Storytelling** Students build upon a topic by having one student form a sentence using a reflexive verb from the given list, then the next student builds upon this topic by adding another reflexive verb. Have them go around the room and create a complete story. They may use a verb more than once.

## Amigos y familia

**Hablar/Escribir** A Margarita le gusta hablar de su familia y de sus amigos. ¡También le gusta hablar de sí misma (*herself*)! Completa sus oraciones para saber lo que dice. *(Hint: What does Margarita say?)*

1. Mi familia y yo (asustarse) de las películas de terror.
2. Yo (aburrirse) con mis amigos en el centro comercial.
3. Tú (sonreírse) cuando ves a tus compañeros.
4. Mis abuelos (divertirse) cuando (reunirse) con los jóvenes.
5. Yo (disculparse) cuando (portarse) mal.
6. Mi hermano (enojarse) con su prima.
7. Mis amigos (preocuparse) por la clase de ciencia.
8. Mi hermanito (caerse) al trepar a un árbol.
9. Después de un día de compras, yo (cansarse).
10. Mi mamá (preocuparse) cuando salimos de noche.

**MÁS PRÁCTICA** *cuaderno* p. 46

**PARA HISPANOHABLANTES** *cuaderno* p. 44

## En el parque

**Hablar/Escribir** Antonio y sus amigos están en el parque. ¿Qué hacen? Usa estas expresiones en tus respuestas. *(Hint: Tell what everyone is doing.)*

divertirse | reunirse | sonreírse | sentarse | caerse | despedirse | portarse bien | cansarse

**Objective:** Controlled practice
Reflexives

**Answers**
1. Mi familia y yo (no) nos asustamos de las películas de terror.
2. Yo (no) me aburro con mis amigos en el centro comercial.
3. Tú (no) te sonríes cuando ves a tus compañeros.
4. Mis abuelos (no) se divierten cuando se reúnen con los jóvenes.
5. Yo (no) me disculpo cuando me porto mal.
6. Mi hermano (no) se enoja con su prima.
7. Mis amigos (no) se preocupan por la clase de ciencia.
8. Mi hermanito (no) se cae al trepar a un árbol.
9. Después de un día de compras, yo (no) me canso.
10. Mi mamá (no) se preocupa cuando salimos de noche.

**Objective:** Transitional practice
Reflexives

**Answers**
*Answers will vary. Answers could include:*
1. Las niñas se sientan.
2. Los amigos se reúnen.
3. El niño se cae.
4. Las niñas se sonríen.
5. Los niños se cansan.

### Quick Wrap-up

In small groups or pairs have students ask each other: **Cuando tienes tiempo libre, ¿qué haces?** Tell students to use as many reflexive verbs as possible. This could also be done as a whole class activity if you wish to pose the question to several students.

### Teaching Suggestions

Point out that the present tense conjugation of **construir** and the preterite of **caerse** have a spell change (**i** to **y**); the present tense conjugation of **sentarse** has a stem change (**e** to **ie**); and the verbs **reírse**, **sonreírse**, and **reunirse** show accents in the present tense. Refer students to the *Gramática/resumen* section at the end of the book for a complete list of conjugations.

**Retention** Have students create more sentences using reflexive verbs to describe what people in the class do.

### Teaching All Students

**Extra Help** Repeat **Actividad 8**, but this time have students use a different reflexive verb to complete each sentence.

**Native Speakers** Have Spanish speakers list other reflexive verbs they know and create a sentence using each of them.

**Multiple Intelligences**

**Musical/Rhythmic** Working in small groups, have students create a short chant or rap to recall the reflexive verbs and their meanings.

**Visual** Using several large easels and markers, have students draw a quick picture as they give a sentence in a storybuilding activity (p. 110). The pictures can be used as cues for retelling the story in any tense.

## Teaching Resource Options

### Print 

*Más práctica* Workbook PE, pp. 47–48
*Cuaderno para hispanohablantes* PE, pp. 45–46
Block Scheduling Copymasters
Unit 2 Resource Book
*Más práctica* Workbook TE, pp. 7–8
*Cuaderno para hispanohablantes* TE, pp. 13–14
Audioscript, p. 29
Information Gap Activities, p. 17

### Audiovisual

OHT 47 (Quick Start)
Audio Program Cassette 4A / CD 4

### Technology

*Intrigas y aventuras* CD-ROM, Disc 1

## Quick Start Review

Preterite for completed actions

Use OHT 47 or write on board: Answer the following questions about what you did this morning.

¿Qué comiste esta mañana?
¿Qué bebiste?
¿A qué hora saliste de la casa?
¿A qué hora llegaste a la escuela?
¿A qué clase fuiste primero esta mañana?

**Answers**, see p. 99D.

## Teaching Suggestions
### Presenting the Imperfect Tense

- Use the dialog on pp. 104–105 to illustrate the different uses of the imperfect and the preterite. Have students circle all verbs in the past tense and determine why the imperfect or the preterite is used in each case.
- To practice forming the imperfect tense, have students conjugate some of the reflexive verbs from the list on p. 110. For example, **yo me aburría, tú te aburrías, él/ella/Ud. se aburría,** etc.

ACTIVIDAD 10

## ¿Bien o mal?

**Escuchar/Escribir** Escucha lo que dicen los hijos de la familia Villarreal. ¿Quién se porta mejor, Rubén o sus hermanas? En tu casa, ¿se portan bien los chicos? Explica tu respuesta.
*(Hint: Who behaves better?)*

**MÁS COMUNICACIÓN** p. R5

### Juego

***¿Qué dices?***

Escribe la forma correcta de cada verbo. Luego usa las letras de colores para formar tu respuesta.

1. (Paco / sonreírse)
__ __ ____ __ __ __
2. (yo / divertirse)
__ __ ________
3. (Raúl y Silvia /aburrirse)
__ __ ____ __ __ __
4. (tú / caerse)
__ __ ____
5. (María / enojarse )
__ __ __ __ __ __

¿Qué es lo que haces cuando un amigo te cuenta un chiste divertido?

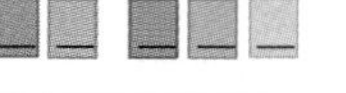

GRAMÁTICA

## Talk About the Past Using the Imperfect

 **¿RECUERDAS?** *p. 36* You've already learned to use the preterite tense to speak about completed actions in the past. Now you'll find out about another past tense, called the **imperfect**.

You can use the **imperfect** in the following ways:

- to speak about background events in a story
- to talk about something you used to do as a matter of habit
- to speak about how old someone was
- to say what time it was

The following chart shows you how to form the imperfect of regular verbs.

Note that -ar verb endings include -aba/-ába.

| -ar | -er | -ir |
|---|---|---|
| cantar | tener | salir |
| cantaba | tenía | salía |
| cantabas | tenías | salías |
| cantaba | tenía | salía |
| cantábamos | teníamos | salíamos |
| cantabais | teníais | salíais |
| cantaban | tenían | salían |

Note that -er and -ir verb endings include -ía.

The following examples use the **imperfect** because they describe continuing actions in the past.

Don Miguel trabajaba en el banco todos las días.
*Don Miguel **worked** in the bank every day.*

—Mi abuelo siempre decía chistes muy divertidos.
*My grandfather always **told** very funny jokes.*

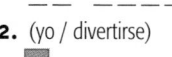

Here are the only verbs that don't follow the regular pattern.

**Eran** las tres.
***It was** three o'clock.*

| ser | ir | ver |
|---|---|---|
| era | iba | veía |
| eras | ibas | veías |
| era | iba | veía |
| éramos | íbamos | veíamos |
| erais | ibais | veíais |
| eran | iban | veían |



## Classroom Community

**Storytelling** Have students form a chain story by taking turns describing what they think their teacher used to do as a child. The first student might say **Jugaba con muñecos de peluche.** The next student adds **Jugaba con muñecos de peluche y trepaba a los árboles,** etc.

**Portfolio** Have students write a short description about their childhood, using the imperfect tense to describe what they used to do: Suggest **"Lo que hacía cuando tenía 10 años"** as a possible title.

### Rubric: Writing

| Criteria | Scale |
|---|---|
| Vocabulary use | 1 2 3 4 5 |
| Creativity | 1 2 3 4 5 |
| Logical organization | 1 2 3 4 5 |

A = 13–15 pts.
B = 10–12 pts.
C = 7–9 pts.
D = 4–6 pts.
F = < 4 pts.

## Todos cambiamos

**Hablar/Escribir** ¿Qué cosas hacían estas personas en el pasado que no hacen ahora? *(Hint: Tell what these people used to do.)*

**modelo**

*No hablo en situaciones nuevas.*

*Antes, hablaba en situaciones nuevas.*

1. Mi abuela no trepa a los árboles.
2. Mis hermanos y yo no nos peleamos.
3. Mi tía no juega con muñecos de peluche.
4. Ustedes no tienen una muñeca favorita.
5. Tú no ves los dibujos animados.
6. Yo no me porto mal.

**MÁS PRÁCTICA**
*cuaderno* pp. 47–48

**PARA HISPANOHABLANTES**
*cuaderno* pp. 45–46

## Un perrito para ti

**Hablar/Escribir** Tu vecino(a) te regala su perrito porque no puede cuidarlo. Para saber más sobre el animal, pregúntale a tu vecino(a) dónde hacía el perrito ciertas cosas. Cambien de papel. *(Hint: Ask about a puppy.)*

**modelo**

*comer*

**Tú:** *¿Dónde comía?*

**Vecino(a):** *Comía fuera de la casa.*

**Nota**

You can use **dentro de** *inside* and **fuera de** *outside* just as you do in English.

Yo estoy **dentro de** mi cuarto. *I am **inside** my room.*

Él dejó su carro **fuera de** la casa. *He left his car **outside** the house.*

1. tomar agua
2. jugar
3. dormir
4. tomar la siesta
5. divertirse con la pelota
6. caminar

## En el Bosque de Chapultepec

**Escuchar/Hablar** Escucha lo que hizo Isabel en el bosque. Luego haz un resumen de lo que escuchaste. *(Hint: Tell what Isabel did.)*

**NOTA CULTURAL**

**El Bosque de Chapultepec** Mucha gente va al Bosque de Chapultepec para disfrutar del aire libre. Camina con el perro, anda en bicicleta, corre y descansa. Este parque famoso tiene lagos, un jardín botánico, restaurantes y nueve museos, incluyendo el Museo Nacional de Antropología.

**Objective:** Open-ended practice
Listening comprehension

*Answers will vary.*

**Objective:** Controlled practice
Imperfect/describing childhood experiences

**Answers**
1. Antes, mi abuela trepaba a los árboles.
2. Antes, mis hermanos y yo nos peleábamos.
3. Antes, mi tía jugaba con muñecos de peluche.
4. Antes, ustedes tenían una muñeca favorita.
5. Antes, tú veías los dibujos animados.
6. Antes, yo me portaba mal.

**Objective:** Transitional practice
Imperfect

*Answers will vary.*

**Objective:** Open-ended practice
Listening comprehension

**Answers**
*Answers will vary but should reflect comprehension of the audio.*
Isabel siempre iba con su mamá y unas vecinas al Bosque de Chapultepec. Ellas tenían un picnic en el bosque. Iban a los juguetes mecánicos. Comían refrescos, dulces, palomitas y la cosa favorita de Isabel –jícama con chile piquín.

## Juego

**Answers**
1. se sonríe
2. me divierto
3. se aburren
4. te caes
5. se enoja

Me río.

## Teaching All Students

**Extra Help** Using the phrases listed in **Actividad 12**, have students form sentences in the imperfect tense, e.g., **Yo veía la televisión porque me gustaba el programa de Plaza Sésamo.**

**Native Speakers** Ask Spanish speakers to write a list of activities that occurred regularly in their homes when they were younger. Or if possible, have them interview an older family member about their life in the past.

**Challenge** Have students categorize the activities they learned in this Etapa according to where they are performed. The categories should be **fuera** and **dentro**.

**Multiple Intelligences**

**Naturalist** Have students describe the geographical features of what they see in the photo of **El Bosque de Chapultepec.**

## Block Schedule

**Variety** Have students make up their own **Juego** using the one in their books as a model.

## Teaching Resource Options

**Print**

*Más práctica* Workbook PE, pp. 41–44
*Cuaderno para hispanohablantes* PE, pp. 41–42
Block Scheduling Copymasters
Unit 2 Resource Book
*Más práctica* Workbook TE, pp. 1–4
*Cuaderno para hispanohablantes* TE, pp. 9–10
Information Gap Activities, p. 18
Audioscript, pp. 30–31

**Audiovisual**

OHT 47 (Quick Start)
Audio Program Cassette 4B / CD 4; (*Para hispanohablantes* Cassette 4B / CD 4)

**Technology**

*Intrigas y aventuras* CD-ROM, Disc 1

## Quick Start Review

Telling ages

Use OHT 47 or write on board: Answer with a complete sentence in Spanish.

¿Cuántos años tiene …
…tu abuelo(a)?
…tu bisabuelo(a)?
…tu hermano(a)?
…tu tío(a)?
…tu primo(a)?

*Answers will vary.*

## Supplementary Vocabulary

Other expressions with **tener** that students may already know are:

**tener frío/calor** to be cold/hot
**tener ganas de** to want to do something

**Actividad 14** **Objective:** Transitional practice
Expressions with **tener**/imperfect

### Answers

1. Yo tenía vergüenza.
2. Yo tenía éxito.
3. Nosotros teníamos sed.
4. Yo tenía envidia.
5. Yo no tenía envidia.
6. Nosotros no teníamos hambre.

### More Practice

For additional practice in **Actividad 14** with the expressions with **tener**:

7. Sus padres trabajaban: el padre era artista y la madre era doctora.
8. Tu hermano no hacía su tarea.
9. Miguel sacaba mejor notas que Carmen.
10. Íbamos muy despacio en el carro.

## Actividad 14 ¿Qué tenías?

**PARA CONVERSAR**
**STRATEGY: SPEAKING**
**Tell when you were always or never (im)perfect** What can you say about yourself with **tener** expressions?
- **Siempre tenía cuidado cuando mi padre se enojaba.**
- **Nunca tenía envidia cuando mis amigos sacaban buenas notas.**

**Hablar/Leer** Tu amigo(a) te cuenta todo lo que le pasaba. Reacciona a lo que te dice, usando una expresión con **tener.** *(Hint: Talk to a friend, using* **tener** *expressions.)*

**modelo**

**Amigo(a):** *Me sentía mal porque yo no ayudaba a mis padres.*
**Tú:** *¿Tenías vergüenza?*
**Amigo(a):** *Sí, yo tenía vergüenza.*

**Nota**

In Spanish, instead of saying "to be hungry" or "to be thirsty," you say **tener hambre** *to have hunger* and **tener sed** *to have thirst.* Here are some other ways to use **tener:**

**tener cuidado** *to be careful*
**tener éxito** *to be successful*
**tener envidia** *to be envious*
**tener vergüenza** *to be ashamed*

1. Me portaba mal en la escuela y mi padre estaba enojado.
2. Yo tenía catorce años cuando era el campeón (*champion*) de matemáticas.
3. Tomábamos mucho jugo después de la escuela.
4. Mi madre le daba mucha atención al bebé.
5. Yo estaba muy alegre porque mi mejor amiga ganó la lotería.
6. Comíamos muy poco.

## Actividad 15 Háblame de tu familia

**Hablar/Escribir** Pregúntales a tus compañeros(as) cómo eran sus parientes. Luego escribe las respuestas en otra hoja de papel. ¡Ojo con las formas de los adjetivos! *(Hint: Ask classmates about their families and write the responses.)*

**modelo**

*abuelos*
**Tú:** *¿Cómo eran tus abuelos cuando eran jóvenes?*
**Compañero(a):** *Mis abuelos eran trabajadores.*

| Tú | Compañero(a) |
|---|---|
| madre/madrastra | amable |
| hermano(a) | animado(a) |
| hermanastro(a) | divertido(a) |
| primos(as) | impaciente |
| novio(a) | sociable |
| cuñado(a) | ¿? |
| ¿? | |

**Vocabulario**

**Unas características**

**amable** *nice*
**animado(a)** *lively, animated*
**divertido(a)** *entertaining, fun*
**impaciente** *impatient*
**obediente** *obedient*
**pobre** *poor*
**rico(a)** *rich*
**sociable** *sociable*
**tímido(a)** *shy*

¿Cómo te describes?

## Classroom Community

**Group Activity** Have students describe a classmate or a former teacher and include words from the given vocabulary list on p. 114. Other students in the group try to guess the identity of the classmate being described. **Alternate:** Have students do a "Show and Tell" activity from their past, bringing in an object and giving 2-3 sentences about it.

**Learning Scenario** Tell students that they are creating a "baby page" for the school yearbook and that they need to identify the picture of each person in the class. Using one of their baby pictures which students have brought in for the Visual activity (p. 115), have them attach a description of themselves to it, using **Unas características** vocabulary on p. 114, as well as any other adjectives they can think of. Number the pictures and have students try to guess the correct person from each description. The student who correctly identifies the most babies gets a prize.

## Tu niñez

**Hablar/Escribir** ¿Qué les vas a decir a tus hijos, nietos o sobrinos de tu niñez? Contesta las preguntas y comparte tus respuestas con tus compañeros(as). Si no sabes qué decir, habla sobre la niñez de un(a) amigo(a). *(Hint: Answer questions about your childhood or the childhood of a friend.)*

**Nota**

When you want to say what there used to be, use **había**, the imperfect form of **hay. Había** is only used in the singular form.

**No había videojuegos.** *There were no video games.*

Cuando eras niño(a)...

1. ¿Dónde vivías?
2. ¿Con quién(es) vivías?
3. ¿Qué juguetes tenías?
4. ¿A qué jugabas? ¿Con quién(es) jugabas?
5. ¿Qué había en tu cuarto?
6. ¿Te gustaba ver la televisión?

## Había una vez en la Ciudad de México

**Hablar** Mira la foto de una celebración que pasó el año pasado en la Ciudad de México. Túrnense para hacer oraciones sobre lo que pasaba en esta foto. ¡Ojo! Cada persona tiene que repetir las oraciones de los demás. *(Hint: Take turns making sentences about the photo, repeating the sentences of the others in your group.)*

**modelo**

**Tú:** *La gente caminaba por las calles.*

**Compañero(a) 1:** *La gente caminaba por las calles y...*

**MÁS COMUNICACIÓN** p. R5

## Refrán

**No sabes en qué palo te trepas.**

Este refrán quiere decir que no sabes lo que va a pasar cuando haces algo. Con un(a) compañero(a), habla de una situación en que este refrán sea apropiado. Luego presenten la situación en clase.

**Objective:** Open-ended practice
Adjectives

*Answers will vary.*

**Objective:** Open-ended practice
Describing childhood experiences

*Answers will vary.*

**Objective:** Open-ended practice
Describing past activities

*Answers will vary.*

### Teaching Suggestions

- As a follow-up to **Actividad 16**, have students work in pairs to compare their answers. You can also have students expand on the questions and continue the interview.
- Use **Actividad 17** as a story-telling game. Go around the room and have students take turns adding to the story using the imperfect tense. When students run out of things to say about the photo in the book, show them other photos to describe.
- Use the **Había una vez** game from the **Ampliación** section on p. 99B as a wrap-up of this **Etapa**.

### Block Schedule

**Personalizing** Have students choose one of the 6 situations in **Actividad 14** that is most likely to be true of them. Have them rewrite the sentence in the **yo** form and add at least 3 more sentences to describe themselves, e.g., **Yo estaba muy alegre porque mi mejor amiga ganó la lotería. Ella quería comprar un carro nuevo y a mí me gustaba la idea. Yo no tenía envidia porque yo también gané la lotería el año pasado...**

### Teaching All Students

**Extra Help** Have students use the adjectives on p. 114 to describe their friends and/or classmates.

**Challenge** Ask students to look up historical events that occurred when they were just born, 1–2 years old, 4–5 years old, 10–12 years old. Have them bring in facts and form a timeline.

**Multiple Intelligences**

**Verbal** Have students practice saying the **Refrán** with a partner, then memorize it and share with the class.

**Visual** Ask student volunteers to bring in pictures of themselves at given ages, e.g., 2, 5, and 10 years old. Use the pictures to cue descriptions and comparisons, and to describe past activities.

### Teaching Resource Options

**Print** 

*Cuaderno para hispanohablantes* PE, pp. 47–48
Block Scheduling Copymasters
Unit 2 Resource Book
*Cuaderno para hispanohablantes* TE, pp. 15–16
Audioscript, p. 29

**Audiovisual**

OHT 47 (Quick Start)
Audio Program Cassette 4A / CD 4

### Quick Start Review

Imperfect/talking about television programs

Use OHT 47 or write on board: Describe 2 stories that you read over and over when you were younger, and explain what you liked. The following words may be useful:

| | |
|---|---|
| Miraba… | Era… |
| Me gustaba… | Leía… |

*Answers will vary.*

### Teaching Suggestions

- **Prereading** Ask students to identify the cognates in the title and in the reading. Present and discuss the Reading Strategy, helping students to relate to knowledge from English classics.
- **Strategy: Use context to guess meaning** Assign groups a paragraph. Have them use context to guess the meaning of any words they do not know and paraphrase their paragraph for the class.
- **Reading** Assign groups, giving each student either a role (narrator, **hormiga**, etc.) or a section to read. Prepare through silent reading, then have each group read the story aloud.
- **Post-reading** Complete the **¿Comprendiste?** and **¿Qué piensas?** questions, then have students illustrate and label a summary of the story.

## En voces

LECTURA

**PARA LEER • STRATEGY: READING**

**Analyze folkloric traditions** Among the oral traditions of ancient people are mythic legends about important origins in their culture. In these stories gods or semidivine heroes bring important gifts to the people through supernatural means. What aspects of **«El monte de nuestro alimento** *(nourishment)*» reflect these characteristics?

- **Personajes sobrenaturales**
- **Sucesos sobrenaturales**
- **El regalo a la gente**

What other stories like this do you know?

# El monte de nuestro alimento

### Una leyenda náhuatl de México

*Antes de la llegada de Colón ya había poblaciones indígenas que tenían sus propias culturas, idiomas y religiones. Entre ellas estaban los aztecas, los mayas y los incas. Esta leyenda viene del náhuatl, el idioma de los aztecas.*

Un día, Quetzalcóatl[1] vio una hormiga[2] en la ciudad de Teotihuacán. La hormiga tenía un grano de maíz.

—Señora hormiga, ¿dónde encontró ese maíz? —preguntó Quetzalcóatl.

—En el monte de nuestro alimento —respondió la hormiga y lo invitó a seguirla.

[1] an Aztec god [2] ant



### Classroom Community

**Paired Activity** Have students work in pairs to read the **Lectura** aloud, paying special attention to the actions of each character.

**Storytelling** Have students think about another popular story, fairy tale, or **leyenda** that they know. In pairs, one student should try to find out what his/her partner's story is by asking questions to narrow it down. Students can give their partners hints if they are having too much trouble figuring it out. Switch roles.

**TPR** On large pieces of paper, draw representations of **Quetzalcóatl** and **la hormiga** and label them. Have students form a large circle and place the two pieces of paper in the middle. Say a characteristic which describes, or an action or event which involves, one of the characters from the story. The first student to raise his/her hand goes to the middle and touches the correct character described. Repeat description if student chooses the wrong character.

Quetzalcóatl siguió a la hormiga hasta el monte pero el dios era demasiado grande para entrar con las hormigas. Entonces se transformó en hormiga y así entró.

Al entrar Quetzalcóatl vio muchísimo maíz. —Toma —dijo la hormiga. Y le dio suficiente para compartir con los otros dioses. Quetzalcóatl le dijo «gracias» a la hormiga y se despidieron. Llevó su maíz y se lo dio a los otros dioses. Luego ellos le dieron de comer a la humanidad.

Algún tiempo después los dioses necesitaron más maíz. Pero era muy difícil para Quetzalcóatl transformarse en hormiga y sacar los granos poco a poco. Entonces trató de llevar el monte entero pero no pudo.

Los dioses le pidieron ayuda al sabio[3] Oxomo. —Con un rayo de Nanáhuatl, el dios del sol, el monte se puede abrir —les dijo.

[3] sage, wise man

Al otro día pidieron la ayuda del dios del sol. Cuando Nanáhuatl lanzaba[4] su rayo, el monte se abrió y cayeron los granos de nuestro alimento, el maíz y el frijol. Los dioses tomaron los granos para la humanidad.

*Todavía hoy en México, el maíz y los frijoles son alimentos básicos de la dieta mexicana.*

[4] cast

## ¿Comprendiste?

1. ¿De qué grupo indígena es el cuento?
2. ¿Qué llevaba la hormiga?
3. ¿Qué hizo Quetzalcóatl con el maíz?
4. ¿Por qué pidieron ayuda los dioses?
5. ¿Qué pasó cuando Nanáhuatl lanzó su rayo?

## ¿Qué piensas?

¿Conoces otros cuentos parecidos a esta leyenda que expliquen algún suceso u objeto en la naturaleza? ¿Cómo crees que pasaron de una generación a otra? ¿Es importante conservarlos para generaciones futuras?



## ¿Comprendiste?

### Answers

1. Es de los aztecas.
2. Llevaba un grano de maíz.
3. Se lo dio a los otros dioses.
4. Porque necesitaron más maíz.
5. El monte se abrió y cayeron el maíz y el frijol.

### Project

Have students find other Latin American legends in the children's section of the public library. They can list the titles and themes of the stories. In class, compile a master list from the students' research. Volunteers may choose to read one of the legends to an elementary school class.

### Cross Cultural Connection

**Strategy** Have students compare and contrast this Nahuatl legend with legends they already know. You may wish to suggest using a web diagram to group topics into related groups.

### Language Note

Many Spanish words come from Nahuatl. Some of these words are **chocolate**, from **xocolatl**; **tomate**, from **tomatl**; and **guacamole**, from **ahuacamolli**. Many Mexican regionalisms are from the Nahuatl language.

## Teaching All Students

**Extra Help** Have students summarize the reading by listing the main characters and their actions.

**Native Speakers** Have Spanish speakers tell about any other **leyendas** they remember. Ask them to give a summary of the **leyenda**, while keeping in mind the vocabulary and comprehension level of the students.

### Multiple Intelligences

**Visual** Ask students to draw characters from a legend they remember.

**Logical/Mathematical** Ask students to divide a piece of paper into the following categories: **presente**, **pretérito**, **imperfecto**, **infinitivo**. Then have them review the reading and list each verb in its appropriate category.

### Block Schedule

**FunBreak** Divide the class into 5 groups. Assign a paragraph of the story to each group and have them illustrate that portion of **El monte de nuestro alimento**. Illustrations can be done on large pieces of paper so each student can have an area to work in. Have each group give a Spanish title to their part of the story. Display the illustrations in the correct order in the classroom.

## Teaching Resource Options

**Print** 

Unit 2 Resource Book
Information Gap Activities, pp. 19–20
Family Involvement, pp. 21–22

**Audiovisual**

OHT 48 (Quick Start)

**Technology**

Electronic Teacher Tools/Test Generator
*Intrigas y aventuras* CD-ROM, Disc 1

## Quick Start Review

Reflexive verbs, present/imperfect

Use OHT 48 or write on board: Conjugate each verb in both the present tense and the imperfect. Be sure to include reflexive pronouns.

asustarse    sentirse (e→ie)

**Answers**, see p. 99D.

## Teaching Suggestions
### What Have Students Learned?

- Have students look at the "Now you can..." notes listed on the left side of pp. 118–119. Point out that if they feel they need to review material before doing the activities, they should consult the "To review" notes.
- Use the video to review vocabulary and structures.

# En uso
## REPASO Y MÁS COMUNICACIÓN

**OBJECTIVES**
- Describe childhood experiences
- Express personal reactions
- Discuss family relationships

*Now you can...*
- discuss family relationships.

*To review*
- possessive adjectives and pronouns, see p. 108.

### ACTIVIDAD 1 ¿Cómo son?

Todos se encuentran con sus parientes en la reunión familiar. ¿Cómo son las personas que ven? *(Hint: Who is at the reunion and what are the people like?)*

**modelo**

*Rosalía: una prima (bonito)*

*Rosalía ve a una prima suya. Su prima es bonita.*

1. ustedes: los cuñados (amable)
2. tú: la novia (sociable)
3. nosotros: unos compañeros (divertido)
4. yo: la madrastra (rico)
5. el bebé: los bisabuelos (animado)
6. Horacio y Anita: el padrastro (pobre)
7. tú: unos sobrinos (tímido)
8. las gemelas: un primo (impaciente)

*Now you can...*
- describe childhood experiences.

*To review*
- possessive adjectives and pronouns, see p. 108.

### ACTIVIDAD 2 ¿Es tuyo?

¿De quién es cada juguete? Contesta las preguntas. *(Hint: Whose toys are these?)*

**modelo**

**Tú:** *Los bloques, ¿son de Rosa? (pequeño)*

**Compañero(a):** *No, no son suyos. Los suyos son más pequeños.*

1. La pelota, ¿es de Jorge? (grande)
2. La muñeca, ¿es de Dolores? (bonito)
3. Las marionetas, ¿son de ustedes? (alto)
4. El bate, ¿es tuyo? (viejo)
5. El muñeco de peluche, ¿es de Miguel? (gordo)
6. La cuerda de saltar, ¿es de ellas? (nuevo)



## Classroom Community

**Paired Activity** Ask students to bring in a picture of their family or an imaginary family. Have them describe the family members to another student, including vocabulary from p. 114.

**Portfolio** Have students plan a family reunion. They can describe the family members who attend and the events that might happen during the reunion. They might use an imaginary family if preferred.

**Rubric: Writing**

| Criteria | Scale |
|---|---|
| Vocabulary use | 1 2 3 4 5 |
| Creativity | 1 2 3 4 5 |
| Logical organization | 1 2 3 4 5 |

A = 13–15 pts.
B = 10–12 pts.
C = 7–9 pts.
D = 4–6 pts.
F = < 4 pts.

*Now you can...*
- express personal reactions.

*To review*
- reflexives, see p. 110.

## ACTIVIDAD 3 Un nuevo director de la escuela

¿Cómo reaccionan estas personas cuando llega el nuevo director? *(Hint: How do people react to the new principal?)*

**modelo**

*los profesores / sonreírse / porque están contentos*

*Los profesores se sonríen porque están contentos.*

1. Andrés / preocuparse / porque el director es amigo de su padrastro
2. mis amigos y yo / sentirse / contentos porque él es divertido
3. tú / darse cuenta / de que no lo conoces
4. Elena / aburrirse / porque no tiene interés en esas cosas
5. Ramón y Susana / asustarse / porque siempre se portan mal en las clases
6. nadie / enojarse / porque el director es amable

*Now you can...*
- describe childhood experiences.

*To review*
- the imperfect tense, see p. 112.

## ACTIVIDAD 4 En mi época...

La señora Pérez te habla de su niñez. Para saber lo que dice, completa los párrafos con la forma apropiada de los verbos indicados. Usa el imperfecto. *(Hint: Find out about her childhood.)*

Cuando yo __1__ (ser) niña, mi familia __2__ (vivir) en un apartamento pequeño en el centro de la ciudad. Mis hermanos y yo __3__ (asistir) a una escuela en otra parte de la ciudad. Nosotros __4__ (tener) que ir en autobús porque la escuela __5__ (estar) bastante lejos de nuestro apartamento.

Después de las clases, mis hermanos y yo __6__ (ir) a la casa de los abuelos para jugar un rato. Yo siempre __7__ (jugar) con unos muñecos de peluche y __8__ (salir) para saltar la cuerda. Mis hermanos __9__ (construir) cosas con bloques o __10__ (trepar) a los árboles.

¿Qué __11__ (hacer) tú cuando __12__ (ser) más joven? ¿También __13__ (ver) mucho a tus abuelos? ¿Con qué juguetes __14__ (jugar)?



### ACTIVIDAD 1 Answers

1. Ustedes ven a los cuñados suyos. Sus cuñados son amables.
2. Tú ves a la novia tuya. Tu novia es sociable.
3. Nosotros vemos a unos compañeros nuestros. Nuestros compañeros son divertidos.
4. Yo veo a la madrastra mía. Mi madrastra es rica.
5. El bebé ve a los bisabuelos suyos. Sus bisabuelos son animados.
6. Horacio y Anita ven al padrastro suyo. Su padrastro es pobre.
7. Tú ves a unos sobrinos tuyos. Tus sobrinos son tímidos.
8. Las gemelas ven a un primo suyo. Su primo es impaciente.

### ACTIVIDAD 2 Answers

1. No, no es suya. La suya es más grande.
2. No, no es suya. La suya es más bonita.
3. No, no son nuestras. Las nuestras son más altas.
4. No, no es mío. El mío es más viejo.
5. No, no es suyo. El suyo es más gordo.
6. No, no es suya. La suya es más nueva.

### ACTIVIDAD 3 Answers

1. Andrés se preocupa porque el director es amigo de su padrastro.
2. Mis amigos y yo nos sentimos contentos porque él es divertido.
3. Tú te das cuenta de que no lo conoces.
4. Elena se aburre porque no tiene interés en esas cosas.
5. Ramón y Susana se asustan porque siempre se portan mal en las clases.
6. Nadie se enoja porque el director es amable.

### ACTIVIDAD 4 Answers

1. era
2. vivía
3. asistíamos
4. teníamos
5. estaba
6. íbamos
7. jugaba
8. salía
9. construían
10. trepaban
11. hacías
12. eras
13. veías
14. jugabas

## Teaching All Students

**Extra Help** A new principal has just been appointed to your school. Have students rewrite the sentences in **Actividad 3** to fit your school setting. Ask them to add additional sentences to describe everyone's reactions.

**Challenge** Have students write sentences using reflexive verbs to describe how they feel when a new teacher comes to their class.

**Multiple Intelligences**

**Verbal** Have students interview a relative/friend on his/her childhood experiences, then write a short summary and present it to the class.

## Block Schedule

**Change of Pace** As a class, brainstorm a list of favorite childhood activities. Then in small groups, have them classify the activities according to age groups, e.g., **bebé, 2–5 años, 6–10 años, 11–16 años**, etc.

## Teaching Resource Options

**Print**

Unit 2 Resource Book
- Cooperative Quizzes pp. 33–34
- Etapa Exam, Forms A and B, pp. 35–44
- *Examen para hispanohablantes* pp. 45–49
- Audioscript, p. 32
- Portfolio Assessment, pp. 50–51
- Multiple Choice Test Questions, pp. 170–172

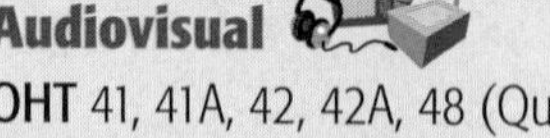

**Audiovisual**

OHT 41, 41A, 42, 42A, 48 (Quick Start)
Audio Program Cassette 19A / CD 19

**Technology**

Electronic Teacher Tools/Test Generator
www.mcdougallittell.com

## Quick Start Review

Question words

Use OHT 48 or write on board: Write four questions you would ask an older family member about his or her youth.

*Answers will vary. Sample answers:*
1. ¿Dónde jugabas?
2. ¿Qué juguetes tenías?

 and 

**Rubric: Speaking**

| Criteria | Scale | |
|---|---|---|
| Fluency | 1 2 3 | A = 8–9 pts. |
| Vocabulary | 1 2 3 | B = 6–7 pts. |
| Pronunciation, rhythm | 1 2 3 | C = 4–5 pts. |
| | | D = 3 pts. |
| | | F = < 3 pts. |

### En tu propia voz

**Rubric: Writing**

| Criteria | Scale | |
|---|---|---|
| Vocabulary use | 1 2 3 4 5 | A = 13–15 pts. |
| Accuracy | 1 2 3 4 5 | B = 10–12 pts. |
| Creativity, appearance | 1 2 3 4 5 | C = 7–9 pts. |
| | | D = 4–6 pts. |
| | | F = < 4 pts. |

## Teaching Note: En tu propia voz

**Writing Strategy** Have students compile as many details as possible before beginning to write their paragraphs.

## Actividad 5 En mi niñez

**PARA CONVERSAR**

**STRATEGY: SPEAKING**

**Add variety to your conversation** To add interest to a conversation, you can
- tell how often: **siempre, mucho, a veces, de vez en cuando, poco, rara vez, nunca.**
- give reasons: **Era difícil / fácil / peligroso / divertido / sociable. Prefería... (No) me gustaba...**

Tú y tu compañero(a) hablan de su niñez. Háganse preguntas sobre lo que hacían para divertirse cuando eran niños(as). *(Hint: What did you do when you were small? Did your friend do the same things?)*

**modelo**

**Tú:** *¿Jugabas con muñecos de peluche?*
**Compañero(a):** *No, no jugaba mucho con muñecos de peluche. ¿Y tú?*
**Tú:** *Sí, siempre jugaba con muñecos de peluche.*
**Compañero(a):** *¿Contabas chistes a veces?*
**Tú:** *No, no contaba chistes porque era tímido(a). ¿Y tú?*
**Compañero(a):** *Sí, contaba muchos chistes. También jugaba a la pelota. ¿Qué hacías tú?*

## Actividad 6 Una reunión familiar

Imagínate que estás en una reunión familiar. Dibuja la situación si quieres. Incluye un mínimo de cinco parientes. Entonces, háblales a tus compañeros(as) de tus parientes. *(Hint: Draw a picture of a family reunion and tell your classmates about your relatives.)*

**modelo**

*En la reunión hay muchos parientes míos. Esta chica es una prima mía. Ella es muy amable, pero su hermano Daniel es impaciente.*

## Actividad 7 En tu propia voz

**ESCRITURA** Entrevista a un(a) pariente(a) o a un(a) amigo(a) sobre su niñez. Luego escribe un párrafo con la información de la entrevista. Escribe sobre su familia, sus actividades y su experiencia en la escuela primaria. *(Hint: Interview someone you know about his or her childhood, and write what the person said.)*

**modelo**

*Mi tío era un niño muy inteligente. No le gustaba la escuela porque se aburría mucho. Después de las clases, se reunía con sus amigos en el parque. Ellos jugaban a la pelota o trepaban a los árboles. A veces...*

## CONEXIONES

**Los estudios sociales** Los aztecas hicieron su propio calendario, usando muchas ideas del calendario maya. Basaron el calendario en el sol, la luna y las estrellas. Su calendario tenía 365 días. Cada 52 años empezaban un calendario nuevo para hacer las correcciones. En la biblioteca o por Internet busca información sobre el calendario azteca. Luego escribe un reportaje sobre el calendario. Comparte información de tu reportaje con tus compañeros(as) de clase.

## Classroom Community

**Paired Activity** Have students work with a partner to form sentences with one cluster of vocabulary words on p. 121, e.g., *Describe Childhood Experiences.*

**Peer Review** The vocabulary is grouped under 4 categories—have students design a mind map to regroup the vocabulary into 6–7 different categories. Encourage them to be creative.

# En resumen

## REPASO DE VOCABULARIO

### DESCRIBE CHILDHOOD EXPERIENCES

**Toys and Games**

| | |
|---|---|
| **el juguete** | *toy* |
| **la marioneta** | *marionette* |
| **la muñeca** | *doll* |
| **el muñeco de peluche** | *stuffed animal* |

**Activities**

| | |
|---|---|
| **caerse** | *to fall down* |
| **construir** | *to construct* |
| **contar (o→ue) chistes** | *to tell jokes* |
| **dibujar** | *to draw* |
| **esconderse** | *to hide* |
| **pelearse** | *to fight* |
| **saltar la cuerda** | *to jump rope* |
| **trepar a los árboles** | *to climb trees* |

**Descriptions and Expressions**

| | |
|---|---|
| **a veces** | *sometimes* |
| **amable** | *nice* |
| **animado(a)** | *lively, animated* |
| **cuando era niño(a)** | *when I/he/she was young* |
| **dentro de** | *inside* |
| **divertido(a)** | *entertaining, fun* |
| **fuera de** | *outside* |
| **impaciente** | *impatient* |
| **obediente** | *obedient* |
| **la risa** | *laugh, laughter* |
| **sociable** | *sociable* |
| **tímido(a)** | *shy* |

### OTHER WORDS AND PHRASES

| | |
|---|---|
| **despedirse (e→i, i) de** | *to say good-bye to* |
| **había** | *there was, there were* |
| **reunirse** | *to get together* |
| **sentarse (e→ie)** | *to sit down* |
| **tener cuidado** | *to be careful* |
| **tener envidia** | *to be envious* |
| **tener éxito** | *to be successful* |
| **tener vergüenza** | *to be ashamed* |

### EXPRESS PERSONAL REACTIONS

| | |
|---|---|
| **aburrirse** | *to get bored* |
| **asustarse de** | *to be scared of* |
| **cansarse** | *to get tired* |
| **darse cuenta de** | *to realize* |
| **disculparse** | *to apologize* |
| **divertirse (e→ie, i)** | *to enjoy oneself* |
| **enojarse con** | *to get angry with* |
| **portarse bien/mal** | *to behave well/badly* |
| **preocuparse por** | *to be worried about* |
| **reírse** | *to laugh* |
| **sentirse (e→ie, i)** | *to feel* |
| **sonreírse** | *to smile* |

### DISCUSS FAMILY RELATIONSHIPS

| | |
|---|---|
| **la amistad** | *friendship, acquaintance* |
| **el bebé** | *baby* |
| **el (la) bisabuelo(a)** | *great grandfather/grandmother* |
| **el (la) compañero(a)** | *classmate, companion* |
| **el (la) cuñado(a)** | *brother-in-law, sister-in-law* |
| **los (las) gemelos(as)** | *twins* |
| **el (la) hermanastro(a)** | *stepbrother, stepsister* |
| **la madrastra** | *stepmother* |
| **el (la) novio(a)** | *boyfriend, girlfriend; groom, bride* |
| **el padrastro** | *stepfather* |
| **el (la) pariente(a)** | *relative* |
| **pobre** | *poor* |
| **rico(a)** | *rich* |
| **el (la) sobrino(a)** | *nephew, niece* |

### Juego

Oso te digo que soy,
con camisa y pantalón.
Amigo de niños también,
me quieren un montón.
¿Quién soy?

## Teaching All Students

**Extra Help** Have one student state the English word and another give the Spanish equivalent.

**Native Speakers** Have Spanish speakers write additional **Juegos** to help the class review the vocabulary.

**Multiple Intelligences**

**Kinesthetic** Write out vocabulary words on index cards, shuffle the deck and hand out cards to students. Form a sentence omitting the vocabulary word and ask students to stand with appropriate word response card, e.g., **Los niños van a ___ en los árboles.** Student stands with card: **esconderse**.



## Interdisciplinary Connections

**Social Studies** Have students research other calendar systems, and compare to the Mayan and Aztec systems.

## Teaching Suggestions

### Vocabulary Review

Have students make flashcards of the words in the **Repaso de vocabulario** on p. 121. Divide students into groups of 3 or 4. Deal 5 cards per group. See how many sentences students can make using the vocabulary cards. The team with the most grammatically correct sentences wins.

## Culture Highlights

See photo on p. 135 for a look at the enormous **Piedra del Sol**, an Aztec calendar at the **Museo Nacional de Antropología**.

## Projects

Have students research 3 museums in Mexico City and compare them. What kind of collections are found in each? When are the museums open? Which one(s) would students like to visit? Explain.

## Juego

**Answer**
muñeco de peluche

## Project: Reviewing Etapa 1

Assign the following out-of-class activities:

- Find out about a current event in Mexico.
- Bring in realia about Mexico City.
- Interview a Spanish speaker about his/her childhood.
- Find information on Diego Rivera or Frida Kahlo or another Mexican artist.

**Extra Credit**

| | |
|---|---|
| Current event | 2 pts. |
| Realia | 2 pts. |
| Interview | 2 pts. |
| Artist information | 2 pts. |

## Block Schedule

**Retention** Have students review their homework assignments for **Etapa 1** to help them prepare for the **Etapa Exam**.

# Planning Guide CLASSROOM MANAGEMENT

## OBJECTIVES

**Communication**
- Narrate in the past *pp. 124–125, 126–127, 138–139*
- Talk about family celebrations *pp. 126–127, 136*
- Talk about activities in progress *pp. 130–133*

**Grammar**
- Present and past progressive tenses *p. 130*
- Ordinals *p. 132*
- Preterite and imperfect *p. 134*

**Culture**
- **La piñata** *p. 132*
- **Museo Nacional de Antropología** *p. 135*
- **¡Temblor!** *pp. 138–139*
- **Diego Rivera** *p. 142*

**Recycling**
- Imperfect tense *p. 129*
- Reflexives *p. 130*
- Telling time *p. 133*

## STRATEGIES

**Listening Strategies**
- Listen for a series of events *p. 126*

**Speaking Strategies**
- Brainstorm to get ideas *p. 132*
- Interact by expressing approval, disapproval, or astonishment *p. 142*

**Reading Strategies**
- Activate prior knowledge *TE p. 138*

**Writing Strategies**
- Use different kinds of descriptive words *Actividad 7, TE p. 143*

**Connecting Cultures Strategies**
- Learn about **El Museo Nacional de Antropología**, *TE p. 135*
- Observe and generalize *p. 138*
- Find out about artist Diego Rivera *TE p. 143*

## PROGRAM RESOURCES

### Print
- *Más práctica* Workbook PE *pp. 49–56*
- Block Scheduling Copymasters *pp. 41–48*
- Unit 2 Resource Book
  - *Más práctica* Workbook TE *pp. 52–59*
  - *Cuaderno para hispanohablantes* TE *pp. 60–67*
  - Information Gap Activities *pp. 68–71*
  - Family Involvement *pp. 72–73*
  - Video Activities *pp. 74–76*
  - Videoscript *pp. 77–78*
  - Audioscript *pp. 79–83*
  - Assessment Program Unit 2 Etapa 2 *pp. 84–102; 173–175*
  - Answer Keys *pp. 179–183*

### Audiovisual
- Audio Program Cassette 5A, 5B / CD 5
- *Canciones* Cassette/CD
- Video Program Videotape 2 / Videodisc 1B
- Overhead Transparencies M1, M2; 49–58

### Technology
- Electronic Teacher Tools/Test Generator
- *Intrigas y aventuras* CD-ROM, Disc 1
-  www.mcdougallittell.com

### Assessment Program Options
- Cooperative Quizzes (Unit 2 Resource Book)
- Etapa Exam Forms A and B (Unit 2 Resource Book)
- *Examen para hispanohablantes* (Unit 2 Resource Book)
- Multiple Choice Test Questions (Unit 2 Resource Book)
- Portfolio Assessment (Unit 2 Resource Book)
- Audio Program Cassette 19A / CD 19
- Electronic Teacher Tools/Test Generator

### Native Speakers
- *Cuaderno para hispanohablantes* PE *pp. 49–56*
- *Cuaderno para hispanohablantes* TE (Unit 2 Resource Book)
- *Examen para hispanohablantes* (Unit 2 Resource Book)
- Audio Program *(Para hispanohablantes)* Cassettes 5B, 19A / CD 5, CD 19
- Audioscript (Unit 2 Resource Book)

# Student Text Listening Activity Scripts

Doña Regina

Isabel

Ricardo

Don Miguel

## Videoscript: Diálogo *pages 126–127*

- Videotape 2, 14:09 • Videodisc 1B
  Search Chapter 5, Play to 6. U2E2, En vivo (Dialog)
- Use the videoscript with **Actividades 1, 2** *page 128*

**Don Miguel:** Siéntense por favor. ¡Ah! Regina. ¡Qué bien! Isabel, Ricardo, les presento a mi esposa Regina.
**Doña Regina:** Es un placer, Isabel..
**Isabel:** Igualmente, señora.
**Doña Regina:** Ricardo...
**Ricardo:** Mucho gusto, señora.
**Doña Regina:** Bienvenidos a nuestra casa. Les sirvo unas limonadas, ¿no? Hoy hace mucho calor.
**Isabel:** Muchas gracias.
**Doña Regina:** Ay, de nada. Con permiso.
**Don Miguel:** Esos adornos son para una reunión de la familia esta noche. Estamos celebrando el cumpleaños de mi nieta menor. ¿Comenzamos la entrevista?
**Isabel:** Sí. Bueno, sé que Ud. vivía en la Ciudad de México en el año de 1985, cuando ocurrió el temblor. ¿Me puede contar qué pasó? ¿Cómo fue? Mi madre me contó cómo afectó a nuestra familia, pero quiero saber más.
**Don Miguel:** Pues, el día antes del temblor fue nuestro aniversario de boda. Esa noche nos reunimos con unos amigos para celebrar. Todo mundo estaba muy feliz. Mi esposa y yo nos enamoramos cuando todavía éramos jóvenes.
**Doña Regina:** Ay, sí. Nos llevábamos muy bien en esos días, y todavía nos llevamos bien. Tenemos mucho en común. Ricardo, ¿me haces el favor de ayudarme con los adornos?
**Ricardo:** Sí, cómo no, señora.
**Doña Regina:** Con permiso.
**Don Miguel:** ¿Dónde estaba?
**Isabel:** Nos contaba de la noche antes de ocurrir el temblor.
**Don Miguel:** Ah, sí, es verdad. Así fue que estuvimos juntos hasta muy tarde, y después fuimos a la casa y nos dormimos. Tienes que darte cuenta, el temblor ocurrió a las siete y diecinueve de la mañana, era temprano. Mucha gente dormía o se preparaba para el nuevo día, y casi todo el mundo estaba en sus casas... Regina y yo estábamos durmiendo. De repente, me desperté y me di cuenta de que algo estaba mal. ¡La tierra temblaba! Regina y yo nos levantamos y en seguida salimos de la casa. Fue cuando vimos el efecto del temblor y cuando nos dimos cuenta de lo terrible que fue.
**Isabel:** ¿Qué les pasó? ¿Qué encontraron?
**Don Miguel:** Para empezar, muchos edificios se cayeron. Había gente por todas partes, sin casa. Mucha gente estaba buscando a sus parientes, a sus amigos. Un compañero mío murió.
**Isabel:** Qué tristeza... Mi familia también tiene una historia. Una prima de mi madre murió.
**Don Miguel:** Mira, sí, fue muy triste. Pero después ocurrió algo increíble, algo maravilloso. Todo el mundo respondió a la emergencia con acciones positivas. Mira estas fotos... Todos ayudaban a sus vecinos. Si una familia oía que otra familia necesitaba algo, hacían todo lo posible para ayudar. Y la ayuda vino a México de otras partes, y del mundo también. Como sabes, muchas personas leyeron del temblor en los periódicos o vieron las noticias en la televisión, y mandaron ayuda.
**Isabel:** Sabe, don Miguel, creo que voy a escribir sobre eso, sobre la solidaridad de la gente y su participación en la reconstrucción de la ciudad.
**Don Miguel:** Es una buena idea, Isabel. Personalmente, yo sentí mucho orgullo por mi gente, la gente de México, durante ese tiempo difícil.
**Isabel:** Gracias, don Miguel. Creo que tengo suficiente información para empezar.
**Doña Regina:** Bueno, pues si ya terminaron, ¿nos ayudan? Estamos poniendo estos adornos.
**Isabel:** ¡Sí, claro!
**Doña Regina:** Aquí tienen los globos... Ricardo, estas velas son para el pastel. Y vamos a romper una piñata esta noche. ¿Me ayudan con la piñata?
**Isabel:** Por supuesto. ¡Qué divertido! Va a ser una fiesta de maravilla.

## Actividad 8 Muchas emociones *page 132*

1. Me acuerdo muy bien del temblor de 1985. Todos los días estaba leyendo en el periódico que había mucha destrucción, muchas casas y edificios se cayeron.
2. Yo estaba ayudando con un rescate dramático. De veras fue un rescate de maravilla. Nosotros estábamos rescatando a una familia entera y lo hicimos. La salvamos.
3. Todos estaban leyendo de los héroes que ayudaban a las víctimas. Cuando fue necesario, todo el mundo ayudó. Por eso hubo tantos héroes.
4. Mis padres me dijeron que la casa de mi abuela se estaba cayendo. Fue terrible. Mi abuela estaba perdiendo todas sus posesiones.
5. Todos los días leímos la lista de los muertos en el periódico. Fue una lástima que muchas personas estaban muriendo por el temblor.
6. Por último, ocurrió una maravilla. Todos estaban ayudando a sus vecinos. Todo el mundo estaba ayudando a reconstruir la ciudad. Yo estaba muy orgulloso.

## Actividad 15 Unas celebraciones *page 136*

1. Ay, ¡qué divertido ver a todos los compañeros despúes de diez años! Muchas personas están diferentes. Por ejemplo, Héctor cambió muchísimo. Antes era tímido y no nos llevábamos bien. Pero esta noche estaba muy animado, bailamos y hablamos mucho. Nos llevamos perfectamente.
2. Cuando la novia elegante andaba por la iglesia y la cantante empezó a cantar, fue precioso. Todo el mundo les deseaba mucha felicidad. Y durante la recepción, cuando la orquesta tocaba, bailé con Fabio. Me gustó todo.
3. Estaba muy feliz con todos los regalos que recibió. Yo le di un disco compacto que quería. Comimos mucho pastel, que estaba sabroso, exquisito.

### Quick Start Review Answers

**p. 124** Preterite/reflexives
1. nos reunimos
2. me senté
3. me di cuenta
4. se sonrió
5. se despidió
6. me divertí

**p. 126** Preterite
1. salió
2. se enamoraron
3. se enojó, se pelearon
4. volvió, se dieron
5. celebraron, llegó

**p. 130** Present tense of estar
*Answers will vary but should include:*
1. Cecilia está…
2. Los niños están…
3. Yo estoy…
4. Tú estás…
5. Nosotros estamos…

**p. 132** Tener expressions
1. Carlos
2. El bebé
3. Maribel
4. Mateo
5. Elena

**p. 140** Describing others
1. … bonita, trabajadora y simpática.
2. … cruel.
3. … feas y perezosas.
4. … guapo y alto.

# Pacing Guide

## Sample Lesson Plan - 50 Minute Schedule

### DAY 1

***Etapa* Opener**
- Quick Start Review (TE, p. 122). 5 MIN.
- Have students look at *Etapa* Opener and answer questions. 5 MIN.

**En contexto: Vocabulario**
- Quick Start Review (TE, p. 124). 5 MIN.
- Have students use context and pictures to learn *Etapa* vocabulary. Answer questions p. 125. 10 MIN.

**En vivo: Diálogo**
- Quick Start Review (TE, p. 126). 5 MIN.
- Review Listening Strategy, p. 126. Play audio or show video for the dialog on pp. 126–127. 10 MIN.
- Replay and have students take on roles of characters. 10 MIN.

**Homework Option**
- Video Activities, Unit 2 Resource Book, pp. 75–76.

### DAY 2

**En acción: Vocabulario y gramática**
- Check homework. 5 MIN.
- Ask students for a summary of *En vivo* dialog to check recall. 5 MIN.
- Have students answer Comprehension Questions (TE, p. 127). 5 MIN.
- Quick Start Review (TE, p. 128). 5 MIN.
- Replay the *En vivo* dialog using the audiovisual resources and have students do *Actividades* 1 and 2 orally. 10 MIN.
- Have students complete *Actividades* 3 and 4 in pairs. 10 MIN.
- Have students do *Actividad* 5 by asking their classmates these questions. You can have students summarize their answers in writing as homework. 10 MIN.

**Homework Option**
- *Más práctica* Workbook, pp. 49–52 as needed. *Cuaderno para hispanohablantes*, pp. 49–50 as needed.

### DAY 3

**En acción (cont.)**
- Check homework. 5 MIN.
- Quick Start Review (TE, p. 130). 5 MIN.
- Present *Gramática:* The Progressive Tenses, p. 130. 10 MIN.
- Review vocabulary in the box on p. 131. 5 MIN.
- Have students do *Actividades* 6 and 7 in writing. 10 MIN.
- Play audio and have students begin *Actividad* 8. 5 MIN.
- Present *Vocabulario* and Speaking Strategy, p. 132. Have students do *Actividad* 9 in small groups. 10 MIN.

**Homework Option**
- Have students complete *Actividad* 9 in writing. *Más práctica* Workbook, pp. 53–54. *Cuaderno para hispanohablantes*, pp. 51–52.

### DAY 4

**En acción (cont.)**
- Check homework. 5 MIN.
- Quick Start Review (TE, p. 132). 5 MIN.
- Review vocabulary on p. 133 and have students do *Actividad* 10 orally or in writing. 5 MIN.
- Quick Start Review (TE, p. 134). 5 MIN.
- Present *Gramática:* Using the Preterite and the Imperfect on p. 134. 10 MIN.
- Have students do *Actividades* 11, 12, and 13 in writing. 15 MIN.
- Have students do *Actividad* 14 in pairs. 5 MIN.

**Homework Option**
- *Más práctica* Workbook, pp. 55–56. *Cuaderno para hispanohablantes*, pp. 53–54.

### DAY 5

**En acción (cont.)**
- Check homework. 5 MIN.
- Quick Start Review (TE, p. 136). 5 MIN.
- Play the audio and have students complete *Actividad* 15. Students can also write their responses to *Actividad* 15 as homework. 10 MIN.
- Have students complete *Actividad* 16 in small groups. 5 MIN.

**En colores: Cultura y comparaciones**
- Quick Start Review (TE, p. 138). 5 MIN.
- Review Connecting Cultures Strategies, p. 138. 5 MIN.
- Read *¡Temblor!* aloud with students. Then call on students to reread selected portions aloud. 15 MIN.

### DAY 6

**En colores (cont.)**
- Have students answer the *¿Comprendiste?* and *¿Qué piensas?* activities in small groups. 20 MIN.
- Have students complete *Actividad* 17 in small groups. 10 MIN.
- Divide class into small groups and have them prepare and role-play the *Hazlo tú* activity on p. 139. 20 MIN.

**Homework Option**
- Have students do *En uso, Actividades* 1–4, pp. 140–141.

### DAY 7

**En uso: Repaso y más comunicación**
- Quick Start Review (TE, p. 140). 5 MIN.
- Check *Actividades* 1, 2, 3, and 4 orally. 15 MIN.
- Review Speaking Strategy, p. 142. Then do *Actividad* 5 orally in pairs and *Actividad* 6 in groups of four. 15 MIN.

**Conexiones**
- Read and discuss. 5 MIN.

**En tu propia voz: Escritura**
- Start writing activity and assign the rest for homework. 10 MIN.

**Homework Option**
- Have students finish *Actividad* 7. *Cuaderno para hispanohablantes*, pp. 55–56.

### DAY 8

- Check homework. 5 MIN.
- Quick Start Review (TE, p. 142). 5 MIN.
- Review grammar questions, etc. as necessary. 5 MIN.
- Complete *Etapa* 2 Exam. 20 MIN.

**Ampliación**
- Use a suggested project, game, or activity (TE pp. 99A–99B). 15 MIN.

**Homework Option**
- Preview next *Etapa* Opener, pp. 144–145.

# Sample Lesson Plan - Block Schedule (90 minutes)

## DAY 1

***Etapa* Opener**

- Quick Start Review (TE, p. 122). 5 MIN.
- Have students look at the *Etapa* Opener and answer questions. 5 MIN.

**En contexto: Vocabulario**

- Quick Start Review (TE, p. 124). 5 MIN.
- Have students use context and pictures to learn *Etapa* vocabulary. Answer questions, p. 125. 10 MIN.

**En vivo: Diálogo**

- Quick Start Review (TE, p. 126). 5 MIN.
- Review Listening Strategy, p. 126. Play audio or show video for the dialog on pp. 126–127. 10 MIN.
- Ask Comprehension Questions (TE, p. 127). Replay. 5 MIN.
- Students role-play in groups while looking at the photos in their texts. Encourage them to come up with logical dialog using familiar vocabulary. 10 MIN.

**En acción: Vocabulario y gramática**

- Quick Start Review (TE, p. 128). 5 MIN.
- Have students do *Actividades* 1 and 2 orally. 10 MIN.
- Have students complete *Actividades* 3 and 4 in pairs. 10 MIN.
- Have students do *Actividad* 5 by asking their classmates these questions. You can have students summarize their answers in writing as homework. 10 MIN.

**Homework Option**

- Have students finish *Actividad* 5.
- Video activities, Unit 2 Resource Book, pp. 75–76.

## DAY 2

**En acción (cont.)**

- Check homework. 10 MIN.
- Quick Start Review (TE, p. 130). 5 MIN.
- Present *Gramática:* The Progressive Tenses, p. 130. 10 MIN.
- Review the vocabulary in the box on p. 131. 5 MIN.
- Have students do *Actividades* 6 and 7 in writing. 10 MIN.
- Present *Vocabulario* and Speaking Strategy, p. 132, and have students do *Actividad* 8 in small groups. 10 MIN.
- Have students complete *Actividades* 9 and 10 in writing. 10 MIN.
- Quick Start Review (TE, p. 132). 5 MIN.
- Present *Gramática:* Using the Preterite and the Imperfect, on p. 134. 10 MIN.
- Have students do *Actividades* 11 and 12 in writing. 10 MIN.
- Use Block Scheduling Copymasters for a change of pace as needed. 5 MIN.

**Homework Option**

- *Más práctica* Workbook, pp. 49–54 as needed. *Cuaderno para hispanohablantes*, pp. 49–52 as needed.

## DAY 3

**En acción (cont.)**

- Check homework. 10 MIN.
- Quick Start Review (TE, p. 134). 5 MIN.
- Have students do *Actividades* 13 and 14 in pairs. 15 MIN.
- Play the audio and have students complete *Actividad* 15. Students can also write their responses to *Actividad* 15 as homework. 10 MIN.
- Have students complete *Actividad* 16 in small groups. 10 MIN.
- Have students complete *Actividad* 17 in pairs. *Actividad* 17 can also be saved for individual homework. Expand with *Más comunicación,* p. R6. 10 MIN.
- Use Block Scheduling Copymasters for a change of pace as needed. 10 MIN.

**Ampliación**

- Use a suggested project, game, or activity (TE, pp. 99A–99B). 20 MIN.

**Homework Option**

- Have students finish *Actividad* 17 in writing. *Más práctica* Workbook, pp. 55–56. *Cuaderno para hispanohablantes*, pp. 53–54.

## DAY 4

**En colores: Cultura y comparaciones**

- Check homework. 10 MIN.
- Quick Start Review (TE, p. 138). 5 MIN.
- Review Connecting Cultures Strategy, p. 138. 5 MIN.
- Read *¡Temblor!* aloud with students 10 MIN.
- Have students answer the *¿Comprendiste?* activities orally. 10 MIN.
- Have students answer the *¿Qué piensas?* activities in writing. 10 MIN.
- Divide class into small groups and have them role-play *Hazlo tú* activity on p. 139. 20 MIN.

**Ampliación**

- Choose a project, activity or game. (TE pp. 99A–99B) 20 MIN.

**Homework Option**

- Have students finish the *¿Qué piensas?* activities, p. 139. *Cuaderno para hispanohablantes*, pp. 55–56.

## DAY 5

**En uso: Repaso y más comunicación**

- Check homework. 10 MIN.
- Quick Start Review (TE, p. 140). 5 MIN.
- Review *Actividades* 1 and 3. Have students do *Actividad* 2 and 4 orally. 15 MIN.
- Review Speaking Strategy, p. 142. Then do *Actividad* 5 orally in pairs and *Actividad* 6 in groups of four. 10 MIN.
- Review grammar questions, etc. as necessary. 10 MIN.
- Complete *Etapa* 2 Exam. 20 MIN.

**Conexiones**

- Read and discuss. 5 MIN.

**En tu propia voz: Escritura**

- Start writing activity. 15 MIN.

**Homework Option**

- Finish writing activity and preview next *Etapa* Opener, pp. 144–145.

▼ Todos preparan la fiesta en la casa de don Miguel.

## Etapa Theme

**Narrating in the past, talking about family celebrations, and talking about activities in progress.**

## Grammar Objectives

- Present and past progressive
- Preterite and imperfect

### Teaching Resource Options

**Print** 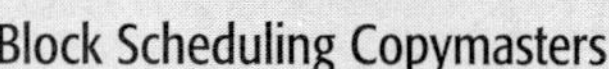

Block Scheduling Copymasters

**Audiovisual** 

OHT 55 (Quick Start)
*Canciones* Cassette / CD Songs 11, 14

### Quick Start Review

**Saber** and **conocer**

Use OHT 55 or write on board: Answer the following questions about the photo with a complete sentence in Spanish. Each response should contain either **saber** or **conocer**.

¿Conoces al señor?
¿Qué sabe hacer el señor?
¿Sabes qué hay dentro de la piñata? ¿Qué?
¿Conoces a la chica que escribe? ¿Cómo se llama?
¿Sabes qué tipo de fiesta preparan? ¿Qué celebran?

*Answers will vary. Sample answers:*
No, no conozco al señor.
Sabe usar las marionetas.
Sí, sé que hay dulces en la piñata.
Sí, la conozco. Se llama Isabel.
Sí, sé que preparan una fiesta de cumpleaños.

### Teaching Suggestions
**Previewing the Etapa**

- Ask students to study the picture on pp. 122–123 (1 min.).
- Divide the class into small groups and ask each group to make up a story based on the photo. Have some groups present their story to the class.
- Use the **¿Qué ves?** questions to guide the imaginary story that students create.

UNIDAD 2

ETAPA 2

# Había una vez...

- Narrate in the past
- Discuss family celebrations
- Talk about activities in progress

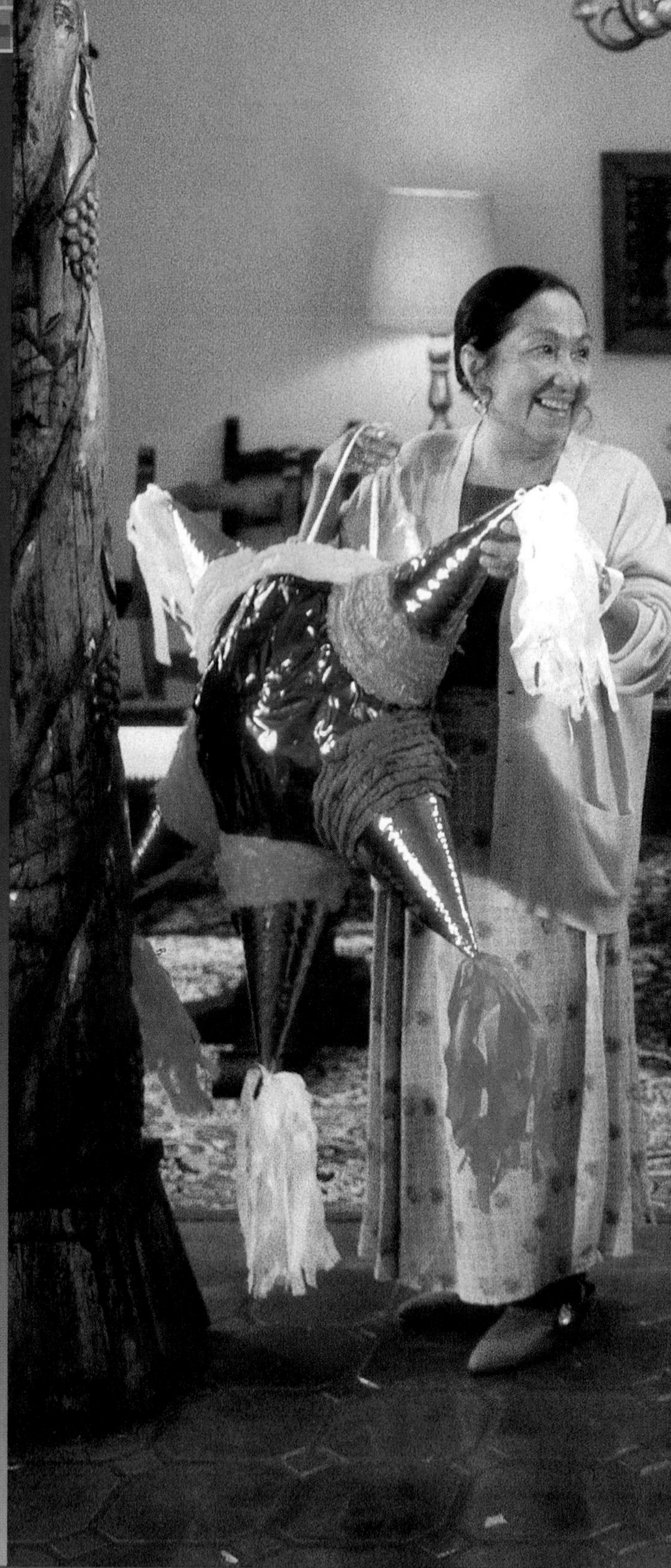

### ¿Qué ves?

Mira la foto y contesta las preguntas.

1. ¿Puedes identificar las personas de esta foto? ¿Quiénes son?
2. ¿Dónde están?
3. ¿Qué hacen?
4. ¿Te gusta recibir tarjetas de cumpleaños?

122

### Classroom Management

**Planning Ahead** Prepare students to discuss family celebrations. Have them bring in family photos of holiday celebrations to display on a bulletin board. You may wish to have students create birthday greeting cards as suggested in the **Ampliación** section on page 99A as a warm-up activity for this **Etapa**. The cards can also be displayed on the bulletin board.

**Peer Teaching** Have students work in pairs to ask each other the **¿Qué ves?** questions on p. 122. Then have them prepare 2 more questions to ask another pair of students.

## Cross Cultural Connection

Ask students to describe a family celebration from their childhood. Have them describe any special family traditions they had to celebrate any particular holiday.

## Teaching Note

You might want to refer students to the new family vocabulary they learned in the last **Etapa** (p. 109).

## Culture Highlights

- **EL CUMPLEAÑOS and EL DÍA DEL SANTO** In Spain and in some Latin American countries people celebrate not only their birthday but also their **día del Santo**, or the day of the saint for whom they were named. For example, men named Juan will celebrate their saint's day on June 24 for San Juan, or people named Patricia or Patrick might celebrate March 17 as their saint's day.
- **PIÑATAS** are a popular entertainment for children's parties. They are hollow shapes, made from *papier maché* and decorated with colorful paper to form animals, stars, or other fun characters. They are filled with candy, small toys, and other treats. Children take turns being blindfolded to try to hit the **piñata** with a stick **(un palito)** to scatter all the treats for the children to gather.

## Teaching All Students

**Extra Help** Review family vocabulary by having students create a family tree on the board with all the members labeled.

**Native Speakers** Ask Spanish speakers to describe how birthdays or **días del santo** are celebrated in their culture.

**Multiple Intelligences**

**Logical/Mathematical** Have students poll the class to find out how many students have birthdays in each month. Have students chart the results.

**Visual** Have students design a **piñata** and other decorations to use in a class celebration.

## Block Schedule

**Change of Pace** Have students design an invitation in Spanish to a class birthday party.

## Teaching Resource Options

**Print** 

Unit 2 Resource Book
- Video Activities, p. 74
- Videoscript, p. 77
- Audioscript, p. 79

**Audiovisual** 

**OHT** 49, 50, 55 (Quick Start)
**Audio Program** Cassette 5A / CD 5
**Video Program** Videotape 2, 10:44 / Videodisc 1B

Search Chapter 4, Play to 5
U2E2, En contexto (Vocabulary)

**Technology** 

*Intrigas y aventuras* **CD-ROM**, Disc 1

## Quick Start Review

Preterite/reflexive verbs

Use OHT 55 or write on board: Conjugate the verbs in each sentence to complete Antonio's story about the party last night. Use the preterite.

1. Nosotros / reunirse / en la casa de Anita
2. Yo / sentarse / cerca de la prima de Anita
3. Yo / darse cuenta de / que era una chica bellísima
4. Conté chistes y ella / sonreírse
5. Pero pronto ella / despedirse / porque tenía que ir
6. Yo no / divertirse / en la fiesta

**Answers**, see p. 121B.

# En contexto

## VOCABULARIO

Mira las fotos que cuentan una historia de amor.

*Una historia de amor*

**A** En esta **historia** de **amor,** la chica (Isabel) y el chico (Ricardo) **se llevan bien.**

**B** Por eso **se enamoraron. Se casaron** y celebraron **una boda de maravilla** con mucha **felicidad.**

**C** Pasaron los años y celebraron… ¡su quinto **aniversario**!

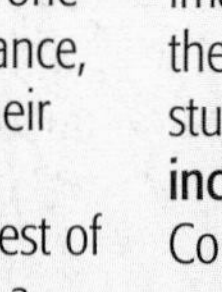



## Classroom Community

**TPR** In groups of 3, have students create a mini story of their own. The story can be about love, like the one they have just read, or about a birthday party, a dance, etc. Have the students use the preterite tense in their story. One person in the group should read the narration while the other two act it out. Have the rest of the students raise their hands each time they hear a verb in the preterite tense. Have as many groups present as time permits.

**Storytelling** «Una fiesta increíble» Have your class imagine that they planned to have a big party, but there was a problem and then it was resolved. One student begins the story: **Nosotros tuvimos una fiesta increíble...** The next person adds another sentence. Continue around the room until the last person resolves the problem.

**F** Por suerte y como es **común** después de una pelea, se dieron **un abrazo...**

**E** Fue **una reunión** muy divertida. Pero después de la fiesta **ocurrió** una pelea por **una mentira** que dijo alguien. Fue **una tristeza.**

**D** Hicieron una gran **fiesta** de aniversario. Enviaron **invitaciones** y vinieron muchas personas. También pusieron muchos **adornos,** como **globos** y **velas,** pero no piñatas. Sólo en los cumpleaños se **rompe la piñata,** no en una fiesta de aniversario.

**G** ...y se dieron **un beso.** ¡**Así fue que** terminó una verdadera historia de amor!

### Preguntas personales

1. ¿Lees historias de amor o de risa?
2. ¿Qué historias de amor conoces?
3. ¿Fuiste a una fiesta de aniversario alguna vez?
4. ¿Qué adornos tenían?
5. ¿Qué tipos de fiestas celebras?



## Teaching All Students

**Extra Help** Have students reread the story on pp. 124–125, changing the verb forms to the **nosotros** form in order to personalize the plot.

**Native Speakers** Have Spanish speakers list the occasions they celebrate in their family. If possible, have them describe a recent family celebration. Be sure to explain any cultural differences.

### Multiple Intelligences

**Interpersonal** Ask students to talk about a favorite birthday or holiday celebration with another student.

**Musical/Rhythmic** Ask students to name love songs that might match the frames of the story on pp. 124–125.

## Teaching Suggestions
### Introducing Vocabulary

- Have students look at pp. 124–125. Use OHT 49–50 and Audiocassette 5A / CD 5 to present the vocabulary.
- Introduce the characters' names and the setting: **¿La muchacha joven se llama Isabel? ¿El chico joven se llama Ricardo? ¿Son hermanos o son esposo y esposa Isabel y Ricardo? ¿Qué celebran Isabel y Ricardo?**
- Use the video vocabulary presentation for review and reinforcement.

## Comprehension Questions

1. En esta historia, ¿se llevan bien los novios? **(Sí)**
2. ¿Quiere el chico salir con muchas chicas diferentes? **(No)**
3. ¿Se enamoran? **(Sí)**
4. Cuando dos personas se casan, ¿celebran una boda? **(Sí)**
5. ¿Es una fiesta de cumpleaños o de aniversario? **(de aniversario)**
6. ¿Pusieron globos o piñatas? **(globos)**
7. ¿Fue divertida o aburrida la fiesta? **(divertida)**
8. ¿Qué ocurrió después de la fiesta? **(una pelea)**
9. ¿Por qué ocurrió la pelea? **(a causa de una mentira)**
10. ¿Qué se dieron después de la pelea? **(un abrazo y un beso)**

## Teaching Note

Have students look at pp. 124–125 and point out the uses of the reflexive verbs. You may review these verbs from Unit 2, **Etapa 1**.

## Gestures

Have students identify gestures and facial expressions that show excitement.

## Block Schedule

**Personalization** Ask students to list at least 3–4 celebrations that they have attended and rank them in order from most favorite (**más favorita**) to least favorite (**menos favorita**).

## Teaching Resource Options

**Print** 

Block Scheduling Copymasters
Unit 2 Resource Book
Video Activities, p. 75
Videoscript, pp. 77–78
Audioscript, p. 79

**Audiovisual** 

OHT 53, 54, 55 (Quick Start)
Audio Program Cassette 5A / CD 5
Video Program Videotape 2, 14:09 / Videodisc 1B

Search Chapter 5, Play to end
U2E2, En vivo (Dialog)

**Technology**

*Intrigas y aventuras* CD-ROM, Disc 1

## Quick Start Review

Preterite/**En contexto** vocabulary

Use OHT 55 or write on board: Imagine you are writing the soap opera update for your local newspaper. Tell what happened on *¡Así es la vida!* Complete each sentence by conjugating the verb in the preterite.

1. Rafael / salir / con Nina, la novia de Carlos
2. Rafael y Nina / enamorarse
3. Carlos / enojarse / con Nina y ellos / pelearse
4. La hija de Paula / volver / a casa después de diez años. Las dos / darse / un abrazo
5. Ana y Luis / celebrar / su primer aniversario pero Edgar / llegar / con malas noticias

**Answers**, see p. 121B.

# En vivo

**DIÁLOGO**

Don Miguel

Doña Regina

Isabel

Ricardo

**PARA ESCUCHAR • STRATEGY: LISTENING**

**Listen for a series of events** Enjoying a story depends on understanding what happened when. Don Miguel's story about the earthquake uses words to indicate time and sequence, and the preterite tense to tell the order of events. What expressions do you hear that help you keep track of the story's chronology?

## En la casa...

1 ▶ **Don Miguel:** Isabel, Ricardo, les presento a mi esposa, Regina.
**Doña Regina:** Es un placer.
**Isabel:** Igualmente, señora.
**Doña Regina:** Les sirvo unas limonadas, ¿no?

5 ▶ **Don Miguel:** ¿Dónde estaba?
**Isabel:** Nos contaba de la noche antes de ocurrir el temblor.
**Don Miguel:** Ah, sí, es verdad.

6 ▶ **Don Miguel:** Así fue que estuvimos juntos hasta muy tarde, y después fuimos a la casa. El temblor ocurrió a las siete y diecinueve de la mañana. Era temprano. Regina y yo estábamos durmiendo.

7 ▶ **Don Miguel:** De repente, me desperté. ¡La tierra temblaba! Un compañero mío murió.
**Isabel:** Qué tristeza. Mi familia también tiene una historia. Una prima de mi madre murió.



## Classroom Community

**Group Activity** Divide the class into 2 groups. Have members of Group 1 interview members of Group 2 about a special occasion in their lives. Then have them switch roles.

**Storytelling** Have students add more scenes (at least 3 more frames) to the **En vivo** dialog. Encourage them to include drawings to support their presentation.

**Portfolio** Ask students to write a paragraph about an event that happened to them in the past (e.g., a family celebration, a natural disaster, etc.).

**Rubric: Writing**

| Criteria | Scale |
|---|---|
| Creativity | 1 2 3 4 5 |
| Use of preterite | 1 2 3 4 5 |
| Logical organization | 1 2 3 4 5 |

A = 13–15 pts.
B = 10–12 pts.
C = 7–9 pts.
D = 4–6 pts.
F = < 4 pts.

2 ▶ **Don Miguel:** Tengo prisa porque esta noche estamos celebrando el cumpleaños de mi nieta. ¿Por qué no comenzamos la entrevista?

3 ▶ **Isabel:** Bueno, usted vivía en la Ciudad de México en el año de 1985, cuando ocurrió el temblor. ¿Me puede contar qué pasó?
**Don Miguel:** El día antes del temblor fue nuestro aniversario de boda. Esa noche nos reunimos con unos amigos.

4 ▶ **Doña Regina:** Nos llevábamos muy bien en esos días, y todavía nos llevamos bien. Tenemos mucho en común. Ricardo, ¿me haces el favor de ayudarme con los adornos?
**Ricardo:** Sí, cómo no, señora.

8 ▶ **Don Miguel:** Pero después ocurrió algo increíble, algo maravilloso. Todo el mundo respondió a la emergencia con acciones positivas. Todos ayudaban a sus vecinos.

9 ▶ **Isabel:** Voy a escribir sobre eso, sobre la solidaridad de la gente y su participación en la reconstrucción de la ciudad. Gracias, don Miguel. Creo que tengo suficiente información para empezar.

10 ▶ **Doña Regina:** ¿Nos ayudan? Estamos poniendo estos adornos. Aquí tienen los globos. Estas velas son para el pastel. Y vamos a romper una piñata.
**Isabel:** ¡Qué divertido! Va a ser una fiesta de maravilla.



## Teaching Suggestions
### Presenting the Dialog

- Prepare students for listening by focusing on the dialog context using yes/no or either/or questions.
- Use the video, audiocassette, or CD to present the dialog. The video version offers expanded language opportunities.
- Introduce the characters' names and the setting: **¿La chica joven es Isabel? ¿Qué es la relación entre don Miguel y doña Regina? ¿Qué hace Isabel con don Miguel?**

### Video Synopsis

Isabel interviews don Miguel and his wife, doña Regina, about their experiences during the 1985 earthquake in Mexico City. For a complete transcript of the video dialog, see p. 121B.

## Comprehension Questions

1. ¿Preparan una fiesta don Miguel y doña Regina? **(Sí)**
2. ¿Van a celebrar un aniversario? **(No)**
3. ¿Ocurrió el temblor en 1985? **(Sí)**
4. ¿Estaba don Miguel en una reunión el día antes del temblor? **(Sí)**
5. ¿Ocurrió el temblor a las siete de la mañana o de la noche? **(de la mañana)**
6. ¿Murió un hijo de don Miguel o un amigo? **(un amigo)**
7. ¿Cómo respondió la gente? **(con acciones positivas / todos ayudaron)**
8. ¿Sobre qué va a escribir Isabel? **(la reconstrucción de la ciudad)**
9. ¿Qué van a poner en el pastel? **(las velas)**
10. ¿Qué van a romper durante la fiesta? **(una piñata)**

## Community Connection

Ask students if they or someone they know has been in an earthquake and have them briefly explain where they were and one thing that happened.

## Teaching All Students

**Extra Help** Have students write a brief summary in Spanish about don Miguel's earthquake story.

**Challenge** Plan a Mexican birthday celebration for the class. Assign students to committees as follows: decorations, refreshments, invitations, and entertainment. Have the committees present their plans to the class for approval, then plan for the big day.

### Multiple Intelligences

**Kinesthetic** Have students imitate any gestures they recognize in the photographs. Have students look at frames 7–8 to identify the gestures that don Miguel uses when telling a story.

**Interpersonal/Verbal** Have students interview an older couple on how they met and how they celebrate their wedding anniversaries. Have students summarize their interview in Spanish for the class.

## Block Schedule

**Retention** Working in small groups, have students reread the dialog and add more information to each scene.

## Teaching Resource Options

**Print** 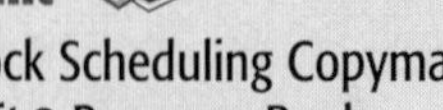

Block Scheduling Copymasters
Unit 2 Resource Book
Video Activities, p. 76
Videoscript, p. 79
Audioscript, p. 80

**Audiovisual** 

OHT 56 (Quick Start)
**Audio Program** Cassette 5A, 5B / CD 5
**Video Program** Videotape 2, 14:09 / Videodisc 1B

**Technology** 

*Intrigas y aventuras* CD-ROM, Disc 1

## Quick Start Review

Imperfect for habitual actions

Use OHT 56 or write on board: Answer the following questions about the birthday parties you used to have when you were younger. Use the imperfect in your responses.

1. ¿A quiénes invitabas a la fiesta?
2. ¿Comían ustedes pastel y helado?
3. ¿Traían regalos los invitados?
4. ¿Recibías muchos juguetes?
5. ¿Rompían ustedes una piñata?

*Answers will vary.*

## Projects

Have students research the most recent earthquakes (via Internet or at the library) in the past 10 years. How many were in Latin America? How many were in the U.S.?

**Objective:** Controlled practice
Listening comprehension/vocabulary

**Answers**

1. b
2. e
3. a
4. c
5. f
6. d

# En acción

## VOCABULARIO Y GRAMÁTICA

**OBJECTIVES**

- Narrate in the past
- Discuss family celebrations
- Talk about activities in progress

### Todo parejo

**Escuchar** Empareja las dos columnas de acuerdo con el diálogo. *(Hint: Match the columns.)*

1. Don Miguel les presentó
2. Doña Regina sirvió
3. Están celebrando
4. El día antes del temblor fue
5. Don Miguel vivía en la Ciudad de México cuando
6. El temblor ocurrió

a. un cumpleaños.
b. a su esposa, Regina.
c. el aniversario de don Miguel y su esposa.
d. a las siete y diecinueve de la mañana.
e. unas limonadas.
f. ocurrió el temblor.

**TAMBIÉN SE DICE** ¿Qué palabra usas para hablar de lo que pasa cuando la tierra tiembla? La palabra más común es **temblor,** pero en muchos países también se usa **terremoto** o, a veces, **sismo.**

### ¿Cierto o falso?

**Escuchar/Escribir** Según el diálogo, ¿son las oraciones **ciertas** o **falsas**? Si son falsas, explica por qué. *(Hint: True or false? If false, explain why.)*

1. En la casa de don Miguel celebran el aniversario de su hija.
2. Ricardo ayuda a doña Regina a preparar para la fiesta.
3. El temblor ocurrió a las siete de la tarde.
4. Don Miguel dice que todo el mundo ayudó a sus vecinos a recuperarse del temblor.
5. Don Miguel y su esposa estaban afuera cuando la tierra temblaba.
6. Isabel va a escribir sobre el temblor.
7. Isabel no tiene suficiente información para empezar su artículo.
8. En la fiesta, van a tener una piñata, unos globos y un pastel.



## Classroom Community

**Time Saver** Do **Actividades 1** and **2** orally with the class, but ask only the odd numbered questions for both. For **Actividades 3** and **4**, you may want to quickly do the first 2 or 3 questions for the class to move things along and to help them understand how the activity works.

**Peer Review/Peer Teaching** Have students work in pairs to do **Actividad 4**. Then extend the activity by having students ask their partner additional questions about what they need for a birthday party in their family.

- *Use present progressive and past progressive*
- *Use preterite and imperfect*

## Una fiesta

**Hablar** Para la fiesta de su nieta, doña Regina no tiene todo lo necesario. Mira su lista y mira la foto. Luego habla con un(a) compañero(a) de qué necesita todavía. *(Hint: Tell what she still needs.)*

**modelo**

*regalos*

**Tú:** *¿Necesita regalos?*

**Compañero(a):** *No, ya tiene regalos.*

Para la fiesta...
~~regalos~~
1. helado
2. adornos
3. globos
4. invitaciones
5. una piñata
6. el pastel

## Una reunión escolar

**Hablar/Escribir** Tú y tus compañeros(as) de la escuela se reúnen después de no verse por mucho tiempo. Contesta las preguntas que se hacen en la reunión. *(Hint: Answer these questions.)*

**modelo**

**Tú:** *Oye, Demetrio, ¿todavía eres miembro del club de deportes?*

**Compañero:** *Antes era miembro, pero ya no.*

1. Oye, Dolores, ¿todavía sales con Salvador?
2. Oye, Juan Manuel, ¿todavía vives en la calle 18?
3. Oye, Ernesto, ¿todavía te gusta la comida mexicana?
4. Oye, Adriana, ¿todavía vas de vacaciones a Valle del Bravo?
5. Oye, Claudia, ¿todavía practicas deportes?
6. Oye, Jorge, ¿todavía vas a clases de artes marciales?
7. Oye, Daniel, ¿todavía estudias en el colegio americano?
8. Oye, Mónica, ¿todavía das clases de inglés?



## Teaching All Students

**Extra Help** Have students identify the frame from pp. 126–127 that completes the phrases in the left column of **Actividad 1**.

**Multiple Intelligences**

**Verbal** Have students add at least 4 more examples to **Actividad 4** in which they ask their classmate if he or she still does some type of activity. Classmate responds: **Antes sí, pero ya no...**

**Interpersonal** Have students work with a partner to talk about an activity that they still like to do, e.g., **Todavía me gusta nadar.**

**Logical/Mathematical** Have students estimate the costs for hosting a friend's birthday party. They should list the items needed and their estimated costs.

**Objective:** Controlled practice
Listening comprehension/vocabulary

**Answers**
1. Falso. Celebran el cumpleaños de su nieta.
2. Cierto.
3. Falso. Ocurrió a las siete de la mañana.
4. Cierto.
5. Falso. Estaban durmiendo en su casa.
6. Falso. Va a escribir sobre la solidaridad de la gente.
7. Falso. Tiene suficiente información.
8. Cierto.

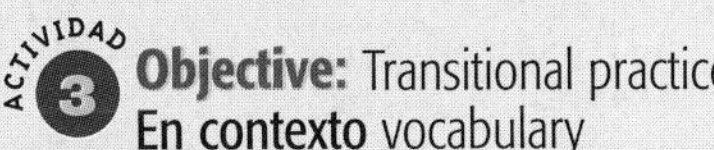

**Objective:** Transitional practice
**En contexto** vocabulary

**Answers**
1. ¿Necesita helado? Sí, necesita helado.
2. ¿Necesita adornos? No, ya tiene adornos.
3. ¿Necesita globos? Sí, necesita globos.
4. ¿Necesita invitaciones? Sí, necesita invitaciones.
5. ¿Necesita una piñata? No, ya tiene una piñata.
6. ¿Necesita el pastel? Sí, necesita el pastel.

**Objective:** Transitional practice
Imperfect tense

Imperfect for habitual actions

**Answers**
1. Antes salía con Salvador, pero ya no.
2. Antes vivía en la calle 18, pero ya no.
3. Antes me gustaba, pero ya no.
4. Antes iba de vacaciones a Valle del Bravo, pero ya no.
5. Antes practicaba deportes, pero ya no.
6. Antes iba a clases de artes marciales, pero ya no.
7. Antes estudiaba en el Colegio Americano, pero ya no.
8. Antes daba clases de inglés, pero ya no.

## Cross Cultural Connection

Ask students to brainstorm for 2 minutes about items they would need for planning a friend's birthday party, then compare and contrast with the preparations don Miguel and doña Regina make.

## Language Note

Another word for **adornos** is **arreglos**. The word **decoraciones** refers to a more general concept of decor. In Mexico, ice cream is often called **nieve** instead of **helado**.

## Block Schedule

**Change of Pace** Place 8–10 objects on a desk. Have students model **Actividad 3** by asking each other if they have the objects displayed. For example, S1 says: **¿Necesitas** [object]? and S2 responds: **No, ya tengo** [object].

## Teaching Resource Options

**Print**

*Más práctica* Workbook PE, pp. 53–54
*Cuaderno para hispanohablantes* PE, pp. 51–52
Block Scheduling Copymasters
Unit 2 Resource Book
*Más práctica* Workbook TE, pp. 56–57
*Cuaderno para hispanohablantes* TE, pp. 62–63

**Audiovisual**

OHT 56 (Quick Start)

**Technology**

*Intrigas y aventuras* CD-ROM, Disc 1

## Quick Start Review

**Present tense of estar**

Use OHT 56 or write on board: Form 4 sentences using a word from each group below. Conjugate the verb **estar** in the present tense.

| | | |
|---|---|---|
| Cecilia | estar | en clase |
| los niños | | en el parque |
| papá | | en la reunión |
| tú | | en la oficina |
| nosotros | | en casa |

Now write 5 sentences telling where members of your family are right now.

**Answers**, see p. 121B.

## Teaching Suggestions
### Presenting the Progressive Tenses

- Remind students that the progressive tense is used more often in English than in Spanish. Spanish also uses the present tense to express an action that is going on right now.
- Write a list of familiar verbs on the board and have students form the present participle. For example, **llevar, celebrar, pasar, estudiar, comer,** etc.
- With the whole class, write a list of things that are occurring at the present moment using the progressive tense. For example, **La profesora está hablando. Los estudiantes están escuchando. Estamos estudiando los verbos.**

ACTIVIDAD 5

### Reacciones

**Hablar** En grupos, hablen de cómo respondiste en las siguientes situaciones. *(Hint: Tell how you responded.)*

**modelo**

*…sacaste una mala nota?*

**Compañero(a):** *¿Cómo respondiste la última vez que sacaste una mala nota?*

**Tú:** *Me sentí mal.*

reírse | sentirse | aburrirse | esconderse | divertirse

¿Cómo respondiste la última vez que…

1. …viste una película en el cine?
2. …leíste las tiras cómicas?
3. …tu equipo favorito perdió un partido?
4. …fuiste a una fiesta?
5. …hiciste mucha tarea?
6. …ganaste un juego?

GRAMÁTICA

## The Progressive Tenses

Remember that you form the **present progressive** by using

the **present tense of estar** + **-ando**, **-iendo**/**-yendo** forms

To make these forms, drop the ending of the infinitive and add **-ando** or **-iendo**/**-yendo**.

*becomes*

| | |
|---|---|
| **hablar** | **hablando** |
| **comer** | **comiendo** |
| **escribir** | **escribiendo** |
| **leer** | **leyendo** |

When the stem of an **-er** or **-ir** verb ends in a **vowel,** there is a spelling change in the ending.

Remember that some **-ir** stem-changing verbs have a stem vowel change.

**pedir** → **pidiendo**
**dormir** → **durmiendo**

The progressive can also be used in the past. To form the **past progressive,** use

the **imperfect tense of estar** + **-ando**, **-iendo**/**-yendo** forms

When do you use the progressive tenses? You only use them for an action that is actually going on at the time of the sentence.

**Present Progressive**

Isabel **está hablando** con don Miguel.
*Isabel **is talking** with Don Miguel.*

**Past Progressive**

Isabel **estaba escribiendo** un artículo sobre el temblor.
*Isabel **was writing** an article about the earthquake.*

## Classroom Community

**Paired Activity** Using the reflexive verbs in **Actividad 5**, have students work in pairs to share a time when something happened to them, e.g., **Me enojé cuando mi hermano salió de casa...**

**Portfolio** Have students write a short description of what is happening in their school (in their town, in the U.S., in the world, etc.) at the present time. Have them consult a newspaper or a news program to get more global information.

**Rubric: Writing**

| Criteria | Scale |
|---|---|
| Correct sentence structure | 1 2 3 4 5 |
| Creativity | 1 2 3 4 5 |
| Logical organization | 1 2 3 4 5 |

A = 13–15 pts.
B = 10–12 pts.
C = 7–9 pts.
D = 4–6 pts.
F = < 4 pts.

## Un reportaje del temblor

**Hablar/Escribir** Un reportero hizo un reportaje de radio durante el temblor de 1985. Completa su descripción con el presente progresivo. *(Hint: Complete the report using the present progressive.)*

**modelo**

*la policía/ayudar a la gente*

*La policía está ayudando a la gente.*

1. yo / recibir los detalles todavía
2. los oficiales / investigar los efectos del temblor
3. la gente / buscar a sus parientes y amigos y otros / limpiar la devastación
4. nosotros / reportar que hubo un temblor en la capital
5. tú / escuchar las noticias de la estación 710

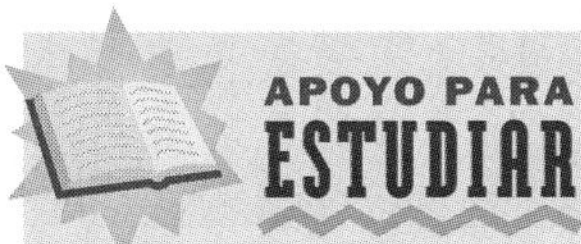

APOYO PARA ESTUDIAR

**The Progressive Tenses**

These verb tenses are similar in English. Remember to use the form of **estar** that fits the subject plus the **-ando** or **-iendo/-yendo** form of the verb. If you want to use **no**, where does it go? Place it before **estar.** For a very strange broadcast, make all of the sentences negative: **La policía no está ayudando a la gente.**

ACTIVIDAD 7 Gramática

## Muchos años después

**Hablar/Escribir** Ahora, muchos años después, el mismo reportero describe aquella noche. Completa su descripción con el imperfecto progresivo. *(Hint: Complete the report using the past progressive.)*

**modelo**

*la mayoría de las familias / dormir*

*La mayoría de las familias estaba durmiendo.*

1. la tierra / temblar
2. para empezar, no sabíamos qué / pasar, pero momentos después, nosotros / exclamar que hubo un temblor
3. nosotros / salir de las casas
4. aunque tenían miedo, muchos valientes / rescatar a gente atrapada
5. yo / escribir el reportaje para informar a todo el mundo

### Vocabulario

Cuando charlas...

**aunque** *even though*
**exclamar** *to exclaim*
**la mayoría** *majority*
**mientras** *while*
**para empezar** *to begin with*
**todo el mundo** *everyone*

¿Cuáles de estas palabras usas en tus conversaciones?

**MÁS PRÁCTICA** *cuaderno* pp. 53–54

**PARA HISPANOHABLANTES** *cuaderno* pp. 51–52

**Objective:** Transitional practice
Reflexive verbs

Preterite

*Answers will vary. Sentences should be in the preterite.*

**Objective:** Controlled practice
Present progressive

**Answers**

1. Yo estoy recibiendo los detalles todavía.
2. Los oficiales están investigando los efectos del temblor.
3. La gente está buscando a sus parientes y amigos y otros están limpiando la devastación.
4. Nosotros estamos reportando que hubo un temblor en la capital.
5. Tú estás escuchando las noticias de la estación 710.

**Objective:** Controlled practice
Past progressive

**Answers**

1. La tierra estaba temblando.
2. Para empezar, no sabíamos qué estaba pasando, pero momentos después, nosotros estábamos exclamando que hubo un temblor.
3. Nosotros estábamos saliendo de las casas.
4. Aunque tenían miedo, muchos valientes estaban rescatando a gente atrapada.
5. Yo estaba escribiendo el reportaje para informar a todo el mundo.

### Quick Wrap-up

Ask students to imagine what people are doing at this moment.

¿Qué está haciendo...
...tu abuela?
...tus padres?
...Alejandro Romero? (pintar)
...Cristian Castro? (cantar)

Continue with people familiar to students.

## Teaching All Students

**Extra Help** Have students list 3 activities that they are presently doing, e.g., **Estoy...** Then have them list 3 activities that classmates were just doing **(Estaban...)**.

**Multiple Intelligences**

**Verbal** Have students take turns stating things that are NOT happening at the present time. Continue around classroom and have each student add a new activity.

**Kinesthetic** Ask a student to act out an activity and then have the class try to guess what s/he is doing, e.g., **Ella está escribiendo.**

**Logical/Mathematical** Have students brainstorm activities for each hour of the day using the present progressive tense. **A las 7:00 nos estamos levantando, a las 8:00 estamos desayunando**, etc.

## Block Schedule

**Change of Pace** Go back to all the **Etapa** openers and have students describe what is happening in each photo using the present progressive tense. See pp. 28–29, 50–51, 72–73, 100–101, and 122–123. Use additional photos if desired.

## Teaching Resource Options

**Print**

Block Scheduling Copymasters
Unit 2 Resource Book
Audioscript, p. 80
Information Gap Activities, p. 68

**Audiovisual**

OHT 56 (Quick Start)
Audio Program Cassette 5A, 5B / CD 5

**Technology**

*Intrigas y aventuras* CD-ROM, Disc 1

## Quick Start Review

**Tener** expressions

Use OHT 56 or write on board: Fill in the blank with the name of the correct person based on the information you are given.

El bebé estaba llorando.
Elena trabajaba mucho. Vendió más casas que todos en su oficina.
Mateo cuidaba bien a los niños. No quería accidentes.
Carlos estaba muy ocupado y no le compró un regalo a su madre.
Ana ganó el campeonato de ciclismo. Maribel llegó segunda.

1. ______ tenía vergüenza.
2. ______ tenía hambre.
3. ______ tenía envidia.
4. ______ tenía cuidado.
5. ______ tenía éxito.

**Answers**, see p. 121B.

ACTIVIDAD 8

### Muchas emociones

**Escuchar/Escribir** Escucha estas seis descripciones del temblor de 1985. Decide si la persona expresa tristeza o felicidad. Luego escribe sobre un momento de tristeza o de felicidad en tu vida. *(Hint: Is each person sad or happy? What about you?)*

NOTA CULTURAL

**La piñata**

*No quiero oro*
*ni quiero plata,*
*yo lo que quiero,*
*es romper la piñata.*

La historia de la piñata es muy antigua —¡algunos dicen que Marco Polo la trajo desde China! Luego los españoles la trajeron a México. Una cosa sí es segura: donde hay una piñata, hay fiesta. Antes, la gente hacía las piñatas cubriendo una olla de barro (*clay*). Hoy en día, las hacen de cartón. Adentro, les ponen dulces y sorpresas.

ACTIVIDAD 9

### ¡Sorpresa!

**PARA CONVERSAR** • **STRATEGY: SPEAKING**

**Brainstorm to get ideas** In your group, brainstorm to get lots of ideas about what you might do for a surprise party. See how long a list you can make. You can be serious or silly; just be in Spanish! Then take turns saying what your tasks will be.

**Hablar** Tú y un grupo de compañeros(as) quieren sorprender a un(a) amigo(a) para su cumpleaños. Usen el presente progresivo y estas expresiones para explicar qué están haciendo. *(Hint: What are you doing?)*

**velas**
**piñata**
**invitaciones**
**pastel**
**adornos**

**modelo**

**Compañero(a):** *Para el cumpleaños, ¿qué estás haciendo?*
**Tú:** *Primero estoy limpiando la casa. Segundo…*

**MÁS COMUNICACIÓN** p. R6

### Vocabulario

**¿Qué haces?**

**la sorpresa** *surprise* **sorprender** *to surprise*

**Números ordinales**

| | | |
|---|---|---|
| **primero(a)** *first* | **quinto(a)** *fifth* | **octavo(a)** *eighth* |
| **segundo(a)** *second* | **sexto(a)** *sixth* | **noveno(a)** *ninth* |
| **tercero(a)** *third* | **séptimo(a)** *seventh* | **décimo(a)** *tenth* |
| **cuarto(a)** *fourth* | | |



## Classroom Community

**Group Activity** Cut up blank paper into narrow strips. Give each group of students 5 strips. Then, have students write a series of 5 activities that they do on a regular basis on the slips of paper using the vocabulary from p. 133. The groups then collect and shuffle strips and exchange their strips with another group. Each group logically sequences the events and reads them aloud to verify sequential order.

**TPR** Line 10 students up in a row and have them identify their place in line. (e.g., **Soy el primer estudiante, María es la segunda**, etc.)

**Game** **¿Quién está haciendo esto?** A student looks around room and describes what another student is doing, e.g., **Él está leyendo un libro**. The class then tries to identify the person.

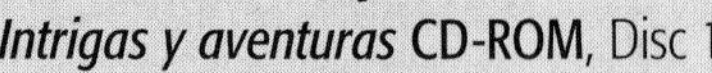

## Un sábado típico

**Hablar/Escribir** Roberto tiene la misma rutina casi todos los sábados. Mira las fotos y el reloj para decir qué está haciendo a cada hora. Exprésate usando el presente progresivo y las palabras útiles. Luego escribe lo que tú estabas haciendo a esas horas el sábado pasado. Usa el imperfecto progresivo. *(Hint: Tell what Roberto was doing. What were you doing?)*

**modelo**

*Por la mañana, Roberto está durmiendo. Son las siete…*
*A las siete, yo estaba…*

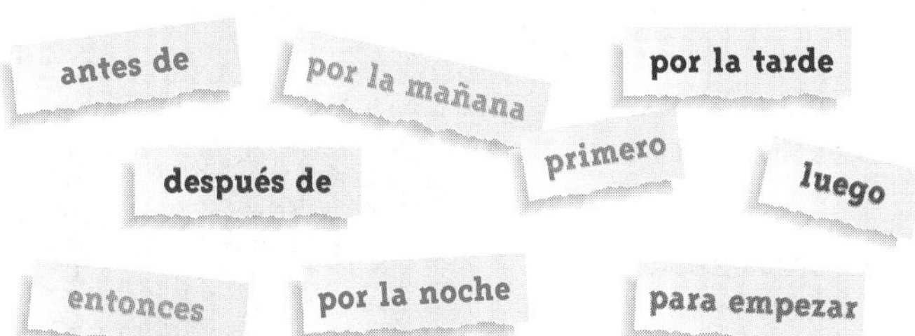


### Vocabulario

**Tus ideas**

- **al contrario** *on the contrary*
- **casi** *almost*
- **diario** *daily*
- **en seguida** *at once*
- **los demás** *the rest of the people*
- **por fin** *finally*
- **siguiente** *next*

¿Cuáles de estas palabras usas para contar una historia?

1. 9:00 de la mañana

2. 10:00

3. 11:00

4. 2:00

5. 5:00

6. 9:30 de la noche



### Teaching Suggestions
#### Presenting Ordinal Numbers

- Remind students that ordinal numbers agree in gender and number with the noun they modify. Also, **primero** and **tercero** are shortened to **primer** and **tercer** before masculine singular nouns.
- Have students list their daily class schedule in order. (e.g., **Mi primera clase es..., mi segunda clase es...**)

**Objective:** Open-ended practice
Listening comprehension/expressing emotions

**Answers** (See script, p. 121B)

1. Expresa tristeza.
2. Expresa felicidad.
3. Expresa felicidad.
4. Expresa tristeza.
5. Expresa tristeza.
6. Expresa felicidad.

**Objective:** Open-ended practice
Talking about activities in progress

**Answers**

*Answers will vary but should use the vocabulary provided and the present progressive.*

### Teaching Note

Review the vocabulary for telling time before doing **Actividad 10**.

**Objective:** Open-ended practice
Talking about activities in progress

Telling time

**Answers**

1. Son las nueve de la mañana. Roberto se está levantando.
2. Son las diez. Roberto está desayunando (comiendo). Está leyendo el periódico por la mañana.
3. Son las once. Roberto está trabajando en el jardín por la mañana.
4. Son las dos. Entonces Roberto está comiendo con la familia.
5. Son las cinco. Roberto está hablando por teléfono. Está escuchando música por la tarde.
6. Son las nueve y media de la noche. Roberto está entrando al cine con sus amigos.

### Teaching All Students

**Extra Help** Change Roberto's daily routine to the imperfect progressive in **Actividad 10** to describe last Saturday.

**Native Speakers** Have Spanish speakers give their daily schedule with time and activity following the model in **Actividad 10**. After Spanish speakers have given their daily schedules, have other students volunteer to give their schedules.

**Multiple Intelligences**

**Intrapersonal** In small groups, have students describe their dreams using the present progressive tense, e.g., **Yo estoy viajando por el mundo...**

**Visual** Have students cut out pictures of people in action from magazines, then describe each picture using the present progressive.

### Block Schedule

**Variety** Have students create a page in their "daily planner" as an activity to practice times and corresponding activities. They can describe the present day using the present progressive and describe a day in the past using the imperfect progressive.

## Teaching Resource Options

**Print** 

*Más práctica* Workbook PE, pp. 55–56
*Cuaderno para hispanohablantes* PE, pp. 53–54
Block Scheduling Copymasters
Unit 2 Resource Book
*Más práctica* Workbook TE, pp. 58–59
*Cuaderno para hispanohablantes* TE, pp. 64–65

**Audiovisual** 

OHT 57 (Quick Start)

**Technology** 

*Intrigas y aventuras* CD-ROM, Disc 1

## Quick Start Review

Preterite/imperfect

Use OHT 57 or write on board: Write the full conjugation of each verb in both the preterite and the imperfect.

| | |
|---|---|
| comer | dormir (o→ue) |
| ir | hablar |

**Answers**
Use the verb charts on pp. R27–R33 to check answers.

## Teaching Suggestions

### Presenting the Preterite and the Imperfect

- Refer students back to pp. 36, 38, 40, 61, 84, 112 to review the formation and uses of the preterite and the imperfect.
- For a visual representation of the preterite vs. the imperfect, draw several vertical lines and identify the first and last as **pasado** and **presente**. Then draw a wavy line from **presente** through **pasado** along the chalkboard. The preterite is represented by the vertical lines that begin and end at a specific moment in time; the imperfect is represented by the continuous wavy lines.
- Remind students that the imperfect is also used to indicate emotion.

GRAMÁTICA

## Talk About the Past Using the Preterite and the Imperfect

**¿RECUERDAS?** *pp. 36, 112* Now you know the two verb forms used for the past tense—the **preterite** and the **imperfect**. Let's look at how each is used.

The **preterite** tells you about an action that started and ended at a definite time.

- **Ocurrió** un temblor.
  *An earthquake* ***took place.***
- El temblor **ocurrió** a las 7:19 de la mañana.
  *The earthquake* ***took place*** *at 7:19 in the morning.*
- Muchos edificios **se cayeron.**
  *Many buildings* ***fell down.***

The earthquake started and ended.

The **imperfect** tells about past actions without saying when they begin or end.

- Todo el mundo **dormía.**
  *Everybody* ***was sleeping.***
- La tierra **temblaba.**
  *The earth* ***was shaking.***
- **Había** gente por todas partes.
  ***There were*** *people everywhere.*

The sentences don't tell you when the action started and ended.

You use both tenses to talk about something that happened **(preterite)** while something else was going on **(imperfect)**.

**Nos enamoramos.**
***We fell in love.***

**Éramos** jóvenes.
***We were*** *young.*

**Nos enamoramos** cuando **éramos** jóvenes.
***We fell in love*** *when* ***we were*** *young.*

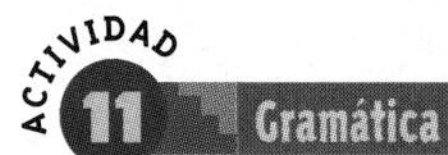

ACTIVIDAD 11 Gramática

### Durante las vacaciones

**Escribir** Escribe lo que pasó durante unas vacaciones en la Ciudad de México. Usa el pretérito, el imperfecto y la palabra **mientras.**
*(Hint: Write what happened.)*

**modelo**

*tú: caminar → encontrarse con unos amigos*
*Mientras caminabas, te encontraste con unos amigos.*

1. yo: almorzar → terminar un libro
2. Emilia: ir de compras → comer un taco
3. ustedes: caminar → ver un pájaro bonito
4. nosotros: leer revistas → oír el teléfono
5. tú: comer → haber un accidente
6. las niñas: almorzar → empezar a llover



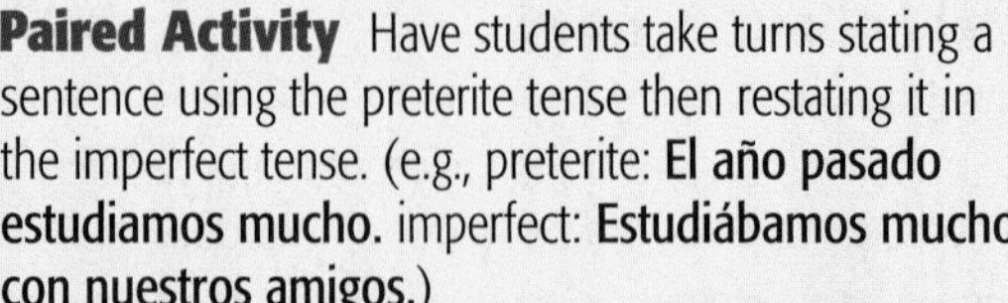

## Classroom Community

**Paired Activity** Have students take turns stating a sentence using the preterite tense then restating it in the imperfect tense. (e.g., preterite: **El año pasado estudiamos mucho.** imperfect: **Estudiábamos mucho con nuestros amigos.**)

**Learning Scenario** Refer back to **«Una historia de amor»** on pp. 124–125 and have students explain why the verbs are in the preterite. Have them rewrite the story using the imperfect. Add words to show that the actions are continuous without referring to a beginning or end.

**Storytelling** Refer back to **Unidad 2 Etapa 2** Opener (pp. 122–123). Have students write a short creative story on what took place in the pictures, using both imperfect and preterite tenses.

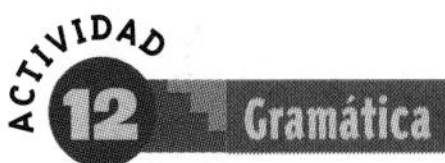

## ¡Feliz aniversario!

**Leer/Escribir** Mateo recibió buenas noticias. Completa la historia con las formas correctas de los verbos para saber las noticias. *(Hint: Choose the correct forms of the verbs.)*

El sábado por la noche Mateo y su esposa María __1__ (celebraron / celebraban) su aniversario cuando Mateo __2__ (sorprendió / sorprendía) a María. Ellos __3__ (ganaron / ganaban) la lotería. ¡Qué sorpresa! __4__ (Estuvieron / Estaban) muy alegres. El día siguiente Mateo __5__ (se dio / se daba) cuenta de que se __6__ (perdió / perdía) el boleto. —Lo siento, mi amor —le __7__ (dijo / decía) con tristeza a su esposa. Pero María __8__ (quiso / quería) investigar un poco más. __9__ (Fue / Era) cuando lo __10__ (encontró / encontraba) debajo de la cama. Esta vez María __11__ (sorprendió / sorprendía) a su esposo. Aquella noche __12__ (celebraron / celebraban) con una cena en un restaurante elegante. Luego __13__ (fueron / iban) al teatro. __14__ (Se divirtieron / Se divertían) muchísimo.

**MÁS PRÁCTICA** *cuaderno* pp. 55–56

**PARA HISPANOHABLANTES** *cuaderno* pp. 53–54

## Unas actividades

**Hablar** Las actividades de Isabel y sus amigos(as) cambian de un día para otro. Explica lo que hacían antes y lo que hicieron ayer. *(Hint: Tell what they used to do and what they did yesterday.)*

**modelo**

*Ricardo: pasar mucho tiempo en Internet*

**Compañero(a):** *¿Qué hacía Ricardo antes?*

**Tú:** *Pasaba mucho tiempo en Internet.*

**Compañero(a):** *¿Qué hizo ayer?*

**Tú:** *Al contrario, ayer no pasó mucho tiempo en Internet.*

1. Tú: olvidar la tarea
2. Isabel y tú: visitar el Museo Nacional de Antropología
3. Juana: no decir la verdad
4. Tú: contar chistes malos
5. Mi prima: dormir hasta muy tarde
6. Ustedes: asistir a clases

**El Museo Nacional de Antropología** en el Bosque de Chapultepec contiene miles de artefactos de las culturas indígenas de México. Uno de los objetos más conocidos del museo es la Piedra del Sol, un enorme calendario azteca.

**Objective:** Controlled practice
Preterite and imperfect

**Answers**

1. Mientras yo almorzaba, terminé un libro.
2. Mientras Emilia iba de compras, comió un taco.
3. Mientras ustedes caminaban, vieron un pájaro bonito.
4. Mientras nosotros leíamos revistas, oímos el teléfono.
5. Mientras tú comías, hubo un accidente.
6. Mientras las niñas almorzaban, empezó a llover.

**Objective:** Controlled practice
Preterite vs. imperfect

**Answers**

1. celebraban
2. sorprendió
3. ganaron
4. Estaban
5. se dio
6. perdió
7. dijo
8. quiso
9. Fue
10. encontró
11. sorprendió
12. celebraron
13. fueron
14. Se divirtieron

**Objective:** Transitional practice
Preterite vs. imperfect

**Answers**

1. ¿Qué hacías tú antes? Olvidaba mi tarea. ¿Qué hiciste ayer? Al contrario, ayer no olvidé mi tarea.
2. ¿Qué hacían Isabel y tú antes? Visitábamos el Museo Nacional de Antropología. ¿Qué hicieron ayer? ... ayer no visitamos el Museo Nacional de Antropología.
3. ¿Qué hacía Juana antes? No decía la verdad. ¿Qué hizo ayer? ... ayer dijo la verdad.
4. ¿Qué hacías tú antes? Contaba chistes malos. ¿Qué hiciste ayer? ... ayer no conté chistes malos (ayer conté chistes buenos).
5. ¿Qué hacía mi prima antes? Dormía hasta muy tarde. ¿Qué hizo ayer? ... ayer no durmió hasta muy tarde.
6. ¿Qué hacían ustedes antes? Asistíamos a clases. ¿Qué hicieron ayer? ... ayer no asistimos a clases.

## Teaching All Students

**Extra Help** Tell students to refer back to **En vivo Diálogo** (pp. 126–127) and with a partner categorize the verbs as follows: present, present progressive, imperfect, preterite, infinitive.

**Native Speakers** Ask Spanish speakers to describe a family celebration with special attention to the use of the preterite and the imperfect.

**Multiple Intelligences**

**Verbal** Working in small groups, the first student states a sentence in the present tense about a family gathering. The second student restates the sentence in the preterite. The third student restates it in the imperfect.

## Block Schedule

**Variety** Have students bring a picture of a favorite family event that they remember well. Have them share the picture and memories with others in small groups.

## Teaching Resource Options

**Print** 

*Más práctica* Workbook PE, pp. 49–52
*Cuaderno para hispanohablantes* PE, pp. 49–50
Block Scheduling Copymasters
Unit 2 Resource Book
*Más práctica* Workbook TE, pp. 52–55
*Cuaderno para hispanohablantes* TE, pp. 60–61
Audioscript, pp. 80–82
Information Gap Activities, p. 69

**Audiovisual** 

OHT 57 (Quick Start)
Audio Program Cassette 5A, 5B / CD 5; (*Para hispanohablantes* Cassette 5B / CD 5)

**Technology**

*Intrigas y aventuras* CD-ROM, Disc 1

## Quick Start Review

Preterite for completed actions

Use OHT 57 or write on board: Write down four things you did yesterday. Use the preterite tense. Here are some verbs to get started:

| | |
|---|---|
| ir | jugar |
| estudiar | mirar |
| escribir | comprar |
| hablar | |

*Answers will vary.*

## Teaching Suggestions

- Review the vocabulary for dates, months of the year, etc. and have students give the date of their birthdays.
- This might also be a good opportunity to have students make birthday greeting cards in Spanish as suggested in the **Ampliación** section on p. 99A.
- As a follow-up to **Actividad 14**, have students present their own agendas for the past week and how they felt about each activity.

## Un mes ocupado

**Hablar/Leer** Isabel escribió cinco actividades en su calendario. Habla de dónde fue y adivina cómo se sentía allí. Usa la lista para encontrar ideas. *(Hint: Talk about where Isabel was and how she probably felt.)*

modelo

**Tú:** *¿Cuál fue su primera actividad?*
**Compañero(a):** *Su primera actividad fue ir al dentista.*
**Tú:** *¿Cómo se sentía?*
**Compañero(a):** *Probablemente se sentía nerviosa.*

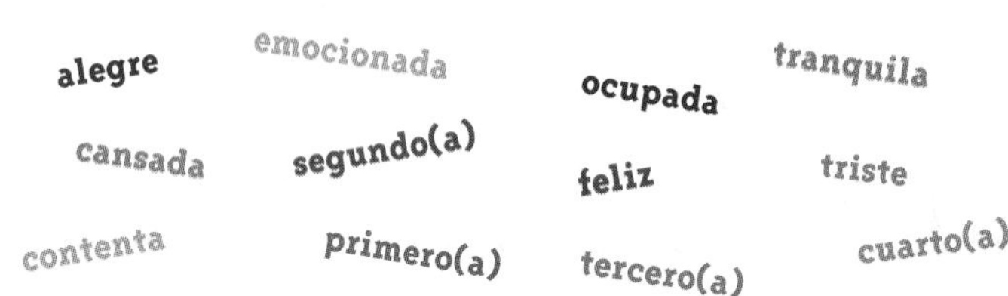

septiembre
7 lunes
el dentista 3:30
8 martes
aniversario de mis abuelos
9 miércoles
reuni n en la escuela 7:00
10 jueves
examen de c lculo
11 viernes
12 sábado
boda de Carlos y Victoria
13 domingo

## Unas celebraciones

**Escuchar/Hablar** Tres personas fueron a varias celebraciones. Escucha sus descripciones. Luego di a qué celebración asistió cada persona. Después descríbele a un grupo de compañeros(as) tuyos(as) una celebración a la que tú asististe. *(Hint: Decide which type of celebration these people attended. Then talk about a celebration that you attended.)*

- una fiesta de graduación
- una fiesta de cumpleaños
- una boda
- una reunión del décimo aniversario de graduación
- una fiesta de Navidad
- una reunión familiar



## Classroom Community

**Portfolio** Have students write in their journal about how they spent last weekend, using both the imperfect and preterite tenses.

**Rubric: Writing**

| Criteria | Scale |
|---|---|
| Verb conjugation | 1 2 3 4 5 |
| Logical organization | 1 2 3 4 5 |
| Vocabulary use | 1 2 3 4 5 |

A = 13–15 pts.
B = 10–12 pts.
C = 7–9 pts.
D = 4–6 pts.
F = < 4 pts.

**Storytelling** Working with groups of 10 students, the first student begins a story with **Primero...**; the second student continues story with **Segundo...**; continue until the 10th person concludes the story.

**Cooperative Learning** In groups of 3, students create a story describing what an imaginary student did last weekend. All students contribute at least one activity in the preterite. Student 1 = recorder, Student 2 = proofreader, Student 3 = narrator.

## Dibujos

**Hablar** Haz cuatro dibujos de algo que te pasó durante algunos de estos períodos de tiempo: el año pasado, anteayer, ayer y anoche. Luego muéstrale los dibujos a un grupo de compañeros(as) y descríbeselos usando el pretérito y el imperfecto. *(Hint: Make and describe four simple drawings.)*

**modelo**

**Tú:** *Anoche, mientras trabajaba en un restaurante de comida rápida, mis amigos me hicieron una visita y pidieron batidos.*

### Vocabulario

**El pasado**

**anoche** *last night*
**anteayer** *day before yesterday*
**el año pasado** *last year*
**ayer** *yesterday*

¿Cuándo tuviste mucha tarea?

## Tu mejor amigo(a)

**Hablar/Escribir** Tú no viste a tu mejor amigo(a) por una semana entera. Ahora le tienes que decir exactamente lo que hiciste. Haz una lista de todo lo que hiciste, siguiendo el modelo. Luego comparte los detalles de tu semana con tu amigo(a), usando las palabras útiles cuando sea necesario. *(Hint: Make a list of everything you did this week. Then share it with a friend.)*

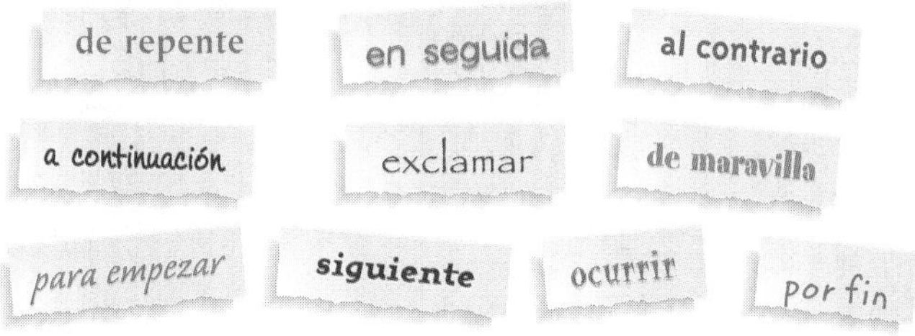


| lunes | martes | miércoles | jueves |
|---|---|---|---|
| 8:00 a.m. ir a la escuela<br>4:00 p.m. dar clases de natación<br>6:00 p.m. cenar en casa de Bobby | 8:00 a.m. ir a la escuela<br>4:00 p.m. dar clases de natación<br>6:00 p.m. cenar con mis papás<br>7:00 p.m. ir al cine | 9:00 a.m. llegar tarde a la escuela<br>4:00 p.m. dar clases de natación<br>7:00 p.m. salir a una reunión del club | 8:00 a.m. |

**MÁS COMUNICACIÓN** p. R6

### Refrán

**Colorín, colorado, este cuento se ha acabado.**

Este refrán se usa al final de un cuento para decir «El cuento se termina». Haz un cuento y preséntaselo a tus compañeros(as) de clase. Al final, usa el refrán.

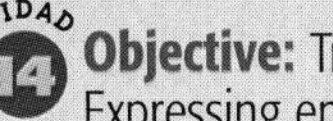

**Objective:** Transitional practice
Expressing emotions

Ordinal numbers

**Answers**

1. ¿Cuál fue su segunda actividad? Su segunda actividad fue el aniversario de sus abuelos. ¿Cómo se sentía? Probablemente se sentía (alegre, contenta, emocionada, feliz).
2. Su tercera actividad fue una reunión en la escuela. ... Probablemente se sentía (cansada, ocupada).
3. Su cuarta actividad fue un examen de cálculo. ... Probablemente se sentía (tranquila, nerviosa).
4. Su quinta actividad fue la boda de Carlos y Victoria. ... Probablemente se sentía (alegre, contenta, emocionada, feliz).

**Objective:** Open-ended practice
Listening comprehension

**Answers** (See script, p. 121B)

1. Estuvo en una reunión del décimo aniversario de su graduación.
2. Estuvo en una boda.
3. Estuvo en una fiesta de cumpleaños.

**Objective:** Open-ended practice
Preterite and imperfect

*Answers will vary.*

**Objective:** Open-ended practice
Preterite and imperfect

*Answers will vary.*

### Supplementary Vocabulary

**la semana pasada** last week
**el mes pasado** last month
**los días de la semana**
**lunes**
**martes**
**miércoles**
**jueves**
**viernes**
**sábado**
**domingo**

### Teaching All Students

**Extra Help** Have students make a time line (either on the board or on a piece of paper) and put the following time expressions in logical order from least to most recent: **el año pasado, el mes pasado, ayer, anteayer, la semana pasada, mañana, hoy.**

**Multiple Intelligences**

**Verbal** Read aloud 2 sentences and ask the class to decide which sentence probably came first, e.g., **Me desperté a las 9:00.** or **Desayuné un poco de cereal.**

### Block Schedule

**"Plan B"** Have students draw a weekly calendar and fill in each day with the activities offered at school. Each day should have a different activity planned.

### Teaching Resource Options

**Print**

*Cuaderno para hispanohablantes* PE, pp. 55–56
Unit 2 Resource Book
*Cuaderno para hispanohablantes* TE, pp. 66–67

**Audiovisual**

**OHT** 57 (Quick Start)

### Quick Start Review

**Hay**/circumlocution

Use OHT 57 or write on board: Describe what you see in the photos of Mexico City on pp. 138–139. If you do not know the exact word in Spanish, use several words you do know to describe what you mean. Write at least 4 sentences.

*Answers will vary.*

### Teaching Suggestions
**Presenting En colores**

- **Prereading** Ask students to guess the topic of the cultural section. Write the list of possibilities on the board.
- Activate students' background knowledge by asking them to discuss what they know about earthquakes or natural disasters.
- **Video** Use the video to expand and enrich the cultural information.

**Reading Strategy**
**Activate Prior Knowledge**

- Ask students to think about news reports they may have seen or read that dealt with an earthquake. Ask them to list the topics that are generally in these types of news reports. Also remind them to review the **¿Comprendiste?** questions first before starting the reading.
- **Post-reading** Ask students what would happen in their area if an earthquake occurred. What kind of damage might there be? How do you think people might react?

# *En colores*
**CULTURA Y COMPARACIONES**

# ¡Temblor!

**PARA CONOCERNOS**

**STRATEGY: CONNECTING CULTURES**

**Observe and generalize** Think of a disaster that you have seen or heard about. How do you think people generally behave at such a time? Make a chart like the one below to show what you have personally observed or what you have read about the actions of people in a particular disaster.

| Desastre | Buenas acciones | Malas acciones |
|---|---|---|
| Temblor de 1985 | La gente se ayuda. | |
| | solidaridad | |

El 19 de septiembre de 1985, a las 7:19 de la mañana el suelo tembló por un minuto y medio en la Ciudad de México. Así fue que en ese instante mientras unos se levantaban y otros dormían, los edificios de la Ciudad de México cayeron encima de sus habitantes. En el sector más afectado, el centro de la ciudad, más del cincuenta por ciento (50%) de los edificios destruidos fueron casas y apartamentos.

Al día siguiente hubo otro temblor casi intenso. Más de 9.500 personas se murieron en el primer temblor y el segundo.



### Classroom Community

**Group Activity** Have students make a list of the preterite and imperfect verbs in the reading. Break the class into small groups and have them determine why the preterite or imperfect was used in each case.

**TPR** Have students act out a natural disaster and ask classmates to guess the type of disaster (hurricane, tornado, blizzard, wind storm, earthquake, severe thunderstorm, lightning strike, drought, rainstorm, etc.). Then discuss the effects of such disasters on the community.

**Storytelling** Ask students to share a natural disaster that they have read about or experienced, such as a hurricane, tornado, earthquake, blizzard, etc. If they are unaware of a disaster, have them look up on the Internet a recent disaster and its effects on the people in the area.

Después del temblor, el gobierno de México cambió las reglas de construcción.

En el rescate los vecinos se ayudaron entre sí.

Al principio todo el mundo estaba paralizado. Pero poco a poco la gente se dio cuenta de la magnitud de la destrucción, y se organizaron brigadas de auxilio. El pánico y el horror del primer momento fueron reemplazados por la solidaridad de la gente que sobrevivió.

Algunos se dedicaron a recolectar ropa, comida y dinero para la gente que sufría de la destrucción. Esta ayuda entre vecinos (de lejos y cerca) continuó por varias semanas.

## ¿Comprendiste?

1. ¿Cuándo ocurrió el temblor en la Ciudad de México?
2. ¿Qué hacían los habitantes cuando empezó el temblor?
3. ¿Cómo reaccionó la gente al temblor y a los efectos?

## ¿Qué piensas?

1. ¿Sentiste los efectos de un temblor alguna vez? ¿Fueron suaves o fuertes los movimientos del terreno?
2. ¿Hubo algún desastre causado por la naturaleza en tu comunidad? ¿Qué pasó? ¿Cómo reaccionó la gente?

## Hazlo tú 

Muchas personas necesitaban ayuda durante el temblor de 1985. En grupos pequeños, presenten una situación en que unas personas necesitan la ayuda de otras personas que no conocen. ¿Qué pasó? ¿Qué van a hacer?



## Cross Cultural Connection

Have students think of a recent earthquake in the U.S. Have them research or brainstorm a list of observations from the U.S. earthquake and compare and contrast them to what they have read about the Mexico City earthquake of 1985. They can then make a Venn diagram to illustrate the similarities and differences.

## ¿Comprendiste?

### Answers

1. El 19 de septiembre de 1985, a las 7:19 de la mañana.
2. Unos se vestían y se preparaban para ir a la escuela, otros dormían.
3. Se ayudaron entre sí con solidaridad.

## Supplementary Vocabulary

| | |
|---|---|
| **el incendio** | fire |
| **el diluvio** | flood |
| **el huracán** | hurricane |

## Critical Thinking

Have students list international groups that might have helped after the earthquake, as well as types of national (Mexican) groups that organized help. Also, ask students what kinds of new construction rules the government might have imposed.

## Culture Highlights

● **LAGO DE TEXCOCO** Mexico City was once an island in Lake Texcoco. The lake area was filled in by the Spanish conquistadors to create more buildable land. Unfortunately, now some buildings in Mexico City are beginning to sink.

## Teaching All Students

**Extra Help** Have students go through the reading and pick out cognates they recognize. Then have them scan the reading for 3 words they don't know and try to guess the meanings from context clues.

**Multiple Intelligences**

**Verbal** Have students write Spanish captions for each of the photos on pp. 138–139.

**Naturalist** Have students research how their community is prepared for natural disasters, e.g., fire, earthquake, flood, or hurricane. Have them research which natural disasters are most likely to happen in their area.

## Block Schedule

**Change of Pace** Ask students to tell where they were at 7:19 that morning. **¿Qué hacías? ¿Dónde estabas?** What would they do if a disaster happened in their town?

## Teaching Resource Options

**Print** 

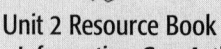

Unit 2 Resource Book
Information Gap Activities, pp. 70–71
Family Involvement, pp. 72–73

**Audiovisual** 

OHT 58 (Quick Start)

**Technology** 

Electronic Teacher Tools/Test Generator
*Intrigas y aventuras* CD-ROM, Disc 1

## Quick Start Review

Describing others/imperfect

Use OHT 58 or write on board: Complete each sentence with an adjective or two to describe the characters in this famous children's story.

| bonito | cruel | trabajador |
|---|---|---|
| feo | alto | simpático |
| guapo | perezoso | |

La Cenicienta era…
La madrastra era…
Las tres hermanastras eran…
El príncipe era…

**Answers**, see p. 121B.

## Teaching Suggestions
### What Have Students Learned?

Have students look at the "Now you can..." notes listed on the left side of pp. 140–141. To review material before doing the activities or taking the test, have them consult the "To review" notes.

# En uso
## REPASO Y MÁS COMUNICACIÓN

**OBJECTIVES**
- Narrate in the past
- Discuss family celebrations
- Talk about activities in progress

*Now you can...*
- talk about activities in progress.

*To review*
- the progressive tenses, see p. 130.

### ACTIVIDAD 1 La fiesta de sorpresa

Todos están ayudando a Silvia a prepararle una fiesta de sorpresa a su hermanita Pepita. ¿Qué están haciendo? *(Hint: How is everyone preparing?)*

**modelo**

*los vecinos: sacar*
*Los vecinos están sacando la basura.*

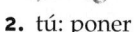

1. Arturo: hacer

2. tú: poner

3. Cecilia: buscar

4. todos nosotros: comprar

5. su madre: preparar

*Now you can...*
- talk about activities in progress.

*To review*
- the progressive tenses, see p. 130.

### ACTIVIDAD 2 ¡Un temblor!

¿Qué estaban haciendo estas personas cuando ocurrió el temblor? *(Hint: What were they doing?)*

**modelo**

*la señora Guzmán / desayunar*
*La señora Guzmán estaba desayunando.*

1. nosotros / salir de la casa
2. el señor Arenas / comer
3. yo / limpiar la casa
4. Berta y José / dormir en casa
5. la vecina / bañarse
6. Eduardo / correr en el parque



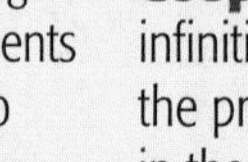
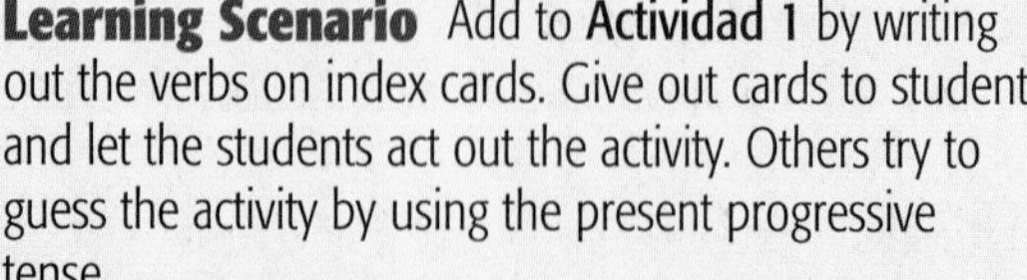

## Classroom Community

**Learning Scenario** Add to **Actividad 1** by writing out the verbs on index cards. Give out cards to students and let the students act out the activity. Others try to guess the activity by using the present progressive tense.

**Cooperative Learning** S1 states a verb in the infinitive form. S2 states a sentence using the verb in the present progressive tense. S3 restates the sentence in the past progressive. S4 checks for appropriate verb forms and tenses.

*Now you can...*
- discuss family celebrations
- narrate in the past.

*To review*
- the preterite and the imperfect, see p. 134.

## Actividad 3 Una boda de maravilla

Rosa y Felipe se casaron anoche. Describe su boda usando el imperfecto y el pretérito en cada oración. *(Hint: Describe the wedding.)*

**modelo**

*El organista tocaba música bonita cuando Rosa entró.*

1. Cuando Rosa (llegar) al altar, Felipe ya (estar) esperándola.
2. Él (sonreír) cuando ella le (dar) su anillo.
3. En el salón de recepción algunas personas (saludar) a los novios mientras los demás (comer).
4. Tú (hablar) con Rosa cuando (llegar) su bisabuelo.
5. Mientras los novios (bailar), yo (sacar) muchas fotos.
6. Todo el mundo (exclamar), «¡Felicidades!» mientras los novios (salir) para Cancún en su carro.

*Now you can...*
- narrate in the past.

*To review*
- the preterite and the imperfect, see p. 134.

## Actividad 4 Me enamoré de Antonia

Un abuelo le cuenta a su nieta cómo él conoció a su esposa. Completa la descripción con el pretérito o el imperfecto. *(Hint: Tell how a grandfather met his wife.)*

Cuando tu abuela y yo __1__ (ser) niños, nuestras familias __2__ (vivir) en el mismo pueblo. Tu abuela __3__ (asistir) a una escuela para niñas con mi hermana Beatriz. Yo, al contrario, __4__ (ir) a una escuela sólo para niños.

Un día __5__ (ocurrir) algo muy especial. Para empezar, Beatriz __6__ (decidir) invitar a su amiga Antonia a su fiesta de cumpleaños. Cuando Antonia __7__ (llegar), yo __8__ (estar) en la cocina ayudando a mi madre. Por fin, mamá y yo __9__ (salir) a servir la limonada. Fue entonces cuando yo __10__ (ver) a tu abuela por primera vez. Ella __11__ (ser) una muchacha alta, delgada y muy bonita. En seguida yo me __12__ (presentar) y nosotros __13__ (empezar) a hablar. El día siguiente __14__ (ir) al teatro. Pronto nos __15__ (dar) cuenta de que __16__ (tener) mucho en común.

Así fue que tu abuela y yo nos __17__ (conocer) y nos __18__ (enamorar). ¿Qué te parece?



### Actividad 1 Answers

1. Arturo está haciendo la limonada.
2. Tú estás poniendo los adornos.
3. Cecilia está buscando los globos.
4. Todos nosotros estamos comprando una piñata.
5. Su madre está preparando el pastel.

### Actividad 2 Answers

1. Nosotros estábamos saliendo de la casa.
2. El señor Arenas estaba comiendo.
3. Yo estaba limpiando la casa.
4. Berta y José estaban durmiendo en casa.
5. La vecina estaba bañándose.
6. Eduardo estaba corriendo en el parque.

### Actividad 3 Answers

1. Cuando Rosa llegó al altar, Felipe ya estaba esperándola.
2. Él sonreía (sonrió) cuando ella le dio su anillo.
3. En el salón de recepción algunas personas saludaron a los novios mientras los demás comían.
4. Tú hablabas con Rosa cuando llegó su bisabuelo.
5. Mientras los novios bailaban, yo saqué muchas fotos.
6. Todo el mundo exclamó, «¡Felicidades!» mientras los novios salían para Cancún en su carro.

### Actividad 4 Answers

1. éramos
2. vivían
3. asistía
4. iba
5. ocurrió
6. decidió
7. llegó
8. estaba
9. salimos
10. vi
11. era
12. presenté
13. empezamos
14. fuimos
15. dimos
16. teníamos
17. conocimos
18. enamoramos

## Teaching All Students

**Extra Help** Have students describe what has happened recently in their school using the imperfect/preterite tenses.

**Native Speakers** As a follow-up to **Actividad** 4, have Spanish-speaking students prepare a short description about how their parents or grandparents met, using the preterite and imperfect tenses. Have volunteers present their stories to the class.

**Multiple Intelligences**

**Interpersonal** Ask students to think about how they met their best friend. Have them share their story with a small group of students, using the imperfect/preterite tenses as needed.

**Visual** Ask students to draw a picture to describe the usage of the imperfect/preterite tenses.

## Block Schedule

**Change of Pace** Have students describe a family member's wedding they have attended recently. If they haven't been to one, have them describe a celebrity's wedding or create an imaginary wedding to describe.

## Teaching Resource Options

**Print**

Unit 2 Resource Book
Cooperative Quizzes, pp. 84–85
Etapa Exam, Forms A and B, pp. 86–95
*Examen para hispanohablantes*, pp. 96–100
Portfolio Assessment, pp. 101–102
Audioscript, p. 83
Multiple Choice Test Questions, pp. 173–175

**Audiovisual**

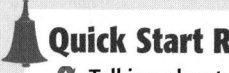

OHT 49, 50, 51, 51A, 52, 52A, 58 (Quick Start)
Audio Program Cassette 19A / CD 19; (*Para hispanohablantes* Cassette 19A / CD 19)

**Technology**

Electronic Teacher Tools/Test Generator
www.mcdougallittell.com

## Quick Start Review

Talking about activities

Use OHT 58 or write on board: Write down 4 activities one does at a typical party. Use the infinitive when jotting down your ideas. For example: **contar chistes**.

*Answers will vary.*

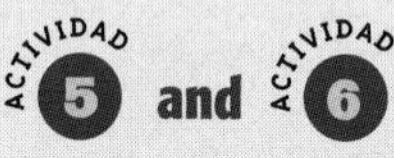

Present progressive

**Rubric: Speaking**

| Criteria | Scale | |
|---|---|---|
| Fluency | 1 2 3 | A = 8–9 pts. |
| Vocabulary | 1 2 3 | B = 6–7 pts. |
| Pronunciation, rhythm | 1 2 3 | C = 4–5 pts. |
| | | D = 3 pts. |
| | | F = < 3 pts. |

**Actividad 7 En tu propia voz**

**Rubric: Writing**

| Criteria | Scale | |
|---|---|---|
| Vocabulary use | 1 2 3 4 5 | A = 13–15 pts. |
| Accuracy | 1 2 3 4 5 | B = 10–12 pts. |
| Creativity, appearance | 1 2 3 4 5 | C = 7–9 pts. |
| | | D = 4–6 pts. |
| | | F = < 4 pts. |

### Actividad 5 ¡Una fiesta!

Mira el dibujo y conversa con tu compañero(a) sobre las actividades de las personas. *(Hint: What are they doing?)*

**modelo**

*Alguien le está dando un regalo al chico.*

### Actividad 6 ¡A celebrar!

**PARA CONVERSAR**

**STRATEGY: SPEAKING**

**Interact by expressing approval, disapproval, or astonishment** React to your partner's statements. Here are some ideas:

- **¡Qué fiesta/felicidad/lástima/maravilla/sorpresa/tristeza/vergüenza!**
- **¡Qué amable/bueno/cómico/divertido/horrible/loco/malo/maravilloso/serio/raro!**
- **¡No me digas! ¡No lo creo!**

Imagínate que es el fin del año escolar. Tú y tus compañeros(as) están en una fiesta en la casa de su profesor(a) de español. ¿Qué están haciendo? *(Hint: Tell what is happening at your teacher's party.)*

**modelo**

*Raúl está bailando sobre la mesa.*

### Actividad 7 *En tu propia voz*

**ESCRITURA** Imagínate que le escribes a tu amigo que vive en México. Escríbele una carta sobre lo que pasó en una fiesta de tu escuela. *(Hint: Write a letter about what happened at a party.)*

## CONEXIONES

**El arte** El muralista Diego Rivera vivió en la Ciudad de México y pintó murales por toda la ciudad. ¿Qué murales pintó y dónde están? Escríbele una carta a un consulado mexicano o una agencia de viajes, pidiéndoles un mapa de la Ciudad de México e información sobre dónde se encuentra el arte de Diego Rivera. Luego usa el mapa para localizar todos los lugares dónde se encuentran los famosos murales: el Parque Alameda, el Palacio Nacional, etc.

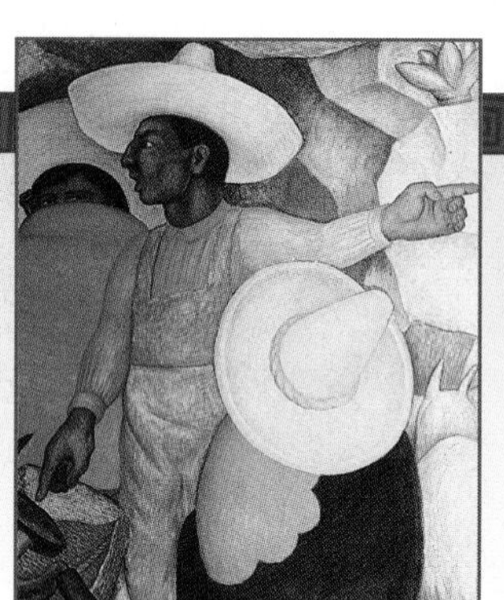



## Classroom Community

**Games** **Concentration Board:** Choose 15 words and have students draw pictures of them. Also write them on index cards. Students must match the pictures and words correctly.

**Storytelling** Based on the vocabulary on p. 143, one student initiates a story and the others continue with the plot. Each student should have a chance to add to the story.

**Cooperative Learning** Divide the class into groups of 3. Give each group a designated set of vocabulary words. Student 1 (S1) is the cardmaker, making an index card for each vocabulary word. Each group (all members) then generates an idea for a "visual hook" to recall vocabulary. S2 is the artist, drawing each "hook" on the appropriate card. S3 is the presenter, sharing the "hooks" with the rest of the class.

# En resumen

## REPASO DE VOCABULARIO

### NARRATE IN THE PAST

**The Past**

| | |
|---|---|
| **anoche** | *last night* |
| **anteayer** | *day before yesterday* |
| **el año pasado** | *last year* |
| **ayer** | *yesterday* |

**Transitional Words**

| | |
|---|---|
| **al contrario** | *on the contrary* |
| **así fue que** | *and so it was that* |
| **aunque** | *even though* |
| **casi** | *almost* |
| **de maravilla** | *marvelous* |
| **en seguida** | *at once* |
| **exclamar** | *to exclaim* |
| **los demás** | *the rest of the people* |
| **la mayoría** | *majority* |
| **mientras** | *while* |
| **ocurrir** | *to occur* |
| **para empezar** | *to begin with* |
| **por fin** | *finally* |
| **siguiente** | *next* |
| **todo el mundo** | *everyone* |

**Ordinal Numbers**

| | |
|---|---|
| **primero(a)** | *first* |
| **segundo(a)** | *second* |
| **tercero(a)** | *third* |
| **cuarto(a)** | *fourth* |
| **quinto(a)** | *fifth* |
| **sexto(a)** | *sixth* |
| **séptimo(a)** | *seventh* |
| **octavo(a)** | *eighth* |
| **noveno(a)** | *ninth* |
| **décimo(a)** | *tenth* |

### DISCUSS FAMILY CELEBRATIONS

| | |
|---|---|
| **los adornos** | *decorations* |
| **el aniversario** | *anniversary* |
| **la boda** | *wedding* |
| **la fiesta** | *party* |
| **los globos** | *balloons* |
| **la invitación** | *invitation* |
| **la reunión** | *gathering* |
| **romper la piñata** | *to break the piñata* |
| **sorprender** | *to surprise* |
| **la sorpresa** | *surprise* |
| **las velas** | *candles* |

### OTHER WORDS AND PHRASES

| | |
|---|---|
| **el abrazo** | *hug* |
| **el amor** | *love* |
| **el beso** | *kiss* |
| **casarse (con)** | *to get married (to)* |
| **común** | *common* |
| **diario** | *daily* |
| **enamorarse (de)** | *to fall in love (with)* |
| **la felicidad** | *happiness* |
| **la historia** | *story* |
| **llevarse bien** | *to get along well* |
| **la mentira** | *lie* |
| **la tristeza** | *sadness* |

### Juego

Si Julia cambia de lugar con José y José cambia con Javier y Jorge cambia con Julia, ¿quién es el primero? ¿el cuarto? ¿el tercero? ¿el segundo?

## Teaching All Students

**Extra Help** In small groups, have students write a short paragraph about something that occurred last week with their friend(s). Remind students to use the imperfect and preterite.

**Multiple Intelligences**

**Logical/Mathematical** Have students design a mind map in which all vocabulary words are used. They may have up to 7 categories.

**Visual** As a variation to **Actividad 5**, have students make drawings of a recent party and use their drawings to describe the party to the class.

## Teaching Note: En tu propia voz

**Writing Strategy** Ask students to divide information in these categories: time, place, weather, kind of music, food, people. Have them select interesting and descriptive words to include in the paragraph.

## Teaching Suggestions
### Vocabulary Review

Have students make flashcards of the words in the **Repaso de vocabulario** on p. 143. Divide students into groups of 3 or 4. Deal 5 cards per group. See how many sentences students can make using the vocabulary cards. The team with the most grammatically correct sentences wins.

## Interdisciplinary Connections

**Art** Have students use the library or the Internet to learn more about Mexican murals. The class can create a bulletin board display or a group project.

## Juego

**Answers**

Javier es el primero; Jorge es el cuarto; Julia es la tercera; José es el segundo.

## Project: Reviewing Etapa 2

Assign the following out-of-class activities:

- Find out about a recent natural disaster in Mexico (e.g., newspaper).
- Interview Spanish speakers about how they celebrated their wedding in a Spanish-speaking country.
- Find information on Mexican holidays via the Internet.

**Extra Credit**

| | |
|---|---|
| Natural disaster | 2 pts. |
| Interview | 2 pts. |
| Mexican holidays | 2 pts. |

## Teaching Note

Tell students that the Rivera painting shown is called **Workers' Meeting *(Reunión de los trabajadores)***.

## Block Schedule

**FunBreak** Try the recipe for **Tacos** found in the **Ampliación** on p. 99B.

# Planning Guide CLASSROOM MANAGEMENT

## OBJECTIVES

**Communication**
- Order in a restaurant *pp. 146–147, 148–149*
- Ask for and pay a restaurant bill *pp. 147, 148–149*
- Talk about things to do in the city *pp. 146–147*

**Grammar**
- Verbs similar to **gustar** *p. 155*
- Double object pronouns *p. 157*

**Culture**
- **El baile folklórico** *p. 151*
- **El Palacio de Bellas Artes** *p. 152*
- **Las telenovelas** *p. 156*
- **Teotihuacán** *pp. 160–161*
- **La comida mexicana** *pp. 162–163*

**Recycling**
- Direct object pronouns *p. 152*
- Indirect object pronouns *p. 154*
- Preterite and imperfect *p. 151*
- The verb **gustar** *p. 155*
- Double object pronouns *p. 157*

## STRATEGIES

**Listening Strategies**
- Listen for useful expressions *p. 148*

**Speaking Strategies**
- Personalize responses *p. 156*
- Resolve misconceptions *p. 166*

**Reading Strategies**
- Identify gaps in knowledge *p. 160*
- Summarize important information *TE p. 163*

**Writing Strategies**
- Organize information chronologically and by category *Actividad 7, TE p. 167*
- Develop your story *pp. 168–169*

**Connecting Cultures Strategies**
- Compare meals and mealtimes *p. 162*
- Learn about dance traditions in Mexico *TE pp. 151–152*
- Compare **Teotihuacán** and early settlements in the U.S. *TE p. 161*

## PROGRAM RESOURCES

### Print
- *Más práctica* Workbook PE *pp. 57–64*
- Block Scheduling Copymasters *pp. 49–56*
- Unit 2 Resource Book
  - *Más práctica* Workbook TE *pp. 103–110*
  - *Cuaderno para hispanohablantes* TE *pp. 111–118*
  - Information Gap Activities *pp. 119–122*
  - Family Involvement *pp. 123–124*
  - Video Activities *pp. 125–127*
  - Videoscript *pp. 128–129*
  - Audioscript *pp. 130–134*
  - Assessment Program Unit 2 Etapa 3 *pp. 135–153; 154–169; 170–178*
  - Answer Keys *pp. 179–183*

### Audiovisual
- Audio Program Cassette 6A, 6B / CD 6
- *Canciones* Cassette/CD
- Video Program Videotape 2 / Videodisc 2A
- Overhead Transparencies M1, M2; GO1–GO5; 59–68

### Technology
- Electronic Teacher Tools/Test Generator
- *Intrigas y aventuras* CD-ROM, Disc 1
-  www.mcdougallittell.com

### Assessment Program Options
- Cooperative Quizzes (Unit 2 Resource Book)
- Etapa Exam Forms A and B (Unit 2 Resource Book)
- *Examen para hispanohablantes* (Unit 2 Resource Book)
- Portfolio Assessment (Unit 2 Resource Book)
- Unit 2 Comprehensive Test (Unit 2 Resource Book)
- *Prueba comprensiva para hispanohablantes,* Unit 2 (Unit 2 Resource Book)
- Multiple Choice Test Questions (Unit 2 Resource Book)
- Audio Program Cassette 19A, 19B / CD 19
- Electronic Teacher Tools/Test Generator

### Native Speakers
- *Cuaderno para hispanohablantes* PE *pp. 57–64*
- *Cuaderno para hispanohablantes* TE (Unit 2 Resource Book)
- *Examen para hispanohablantes* (Unit 2 Resource Book)
- *Prueba comprensiva para hispanohablantes,* Unit 2 (Unit 2 Resource Book)
- Audio Program *(Para hispanohablantes)* Cassettes 6B, 19 / CD 6, CD 19
- Audioscript (Unit 2 Resource Book)

Laura

Isabel

Mesero

# Student Text Listening Activity Scripts

##  Videoscript: Diálogo *pages 148–149*

- Videotape 2, 25:37 • Videodisc 2A
  **Search Chapter 2, Play to 3. U2E3, En vivo (Dialog)**
- Use the videoscript with **Actividades 1, 2** *page 150*

**Isabel:** Éste es mi restaurante favorito, Laura. Sirven la mejor comida mexicana de toda la ciudad.
**Laura:** A mí me encanta la comida mexicana... pero hay algunos platillos en el menú que no conozco.
**Isabel:** ¿Cómo qué? Yo te explico.
**Laura:** ¿Qué son los chilaquiles?
**Isabel:** Bueno, los chilaquiles... aquí los preparan con tortillas fritas, salsa verde, queso blanco, pollo... Te los recomiendo. Son riquísimos.
**Laura:** Es que no tengo mucha hambre. Prefiero algo ligero, tal vez una torta o unos tacos al carbón.
**Isabel:** Si quieres tacos, vamos mañana a una taquería que está cerca de mi casa. Sirven los mejores tacos del mundo.
**Mesero:** ¿Qué desean comer?
**Laura:** Para mí, una torta de pollo con guacamole. Y también me trae frijoles. Gracias.
**Isabel:** ¿Qué me recomienda hoy, las enchiladas o los tamales de mole?
**Mesero:** Los tamales de mole están deliciosos hoy. Se los recomiendo.
**Isabel:** Muy bien, entonces, ¿me los trae, por favor?
**Mesero:** Sí, cómo no. ¿Y qué les traigo de tomar?
**Laura:** Para mí, un agua de fruta ¿Qué aguas tiene?
**Mesero:** Hoy tenemos agua de melón, de papaya, y de sandía.
**Laura:** Un agua de sandía, por favor.
**Mesero:** ¿Y para Ud., señorita?
**Isabel:** Para mí, una botella de agua, gracias.
**Mesero:** Sí, cómo no.
**Isabel:** Ah, y señor, a mí me faltan unos cubiertos y una servilleta.
**Mesero:** En un momento.
**Isabel:** Así que por fin pasó la lluvia en Atlanta y pudiste salir. ¿Cuánto tiempo esperaste en el aeropuerto?
**Laura:** Ay, fue horrible. Esperé cuatro horas. Y después cancelaron el vuelo y fui a un hotel. Por eso no pude salir anoche. Tuve que esperar hasta esta mañana.
**Isabel:** Bueno, ahora estás aquí. Más vale tarde que nunca, ¿verdad?
**Laura:** Sí, pero sentí mucho no estar contigo para la entrevista con don Miguel. ¿Cómo estuvo?
**Isabel:** Ay, todo salió muy bien. Creo que vas a estar muy contenta.
**Mesero:** ¿Se les ofrece algo más?
**Isabel:** No, gracias, nada más. Nos trae la cuenta, por favor.
**Mesero:** Sí, cómo no. Se la traigo en seguida.
**Isabel:** Bueno, Laura, ¿qué te interesa hacer aquí en la Ciudad de México? Debemos hacer algo divertido mañana.
**Laura:** A ver... sabes, me fascina el teatro. Podemos ir a una obra de teatro. ¿Qué te parece?
**Isabel:** ¡Sí! Hay una nueva obra musical. Me gustaría mucho verla. La cantante que tiene el papel principal es extraordinaria.
**Laura:** Pues, me parece excelente. Podemos ir a comprar los boletos esta tarde. Y podemos también dar una vuelta por la ciudad, ¿no? Me interesa ver más de la Ciudad de México.
**Mesero:** Aquí tienen la cuenta. Muchas gracias.
**Laura:** A usted. No, Isa. Yo voy a pagarla.
**Isabel:** ¿Seguro? Bueno, muchísimas gracias, Laura.
**Laura:** De nada, Isabel. Gracias a ti por hacer la entrevista ayer. Oye, quiero dejarle una buena propina. El mesero fue muy amable. ¿Cuánto dejo?
**Isabel:** A ver... ¿cuánto fue?

## Actividad 8 ¡A comer! *page 154*

**Isabel:** ¿Qué vas a pedir tú, Laura?
**Laura:** Yo quiero una torta de pollo y unos frijoles.
**Isabel:** Yo creo que voy a pedir los tamales de mole.
**Mesero:** Buenas tardes, señoritas. Para empezar, les traigo unas tortillas con guacamole.
**Laura:** Gracias.
**Mesero:** ¿Desean algo de tomar?
**Isabel:** Por favor, sólo agua para mí. ¿Y tú, Laura?
**Laura:** Agua de sandía, por favor.
**Mesero:** ¿Y qué desean comer?
**Laura:** Primero tú, Isabel.
**Isabel:** Bueno. Los tamales de mole, por favor.
**Laura:** Y para mí, la torta de pollo y unos frijoles, por favor.
**Mesero:** Muy bien.

## Actividad 16 Las recomendaciones *page 159*

1. El estreno que vi es horrible. Me molesta la violencia y los actores no me convencen.
2. Siempre me fascinan las aventuras. La acción es muy emocionante, por eso las aventuras me interesan mucho.
3. Es la mejor obra de teatro del año. Me encantan los musicales. Los cantantes me parecen fenomenales. Ustedes deben verla.
4. Los comediantes son cómicos... sí, muy cómicos. No me importa el precio del boleto porque vale el dinero. Nos reímos toda la noche. ¡Qué divertido!
5. El drama me pareció aburrido. No me interesó. Es que le faltaba un buen tema.

### Quick Start Review Answers

**p. 148** Ordinal numbers

**Primero, tienes que poner los cubiertos y las… Segundo, ...traer el menú. Tercero, debes preguntar, «¿Qué desean comer?» Cuarto, recomiendas la especialidad... Quinto, debes servir la comida. Sexto, debes preguntar, «¿Se les ofrece...» Séptimo, ... traer la cuenta.**

**p. 152** Direct objects

1. **el menú**
2. **los chilaquiles con pollo y salsa verde**
3. **las servilletas**
4. **la cuenta**
5. **una propina**

**p. 154** Direct object pronouns

1. **Sí, (No, no) la traje.**
2. **Sí, (No, no) la hice.**
3. **Sí, (No, no) lo tengo.**
4. **Sí, (No, no) lo puedes usar.**
5. **Sí, (No, no) lo comí.**

**p. 156** Indirect object pronouns

1. **Le compré los casetes.**
2. **Le compré la torta.**
3. **Te compré el boleto.**
4. **Les compré la pintura.**
5. **Me compré una rosa.**

**p. 158** Present progressive

1. **Sí, estoy poniéndolos.**
2. **Sí, estoy sacándolos.**
3. **Sí, estoy lavándolos.**
4. **Sí, estoy abriéndola.**

**p. 160** Countries

**Stonehenge/Inglaterra**
**Machu Picchu/Perú**
**Chichén-Itzá/México**
**Pompeya/Italia**

**p. 164** Direct object pronouns

1. **Sí, la compré.**
2. **Sí, lo compré.**
3. **Sí, las compré.**
4. **Sí, lo compré.**
5. **Sí, la compré.**
6. **Sí, las compré.**

# Pacing Guide

## Sample Lesson Plan - 50 Minute Schedule

### DAY 1

***Etapa* Opener**
- Quick Start Review (TE, p. 144). 5 MIN.
- Have students look at the *Etapa* opener and answer questions. 5 MIN.

**En contexto: Vocabulario**
- Quick Start Review (TE, p. 146). 5 MIN.
- Discuss picture, have students use context and pictures to learn *Etapa* vocabulary. Answer questions, TE p. 147. 10 MIN.

**En vivo: Diálogo**
- Quick Start Review (TE, p. 148). 5 MIN.
- Review Listening Strategy, p. 148. Play audio or show video for the dialog shown on pp. 148–149. 5 MIN.
- Replay twice. Read aloud, students taking on roles of characters. 10 MIN.
- Students role-play in groups while looking at the photos in their texts. Encourage them to come up with logical dialog using familiar vocabulary. 5 MIN.

**Homework Option**
- Video Activities, Unit 2 Resource Book, pp. 125–127.

### DAY 2

**En acción: Vocabulario y gramática**
- Check homework. 5 MIN.
- Quick Start Review (TE, p. 150). 5 MIN.
- Ask students for a summary of *En vivo* dialog to check recall. 5 MIN.
- Replay the *En vivo* dialog using the audiovisual resources and have students do *Actividades* 1 and 2 orally. 10 MIN.
- Have students complete *Actividades* 3 and 4, then *Actividad* 5 in pairs. 10 MIN.
- Use a game or expansion activity (TE, pp. 150–151) to reinforce retention of vocabulary and dialog structures. 10 MIN.
- Review *Nota cultural,* p. 152. 5 MIN.

**Homework Option**
- *Más práctica* Workbook, pp. 57–60 as needed. *Cuaderno para hispanohablantes*, pp. 57–59 as needed.

### DAY 3

**En acción (cont.)**
- Check homework. 5 MIN.
- Quick Start Review (TE, p. 152). 5 MIN.
- Present *Gramática:* Direct Object Pronouns, p. 152. 10 MIN.
- Review the vocabulary in the box on p. 153. 5 MIN.
- Have students do *Actividades* 6 and 7 in pairs. 15 MIN.
- Play the audio and do *Actividad* 8 orally. Students can also write their summary. 10 MIN.

**Homework Option**
- Have students complete *Actividades* 6 and 7 in writing. *Más práctica* Workbook, p. 161.

### DAY 4

**En acción (cont.)**
- Check homework. 5 MIN.
- Quick Start Review (TE, p. 154). 5 MIN.
- Present *Gramática*: Indirect Object Pronouns and *Vocabulario* on p. 154–155. 10 MIN.
- Have students do *Actividades* 9 and 10. 10 MIN.
- Present *Vocabulario* and Speaking Strategy, p. 156. Have students complete *Actividad* 11 in pairs. 10 MIN.
- Have students do *Actividad* 12 in class by interviewing 5 classmates. 10 MIN.

**Homework Option**
- Have students do *Actividad* 15 in writing. *Más práctica* Workbook, p. 62. *Cuaderno para hispanohablantes*, p. 60.

### DAY 5

**En acción (cont.)**
- Check homework. 5 MIN.
- Quick Start Review (TE, p. 156). 5 MIN.
- Present *Gramática:* Double Object Pronouns. 10 MIN.
- Have students complete *Actividades* 13 and 14 orally. 10 MIN.
- Play audio for students and do *Actividad* 16 orally with the whole class. 10 MIN.
- Have students complete *Actividad* 17 in small groups. 10 MIN.

**Homework Option**
- Have students do *Actividad* 15, p. 159.
- *Más práctica* Workbook, pp. 63–64. *Cuaderno para hispanohablantes*, pp. 61–62.

### DAY 6

**En voces: Lectura**
- Check homework. 5 MIN.
- Quick Start Review (TE, p. 160). 5 MIN.
- Review Reading Strategy, p. 160, and have students read silently. 5 MIN.
- Have students read *Teotihuacán: Ciudad misteriosa* aloud taking turns. 10 MIN.
- Call on volunteers to answer *¿Comprendiste?* questions and start answering *¿Qué piensas?* questions. 10 MIN.

**En uso: Repaso y más comunicación**
- Quick Start Review (TE, p. 164). 5 MIN.
- Complete *Actividades* 1–4 in writing, pp. 164–165. 10 MIN.

**Homework Option**
- Finish answering *¿Qué piensas?* questions, p. 161.
- Review for *Etapa* 3 exam.

### DAY 7

**En uso: Repaso y más comunicación**
- Check homework and review grammar questions as necessary. 10 MIN.
- Review Speaking Strategy, p. 166. Then do *Actividad* 5 in pairs and *Actividad* 6 in groups. 10 MIN.
- Complete *Etapa 3* Exam 20 MIN.
- Begin *Actividad* 7 writing activity. 10 MIN.

**Homework Option**
- Finish *Actividad* 7. Review for Unit 2 Exam.

### DAY 8

**En colores: Cultura y comparaciones**
- Review Connecting Cultures Strategy, p. 162. 3 MIN.
- Read *¡Buen provecho! La comida mexicana* aloud with students. 7 MIN.
- Answer *¿Comprendiste?* and *¿Qué piensas?* questions orally. 5 MIN.
- Review grammar questions as needed for Unit 2. 5 MIN.
- Complete Unit 2 Exam. 30 MIN.

**Homework Option**
- Complete *En tu propia voz,* pp. 168–169.

# Sample Lesson Plan - Block Schedule (90 minutes)

## DAY 1

### Etapa Opener

- Quick Start Review (TE, p. 144). 5 MIN.
- Have students look at the *Etapa* Opener and answer questions. 10 MIN.

### En contexto: Vocabulario

- Quick Start Review (TE, p. 146). 5 MIN.
- Discuss photos, have students use context and photos to learn *Etapa* vocabulary. Answer questions, p. 147. 10 MIN.

### En vivo: Diálogo

- Quick Start Review (TE, p. 148). 5 MIN.
- Review Listening Strategy, p. 148. Play audio or show video for the dialog shown on pp. 148–149. 5 MIN.
- Ask Comprehension Questions (TE, p. 149). 5 MIN.
- Replay twice. Read aloud. Students take roles of characters. 10 MIN.
- Students role-play in groups while looking at the photos in their texts. 5 MIN.
- Use Block Scheduling Copymasters for variety. 5 MIN.

### En acción: Vocabulario y gramática

- Quick Start Review (TE, p. 150). 5 MIN.
- Have students do *Actividades* 1 and 2 orally. 10 MIN.
- Have students complete *Actividades* 3, 4, and 5 in pairs. 10 MIN.

### Homework Option

- Video Activities, Unit 2 Resource Book, pp. 125–127.

## DAY 2

### En acción (cont.)

- Check homework. 10 MIN.
- Quick Start Review (TE, p. 152). 5 MIN.
- Present *Gramática:* Direct Object Pronouns, p. 152. 10 MIN.
- Review the vocabulary in the box on p. 153. 5 MIN.
- Have students do *Actividades* 6 and 7 orally. 10 MIN.
- Play the audio and do *Actividad* 8 orally. 10 MIN.
- Present *Gramática*: Indirect Object Pronouns, p. 154. 10 MIN.
- Have students do *Actividades* 9 and 10 in writing. 10 MIN.
- Present Speaking Strategy, p. 156 and have students do *Actividad* 11 in pairs and *Actividad* 12 in small groups. 15 MIN.
- Use *Más comunicación* activity, p. R7, for variety. 5 MIN.

### Homework Option

- *Más práctica* Workbook, pp. 57–62 as needed. *Cuaderno para hispanohablantes*, pp. 57–60 as needed.

## DAY 3

### En acción (cont.)

- Quick Start Review (TE, p. 156). 5 MIN.
- Present *Gramática*: Double Object Pronouns, p. 157. 10 MIN.
- Quick Start Review (TE, p. 158). 5 MIN.
- Have students complete *Actividades* 13 and 14 orally. 10 MIN.
- Present *Vocabulario,* p. 159, then have students complete *Actividad* 15 in writing. 10 MIN.
- Play audio for students and do *Actividades* 16 and 17 orally with the whole class. 10 MIN.

### En voces: Lectura

- Quick Start Review (TE, p. 160). 5 MIN.
- Review Reading Strategy, p. 160. 5 MIN.
- Have students read *Teotihuacán: Ciudad misteriosa* silently, then have students read it aloud in turns. 10 MIN.
- Call on volunteers to answer *¿Comprendiste?* questions. Refer back to the reading if students give the incorrect answer. 10 MIN.
- Have students begin *Actividad* 7. 10 MIN.

### Homework Option

- Have students finish *Actividad* 7. *Más práctica* Workbook, pp. 63–64. *Cuaderno para hispanohablantes*, pp. 61–62.
- Prepare for *Etapa* 3 Exam.

## DAY 4

### En colores: Cultura y comparaciones

- Check homework. 10 MIN.
- Quick Start Review (TE, p. 162). 5 MIN.
- Present Connecting Cultures Strategy, p. 162. 10 MIN.
- Read *¡Buen provecho! La comida mexicana* aloud with students. 10 MIN.
- Have students answer the *¿Comprendiste?* questions orally. 10 MIN.

### En uso: Repaso y más comunicación

- Quick Start Review (TE, p. 164). 5 MIN.
- Review Now You Can… and do *Actividades* 1–4 orally. 15 MIN.
- Present Speaking Strategy, p. 166, then have students do *Actividad* 5 and 6 in groups of four. 10 MIN.
- Complete *Etapa* 3 Exam. 20 MIN.

### Homework Option

- Write answers to *¿Qué piensas?* questions. Read *Tu en la comunidad,* p. 166. Prepare for Unit 2 Exam.

## DAY 5

### En uso: Repaso y más comunicación

- Check homework. 10 MIN.
- Quick Start Review (TE, p. 166). 5 MIN.
- Review grammar from the unit as necessary. 10 MIN.
- Complete Unit 2 Exam. 30 MIN.

### En tu propia voz: Escritura

- Begin writing activity, pp. 168–169. 15 MIN.

### Ampliación

- Use a suggested project, game, or activity (TE pp. 99A–99B). 20 MIN.

### Homework Option

- Finish writing activity and preview *Unidad* 3 Opener, pp. 168–169.

▼ Isabel y Laura comen en un restaurante.

## Etapa Theme

**Eating in a restaurant, talking about things to do in the city**

## Grammar Objectives

- Direct and Indirect Object Pronouns
- Double Object Pronouns
- Verbs similar to **gustar**

### Teaching Resource Options

**Print** 

Block Scheduling Copymasters

**Audiovisual** 

**OHT** 65 (Quick Start)
*Canciones* Cassette / CD Song 9

### Quick Start Review

Talking about restaurants and food

Use OHT 65 or write on the board: Each of the following sentences has one error. Look at the photos on pp. 144–145 and rewrite them so that they are correct.

1. Laura e Isabel están en un restaurante francés.
2. El señor que sirve la comida es un auxiliar de vuelo.
3. Las especialidades de la casa son tamales de mole, chilaquiles al horno, sopa azteca, pollo en salsa roja y flan.

**Answers**

1. Laura e Isabel están en un restaurante mexicano.
2. El señor que sirve la comida es un mesero.
3. Las especialidades de la casa son tamales de mole, chilaquiles al horno, sopa azteca, pollo en salsa verde y flan.

### Teaching Suggestions
**Previewing the Etapa**

- Ask students to study the photo on pp. 144–145 (1 min.).
- Ask students to list other examples of Mexican foods they have eaten.
- Have students list 3 similarities and 3 differences between this restaurant scene and another restaurant they may be familiar with.
- Have students create imaginary conversations between the people at each table.

UNIDAD 2

ETAPA 3

# Hoy en la ciudad

- Order in a restaurant
- Ask for and pay a restaurant bill
- Talk about things to do in the city

### ¿Qué ves?

Mira la foto y contesta las preguntas.

1. ¿Dónde están Isabel y Laura?
2. ¿Qué cosas están en la mesa?
3. ¿Qué trae el mesero?
4. ¿Te gustaría alguna de las especialidades de la casa?

### Classroom Management

**Planning Ahead** Prepare students to discuss ordering in restaurants by bringing in menus from restaurants that serve food from Spanish-speaking countries. Have students brainstorm words and expressions they may already know about food and restaurants. Also, start collecting grocery labels and photos of common foods to illustrate the chapter vocabulary.

**Time Saver** The day before you are ready to present the **En contexto** vocabulary on pp. 146–147, ask students to preview the pages. Assign each student a vocabulary word for which he/she will make an illustrated flashcard. Tell them to come to class the next day with their flashcards and have them immediately open their books to pp. 146–147.

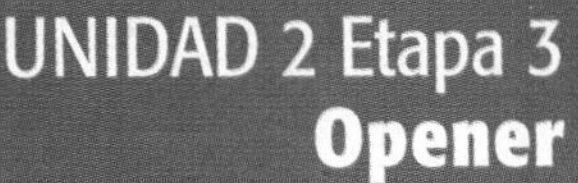

## Cross Cultural Connection

If possible, arrange to have menus of local Mexican, Chinese, Greek, Italian, or other ethnic restaurants. Poll the class on likes and dislikes of different ethnic foods. Ask questions like **¿A quién le gusta la comida mexicana? ¿la comida china?**, etc. Have students give examples of their favorite dishes. Summarize the results on a chart and display in the class.

## Culture Highlights

- **TAMALES** Meat (usually chicken or pork) with mole (a chile and chocolate sauce) covered in cornmeal dough and wrapped in cornhusks (sometimes plantain leaves) and steamed.
- **CHILAQUILES AL HORNO** Tortillas baked in tomato and chile sauce with cheese and cream.
- **SOPA AZTECA** Chicken soup, sometimes known as "tortilla soup," mostly broth, served with tortilla chips, guacamole, chopped chilis, and chopped cilantro as condiments.
- **POLLO EN SALSA VERDE** Chicken in a green chile sauce, often served with rice and beans.
- **FLAN** A rich egg custard in caramel sauce.

## Teaching Note

You may wish to tell students that the photo was taken at the **La Piazza** restaurant in Mexico City.

## Teaching All Students

**Extra Help** Help students identify the people and items in the restaurant scene by pointing to people/objects and having students repeat each word/phrase.

**Native Speakers** Have Spanish speakers describe their favorite foods or recipes, especially those from their country of origin.

**Multiple Intelligences**

**Visual** Have students design a menu for the restaurant in this photo that includes a creative name, food offerings, and prices. Then recreate the restaurant scene in your classroom with tables, place settings, and customers/waiters.

**Naturalist** Have students research the availability of foods on the menu: would they be fresh or frozen, etc.

## Block Schedule

**Peer Teaching** Have students bring in the recipe of a favorite food. They must describe it to the class by listing the ingredients and telling how it is made. You can turn this into a guessing game by having the class guess each student's favorite food after hearing the description.

## UNIDAD 2 Etapa 3
## Vocabulary Input

### Teaching Resource Options

**Print** 

Unit 2 Resource Book
Video Activities, p. 125
Videoscript, p. 128
Audioscript, p. 130

**Audiovisual** 

**OHT** 59–60, 65 (Quick Start)
**Audio Program** Cassette 6A / CD 6
**Video Program** Videotape 2, 21:34 / Videodisc 2A

Search Chapter 1, Play to 2
U2E3, En contexto (Vocabulary)

**Technology** 

*Intrigas y aventuras* CD-ROM, Disc 1

### Quick Start Review

**Servir**/preterite

Use OHT 65 or write on board: Tell what these people served for dinner last night. Use the preterite of **servir** and remember the spelling change.

1. yo / pizza
2. tú / hamburguesas
3. ellos / enchiladas
4. papá / arroz con pollo
5. abuela / una sopa de verduras
6. mis primos / pasta

**Answers**

1. serví
2. serviste
3. sirvieron
4. sirvió
5. sirvió
6. sirvieron

# En contexto

## VOCABULARIO

Mira las ilustraciones de Laura e Isabel en la Ciudad de México.

**A** Fui a **cenar** con Laura, de la revista *Onda Internacional*. Al entrar al restaurante, el mesero nos preguntó: –¿**Qué desean** comer?

Contestamos: –**¿Qué nos recomienda?**

**B** El mesero nos dijo: –Aquí sirven unos sándwiches o **tortas** de pollo y **frijoles.** Para comer la torta no necesitas **cubiertos,** pero para comer los frijoles sí. También se necesita **una servilleta.** ¡No hay que ensuciar **el mantel**!



### Classroom Community

**TPR** Have students brainstorm a list of Mexican foods they know. Then, as you call out each food item, have them stand up if they like the food and stay seated if they don't like it. You can also review the use of **gustar**.

**Group Activity** Have students work in groups of three to reenact the **En contexto** restaurant scene with Isabel, Laura, and the **mesero**.

**Learning Scenario** Hand out a blank sheet of paper to each student. Students draw their favorite restaurant (the inside or the outside of the building). Answer the following: **¿Cómo se llama tu restaurante favorito? ¿Con quién(es) comes? ¿Hay algo único en este restaurante? ¿Cuándo fue la última vez que comiste allí?** (Hold on to pictures and use later on when creating class menus.)

**C** Aquí brindamos con los vasos: —¡**Salud!**

**D** Después de comer, el mesero nos preguntó: —**¿Se les ofrece algo más?** Ya queríamos ir. Entonces pedimos **la cuenta** y **dejamos la propina.**

**E** Luego queríamos ir a **una obra de teatro** que no era muy seria. Decidimos ir a **un musical romántico** para escuchar a **una cantante** famosa.

**F** Pero… ¡todavía teníamos hambre! Fuimos a **una taquería** a comer **tacos…** Ay, ¡qué sabrosos!

## Preguntas personales

1. ¿Te gusta salir a comer en restaurantes?
2. Cuando sales a comer, ¿qué comida te gusta?
3. ¿Alguna vez comiste tacos? ¿Te gustan?
4. ¿Vas al cine o al teatro? ¿Te gusta?
5. ¿Qué obras de teatro conoces?
6. ¿Qué cantantes famosos conoces?





## Teaching Suggestions
### Introducing Vocabulary

- Have students look at pp. 146–147. Use OHTs 59–60 and Audiocassette 6A / CD 6 to present the vocabulary.
- Use the video vocabulary presentation for review and reinforcement.

## Comprehension Questions

1. ¿Comen Isabel y Laura en la casa de Laura? **(No)**
2. ¿Recomienda el mesero algo de comer? **(Sí)**
3. ¿Necesitan cubiertos para comer sándwiches? **(No)**
4. La cosa que cubre la mesa, ¿es la servilleta o el mantel? **(el mantel)**
5. ¿Es la torta un sándwich o un refresco? **(un sándwich)**
6. ¿Luego quieren ir Isabel y Laura al cine o al teatro? **(al teatro)**
7. ¿Es un drama o un musical? **(un musical)**
8. ¿Qué dicen cuando brindan con los vasos? **(¡Salud!)**
9. Después de comer, ¿qué piden? **(la cuenta)**
10. ¿Adónde fueron a comer tacos? **(a una taquería)**

## Language Note

Although both **torta** and **sándwich** are used to refer to sandwiches, a **torta** is usually made on a roll, while a **sándwich** is usually made on slices of "pan Bimbo" or other commercially prepared brands. In Spain, a **torta** is called a **bocadillo**.

## Teaching All Students

**Extra Help** Have students work with partners to discuss the action in each picture in **En contexto**.

**Native Speakers** Have Spanish speakers list their favorite native foods. Have them describe a typical meal at home vs. a typical meal in a restaurant.

### Multiple Intelligences

**Verbal** Clip pictures of various food items from magazines. Show pictures to the class and ask the following: **¿Te gusta este plato? ¿Dónde se puede comer este plato? ¿Vas a recomendarle este plato a tu amigo(a) favorito(a)? ¿Quién puede preparar este plato en casa?**

**Visual** Have students cut out pictures of a variety of food items and bring to class. Have them work in small groups to form a food collage and label it in Spanish.

## Block Schedule

**Variety** Have students share with a partner the name of their favorite restaurant and the meal that they like to order there. **Me gusta ___ y prefiero comer ___.**

### Teaching Resource Options

**Print** 

Block Scheduling Copymasters
Unit 2 Resource Book
Video Activities, pp. 125–126
Videoscript, pp. 128–129
Audioscript, p. 130

**Audiovisual**

OHT 63, 64, 65 (Quick Start)
Audio Program Cassette 6A / CD 6
Video Program Videotape 2, 25:37 / Videodisc 2A

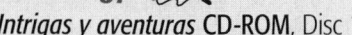

Search Chapter 2, Play to 3
U2E3, En vivo (Dialog)

**Technology**

*Intrigas y aventuras* CD-ROM, Disc 1

### Quick Start Review

Ordinal numbers

Use OHT 65 or write on board: Imagine that you work at a restaurant and are giving a new waiter instructions. Put the following statements in order and start each statement with an ordinal number such as: **primero, segundo…**

Debes servir la comida.
Recomiendas la especialidad de la casa.
Tienes que poner los cubiertos y las servilletas en la mesa.
Debes preguntar «¿Qué desean comer?»
Tienes que traer el menú.
Tienes que traer la cuenta.
Debes preguntar «¿Se les ofrece algo más?»

**Answers**, see p. 143B.

# En vivo

## DIÁLOGO

Laura

Isabel

Mesero

**PARA ESCUCHAR** • STRATEGY: LISTENING

**Listen for useful expressions** When traveling in another country, observe the local customs of politeness. What expressions can you borrow from Isabel and Laura when you are in a restaurant?

## En un restaurante…

1 ▶ Laura: Me encanta la comida mexicana, pero hay algunos platillos en el menú que no conozco.
Isabel: ¿Como qué? Yo te explico.
Laura: ¿Qué son los chilaquiles?

5 ▶ Mesero: ¿Qué les traigo de tomar?
Laura: Un agua de sandía, por favor.
Isabel: Una botella de agua, gracias. Y señor, me faltan unos cubiertos y una servilleta.

6 ▶ Laura: Sentí mucho no estar contigo para la entrevista con don Miguel. ¿Cómo estuvo?
Isabel: Todo salió muy bien. Creo que vas a estar muy contenta.

7 ▶ *(después de comer)*
Mesero: ¿Se les ofrece algo más?
Isabel: No, gracias, nada más. Nos trae la cuenta, por favor.
Mesero: Sí, cómo no. Se la traigo en seguida.



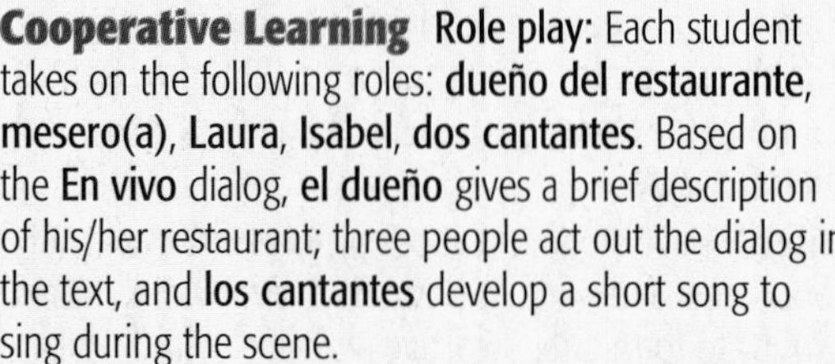

### Classroom Community

**Cooperative Learning** Role play: Each student takes on the following roles: **dueño del restaurante, mesero(a), Laura, Isabel, dos cantantes**. Based on the **En vivo** dialog, **el dueño** gives a brief description of his/her restaurant; three people act out the dialog in the text, and **los cantantes** develop a short song to sing during the scene.

**Learning Scenario** Create a restaurant environment in your classroom. Assign the following tasks to small groups: 1) create a name for the restaurant/design a sign; 2) design the menu and decide what food to serve; 3) arrange tables for restaurant seating; 4) assign waiters/waitresses and customers; 5) plan entertainment; and 6) design a customer survey.

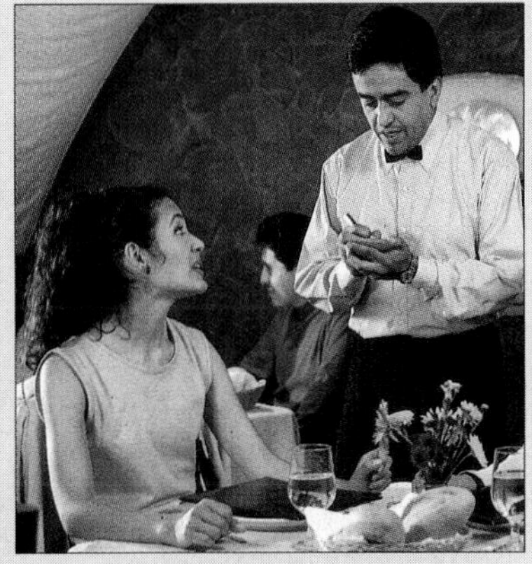

2► Isabel: Los chilaquiles… aquí los preparan con tortillas, salsa verde, queso, pollo…
Laura: No tengo mucha hambre. Prefiero una torta o unos tacos.

3► Isabel: Si quieres tacos, vamos mañana a una taquería.
Mesero: ¿Qué desean comer?
Laura: Para mí, una torta de pollo con guacamole. Y también me trae frijoles. Gracias.

4► Isabel: ¿Qué me recomienda hoy?
Mesero: Los tamales de mole están deliciosos. Se los recomiendo.
Isabel: Muy bien, entonces, ¿me los trae, por favor?

8► Isabel: ¿Qué te interesa hacer?
Laura: Podemos ir a una obra de teatro.
Isabel: Hay una nueva obra musical. La cantante que tiene el papel principal es extraordinaria.

9► Mesero: Aquí tienen la cuenta. Muchas gracias.
Laura: Yo voy a pagarla.
Isabel: Muchísimas gracias, Laura.
Laura: De nada. Gracias a ti por hacer la entrevista ayer.

10► Laura: Oye, quiero dejarle una buena propina. El mesero fue muy amable. ¿Cuánto dejo?
Isabel: A ver… ¿cuánto fue?



## Teaching Suggestions
### Presenting the Dialog

- Introduce the characters' names and the setting: **Laura trabaja en la revista *Onda Internacional*. Isabel hizo una entrevista para la revista. Isabel y Laura comen en un restaurante mexicano.**
- Use the video, audiocassette, or CD to present the dialog.

### Video Synopsis

Isabel and Laura get together for dinner at a restaurant in Mexico City. They also discuss going to the theater. For a complete transcript of the video dialog, see p. 143B.

## Comprehension Questions

1. ¿Van Isabel y Laura a un restaurante mexicano? **(Sí)**
2. ¿Conoce Laura todos los platos del menú? **(No)**
3. ¿Se hacen los chilaquiles con tortillas? **(Sí)**
4. ¿Tiene mucha hambre Laura? **(No)**
5. ¿Pide Laura un taco o una torta de pollo? **(una torta de pollo)**
6. ¿Recomienda el mesero los chilaquiles o los tamales de mole? **(los tamales de mole)**
7. ¿Toma Laura un agua de sandía o un café? **(un agua de sandía)**
8. ¿Adónde van después de cenar? **(al teatro)**
9. ¿Quién paga la cuenta? **(Laura)**
10. ¿Qué le dejan al mesero? **(una propina)**

## Gestures

Have students identify any gestures they recognize in the photographs. Have students try to describe each of the waiter's gestures in frames 3–5 and 9.

## Teaching All Students

**Extra Help** ¿Quién lo dice? Read a line from the dialog and ask the class to identify the character.

**Challenge** Have students compare and contrast American foods and Mexican foods.

**Multiple Intelligences**

**Verbal** Have students write a short description of one of the characters, based on the dialog.

**Logical/Mathematical** Have students list in Spanish the types of questions a waiter usually asks in a restaurant.

**Visual** Have students describe one of the scenes and ask a partner to identify it.

## Block Schedule

**Variety** Have students work in small groups to reread and expand each scene.

## Teaching Resource Options

**Print** 

Block Scheduling Copymasters
Unit 2 Resource Book
Video Activities, p. 127
Videoscript, pp. 128–129
Audioscript, p. 130

**Audiovisual**

OHT 66 (Quick Start)
Audio Program Cassette 6A / CD 6
Video Program Videotape 2, 25:37 / Videodisc 2A

**Technology** 

*Intrigas y aventuras* CD-ROM, Disc 1

## Quick Start Review

Describing food

Use OHT 66 or write on board: Complete these sentences about the last time you went to a restaurant.

Yo fui a un restaurante… (¿qué tipo? mexicano, indio…)
Fui con…
Yo pedí…
De postre pedí…
La comida era…

*Answers will vary.*

**Actividad 1 Objective:** Controlled practice
Listening comprehension/vocabulary

**Answers**

1. Laura
2. Laura
3. el mesero
4. Isabel
5. Isabel
6. Laura
7. Isabel
8. el mesero
9. Laura
10. Laura

**Actividad 2 Objective:** Controlled practice
Listening comprehension/vocabulary

**Answers**

1. hambre
2. una taquería
3. unos cubiertos
4. la cuenta
5. una obra de teatro
6. propina

# En acción

## VOCABULARIO Y GRAMÁTICA

**OBJECTIVES**

- Order in a restaurant
- Ask for and pay a restaurant bill
- Talk about things to do in the city

Actividad 1

### ¿Quién?

**Escuchar** ¿A quién se refiere cada frase: a Isabel, a Laura o al mesero? *(Hint: Whom are these sentences about?)*

1. Hay platos en el menú que no conoce.
2. Prefiere una torta.
3. Recomienda los tamales.
4. Quiere tomar una botella de agua.
5. Le faltan cubiertos.
6. Sintió mucho no estar en la entrevista.
7. Le gustaría ver el nuevo musical.
8. Les trae la cuenta en seguida.
9. Paga la cuenta.
10. Quiere dejar una buena propina.

Actividad 2

### Palabras perdidas

**Escuchar/Escribir** Usa estas palabras para completar la descripción del diálogo. *(Hint: Complete each description.)*

una taquería | hambre | la cuenta | una obra de teatro | unos cubiertos | propina

1. Laura no tiene mucha _____.
2. Mañana Isabel y Laura van a ir a _____ para comer.
3. No había ni una servilleta ni _____ en la mesa.
4. Isabel y Laura sólo querían _____.
5. Ellas pensaron ir a _____ para divertirse.
6. Laura quería dejar una buena _____ porque el mesero era amable.



## Classroom Management

**Time Saver** Have copies of the answers to **Actividades 1** and **2** ready to distribute. Give them to students after completion of these activities. Students then exchange papers and check/correct.

**Peer Teaching** Have students work in pairs to do **Actividad 1**. Then extend the activity by having students work with their partner to locate the line in the dialog that gives the answer.

- *Review: Use direct object pronouns*
- *Review: Use indirect object pronouns*
- *Use double object pronouns*

## ¡A divertirse en la ciudad!

**Escribir** Laura cuenta de su primer día en la Ciudad de México. Termina su historia con el pretérito o el imperfecto. *(Hint: Complete the story with the preterite or the imperfect.)*

El primer día que __1__ (estar) en México, __2__ (ir) al Bosque de Chapultepec. __3__ (Hacer) mucho sol. __4__ (Haber) mucha gente en el parque. Los niños __5__ (estar) trepando a los árboles. Mientras __6__ (caminar) por el parque, __7__ (ver) el Árbol de Moctezuma y el Castillo de Chapultepec. __8__ (Llegar) al Museo Nacional de Antropología y __9__ (entrar). __10__ (Andar) de salón a salón. Luego __11__ (ir) a ver unos bailarines folklóricos. ¡__12__ (Pasar) un día maravilloso!

## ¿A qué corresponde?

**Hablar/Leer** ¿A qué corresponde cada oración: el restaurante o el teatro? *(Hint: Say which: the restaurant or the theater?)*

1. Leí que la cantante es extraordinaria.
2. Vamos a cenar a las nueve.
3. ¿Qué desea beber?
4. ¿Qué me recomienda para tomar?
5. ¿Se les ofrece algo más?
6. Dicen que la obra es muy romántica.
7. El musical abre mañana.
8. Cuando hay buen servicio, siempre dejo una buena propina.

El restaurante

El teatro

### NOTA CULTURAL

**El baile folklórico** de México varía mucho entre las regiones del país. Una persona puede ver los bailarines en los centros culturales de los diferentes estados. Pero una cosa es cierta –los trajes de los bailarines siempre son elegantes y de muchos colores.

## Culture Highlights

- **ÁRBOL DE MOCTEZUMA** The measurements of the tree are 76.5 yards in height by 21.8 yards in circumference.
- **CHAPULTEPEC** The five museums in Bosque de Chapultepec include the **Museo Nacional de Antropología**, **Museo Nacional de Historia**, **Museo de Arte Moderno**, **Museo de Tecnología**, and the **Museo de Historia Natural**. There is also a zoo, an amusement park, and facilities for boating and horseback riding.

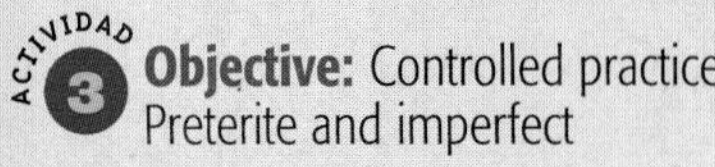

**Objective:** Controlled practice
Preterite and imperfect

### Answers

| | |
|---|---|
| 1. estuve | 7. vi |
| 2. fui | 8. Llegué |
| 3. Hacía | 9. entré |
| 4. Había | 10. Anduve |
| 5. estaban | 11. fui |
| 6. caminaba | 12. Pasé |

**Objective:** Transitional practice
**En contexto** vocabulary

### Answers

| | |
|---|---|
| 1. el teatro | 5. el restaurante |
| 2. el restaurante | 6. el teatro |
| 3. el restaurante | 7. el teatro |
| 4. el restaurante | 8. el restaurante |

## Interdisciplinary Connections

**Theater** Consult the drama or music department to find out about any theatrical or musical productions at your school. Have students attend and write a short review in Spanish.

## Teaching All Students

**Extra Help** Have students create 3-5 sentences using the vocabulary in **Actividad 2**.

**Challenge** Based on **Actividad 4**, ask students to think of two more places in the city (e.g., **el parque, la escuela**). Have them write 6–8 sentences to describe these two places. Then ask volunteers to read their sentences so others may identify the place mentioned.

### Multiple Intelligences

**Verbal** Have students give a reason why the characters say the lines in **Actividad 1**, e.g., **Hay platos en el menú que no conoce porque (él nunca comió allí)**...

## Block Schedule

**Retention** Have students write additional sentences that correspond either to **el restaurante** or **el teatro**, as in **Actividad 4**. (For additional activities, see **Block Scheduling Copymasters**.)

## Teaching Resource Options

**Print** 

*Más práctica* Workbook PE, p. 61
*Cuaderno para hispanohablantes* PE, p. 59
Block Scheduling Copymasters
Unit 2 Resource Book
*Más práctica* Workbook TE, p. 107
*Cuaderno para hispanohablantes* TE, p. 113

**Audiovisual**

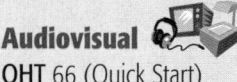

OHT 66 (Quick Start)

**Technology**

*Intrigas y aventuras* CD-ROM, Disc 1

## Quick Start Review

Identifying the direct object

Use OHT 66 or write on board: Underline the direct object in each sentence. Remember the direct object answers the question "what?" in relation to the verb.

1. Tengo el menú.
2. Preparan los chilaquiles con pollo y salsa verde.
3. ¿Pusiste las servilletas en la mesa?
4. El mesero trajo la cuenta en seguida.
5. Le dejaron una propina al mesero.

**Answers**, see p. 143B.

## Teaching Suggestions
### Presenting Direct Object Pronouns

- Have students refer back to the dialog on pp. 148–149 and identify the direct object pronouns and the item to which they refer.
- Remind students to add an accent when attaching a pronoun to **-ndo** forms.

**Objective:** Open-ended practice
**En contexto** vocabulary/circumlocution

## Culture Highlights

- The **Ballet Folklórico** and the **Orquesta Sinfónica de México** perform in the **Palacio de Bellas Artes** in Mexico City.

ACTIVIDAD 5

## Adivínala

**Hablar** Escoge una palabra o frase de la lista. Luego ayuda a un(a) compañero(a) a adivinar tu palabra. *(Hint: Give clues to help your partner guess each word.)*

**modelo**

*una obra de teatro*
**Tú:** *Es algo con actores y actrices que ves en el teatro.*
**Compañero(a):** *Es una obra de teatro.*

una obra de teatro
una taquería
una servilleta
una torta
un(a) cantante
unos cubiertos
un musical

### NOTA CULTURAL

En el magnífico Palacio de Bellas Artes se presentan obras de teatro y obras musicales de todo tipo. El telón (*stage curtain*) es un mosaico de casi un millón de pedazos de cristal que representa dos volcanes mexicanos.

## REPASO
### Direct Object Pronouns

Remember that you use **direct object pronouns** when you don't want to keep repeating the **direct object nouns.**

Comemos **tamales.** *We eat* ***tamales.*** — *becomes* — **Los** comemos. *We eat* ***them.***

Llamamos al **mesero.** *We called the* ***waiter.*** — *becomes* — **Lo** llamamos. *We called* ***him.***

Note that **mesero** is the **direct object** even though it takes a personal **a**.

**Direct Object Pronouns**

| | |
|---|---|
| me | nos |
| te | os |
| lo/la | los/las |

Direct object pronouns are usually placed before **conjugated verbs**. They may follow **infinitives** and **-ndo forms**.

**Lo llamamos.** *We called* ***him.***

When you put the pronoun after the **infinitive** or **-ndo** form, it attaches to the verb.

**Lo vamos** a llamar. *We're going to call* ***him.*** ←→ Vamos a **llamarlo**. (*attaches*)

**Lo estamos** llamando. *We're calling* ***him.*** ←→ Estamos **llamándolo**. (*attaches*)

La mesera puso la **mesa** con cubiertos. *The waitress set the* ***table*** *with silverware.* — *becomes* — **La puso** con cubiertos. *She set* ***it*** *with silverware.*



## Classroom Community

**Paired Activity** Have students work in pairs to create a shopping list from the vocabulary box on p. 153.

**Storytelling** Based on vocabulary in the box on p. 153, have students form a short dialog in which one person acts as a grocer (**el abacero/la abacera**) and the other acts as a customer (**el/la cliente**).

**Group Activity** Divide the class into groups of 3. Have them brainstorm a list of 5 foods they might see on a menu and write them down. Have the students role-play 2 customers asking a waiter for recommendations. Students switch roles after 3 items.

S1: **¿Recomiendas la sopa?**
S2: **Sí, la recomiendo./No, no la recomiendo.**

## ¿Lo comió?

**Hablar** Pregúntale a un(a) compañero(a) si comió o tomó lo siguiente durante la semana pasada. *(Hint: Ask a classmate the following.)*

**modelo**

*comer frijoles*

**Tú:** *¿Comiste frijoles?*

**Compañero(a):** *Sí, (No, no) los comí.*

1. tomar un batido de chocolate
2. comer una zanahoria
3. comer arroz
4. comer unas salchichas
5. tomar jugo de manzana
6. comer pan con mantequilla

**MÁS PRÁCTICA** *cuaderno* p. 61

**PARA HISPANOHABLANTES** *cuaderno* p. 59

## La sopa del día

**Hablar** Imagínate que preparas una sopa riquísima. Pregúntale a un(a) compañero(a) si quiere poner estos ingredientes en la sopa. *(Hint: Does your friend like these ingredients?)*

**modelo**

*el queso*

**Tú:** *¿Quieres poner el queso en la sopa?*

**Compañero(a):** *Sí, (No, no) lo quiero poner en la sopa. (Sí, [No, no] quiero ponerlo en la sopa.)*

1. las papas
2. el aceite
3. las verduras
4. la carne de res
5. el azúcar
6. la sal y la pimienta
7. las cerezas
8. los tomates
9. las cebollas
10. la pasta
11. la harina
12. el pescado

### Vocabulario Unas comidas

¿Cuál es tu comida preferida?



## Teaching Suggestions

### Presenting Vocabulary for Unas comidas

- Bring in a shopping cart of plastic foods or use supermarket advertisements to further illustrate the foods listed here. Hold the items up and have students identify them.
- Have students collect and bring in illustrations of food and decorate a bulletin board.

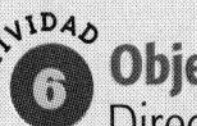

**Objective:** Controlled practice
Direct object pronouns

Food/preterite

**Answers**

1. ¿Tomaste un batido de chocolate? Sí, (No, no) lo tomé.
2. ¿Comiste una zanahoria? Sí, (No, no) la comí.
3. ¿Comiste arroz? Sí, (No, no) lo comí.
4. ¿Comiste unas salchichas? Sí, (No, no) las comí.
5. ¿Tomaste jugo de manzana? Sí, (No, no) lo tomé.
6. ¿Comiste pan con mantequilla? Sí, (No, no) lo comí.

**Objective:** Transitional practice
Direct object pronouns

Food

**Answers**

*Answers may vary.*

1. ¿Quieres poner las papas en la sopa? Sí, (No, no) quiero ponerlas (las quiero poner) en la sopa.
2. … quiero ponerlo…
3. … quiero ponerlas…
4. … quiero ponerla…
5. … quiero ponerlo…
6. … quiero ponerlas…
7. … quiero ponerlas…
8. … quiero ponerlos…
9. … quiero ponerlas…
10. … quiero ponerla…
11. … quiero ponerla…
12. … quiero ponerlo…

## Teaching All Students

**Extra Help** Referring to the list in **Actividad 7**, have students quickly identify the pronoun to match a given vocabulary word, e.g., **las papas–las**.

**Native Speakers** Have Spanish speakers give other Spanish names for the foods listed in the vocabulary box. For example, most of the Spanish-speaking world uses **papa** for *potato,* but Spain uses **patata**.

**Multiple Intelligences**

**Verbal** Have students state if they have the items listed in the vocabulary box at home, e.g., **¿Tienes aceite en casa?** Students respond: **No, no lo tengo/Sí, lo tengo.**

## Block Schedule

**Variety** As a variation to **Actividad 7**, have students create a fruit salad using the vocabulary they are learning here. Tell them they can include fruit that they have learned previously.

## Teaching Resource Options

**Print** 

*Más práctica* Workbook PE, p. 62
*Cuaderno para hispanohablantes* PE, p. 60
Block Scheduling Copymasters
Unit 2 Resource Book
*Más práctica* Workbook TE, p. 108
*Cuaderno para hispanohablantes* TE, p. 114
Audioscript, p. 132

**Audiovisual**

OHT 66 (Quick Start)
Audio Program Cassette 6A, 6B / CD 6

## Quick Start Review

Direct object pronouns

Use OHT 66 or write on board: Answer the following questions in Spanish, using a direct object pronoun in your response.

1. ¿Trajiste la mochila hoy?
2. ¿Hiciste la tarea anoche?
3. ¿Tienes tu cuaderno hoy?
4. ¿Puedo usar tu libro?
5. ¿Desayunaste esta mañana?

**Answers**, see p. 143B.

## Teaching Suggestions
### Presenting Indirect Object Pronouns

- Tell students that indirect object pronouns answer the following questions: **to whom?** and **for whom?**
- Remind students that they have already used indirect object pronouns with the verb **gustar** in Level 1.

ACTIVIDAD 8 **Objective:** Open-ended practice
Listening comprehension

**Answers** (See script, p. TE 143B.)

1. la torta de pollo y frijoles
2. los tamales de mole
3. unas tortillas con guacamole
4. agua
5. agua de sandía

ACTIVIDAD 8 

## ¡A comer!

**Escuchar/Hablar** Escucha lo que dicen Isabel y Laura de la comida en este menú. Luego contesta las preguntas. *(Hint: Listen to the audiotape. Then answer the questions.)*

1. ¿Qué va a pedir Laura?
2. ¿Qué va a pedir Isabel?
3. ¿Qué trae el mesero?
4. ¿Qué toma Isabel?
5. ¿Qué toma Laura?

*Especialidades del día*

*Tamales de mole* — *56 pesos*
*Torta de pollo con guacamole* — *40 pesos*
*Frijoles* — *30 pesos*
*Chilaquiles* — *38 pesos*
*Agua de sandía* — *7 pesos*
*Tacos de carne* — *56 pesos*
*Flan* — *22 pesos*

REPASO

## Indirect Object Pronouns

Remember that, as with direct object pronouns, you use **indirect object pronouns** when you don't want to keep repeating the **indirect object nouns.**

*direct object* · *indirect object* · *indirect object pronoun* · *direct object*

Compró **regalos** para sus **amigos.** → **Les** compró **regalos.**
*She bought **presents** for her **friends.*** — *She bought **presents for them.***

If there's an **indirect object,** there's usually also a **direct object.**

The first and second person indirect object pronouns are the same as the direct object pronouns: **me, te, nos,** and **os.**

**Indirect Object Pronouns**

| | |
|---|---|
| me | nos |
| te | os |
| le | les |

Like direct object pronouns, **indirect object pronouns** are usually placed before **conjugated verbs**, and may be attached to **infinitives** and **-ndo forms**.

El mesero **dio** la **cuenta** a **Laura.** *becomes* El mesero **le dio** la **cuenta.**
*The waiter **gave Laura** the bill.* — *The waiter **gave her** the bill.*

*attaches*
El mesero va a **darle** la **cuenta.**
*The waiter is going **to give her** the bill.*

*attaches*
El mesero está **dándole** la **cuenta.**
*The waiter is **giving her** the bill.*

## Classroom Community

**Group Activity** Have students write the sentences from **Actividad 9** with the appropriate indirect object pronouns. Cut the sentences into individual words and give the words from one sentence to a group of students. They should correctly organize the words into a complete sentence in a given time period, e.g., **La / mesera / nos / sirvió / los tamales.**

**Learning Scenario** Divide the class into groups of 3. Students imagine they are at a restaurant in a Spanish-speaking country. Student 1 (S1) speaks Spanish. S2 does not speak Spanish. The waiter, S3, needs to understand S2's order. Have students write and perform a skit which demonstrates this "language problem" being effectively solved.

## ¿A quién?

**Escribir** Isabel fue al centro ayer. Completa las oraciones sobre su visita usando **me, te, le, nos** o **les.** *(Hint: Complete the sentences.)*

**modelo**

*La mesera trajo las bebidas. (a nosotras)*
*La mesera nos trajo las bebidas.*

1. La mesera sirvió los tamales. (a nosotros)
2. La vendedora dijo el precio de la camisa. (a mí)
3. Tú diste flores. (a ella)
4. La señorita ofreció los boletos a un buen precio. (a ustedes)
5. Recomendamos el musical. (a nuestros amigos)
6. Mandé una tarjeta postal. (a ti)
7. Yo dejé una propina. (al mesero)
8. Un señor preguntó la hora. (a usted)

**MÁS PRÁCTICA** *cuaderno* p. 62
**PARA HISPANOHABLANTES** *cuaderno* p. 60

## En la ciudad

**Leer/Escribir** Lee las descripciones de algunas situaciones en la ciudad y completa las oraciones. *(Hint: Read the descriptions and complete the sentences.)*

**modelo**

*Vas a la galería de arte todas las semanas. (fascinar el arte)*
*Te fascina el arte.*

**Nota**

Remember that with **gustar,** the subject (the thing liked) follows the verb, and the indirect object **(me, te, le, nos, os, les)** comes before the subject.

**Me gusta** el pescado, pero **no me gustan** las salchichas.
***I like** fish, but **I don't like** hot dogs.*

Other verbs that follow the same rule are listed in the vocabulary box.

1. La señora Rojas admira mucho a su cantante favorito. (encantar los musicales)
2. En el restaurante, ustedes piden sopa y sólo tienen un tenedor. (faltar una cuchara)
3. Voy al teatro todos los viernes. (fascinar las obras de teatro)
4. Tomamos el autobús. (importar los precios de los taxis)
5. Catalina siempre compra un periódico. (interesar las noticias)
6. Queremos ver el nuevo musical, pero los boletos son caros. (faltar dinero)

### Vocabulario

**Verbs Similar to gustar**

**encantar** *to delight*
**faltar** *to lack*
**fascinar** *to fascinate, to love (sports, food, etc.)*
**importar** *to be important to, to matter*
**interesar** *to interest*
**molestar** *to bother*

¿Te fascina el cine?



### Teaching Suggestions

- Be sure to review the vocabulary in the box at the bottom of page 155 before doing **Actividad 10**.
- Review the use of **gustar** using foods learned in this chapter. For example, **¿Te gustan los tacos? ¿Te gusta el pescado? A los estudiantes les gusta la pizza.**
- When presenting **gustar** and similar verbs, be sure to remind students that the verb agrees with the subject (the thing liked) as in, **Me gustan los frijoles pero no me gusta el pollo.**

**Objective:** Controlled practice
Indirect object pronouns

Preterite

**Answers**

1. La mesera nos sirvió los tamales.
2. La vendedora me dijo el precio de la camisa.
3. Tú le diste flores.
4. La señorita les ofreció los boletos a un buen precio.
5. Les recomendamos el musical.
6. Te mandé una tarjeta postal.
7. Yo le dejé una propina.
8. Un señor le preguntó la hora.

**Objective:** Transitional practice
Verbs similar to **gustar**

**Answers**

1. Le encantan los musicales.
2. Les falta una cuchara.
3. Me fascinan las obras de teatro.
4. Nos importan los precios de los taxis.
5. Le interesan las noticias.
6. Nos falta dinero.

### Teaching All Students

**Extra Help** Have students list the direct and indirect object pronouns, summarizing their placement before and after verbs. Have them give an example of how they are used in each way.

**Native Speakers** Have Spanish speakers give sample sentences using the verbs similar to **gustar** on p. 155.

**Multiple Intelligences**

**Kinesthetic** Choose one of the answers to **Actividad 10** or another descriptive sentence using an indirect/direct object pronoun. Write each word on a separate strip of paper. Give strips to individual students. The students stand in front of room and the class has to rearrange the words to form a sentence.

### Block Schedule

**Variety** First have the class generate a list of foods they wish to discuss. Students then ask each other about their favorite foods and report the results to be tallied on the board. After the results are in, ask students where they go to eat their favorite foods. **¿Dónde sirven el mejor helado?**

### Teaching Resource Options

**Print** 

*Más práctica* Workbook PE, pp. 63–64
*Cuaderno para hispanohablantes* PE, pp. 61–62
Block Scheduling Copymasters
Unit 2 Resource Book
*Más práctica* Workbook TE, pp. 109–110
*Cuaderno para hispanohablantes* TE, pp. 115–116
Information Gap Activities, p. 119

**Audiovisual** 

OHT 67 (Quick Start)

**Technology** 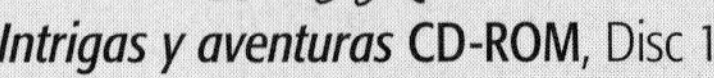

*Intrigas y aventuras* CD-ROM, Disc 1

### Quick Start Review

Indirect object pronouns

Use OHT 67 or write on board: Answer the questions following the cue given. In your answer substitute an indirect object pronoun for the indirect object.

¿Qué compraste para Vivián?
(un libro) Le compré un libro.

1. ¿Qué compraste para Luis? (los casetes)
2. ¿Qué compraste para Carmen? (la torta)
3. ¿Qué compraste para mí? (el boleto)
4. ¿Qué compraste para mis padres? (la pintura)
5. ¿Qué compraste para ti? (una rosa)

**Answers**, see p. 143B.

### Teaching Suggestion

Before doing **Actividad 11**, have students brainstorm their favorite actors/actresses, comedians, movies, and/or television shows.

**Objective:** Open-ended practice
Expressing opinions

Indirect object pronouns/ family vocabulary

*Answers will vary. Sentences should include indirect object pronouns.*

## Actividad 11 ¡Opiniones!

**PARA CONVERSAR** • **STRATEGY: SPEAKING**

**Personalize responses** Perhaps you see a great many films and even some plays. You've probably also read or seen reviews of these productions. Do you usually agree with the critics? Here's a chance for you to express your own personal preferences and feelings about show business.

**Hablar** Habla con un(a) compañero(a) de las opiniones de las siguientes personas sobre el mundo del espectáculo. *(Hint: Talk with a classmate about opinions related to show business.)*

**modelo**

**Tú:** *¿A tus amigos les fascinan las series de ciencia ficción?*
**Compañero(a):** *No, no (Sí,) les fascinan.*

| | | | |
|---|---|---|---|
| a ti | me | encantar | el actor/la actriz (*nombre*) |
| a tu mejor amigo(a) | te | fascinar | las películas de aventuras |
| a tu madre/padre | le | gustar | las series de ciencia ficción |
| a tu profesor(a) de [clase] | nos | importar | el (la) comediante (*nombre*) |
| a tus amigos(as) | os | interesar | las escenas de horror y violencia |
| a tu hermano(a) | les | molestar | el estreno (*nombre de la película*) |
| a ti y tus amigos(as) | | | las telenovelas |
| ¿? | | | la obra de teatro *Les Misérables* |

**NOTA CULTURAL**

**Las telenovelas** ¿Te gusta ver la tele? Entonces debes saber que en el mundo hispano a mucha gente le gusta ver las telenovelas. Son diferentes porque sólo duran unos meses en contraste con las de Estados Unidos, que duran décadas.

### Vocabulario

**El mundo del espectáculo**

**el actor/la actriz** *actor, actress*
**las aventuras** *adventures*
**la ciencia ficción** *science fiction*
**la comedia** *comedy*
**el (la) comediante** *comedian*
**la escena** *scene*
**el estreno** *new release*
**el horror** *horror*
**el papel** *role*
**la serie** *series*
**la telenovela** *soap opera*
**el tema** *theme, subject*

¿Cuáles te encantan?



### Classroom Community

**Group Activity** Have students describe one of the words in the vocabulary box on p. 156 and ask other students to identify it.

**Pair Work** Divide the class into pairs. Student 1 (S1) makes a list of 3 direct object pronouns. S2 makes a list of 3 indirect object pronouns. S1 and S2 then forms sentences that use both a direct and indirect object pronoun. S1 proofreads the sentences and S2 reads them to the class.

**Portfolio** Have students write in their journal about their favorite actor/actress and the role he/she plays.

**Rubric: Writing**

| Criteria | Scale |
|---|---|
| Vocabulary use | 1 2 3 4 5 |
| Accuracy | 1 2 3 4 5 |
| Creativity | 1 2 3 4 5 |

A = 13–15 pts.
B = 10–12 pts.
C = 7–9 pts.
D = 4–6 pts.
F = < 4 pts.

ACTIVIDAD 12

## ¿Qué te interesa?

**Hablar** Usa las palabras útiles para charlar con unos(as) compañeros(as) sobre lo que les interesa hacer en la ciudad.
*(Hint: Talk about interests.)*

**modelo**

**Tú:** *Cuando das una vuelta, ¿qué te interesa hacer?*

**Compañero(a):** *Me interesa ir a los museos. ¿Y a ti?*

**Nota**

When you are in the city, you could take a stroll **(dar una vuelta).**

Podemos también **dar una vuelta** por la ciudad, ¿no?

*We can also **take a stroll** around the city, right?*

**MÁS COMUNICACIÓN** p. R7

GRAMÁTICA

## Double Object Pronouns

**¿RECUERDAS?** *pp. 152, 154* You have learned about both **direct** and **indirect** object pronouns. They both go before the **conjugated verb**.

What happens if you want to have both **direct** and **indirect** object pronouns in the same sentence? The **indirect** object goes **first.**

indirect object → **Te**, direct object → **los**

**Te los compramos.**
*We bought **them for you.***

indirect object → **me**, direct object → **los**

El mesero **me los dio.**
*The waiter gave **them to me.***

Remember that when a **conjugated verb** appears with an **infinitive** or an **-ndo form,** you have two choices. You can put the pronouns before the **conjugated verb**, or you can attach them to the **infinitive** or **-ndo form.** Either way, the sentences mean the same thing:

**Me los vas a comprar.**
***You are going to buy them for me.***

**Vas a comprármelos.**
***You are going to buy them for me.***

**Me los estás comprando.**
***You are buying them for me.***

**Estás comprándomelos.**
***You are buying them for me.***

There is a special rule for verbs with two pronouns when both are **third person:** change the **indirect** object pronoun to **se.**

**Le** pedí una **servilleta** al **mesero.**
*I asked the **waiter** for a **napkin.***

indirect object → **Se**, direct object → **la**

**Se la pedimos.**
*We asked **him** for **it.***

### Teaching Suggestions
### Presenting Double Object Pronouns

- Remind students about the substitution and placement rules they already know for direct and indirect object pronouns. Practice substitution of pronouns for objects.
- Remind students that **se** is used when there are two third person object pronouns, and it is also the third person reflexive pronoun, as in **Ellos se levantan a las ocho.**
- Remind students to add accents with double object pronouns when attaching them to an infinitive or **-ndo** form.

ACTIVIDAD 12 **Objective:** Open-ended practice
Indirect object pronouns

Things to do in the city

*Answers will vary. They may include:*
**Me interesa ir de compras. Me interesa ir a la Alameda. Me interesa comer helado. Me interesa ir al cine.**

### Culture Highlights

**SHOPPING IN MEXICO CITY** The more elegant shops are found in the Polanco area or in La Zona Rosa in the West End of Mexico City. Outdoor markets are scattered around the city, the more popular ones being Mercado San Juan, Plaza Ciudadela, and Mercado San Ángel.

**PARQUE ALAMEDA** is a park with gardens, fountains, and walking paths. It was once the site of the Aztec market.

### Community Connection

Spanish-speaking actors have become more popular in the U.S. recently. Have students try to make a list of those they know. Point out Antonio Banderas (**español**), Edward James Olmos (**chicano**), Rosie Pérez (**puertorriqueña**), Jennifer López (**puertorriqueña**), Andy García (**cubanoamericano**), etc.

### Teaching All Students

**Extra Help** Have students write 5 more sentences based on the expressions given in **Actividad 11**.

**Native Speakers** Have Spanish speakers describe any plays or movies they have seen in Spanish using the vocabulary on p. 156.

**Multiple Intelligences**

**Interpersonal** Have students brainstorm a list of recent movies that fit the categories **aventura, comedia, ciencia ficción,** and **horror**. Then have students work in pairs to determine if they like or dislike the movies listed (e.g., **Me gusta/No me gusta, Me encanta,** etc.).

### Block Schedule

**Retention** Divide students into pairs. Have them use the verbs **gustar, molestar, encantar,** and **interesar** to discuss television show preferences. (For additional activities, see **Block Scheduling Copymasters.**)

## Teaching Resource Options

**Print** 

*Más práctica* Workbook PE, pp. 57–60
*Cuaderno para hispanohablantes* PE, pp. 57–58
Block Scheduling Copymasters
Unit 2 Resource Book
*Más práctica* Workbook TE, pp. 103–106
*Cuaderno para hispanohablantes* TE, pp. 111–112
Information Gap Activities, p. 120
Audioscript, pp. 131–133

**Audiovisual** 

OHT 67 (Quick Start)
Audio Program Cassette 6A, 6B / CD 6; (*Para hispanohablantes* Cassette 6B / CD 6)

**Technology**

*Intrigas y aventuras* CD-ROM, Disc 1

## Quick Start Review

Present progressive

Use OHT 67 or write on board: Imagine it is the grand opening of a new restaurant and your boss frantically asks you the following questions. You are one step ahead of her and answer each time that you are already doing it. Follow the model.

¡Las ventanas están sucias!
Sí, estoy limpiándolas.

1. ¿Pusiste los manteles en las mesas?
2. Debes ayudar a Lupe con los adornos.
3. Necesitamos lavar los cubiertos.
4. ¿Abriste la puerta?

**Answers**, see p. 143B.

## Teaching Suggestions

- When doing **Actividad 13**, have students analyze each sentence before condensing it. Circle the direct objects and underline the indirect objects, then write down the corresponding pronouns.

## A dar una vuelta

**Escribir** Isabel da una vuelta por la ciudad. Mira lo que dicen varias personas. Condensa las oraciones usando doble pronombres. *(Hint: Use double object pronouns to condense the sentences.)*

**modelo**

*La mesera les sirve los tacos a las señoras.*
*La mesera se los sirve.*

1. Tú les das dinero a los pobres.
2. ¿Me vas a escribir muchas cartas?
3. Mis nietos me dan muchos abrazos a mí.
4. Siempre me dicen la verdad.
5. Le estoy explicando la información a la señora.
6. Compramos boletos para nuestros amigos.
7. Ese chavo compra una bolsa para su novia.
8. El cine vende boletos más baratos para estudiantes.

**TAMBIÉN SE DICE**

En México se usa la palabra **chavo(a)** para referirse a **un(a) chico(a)** o **un(a) muchacho(a).** Si ves la tele en español tal vez escuchaste la palabra antes porque hay un programa famoso para niños que se llama «El chavo del ocho».

## Muchos favores

**Leer/Escribir** Hoy todo el mundo te pide favores. ¿Qué te pide? *(Hint: What favors does everyone want from you? Match the columns.)*

**modelo**

*Nosotros queremos más postre.*
*¿Nos lo pasas, por favor?*

**Nota**

The verb **ofrecer** *to offer* is often used with an indirect object pronoun.
Me **ofrecieron** un trabajo. *They **offered** me a job.*

1. No entiendo el tema de la obra de teatro.
2. Me gustaría unas enchiladas.
3. Tu hermanito necesita zapatos nuevos.
4. Tu amigo perdió los boletos para el concierto.
5. Tu mamá quiere otra taza de café.
6. No recordamos el nombre de una nueva comediante.

a. ¿Se los buscas?
b. ¿Me lo explicas?
c. ¿Me las preparas?
d. ¿Nos lo dices?
e. ¿Se la ofreces?
f. ¿Se los compras?

**MÁS PRÁCTICA** *cuaderno* pp. 63–64
**PARA HISPANOHABLANTES** *cuaderno* pp. 61–62



## Classroom Community

**Paired Activity** Have pairs of students critique movies listed in your local newspaper by stating whether or not they are interested in seeing them and explain why, e.g., **Me interesa ver __ porque __.**

**Learning Scenario** Imagine that a local newspaper is looking for Spanish reviews of favorite movies for its entertainment section. Using the vocabulary on p. 159, students work in groups to write a review of a preferred movie of their choice. One student should play the newspaper editor, another the "fact checker," a third and fourth should draft the review.

## ¿Un estreno fenomenal?

**Escribir** Con tus compañeros(as), mira el anuncio. Luego prepara una crítica de la película, usando las palabras de la lista. *(Hint: Write a movie review.)*

### Vocabulario

Para tu crítica…

| | |
|---|---|
| **bastante** *enough* | **mojado(a)** *wet* |
| **demasiado(a)** *too much* | **seco(a)** *dry* |
| **llenar** *to fill* | **vacío(a)** *empty* |
| **lleno(a)** *full* | |

¿Qué palabras pertenecen a esta película?

## Las recomendaciones

**Escuchar/Escribir** Escucha las siguientes descripciones de varios programas y decide si las personas que hablan se los recomiendan a sus amigos(as) o no. *(Hint: Do the speakers recommend the performances?)*

**modelo**

*el tema*
*No se lo recomienda.*

1. el estreno
2. las aventuras
3. la obra de teatro
4. los comediantes
5. el drama

## En un restaurante elegante

**Hablar** Con dos compañeros(as), presenta una escena en un restaurante elegante. Sé creativo(a). *(Hint: Present a creative restaurant scene.)*

**MÁS COMUNICACIÓN** p. R7

### Refrán

**Se me hace la boca agua.**

Este refrán quiere decir que unas comidas son tan deliciosas que tenemos hambre cuando las vemos. Con un(a) compañero(a), hagan una lista de las comidas que «se les hace la boca agua».

## Teaching All Students

**Extra Help** To practice pronoun positioning, have students change the answers in **Actividad 13** to the negative or interrogative form.

**Challenge** Have students brainstorm additional words or expressions to use when reviewing or describing a movie.

**Native Speakers** Have Spanish-speaking students give other **refranes** they may know. There are many that have to do with food, such as, **"Pan y cebolla a gusto, saben a gloria."**

### Multiple Intelligences

**Verbal** Have students write a simple response to the questions from **Actividad 14**, e.g., **¿Se los buscas? Sí, se los busco.**

## Teaching Suggestions

- As a variation for **Actividad 15**, have students choose their own movie to critique.
- Use the dialog on pp. 148–149 as a model for the restaurant scene that students will create in **Actividad 17**.

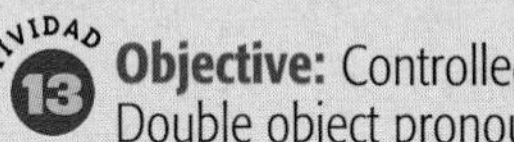

**Objective:** Controlled practice
Double object pronouns

**Answers**
1. Tú se lo das.
2. ¿Me las vas a escribor? (Vas a escribírmelas.)
3. Mis nietos me los dan.
4. Siempre me la dicen.
5. Se la estoy explicando. (Estoy explicándosela.)
6. Se los compramos.
7. Se la compra.
8. Se los vende más baratos.

**Objective:** Controlled practice
Double object pronouns

**Answers**
1. b. ¿Me lo explicas?
2. c. ¿Me las preparas?
3. f. ¿Se los compras?
4. a. ¿Se los buscas?
5. e. ¿Se la ofreces?
6. d. ¿Nos lo dices?

**Actividad 15 Objective:** Open-ended practice
Writing/discussing movies

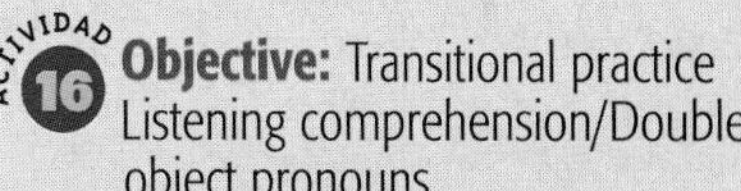

**Actividad 16 Objective:** Transitional practice
Listening comprehension/Double object pronouns

**Answers** (See script, p. 143B.)
1. No se lo recomienda.
2. Se las recomienda.
3. Se la recomienda.
4. Se los recomienda.
5. No se lo recomienda.

**Actividad 17 Objective:** Open-ended practice
Ordering in a restaurant

**En contexto** vocabulary

## Block Schedule

**FunBreak** After completing **Actividad 16**, try the second project in the **Ampliación** section on page 98A. Have students film or record an audiovisual guide for eating in a Mexican restaurant. (i.e., how to read a menu, how to order, how to eat a taco, how to pay the bill, etc.)

## Teaching Resource Options

**Print**

Block Scheduling Copymasters
Unit 2 Resource Book
Videoscript, p. 129
Audioscript, p. 131

**Audiovisual**

OHT 67
Audio Program Cassette 6A / CD 6
*Canciones* Cassette / CD Song 9
Video Program Videotape 2, 30:22 / Videodisc 2A

Search Chapter 3, Play to 4
U2E3, En voces (Culture), Spanish

Search Chapter 3, Play to 4
U2E3, En voces (Culture), English

## Quick Start Review

Countries

Use OHT 67 or write on board: Match the items in the first column with the appropriate country.

| | |
|---|---|
| Stonehenge | México |
| Machu Picchu | Perú |
| Pompeya | Italia |
| Chichén-Itzá | Inglaterra |

Are there any mysteries associated with any of these sites?

**Answers**, see p. 143B.

## Teaching Suggestions
### Presenting En voces

- **Pre-reading** Activate students' background knowledge by asking them to discuss what they know about ancient civilizations of Mexico.
- **Reading** Have students listen to the audiocassette or CD.
- **Post-reading** Have students sketch a map of Teotihuacán.
- **Strategy: Identify gaps in knowledge** Have students work in small groups to make a 2-column chart of known and unknown facts about Teotihuacán. Have students view the cultural presentation on videotape to expand the reading.

# En voces
**LECTURA**

**PARA LEER** • **STRATEGY: READING**

**Identify gaps in knowledge** Careful writing is clear about what is known and what is speculation or a guess. As you read about Teotihuacán, jot down what is known and not known about this **ciudad misteriosa.** Make a chart like the one started here.

| Teotihuacán | |
|---|---|
| conocido | desconocido |
| el plan maestro | origen |

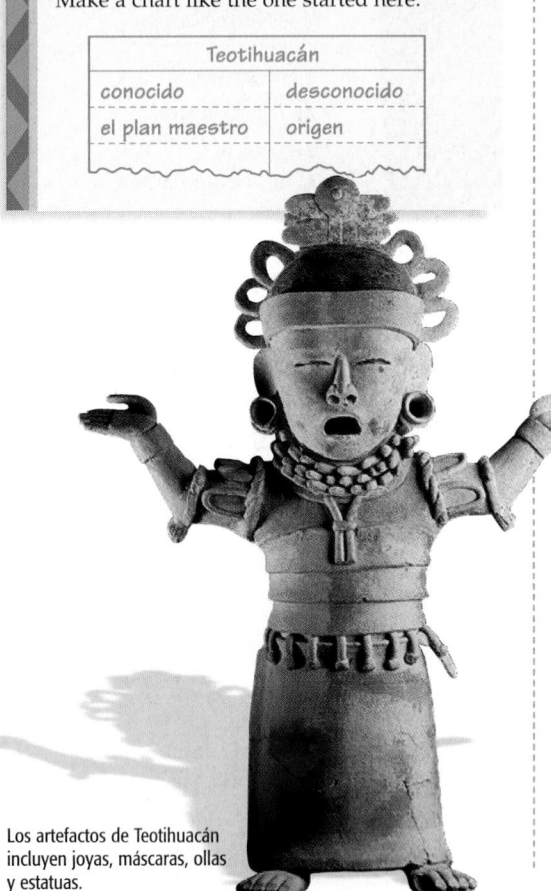

Los artefactos de Teotihuacán incluyen joyas, máscaras, ollas y estatuas.

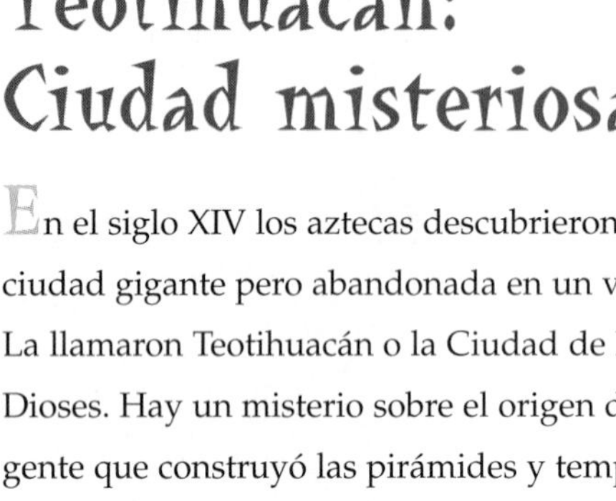

## Teotihuacán: Ciudad misteriosa

En el siglo XIV los aztecas descubrieron una ciudad gigante pero abandonada en un valle. La llamaron Teotihuacán o la Ciudad de los Dioses. Hay un misterio sobre el origen de la gente que construyó las pirámides y templos de esta ciudad. Por las esculturas y cerámicas que dejaron parece que ellos fueron una gente pacífica[1].

Parece que Teotihuacán fue diseñada por un plan maestro[2]. Tiene una avenida central, la Avenida de los Muertos. Aquí están las pirámides principales. Desde la avenida las calles secundarias salen en forma cuadriculada[3]. Alrededor de la avenida central hay ruinas de casas lujosas y en los sectores exteriores, casas más sencillas.

En un lado de la Avenida de los Muertos hay un sector grande que probablemente fue un mercado. Los arqueólogos piensan que aquí

[1] peaceful [2] master plan [3] square



## Classroom Community

**Cooperative Learning** Divide the class into 4 groups. Have students research aspects of Teotihuacán mentioned in this reading. Group 1 researches more on temples and pyramids. Group 2 researches the people who lived there. Group 3 researches artifacts. Group 4 researches the mysterious abandonment of the temples and pyramids. Cue students to use the Internet or library resources. Groups then share their findings with the class.

**Storytelling** Have students work in small groups to tell a story about another mysterious city or civilization they may know. If the group can't think of one, they can create an imaginary story.

*Avenida de los Muertos, Teotihuacán*

Si vas al Museo Nacional de Antropología, puedes ver esta máscara de jade y coral de Teotihuacán.

llegaron negociantes de otras partes de México a comprar la obsidiana[4] y la cerámica fabricada en Teotihuacán, y a vender sus propios productos.

Teotihuacán fue el centro urbano más grande e importante en el Valle Central de México durante la época precolombina. Llegó a tener una población de más de 150.000 personas alrededor del siglo III o IV[5]. Pero aproximadamente en el año 750, por razones desconocidas hasta hoy, la ciudad fue quemada o destruida[6] y, al final, abandonada.

[4] hard, black, volcanic rock
[5] third or fourth century
[6] burned or destroyed

## ¿Comprendiste?

1. ¿De dónde viene el nombre Teotihuacán?
2. ¿Por qué parece que Teotihuacán fue diseñada por un plan maestro?
3. ¿Qué productos estaban de venta en el mercado?
4. ¿Sabemos exactamente por qué la civilización desapareció? Explica tu respuesta.

## ¿Qué piensas?

1. ¿Puedes hacer unas comparaciones entre Teotihuacán y tu ciudad?
2. ¿Tienen las calles de tu ciudad un plano regular o irregular? ¿Qué son los edificios importantes? ¿Cómo son las casas? ¿Dónde están con relación al centro?



## Culture Highlights

- **LOS AZTECAS** were a brilliant indigenous civilization that flourished in central Mexico until the Spanish conquest in 1519. The Aztecs had an advanced civilization with a monarchy or monarchial government, classed society, and cultural riches in architecture, literature, pottery, and jewelry.
- **TEOTIHUACÁN** is located about 45 km from Mexico City and has some of the most remarkable ruins from a mysterious civilization dating back to 300 B.C. Teotihuacán was abandoned so completely that it was the Aztecs who named all the locations when they settled there later in the 14th century.
- **QUETZACÓATL** is the God of Air and Wind, known as the "feathered serpent" to the Toltecs and Mayans. It is said that the Aztec leader Moctezuma II mistook Cortés, the Spanish conqueror, for Quetzacóatl, which helped lead to the Aztecs' destruction.

## ¿Comprendiste?

### Answers

1. Significa la Ciudad de los Dioses.
2. Porque tiene una avenida central y desde la avenida las calles secundarias salen en forma cuadrangular.
3. La obsidiana y la cerámica y otros productos.
4. No sabemos exactamente por qué desapareció la civilización. *Explanations will vary.*

## Cross Cultural Connections

**Strategy** Have students research some early Native American archaeological sites in the U.S. and compare them to Teotihuacán.

## Teaching All Students

**Extra Help** Have students listen to the Audio Program reading, then reread the reading themselves in small groups. Then ask each group to summarize a paragraph in one or two sentences and share them with the class.

**Multiple Intelligences**

**Verbal** Have students describe any ruins or archaeological sites they have visited.

**Logical/Mathematical** Have students design a map based on the description of Teotihuacán in this reading. Then have them draw a similar map outlining their city or town and label the important buildings and streets.

## Block Schedule

**Variety** After drawing a map of Teotihuacán, have students compare it to their own state capital. (For additional activities, see **Block Scheduling Copymasters**.)

## Teaching Resource Options

**Print** 

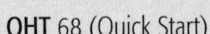

*Cuaderno para hispanohablantes* PE, pp. 63–64

Unit 2 Resource Book
*Cuaderno para hispanohablantes* TE, pp. 117–118

**Audiovisual**

OHT 68 (Quick Start)

## Quick Start Review

Preterite/telling time

Use OHT 68 or write on board: Answer the following questions with a complete sentence in Spanish.

1. ¿A qué hora desayunaste esta mañana? ¿Qué comiste?
2. ¿A qué hora comiste el almuerzo? ¿Qué comiste?
3. ¿A qué hora comiste la cena anoche? ¿Qué comiste?

*Answers will vary.*

## Teaching Suggestions
### Presenting En colores

- **Pre-reading** Activate students' background knowledge by asking them to list the Mexican foods they have eaten. Also ask them to discuss their own meal times and special customs.
- **Strategy: Compare meals and mealtimes** Students can create a Venn diagram to compare and contrast Mexican eating habits, based on this reading, and U.S. eating habits, based on students' interviews or their own experiences.

## Cross Cultural Connections

Divide the class in half. Ask half of the students to compare foods they eat with what their parents eat and the other half to compare what they eat with foods their grandparents used to eat. Have students draw a Venn diagram to compare and contrast the different foods and eating customs.

# En colores
## CULTURA Y COMPARACIONES

*La cochinita pibil, puerco asado en una hoja de plátano y servido en tacos o tamales, es típico del sur de México.*

### PARA CONOCERNOS
**STRATEGY: CONNECTING CULTURES**

**Compare meals and mealtimes** Interview three people of different ages or backgrounds to find out at what time of day they eat their main meal and the name for that meal. Make a chart like the one here and then compare your answers.

| Nombre | Edad | Comida principal | Hora |
| --- | --- | --- | --- |
| Adriana | 15 | almuerzo | 1:00 p.m. |
| | | | |

# ¡BUEN PROVECHO! LA COMIDA MEXICANA

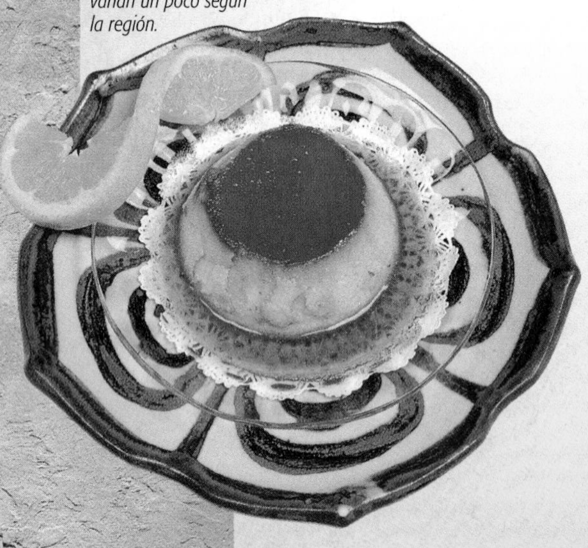

*El flan es un postre que se ve por todo el país. Los ingredientes varían un poco según la región.*

La cocina[1] mexicana es una de las más variadas del mundo. La mayor parte de platos mexicanos tienen su origen en el mundo precolombino, pero hay otros que son variantes de platos españoles. En Estados Unidos se comen algunos platos mexicanos típicos como los tacos, las enchiladas, el guacamole y la salsa picante.

La cocina mexicana es a base de maíz[2]. De la harina de maíz se hacen las tortillas, el

[1] cuisine [2] corn



## Classroom Community 

**Paired Activity** Have students reread the text and list the most important aspect in each paragraph.

**Learning Scenario** Divide the class into two groups. One group will describe the meals for a typical day in Mexico based on the reading. The other group will describe the meals for a typical day in their present-day lives. Be sure to include all three meals.

**Group Activity** On a set of index cards write down the following words: **desayuno en mi casa, almuerzo en mi casa, merienda en la escuela, cena en mi casa, comida con la familia, fiesta de cumpleaños, picnic en el fin de semana**. Divide the class into several small groups. Have each group choose a card and then determine the elements of the meal.

***Los chiles rellenos*** de este tipo se vende mucho en Veracruz, una ciudad en el centro de México.

***Las flautas*** A estos tacos fritos se les llaman «flautas» porque tienen la forma del instrumento musical. Los sirven por todo México.

***El mole negro*** Puedes pedir mole negro, un platillo que incluye una salsa con más de 20 ingredientes, cuando visitas Oaxaca, una ciudad en el sur del país.

equivalente mexicano del pan. Las tortillas son un elemento importante en muchas recetas. Otros alimentos importantes en México son el arroz, los frijoles, el chocolate, los chiles y los tomates.

En cuanto a[3] las costumbres de comida, lo que es tradicional en México es un desayuno y, generalmente alrededor de las dos de la tarde, un almuerzo fuerte (la comida principal del día) que se llama *la comida*. Típicamente, la cena es ligera[4], como un yogur o un sándwich.

[3] as for [4] light

## ¿Comprendiste?

1. ¿Qué orígenes tiene la comida mexicana?
2. ¿Qué platos mexicanos se comen en Estados Unidos?
3. ¿Cuál es el alimento básico en México?
4. Describe las tres comidas del día en México.

## ¿Qué piensas?

1. ¿Cuáles son los alimentos que se usan en más de un plato?
2. ¿Por qué crees que algunos platos mexicanos son de origen precolombino y otros de origen español?

## Hazlo tú 

Con unos(as) compañeros(as), busquen unas recetas mexicanas. Estúdienlas para ver cuáles pueden hacer en Estados Unidos. Escojan una, háganla y preséntensela a la clase. Sírvanles el plato a sus compañeros(as), contándoles de qué región viene y cómo se hace. ¡Buen provecho!



## Reading Strategy

Summarize each paragraph to be sure important information is clearly understood.

## Culture Highlights

- **TACOS** are often filled with meat or chicken mixed with beans, and stuffed in a soft corn tortilla shell. **Flautas** are tacos that are rolled and then fried. There are many taquerías on the streets of Mexico that serve these "fast foods."

## ¿Comprendiste?

**Answers**

1. Tiene su origen en el mundo precolombino.
2. los tacos, las enchiladas, el guacamole y la salsa picante
3. maíz
4. En México se come un desayuno, un almuerzo fuerte y una cena ligera.

## Community Connections

Have students try to find local job opportunities that may include the use of Spanish and post a list on the bulletin board.

## Teaching All Students

**Native Speakers** Ask Spanish speakers to describe a typical meal schedule in the country their family comes from.

**Multiple Intelligences**

**Intrapersonal** Have students describe the pictures of food on p. 163. Which meal appeals most to them? Have students describe how it would feel to follow a typical Mexican meal schedule. How would it affect their present lifestyle?

## Block Schedule

**Change of Pace** Have students create a shopping list for the foods they would need for one of the meals listed in the **Group Activity** note in **Classroom Community** at the bottom of p. 162. Have students come up with other meal situations and create corresponding shopping lists.

## Teaching Resource Options

**Print** 

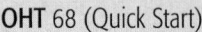

Block Scheduling Copymasters
Unit 2 Resource Book
Information Gap Activities, pp. 121–122
Family Involvement, pp. 123–124

**Audiovisual** 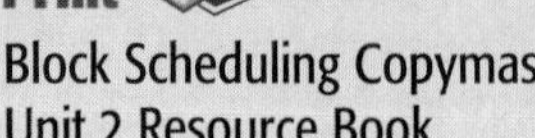

OHT 68 (Quick Start)

**Technology** 

Electronic Teacher Tools/Test Generator
*Intrigas y aventuras* CD-ROM, Disc 1

## Quick Start Review

Food/direct object pronouns

Use OHT 68 or write on board: Imagine your mother wants to make sure you bought everything on the grocery list. Answer her using a direct object pronoun. Follow the model.

¿Compraste los tomates?
Sí, los compré.

1. la harina
2. el pan
3. las manzanas
4. el pescado
5. la carne de res
6. las verduras

**Answers**, see p. 143B.

## Teaching Suggestions
### What Have Students Learned?

- Have students look at the "Now you can..." notes listed on the left side of pp. 164–165. Point out that if they feel they need to review material before doing the activities, they should consult the "To review" notes.
- Use the video to review vocabulary and structures.

# En uso
## REPASO Y MÁS COMUNICACIÓN

**OBJECTIVES**
- Order in a restaurant
- Ask for and pay a restaurant bill
- Talk about things to do in the city

*Now you can...*
- order in a restaurant.

*To review*
- direct object pronouns, see p. 152.

### ACTIVIDAD 1 ¿Me ayudas?

Estás comiendo en un restaurante con un niño pequeño. Explícale cómo comer las siguientes cosas. *(Hint: Tell a child how to eat the different foods.)*

**modelo**
*¿Cerezas o tomate?*
*¿Los tacos? Puedes comerlos con tomate.*

1. ¿El cuchillo o la cuchara? 
2. ¿Sal o azúcar? 
3. ¿La cuchara o las manos? 
4. ¿Las manos o el tenedor? 
5. ¿Mantequilla o mantequilla de cacahuate? 
6. ¿Aceite o harina? 

*Now you can...*
- talk about things to do in the city.

*To review*
- indirect object pronouns, see p. 154.
- verbs similar to **gustar**, see p. 155.

### ACTIVIDAD 2 ¡Vamos al centro!

Todos están hablando de actividades en la ciudad. ¿Qué dicen? *(Hint: Tell people's opinions of city activities.)*

**modelo**
*Juan y yo (interesar) visitar los museos*
*A Juan y a mí nos interesa visitar los museos.*

1. mis padres (encantar) las galerías de arte
2. yo (gustar) los actores mexicanos
3. tú (importar) ver los estrenos
4. nosotros (molestar) pagar los precios de los boletos
5. Tomás y Berta (fascinar) las obras de teatro
6. ustedes (faltar) dinero para salir

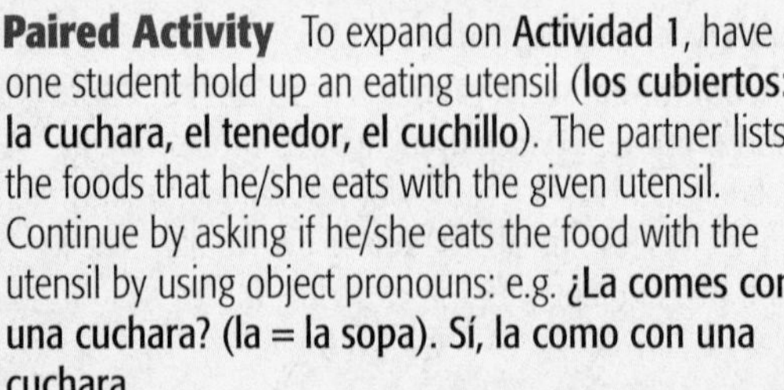

## Classroom Community

**Paired Activity** To expand on **Actividad 1**, have one student hold up an eating utensil (**los cubiertos: la cuchara, el tenedor, el cuchillo**). The partner lists the foods that he/she eats with the given utensil. Continue by asking if he/she eats the food with the utensil by using object pronouns: e.g. **¿La comes con una cuchara? (la = la sopa). Sí, la como con una cuchara.**

**Learning Scenario** Working in pairs, imagine that you (Student 1) are in Mexico City eating dinner at a restaurant with your little brother or sister (Student 2). Using **Actividad 1** as a model, create a dialog in which you (S1) help your sibling (S2) understand how to eat various items on the menu. Present the dialog to the class.

*Now you can...*
- order in a restaurant.

*To review*
- indirect object pronouns, see p. 154.
- double object pronouns, see p. 157.

## Actividad 3 ¿Qué nos recomienda?

Raúl y sus amigos piden la comida en un restaurante mexicano. ¿Qué les recomiendan los meseros? ¿Cómo se lo van a servir? *(Hint: Tell what the waiters recommend and how it will be served.)*

**modelo**

*María: la sopa (una torta)*

*Le recomiendan la sopa. Van a servírsela con una torta.*

1. nosotros: los tacos (salsa picante)
2. yo: el pescado (cebolla)
3. Gabriel: las verduras (sal y pimienta)
4. Salvador y yo: el melón (azúcar)
5. tú: el pollo (tortillas)
6. ustedes: la carne de res (frijoles)
7. yo: las papas asadas (mantequilla)
8. Alex y Sandra: la pasta (queso)

*Now you can...*
- order in a restaurant.
- ask for and pay a restaurant bill.

*To review*
- double object pronouns, see p. 157.

## Actividad 4 ¿Qué desean?

Imagínate que trabajas en un restaurante como mesero(a). Contesta que sí a las preguntas de los clientes. *(Hint: You are a waiter or waitress at a restaurant. Answer yes to the customers' questions.)*

**modelo**

*¿Me trae unos cubiertos, por favor?*

*Sí, se los traigo.*

1. ¿Me trae el menú, por favor?
2. ¿Nos recomienda las enchiladas?
3. ¿Le sirve un café a mi esposa, por favor?
4. ¿Nos trae más pan, por favor?
5. ¿Les sirve más limonada a mis hijos, por favor?
6. ¿Me trae la cuenta, por favor?
7. ¿Le doy la tarjeta de crédito a usted?
8. ¿Le dejo la propina en la mesa?

### Actividad 1 Answers

1. ¿La sopa? Puedes comerla con la cuchara.
2. ¿El pescado? Puedes comerlo con sal.
3. ¿La torta? Puedes comerla con las manos.
4. ¿La zanahoria? Puedes comerla con las manos.
5. ¿Las papas? Puedes comerlas con mantequilla.
6. ¿La ensalada? Puedes comerla con aceite.

### Actividad 2 Answers

1. A mis padres les encantan las galerías de arte.
2. A mí me gustan los actores mexicanos.
3. A ti te importa ver los estrenos.
4. A nosotros nos molesta pagar los precios de los boletos.
5. A Tomás y a Berta les fascinan las obras de teatro.
6. A ustedes les falta dinero para salir.

### Actividad 3 Answers

1. Nos recomiendan los tacos. Van a servírnoslos con salsa picante.
2. Me recomiendan el pescado. Van a servírmelo con cebolla.
3. Le recomiendan las verduras. Van a servírselas con sal y pimienta.
4. Nos recomiendan el melón. Van a servírnoslo con azúcar.
5. Te recomiendan el pollo. Van a servírtelo con tortillas.
6. Les recomiendan la carne de res. Van a servírsela con frijoles.
7. Me recomiendan las papas asadas. Van a servírmelas con mantequilla.
8. Les recomiendan la pasta. Van a servírsela con queso.

### Actividad 4 Answers

1. Sí, se lo traigo.
2. Sí, se las recomiendo.
3. Sí, se lo sirvo.
4. Sí, se lo traigo.
5. Sí, se la sirvo.
6. Sí, se la traigo.
7. Sí, me la da.
8. Sí, me la deja en la mesa.

## Teaching All Students

**Extra Help** Have students review the food vocabulary they have learned by going through the *Etapa* and identifying all the food items in photos or pictures.

**Challenge** Ask pairs of students to write out 3 foods they recommend from the school cafeteria. **Nosotros recomendamos la sopa.** Then, have students switch lists with another pair of students and add what they will serve with the recommendation given, e.g., **Se la servimos con una cuchara.**

### Multiple Intelligences

**Logical/Mathematical** In a small group, have students list 8–10 items that they like to order in a restaurant. Give the list to another group to categorize as breakfast, lunch, or dinner items. Encourage them to be creative.

## Block Schedule

**Variety** Have students use an actual menu from a Mexican restaurant as an expansion of **Actividad 3**. Or you can have students create their own Mexican restaurant menu.

## Teaching Resource Options

### Print

Unit 2 Resource Book
- Audioscript, pp. 133–134
- Cooperative Quizzes, pp. 135–136
- Etapa Exam, Forms A and B, pp. 137–146
- *Examen para hispanohablantes,* pp. 147–151
- Portfolio Assessment, pp. 152–153
- Unit 2 Comprehensive Test, pp. 154–161
- *Prueba comprensiva para hispanohablantes,* Unit 2, pp. 162–169
- Multiple Choice Test Questions, pp. 176–178

### Audiovisual

**OHT** 59, 60, 61, 61A, 62, 62A, 68 (Quick Start)
**Audio Program** Cassette 19A, 19B / CD 19; (*Para hispanohablantes* Cassette 19A, 19B / CD 19)

### Technology

Electronic Teacher Tools/Test Generator
www.mcdougallittell.com

## Quick Start Review

Leisure activities

Use OHT 68 or write on board: Based on what you have learned about Mexico City, write down five activities a tourist might do in the city. Use the infinitive. For example: **ir a una galería de arte.**

*Answers will vary. Answers could include:*
**comer en un restaurante, ir al parque, visitar un museo, asistir el teatro, ver una película, ir a una taquería.**

### Rubric: Speaking

| Criteria | Scale | |
|---|---|---|
| Fluency | 1 2 3 | A = 8–9 pts. |
| Vocabulary | 1 2 3 | B = 6–7 pts. |
| Pronunciation, rhythm | 1 2 3 | C = 4–5 pts. |
| | | D = 3 pts. |
| | | F = < 3 pts. |

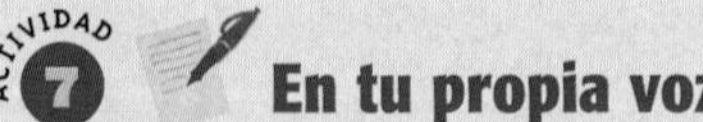

### Rubric: Writing

| Criteria | Scale | |
|---|---|---|
| Vocabulary use | 1 2 3 4 5 | A = 13–15 pts. |
| Accuracy | 1 2 3 4 5 | B = 10–12 pts. |
| Creativity, appearance | 1 2 3 4 5 | C = 7–9 pts. |
| | | D = 4–6 pts. |
| | | F = < 4 pts. |

## Actividad 5 ¿Me pasas...?

**PARA CONVERSAR**
**STRATEGY: SPEAKING**
**Resolve misconceptions** Your partner may ask for something you don't have. To resolve the misunderstanding, offer what you do have: **No tengo X, pero puedo pasarte Y.**

Estás comiendo en un restaurante con tu amigo(a). Dibuja cuatro cosas, comidas o cubiertos, en papeles separados. Entonces, pídeselas a tu amigo(a). *(Hint: You and a partner draw restaurant items and ask each other for them.)*

**modelo**

**Tú:** *Las cerezas… ¿me las pasas, por favor?*
**Amigo(a):** *¡Cómo no! Te las paso en seguida.*

## Actividad 6 ¡Problemas!

Tú y dos compañeros(as) están en un restaurante. Una persona hace el papel del (de la) mesero(a) y las otras hacen el papel de los clientes. El (La) pobre mesero(a) tiene problemas porque un cliente lo critica todo y el otro le hace muchas preguntas. *(Hint: A server is trying to please two difficult customers. Act out the scene.)*

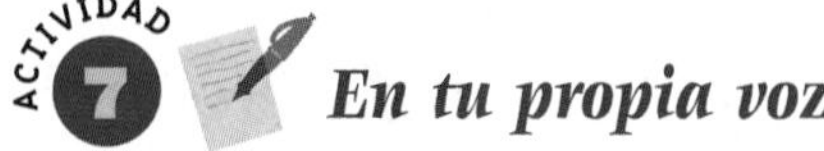

## Actividad 7 En tu propia voz

**ESCRITURA** Imagínate que estás de vacaciones con tu familia. Escríbele una tarjeta postal a un(a) amigo(a). Incluye las reacciones de varios miembros de la familia a cinco actividades que hicieron durante el viaje. *(Hint: Write a postcard describing a vacation.)*

México
XOCHIMILCO
Querida Sonia:
Me gusta mucho México. Me fascinan los museos pero a mamá no le gusta visitarlos. Prefiere ir al teatro. Le encantan las obras musicales. Los cantantes mexicanos son muy buenos.
¡Saludos! —Catarina
Sonia Díaz
2 Main St.
Rye, NY 01580
U.S.A.


## TÚ EN LA COMUNIDAD

**Sharon** es una estudiante de Massachusetts. Cuando estaba trabajando de consejera (*counselor*) en un campamento, hablaba español con algunos niños que no podían expresarse en inglés. También habla español con parientes, amigos y gente de la comunidad. ¿Con quién practicas el español?

## Classroom Community

**Paired Activity** As a quick check on vocabulary, have students review each word in the vocabulary list on p. 167 with a partner to see if they know the meanings.

**Storytelling** Divide the class into 3 groups. Each group is assigned a cluster of vocabulary words from the list (Order in a restaurant/Things to do in the city/Other words). Each group uses their cluster of vocabulary to tell a short story or prepare a dialog, and then shares it with the class.

# En resumen

## REPASO DE VOCABULARIO

### ORDER IN A RESTAURANT

**At the Restaurant**

| | |
|---|---|
| **el aceite** | *oil* |
| **la carne de res** | *beef* |
| **las cebollas** | *onions* |
| **las cerezas** | *cherries* |
| **los cubiertos** | *silverware* |
| **los frijoles** | *beans* |
| **la harina** | *flour* |
| **el mantel** | *tablecloth* |
| **las manzanas** | *apples* |
| **el pan** | *bread* |
| **las papas** | *potatoes* |
| **la pasta** | *pasta* |
| **las peras** | *pears* |
| **el pescado** | *fish* |
| **la pimienta** | *pepper* |
| **la sal** | *salt* |
| **las salchichas** | *hot dogs, sausages* |
| **la servilleta** | *napkin* |
| **el taco** | *taco* |
| **la taquería** | *taco restaurant* |
| **los tomates** | *tomatoes* |
| **la torta** | *sandwich* |
| **las verduras** | *vegetables* |
| **las zanahorias** | *carrots* |

**Common Expressions**

| | |
|---|---|
| **¿Qué desea(n)?** | *What would you like?* |
| **¿Qué me (nos) recomienda?** | *What do you recommend?* |
| **¡Salud!** | *Cheers!* |
| **¿Se le(s) ofrece algo más?** | *May I offer you anything more?* |

### ASK FOR/PAY A RESTAURANT BILL

| | |
|---|---|
| **la cuenta** | *bill* |
| **dejar la propina** | *to leave the tip* |

### THINGS TO DO IN THE CITY

**People**

| | |
|---|---|
| **el actor** | *actor* |
| **la actriz** | *actress* |
| **el (la) cantante** | *singer* |
| **el (la) comediante** | *comedian* |

**Activities and Events**

| | |
|---|---|
| **las aventuras** | *adventures* |
| **la ciencia ficción** | *science fiction* |
| **la comedia** | *comedy* |
| **dar una vuelta** | *to take a walk, stroll, or ride* |
| **la escena** | *scene* |
| **el estreno** | *new release* |
| **el horror** | *horror* |
| **el musical** | *musical* |
| **la obra de teatro** | *theatrical production* |
| **romántico(a)** | *romantic* |
| **la serie** | *series* |
| **la telenovela** | *soap opera* |
| **el tema** | *theme, subject* |

### OTHER WORDS AND PHRASES

| | |
|---|---|
| **bastante** | *enough* |
| **cenar** | *to eat dinner* |
| **demasiado(a)** | *too much* |
| **llenar** | *to fill* |
| **lleno(a)** | *full* |
| **mojado(a)** | *wet* |
| **ofrecer** | *to offer* |
| **el papel** | *role* |
| **seco(a)** | *dry* |
| **vacío(a)** | *empty* |

**Verbs Similar to** gustar

| | |
|---|---|
| **encantar** | *to delight* |
| **faltar** | *to lack* |
| **fascinar** | *to fascinate, to love (sports, food, etc.)* |
| **importar** | *to be important to, to matter* |
| **interesar** | *to interest* |
| **molestar** | *to bother* |

**Juego**

*¿Qué soy yo?*

Puedo ser feliz o triste, y tal vez romántica. Te puedo llevar a muchos lugares. Alguien me escribió y otros me presentan. Necesito personas que se ven, personas que no se ven y personas que ven para salir bien. Tal vez necesitas boletos para verme. ¿Qué soy yo?



## Teaching Note: En tu propia voz

**Writing Strategy** Encourage students to think about 5 events during a 5-day vacation trip, and the possible reactions or emotions to each one. Then have them organize the information in a paragraph.

## Teaching Suggestions
### Vocabulary Review

- Have students categorize the food words in the first column of the **Repaso de Vocabulario** on page 167.
- Have students give examples of the people and events listed in the second column.

## Juego

**Answer:** una obra de teatro

## Critical Thinking

After solving the **Juego**, have students work in groups to develop their own new **Juego**.

## Community Connections

Have students find out if there are opportunities working with children where a knowledge of Spanish would be useful.

## Project: Reviewing Etapa 3

Assign the following activities:

- Write a review of a Mexican restaurant
- Interview a Spanish speaker about what he or she likes to do in the city
- Find information on the Aztec civilization via the Internet

**Extra Credit**

| | |
|---|---|
| Mexican restaurant review | 2 pts. |
| Interview | 2 pts. |
| Aztec civilization | 2 pts. |

## Teaching All Students

**Extra Help** Have students regroup the vocabulary words to fit a pattern for them to study the meanings. Encourage them to be creative. They may have up to 7 categories.

**Native Speakers** Have Spanish speakers create other **Juegos** to help students review the vocabulary.

**Multiple Intelligences**

**Verbal** Have students create a logical sentence using as many vocabulary words as possible.

**Musical/Rhythmic** Play the *Canciones* Cassette/CD for the class. Have students choose appropriate music for these situations: eating in a Mexican restaurant, eating in an elegant restaurant, during a romantic movie, and during a horror movie.

## Block Schedule

**Peer Teaching** Based on student responses to the review on p. 164, divide the class into pairs in which one student teaches/reviews with a partner a concept he or she understands well. Take turns and/or switch pairs as needed.

### Teaching Resource Options

**Print**
Block Scheduling Copymasters

**Audiovisual**
OHT GO1–GO5; 68 (Quick Start)

**Technology**
*Intrigas y aventuras* CD-ROM, Disc 1
www.mcdougallittell.com

### Quick Start Review

Preterite/imperfect

Use OHT 68 or write on board: Give the preterite and the imperfect for the following:

1. yo soy
2. tú miras
3. nosotros llamamos

**Answers**
1. yo fui; yo era
2. tú miraste; tú mirabas
3. nosotros llamamos; nosotros llamábamos

### Teaching Suggestion
**Prewriting**
- Have students generate a list of children's stories they remember from their childhood. Choose one well-known story and have the students identify the characters, setting, plot, background, and structure, ending with a story map.
- Bring in several examples of Spanish children's books for students to review.
- Point out the **PASS** list at the beginning of the page.

**Post-writing**
- Have students exchange stories with a partner and concentrate on reviewing the plot structure and the ending. Have them make suggestions to make the plot clearer and the ending more appropriate or interesting.
- Since most children's stories are read aloud, have students form small groups to read their stories aloud.

UNIDAD 2

# *En tu propia voz*
**ESCRITURA**

## Escribe un cuento

The Spanish classes at your school were invited to write and illustrate children's picture books in Spanish for local elementary schools. Write a short story that would appeal to young children.

**Purpose:** Provide books in Spanish for local children
**Audience:** Elementary schoolchildren
**Subject:** Story writing
**Structure:** Picture book

El cumpleaños de Quique

**PARA ESCRIBIR • STRATEGY: WRITING**

**Develop your story** An interesting, well-planned story will hold your reader's attention. Remember to thoroughly develop your ideas for characters and plot.

## Modelo del estudiante

Había una vez una granja pequeña en México. En la granja vivía un cerdito pequeño, Quique. Quique era muy amable: obediente, sociable y animado. Le gustaba contar chistes y jugar con los otros animales.

*The writer tells where the story takes place.*

*The writer describes the main character of the story.*

El día de su cumpleaños empezó muy mal para Quique. Se levantó tarde por la mañana y no había más desayuno. –No hay problema –dijo Quique–. Voy a celebrar con mis amigos.

Entonces, salió del corral en busca de los otros animales, pero no había nadie por ninguna parte. El pobre cerdito estaba muy triste.

Quique regresó al corral, solito. De repente, todos sus amigos saltaron de los rincones del corral y gritaron: –¡Feliz cumpleaños, Quiquito!

*The story contains a series of events that make up the plot.*

–¡Qué sorpresa! –exclamó Quique alegremente. Luego todos los animales celebraron con una fiesta magnífica y Quique rompió la piñata.

*The story has a happy ending.*

### Classroom Community

**Paired Activity** Have students work with a partner to brainstorm a list of memorable storybook characters. Then have students describe each character briefly (including physical and personality traits).

**Storytelling** Bring in children's picture books and cover up the English words. Have students work in groups to tell the story in Spanish. Use this oral storytelling exercise as a warm-up for students to make up their own story in Spanish.

## Estrategias para escribir

### Antes de escribir...

A good children's story contains a setting (time, place), a few characters, and a basic plot (series of events). The action of the story moves along quickly, usually toward a happy ending. Before you write, create a story map like this one to plan and organize your ideas.

| | |
|---|---|
| Personaje central: | un pato tímido |
| Lugar: | un río de Nueva York |
| Situación: | El pato no sabía nadar. No podía ir de vacaciones con la familia. |
| Lo que pasa: | 1. Consultó con otros.<br>2. Miraba a sus hermanos.<br>3. Practicaba cada mañana.<br>4.<br>5. |
| Fin: | Aprendió a nadar. |

### Revisiones

Share your draft with a partner. Then ask

- *Do the characters' words and actions make sense?*
- *Is there a real problem or situation that moves the story along?*
- *Does the story come to a natural or interesting stopping point?*

Revise your draft based on your partner's answers.

### La versión final

Before you create the final draft of your story, check your writing and use proofreading symbols (p. 97) to correct any errors you find. Look over your work with the following questions in mind:

- *Did I use the preterite in the right places?*

**Try this:** Find each preterite form and make sure it refers to a completed action in the past. If not, change to the imperfect.

- *Did I use the imperfect correctly?*

**Try this:** Locate each imperfect form. Does each refer to an ongoing action or description in the past? If not, change to the preterite.

Cerca de un río de Nueva York vivía un pato tímido con su familia. Todos los días el pato Danilo miraba las nubes o corrió de un lugar a otro. Sus hermanos siempre jugaron en el río, pero Danilo no.

Un día los padres llamó a sus hijos y les dijeron sus planes para ir de vacaciones.

Share your writing on www.mcdougallittell.com



## Supplementary Vocabulary

| | |
|---|---|
| **Había una vez** | Once upon a time |
| **tener lugar** | to take place |
| **por fin** | finally |

## Rubric: Writing

Let students know ahead of time which elements of their writing you will be evaluating. A global evaluation is more helpful to students than a correction of every mistake made. Consider the following in scoring compositions.

| | Sentences |
|---|---|
| 1 | Most not logical |
| 2 | In logical order |
| 3 | Flow purposefully |
| | **Details** |
| 1 | Few details |
| 2 | Sufficient basic details |
| 3 | Clear and vivid details |
| | **Organization** |
| 1 | Not well organized |
| 2 | Some organization |
| 3 | Strong organization |
| | **Accuracy** |
| 1 | Errors prevent comprehension |
| 2 | Some spelling and agreement errors throughout |
| 3 | Very few errors |

| Criteria | Scale | |
|---|---|---|
| Logical sentence order | 1 2 3 | A = 10–12 pts. |
| Clear and vivid detail | 1 2 3 | B = 7–9 pts. |
| Organization | 1 2 3 | C = 4–6 pts. |
| Accuracy | 1 2 3 | D = 3 pts. |
| | | F = < 3 pts. |

## Teaching All Students

**Extra Help** Review structures with students before writing:

- Use of **ser** to describe physical and personality traits
- Use of adjectives that agree in gender and number with the subject
- Use of preterite regular and irregular verbs
- Use of imperfect regular and irregular verbs

**Challenge** Have students come up with examples for each of the 4 structures reviewed in the Extra Help section.

**Native Speakers** Have Spanish speakers bring in any Spanish children's books they read as children. Or have them tell any stories they remember from their childhood to the rest of the class.

## Block Schedule

**FunBreak** Have students illustrate their stories with drawings, paintings, or pictures from magazines. Create actual books to share with children. (For additional activities, see **Block Scheduling Copymasters**.)

## Unit Theme

**Discussing ways to stay fit and healthy, talking about daily routine and chores, and talking about the beach.**

**Communication**
- Talking about fitness, health, and illness
- Making suggestions
- Talking about daily routine, personal care, and chores
- Telling someone what to do
- Saying if something has already been done
- Discussing beach activities
- Describing time periods
- Giving advice

**Cultures**
- Learning about the geography and political status of Puerto Rico
- Learning about baseball in Puerto Rico
- Learning about the music and dance of Puerto Rico
- Learning about the **jíbaros** of Puerto Rico

**Connections**
- Connecting to Science: Investigating Puerto Rico's **Bahía Fosforescente**
- Connecting to History: Learning about the history of pirates and the **jíbaros**

**Comparisons**
- Comparing the beaches in Puerto Rico and the United States
- Comparing health and illness
- Comparing sports and fitness

**Communities**
- Using Spanish at the doctor's office
- Using Spanish for personal enjoyment

### Teaching Resource Options

**Print** 

Block Scheduling Copymasters

**Audiovisual** 

OHT 69, 70, 71, 72
*Canciones* Cassette / CD Songs 1, 5, 6, 8, 13
Video Program Videotape 3, 0:00 / Videodisc 2A

Search Chapter 4, Play to 5
U3, Cultural Introduction

UNIDAD

# SAN JUAN
## PUERTO RICO

SOL Y SOMBRA

**OBJECTIVES**

ETAPA 1 ¿Estás en forma?
- Discuss ways to stay fit and healthy
- Make suggestions
- Talk about daily routine and personal care

ETAPA 2 Preparaciones
- Discuss beach activities
- Tell someone what to do
- Talk about chores
- Say if something has already been done

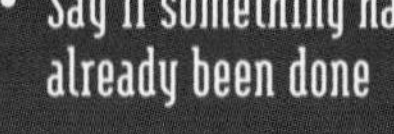

ETAPA 3 ¿Cómo te sientes?
- Describe time periods
- Talk about health and illness
- Give advice

EL OBSERVATORIO DE ARECIBO

ARECIBO

MAYAGÜEZ

PONCE

**EL OBSERVATORIO DE ARECIBO** Puedes encontrar el radiotelescopio más grande del mundo en Arecibo, Puerto Rico. ¿Qué se puede estudiar desde un observatorio?

**LOS PASTELES** Estos deliciosos tamales se hacen de plátanos verdes o yautías (un vegetal parecido a la papa) y carne. Son una comida típica de Puerto Rico. ¿Conoces otro plato como éste?

170

### Classroom Community

**Group Activity** Have students work in small groups to describe the pictures on pp. 170–171. Ask volunteers to write on the board any other people, places, or facts they know about Puerto Rico and Puerto Ricans.
**Alternate:** Have students in each group prepare 3–4 questions about Puerto Rico to ask other groups.

**Cooperative Learning** Divide class into groups of 3. Based on the objectives listed on p. 170 for **Etapa 1**, have each group come up with their own list of ways they stay fit and healthy. Student 1 (S1) is the recorder, Student 2 (S2) is the proofer, and Student 3 (S3) is the presenter. Each group then presents their list and comparisons are made.

## ALMANAQUE

**Población:** 3.522.000
**Altura:** nivel del mar
**Clima:** 23°C (73°F), enero; 27°C (81°F), julio
**Moneda:** el dólar
**Comida típica:** pasta de guayaba, arroz con gandules, pernil, pasteles
**Gente famosa de Puerto Rico:** Gigi Fernández (deportista), Luis Muñoz Marín (político), Francisco Oller (pintor), Luis Rafael Sánchez (escritor)

**¿Vas a San Juan?** Si eres estadounidense y viajas a Puerto Rico, no necesitas tu pasaporte. Puerto Rico es parte de Estados Unidos.

INTERNET Ve a www.mcdougallittell.com para más información sobre San Juan.

**PIRATAS** Realmente existían los piratas y fueron un peligro para los barcos españoles que navegaban en el Atlántico. Para defenderse contra los piratas, el gobierno español construyó un fuerte masivo en San Juan. ¿Qué otra información sabes sobre los piratas?

**LA CEIBA DE PONCE** es uno de los árboles más antiguos de Puerto Rico. Está en la ciudad de Ponce, llamada así por Ponce de León. Aquí ves una pintura del árbol. La pintó Francisco Oller, uno de los pintores puertorriqueños más famosos. ¿Qué otros pintores conoces?

SAN JUAN
EL YUNQUE
PUERTO RICO
HUMACAO

**EL YUNQUE,** un magnífico bosque tropical, es el único en Estados Unidos. Allí caen más de 200 pulgadas (*inches*) de lluvia al año. Toda esta lluvia contribuye a la vida de los animales y plantas que viven allí. ¿Qué clase de animales y plantas crees que puedes encontrar en El Yunque?

**MARC ANTHONY** Tal vez lo viste en películas como *Hackers*. Marc Anthony, cantante y actor puertorriqueño, es uno de los cantantes de salsa más importantes. ¿Qué otros actores o cantantes latinos conoces?

EL CARIBE

171

## Teaching All Students

**Extra Help** Have students read aloud a caption and let their partner summarize what they read in one or two sentences. Then have them switch roles.

**Challenge** Ask students to design an **Almanaque** for their area and compare it to Puerto Rico's.

**Native Speakers** If any Spanish speakers have family from Puerto Rico, ask them to talk about their home town in Puerto Rico. Ask them to bring in photos or artifacts from Puerto Rico for extra credit.

**Multiple Intelligences**

**Naturalist** Ask interested students to research the animals and plants found in **El Yunque** rain forest in Puerto Rico. They can research via the Internet or in their local library.

**Verbal** Ask students to choose one caption and respond to the given question by referring to information from the library or the Internet.

## Teaching Suggestions
### Previewing the Unit

You may wish to use the video to preview the unit. Tell students that this unit centers around Puerto Rico. Ask students to brainstorm what they know about Puerto Rico. What do they know about the political status of Puerto Rico?

## Culture Highlights

- **EL OBSERVATORIO DE ARECIBO** has the largest radar/radio telescope in the world, with a dish measuring 20 acres in a sinkhole the size of 13 football fields. It is used to study planets, comets, asteroids, and galaxies, as well as pulsars and quasars. The movie *Contact* was filmed there.
- **EL YUNQUE** is part of the U.S. National Parks system and is one of the most accessible and well-maintained tropical rain forests in the world. (See the **En colores** reading, pp. 210–211.)
- **PONCE** is the second largest city in Puerto Rico after the capital of San Juan, with a population of 300,000. It is an important commercial and cultural center. Ponce is home to one of the Caribbean's most important art museums, **El Museo de Arte de Ponce**.
- **PONCE DE LEÓN** discovered San Juan, Puerto Rico, in the 16th century. He made a home in what is now Old San Juan. His family home, Casa Blanca, is still there today.
- **MARC ANTHONY** is a **salsero** born and raised in New York City by Puerto Rican parents. His recent albums include *Contra la corriente* (1997), *Todo a su tiempo* (1995), and *Otra nota* (1993).
- **SALSA** is dance music with Afro-Cuban influences that is popular in Puerto Rico and the rest of Latin America. **Salseros** include Tito Puente, Celia Cruz, Johnny Pacheco, Eddie Palmieri, Rubén Blades, Willi Colón, Luis Enrique, and Jerry Rivera.

## Block Schedule

**Variety** Bring in travel guides and other books about Puerto Rico. Have groups of students find five interesting facts about the island to present to the class.

# Planning Ahead...

# Ampliación

These activities may be used at various points in the Unit 3 sequence.

For Block Schedule, you may find that these projects will provide a welcome change of pace while reviewing and reinforcing the material presented in the unit. See the Block Schedule Copymasters.

## PROJECTS

**Create an exercise guidebook** for students who are trying to change their lifestyles. Break the class into two groups. Half the class will write a list of simple commands for changing to a more healthy lifestyle through exercise. The other half will write a list of commands for changing to a healthier daily routine. Add illustrations, photos, or healthy recipes to make your guidebook more useful.

PACING SUGGESTION: Upon completion of Etapa 1.

**Create a Spanish communication guide to the emergency room** of your local hospital or medical clinic. Divide students into small groups and have some groups make a list of useful questions in Spanish for the hospital workers to ask when attending a Spanish-speaking patient. Have the other groups make a list of Spanish expressions that the patients might use when describing an injury or illness. Have students use the vocabulary on pp. 227, 229, and parts of the *En vivo* dialog as model expressions. Students may wish to donate their final project to a local hospital or medical clinic, or to the school nurse.

PACING SUGGESTION: Upon completion of Etapa 3.

## STORYTELLING

**Los quehaceres domésticos de Juan** After reviewing the vocabulary for chores and informal commands, model a mini-story (using puppets, student actors, sports equipment, or pictures from the text) that students will revise, retell, and expand:

> Juan llegó del colegio un día y su mamá tenía una lista de quehaceres para él. Ella le dijo, "Juan, ven conmigo porque vamos a limpiar la casa entera esta tarde. Juan le preguntó, "Qué debo hacer?" Ella le contestó, "Primero, limpia tu cuarto y pasa la aspiradora allí. Luego, limpia los cuartos de baño y saca la basura. Y luego..."

Pause as the story is being told so that students may fill in words and act out gestures. Students should then write, narrate, and read aloud a longer main story. This new version should include vocabulary from Unidad 3. Students can write, illustrate, and act out additional new stories based on this storytelling experience.

**Mis quehaceres domésticos** Ask students to tell a story about daily or weekly chores they have to do at home. You may want to have students make lists of chores and compare with a partner as an advance organizer activity.

PACING SUGGESTION: Upon completion of Etapa 2.

## BULLETIN BOARDS / POSTERS

**Bulletin Board Plan ahead:** Contact local travel agents for information about the beach life, sports, and exercise options in Puerto Rico. Have students discuss their favorite warm weather activities while reviewing the bulletin board.

**Posters Have students create** • **Nutrition tips** posters • **Athletic club** posters • **Travel** posters for the beaches of Puerto Rico • **Check-off list** for routine household chores • Poster of **Parts of the body** labeled in Spanish

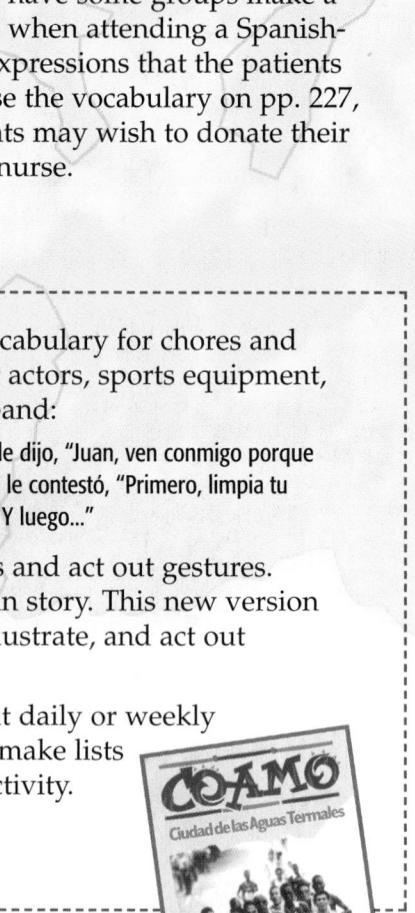

## GAMES

### Voy a la playa y voy a llevar...

**Prepare ahead:** Bring in a beach bag and pictures of items that one might take to the beach, such as **toalla**, **gafas de sol**, **libro**, **sombrero**, etc. You can also use the actual items.

Put the pictures or items and the beach bag in the center of the room, then start the game. One by one, a student will say, **"Voy a la playa y voy a llevar ____."** Then he or she places the item in the beach bag. The next student repeats what the first was taking and adds one more item. The game continues until all items are in the beach bag and one student correctly lists all the items in the proper order.

PACING SUGGESTION: Upon completion of Etapa 2.

## MUSIC

Puerto Rican music is a mixture of three major influences:

- Spanish: Stringed instruments, like **la guitarra** or **la mandolina**;
- African: Dance rhythms created from the drums, or **el tambor**;
- Indian: Musical instruments made from seeds or vegetables, like **las maracas** or **el güiro**.

**El güiro** is a musical instrument native to Puerto Rico that is made from the hollow, dry **güiro** fruit, similar to a gourd. The **güiro** is played with a fork-like utensil in a scraping motion along its ridges. You will hear the **güiro** in much of the Caribbean dance music, such as salsa or merengue. Try to bring in some sample music from Celia Cruz, Tito Puente, Willie Colón, or Juan Luis Guerra and 440, and have students try to distinguish between the different dances. Play the *Canciones* Cassette/CD for the class. As students listen to the music, have them try to identify the various instruments. See if they can differentiate between the *salsa* and the *merengue.*

## HANDS-ON CRAFTS

Have students make their own set of **maracas** using papier maché and filling them with uncooked rice and/or beans. Prepare ahead: Newspapers torn in strips, flour and water to make a paste, small balloons to make molds for the **maracas**, and paints to decorate them.

Have students dip the newspaper strips in the flour paste and wrap them around the balloons in criss-crossed layers, leaving a small hole. After the shapes are completely dry, pop the balloons and have students decorate the **maracas** with paints. Then fill them with uncooked rice and/or beans, and cover the small holes with tape.

## RECIPE

In keeping with the unit theme of health and nutrition, have students create a fruit salad, if possible, made from tropical fruits found in Puerto Rico. Students can use the fruits listed in the recipe, or create their own combination. To review commands, students can give a short speech on how to make this recipe.

# Receta

***Ensalada de fruta***
*1 piña*
*2 chinas (naranjas)*
*2 guineos (bananas)*
*2 mangos*
*1 papaya*
*media taza de coco rallado*

*Lave todas las frutas. Quite la cáscara de la piña y córtela en rodajas, quitando el corazón. Corte las rodajas de piña en pedazos pequeños. Quite la cáscara de las chinas, la papaya y los mangos y córtelos en pedazos. Pele los guineos y córtelos en pedazos pequeños. Combine toda la fruta y mezcle bien. Por último, ponga el coco rallado encima y sirva la ensalada en platos pequeños.*

# Planning Guide CLASSROOM MANAGEMENT

## OBJECTIVES

**Communication**
- Discuss ways to stay fit and healthy *pp. 174–175, 176–177*
- Make suggestions *pp. 176–177, 182–184*
- Talk about daily routine and personal care *pp. 181, 185*

**Grammar**
- Pronoun placement *p. 180*
- Giving commands using the **usted/ustedes** form *p. 182*
- **Usted** commands and pronoun placement *pp. 184–185*

**Culture**
- History and important cities of Puerto Rico *pp. 170–171 (Unit Opener)*
- **El béisbol en Puerto Rico** *p. 180*
- **El viejo San Juan** *p. 186*
- **Puerto Rico: Lugar maravilloso** *pp. 188–189*

**Recycling**
- Double object pronouns *p. 179*
- Expressions of frequency *p. 179*
- Reflexive verbs *pp. 181, 186*
- Ordinal numbers *p. 181*

## STRATEGIES

**Listening Strategies**
- Listen and sort details *p. 176*

**Speaking Strategies**
- Use gestures to convey meaning *p. 187*
- React to daily routines *p. 192*

**Reading Strategies**
- Observe organization of ideas *p. 188*

**Writing Strategies**
- Organize information by category *Actividad 7, TE p. 192*

**Connecting Cultures Strategies**
- Compare and contrast places in Puerto Rico and local communities *TE p. 189*
- Identify influences of geography and climate *TE p. 189*

## PROGRAM RESOURCES

### Print

- *Más práctica* Workbook PE *pp. 65–72*
- Block Scheduling Copymasters *pp. 57–64*
- Unit 3 Resource Book
  - *Más práctica* Workbook TE *pp. 1–8*
  - *Cuaderno para hispanohablantes* TE *pp. 9–16*
  - Information Gap Activities *pp. 17–20*
  - Family Involvement *pp. 21–22*
  - Video Activities *pp. 23–25*
  - Videoscript *pp. 26–27*
  - Audioscript *pp. 28–32*
  - Assessment Program, Unit 3 Etapa 1 *pp. 33–51; 170–172*
  - Answer Keys *pp. 187–188*

### Audiovisual

- Audio Program Cassette 7A, 7B / CD 7
- *Canciones* Cassette/CD
- Video Program Videotape 3 / Videodisc 2A
- Overhead Transparencies M1, M3; GO1; 69–82

### Technology

- Electronic Teacher Tools/Test Generator
- *Intrigas y aventuras* CD-ROM, Disc 1
- 

  www.mcdougallittell.com

### Assessment Program Options

- Cooperative Quizzes (Unit 3 Resource Book)
- Etapa Exam Forms A and B (Unit 3 Resource Book)
- *Examen para hispanohablantes* (Unit 3 Resource Book)
- Portfolio Assessment (Unit 3 Resource Book)
- Multiple Choice Test Questions (Unit 3 Resource Book)
- Audio Program Cassette 19B / CD 19
- Electronic Teacher Tools / Test Generator

### Native Speakers

- *Cuaderno para hispanohablantes* PE *pp. 65–72*
- *Cuaderno para hispanohablantes* TE (Unit 3 Resource Book)
- *Examen para hispanohablantes* (Unit 3 Resource Book)
- Audio Program *(Para hispanohablantes)* Cassettes 7B, 19B / CD 7, CD 19
- Audioscript (Unit 3 Resource Book)

# Student Text Listening Activity Scripts

## Videoscript: Diálogo *pages 176–177*

• Videotape 3, 3:55 • Videodisc 2A
Search Chapter 6, Play to end. U3E1, En vivo (Dialog)
• Use the videoscript with **Actividades 1, 2** *page 178*

Francisco: (V/O) Queridos lectores, ¡saludos desde San Juan, Puerto Rico! Llegué anoche. ¡Qué bella es la isla! Como saben, mi madre es puertorriqueña, así que tengo la suerte de poder visitar a mi familia mientras estoy aquí. Mañana tengo una cita con Elena Suárez. Es la estrella de un programa de televisión de ejercicio y salud aquí en Puerto Rico.

Elena: Sí, es súper popular. Lo pasan en el canal siete todos los sábados.

Juana: Con permiso, ¿es Ud. Elena Suárez? ¿La del programa de televisión?

Elena: Sí, soy yo.

Juana: Ay, me encanta su programa! Venga, por favor, a conocer a mi esposo.

Miguel: Siéntese, por favor, siéntese. Sabe, su programa es maravilloso. Lo veo todos los sábados. Es parte de mi rutina. Los sábados por la mañana, me levanto temprano y me lavo la boca. Luego me baño y me pongo la ropa. Después, me seco el pelo y me peino. Entonces pongo la televisión y veo su programa. Como Ud. aconsejó, ahora tratamos de comer más alimentos sanos, como frutas, pescado y arroz.

Juana: Sí, y estamos tratando de eliminar tanto estrés como posible. Y los ejercicios que Ud. hace ayudan mucho. Los hago todos los días.

Elena: Me alegra oírlo, señora. Siga con los ejercicios; así Ud. se va a mantener sana y joven por muchos años.

Juana: Ay, qué amable. ¿De veras me veo joven?

Elena: ¿Cómo no? Si una persona vive bien, es optimista y llena de energía, siempre va a ser joven.

Miguel: Por favor, señorita Suárez, dénos su autógrafo. Ponga, por favor, "a Miguel y Juana, de su amiga Elena Suárez".

Juana: No, no. Por favor, ponga "a Juana y Miguel".

Elena: Con mucho gusto. Discúlpenme, pero tengo que irme. Gracias por ver mi programa.

Juana: No, no, discúlpenos a nosotros. Pero...

Elena: ¿Sí?

Juana: Háganos un favor. Por favor, diga la frase con la que Ud. siempre cierra su programa.

Elena: Ay, señora, me gustaría pero aquí no puedo decirla.

Juana: ¡Ay bendito! Por favor, dígala.

Elena: Muy bien. "Adiós, queridos televidentes, y acuérdense, para mantenerse sanos, lleven una dieta balanceada y nutritiva, no fumen nunca, y... ¡hagan ejercicio!"

Francisco: ¿Y eso pasa con frecuencia?

Elena: No, no, sólo de vez en cuando. Bueno, Francisco. Vas a venir a ver la producción de mi programa, ¿no?

Francisco: Sí, con mis tíos y mi prima.

Elena: Pues, si quieren, ellos también pueden venir. Mi programa de televisión es para el público en general, personas como tú y tu familia. Ustedes pueden participar.

Francisco: ¿Cómo es? ¿Qué tenemos que hacer?

Elena: Es bien sencillo. Primero, nos estiramos un poco, después hacemos los ejercicios. Y luego hay una parte sobre la dieta y la buena alimentación, y el bienestar y la vida saludable en general.

Francisco: Pues, me encantaría. Y voy a invitar a mi familia.

Elena: Y pónganse ropa ligera.

Francisco: Muy bien, nos ponemos ropa ligera. ¿Tienes algún otro consejo?

Elena: Sí, les aconsejo traer toallas. Van a sudar mucho y quemar muchas calorías.

Francisco: Ah, ¿sí? Muy bien. ¿Cuántas?

Elena: ¿Cuántas qué? ¿Toallas o calorías?

## Actividad 8 ¿Lógico o no? *page 182*

1. Por la mañana, me gusta levantarme temprano y relajarme un poco antes de ir a la escuela.
2. Es necesario maquillarse antes de acostarse.
3. Por la mañana, lo primero que tienes que hacer es quitarte el pijama y después ponerte la ropa.
4. Cuando Susana necesita levantarse temprano, se acuesta muy tarde.
5. Cuando me voy a duchar, me gusta ponerme los zapatos.
6. Después de entrenarse, ellos se van a bañar.
7. Para mantenernos sanos, vamos a estirarnos, hacer ejercicio y comer una dieta saludable.
8. Me falta energía. Quiero acostarme temprano.

## Actividad 14 ¿Qué venden? *page 186*

1. ¿Tiene usted pelo lacio? ¿Quiere pelo más sano y fuerte? O tal vez tiene pelo rizado y quiere conservar el volumen. Pues, séquese el pelo con «Súper Pelo» y tenga pelo con volumen, pelo con estilo. Láveselo con su champú favorito y séqueselo con «Súper Pelo». Su pelo le va a decir «¡Gracias!»
2. Sabemos que ustedes hacen actividades para su bienestar. Se entrenan con frecuencia, hacen ejercicios y levantan pesas. Así que necesitan protección fuerte, protección que dure todo el día. Pónganse «Refrescante» y vístanse con seguridad.
3. ¿Está pálida? ¿Quiere tener ojos más grandes? ¿Busca usted colores naturales? Tenemos la solución. Maquíllese con «Bellísima». Maquíllese con colores naturales pero vivos. ¡«Bellísima»! Cómprelo hoy y mírese en el espejo.
4. Ella se pone un perfume que lo vuelve loco. Es romántico. Es especial. Pero, ¿qué hace usted? Haga usted lo mismo para ella. Compre «Aficionado». Es romántico. Es especial. A ella le gustaría. Póngaselo y huela bien. «Aficionado».
5. Nadie quiere tener dientes amarillos. Se los lava y se los lava, pero todavía están... amarillos. Usted no tiene la culpa. Necesita un producto especial para ese problema... «Perlitas». Lávese la boca con «Perlitas» para tener una sonrisa maravillosa.
6. Usted sabe lo que es tener un día malo con su pelo. ¡No lo haga otra vez! Lávese el pelo con «Pelo Hermoso» y vea la diferencia. No se lave el pelo con otro producto. «Pelo Hermoso» es para usted.

# Pacing Guide

## Sample Lesson Plan - 50 Minute Schedule

### DAY 1

***Unit Opener***
- Anticipate/Activate prior knowledge: Present the *Almanaque* and the cultural notes. Use Map OHTs as needed. 10 MIN.

***Etapa Opener***
- Quick Start Review (TE, p. 172). 5 MIN.
- Have students look at the *Etapa* Opener and answer *¿Qué ves?* questions. 5 MIN.

***En contexto: Vocabulario***
- Quick Start Review (TE, p. 174). 3 MIN.
- Have students use context and pictures to learn *Etapa* vocabulary. Answer questions, p. 175. 10 MIN.

***En vivo: Diálogo***
- Quick Start Review (TE, p. 176). 2 MIN.
- Review Listening Strategy, p. 176. Play audio or show video for the dialog shown on pp. 176–177. 7 MIN.
- Replay and have students take on roles of characters. 8 MIN.

***Homework Option***
- Video Activities, Unit 3 Resource Book, pp. 23–25

### DAY 2

***En acción: Vocabulario y Gramática***
- Check homework. 5 MIN.
- Quick Start Review (TE, p. 178). 5 MIN.
- Ask students for a summary of *En vivo* dialog to check recall. 5 MIN.
- Have students answer Comprehension Questions (TE, p. 177). 5 MIN.
- Replay the *En vivo* dialog using the audiovisual resources and have students do *Actividades* 1 and 2 orally. 10 MIN.
- Have students complete *Actividades* 3 and 4. 10 MIN.
- Present grammar review box, p. 180, then have students complete *Actividad* 5 orally. 10 MIN.

***Homework Option***
- *Más práctica* Workbook, pp. 69–70 as needed. *Cuaderno para hispanohablantes*, pp. 67–68.

### DAY 3

***En acción (cont.)***
- Check homework. 5 MIN.
- Quick Start Review (TE, p. 180). 5 MIN.
- Review the vocabulary in the box on p. 181, then have students complete *Actividades* 6 and 7 in pairs. 10 MIN.
- Play the audio and have students complete *Actividad* 8. 8 MIN.
- Present *Gramática:* Give Formal Commands Using *usted/ustedes*, p. 182. 10 MIN.
- Have students do *Actividad* 9 orally and *Actividad* 10 in pairs. Expand with *Más comunicación* activity, p. R8. 12 MIN.

***Homework Option***
- Have students prepare *Actividad* 11 in writing. *Más práctica* Workbook, p. 71. *Cuaderno para hispanohablantes*, p. 69.

### DAY 4

***En acción (cont.)***
- Check homework. 5 MIN.
- Quick Start Review (TE, p. 182) 5 MIN.
- Have students complete *Actividad* 11 in small groups. 10 MIN.
- Present *Gramática:* Formal *usted/ustedes* Commands and Pronoun Placement, p. 184. 10 MIN.
- Have students complete *Actividad* 12. 5 MIN.
- Review the vocabulary box on p. 185 and have students complete *Actividad* 13. 5 MIN.
- Play audio and have students complete *Actividad* 14. 5 MIN.
- Have students complete *Actividad* 15 in groups. 5 MIN.

***Homework Option***
- *Más práctica* Workbook, p. 72. *Cuaderno para hispanohablantes*, p. 70.

### DAY 5

***En acción (cont.)***
- Check homework. 5 MIN.
- Quick Start Review (TE, p. 186). 5 MIN.
- Have students do *Actividad* 16. 5 MIN.
- Present Speaking Strategy, p. 187, and have students do *Actividad* 17. 10 MIN.
- Have students complete *Actividad* 18 in small groups and possibly present *anuncios* to the class. 10 MIN.

***En voces: Lectura***
- Review Reading Strategy, p. 188, and have students read silently. 5 MIN.
- Have volunteers read the selection and answer questions. 10 MIN.

***Homework Option***
- Have students answer *¿Comprendiste?* and *¿Qué piensas?* questions in writing.

### DAY 6

***En uso: Repaso y más comunicación***
- Check homework. 10 MIN.
- Quick Start Review (TE, p. 190). 5 MIN.
- Do *Actividades* 1 and 2 orally. 10 MIN.
- Do *Actividades* 3 and 4 in writing. 10 MIN.
- Review Speaking Strategy, p. 190. Then do *Actividad* 5 orally in pairs. 10 MIN.
- Read and discuss *Conexiones*. 5 MIN.

***Homework Option***
- Have students do *Actividades* 1 and 2 in writing. *Cuaderno para hispanohablantes*, pp. 71–72.

### DAY 7

***En uso (cont.)***
- Check homework. 5 MIN.
- Quick Start Review (TE, p. 192). 5 MIN.
- Have students do *Actividad* 6 in groups of four. 10 MIN.

***En tu propia voz: Escritura***
- Begin *Actividad* 7. 10 MIN.

***Ampliación***
- Use a suggested project, game, or activity (TE pp. 171A–171B). 20 MIN.

***Homework Option***
- Complete *Actividad* 7. Review for *Etapa* 1 Exam.

### DAY 8

***En resumen: Repaso de vocabulario***
- Check homework. 5 MIN.
- Review grammar questions, etc. as necessary. 10 MIN.
- Complete *Etapa* 1 Exam. 20 MIN.

***Ampliación***
- Use a suggested project, game, or activity (TE pp. 171A–171B). 15 MIN.

***Homework Option***
- Preview next *Etapa* Opener, pp. 194–195.

# Sample Lesson Plan - Block Schedule (90 minutes)

## DAY 1

***Unit Opener***

- Anticipate/Activate prior knowledge: Present the *Almanaque* and the cultural notes. Use Map OHTs as needed. 10 MIN.

***Etapa Opener***

- Quick Start Review (TE, p. 172). 5 MIN.
- Have students look at the *Etapa* Opener and answer *¿Qué ves?* questions. 10 MIN.

***En contexto: Vocabulario***

- Quick Start Review (TE, p. 174). 5 MIN.
- Have students use context and pictures to learn *Etapa* vocabulary. Answer questions, p. 175. 10 MIN.

***En vivo: Diálogo***

- Quick Start Review (TE, p. 176). 5 MIN.
- Review Listening Strategy, p. 176. Play audio or show video for the dialog shown on pp. 176–177. 10 MIN.
- Replay and have students take on roles of characters. 10 MIN.
- Ask Comprehension Questions (TE, p. 177). 5 MIN.
- Use Block Scheduling Copymasters for variety. 10 MIN.

***En acción: Vocabulario y Gramática***

- Quick Start Review (TE, p. 178). 5 MIN.
- Have students do *Actividades* 1 and 2 orally. 5 MIN.

***Homework Option***

- Video Activities, Unit 3 Resource Book, pp. 23–25.

## DAY 2

***En acción (cont.)***

- Check homework. 10 MIN.
- Quick Start Review (TE, p. 180). 5 MIN.
- Have students complete *Actividades* 3 and 4. 10 MIN.
- Present grammar review box, p. 180, then have students complete *Actividad* 5 orally. 10 MIN.
- Review the vocabulary in the box on p. 181, then have students complete *Actividades* 6 and 7 in pairs. 12 MIN.
- Play the audio and have students complete *Actividad* 8. 10 MIN.
- Present *Gramática:* Give Formal Commands Using *usted/ustedes,* p. 182. 10 MIN.
- Have students do *Actividad* 9 orally and *Actividad* 10 in pairs. Expand with *Más comunicación* activity, p. R8. 13 MIN.
- Have students prepare *Actividad* 11 in writing and present it in small groups. 10 MIN.

***Homework Option***

- *Más práctica* Workbook, pp. 69–71. *Cuaderno para hispanohablantes*, pp. 67–69.

## DAY 3

***En acción (cont.)***

- Check homework. 10 MIN.
- Quick Start Review (TE, p. 184). 5 MIN.
- Present *Gramática* box on p. 184. 10 MIN.
- Have students do *Actividad* 12. 5 MIN.
- Review *Vocabulario* on p. 185 and have students complete *Actividad* 13. 10 MIN.
- Play the audio and do *Actividad* 14 orally with the whole class. 7 MIN.
- Have students complete *Actividad* 15 in groups. 8 MIN.
- Have students do *Actividad* 16 in pairs. 5 MIN.
- Present Speaking Strategy, p. 187, and do *Actividad* 17 in small groups. 10 MIN.
- Have students complete *Actividad* 18 in pairs and possibly present *anuncios* to the class. 10 MIN.
- Use Block Scheduling Copymasters for a change of pace as needed. 10 MIN.

***Homework Option***

- *Más práctica* Workbook, p. 72. *Cuaderno para hispanohablantes*, p. 70.

## DAY 4

***En voces: Lectura***

- Check homework. 5 MIN.
- Quick Start Review (TE, p. 188). 5 MIN.
- Review Reading Strategy, p. 188. 5 MIN.
- Have students read *Puerto Rico: Lugar maravilloso* silently. 10 MIN.
- Have students read *Lectura* aloud in turns. 10 MIN.
- Call on volunteers to answer *¿Comprendiste?* questions. Refer back to the reading if students give the incorrect answer. 10 MIN.
- Have students do the *¿Qué piensas?* activity in writing, then discuss in class. 10 MIN.
- Optional: Storytelling. Have students retell main points in their own words. 10 MIN.

***Ampliación***

- Use a suggested project, game, or activity (TE pp. 171A–171B). 25 MIN.

***Homework Option***

- Review for *Etapa* 1 Exam. *Cuaderno para hispanohablantes*, pp. 71–72.
- Have students write *Actividades* 1–4.

## DAY 5

***En uso: Repaso y más comunicación***

- Quick Start Review (TE, p. 190). 5 MIN.
- Go over *Actividades* 1, 2, 3 and 4 orally. 15 MIN.
- Review Speaking Strategy, p. 192. Then do *Actividad* 5 orally in pairs and *Actividad* 6 in groups of four. 15 MIN.

***Conexiones***

- Read and discuss. 5 MIN.
- Review grammar questions, etc. as necessary. 10 MIN.
- Complete *Etapa* 1 Exam. 20 MIN.

***En tu propia voz: Escritura***

- Do *Actividad* 7. Call on volunteers to share with class. 20 MIN.

***Homework Option***

- Preview next *Etapa* Opener, pp. 194–195.

▼ Elena y Francisco corren por la cuidad.

UNIDAD 3 Etapa 1
**Opener**

## Etapa Theme

**Discussing ways to stay fit and healthy, making suggestions, and talking about daily routine and personal care.**

## Grammar Objectives

- Pronoun placement
- **Usted/ustedes** commands and pronoun placement

### Teaching Resource Options

**Print** 

Block Scheduling Copymasters

**Audiovisual** 

OHT 79 (Quick Start), GO1
*Canciones* Cassette / CD Songs 5, 6, 8

### Quick Start Review

Greeting others/introducing yourself

Use OHT 79 or write on board: Francisco is about to interview Elena Suárez. Write a short dialog in which he greets her, introduces himself, asks how she is, and comments on exercise. Include Elena's responses.

*Answers will vary.*

### Teaching Suggestions
**Previewing the Etapa**

- Ask students to study the picture on pp. 172–173.
- Ask students to identify what the people are wearing in the picture.
- Have students predict what activities the people are planning to do.
- Have students review colors as they give their answers.

### Supplementary Vocabulary

| | |
|---|---|
| **hacer ejercicios aeróbicos** | to do aerobics |
| **hacer artes marciales** | to do martial arts |
| **hacer yoga** | to do yoga |
| **levantar pesas** | to lift weights |
| **llevar una vida sana** | to lead a healthy life |

UNIDAD 3

# ¿Estás en forma?

- Discuss ways to stay fit and healthy
- Make suggestions
- Talk about daily routine and personal care

### ¿Qué ves?

Mira la foto del Viejo San Juan. Luego contesta las preguntas.

1. ¿Quiénes son las personas de esta foto?
2. ¿Qué hacen?
3. ¿Dónde puedes leer de actividades para hacer en San Juan?

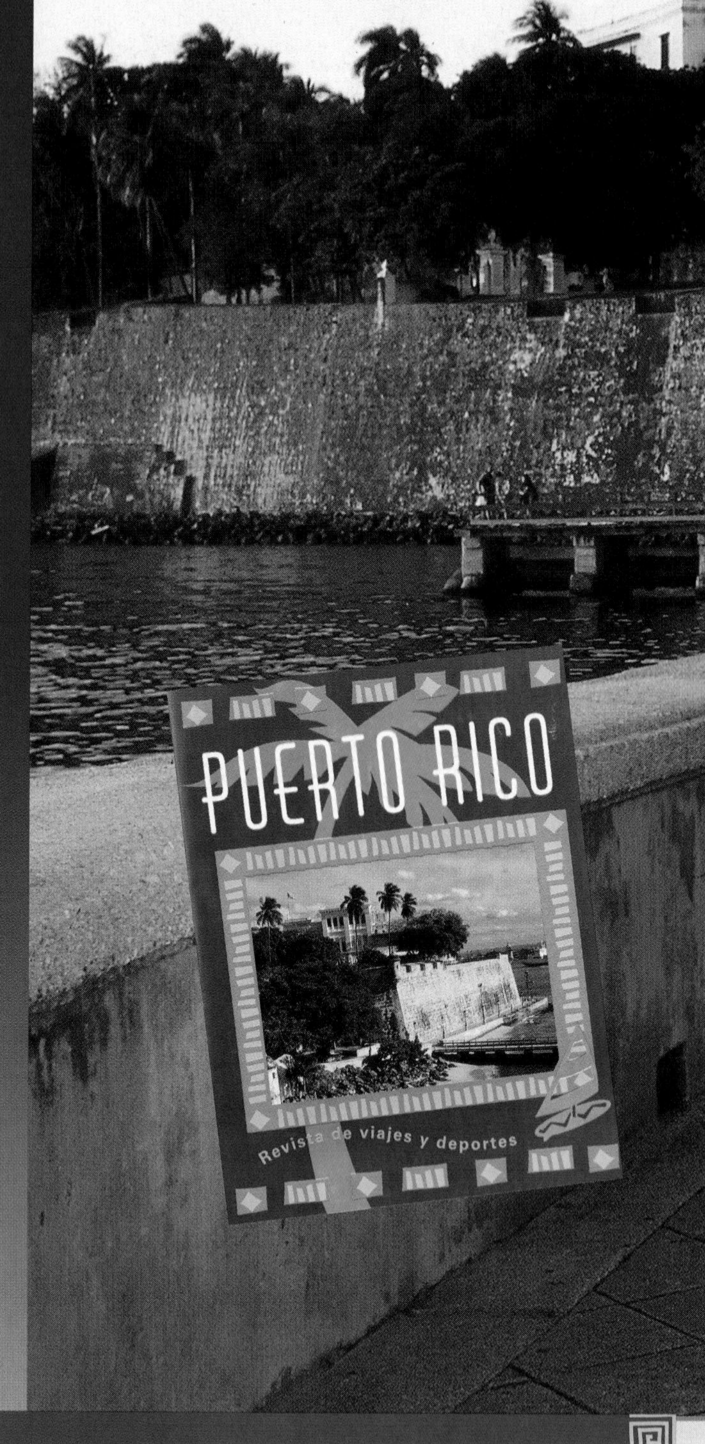


172

### Classroom Management

**Planning Ahead** Prepare students to discuss health and fitness. Have students brainstorm a list of body parts they already know. Have them list the healthiest foods from the vocabulary they studied in the previous unit. Collect magazine advertisements that show different sports or fitness activities. (Mount and laminate for future use if possible.)

**Peer Teaching** Have students work in pairs to list 5 things in the photo that are similar to their own area, and then list 5 things that are different. Suggest that students use a Venn diagram for discussion. (You may wish to use the Graphic Organizer Overhead Transparencies as the basis for the diagram.)

## Cross Cultural Connections

Where do people go running in your community? Compare your local running spots to the place where Elena and Francisco are planning to run, as seen in the photo on pp. 172–173.

## Culture Highlights

- **EL MORRO** is a massive fort that features a maze of tunnels, dungeons, and outposts, as well as 18-foot-thick walls. It was built by the Spanish starting in 1521 to protect the port city of San Juan from other European invaders and pirates.
- **EL VIEJO SAN JUAN** is the oldest part of Puerto Rico, with beautiful colonial architecture and many historical sites. The pastel-colored houses, courtyard gardens, narrow streets, and wrought-iron balconies make it a very picturesque part of town.

## Teaching All Students

**Extra Help** Ask students to list 5 adjectives to describe Francisco and 5 adjectives to describe Elena.

**Native Speakers** Have Spanish speakers describe their exercise/fitness routine to the class in Spanish. All students will then have a model to describe their own routines. Have them compare their own routines to Francisco's.

### Multiple Intelligences

**Intrapersonal** Take one minute to allow students to "take in" the scenery and information in the pictures and jot down their observations. Ask volunteers to share their observations.

**Musical/Rhythmic** Students might enjoy listening to *"En mi viejo San Juan,"* Song 6 on the ***Canciones*** Cassette/CD.

## Block Schedule

**FunBreak** If any of your Spanish speakers know how to dance merengue, have them bring in music and demonstrate for the class. (For additional activities, see **Block Scheduling Copymasters**.)

## Teaching Resource Options

**Print** 

Unit 3 Resource Book
- Video Activities, p. 23
- Videoscript, p. 26
- Audioscript, p. 28

**Audiovisual** 

**OHT** 73, 74, 79 (Quick Start)
**Audio Program** Cassette 7A / CD 7
**Video Program** Videotape 3, 1:29 / Videodisc 2A

Search Chapter 5, Play to 6
U3E1, En contexto (Vocabulary)

**Technology** 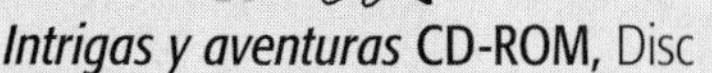

*Intrigas y aventuras* CD-ROM, Disc 1

## Quick Start Review

Food

Use OHT 79 or write on board: Make two columns labeled **frutas** and **verduras**. List all the fruits and vegetables you know in Spanish (at least 5 in each category).

*Answers will vary.*

## Teaching Suggestions
### Introducing Vocabulary

- Have students look at pages 174–175. Use OHT 73 and 74 and Audiocassette 7A / CD 7 to present the vocabulary.
- Ask the Comprehension Questions in the margin of the Teacher's Edition.
- Introduce the characters' names and the setting: **La mujer se llama Elena. El muchacho se llama Francisco. ¿Qué hacen Elena y Francisco? ¿Dónde están?**
- Use the video vocabulary presentation and the TPR activity for review and reinforcement.

# En contexto

## VOCABULARIO

Lee lo que dice Francisco sobre cómo mantenerse saludable.

*¡Hola!* Si quieres **mantenerte sano,** sigue mis **consejos.**

Consejos para mantenerse sano

Dieta balanceada

Leche

**A** Para tener mucha **energía** y estar **saludable,** les **aconsejo** seguir **una dieta balanceada.**

**B** En tu **alimentación,** come comidas o **alimentos** de **calorías nutritivas,** sin mucho azúcar.



## Classroom Community

**TPR** Have students act out the following verbs and phrases as you say them in Spanish: **tener mucha energía, comer comidas nutritivas, entrenarse, estirarse, relajarse, hacer ejercicios.**

**Paired Activity** Have students work in pairs to ask each other the **Preguntas personales** to reinforce and practice the new vocabulary, then report their partner's responses to another person.

**Group Activity** Working in groups of five, have each student choose a caption (A–E) to read aloud and describe the meaning of each highlighted vocabulary word in Spanish. Then have each group select 2 descriptions to present to the class.

Consejos para mantenerse sano
Ejercicio
ENTRENARSE
ESTIRARSE Y RELAJARSE
ATLETISMO

**D** A veces **me entreno** con mis amigos, pero a veces me entreno solo. Siempre **sudo** mucho.

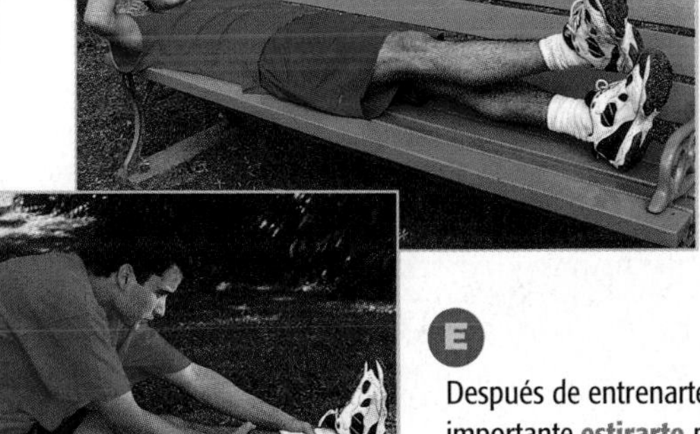

**E** Después de entrenarte, es importante **estirarte** para **relajarte…** como yo estoy haciendo.

Así vas a lograr tu **bienestar** y **crecer** fuerte y sano, sin tener **estrés.**

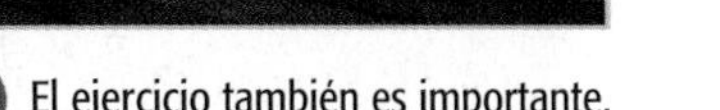

**C** El ejercicio también es importante. Tal vez te gusta **el atletismo.**

### Preguntas personales

1. ¿Qué te gusta comer cada día? ¿Es balanceada tu dieta?
2. ¿Haces ejercicio? ¿Qué tipo?
3. ¿Prefieres entrenarte solo(a) o con tus amigos(as)? ¿Por qué?
4. ¿Cómo te sientes cuando haces ejercicio? Explica tu respuesta.



## Comprehension Questions

1. ¿Explica Francisco cómo mantenerse sano? (Sí.)
2. ¿Tiene mucha energía una persona perezosa? (No.)
3. ¿Influye la comida en nuestra salud? (Sí.)
4. ¿Es importante comer muchas cosas con azúcar o sin azúcar? (sin azúcar)
5. ¿Incluye una dieta balanceada muchas comidas diferentes o pocas comidas? (muchas comidas diferentes)
6. ¿Tiene calorías nutritivas una zanahoria o una galleta? (una zanahoria)
7. ¿Sudas más cuando nadas o cuando corres? (Answer many vary between cuando corro or cuando nado.)
8. ¿Qué come Francisco en la foto? (una manzana)
9. ¿Qué hace Francisco después de entrenarse? (estirarse, relajarse)
10. ¿Es importante el atletismo en nuestra escuela? ¿En qué deportes puede participar un estudiante? (Answers will vary.)

## Language Notes

- Have students look at pages 174–175, review the context, and try to guess what the word **consejos** means. Ask students to give other examples of **consejos**. At this point they only need to use the infinitive form. For example, **Consejos para ser un buen estudiante: estudiar mucho, hacer la tarea todos los días, dormir bien, comer bien, asistir a clase todos los días**, etc.
- The word **atletismo** refers to running or jogging. Another expression used in Spain is **hacer footing** or even **correr**.
- Tell students that **mantener** is conjugated like **tener**, and **crecer** like **conocer**.

## Teaching All Students

**Extra Help** Give students a list of the active vocabulary words, and have them form at least 5 complete sentences using them. Have students take turns reading their sentences aloud to a partner.

**Native Speakers** Have Spanish speakers write a list of **consejos** they might hear at home from their Spanish-speaking relatives on the board. Have them read them aloud with the appropriate tone and gestures.

**Multiple Intelligences**

**Visual** Have students draw/cut out pictures to represent new vocabulary words in this **Etapa**. Have them work together to make a collage for display in the classroom and for use in reviewing the vocabulary.

**Naturalist** Have students research foods that are grown in Puerto Rico that are part of **una dieta balanceada.**

## Block Schedule

**FunBreak** Divide the class into groups. Have each group make posters illustrating the **Consejos** discussed in the **Language Notes** above.

## Teaching Resource Options

**Print** 

Block Scheduling Copymasters
Unit 3 Resource Book
Video Activities, pp. 24–25
Videoscript, pp. 26–27
Audioscript, p. 28

**Audiovisual** 

OHT 77, 78, 79 (Quick Start)
Audio Program Cassette 7A / CD 7
Video Program Videotape 3, 3:55 / Videodisc 2A

Search Chapter 6, Play to end
U3E1, En vivo (Dialog)

**Technology** 

*Intrigas y aventuras* CD-ROM, Disc 1

## Quick Start Review

Present progressive

Use OHT 79 or write on board: Tell what the following people are doing right now at the health spa.

Ex: Roberto está saltando la cuerda.

1. Tara / practicar los artes marciales
2. Toni / hacer el ciclismo
3. los gemelos / nadar
4. Anita / correr
5. Simón y Marcos / jugar al baloncesto

**Answers**

1. está practicando
2. está haciendo
3. están nadando
4. está corriendo
5. están jugando

## Teaching Suggestions
### Presenting the Dialog

- Prepare students for listening by focusing on the dialog context using yes/no or either/or questions.
- Use the video, audiocassette, or CD to present the dialog.

# En vivo

## DIÁLOGO

Francisco

Elena

Juana

Miguel

**PARA ESCUCHAR • STRATEGY: LISTENING**

**Listen and sort details** Elena's **consejos** (advice) are in three categories: **ejercicio** (exercise), **dieta** (diet), and **actitudes** (attitudes). Listen for these three categories. What words do you hear?

### En San Juan...

1 ▶ Francisco: (*escribiendo su artículo*) Elena Suárez es la estrella de un programa de televisión de ejercicio y salud. La voy a entrevistar. Vamos a correr un poco y luego hablar de la entrevista.

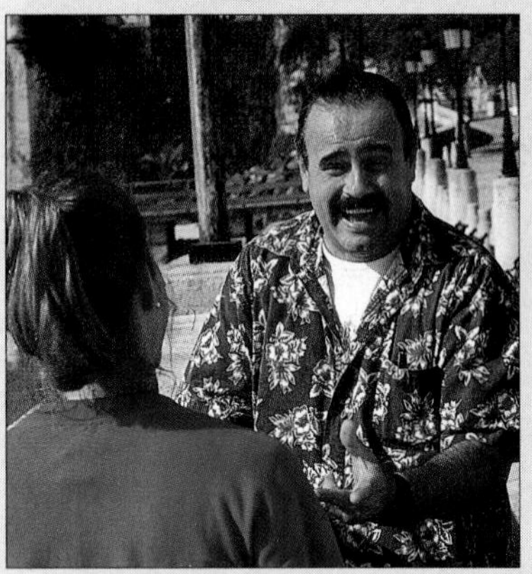

5 ▶ Miguel: Entonces veo su programa. Estábamos mirándolo el sábado pasado cuando usted habló de la dieta y el estrés. Sus consejos nos ayudaron mucho.
Elena: Muchas gracias, muy amable.

6 ▶ Miguel: Ahora tratamos de comer más alimentos sanos.
Juana: Sí, y estamos tratando de eliminar el estrés. Y los ejercicios ayudan mucho. Los hago todos los días.
Elena: Me alegra oírlo, señora.

7 ▶ Miguel: Por favor, señorita Suárez, dénos su autógrafo. Ponga, por favor, «a Miguel y Juana, de su amiga Elena Suárez».
Juana: Por favor, diga la frase con la que usted cierra su programa.



## Classroom Community

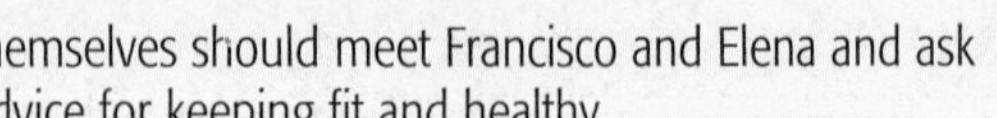

**TPR** Divide the class into 3 groups to represent Elena's 3 types of advice: **ejercicio**, **dieta**, and **actitudes**. Play or read the dialog for the class. Each time students hear their type of advice they should stand. (e.g., When they hear **"Ahora tratamos de comer más alimentos sanos"** the **dieta** students stand.)

**Storytelling** Have students continue the dialog by writing and illustrating at least 3 more frames. They themselves should meet Francisco and Elena and ask advice for keeping fit and healthy.

**Games** **Plan ahead:** Make copies of the **En vivo** dialog from the Videoscript, crossing out completely the characters' names. Put the names of the 4 characters on the board. Ask students to take turns matching the dialog with the characters, without using the textbook.

2▶ Francisco: Y tu programa de televisión es muy popular aquí, ¿no?
Elena: Sí, súper popular. Lo pasan en el canal siete todos los sábados.

3▶ Juana: Con permiso… ¿Es usted Elena Suárez? ¿La del programa de televisión?
Elena: Sí, soy yo.
Juana: ¡Ay, me encanta su programa! Venga, por favor, a conocer a mi esposo.

4▶ Miguel: Sabe, su programa es maravilloso. Lo veo todos los sábados. Los sábados por la mañana, me levanto temprano y me lavo la boca. Luego…
Juana: ¡Miguel! A la señorita Suárez no le interesa tu rutina.

8▶ Elena: «Adiós, queridos televidentes, y acuérdense –para mantenerse sanos, lleven una dieta balanceada y nutritiva, no fumen nunca, y ¡hagan ejercicio!»

9▶ Elena: Bueno, Francisco. Vas a venir a ver la producción de mi programa, ¿no? ¿Y estás con tu familia aquí?
Francisco: Sí, con mis tíos y mi prima.
Elena: Ellos también pueden venir. Ustedes pueden participar.

10▶ Francisco: ¿Qué tenemos que hacer?
Elena: Primero, nos estiramos un poco, después hacemos los ejercicios. Y hay una parte sobre la dieta y la alimentación, el bienestar y la vida saludable. Pónganse ropa ligera.



## Teaching All Students

**Extra Help** Ask students to complete the following sentences: 1. Elena Suárez es... 2. Su programa es... 3. Según Elena, para mantenerse sano, debe... 4. La producción de su programa es...

**Native Speakers** Ask for volunteers to model a simple exercise or stretch in Spanish. Allow other students to practice the exercise/stretch, repeating the directions after the student who is leading the exercise. You can also ask if students have any exercise videos in Spanish that they could bring in and show to the class.

### Multiple Intelligences

**Interpersonal** Divide the class into groups of 4. Have each group take on the roles of Francisco, Elena, Juana and Miguel and role-play the scenes in the **En vivo** dialog. Have them add a different ending to the dialog.

## Video Synopsis

Francisco is interviewing Elena Suárez, hostess of a television exercise program in Puerto Rico. As they are talking they encounter two fans, Juana and Miguel. For a complete transcript of the video dialog, see p. 171D.

## Comprehension Questions

1. ¿Está bien informada Elena Suárez sobre el ejercicio y la salud? **(Sí.)**
2. ¿Tiene un programa de televisión? **(Sí.)**
3. ¿Les da consejos Elena a los televidentes? **(Sí.)**
4. ¿Mira Miguel el programa todos los lunes? **(No.)**
5. ¿Recomienda Elena eliminar el estrés o la carne de res? **(el estrés)**
6. ¿Quieren Miguel y Juana el video de Elena o su autógrafo? **(su autógrafo)**
7. ¿Recomienda Elena el ejercicio para formar músculos o para mantenerse sano? **(para mantenerse sano)**
8. ¿Qué van a hacer Francisco y su familia? **(participar en el programa de Elena)**
9. ¿Cuál es la primera actividad que hacen en el programa? **(se estiran)**
10. ¿Qué hacen después? **(hacen ejercicios)**

## Cross Cultural Connections

Ask students if they know of any exercise/fitness programs on television. Who are the celebrities? What kind of information might be on these programs? Who watches them? How do they compare to the description of the Elena Suárez program described here?

## Gestures

Have students identify any gestures they recognize in the photographs. What are Miguel's gestures in frames 5–7 and what do they mean? Remind students that paying attention to nonverbal communication clues can increase comprehension.

## Block Schedule

**Retention** To review the grammar from Unit 2, have students point out the uses of the direct and indirect object pronouns in this dialog. You can also point out the uses of the command forms that students will be learning in Unit 3.

### Teaching Resource Options

**Print** 

Block Scheduling Copymasters
Unit 3 Resource Book
Video Activities, pp. 24–25
Videoscript, pp. 26–27
Audioscript, p. 28

**Audiovisual** 

OHT 80 (Quick Start)

Audio Program Cassette 7A / CD 7
Video Program Videotape 3, 3:55 / Videodisc 2A

**Technology** 

*Intrigas y aventuras* CD-ROM, Disc 1

### Quick Start Review

Verbs similar to **gustar**

Use OHT 80 or write on board: Write sentences using phrases from each column and these verbs: **encantar, fascinar, importar, interesar**.

| | |
|---|---|
| A Elena | ver a Elena |
| A Francisco | mantenerse sano |
| A Miguel | hacer entrevistas |
| A Juana | mirar el programa de Elena |

*Answers will vary.*

### Teaching Suggestions

Before students write the answers in sentence form for **Actividad 4**, have them scan the sentences and write down which pronouns they are going to use in each item.

# En acción
## VOCABULARIO Y GRAMÁTICA

**OBJECTIVES**
- Discuss ways to stay fit and healthy
- Make suggestions
- Talk about daily routine and personal care

ACTIVIDAD 1

### ¿Quién habla?

**Escuchar** Según el diálogo, ¿quién habla? *(Hint: Say who speaks.)*

Francisco  — Elena  — Juana  — Miguel

1. «Vamos a correr un poco y luego hablar de la entrevista.»
2. «¡Ay, me encanta su programa!»
3. «Los sábados por la mañana, me levanto temprano y me lavo la boca.»
4. «Sus consejos nos ayudaron mucho.»
5. «Adiós, queridos televidentes, y acuérdense…»

ACTIVIDAD 2 

### No es cierto

**Escuchar/Escribir** Todas estas oraciones son falsas. Escribe la verdad según el diálogo. *(Hint: Change these false sentences to true ones.)*

1. El programa de Elena Suárez está en la televisión los jueves.
2. Inmediatamente después de levantarse, Miguel ve el programa.
3. Juana sólo hace ejercicios los sábados.
4. Según Elena, no es importante comer alimentos nutritivos.
5. En el autógrafo, Miguel quiere poner el nombre de su esposa primero.
6. Después del autógrafo, Miguel y Juana le piden unos consejos a Elena.
7. El programa de Elena es a las dos de la tarde.
8. Elena dice que la familia de Francisco no puede venir a ver el programa.

**TAMBIÉN SE DICE**

En Puerto Rico, mucha gente usa la palabra **súper** en lugar de **muy**. Por ejemplo, Elena dice «súper popular». Pero si quieres decir que algo es muy bueno, puedes usar las palabras **chévere, fenomenal, genial, fantástico, maravilloso** o **buenísimo.**



### Classroom Management

**Streamlining** Have students review the story in the dialog by acting it out. Ask for 4 volunteers to portray Francisco, Elena, Juana, and Miguel and reenact the dialog. Then do **Actividades 1** and **2** orally.

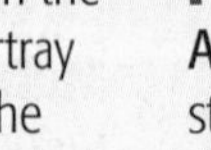

**Peer Teaching** Have students work in pairs to do **Actividad 2**. Then extend the activity by having students work with their partner to locate the line in the dialog that gives the answer.

* Review: Pronoun placement
* Use formal **usted** commands

## Consejos

**Hablar/Escribir** Tus compañeros(as) necesitan consejos sobre cómo mantenerse sanos(as). Dales unos buenos consejos.
*(Hint: Give advice.)*

**modelo**

*dormir más de siete horas cada noche*

*Debes dormir más de siete horas cada noche. (No debes dormir más de siete horas cada noche.)*

1. comer alimentos nutritivos
2. sudar mucho cuando haces ejercicio
3. comer muchos dulces y comida rápida
4. estirarte antes y después de hacer ejercicio
5. vivir una vida balanceada
6. participar en el atletismo
7. entrenarte todos los días
8. pensar en la alimentación en tu dieta
9. usar comida para bajar el estrés
10. relajarte un poco todos los días

## ¿Siempre o nunca?

**Hablar/Escribir** Tu compañero(a) quiere saber con qué frecuencia haces estas cosas. ¿Qué le dices? *(Hint: How often do you do these activities?)*

**modelo**

*darle regalos a tu hermano*

**Compañero(a):** *¿Con qué frecuencia le das regalos a tu hermano?*

**Tú:** *Siempre se los doy.*

1. dejarle una buena propina al (a la) mesero(a)
2. contarle chistes a tu hermano(a) en un restaurante
3. comprar un refresco para mí
4. darles servilletas a los miembros de tu familia
5. pagarles la cuenta a tus amigos
6. recomendarle un plato a un(a) compañero(a)
7. pedirles dinero a tus padres para cenar en un restaurante
8. preparar comida para tu familia



## Teaching All Students

**Extra Help** Have students list 3 ways that they stay fit and healthy and review the answers on the board.

**Multiple Intelligences**

**Verbal** Using the chart from **Actividad 4**, ask students to write what they do for each of the time slots, e.g., **Nunca estudio durante el día. Siempre estudio por la noche. Rara vez hablo por teléfono después de las diez de la noche...**

**Logical/Mathematical** Ask students to rank the items listed in **Actividad 3** in order from most important (12) to least important (1). Compare the results with the whole class.

**Objective:** Controlled practice
Listening comprehension

**Answers**

1. Francisco
2. Juana
3. Miguel
4. Miguel
5. Elena

**Objective:** Transitional practice
Listening comprehension

**Answers** *(Answers may vary)*

1. Está en la televisión los sábados.
2. Miguel se lava la boca.
3. Hace ejercicio todos los días.
4. Es importante.
5. Quiere poner su nombre primero.
6. Ellos le piden la frase.
7. Es por la mañana.
8. Pueden venir a ver y participar.

## Language Note

Before doing **Actividad 3**, explain to students that the verb **deber** + another verb in the infinitive means *should do something*. For example, **debes dormir** means *you should sleep*.

**Objective:** Transitional practice
**En contexto** vocabulary

**Answers**

Students should answer in complete sentences.

1. Debes ...
2. Debes ...
3. No debes ...
4. Debes ...
5. Debes ...
6. Debes ...
7. Debes ...
8. Debes ...
9. No debes ...
10. Debes ...

**Objective:** Transitional practice
Double object pronouns
Expressions of frequency

**Answers** *(Answers will vary)*

1. Siempre se la dejo.
2. De vez en cuando se los cuento.
3. Rara vez te lo compro.
4. Siempre se las doy.
5. De vez en cuando se la pago.
6. Siempre se lo recomiendo.
7. Nunca se lo pido.
8. Se la preparo mucho.

## Block Schedule

**Variety** Divide the class into groups. Have each group choose a character and draw a picture, then write a plan for staying fit and healthy, a daily routine, and personal care for that character. (For additional activities, see **Block Scheduling Copymasters.**)

## Teaching Resource Options

**Print** 

*Más práctica* Workbook PE, pp. 69–70
*Cuaderno para hispanohablantes* PE, pp. 67–68
Block Scheduling Copymasters
Unit 3 Resource Book
*Más práctica* Workbook TE, pp. 5–6
*Cuaderno para hispanohablantes* TE, pp. 11–12

**Audiovisual** 

OHT 80 (Quick Start)

**Technology**

*Intrigas y aventuras* CD-ROM, Disc 1

## Quick Start Review

Review of tenses

Use OHT 80 or write on board: You have learned many verb tenses so far in your study of Spanish. Rewrite the following sentences using the appropriate tense. The cues will help you determine which tense to use.

Yo / hacer ejercicio

1. Hoy…
2. En este momento…
3. Ayer…
4. El año pasado cada día…
5. Mañana…

**Answers**

1. Hoy hago ejercicio.
2. En este momento estoy haciendo ejercicio.
3. Ayer hice ejercicio.
4. El año pasado cada día hacía ejercicio.
5. Mañana voy a hacer ejercicio.

## Teaching Suggestions

### Presenting Pronoun Placement

- Present this grammar note as a review of pronouns. Remind students about different types of pronouns by identifying them in the sentences.
- Remind students that the formula *ir a + infinitive* is used to express an action in the future.

## Pronoun Placement

Where do you put direct or indirect object pronouns? Sometimes they are placed **before** the verb, and sometimes they **attach** to the verb.

Is the verb **conjugated**? You can put the pronoun **before** the verb.

Sus consejos nos **ayudaron** mucho.
*Your advice **helped us** a lot.*

Is the verb in the **infinitive** or in the **-ndo** form? You can **attach** the pronoun to the verb.

***attached***

Voy a **entrevistar**la.
*I am going **to interview her.***

Estábamos **mirándo**lo el sábado pasado.
*We were **watching it** last Saturday.*

Remember that a written accent is often needed to retain correct pronunciation.

**El béisbol** es el deporte más popular de Puerto Rico. Cuando la temporada profesional se termina en Estados Unidos, comienza la liga del invierno en Puerto Rico, que corre desde finales de octubre hasta principios de febrero.

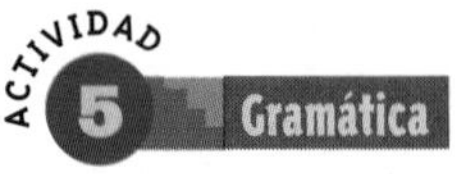

## No dejes para mañana...

**Escribir** Tu profesor(a) de educación física te pregunta qué vas a hacer hoy para estar en forma, pero siempre le dices que vas a hacerlo mañana.
*(Hint: Say what you'll do.)*

**modelo**

*¿Haces ejercicio hoy?*
*No, voy a hacerlo mañana.*
*(No, lo voy a hacer mañana.)*

1. ¿Comes alimentos saludables?
2. ¿Te entrenas hoy?
3. ¿Comes comidas con pocas calorías?
4. ¿Andas en bicicleta hoy?
5. ¿Practicas el atletismo hoy?
6. ¿Te estiras hoy?
7. ¿Bajas el estrés?
8. ¿Te relajas un poco hoy?

**MÁS PRÁCTICA** *cuaderno* pp. 69–70

**PARA HISPANOHABLANTES** *cuaderno* pp. 67–68



## Classroom Community

**TPR** To practice pronoun placement, write the words to several model sentences on separate pieces of paper. Give each student a word. Direct them to stand in the correct order to form sentences using proper pronoun placement.

**Paired Activity** Scramble words for each response in **Actividad 5**. Ask pairs of students to take turns unscrambling them and forming complete sentences.

**Cooperative Learning** Divide the class into groups of 4 or 5. Give each student a particular time of the morning (S1=6:30, S2=6:40, etc.). Students form a short story telling what they will do tomorrow morning. Groups present to the class with each student saying his/her part. (**Modelo:** S1 says: **A las seis y media, voy a despertarme.** etc.)

ACTIVIDAD 6

## Primero

**Hablar** Pregúntale a tu compañero(a) en qué orden estas personas van a hacer las actividades mañana. *(Hint: Tell in what order these people will do these activities tomorrow.)*

**modelo**

*tú: lavarse los dientes / ponerse la ropa*

**Compañero(a):** *¿Qué vas a hacer primero mañana, lavarte los dientes o ponerte la ropa?*

**Tú:** *Voy a lavarme los dientes primero. (Me voy a lavar los dientes primero.)*

1. nosotros: despertarse / levantarse
2. tu hermano(a): cepillarse el pelo / lavarse el pelo
3. ustedes: acostarse / quitarse la ropa
4. unos amigos: secarse / bañarse
5. tu padre: ponerse la ropa / afeitarse
6. tú: peinarse / secarse el pelo
7. tú: arreglarse / acostarse

### Vocabulario

**Las preparaciones**

**acostarse (o → ue)** *to lie down, to go to bed*
**arreglarse** *to get ready*
**cepillarse el pelo** *to brush one's hair*
**quitarse la ropa** *to take off one's clothes*

**Ya sabes**

**afeitarse** *to shave oneself*
**bañarse** *to take a bath*
**despertarse (e → ie)** *to wake up*
**ducharse** *to take a shower*
**lavarse** *to wash oneself*
**lavarse los dientes** *to brush one's teeth*
**levantarse** *to get up*
**maquillarse** *to put on makeup*
**peinarse** *to comb one's hair*
**ponerse la ropa** *to get dressed*
**secarse** *to dry oneself*

¿Qué actividad haces primero?

ACTIVIDAD 7

## El día de deportes

**Hablar** Tú y tus amigos están planeando un día de deportes en el parque. Pregúntale a tu padre qué necesitan ustedes. Luego cambien de papel. *(Hint: What do you need for your sports day?)*

**modelo**

**Hijo(a):** *¿Traigo los patines?*

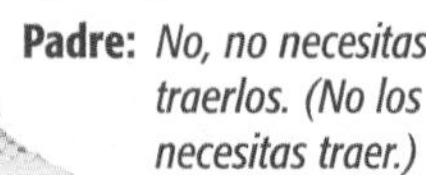

**Padre:** *No, no necesitas traerlos. (No los necesitas traer.)*

1. 
2. 
3. 
4. 
5. 
6. 

ACTIVIDAD 5 **Objective:** Controlled practice
Pronoun placement

**Answers**
1. No, voy a comerlos mañana. (No, los voy a comer mañana.)
2. No, voy a entrenarme mañana.
3. No, no voy a comerlas mañana.
4. No, voy a andar en bicicleta mañana.
5. No, voy a practicarlo mañana.
6. No, voy a estirarme mañana.
7. No, voy a bajarlo mañana.
8. No, voy a relajarme mañana.

ACTIVIDAD 6 **Objective:** Transitional practice
Pronoun placement/reflexive verbs
Ordinal numbers

**Answers**
1. ¿Qué vamos a hacer primero mañana, despertarnos o levantarnos? Vamos a despertarnos primero. (Nos vamos a despertar primero.)
2. ¿Qué va..., cepillarse el pelo o lavarse el pelo? Va a lavarse el pelo primero.
3. ¿Qué van..., acostarse o quitarse la ropa? Vamos a quitarnos la ropa primero.
4. ¿Qué van..., secarse o bañarse? Van a bañarse primero.
5. ¿Qué va..., ponerse la ropa o afeitarse? Va a afeitarse primero.
6. ¿Qué vas..., peinarte o secarte el pelo? Voy a secarme el pelo primero.
7. ¿Qué vas..., arreglarte o acostarte? Voy a arreglarme primero.

### Language Note

Remind students of regional differences such as **jugo/zumo**, **naranjas/chinas**, and **pelota/bola**.

ACTIVIDAD 7 **Objective:** Transitional practice
Pronoun placement

**Answers** *(Answers may vary)*
1. ¿Traigo el jugo? Sí, lo necesitas traer. (Sí, necesitas traerlo.)
2. ¿Traigo los guantes de béisbol? (los)
3. ¿Traigo los uniformes? (los)
4. ¿Traigo las naranjas? (las)
5. ¿Traigo el bate de béisbol? (lo)
6. ¿Traigo los cascos de béisbol? (los)

## Teaching All Students

**Extra Help** Ask students to state when they will do the following: e.g., **¿Vas a acostarte temprano? – Sí, voy a acostarme a las diez. 1. ¿Vas a bañarte por la mañana o la tarde? 2. ¿Vas a lavarte los dientes antes de salir? 3. ¿Vas a levantarte a las cinco de la mañana? 4. ¿Vas a peinarte?**

**Native Speakers** Have Spanish speakers give other Spanish names for the items listed in **Actividad 6**. Encourage all students to see the diversity of the Spanish language throughout the different regions.

### Multiple Intelligences

**Visual** In small groups have students draw a visual hook of verb(s).

**Logical/Mathematical** Have students put the list of reflexive verbs on p. 181 in a logical order based on the order in which they get ready in the morning.

## Teaching Suggestions
### Presenting Reflexive Verbs

Remind students that they have already learned about reflexive verbs in Unit 2. These new reflexive verbs on p. 181 have to do with daily routines. Model your own daily routine for students, using these verbs.

## Teaching Resource Options

**Print**

*Más práctica* Workbook PE, p. 71
*Cuaderno para hispanohablantes* PE, p. 69
Block Scheduling Copymasters
Unit 3 Resource Book
*Más práctica* Workbook TE, p. 7
*Cuaderno para hispanohablantes* TE, p. 13
Information Gap Activities, p. 17
Audioscript, pp. 28–29

**Audiovisual**

OHT 80 (Quick Start)
Audio Program Cassette 7A / CD 7

**Technology**

*Intrigas y aventuras* CD-ROM, Disc 1

## Quick Start Review

Present tense

Use OHT 80 or write on board: Give the **yo** form present tense for the following verbs:

| | | |
|---|---|---|
| hablar | pedir | salir |
| vivir | jugar | decir |
| comer | tener | poner |
| dormir | hacer | venir |

**Answers**
See Verb Charts, pp. R29–R35.

## Teaching Suggestions
### Presenting Formal Commands Using usted/ustedes

- Remind students that verbs with spelling changes in the **yo** form and stem-changes will make the same changes in the **usted/ustedes** command forms.
- Note that **dé** has an accent to distinguish it from the preposition **de**.

## Juego

**Answer**
Es mi trompeta.

ACTIVIDAD 8

### ¿Lógico o no?

**Escuchar/Escribir** Escucha las descripciones dos veces. La segunda vez, indica si son lógicas o ilógicas. *(Hint: Are the descriptions logical?)*

1. _____
2. _____
3. _____
4. _____
5. _____
6. _____
7. _____
8. _____

MÁS COMUNICACIÓN p. R8

### Juego

Tu tío Tito te dio tu trompeta y te dijo: —La vas a tocar todos los días con tu tía Tania.

¿De quién es la trompeta?

GRAMÁTICA

## Give Formal Commands Using usted/ustedes

For **affirmative tú commands,** you know that you use the third person singular form of the verb in the present tense. But what do you use for **usted commands**?

- For **-ar** verbs, take the **yo form** of the verb and change the ending to **-e**.

  siento *becomes* siente

  No **siente** al niño delante de la televisión.
  *Don't **sit** the child in front of the television.*

- For **-er** and **-ir** verbs, take the **yo form** of the verb and change the ending to **-a**.

  como *becomes* coma

  **Coma** comidas nutritivas.
  ***Eat** nutritious foods.*

For **ustedes commands,** use plural endings.

hablo *becomes* hablen

**Hablen** español, por favor.
***Speak** Spanish, please.*

escribo *becomes* escriban

**Escriban** las respuestas.
***Write** the answers.*

Some common verbs have irregular **usted commands**:

| | dar | estar | ir | saber | ser |
|---|---|---|---|---|---|
| **usted** | dé | esté | vaya | sepa | sea |
| **ustedes** | den | estén | vayan | sepan | sean |

Elena dice:
—Por favor, **vayan** a hacer ejercicio hoy, no mañana.
*Please, **go** exercise today, not tomorrow.*

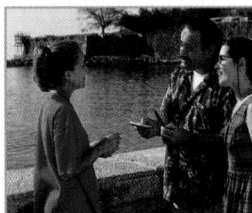

Verbs ending in **-car**, **-gar**, and **-zar** have a spelling change to preserve pronunciation: empezar→empiece



## Classroom Community

**Paired Activity** Ask students to work in pairs and list the advice they hear their parents give in the **ustedes** command form. Ask students to jot down 4–5 things that they hear most often. Then have pairs compare lists.

**Group Activity** Divide the class into groups of 4. Ask students to make a list of suggestions in the **usted** command form for how to be a better student.

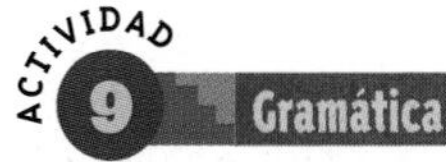


## ¡Mejore su clase!

**Escribir** Imagínate que le aconsejas a un(a) profesor(a) cómo mejorar su clase. Escribe mandatos afirmativos o negativos. *(Hint: Write affirmative or negative commands.)*

**modelo**

*cantar (más / menos) en clase*

*Cante más en clase.*

*(No cante más en clase.)*

1. hablar (más / menos)
2. escuchar a los estudiantes
3. dar (más / menos) tarea
4. leer (más / menos) en clase
5. escribir (más / menos) en el pizarrón
6. traer comida para los estudiantes
7. tocar música en clase
8. llegar a tiempo todos los días

**MÁS PRÁCTICA** *cuaderno* p. 71

**PARA HISPANOHABLANTES** *cuaderno* p. 69

## Para su bienestar

**Hablar/Escribir** Imagínate que trabajas en un club y un señor te pide consejos. ¿Qué le dices? *(Hint: Give advice.)*

**modelo**

*¿Cuántas horas debo dormir? (ocho o nueve horas)*

**Señor:** *¿Cuántas horas debo dormir?*

**Tú:** *Duerma ocho o nueve horas cada noche.*

1. ¿Hago ejercicios aeróbicos? (casi todos los días)
2. ¿Qué como? (alimentos nutritivos)
3. ¿Bebo café? (muy poco)
4. ¿Voy al club? (con frecuencia)
5. ¿Practico el atletismo? (para aliviar el estrés)
6. ¿Juego al béisbol? (después de estirarse)

## Los diez consejos

**Hablar/Escribir** En un grupo, escriban una lista de diez consejos en orden de importancia para los adultos. Léanle la lista al resto de la clase, empezando con el último consejo. *(Hint: Write a "top ten" list of advice for adults, and read it backwards to the class.)*

**modelo**

1. Compren un carro nuevo.
2. Tengan paciencia.
3. Denles mucho dinero a sus hijos.



## Teaching All Students

**Extra Help** Give students a list of infinitive verbs (on the board or on paper), and ask them to form **usted/ustedes** command forms. Include verbs from Units 1 and 2.

**Challenge** Ask students to list verbs that do *not* end in **o** in the **yo** form of the present tense (**soy, estoy, doy, voy, sé**). Now have them change the verbs to **usted** command forms. These 5 verbs are the irregular **usted(es)** commands.

**Multiple Intelligences**

**Kinesthetic** Have students take an "exercise break" in class. Have them do jumping jacks or stretches while counting in Spanish.

**Musical/Rhythmic** Have students create a background rhythm to reinforce the rhyming command forms **dé/esté, vaya/haya, sea/sepa**.

## Teaching Suggestions

Encourage students to use a sense of humor when doing **Actividad 11**. Collect the most creative pieces of advice and post them on a bulletin board.

**Objective:** Transitional practice
Listening comprehension/reflexives

**Answers** (See script, p. 171D.)

1. lógica
2. ilógica
3. lógica
4. ilógica
5. ilógica
6. lógica
7. lógica
8. lógica

**Objective:** Controlled practice
**Usted** commands

**Answers**

1. Hable más/menos en clase.
2. Escuche a sus estudiantes.
3. Dé más/menos tarea.
4. Lea más/menos en clase.
5. Escriba más/menos en el pizarrón.
6. Traiga comida para los estudiantes.
7. Toque música en clase.
8. Llegue a tiempo todos los días.

**Objective:** Transitional practice
**Usted** commands

**Answers**

1. Haga ejercicios aeróbicos casi todos los días.
2. Coma alimentos nutritivos.
3. Beba muy poco café.
4. Vaya al club con frecuencia.
5. Practique el atletismo para aliviar el estrés.
6. Juegue al béisbol después de estirarse.

**Objective:** Open-ended practice
**Ustedes** commands

*Answers will vary.*

## Quick Wrap-up

Have students write commands for visitors to their area.

For example: **Si les gusta la comida italiana, coman en el restaurante Roma. La pasta es sabrosa y no es muy cara.** Other introductory phrases might be: **Si les gusta bailar..., tomar fotos, la música, ir de compras.**

## Block Schedule

**Variety** As a variation to **Actividad 9**, have students write a list of suggestions for their school principal to create a better learning environment.

# UNIDAD 3 Etapa 1
## Vocabulary/Grammar

### Teaching Resource Options

**Print**

*Más práctica* Workbook PE, p. 72
*Cuaderno para hispanohablantes* PE, p. 70
Block Scheduling Copymasters
Unit 3 Resource Book
*Más práctica* Workbook TE, p. 8
*Cuaderno para hispanohablantes* TE, p. 14

**Audiovisual**

OHT 81 (Quick Start)

**Technology**

*Intrigas y aventuras* CD-ROM, Disc 1

### Quick Start Review

Food

Use OHT 81 or write on board: Imagine you are the nutrition editor for your paper and you are giving readers advice on food. Write two affirmative commands and one negative command using the verbs **comer** or **beber**.

For example: **Coman el pescado./No coman mucho helado.**

*Answers will vary.*

### Teaching Suggestions
#### Presenting Commands and Pronoun Placement

Students may have trouble remembering where pronouns should go with commands. Try this mnemonic device: Affirmative > After > Attached > Accent. (Refer students to *Apoyo Para Estudiar* on p. 185.)

### Language Note

In the dialog, Juana uses the expression **Con permiso**. Another way to say *pardon me* is **Perdóneme**.

**Objective:** Controlled practice **Ustedes** commands/pronoun placement

**Answers**

1. Diviértanse con una rutina de ejercicio.
2. No se duerman tarde todos los días.
3. Lávense los dientes.
4. Relájense.
5. No se acuesten muy tarde.
6. Pónganse ropa ligera.

## GRAMÁTICA: Commands and Pronoun Placement

There are easy rules for pronoun placement in sentences with **commands.**

- In **affirmative** commands, the **pronoun follows** the **verb** and is attached to it.
- In **negative** commands, the **pronoun** goes **before** the **verb.**

**Usted command:**

*attached*

Por favor, señorita Elena, **escríbanos** aquí su autógrafo.
*Please, Elena,* ***write*** *your autograph* ***for us*** *here.*

*before*

No, **no nos escriba** su autógrafo con esa pluma.
*No,* ***don't write*** *your autograph* ***for us*** *with that pen.*

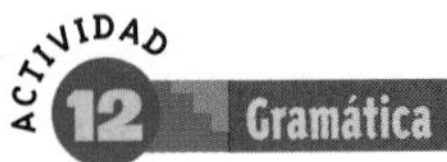

Remember to add written **accents** to maintain stress on the correct syllable.

**Tú command:**

**Háblame** antes del programa.
***Talk to me*** *before the show.*

**No me hables** antes del programa.
***Don't talk to me*** *before the show.*

### ACTIVIDAD 12 Gramática

### ¡Salud!

**Hablar/Escribir** Elena sabe mucho sobre cómo mantenerse saludable. Tomó unos apuntes de lo que piensa aconsejarle a la gente. Cambia cada apunte del infinitivo al imperativo. *(Hint: Give commands.)*

**modelo**

*mantenerse sanos con comida nutritiva (sí)*
*Manténganse sanos con comida nutritiva.*

1. divertirse con una rutina de ejercicio (sí)
2. dormirse tarde todos los días (no)
3. lavarse los dientes (sí)
4. relajarse (sí)
5. acostarse muy tarde (no)
6. ponerse ropa ligera (sí)



### Classroom Community

**Paired Activity** Have students talk about their favorite brands of toothpaste, soap, shampoo, and perfumes with a partner. Have them suggest to their partners that they try their brands. e.g., **Mi jabón favorito es ____. Debes bañarte con ____.**

**Learning Scenario** Divide the class into groups of 3 or 4. There is a slight problem today! You (the teacher) have a sore throat and cannot speak well. Tell the students that they are going to be teaching the **Gramática** on p. 184 to the class. To do this, they need to come up with 5 examples of the command being used in the affirmative and 5 in the negative. Be sure to do this activity only after you have presented it, and after you are sure the students have a firm grasp of the material.

## ¿Qué deben comprar?

**Leer/Escribir** ¿Deben las siguientes personas comprar el artículo mencionado? Usa mandatos afirmativos y negativos para hacerles recomendaciones. *(Hint: Should these people buy these items?)*

**modelo**

*Tenemos pelo sucio. (el perfume)*
*No lo compren.*

1. En la mañana el sabor en la boca es feo. (la pasta de dientes)
2. Corro y levanto pesas. (el desodorante)
3. Tenemos las manos bastante secas. (el maquillaje)
4. Tenemos el pelo muy sucio. (el champú)
5. Queremos tener pelo más rizado. (los cepillos de dientes)
6. Necesito un regalo para una señorita elegante. (el perfume)

**MÁS PRÁCTICA** *cuaderno* p. 72
**PARA HISPANOHABLANTES** *cuaderno* p. 70

**Pronoun placement with affirmative commands**

When you attach any object pronoun (direct, indirect, or reflexive) to an affirmative command of two or more syllables, add a written accent to the stressed syllable of the verb. Examples: **Escríbalo. Tráigame. Siéntese. Póngase la gorra. Acuéstese.** But… **Hazlo. Ponlos.**

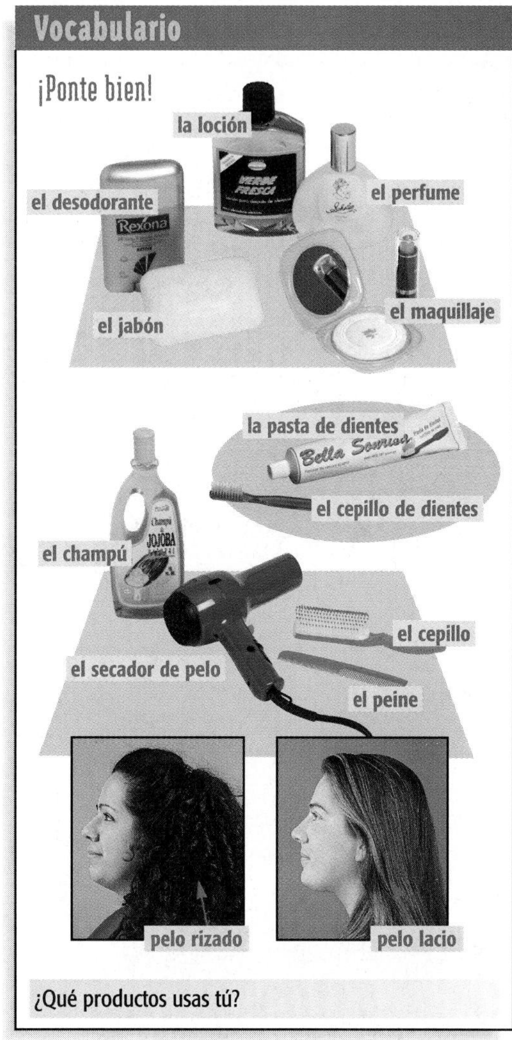


## Teaching Suggestions

- Teach the vocabulary in the **Vocabulario** box before doing **Actividad 13**. You can bring in actual toiletries to use when presenting the vocabulary. You can also have students collect magazine photos or advertisements of these products.
- Have students review the words in the **Vocabulario** box and pick out the cognates.

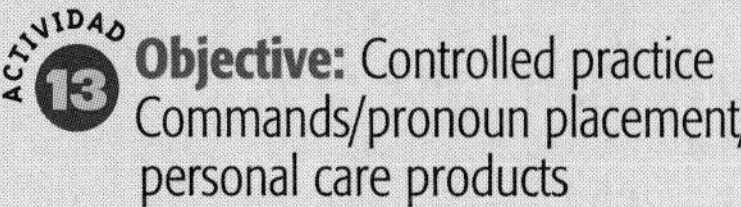


**Objective:** Controlled practice Commands/pronoun placement/personal care products

### Answers

1. Cómprala. (Cómprela.)
2. Cómpralo. (Cómprelo.)
3. No lo compren.
4. Cómprenlo.
5. No los compren.
6. Cómpralo. (Cómprelo.)

## Block Schedule

**Change of Pace** Bring in as many of the items as possible from the **Vocabulario** on p. 185. (For items such as **la loción, la pasta de dientes, el champú,** etc., try to get products that have labels in Spanish. If you don't have any, try asking other Spanish teachers in the school if they have collected such products in their travels.) In groups of 3 or 4, students should create a skit in Spanish that describes what they need to get ready to go to school in the morning. (**Modelo:** *All students*: **Vamos a la escuela.** *Student 1*, **"Necesito el jabón."** S1 pantomimes using this item as the sentence is being presented.) All students in each group should pantomime use of a different product. Each group presents their skit to the class.

**Variation:** This could also be a good time to practice commands. Instead of simply saying, **"Necesito....",** Students say **"Déme..."**

For additional activities, see **Block Scheduling Copymasters**.



## Teaching All Students

**Extra Help** Give students 7–8 command forms, and have them write out the corresponding affirmative/negative form, e.g., **Acuéstense. / No se acuesten. Báñate. / No te bañes.**

**Native Speakers** Ask Spanish speakers to talk about their daily personal care routine and the products they use. If they have access to Spanish-language newspapers and magazines, ask them to bring in advertisements of personal care products to share with the class.

### Multiple Intelligences

**Verbal** Ask students to list 5 commands in the affirmative and 5 different verbs in the negative that refer to a person's daily routine.

## Teaching Resource Options

**Print**

*Más práctica* Workbook PE, pp. 65–68
*Cuaderno para hispanohablantes* PE, pp. 65–66
Block Scheduling Copymasters
Unit 3 Resource Book
*Más práctica* Workbook TE, pp. 1–4
*Cuaderno para hispanohablantes* TE, pp. 9–10
Information Gap Activities, p. 18
Audioscript, pp. 29, 30–32

**Audiovisual**

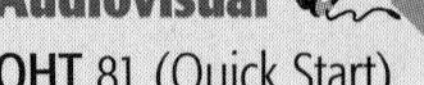

OHT 81 (Quick Start)
Audio Program Cassette 7A, 7B / CD 7; (*Para hispanohablantes* Cassette 7B / CD 7)

**Technology**

*Intrigas y aventuras* CD-ROM, Disc 1

## Quick Start Review

**Talking about entertainment**

Use OHT 81 or write on board: Read the preferences of each person and give advice on which type of movie or show to attend. Use the **usted** command of the verb **ir**. For example: **Me gusta la ciencia. Vaya a ver una película de ciencia ficción.**

1. Me gustan las historias de amor.
2. Me gusta la acción.
3. Me gusta asustarme.
4. Me gusta la música.

a. un musical
b. una película de horror
c. una película de aventuras
d. una película romántica

**Answers**
1. d; 2. c; 3. b; 4. a

## Teaching Suggestions

This may be a good opportunity to review body parts and commands by playing a game of **Simón dice**. Hint: Prepare a list of commands ahead of time to read to the class.

## ¿Qué venden?

**Escuchar** Escucha los seis anuncios del radio. ¿Qué producto quieren vender en cada anuncio? *(Hint: Tell what product is being advertised.)*

**NOTA CULTURAL**

**El Viejo San Juan** Puerto Rico recibe mucha influencia de Estados Unidos, sobre todo en sus productos. Pero también tiene influencia de otros lugares. Esto se puede ver en los edificios del Viejo San Juan, que tienen un estilo colonial español que llegó con Ponce de León en el siglo XVI.

## Consejos locos

**Hablar/Escribir** Con otros(as) compañeros(as), usa el imperativo de algunos verbos reflexivos para escribir cinco frases creativas que pueden actuar en clase. *(Hint: Give five commands with reflexive verbs for classmates to act out.)*

**modelo**

*Siéntense y levántense cinco veces.*
*Lávense los dientes con un lápiz.*
*Dúchense con agua fría.*
*Péinense.*
*Maquíllense.*

## ¡Háganlo!

**Hablar** Tú y tu compañero(a) de clase van a enseñarles a unos niños de la escuela primaria a hacer algo. Decidan qué van a enseñar usando las ideas de abajo. Luego practíquenlo con sus compañeros(as) de clase. *(Hint: Teach children to do something new.)*

andar en patineta
cuidar a un niño
lavarse los dientes
saludar en español
hacer un sándwich



## Classroom Community

**Storytelling** Ask students to write a short story about a famous person's daily personal care routine, using the vocabulary words on pp. 181 and 185.

**Portfolios** Based on vocabulary items on pp. 181 and 185, have students write about their own daily personal care routine. Have them include as many products as possible.

**Rubric: Writing**

| Criteria | Scale |
|---|---|
| Vocabulary use | 1 2 3 4 5 |
| Logical sentence order | 1 2 3 4 5 |
| Grammar/spelling/accuracy | 1 2 3 4 5 |

A = 13–15 pts.
B = 10–12 pts.
C = 7–9 pts.
D = 4–6 pts.
F = < 4 pts.

## Tu rutina

**PARA CONVERSAR**

**STRATEGY: SPEAKING**

**Use gestures to convey meaning**

The more senses you use when you communicate, the more sense you make. Use physical actions, as well as words, when talking about your daily routine.

**Hablar** Con un grupo de compañeros(as), habla de tu rutina diaria. *(Hint: Talk about your daily routine.)*

1. ¿A qué hora te levantas? ¿A qué hora te acuestas?
2. ¿Qué haces después de levantarte?
3. ¿Qué comes y bebes por la mañana? ¿por la noche?
4. ¿Cómo te mantienes saludable?
5. ¿Cómo te relajas?

## Los anuncios

**Hablar/Escribir** Con un(a) compañero(a), haz un anuncio (cartel, video o presentación) para un producto de arreglo personal. Acuérdate de incluir lo siguiente. *(Hint: Create an ad for a personal care product.)*

- un mandato negativo (**usted** o **ustedes**)
- dos mandatos afirmativos (**usted** o **ustedes**)
- dos verbos reflexivos
- persuasión
- creatividad
- calidad

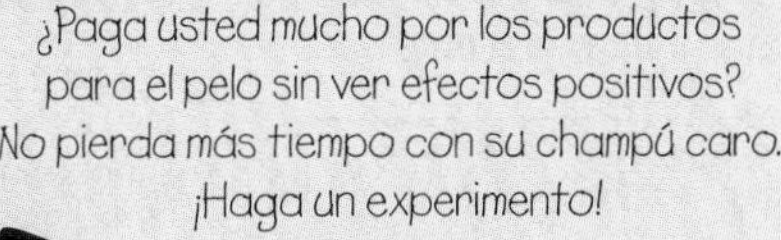

Champú El brillo
Cabello de lujo a bajo precio
¿Paga usted mucho por los productos para el pelo sin ver efectos positivos?
No pierda más tiempo con su champú caro.
¡Haga un experimento!
Lávese el pelo todos los días con Champú El brillo.
¡Acuérdese! Si usted quiere tener cabello de lujo a bajo precio,
use Champú El brillo.


MÁS COMUNICACIÓN p. R8

**Refrán**

**El ejercicio hace al maestro.**

Este refrán quiere decir que si sigues tratando, un día lo vas a hacer. En grupos pequeños, inventen un juego para tu clase donde los otros estudiantes tienen que tratar algo muchas veces antes de completar la actividad con éxito.

## Teaching All Students

**Extra Help** Have students write out their answers to **Actividad 16** before sharing them with classmates in small groups.

**Native Speakers** Have Spanish-speaking students give other Spanish **refranes** they know that have similar themes. Ask them to describe situations in Spanish that illustrate this **refrán** in which lots of practice brings success.

**Multiple Intelligences**

**Verbal** Have students create a slogan for a health and fitness product that they use. Let them try to "sell" their product by convincing another student to try their brand.

**Visual** Have students choose a product in **Actividad 15** and create a **«cupón»** (manufacturer's discount coupon) or other marketing tool to sell the product.

## Teaching Suggestions

**Speaking Strategy** Have students mime their routines in **Actividad 16** and have the class guess the activity.

**Objective:** Transitional practice
Listening comprehension/personal care products

**Answers** (See script, p. 171D.)
1. el secador de pelo
2. el desodorante
3. el maquillaje
4. la loción
5. la pasta de dientes
6. el champú

**Objective:** Open-ended practice
Usted commands

Reflexive verbs

*Answers will vary.*

**Objective:** Open-ended practice
Usted commands

*Answers will vary.*

**Objective:** Open-ended practice
Discussing daily routine

**Rubric: Speaking**

| Criteria | Scale | |
|---|---|---|
| Vocabulary use | 1 2 3 4 5 | A = 17–20 pts. |
| Gesture use | 1 2 3 4 5 | B = 13–16 pts. |
| Fluency, intonation | 1 2 3 4 5 | C = 9–12 pts. |
| Accuracy | 1 2 3 4 5 | D = 5–8 pts. |
| | | F = < 5 pts. |

**Objective:** Open-ended practice
Usted commands/reflexives

**Rubric: Speaking or Writing**

| Criteria | Scale | |
|---|---|---|
| Vocabulary use | 1 2 3 4 5 | A = 17–20 pts. |
| Correct verb use | 1 2 3 4 5 | B = 13–16 pts. |
| Logical organization | 1 2 3 4 5 | C = 9–12 pts. |
| Creativity | 1 2 3 4 5 | D = 5–8 pts. |
| | | F = < 5 pts. |

## Block Schedule

**FunBreak** Bring in Spanish magazine advertisements. Divide the class into two teams and present a member from each team with an advertisement. The first to name the product in Spanish gets a point.

## Teaching Resource Options

**Print** 

*Cuaderno para hispanohablantes* PE, pp. 71–72
Unit 3 Resource Book
*Cuaderno para hispanohablantes* TE, pp. 15–16
Audioscript, pp. 29–30

**Audiovisual** 

**Audio Program** Cassette 7A / CD 7
**OHT** 81 (Quick Start)
*Canciones* Cassette / CD Song 6

## Quick Start Review

Indirect object pronouns

Use OHT 81 or write on board: Look at the pictures of Puerto Rico and imagine you are a tourist. Write four sentences telling what you like about the island. Use the verbs **encantar, gustar, fascinar, interesar**. You might like to talk about:

| | |
|---|---|
| las plantas exóticas | la historia |
| el bosque tropical | la comida |
| las playas | |

*Answers will vary.*

## Teaching Suggestions
### Presenting En voces

- **Prereading** Begin by asking students to guess the topic of the reading. Write the list of possibilities on the board.
- **Strategy: Observe Organization of Ideas** Have students jot down notes as they read each paragraph to help them determine the key ideas.
- **Reading** Have students listen to the reading on the Audio Program.
- **Post-reading** Ask students to write at least 3 questions they would like answered about Puerto Rico.

## Dictation

Have students silently reread the first paragraph of the reading, then close their books. Dictate the paragraph and have students check their work.

# En voces
LECTURA

**PARA LEER**
**STRATEGY: READING**
**Observe organization of ideas** In a short reading, the number of paragraphs is often a clue to the number of key ideas. First, read the entire article quickly to get a general overview. Then reread each paragraph. On a copy of the chart below, give a title to each one.

| Párrafo | Título |
|---|---|
| #1 | |
| #2 | |
| #3 | |
| #4 | |
| #5 | |
| #6 | |

# Puerto Rico: Lugar maravilloso

Puerto Rico es un lugar maravilloso para pasar las vacaciones porque tiene de todo. Tiene paisaje[1], deportes e historia. Y como es una isla pequeña puedes hacerlo todo en pocos días.

Si te gusta la naturaleza[2], no hay mejor lugar. En el interior de la isla hay varias reservas forestales y unas cuevas[3] muy importantes donde viven murciélagos[4] y donde se encuentran paredes de cristal.

Con el océano Atlántico al norte y el mar Caribe al sur, Puerto Rico tiene muchas playas. Algunas de las más famosas están cerca de San Juan en la costa atlántica, como Isla Verde, Luquillo y Condado. Para la gente que prefiere los deportes acuáticos, es posible hacer surfing, o bucear[5]. Se puede explorar la isla por mar en un barco o a caballo en las playas y las montañas. Y si no te interesa ninguno de esos deportes, el béisbol también es muy popular en Puerto Rico.

[1] landscape [2] nature [3] caves [4] bats [5] scuba diving



## Classroom Community

**Learning Scenario** Have students design a brochure for Puerto Rico. Use the information given in the text as well as any information they may find on the Internet. Then let them act as a travel agent and try to sell their trip to Puerto Rico to a small group.

**Portfolio** Based on what they have learned about Puerto Rico, ask students if they would like to visit the island. Why or why not? Have them write their response in their journal.

**Rubric: Writing**

| Criteria | Scale |
|---|---|
| Accuracy of information | 1 2 3 4 5 |
| Logical organization | 1 2 3 4 5 |
| Vocabulary use | 1 2 3 4 5 |

A = 13–15 pts.
B = 10–12 pts.
C = 7–9 pts.
D = 4–6 pts.
F = < 4 pts.

Después de disfrutar las maravillas naturales de la isla, es hora de conocer San Juan. El centro de la capital, el Viejo San Juan, es un barrio de mucho ambiente[6] con casas, iglesias y edificios de la época colonial española. Hay muchas cosas que ver, como la catedral, la fortaleza San Felipe del Morro y los excelentes museos.

En el San Juan moderno está el Jardín Botánico de la Universidad de Puerto Rico. Aquí puedes ver todo tipo de flora puertorriqueña, hasta plantas exóticas y especies en peligro de extinción.

Si acaso después de ver tantas atracciones tienes hambre, puedes comer un plato típico de la isla como el asopao o el arroz con habichuelas. ¡Buen provecho!

[6] atmosphere

el asopao

## ¿Comprendiste?

1. ¿Por qué es Puerto Rico un buen lugar para pasar las vacaciones?
2. ¿Qué hay en el interior de la isla?
3. ¿Qué puedes hacer en la isla si te gusta el mar?
4. ¿Qué puedes ver en el Viejo San Juan?
5. ¿Qué lugar puedes visitar en el San Juan moderno?

## ¿Qué piensas?

1. Repasa tus apuntes sobre la organización del artículo. ¿De qué se trata cada párrafo?
2. ¿Por qué crees que el béisbol y el surfing son pasatiempos populares en Puerto Rico?
3. Tienes una semana en Puerto Rico. ¿Cómo vas a pasar tu tiempo? ¿Qué te gustaría hacer? ¿Por qué?



## Culture Highlights

- **EL ASOPAO** is a soupy rice dish made with rice, chicken, vegetables, and seasonings. It can be served for lunch or dinner.
- **EL MOFONGO** is another typical Puerto Rican specialty. It consists of cooked plantains that are mashed and seasoned with garlic. It is served as a side dish to any rice, chicken, or meat main course.
- **PUERTO RICO** is an island of 8,959 square kilometers, about the size of Rhode Island. One-third of the population lives in the San Juan metropolitan area.
- **LUQUILLO BEACH** is one of the most scenic beaches in Puerto Rico, with its mile-long groves of majestic coconut palm trees.

## Cross Cultural Connections

**Strategy** Compare and contrast the information given about Puerto Rico with local places to visit, using a Venn diagram. Students may also identify influences of geography and climate, using what they already know from science and social studies. You may ask students to use the **¿Comprendiste?** questions to focus their inquiry.

## ¿Comprendiste?

### Answers

1. Porque tiene de todo: paisaje, deportes e historia en una isla pequeña.
2. Hay varias reservas forestales y unas cuevas muy importantes.
3. Puedes ir a la playa, hacer surfing, bucear o explorar la isla en un barco.
4. Puedes ver la catedral y la fortaleza San Felipe del Morro, y visitar excelentes museos.
5. Puedes visitar el Jardín Botánico de la Universidad de Puerto Rico.

## Teaching All Students

**Extra Help** Have students read aloud with a partner. Have them listen well for their partner's correct pronunciation.

**Challenge** Ask students to locate all the places mentioned in this reading on a map of Puerto Rico or San Juan.

### Multiple Intelligences

**Logical/Mathematical** Using a globe, let students measure the distance from their town/city to Puerto Rico using a piece of string/yarn. Compare that distance to the distance from their town/city to other Spanish-speaking countries.

**Interpersonal** Have students tell each other what they would like to do on a Puerto Rican vacation based on what they have learned in this **Etapa**.

## Block Schedule

**Retention** Have students reread **Puerto Rico: Lugar maravilloso**, then write a short paragraph in Spanish describing the highlights of their own city or town.

# UNIDAD 3 Etapa 1
## Review

### Teaching Resource Options

**Print**

Block Scheduling Copymasters
Unit 3 Resource Book
Information Gap Activities, pp. 19–20
Family Involvement, pp. 21–22

**Audiovisual**

OHT 82 (Quick Start)

**Technology**

Electronic Teacher Tools/Test Generator
*Intrigas y aventuras* CD-ROM, Disc 1

### Quick Start Review

Personal care products

Use OHT 82 or write on the board: Make a list of five items a person might buy at a pharmacy or in the personal care section of a grocery store.

*Answers could include:*
**el champú, la pasta de dientes, el perfume, el desodorante, la loción**

### Teaching Suggestions

- Have students look at the "Now you can..." notes listed on the left side of pp. 190–191. Point out that if they feel they need to review material before doing the activities, they should consult the "To review" notes.
- Use the video to review vocabulary and structures.

# En uso
## REPASO Y MÁS COMUNICACIÓN

**OBJECTIVES**
- Discuss ways to stay fit and healthy
- Make suggestions
- Talk about daily routine and personal care

*Now you can...*
- talk about daily routine and personal care.

*To review*
- pronoun placement, see p. 180.

### ACTIVIDAD 1 ¡No lo encuentro!

Una señora está arreglándose y no puede encontrar muchas cosas. ¿Qué dice? *(Hint: Tell what she says when she can't find what she needs.)*

**modelo**

*¿Dónde está mi cepillo? ¡No lo encuentro y tengo que usarlo!*

*Now you can...*
- talk about daily routine and personal care.

*To review*
- pronoun placement, see p. 180.

### ACTIVIDAD 2 Un momento...

Francisco está arreglándose para la entrevista. ¿Qué le dice a su prima cuando toca a la puerta del baño? *(Hint: Tell what Francisco says when his cousin knocks on the bathroom door.)*

**modelo**

*bañarse*
*Un momento. Me estoy bañando. (Estoy bañándome.)*

1. lavarse el pelo
2. secarse
3. afeitarse
4. bañarse
5. lavarse los dientes
6. peinarse
7. ponerse la ropa
8. cepillarse el pelo



### Classroom Community

**Cooperative Learning** Assign a small group of students to a "Now you can..." or a "To review..." from the marginal annotations on pp. 190–191. Each group reviews concept(s) and plans a short presentation to the entire class. This will summarize the entire lesson.

**Game** Have pairs of students write matching vocabulary words on pairs of index cards, e.g., **lavarse** and **jabón**. Each pair joins another and combines cards, spreading them face down. Students take turns trying to find matching cards.

*Now you can...*
- discuss ways to stay fit and healthy.
- make suggestions.

*To review*
- formal **usted/ustedes** commands, see p. 182.

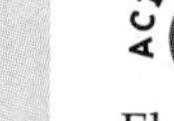

## ¡Manténganse sanos!

Elena les da consejos a sus admiradores. ¿Qué les dice?
*(Hint: Tell what advice Elena gives to her fans.)*

**modelo**

*hacer ejercicio para bajar el estrés*
*Hagan ejercicio para bajar el estrés.*

1. participar en varios deportes
2. correr para quemar calorías
3. caminar en el parque para relajarse
4. llevar una dieta balanceada
5. tomar suficiente agua
6. dormir ocho horas
7. vivir una vida saludable
8. estirarse para relajarse

*Now you can...*
- discuss ways to stay fit and healthy.
- make suggestions.

*To review*
- commands and pronoun placement, see p. 184.

## Unas respuestas

Elena contesta las preguntas de sus admiradores. ¿Qué dice?
*(Hint: Tell how Elena answers her fans' questions.)*

**modelo**

| | |
|---|---|
| *¿Debo comer papas fritas?* | *No, no las coma.* |
| *¿Debo mantenerme sano?* | *Sí, manténgase sano.* |

1. ¿Debo comer frutas?
2. ¿Debo entrenarme todos los días?
3. ¿Debo beber mucho café?
4. ¿Debo estirarme antes de correr?
5. ¿Debo tomar muchos refrescos?
6. ¿Debo comer muchos dulces?
7. ¿Debo practicar deportes?
8. ¿Debo hacer ejercicio con frecuencia?
9. ¿Debo acostarme muy tarde?
10. ¿Debo tomar mucha agua?
11. ¿Debo relajarme después de correr?
12. ¿Debo levantar pesas?

### Answers

1. secador de pelo/lo
2. maquillaje/lo
3. perfume/lo
4. jabón/lo
5. desodorante/lo
6. pasta de dientes/la
7. cepillo de dientes/lo
8. peine/lo

### Answers

1. Un momento. Me estoy lavando el pelo. (Estoy lavándome el pelo.)
2. Un momento. Me estoy secando.
3. Un momento. Me estoy afeitando.
4. Un momento. Me estoy bañando.
5. Un momento. Me estoy lavando los dientes.
6. Un momento. Me estoy peinando.
7. Un momento. Me estoy poniendo la ropa.
8. Un momento. Me estoy cepillando el pelo.

### Answers

1. Participen en varios deportes.
2. Corran para quemar calorías.
3. Caminen en el parque para relajarse.
4. Lleven una dieta balanceada.
5. Tomen suficiente agua.
6. Duerman ocho horas.
7. Vivan una vida saludable.
8. Estírense para relajarse.

### Answers

1. Sí, cómalas.
2. Sí, entrénese todos los días.
3. No, no lo beba mucho.
4. Sí, estírese antes de correr.
5. No, no los tome.
6. No, no los coma.
7. Sí, practíquelos.
8. Sí, hágalo con frecuencia.
9. No, no se acueste muy tarde.
10. Sí, tómela.
11. Sí, relájese después de correr.
12. Sí, levántelas.

## Teaching All Students

**Extra Help** Ask students to write 5 things that they want their teacher to do today, e.g., **Ayúdeme con la tarea.** Write 5 things that they do not want their teacher to do today, e.g., **No duerma en clase.**

**Native Speakers** Have those Spanish speakers who know how to dance **salsa** teach the class. They can demonstrate steps and give instructions using formal commands, e.g., **Muévanse los pies, Sigan el ritmo.** They can teach another type of dance if they don't know **salsa**.

### Multiple Intelligences

**Verbal** Write sentence halves from **Actividad 3** on cards. Give to students and have them find their partners to form complete commands.

## Block Schedule

**Variety** As a follow-up to **Actividad 3**, have students add to the list of Elena's advice based on eating and drinking habits, and personal care routines. (For additional activities, see **Block Scheduling Copymasters**.)

## Teaching Resource Options

**Print**

Unit 3 Resource Book
- Cooperative Quizzes 33–34
- Etapa Exam, Forms A and B, pp. 35–44
- *Examen para hispanohablantes,* pp. 45–49
- Audioscript, p. 32
- Portfolio Assessment, pp. 50–51
- Multiple Choice Test Questions, pp. 170–172

**Audiovisual**

OHT 75, 75A, 76, 76A, 82 (Quick Start)
Audio Program Cassette 19B / CD 19; (*Para hispanohablantes* Cassette 19B / CD 19)

**Technology**

Electronic Teacher Tools/Test Generator
www.mcdougallittell.com

## Quick Start Review

**En contexto** vocabulary

Use OHT 82 or write on board: Brainstorm a list of four things a person might do to stay healthy. Use the infinitive form of the verb as you make your list.

*Answers could include:* **entrenarse, estirarse, relajarse, llevar una dieta balanceada**

**Actividad 5 and Actividad 6**

**Rubric: Speaking**

| Criteria | Scale | |
|---|---|---|
| Fluency | 1 2 3 4 5 | A = 13–15 pts. |
| Vocabulary | 1 2 3 4 5 | B = 10–12 pts. |
| Pronunciation, rhythm | 1 2 3 4 5 | C = 7–9 pts. |
| | | D = 4–6 pts. |
| | | F = < 4 pts. |

**En tu propia voz**

**Rubric: Writing**

| Criteria | Scale | |
|---|---|---|
| Vocabulary use | 1 2 3 4 5 | A = 13–15 pts. |
| Accuracy | 1 2 3 4 5 | B = 10–12 pts. |
| Creativity, appearance | 1 2 3 4 5 | C = 7–9 pts. |
| | | D = 4–6 pts. |
| | | F = < 4 pts. |

### Teaching Note: En tu propia voz

**Writing Strategy** Have students organize their suggestions by category, such as nutrition advice, exercise recommendations, and tips for stress reduction.

## Actividad 5 Nuestras rutinas

**PARA CONVERSAR**

**STRATEGY: SPEAKING**

**React to daily routines** As you compare daily routines, you will find similarities and differences. You often signal your general response before specifically telling how alike or different your schedules are.

To do this, use expressions like **yo también / ni yo tampoco / yo no / lo mismo para mí / no, al contrario / ¿de veras? / ¡no me digas!**

Haz una tabla con siete actividades y las horas correspondientes. Luego, en pares, háganse preguntas para comparar sus rutinas. *(Hint: Make a chart and compare routines.)*

**modelo**

**Tú:** *Me despierto a las seis. ¿Y tú?*

**Compañero(a):** *Yo también, pero no me levanto hasta las seis y cinco. ¿A qué hora te levantas?*

| Rutina diaria | | |
|---|---|---|
| Hora | Actividad | Horario de mi compañero(a) |
| 6:00 | me despierto | 6:00 |
| 6:15 | me levanto | 6:05 |
| 6:20 | me baño | 6:10 |

## Actividad 6 ¡Hagan ejercicio!

Tú eres maestro(a) de ejercicios aeróbicos. Dales consejos a otros compañeros(as) y contesta sus preguntas sobre la salud. *(Hint: Give advice.)*

**modelo**

**Tú:** *Relájense después de hacer ejercicio. Caminen en el parque.*

**Compañero(a):** *¿Debemos hacer ejercicio todos los días?*

**Tú:** *Sí, háganlo todos los días para mantenerse fuertes y sanos.*

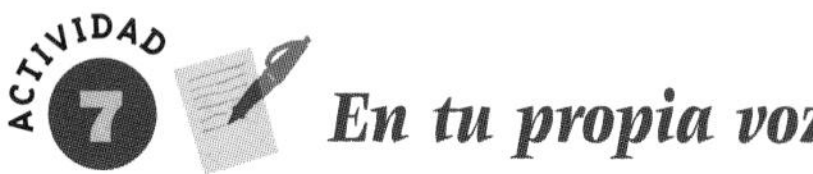

## Actividad 7 En tu propia voz

**ESCRITURA** Imagínate que trabajas para un programa de salud y un señor te pide consejos. Hazle una lista de consejos apropiados. Incluye tres mandatos afirmativos y tres mandatos negativos. *(Hint: Give health advice.)*

**modelo**

*1. Haga ejercicio todos los días.*

*2. No coma…*

### CONEXIONES

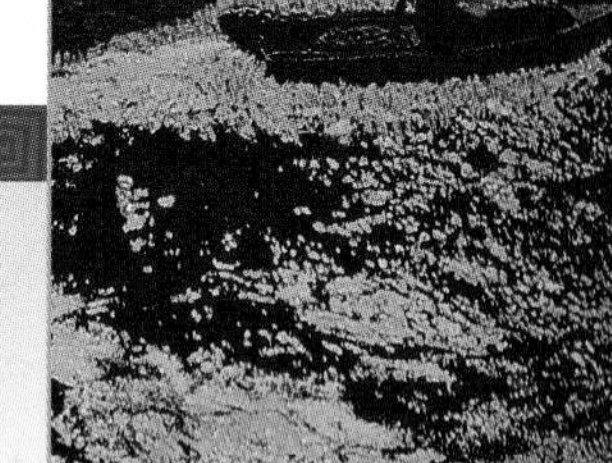

**Las ciencias** En Puerto Rico, hay un pueblo que se llama La Parguera al pie de la Bahía Fosforescente. Hay una luminosidad (*glow*) que viene del agua. ¿Qué significa **fosforescente**? ¿Por qué se ilumina el agua de esta bahía? ¿Bajo qué circunstancias puedes ver esta luminosidad? Investiga estas preguntas y comparte las respuestas con la clase.



### Classroom Community

**TPR** Have students act out the verbs in the Daily Routine section of the vocabulary list for fellow students to guess.

**Storytelling** Have students form a chain story by asking each student to make a sentence using one word from the vocabulary list. Each student should contribute at least one sentence to the theme of the story.

# En resumen

## REPASO DE VOCABULARIO

### DISCUSS WAYS TO STAY FIT AND HEALTHY

**Diet and Exercise**

| | |
|---|---|
| **el bienestar** | *well-being* |
| **crecer** | *to grow* |
| **la energía** | *energy* |
| **mantenerse sano(a)** | *to be healthy* |
| **relajarse** | *to relax* |
| **saludable** | *healthy* |

**Diet**

| | |
|---|---|
| **la alimentación** | *nourishment* |
| **el alimento** | *food* |
| **balanceado(a)** | *balanced* |
| **la caloría** | *calorie* |
| **la dieta** | *diet* |
| **nutritivo(a)** | *nutritious* |

**Exercise**

| | |
|---|---|
| **el atletismo** | *athletics* |
| **entrenarse** | *to train* |
| **estirarse** | *to stretch* |
| **el estrés** | *stress* |
| **sudar** | *to sweat* |

### MAKE SUGGESTIONS

| | |
|---|---|
| **aconsejar** | *to advise* |
| **el (los) consejo(s)** | *advice* |

### Juego

Lee las pistas y di qué necesitan Marta, Antonio y Beatriz.

Marta se lavó el pelo.

Antonio debe levantarse.

Beatriz quiere ducharse.

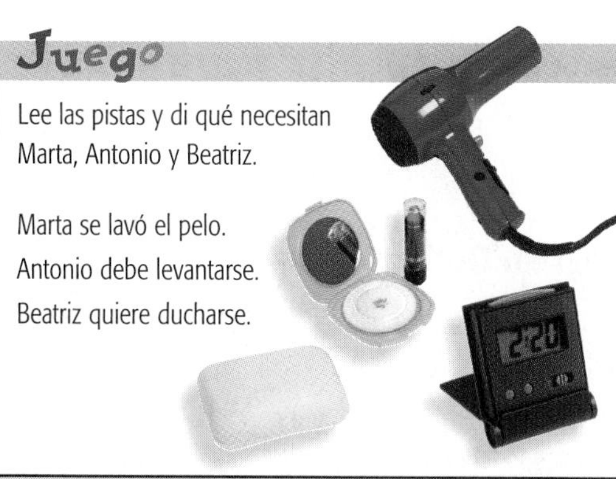


### TALK ABOUT DAILY ROUTINE AND PERSONAL CARE

**Daily Routine**

| | |
|---|---|
| **acostarse (o → ue)** | *to lie down, to go to bed* |
| **arreglarse** | *to get ready* |
| **cepillarse el pelo** | *to brush one's hair* |
| **quitarse la ropa** | *to take off one's clothes* |

**Ya sabes**

| | |
|---|---|
| **afeitarse** | *to shave oneself* |
| **bañarse** | *to take a bath* |
| **despertarse (e → ie)** | *to wake up* |
| **ducharse** | *to take a shower* |
| **lavarse** | *to wash oneself* |
| **lavarse los dientes** | *to brush one's teeth* |
| **levantarse** | *to get up* |
| **maquillarse** | *to put on makeup* |
| **peinarse** | *to comb one's hair* |
| **ponerse la ropa** | *to get dressed* |
| **secarse** | *to dry oneself* |

**Personal Care**

| | |
|---|---|
| **el desodorante** | *deodorant* |
| **lacio** | *straight (hair)* |
| **la loción** | *after-shave lotion* |
| **el maquillaje** | *makeup* |
| **el perfume** | *perfume* |
| **rizado** | *curly (hair)* |

**Ya sabes**

| | |
|---|---|
| **el cepillo** | *hairbrush* |
| **el cepillo de dientes** | *toothbrush* |
| **el champú** | *shampoo* |
| **el jabón** | *soap* |
| **la pasta de dientes** | *toothpaste* |
| **el peine** | *comb* |
| **el secador de pelo** | *hair dryer* |



## Teaching All Students

**Extra Help** Have students review **Etapa 1** by searching for vocabulary words in the dialog and the readings.

**Native Speakers** Ask Spanish speakers to read aloud the words in the vocabulary list for the class, paying special attention to pronunciation. Have the rest of the class repeat each word after the Spanish speaker.

**Multiple Intelligences**

**Visual** Assign words to students so they may make a visual hook to represent the meaning of the vocabulary items. Share hooks and display them around the classroom.



## Teaching Suggestions
### Vocabulary Review

Before class, write vocabulary words on index cards. Have students take turns choosing cards and drawing representations of words on the board for the class to guess.

## Interdisciplinary Connections

**Science** After reading and discussing **Conexiones**, have students research phosphorescence with the help of the science department. Have them work in groups to prepare reports to present to the class.

## Critical Thinking

Ask students to choose one of the 2 main vocabulary themes–staying fit or daily routine and personal care–and make a mind map of vocabulary words by separating the words into 5 or more logical categories.

## Juego

**Answers**

**Marta necesita el secador de pelo; Antonio necesita el despertador; Beatriz necesita el jabón.**

## Project: Reviewing Etapa 1

Assign the following out-of-class activities:

- Interview a Spanish speaker about what they do to stay fit
- Bring in tourist information about sports and fitness opportunities while vacationing in Puerto Rico
- Find out about the political status of Puerto Rico
- Find information on health clubs in Puerto Rico via the Internet

**Extra Credit**

| | |
|---|---|
| Interview | 2 pts. |
| Tourist information | 2 pts. |
| Puerto Rico's political status | 2 pts. |
| Health Clubs in Puerto Rico | 2 pts. |

## Block Schedule

**Peer Teaching** Have volunteers present mini-reviews of **Etapa** objectives in preparation for the exam.

# Planning Guide CLASSROOM MANAGEMENT

## OBJECTIVES

| | |
|---|---|
| **Communication** | • Tell someone what to do *pp. 198–199, 202, 204, 210–211*<br>• Talk about chores *pp. 198–199, 203*<br>• Say if something has already been done *pp. 198–199, 208*<br>• Discuss beach activities *pp. 196–197, 201, 209* |
| **Grammar** | • Affirmative **tú** commands *p. 202*<br>• Negative **tú** commands *p. 204*<br>• Adverbs ending in **-mente** *p. 206* |
| **Culture** | • **Los jóvenes y los quehaceres en los países hispanos** *p. 203*<br>• **El manatí** *p. 208*<br>• **El Yunque: Parque Nacional** *pp. 210–211* |
| **Recycling** | • Talking about daily routine and personal care *p. 201*<br>• Pronoun placement *p. 208* |

## STRATEGIES

| | |
|---|---|
| **Listening Strategies** | • Listen and categorize information *p. 198* |
| **Speaking Strategies** | • Improvise *p. 205*<br>• Encourage or discourage certain behaviors *p. 214* |
| **Reading Strategies** | • Gather and sort information *TE p. 210*<br>• Observe organization *TE p. 210* |
| **Writing Strategies** | • Using details to enrich a description *Actividad 7, TE p. 215* |
| **Connecting Cultures Strategies** | • Recognize unique natural wonders *pp. 210–211* |

## PROGRAM RESOURCES

### Print

- *Más práctica* Workbook PE *pp. 73–80*
- Block Scheduling Copymasters *pp. 65–72*
- Unit 3 Resource Book
  - Más práctica Workbook TE *pp. 52–59*
  - *Cuaderno para hispanohablantes* TE *pp. 60–67*
  - Information Gap Activities *pp. 68–71*
  - Family Involvement *pp. 72–73*
  - Video Activities *pp. 74–76*
  - Videoscript *pp. 77–79*
  - Audioscript *pp. 80–83*
  - Assessment Program, Unit 3 Etapa 2 *pp. 84–102; 173–175*
  - Answer Keys *pp. 188–189*

### Audiovisual

- Audio Program Cassette 8A, 8B / CD 8
- *Canciones* Cassette/CD
- Video Program Videotape 3 / Videodisc 2B
- Overhead Transparencies M1, M3; 83–92

### Technology

- Electronic Teacher Tools/Test Generator
- *Intrigas y aventuras* CD-ROM, Disc 1
-  www.mcdougallittell.com

### Assessment Program Options

- Cooperative Quizzes (Unit 3 Resource Book)
- Etapa Exam Forms A and B (Unit 3 Resource Book)
- *Examen para hispanohablantes* (Unit 3 Resource Book)
- Portfolio Assessment (Unit 3 Resource Book)
- Multiple Choice Test Questions (Unit 3 Resource Book)
- Audio Program Cassette 19B / CD 19
- Electronic Teacher Tools / Test Generator

### Native Speakers

- *Cuaderno para hispanohablantes* PE *pp. 73–80*
- *Cuaderno para hispanohablantes* TE (Unit 3 Resource Book)
- *Examen para hispanohablantes* (Unit 3 Resource Book)
- Audio Program *(Para hispanohablantes)* Cassettes 8B, 19B / CD 8, CD 19
- Audioscript (Unit 3 Resource Book)

Tía Julia

Tío Rodrigo

Francisco

Susana

# Student Text Listening Activity Scripts

##  Videoscript: Diálogo *pages 198–199*

- Videotape 3, 13:08 • Videodisc 2B
  **Search Chapter 2, Play to 3. U3E2, En vivo (Dialog)**
- Use the videoscript with **Actividades 1, 2** *page 200*

**Tía Julia:** ¿Dónde están todos? Ya estamos atrasados. ¡Rodrigo!
**Tío Rodrigo:** ¿Sí, mi amor?
**Tía Julia:** Los platos. No me dejes los platos sucios. Lavar los platos es tu quehacer, no el mío.
**Tío Rodrigo:** Sí, ya lo sé, ya lo sé, y me encanta lavarlos, mi amor.
**Tía Julia:** Rodrigo, ¡lava los platos antes de salir de esta casa!
**Tío Rodrigo:** Sí, claro, claro.
**Susana:** Voy a salir en televisión. ¡Voy a ser una estrella!
**Tía Julia:** Susana, por favor, no corras por la casa. Ah, Susana, ¿ya hiciste la cama?
**Susana:** No, no la hice.
**Tía Julia:** Pues, mi hija, vete y haz la cama inmediatamente. ¡Y limpia tu cuarto también!
**Susana:** Sí, mamá. Pero las estrellas no tienen que hacer la cama.
**Tía Julia:** Si son estrellas que viven en mi casa, sí hacen la cama. Ah, Susana, gracias por traer mi sombrero.
**Francisco:** Buenos días, tía Julia. ¿Ya estás lista para ir a la playa?
**Tía Julia:** Ay, desgraciadamente no. ¡Qué revolú hay en esta casa!
**Francisco:** ¿Cómo te ayudo?
**Tía Julia:** Ay, gracias, mi hijo. Por favor, pasa la aspiradora en la sala. Y después, si hay tiempo, saca la basura.
**Francisco:** Cómo no, tía.
**Tía Julia:** ¡Rodrigo! ¡No comas el queso! Es para el almuerzo. ¡Rodrigo! ¡No hagas eso! ¡Ay, Rodrigo, ¡no! ¡Ay, qué loco eres! ¡Deja! ¡Deja! No seas malo.
**Tío Rodrigo:** Aquí está la cartera. Y, querida esposa, acabo de lavar los platos.
**Tía Julia:** Gracias, Rodrigo. Bien, tenemos loción protectora, toallas, gafas de sol, sandalias para mí y para Susana... Rodrigo, ¿dónde están tus sandalias ? A ver, ¿qué más necesitamos? Necesitamos la sombrilla de playa.
**Susana:** Estoy lista. Acabo de hacer la cama y limpiar mi cuarto.
**Tío Rodrigo:** Gracias, hija. Susana, hazme un favor. Ve a mi cuarto. Tráeme mis sandalias. Normalmente están al lado de la cama. Rápido, por favor.
**Susana:** Sí, papi.
**Tío Rodrigo:** Ah, Susana, ¿mi gorro?... ¿Qué más hago, Julia?
**Tía Julia:** A ver... ah, ¡sí! Pon la neverita con los sándwiches y el agua en el carro. Y la sombrilla de playa también.
**Tío Rodrigo:** Sí, mi amor.
**Tía Julia:** Susana, no pongas las sandalias en la mesa. Están sucias. Dámelas. Tenemos todo lo que necesitamos para ir a la playa. Tenemos el almuerzo, la casa está limpia...
**Tío Rodrigo:** (V/O) ¡Julia! Vamos, no queremos llegar tarde. ¡Date prisa!
**Francisco:** ¡Qué precioso está el mar! Y la arena es tan suave.
**Tío Rodrigo:** Sí, tenemos playas bien lindas aquí en Puerto Rico. Con la arena suave, las olas, las palmas, es un paraíso tropical.
**Susana:** ¡Mira el caracol, papi! ¿No es bonito? Lo encontré en la orilla.
**Tío Rodrigo:** Sí, es un caracol muy bonito. Ah, Susana, por favor, ponte la loción protectora. ¡En seguida! Tú también, Francisco. Debes proteger la piel. El sol aquí es muy fuerte y no quieres una quemadura.
**Susana:** ¡Miren! ¡Allí está Elena Suárez y su equipo de televisión! Voy a ser estrella, voy a ser estrella....

##  Actividad 7 Los quehaceres *page 203*

**MODELO:**
**Tú oyes:** La mesita está sucia y tu abuela va a estar aquí muy pronto. Quita el polvo, por favor.
**Tú dices:** No tengo lo que necesito para hacer el trabajo.

1. Tenemos un montón de ropa sucia. Lávala y sécala, por favor.
2. Estoy ocupada y necesito tu ayuda. Primero, saca la basura.
3. Hace sol. Corta el césped, por favor.
4. ¡Ay, tu tía llega dentro de quince minutos! Pasa la aspiradora.
5. Mira, la comida del perro está en el piso. Por favor, barre el piso.
6. Vamos al teatro. Plancha tu ropa inmediatamente.

##  Actividad 15 ¿Ya? *page 208*

**MODELO:**
**Tú oyes:**
**Tía Julia:** ¡Susana, quítate los zapatos antes de entrar en la sala!
**Susana:** Ya me los quité, mami. Acabo de ponerlos en mi cuarto.
**Tú dices:** Sí, Susana acaba de hacerlo.

1. **Tío Rodrigo:** Ponte la loción protectora, Francisco. No te quemes la piel.
   **Francisco:** Voy a hacerlo. Sí, voy a hacerlo, pero no sé dónde está.
2. **Tía Julia:** Francisco, hazme un favor. Pon el agua en la neverita.
   **Francisco:** Acabo de ponerla en la neverita. ¿Hay algo más que necesites, tía?
3. **Tío Rodrigo:** ¿Ya hiciste la cama, Susana? Salimos en cinco minutos.
   **Susana:** Pues, quiero hacerla pronto, papi, pero estoy mirando mi programa favorito.
4. **Tía Julia:** Rodrigo, lava las toallas, por favor. Vamos a la playa mañana y todas las toallas están sucias.
   **Tío Rodrigo:** No te preocupes, Julia, ya las lavé y estoy secándolas ahora.
5. **Tío Rodrigo:** Saca una foto de la palmera, Julia. Con el sol y el agua así, se ve muy bonita.
   **Tía Julia:** Acabo de sacarla. Tienes razón, es una maravilla.
6. **Tía Julia:** Susana, ponte los pantalones cortos y ven aquí. Tengo tus sandalias.
   **Susana:** Sí, mami, me los tengo que poner. Me pongo los pantalones cortos y después vengo por mis sandalias.

# Pacing Guide

## Sample Lesson Plan - 50 Minute Schedule

### DAY 1

***Etapa* Opener**
- Quick Start Review (TE p. 194). 5 MIN.
- Anticipate/Activate prior knowledge: have students look at *Etapa* Opener and answer *¿Qué ves?* questions. 10 MIN.

**En contexto: Vocabulario**
- Quick Start Review (TE p. 196). 5 MIN.
- Discuss pictures, have students use context and pictures to learn *Etapa* vocabulary. Answer questions, p. 197. 10 MIN.

**En vivo: Diálogo**
- Quick Start Review (TE p. 198). 5 MIN.
- Review Listening Strategy, p. 198. Play audio or show video for the dialog shown on pp. 198–199. 7 MIN.
- Read aloud, students taking on roles of characters. 8 MIN.

**Homework Option**
- Video Activities, Unit 3 Resource Book, pp. 74–76.

### DAY 2

**En acción: Vocabulario y Gramática**
- Check homework. 5 MIN.
- Quick Start Review (TE p. 200). 5 MIN.
- Ask students for a summary of *En vivo* dialog to check recall. 5 MIN.
- Ask Comprehension Questions (TE, p. 199). 5 MIN.
- Replay the *En vivo* dialog using the audiovisual resources and have students do *Actividades* 1 and 2 orally. 10 MIN.
- Have students complete *Actividades* 3 and 4 in pairs. 10 MIN.
- Present grammar review box, p. 202. Then have students complete *Actividad* 5 and *Actividad* 6. You may also want to review the *Vocabulario* box on p. 203. 10 MIN.

**Homework Option**
- *Más práctica* Workbook, p. 77 as needed. *Cuaderno para hispanohablantes*, p. 75.

### DAY 3

**En acción (cont.)**
- Check homework. 5 MIN.
- Quick Start Review (TE p. 204). 5 MIN.
- Play the audio and have students complete *Actividad* 7 in writing. 10 MIN.
- Present *Gramática:* Negative *tú* Commands, p. 204. 10 MIN.
- Have students do *Actividad* 8 in writing. 5 MIN.
- Present Speaking Strategy, p. 205, have students do *Actividades* 9 and 10 in pairs. Expand with *Más comunicación*, p. R9. 15 MIN.

**Homework Option**
- *Más práctica* Workbook, pp. 78–79. *Cuaderno para hispanohablantes*, pp. 76–77.

### DAY 4

**En acción (cont.)**
- Check homework. 5 MIN.
- Quick Start Review (TE p. 206). 5 MIN.
- Present *Gramática:* Adverbs ending in *-mente,* and *Vocabulario,* on p. 206. 10 MIN.
- Have students complete *Actividad* 11 in writing. 5 MIN.
- Have students complete *Actividad* 12 in pairs. 5 MIN.
- Have students prepare *Actividad* 13 and then survey 5 classmates. 10 MIN.
- Discuss *Nota gramatical* on p. 208 and have students complete *Actividad* 14 in writing. 10 MIN.

**Homework Option**
- *Más práctica* Workbook, p. 80. *Cuaderno para hispanohablantes*, p. 78.

### DAY 5

**En acción (cont.)**
- Check homework. 5 MIN.
- Quick Start Review (TE, p. 208). 5 MIN.
- Play the audio and do *Actividad* 15 orally with the whole class. 8 MIN.
- Have students complete *Actividad* 16 in pairs. 7 MIN.
- Have students complete *Actividad* 17 in groups. Expand with *Más comunicación*, p. R9. 10 MIN.

**Ampliación**
- Use a suggested project, game, or activity (TE pp. 171A–171B). 15 MIN.

**Homework Option**
- Have students do *Actividad* 17 in writing.

### DAY 6

**En colores: Cultura y comparaciones**
- Check homework. 5 MIN.
- Read and discuss *Refrán.* 5 MIN.
- Quick Start Review (TE, p. 210). 5 MIN.
- Review Connecting Cultures Strategy, p. 210. 5 MIN.
- Read *El Yunque: Parque Nacional* aloud with students. 10 MIN.
- Have students answer the *¿Comprendiste?* and *¿Qué piensas?* activities orally. 10 MIN.
- Divide the class into small groups and have them role-play *Hazlo tú* activity. 10 MIN.

**Homework Option**
- Have students finish the *¿Qué piensas?* questions in writing, p. 211. *Cuaderno para hispanohablantes*, pp. 79–80.

### DAY 7

**En uso: Repaso y más comunicación**
- Check homework. 5 MIN.
- Quick Start Review (TE, p. 212). 5 MIN.
- Do *Actividades* 1, 2, 3, and 4 orally. 10 MIN.
- Review Speaking Strategy, p. 214. Then do *Actividad* 5 orally in pairs and *Actividad* 6 in groups of four. 15 MIN.

**En tu propia voz: Escritura**
- Start *Actividad* 7. 15 MIN.

**Homework Option**
- Finish *Actividad* 7. Review for *Etapa* 2 Exam.

### DAY 8

**Tú en la comunidad**
- Check homework. 5 MIN.
- Read and discuss. 5 MIN.
- Review grammar questions, etc. as necessary. 10 MIN.
- Complete *Etapa* 2 Exam. 20 MIN.

**Ampliación**
- Use a suggested project, game, or activity (TE pp. 171A–171B). 10 MIN.

**Homework Option**
- Preview next *Etapa* Opener, pp. 216–217.

# Sample Lesson Plan - Block Schedule (90 minutes)

## DAY 1

***Etapa* Opener**
- Quick Start Review (TE p. 194). 5 MIN.
- Anticipate/Activate prior knowledge: have students look at the *Etapa* Opener and answer *¿Qué ves?* questions. 10 MIN.

**En contexto: Vocabulario**
- Quick Start Review (TE p. 196). 5 MIN.
- Have students use context and pictures to learn *Etapa* vocabulary. Answer questions, p. 197. 10 MIN.

**En vivo: Diálogo**
- Quick Start Review (TE p. 198). 5 MIN.
- Review Listening Strategy, p. 198. Play audio or show video for the dialog shown on pp. 198–199. 10 MIN.
- Replay. Read aloud, students taking roles of characters. Ask Comprehension Questions (TE, p. 199). 10 MIN.
- Students role-play in groups while looking at the photos in their texts. Encourage them to come up with logical dialog using familiar vocabulary. 10 MIN.

**En acción: Vocabulario y Gramática**
- Quick Start Review (TE, p. 200). 5 MIN.
- Have students do *Actividades* 1 and 2 orally. 10 MIN.
- Have students complete *Actividades* 3 and 4 in pairs. 10 MIN.

**Homework Option**
- Video Activities, Unit 3 Resource Book, pp. 74–76.

## DAY 2

**En acción (cont.)**
- Check homework. 5 MIN.
- Quick Start Review (TE p. 202). 5 MIN.
- Present grammar review box, p. 202, and then have students complete *Actividad* 5 and *Actividad* 6. You may also want to review the *Vocabulario* box on p. 203. 15 MIN.
- Play the audio and have students complete *Actividad* 7 in writing. 10 MIN.
- Present *Gramática:* Negative *tú* Commands, p. 204. 10 MIN.
- Have students do *Actividad* 8 in writing. 5 MIN.
- Present Speaking Strategy, p. 205, and do *Actividades* 9 and 10 in pairs. Expand with *Más comunicación,* p. R9. 15 MIN.
- Present *Gramática:* Adverbs ending in *-mente,* p. 206. 5 MIN.
- Review the vocabulary box on p. 206 and have students complete *Actividad* 11 in writing. 10 MIN.
- Have students complete *Actividad* 12 in pairs. 5 MIN.
- Use Block Scheduling Copymasters for variety. 5 MIN.

**Homework Option**
- Have students complete *Actividad* 11 in writing if necessary. *Más práctica* Workbook, pp. 77–80 as needed. *Cuaderno para hispanohablantes*, pp. 75–78 as needed.

## DAY 3

**En acción (cont.)**
- Check homework. 10 MIN.
- Quick Start Review (TE p. 208). 5 MIN.
- Have students prepare *Actividad* 13 and then survey 5 classmates. 10 MIN.
- Discuss *Nota* and have students complete *Actividad* 14. 10 MIN.
- Play the audio and do *Actividad* 15 orally with the whole class. 10 MIN.
- Have students complete *Actividad* 16 in pairs. Save time for some students to read their lists to the class. 10 MIN.
- Have students complete *Actividad* 17 in groups. 10 MIN.
- Use Block Scheduling Copymasters for a change of pace. 5 MIN.

**Ampliación**
- Use a suggested project, game, or activity (TE pp. 171A–171B). 20 MIN.

**Homework Option**
- Have students complete *Actividad* 17 in writing.

## DAY 4

**En colores: Cultura y comparaciones**
- Check homework. 10 MIN.
- Quick Start Review (TE, p. 210). 5 MIN.
- Review Connecting Cultures Strategy, p. 210. 10 MIN.
- Read *El Yunque: Parque Nacional* aloud with students. 10 MIN.
- Have students answer the *¿Comprendiste?* questions orally. 10 MIN.
- Have students answer the *¿Qué piensas?* questions in writing. 10 MIN.
- Divide the class into small groups and have them role-play *Hazlo tú* activity. 15 MIN.

**Ampliación**
- Use a suggested project, game, or activity (TE pp. 171A–171B). 20 MIN.

**Homework Option**
- Have students do *Actividades* 1–4 in *En uso. Cuaderno para hispanohablantes*, pp. 79–80.

## DAY 5

**En uso: Repaso y más comunicación**
- Quick Start Review (TE, p. 212). 5 MIN.
- Go over *Actividades* 1, 2, 3, and 4 orally. 15 MIN.
- Review Speaking Strategy, p. 214. Then do *Actividad* 5 orally in pairs and *Actividad* 6 in groups of four. 15 MIN.

**Tú en la comunidad**
- Read and discuss. 5 MIN.
- Review grammar questions, etc. as necessary. 10 MIN.
- Complete *Etapa* 2 Exam. 20 MIN.

**En tu propia voz: Escritura**
- Do *Actividad* 7. 20 MIN.

**Homework Option**
- Preview next *Etapa* Opener, pp. 216–217.

▼ Susana quiere ser estrella de televisión.

UNIDAD 3 Etapa 2
**Opener**

### Etapa Theme

**Telling someone what to do, talking about home chores, and discussing the beach.**

### Grammar Objectives

- Affirmative and negative **tú** commands
- Adverbs ending in **-mente**

### Teaching Resource Options

**Print** 

Block Scheduling Copymasters

**Audiovisual** 

**OHT** 89 (Quick Start)

### Quick Start Review

Reflexive pronouns and verbs

Use OHT 89 or write on board: Form sentences in the present tense based on the photo. Use whatever the photo suggests as the subject of your sentence and add details if possible.

1. sentarse
2. sonreírse
3. divertirse
4. relajarse
5. no aburrirse

*Answers will vary.*

### Teaching Suggestions
**Previewing the Etapa**

- Ask students to study the picture on pp. 194–195.
- Ask students to identify what they see in the picture—the people, the items, the clothes.
- Have students try to guess what the items are in the list.
- Use the **¿Qué ves?** questions for further discussion.

UNIDAD 3

# Preparaciones

- Discuss beach activities
- Tell someone what to do
- Talk about chores
- Say if something has already been done

## ¿Qué ves?

Mira la foto de la playa y contesta las preguntas.

1. ¿Conoces a algunas personas de la foto? ¿A quién(es)?
2. ¿Qué hacen estas personas?
3. ¿Por qué crees que están allí?
4. ¿Qué puedes llevar a la playa?

194

### Classroom Management

**Planning Ahead** Prepare students to discuss the beach. Collect travel advertisements that show different beach scenes. Have students brainstorm a list of activities they might do at the beach. You may want to pack a beachbag or a cooler full of items one would take to the beach to help present the vocabulary.

**Peer Review** Have students play "I Spy" or in Spanish, **"Veo, veo,"** by taking turns describing items in the picture for their partner to guess. S1 chooses an item secretly and says **"Veo, veo."** S2 says **"¿Qué ves?"** and then S1 describes the object, **"Veo una cosa que te pones en los pies."** S2 points to the sneakers.

## Cross Cultural Connections

Ask students where people go to the beach in their community. Where are the popular swimming areas in their town or city? Have them compare their local swimming areas to the Puerto Rico beach in the photo on pp. 194–195. Ask them to explain where they prefer to go swimming and why.

## Culture Highlights

- **PUERTO RICO** lies between the Caribbean Sea to the south and the Atlantic Ocean to the north. The beaches of San Juan are on the Atlantic Ocean and tend to have bigger waves and more active surf.
- **SCUBA DIVING** is a popular sport in Puerto Rico, especially in the Phosphorescent Bay, off La Parguera, on the western side of the island. Any movement in the water can cause the micro-organisms to light up. Other popular diving spots include the Parguera Wall, about 20 miles offshore, and the smaller islands of Vieques and Culebra.

## Supplementary Vocabulary

| | |
|---|---|
| **la bronceadura** | suntan |
| **broncearse** | to get a suntan |
| **bucear** | to scuba dive |
| **el buceo** | scuba diving |
| **la crema bronceadora, el bronceador** | suntan lotion |

## Block Schedule

**FunBreak** Allow students to study the picture for 2 minutes and then close books. Divide the class into two teams. Call out a color and have each team list what they can recall seeing in that color. The team with the most items wins that round. Continue using a variety of colors. (For additional activities, see **Block Scheduling Copymasters**.)

## Teaching All Students

**Extra Help** Ask students to list in Spanish 4–5 activities they like to do at the beach.

### Multiple Intelligences

**Visual** Prepare ahead: Make copies of the opening page and cut each copy into 4 sections. Give each student a quarter section of the picture. Students find others to form a complete picture by describing what they have or what they need to have a "whole" picture.

**Intrapersonal** Ask students to write 4–5 sentences in their journal about how the picture makes them feel.

**Naturalist** Have students research the beaches of Puerto Rico, comparing physical locations and characteristics, and prepare a chart and map for the class.

## Teaching Resource Options

**Print**

Unit 3 Resource Book
Video Activities, p. 74
Videoscript, p. 77
Audioscript, p. 80

**Audiovisual**

**OHT** 83, 84, 89 (Quick Start)
**Audio Program** Cassette 8A / CD 8
**Video Program** Videotape 3, 10:41 / Videodisc 2B

Search Chapter 1, Play to 2
U3E2, En contexto (Vocabulary)

**Technology**

*Intrigas y aventuras* CD-ROM, Disc 1

## Quick Start Review

Present tense/discussing leisure time

Use OHT 89 or write on board: Write four sentences telling what you and your family and friends do at the beach.

| | |
|---|---|
| leer | pasear |
| dibujar | nadar |
| escuchar música | tocar la guitarra |
| hablar | escribir cartas |
| correr | |

*Answers will vary.*

## Supplementary Vocabulary

| | |
|---|---|
| **nadar** | to swim |
| **pescar** | to go fishing |
| **los refrescos** | cold drinks |
| **tomar el sol** | to sunbathe |
| **el traje de baño** | bathing suit |

# En contexto

## VOCABULARIO

Aquí Francisco y Susana se divierten en una de las hermosas playas de Puerto Rico.

**A** En este día hermoso, Susana y Francisco están en **la orilla** del **océano** Atlántico. ¡Están preparados!

Susana llevó **la sombrilla de playa** y **la loción protectora** para **proteger la piel** de **quemaduras.** Si no usan loción protectora, el sol los puede **quemar** porque es muy fuerte.

Francisco llevó **una toalla** para sentarse en **la arena.** Como la arena está muy caliente, tienen **sandalias.**

Francisco y Susana también llevaron **una neverita** con refrescos y piensan encontrar **caracoles** para tener de recuerdo.

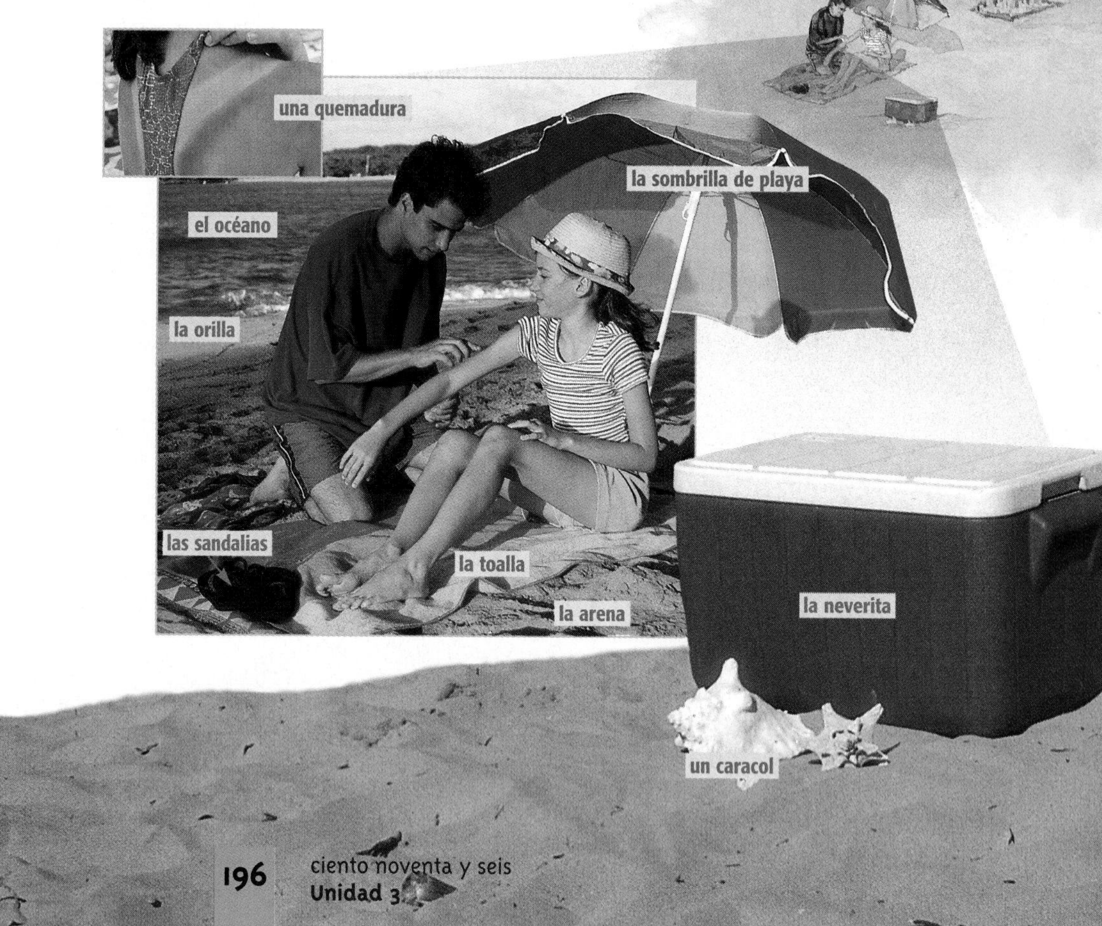




## Classroom Community

**TPR** Write each of the following expressions on a piece of paper: **ponerse loción protectora, la arena está caliente, encuentran caracoles, pescar, disfrutar de las olas, tomar el sol.** Have volunteers read a paper and act out the expression. The rest of the class can guess the activity.

**Paired Activity** Let students read aloud each caption with a partner and write a question about each one. Collect questions and have students or the teacher read to the entire class as a way to reinforce vocabulary.

**Group Activity** Divide class into 4 groups. Ask students to briefly describe each picture, with each group describing a different category: **las personas, la tierra, la temperatura** and **las cosas.**

**B** **El agua de coco** es deliciosa y quita la sed que da el sol. El coco crece en **la palma.** En Puerto Rico, Susana y Francisco ven muchos **palmares,** o grupos de palmas.

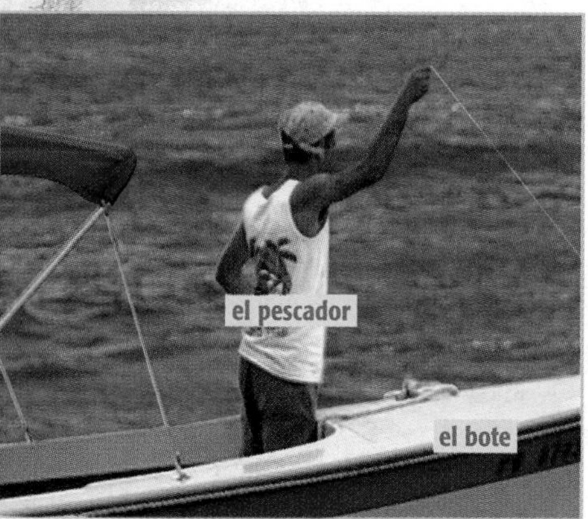

**C** También ellos ven a **un pescador** que disfruta de **las olas** en su **bote** mientras pesca.

### Preguntas personales

1. ¿Te gusta ir a la playa? ¿Cuál es tu playa favorita?
2. ¿Qué playa está cerca de donde vives?
3. Cuando vas a la playa, ¿qué llevas?
4. Cuando estás en la playa, ¿prefieres nadar o buscar caracoles? ¿Por qué?



## Teaching Suggestions
### Introducing Vocabulary

- Have students look at pages 196–197. Use OHT 83 and 84 and Audiocassette 8A/CD 8 to present the vocabulary.
- Introduce the characters and the setting: **La muchacha se llama Susana. El muchacho se llama Francisco. ¿Qué hacen Susana y Francisco? ¿Dónde están? ¿Qué llevan?**
- Ask the Comprehension Questions in order of yes/no (questions 1–3), either/or (questions 4–7) and simple word or phrase (question 8–10). You may expand by adding similar questions.

## Comprehension Questions

1. ¿Están Francisco y Susana en la playa? **(Sí)**
2. ¿Está la playa en el Océano Pacífico? **(No)**
3. ¿Trae Susana la loción protectora? **(Sí)**
4. ¿Se sientan en sillas o en la arena? **(en la arena)**
5. ¿Llevan sandalias o zapatos? **(sandalias)**
6. ¿Llevan los refrescos en una bolsa o en una neverita? **(una neverita)**
7. ¿Beben agua de coco o limonada? **(agua de coco)**
8. ¿Dónde crece el coco? **(en la palma)**
9. ¿Cómo se llama un grupo de palmas? **(palmares)**
10. ¿Qué hace el señor en el bote? **(Disfruta de las olas y pesca.)**

## Culture Highlights

- **EL AGUA DE COCO** is served cold in a freshly carved coconut shell with a straw. When the coconut is dried, the liquid becomes milkier and is called **leche de coco.**

## Teaching All Students

**Extra Help** Use a beachbag or cooler filled with actual items one would take to the beach to help present or review the vocabulary. Have students list 5 items that they would take to the beach.

**Native Speakers** Have those Spanish speakers who have been to Puerto Rico, especially to the beaches, describe their experiences and point out on a map where the best beaches are.

**Multiple Intelligences**

**Musical/Rhythmic** Play the **Canciones** Cassette/CD for the class. Ask students to pick a song that reminds them of being at the beach. Have students share with others the reason they chose the song.

## Block Schedule

**Peer Teaching** Have students interview a partner using the **Preguntas personales** on p. 197. Summarize the answers on a chart on the board to find the **la playa favorita** and **la actividad favorita en la playa** for the class. (For additional activities, see **Block Scheduling Copymasters.**)

## Teaching Resource Options

**Print** 

Block Scheduling Copymasters
Unit 3 Resource Book
Video Activities, pp. 75–76
Videoscript, pp. 77–78
Audioscript, p. 80

**Audiovisual**

**OHT** 87, 88, 89 (Quick Start)
**Audio Program** Cassette 8A / CD 8
**Video Program** Videotape 3, 13:08 / Videodisc 2B

Search Chapter 2, Play to 3
U3E2, En vivo (Dialog)

**Technology** 

*Intrigas y aventuras* CD-ROM, Disc 1

## Quick Start Review

Direct object pronouns

Use OHT 89 or write on board: You are on the beach and your friend asks if you have brought these items. Answer with a direct object pronoun. For example:

¿Trajiste la loción protectora?
Sí, la traje.

1. ¿Trajiste las toallas?
2. ¿Trajiste los refrescos?
3. ¿Trajiste el radio?
4. ¿Trajiste nuestra revista favorita?
5. ¿Trajiste la cámara?

**Answers**

1. Sí, (No, no) las traje.
2. Sí, (No, no) los traje.
3. Sí, (No, no) lo traje.
4. Sí, (No, no) la traje.
5. Sí, (No, no) la traje.

## Gestures

Ask students to look at frames 2, 3, 6, 7 and 8. Ask them if they can detect a certain tone or attitude associated with these gestures. Then, have students read the text and see if their predictions were accurate.

# En vivo

**DIÁLOGO**

Tía Julia

Tío Rodrigo

Susana

Francisco

**PARA ESCUCHAR** • STRATEGY: LISTENING

**Listen and categorize information** Categorizing information often helps provide a framework for examining a subject. Tía Julia is trying to get everyone to share certain responsibilities. Listen and think of two categories into which these tasks would fit. What did you come up with?

## La casa de los tíos

1 ▶ **Tía Julia:** ¿Dónde están todos? Ya estamos atrasados. ¡Rodrigo!
**Tío Rodrigo:** ¿Sí, mi amor?
**Tía Julia:** No me dejes los platos sucios. Lavar los platos es tu quehacer, no el mío.

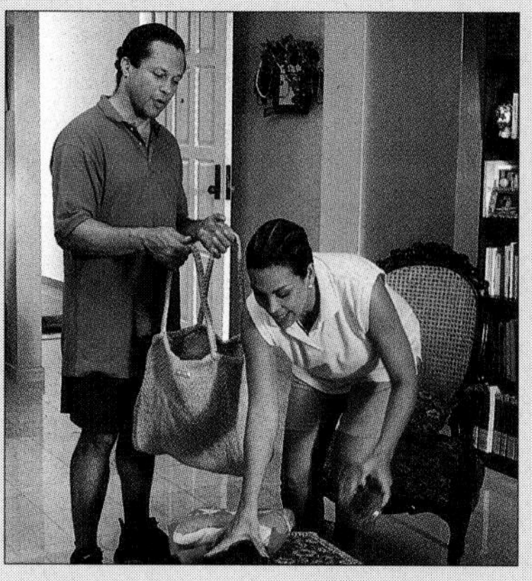

5 ▶ **Tío Rodrigo:** Aquí está la cartera. Y acabo de lavar los platos.
**Tía Julia:** Gracias, Rodrigo. Bien. Tenemos loción protectora, toallas, gafas de sol, sandalias.

6 ▶ **Tío Rodrigo:** ¿Qué más hago, Julia?
**Tía Julia:** A ver... ah, ¡sí! Pon la neverita con los sándwiches y el agua en el carro. Y la sombrilla de playa también.

7 ▶ **Tía Julia:** Tenemos todo lo que necesitamos para ir a la playa. Tenemos el almuerzo. La casa está limpia...
**Tío Rodrigo:** ¡Julia! Vamos, no queremos llegar tarde. ¡Date prisa!



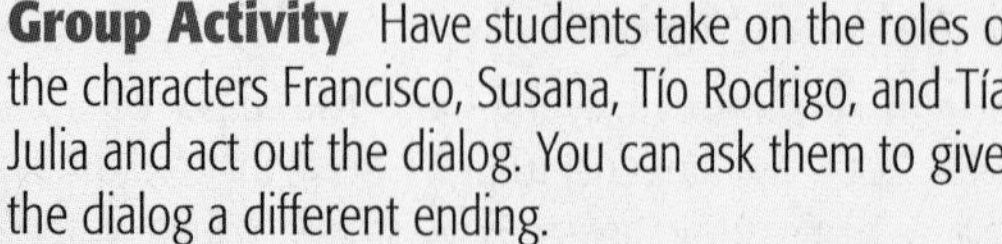

## Classroom Community

**Group Activity** Have students take on the roles of the characters Francisco, Susana, Tío Rodrigo, and Tía Julia and act out the dialog. You can ask them to give the dialog a different ending.

**TPR** Assign each student in the class a vocabulary word from the **En contexto** on pp. 196–197. Students should prepare a visual representation on poster board of their given word using either magazine clippings, drawings or photos. Then give "movement" commands such as: **"Caracol, ¡levántate! / Sandalias, ¡ven aquí! / Palma, camina al lado del caracol."** The student with the appropriate vocabulary word should perfom the command given. After 10 commands, have students exchange words and repeat the exercise.

2► Tío Rodrigo: Sí, ya lo sé, y me encanta lavarlos.
Tía Julia: Rodrigo, ¡lava los platos antes de salir de esta casa!
Tío Rodrigo: Sí. Claro, claro.

3► Susana: ¡Voy a ser una estrella!
Tía Julia: Susana, por favor, no corras por la casa. ¿Ya hiciste la cama?
Susana: No, no la hice.
Tía Julia: Vete y haz la cama inmediatamente. ¡Y limpia tu cuarto!

4► Francisco: Buenos días. ¿Ya estás lista?
Tía Julia: Ay, no. ¡Qué revolú hay en esta casa!
Francisco: ¿Cómo te ayudo?
Tía Julia: Por favor, pasa la aspiradora en la sala y saca la basura.

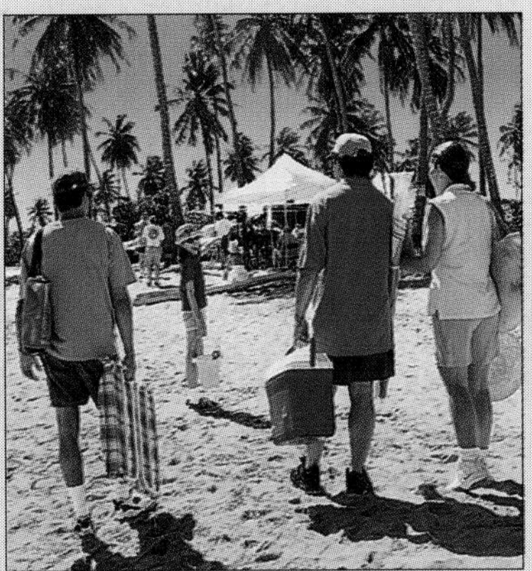

8► Francisco: ¡Qué precioso está el mar! Y la arena es tan suave.
Tío Rodrigo: Sí, tenemos playas bien lindas aquí. Con la arena suave, las olas y las palmas, es un paraíso tropical.

9► Susana: ¡Mira el caracol, papi! ¿No es bonito? Lo encontré en la orilla.
Tío Rodrigo: Sí, es muy bonito. Susana, por favor, ponte la loción protectora.

10► Susana: ¡Miren! ¡Allí está Elena Suárez y su equipo de televisión! Voy a ser estrella. Voy a ser estrella…



## Teaching Suggestions
### Presenting the Dialog

- Prepare students for listening by using the visuals to focus on the dialog context. Have them review the photos and try to guess what is happening.
- Introduce the characters and the setting: Francisco travels to Puerto Rico to visit his uncle and aunt, Tío Rodrigo and Tía Julia. Francisco's younger cousin is Susana.

## Video Synopsis

Use the video, audiocassette, or CD to present the dialog. Francisco is going to the beach with his uncle, aunt, and cousin. He arrives at their house to help prepare for the day trip. For a transcript of the video dialog, see p. 193B.

## Comprehension Questions

1. ¿Está muy ocupada Tía Julia? **(Sí)**
2. ¿Lavó los platos Tía Julia? **(No)**
3. ¿Hizo la cama Susana? **(No)**
4. ¿Los ayuda Francisco? **(Sí)**
5. ¿Llevan muchas cosas a la playa o solamente uno o dos cosas? **(muchas cosas)**
6. ¿Llevan sándwiches o ensalada en la neverita? **(sándwiches)**
7. ¿Llevan un paraguas o una sombrilla de playa? **(una sombrilla de playa)**
8. ¿Cómo es la playa? **(linda, tiene arena suave, agua preciosa y palmas)**
9. ¿Qué encontró Susana en la playa? **(un caracol)**
10. ¿Qué se ponen para proteger la piel? **(la loción protectora)**

## Teaching All Students

**Extra Help** To review the grammar from Unit 2, ask students to point out direct and indirect object pronouns in this dialog. You can also point out the informal command forms that students will be learning in this unit.

**Native Speakers** Ask Spanish speakers about the beaches in their native country. Have them share what their beaches look, feel, and sound like and how they compare to some of the beaches in the U.S.

**Multiple Intelligences**

**Verbal** **¿Quién soy yo?** Ask students to describe a character in the dialog for others to identify.

**Intrapersonal** Have students compare themselves or a family member to one of the characters in the dialog. Who are they or their family member most like? Why?

## Block Schedule

**FunBreak** Prepare a "virtual reality" trip to the beach. Use audiocassettes of waves, decorate the classroom with beach pictures, and have students "describe"/imagine what they would see and do.

## Teaching Resource Options

**Print**

Block Scheduling Copymasters
Unit 3 Resource Book
Video Activities, pp. 75–76
Videoscript, pp. 77–78
Audioscript, p. 80

**Audiovisual**

OHT 90 (Quick Start)
Audio Program Cassette 8A / CD 8
Video Program Videotape 3, 13:08 / Videodisc 2B

**Technology**

*Intrigas y aventuras* CD-ROM, Disc 1

### Quick Start Review

Indirect object pronouns

Use OHT 90 or write on the board: Match the person to the phrase and complete the sentence. For example:

(fascinar) ser estrella
A Susana le fascina ser estrella.
Tía Julia, Tío Rodrigo, Francisco, todos

1. (no encantar) lavar los platos
2. (importar) ayudar a Tía Julia
3. (molestar) una casa sucia
4. (gustar) ir a la playa

**Answers**

1. A Tío Rodrigo no le encanta lavar los platos.
2. A Francisco le importa ayudar a Tía Julia.
3. A Tía Julia le molesta una casa sucia.
4. A todos les gusta ir a la playa.

**Objective:** Controlled practice
Listening comprehension

**Answers**

1. a, f
2. c
3. e
4. a, f
5. d
6. b

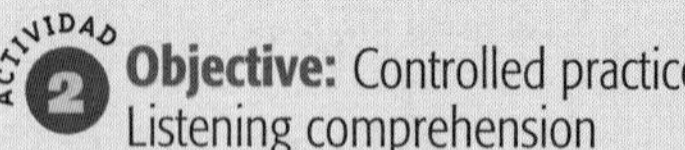

**Objective:** Controlled practice
Listening comprehension

**Answers**

1. b
2. b
3. c
4. b
5. d

# En acción
## VOCABULARIO Y GRAMÁTICA

**OBJECTIVES**
- Discuss beach activities
- Tell someone what to do
- Talk about chores
- Say if something has already been done

ACTIVIDAD 1

### Frases revueltas

**Escuchar** Combina frases de las dos columnas para describir el diálogo. *(Hint: Match phrases to describe the dialog.)*

1. Tío Rodrigo debe
2. Susana quiere
3. Susana necesita
4. Tía Julia dice que tío Rodrigo debe
5. Tía Julia dice que Francisco puede
6. Susana debe ponerse

a. lavar los platos.
b. loción protectora en la piel.
c. ser una estrella.
d. pasar la aspiradora.
e. hacer la cama.
f. poner la neverita en el carro.

**TAMBIÉN SE DICE** Tía Julia usa la frase **¡Qué revolú!** para hablar de la falta de organización de su casa. Esta frase, que es popular en Puerto Rico, viene de la palabra **revolución.** Quiere decir que un lugar está muy sucio o desordenado.

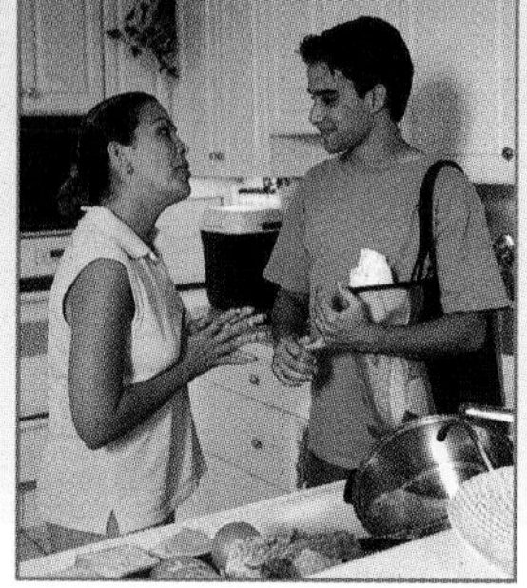

ACTIVIDAD 2

### ¿Ocurrió?

**Escuchar/Leer** Lee las oraciones e indica cuál no ocurrió en el diálogo. *(Hint: Which didn't occur?)*

1. Tío Rodrigo…
   a. le trae la cartera a su esposa
   b. generalmente prepara los sándwiches
   c. ayuda en casa
   d. lava los platos
2. Susana…
   a. está contenta porque va a salir en la televisión
   b. tiene que pasar la aspiradora
   c. corre en la casa
   d. tiene que hacer la cama
3. Francisco…
   a. le ofrece ayuda a tía Julia
   b. saca la basura
   c. pone la neverita en el carro
   d. admira la playa
4. Tía Julia…
   a. organiza el viaje a la playa
   b. necesita lavar los platos
   c. dice que no está lista para ir a la playa
   d. prepara el almuerzo
5. Francisco y su familia…
   a. limpian la casa
   b. hacen los quehaceres
   c. van a la playa
   d. comen una cena grande



### Classroom Management

**Streamlining** Have students reenact the story in the dialog. Ask for 4 volunteers to portray Francisco, Tío Rodrigo, Tía Julia, and Susana and act out the chores they are responsible for in the dialog. Then do **Actividades 1** and **2** orally.

**Peer Review** Have students work in pairs to do **Actividad 1**. Have partners check their work by locating the line in the dialog that gives the answer.

- Review: Use affirmative *tú* commands
- Use negative *tú* commands
- Review: Use adverbs ending in *-mente*

## Por la mañana

**Hablar** ¿Qué hace Chela, la amiga de Francisco? Compara su rutina con la tuya. *(Hint: Describe her routine and compare it with yours.)*

6:00

**modelo**

**Tú:** *Chela se despierta a las seis. ¿A qué hora te despiertas?*

**Compañero(a):** *Me despierto a las siete. ¿Y tú?*

**Tú:** *Me despierto a las cinco y media.*

## ¿Qué prefieres?

**Hablar** Imagínate que tú y un(a) compañero(a) van a la playa. ¿Qué dicen? *(Hint: Talk about beach preferences.)*

**modelo**

*sentarse en la sombra / sentarse al sol*

**Tú:** *¿Prefieres sentarte en la sombra o sentarte al sol?*

**Compañero(a):** *Prefiero sentarme al sol.*

1. ir a una playa de rocas / ir a una playa de arena
2. nadar / tomar el sol
3. usar una sombrilla de playa para proteger la piel / usar loción protectora
4. nadar en olas grandes / nadar en olas pequeñas
5. llevar una toalla bonita / llevar una toalla grande
6. buscar caracoles / nadar
7. llevar comida en una neverita / comprar comida en un café
8. caminar a orillas del mar / andar en bote por el océano



### Teaching Suggestions

- **Actividad 3** recycles vocabulary from the previous **Etapa**. As a follow-up, have students describe their routine for preparing to go to the beach, as modeled in the dialog on pp. 198–199.
- As a variation of **Actividad 3**, have students describe yesterday's routine using the past tenses.
- Have students summarize their findings in **Actividad 4** by sharing their results from their partner interview on the board.

**Objective:** Transitional practice
Describing daily routine

Telling time

**Answers**

*Answers will vary but will reflect correct usage of reflexive verbs.*

1. Se levanta a las seis y cuarto.
2. Se seca el pelo a las siete menos cuarto (seis cuarenta y cinco).
3. Se maquilla a las siete.
4. Desayuna a las siete y cuarto.
5. Se lava los dientes a las siete y media.
6. Sale a las ocho menos cuarto (siete cuarenta y cinco).

**Objective:** Transitional practice
**En contexto** vocabulary

**Answers**

*Answers will vary but should include **prefieres** in the question and **prefiero** in the answer.*

### Language Note

The word **revolú** is a common expression in Puerto Rico that refers to a mess or something that is disorganized. Point out to students that Puerto Rico has many colloquial expressions that are unique to the island.

### Teaching All Students

**Extra Help** Ask students to talk about chores by forming complete sentences using the following verbs: **Tengo que, quiero, necesito, debo, puedo, prefiero...**

**Native Speakers** Ask Spanish speakers to comment on the **También se dice** note on p. 200. Do they also use this expression **(¡Qué revolú!)** to express a lack of organization? If not, what do they say?

**Multiple Intelligences**

**Interpersonal** Have students interview a friend about his/her daily routine and take notes. As an entire class, compare daily routines by making a class chart.

**Visual** Have students cut out and label magazine pictures of people completing daily activities. Have them describe the pictures to others in the class. You can have students make a collage of all the pictures to display on a bulletin board.

### Block Schedule

**Variety** Make a chart of student daily activities. Ask students to share what they typically do and when. Hang the chart on the wall.

## Teaching Resource Options

**Print** 

*Más práctica* Workbook PE, pp. 77–78
*Cuaderno para hispanohablantes* PE, pp. 75–76
Block Scheduling Copymasters
Unit 3 Resource Book
*Más práctica* Workbook TE, pp. 56–57
*Cuaderno para hispanohablantes* TE, pp. 62–63
Audioscript, p. 80

**Audiovisual**

OHT 90 (Quick Start)
Audio Program Cassette 8A / CD 8

**Technology** 

*Intrigas y aventuras* CD-ROM, Disc 1

## Quick Start Review

Formal commands: plural

Use OHT 90 or write on board: Imagine you are a travel agent giving advice to two clients about a trip to a beach resort. Change the infinitive in each sentence to an **ustedes** command.

1. Viajar en aerolínea México.
2. No traer mucho equipaje.
3. Beber el agua de coco.
4. Ponerse mucha loción protectora.
5. Ir al restaurante Rosa.

**Answers**
1. Viajen...
2. No traigan...
3. Beban...
4. Pónganse...
5. Vayan...

## Teaching Suggestions
### Presenting Affirmative Tú Commands

Remind students that pronouns belong attached to the end of an affirmative command, as in **Lávalos** for **Lava los platos**. An accent may need to be added when a pronoun is attached.

## Affirmative tú Commands

 **¿RECUERDAS?** *p. 184* You have already reviewed pronoun placement with commands. Remember, to form **affirmative tú commands,** all you do is use the third person singular **(él/ella/usted)** form of the verb in the present tense.

| third person, present tense | tú command |
|---|---|
| Rodrigo **pasa** la aspiradora los sábados, pero nunca **saca** la basura.<br>*Rodrigo **vacuums** on Saturdays, but he never **takes out** the trash.* | Por favor, **pasa** la aspiradora en la sala, y después **saca** la basura.<br>*Please **vacuum** in the living room, and then **take out** the trash.* |

Remember that **hacer, ser,** and **ir** are irregular in the **tú command** form.

**hacer**

Vete, hija, y **haz** la cama inmediatamente.
*Go, daughter, and **make** the bed right away.*

**ser, ir**

**Sé** bueno. **Ve** a mi cuarto y **tráeme** mis sandalias.
*Be good. **Go** to my room and **bring me** my sandals.*

Remember that object pronouns attach to **affirmative commands.**

These five verbs have **tú command** forms that are also irregular. For each, take the present tense of the **yo** form and drop the **-go** ending.

| | yo form | tú command |
|---|---|---|
| **decir** | di**go** | di |
| **poner** | pon**go** | pon |
| **salir** | sal**go** | sal |
| **tener** | ten**go** | ten |
| **venir** | ven**go** | ven |

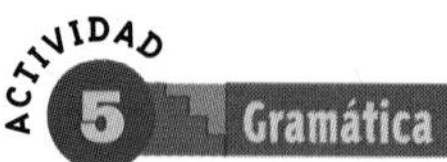

ACTIVIDAD 5 Gramática

### ¡A la playa!

**Escribir** Tu hermana menor va a la playa con sus amigos. Escríbele una lista de cosas que debe hacer. *(Hint: Write affirmative commands.)*

**modelo**

*traer bastante agua*
*Trae bastante agua.*

1. despedirse de su papá
2. proteger la piel
3. ponerse loción protectora
4. tener cuidado
5. escuchar la radio
6. llegar a casa a las siete
7. traer un almuerzo saludable
8. salir con los amigos
9. usar las sandalias
10. terminar la tarea

**MÁS PRÁCTICA** *cuaderno* p. 77
**PARA HISPANOHABLANTES** *cuaderno* p. 75



## Classroom Community

**Paired Activity** Have students ask a partner to do 5 activities, using the **tú** command form, e.g., **levántate, escríbelo en espanol...**

**Cooperative Learning** Divide the class into groups of 4. The group makes a list of all verbs they know that have irregular command forms. **(dar, decir, hacer, ir, poner, salir, ser, tener, venir)** Student 1 is the recorder and writes them down. Student 2 tells Student 3 what to do using an irregular **tú** command. Student 3 then tells Student 4 what to do using a different command. Student 1 writes down all commands, and Student 4 presents the list to the class. Compare lists.

## La casa sucia

**Hablar** Después de una fiesta, tu hermano(a) te ayuda a limpiar la casa. ¿Qué le dices? *(Hint: Give the commands.)*

**modelo**

*lavar los platos*
**Hermano(a):** *¿Lavo los platos?*
**Tú:** *Sí, lávalos.*

1. barrer el piso
2. hacer la limpieza
3. pasar la aspiradora
4. limpiar el cuarto
5. cortar el césped
6. preparar la comida
7. quitar el polvo
8. sacar la basura
9. planchar la ropa
10. hacer la cama

### Vocabulario

#### Los quehaceres

**barrer el piso** *to sweep the floor*
**cortar el césped** *to cut the grass*
**hacer la limpieza** *to do the cleaning*

#### Ya sabes

**lavar los platos** *to wash the dishes*
**limpiar el cuarto** *to clean the room*
**limpio(a)** *clean*
**pasar la aspiradora** *to vacuum*
**planchar** *to iron*
**los quehaceres** *chores*
**quitar el polvo** *to dust*
**sacar la basura** *to take out the trash*
**sucio(a)** *dirty*

¿Qué haces en tu casa para ayudar?

## Los quehaceres

**Escuchar/Hablar** Escucha estos seis mandatos de tu mamá y mira el dibujo. Luego dile a tu mamá si tienes todo lo que necesitas para hacer lo que ella quiere. *(Hint: Do you have the necessary items?)*

### NOTA CULTURAL

**Después de las clases** ¿Tienes que hacer los quehaceres de la casa antes de salir con tus amigos? Como en Estados Unidos, en los países hispanos los jóvenes hacen varias actividades después de las clases. Muchos practican deportes o salen con amigos al parque o a un café. Otros regresan a la casa para ayudar con los quehaceres. ¡Y todos tienen que hacer la tarea para la escuela!



## Teaching All Students

**Extra Help** Ask students to form **tú** commands for each of the verbs listed in the **Los quehaceres** vocabulary list on p. 203.

**Native Speakers** Have Spanish speakers comment on the **Nota cultural** on this page. Ask them to list other household chores in Spanish. They may also have different expressions for some of the chores listed in the box.

**Multiple Intelligences**

**Verbal** Have students list 5 daily activities and give their list to another student who changes the verbs to the **tú** command form.

**Musical/Rhythmic** Have students develop a short rap/chant to recall the 9 irregular **tú** commands, e.g. **Hacer haz, haz, ser sé, sé, e ir ve, ve. Decir di, di, poner pon, pon. Los mandatos de "tú" son, son.**

## Teaching Suggestions

- Use TPR to practice familiar commands (**siéntate, levántate, habla en español**, etc.)
- Ask students to say what is happening. (You are giving commands.)
- Then have students look at how the commands are formed.

**Objective:** Controlled practice
Affirmative **tú** commands

**Answers**

1. Despídete de tu papá.
2. Protege la piel.
3. Ponte loción protectora.
4. Ten cuidado.
5. Escucha la radio.
6. Llega a casa a las siete.
7. Trae un almuerzo saludable.
8. Sal con los amigos.
9. Usa las sandalias.
10. Termina la tarea.

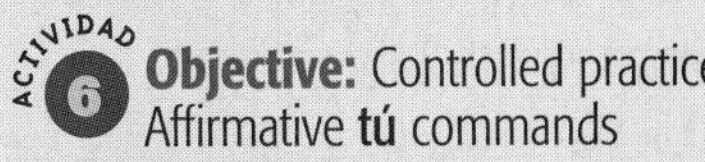

**Objective:** Controlled practice
Affirmative **tú** commands

**Answers**

1. Sí, bárrelo.
2. Sí, hazla.
3. Sí, pásala.
4. Sí, límpialo.
5. Sí, córtalo.
6. Sí, prepárala.
7. Sí, quítalo.
8. Sí, sácala.
9. Sí, plánchala.
10. Sí, hazla.

**Objective:** Transitional practice
Listening comprehension/chores

**Answers** (See script, p. 193B.)

1. Sí, tengo lo que necesito.
2. Sí, tengo lo que necesito.
3. No tengo lo que necesito.
4. Sí, tengo lo que necesito.
5. No tengo lo que necesito.
6. Sí, tengo lo que necesito.

## Language Note

Other words for *grass* are **la hierba, el zacate,** and **la grama.** A lawnmower is **la cortadora, el cortahierba,** or **el cortacésped.**

## Block Schedule

**Retention** To present the vocabulary on household chores on p. 203, have students either act out or illustrate each chore. Then have them personalize the list of chores by naming the person in their household that does each chore. (For additional activities, see **Block Scheduling Copymasters.**)

## Teaching Resource Options

**Print**

*Más práctica* Workbook PE, pp. 78–79
*Cuaderno para hispanohablantes* PE, pp. 76–77
Block Scheduling Copymasters
Unit 3 Resource Book
*Más práctica* Workbook TE, pp. 57–58
*Cuaderno para hispanohablantes* TE, pp. 63–64
Information Gap Activities, p. 68

**Audiovisual**

OHT 90 (Quick Start)

**Technology**

*Intrigas y aventuras* CD-ROM, Disc 1

## Quick Start Review

Formal commands: singular

Use OHT 90 or write on board: Give both the affirmative and negative usted commands for the following verbs.

1. hablar
2. escribir
3. salir
4. poner
5. ir
6. sentarse

**Answers**

1. Hable. / No hable.
2. Escriba. / No escriba.
3. Salga. / No salga.
4. Ponga. / No ponga.
5. Vaya. / No vaya.
6. Siéntese. / No se siente.

## Teaching Suggestions
### Presenting Negative Tú Commands

Variation on **Actividad 8**: Give a friend advice on how to eat better and lead a more healthy lifestyle. Students can use affirmative or negative **tú** commands while reviewing vocabulary from **Etapa 1**.

## Negative tú Commands

**¿RECUERDAS?** *p. 202* You already know how to form **affirmative tú commands.** However, when you're telling people not to do something you use another form, a **negative tú command.**

To form the **negative tú command,** you take the **yo form** of the verb in the present tense and:

- Change the ending to **-es** for **-ar** verbs

**dejar** dejo ¡**No** me dejes los platos sucios!
*Don't leave me the dirty dishes!*

Remember that in **negative commands,** the pronoun is placed before the verb.

- Change the ending to **-as** for **-er** and **-ir** verbs

**creer** creo Rodrigo, **no** creas que voy a olvidar los platos.
*Rodrigo, don't think I'm going to forget the dishes.*

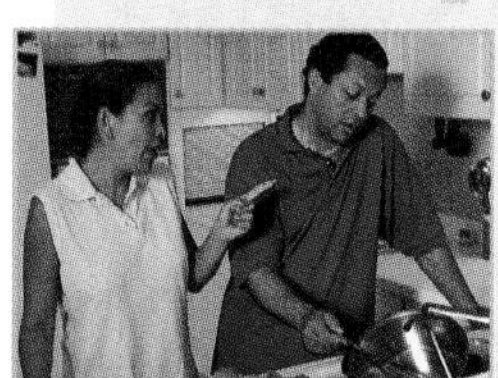

Remember that some verbs will require spelling changes to keep pronunciation consistent:
llego → llegues

These verbs have **negative tú commands** that are irregular.

| | negative tú command |
|---|---|
| dar | no des |
| estar | no estés |
| ir | no vayas |
| saber | no sepas |
| ser | no seas |

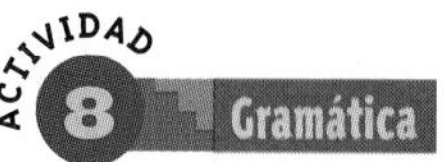


## ¡No te preocupes!

**Hablar/Escribir** La abuela de Francisco se preocupa mucho. ¿Qué le aconsejó a Francisco antes de su viaje? Usa el mandato negativo de **tú.**
*(Hint: Write negative commands.)*

**modelo**

*beber el agua*
*No bebas el agua.*

1. nadar en el mar por la noche
2. llevar mucho equipaje
3. ser malo
4. comer mucho azúcar
5. ir con personas que no conoces
6. estar nervioso
7. acostarse tarde todas las noches
8. darles tu dinero a los demás
9. hablar con personas que no conoces
10. perder las maletas

**MÁS PRÁCTICA** *cuaderno* pp. 78–79

**PARA HISPANOHABLANTES** *cuaderno* pp. 76–77



## Classroom Community

**TPR** In pairs, the "commander" gives an affirmative **tú** command, e.g., **Camina**, for the "actor" to act out, then gives a negative command using the same verb, e.g., **No camines**, and the actor stops. Students switch roles.

**Storytelling** Have the class create a humorous story about chores. One student is a recorder. Start with, **"Era un día hermoso, pero Pablo tenía mucho que hacer."** Each student adds a sentence, and the recorder writes them down. Make any corrections, copy, and distribute to students.

**Game** Divide the class into groups. Have students form negative **tú** commands by using verbs that begin with as many letters of the alphabet as possible, e.g., **no abras la ventana, no bebas mucho café, no cocines...** The group with the most commands wins.

## Una solución

**PARA CONVERSAR**

**STRATEGY: SPEAKING**

**Improvise** Develop spontaneity when speaking Spanish. Here you can practice speaking "on impulse" by giving an unexpected or illogical solution (**¿Corto el césped?**) to the problem (**Mi cuarto está sucio.**).

**Hablar/Leer** Con un(a) compañero(a) lee los problemas y las soluciones. Usa el mandato negativo para decir que las soluciones son ilógicas. Luego da una mejor solución. *(Hint: Read the problems, and then solve them correctly.)*

**modelo**

*Mi cuarto está sucio. (cortar el césped)*

**Compañero(a):** *Mi cuarto está sucio. ¿Corto el césped?*

**Tú:** *No, no cortes el césped. Limpia tu cuarto.*

En la casa...

1. Mi casa es un desastre. (planchar la ropa)
2. El piso no está limpio. (quitar el polvo)
3. La basura está llena. (hacer la cama)

En la playa...

4. No quiero una quemadura. (hacer un castillo de arena)
5. Quiero tomar el sol. (sentarse debajo de una palma)
6. La arena me está quemando los pies. (ponerse un traje de baño)

## ¿Qué hago?

**Hablar** Tú tienes muchos problemas y hablas con el (la) consejero(a) de tu escuela. ¿Qué te dice? *(Hint: Discuss problems.)*

**modelo**

*estar aburrido*

**Tú:** *Estoy aburrido(a).*

**Consejero(a):** *Lee un libro interesante.*

| Tú | Consejero(a) |
|---|---|
| sacar malas notas | leer un libro interesante |
| no poder dormir | buscar un trabajo |
| estar aburrido(a) | no ver la televisión |
| no tener dinero | no escuchar la radio |
| no hacer la tarea | participar en más actividades |
| estar triste | no trabajar tanto |
| nunca ir a la escuela | poner música tranquila |
| no tener suficientes amigos | levantarse temprano |
| | ir a la escuela |
| | cambiar de horario |

MÁS COMUNICACIÓN p. R9

**ACTIVIDAD 8** **Objective:** Controlled practice
Negative **tú** commands

**Answers**

1. No nades en el mar por la noche.
2. No lleves mucho equipaje.
3. No seas malo.
4. No comas mucha azúcar.
5. No vayas con personas que no conoces.
6. No estés nervioso.
7. No te acuestes tarde todas las noches.
8. No le des tu dinero a los demás.
9. No hables con personas que no conoces.
10. No pierdas las maletas.

**Objective:** Transitional practice
Negative **tú** commands

**Answers**

1. No, no planches la ropa. Limpia la casa.
2. No, no quites el polvo. Barre el piso.
3. No, no hagas la cama. Saca la basura.
4. No, no hagas un castillo de arena. Ponte loción protectora.
5. No, no te sientes debajo de una palmera. Siéntate en el sol.
6. No, no te pongas un traje de baño. Ponte sandalias.

**Objective:** Open-ended practice
Giving advice

**Answers**

*Answers will vary but will reflect correct usage of familiar commands.*

Lee/No leas
Busca/No busques
Ve/No veas
Escucha/No escuches
Participa/No participes
Trabaja/No trabajes
Pon/No pongas
Levántate/No te levantes
Ve/No vayas
Cambia/No cambies



## Teaching All Students

**Extra Help** Ask students to write 5 negative **tú** commands they usually hear when they are with their friends or family.

**Native Speakers** Ask Spanish speakers to share 3–4 typical commands that they hear or see often in Spanish advertisements. Have them bring in Spanish magazines or newspapers or describe Spanish radio or television ads that use commands.

**Multiple Intelligences**

**Logical/Mathematical** Have students create a mind map of command forms—include formal and familiar, negative and affirmative and all irregular forms. Have students share their mind maps with the class.

## Block Schedule

**Change of Pace** Have students write a list of affirmative and negative commands for appropriate behavior in your school cafeteria, in gym class, in study hall, at the prom, or during other school activities. You can have students create posters of the "rules" and post them on a bulletin board. (For additional activities, see **Block Scheduling Copymasters**.)

# UNIDAD 3 Etapa 2
# Vocabulary/Grammar

## Teaching Resource Options

### Print

*Más práctica* Workbook PE, p. 80
*Cuaderno para hispanohablantes* PE, pp. 78
Block Scheduling Copymasters
Unit 3 Resource Book
*Más práctica* Workbook TE, p. 59
*Cuaderno para hispanohablantes* TE, p. 65

### Audiovisual

OHT 91 (Quick Start)

### Technology

*Intrigas y aventuras* CD-ROM, Disc 1

## Quick Start Review

Saying how often you do something

Use OHT 91 or write on board: Write four sentences in the present tense saying how often you do these household tasks.

todos los días • mucho • de vez en cuando • rara vez • nunca

| | |
|---|---|
| cortar el césped | quitar el polvo |
| limpiar mi cuarto | lavar los platos |
| hacer mi cama | planchar |

*Answers will vary.*

## Teaching Suggestions
### Presenting Adverbs Ending in -mente

- Have students brainstorm a list of additional adjectives to convert into adverbs. They can refer to the end-of-chapter vocabulary lists for ideas. Write both the adjective form and adverb form on the board. You can then have students take turns forming the adverb.
- Point out that **afortunadamente** is the opposite of **desafortunadamente**.
- You can have students go back to any activity that consists of a list of commands and match an adverb to the command. Use **Actividades 5, 6, 8, 9, 10** on pp. 203–205.

## Adverbs Ending in -mente

Remember that some **adverbs** tell you how an action takes place: *quickly, slowly, reluctantly*. In English adverbs often end in **-ly**. In Spanish they often end in **-mente.**

Caminó **lentamente.**
*He walked **slowly**.*

To make **adverbs** of this type, add **-mente** to the **feminine** form of the **adjective.**

From **desafortunado/ desafortunada**:

¿Estás lista para la playa?
**Desafortunadamente**, no.
*Are you ready for the beach? **Unfortunately**, no.*

If the adjective doesn't have masculine and feminine forms, but just a **single** form, add **-mente** to the **single** form.

From **frecuente**:

Hablo en clase **frecuentemente**.
*I **frequently** speak in class.*

And don't forget the accents! They go where they would if there were no **-mente.**

***Since** feliz **has no accent,** felizmente **doesn't either.***

**Felizmente**, los adverbios se hacen muy **fácilmente**.
*Happily, adverbs are made **easily**.*

***But since** fácil **has an accent,** fácilmente **does too.***

### Vocabulario

**Adverbs Ending in -mente**

**especialmente** *especially*
**inmediatamente** *immediately*
**normalmente** *normally*
**rápidamente** *quickly*
**recientemente** *recently*
**típicamente** *typically*
**tranquilamente** *calmly*

¿Cómo haces las cosas?



## Classroom Community

**Paired Activity** Ask pairs of students to write sentences using the words in the vocabulary box on p. 206.

**Portfolio** Have students create a collage of daily activities and chores. They can label how they do each one with a **-mente** adverb.

**Rubric: Writing**

| Criteria | Scale |
|---|---|
| Creativity, appearance | 1 2 3 4 5 |
| Vocabulary use | 1 2 3 4 5 |
| Accuracy | 1 2 3 4 5 |

A = 13–15 pts.
B = 10–12 pts.
C = 7–9 pts.
D = 4–6 pts.
F = < 4 pts.

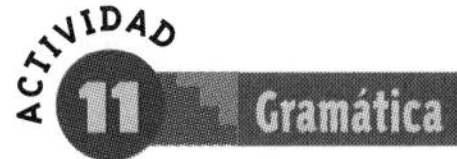


## En Puerto Rico

**Leer/Escribir** Completa las observaciones de Francisco en Puerto Rico con adverbios que terminen en **-mente.** Usa un adverbio diferente para cada oración. *(Hint: Complete Francisco's observations.)*

| | |
|---|---|
| típicamente | frecuentemente |
| normalmente | especialmente |
| tranquilamente | lentamente |
| desafortunadamente | inmediatamente |

**modelo**

*Mi familia _____ va a la playa los fines de semana.*
*Mi familia normalmente va a la playa los fines de semana.*

1. En el Viejo San Juan, los edificios son _____ antiguos.
2. A mis parientes les gusta nadar en el océano Atlántico, _____ cuando hace mucho calor.
3. Tío Rodrigo _____ asiste a un partido de béisbol.
4. Por las tardes, muchas personas caminan _____ por la orilla del océano.
5. La economía de algunos países _____ tiene problemas.
6. Los puertorriqueños _____ hablan español e inglés.

**MÁS PRÁCTICA** *cuaderno* p. 80
**PARA HISPANOHABLANTES** *cuaderno* p. 78

## ¿Cómo lo haces?

**Hablar** Habla con un(a) compañero(a) de tu manera de hacer las siguientes actividades, usando adverbios con **-mente.** *(Hint: Talk with a classmate.)*

**modelo**

*hablar español (fácil / difícil)*
**Compañero(a):** *¿Cómo hablas español?*
**Tú:** *Hablo español fácilmente.*

1. dormir (profundo / ligero)
2. correr (rápido / lento)
3. viajar (frecuente / raro)
4. esperar (paciente / impaciente)
5. aprender las matemáticas (fácil / difícil)
6. levantarse por la mañana (rápido / lento)

## Unas actividades

**Hablar/Escribir** Describe cómo haces cinco actividades, utilizando una palabra que termine en **-mente.** Después pregúntales a cinco compañeros(as) si lo hacen así también. Luego haz una tabla con los resultados. *(Hint: Describe doing activities and poll classmates. Chart results.)*

| Actividades | Yo | Pablo |
|---|---|---|
| esquiar | Esquío rápidamente. | |
| bailar | Bailo locamente. | |
| hablar | Hablo en clase frecuentemente. | |
| llevar | Llevo sandalias normalmente. | |
| cortar | Me corté el pelo recientemente. | |
| | | |



## Teaching Suggestions

In **Actividad 13**, place students in pairs and ask them to create 5 different sentences that follow the models. Then they should each ask 5 classmates about each activity and chart the results of how many classmates do those same activities in the same way.

**Objective:** Controlled practice
Adverbs with **-mente**

### Answers
1. típicamente
2. especialmente
3. frecuentemente
4. lentamente/tranquilamente
5. desafortunadamente
6. normalmente

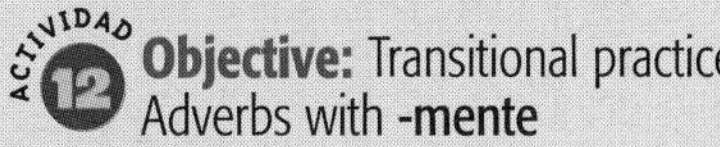
**Objective:** Transitional practice
Adverbs with **-mente**

### Answers
*Answers will vary.*
1. Duermo profundamente/ligeramente.
2. Corro rápidamente/lentamente.
3. Viajo frecuentemente/raramente.
4. Espero pacientemente/impacientemente.
5. Aprendo las matemáticas fácilmente/difícilmente.
6. Me levanto por las mañanas rápidamente/lentamente.

### More Practice
7. comer (lento / rápido)
   Como lentamente/rápidamente.
8. hacer la tarea (fácil/difícil)
   Hago la tarea fácilmente/difícilmente.
9. ir a la playa (frecuente/raro)
   Voy a la playa frecuentemente/raramente.
10. limpiar la casa (normal/típico)
    Limpio la casa normalmente/típicamente.

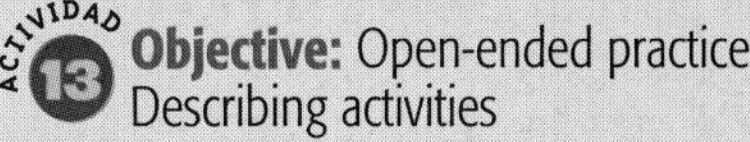
**Objective:** Open-ended practice
Describing activities

*Answers will vary but all should reflect correct usage of **-mente** adverbs.*

## Teaching All Students

**Extra Help** Have students list 10 adjectives in the feminine form and then form the corresponding **-mente** adverbs. Then ask students to write sample sentences using the new adverbs.

**Native Speakers** Ask Spanish speakers to describe and act out their family's daily or weekly chores using vocabulary from this chapter and adverbs using **-mente**.

### Multiple Intelligences

**Verbal** Have all students contribute to a chain story. S1 begins telling a story with **lentamente** or **afortunadamente**. S2 continues, beginning with **rápidamente** or **desafortunadamente**. S3 continues with **normalmente**, etc. Go around the room until each student has contributed. Choose one student to record the story and read it back to the class.

## Block Schedule

**Variety** As an expansion on **Actividad 11**, have students create their own sentences to describe a recent beach vacation. (For additional activities, see **Block Scheduling Copymasters.**)

## Teaching Resource Options

**Print** 

*Más práctica* Workbook PE, pp. 73–76
*Cuaderno para hispanohablantes* PE, pp. 73–74
Block Scheduling Copymasters
Unit 3 Resource Book
*Más práctica* Workbook TE, pp. 52–55
*Cuaderno para hispanohablantes* TE, pp. 60–61
Information Gap Activities, p. 69
Audioscript, pp. 81–83

**Audiovisual** 

OHT 91 (Quick Start)
Audio Program Cassette 8A, 8B / CD 8; (*Para hispanohablantes* Cassette 8B / CD 8)

**Technology** 

*Intrigas y aventuras* CD-ROM, Disc 1

## Quick Start Review

Pronoun placement/talking about daily routine

Use OHT 91 or write on board: Tell about what you have to do every morning to get ready for school. For example: **Tengo que levantarme a las seis.**

Verbs you might use: **arreglarse el pelo, despertarse, ducharse, levantarse, peinarse, ponerse la ropa**

*Answers will vary.*

## Teaching Suggestions

Another way to answer **¿Ya hiciste la cama?** is to say **Sí, ya la hice.** There is a slight difference between **Sí, acabo de hacerla** and **Sí, ya la hice.** The former means that the activity was just completed very recently; the latter means that it was already done, maybe a little while ago.

## Dictation

Have students write the following sentences to reinforce pronoun placement:

**Me entrené ayer.**
**Tengo que entrenarme.**
**Me entreno por la mañana.**
**Estoy entrenándome.**
**Acabo de entrenarme.**

ACTIVIDAD 14

## En la playa

**Hablar** Estás en la playa con tus parientes y tus amigos. Ellos acaban de hacer estas actividades. Díselo a tu compañero(a). *(Hint: Tell your classmate about the following people.)*

**modelo**

*tú / ponerse loción protectora*

**Compañero(a):** *¿Ya te pusiste loción protectora?*

**Tú:** *Sí, acabo de ponerme loción protectora. (Sí, acabo de ponérmela.)*

**Nota**

When saying what you have already done, use **ya.** To say what you have just done, use **acabar de** + an infinitive.

**¿Ya hiciste la cama?** *Did you **already** make your bed?*

**Sí, acabo de hacerla.** *Yes, **I (have) just** made it.*

1. tú / abrir la sombrilla de playa
2. tu madre / buscar caracoles
3. tus compañeros(as) / hablar con un pescador
4. ustedes / proteger la piel
5. yo / contarte un chiste
6. tu amigo(a) / salir en bote
7. tus amigos(as) / beber agua de coco
8. tú / sacar un refresco de la neverita

**El manatí** ¿Sirenas (*mermaids*) en Puerto Rico? Hace muchos años, los marineros vieron por primera vez el manatí y pensaron que era una mujer con cola de pez. Y así continúa el mito de la sirenita.

ACTIVIDAD 15

## ¿Ya?

**Escuchar/Hablar** Escucha las siguientes conversaciones e indica si la segunda persona ya hizo el favor o si va a hacerlo. *(Hint: Tell whether the second person already completed the task or is going to.)*

**Acaba de hacerlo.**

**Va a hacerlo.**

**modelo**

*Susana*

*Sí, Susana acaba de hacerlo.*

1. Francisco
2. Francisco
3. Susana
4. tío Rodrigo
5. tía Julia
6. Susana



## Classroom Community

**Paired Activity** Ask pairs of students to share 3 things that they have already done today, e.g., **Ya desayuné en casa.**

**Group Activity** For a variation to **Actividad 15,** have students write a list of suggestions for a new Spanish teacher at the school. Be sure they address the teacher with formal commands.

**Game** Divide the class into two teams. Using the responses to **Actividad 14,** scramble the words on an overhead transparency and have students take turns unscrambling them to make logical sentences. Let them give a reason why the action was already done—encourage them to be creative. Each team collects points for unscrambling each sentence. The team with the most points after 10 minutes wins.

## Unas sugerencias

**Hablar/Escribir** Con un(a) compañero(a), escriban una lista de sugerencias para un(a) estudiante que va a tomar la clase de español el año que viene. Léele la lista a la clase. *(Hint: Write suggestions for a student who will be taking Spanish next year.)*

- Llega a clase a tiempo.
- No hables inglés en clase.
- Escucha mucha música latina.
- Trata de hablar mucho español. (No es necesario hablar perfectamente.)
- No duermas en clase.

## La playa de Puerto Rico

**Hablar** Mira la foto de la playa de Puerto Rico. Túrnense para hacer oraciones sobre lo que pasa. ¡Ojo! Cada persona tiene que repetir las oraciones de los demás. *(Hint: Take turns making sentences about the photo, repeating the sentences of others in your group.)*

**modelo**

*Hay arena.*

*Hay arena y un palmar.*

**MÁS COMUNICACIÓN** p. R9

## Refrán

***No dejes para mañana lo que puedes hacer hoy.***

En grupos pequeños, hagan una lista de cosas que deben hacer hoy en lugar de mañana. Luego comparen su lista con la lista de otro grupo.

## Teaching All Students

**Extra Help** Based on the list of **«Unas sugerencias»** in **Actividad 15**, ask students to state that they have just done each affirmative item, e.g., **Acabo de llegar a clase a tiempo.**

**Challenge** In small groups, have students draw/design a picture of the beach, adding in 10 items that really do *not* pertain to the beach. Swap pictures with another group and identify what does not belong.

**Multiple Intelligences**

**Kinesthetic** Have students list activities they typically see at the beach. Then have students take turns acting out the activities on the list for other students to guess.

**Objective:** Transitional practice
**Acabar de/En contexto** vocabulary

**Answers**

*Answers will vary.*

1. ¿Ya abriste la sombrilla de playa? Sí, acabo de abrir la sombrilla de playa. (Sí, acabo de abrirla.)
2. ¿Tu madre ya buscó caracoles? Sí, acaba de buscar caracoles. (... de buscarlos.)
3. ¿Tus compañeros ya hablaron con un pescador? Sí, acaban de hablar con un pescador. (... de hablarle.)
4. ¿Ustedes ya se protegieron la piel? Sí, acabamos de protegernos la piel. (... de protegérnosla.)
5. ¿Ya me contaste un chiste? Sí, acabo de contarte un chiste.
6. ¿Tu amigo(a) ya salió en bote? Sí, acaba de salir en bote.
7. ¿Tus amigas ya bebieron agua de coco? Sí, acaban de beber agua de coco. (... de beberla.)
8. ¿Ya sacaste un refresco de la neverita? Sí, acabo de sacar un refresco de la neverita.

**Objective:** Transitional practice
Listening comprehension/**acabar de**

**Answers** (See script, p. 193B.)

1. Va a hacerlo.
2. Acaba de hacerlo.
3. Va a hacerlo.
4. Acaba de hacerlo.
5. Acaba de hacerlo.
6. Va a hacerlo.

**Objective:** Open-ended practice
Making suggestions

*Answers will vary but should reflect correct conjugation of informal commands.*

**Objective:** Open-ended practice
Discussing the beach

*Answers will vary.*

## Block Schedule

**Variety** Bring in magazine clippings or photos of beach scenes or of household product advertisements. Have students describe the action in the photos using adverbs. You can make a game by dividing the class into two teams and alternate presenting a member from each team with a photo or advertisement to describe correctly. The team with the most correct sentences at the end of 10 minutes wins. (For additional activities, see **Block Scheduling Copymasters**.)

## Teaching Resource Options

**Print** 

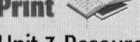

Unit 3 Resource Book
Videoscript, p. 79

**Audiovisual** 

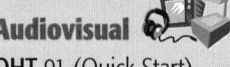

OHT 91 (Quick Start)
**Video Program** Videotape 3, 19:13 / Videodisc 2B

Search Chapter 3, Play to 4
U3E2, En colores (Culture), Spanish

Search Chapter 3, Play to 4
U3E2, En colores (Culture), English

## Quick Start Review

Asking questions

Use OHT 91 or write on board: Look at the picture and write down three questions in Spanish you might ask the tour guide from **El Yunque**.

*Answers will vary.*

## Teaching Suggestions

### Presenting En colores

- **Prereading** Begin by asking students to guess the topic of the reading, based on the photos. Write the list of possibilities on the board.
- **Strategy: Recognize unique natural wonders** Have students describe what they know about rain forests by writing the three headings in their notebooks: **el clima, los animales, las plantas.** As they start to read, have students jot down notes under each heading.

## Reading Strategy

Remind students to gather and sort information as they read. They may also find it helpful to observe organization: can they think of two or more categories under which the information can be classified?

# En colores

## CULTURA Y COMPARACIONES

# El Yunque

### PARA CONOCERNOS

**STRATEGY: CONNECTING CULTURES**

**Recognize unique natural wonders** **El Yunque** is the only rain forest (**bosque tropical**) in the Northern Hemisphere. It is part of the U.S. National Forest Service. From your reading and your own knowledge, define the major characteristics of a rain forest.

| Características de un bosque tropical |
| --- |
| Clima: |
| Animales: |
| Plantas: |

What other U.S. national parks can you name?

Bienvenidos a El Yunque, el único bosque tropical del Servicio Forestal Nacional de Estados Unidos. El parque queda a 25 millas de San Juan. Hoy vamos a conocerlo. Este maravilloso parque te va a sorprender.

¡Hay tantas cosas interesantes en El Yunque! Hay una variedad tremenda de plantas. En el parque encuentras 240 clases de árboles y varias clases de plantas y flores. Toma fotos de los magníficos cedros[1], el bambú y los helechos[2]. Trepa a un árbol. Y nota el perfume tan agradable de las flores. Es el perfume de las pequeñas orquídeas que crecen por todas partes. Escucha bien

[1] cedars [2] ferns

*Esta guía te cuenta de El Yunque.*



## Classroom Community

**TPR** Have students take turns playing the role of tour guide of **El Yunque**. Ask them to read aloud the presentation, using lots of body movement and facial expressions.

**Learning Scenario** Have half the students play the role of tourists who make a list of questions they would like to ask the forest ranger about **El Yunque**. Have the other students act as the ranger and answer the questions. Students may research the Internet for the answers and present their findings to the class.

# Bosque Nacional

el canto de los pájaros. El Yunque es un refugio de aves[3] donde puedes ver el casi extinto loro[4] puertorriqueño. No hagas ruido y vas a oír el coquí, la rana indígena que recibió su nombre del sonido que hace, «coquí-coquí-coquí».

Ahora vamos a caminar por un sendero[5] y subir hasta El Toro. A unos 3.530 pies de altura, El Toro es el pico más elevado del parque. ¡No te canses! Después seguimos hasta las cataratas[6]. ¡Ten cuidado! ¡No te caigas al agua!

[3] bird sanctuary [4] parrot [5] path [6] waterfalls

No te preocupes si empieza a llover durante tu visita. En el parque hay muchos lugares de recreo y centros de información donde puedes buscar refugio. No te vayas de El Yunque sin ir al Centro Forestal tropical, El Portal, para ver exhibiciones y una película sobre El Yunque. Siéntate en el patio y disfruta el panorama de este paraíso tropical.

## ¿Comprendiste?

1. ¿Qué es El Yunque? ¿Dónde está?
2. ¿Qué árboles y plantas puedes ver en El Yunque?
3. ¿Qué animales viven en El Yunque?
4. ¿A qué lugares te llevan los senderos?
5. ¿Qué haces si empieza a llover?

## ¿Qué piensas?

Compara otro parque nacional en Estados Unidos con El Yunque.

## Hazlo tú

Ya hiciste una excursión por El Yunque. Ahora, piensa en alguna parte de tu escuela y prepara una excursión de este lugar.

## Culture Highlights

- **EL YUNQUE** covers about 28,000 acres in the northeast part of Puerto Rico. Typical annual rainfall is about 100 billion gallons of water.
- **EL LORO PUERTORRIQUEÑO** is the protected red, blue, and green parrot found only in certain parts of the island, especially **El Yunque**.
- **EL COQUÍ** The **coquí** is a singing tree frog native to Puerto Rico that serves as its unofficial mascot. Rarely seen, it makes a beautiful **"coquí, coquí"** sound.
- **LAS ORQUÍDEAS** There are over 20 species of wild orchids found in **El Yunque** Rain Forest.

## Interdisciplinary Connections

**Social Studies** Have students list any national parks they have visited in the U.S. Then have them list some state parks in their area. They may use the Internet for more information. Have them choose one park and compare and contrast it to what they have read about **El Yunque**. Possible categories to compare/contrast are: activities, wildlife, foliage, average rainfall, size, and location.

## ¿Comprendiste?

**Answers**

1. El Yunque es el único bosque tropical del Servicio Forestal Nacional de los Estados Unidos. Está a 25 millas de San Juan.
2. En El Yunque puedes ver los cedros, el bambú y los helechos.
3. El loro puertorriqueño y el coquí viven en El Yunque.
4. Los senderos te llevan a El Toro, el pico más elevado del parque, y a las cataratas.
5. Si empieza a llover, puedes buscar refugio en los lugares de recreo y los centros de información.

## Teaching All Students

**Extra Help** Ask students to scan the reading and locate all the cognates and other words they recognize.

**Challenge** List some names of national parks in the U.S. Assign a park to small groups to research. Have students design a travel brochure for Spanish-speaking tourists for their assigned park and give a short presentation to the class.

**Multiple Intelligences**

**Naturalist** Have students count the examples of plants and wildlife that were mentioned in the reading. Then ask them to categorize them into **plantas**, **animales**, **pájaros**, and **árboles**.

## Block Schedule

**Retention** Have students write a list of 5–7 **tú** commands about what to do or not to do while visiting **El Yunque**. Then have them write another 5–7 commands about what to do or not to do while visiting a state park near their home. Compare the lists. Students can review the **En colores** reading to get ideas.

## Teaching Resource Options

**Print**

Block Scheduling Copymasters
Unit 3 Resource Book
Information Gap Activities, pp. 70–71
Family Involvement, pp. 72–73

**Audiovisual**

OHT 92 (Quick Start)

**Technology**

Electronic Teacher Tools/Test Generator
*Intrigas y aventuras* CD-ROM, Disc 1

## Quick Start Review

Informal commands

Use OHT 92 or write on board: Give both the affirmative and negative **tú** command for the following verbs.

1. comer 3. ayudar 5. ir
2. lavar 4. poner 6. hacer

**Answers**

1. Come. / No comas.
2. Lava. / No laves.
3. Ayuda. / No ayudes.
4. Pon. / No pongas.
5. Ve. / No vayas.
6. Haz. / No hagas.

## Teaching Suggestions
### What Have Students Learned?

- Have students look at the "Now you can..." notes listed on the left side of pages 212–213. Point out that if they feel they need to review material before doing the activities, they should consult the "To review" notes.
- Use the video to review vocabulary and structures.

# En uso
## REPASO Y MÁS COMUNICACIÓN

**OBJECTIVES**

- Discuss beach activities
- Tell someone what to do
- Talk about chores
- Say if something has already been done

*Now you can...*
- talk about chores.

*To review*
- affirmative **tú** commands, see p. 202.

### ACTIVIDAD 1 Responsabilidades

Francisco tiene algunas responsabilidades en la casa de sus tíos. ¿Qué le dice su tía? Usa cada verbo una vez. *(Hint: Tell what Francisco's aunt wants him to do.)*

**modelo**

*_____ la cena.*
*Prepara la cena.*

ser | tener | secar | preparar | hacer | ir | poner | barrer

1. _____ responsable.
2. _____ paciencia con tu prima.
3. _____ al supermercado para comprar leche.
4. _____ la mesa.
5. _____ la limpieza.
6. _____ el piso.
7. _____ los platos.
8. _____ el desayuno.

*Now you can...*
- tell someone what to do.

*To review*
- affirmative **tú** commands, see p. 202.
- negative **tú** commands, see p. 204.

### ACTIVIDAD 2 ¡Mira los caracoles!

Susana quiere ir a la playa. ¿Qué le dice Francisco? *(Hint: Tell what Francisco says to Susana.)*

**modelo**

*llevar toallas*
*Lleva toallas. (No lleves toallas.)*

1. tomar mucho sol
2. proteger la piel
3. ponerse loción protectora
4. jugar en las olas grandes
5. ir sola
6. usar gorra
7. nadar después de comer
8. hacer castillos de arena
9. sentarse debajo de una sombrilla de playa
10. mirar al pescador



## Classroom Community

**Portfolio** Based on what they have learned about **El Yunque** have students write in their journal about why they would or would not like to visit this park.

**Rubric: Writing**

| Criteria | Scale |
|---|---|
| Accuracy of information | 1 2 3 4 5 |
| Logical organization | 1 2 3 4 5 |
| Vocabulary use | 1 2 3 4 5 |

A = 13–15 pts.
B = 10–12 pts.
C = 7–9 pts.
D = 4–6 pts.
F = < 4 pts.

**Peer Review** Assign a "Now you can" to a group of students. Each group reviews concept(s) and presents material to class as a review, e.g., oral presentation, worksheet, game, practice test, etc.

**Paired Activity** As a variation to **Actividad 1**, have students work in pairs to write a list of commands their parents may use when speaking to them. As a variation to **Actividad 2**, write a list of commands to prepare a friend to go to the **El Yunque** rain forest.

*Now you can...*
- discuss beach activities.

*To review*
- adverbs ending in **-mente**, see p. 206.

## ACTIVIDAD 3 Una postal

Franciso les escribe una postal a sus abuelos. ¿Qué dice? *(Hint: Complete Francisco's postcard.)*

**modelo**

*(Reciente) fui a la playa con mis tíos.*
*Recientemente fui a la playa con mis tíos.*

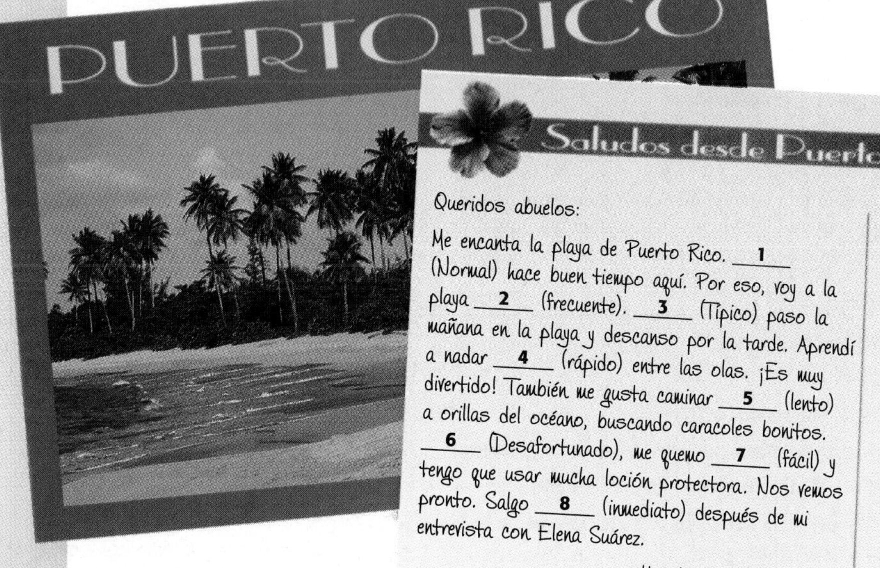


Queridos abuelos:

Me encanta la playa de Puerto Rico. __1__ (Normal) hace buen tiempo aquí. Por eso, voy a la playa __2__ (frecuente). __3__ (Típico) paso la mañana en la playa y descanso por la tarde. Aprendí a nadar __4__ (rápido) entre las olas. ¡Es muy divertido! También me gusta caminar __5__ (lento) a orillas del océano, buscando caracoles bonitos. __6__ (Desafortunado), me quemo __7__ (fácil) y tengo que usar mucha loción protectora. Nos vemos pronto. Salgo __8__ (inmediato) después de mi entrevista con Elena Suárez.

Un abrazo, Francisco

*Now you can...*
- say if something has already been done.

*To review*
- **ya** and **acabar de,** see p. 208.

## ACTIVIDAD 4 ¿Más quehaceres?

Hay una fiesta en tu casa mañana y ayudas a tu mamá con la limpieza. Contesta sus preguntas. *(Hint: Answer your mother's questions.)*

**modelo**

*¿Ya sacaste la basura? (sí)* *Sí, acabo de sacarla.*

1. ¿Ya pasaste la aspiradora? (sí)
2. ¿Ya pusiste la mesa? (no)
3. ¿Ya quitaste el polvo? (sí)
4. ¿Ya lavaste los platos? (no)
5. ¿Ya limpiaste el baño? (no)
6. ¿Ya cortaste el césped? (sí)



### ACTIVIDAD 1 Answers

1. Sé
2. Ten
3. Ve
4. Pon
5. Haz
6. Barre
7. Seca
8. Haz

### ACTIVIDAD 2 Answers

1. No tomes mucho sol.
2. Protege la piel.
3. Ponte loción protectora.
4. No juegues en las olas grandes.
5. No vayas sola.
6. Usa la gorra.
7. No nades después de comer.
8. Haz castillos de arena bonitos.
9. Siéntate debajo de una sombrilla de playa.
10. Mira al pescador.

### ACTIVIDAD 3 Answers

1. Normalmente
2. frecuentemente
3. Típicamente
4. rápidamente
5. lentamente
6. Desafortunadamente
7. fácilmente
8. inmediatamente

### ACTIVIDAD 4 Answers

1. Sí, acabo de pasarla.
2. No, no la puse.
3. Sí, acabo de quitarlo.
4. No, no los lavé.
5. No, no lo limpié.
6. Sí, acabo de cortarlo.

### Critical Thinking

Ask students what they think are the dangers involved in the destruction of the rain forests around the world. Are they familiar with any of the work done by environmental groups to save the rain forests? What do they think of it? Bring in some environmental brochures and distribute them among the class in order to stimulate conversation.

### Teaching All Students

**Extra Help** Ask students to rewrite **Actividad 1** by using negative **tú** commands.

**Challenge** Have students write a letter to a friend or family member that models the postcard in **Actividad 3**. Students can also describe a recent vacation if they prefer.

**Multiple Intelligences**

**Verbal** Have groups of students review informal commands by listing the 9 irregular affirmative and the 5 irregular negative **tú** commands, making a chart, and posting it in class.

### Block Schedule

**FunBreak** This may be a good time to play one of the games described in the **Ampliación** section on p. 171B. Try the game called **Voy a la playa y voy a llevar...** (For additional activities, see **Block Scheduling Copymasters.**)

## Teaching Resource Options

### Print

Unit 3 Resource Book
- **Cooperative Quizzes**, pp. 84–85
- **Etapa Exam**, Forms A and B, pp. 86–95
- ***Examen para hispanohablantes*** pp. 96–100
- **Audioscript**, p. 83
- **Portfolio Assessment**, pp. 101–102
- **Multiple Choice Test Questions**, pp. 173–175

### Audiovisual

**OHT** 85, 85A, 86, 86A, 92 (Quick Start)
**Audio Program** Cassette 19B / CD 19;
(***Para hispanohablantes*** Cassette 19B / CD 19)

### Technology

**Electronic Teacher Tools/Test Generator**
**www.mcdougallittell.com**

## Quick Start Review

**Describing**

Use OHT 92 or write on board: List the adjectives that might apply to a description of the beach. Then write a sentence about a beach you know.

| | | |
|---|---|---|
| bonito | excelente | blanco |
| divertido | enorme | lujoso |
| perfecto | pequeño | extraño |
| valiente | inteligente | sabroso |

*Answers will vary.*

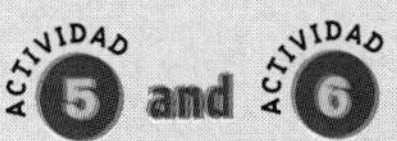

**Actividad 5 and Actividad 6**

**Household chores**

**Rubric: Speaking**

| Criteria | Scale | |
|---|---|---|
| Fluency | 1 2 3 4 5 | A = 13–15 pts. |
| Vocabulary | 1 2 3 4 5 | B = 10–12 pts. |
| Pronunciation, rhythm | 1 2 3 4 5 | C = 7–9 pts. |
| | | D = 4–6 pts. |
| | | F = < 4 pts. |

**Actividad 7 En tu propia voz**

**Rubric: Writing**

| Criteria | Scale | |
|---|---|---|
| Vocabulary use | 1 2 3 4 5 | A = 13–15 pts. |
| Accuracy | 1 2 3 4 5 | B = 10–12 pts. |
| Creativity, appearance | 1 2 3 4 5 | C = 7–9 pts. |
| | | D = 4–6 pts. |
| | | F = < 4 pts. |

## Actividad 5 ¡A la playa!

**PARA CONVERSAR**

**STRATEGY: SPEAKING**

**Encourage or discourage certain behaviors** With your partner, brainstorm typical ways children act. Then decide in your role-play which ones you will encourage and which ones you will discourage. How can you make good choices more appealing? The model gives you some ideas.

Vas a llevar a un(a) niño(a) a la playa. ¿Qué dicen ustedes antes de salir? *(Hint: Role-play a conversation between you and a child you are taking to the beach.)*

**modelo**

**Niño(a):** *¿Llevo la toalla?*
**Tú:** *Sí, llévala.*
**Niño(a):** *¿Me pongo perfume?*
**Tú:** *No, no te pongas perfume. Ponte loción protectora.*
**Niño(a):** *¿Puedo jugar entre las olas grandes?*
**Tú:** *No, no juegues entre las olas grandes. Juega entre las olas pequeñas.*

## Actividad 6 ¡Qué desastre!

Tú y tus amigos tuvieron una fiesta anoche y dejaron la casa muy sucia. Esta noche tus padres tienen una fiesta. ¿Qué dicen todos? Cambien de papel. *(Hint: Role-play a conversation between you and your parents about cleaning the house for a party.)*

**modelo**

**Mamá:** *¡Lava los platos inmediatamente!*
**Tú:** *Está bien, mamá. Voy a lavarlos ahora.*
**Papá:** *¿Ya limpiaste el baño?*
**Tú:** *Sí, papá. Acabo de limpiarlo.*

## Actividad 7 En tu propia voz

**ESCRITURA** Un(a) amigo(a) tuyo(a) va a hacer un viaje a Puerto Rico. Escríbele una carta que incluya una descripción de la playa y varias recomendaciones. *(Hint: Write a letter to a friend who plans to visit Puerto Rico.)*

**modelo**

*Querida Linda:*

*Puerto Rico es muy bonito, especialmente la playa. En la playa hay... Si vas a la playa, lleva...*

*San Juan tiene muchos edificios antiguos. Visita...*

## TÚ EN LA COMUNIDAD

**Tom** tiene diecisiete años y es estudiante en Washington. Ahora aprende español en la escuela. Algunas veces habla español en casa con sus primos y hermanitos. Por la tarde trabaja en una heladería. Cuando los clientes hispanos que no hablan inglés van a la heladería, Tom trata de ayudarlos y les habla en español. ¿Usas tu español cuando quieres ayudar a la gente hispana que no entiende bien el inglés?

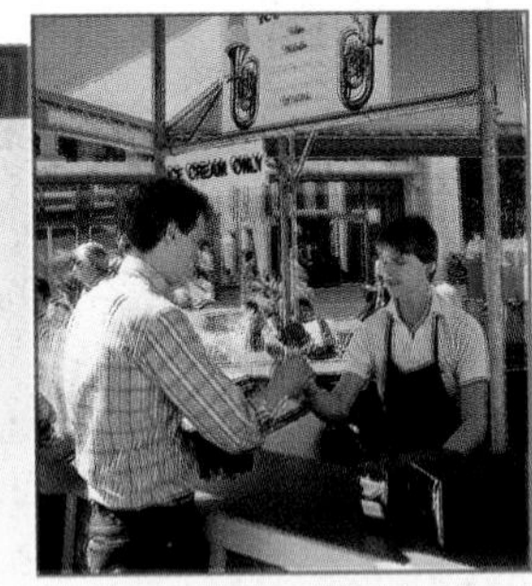



## Classroom Community

**TPR** Divide the class into 2 teams. Using the **Quehaceres** vocabulary words, have volunteers from each team act out the chores for their team to guess (for 1 point.) If they create a logical sentence using the chore and **-mente** adverb, they get an extra point.

**Paired Activity** Have students review vocabulary with a partner. For the words that are the most challenging to remember, have students make flashcards.

**Game Cadenas** Form a short story with all the vocabulary words by asking each student to add one sentence. Each sentence does *not* have to incorporate a vocabulary word, but the goal is to use *all* the words in the story. The teacher may write the story on an overhead transparency.

# En resumen

## REPASO DE VOCABULARIO

### TELL SOMEONE WHAT TO DO

| | |
|---|---|
| **barrer el piso** | *to sweep the floor* |
| **cortar el césped** | *to cut the grass* |
| **hacer la limpieza** | *to do the cleaning* |

 **Ya sabes**

| | |
|---|---|
| **lavar los platos** | *to wash the dishes* |
| **limpiar el cuarto** | *to clean the room* |
| **pasar la aspiradora** | *to vacuum* |
| **planchar** | *to iron* |
| **quitar el polvo** | *to dust* |
| **sacar la basura** | *to take out the trash* |

### TALK ABOUT CHORES

| | |
|---|---|
| **limpio(a)** | *clean* |
| **los quehaceres** | *chores* |
| **sucio(a)** | *dirty* |

### SAY IF SOMETHING HAS ALREADY BEEN DONE

| | |
|---|---|
| **acabar de** | *to have just* |
| **ya** | *already* |

### Juego

Francisco le escribe por correo electrónico a su amigo y le gusta jugar con letras. ¿Qué escribió Francisco?

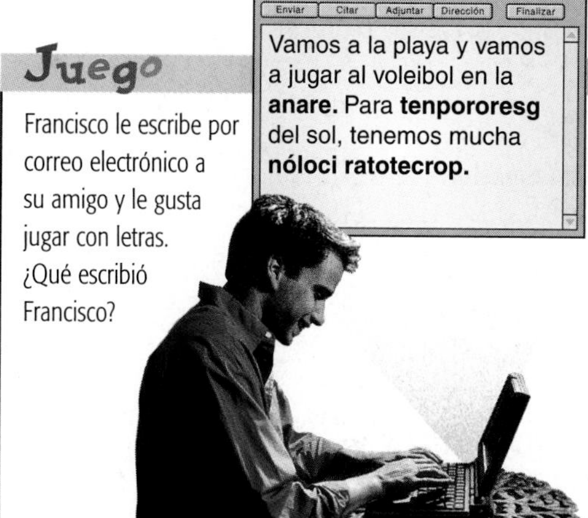

Enviar
Citar
Adjuntar
Dirección
Finalizar
Vamos a la playa y vamos a jugar al voleibol en la **anare.** Para **tenpororesg** del sol, tenemos mucha **nóloci ratotecrop.**


### DISCUSS BEACH ACTIVITIES

**What You See**

| | |
|---|---|
| **la arena** | *sand* |
| **el bote** | *boat* |
| **el caracol** | *shell* |
| **el océano** | *ocean* |
| **las olas** | *waves* |
| **la orilla** | *edge, shore* |
| **la palma** | *palm tree* |
| **el palmar** | *palm tree grove* |
| **el (la) pescador(a)** | *fisherman* |

**At the Beach**

| | |
|---|---|
| **el agua de coco** | *coconut milk* |
| **la loción protectora** | *sunscreen* |
| **la neverita** | *cooler* |
| **la piel** | *skin* |
| **proteger** | *to protect* |
| **la quemadura** | *burn* |
| **quemar** | *to burn* |
| **las sandalias** | *sandals* |
| **la sombrilla de playa** | *beach umbrella* |
| **la toalla** | *towel* |

### ADVERBS ENDING IN -MENTE

| | |
|---|---|
| **desafortunadamente** | *unfortunately* |
| **especialmente** | *especially* |
| **fácilmente** | *easily* |
| **frecuentemente** | *frequently* |
| **inmediatamente** | *immediately* |
| **lentamente** | *slowly* |
| **normalmente** | *normally* |
| **rápidamente** | *quickly* |
| **recientemente** | *recently* |
| **típicamente** | *typically* |
| **tranquilamente** | *calmly* |



## Teaching All Students

**Extra Help** Have students form complete sentences, using words from the vocabulary list.

**Native Speakers** Assign students 1 to 2 vocabulary sections to help the rest of the class review. Allow the class to review the section(s) for 30 seconds, then tell them to close their books. Students read each word or expression from their section(s) out of order. The class must write down the Spanish word(s) in one column and the translation in another.

**Multiple Intelligences**

**Logical/Mathematical** State 3 words from the vocabulary list, choosing 2 that have something in common and 1 intruder word. Students identify intruder word. Then have students create their own 3-word combinations for fellow classmates to distinguish the intruder.

## Teaching Note: En tu propia voz

**Writing Strategy** Remind students that descriptive details will make their letter more interesting. The topic sentence of each paragraph should be supported with specific information.

## Teaching Suggestions

### Vocabulary Review

Have students make separate flashcards of the verbs and nouns in the list titled "Tell Someone What to Do" in the **Repaso de Vocabulario** on p. 215. Make separate cards for **barrer, cortar, hacer...,** etc. and separate cards for **el piso, el césped, la limpieza,** etc. Break students into groups of 3 or 4 and have each group take turns matching the verb to the appropriate noun, as with **barrer el piso**.

## Community Connections

Have students work in groups to write and illustrate short guides in Spanish for local tourist attractions.

## Juego

**Answers**

Vamos a la playa y vamos a jugar al voleibol en la **arena**. Para **protegernos** del sol, tenemos mucha **loción protectora**.

## Project: Reviewing Etapa 2

Assign the following out-of-class activities:

- Interview a Spanish speaker about what household chores he/she does.
- Bring in tourist information about beach vacations in Puerto Rico.
- Find out more about **El Yunque**.
- Find more information on the most popular sports and activities for young people in Puerto Rico.

**Extra Credit**

| | |
|---|---|
| Interview | 2 pts. |
| Tourist information | 2 pts. |
| El Yunque | 2 pts. |
| Sports & activities | 2 pts. |

## Block Schedule

**FunBreak** Have students make their own scrambled-word **juegos** for partners to solve.

*pages 216–239*

# Planning Guide CLASSROOM MANAGEMENT

## OBJECTIVES

**Communication**
- Describe time periods *pp. 220–221, 224–225*
- Talk about health and illness *pp. 218–219, 220–221, 227, 229*
- Give advice *pp. 220–221, 228–230*

**Grammar**
- **Hacer** with expressions of time *p. 224*
- The subjunctive with impersonal expressions *pp. 226, 228*
- **Doler** *p. 223*

**Culture**
- **Los huracanes en Puerto Rico** *p. 222*
- **La celebración de Carnaval** *p. 225*
- **El estatus político de Puerto Rico** *pp. 232–233*
- **Una voz de la tierra** *pp. 234–235*

**Recycling**
- Talk about household chores *p. 223*
- Use the preterite *p. 225*
- Vacation vocabulary *p. 231*
- Talk about the past *p. 233*

## STRATEGIES

**Listening Strategies**
- Listen sympathetically *p. 220*

**Speaking Strategies**
- Give feedback *p. 231*
- Use language for problem-solving *p. 238*

**Reading Strategies**
- Activate associated knowledge *p. 232*

**Writing Strategies**
- Support an opinion with facts and examples *Actividad 7, TE p. 239*
- Compare and contrast to make strong descriptions *p. 240*

**Connecting Cultures Strategies**
- Discover many cultures inside one country *p. 234*
- Make a historical timeline *TE p. 233*
- Compare places *TE p. 233*

## PROGRAM RESOURCES

### Print
- *Más práctica* Workbook PE *pp. 81–88*
- Block Scheduling Copymasters *pp. 73–80*
- Unit 3 Resource Book
  - *Más práctica* Workbook TE *pp. 103–110*
  - *Cuaderno para hispanohablantes* TE *pp. 111–118*
  - Information Gap Activities *pp. 119–122*
  - Family Involvement *pp. 123–124*
  - Video Activities *pp. 125–127*
  - Videoscript *pp. 128–129*
  - Audioscript *pp. 130–134*
  - Assessment Program, Unit 3 Etapa 3 *pp. 135–169; 176–186*
  - Answer Keys *pp. 189–192*

### Audiovisual
- Audio Program Cassette 9A, 9B / CD 9
- *Canciones* Cassette/CD
- Video Program Videotape 3 / Videodisc 2B
- Overhead Transparencies M1, M3; GO1–GO5; 93–102

### Technology
- Electronic Teacher Tools/Test Generator
- *Intrigas y aventuras* CD-ROM, Disc 1
-  www.mcdougallittell.com

### Assessment Program Options
- Cooperative Quizzes (Unit 3 Resource Book)
- Etapa Exam Forms A and B (Unit 3 Resource Book)
- *Examen para hispanohablantes* (Unit 3 Resource Book)
- Portfolio Assessment (Unit 3 Resource Book)
- Unit 3 Comprehensive Test (Unit 3 Resource Book)
- *Prueba comprensiva para hispanohablantes,* Unit 3 (Unit 3 Resource Book)
- Multiple Choice Test Questions (Unit 3 Resource Book)
- Midyear Exam (Unit 3 Resource Book)
- Audio Program Cassette 19B / CD 19
- Electronic Teacher Tools / Test Generator

### Native Speakers
- *Cuaderno para hispanohablantes* PE *pp. 81–88*
- *Cuaderno para hispanohablantes* TE (Unit 3 Resource Book)
- *Examen para hispanohablantes* (Unit 3 Resource Book)
- *Prueba comprensiva para hispanohablantes,* Unit 3 (Unit 3 Resource Book)
- Audio Program *(Para hispanohablantes)* Cassettes 9B, 19B / CD 9, CD 19
- Audioscript (Unit 3 Resource Book)

Francisco | Elena | Tío Rodrigo | Tía Julia | Susana

# Student Text Listening Activity Scripts

## Videoscript: Diálogo *pages 220–221*

- Videotape 3, 25:35 • Videodisc 2B
  **Search Chapter 5, Play to end. U3E3, En vivo (Dialog)**
- Use the videoscript with **Actividades 1, 2** *page 222*

**Elena:** Aquí están. ¡Bienvenidos!
**Francisco:** Gracias. Elena, te presento a mi familia. Mi tía Julia, mi tío Rodrigo y mi prima Susana.
**Elena:** Es un placer.
**Tía Julia:** Encantada. Me gusta mucho su programa. Hace tres años que nuestra familia lo ve... ¡todos los sábados!
**Elena:** Muchas gracias, muy amable.
**Tío Rodrigo:** Mucho gusto, señorita Suárez.
**Susana:** Hola.
**Elena:** Gracias por venir a participar. Vengan, les explico todo. Es importante que ustedes entiendan lo que van a hacer.
**Asistente:** (V/O) Preparados, muy bien. Silencio...
**Director:** y cámara... ¡y acción!
**Elena:** ¡Bienvenidos al show de Elena Suárez! ¿Están todos listos? ¡Muy bien! Primero, vamos a estirar el cuerpo. Comenzamos con el cuello. Despacio, despacio, despacio. Ahora los hombros. Muy bien, muy bien. Y ahora las piernas. Estiren las manos hacia el pie derecho. Respiren. Otro lado. Respiren. Otro lado. Respiren. Cambiamos. Uno, dos, tres, cuatro, cinco, seis, siete...
**Director:** (V/O) ¡Corte!
**Tío Rodrigo:** Elena, déjame ver. Soy doctor.
**Elena:** Ay, me duele mucho.
**Tío Rodrigo:** A ver, ¿dónde? ¿Es la rodilla o el tobillo?
**Elena:** Es el tobillo... ¡Ahí! Ahí me duele.
**Tío Rodrigo:** Elena, es necesario que te examine el tobillo. Vamos, te llevo a mi consultorio.
**Elena:** Ay, qué pena. Hace cuatro años que grabamos este programa, y ni un accidente. Y ahora esto. ¡Qué mala suerte!
**Tío Rodrigo:** Tengo malas noticias, Elena. Tienes una fractura de tobillo. Se ve muy claro en la radiografía.
**Elena:** ¿Una fractura? Ay, no. ¿Qué voy a hacer? Mi programa de televisión...
**Tío Rodrigo:** Voy a ponerte un yeso. No hay otra opción. Es necesario que el tobillo se recupere. El tobillo te va a doler mucho hoy y mañana. Esta receta es para unas pastillas. Son para el dolor. Es posible que te molesten un poco el estómago. Y es importante que no camines por unos días.
**Elena:** Ay, doctor, hace quince años que no me rompo un hueso. ¡Qué mala suerte!
**Tío Rodrigo:** Sí, muy mala suerte. ¡Pero por lo menos estaba yo en la playa! No tuviste que ir a la sala de emergencia.
**Francisco:** (V/O) ¿Tío? ¿Elena?
**Tío Rodrigo:** Pasa, Francisco, pasa.
**Francisco:** Estamos todos afuera, en la sala de espera. Estamos muy preocupados. ¿Cómo estás, Elena?
**Elena:** Pues, no muy bien. Tengo una fractura de tobillo. Me lastimé.
**Francisco:** Ay, qué horrible. ¿Te duele mucho?
**Elena:** Sí, me duele. Pero tu tío es un excelente doctor, y me puso este yeso. Francisco, lo siento mucho. Es una pena que no puedas participar en mi programa. Pero todavía podemos hacer la entrevista para tu artículo, ¿verdad? ¿Por qué no la hacemos por teléfono mañana? Puedes llamarme por la tarde. ¿Tienes mi número?
**Francisco:** Sí, lo tengo en mi cuaderno. Muchas gracias. Pero mi prima Susana está muy triste. Ella quería ser estrella de televisión.
**Elena:** No hay problema. Después de recuperarme voy a seguir con mi programa. Susana y toda la familia pueden venir a participar. ¡Es bueno que ellos vivan aquí en Puerto Rico!
**Tío Rodrigo:** Muchas gracias, Elena. La nena va a estar muy feliz.
**Francisco:** Bueno, me voy. Nos hablamos mañana.
**Elena:** Hasta mañana.
**Francisco:** A pesar del accidente en la playa, lo pasé muy bien aquí en Puerto Rico. Finalmente, mi entrevista con Elena fue un éxito. Su programa es maravilloso. Es importante que todos mantengan la salud, y que hagan ejercicio. Así van a tener una vida—como se dice en Puerto Rico—¡muy chévere! Bueno, hasta la próxima vez... Francisco.

## Actividad 7 En el consultorio *page 225*

1. **Patient:** Doctora, estaba andando en patineta y me caí.
   **Doctor:** ¿Cuánto tiempo hace que te caíste?
   **Patient:** Pues, hace una semana y me duele la muñeca.
   **Doctor:** ¿Una semana? Bueno, necesitas una radiografía de la muñeca.
2. **Patient:** No tengo una enfermedad, pero me duelen los dientes.
   **Doctor:** ¿Hace cuánto tiempo que te duelen?
   **Patient:** Hace dos días, doctora, sólo dos días pero me duele mucho.
   **Doctor:** Te puedo dar una receta para unas pastillas. Son para el dolor. Y ahora, necesito examinarte los dientes.
   **Patient:** Muchas gracias, doctora.
3. **Patient:** Me es difícil respirar y me duele la cabeza.
   **Doctor:** Ah, usted tiene dolor de cabeza. ¿Exactamente dónde le duele?
   **Patient:** Hace tres días que me duelen los oídos y toda la cabeza.
   **Doctor:** Ah, debe tomar estas pastillas y descansar bastante.
4. **Patient:** Me rompí la pierna cuando estaba de vacaciones y la doctora me mandó hablar con usted al regresar.
   **Doctor:** ¿Hace cuánto tiempo que te puso el yeso?
   **Patient:** Hace cinco días que me puso el yeso en la pierna.
   **Doctor:** Bueno... hace cinco días... Todavía debes elevar la pierna lo más posible.

## Actividad 14 ¿Es buen doctor? *page 230*

1. **Patient:** ¿Sabe usted qué me pasó? Estaba jugando al básquetbol y me lastimé la rodilla. ¿Qué me recomienda?
   **Doctor:** Es importante que tomemos una radiografía.
2. **Patient:** Uy, doctora, no me siento bien. Tengo fiebre, tos, dolor de garganta y me duele el cuello. ¿Qué enfermedad tengo?
   **Doctor:** Respira profundamente, por favor. *(Patient breathes.)* Es probable que tengas gripe.
3. **Patient:** Es que me duele el diente. Hace tres días que me duele.
   **Dentist:** Es lógico que te saque todos los dientes. Ya no necesitas los dientes, ¿verdad?
4. **Patient:** Me duelen los oídos y estoy resfriada. ¿Debo tomar aspirina?
   **Doctor:** Es mejor que también tomes medicina especialmente para la infección.

# Pacing Guide

## Sample Lesson Plan - 50 Minute Schedule

### DAY 1

***Etapa* Opener**
- Quick Start Review (TE, p. 216). 5 MIN.
- Anticipate/Activate prior knowledge: Have students look at *Etapa* Opener and answer *¿Qué ves?* questions. 10 MIN.

**En contexto: Vocabulario**
- Quick Start Review (TE, p. 218). 5 MIN.
- Discuss pictures, have students use context and pictures to learn *Etapa* vocabulary. Answer questions, p. 219. 10 MIN.

**En vivo: Diálogo**
- Quick Start Review (TE, p. 220). 5 MIN.
- Review Listening Strategy, p. 220. Play audio or show video for the dialog on pp. 220–221. 5 MIN.
- Replay. Read aloud, students take on roles of characters. Ask Comprehension Questions (TE, p. 221). 10 MIN.

**Homework Option**
- Video Activities, Unit 3 Resource Book, pp. 125–127.

### DAY 2

**En acción: Vocabulario y Gramática**
- Check homework. 5 MIN.
- Quick Start Review (TE, p. 222). 2 MIN.
- Ask students for a summary of *En vivo* dialog to check recall. 3 MIN.
- Replay the *En vivo* dialog using the audiovisual resources and have students do *Actividades* 1 and 2 orally. 10 MIN.
- Have students complete *Actividades* 3 and 4 in pairs. 10 MIN.
- Present *Gramática: Hacer* with Expressions of Time, p. 224. 10 MIN.
- Have students do *Actividad* 5 in writing. 5 MIN.
- Have students complete *Actividad* 6 in pairs. 5 MIN.

**Homework Option**
- *Más práctica* Workbook, p. 85. *Cuaderno para hispanohablantes*, pp. 83.

### DAY 3

**En acción (cont.)**
- Check homework. 5 MIN.
- Quick Start Review (TE, p. 224). 5 MIN.
- Review *Gramática: Hacer* with Expressions of Time. Play the audio and have students complete *Actividad* 7. Expand with *Más comunicación,* p. R10. 12 MIN.
- Present *Gramática:* Present Subjunctive with Impersonal Expressions, on p. 226. 10 MIN.
- Have students do *Actividad* 8 in writing. 8 MIN.
- Present *Vocabulario* box on p. 227 and have students complete *Actividad* 9 in pairs. 10 MIN.

**Homework Option**
- *Más práctica* Workbook, pp. 86–87. *Cuaderno para hispanohablantes*, pp. 84–85.

### DAY 4

**En acción (cont.)**
- Check homework. 5 MIN.
- Quick Start Review (TE, p. 226). 5 MIN.
- Review the *Gramática,* p. 226 and have students complete *Actividad* 10 in groups. 10 MIN.
- Present *Vocabulario* box and *Nota* on p. 228 and have students complete *Actividades* 11 and 12. 20 MIN.
- Present *Vocabulario* box on p. 229, then have students complete *Actividad* 13 in pairs. 10 MIN.

**Homework Option**
- Have students do *Actividad* 12 as written homework. *Más práctica* Workbook, p. 88. *Cuaderno para hispanohablantes*, p. 86.

### DAY 5

**En acción (cont.)**
- Check homework. 5 MIN.
- Quick Start Review (TE, p. 228). 5 MIN.
- Review *Vocabulario* box on p. 229. Play the audio and do *Actividad* 14 in writing. 10 MIN.
- Have students complete *Actividad* 15 in small groups. 10 MIN.
- Present Speaking Strategy, p. 231, and have students complete Actividad 16 in pairs and possibly present travel plans to the class. 10 MIN.
- Have students complete *Actividad* 17 in small groups. Expand with *Más comunicación,* p. R10. 10 MIN.

**Homework Option**
- Have students complete *Actividad* 16 in writing.

### DAY 6

**En voces: Lectura**
- Check homework. 5 MIN.
- Quick Start Review (TE, p. 232). 5 MIN.
- Review Reading Strategy, p. 232 and have students read silently. 5 MIN.
- Have volunteers read the selection aloud and answer the questions, p. 233. 10 MIN.

**En colores: Cultura y comparaciones**
- Quick Start Review (TE, p. 234). 5 MIN.
- Review Connecting Cultures Strategy, p. 234. 5 MIN.
- Read the selection aloud with students and have volunteers answer the questions, p. 235. 10 MIN.
- Review *En uso* for *Etapa* 3 Exam. 5 MIN.

**Homework Option:**
- Prepare *En uso Actividades* 1–4. Review for *Etapa* 3 Exam.

### DAY 7

**En uso: Repaso y más comunicación**
- Check homework. 5 MIN.
- Quick Start Review (TE, p. 236). 5 MIN.
- Review *Actividades* 1–4 orally. 10 MIN.
- Present Speaking Strategy, p. 238. Do *Actividad* 5 in pairs and *Actividad* 6 in groups. 10 MIN.

**En resumen: Repaso de vocabulario**
- Review grammar questions, etc. as necessary. 5 MIN.
- Complete *Etapa* 3 Exam. 20 MIN.

**En tu propia voz: Escritura**
- Do *Actividad* 7. 5 MIN.

**Homework Option:**
- Review for Unit 3 Comprehensive Test.

### DAY 8

**En resumen: Repaso de vocabulario**
- Quick Start Review (TE, p. 238). 5 MIN.

**En tu propia voz: Escritura**
- Start writing activity, pp. 240–241. 10 MIN.

**Unit 3 Comprehensive Test**
- Review grammar questions, etc. as necessary. 5 MIN.
- Complete Unit 3 Comprehensive Test. 30 MIN.

**Homework Option:**
- Have students complete writing activity. Preview *Unidad* 4 Opener, pp. 240–241.

# Sample Lesson Plan - Block Schedule (90 minutes)

## DAY 1

***Etapa* Opener**
- Quick Start Review (TE, p. 216). 5 MIN.
- Anticipate/Activate prior knowledge: have students look at the *Etapa* Opener and answer *¿Qué ves?* questions. 10 MIN.

**En contexto: Vocabulario**
- Quick Start Review (TE, p. 218). 5 MIN.
- Have students use context and pictures to learn *Etapa* vocabulary. Answer questions, p. 219. 10 MIN.

**En vivo: Diálogo**
- Quick Start Review (TE, p. 220). 5 MIN.
- Review Listening Strategy, p. 220. Play audio or show video for the dialog shown on pp. 220–221. 10 MIN.
- Replay. Read aloud, students taking roles of characters. Ask Comprehension Questions (TE, p. 221). 10 MIN.
- Use Block Scheduling Copymasters for variety. 10 MIN.

**En acción: Vocabulario y Gramática**
- Quick Start Review (TE, p. 222). 5 MIN.
- Play the *En vivo* dialog using the audiovisual resources and have students do *Actividades* 1 and 2 orally. 10 MIN.
- Have students complete *Actividades* 3 and 4 in pairs. 10 MIN.

**Homework Option**
- Video Activities, Unit 3 Resource Book, pp. 125–127.

## DAY 2

**En acción (cont.)**
- Check homework. 5 MIN.
- Quick Start Review (TE, p. 224). 3 MIN.
- Present *Gramática: Hacer* with Expressions of Time, p. 224. 10 MIN.
- Have students do *Actividad* 5 in writing and *Actividad* 6 in pairs. 10 MIN.
- Play the audio and have students complete *Actividad* 7. Expand with *Más comunicación*, p. R10. 12 MIN.
- Quick Start Review (TE, p. 226). 5 MIN.
- Present *Gramática:* Present Subjunctive with Impersonal Expressions on p. 226. 10 MIN.
- Present the *Vocabulario* on p. 227 and have students do *Actividad* 9 in pairs. 10 MIN.
- Have students prepare *Actividad* 10 in small groups. 10 MIN.
- Present *Vocabulario* and *Nota* on p. 228 and have students complete *Actividad* 11 in writing. 10 MIN.
- Have students begin *Actividad* 12 in writing. 5 MIN.

**Homework Option**
- Have students finish *Actividad* 12 in writing. *Más práctica* Workbook, pp. 85–87. *Cuaderno para hispanohablantes*, pp. 83–85.

## DAY 3

**En acción (cont.)**
- Check homework. 5 MIN.
- Quick Start Review (TE, p. 228). 5 MIN.
- Present *Vocabulario* box on p. 229, then have students complete *Actividad* 13 in pairs. 10 MIN.
- Play the audio and do *Actividad* 14 in writing. 10 MIN.
- Have students complete *Actividad* 15 in small groups. 10 MIN.
- Present Speaking Strategy, p. 231. Have students complete *Actividad* 16 in pairs and possibly present travel plans to the class. 10 MIN.
- Have students complete *Actividad* 17 in small groups. Expand with *Más comunicación*, p. R10. 10 MIN.

**En voces: Lectura**
- Review Reading Strategy, p. 232 and have students read silently. 5 MIN.
- Have volunteers read the selection aloud and answer the questions, p. 233. 10 MIN.

**En uso: Repaso y más comunicación**
- Do *Actividades* 1, 2, 3, and 4 orally. 15 MIN.

**Homework Option**
- *Más práctica* Workbook, p. 88. *Cuaderno para hispanohablantes*, pp. 86–88. Review for *Etapa* 3 Exam.

## DAY 4

**En colores: Cultura y comparaciones**
- Check homework. 5 MIN.
- Quick Start Review (TE, p. 234). 5 MIN.
- Review Connecting Cultures Strategy, p. 234. 5 MIN.
- Read selection aloud with students. 10 MIN.
- Have students answer the questions orally. 10 MIN.
- Divide students into small groups and have them role-play *Hazlo tú* activity. 10 MIN.

**En uso: Repaso y más comunicación**
- Present Speaking Strategy, p. 238. Do *Actividad* 5 in pairs and *Actividad* 6. 10 MIN.
- Do *Actividad* 7. 5 MIN.

**En resumen: Repaso de vocabulario**
- Review grammar questions, etc. as necessary. 10 MIN.
- Complete *Etapa* 3 Exam. 20 MIN.

**Homework Option:**
- Review for Unit 3 Comprehensive Test.

## DAY 5

**En resumen: Repaso de vocabulario**
- Quick Start Review (TE, p. 238). 5 MIN.

**En tu propia voz: Escritura**
- Start writing activity, pp. 240–241. 10 MIN.

**Ampliación**
- Use a suggested project, game, or activity (TE pp. 171A–171B). 10 MIN.

**Unit 3 Comprehensive Test**
- Review grammar questions, etc. as necessary. 15 MIN.
- Complete Unit 3 Comprehensive Test. 30 MIN.

**Ampliación**
- Use a suggested project, game, or activity (TE pp. 171A–171B). 20 MIN.

**Homework Option:**
- Finish writing activity and preview *Unidad* 4 Opener, pp. 240–241.

▼ ¡Todos hacen ejercicio con Elena Suárez!

### Etapa Theme

**Describing time periods, talking about health and illness, and giving advice.**

### Grammar Objectives

- **Hacer** with expressions of time
- Subjunctive with impersonal expressions

### Teaching Resource Options

**Print** 

Block Scheduling Copymasters

**Audiovisual**

OHT 99 (Quick Start)
*Canciones* Cassette / CD Songs 5, 8

### Quick Start Review

Discussing the beach

Use OHT 99 or write on board: Name as many things in Spanish as you can in the scene on page 216.

*Answers will vary.*

| | |
|---|---|
| el mar | las olas |
| la arena | los caracoles |

### Teaching Suggestions
**Previewing the Etapa**

- Ask students to study the picture on pp. 216–217.
- Ask students to guess what might be happening in the photo.
- Use the **¿Qué ves?** questions to expand discussion.

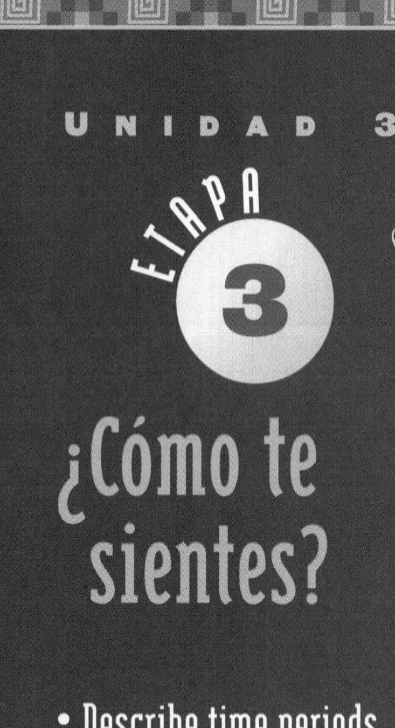

UNIDAD 3

ETAPA 3

# ¿Cómo te sientes?

- Describe time periods
- Talk about health and illness
- Give advice

### ¿Qué ves?

Mira la foto. ¿Qué ves?

1. Haz una lista de todo lo que ves.
2. ¿Dónde están estas personas?
3. ¿Qué hacen?
4. ¿Cómo se llama el programa?

216

### Classroom Management

**Planning Ahead** Prepare students to discuss exercise programs. Ask them if they know of any exercise programs on television or on home videos. Are these programs shot on location or in a studio? Who are the famous exercise leaders today? Have students poll each other to see how many have exercise videos or programs.

**Time Saver** If time is short, have students read the **Etapa** objectives and discuss how they might relate to the picture on pp. 216–217.

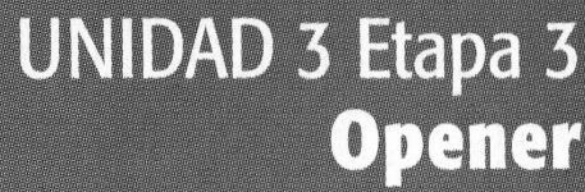


## Culture Highlights

● **BEACHES OF PUERTO RICO** The beaches closest to San Juan are Isla Verde, Condado, and Ocean Park. Other beaches include Luquillo Beach and Dorado Beaches on the Atlantic coast, and Boquerón Beach and Guánica Beach on the Caribbean.

## Supplementary Vocabulary

Introduce exercise and water sports vocabulary.

| | |
|---|---|
| **los abdominales** | sit-ups |
| **las flexiones de barra** | pull-ups |
| **las flexiones en el suelo** | push-ups |
| **patear** | to kick |
| **correr en su lugar** | to run in place |
| **tirar** | to throw |
| **atrapar, agarrar** | to catch |
| **practicar motonáutica** | to jetski |
| **navegar** | to sail |
| **practicar el surfing a vela** | to windsurf |

## Critical Thinking

Have students think about and discuss any advances in medical science they know of: penicillin, for example. What have these new treatments meant for humanity? After discussion, have students choose a medical breakthrough and research the scientist, date of discovery, the diseases it cures, etc. By recording and illustrating their findings they could create an *Enciclopedia de descubrimientos médicos.*

## Teaching All Students

**Extra Help** Have students work in pairs to write additional **¿Qué ves?** questions for other classmates to answer.

### Multiple Intelligences

**Verbal** Ask students to write a short description about one character in the picture. Have them read their description aloud to see if a partner can identify who they are describing.

**Naturalist** Have students describe the weather, the time of day, and the location of the picture. Have them research the plants and wildlife that might live near the beaches of Puerto Rico.

## Block Schedule

**Retention** Ask students to take on the role of a character in the picture. Have them act out what they might say and do. (For additional activities, see **Block Scheduling Copymasters.**)

### Teaching Resource Options

**Print**

Unit 3 Resource Book
Video Activities, p. 125
Videoscript, p. 128
Audioscript, p. 130

**Audiovisual**

**OHT** 93, 94, 99 (Quick Start)
**Audio Program** Cassette 9A / CD 9
**Video Program** Videotape 3, 21:43 / Videodisc 2B

Search Chapter 4, Play to 5
U3E3, En contexto (Vocabulary)

**Technology**

*Intrigas y aventuras* **CD-ROM,** Disc 1

### Quick Start Review

**Adverbs**

Use OHT 99 or write on board: Imagine that Francisco is talking to his doctor. Change the following adjectives to adverbs using **-mente**.

1. (Normal) sigo una dieta balanceada.
2. No como (rápido).
3. Como verduras (frecuente).
4. (Típico) hago ejercicio tres días a la semana.
5. (Desafortunado) no me siento bien hoy.

**Answers**

1. Normalmente
2. rápidamente
3. frecuentemente
4. Típicamente
5. Desafortunadamente

### Language Note

Tell students that **la muñeca** means both *wrist* and *doll*.

# En contexto

## VOCABULARIO

Mira las fotos y las ilustraciones para ver lo que le pasó a Francisco.

**A** **¡Socorro!** Francisco tiene que ir al doctor. Y, ¿sabes qué? El doctor tiene que hacerle **una radiografía** porque no sabe qué **enfermedad** tiene. Se ve en **la cara** que le **duele** alguna parte de su **cuerpo**. Tal vez comió demasiados dulces y tiene dolor de **estómago** o le duele **la cabeza**. Quizás le duele **el codo** o **la mano** porque estaba jugando al tenis. ¿Quién sabe? Le puede doler **la rodilla, la pierna, el tobillo** o **el pie** porque corre mucho.

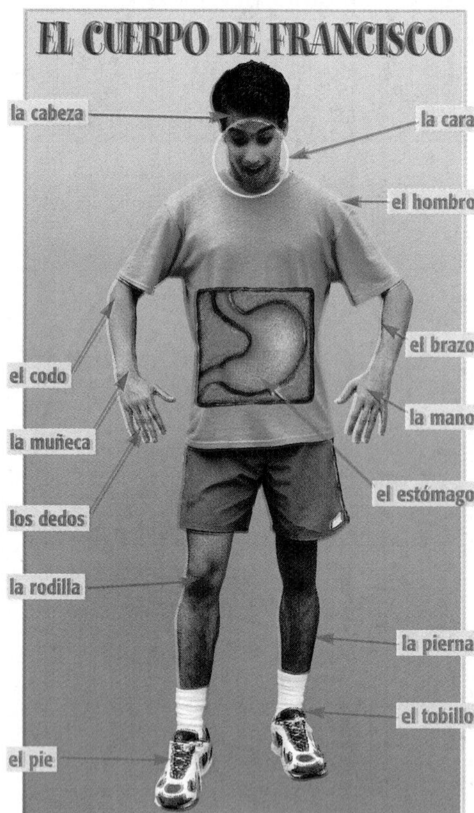

### Classroom Community

**Paired Activity** Have students interview a partner using the **Preguntas personales** on p. 219. Summarize the answers on a chart on the board to find out how many students have worn a **yeso** (cast) and on which part of the body.

**TPR** **«Simón dice...»** Play "Simon says" using parts of the body.

**Group Activity** Write the following verbs and body parts on index cards and have the class match actions to body parts. You can divide the class into 2 teams and make it a contest to see which team finds the most matches. Some cards can be used more than once.

**la nariz, la boca, las orejas, los ojos, los dientes, la cabeza, las manos, los pies**

**respirar, oír, hablar, ver, comer, pensar, escribir, correr, cantar, tocar, caminar**

**B**

El doctor lo revisa y Francisco no tiene problemas en los ojos para ver, ni en **la nariz** para **respirar,** ni en **las orejas** ni en **el oído** para escuchar. La boca y **los dientes** están bien. Quiere decir que no comió demasiados dulces. No le duele ni **la garganta** ni **el cuello** tampoco.

**C**

¡Ay! Cuando el doctor le toca **el brazo,** le duele mucho. Parece que le duelen **el hombro, la muñeca** y **los dedos** porque se cayó mientras jugaba al tenis. Así que en **el consultorio** le ponen **un yeso.**

el yeso

**D**

También le dan **una receta** para mejorarse más rápido. Pero pobre Francisco, ¡no le gusta tomar **las pastillas**!

## Preguntas personales

1. ¿Alguna vez te sacaron una radiografía? ¿De qué parte del cuerpo?
2. ¿Alguna vez te pusieron un yeso? ¿Por qué?
3. ¿Qué haces si te duele la garganta?
4. ¿Cómo puedes ayudar a alguien que tiene un yeso en el brazo?
5. ¿Recuerdas alguna vez que gritaste «socorro»? Explica.



## Teaching Suggestions
### Introducing Vocabulary

- Have students look at pp. 218–219. Use OHT 93 and 94 and Audiocassette 9A / CD 9 to present the vocabulary.
- Ask the Comprehension Questions in the margin of the Teacher's Edition. You may write the questions on the board and have students work in small groups to answer them.
- Introduce the characters and the setting: **¿Dónde está Francisco? ¿Qué le pasa a Francisco?**

## Comprehension Questions

1. ¿El dcotor tiene que hacerle una radiografía a Francisco? **(Sí)**
2. ¿Tenemos dos codos? **(Sí)**
3. ¿Tenemos dos cuellos? **(No)**
4. Cuando quieres responder en clase, ¿levantas la mano o el pie? **(la mano)**
5. Cuando juegas al fútbol, ¿usas las manos o los pies? **(los pies)**
6. Si quieres levantar pesas, ¿usas los brazos o los dientes? **(los brazos)**
7. ¿Se lleva un arete en el cuello o en la oreja? **(en la oreja)**
8. ¿Qué le duelen a Francisco? **(el brazo, el hombro, la muñeca y los dedos)**
9. ¿Qué le pusieron en el brazo? **(un yeso)**
10. ¿Qué le da el doctor a Francisco para recuperarse más rápido? **(una receta)**

## Culture Highlights

**HEALTH CONSCIOUSNESS** exists in Puerto Rico as it does in the U.S. Some of the more popular exercise activities include **caminar, alzar/levantar pesas, bailar, montar en bicicleta, correr, hacer aeróbicos,** and **nadar.**

## Teaching All Students

**Extra Help** Point to parts of the body and ask students to identify body part, e.g., **¿Es la boca o la nariz?**

**Native Speakers** Have Spanish-speaking students describe an experience they have had in a doctor's office or at a hospital. Did they speak Spanish or English? Were there translators available?

**Multiple Intelligences**

**Musical/Rhythmic** You can review the parts of the body by singing and making gestures to the song, **Cabeza, hombros, rodillas, pies, rodillas, pies. (Repeat) Y ojos, orejas, boca y nariz. Cabeza, hombros, rodillas, pies, rodillas, pies.**

**Naturalist** Ask students to state what each part of our body is for, e.g., **La nariz es para respirar...**

## Block Schedule

**Change of Pace** Have your students count how many classmates have broken a bone (or bones) in their body. What part of the body was broken the most? How were the bones broken, from playing, working, or from an accident?

## Teaching Resource Options

**Print** 

Block Scheduling Copymasters
Unit 3 Resource Book
Video Activities, pp. 126–127
Videoscript, pp. 128–129
Audioscript, p. 130

**Audiovisual**

OHT 97, 98, 99 (Quick Start)
Audio Program Cassette 9A / CD 9
Video Program Videotape 3, 25:35 / Videodisc 2B

Search Chapter 5, Play to End
U3E3, En vivo (Dialog)

**Technology**

*Intrigas y aventuras* CD-ROM, Disc 1

## Quick Start Review

**En contexto** vocabulary

Use **OHT** 99 or write on board: Name the body part these items suggest.

las gafas de sol — el sombrero
el anillo — los zapatos
el peine

**Answers**
los ojos, la mano, el pelo, la cabeza, los pies

## Teaching Suggestions
### Presenting the Dialog

- Introduce the characters and the setting: Francisco accompanies his uncle, aunt, and younger cousin Susana to the beach in Puerto Rico.
- Have students discuss the locations of the different parts of the dialog. What gives them clues to guess the different locations?

# En vivo
## DIÁLOGO

Elena

Francisco

Tía Julia

Tío Rodrigo

Susana

**PARA ESCUCHAR • STRATEGY: LISTENING**

**Listen sympathetically** Listening sympathetically is an important part of being a good listener. Because of an accident in this scene, you can hear many ways of expressing pain or concern—your own or someone else's. What expressions for pain or concern do you hear?

## El día del show

1 ▶ Elena: ¡Bienvenidos!
Francisco: Gracias. Te presento a mi familia.
Tía Julia: Encantada.
Tío Rodrigo: Mucho gusto.
Susana: Hola.

5 ▶ Elena: ¡Ahí! Me duele ahí.
Tío Rodrigo: Elena, es necesario que te examine el tobillo.
Elena: Ay, ¡qué pena! Hace cuatro años que grabamos este programa, y ni un accidente.

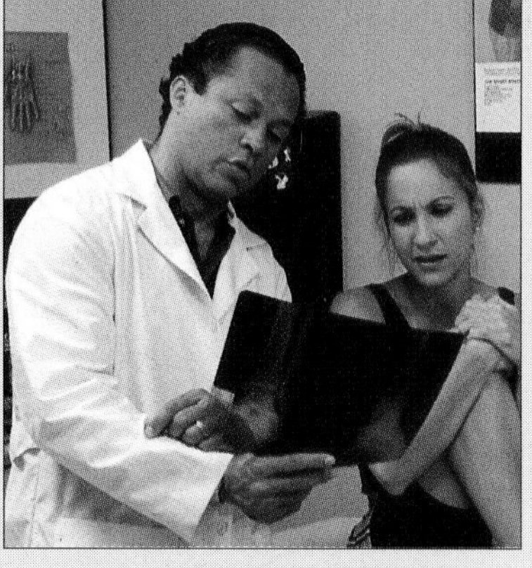

6 ▶ *(En el consultorio)*
Tío Rodrigo: Elena, tienes una fractura de tobillo. Se ve muy claro en la radiografía.
Elena: ¿Una fractura? ¿Qué voy a hacer?
Tío Rodrigo: Voy a ponerte un yeso. Es necesario que el tobillo se recupere.

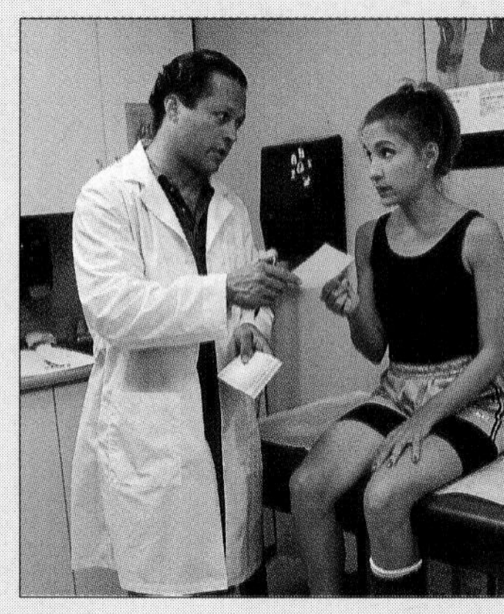

7 ▶ Tío Rodrigo: El tobillo te va a doler mucho hoy y mañana. Esta receta es para unas pastillas. Son para el dolor. Y es importante que no camines por unos días.



## Classroom Community

**TPR** Working in groups of five, have students take on the role of each character and read the dialog aloud. Encourage them to use lots of expressions, gestures, and actions to act out the dialog.

**Portfolio** Ask students if they have ever broken an arm/leg, had to go to the emergency room, fallen down and hurt themselves, or been in a car accident. If so, ask them to explain in their journal. They can also describe an accident that happened to someone else.

**Rubric: Writing**

| Criteria | Scale |
| --- | --- |
| Logical sentences | 1 2 3 4 5 |
| Vocabulary use | 1 2 3 4 5 |
| Accuracy | 1 2 3 4 5 |

A = 13–15 pts.
B = 10–12 pts.
C = 7–9 pts.
D = 4–6 pts.
F = < 4 pts.

2► *(Comienza el show.)*
Elena: Gracias por venir a participar. Vengan, les explico todo. Es importante que ustedes entiendan lo que van a hacer.

3► Elena: ¡Bienvenidos al Show de Elena Suárez! ¿Están todos listos? ¡Muy bien! Primero, vamos a estirar el cuerpo. Comenzamos con el cuello. Ahora los hombros. Las piernas. Estiren las manos hacia el pie derecho. Respiren.

4► *(Elena se cae.)*
Tío Rodrigo: Déjame ver. Soy doctor.
Elena: Ay, me duele mucho.
Tío Rodrigo: A ver. ¿Dónde? ¿Es la rodilla o el tobillo?
Elena: Es el tobillo.

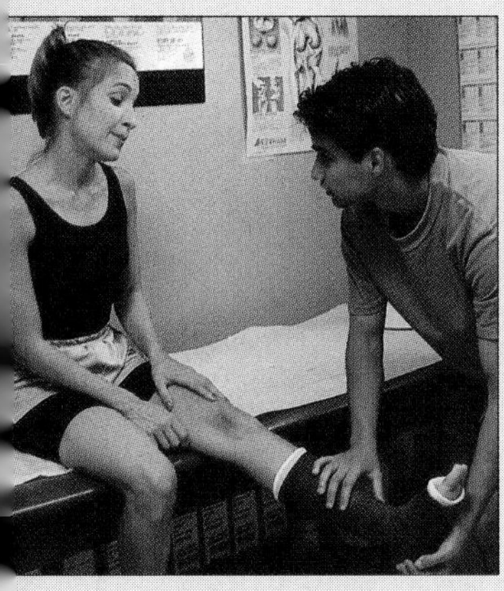

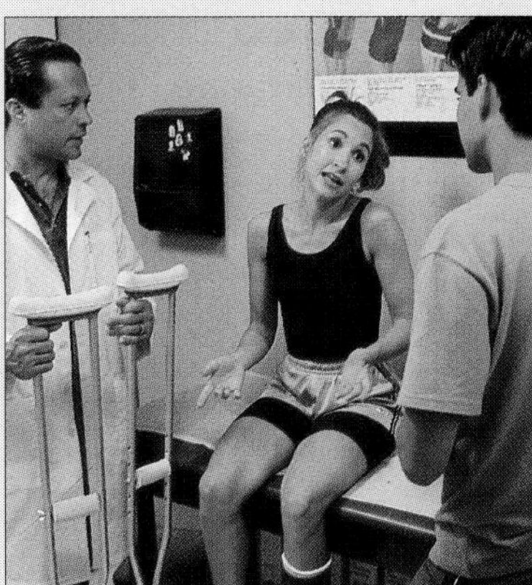

8► *(Alguien toca a la puerta.)*
Tío Rodrigo: Pasa, Francisco.
Francisco: Estamos todos en la sala de espera. Estamos muy preocupados. ¿Cómo estás?
Elena: No muy bien. Me lastimé.

9► Elena: Francisco, lo siento mucho. Es una pena que no puedas participar en mi programa. Pero podemos hacer la entrevista por teléfono mañana.
Francisco: Sí. Muchas gracias. Pero Susana está triste. Ella quería ser estrella.

10► Elena: No hay problema. Después de recuperarme voy a seguir con mi programa. Susana y toda la familia pueden participar.
Tío Rodrigo: Gracias, Elena.
Francisco: Bueno, nos hablamos mañana.



## Teaching All Students

**Extra Help** Ask students to list the instructions given by the doctor (Tío Rodrigo) to Elena.

**Native Speakers** Ask Spanish speakers to list expressions of sympathy they might say to a person if he/she were injured or sick.

**Multiple Intelligences**

**Intrapersonal** Ask students to take on the role of Elena in the dialog. Have them write a short description of how they feel (how Elena feels) in each scene.

## Video Synopsis

Use the video, audiocassette, or CD to present the dialog. The video version offers expanded language opportunities. Francisco goes to the beach with his uncle, aunt, and cousin to participate in Elena's exercise show. For a transcript of the video dialog, see p. 215B.

## Comprehension Questions

1. ¿Se estira Elena antes de hacer los ejercicios? **(Sí)**
2. ¿Estira las piernas primero? **(No)**
3. ¿Se lastimó Elena? **(Sí)**
4. ¿Es doctor Tío Rodrigo? **(Sí)**
5. ¿Le duele la rodilla o el tobillo? **(el tobillo)**
6. ¿Necesita Elena un yeso o una operación? **(un yeso)**
7. ¿Va a recuperarse del tobillo en dos horas o le va a doler por dos días? **(Le va a doler por dos días.)**
8. ¿Por qué le da una receta? **(para el dolor)**
9. ¿Por qué está triste Susana? **(Quería ser estrella.)**
10. ¿Qué va a hacer Elena después de recuperarse? **(seguir con el programa)**

## Language Notes

Point out to students that Tío Rodrigo refers to himself as a **doctor**, his title. As a profession, the word is often **médico**.

## Gestures

Have students identify any gestures they recognize in the photos. Elena's facial expressions are especially helpful to guess what is happening. Ask what gestures they see in frames 3–5. What do they think happened between frames 3 and 4?

## Block Schedule

**Change of Pace** Before presenting the actual dialog, break the class into small groups and have them cover the printed dialog on pp. 220–221. Assign each group several frames and have them create their own dialog to match the action in the photos. Then have them compare the dialog they created themselves to the printed version. (For additional activities, see **Block Scheduling Copymasters**.)

### Teaching Resource Options

**Print** 

Block Scheduling Copymasters
Unit 3 Resource Book
Video Activities, pp. 126–127
Videoscript, pp. 128–129
Audioscript, p. 130

**Audiovisual** 

**OHT** 100 (Quick Start)
**Audio Program** Cassette 9A / CD 9
**Video Program** Videotape 3, 13:08 / Videodisc 2B

**Technology** 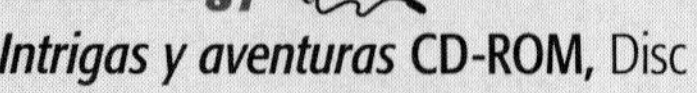

*Intrigas y aventuras* **CD-ROM,** Disc 1

### Quick Start Review

**Preterite**

Use OHT 100 or write on board: Conjugate the verb in each sentence in the preterite tense to tell what happened in the dialog.

1. **Francisco y su familia (ir) al programa de Elena.**
2. **Primero ellos (estirar) el cuerpo.**
3. **Elena (lastimarse).**
4. **Tío Rodrigo le (poner) un yeso.**
5. **Francisco (decidir) hacer la entrevista por teléfono.**

**Answers**
1. fueron; 2. estiraron; 3. se lastimó; 4. puso; 5. decidió

**Objective:** Controlled practice
Listening comprehension

**Answers**
*Answers will vary.*
1. "Ay, me duele mucho."
2. "Déjame ver. Soy doctor."
3. "Ay, ¡qué pena! Hace cuatro años que grabamos este programa, y ni un accidente."
4. "Elena, tienes una fractura de tobillo. Se ve muy claro en la radiografía."
5. "Esta receta es para unas pastillas. Son para el dolor."
6. "Después de recuperarme voy a seguir con mi programa. Susana y toda la familia pueden participar."

# En acción
## VOCABULARIO Y GRAMÁTICA

**OBJECTIVES**
- Describe time periods
- Talk about health and illness
- Give advice

ACTIVIDAD 1 

### ¿Cómo lo sabes?

**Escuchar/Escribir** Todas estas oraciones son ciertas. Busca las líneas del diálogo que lo muestren. *(Hint: Find the lines of the dialog that prove these sentences are true.)*

**modelo**

*A Elena le gusta que la familia de Francisco vaya a participar en el programa.*
*«Gracias por venir a participar.»*

1. Elena tiene un problema.
2. Tío Rodrigo ayuda a Elena.
3. A Elena no le ocurren muchos accidentes en su programa.
4. La radiografía confirma las malas noticias.
5. Tío Rodrigo le da algo para el dolor.
6. Elena tiene una solución para el problema de Susana.

**NOTA CULTURAL**

**Los huracanes** Por la situación geográfica de la isla de Puerto Rico, llegan huracanes allí. Después del huracán Georges, llegó ayuda de muchas partes –incluyendo la Cruz Roja y la Guardia Nacional de Estados Unidos.

ACTIVIDAD 2 

### ¿Quién?

**Escuchar/Hablar** Francisco, Elena y la familia de Francisco están charlando. Según lo que ya sabes de ellos, decide quién hace cada comentario. *(Hint: Who would say this?)*

Elena

Francisco

Tía Julia

Tío Rodrigo

Susana

1. «Fuimos al consultorio de mi tío.»
2. «¿Puedo hablar con Elena Suárez, por favor? Habla… »
3. «Voy a recetarte una medicina para el dolor.»
4. «Voy a salir en la tele.»
5. «Me duele un montón.»
6. «Ay mi'ja, no corras por la playa.»
7. «No puedo hacer el show por alrededor de un mes.»
8. «Primo, ¿ya hablaste con la estrella?»



### Classroom Management 

**Streamlining** Have students add to the list of activities in **Actividad 4** and write them on the board. As a class determine what part of the body hurts in each situation.

**Peer Review** Have students work in pairs to review the content of the dialog. Have them tell the story in their own words. As a variation, they can tell the story from Susana's or Tío Rodrigo's point of view.

**Planning Ahead** As a review before starting **Actividad 3**, write the numbers 1–6 on the board with a blank line next to each. Have students go to the board and write the corresponding Spanish word(s) for the action being shown in each photo. As an alternative, orally quiz the students on how to say each action being depicted before starting.

- *Use* ***hacer*** *with expressions of time*
- *Use the subjunctive with impersonal expressions*

## Actividad 3 — Los quehaceres en tu casa

**Hablar** Con un(a) compañero(a), habla de quién hace los quehaceres en tu casa. *(Hint: Talk about who does these chores.)*

**modelo**

**Compañero(a):** *¿Quién plancha la ropa?*

**Tú:** *Yo plancho la ropa. (Toda la familia plancha la ropa.)*

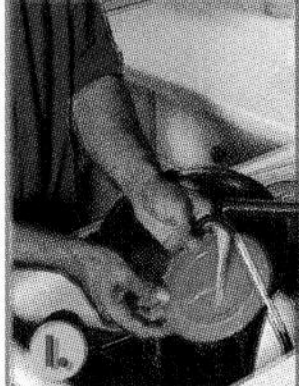

## Actividad 4 — ¿Qué te duele?

**Hablar** Imagínate que algo le duele a tu compañero(a) a causa de las siguientes actividades. Descríbele lo que le duele. *(Hint: Describe what hurts.)*

**modelo**

*Corrí diez kilómetros ayer.*

**Compañero(a):** *Corrí diez kilómetros ayer.*

**Tú:** *Te duelen las piernas.*

**Nota**

When you want to describe what hurts, use **doler** **(o → ue). Doler** is always used with indirect object pronouns: **me, te, le, nos,** and **les,** to tell who is hurting.

¿Te **duele** mucho? *Does it* ***hurt*** *(you) a lot?*

Sí, me **duele** el tobillo. *Yes, my ankle* ***hurts*** *(me).*

1. Caminé en la arena caliente sin zapatos.
2. Acabo de leer un libro largo.
3. Me caí de mi bicicleta.
4. Yo escuchaba la radio muy alto.
5. Escribí en la computadora por muchas horas ayer.
6. Comí demasiado anoche.
7. No me puse loción protectora y hacía mucho sol.
8. Tuve un accidente cuando estaba jugando al fútbol.



### Teaching Suggestions

- **Actividad 3** recycles vocabulary from the previous **Etapa**. As a follow-up, have students tell which parts of the body they use for each household chore in each picture. As a variation on **Actividad 3**, have students describe yesterday's chores using past tenses.
- Before doing **Actividad 4**, be sure to present and practice the verb **doler**.

**Objective:** Controlled practice
Listening comprehension

**Answers**

1. Francisco
2. Francisco
3. Tío Rodrigo
4. Susana
5. Elena
6. Tía Julia
7. Elena
8. Susana

**Objective:** Transitional practice
Discussing household chores

Household chores

**Answers**

1. ¿Quién lava los platos?
   Yo lavo los platos. (Toda la familia lava los platos.)
2. ¿Quién sirve la comida?
   Yo sirvo la comida. (Toda la familia sirve la comida.)
3. ¿Quién corta el césped?
   Yo corto el césped. (Toda la familia corta el césped.)
4. ¿Quién barre el piso?
   Yo barro el piso. (Toda la familia barre el piso.)
5. ¿Quién pasa la aspiradora?
   Yo paso la aspiradora. (Toda la familia pasa la aspiradora.)
6. ¿Quién saca la basura?
   Yo saco la basura. (Toda la familia saca la basura.)

**Objective:** Transitional practice
**Doler**/parts of body

**Answers**

*Answers will vary.*

1. Te duelen los pies.
2. Te duelen los ojos.
3. Te duele la cabeza.
4. Te duelen los oídos.
5. Te duelen las manos.
6. Te duele el estómago.
7. Te duele la espalda.
8. Te duele la pierna.

### Block Schedule

**TPR** Have students draw/cut out pictures of people doing household chores. Hold up pictures and ask students who is responsible for each chore in their homes. (For additional activities, see **Block Scheduling Copymasters**.)

### Teaching All Students

**Extra Help** Have students work in pairs to prioritize the household chores in **Actividad 3** from the most important to the least important to them.

**Challenge** Based on the 8 statements in **Actividad 4**, have students state what should be done in each instance, e.g., 1. **Debes descansar en el sofá.**

**Multiple Intelligences**

**Verbal** Have students describe what is hurting them, e.g., **Me duele la garganta.** Their partner prescribes a treatment, e.g., **No debes hablar tanto.**

**Interpersonal** Ask students to list three things that they have done. Two statements should be true and one should be false. Have the class determine which is the false statement.

## Teaching Resource Options

**Print** 

*Más práctica* Workbook PE, p. 85
*Cuaderno para hispanohablantes* PE, p. 83
Block Scheduling Copymasters
Unit 3 Resource Book
*Más práctica* Workbook TE, p. 107
*Cuaderno para hispanohablantes* TE, p. 113
Information Gap Activities, p. 119
Audioscript, p. 130

**Audiovisual** 

OHT 100 (Quick Start)
Audio Program Cassette 9A / CD 9

**Technology** 

*Intrigas y aventuras* CD-ROM, Disc 1

## Quick Start Review

Household chores

Use OHT 100 or write on board: Imagine you are planning your Saturday morning. Write a list of four chores to do and the time it takes to do each one. Write out the numbers when stating the time. For example:

barrer el piso    quince minutos

*Answers will vary.*

## Teaching Suggestions

### Presenting Hacer with Expressions of Time

- Inform students that when asking a question, they can use either **¿Cuánto tiempo hace que** + verb? or **¿Hace cuánto tiempo que** + verb? Both mean the same.
- For an expansion of **Actividad 5**, have students form both a question (using **¿Cuánto tiempo hace que** + present tense?) and a statement (using **Hace** + period of time + **que** + present tense) for each item.
- Students may need to review body parts before doing **Actividad 7**; refer them to pp. 218–219.

## Hacer with Expressions of Time

In Spanish, if someone asks, "How long has this been going on?" or "How long has it been?" you answer with the verb **hacer:**

**hace** + **the period of time** + **que** + **the present tense**

Ay, Elena, **hace cuatro años que quiero** venir a tu programa.
*Oh, Elena, **I've been wanting** to come to your program **for four years.***

Ay, doctor, **hace una hora que** lo **espero.**
*Oh, doctor, **I've been waiting** for you **for an hour.***

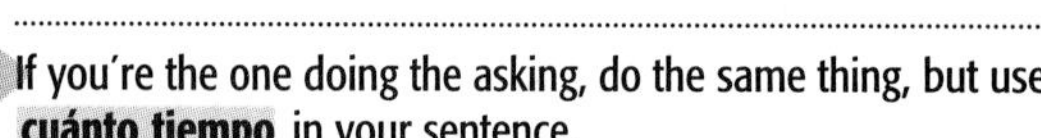

If you're the one doing the asking, do the same thing, but use **cuánto tiempo** in your sentence.

**¿Cuánto tiempo** + **hace** + **que** + **the present tense?**

**¿Cuánto tiempo hace que quieres** venir al programa?
***How long have you been wanting** to come to the program?*

If you are talking about the **past,** use the **preterite** and **hace** to say *ago.*

**hace** + **the period of time** + **que** + **the preterite**

**Hace un año que fui** a Puerto Rico.
***I went** to Puerto Rico **a year ago.***

To say *ago,* you can also put the verb first. When the verb comes first, you do not need **que.** Use

**the preterite** + **hace** + **the period of time**

La **conocí hace tres meses**.
***I met** her **three months ago.***

This construction refers to events that happened some time **ago.**

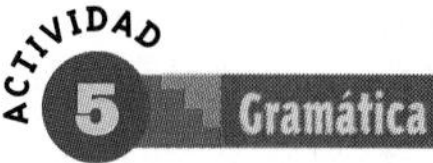

### Actividad 5 Gramática

## ¿Cuánto tiempo hace...?

**Hablar/Escribir** ¿Cuánto tiempo hace que las siguientes personas hacen estas actividades? *(Hint: Tell how long these people have been doing these activities.)*

**modelo**

*Susana: saber leer (dos años)*
*Hace dos años que Susana sabe leer.*

1. Francisco: estar en Puerto Rico (dos semanas)
2. nosotros: vivir aquí (cinco meses)
3. tú: estudiar español (más de un año)
4. Elena Suárez: grabar el programa sin accidentes (cuatro años)
5. yo: estar en clase (diez minutos)
6. la familia de Francisco: mirar el programa de Elena (tres años)
7. ustedes: hablar por teléfono (cuarenta minutos)
8. yo: conocer a Javier (cuatro años)

**MÁS PRÁCTICA** *cuaderno* p. 85
**PARA HISPANOHABLANTES** *cuaderno* p. 83



## Classroom Community

**Paired Activity** Have students work in pairs to determine who has the most experience in the following situations. They should ask each other the following questions: **¿Cuánto tiempo hace que estudias español? ¿Cuánto tiempo hace que vives en este pueblo/esta ciudad? ¿Cuánto tiempo hace que asistes a esta escuela?**

**Storytelling** Ask students to tell a story about a time when they witnessed an accident. The first sentence should use **hacer** with time. Have them describe what happened, if anyone was hurt, and if anyone had to go to the hospital or see a doctor.

**TPR** Have students act out something that hurts them. Others give advice on how to relieve the pain.

## ¿Cuándo lo hiciste?

**Hablar** Habla con un(a) compañero(a) sobre cuándo hiciste las siguientes actividades. Usa **hace ... que** y el pretérito para contestar. *(Hint: Tell how long ago you did the following.)*

**modelo**

*comer pizza*

**Compañero(a):** *¿Cuánto tiempo hace que comiste pizza? (¿Hace cuánto tiempo que comiste pizza?)*

**Tú:** *Hace tres días que comí pizza. (Comí pizza hace tres días.)*

1. bailar
2. comprar un regalo
3. hacer la tarea
4. comer comida china
5. ver una buena película
6. ayudar a alguien
7. limpiar tu cuarto
8. ir a una fiesta
9. practicar un deporte
10. estar enfermo(a)

## En el consultorio

**Escuchar/Escribir** Escucha lo que dicen los pacientes y su doctora. ¿Hace cuánto tiempo que tienen el problema y qué parte(s) del cuerpo les afecta? *(Hint: Tell how long these people have had the problem and which body part is affected.)*

1. ______ ______
2. ______ ______
3. ______ ______
4. ______ ______

| | |
|---|---|
| un día | el estómago |
| dos días | los dientes |
| tres días | los oídos y la cabeza |
| cinco días | la muñeca |
| una semana | la pierna |

### NOTA CULTURAL

**La celebración de Carnaval** Cada viernes por la noche en San Juan la gente disfruta de la vida nocturna. Además de los viernes, se conoce San Juan por su famosa celebración de Carnaval. Como parte de esta tradición de la cultura española y africana, mucha gente se pone máscaras.

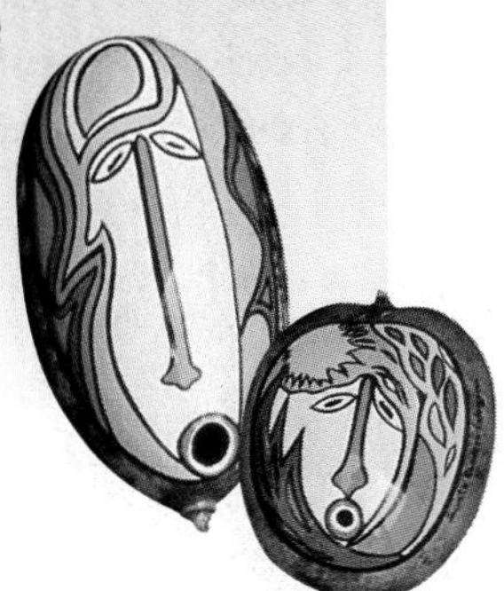



## Teaching All Students

**Extra Help** Have students complete the following sentences with either a present or preterite tense verb, depending on the intended message: **Hace un minuto que... Hace una hora que..., Hace un día que..., Hace una semana que..., Hace un año que....**

**Multiple Intelligences**

**Verbal** Ask students to share how long ago they completed the following activities: **comer una hamburguesa, leer una novela, ir al cine, comprar algo nuevo, mirar un buen programa en la televisión, hablar por teléfono, caminar por su barrio, escuchar el radio.**

**Intrapersonal** Ask students to write four things that they did a while ago using the expression **hace... que**.

**Objective:** Controlled practice
**Hacer** + expressions of time

### Answers

1. Hace dos semanas que Francisco está en Puerto Rico.
2. Hace cinco meses que vivimos aquí.
3. Hace más de un año que (tú) estudias español.
4. Hace cuatro años que Elena Suárez graba el programa sin accidente.
5. Hace diez minutos que (yo) estoy en clase.
6. Hace tres años que la familia de Francisco mira el programa de Elena.
7. Hace cuarenta minutos que (ustedes) hablan por teléfono.
8. Hace cuatro años que (yo) conozco a Javier.

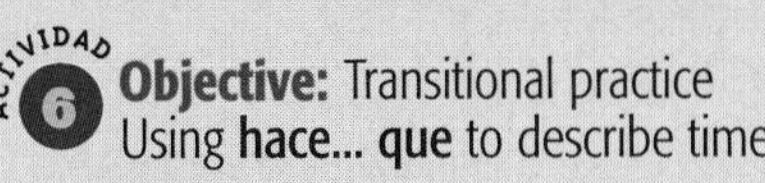

**Objective:** Transitional practice
Using **hace... que** to describe time
Preterite

### Answers

*Answers will vary.*

1. ¿Cuánto tiempo hace que bailaste? (¿Hace cuánto tiempo que bailaste?) Hace [dos meses] que bailé. (Bailé hace [dos meses].)
2. compraste [...] compré
3. hiciste [...] hice
4. comiste [...] comí
5. viste [...] vi
6. ayudaste [...] ayudé
7. limpiaste [...] limpié
8. fuiste [...] fui
9. practicaste [...] practiqué
10. estuviste [...] estuve

ACTIVIDAD 7

**Objective:** Transitional practice
Listening comprehension/**Hacer** + expressions of time

### Answers (See script, p. 215B.)

1. Hace una semana que tiene el problema. Le duele la muñeca.
2. Hace dos días... Le duelen los dientes.
3. Hace tres días... Le duelen los oídos y la cabeza.
4. Hace cinco días... Le duele la pierna.

## Cross Cultural Connections

Have students describe any holidays or events where masks or costumes are used in the U.S. Have them compare this tradition to the **Carnaval** tradition in San Juan.

## Block Schedule

**Change of Pace** Encourage students to research health and fitness opportunities in Puerto Rico via the Internet or with a local travel agency. (For additional activities, see **Block Scheduling Copymasters**.)

## Teaching Resource Options

**Print** 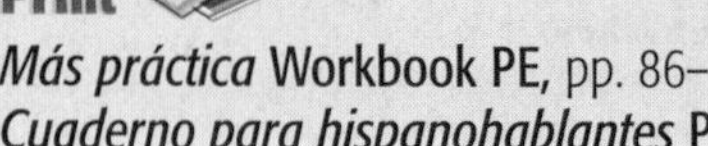

*Más práctica* Workbook PE, pp. 86–87
*Cuaderno para hispanohablantes* PE, pp. 84–85
Block Scheduling Copymasters
Unit 3 Resource Book
*Más práctica* Workbook TE, pp. 108–109
*Cuaderno para hispanohablantes* TE, pp. 114–115

**Audiovisual**

OHT 100 (Quick Start)

**Technology**

*Intrigas y aventuras* CD-ROM, Disc 1

## Quick Start Review

Familiar negative commands

Use OHT 100 or write on board: Write the negative **tú** command for the following verbs.

1. correr
2. dormir
3. ir
4. salir
5. ser
6. seguir

**Answers**

1. no corras; 2. no duermas; 3. no vayas; 4. no salgas; 5. no seas; 6. no sigas

## Teaching Suggestions
### Presenting the Subjunctive with Impersonal Expressions

- The subjunctive can sometimes be overwhelming for students. Try to present this new "mood" as a way to express your opinion about an action.
- Remind students that the word *indicative* applies to all the verb tenses they have learned thus far except commands.
- Explain that since the subjunctive uses the same stem as the present indicative **yo** form, any verbs that have an irregular **yo** form will also have an irregular subjunctive form. For example, **Yo vengo** and **Es necesario que ella venga a ver al doctor.**
- Point out that **Es necesario** + the subjunctive is a way to give advice to someone.

## GRAMÁTICA: The Subjunctive with Impersonal Expressions

**¿RECUERDAS?** *p. 182* You already know how to form usted commands. You form the subjunctive the same way. For -ar verbs, take the **yo** form, drop the **o,** and add endings with -e. For -er and -ir verbs, take the **yo** form, drop the **o,** and add endings with -a.

You use the indicative to make a plain statement of fact. You use the subjunctive after verbs and expressions that involve uncertainty.

**Indicative:**
**Haces** ejercicio.
***You do** exercise.*

**Subjunctive:**
**Es necesario que hagas** ejercicio.
***It is necessary that you do** exercise.*

**Impersonal expressions,** such as **es necesario que,** influence the verb and show uncertainty. These expressions are often followed by the subjunctive.

**The present subjunctive of regular verbs**

| | -ar hablar | -er comer | -ir escribir |
|---|---|---|---|
| yo | hable | coma | escriba |
| tú | hables | comas | escribas |
| él, ella, usted | hable | coma | escriba |
| nosotros(as) | hablemos | comamos | escribamos |
| vosotros(as) | habléis | comáis | escribáis |
| ellos, ellas, ustedes | hablen | coman | escriban |

Remember that, as with usted commands, you have to change the spelling for some verbs to keep the pronunciation the same.

**llegar** → **llegue**  **buscar** → **busque**  **cruzar** → **cruce**

### ACTIVIDAD 8 Gramática
## ¿Es necesario?

**Hablar/Escribir** Presenta tu opinión, haciendo oraciones afirmativas o negativas con **es necesario que** y el subjuntivo.
*(Hint: Give your opinion.)*

**modelo**

*yo: cocinar bien*
*Es necesario que (yo) cocine bien.*
*(No es necesario que yo cocine bien.)*

1. los profesores: hacer la clase divertida
2. los hijos: ayudar en casa
3. yo: ganar mucho dinero
4. mi doctor(a): tener buena personalidad
5. los estudiantes: estudiar mucho
6. nosotros: trabajar
7. tu amigo(a) (*nombre*): asistir a la escuela regularmente
8. yo: tener muchos(as) amigos(as)

**MÁS PRÁCTICA** *cuaderno* pp. 86–88

**PARA HISPANOHABLANTES** *cuaderno* pp. 84–86



## Classroom Community

**Group Activity** Ask small groups of students to list 9–10 things that are necessary in order to be a good student. They should begin each statement with **Es necesario que...** Share the results with the class.

**Portfolio** Based on the students' responsibilities at home, ask them to write 4–5 sentences stating what they need to do: **Es necesario que yo...**

**Rubric: Writing**

| Criteria | Scale |
|---|---|
| Vocabulary use | 1 2 3 4 5 |
| Accuracy | 1 2 3 4 5 |
| Logical organization | 1 2 3 4 5 |

A = 13–15 pts.
B = 10–12 pts.
C = 7–9 pts.
D = 4–6 pts.
F = < 4 pts.

## ¿Qué le recomiendas?

**Hablar/Leer** Tu compañero(a) te cuenta un problema. ¿Qué le recomiendas? Usa **es necesario que** y el subjuntivo en tu respuesta. *(Hint: Give advice.)*

**modelo**

**Compañero(a):** *Me lastimé el brazo. (tomarte una radiografía / respirar profundamente)*

**Tú:** *Es necesario que te tomes una radiografía.*

1. Me duele la cabeza. (ponerte un yeso / tomar aspirina)
2. Tengo tos y fiebre. (estirarte para estar más cómodo(a) / tomar medicina)
3. Tengo una infección. (tomar jugo / tomar medicina)
4. ¡Socorro! Me corté el dedo y me lastimé. (ponerte presión / tomar vitaminas)
5. Estoy resfriado(a). (tomar sopa de pollo / hacer mucho ejercicio)
6. Tengo gripe y me van a dar una inyección. (gritar / no llorar)

### Vocabulario

**Las enfermedades**

**el dolor de cabeza** *headache*
**estar resfriado(a)** *to have a cold*
**la fiebre** *fever*
**la gripe** *flu*
**la infección** *infection*
**la tos** *cough*

**Para mejorarse**

**la aspirina** *aspirin*
**la inyección** *injection*
**la medicina** *medicine*

**¿Cómo te sientes?**

**cómodo(a)** *comfortable*
**cortarse** *to cut oneself*
**gritar** *to scream*
**lastimarse** *to hurt oneself*
**llorar** *to cry*

¿Qué tienes y cómo te vas a mejorar?

## Para mantenerse sanos

**Hablar/Escribir** En grupos pequeños, hagan un póster con diez oraciones sobre lo que tú y tus amigos(as) necesitan hacer para **no** ir al consultorio. *(Hint: List what you need to do to avoid going to the doctor's office.)*

Para no ir al consultorio...
Es necesario que uses un casco.
Es necesario que hagamos ejercicio frecuentemente.
Es necesario que tomemos jugos.


MÁS COMUNICACIÓN p. R10



### Teaching Suggestions

Present and practice the vocabulary in the box on page 227 before doing **Actividades 9** and **10**.

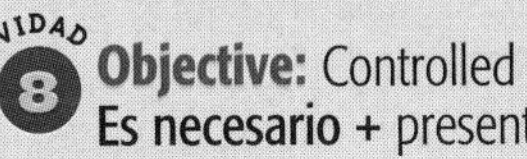

**Objective:** Controlled practice
**Es necesario** + present subjunctive

**Answers**
1. (No) Es necesario que los profesores hagan la clase divertida.
2. … los hijos ayuden en casa.
3. … (yo) gane mucho dinero.
4. … mi doctor(a) tenga una buena personalidad.
5. … los estudiantes estudien mucho.
6. … nosotros trabajemos mucho.
7. … tu amigo(a) [nombre] asista a la escuela regularmente.
8. … (yo) tenga muchos(as) amigos(as).

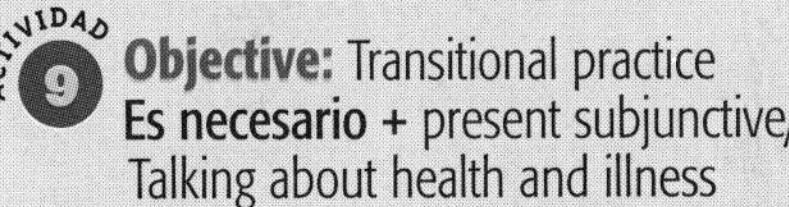

**Objective:** Transitional practice
**Es necesario** + present subjunctive/ Talking about health and illness

**Answers**
1. Es necesario que tomes aspirina.
2. Es necesario que tomes medicina.
3. Es necesario que tomes medicina.
4. Es necesario que te pongas presión.
5. Es necesario que tomes sopa de pollo.
6. Es necesario que no llores.

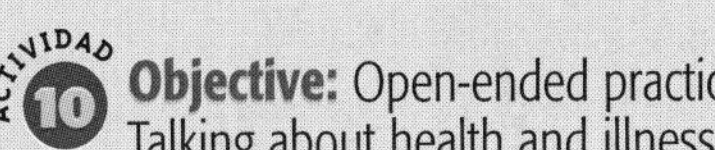

**Objective:** Open-ended practice
Talking about health and illness

### Quick Wrap-up

While students are working on **Actividad 10**, write these statements on the board:

**pedir información de las universidades**
**leer toda la información**
**visitar una variedad de universidades**
**hablar con los estudiantes y profesores allí**

How does a student find a good college? Have students rewrite or restate the statements using **es necesario** and the subjunctive.

### Teaching All Students

**Extra Help** Ask students to write five things that are necessary to do every day. Have them begin each sentence with **Es necesario que tú...**

**Native Speakers** Students can describe what is necessary to do when they have one or more of the *enfermedades* listed in the **Vocabulario** box on p. 227. The other students can also talk about and compare the remedies they use in the same situations.

**Multiple Intelligences**

**Visual** Ask students to draw/cut out pictures of each vocabulary word in the vocabulary box on p. 227. Have them create a collage and label it in Spanish.

**Verbal** Ask students to create a short dialog between a doctor and a patient using the new vocabulary from the box on p. 227.

### Block Schedule

**Process Time** Be sure to practice the formation of the subjunctive before doing the activities. Write some familiar verbs on the board and have students conjugate them in their notebooks. Use regular **-ar**, **-er**, and **-ir** verbs like **vivir, comer, mirar, correr, ayudar, estudiar**, etc.

## Teaching Resource Options

**Print** 

*Más práctica* Workbook PE, p. 88
*Cuaderno para hispanohablantes* PE, p. 86
Block Scheduling Copymasters
Unit 3 Resource Book
*Más práctica* Workbook TE, p. 110
*Cuaderno para hispanohablantes* TE, p. 116

**Audiovisual**

OHT 101 (Quick Start)

**Technology**

*Intrigas y aventuras* CD-ROM, Disc 1

## Quick Start Review

Formation of the subjunctive

Use OHT 101 or write on board: Give the full conjugation of these verbs in the subjunctive.

hablar vivir hacer
comer dormir

**Answers**

See verb charts, pp. R29–R35.

## Teaching Suggestions

Review the **Nota** in **Actividad 11**. Then ask students to create new sentences using the list of impersonal expressions in the vocabulary box on p. 228. They can use the characters from the video/dialog in their sentences. For example, **Es importante que Elena no camine en el tobillo.** Then have them create the corresponding sentences in the indicative, e.g., **Elena no camina en el tobillo.**

ACTIVIDAD 11

## Opiniones

**Hablar/Escribir** ¿Qué opinas? Usa una expresión impersonal y el subjuntivo para dar tus opiniones sobre lo siguiente. *(Hint: Give your opinion.)*

**modelo**

*los estudiantes / usar Internet en sus estudios*

*Es importante que los estudiantes usen Internet en sus estudios.*

**Nota**

Remember that the subjunctive is used after many **impersonal expressions** like **es necesario que.** These expressions (below) come in handy to tell people about what you think is necessary, good, or important. See the difference between the **present indicative** and the **present subjunctive:**

**Indicative** Ellos **viven** aquí en Puerto Rico. *They live here in Puerto Rico.*

**Subjunctive** **Es bueno que** ellos **vivan** aquí en Puerto Rico. *It's good that they live here in Puerto Rico.*

1. yo / preparar para los exámenes
2. tú / escuchar a la profesora
3. nosotros(as) / comer en clase
4. ustedes / gritar en clase
5. los jóvenes / recibir dinero al sacar buenas notas
6. yo / hablar español bien
7. mi amiga / limpiar su cuarto
8. mis amigos / tener su propio teléfono

ACTIVIDAD 12

## ¿Qué te importa?

**Hablar/Escribir** ¿Qué es importante en tu vida y las vidas de tus amigos(as)? Completa las siguientes frases con unas opiniones personales. *(Hint: Complete the phrases.)*

1. Es necesario que...
2. Es malo que...
3. Es una lástima que...
4. Es bueno que...
5. Es mejor que...
6. Es posible que...

### Vocabulario

**Expresa tu opinión**

**Es bueno que...** *It's good that...*
**Es importante que...** *It's important that...*
**Es lógico que...** *It's logical that...*
**Es malo que...** *It's bad that...*
**Es mejor que...** *It's better that...*
**Es peligroso que...** *It's dangerous that...*
**Es posible que...** *It's possible that...*
**Es probable que...** *It's probable that...*
**Es raro que...** *It's rare (strange) that...*
**Es ridículo que...** *It's ridiculous that...*
**Es triste que...** *It's sad that...*
**Es una lástima que...** *It's a pity that...*

¿Qué dices para expresar tu opinión?



## Classroom Community

**Storytelling** Working in groups of three, S1 begins story with **Es bueno que ...**, S2 continues with **Es malo que...** S3 keeps the story flowing and adds comments whenever necessary—she/he does not have to use an impersonal expression. Students build on the story by beginning each sentence with one of the two expressions.

**TPR** Pretend that someone had an accident. Have several students act out an emergency trip to the hospital while others use as much vocabulary as possible to describe the scenario. Include the following characters: driver, victim, receptionist, doctor.

## Recomendaciones

**Hablar/Leer** Tienes un problema. Explíquelo a tu compañero(a). ¿Qué te recomienda? *(Hint: Give recommendations.)*

**modelo**

*Mi infección está peor.*

**Tú:** *Mi infección está peor.*

**Compañero(a):** *Es lógico que escuches el consejo de la enfermera.*

**Tú**

- Mi infección está peor.
- Tengo tos.
- Me corté el dedo. Hay mucha sangre.
- Me rompí la pierna.
- Tengo dolor de cabeza.
- Estoy resfriado(a).
- Sufrí un accidente.

**Compañero(a)**

- Es necesario que (comprar) 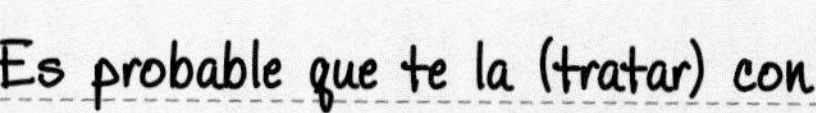 .
- Es probable que te la (tratar) con 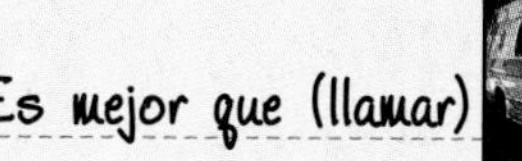 .
- Es mejor que (llamar) 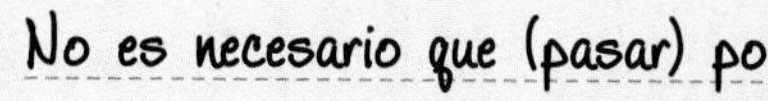 .
- No es necesario que (pasar) por  .



- Es ridículo que (recibir) 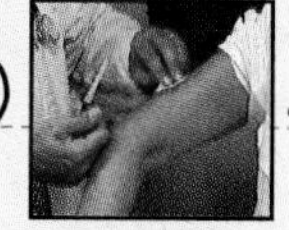 .
- Es posible que 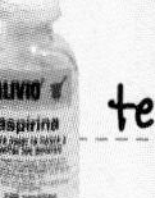 te (ayudar).
- Es lógico que (escuchar) el consejo de  .

### Vocabulario

**El hospital**

**la ambulancia** *ambulance*
**la consulta** *consultation*
**el (la) enfermero(a)** *nurse*
**recuperarse** *to get better*
**la sala de emergencia** *emergency room*
**la sangre** *blood*
**tratar** *to treat*

¿Qué haces cuando vas al hospital?



## Teaching All Students

**Extra Help** Ask students to write a sentence using each of the impersonal expressions.

**Multiple Intelligences**

**Interpersonal** Using the list of impersonal expressions, ask students to give advice to a friend who: will be moving soon, just forgot to pass in the homework, has to go to the doctor's today, decided to ask another student on a date.

**Verbal** Write split sentences with impersonal expressions on pairs of cards, e.g., **Es importante que todos** and **hagan ejercicio**. Give each student a card and have them find their partners to form complete sentences. Then have pairs take turns reading their sentences to the class.

 **Objective:** Transitional practice
Subjunctive + impersonal expressions

**Answers**

*Answers will vary.*

1. [Es importante que] (yo) prepare para los exámenes.
2. [Es importante que] tú escuches a la profesora.
3. [Es malo que] nosotro(a)s comamos en clase.
4. [Es ridículo que] ustedes griten en clase.
5. [Es bueno que] los jóvenes reciban dinero al sacar buenas notas.
6. [Es importante que] (yo) hable español bien.
7. [Es raro que] mi amiga limpie su cuarto.
8. [Es ridículo que] mis amigos tengan su propio teléfono.

 **Objective:** Open-ended practice
Expressing opinions with impersonal expressions

*Answers will vary.*

 **Objective:** Open-ended practice
Discussing health and illness/giving advice

*Answers will vary.*

### Quick Wrap-up

Divide students into groups of three. Have them pick three impersonal expressions on p. 228 and use them to state something about the school. For example: **Es ridículo que sirvan pescado en la cafetería. Nadie lo come.** Groups then share their statements with the class. (**Estoy de acuerdo** could also be reviewed.)

### Block Schedule

**Retention** As an expansion on **Actividad 11**, ask students to add to the list of opinions using impersonal expressions and the subjunctive. They can write about household chores, a visit to the hospital, or a trip to the beach. (For additional activities, see **Block Scheduling Copymasters.**)

## Teaching Resource Options

**Print**

*Más práctica* Workbook PE, pp. 81–84
*Cuaderno para hispanohablantes* PE, pp. 81–82
Block Scheduling Copymasters
Unit 3 Resource Book
*Más práctica* Workbook TE, pp. 103–106
*Cuaderno para hispanohablantes* TE, pp. 111–112
Information Gap Activities, p. 120
Audioscript, pp. 131–133

**Audiovisual**

OHT 101 (Quick Start)
Audio Program Cassette 9A, 9B / CD 9; (*Para hispanohablantes* Cassette 9B / CD 9)

**Technology**

*Intrigas y aventuras* CD-ROM, Disc 1

## Quick Start Review

Formal commands

Use OHT 101 or write on board: Imagine you are a doctor giving advice to a patient. Change the verbs in the following phrases into **usted** commands.

1. evitar el estrés
2. comer alimentos nutritivos
3. beber ocho vasos de agua cada día
4. hacer ejercicio frecuentemente
5. tomar dos aspirinas

**Answers**

1. ...evite... 2. ...coma... 3. ...beba... 4. ...haga... 5. ...tome...

## Teaching Suggestions

- Before doing **Actividad 15**, you may need to review how to say the years in Spanish so students can create time lines of their lives. You can model your own time line before students create their own. Or refer students to pp. 232–233 for a time line model about important events in Puerto Rico's history.
- Have students work in pairs to create a dialog in **Actividad 16**. Ask for volunteers to present their dialogs to the class.

ACTIVIDAD
14

## ¿Es buen doctor?

**Escuchar/Escribir** Escucha estas cuatro conversaciones entre los doctores y sus pacientes en Puerto Rico. Usa una expresión impersonal diferente cada vez para recomendar o no recomendar al doctor. *(Hint: Recommend or don't recommend the doctor.)*

**modelo**

*Es mejor que…*
*Es mejor que busques a otro doctor.*

**TAMBIÉN SE DICE**

En Puerto Rico la gente usa la palabra **montón** para decir **mucho**. Dicen, por ejemplo, «Me duele un montón», o «Tengo un montón de cosas que hacer». En otros países hispanos, puedes oír **un chorro**, **un toco**, **una barbaridad** o **un pedazo**.

ACTIVIDAD
15

## Una línea cronológica

**Hablar/Escribir** Haz una línea cronológica con cinco o más eventos importantes de tu vida. Túrnate con tus compañeros(as) para decir cuánto tiempo hace que pasaron las actividades que anotaste. *(Hint: Make a time line. Then talk to your classmates.)*

**modelo**

**Tú:** *Hace doce años que fui a San Diego.*
**Compañero(a) 1:** *Hace dos años que manejé.*
**Compañero(a) 2:** *Hace ocho años que esquié.*

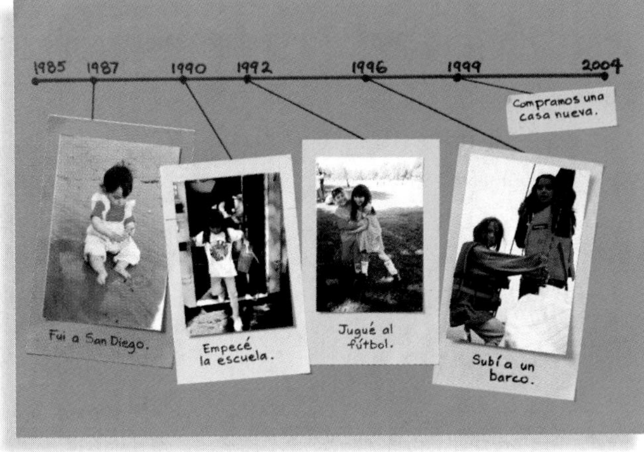
1985
1987
1990
1992
1996
1999
2004
Compramos una casa nueva.
Fui a San Diego.
Empecé la escuela.
Jugué al fútbol.
Subí a un barco.

## Classroom Community

**Paired Activity** Working with a partner, S1 begins with **¿Cuánto tiempo hace que tú [activity]...?** S2 responds and asks how long the partner has done another activity. Complete four rounds of questioning.

**Cooperative Learning** In groups, have students plan a trip to Puerto Rico. Using the Unit Opener as a guide, S1 and S2 should decide what they want to visit and write short descriptions of each place. S3 should make a timeline of the itinerary. S4 should draw or find pictures to illustrate the timeline. Groups assemble their information and present their plans to the class.

**Group Activity** Have students prepare a debate, with pro and con sides, using impersonal expressions. Each group presents its debate to the class.

## ¡Vamos a Puerto Rico!

**PARA CONVERSAR**

**STRATEGY: SPEAKING**

**Give feedback** Ask for and give feedback when practicing with a partner. When you hear yourself make an error, correct it. Seek information from your partner about errors you might not have noticed. Making mistakes is something we all do. What is important is learning from them.

**Hablar** Estás planeando un viaje a Puerto Rico. Usa las fotos para hablar con un(a) compañero(a) sobre lo que vas a hacer allí. *(Hint: Use the pictures to talk about a trip to Puerto Rico.)*

## ¿Cómo te sientes?

**Hablar** Habla con un grupo de compañeros(as) sobre cómo te sientes hoy y la última vez que te sentías mal. *(Hint: Talk about how you feel today and the last time you felt ill.)*

**modelo**

**Tú:** *Hoy me siento bien, pero la semana pasada tenía dolor de garganta….*

**MÁS COMUNICACIÓN** p. R10

### Refrán

**Sana, sana, colita de rana, si no sanas hoy sanarás mañana.**

En su niñez, muchos hispanohablantes escucharon este refrán cuando se lastimaban o se cortaban. ¿Significa algo para ti? ¿Puedes pensar en algún refrán parecido en inglés? Con un(a) compañero(a), inventa otro refrán en español que los adultos pueden decirles a los niños cuando se lastiman.

**Objective:** Open-ended practice
Listening comprehension/giving advice

**Answers** (See script, p. 215B.)
*Answers will vary.*
1. Es bueno que veas a este doctor.
2. Es importante que escuches a la doctora.
3. Es ridículo que vayas a ver a esta doctora.
4. Es mejor que escuches al doctor.

**Objective:** Open-ended practice
Describing time periods

*Answers will vary.*

**Objective:** Open-ended practice
Making/reacting to suggestions

Vacation vocabulary

*Answers will vary.*

**Objective:** Open-ended practice
Discussing health and illness

*Answers will vary.*

### Speaking Strategy: Give Feedback

Have students work in pairs to give each other feedback on their personal timelines.

**Rubric: Speaking**

| Criteria | Scale |
|---|---|
| Feedback | 1 2 3 4 5 |
| Vocabulary | 1 2 3 4 5 |
| Pronunciation, rhythm | 1 2 3 4 5 |

A = 13–15 pts.
B = 10–12 pts.
C = 7–9 pts.
D = 4–6 pts.
F = < 4 pts.

### Teaching All Students

**Extra Help** Have students go back to the dialog on pp. 220–221 and identify the impersonal expressions they recognize.

**Native Speakers** Ask Spanish speakers to give constructive feedback to fellow classmates when they work in pairs or small groups.

**Multiple Intelligences**

**Kinesthetic** Based on vocabulary, ask the students to demonstrate that they have a body ache and have another student give advice on how to stop the pain by using an impersonal expression.

**Logical/Mathematical** Ask students to make a mind map of the subjunctive tense forms and its usages with impersonal expressions.

### Block Schedule

**Variety** Refer to pp. 216–217 and ask students to form a dialog among the characters, using at least 5 impersonal expressions. (For additional activities, see **Block Scheduling Copymasters**.)

### Teaching Resource Options

**Print** 

*Cuaderno para hispanohablantes* PE, pp. 87–88

Unit 3 Resource Book

*Cuaderno para hispanohablantes* TE, pp. 117–118

Audioscript, p. 131

**Audiovisual** 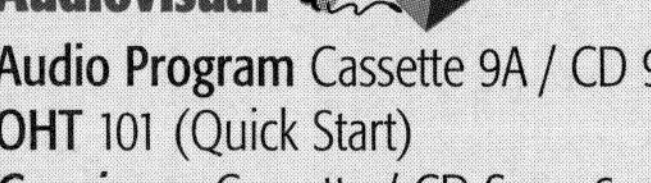

Audio Program Cassette 9A / CD 9

OHT 101 (Quick Start)

*Canciones* Cassette / CD Song 6

### Quick Start Review

Giving information

Use OHT 101 or write on board: Conjugate the verbs in the preterite to complete the following headlines.

1. Sesenta por ciento de los estadounidenses (votar) ayer.
2. El presidente Rey (ganar) por segunda vez. ¡Cuatro años más!
3. El Partido Republicano (mantener) una mayoría en el Congreso.
4. El comité que (investigar) las acciones del líder del Partido Democrático (hacer) público su reportaje hoy.

**Answers**

1. votaron; 2. ganó; 3. mantuvo; 4. investigó / hizo

### Teaching Suggestions
**Presenting En voces**

- **Prereading** Ask students what they know about the political relationship between the United States and Puerto Rico. Write their observations on the board. Then ask students to guess the topic of the reading, based on the photos and the time line. Write the list of possibilities on the board.
- **Strategy: Activate Associated Knowledge** Ask students if they know of any other territories or commonwealths of the U.S. Have students locate them on a globe or map.
- **Reading** Ask students to scan for the cognates in the reading as this will aid their comprehension.

# En voces

**LECTURA**

# El estatus político de Puerto Rico

**PARA LEER**

**STRATEGY: READING**

**Activate associated knowledge** In social studies classes, you have heard political terms like **colony, territory, commonwealth, state, nation, republic.** Look up the definitions of these words. As you read this article and refer to the time line, decide which term describes Puerto Rico during each period of its history.

**1898**
**España cede Puerto Rico a Estados Unidos.**

**1917**
**Los puertorriqueños obtienen nacionalidad estadounidense.**

**1948**
**Luis Muñoz Marín, jefe del Partido Popular Democrático, gana la primera elección para gobernador de Puerto Rico.**

**1952**
**Puerto Rico se convierte en un Estado Libre Asociado.**

**1993**
**En un referéndum sobre el estatus político, los puertorriqueños votan por continuar la situación actual.**

*Carlos Antonio Romero-Barceló, el Comisionado Residente*

*Luis Muñoz Marín, jefe del Partido Popular Democrático*



### Classroom Community

**Learning Scenario** Have students poll 5–10 people in their neighborhood to give an opinion on the future status of Puerto Rico. Should Puerto Rico become a state, an independent country, or maintain the commonwealth status? Inform students that they may need to educate some people on the special commonwealth status of Puerto Rico. Ask students to bring the results to class and compare the results with those of their classmates.

**Portfolio** Have students research and write a paragraph on the political status of Puerto Rico, including their own opinion.

**Rubric: Writing**

| Criteria | Scale |
|---|---|
| Logical sentences | 1 2 3 4 5 |
| Vocabulary use | 1 2 3 4 5 |
| Accuracy | 1 2 3 4 5 |

A = 13–15 pts.
B = 10–12 pts.
C = 7–9 pts.
D = 4–6 pts.
F = < 4 pts.

La situación política de Puerto Rico ha tenido[1] dos etapas formativas. La primera fue el período del gobierno español, que comenzó en 1493 y duró hasta 1898, cuando hubo un conflicto entre España y Estados Unidos. Después, España tuvo que ceder Puerto Rico a Estados Unidos.

Como puedes ver en la cronología, este siglo ha sido[2] uno de cambios y negociaciones sobre el estatus político de Puerto Rico. Luis Muñoz Marín, el líder del Partido Popular Democrático (PPD), negoció[3] el Estado Libre Asociado en 1952. El PPD quiere una asociación con Estados Unidos, pero manteniendo el idioma y la autonomía[4] local del gobierno. Hay otros dos partidos[5]: el Partido Nuevo Progresista (PNP) y el Partido Independentista Puertorriqueño (PIP). El PNP quiere la estadidad[6] para Puerto Rico, mientras que el PIP está a favor de la independencia.

[1] has had [2] century has been [3] negotiated

Hoy en día, aunque los puertorriqueños son estadounidenses y tienen un representante en el Congreso (el Comisionado Residente), no pueden votar en elecciones presidenciales. Por eso y otras razones, el debate sigue sobre la cuestión del estatus político de Puerto Rico. Queda por ver lo que pasa.

[4] autonomy, freedom [5] political parties [6] statehood

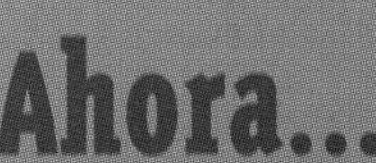

## Ahora...

**Los partidos políticos siguen el debate sobre el estatus político de Puerto Rico.**

### ¿Comprendiste?

1. ¿Qué país conquistó a la gente indígena de Puerto Rico?
2. ¿Quién es Luis Muñoz Marín?
3. ¿Qué nacionalidad tienen los puertorriqueños?
4. ¿Cuál es el estatus político actual de Puerto Rico?
5. ¿Cuál fue el resultado del referéndum de 1993?

### ¿Qué piensas?

Imagínate que eres puertorriqueño(a) y vas a votar en el referéndum. ¿A favor de qué estatus político vas a votar? ¿Por qué?



### Culture Highlights

● **PUERTO RICO, A FREE-ASSOCIATED STATE** or commonwealth, enjoys a special relationship with the U.S., which oversees its national defense, currency, foreign relations, postal service, and customs administration. Puerto Rico handles its own internal affairs, such as education and local government. Puerto Rico differs from the 50 states in its local taxation system, its lack of vote in Congress or for the U.S. president, its exemption from federal taxes, and lack of certain revenues from the federal government. Puerto Rico has one representative in Congress with a voice but no vote. Official languages of Puerto Rico are both English and Spanish.

### Cross Cultural Connection

Have students compare their state timeline (see *Visual* below) to the one for Puerto Rico on pp. 232-233.

### ¿Comprendiste?

**Answers**

1. España conquistó a la gente indígena de Puerto Rico.
2. Fue el primer gobernador de Puerto Rico.
3. Tienen nacionalidad estadounidense.
4. Es un Estado Libre Asociado.
5. En el referéndum de 1993, el pueblo puertorriqueño votó a favor de continuar la situación actual.

### Critical Thinking

Ask students if they know what it takes to become a state. What does Puerto Rico need to do to become the fifty-first state? What are some of the changes that Puerto Ricans may experience if they become a state? What changes may occur if they become independent?

## Teaching All Students

**Extra Help** Divide the class into small groups and ask each group to summarize the main facts in each paragraph of the reading. One group can summarize the timeline above the reading. Share summaries.

**Native Speakers** If any Spanish speakers are from Puerto Rico or if they know any Puerto Ricans, ask them to share their personal opinions (or interview a native Puerto Rican) about the political status of Puerto Rico.

**Multiple Intelligences**

**Visual** Have students make a timeline to show the important historical events of their home state. They can research the history and special events via the Internet.

## Block Schedule

**Retention** Prepare Ahead: Make copies of the reading for students (you may chose to make copies for groups), and ask students to cut up each sentence. Mix up the sentences. Have students reorganize them to form a complete story without using their text.

### Teaching Resource Options

**Audiovisual**
OHT 102 (Quick Start)

### Quick Start Review

Discuss what others do

Use OHT 102 or write on board: Look at the photos that accompany the reading and describe the activities pictured in Spanish.

*Answers will vary.*

### Teaching Suggestions
#### Presenting En colores

- Have students look at the photographs and read and discuss the **Connecting Cultures Strategy** before beginning the Culture reading.
- **Reading Strategy** Ask students to activate associated knowledge (p. 232) as they read about the **jíbaros** of Puerto Rico. For example, there are similar musical traditions in rural areas of the U.S.

### Cross Cultural Connections

The **jíbaros** of Puerto Rico live and work in the mountainous countryside. Ask students to describe similar groups from the U.S. countryside. Where do they live? What are their customs? What is their role in literature and culture?

### Critical Thinking

Ask students to think about stereotypes, noting that when we first learn about another culture, we generalize because we lack experience with it. Over-generalizing leads to stereotyping, or failing to distinguish among individual behaviors within a group. Ask students if they have experienced or witnessed stereotyping. Discuss.

# En colores
## CULTURA Y COMPARACIONES

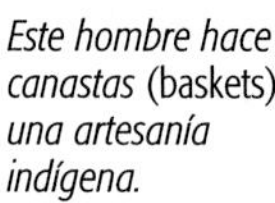

*Este hombre hace canastas (baskets), una artesanía indígena.*

### PARA CONOCERNOS
**STRATEGY: CONNECTING CULTURES**
**Discover many cultures inside one country**

Expressions like *the American culture, the Hispanic culture,* or *the Puerto Rican culture* oversimplify by ignoring the diversity a culture contains. As you read «**Una voz de la tierra**» (*A voice from the land*) you will see that in one country there are many cultures different in dress, music, customs, and language. Use this chart to identify a cultural group within the U.S. that you know.

| Nombre: |
| --- |
| Lugar: |
| Tradiciones: |

How do diverse cultural traditions enrich our national life?

# Una voz de la tierra

*Monumento al jíbaro puertorriqueño*

### NOTA CULTURAL

**La cultura de los jíbaros** se expresa principalmente a través de la música. Además de bailar, estos campesinos usan instrumentos españoles y africanos en su música. Hasta crearon el cuatro, un tipo de guitarra especial.

### Classroom Community

**Learning Scenario** Have students make a Venn diagram. On one side list the characteristics of the **jíbaros** and on the other, characteristics of country people as students know them. List any similarities in the middle.

**Paired Activity** In pairs, students can use a Venn diagram to compare and contrast the life of a **jíbaro** in the mountains with the life of someone who decides to **ganarse la vida en San Juan**. What are the pros and cons of each environment? Are there any similarities? Which do they think they would prefer?

**Cooperative Learning** Using one sheet of paper, S1 writes a question about the **jíbaros** in the indicative, S2 answers the question in the indicative, S3 changes the question to the subjunctive by using an impersonal expression, and S4 answers the question using an impersonal expression and the subjunctive.

Manuel A. Alonso escribió *El Gíbaro* (1849) que honra[1] a los campesinos de Puerto Rico. Desde entonces el jíbaro se ha convertido[2] en uno de los símbolos folklóricos de Puerto Rico.

El jíbaro representa a los campesinos que vivieron en la Cordillera Central durante el siglo[3] XIX y principios del XX. Allí desarrollaron[4] una cultura que tiene como temas centrales el trabajo en la tierra, la naturaleza y la alegría de compartir con los demás.

Una canción muy famosa, «El jibarito», por Rafael Hernández fue escrita[5] durante una fuerte depresión en los años treinta. En esta época, muchos campesinos tuvieron que abandonar sus fincas para trabajar en ciudades. A partir de los cincuenta, muy pocas personas cultivaron la tierra.

Hoy, el jíbaro es un símbolo popular. Ninguna fiesta navideña está completa sin una décima[7] o un cuatro templado[8]. Si viajas a Puerto Rico y oyes una canción que empieza, «Ay, le lolai, le lo lé…», escuchas una voz de la tierra, la voz del jíbaro.

[1] that honors [2] has become [3] century [4] developed [5] was written

[7] ballad [8] a tuned cuatro (type of guitar)

## ¿Comprendiste?

1. ¿Qué es el jíbaro?
2. ¿Qué temas son los temas centrales de la cultura campesina?
3. ¿Cómo se expresó esta cultura?
4. ¿En qué época se escribió «El jibarito»? ¿De qué crees que habla? ¿Por qué?

## ¿Qué piensas?

¿Te parece que en Estados Unidos muchas personas abandonan el campo para trabajar en ciudades? ¿Por qué?

## Hazlo tú 

En grupos pequeños, piensen en símbolos folklóricos de Estados Unidos. Escojan un símbolo folklórico e investíguenlo. ¿Está relacionado con una región? ¿Expresa una cultura? ¿Cuál es su manera de expresión? Preparen un informe pequeño y compártanlo con la clase.



## Culture Highlights

- **MANUEL A. ALONSO** (1822–1889) wrote about the customs and daily lives of the Puerto Rican people. He studied medicine in Spain, then practiced in Caguas, Puerto Rico. His most famous work is *El Gíbaro,* written in 1849.
- **EL GÜIRO** is a musical instrument native to Puerto Rico that is made from the hollow, dry **güiro** fruit, similar to a gourd. The **güiro** is played with a fork-like utensil in a scraping motion along its ridges. It is sometimes called a **güicharo**.
- **LAS MARACAS,** musical instruments made from gourds with seeds inside, are an example of the Indian influence in Puerto Rican music.
- **LA BOMBA** is a type of drum native to Puerto Rico that is used in much of the native Puerto Rican music. For more information on native Puerto Rican instruments, such as the **güiro,** the **maracas,** and the **bomba,** see the Music note in the **Ampliación** section on p. 171B.

## ¿Comprendiste?

**Answers**

*Answers will vary.*

1. El jíbaro es el campesino puertorriqueño.
2. Los temas centrales son el trabajo en la tierra, la naturaleza y la alegría de compartir con los demás.
3. Se expresó esta cultura a través de la música.
4. Se escribió durante una depresión de los años treinta. Habla de los problemas del jíbaro porque fue un tiempo muy difícil para ellos.

## Block Schedule

**Peer Teaching** In groups of 3, students choose one of the cultural groups they have written about in the Connecting Cultures diagram. Have them add as much information as possible about the culture and then present the information to the class. You might also suggest that each group bring in a snack particular to their cultural group to share with the class after the presentations.

## Teaching All Students

**Extra Help** Divide the students into three groups. Assign a paragraph to each group. Have students summarize the paragraph and explain it to the class.

**Native Speakers** If any Spanish speakers are from Puerto Rico, ask them about the role of the **jíbaro** in Puerto Rican culture and if they know any of their songs or music. Have them bring in samples or give a short presentation to the class.

**Multiple Intelligences**

**Musical/Rhythmic** Bring in samples of U.S. and Puerto Rican regional folk music to play in class. Have students explain how it is different from current popular music.

**Visual** Based on the description given of the **jíbaros,** ask students to draw a picture of what they think a **jíbaro** and his/her home would look like.

## Teaching Resource Options

**Print**

Block Scheduling Copymasters
Unit 3 Resource Book
Information Gap Activities, pp. 121–122
Family Involvement, pp. 123–124

**Audiovisual**

OHT 102 (Quick Start)

**Technology**

Electronic Teacher Tools/Test Generator
*Intrigas y aventuras* CD-ROM, Disc 1

## Quick Start Review

**En contexto** vocabulary

Use OHT 102 or write on board: Name the parts of the body these verbs suggest.

1. escuchar
2. bailar
3. tocar la guitarra
4. comer
5. respirar
6. reírse

**Answers**

1. las orejas; los oídos 2. las piernas; los pies 3. las manos; los dedos 4. la boca; los dientes 5. la boca; la nariz 6. la boca

## Teaching Suggestions

### What Have Students Learned?

- Have students look at the "Now you can..." notes listed on the left side of pages 236–237. Point out that if they feel they need to review material before doing the activities, they should consult the "To review" notes.
- Use the video to review vocabulary and structures.

ETAPA 3

# En uso

## REPASO Y MÁS COMUNICACIÓN

**OBJECTIVES**

- Describe time periods
- Talk about health and illness
- Give advice

*Now you can...*

- describe time periods.
- talk about health and illness.

*To review*

- **hacer** with expressions of time, see p. 224.

ACTIVIDAD 1

### ¡Nos duele todo!

Estás en el consultorio del tío Rodrigo. ¿Qué comentarios oyes?
*(Hint: Tell what you hear in the doctor's office.)*

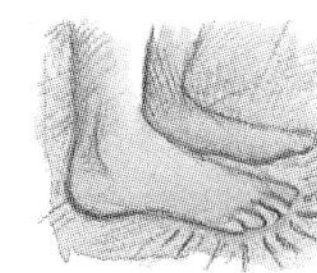

**modelo**

*José: dos semanas*
*Hace dos semanas que le duele el pie.*

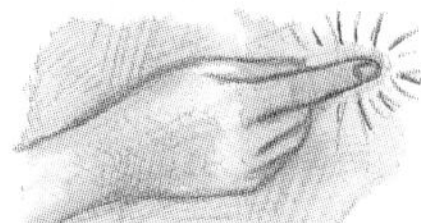

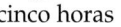

1. tú: cinco horas

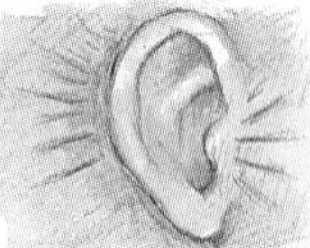

2. mi madre: cuatro días

3. Clara y Pablo: quince horas

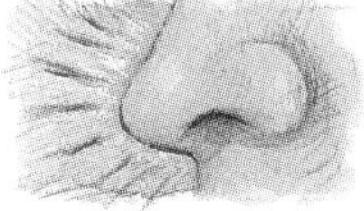

4. yo: una semana

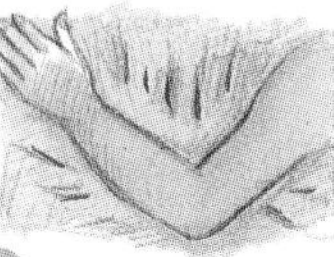

5. nosotros: veinte horas

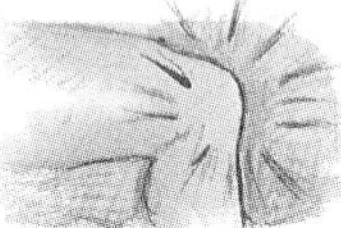

6. Rita y yo: diez horas

*Now you can...*

- describe time periods.
- talk about health and illness.

*To review*

- **hacer** with expressions of time, see p. 224.

ACTIVIDAD 2

### Hace tres días que...

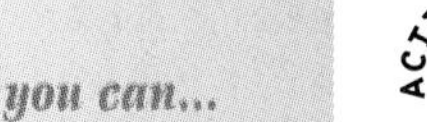

Tú y tus compañeros(as) están hablando de los accidentes y de las enfermedades. ¿Cuánto tiempo hace que estas cosas pasaron?
*(Hint: Tell how long ago these things happened.)*

**modelo**

*el (la) doctor(a): ponerte una inyección*
*Hace dos semanas que el (la) doctor(a) me puso una inyección.*

1. tú: cortarte el dedo
2. la doctora: ponerte un yeso
3. tus vecinos: ir a la sala de emergencia
4. tu abuelo: recuperarse
5. la doctora: darte una receta
6. un enfermero: hacerte una radiografía
7. tú y tus amigos: lastimarse
8. tú: tomar una medicina



## Classroom Community

**Peer Review** Cooperative Learning: Assign "Now you can" or "To review"—each group reviews the concept(s) and presents to the class. Encourage them to include visuals, worksheets, and a quiz.

**Portfolio** Have students give a detailed description of an actual physical ailment that is bothering them now. Or have them describe the health or illness of someone they know.

**Rubric: Writing**

| Criteria | Scale |
|---|---|
| Logical sentences | 1 2 3 4 5 |
| Vocabulary use | 1 2 3 4 5 |
| Accuracy | 1 2 3 4 5 |

A = 13–15 pts.
B = 10–12 pts.
C = 7–9 pts.
D = 4–6 pts.
F = < 4 pts.

*Now you can...*
- give advice.

*To review*
- the subjunctive with impersonal expressions, see pp. 226, 228.

## Me siento mal

Tu amigo(a) tiene gripe. ¿Qué le dices? *(Hint: Give advice.)*

**modelo**

*tomar sopa de pollo (¿triste o mejor?)*
*Es mejor que tomes sopa de pollo.*

1. correr mucho (¿bueno o malo?)
2. tomar medicina (¿peligroso o importante?)
3. salir de la casa (¿malo o probable?)
4. hacer mucho ejercicio (¿mejor o peligroso?)
5. beber jugo (¿bueno o raro?)
6. descansar mucho (¿ridículo o lógico?)
7. visitar al doctor (¿necesario o posible?)
8. tener fiebre (¿importante o una lástima?)

*Now you can...*
- talk about health and illness.

*To review*
- the subjunctive with impersonal expressions, see pp. 226, 228.

## ¡Es interesante!

Tú y tus compañeros(as) están hablando de la salud. ¿Qué dicen? Usa las expresiones de la lista. *(Hint: Tell what you and your friends say.)*

| | |
|---|---|
| Es bueno que | Es probable que |
| Es malo que | Es raro que |
| Es peligroso que | Es triste que |

**modelo**

*los doctores: ponerles un yeso a las personas con fracturas*
*Es probable que los doctores les pongan un yeso a las personas con fracturas.*

1. yo: tener dolor de cabeza
2. los enfermeros: escribir las recetas
3. la ambulancia: llegar tarde
4. los niños: gritar en el consultorio
5. tú: lastimarte muy poco
6. los pacientes: llorar en la sala de emergencia
7. el doctor: ver sangre todos los días
8. nosotros: esperar mucho en el consultorio



### Actividad 1 Answers

1. Hace cinco horas que te duele el dedo.
2. Hace cuatro días que a mi madre le duele la oreja.
3. Hace quince horas que a Clara y a Pablo les duele la cabeza.
4. Hace una semana que me duele la nariz.
5. Hace veinte horas que nos duelen los brazos.
6. Hace diez horas que a Rita y a mí nos duelen las rodillas.

### Actividad 2 Answers

*The time periods in answers will vary but should reflect correct usage of **hacer** + expressions of time.*

1. Hace [dos semanas] que te cortaste el dedo.
2. Hace [un mes] que la doctora te puso un yeso.
3. Hace [tres horas] que tus vecinos fueron a la sala de emergencia.
4. Hace [dos años] que tu abuelo se recuperó.
5. Hace [una semana] que la doctora te dio una receta.
6. Hace [diez minutos] que un enfermero te hizo una radiografía.
7. Hace [cinco días] que tú y tus amigos se lastimaron.
8. Hace [seis horas] que tomaste una medicina.

### Actividad 3 Answers

1. Es malo que corras mucho.
2. Es importante que tomes medicina.
3. Es malo que salgas de la casa.
4. Es peligroso que hagas mucho ejercicio.
5. Es bueno que bebas jugo.
6. Es lógico que descanses mucho.
7. Es necesario que visites al doctor.
8. Es una lástima que tengas fiebre.

### Actividad 4 Answers

*Answers may vary but should reflect correct conjugation of the subjunctive after an impersonal expression.*

1. [Es raro que] (yo) tenga dolor de cabeza.
2. [Es peligroso que] los enfermeros escriban las recetas.
3. [Es malo que] la ambulancia llegue tarde.
4. [Es malo que] los niños griten en el consultorio.
5. [Es bueno que] (tú) te lastimes muy poco.
6. [Es triste que] los pacientes lloren en la sala de emergencia.
7. [Es probable que] el doctor vea sangre todos los días.
8. [Es raro que] (nosotros) esperemos mucho en el consultorio.

## Teaching All Students

**Extra Help** Give students a list of impersonal expressions. Ask them to form complete sentences to give another student advice on improving his/her performance in Spanish class.

**Challenge** Have student scan the front page of a Spanish newspaper and write 5 complete sentences that use an impersonal expression (from p. 228) followed by the subjunctive, based on what they read.

### Multiple Intelligences

**Verbal** Have students count down the activities they just completed over the past hours, e.g., **Hace seis horas que..., Hace cinco horas que....**

**Visual** Show students pictures of people doing various activities and ask **¿Cuánto tiempo hace que (hiciste la actividad)?** Students respond with **Hace... que.**

## Block Schedule

**Variety** After giving advice to a friend with the flu in **Actividad 3**, have students create a list of advice for a friend who has a bad stomachache. (For additional activities, see **Block Scheduling Copymasters**.)

## Teaching Resource Options

### Print

Unit 3 Resource Book
- Audioscript, pp. 133–134
- Cooperative Quizzes, pp. 135–136
- Etapa Exam, Forms A and B, pp. 137–146
- *Examen para hispanohablantes,* pp. 147–151
- Portfolio Assessment, pp. 152–153
- Multiple Choice Test Questions, pp. 176–178
- Unit 3 Comprehensive Test, pp. 154–161
- *Prueba comprensiva para hispanohablantes,* Unit 3, pp. 162–169
- Midyear Exam, pp. 179–186

### Audiovisual

OHT 95, 95A, 96, 96A, 102 (Quick Start)
Audio Program Cassette 19B / CD 19;
(*Para hispanohablantes* Cassette 19B / CD 19)

### Technology

Electronic Teacher Tools/Test Generator
www.mcdougallittell.com

## Quick Start Review

Talking about illness

Use OHT 102 or write on board: Write a description of how you feel when you have the flu. What are the common symptoms? You might use the phrases **me siento** or **me duele**, along with other words you have learned in this unit.

*Answers will vary.*

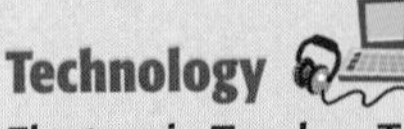

### Rubric: Speaking

| Criteria | Scale | |
|---|---|---|
| Fluency | 1 2 3 4 5 | A = 13–15 pts. |
| Vocabulary | 1 2 3 4 5 | B = 10–12 pts. |
| Pronunciation, rhythm | 1 2 3 4 5 | C = 7–9 pts. |
| | | D = 4–6 pts. |
| | | F = < 4 pts. |

### Actividad 7 En tu propia voz

### Rubric: Writing

| Criteria | Scale | |
|---|---|---|
| Vocabulary use | 1 2 3 4 5 | A = 13–15 pts. |
| Accuracy | 1 2 3 4 5 | B = 10–12 pts. |
| Creativity, appearance | 1 2 3 4 5 | C = 7–9 pts. |
| | | D = 4–6 pts. |
| | | F = < 4 pts. |

## Actividad 5 Me duele...

**PARA CONVERSAR**

**STRATEGY: SPEAKING**

**Use language for problem-solving** When you begin this role-play, observe the stages of effective problem-solving: (1) Patient gives information about the symptoms; (2) Doctor asks clarifying questions; patient answers; (3) Doctor proposes solution; (4) Patient asks clarifying questions; (5) Doctor advises patient on best course of action; (6) Patient seeks a second opinion by repeating the above process. You can treat this role-play seriously or humorously.

Selecciona un problema de abajo y explícaselo a tu compañero(a). Tu compañero(a) te puede dar consejos y una receta. Después busca una segunda opinión de otro(a) doctor(a). *(Hint: Role-play one of the situations on the list.)*

- una fractura de tobillo
- dolor de cabeza
- dolor de estómago
- dolor de garganta y mucha tos
- fiebre y dolor en todo el cuerpo
- la gripe

## Actividad 6 ¿Cierto o falso?

Completa la tabla con seis actividades ciertas y falsas. Léelas para que tus compañeros(as) adivinen cuáles son ciertas y cuáles son falsas. *(Hint: Complete the chart with six activities. Read them aloud for your classmates to guess if they are true or false.)*

**modelo**

| Actividades del presente | Actividades del pasado |
|---|---|
| 1. Toco el piano. | 1. Fui al consultorio del doctor. |
| 2. | 2. |
| 3. | 3. |

**Tú:** *Hace cinco años que toco el piano.*
**Estudiante 1:** *Cierto.*
**Estudiante 2:** *Falso.*
**Tú:** *Cierto. Hace cinco años que toco el piano. Lo toco muy bien.*

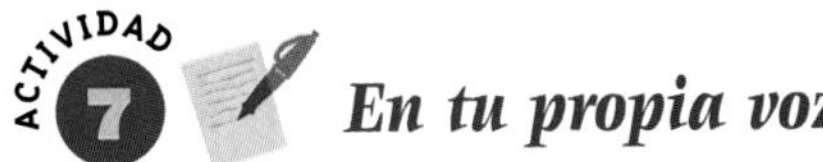

## Actividad 7 En tu propia voz

**Escritura** Imagínate que eres doctor(a). Otro(a) doctor(a) pide tu opinión sobre un caso y acabas de examinar el (la) paciente. Escríbele una carta al (a la) otro(a) doctor(a) que incluya una descripción del problema y tus recomendaciones. *(Hint: Write a letter about a patient's problem and include your recommendations.)*

## CONEXIONES

**La historia** ¿Qué significa realmente la palabra *pirata*? ¿Qué hacían los piratas y por qué? ¿Qué hacían con estas monedas? Haz una investigación de la historia de los piratas. Luego comprueba lo que saben tus compañeros(as), haciéndoles preguntas sobre la información que encontraste.

*Estos doblones son de la época de Carlos III.*



## Classroom Community

**Learning Scenario** In pairs, have students play the roles of patient and doctor. The patient tells the doctor he doesn't feel well. By asking questions, and by process of elimination, the doctor must figure out what is wrong with the patient. Once the doctor has determined the ailment, he must prescribe a treatment. Switch roles.

**Storytelling** Ask each student to contribute to a class story. Each student takes a turn and forms a sentence using a vocabulary word/expression from the list on p. 239. Mark off the words so that *all* vocabulary is used. Form a creative story.

# En resumen

## REPASO DE VOCABULARIO

### DESCRIBE TIME PERIODS

| | |
|---|---|
| ¿Cuánto tiempo hace que...? | *How long has it been since...?* |
| hace ... que | *ago* |

### GIVE ADVICE

| | |
|---|---|
| Es bueno que... | *It's good that...* |
| Es importante que... | *It's important that...* |
| Es lógico que... | *It's logical that...* |
| Es malo que... | *It's bad that...* |
| Es mejor que... | *It's better that...* |
| Es necesario que... | *It's necessary that...* |
| Es peligroso que... | *It's dangerous that...* |
| Es posible que... | *It's possible that...* |
| Es probable que... | *It's probable that...* |
| Es raro que... | *It's rare (strange) that...* |
| Es ridículo que... | *It's ridiculous that...* |
| Es triste que... | *It's sad that...* |
| Es una lástima que... | *It's a pity that...* |

### TALK ABOUT HEALTH AND ILLNESS

**The Body**

| | |
|---|---|
| la boca | *mouth* |
| el brazo | *arm* |
| la cabeza | *head* |
| la cara | *face* |
| el codo | *elbow* |
| el cuello | *neck* |
| el cuerpo | *body* |
| los dedos | *fingers* |
| los dientes | *teeth* |
| el estómago | *stomach* |
| la garganta | *throat* |
| el hombro | *shoulder* |
| la mano | *hand* |
| la muñeca | *wrist* |
| la nariz | *nose* |
| el oído | *inner ear* |
| los ojos | *eyes* |
| la oreja | *ear* |
| el pie | *foot* |
| la pierna | *leg* |
| la rodilla | *knee* |
| la sangre | *blood* |
| el tobillo | *ankle* |

**Health Problems and Solutions**

| | |
|---|---|
| la ambulancia | *ambulance* |
| la aspirina | *aspirin* |
| cómodo(a) | *comfortable* |
| la consulta | *consultation* |
| el consultorio | *office (doctor's)* |
| cortarse | *to cut oneself* |
| doler (o→ue) | *to hurt, to suffer* |
| el dolor de cabeza | *headache* |
| la enfermedad | *sickness* |
| el (la) enfermero(a) | *nurse* |
| estar resfriado(a) | *to have a cold* |
| la fiebre | *fever* |
| la gripe | *flu* |
| gritar | *to scream* |
| la infección | *infection* |
| la inyección | *injection* |
| lastimarse | *to hurt oneself* |
| llorar | *to cry* |
| la medicina | *medicine* |
| las pastillas | *pills* |
| la radiografía | *x-ray* |
| la receta | *prescription* |
| recuperarse | *to get better* |
| respirar | *to breathe* |
| la sala de emergencia | *emergency room* |
| ¡Socorro! | *Help!* |
| la tos | *cough* |
| tratar | *to treat* |
| el yeso | *cast* |

### Juego

Estas tres personas están en un consultorio. A Ernesto le duele el estómago, a Javier le duelen las piernas. ¿Qué le duele a Andrea? Usa el dibujo para decir qué le duele.

## Teaching All Students

**Extra Help** Ask students to find magazine pictures (or draw them) for the health and illness vocabulary and put them on index cards. As a review, students can hold up a picture card and others can identify the Spanish word, then form questions and/or sentences.

**Multiple Intelligences**

**Musical/Rhythmic** Ask students to develop a song or poem to include as many vocabulary items as possible. Hint: You may assign a section of vocabulary words.



### Teaching Note: En tu propia voz

**Writing Strategy** Tell students to support their opinion with facts and examples. Have them explain how their recommendations will help the patient.

### Teaching Suggestions

- Bring in any articles, books, pictures, etc., that you can find on pirates to elicit interest in the **Conexiones** project.
- Orally present students with scenarios that require them to use the expressions from the "Give Advice" section of the vocabulary list.

### Juego

**Answer**

A Andrea le duele la muñeca.

### Interdisciplinary Connections

**History** Have students research the historical importance of pirates in the history of Puerto Rico and compare to information about pirates in the U.S.

**Health** This may be a good time to do the second project described in the **Ampliación** section on p. 171B. Students are asked to create a Spanish communication guide for their local hospital or medical facility to use when hospital workers treat a Spanish-speaking patient.

### Project: Reviewing Etapa 3

Assign the following out-of-class activities:

- Interview a Spanish speaker about exercise routines
- Bring in an article about the political status of Puerto Rico
- Find out about the major hospitals in Puerto Rico via the Internet
- Find more information on the current leaders in Puerto Rico's government

**Extra Credit**

| | |
|---|---|
| Interview | 2 pts. |
| Puerto Rico's status | 2 pts. |
| Hospitals in Puerto Rico | 2 pts. |
| Politicians in Puerto Rico | 2 pts. |

### Block Schedule

**Retention** Borrow a skeleton from the biology department, or bring in a cardboard Halloween skeleton. Point to the different body parts on the skeleton and have students name them in Spanish.

### Teaching Resource Options

**Print**

Block Scheduling Copymasters

**Audiovisual**

OHT GO1, 102 (Quick Start)

**Technology**

*Intrigas y aventuras* CD-ROM, Disc 1

www.mcdougallittell.com

### Quick Start Review

Comparatives

Use OHT 102 or write on the board: Use these words and phrases to compare this school with your previous school.

más… que tanto… como
menos… que mejor

*Answers will vary.*

### Teaching Suggestions

**Prewriting**

- Have students review the places in Puerto Rico covered in their textbook. See the **En voces** and **En colores** readings on pp. 188-189, 210-211, 232-235 for ideas. Students can also research the Internet or their local library to find out more about Puerto Rican areas of interest.
- Point out the **PASS** list at the beginning of the page: **P**urpose, **A**udience, **S**ubject, **S**tructure. This will be their PASS key to a well-structured writing assignment in every unit.

**Post-writing**

- Have students exchange paragraphs and practice their proofreading skills. Have them read their partner's paragraph aloud to hear as well as see any possible errors. Have them offer suggestions to improve the paragraph.

UNIDAD

3

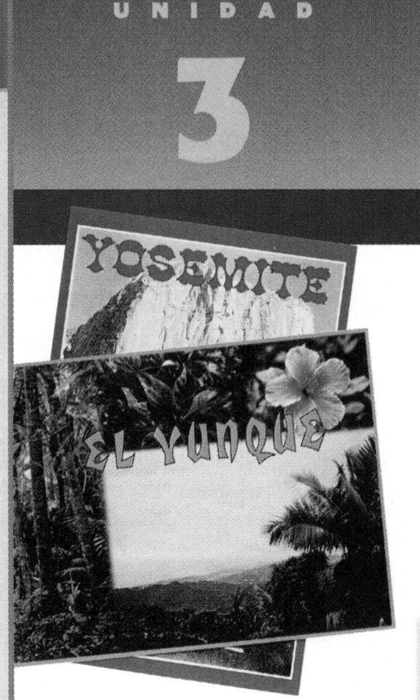


# En tu propia voz

**ESCRITURA**

## ¡Qué contraste!

Your class will be corresponding with a class in Puerto Rico. Tell your new pen pal about your state by comparing and contrasting a place near you with a place in Puerto Rico.

**Purpose:** Compare Puerto Rican and local places
**Audience:** Puerto Rican pen pal
**Subject:** Two different places
**Structure:** Friendly letter

**PARA ESCRIBIR** • **STRATEGY: WRITING**

**Compare and contrast to make strong descriptions** A well-written description will provide your reader with a strong mental image. Compare and contrast the location you present with one that is familiar to the reader.

### Modelo del estudiante

12310 E. Lester St
Fresno, CA 93720
17 de enero

Querido Mario:

Quiero contarte un poco sobre el lugar donde vivo. Me encanta ir al Parque
Nacional Yosemite, no muy lejos de mi casa. Yosemite es un poco similar al Bosque
Nacional El Yunque, en Puerto Rico. Pero sé que lo que ves en los dos lugares es muy
diferente.

The writer introduces the two subjects, Yosemite National Park and El Yunque.

En El Yunque, la gente puede caminar mucho y ver la naturaleza. Hay plantas y
animales tropicales. El tiempo no cambia mucho durante el año. Es un lugar muy
bonito.

The author provides information about El Yunque.

En Yosemite, como en El Yunque, la gente camina y ve la naturaleza. Las plantas
y animales son diferentes, porque hay cuatro estaciones allí. Hay árboles muy altos,
como pinos y otros que tienen hojas que cambian de color y se caen en el otoño. En
el invierno hay nieve. Si hay mucha nieve, hay más agua para correr sobre las piedras.
Todo el año la gente viene a ver las rocas enormes, las cataratas, que forman el valle
de Yosemite. ¡Es magnífico!

The author gives a detailed description of Yosemite, the place that is more familiar.

Yosemite y El Yunque son básicamente similares. Los dos lugares protegen
la naturaleza, y la gente que los visita puede caminar mucho y ver las plantas y lo
... es diferente en cada lugar, pues las plantas y los animal

The writer refers to details to compare and contrast the two places.

### Classroom Community

**Paired Activity** Have students work with a partner to review their Venn diagrams. Have each student give his/her partner suggestions on how to improve the descriptions of the similarities and differences.

**Group Activity** Have students write a brief description of a local place they want to use in their comparison/contrast paragraph. Have students read their descriptions aloud and have the rest of their group try to guess the location.

**Portfolio** Have students save this paragraph for their portfolios. Subsequent writing projects will show their progress in Spanish.

## Estrategias para escribir

### Antes de escribir...

Remember that the purpose of this friendly letter is to provide your pen pal with information about a place in your state. Choose a place you know well that has something in common with a place in Puerto Rico that you've learned about. Then brainstorm similarities and differences, using a Venn diagram to record your ideas.

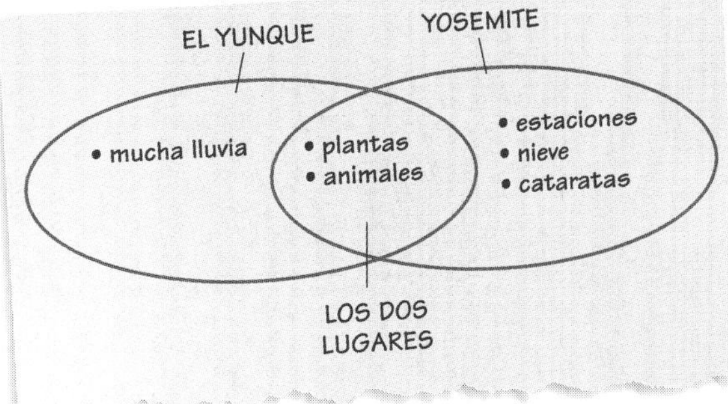


Write your first draft freely and naturally. Write as if you were face to face with your pen pal, sharing the information. Be sure to cover all the ideas listed on your Venn diagram.

### Revisiones

Share your draft with a partner. Then ask

- *Is the subject clearly stated?*
- *What details could I add?*
- *After reading the letter, would you want to visit this spot?*

Make revisions to your draft based on your partner's answers to these questions.

Me gusta mucho ir a la playa.
Pero creo que ~~una~~ playa de las/s
Puerto Rico ~~sea~~ más bonita son/s
que la playa de mi pueblo de
Nueva Inglaterra. Tienen mucho en
común pero son muy diferentes.
En el verano la playa de mi
pueblo es bonita. El agua refleja
el cielo y la arena te invita a
relajarse. Pero pronto ves que te
~~encima de~~ la arena hay muchísimas
piedras...

### La versión final

Before completing the final draft of your friendly letter, correct any errors using the proofreading symbols (p. 97). Keep the following question in mind:

- *Did I put pronouns in the right places?*

**Try this:** Are you sure that reflexive, indirect object, and direct object pronouns are placed correctly? Circle these pronouns and then review the rules for proper placement.

Share your writing on www.mcdougallittell.com



### Supplementary Vocabulary

| | |
|---|---|
| **más ... que** | more ... than |
| **menos ... que** | less ... than |
| **mejor** | better |
| **peor** | worse |
| **tanto(a) ... como** | as much ... as |
| **tantos(as) ... como** | as many ... as |

### Rubric: Writing

Let students know ahead of time which elements of their writing you will be evaluating. A global evaluation is more helpful to students than a correction of every mistake made. Consider the following in scoring compositions.

| | |
|---|---|
| **Sentences** | |
| 1 | Most not logical |
| 2 | In logical order |
| 3 | Flow purposefully |
| **Details** | |
| 1 | Few details |
| 2 | Sufficient basic details |
| 3 | Clear and vivid details |
| **Organization** | |
| 1 | Not well organized |
| 2 | Some organization |
| 3 | Strong organization |
| **Accuracy** | |
| 1 | Errors prevent comprehension |
| 2 | Some spelling and agreement errors throughout |
| 3 | Very few errors |

| Criteria | Scale | |
|---|---|---|
| Logical sentence order | 1 2 3 | A = 10–12 pts. |
| Clear and vivid detail | 1 2 3 | B = 7–9 pts. |
| Organization | 1 2 3 | C = 5–6 pts. |
| Accuracy | 1 2 3 | D = 4 pts. |
| | | F = < 4 pts. |

## Teaching All Students

**Extra Help** Review the following structures with students before writing:

- Use of adjectives that agree in gender and number with the subject
- Use of demonstrative adjectives and pronouns
- Use of reflexive verbs
- Placement of pronouns (reflexive, indirect and direct object pronouns)

**Challenge** Have students compare and contrast what they know about Puerto Rican food and North American food in a Venn diagram. You can also ask students to write a paragraph based on the information in the diagram.

**Native Speakers** If you have Spanish speakers from Puerto Rico in your class, have them give a complete description of their favorite places on the island before the class gets started on their paragraphs.

### Block Schedule

**Variety** Have students compare and contrast their Spanish class with another class. They should follow the same steps as outlined here, i.e., brainstorm ideas, create a Venn diagram, then write the paragraph.

## Unit Theme

**Traveling in Spain, describing different housing situations, and shopping for clothes.**

**Communication**
- Talking about travel plans
- Describing rooms
- Describing your city or town
- Making suggestions, comparisons
- Asking for and giving directions
- Talking about shopping for clothes
- Asking for/giving opinions; persuading
- Discussing saving/spending money

**Cultures**
- Learning about lodging options and different housing situations in Spain
- Learning about different places to shop in Spain and Latin America
- Learning about some Spanish artists

**Connections**
- Connecting to Art: Finding out about artists of the Spanish School
- Connecting to Technology: Creating a web page for your community
- Connecting to Geography: Navigating one's way in a city

**Comparisons**
- Comparing the cities and towns in Spain and the U.S.
- Comparing shopping customs

**Communities**
- Using Spanish in the workplace
- Using Spanish for personal interest

## Teaching Resource Options

**Print** 

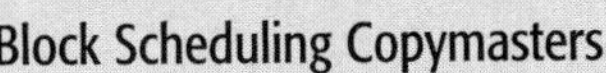

Block Scheduling Copymasters

**Audiovisual** 

**OHT** M1, M5; 103, 104, 105, 106
*Canciones* Cassette / CD Songs 2, 10, 12
**Video Program** Videotape 4, 0:00 / Videodisc 3A

Search Chapter 1, Play to 2
U4 Cultural Introduction

UNIDAD 4
OBJECTIVES
ETAPA 1
En la pensión
• Talk about travel plans
• Persuade others
• Describe rooms, furniture, and appliances
ETAPA 2
Conoce la ciudad
• Describe your city or town
• Make suggestions
• Ask for and give directions
ETAPA 3
Vamos de compras
• Talk about shopping for clothes
• Ask for and give opinions
• Make comparisons
• Discuss ways to save and spend money
242


# MADRID
# ESPAÑA
## UN VIAJE

**EL PRADO** En 1818, el rey Fernando VII y la reina María Isabel de Braganza querían redecorar el Palacio Real y decidieron mover sus enormes pinturas al vacante Palacio del Prado. Y así empezó el famoso Museo del Prado. ¿Qué otros museos conoces?

PORTUGAL

**LA GUITARRA** acústica tiene más de 2.000 años. Se cree que los egipcios la inventaron y que los árabes la trajeron a España. ¿Cuándo crees que se inventó la guitarra eléctrica?

OCÉANO ATLÁNTICO

ISLAS CANARIAS

## Classroom Community

**Cooperative Learning** Ask students to divide into groups and choose one of the **Gente famosa de España** in the **Almanaque** on p. 243. Have each group research an important accomplishment of their famous person. All students should contribute at least one piece of information. S1 acts as the recorder, S2 reads the presentation to the class, and S3 adds one or more **españoles famosos** to the list.

**Paired Activity** Tape or draw a large map of Spain (one without city names) on the board. On pieces of paper, write names of Spanish cities and towns and place them in a container. Each pair of students chooses two and locates them using an atlas. They then go to the board and tape their cities/towns at the correct locations. Give students a geographical quiz.

## ALMANAQUE

**Población:** 2.910.000
**Altura:** 656 metros (2.150 pies)
**Clima:** 5°C (41°F), diciembre; 24°C (76°F), julio
**Moneda:** la peseta
**Comida típica:** paella, cocido madrileño, horchata, churros con chocolate
**Gente famosa de España:** Severiano Ballesteros (golfista), Antonio Banderas (actor), Miguel de Cervantes (escritor), Felipe II (rey), Francisco de Goya (artista), Ana María Matute (escritora), Joaquín Sabina (cantante), Diego Velázquez (artista)
**¿Vas a Madrid?** Si un madrileño te pregunta si hablas «castellano», debes decirle que sí. Español y castellano son lo mismo.

INTERNET Ve a www.mcdougallittell.com para más información sobre Madrid.

**PAELLA** Este plato de mariscos, pollo, chorizo y arroz tiene muchas variaciones a través de España. Para cocinarla, tienes que usar una olla especial que se llama una paellera. ¿Alguna vez probaste paella? ¿Te gustó?

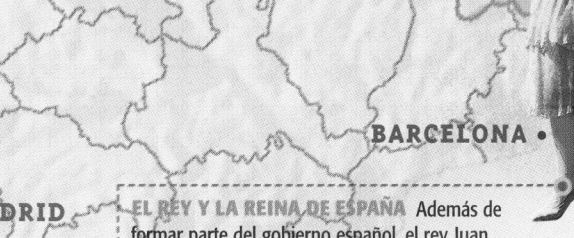

**EL REY Y LA REINA DE ESPAÑA** Además de formar parte del gobierno español, el rey Juan Carlos y la reina Sofía participan en varios aspectos de la vida de su país. ¿Cuáles piensas que son algunos de éstos?

**ANTONIO BANDERAS** Esta estrella del cine en Estados Unidos y Europa comenzó a hacer teatro a los catorce años. Ahora, participa en películas en inglés y español. ¿Cuáles de sus películas conoces?

**EL GRECO (1541–1614)** nació en Grecia y estudió arte en Italia, pero completó la mayoría de su obra en España. Se lo considera uno de los artistas más importantes del mundo. Este cuadro *Vista de Toledo,* muestra la ciudad española en la que vivió por 37 años. ¿Qué te parece?

## Teaching All Students

**Extra Help** Ask students to read aloud each caption with a partner and ask each other basic questions about what they read.

**Native Speakers** Ask Spanish speakers what they know about Spain's influence on their native country. If any students have connections to Spain, have them share them with the class.

**Multiple Intelligences**

**Visual** Have students draw a Venn Diagram comparing the items about Madrid in the **Almanaque** with corresponding information for their area.

**Kinesthetic** Have students write 2–3 true/false statements about the captions and read each one aloud. Students stand up if it is true or remain seated if it is false.



## Teaching Suggestions
### Previewing the Unit

- You may wish to use the video to preview the unit.
- Tell students that this unit centers on Spain. Ask students to share what they already know about Spain and the Spanish culture.
- Show students a map of Spain and ask what cities they are already familiar with.

## Culture Highlights

- **EL PRADO** A museum that includes the works of Spain's three great masters: Francisco Goya, Diego Velázquez, and El Greco plus many masterpieces by Flemish and Italian artists.
- **LA GUITARRA** Today's 6-string guitar is still called the "Spanish guitar" because it was developed in Spain. **Castañuelas**, or *castanets* in English, accompany the guitar in flamenco performances.
- **PAELLA** It is said that the first **paella** was served in Valencia. The typical Valencian **paella** consists of rice, seafood, chicken, and vegetables.
- **EL REY Y LA REINA DE ESPAÑA** King Juan Carlos has a role in overseeing the government institutions in Spain's parliamentary monarchy. He and his wife, Sofía, have three children.
- **ANTONIO BANDERAS** Some recent American movies with Antonio Banderas include *Mask of Zorro* and *Evita.*
- **EL GRECO** (1541–1614) was a Greek-born artist named Domenikos Theotokopoulus who lived and worked in Toledo, Spain. He is considered one of the world's first modern painters due to his spiritual style that differed from realism.
- **MONEDA** In 1999 the euro replaced the peseta as the official currency of Spain. However, euro notes and coins will not be issued until 2002.

## Block Schedule

**Warm-Up** Students should flip through the unit to familiarize themselves with the coming topics. Have them answer questions about the unit.

# Ampliación

These activities may be used at various points in the Unit 4 sequence.

For Block Schedule, you may find that these projects will provide a welcome change of pace while reviewing and reinforcing the material presented in the unit.

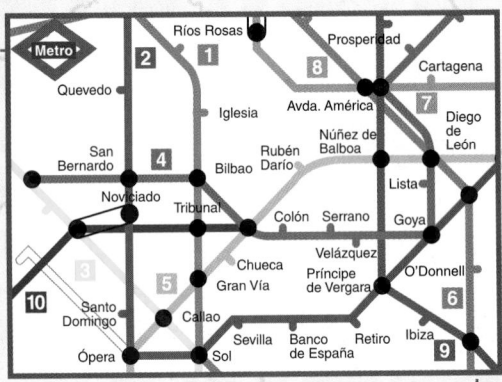

## PROJECTS

**¿Prefieres la ciudad o el campo?** Divide the class into two or three groups. Have one group try to persuade the class to live in the city, the second group try to persuade the class to live in the country, and the third group (optional) try to persuade the class to live in the suburbs. Each group should list the top ten reasons to live in each location, then create an advertisement to convince others.

PACING SUGGESTION: Upon completion of Etapa 1 or 2.

**Create a shopping guide** for where to buy clothing in your community. Divide the class into small groups and assign each group a type of clothing to research. They must decide on a store then give directions on how to get there. Put all the information together and create a shopping guide for visiting Spanish-speakers.

PACING SUGGESTION: Upon completion of Etapa 2 or 3.

## STORYTELLING

**De compras en el centro** After reviewing the vocabulary for asking for and giving directions, model a mini-story that students will retell and revise:

> Un día Miguel quería ir de compras. Preguntó a su padre, "Papá, ¿cómo se va al centro comercial?" Él le preguntó, "¿Vas a caminar o vas en autobús?" Le dijo, "Quiero ir en la manera más rápida." "Pues, tienes que ir en autobús" dijo el papá. "Ve a la calle Mayor y espera el autobús número 9. Sube el autobús y ve hasta la parada del centro comercial. Al volver, puedes tomar el mismo autobús para volver a casa de nuevo."

As you give your model, be sure to pause as the story is being told so that students may fill in words and act out gestures. Students should then write, narrate, and read aloud a longer main story. This new version should include vocabulary from **Unidad 4**.

**¿Cómo se va a...?** Ask students to give directions to the last place they went shopping.

PACING SUGGESTION: Upon completion of Etapa 2.

## BULLETIN BOARDS / POSTERS

**Bulletin Board** **Plan ahead:** Contact a travel agency or the Tourist Office of Spain for maps and brochures on different cities in Spain. Create a collage of places to visit in Spain. Have students review the collage and decide where they might like to visit and why.

**Posters** **Have students create** • **A map** of their house • **Store advertisement** posters with items and their prices • **Travel posters** for Madrid, Spain • **Map of the local area** so students can use it to give directions • **Currency exchange** rate table for U.S. dollar vs. Spanish *peseta,* euro, Mexican *peso,* among others.

## GAMES

**¿Cuánto vale?**

**Prepare ahead:** Gather play money and pictures of clothing and assign a price to each one. Divide the class in half and assign one half to be the buyers and the other half the sellers. Give the sellers the pictures of clothing items. Give the buyers each 10,000 *pesetas* (play money) and have them try to buy some new clothes. The sellers must try to get as much money for their item as possible, while the buyers must try to buy as many items as possible. Give the class 10 minutes for the buying/selling round. The two winners are the buyer with the most clothing and the seller with the most money.

PACING SUGGESTION: Upon completion of Etapa 3.

## MUSIC

**La tuna** is a group of strolling musicians made up of university students, a tradition that dates back to the 13th century. These musicians dress in medieval costumes and play tambourines, guitars, and **bandurrias** (smaller, guitar-like instruments) while singing traditional Castilian songs with humor and style. **Las tunas** still entertain at parties and restaurants in many parts of Spain. Show pictures of **la tuna** or play some old Spanish songs and have students try to name similar types of strolling musicians they might see in their country. Play the *Canciones* Cassette/CD for the class.

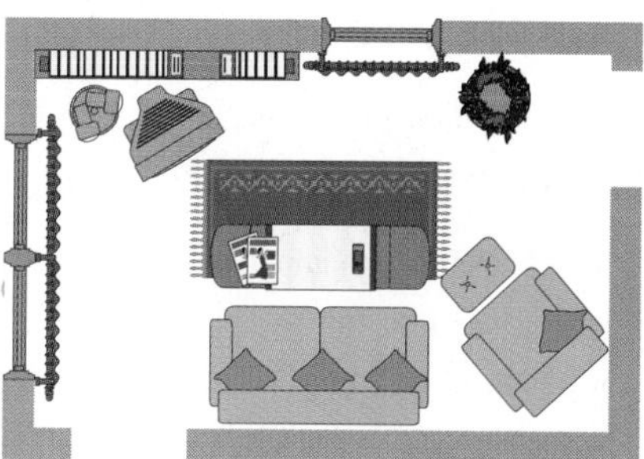

## HANDS-ON CRAFTS

Work with the art department to create models or floor plans of students' homes. Have students give Spanish labels to each part of their house. The models can be created in any medium and can be displayed in the class or in another centralized location. The floor plans can be displayed on a bulletin board.

## Receta

***Tortilla española***
*4 huevos*
*1 cucharadita de sal*
*1/2 taza y 3 cucharadas de aceite de oliva*
*4 patatas grandes, cortadas en tajadas*
*1 cebolla grande, cortada en tajadas*

*En una sartén, caliente la taza de aceite. Añada las cebollas y las patatas y cocínelas hasta que se ablanden. Quite las patatas y la cebolla de la sartén y reserve sólo tres cucharadas de aceite. Limpie bien la sartén para usarla de nuevo con la tortilla. Bata los huevos y agregue la sal. Añada los huevos, las cebollas y las patatas y cocine a fuego bajo hasta que se seque y dore un poco la parte de abajo. No lo mueva mucho. Colóquele encima un plato grande, y voltee todo junto rápidamente. Ponga la tortilla nuevamente en la sartén y continúe cocinando el otro lado hasta dorarlo ligeramente también. Ponga la sal encima de la tortilla cocida. Sírvala con pan.*

## RECIPE

**La tortilla española** is a staple in the Spanish diet. It is served as a light supper **(la cena)** or in a sandwich **(el bocadillo)** as a snack **(la merienda)**. The typical **tortilla española** is made of eggs, potato, and onion.

# Planning Guide CLASSROOM MANAGEMENT

## OBJECTIVES

| | |
|---|---|
| **Communication** | • Talk about travel plans *pp. 246–247, 248–249*<br>• Persuade others *pp. 248–249, 252–253*<br>• Describe rooms, furniture, and appliances *pp. 247, 254, 257* |
| **Grammar** | • The subjunctive to express hopes and wishes *pp. 252–253*<br>• Irregular subjunctive forms *pp. 255–256* |
| **Culture** | • La Plaza de la Cibeles *p. 253*<br>• Alojamiento en Madrid *pp. 257, 260–261* |
| **Recycling** | • The subjunctive with impersonal expressions<br>• Places to go shopping<br>• Giving formal commands |

## STRATEGIES

| | |
|---|---|
| **Listening Strategies** | • Listen and check details *p. 248* |
| **Speaking Strategies** | • Persuade *p. 259*<br>• Make and express decisions *p. 264* |
| **Reading Strategies** | • Compare related details *p. 260* |
| **Writing Strategies** | • Use different kinds of descriptive words *Actividad 7, TE p. 264* |
| **Connecting Cultures Strategies** | • Comparing hotels in Spain and the U.S. *p. 260*<br>• Research Spanish artists *p. 264* |

## PROGRAM RESOURCES

### Print

- *Más práctica* Workbook PE *pp. 89–96*
- Block Scheduling Copymasters *pp. 81–88*
- Unit 4 Resource Book
  - *Más práctica* Workbook TE *pp. 1–8*
  - *Cuaderno para hispanohablantes* TE *pp. 9–16*
  - Information Gap Activities *pp. 17–20*
  - Family Involvement *pp. 21–22*
  - Video Activities *pp. 23–25*
  - Videoscript *pp. 26–27*
  - Audioscript *pp. 28–32*
  - Assessment Program, Unit 4 Etapa 1 *pp. 33–51; pp. 170–172*
  - Answer Keys *pp. 179–180*

### Audiovisual

- Audio Program Cassette 10A, 10B / CD 10
- *Canciones* Cassette/CD
- Video Program Videotape 4 / Videodisc 3A
- Overhead Transparencies M1, M5; 104; 107–116

### Technology

- Electronic Teacher Tools/Test Generator
- *Intrigas y aventuras* CD-ROM, Disc 2
-  www.mcdougallittell.com

### Assessment Program Options

- Cooperative Quizzes (Unit 4 Resource Book)
- Etapa Exam Forms A and B (Unit 4 Resource Book)
- *Examen para hispanohablantes* (Unit 4 Resource Book)
- Portfolio Assessment (Unit 4 Resource Book)
- Multiple Choice Test Questions (Unit 4 Resource Book)
- Audio Program Cassette 20 / CD 20
- Electronic Teacher Tools/Test Generator

### Native Speakers

- *Cuaderno para hispanohablantes* PE *pp. 89–96*
- *Cuaderno para hispanohablantes* TE (Unit 4 Resource Book)
- *Examen para hispanohablantes* (Unit 4 Resource Book)
- Audio Program (*Para hispanohablantes*) Cassettes 10B, 20A / CD 10, CD 20
- Audioscript (Unit 4 Resource Book)

Isabel | Angelina | Felipe | Señor Zavala | Andrea

# Student Text Listening Activity Scripts

## Videoscript: Diálogo *pages 248–249*

- Videotape 4, 5:18 • Videodisc 3A
  Search Chapter 3, Play to 4. U4E1, En vivo (Dialog)
- Use the videoscript with **Actividades 1, 2** *page 250*

**Isabel:** Gracias por todo, Felipe. Y gracias a ustedes también. Fue un placer estar en su casa.
**Angelina:** El placer fue nuestro, Isabel. Sabes que Ana María no quiere que te vayas. Es una lástima que nosotros tengamos que salir mañana para Cádiz.
**Felipe:** Sí, qué lástima. Pero te va a gustar mucho la pensión de mi tío. Es una pensión muy buena. Y mi tío es muy buena gente. Pero como vas a ver, él habla muchísimo.
**Isabel:** Estoy segura que me va a gustar.
**Felipe:** Sabes, Isabel, el artículo que escribiste para *Onda Internacional* es excelente. Escribes muy bien.
**Isabel:** Gracias, Felipe, pero me ayudaste mucho.
**Felipe:** No tanto, Isabel. Tienes mucho talento. Si te interesa ser periodista, es bueno que escribas. Escribe un poco todos los días. Es la mejor práctica. Bueno, ¿estás lista? Dame tu maleta.
**Isabel:** Gracias. ¡Adiós!
**Angelina:** ¡Adiós!
**Ana María:** ¡Adiós!
**Felipe:** ¡Hasta luego!
**Sr. Zavala:** Sí, muy bien... Tienen una reserva para una habitación doble con baño. Si nos hacen el favor de presentarse en recepción antes de la seis de la tarde... Muy bien. Hasta el viernes, entonces. Adiós.

Debes de ser Isabel Palacios. Felipe me llamó y me dijo que ibas a venir. Yo soy su tío, Enrique Zavala.
**Isabel:** Mucho gusto, Sr. Zavala.
**Sr. Zavala:** Igualmente, Isabel. Vamos, te acompaño a tu habitación. Lo siento, pero estamos muy ocupados hoy y el maletero está enfermo. ¡Así que yo soy el maletero hoy!
Vamos en el ascensor; tu habitación está en el tercer piso. Pero si tienes muchas energías, las escaleras están por allí. Nuestra pensión es pequeña, pero creo que es muy cómoda. ¿Eres de México, no? ¿Y vas a pasar aquí unos días más en Madrid? Muy bien. Madrid es una ciudad maravillosa. Es importante que vayas al Prado. Es un museo excelente. Tremendo. Y es esencial que des una vuelta por la Gran Vía, y veas la Plaza Mayor. Hay tanto que ver. Ojalá que tengas tiempo de visitar el Parque del Buen Retiro. También debes ir a....
Y es necesario que te pongas unos zapatos muy cómodos porque vas a caminar mucho. Madrid es una ciudad perfecta para caminar. Ésta es tu llave. Cuando los huéspedes salen del hotel, es muy importante que dejen la llave en la recepción. Así la llave no se pierde nunca, ¿verdad? E Isabel, insisto en que nos digas adónde vas. Mi esposa y yo somos responsables de ti. Y es importante que sepas que si tienes algún problema o dificultad, puedes llamarnos a cualquier hora. Mira, ésta es tu habitación.
Ésta es una de nuestras mejores habitaciones. Muy bonita la habitación, ¿no? Mi esposa y yo decoramos toda la pensión. Ella buscó todos los muebles. Mira, ésta es la cama. Creo que es muy cómoda.
**Isabel:** Sr. Zavala...
**Sr. Zavala:** ¿Sí, Isabel? Dime.
**Isabel:** Gracias por todo, Sr. Zavala. Usted es muy amable y me encanta la habitación. Pero perdóneme, por favor. Estoy muy cansada y me gustaría descansar un ratito.
**Sr. Zavala:** Claro que sí, Isabel. Ya me voy. Pero Isabel, ¿por qué no me dijiste que estabas cansada? Hasta luego.
**Isabel:** Adiós.
Aquí tiene la llave de mi habitación. Voy a dar una vuelta y explorar un poco.
**Sr. Zavala:** Gracias, Isabel. ¿Adónde vas?
**Isabel:** Voy a la Plaza Mayor y a la Gran Vía. Y después, no sé. ¿Tiene alguna sugerencia?
**Sr. Zavala:** Sí, te sugiero que vayas al Palacio Real. Es impresionante. Y después, es lógico que pases por la Puerta del Sol. Ah, aquí tienes una tarjeta con el número de teléfono de la pensión. Y también tiene la dirección, ¿ves? Si necesitas algo, llámame. Ah, ¿tienes dinero suficiente para un taxi? ¿Y para comer algo? ¿Y te pusiste zapatos cómodos?
**Isabel:** Sí, Sr. Zavala. Lo llamo si necesito algo... y tengo dinero... y mis zapatos son muy cómodos.
**Sr. Zavala:** Después de caminar mucho, es muy divertido sentarse en un café cerca de la Plaza Mayor. Te recomiendo el Café Reina Sofía. Tienen pasteles deliciosos. Ah, perdón. El teléfono. ¿Diga?
**Isabel:** Adiós, Sr. Zavala. Hasta luego.
**Andrea:** Disculpa, ¿me puedo sentar aquí?
**Isabel:** ¡Claro que sí! Siéntate, por favor.
**Andrea:** Muchas gracias. Me llamo Andrea Machado.
**Isabel:** Soy Isabel Palacios.
**Andrea:** Encantada.
**Isabel:** Igualmente.
**Andrea:** ¿De dónde eres?
**Isabel:** Soy de México, de la Ciudad de México.
**Andrea:** Ah, nunca he estado en la Ciudad de México.
**Isabel:** Tienes que visitarla. Es una ciudad muy grande.

## Actividad 9 ¿Loca o normal? *page 255*

*Estas personas van a redecorar varias partes de la casa. Escucha cada descripción. ¿Es loca o normal?*

1. Quiero que compremos una mesa grande y ocho sillas bonitas para el comedor.
2. Mi esposo sugiere que pongamos un espejo grande sobre el lavabo en el baño.
3. Ojalá que plantemos muchas flores bonitas en el jardín cerca del armario.
4. Insisto en que pongamos una bañera bonita en la sala.
5. Espero que la habitación de Alfredo tenga un armario grandísimo y una cama elegante.
6. Mi familia quiere que tengamos camas grandes en la cocina.
7. Mi mamá desea que compremos unas pinturas alegres para la habitación de Ana.
8. Prefiero que el sofá nuevo esté en el garaje.
9. Los vecinos quieren que decoremos el apartamento con muebles viejos y basura.

## Actividad 13 ¿Dónde quieren hospedarse? *page 257*

*Estas personas están describiendo dónde quieren hospedarse. ¿Qué dibujo corresponde a cada descripción? Luego explícale a un compañero o una compañera dónde te gustaría hospedarte a ti.*

1. Me gusta cocinar, entonces quiero hospedarme en una habitación moderna con una cocina. Es necesario que haya una estufa, un horno, un horno microondas y especialmente un lavaplatos. Y claro, debe tener un baño.
2. Quiero que sea una habitación con muebles antiguos y paredes bonitas. No es necesario que la habitación tenga baño. Si hay servicios en el pasillo, está bien.
3. No es importante que tengamos una habitación extravagante, pero necesitamos dos camas. E insistimos en que haya un patio. Nos gusta tomar nuestro desayuno en el jardín.
4. Es necesario que yo viaje a varias partes del mundo por mi trabajo. Entonces, quiero que la habitación sea práctica y cómoda. Prefiero que haya una cama grande, un sillón y un escritorio con una lámpara y un teléfono. También deseo que haya una televisión.

# Pacing Guide

## Sample Lesson Plan - 50 Minute Schedule

### DAY 1

***Unit Opener***
- Anticipate/Activate prior knowledge: Present the *Almanaque* and the cultural notes on p. 242–243. Use Map OHTs as needed. 10 MIN.

***Etapa Opener***
- Quick Start Review (TE p. 244). 5 MIN.
- Have students look at the *Etapa* Opener and answer *¿Qué ves?* questions. 5 MIN.

***En contexto: Vocabulario***
- Quick Start Review (TE p. 246). 3 MIN.
- Have students use context and pictures to learn *Etapa* vocabulary. Answer questions p. 247. 10 MIN.

***En vivo: Diálogo***
- Quick Start Review (TE p. 248). 2 MIN.
- Review Listening Strategy, p. 248. Play audio/show video for the dialog. 7 MIN.
- Have students take on roles of characters. 8 MIN.

***Homework Option***
- Video Activities, Unit 4 Resource Book, pp. 23–25.

### DAY 2

***En acción: Vocabulario y Gramática***
- Check homework. 5 MIN.
- Quick Start Review (TE p. 250). 5 MIN.
- Ask students for a summary of *En vivo* dialog to check recall. 5 MIN.
- Have students answer Comprehension Questions (TE p. 249). 5 MIN.
- Replay the *En vivo* dialog using the audiovisual resources and have students do *Actividades* 1 and 2 orally. 8 MIN.
- Have students complete *Actividades* 3 and 4. 7 MIN.
- Present *Gramática*: The Subjunctive to Express Hopes and Wishes, p. 252, and *Vocabulario*. Have students complete *Actividades* 5 and 6 in writing. 15 MIN.

***Homework Option***
- *Más práctica* Workbook, p. 93. *Cuaderno para hispanohablantes*, p. 91.

### DAY 3

***En acción (cont.)***
- Check homework. 5 MIN.
- Quick Start Review (TE p. 254). 5 MIN.
- Present the vocabulary in the box on p. 254, then have students complete *Actividad* 7 in writing and *Actividad* 8 in pairs. 15 MIN.
- Play the audio and have students complete *Actividad* 9. 10 MIN.
- Present *Gramática*: Irregular Subjunctive Forms, p. 255. 10 MIN.
- Have students do *Actividad* 10 in writing. 5 MIN.

***Homework Option***
- *Más práctica* Workbook, p. 94. *Cuaderno para hispanohablantes*, p. 92.

### DAY 4

***En acción (cont.)***
- Check homework. 5 MIN.
- Quick Start Review (TE p. 256). 5 MIN.
- Present the vocabulary box on p. 257 and have students complete *Actividad* 11 in pairs and *Actividad* 12 in small groups. 10 MIN.
- Play audio and have students complete *Actividad* 13. Expand with *Más comunicación*, p. R11. 10 MIN.
- Have students complete *Actividad* 14 in pairs. 10 MIN.
- Have students study the Metro map on p. 258 and complete *Actividad* 15 in pairs. 10 MIN.

***Homework Option***
- *Más práctica* Workbook, pp. 95–96. *Cuaderno para hispanohablantes*, pp. 93–94.

### DAY 5

***En acción (cont.)***
- Check homework. 5 MIN.
- Quick Start Review (TE p. 258). 5 MIN.
- Present Speaking Strategy, p. 259, and have students do *Actividad* 16 in pairs. 10 MIN.
- Have students complete *Actividad* 17 in small groups and possibly present their ideal homes to the class. Expand with *Más comunicación*, p. R11. 15 MIN.

***En voces: Lectura***
- Review Reading Strategy, p. 260, and have students read silently. 5 MIN.
- Have students read *Felices sueños* aloud taking turns. Call on volunteers to answer *¿Comprendiste?* questions. 10 MIN.

***Homework Option***
- Have students answer the *¿Comprendiste?* and *¿Qué piensas?* questions as written homework. *Cuaderno para hispanohablantes*, p. 90.

### DAY 6

***En uso: Repaso y más comunicación***
- Review the *¿Comprendiste?* and *¿Qué piensas?* questions as a class. 10 MIN.
- Quick Start Review (TE p. 262). 5 MIN.
- Do *Actividades* 1 and 2 orally. 10 MIN.
- Do *Actividades* 3 and 4 in writing. 10 MIN.
- Review Speaking Strategy, p. 264. Then do *Actividad* 5 orally in pairs. 10 MIN.
- Review the *Notas culturales,* pp. 253, 257. 5 MIN.

***Homework Option***
- Have students prepare 5 review questions.
- *Cuaderno para hispanohablantes*, pp. 95–96.

### DAY 7

***En uso (cont.)***
- Check homework. 5 MIN.
- Quick Start Review (TE p. 264). 5 MIN.
- Have students do *Actividad* 6 in groups of four. 10 MIN.

***En tu propia voz: Escritura***
- Start writing activity. 10 MIN.

***Ampliación***
- Use a suggested project, game, or activity (TE pp. 243A–243B). 20 MIN.

***Homework Option***
- Complete writing activity. Review for *Etapa* 1 Exam.

### DAY 8

***En resumen: Repaso de vocabulario***
- Check homework. 5 MIN.

***Conexiones***
- Read and discuss. 5 MIN.
- Review grammar questions, etc., as necessary. 10 MIN.
- Complete *Etapa* 1 Exam. 20 MIN.

***Ampliación***
- Use a suggested project, game, or activity (TE pp. 243A–243B). 10 MIN.

***Homework Option***
- Preview next *Etapa* Opener, pp. 266–267.

# Sample Lesson Plan - Block Schedule (90 minutes)

## DAY 1

***Unit Opener***

- Anticipate/Activate prior knowledge: Present the *Almanaque* and the cultural notes on pp. 242–243. Use Map OHTs as needed. 10 MIN.

***Etapa Opener***

- Quick Start Review (TE p. 244). 5 MIN.
- Have students look at the *Etapa* Opener and answer questions. 10 MIN.

***En contexto: Vocabulario***

- Quick Start Review (TE p. 246). 5 MIN.
- Have students use context and photos to learn *Etapa* vocabulary. Answer questions p. 247. 10 MIN.

***En vivo: Diálogo***

- Quick Start Review (TE p. 248). 5 MIN.
- Review Listening Strategy, p. 248. Play audio or show video for the dialog shown on pp. 248–249. 10 MIN.
- Replay and have students take on roles of characters. 10 MIN.
- Ask Comprehension Questions (TE p. 249) 10 MIN.

***En acción: Vocabulario y Gramática***

- Quick Start Review (TE p. 250). 5 MIN.
- Have students do *Actividades* 1 and 2 orally. 10 MIN.

***Homework Option***

- Have students prepare two T/F or yes/no questions about the dialog.
- Video Activities, Unit 4 Resource Book, pp. 23–25.

## DAY 2

***En acción (cont.)***

- Check homework. 10 MIN.
- Quick Start Review (TE p. 252). 5 MIN.
- Have students complete *Actividades* 3 and 4 in pairs. 10 MIN.
- Present *Gramática:* The Subjunctive to Express Hopes and Wishes and the vocabulary box, p. 252, and then have students complete *Actividades* 5 and 6 in writing. 15 MIN.
- Present the *Vocabulario,* p. 254. Have students complete *Actividad* 7 in writing and *Actividad* 8 in pairs. 15 MIN.
- Play the audio and have students complete *Actividad* 9. 10 MIN.
- Present *Gramática*: Irregular Subjunctive Forms, p. 255. 10 MIN.
- Have students do *Actividad* 10 in writing and *Actividad* 11 in pairs. 10 MIN.
- Use Block Scheduling Copymasters for variety. 5 MIN.

***Homework Option***

- *Más práctica* Workbook, pp. 93–94. *Cuaderno para hispanohablantes*, pp. 91–92.

## DAY 3

***En acción (cont.)***

- Check homework. 10 MIN.
- Quick Start Review (TE p. 256). 5 MIN.
- Present the vocabulary box on p. 257 and have students complete *Actividad* 12 orally. 10 MIN.
- Play the audio and do *Actividad* 13 orally with the whole class. Expand with *Más comunicación,* p. R11. 15 MIN.
- Have students complete *Actividad* 14 in pairs. 10 MIN.
- Have students study the Metro map on p. 258 and do *Actividad* 15 in pairs. 10 MIN.
- Present Speaking Strategy, p. 259, and do *Actividad* 16 in pairs. 10 MIN.
- Have students complete *Actividad* 17, then have some volunteers describe their dream house to the class. Expand with *Más comunicación,* p. R11. 15 MIN.
- Use Block Scheduling Copymasters, pp. 81–88, for a change of pace as needed. 5 MIN.

***Homework Option***

- *Más práctica* Workbook, pp. 95–96. *Cuaderno para hispanohablantes*, pp. 93–94.

## DAY 4

***En voces: Lectura***

- Check homework. 10 MIN.
- Quick Start Review (TE p. 260). 5 MIN.
- Review Reading Strategy, p. 260. 5 MIN.
- Have students read *Felices sueños* silently. 10 MIN.
- Have students read the *Lectura* aloud in turns. 10 MIN.
- Call on volunteers to answer *¿Comprendiste?* questions. Refer back to the reading if students give the incorrect answer. 10 MIN.
- Have students do the *¿Qué piensas?* activity in writing, then discuss in class. 10 MIN.

***En uso: Repaso y más comunicación***

- Quick Start Review (TE p. 262). 5 MIN.
- Use Teaching Suggestions (TE p. 262). 10 MIN.
- Do *Actividades* 1, 2, 3, and 4 orally. 15 MIN.

***Homework Option***

- *Cuaderno para hispanohablantes*, pp. 90, 95–96.
- Review for *Etapa* 1 Exam.

## DAY 5

***En uso: Repaso y más comunicación (cont.)***

- Quick Start Review (TE p. 264). 5 MIN.
- Review Speaking Strategy, p. 264. Then do *Actividad* 5 orally in pairs and *Actividad* 6 in groups of four. 15 MIN.

***Conexiones***

- Read and discuss. 5 MIN.

***En resumen: Repaso de vocabulario***

- Review grammar questions, etc., as necessary. 10 MIN.
- Complete *Etapa* 1 Exam. 20 MIN.

***En tu propia voz: Escritura***

- Do *Actividad* 7. Have volunteers present letters. 20 MIN.

***Ampliación***

- Use a suggested project, game, or activity (TE pp. 243A–243B). 15 MIN.

***Homework Option***

- Finish writing activity and preview next *Etapa* Opener, pp. 266–267.

▼ Isabel se despide de Felipe y su familia.

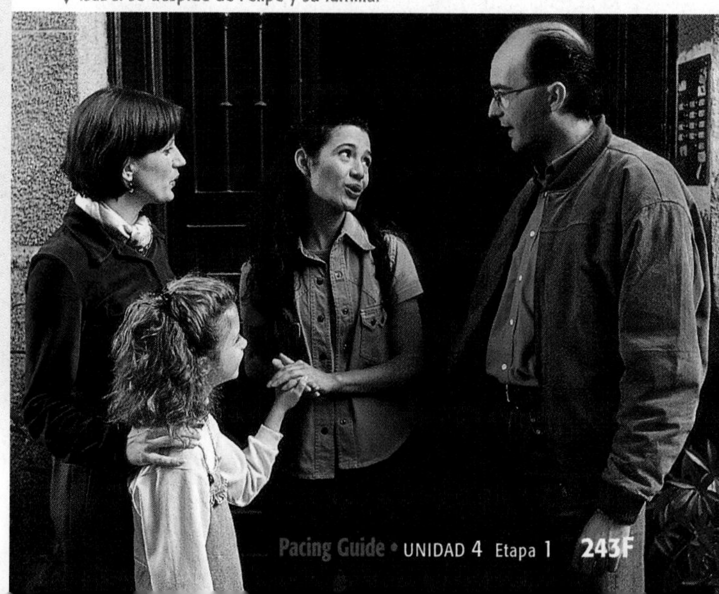

## Etapa Theme

**Talking about travel plans, persuading others, and describing rooms, furniture, and appliances**

## Grammar Objectives

- Subjunctive to express hopes and wishes
- Irregular subjunctive forms

### Teaching Resource Options

**Print** 

Block Scheduling Copymasters

**Audiovisual**

**OHT** 104, 113 (Quick Start)

*Canciones* Cassette / CD Song 12

### Quick Start Review

Discussing likes and dislikes

Use OHT 113 or write on board: Look at the picture and pick out a few features that interest you. Notice the architecture and some of the artistic elements. Think of some descriptive words in Spanish and complete two of the following statements.

**Me interesa...**
**Me fascina...**
**No me gusta...**

*Answers will vary.*

### Teaching Suggestions
**Previewing the Etapa**

Ask students to study the photo on pp. 244–245 and brainstorm about what activities Isabel may be planning to do.

UNIDAD 4

ETAPA 1

# En la pensión

- Talk about travel plans
- Persuade others
- Describe rooms, furniture, and appliances

### ¿Qué ves?

Mira la foto. ¿Qué ves?

1. ¿Dónde crees que está Isabel?
2. ¿Qué tiene en las manos?
3. ¿Qué significa **pensión**?
4. ¿Dónde puedes encontrar información sobre hoteles en Madrid?

244

### Classroom Management

**Planning Ahead** Prepare students to discuss travel plans in their city and in other cities. Collect travel brochures and tour advertisements for Madrid and other Spanish cities. Also collect any travel information on your own area.

**Peer Review** Have students work in pairs to answer the **¿Qué ves?** questions. Then have them create additional questions about the photo to ask another pair of students.

## Culture Highlights

- **MADRILEÑO(A)** A **madrileño(a)** is a person from Madrid. Ask students what they call people from their city or town.
- **UNA PENSIÓN** In Spain a **pensión** is a guest house that is a more modest accommodation than a hotel. It has a family-like atmosphere since the owners do the cooking and cleaning of the rooms. Rates may include room and board.
- **AZULEJOS** Point out the painted tilework on the outside of the building, which is located just off the Plaza Ana in the center of Madrid. These **azulejos** are very common decorations in Spain, depicting Spanish scenes or forming geometric designs. The scene on p. 245 is the Plaza de España in Sevilla.

## Cross Cultural Connections

People from Spain will identify themselves first by the region or city they are from before they identify themselves as **español(a).** Ask students which is more important to them, the city they come from, or the state or country?

## Critical Thinking

Ask students to outline where people visit when they come to your town/city or state. Compare and contrast the attractions, ranking them in order of interest and comparing them to the places they learn about in Madrid in this **Etapa**.

## Block Schedule

**Process Time** Have students use the **¿Qué ves?** questions to lead into discussions in groups of 3 or 4. Ask them to talk about trips they have taken and if they have stayed in hotels. Encourage them to look ahead in the chapter for vocabulary. (For additional activities, see **Block Scheduling Copymasters.**)

## Teaching All Students

**Extra Help** Ask students to work with a partner to create a list of all the vocabulary words they associate with the picture on pp. 244–245. Have students write all the words on the board for the whole class to see.

**Native Speakers** Ask Spanish speakers if they have stayed in a hotel or pension in another country. If so, have them describe the experience to the class.

**Multiple Intelligences**

**Visual** Ask students to describe a mural or painted tilework they have seen, similar to the scenes on pp. 244–245.

**Verbal** Ask students to create a monologue to describe Isabel's first impressions upon arrival at Pensión Zavala.

### Teaching Resource Options

**Print** 

Unit 4 Resource Book
- Video Activities, p. 23
- Videoscript, p. 26
- Audioscript, p. 28

**Audiovisual** 

**OHT** 107, 108, 113 (Quick Start)
**Audio Program** Cassette 10A / CD 10
**Video Program** Videotape 4, 1:26 / Videodisc 3A

Search Chapter 2, Play to 3
U4E1, En contexto (Vocabulary)

**Technology** 

*Intrigas y aventuras* **CD-ROM**, Disc 2

### Quick Start Review

Talking about health

Use OHT 113 or write on board: Imagine you are on vacation in a big city and have spent all day sightseeing. Upon returning to the hotel you are tired and your body aches. Write four sentences that begin with the phrase **Me duele(n)**.

*Answers will vary.*

### Teaching Suggestions
#### Introducing Vocabulary

- Have students look at pp. 246–247. Use OHT 107–108 and Audiocassette 10A / CD 10 to present the vocabulary.
- Ask the Comprehension Questions in the margin of the Teacher's Edition on p. 247. You may write the questions on the board and have students work in small groups to answer them.
- Use the video vocabulary presentation for review and reinforcement.

# En contexto

## VOCABULARIO

Isabel va a empezar sus vacaciones en Madrid.

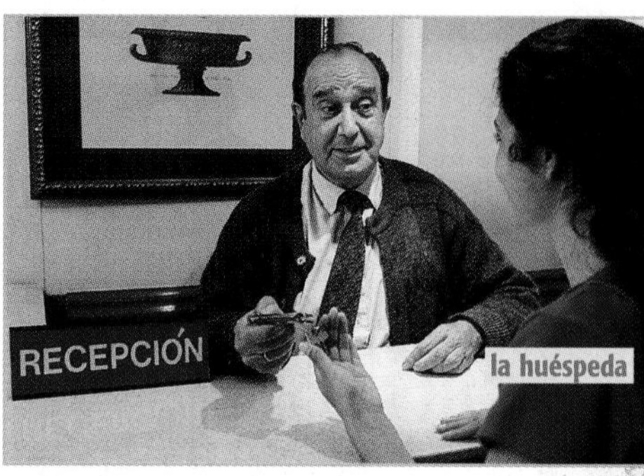


**A** Isabel toma un taxi a **la pensión** donde va a **hospedarse.** Esta pensión es popular entre **los extranjeros,** como Isabel, que vienen para hacer **turismo.** En **la recepción,** el señor busca **la reserva** de **la huéspeda** nueva. Luego, le da a Isabel **una llave.**

**B** **El maletero** ayuda a los huéspedes con sus maletas. La recepción está en **la planta baja,** pero Isabel y el maletero tienen que subir al tercer **piso.** Toman **el ascensor** en vez de **las escaleras.** ¡Es más fácil!

### Classroom Community

**Paired Activity** Ask students to read aloud each section with a partner and make a list of the new vocabulary words. Then have students prepare a short dialog on the following: Imagine you are traveling with your cranky cousin who does nothing but complain about aches and pains. Have students present their dialogs to the class.

**Group Activity** Divide students into small groups and ask each group to create a list of places their members have visited and where they stayed. For example, Florida: hotel, Yosemite National Park: tent, etc. Have the group with the longest list share it with the class.

**C** **La habitación** tiene varios **muebles: una cama, una mesa, una silla** y **una lámpara.** Sobre la mesa hay **un despertador,** pero Isabel no lo necesita —¡está de vacaciones!

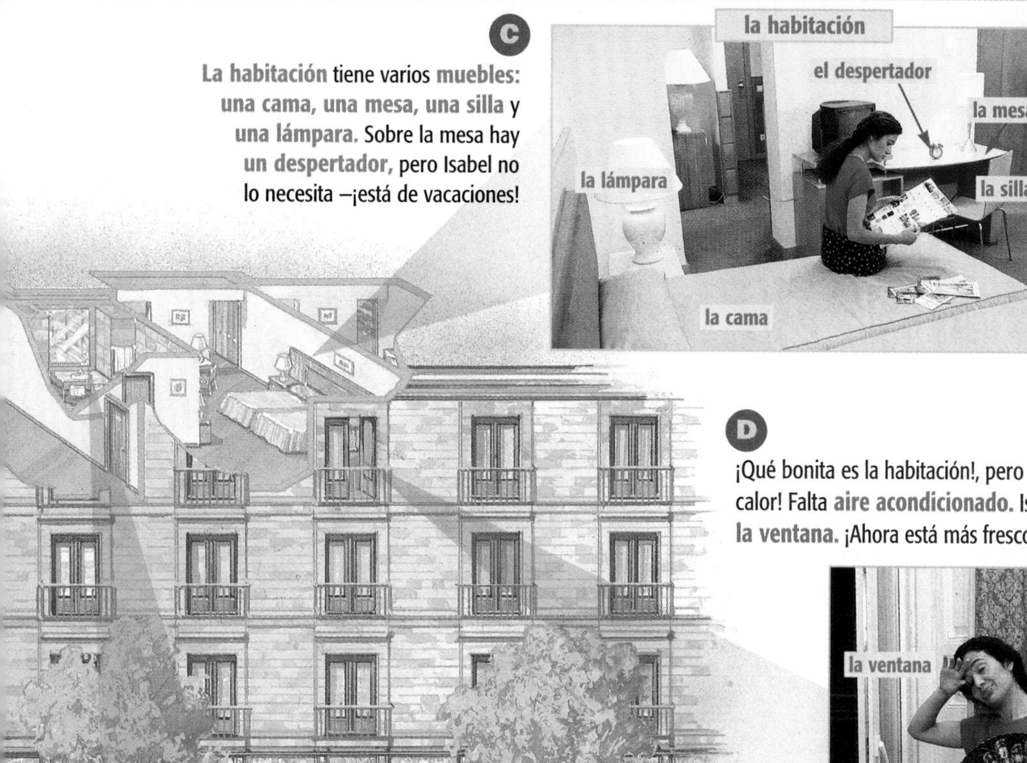


**D** ¡Qué bonita es la habitación!, pero ¡uf, qué calor! Falta **aire acondicionado.** Isabel abre **la ventana.** ¡Ahora está más fresco!

la ventana

**E** Antes de salir, Isabel se mira en **el espejo** que está en **el baño** y se peina. Para los huéspedes con habitaciones sin baño, hay **servicios** en el pasillo.

## Preguntas personales

1. ¿Te gusta viajar?
2. ¿Prefieres una habitación en el primer piso o en los pisos de arriba?
3. ¿Qué te gusta tener en tu habitación?
4. ¿Qué cosas debe tener una buena pensión?
5. Si eres huésped(a) de una pensión, tienes que dejar este objeto en la recepción antes de salir. ¿Cómo se llama?



## Teaching All Students

**Extra Help** List the new vocabulary words on a transparency or on the board and give a short definition for each one. Have students guess the item described.

**Native Speakers** Ask Spanish speakers to describe their home. They may also illustrate the floor plan.

**Multiple Intelligences**

**Logical/Mathematical** Using the new vocabulary words as your word bank, ask students to fill in a Bingo sheet with any of the words. Randomly call out the words; students check off the ones called until someone wins.



### Comprehension Questions

1. ¿Se hospeda Isabel en un hotel enorme? **(No.)**
2. ¿Es popular esta pensión entre los extranjeros? **(Sí.)**
3. ¿La ayuda el maletero con las maletas? **(Sí.)**
4. ¿Está la habitación en la planta baja o en el tercer piso? **(en el tercer piso)**
5. ¿Toman las escaleras o el ascensor? **(el ascensor)**
6. ¿Hay una o dos camas en la habitación? **(una cama)**
7. ¿Qué otros muebles hay en la habitación? **(dos mesas, una silla, una lámpara)**
8. ¿Por qué abre la ventana Isabel? **(hace calor/falta aire acondicionado)**
9. ¿Usas un despertador? **(Answers will vary.)**
10. ¿Dónde están los servicios para las habitaciones sin baño? **(en el pasilllo)**

### Community Connection

Ask students what kinds of accommodations tourists can find in their town/city. Have them research what kinds of facilities are offered at each type of accommodation.

### Language Notes

- Another more colloquial expression for **el maletero** is **el botones**.
- Explain the way the floors are numbered in many European countries. For example, the ground floor is **la planta baja**, instead of the **primer piso**. Then the floors are numbered **primer piso**, **segundo piso**, **tercer piso**, etc.

### Project

Have students draw their bedroom and label the different things found there.

### Block Schedule

**Retention** Go through the unit with the class, point out the objectives, and ask students what they think they will be learning. Have them make a personal list of ideas, vocabulary, or information that they want to gain by the end of the unit.

## Teaching Resource Options

### Print 

Block Scheduling Copymasters
Unit 4 Resource Book
Video Activities, pp. 24–25
Videoscript, pp. 26–27
Audioscript, p. 28

### Audiovisual

OHT 111, 112, 113 (Quick Start)
Audio Program Cassette 10A / CD 10
Video Program Videotape 4, 5:18 / Videodisc 3A

Search Chapter 3, Play to 4
U4E1, En vivo (Dialog)

### Technology

*Intrigas y aventuras* CD-ROM, Disc 2

## Quick Start Review

**En contexto** vocabulary

Use OHT 113 or write on board: Describe your room at home using vocabulary you have learned so far.
**¿Qué muebles hay en la habitación? ¿Compartes la habitación con tu hermano(a)? ¿Hay una televisión en la habitación? ¿un teléfono? ¿un espejo? ¿un radiocasete? ¿unas plantas? ¿unas fotos? ¿una escultura?**
*Answers will vary.*

## Teaching Suggestions
### Presenting the Dialog

- Prepare students for listening by focusing on the strategy in the **Para escuchar** box. Write the list of places on the board and check off those that are mentioned in the **diálogo**.
- Use the video, audiocassette, or CD to present the dialog. The video version offers expanded language opportunities.

# En vivo
## DIÁLOGO

Isabel

Angelina

Felipe

Señor Zavala

Andrea

**PARA ESCUCHAR • STRATEGY: LISTENING**

**Listen and check details** When you hear a key word, listen carefully for more information. Señor Zavala recommends many places for Isabel to visit. Which of these does he mention? Can you give their names?

- museo
- plaza
- joyería
- mercado
- palacio
- café

## En Madrid...

1 ▶ **Isabel:** Gracias por todo. Fue un placer estar en su casa.
**Angelina:** El placer fue nuestro.
**Felipe:** Te va a gustar mucho la pensión de mi tío. Bueno, ¿estás lista?

5 ▶ **Señor Zavala:** Cuando los huéspedes salen del hotel, es importante que dejen la llave en la recepción. Isabel, insisto en que nos digas adónde vas. Mi esposa y yo somos responsables de ti.

6 ▶ **Señor Zavala:** Ésta es una de nuestras mejores habitaciones. Muy bonita la habitación, ¿no? Mi esposa y yo decoramos toda la pensión. Ella buscó todos los muebles. Mira, ésta es la cama. Creo que es muy cómoda.

7 ▶ **Isabel:** Señor Zavala…
**Señor Zavala:** ¿Sí, Isabel? Dime.
**Isabel:** Perdóneme. Estoy cansada y me gustaría descansar un ratito.
**Señor Zavala:** Claro que sí, Isabel. Ya me voy.



## Classroom Community

**Storytelling** Ask students to write a continuation of Scene 10. Encourage them to be creative and use as many new vocabulary words as possible.

**TPR** Set up a hotel lobby scene in the classroom. Assign the roles of **recepcionista, maletero, huésped (huéspeda)** and ask students to act out the check-in procedure at the hotel or pensión, first with gestures only, then using sentences based on the dialog if desired.

**Learning Scenario** Give students a list of possible problems they might encounter in a hotel, e.g., **la llave no funciona, no hay agua caliente, la habitación está sucia, no hay habitación pero el (la) turista tenía reserva,** etc. Write the problems on separate papers and distribute them to small groups. Have each group find a solution for their problem in the form of a dialog.

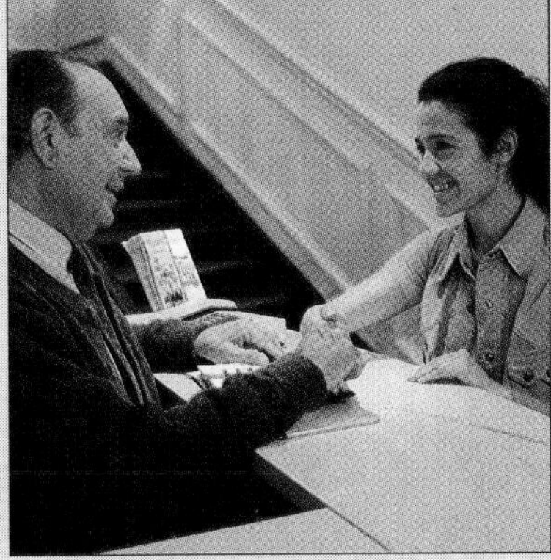

2► *(En la pensión)*
Señor Zavala: Si nos hacen el favor de presentarse en recepción antes de las seis de la tarde. Muy bien. Hasta el viernes, entonces. Adiós.

3► Señor Zavala: Debes de ser Isabel Palacios. Soy Enrique Zavala.
Isabel: Mucho gusto, señor Zavala.
Señor Zavala: Igualmente. Te acompaño a tu habitación. Lo siento; el maletero está enfermo. ¡Así que yo soy el maletero hoy!

4► Señor Zavala: Vamos en el ascensor. Tu habitación está en el tercer piso. Las escaleras están por allí. Madrid es maravillosa. Es importante que vayas al Prado. Es un museo excelente.

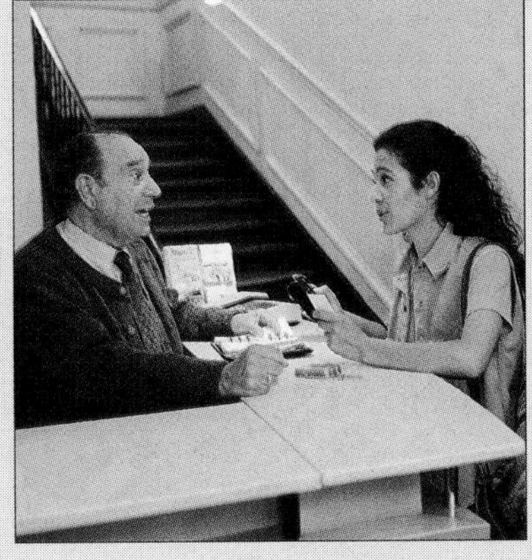

8► Isabel: Aquí tiene la llave de mi habitación.
Señor Zavala: ¿Adónde vas?
Isabel: Voy a la Plaza Mayor y a la Gran Vía. Después, no sé. ¿Tiene alguna sugerencia?

9► Señor Zavala: Sugiero que vayas al Palacio Real. Es impresionante. Después de caminar mucho, es divertido sentarse en un café. Te recomiendo el Café Reina Sofía. Tienen pasteles deliciosos.
Isabel: Adiós. ¡Hasta luego!

10► *(En la Plaza Mayor)*
Andrea: ¿Me puedo sentar aquí?
Isabel: ¡Claro que sí! Siéntate.
Andrea: Muchas gracias. Me llamo Andrea Machado.
Isabel: Soy Isabel Palacios.



## Teaching All Students

**Extra Help** Have students read through the dialog and point out the uses of the command forms they learned in Unit 3.

**Native Speakers** Ask Spanish speakers about the customs for checking into a hotel or pension in their native country. Ask them to compare the customs to those in this country.

### Multiple Intelligences

**Verbal** Have students scan the dialog and write a list of the new vocabulary words used.

**Interpersonal** Ask students to briefly describe the most interesting character (the most sincere, the easiest to understand, etc.) in the dialog.

## Video Synopsis

Isabel checks into a pension that belongs to Señor Zavala, the uncle of her mentor, Felipe. Señor Zavala gives Isabel many recommendations for things to see in Madrid. At a café she meets Andrea, a native **madrileña**. For a complete transcript of the video dialog, see p. 243D.

## Comprehension Questions

1. ¿Se despide Isabel de Felipe y Ana María? **(Sí.)**
2. ¿Conoce Felipe al Sr. Zavala? **(Sí, es su tío.)**
3. ¿Les ayuda el maletero con la maleta? **(No.)**
4. ¿Suben al tercer piso en el ascensor? **(Sí.)**
5. ¿Recomienda el Sr. Zavala el Prado o el Louvre? **(el Prado)**
6. Cuando un huésped sale del hotel, ¿lleva la llave o la deja en la recepción? **(La deja en la recepción.)**
7. ¿Prefiere Isabel hablar con el Sr. Zavala o descansar? **(descansar)**
8. Después de descansar, ¿adónde va Isabel? **(a la Plaza Mayor y a la Gran Vía)**
9. ¿Qué recomienda el Sr. Zavala? **(el Palacio Real y el Café Reina Sofía)**
10. ¿Quién se sienta con Isabel? **(Andrea)**

## Culture Highlights

- **LA PLAZA MAYOR** is the heart of Madrid. Built between 1617 and 1619, it is a prime example of Renaissance style in one of the largest public squares in Europe. Once used as a city market, today sidewalk cafés and shops make it an important meeting place.
- **EL PALACIO REAL** was built in the early 1700s by Felipe V. The palace has 2,800 rooms and is of the classic Italian baroque style.

## Gestures

Have students describe Isabel's facial expressions in each of the photographs. Remind students that paying attention to nonverbal communication clues can increase comprehension.

## Block Schedule

**Process Time** Try to have the class read the dialog before they arrive. They will pick out important words and know them before actually hearing them.

## Teaching Resource Options

**Print** 

Unit 4 Resource Book
Video Activities, pp. 24–25
Videoscript, pp. 26–27
Audioscript, p. 28

**Audiovisual**

OHT 114 (Quick Start)
**Audio Program** Cassette 10A / CD 10
**Video Program** Videotape 4, 5:18 / Videodisc 3A

**Technology**

*Intrigas y aventuras* CD-ROM, Disc 2

## Quick Start Review

**Hacer** with expressions of time

Use OHT 114 or write on board: Imagine that the Puentes family wants to go somewhere new on vacation. They decide to list all the places they have already been. Expand the following sentences to tell where they went in the past.

1. hace / 2 años / nosotros / ir / Portugal
2. hace / 5 años / nosotros / viajar / Brasil
3. hace / 1 año / visitar / China
4. hace / 3 años / hacer un viaje / Canadá

Now write two more sentences in the same pattern, telling where you or a fictitious world traveler has been.

**Answers**

1. Hace 2 años que fuimos a Portugal. *Verbs only:* 2. viajamos, 3. visitamos, 4. hicimos

## Teaching Suggestion
### Comprehension Check

Have students write as many sentences as they can to describe the 4 characters in **Actividad 1** in as much detail as possible. (e.g., **Isabel es turista. Visita a Madrid. Se queda en la pensión del Señor Zavala. Conoce a Andrea en un café.**)

# En acción
## VOCABULARIO Y GRAMÁTICA

**OBJECTIVES**
- Talk about travel plans
- Persuade others
- Describe rooms, furniture, and appliances

ACTIVIDAD 1

### ¿Quién habla?

**Escuchar** ¿Quién habla: Isabel, Felipe, el señor Zavala o Andrea? *(Hint: Who speaks?)*

Isabel

Felipe

Señor Zavala

Andrea

1. «Sugiero que vayas al Palacio Real.»
2. «Estoy cansada y me gustaría descansar un ratito.»
3. «Te va a gustar mucho la pensión de mi tío.»
4. «Voy a la Plaza Mayor y a la Gran Vía.»
5. «¿Me puedo sentar aquí?»
6. «¡Así que yo soy el maletero hoy!»

**TAMBIÉN SE DICE** Aunque por todo el mundo hispano se habla el mismo idioma, los españoles tienen un acento distinto. Escucha al señor Zavala. Vas a notar que él pronuncia los sonidos de la **z**, la **ce** y la **ci** como los estadounidenses pronuncian **th**.

ACTIVIDAD 2

### ¿Cuál corresponde?

**Escuchar** Completa las oraciones con las palabras apropiadas según el diálogo. *(Hint: Complete the sentences.)*

la llave | una extranjera | el maletero | el despertador | la pensión | unos pasteles | los muebles | la casa | el ascensor | la habitación

1. Primero, Isabel se quedó en _____ de Felipe.
2. Luego, ella se hospedó en _____ del señor Zavala.
3. El señor Zavala le mostró su habitación porque _____ estaba enfermo.
4. Ellos subieron en _____, no por las escaleras.
5. El señor Zavala dijo que el Café Reina Sofía tiene _____ deliciosos.
6. La esposa del señor Zavala buscó todos _____ de la pensión.
7. _____ de Isabel tiene baño.
8. Isabel dejó _____ en la recepción antes de salir.



## Classroom Management

**Peer Review** Have students work in pairs to do **Actividad 3**. Then extend the activity by having students work with their partner to compare the items they have in their actual rooms at home or in a dream room. Have them first write a list of the items in each room, then compare the lists.

**Time Saver** Prepare copies of the answers to **Actividades 1–4** and distribute them to students. Allow students to correct their own work.

**Game** Cut out pictures of rooms, furniture, and appliances from catalogs/magazines and tape them to the board. Hold up a card with the name of each item and say it aloud. The first student to raise his/her hand goes to the board and writes the word under the correct picture. Challenge students by using some items which they may not know, but which they could possibly figure out.

- *Use the subjunctive to express hopes and wishes*
- *Use irregular subjunctive forms*

## Dos habitaciones

**Hablar/Escribir** En pares, vean los dibujos de estas dos habitaciones de una pensión en Madrid. Una habitación es tuya y la otra es de tu compañero(a). Compárenlas y hagan una lista de lo que tienen y de lo que no tienen en común. *(**Hint:** Make a list of similarities and differences.)*

**modelo**

| Habitación A | Habitación B |
|---|---|
| 1. No tiene baño. | Tiene baño. |
| 2. | |
| 3. | |

## Es mejor que...

**Hablar/Escribir** Una agente de viajes te apunta los siguientes consejos sobre tu viaje a España. Pero sus apuntes se mezclaron. Completa las oraciones con el subjuntivo y ponlas en orden. *(**Hint:** Complete and order the sentences.)*

**modelo**

*Es posible que (tomar) el ascensor a tu habitación.*

*Es posible que tomes el ascensor a tu habitación.*

**a.** Es bueno que el maletero (llevar) tu equipaje.
**b.** Es lógico que (llamar) a la pensión para hacer una reserva.
**c.** Es posible que (cenar) en un café cerca de la pensión.
**d.** Es mejor que (descansar) un poco antes de conocer la ciudad.
**e.** Al llegar, es importante que (hablar) con la recepción.
**f.** Es necesario que (decidir) las fechas de tu viaje.



## Teaching All Students

**Extra Help** Ask students to give suggestions using the subjunctive forms about class activities, e.g., **Es mejor que nosotros hablemos más en inglés. (¡Claro que no!)**, etc.

**Native Speakers** Ask Spanish speakers to comment on Señor Zavalas' Castilian accent they hear on the tape or video. Ask them to compare it to the Spanish they usually hear. Ask them to point out any other accents or regional differences they may know.

### Multiple Intelligences

**Visual** Ask students to list places where they have stayed on vacation. Then have them compare each place by forming a diagram to show similarities and differences.

**Musical/Rhythmic** Ask students to develop a short rap using vocabulary words they have just learned. For example, **Cuando voy a la pensión, busco una habitación con una cama y una ventana.**

**Actividad 1** **Objective:** Controlled practice
Listening comprehension/vocabulary

**Answers**

1. el señor Zavala
2. Isabel
3. Felipe
4. Isabel
5. Andrea
6. el señor Zavala

**Actividad 2** **Objective:** Controlled practice
Listening comprehension/vocabulary

**Answers**

1. la casa
2. la pensión
3. el maletero
4. el ascensor
5. unos pasteles
6. los muebles
7. La habitación
8. la llave

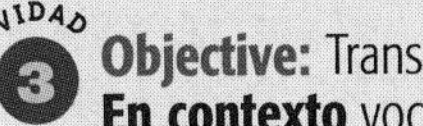

**Actividad 3** **Objective:** Transitional practice
**En contexto** vocabulary

**Answers**

*Answers will vary.*

**Tienen en común:** ventanas abiertas, mesas, despertadores, lámparas
**No tienen en común:** cama pequeña/grande, sin baño/con baño, horas diferentes en el despertador, lámpara pequeña/grande, suelo verde/azul

**Actividad 4** **Objective:** Transitional practice
Subjunctive with impersonal expressions

**Answers**

a. lleve
b. llames
c. cenes
d. descanses
e. hables
f. decidas

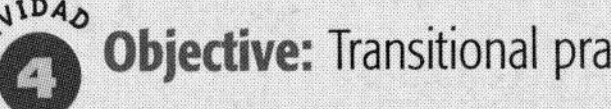

### Culture Highlights

**EL CASTELLANO** Señor Zavala speaks **castellano** (or Castilian), the modern standard Spanish. It is spoken throughout Spain and is the official language of the country. Point out to students that **castellano** is often a second language since several regions of Spain have their own languages, such as **catalán**, **gallego**, and **vasco**.

### Block Schedule

**Variety** Gather magazine photos of different bedrooms. Divide the class into pairs and give each partner a photo of a different room. Without showing their photo, they must describe their particular room and listen to a partner's description until they can compile a list of similarities and differences between the 2 rooms.

## Teaching Resource Options

**Print** 

*Más práctica* Workbook PE, pp. 93–94
*Cuaderno para hispanohablantes* PE, pp. 91–92
Block Scheduling Copymasters
Unit 4 Resource Book
*Más práctica* Workbook TE, pp. 5–6
*Cuaderno para hispanohablantes* TE, pp. 11–12

**Audiovisual** 

OHT 114 (Quick Start)

**Technology** 

*Intrigas y aventuras* CD-ROM, Disc 2

## Quick Start Review

Subjunctive: regular verbs

Use OHT 114 or write on board: Write five sentences of your choice using words from each group below.

Es importante que...

| | |
|---|---|
| tú | comer alimentos sanos |
| ellos | estudiar |
| | leer mucho |
| | escribir en español |
| | caminar con el perro |
| | entrenarse |

*Answers will vary. Verbs should be in the subjunctive.*

## Teaching Suggestions

- **Presenting the Subjunctive to Express Hopes and Wishes** You may first want to review the forms of the subjunctive. Remind students that they have already learned to use the subjunctive for expressing opinions in Unit 3.
- Have students study the words and phrases that express hopes and wishes in the box at the bottom of p. 252. Ask them to make a list of the situations when they might use these.

GRAMÁTICA

## The Subjunctive to Express Hopes and Wishes

**¿RECUERDAS?** *p. 226* You use the subjunctive after **impersonal expressions** involving uncertainty.

You have already learned these verb endings for the subjunctive:

| -ar | -er | -ir |
|---|---|---|
| **habl**ar | **aprend**er | **viv**ir |
| **habl**e | **aprend**a | **viv**a |
| **habl**es | **aprend**as | **viv**as |
| **habl**e | **aprend**a | **viv**a |
| **habl**emos | **aprend**amos | **viv**amos |
| **habl**éis | **aprend**áis | **viv**áis |
| **habl**en | **aprend**an | **viv**an |

You also use the subjunctive to express a **hope** or a **wish**, such as when you want someone else to do something.

***He knows what he wants ... but he's not sure she will take the elevator.***

El señor Zavala **quiere que** Isabel tome el ascensor.
*Señor Zavala **wants** Isabel **to take** the elevator.*

***The indicative, sugiere, indicates a statement of fact...***

El señor Zavala **sugiere que** Isabel visite el Prado.
*Señor Zavala **suggests that** Isabel **visit** the Prado.*

***...but the subjunctive, visite, indicates uncertainty.***

Check the box at right for a list of words and phrases that express hopes and wishes. These expressions are often followed by the word **que** and the subjunctive.

### Vocabulario

#### Expressing Hopes and Wishes

**insistir (en)** *to insist*
**ojalá que** *I hope that, hopefully*
**sugerir (e→ie, i)** *to suggest*

 Ya sabes

**desear** *to desire*
**esperar** *to hope*
**necesitar** *to need*
**preferir (e→ie, i)** *to prefer*
**querer (e→ie)** *to want*

¿Qué palabras usas si quieres darle un consejo a alguien?



## Classroom Community

**Paired Activity** Ask students to form a sentence using the words to express hopes/wishes and share it with a partner. Based on the sentence, the partner should respond accordingly, e.g., **Yo sugiero que tú visites la biblioteca después de la escuela. Voy a la biblioteca hoy. Yo insisto en que tú estudies más**, etc.

**Portfolios** Ask students to write a short paragraph of 5–6 sentences in their journals using the new vocabulary phrases to express hopes and wishes about an upcoming trip or vacation.

**Rubric: Writing**

| Criteria | Scale |
|---|---|
| Vocabulary use | 1 2 3 4 5 |
| Accuracy | 1 2 3 4 5 |
| Creativity, appearance | 1 2 3 4 5 |

A = 13–15 pts.
B = 10–12 pts.
C = 7–9 pts.
D = 4–6 pts.
F = < 4 pts.

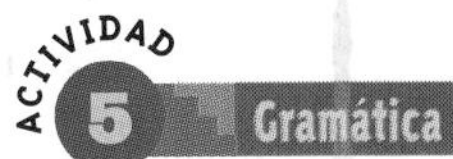


## ¡Saludos desde Madrid!

**Escribir** Usa el subjuntivo para completar la tarjeta postal que escribe Isabel. *(Hint: Complete the postcard.)*

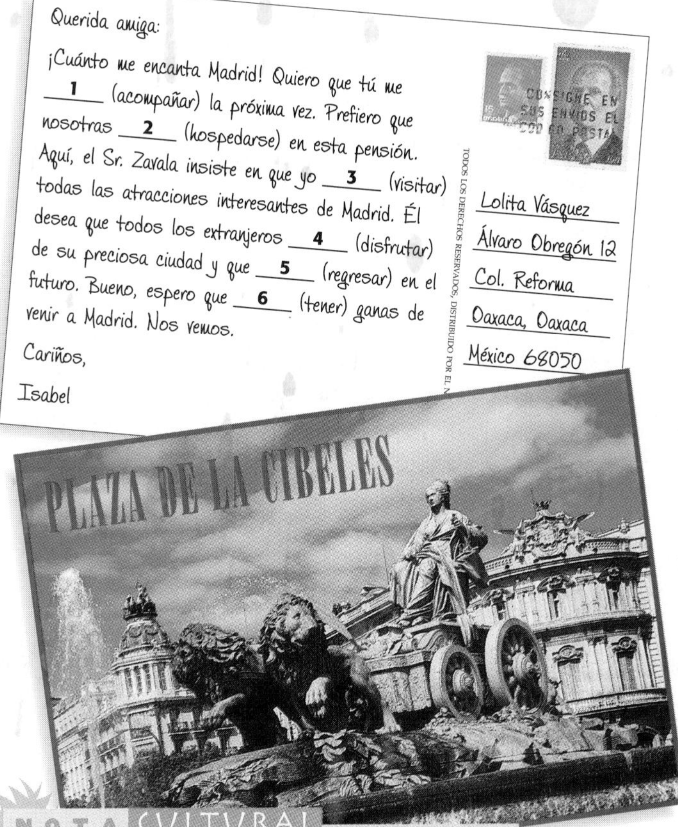

Querida amiga:

¡Cuánto me encanta Madrid! Quiero que tú me __1__ (acompañar) la próxima vez. Prefiero que nosotras __2__ (hospedarse) en esta pensión. Aquí, el Sr. Zavala insiste en que yo __3__ (visitar) todas las atracciones interesantes de Madrid. Él desea que todos los extranjeros __4__ (disfrutar) de su preciosa ciudad y que __5__ (regresar) en el futuro. Bueno, espero que __6__ (tener) ganas de venir a Madrid. Nos vemos.

Cariños,

Isabel

Lolita Vásquez
Álvaro Obregón 12
Col. Reforma
Oaxaca, Oaxaca
México 68050



### NOTA CULTURAL

**La Plaza de la Cibeles** Enfrente del Banco de España se encuentra la bella Plaza de la Cibeles. En el centro de la plaza hay una fuente dedicada a Cibeles, una diosa griega. Es quizás la fuente más famosa de España. El centro financiero de Madrid, en la calle de Alcalá, comienza en esta plaza.

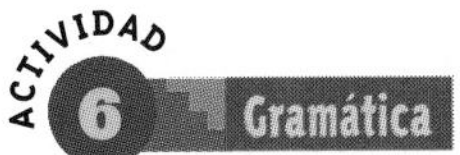


## ¡Tantos deseos!

**Escribir** Expresa los deseos de estas personas. *(Hint: Write sentences expressing wishes.)*

**modelo**

*Ojalá que yo (tener) tarea hoy.*

*Ojalá que yo (no) tenga tarea hoy.*

1. Los profesores insisten en que los estudiantes (gritar) durante la clase.
2. Ojalá que (hacer) sol hoy.
3. Mis padres sugieren que yo (limpiar) mi cuarto de vez en cuando.
4. Ojalá que mi amigo(a) y yo (visitar) Madrid en el futuro.
5. Mis padres quieren que yo (asistir) a la universidad.
6. Prefiero que mi mejor amigo(a) (hablar) español.
7. Los estudiantes necesitan que los profesores (comprender) bien la gramática.
8. Mis amigos y yo esperamos que nuestros hermanos (portarse) mal.

**MÁS PRÁCTICA** *cuaderno* pp. 93–94

**PARA HISPANOHABLANTES** *cuaderno* pp. 91–92

**Objective:** Controlled practice
Subjunctive to express hopes and wishes

### Answers

1. acompañes
2. nos hospedemos
3. visite
4. disfruten
5. regresen
6. tengas

**Objective:** Controlled practice
Subjunctive to express hopes and wishes

### Answers

1. Los profesores insisten en que los estudiantes (no) griten durante la clase.
2. Ojalá que (no) haga sol hoy.
3. Mis padres sugieren que yo (no) limpie mi cuarto de vez en cuando.
4. Ojalá que mi amigo(a) y yo (no) visitemos Madrid en el futuro.
5. Mis padres quieren que yo (no) asista a la universidad.
6. Prefiero que mi mejor amigo(a) (no) hable español.
7. Los estudiantes necesitan que los profesores (no) comprendan bien la gramática.
8. Mis amigos y yo esperamos que nuestros hermanos (no) se porten mal.

### Culture Highlights

- **LA PLAZA DE LA CIBELES** The fountain in the **Plaza de Cibeles** is beautifully lit at night and is located in front of the main post office in Madrid, **El Palacio de Comunicaciones**.

### Language Note

**Ojalá que** is an expression that comes from Arabic and means "may Allah grant that." It is always followed by a verb in the subjunctive.

## Teaching All Students

**Extra Help** Ask students to list the uses of the subjunctive they have learned so far and give examples.

**Challenge** Ask students to bring in more information related to the **Nota cultural** and share it with classmates, e.g., who was Cybele in Greek mythology? What is the significance of the lions in the statue?

**Native Speakers** Have Spanish speakers give sample sentences using the words and phrases to express hopes and wishes in the **Vocabulario** box on p. 252. Ask them to point out the expressions they might use most often.

### Block Schedule

**Change of Pace** Actividad 5 provides practice in context. Photocopy the activity so students can do it as a worksheet, writing on it as they read. Then have them make up similar paragraphs for additional practice. (For additional activities, see **Block Scheduling Copymasters**.)

## Teaching Resource Options

**Print** 

Block Scheduling Copymasters
Unit 4 Resource Book
Audioscript, p. 29

**Audiovisual** 

OHT 114 (Quick Start)
Audio Program Cassette 10A / CD 10

**Technology** 

*Intrigas y aventuras* CD-ROM, Disc 2

## Quick Start Review

Subjunctive

Use OHT 114 or write on board: Express an opinion on the following statements. Use an impersonal expression in each sentence you write. If you need help, turn to p. 228. For example: **La cafetería sirve pescado. Es raro que la cafetería sirva pescado.**

**Ella no se pone loción protectora.**
**Ellos cuentan chistes en clase.**
**Luis tiene fiebre.**
**Mi hermano hace la limpieza.**
**Tú te mantienes sana.**

*Answers will vary.*

## Teaching Suggestions

### Presenting Vocabulary

Have students draw a sketch of their homes and ask them to identify the items from the **Vocabulario** list on p. 254.

## Supplementary Vocabulary

| | |
|---|---|
| **la lavadora** | washing machine |
| **la secadora** | dryer |
| **el escritorio** | desk |
| **la alfombra** | carpet, rug |
| **el estante** | bookcase |

## Una nueva casa

**Hablar/Escribir** Tienes una nueva casa y unos amigos te ayudan con tus cosas. Di dónde ponerlas. *(Hint: Tell where to put items.)*

**modelo**

*ustedes:*

*Quiero que ustedes pongan la mesa en el comedor.*

1. Javier: 
2. tú: 
3. Elena: 
4. Miguel: 
5. nosotros: 

## ¿Qué prefieres?

**Hablar** Imagínate que tú y un(a) compañero(a) van a hacer un viaje. Él (Ella) te pregunta sobre tus preferencias. ¿Qué le dices? *(Hint: Talk about preferences.)*

**modelo**

*comer en un restaurante en el hotel / comer en un restaurante fuera del hotel*

**Compañero(a):** *¿Prefieres que comamos en un restaurante en el hotel o fuera del hotel?*

**Tú:** *Quiero que comamos en un restaurante fuera del hotel.*

1. hospedarse en un hotel grande / hospedarse en una pensión pequeña
2. hacer reservas / no hacer reservas
3. dejar la llave en la recepción / llevar la llave con nosotros
4. tener una habitación en un piso alto / tener una habitación en el primer piso
5. el (la) maletero(a) llevar las maletas / llevar nuestras propias maletas
6. subir por las escaleras / tomar el ascensor
7. usar los servicios en el pasillo / tener un baño en la habitación
8. quedarse en la ciudad / quedarse en el campo

### Vocabulario

#### Habitaciones y muebles

**el armario** *closet, wardrobe*
**la bañera** *bathtub*
**la cocina** *kitchen*
**el comedor** *dining room*
**el garaje** *garage*
**el jardín** *garden*
**el lavabo** *bathroom sink*
**la pared** *wall*
**la puerta** *door*
**la sala** *living room*
**el sillón** *armchair*
**el sofá** *sofa*
**el suelo** *floor*

¿Qué tienes en tu casa?



## Classroom Community

**TPR** Ask students to act out the actions associated with each of the vocabulary words in the box on p. 254. Have others try to guess the room or furniture.

**Portfolio** Ask students to write a short paragraph describing the types of rooms in their homes using the new vocabulary words. Have them choose one room and describe it in more detail.

**Rubric: Writing**

| Criteria | Scale |
|---|---|
| Vocabulary use | 1 2 3 4 5 |
| Accuracy | 1 2 3 4 5 |
| Creativity, appearance | 1 2 3 4 5 |

A = 13–15 pts.
B = 10–12 pts.
C = 7–9 pts.
D = 4–6 pts.
F = < 4 pts.

## ¿Loca o normal?

**Escuchar** Estas personas van a redecorar varias partes de la casa. Escucha cada descripción. ¿Es loca o normal? *(Hint: Are the descriptions crazy or normal?)*

1. el comedor
2. el baño
3. el jardín
4. la sala
5. la habitación de Alfredo
6. la cocina
7. la habitación de Ana
8. el garaje
9. el apartamento

## GRAMÁTICA: Irregular Subjunctive Forms

 **¿RECUERDAS?** *p. 226* You've learned how to form the subjunctive of regular verbs.

However, some verbs have **irregular subjunctive** forms. Use the chart to get to know them.

| dar | estar | ir | saber | ser |
|---|---|---|---|---|
| **dé** | **esté** | **vaya** | **sepa** | **sea** |
| **des** | **estés** | **vayas** | **sepas** | **seas** |
| **dé** | **esté** | **vaya** | **sepa** | **sea** |
| **demos** | **estemos** | **vayamos** | **sepamos** | **seamos** |
| **deis** | **estéis** | **vayáis** | **sepáis** | **seáis** |
| **den** | **estén** | **vayan** | **sepan** | **sean** |

Es importante que **sepas** que si tienes algún problema o dificultad, puedes llamarnos a cualquier hora.
*It's important that **you know** that if you have any trouble or difficulty, you can call us at any time.*

The only other verb with an **irregular subjunctive** is **haber.**

Estoy muy cansada. Ojalá que **haya** tiempo para descansar.
*I'm very tired. I hope **there will be** time to rest.*

The indicative **hay** becomes **haya** in the subjunctive.



### Teaching Suggestions
#### Presenting Irregular Subjunctive Forms

Have students write out these irregular subjunctive forms in their notebooks. They are common verbs that are used often and students will refer to them frequently.

 **Objective:** Transitional practice
Subjunctive/rooms and furniture

**Answers**
*Answers will vary.*
1. Sugiero que Javier ponga el sillón en la sala.
2. Sugiero que tú pongas el lavabo en el baño.
3. Sugiero que Elena ponga los zapatos en el armario.
4. Sugiero que Miguel ponga la bicicleta en el garaje.
5. Sugiero que nosotros pongamos el sofá en la sala.

 **Objective:** Transitional practice
Expressing preferences

**En contexto** vocabulary

**Answers**
*Answers will vary but should include correct usage of subjunctive verbs in the **nosotros** form.*

 **Objective:** Open-ended practice
Listening comprehension

**Answers** (See script, p. TE 243D.)
1. normal
2. normal
3. loca
4. loca
5. normal
6. loca
7. normal
8. loca
9. loca

### Interdisciplinary Connection

**Art** Have students make models of their homes or rooms as described in the Hands-on Crafts in the **Ampliación** section on p. 243B.

### Teaching All Students

**Extra Help** Based on the vocabulary, ask students to give a suggestion about the use(s) of each item, e.g., **Yo recomiendo que no duermas en el sofá.**

**Native Speakers** Have Spanish speakers point out any different words that may be used for the rooms or furniture listed in the **Vocabulario** box on p. 254. For example, **habitación, dormitorio, recámera,** and **cuarto** are all words for bedroom in different Spanish-speaking regions.

**Multiple Intelligences**

**Visual** Have students describe their homes to a partner. The partner draws his/her interpretation in a floor plan or diagram based on the description. Then have partners switch roles.

**Intrapersonal** Ask students to share a favorite place in their home where they like to sit and explain why.

### Block Schedule

**FunBreak** Have students work in pairs to create a floor plan of a dream house and decorate it as they choose. Encourage them to give each other descriptions and suggestions for where to put things. (For additional activities, see **Block Scheduling Copymasters.**)

## Teaching Resource Options

**Print** 

*Más práctica* Workbook PE, pp. 95–96
*Cuaderno para hispanohablantes* PE, pp. 93–94
Block Scheduling Copymasters
Unit 4 Resource Book
*Más práctica* Workbook TE, pp. 7–8
*Cuaderno para hispanohablantes* TE, pp. 13–14
Information Gap Activities, p. 17
Audioscript, p. 29

**Audiovisual** 

OHT 115 (Quick Start)
Audio Program Cassette 10A / CD 10

**Technology** 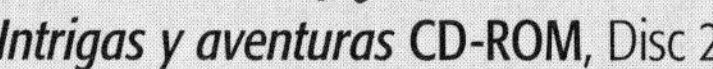

*Intrigas y aventuras* CD-ROM, Disc 2

## Quick Start Review

Formal commands

Use OHT 115 or write on board: First, think of a place you have been to or know about. Then write three sentences telling a tourist where to stay, what attractions to visit, and where to go for entertainment. Use **Ud.** commands and any verbs you wish, such as: **ir, visitar, disfrutar, divertirse, andar, comer, relajarse.**

*Answers will vary.*
***Sample answer:*** Vaya a Arizona y visite el «Grand Canyon».

## Teaching Suggestions

- **Extra Practice** Even though **Actividades 11** and **12** are designated as speaking activities, it would be helpful if students wrote out their answers for extra practice in using the subjunctive.
- **Presenting Vocabulary** Have students bring in magazine photos of a kitchen and identify the items they see in Spanish. Or students can sketch their own kitchen at home and identify the items in it.

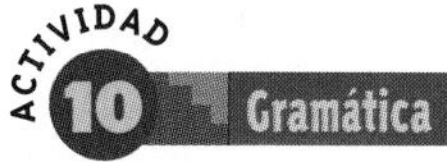

### Consejos

**Escribir** Al señor Zavala le gusta darles recomendaciones a sus huéspedes. Usa una expresión de la lista y el subjuntivo para saber lo que dice. *(Hint: Express Señor Zavala's recommendations.)*

| | |
|---|---|
| **Insisto en que...** | **Espero que...** |
| **Ojalá que...** | **Quiero que...** |
| **Sugiero que...** | **Prefiero que...** |

**modelo**

*ustedes (ir) al Palacio Real*
*Ojalá que ustedes vayan al Palacio Real.*

1. los huéspedes le (dar) la llave al recepcionista
2. tú (ir) a un restaurante español
3. usted (ser) paciente
4. ustedes (saber) el número de teléfono de la pensión
5. tú no (estar) enfermo hoy
6. ustedes (ir) a la Plaza Mayor

**MÁS PRÁCTICA** *cuaderno* pp. 95–96
**PARA HISPANOHABLANTES** *cuaderno* pp. 93–94

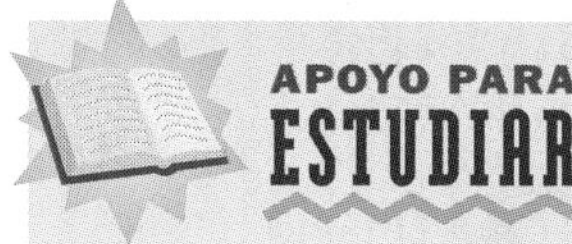

**APOYO PARA ESTUDIAR**

**Irregular subjunctive forms**

Where have you seen these forms of **dar, estar, ir, saber,** and **ser** before? They are the same as the **usted(es)** commands and the negative **tú** commands. When you write, be sure to put the accents on **dé** and **esté**. That avoids confusion with **de** (*of*) and **este** (*this*).

### De compras en Madrid

**Hablar/Leer** Imagínate que estás en Madrid. Tu compañero(a) te pregunta dónde estas personas pueden comprar varias cosas. Sigue el modelo. *(Hint: Suggest where to buy the following items.)*

**modelo**

*yo: sandalias*
**Compañero(a):** *Busco sandalias nuevas.*
**Tú:** *Sugiero que vayas a la Zapatería Rojas.*

1. mis amigos: un radiocasete
2. mi hermano: artesanía
3. mi tía y yo: un collar de plata
4. nosotros: tarjetas postales
5. mi familia: un libro de la historia de España
6. mi amigo: unos patines



## Classroom Community

**Cooperative Learning** Have students work in groups of 4 to choose a vacation destination that meets their group's requirements. S1 and S2 write 3 sentences beginning with **Ojalá** expressing their hopes for the trip. For example: **Ojalá que la playa sea bonita. Ojalá que el hotel tenga...** Then S3 and S4 read the sentences and try to pick a vacation destination that matches the requirements. Then students switch roles.

**Storytelling** Based on the picture in **Actividad 11**, ask students to create a short story about a day of running errands at various stores.

**Group Activity** Ask students to cut out magazine pictures of houses showing rooms, appliances, and furniture. Have them make collages of different rooms and label vocabulary words in Spanish.

## En la cabaña

**Hablar/Escribir** Laura pasa el fin de semana en una cabaña en el campo. Algunos aparatos no funcionan. ¿Qué espera Laura que todavía funcione? *(Hint: Which does Laura hope still works?)*

**modelo**

*Quiero hacer un pastel.*
*Ojalá que funcione el horno.*

1. Quiero tomar refrescos fríos.
2. Vamos a mirar videos.
3. Mi amiga trae el helado.
4. Voy a cocinar paella.
5. No quiero tener frío.
6. No queremos pasar mucho tiempo lavando platos.

### Vocabulario

**En la casa**

- **la calefacción** *heat, heating*
- **el congelador** *freezer*
- **la electricidad** *electricity*
- **la estufa** *stove*
- **funcionar** *to work, to run*
- **el horno** *oven*
- **el horno microondas** *microwave oven*
- **el lavaplatos** *dishwasher*
- **el refrigerador** *refrigerator*

¿Qué tienes en tu cocina?

## ¿Dónde quieren hospedarse?

**Escuchar/Hablar** Estas personas están describiendo dónde quieren hospedarse. ¿Qué dibujo corresponde a cada descripción? Luego explícale a un(a) compañero(a) dónde te gustaría hospedarte a ti. *(Hint: Which picture goes with each description?)*

1. ____ 2. ____ 3. ____ 4. ____

a.

b.

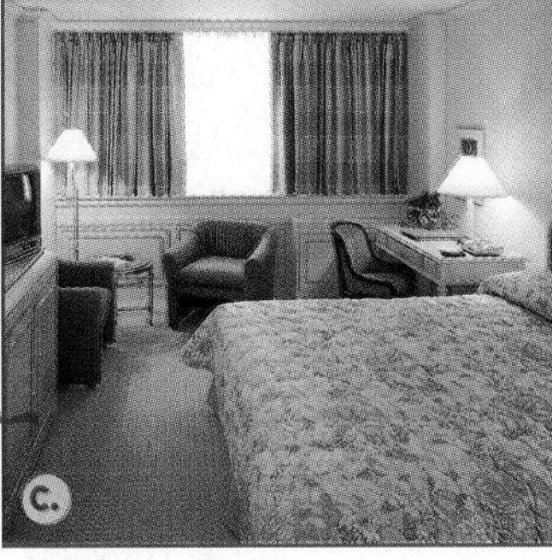
c.

d.

**MÁS COMUNICACIÓN** p. R11

### NOTA CULTURAL

**Alojamiento** Si buscas alojamiento (*lodging*), en Madrid hay muchas opciones. Hay **hoteles** (¡los de cinco estrellas son muy cómodos!) y los **paradores** del gobierno (muchos de éstos son edificios históricos). También hay **hostales** y **pensiones,** que son más pequeños, pero también son más baratos.

**Objective:** Controlled practice
Irregular subjunctives

**Answers**
*Answers will vary.*
1. [Prefiero que] los huéspedes le den la llave al recepcionista.
2. [Sugiero que] tú vayas a un restaurante español.
3. [Espero que] usted sea paciente.
4. [Insisto en que] ustedes sepan el número de teléfono de la pensión.
5. [Ojalá que] tú no estés enfermo(a) hoy.
6. [Quiero que] ustedes vayan a la Plaza Mayor.

**Objective:** Transitional practice
Irregular subjunctives
Places to shop

**Answers**
1. Sugiero que vayan a la Supertienda de Música y Videos.
2. Sugiero que vaya a Regalolandia.
3. Sugiero que vayan a la Joyería Plata Viva.
4. Sugiero que vayan a la Papelería Fina.
5. Sugiero que vaya a la Librería Crisol.
6. Sugiero que vaya al Mundo de Deportes.

**Objective:** Transitional practice
Talking about appliances

**Answers**
1. Ojalá que funcione el refrigerador.
2. Ojalá que funcione el televisor/la videograbadora.
3. Ojalá que funcione el congelador.
4. Ojalá que funcione la estufa.
5. Ojalá que funcione la calefacción.
6. Ojalá que funcione el lavaplatos.

ACTIVIDAD 13

**Objective:** Open-ended practice
Listening comprehension

**Answers** (See script, p. TE 243D.)
1. d 2. a 3. b 4. c

### Teaching All Students

**Extra Help** Ask students to form a short phrase using each of the six irregular verbs in the subjunctive tense. NOTE: The irregular verbs are listed in the **Apoyo para estudiar** box on p. 256.

**Native Speakers** Ask Spanish-speaking students to present the vocabulary on p. 257. Have them pronounce each word carefully and give definitions in Spanish.

**Multiple Intelligences**

**Visual** Ask students to generate a visual that defines each of the vocabulary words.

**Verbal** Ask students to describe to a partner their idea of a perfect vacation accommodation. Encourage them to be creative.

### Block Schedule

**Retention** Have students write definitions to the new vocabulary words. For example, **el horno microondas calienta la comida rápidamente.** This will also provide reinforcement of other vocabulary and "hooks" for increased retention. (For additional activities, see **Block Scheduling Copymasters.**)

## Teaching Resource Options

**Print** 

*Más práctica* Workbook PE, pp. 89–92
*Cuaderno para hispanohablantes* PE, pp. 89–90
Block Scheduling Copymasters
Unit 4 Resource Book
*Más práctica* Workbook TE, pp. 1–4
*Cuaderno para hispanohablantes* TE, pp. 9–10
Information Gap Activities, p. 18
Audioscript, pp. 30–31

**Audiovisual**

OHT 109, 109A, 115 (Quick Start)
Audio Program Cassette 10A, 10B / CD 10; (*Para hispanohablantes* Cassette 10B / CD 10)

**Technology**

*Intrigas y aventuras* CD-ROM, Disc 2

## Quick Start Review

**Furniture**

Use OHT 115 or write on board: Write one or two things you might find in each of the following rooms.
**sala, cocina, comedor, habitación (bedroom)**

*Answers will vary.*
***Sample answers:*** sala: el sillón, el sofá; cocina: la estufa, el horno, el lavaplatos; comedor: la mesa, las sillas; la habitación: la cama, la lámpara

**Objective:** Transitional practice
Making suggestions

### Answers

*Answers will vary but should reflect correct use of the subjunctive.*

## Culture Highlights

● **EL METRO DE MADRID** Madrid's subway is open from 6:00 A.M. until 1:30 A.M. There are 10 metro lines that cross the city. This map shows only a small part of the extensive system. Each metro line is a separate color, and the number of each line is indicated in a square of the same color.

ACTIVIDAD 14

## Unas sugerencias

**Hablar** Conversa con un(a) compañero(a) sobre los problemas de tus amigos(as). Tu compañero(a) te da una sugerencia para cada uno(a). *(Hint: Make suggestions.)*

**modelo**

*no poder estudiar en casa*
**Tú:** *Mónica no puede estudiar en casa.*
**Compañero(a):** *Sugiero que vaya a la biblioteca.*

Insisto en que... Espero que...
Ojalá que... Quiero que...
Sugiero que... Prefiero que...

| Tú | Compañero(a) |
|---|---|
| no poder estudiar en casa | ser más responsable |
| nunca hacer la tarea | comprar un despertador |
| nunca escuchar al (a la) maestro(a) | ir a la biblioteca |
| siempre llegar tarde | estudiar con unos(as) amigos(as) después de la escuela |
| nunca estudiar para los exámenes | ser más cortés |
| siempre dormir en clase | descansar más en casa |
| siempre hablar cuando debe estar estudiando | hablar con el (la) maestro(a) |

ACTIVIDAD 15

## El metro de Madrid

**Hablar/Leer** Imagínate que vives en Madrid. Un turista te pregunta cómo llegar a varios lugares en metro. Usa el plano para darle instrucciones. *(Hint: Give directions.)*

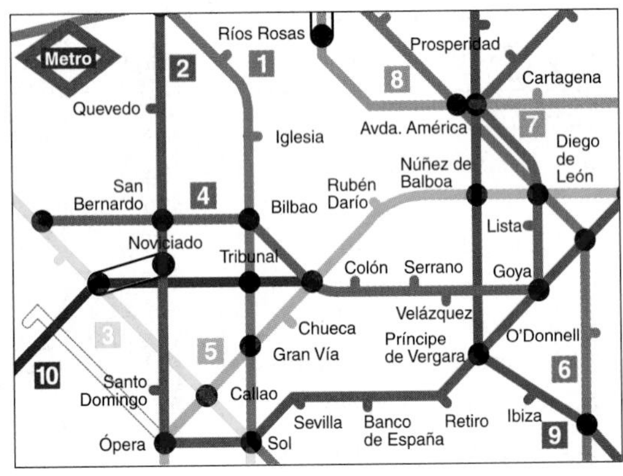


**modelo**

*de Bilbao a Ópera*
**Turista:** *¿Cómo llego desde Bilbao a Ópera?*
**Tú:** *Tome la línea 1 en Bilbao y baje en la estación Gran Vía. Allí tome la línea 5 hasta Ópera.*

1. de Retiro a Lista
2. de Sevilla a Iglesia
3. de Velázquez a Núñez de Balboa
4. de Quevedo a Chueca



## Classroom Community

**Group Activity** Write 8–10 subjunctive expressions on a transparency or on the board. (See pp. 226 and 252.) Ask students to write an appropriate ending, e.g., **Es posible que... (vayas a la cafetería).** Time the activity for fun.

**Learning Scenario** Imagine that your class holds a winning lottery ticket. Students express their wishes/desires on how they want to spend the money, e.g., S1: **Quiero que nosotros hagamos un viaje a Europa.** S2: **Deseo que compremos una nueva computadora para la clase.** etc. After students have listed 7–10 suggestions, have the class vote on the most popular wish.

## ¿Al campo o a la ciudad?

**PARA CONVERSAR**

**STRATEGY: SPEAKING**

**Persuade** Winning someone over to your course of action can be done by reason (**no tenemos un coche**), by emotion (**nos divertimos**), or by a reward (**pago el almuerzo**). What works best for you? Use it here.

**Hablar** Vas a viajar con un(a) compañero(a) este fin de semana, pero ustedes tienen un problema. Uno de ustedes quiere ir al campo, y el otro a la ciudad. Convéncelo(a) de que te acompañe. *(Hint: Convince your classmate.)*

**modelo**

**Tú:** *Quiero que pasemos el fin de semana en la ciudad. Va a haber muchas cosas divertidas para hacer.*

**Compañero(a):** *Pues, yo sugiero que vayamos al campo. Va a hacer sol y prefiero que estemos al aire libre.*

## La casa perfecta

**Hablar/Escribir** Haz un dibujo simple de tu casa ideal y en otro papel haz una descripción completa de la misma casa. Luego, con un grupo de compañeros(as), muestra los dibujos del grupo y lee tu descripción. ¿Pueden tus compañeros(as) identificar tu casa? *(Hint: Draw and describe your ideal house. Can classmates pick out your picture?)*

**modelo**

*«Mi casa ideal»*

*Mi casa ideal va a ser muy grande. Quiero que sea de tres pisos y que tenga cinco habitaciones. Cada habitación va a tener una cama muy grande y una lámpara bonita. Aunque me gusta mucho la ciudad, prefiero que la casa esté en el campo porque….*

**MÁS COMUNICACIÓN** p. R11

### Refrán

**Quien va a Sevilla pierde su silla.**

Mira el dibujo y habla con tus compañeros(as). ¿Qué crees que significa este refrán? ¿Puedes describir una situación en la que tú perdiste algo porque te fuiste?

**Objective:** Open-ended practice
Giving directions

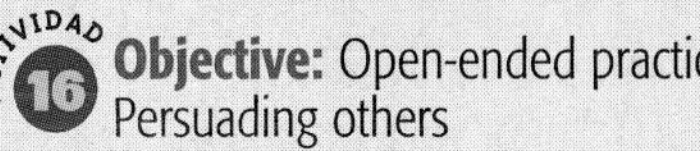

**Usted commands**

### Answers

*Answers may vary.*

1. Tome la Línea 2 en Retiro y baje en la estación Goya. Allí tome la Línea 4 una parada hasta Lista.
2. Tome la Línea 2 en Sevilla y baje en la estación Sol. Allí tome la Línea 1 cuatro paradas hasta Iglesia.
3. Tome la Línea 4 en Velázquez y baje en la estación Diego de León. Allí tome la Línea 5 una parada hasta Núñez de Balboa.
4. Tome la Línea 2 en Quevedo y baje en la estación Ópera. Allí tome la Línea 5 tres paradas hasta Chueca.

Actividad 16 **Objective:** Open-ended practice
Persuading others

*Answers will vary.*

Actividad 17 **Objective:** Open-ended practice
Describing a home

*Answers will vary.*

### Teaching Suggestions

After completing **Actividad 16**, have students expand their discussion on the country vs. the city by doing the first project as described in the **Ampliación** section on p. 243A.

### Quick Wrap-up

Have students work in groups of 3 to write a real estate ad for an exquisite house. Bring in some ads from your local paper to serve as models. This activity will practice household vocabulary as well as descriptive writing. Encourage students to include commands and the subjunctive.

### Teaching All Students

**Extra Help** Write 8–10 phrases that express hopes and wishes. Ask students to form sentences by adding subjunctive clauses.

**Native Speakers** Have Spanish-speaking students give other similar **refranes** they may know.

**Challenge** Ask students to write several new proverbs in Spanish.

**Multiple Intelligences**

**Kinesthetic** Give the students a map of the school grounds and label a central location (as a starting point). Give oral directions without mentioning where you are sending them. Do all students end up at the same place?

### Block Schedule

**Variety** Remember to provide movement in each lesson. For pair work like **Actividades 14** and **15**, have students pick a partner from across the room or behind them so they have to move or at least to rotate.

## Teaching Resource Options

**Print** 

*Cuaderno para hispanohablantes* PE, pp. 95–96
Unit 4 Resource Book
*Cuaderno para hispanohablantes* TE, pp. 15–16
Audioscript, pp. 29–30

**Audiovisual**

**Audio Program** Cassette 10A / CD 10
**OHT** 115 (Quick Start)

## Quick Start Review

Talking about lodging

Use OHT 115 or write on board: Imagine you are planning to build a new hotel. Where is the best place to attract many tourist and hotel guests? Make a list in Spanish of three things you would look for in the ideal location for a new hotel.

*Answers will vary.*
*Sample answers:* transporte público (metro, taxi, etc.), cerca de atracciones turísticas o tiendas, cerca de la playa

## Teaching Suggestions

- **Prereading** Have students brainstorm a list of characteristics they would look for if they were choosing a hotel.
- **Strategy: Compare related details** Have students copy the chart into their notebooks and check off the features of each hotel. Ask them to write at least 3 sentences comparing the two hotels.
- **Reading** Have students jot down a complete list of items and characteristics of each hotel in a 2-column list.
- **Post-reading** Now have students compare the class list of desired characteristics in a hotel to the descriptions of Hotel Borbones and Hotel Argüelles. Which one best suits the class list?

# En voces

LECTURA

**PARA LEER • STRATEGY: READING**

**Compare related details** Brochures often tell enough to get your interest but may leave out information you need to know. Use a chart to compare the two hotels described in **«Felices sueños»** (*Sweet Dreams*). What else would you like to know in choosing one of these hotels for your stay in Madrid?

| | Argüelles | Borbones |
|---|---|---|
| habitaciones con baño | | |
| apartamentos | | |
| restaurante | | |
| jardín | | |

# Felices sueños

Si prefieren un hotel de precio módico, el Argüelles es ideal. Sus habitaciones son cómodas y limpias, y todas tienen baño. También ofrece apartamentos con sala y cocina, equipados con calefacción, televisión, estufa, horno microonda y refrigerador.

Para los huéspedes que desean comer en un restaurante, el Café Rosa en la planta baja está abierto todos los días.

## El Hotel Argüelles

El hotel está en un lugar perfecto para los extranjeros: cerca de la Gran Vía, en el Madrid moderno. Hay una estación de metro cercana y una parada de autobús en la esquina. Y la famosa Gran Vía tiene restaurantes, cines y muchísimas tiendas.

El Hotel Argüelles es sencillo[1] y práctico, y tiene todo lo que necesitan sus huéspedes para estar contentos en Madrid.

[1] simple



## Classroom Community

**Group Activity** Divide the class into two groups. Ask one group to list the similarities between the two hotels and the other group to list the differences. Share lists.

**Portfolios** Ask students to write a short description of a hotel where they (or a family member) have (has) stayed.

**Rubric: Writing**

| Criteria | Scale |
|---|---|
| Vocabulary use | 1 2 3 4 5 |
| Accuracy | 1 2 3 4 5 |
| Creativity, appearance | 1 2 3 4 5 |

A = 13–15 pts.
B = 10–12 pts.
C = 7–9 pts.
D = 4–6 pts.
F = < 4 pts.

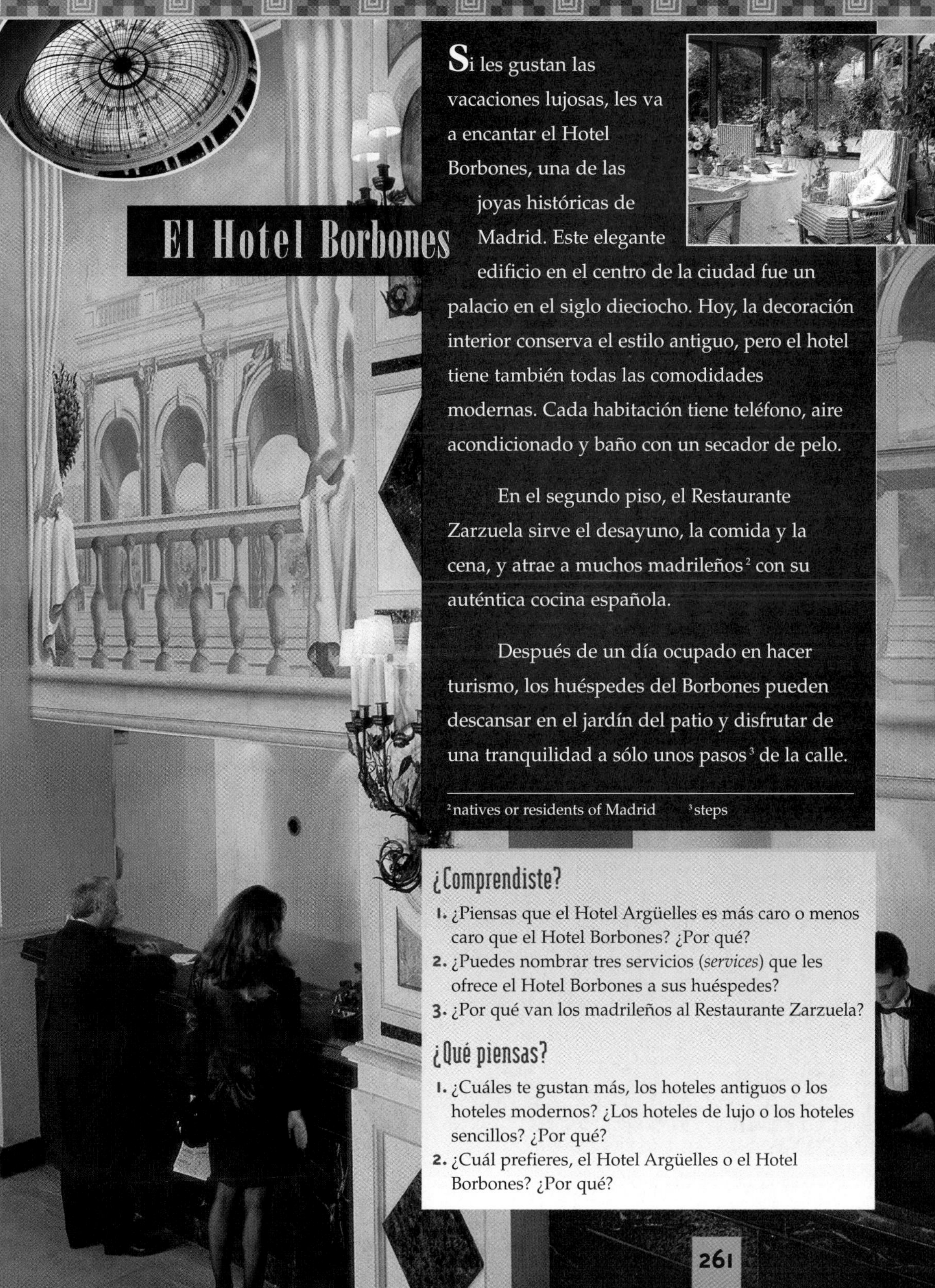

# El Hotel Borbones

Si les gustan las vacaciones lujosas, les va a encantar el Hotel Borbones, una de las joyas históricas de Madrid. Este elegante edificio en el centro de la ciudad fue un palacio en el siglo dieciocho. Hoy, la decoración interior conserva el estilo antiguo, pero el hotel tiene también todas las comodidades modernas. Cada habitación tiene teléfono, aire acondicionado y baño con un secador de pelo.

En el segundo piso, el Restaurante Zarzuela sirve el desayuno, la comida y la cena, y atrae a muchos madrileños[2] con su auténtica cocina española.

Después de un día ocupado en hacer turismo, los huéspedes del Borbones pueden descansar en el jardín del patio y disfrutar de una tranquilidad a sólo unos pasos[3] de la calle.

[2] natives or residents of Madrid [3] steps

## ¿Comprendiste?

1. ¿Piensas que el Hotel Argüelles es más caro o menos caro que el Hotel Borbones? ¿Por qué?
2. ¿Puedes nombrar tres servicios (*services*) que les ofrece el Hotel Borbones a sus huéspedes?
3. ¿Por qué van los madrileños al Restaurante Zarzuela?

## ¿Qué piensas?

1. ¿Cuáles te gustan más, los hoteles antiguos o los hoteles modernos? ¿Los hoteles de lujo o los hoteles sencillos? ¿Por qué?
2. ¿Cuál prefieres, el Hotel Argüelles o el Hotel Borbones? ¿Por qué?



## Culture Highlights

● **LODGING IN SPAIN** Tourists have several lodging options when traveling in Spain. There are hotels that range from modest (one-star) to luxury hotels (rated five-star deluxe). There are state-run **Paradores de Turismo**, inns in historic buildings around Spain. There are also **pensiones**, more modest family-run guest houses. Younger tourists will find youth hostels, and campers can choose from over 1,200 official campgrounds.

## Cross Cultural Connections

Have students make a list to describe an elegant hotel and a new modern hotel in the area. How are these hotels similar to or different from the Madrid hotels described here? Have students interview someone who has traveled both in Spain and the U.S. and discuss the amenities typically found in U.S. hotels that are missing in Spanish hotels, and those available in Spain but not in the U.S.

## Community Connection

Based on this reading, have students create an advertisement for a hotel or inn in the area. Remind them that they are trying to persuade tourists to visit their town/city.

## ¿Comprendiste?

**Answers**

*Answers will vary.*

1. El Hotel Argüelles es menos caro que el Hotel Borbones porque ofrece menos servicios y la descripción dice que tiene precios módicos.
2. En el Hotel Borbones cada habitación tiene teléfono, aire acondicionado y baño con secador de pelo. También tiene restaurante y un jardín de patio.
3. Los madrileños van al Restaurante Zarzuela por su auténtica comida española.

## Teaching All Students

**Extra Help** Before students start to read, have them scan the reading and make a list of the words they don't know. Then after they finish the reading and the associated exercises, have them review the list of unknown words and try to define them from context.

**Challenge** Ask students to write a short paragraph on the hotel that they would most like to visit and why.

**Multiple Intelligences**

**Verbal** Distribute brochures of hotels. Ask groups to write a short description of their hotel and share with the class.

**Logical/Mathematical** Divide the class into small groups; give each group information on 2 different hotels. Have students compare prices and features of the hotels and determine which hotel gives more value for the price.

## Block Schedule

**Variety** Have students work in groups using Madrid guidebooks to find out the significance of the hotel names. (**Argüelles** is a Madrid neighborhood and Metro stop. **Borbones** are the Spanish royal family.)

### Teaching Resource Options

**Print** 

Unit 4 Resource Book
Information Gap Activities, pp. 19–20
Family Involvement, pp. 21–22

**Audiovisual** 

OHT 110, 110A, 116 (Quick Start)

**Technology** 

Electronic Teacher Tools/Test Generator
*Intrigas y aventuras* CD-ROM, Disc 2

### Quick Start Review

Furniture

Use OHT 116 or write on board: Imagine that Ana and Leo are about to be married and make a list of the furniture they would like for their home. List four items in Spanish and include an adjective or two to describe them. For example: **un sofá elegante**

*Answers will vary.*
*Sample answer:* una mesa enorme con sillas elegantes, un sofá lujoso, lámparas de estilo moderno

### Teaching Suggestions
**What Have Students Learned?**

- Have students look at the "Now you can..." notes listed on the left side of pp. 262–263. Point out that if they feel they need to review material before doing the activities, they should consult the "To review" notes.
- Use the video to review vocabulary and structures.

### Actividad 1 Answers

1. pensión
2. reserva
3. habitación
4. piso
5. ascensor
6. maletero
7. llave
8. aire acondicionado
9. muebles
10. lámpara

ETAPA 1

# En uso
## REPASO Y MÁS COMUNICACIÓN

**OBJECTIVES**
- Talk about travel plans
- Persuade others
- Describe rooms, furniture, and appliances

*Now you can...*
- talk about travel plans.

*To review*
- travel vocabulary, see pp. 246–247.

### ACTIVIDAD 1 En la pensión

Tú y tu familia van a hospedarse en la pensión del señor Zavala. ¿Qué les dice? *(Hint: Tell what Señor Zavala says.)*

Bienvenidos a nuestra __1__ (pared / pensión). Veo que ustedes tienen una __2__ (reserva / llave) para una __3__ (recepción / habitación) en el tercer __4__ (piso / paseo). Vamos a su habitación en el __5__ (ascensor / armario). Hoy yo soy el __6__ (extranjero / maletero).
Aquí está su habitación y ésta es la __7__ (planta baja / llave). Espero que no haga mucho calor esta semana porque no hay __8__ (aire acondicionado / lavaplatos). Pero sí tenemos muchos __9__ (huéspedes / muebles) bonitos: una mesa, dos sillas, una __10__ (lámpara / sala)...

*Now you can...*
- talk about travel plans.
- persuade others.

*To review*
- the subjunctive to express hopes and wishes, see p. 252.

### ACTIVIDAD 2 ¡Vamos a Madrid!

Unos estudiantes están hablando de su futuro viaje a Madrid. ¿Qué dicen? *(Hint: Tell what they say.)*

**modelo**

*la profesora / insistir en / los estudiantes / portarse bien*
*La profesora insiste en que los estudiantes se porten bien.*

1. yo / preferir / la pensión / tener aire acondicionado
2. nosotros / querer / la profesora / hacer las reservas
3. ojalá / la calefacción / funcionar bien
4. la profesora / preferir / el maletero / llevar las maletas
5. nadie / desear / nosotros / hospedarse en una pensión sin electricidad
6. algunos estudiantes / insistir en / las habitaciones tener baño

### Classroom Community

**Peer Teaching** Divide the class into 6 groups. Assign a "Now you can" or "To review" objective from the inside margins of pp. 262–263 to each group. Students should give a brief definition/description of the concept, prepare a visual hook (aid), and write a short quiz for the entire class. Allow each group 5–7 minutes to present their concept.

**Storytelling** Ask students to tell a story based on one of the objectives, e.g., talking about travel plans; persuading others; describing rooms, furniture, and appliances. Students can prepare their story by writing notes, then share it with a partner.

*Now you can...*
- talk about travel plans.
- persuade others.
- describe rooms, furniture, and appliances.

*To review*
- irregular subjunctive forms, see p. 255.

## Prefiero que...

Vas de viaje con tu familia. Expresa tus preferencias. *(Hint: Express preferences.)*

**modelo**

*Hay un restaurante en la planta baja.*
*Prefiero que haya un restaurante en la planta baja.*

1. Los otros huéspedes son simpáticos.
2. Nos dan una habitación con horno microondas.
3. El maletero sabe hablar inglés.
4. Vamos de compras ahora.
5. Hay un jardín cerca de nuestro hotel.
6. Le damos una buena propina al maletero.
7. La pensión está cerca del metro.
8. Hay servicios cerca de la recepción.

*Now you can...*
- persuade others.
- describe rooms, furniture, and appliances.

*To review*
- the subjunctive to express hopes and wishes, see p. 252.

## ¿Dónde lo ponemos?

Estás en tu nueva casa. Explícales a los trabajadores dónde poner los muebles: en el baño, en la cocina, en el comedor, en la habitación o en la sala. *(Hint: Tell where to put items.)*

**modelo**

*Quiero que pongan la lámpara en la habitación.*

### Answers

1. Yo prefiero que la pensión tenga aire acondicionado.
2. Nosotros queremos que la profesora haga las reservas.
3. Ojalá que la calefacción funcione bien.
4. La profesora prefiere que el maletero lleve las maletas.
5. Nadie desea que nosotros nos hospedemos en una pensión sin electricidad.
6. Algunos estudiantes insisten en que las habitaciones tengan baño.

### Answers

1. Prefiero que los otros huéspedes sean simpáticos.
2. Prefiero que nos den una habitación con horno microondas.
3. Prefiero que el maletero sepa hablar inglés.
4. Prefiero que vayamos de compras ahora.
5. Prefiero que haya un jardín cerca de nuestro hotel.
6. Prefiero que le demos una buena propina al maletero.
7. Prefiero que la pensión esté cerca del metro.
8. Prefiero que haya servicios cerca de la recepción.

### Actividad 4 Answers

*Answers may vary.*

1. Quiero que pongan el horno microondas en la cocina.
2. Quiero que pongan el lavabo en el baño.
3. Quiero que pongan el armario en la habitación.
4. Quiero que pongan la silla en el comedor.
5. Quiero que pongan la mesa en el comedor.
6. Quiero que pongan el refrigerador en la cocina.
7. Quiero que pongan el sillón en la sala.
8. Quiero que pongan el espejo en el baño (en la habitación).

## Teaching All Students

**Extra Help** Write each of the "Now you can…" and "To review" concepts on a piece of paper. Put slips in a hat/box. Ask students to choose a slip and give an example of how the concept is used.

**Multiple Intelligences**

**Musical/Rhythmic** Ask students to choose different lobby music for each of the hotels described in the **En voces** reading.

**Logical/Mathematical** Ask students to reread the **En voces** reading on pp. 260–261 and count the descriptive adjectives or phrases used in the 2 hotel descriptions. Make a chart to determine which description is more complete and what information is left out of the descriptions.

## Block Schedule

**Time Saver** Instead of having the entire class go over the **En uso** activities as a group, divide them into several groups and have a leader go through the exercises. This promotes discussion and gets students to tune in to the review. (For additional activities, see **Block Scheduling Copymasters.**)

## Teaching Resource Options

### Print 

Unit 4 Resource Book
- **Cooperative Quizzes,** pp. 33–34
- **Etapa Exam,** Forms A and B, pp. 35–44
- ***Examen para hispanohablantes,*** pp. 45–49
- **Audioscript,** p. 32
- **Portfolio Assessment,** pp. 50–51
- **Multiple Choice Test Questions,** pp. 170–171

### Audiovisual 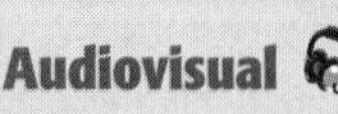

**OHT** 116 (Quick Start)
**Audio Program** Cassette 20A / CD 20; (***Para hispanohablantes*** Cassette 20A / CD 20)

### Technology 

Eletronic Teacher Tools/Test Generator
www.mcdougallittell.com

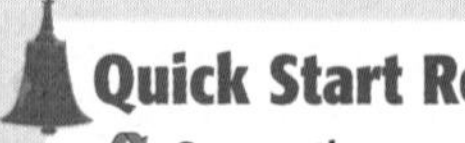

## Quick Start Review

**Suggesting, persuading**

Use OHT 116 or write on board: Write 3 recommendations for tourism in your area. Use phrases such as **Recomiendo que...** and **Sugiero que...**

*Answers will vary.*
*Sample answer:* Recomiendo que usted visite el museo de arte moderno. Hay varias obras famosas allí.

**Actividad 5 and Actividad 6**

**Rubric: Speaking**

| Criteria | Scale | |
|---|---|---|
| Pronunciation | 1 2 3 4 5 | A = 13–15 pts. |
| Accuracy | 1 2 3 4 5 | B = 10–12 pts. |
| Intonation | 1 2 3 4 5 | C = 7–9 pts. |
| | | D = 4–6 pts. |
| | | F = < 4 pts. |

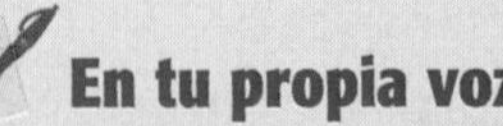

**Actividad 7 En tu propia voz**

**Rubric: Writing**

| Criteria | Scale | |
|---|---|---|
| Vocabulary use | 1 2 3 4 5 | A = 13–15 pts. |
| Accuracy | 1 2 3 4 5 | B = 10–12 pts. |
| Creativity, appearance | 1 2 3 4 5 | C = 7–9 pts. |
| | | D = 4–6 pts. |
| | | F = < 4 pts. |

## Actividad 5 Preferencias

**PARA CONVERSAR**

**STRATEGY: SPEAKING**

**Make and express decisions** Traveling with others requires planning (**planear**) and compromise (**llegar a un acuerdo**). Anticipate decisions: where to stay (**dónde hospedarse**), what to do (**cómo pasar el tiempo**), how to get there (**cómo viajar**). Use persuasion to resolve differences (**sugiero, recomiendo**). Finally, report the results (**estamos** o **no estamos de acuerdo que...**)

Tú y tu amigo(a) van a hacer un viaje a Madrid. Conversen sobre sus preferencias. Luego, preséntenle sus resultados a la clase. *(Hint: Express travel preferences. Then present results.)*

**¿hacer reservas?**
**¿visitar los museos?**
**¿usar el metro?**
**¿tener una habitación con baño?**
**¿...?**

**modelo**

**Tú:** *¿Prefieres que hagamos reservas?*
**Amigo(a):** *Sí, y ojalá que nos hospedemos en una pensión.*
**Tú:** *¿En una pensión? Prefiero que nos hospedemos en...*

## Actividad 6 Bienvenidos a...

Están en una pensión en Madrid. Una persona trabaja en la recepción y las otras son huéspedes(as). El (La) recepcionista les muestra la habitación a los huéspedes(as) y les sugiere actividades turísticas. Cambien de papel. *(Hint: Role-play a scene.)*

**modelo**

**Recepcionista:** *Bienvenidos a la pensión Buena Vida. ¿Tienen una reserva?*
**Huésped(a) 1:** *Sí, para dos.*
**Huésped(a) 2:** *Preferimos que la habitación tenga baño.*
**Recepcionista:** *Tenemos cuatro habitaciones con baño...*

## Actividad 7 En tu propia voz

**ESCRITURA** Imagínate que Isabel viene a visitarte. Escríbele una carta invitándola a hospedarse en tu casa. Describe la casa y su habitación con muchos detalles. También recomiéndale algunas actividades. *(Hint: Write a note inviting Isabel to visit you. Describe your house and recommend activities.)*

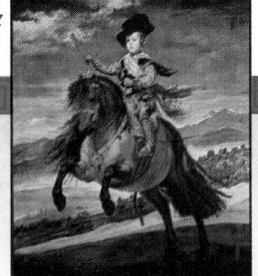

*El Príncipe don Baltasar Carlos,* por Velázquez

**CONEXIONES**

**El arte** Eres un(a) guía en el Museo del Prado. Escoge dos pinturas de El Greco, Goya, Velázquez u otro artista de la escuela española y explícaselas a un grupo de turistas (la clase). Empieza con una descripción de la vida del artista. Busca información en Internet o en la biblioteca. Y no te olvides, ¡es posible que los turistas te hagan algunas preguntas!



## Classroom Community

**Group Activity** Have students make a set of flashcards for the vocabulary words. Students take turns holding up cards and others form sentences with each word. Then divide the class into groups and have each group place 5–6 cards in the center and form a creative sentence with all the words.

**Games Name That Artist:** Based on the **El arte** activity, bring in pictures of works by each artist, (El Greco, Goya or Velázquez, Miró, Picasso, Dalí) and briefly review their styles. Divide the class into two teams and ask students to try to name the artist as you show them a picture.

# En resumen

## REPASO DE VOCABULARIO

### DESCRIBE ROOMS, FURNITURE, AND APPLIANCES

**In and Around the House**

| | |
|---|---|
| **el armario** | *closet, wardrobe* |
| **la bañera** | *bathtub* |
| **el baño** | *bathroom* |
| **la cocina** | *kitchen* |
| **el comedor** | *dining room* |
| **el garaje** | *garage* |
| **la habitación** | *room, bedroom* |
| **el jardín** | *garden* |
| **el lavabo** | *bathroom sink* |
| **la pared** | *wall* |
| **el piso** | *floor, story* |
| **la puerta** | *door* |
| **la sala** | *living room* |
| **el suelo** | *floor* |
| **la ventana** | *window* |

**Furniture**

| | |
|---|---|
| **la cama** | *bed* |
| **el espejo** | *mirror* |
| **la lámpara** | *lamp* |
| **la mesa** | *table* |
| **los muebles** | *furniture* |
| **la silla** | *chair* |
| **el sillón** | *armchair* |
| **el sofá** | *sofa* |

**Appliances**

| | |
|---|---|
| **el aire acondicionado** | *air conditioning* |
| **la calefacción** | *heat, heating* |
| **el congelador** | *freezer* |
| **el despertador** | *alarm clock* |
| **la electricidad** | *electricity* |
| **la estufa** | *stove* |
| **funcionar** | *to work, to run* |
| **el horno** | *oven* |
| **el horno microondas** | *microwave oven* |
| **el lavaplatos** | *dishwasher* |
| **el refrigerador** | *refrigerator* |

### TALK ABOUT TRAVEL PLANS

| | |
|---|---|
| **el ascensor** | *elevator* |
| **las escaleras** | *stairs, staircase* |
| **el (la) extranjero(a)** | *foreigner* |
| **hospedarse (en)** | *to stay (at)* |
| **el (la) huésped(a)** | *guest* |
| **la llave** | *key* |
| **el (la) maletero(a)** | *porter* |
| **la pensión** | *pension, boarding house* |
| **la planta baja** | *ground floor* |
| **la recepción** | *reception, front desk* |
| **la reserva** | *reservation* |
| **los servicios** | *bathrooms* |
| **el turismo** | *tourism* |

### PERSUADE OTHERS

| | |
|---|---|
| **insistir (en)** | *to insist* |
| **ojalá que** | *I hope that, hopefully* |
| **sugerir (e→ie, i)** | *to suggest* |

**Ya sabes**

| | |
|---|---|
| **desear** | *to desire* |
| **esperar** | *to hope* |
| **necesitar** | *to need* |
| **preferir (e→ie, i)** | *to prefer* |
| **querer (e→ie)** | *to want* |

### Juego

Gregorio perdió el control de la televisión. Está en la cocina. ¿Dónde lo dejó?

## Teaching All Students

**Extra Help** Ask students to work with a partner and review the meanings of each vocabulary word. They should keep a record of the words that are most difficult for them. Review these words with the entire class.

**Multiple Intelligences**

**Visual** Ask students to form a visual using as many of the vocabulary words as they can. They may make a mind map, a drawing, etc.

**Logical/Mathematical** Ask students to form "new" categories for the first column of the vocabulary list. For example, categorize the words by where they are found (e.g., rooms of the house, first floor vs. second floor, etc.). Be creative!

## Teaching Note: En tu propia voz

**Writing Strategy** Tell students to give a variety of descriptions in their letter. They might include what the weather is like where they live and what they do for fun with their friends.

## Teaching Suggestions

Using pictures from store catalogs, have students label all the appliances that require electricity.

## Interdisciplinary Connection

**Art** Have students work with the art department to make drawings or paintings in the style of El Greco, Goya, and Velázquez.

## Cultural Highlights

- **FRANCISCO JOSÉ DE GOYA** (1746–1828) was a court painter to Carlos IV. Many of his paintings have a political tone, such as *El 2 de mayo* and *El 3 de mayo*. His "black" paintings reflect his mood as he suffered from deafness. Other works by Goya include *La Maja vestida*, *La Maja desnuda,* and *La familia de Carlos IV.*

## Juego

**Answer**

Está detrás de la televisión.

## Project: Reviewing Etapa 1

Assign the following out-of-class activities:

- Interview a Spanish speaker about the different rooms in his or her home.
- Bring in tourist information about Madrid.
- Find information on hotel accommodations in Madrid via the Internet.
- Find out about family housing in Madrid.

**Extra Credit**

| | |
|---|---|
| Interview | 2 pts. |
| Tourist information | 2 pts. |
| Hotels in Madrid | 2 pts. |
| Housing in Madrid | 2 pts. |

## Block Schedule

**Retention** Have students use vocabulary words to identify things at school and where they are located. For example, **Hay dos puertas en cada clase de la escuela.**

# Planning Guide CLASSROOM MANAGEMENT

## OBJECTIVES

**Communication**
- Describe your city or town *pp. 268–269*
- Make suggestions *pp. 270–271, 274–276*
- Ask for and give directions *pp. 277, 280*

**Grammar**
- **Ni** used to mean *not even, neither,* or *nor* *p. 273*
- Subjunctive stem changes: **-ar**, **-er** verbs *p. 274*
- Stem-changing **-ir** verbs in the subjunctive *pp. 276–277*
- The subjunctive and the infinitive *p. 278*
- **Cuando** and **donde** as connectors *p. 280*

**Culture**
- La Plaza Mayor *p. 272*
- El paseo *p. 275*
- Los Gipsy Kings *pp. 282–283*
- Los gitanos *p. 282*

**Recycling**
- The subjunctive with impersonal expressions
- Stem-changing verbs
- The subjunctive with expressions of hope or wishes
- Direct object pronouns

## STRATEGIES

**Listening Strategies**
- Listen and distinguish *p. 270*

**Speaking Strategies**
- Ask for and give directions *p. 280*
- Work cooperatively *p. 286*

**Reading Strategies**
- Scan for nationalities *TE p. 282*

**Writing Strategies**
- Engage the reader by addressing him or her personally *Actividad 6, TE p. 286*

**Connecting Cultures Strategies**
- Identify characteristics of successful musical groups *p. 282*
- Compare public transportation in Spain and the U.S. *TE p. 271*

## PROGRAM RESOURCES

### Print

- *Más práctica* Workbook PE *pp. 97–104*
- Block Scheduling Copymasters *pp. 89–96*
- Unit 4 Resource Book
  - *Más práctica* Workbook TE *pp. 52–59*
  - *Cuaderno para hispanohablantes* TE *pp. 60–67*
  - Information Gap Activities *pp. 68–71*
  - Family Involvement *pp. 72–73*
  - Video Activities *pp. 74–76*
  - Videoscript *pp. 77–79*
  - Audioscript *pp. 80–83*
  - Assessment Program, Unit 4 Etapa 2 *pp. 84–102; pp. 173–175*
  - Answer Keys *pp. 180–181*

### Audiovisual

- Audio Program Cassette 11A, 11B / CD 11
- *Canciones* Cassette/CD
- Video Program Videotape 4 / Videodisc 3A
- Overhead Transparencies M1, M5; 105, 117–126

### Technology

- Electronic Teacher Tools/Test Generator
- *Intrigas y aventuras* CD-ROM, Disc 2
-  www.mcdougallittell.com

### Assessment Program Options

- Cooperative Quizzes (Unit 4 Resource Book)
- Etapa Exam Forms A and B (Unit 4 Resource Book)
- *Examen para hispanohablantes* (Unit 4 Resource Book)
- Portfolio Assessment (Unit 4 Resource Book)
- Multiple Choice Test Questions (Unit 4 Resource Book)
- Audio Program Cassette 20A / CD 20
- Electronic Teacher Tools/Test Generator

### Native Speakers

- *Cuaderno para hispanohablantes* PE *pp. 97–104*
- *Cuaderno para hispanohablantes* TE (Unit 4 Resource Book)
- *Examen para hispanohablantes* (Unit 4 Resource Book)
- Audio Program *(Para hispanohablantes)* Cassettes 11B, 20A / CD 11, CD 20
- Audioscript (Unit 4 Resource Book)

Andrea

Isabel

# Student Text Listening Activity Scripts

##  Videoscript: Diálogo *pages 270–271*

• Videotape 4, 15:36 • Videodisc 3A

Search Chapter 5, Play to end.
U4E2, En vivo (Dialog)

• Use the videoscript with **Actividades 1, 2** *page 272*

**Isabel:** Escribí mi ensayo para el concurso sobre la vida en las plazas. Fue una sorpresa enorme cuando me llamaron y me contaron quién ganó —¡yo!
**Andrea:** Ay, qué envidia. A mí me encanta viajar. ¿Y qué hiciste aquí en Madrid?
**Isabel:** Escribí un artículo sobre los museos de Madrid. Hay tantos —el Museo del Prado, el Centro de Arte Reina Sofía, el Museo Thyssen-Bornemisza, el Casón del Buen Retiro...
**Andrea:** ¡Ay, tú conoces mejor que yo los museos de Madrid!
**Isabel:** Son fabulosos. Pero sabes, después de tantos días en los museos, quiero ver más de la ciudad. Quiero ver los monumentos y las plazas, los edificios, la gente. No quiero ver ni un museo más.
**Andrea:** Pues empezaste en la mejor de las plazas, en mi opinión. La Plaza Mayor es maravillosa. Y si quieres ver gente, te aconsejo que vayas a dar una vuelta por la Puerta del Sol.
**Isabel:** Sí, buena idea. Oye, Andrea, ¿me haces un favor? Quiero que me saques una foto.
**Andrea:** Claro que sí. Ponte allí. La voy a sacar desde aquí.
Un poco más a tu izquierda, ahora un poco a tu derecha, a tu izquierda, a tu derecha...
**Isabel:** ¡Andrea!
**Andrea:** Je, je, je. Estoy bromeando. No te muevas. Está perfecto.
**Isabel:** Gracias, Andrea. Sabes, tengo que irme. Fue un placer conocerte.
**Andrea:** Igualmente, Isabel.
**Isabel:** Oye, Andrea, ¿cómo llego al Palacio Real? Tengo ganas de verlo.
**Andrea:** ¿Caminando? Es fácil. Subes por la calle Santiago, hacia el oeste. Después, sigues caminando hasta el cruce con la calle Bailén, y desde allí, puedes ver el palacio.
**Isabel:** Gracias.
**Andrea:** Sabes, Isabel, hace mucho tiempo que no voy al palacio. ¿Quieres que te acompañe?
**Isabel:** ¡Me encantaría!
**Andrea:** Además, no quiero que te pierdas.
**Isabel:** ¿Perderme yo? ¡Ja!...
**Andrea:** Pero sabes, hace tanto tiempo que no voy al palacio. ¡Es posible que nos perdamos las dos! ¡Vamos!... ¿Isabel, cómo es la Ciudad de México? ¿Es muy diferente de Madrid?
**Isabel:** Bueno, claro, tiene sus diferencias. México es mucho más grande. En mi opinión, es más difícil andar por la Ciudad de México. Todo está más lejos. Yo siempre voy en metro o en micro.
**Andrea:** ¿En micro? ¿Qué es un micro?
**Isabel:** Es como un autobús, pero los micros son más pequeños. Y siempre van llenísimos.
**Andrea:** Normalmente, yo también voy en metro si tengo prisa o si queda lejos. ¿Y qué otras diferencias hay entre la Ciudad de México y Madrid?
**Isabel:** No sé... La construcción de los edificios es diferente. Hay más edificios antiguos aquí. Pero las dos ciudades tienen mucho en común. Tienen calles, aceras, edificios, puentes, semáforos, y claro, siempre tienes que buscar estacionamiento.
**Andrea:** ¿Y cómo son los conductores de los coches en la Ciudad de México? ¿Son tan locos como aquí?
**Isabel:** ¡Son iguales en todas las ciudades! Los peatones tienen que tener cuidado.
**Andrea:** Mira, el Palacio Real. ¿Entramos? Y después, te aconsejo que compres unas tarjetas postales para mandar a México. Hay un quiosco cerca del Palacio donde puedes comprar postales.
**Isabel:** Muy bien. Oye, voy a preguntar en la taquilla si venden entradas más baratas para estudiantes... ¡Qué tarjetas postales más bonitas! Voy a mandar ésta a mi amigo Ricardo. Oye, ¿dónde hay un buzón?
**Andrea:** Estoy segura de que hay un buzón por aquí. Oye, Isabel, ahora que somos amigas, ¡insisto en que me mandes una tarjeta postal después de regresar a México! Luego te doy mi dirección, ¿vale?
**Isabel:** ¿Quieres una de éstas? ¿Del Palacio Real?
**Andrea:** ¡No, no quiero una tarjeta postal del Palacio Real, sino una de la Ciudad de México! ¡No lo olvides! Oye, sugiero que demos una vuelta por la Gran Vía. Mi heladería favorita está en la Gran Vía.
**Isabel:** ¡Perfecto! Me encanta el helado.
**Andrea:** Y recomiendo que pidas el de chocolate. Es maravilloso. Yo voy a pedir el helado de limón... ¿Y quién es la otra persona que ganó el concurso?
**Isabel:** No sé quién es. Pero sé que es un muchacho de los Estados Unidos.
**Andrea:** ¿De los Estados Unidos? Pero yo pensaba que *Onda Internacional* es una revista para hispanohablantes.
**Isabel:** Sí, lo es, pero hay muchas personas en los Estados Unidos que hablan español.
**Andrea:** Isabel, este vecindario tiene tiendas excelentes. Y mira, ¡hay rebajas! ¿Entramos?
**Isabel:** Sí, ¿por qué no? Pero después tengo que regresar a la pensión. No quiero que el Sr. Zavala se preocupe. ¿Hay una parada de metro cerca de aquí?
**Andrea:** Sí, hay una parada muy cerca. ¿Pero quién es el Sr. Zavala?
**Isabel:** Es el dueño de la pensión. Es muy buena onda, pero habla muchísimo.
**Andrea:** ¿Buena onda?
**Isabel:** Significa que es una persona muy simpática. Es una expresión muy común en México.
**Andrea:** Ves, aprendí algo nuevo. Aquí en España decimos "buena gente". Significa la misma cosa. Bueno, ¿entramos?

## Actividad 7 Una calle de Madrid *page 275*

*Escucha las seis descripciones e indica si corresponden o no a la foto.*

1. En este momento el autobús está al lado de la parada de metro.
2. La mujer que lleva un abrigo rojo bajó del metro en la estación Sol.
3. Es bueno que los peatones puedan caminar por la acera.
4. Hay una heladería junto a la tintorería. Me gustaría tomar un helado.
5. ¡Qué lástima! Quiero mandar mis postales y no veo ni el correo ni un buzón.
6. Estos tres hombres van a tomar el metro. Están entrando en la estación Ópera.

## Actividad 13 En mi vecindario *page 279*

*Andrea te dice cómo llegar a estos lugares desde su casa. Mira el mapa. ¿Son correctas sus direcciones?*

1. ¿Quieres saber dónde vive mi mejor amiga? Pues, de mi casa necesitas subir por la Calle Ana María y debes doblar a la derecha en la Avenida Azucenas. Tienes que seguir hasta la Calle Fereluz. Entonces, quiero que dobles a la izquierda y que camines una cuadra. Dobla a la derecha en la Avenida Benjamín. Su apartamento está a la izquierda.
2. El parque está muy cerca de mi casa. Recomiendo que subas por la Calle Ana María y que dobles a la derecha en el cruce con la Avenida Azucenas. Sigue la Avenida Azucenas hasta el cruce con la Calle Fereluz. El parque está al lado del mercado.
3. ¿Cómo llegas a la parada de autobuses desde mi casa? Pues, debes subir por la Calle Ana María. Dobla a la derecha en la Avenida Benjamín y sigue una cuadra hacia el este. Entonces, debes doblar a la izquierda en la Calle Fereluz. Sugiero que llegues a tiempo.
4. Bueno, desde mi casa es fácil llegar a la escuela. Necesitas subir por la Calle Ana María dos cuadras hacia el norte. Después de cruzar la Avenida Benjamín, mira a la derecha y vas a ver la escuela.
5. ¿Buscas una ganga? Pues, sugiero que vayas a la tienda de rebajas. No es difícil llegar allá. De mi casa, recomiendo que subas por la Calle Ana María. En el cruce, debes doblar a la derecha y bajar por la Avenida Azucenas dos cuadras. Mira hacia el norte y vas a ver la tienda.

# Pacing Guide

## Sample Lesson Plan - 50 Minute Schedule

### DAY 1

**Etapa Opener**
- Quick Start Review (TE p. 266). 5 MIN.
- Anticipate/Activate prior knowledge: have students look at *Etapa* Opener and answer questions. 10 MIN.

**En contexto: Vocabulario**
- Quick Start Review (TE p. 268). 5 MIN.
- Discuss pictures. Have students use context and pictures to learn *Etapa* vocabulary. Answer questions, p. 269. 10 MIN.

**En vivo: Diálogo**
- Quick Start Review (TE p. 270). 5 MIN.
- Review Listening Strategy, p. 270. Play audio or show video for the dialog shown on pp. 270–271. 8 MIN.
- Read aloud, students taking on roles of characters. 7 MIN.

**Homework Option**
- Video Activities, Unit 4 Resource Book, pp. 74–76.

### DAY 2

**En acción: Vocabulario y Gramática**
- Check homework. 5 MIN.
- Quick Start Review (TE p. 272). 3 MIN.
- Ask students for a summary of *En vivo* dialog to check recall. 4 MIN.
- Ask Comprehension Questions (TE p. 271). 5 MIN.
- Replay the *En vivo* dialog using the audiovisual resources and have students do *Actividades* 1 and 2 orally. 8 MIN.
- Have students complete *Actividades* 3 and 4 in pairs. 10 MIN.
- Present *Gramática*: Subjunctive Stem Changes: **-ar**, **-er** Verbs, p. 274, and then have students complete *Actividad* 5 and *Actividad* 6 first in writing, then review orally. 15 MIN.

**Homework Option**
- *Más práctica* Workbook, p. 101. *Cuaderno para hispanohablantes*, p. 99.

### DAY 3

**En acción (cont.)**
- Check homework. 5 MIN.
- Quick Start Review (TE p. 274). 5 MIN.
- Play the audio and have students complete *Actividad* 7 in writing. 5 MIN.
- Present *Gramática*: Stem-Changing **-ir** Verbs in the Subjunctive, p. 276. 10 MIN.
- Have students do *Actividad* 8 in writing. 10 MIN.
- Present the vocabulary box on p. 277 and have students do *Actividad* 9 in pairs. 15 MIN.

**Homework Option**
- Have students prepare *Actividad* 10 in writing. *Más práctica* Workbook, p. 102. *Cuaderno para hispanohablantes*, p. 100.

### DAY 4

**En acción (cont.)**
- Check homework and do *Actividad* 10 in pairs. 8 MIN.
- Quick Start Review (TE p. 278). 5 MIN.
- Present *Gramática*: The Subjunctive and the Infinitive, on p. 278. 10 MIN.
- Have students complete *Actividades* 11 and 12 in writing. 10 MIN.
- Play audio and have students complete *Actividad* 13. 7 MIN.
- Have students complete *Actividad* 14 in small groups. 10 MIN.

**Homework Option**
- *Más práctica* Workbook, p. 103. *Cuaderno para hispanohablantes*, p. 101.

### DAY 5

**En acción (cont.)**
- Check homework. 5 MIN.
- Quick Start Review (TE p. 280). 5 MIN.
- Present Speaking Strategy, p. 280, and have students complete *Actividad* 15 in pairs. 10 MIN.
- Have students work in small groups to prepare *Actividad* 16. Ask volunteers to present their project to the class. 10 MIN.
- Have students complete *Actividad* 17 in pairs. Expand with *Más comunicación*, p. R12. 12 MIN.

**Ampliación**
- Use a suggested project, game, or activity (TE pp. 243A–243B). 8 MIN.

**Homework Option**
- *Más práctica* Workbook, p. 104. *Cuaderno para hispanohablantes*, p. 102.

### DAY 6

**En colores: Cultura y comparaciones**
- Check homework. 5 MIN.
- Quick Start Review (TE p. 282). 5 MIN.
- Review Connecting Cultures Strategy, p. 282. 10 MIN.
- Read *Vamos a bailar–Gipsy Kings* aloud with students. 10 MIN.
- Have students answer the *¿Comprendiste?* and *¿Qué piensas?* questions orally. 10 MIN.
- Divide the class into small groups and have them do research for the *Hazlo tú* activity. 10 MIN.

**Homework Option**
- Have students finish the *¿Qué piensas?* questions and *Hazlo tú* activity in writing, p. 283. *Cuaderno para hispanohablantes*, p. 98.

### DAY 7

**En uso: Repaso y más comunicación**
- Check homework. 5 MIN.
- Quick Start Review (TE p. 284). 5 MIN.
- Do *Actividades* 1, 2, and 3 orally. 15 MIN.
- Review Speaking Strategy, p. 286. Then do *Actividad* 4 orally in pairs and *Actividad* 5 in groups. 15 MIN.

**En tu propia voz: Escritura**
- Start writing activity. 10 MIN.

**Homework Option**
- Finish writing activity. *Cuaderno para hispanohablantes*, pp. 103–104. Review for *Etapa* 2 Exam.

### DAY 8

**Conexiones**
- Check homework. 5 MIN.
- Read and discuss. 5 MIN.

**En resumen: Repaso de vocabulario**
- Review grammar questions, etc., as necessary. 10 MIN.
- Complete *Etapa* 2 Exam. 20 MIN.

**Ampliación**
- Use a suggested project, game, or activity (TE pp. 243A–243B). 10 MIN.

**Homework Option**
- Preview next *Etapa* Opener, pp. 288–289.

# Sample Lesson Plan - Block Schedule (90 minutes)

## DAY 1

***Etapa* Opener**
- Quick Start Review (TE p. 266). **5 MIN.**
- Anticipate/Activate prior knowledge: have students look at the *Etapa* Opener and answer questions. **10 MIN.**

**En contexto: Vocabulario**
- Quick Start Review (TE p. 268). **5 MIN.**
- Have students use context and pictures to learn *Etapa* vocabulary. Answer questions, p. 269. **10 MIN.**

**En vivo: Diálogo**
- Quick Start Review (TE p. 270). **5 MIN.**
- Review Listening Strategy, p. 270. Play audio or show video for the dialog shown on pp. 270–271. **10 MIN.**
- Read aloud, students taking roles of characters. Ask Comprehension Questions (TE p. 271) **10 MIN.**
- Students role-play in groups while looking at the photos in their texts. Encourage them to come up with logical dialog using familiar vocabulary. **10 MIN.**

**En acción: Vocabulario y Gramática**
- Quick Start Review (TE p. 272). **5 MIN.**
- Have students do *Actividades* 1 and 2 orally. **10 MIN.**
- Have students complete *Actividades* 3 and 4 in pairs. **10 MIN.**

**Homework Option**
- *Más práctica* Workbook, pp. 97–100. *Cuaderno para hispanohablantes*, p. 97. Video Activities, Unit 4 Resource Book, pp. 75–76.

## DAY 2

**En acción (cont.)**
- Check homework. **10 MIN.**
- Quick Start Review (TE p. 274). **5 MIN.**
- Present *Gramática*: Subjunctive Stem Changes: **-ar**, **-er** Verbs, p. 274, and then have students complete *Actividad* 5 and *Actividad* 6 first in writing, then review orally in pairs. **15 MIN.**
- Play the audio and have students complete *Actividad* 7 in writing. **5 MIN.**
- Present *Gramática*: Stem-changing **-ir** Verbs in the Subjunctive, p. 276. **10 MIN.**
- Have students do *Actividad* 8 in writing. **10 MIN.**
- Present the vocabulary box on p. 277 and do *Actividades* 9 and 10 in pairs. **15 MIN.**
- Quick Start Review (TE p. 278). **5 MIN.**
- Present *Gramática*: The Subjunctive and the Infinitive, on p. 278. **5 MIN.**
- Have students complete *Actividades* 11 and 12 in writing. **10 MIN.**

**Homework Option**
- Have students complete *Actividades* 11 and 12 in writing if necessary. *Más práctica* Workbook, pp. 101–102. *Cuaderno para hispanohablantes*, pp. 99–100.

## DAY 3

**En acción (cont.)**
- Check homework. **10 MIN.**
- Play audio and have students complete *Actividad* 13. **10 MIN.**
- Quick Start Review (TE p. 280). **5 MIN.**
- Have students complete *Actividad* 14 in small groups. **10 MIN.**
- Present Speaking Strategy, p. 280, and have students complete *Actividad* 15 in pairs. **10 MIN.**
- Have students work in small groups to prepare *Actividad* 16. Save time for some students to present their projects to the class. **15 MIN.**
- Have students complete *Actividad* 17 in pairs. Expand with *Más comunicación,* p. R12. **5 MIN.**
- Use Block Scheduling Copymasters for variety. **5 MIN.**

**Ampliación**
- Use a suggested project, game, or activity (TE pp. 243A–243B). **20 MIN.**

**Homework Option**
- *Más práctica* Workbook, pp. 103–104. *Cuaderno para hispanohablantes*, pp. 101–102.

## DAY 4

**En colores: Cultura y comparaciones**
- Check homework. **10 MIN.**
- Quick Start Review (TE p. 282). **5 MIN.**
- Review Connecting Cultures Strategy, p. 282. **10 MIN.**
- Read *Vamos a bailar–Gipsy Kings* aloud with students. **10 MIN.**
- Have students answer the *¿Comprendiste?* questions orally. **10 MIN.**
- Have students answer the *¿Qué piensas?* questions in writing. **10 MIN.**
- Divide the class into small groups and have them do research for the *Hazlo tú* activity. **15 MIN.**

**En uso: Repaso y más comunicación**
- Quick Start Review (TE p. 284). **5 MIN.**
- Do *Actividades* 1, 2, and 3 orally. **15 MIN.**

**Homework Option**
- Have students finish the *¿Qué piensas?* questions and *Hazlo tú* activity in writing, p. 283. *Cuaderno para hispanohablantes*, pp. 98, 103–104.

## DAY 5

**En uso: Repaso y más comunicación (cont.)**
- Check homework. **10 MIN.**
- Quick Start Review (TE p. 286). **5 MIN.**
- Review Speaking Strategy, p. 286. Then do *Actividad* 4 orally in pairs and *Actividad* 5 in groups of four. **15 MIN.**

**Conexiones**
- Read and discuss. **5 MIN.**

**En resumen: Repaso de vocabulario**
- Review grammar questions, etc., as necessary. **10 MIN.**
- Complete *Etapa* 2 Exam. **20 MIN.**

**En tu propia voz: Escritura**
- Start writing activity. **10 MIN.**

**Ampliación**
- Use a suggested project, game, or activity (TE pp. 243A–243B). **15 MIN.**

**Homework Option**
- Finish writing activity and preview next *Etapa* Opener, pp. 288–289.

▼ Andrea e Isabel hablan en frente del Palacio Real.

## UNIDAD 4 Etapa 2
## Opener

### Etapa Theme

**Describing your city or town, making suggestions, asking for and giving directions**

### Grammar Objectives

- Subjunctive of stem-changing verbs
- Subjunctive and infinitive

### Teaching Resource Options

**Print** 

Block Scheduling Copymasters

**Audiovisual**

OHT 105, 123 (Quick Start)

### Quick Start Review

Talking about food, describing

Use OHT 123 or write on board: Fill in the blanks according to what you see in the photo.

1. Las dos chicas comen en un ___.
2. Las personas en el café ___.
3. La arquitectura no es de estilo moderno, en mi opinión es ___.

**Answers**

1. café
2. *Answers will vary. Possible answers:* comen, beben, hablan, se sientan
3. *Answers will vary. Possible answers:* histórico, tradicional, antiguo, bonito

### Teaching Suggestions
#### Previewing the Etapa

- Ask students to study the photo on pp. 266–267 and describe what they see.
- Ask them to describe a **plaza** in Spanish. Then ask them to list the activities one might see happening in a **plaza**.

UNIDAD 4

# ETAPA 2

# Conoce la ciudad

- Describe your city or town
- Make suggestions
- Ask for and give directions

### ¿Qué ves?

Mira la foto y contesta las preguntas.

1. ¿En qué parte de Madrid están Isabel y su compañera?
2. ¿Cómo se llama la chica que está con Isabel?
3. ¿A qué otras personas ves? ¿Qué hacen?
4. ¿Qué tienen en común el plano y la foto?

Plano de los transportes del Centro de Madrid
2


266

### Classroom Management

**Peer Review** To prepare for the *Storytelling* activity, have each student compile a descriptive list of what s/he sees in the photo. Students should then exchange papers and correct each other's work.

**Storytelling** Working in groups of 3, have students tell a story about what they see in the photos. Encourage them to be creative!

**Group Activity** Create a café scene in the classroom and assign students to Table 1, Table 2, etc. Assign 1 or 2 students the role of **mesero(a)**. Have each table of students create their own dialog simultaneously.

## Cross Cultural Connections

Ask students where people may go to meet friends in your community. Have them compare their local meeting places to the Plaza Mayor in Madrid, as seen on pp. 266–267.

## Culture Highlights

- **CHURROS Y CHOCOLATE** Isabel and Andrea are having **churros y chocolate**. **Churros** are tube-shaped fried dough served hot with a thick, sweet hot chocolate drink. This can be a snack or a breakfast.
- **COCIDO MADRILEÑO** has three basic ingredients–meat, legumes, and vegetables. It is served for the midday meal in three courses: first the broth, then the vegetables, and finally the meat. A similar meal is called **potaje** in Andalucia and **escudella** in Cataluña.
- **HORCHATA** is a cold, refreshing drink made from sweetened **chufa,** a white root native to Valencia.

## Teaching All Students

**Extra Help** State a color and ask students to name the items of this color in the photo on pp. 266–267.

**Native Speakers** Have Spanish speakers describe their favorite meeting place in Spanish as a model for other students. If they have come from another country, have them describe a popular meeting place there.

### Multiple Intelligences

**Verbal** Have students play "I spy" or **Veo, veo** with items they see in the picture. S1 says **"Veo una estatua"** and S2 points to the horse statue. Continue playing until everyone has participated.

**Visual** Have students give directions to a favorite meeting place on the school grounds. Students can draw a map to support their verbal directions.

## Block Schedule

**Warm-Up** Have the students get into groups of 4 or 5. Encourage them to speak in Spanish as they discuss life in a city, in the suburbs, or in the country. Prompt them with questions about sitting in the Plaza Mayor and meeting friends. (For additional activities, see **Block Scheduling Copymasters**.)

**Print** 

Unit 4 Resource Book
Video Activities, p. 74
Videoscript, p. 77
Audioscript, p. 80

**Audiovisual**

OHT 117, 118, 123 (Quick Start)
**Audio Program** Cassette 11A / CD 11
**Video Program** Videotape 4, 12:44 / Videodisc 3A

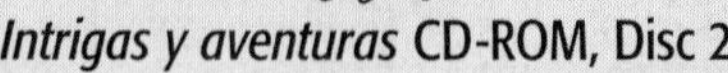

Search Chapter 4, Play to 5
U4E2, En contexto (Vocabulary)

**Technology**

*Intrigas y aventuras* CD-ROM, Disc 2

## Quick Start Review

Furniture

Use OHT 123 or write on board: Isabel and Andrea decide to take a walk in the city. Name six pieces of furniture they might see displayed in **Mueblería Rivas**.

*Answers will vary.*

## Teaching Strategy
### Introducing Vocabulary

- Have students look at pp. 268–269. Use OHT 117–118 and Audiocassette 11A/CD 11 to present the vocabulary.
- Ask the **Comprehension Questions** (TE p. 269). You may write the questions on the board and have students work in small groups to answer them. Follow up with the **Preguntas personales** on p. 269.
- Use the video vocabulary presentation for review and reinforcement.

## Language Note

Point out that **obtener** is conjugated like **tener**.

# En contexto
## VOCABULARIO

Isabel y Andrea van a dar una vuelta y explorar un poco.

el semáforo
la acera
JUGUETERÍA

**A** Si tienes coche, puedes llegar a este **vecindario** por **el puente.** Pero Isabel y Andrea vinieron en metro. Ellas ven a otros **peatones** caminando por **las aceras.** Es bueno que miren **los semáforos** antes de cruzar la calle —¡hay mucho tráfico aquí!

**B** Para este **conductor** es difícil encontrar **un estacionamiento.**

la juguetería

**C** En esta **juguetería** se pueden **obtener** regalos para niños. Cuando la tienda tiene **rebajas,** los precios son buenos. Andrea e Isabel compran unos juguetes muy baratos. ¡Qué **gangas**!



## Classroom Community

**TPR** Create labels for the different places introduced in the new vocabulary and post them around the classroom (e.g., **la juguetería, la taquilla, la heladería, la tintorería, el quiosco, la parada del metro**). You may want to clear out desks and chairs if possible. Have students go to the appropriate label as you say each place in Spanish.

**Paired Activity** Ask students to work with a partner and read aloud the captions A–F. S1 reads the caption and S2 points to the vocabulary item(s) in the corresponding photo.

D Todo lo que necesitas para pasar una tarde perfecta está cerca: **la taquilla** para comprar boletos para un concierto; **la tintorería** para limpiar la ropa que vas a llevar; y **la heladería** para después del concierto. A Isabel le gusta el helado de chocolate, pero Andrea prefiere el de limón.

E Durante su paseo, Isabel y Andrea encuentran muchos **quioscos** de revistas y periódicos. Isabel tiene hambre y **revisa** una revista para buscar la dirección de un restaurante.

F Al encontrar **un buzón,** ¡Isabel se da cuenta de que **olvidó** las postales que iba a enviar! Tiene que **regresar.** ¡Qué lástima! Afortunadamente hay **una parada** de metro cerca.

## Preguntas personales

1. ¿Hay una juguetería en tu vecindario? ¿Una heladería? ¿Qué edificios hay?
2. ¿Compras más o compras menos cuando las tiendas tienen rebajas? ¿Puedes encontrar gangas cerca de tu casa?
3. Si tu abrigo está sucio, ¿lo llevas a una taquilla o una tintorería?
4. ¿Cuál es tu lugar favorito del vecindario donde vives? ¿Por qué?
5. Descríbele tu vecindario a un(a) visitante del extranjero.



## Teaching All Students

**Extra Help** Write the name of each store or place on the board. Then have students list the names of stores from their community that match each heading.

**Native Speakers** Have Spanish speakers describe a city they know using the new vocabulary words on pp. 268–269. If any students come from another country, have them describe a foreign city, if possible.

**Multiple Intelligences**

**Naturalist** Have students research what attractions in Madrid might appeal to tourists interested in nature, animals, or biology.

**Intrapersonal** Divide the class into groups by assigning one of the following to each group: **la juguetería, la taquilla, la tintorería, la heladería, el quiosco.** Ask students to analyze reasons why they would go the assigned place.



### Comprehension Questions

1. ¿Dan una vuelta por la ciudad Isabel y Andrea? **(Sí.)**
2. ¿Caminan los peatones en la calle? **(no, en las aceras)**
3. ¿Hay mucho tráfico? **(Sí.)**
4. ¿Es difícil o fácil encontrar un estacionamiento en la ciudad? **(difícil)**
5. Cuando una tienda tiene rebajas, ¿son muy altos los precios o hay gangas? **(Hay gangas.)**
6. ¿Venden tacos o boletos en una taquilla? **(boletos)**
7. ¿Sugieres que vayamos a la heladería para el desayuno o un postre? **(un postre)**
8. ¿Dónde venden revistas y periódicos? **(en el quiosco)**
9. ¿Qué revistas lees tú? **(Answers will vary.)**
10. ¿Hay una parada de autobús cerca de tu casa? **(Answers will vary.)**

### Teaching Strategy

Ask the students simple **Sí/No** questions pertaining to the text, e.g., **¿Es necesario que miren los semáforos antes de cruzar la calle? (Sí), ¿Está feliz el conductor? (No), ¿Son buenos los precios cuando la tienda tiene rebajas? (Sí), ¿Puede comprar boletos para un concierto en la tintorería? (No, en la taquilla), ¿A Isabel le gusta el helado de vainilla? (No, de chocolate), ¿Revisa Andrea un periódico para la dirección de un restaurante nuevo? (No, una revista), ¿Pone Isabel las postales en el buzón? (No).**

### Critical Thinking

Ask students to compare the neighborhood described in **En contexto** to their own. They may draw pictures or write a brief description of each.

### Block Schedule

**Retention** Have students keep an ongoing list of definitions for places in a city. Encourage them to come up with additional words they think they might need to describe a city. What other stores or places do they frequent?

## Teaching Resource Options

### Print

Unit 4 Resource Book
- Video Activities, pp. 75–76
- Videoscript, pp. 77–79
- Audioscript, p. 80

### Audiovisual

**OHT** 121–122, 123 (Quick Start)
**Audio Program** Cassette 11A / CD 11
**Video Program** Videotape 4, 15:36 / Videodisc 3A

Search Chapter 5, Play to end
U4E2, En vivo (Dialog)

### Technology

*Intrigas y aventuras* CD-ROM, Disc 2

## Quick Start Review

Describing the city

Use OHT 123 or write on board: Look at the photos from the dialog and write a list in Spanish of six things you see.

*Answers will vary.*

## Teaching Strategy
### Presenting the Dialog

- Prepare students for listening by focusing on the dialog context using yes/no or either/or questions.
- Use the video, audiocassette, or CD to present the dialog. The video version offers expanded language opportunities.

# En vivo

## DIÁLOGO

Andrea

Isabel

**PARA ESCUCHAR** • **STRATEGY: LISTENING**

**Listen and distinguish** Listen to what Andrea and Isabel say about Madrid and Mexico City. Where are the following found?

- **metro**
- **micro**
- **conductores locos**
- **buena onda**
- **buena gente**

## Nuevas amigas

1► **Andrea:** ¿Qué hiciste aquí?
**Isabel:** Escribí un artículo sobre los museos de Madrid. Son fabulosos. Pero quiero ver más de la ciudad – las plazas, los edificios, la gente. No quiero ver ni un museo más.

5► **Andrea:** ¿Qué es un micro?
**Isabel:** Es como un autobús, pero los micros son más pequeños.
**Andrea:** Normalmente, yo también voy en metro si tengo prisa.

6► **Andrea:** ¿Cómo son los conductores de los coches en la Ciudad de México? ¿Son tan locos como aquí?
**Isabel:** ¡Son iguales en todas las ciudades! Los peatones tienen que tener cuidado.

7► **Andrea:** Mira, el Palacio Real. ¿Entramos? Después puedes comprar postales.
**Isabel:** Oye, voy a preguntar en la taquilla si venden entradas más baratas para estudiantes.



## Classroom Community

**TPR** Play or read the dialog for the class. Divide the class into 2 groups; one half is Mexico and the other is Spain. Each time students hear a description of Mexico, the Mexico side should stand. Each time students hear a description of Spain, the Spain side should stand.

**Group Activity** **Prepare Ahead:** Make copies of the dialog and cut into segments. Give groups of students a copy of the entire dialog and have them place the lines in the appropriate order (without using the text).

**Portfolio** Have students pretend to be Isabel as she describes a day in Madrid in her travel journal.

**Rubric: Writing**

| Criteria | Scale |
|---|---|
| Accuracy | 1 2 3 4 5 |
| Logical organization | 1 2 3 4 5 |
| Vocabulary use | 1 2 3 4 5 |

A = 13–15 pts.
B = 10–12 pts.
C = 7–9 pts.
D = 4–6 pts.
F = < 4 pts.

2► Isabel: Andrea, ¿me haces un favor? Quiero que me saques una foto.
Andrea: Claro que sí. Ponte allí. La voy a sacar desde aquí. No te muevas. Está perfecto.

3► Isabel: Oye, ¿cómo llego al Palacio Real? Tengo ganas de verlo.
Andrea: ¿Quieres que te acompañe?
Isabel: ¡Me encantaría!
Andrea: Además, no quiero que te pierdas.

4► Andrea: ¿Cómo es la Ciudad de México? ¿Es muy diferente de Madrid?
Isabel: Claro, tiene sus diferencias. México es mucho más grande. Es más difícil andar por la Ciudad de México. Yo siempre voy en metro o en micro.

8► Andrea: Hay un buzón por aquí. ¡Insisto en que me mandes una tarjeta postal de México! ¡No lo olvides! Oye, sugiero que demos una vuelta por la Gran Vía.

9► Andrea: ¡Hay rebajas! ¿Entramos?
Isabel: Sí, pero después tengo que regresar. No quiero que el señor Zavala se preocupe. Es el dueño de la pensión. Es buena onda, pero habla muchísimo.

10► Andrea: ¿Buena onda?
Isabel: Significa que es una persona simpática. Es una expresión común en México.
Andrea: Aquí en España decimos «buena gente». Significa la misma cosa.



## Teaching All Students

**Extra Help** Read aloud one of the characters' lines and ask students to identify the character.

**Native Speakers** Have Spanish speakers discuss any expressions they might use for bus (**micro, combi, guagua, autobús**) and for describing a nice person (**es buena onda, es buena gente, es simpática, es genial,** etc.). Remind all students about the richness of the Spanish language due to all the regional differences.

**Multiple Intelligences**

**Verbal** Ask students to write a short description of Isabel and Andrea based on the dialog. Then have them work in pairs to compare the two characters.

## Video Synopsis

Andrea and Isabel meet in the Plaza Mayor and get to know each other. Together they visit the Palacio Real. For a complete transcript of the video dialog, see p. 265B.

## Comprehension Questions

1. ¿Sólo le interesa a Isabel visitar museos en Madrid? **(No)**
2. ¿Deciden ir al Palacio Real Isabel y Andrea? **(Sí)**
3. ¿Es más pequeña que Madrid la Ciudad de México? **(No)**
4. ¿Es un micro un tipo de autobús o bicicleta? **(un autobús)**
5. ¿Van al Prado o al Palacio Real? **(al Palacio Real)**
6. ¿Tienen cuidado los conductores en la cuidad o son locos? **(Son locos.)**
7. ¿Ponen postales en el buzón o en la taquilla? **(en el buzón)**
8. ¿Adónde va Isabel después de ir de compras? **(Va a regresar a la pensión.)**
9. ¿Qué significa «buena onda» en México? **(una persona simpática)**
10. ¿Cuál es la expresión para una persona simpática en España? **(buena gente)**

## Cross Cultural Connections

Ask students to discuss the public transportation they use most often. Then have them summarize what they learned about the public transportation in Madrid and Mexico City from the dialog. Ask students to work in small groups to compare their experiences with public transportation to those of Andrea and Isabel.

## Gestures

Without reading the captions, have students guess what is going on in frames 1, 2, 3, 8, 9, and 10.

## Block Schedule

**Process Time** Set up different learning stations around the room and allow students to work through the activities at each station at their own pace. Be sure to include an oral station, a reading station, and a writing station.

## Teaching Resource Options

**Print** 

Unit 4 Resource Book
Video Activities, pp. 75–76
Videoscript, pp. 77–79
Audioscript, p. 80

**Audiovisual** 

OHT 124 (Quick Start)
Audio Program Cassette 11A / CD 11
Video Program Videotape 4, 15:36 / Videodisc 3A

**Technology**

*Intrigas y aventuras* CD-ROM, Disc 2

## Quick Start Review

Describing buildings and stores

Use OHT 124 or write on board: Isabel and Andrea see a **juguetería** and a **tintorería** as they stroll through the city. Name some other buildings and stores you know. How many can you list that end in **-ería**?

*Answers may include:* la carnicería, la joyería, la librería, la panadería, la papelería, la pastelería, la taquería, la zapatería

## Projects

Ask students to work in small groups to draw a map of their community and label as many buildings and items as they can.

**Actividad 1 Objective:** Controlled practice
Listening comprehension/vocabulary

**Answers**

1. los museos de Madrid
2. Palacio Real
3. en metro o en micro
4. pequeño
5. tener cuidado
6. México / Isabel
7. rebajas
8. la Gran Vía

**Actividad 2 Objective:** Controlled practice
Listening comprehension/vocabulary

**Answers**

1. Andrea
2. Isabel
3. Isabel
4. Andrea
5. Isabel
6. Andrea

# En acción
## VOCABULARIO Y GRAMÁTICA

**OBJECTIVES**
- Describe your city or town
- Make suggestions
- Ask for and give directions

### Actividad 1 ¿Qué pasó?

**Escuchar/Escribir** Completa las oraciones para explicar lo que pasó en el diálogo. *(Hint: Complete the sentences.)*

1. Isabel escribió un artículo sobre…
2. Isabel quiere que Andrea la acompañe al…
3. Generalmente, la manera en que Isabel va por la Ciudad de México es…
4. Un micro es como un autobús pero es más…
5. En todas las ciudades, los peatones tienen que…
6. Andrea quiere una tarjeta postal de…
7. Isabel y Andrea quieren entrar en la tienda porque hay…
8. Andrea sugiere que den una vuelta por…

**NOTA CULTURAL**

**La Plaza Mayor** Hace muchos años, la Plaza Mayor era el centro municipal de Madrid. Aquí se casaron princesas y fueron coronados reyes. Ahora la plaza está llena de tiendas y cafés, y es un lugar favorito entre los extranjeros y los españoles. No puedes conducir por la Plaza Mayor; solamente se permiten los peatones.

### Actividad 2 ¿Isabel o Andrea?

**Escuchar/Hablar** Isabel y Andrea están hablando. Según lo que ya sabes de ellas, decide quién hace cada comentario. *(Hint: Who would say this?)*

Isabel

Andrea

1. «La última vez que estuve en la Plaza Mayor estaba lloviendo.»
2. «Tengo que mandarles postales a todos mis amigos en la Ciudad de México.»
3. «Cuando mandé mi artículo, no pensé que iba a ganar.»
4. «Tú eres muy buena gente.»
5. «El señor Zavala me dio una habitación muy buena.»
6. «Hay una parada de metro cerca de esta tienda.»



## Classroom Management

**Streamlining** Have students review the story in the dialog by acting it out. Ask for 2 volunteers to be Andrea and Isabel. Then do **Actividades 1** and **2** orally.

**Peer Review** Have students work in pairs to do **Actividad 2**. Then extend the activity by having students work with their partner to put each comment in a logical order according to the dialog. Have each pair of students compare answers with another pair of students.

- *Use stem-changing verbs in the subjunctive*
- *Use the subjunctive and the infinitive*

## ♻ Una lección

**Hablar/Escribir** Imagínate que le enseñas a un(a) amigo(a) a manejar. Dile si las siguientes cosas son necesarias o no. Usa **(No) es importante, (No) es necesario** o **(No) es lógico** en tus respuestas. *(Hint: Give advice.)*

**modelo**

*tener un coche nuevo*

*No es necesario que tengas un coche nuevo.*

1. ser inteligente
2. estar paciente
3. tener prisa
4. manejar por las aceras
5. ver los peatones
6. saber las reglas de manejar
7. mirar en el espejo
8. gritarles a los otros conductores
9. darle las llaves del coche a alguien que no conoces
10. ir rápidamente cuando ves niños en la calle

## En tu vecindario

**Hablar** Mira las fotos y habla con un(a) compañero(a) de lo que hay en tu vecindario. *(Hint: Talk about your neighborhood.)*

**modelo**

**Compañero(a):** *¿Hay buzones amarillos en tu vecindario?*

**Tú:** *Sí, hay buzones amarillos. (No, no hay ni un buzón amarillo.)*

**Nota**

**Ni** can mean *not even, neither,* or *nor,* and is usually combined with another negative word, such as **no.** Observe how it is used in these examples:

No quiero ver **ni** un museo más. *I do not want to see **(not) even** one more museum.*

No visité **ni** las plazas **ni** los edificios históricos. *I visited **neither** the plazas **nor** the historic buildings.*

1.

2.

3.

4.

5.

6.



## Teaching All Students

**Extra Help** Ask students to brainstorm what they see in their neighborhoods. Write the items on a transparency or on the board to be used later.

**Challenge** Have students write a short story about an ideal neighborhood: **Un vecindario ideal.**

**Native Speakers** Have Spanish speakers give directions on how to take a sightseeing tour of their neighborhood.

**Multiple Intelligences**

**Kinesthetic** Have students stand up. Give them 5–7 directions to carry out, e.g., **Levántense, anden tres pasos, sigan derecho hasta la pared....** Commands may be given in clusters of two or three to increase auditory memory. Have a prize waiting at the end.



## Teaching Suggestions

- Extend **Actividad 3** by having students use the expressions **(No) es importante, (No) es necesario, (No) es lógico** to give a friend advice on using public transportation in their city/town.
- As a warm-up for **Actividad 4**, write all the vocabulary words on the board and have students locate an example of each item in the community.

**Objective:** Transitional practice
♻ Subjunctive with impersonal expressions

**Answers**

*Answers will vary.*

1. [Es importante que] seas inteligente.
2. [Es necesario que] estés paciente.
3. [No es necesario que] tengas prisa.
4. [No es lógico que] manejes por las aceras.
5. [Es lógico que] veas los peatones.
6. [Es importante que] sepas las reglas de manejar.
7. [Es necesario que] mires en el espejo.
8. [No es necesario que] les grites a los otros conductores.
9. [No es lógico que] le des las llaves del coche a alguien que no conoces.
10. [No es lógico que] vayas rápidamente cuando ves niños en la calle.

**Objective:** Transitional practice
Describing your city or town

**Answers**

*Answers will vary.*

1. ¿Hay aceras en tu vecindario? Sí, hay aceras. (No, no hay ni una acera.)
2. ¿Hay semáforos en tu vecindario?
3. ¿Hay puentes en tu vecindario?
4. ¿Hay quioscos en tu vecindario?
5. ¿Hay heladerías en tu vecindario?
6. ¿Hay palacios en tu vecindario?

## Language Notes

Before doing **Actividad 4**, point out that just as **ni, ni** is used to mean *neither/nor*, **o, o** is used to mean *either/or* (e.g., **Quiero visitar o las plazas o los edificios históricos**).

## Block Schedule

**Variety** The activities on pp. 272–273 may be used in learning stations around the room with little modification. **Actividad 3** can be set up as an advice column, while **Actividades 1** and **2** can assess comprehension.

## Teaching Resource Options

**Print** 

*Más práctica* Workbook PE, p. 101
*Cuaderno para hispanohablantes* PE, p. 99
Block Scheduling Copymasters
Unit 4 Resource Book
*Más práctica* Workbook TE, p. 56
*Cuaderno para hispanohablantes* TE, p. 62
Audioscript, p. 81

**Audiovisual**
OHT 124 (Quick Start)
Audio Program Cassette 11A / CD 11

**Technology**
*Intrigas y aventuras* CD-ROM, Disc 2

## Quick Start Review

Stem-changing verbs: present tense

Use OHT 124 or write on board: Conjugate these verbs in the present tense.

| jugar | entender |
|---|---|
| acostarse | sentarse |

**Answers**
juego, juegas, juega, jugamos, jugáis, juegan
me acuesto, te acuestas, se acuesta, nos acostamos, os acostáis, se acuestan
entiendo, entiendes, entiende, entendemos, entendéis, entienden
me siento, te sientas, se sienta, nos sentamos, os sentáis, se sientan

## Teaching Suggestions
### Presenting Stem-Changing Verbs in the Subjunctive

Have students write out the conjugations of several stem-changing verbs in the subjunctive (e.g., **querer, entender, recordar, perder, cerrar, volver, despertarse, contar**).

## Subjunctive Stem Changes: -ar, -er Verbs

**¿RECUERDAS?** *p. 21* You have already learned about stem-changing verbs in the present indicative. The stems of these verbs change in all persons except **nosotros** and **vosotros.**

Note that **-ar** and **-er** stem-changing verbs undergo the same stem changes in the subjunctive as they do in the present indicative.

**pensar** *to think, to plan*
**e → ie**

| | |
|---|---|
| piense | pensemos |
| pienses | penséis |
| piense | piensen |

**poder** *to be able, can*
**o → ue**

| | |
|---|---|
| pueda | podamos |
| puedas | podáis |
| pueda | puedan |

***stem changes from o to ue***

Ojalá que Andrea pueda sacar una buena foto de Isabel.
*I hope that Andrea **can** take a good picture of Isabel.*

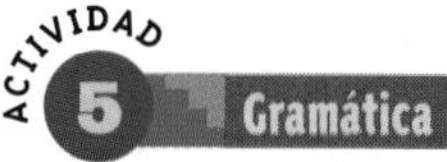

ACTIVIDAD 5 Gramática

## Recomendaciones

**Hablar/Escribir** ¿Qué quiere el señor Zavala que haga o no haga Isabel en Madrid?
*(Hint: What does Señor Zavala want Isabel to do or not do?)*

**modelo**

*sentarse sola en el parque*

*(No) quiere que se siente sola en el parque.*

1. cerrar la habitación con llave
2. perderse en la ciudad
3. entender cómo hablan los españoles
4. recordar la dirección de la pensión
5. acostarse tarde
6. contarles a los Zavala de sus aventuras

**MÁS PRÁCTICA** *cuaderno* p. 101
**PARA HISPANOHABLANTES** *cuaderno* p. 99

## Juego

Escribe la forma correcta del verbo. Luego, pon en orden las letras de colores para responder a la pregunta.

1. Ojalá que nosotros no nos _ _ _ _ _ _ _ en Madrid. (perder)
2. Espero que los boletos no _ _ _ _ _ _ mucho. (costar)
3. Insisto en que ustedes se _ _ _ _ _ _ _ _ _ _ temprano. (despertar)
4. Quiero que tú _ _ _ _ _ _ a España algún día. (volver)

¿Cuál es la palabra de cuatro letras que, al quitarle una, queda (*remains*) también una?

_ _ _ _



## Classroom Community

**Games** Have students work in small groups to create other word games modeled after the **Juego** on p. 274. Then have groups swap their **Juegos** with another group and complete them. Be sure to check the answers.

**Paired Activity** Have students work with a partner to answer the following question, using **Actividad 5** as a model: **¿Qué quiere el(la) profesor(a) que hagan los estudiantes de español?** Have some students write their answers on the board.

## De fiesta

**Hablar/Escribir** Andrea habla con sus amigos de la fiesta que va a haber este fin de semana. ¿Qué dice? *(Hint: Comment on the party this weekend.)*

Recomiendo que

Ojalá que

Es malo que

**modelo**

*los padres: traer los refrescos*

*Ojalá que los padres traigan los refrescos.*

1. nosotros: sentarse en el sofá
2. tú: poder bailar salsa
3. ellos: pensar llegar a tiempo
4. nosotros: perder las direcciones
5. ustedes: poder cocinar
6. yo: querer ir
7. mi hermana: contar chistes
8. mis amigos: poder llegar a tiempo
9. nosotros: volver al supermercado
10. tú: encontrar las llaves del coche
11. él: recordar la fecha de la fiesta
12. ustedes: pensar acompañarnos

## Una calle de Madrid

**Escuchar** Escucha las seis descripciones e indica si corresponden o no a la foto. *(Hint: Listen to the descriptions and tell if they relate to the photo.)*

1. _____
2. _____
3. _____
4. _____
5. _____
6. _____

**NOTA CULTURAL**

**El paseo** En Madrid, como en las otras ciudades de España, la gente sale a dar el paseo por las tardes, caminando por las calles y parándose a hablar con amigos. Van por calles que llevan nombres de personas o sucesos importantes de la historia de España. ¿Sabes quién era Pedro Calderón de la Barca?

## Culture Highlights

- **PEDRO CALDERÓN DE LA BARCA** was an important Spanish playwright of the 17th century. His most important works include the comedy *La vida es sueño.*

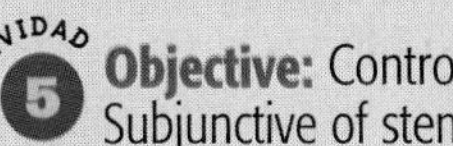

**Objective:** Controlled practice
Subjunctive of stem-changing verbs

**Answers**

*Answers will vary.*

1. (No) quiere que cierre la habitación con llave.
2. (No) quiere que se pierda en la ciudad.
3. (No) quiere que entienda cómo hablan los españoles.
4. (No) quiere que recuerde la dirección de la pensión.
5. (No) quiere que se acueste tarde.
6. (No) quiere que les cuente a los Zavala de sus aventuras.

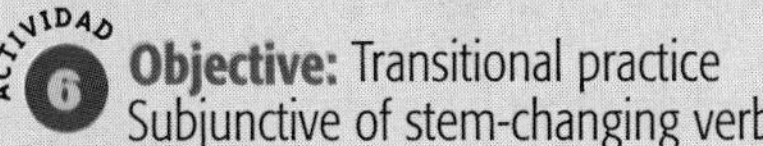

**Objective:** Transitional practice
Subjunctive of stem-changing verbs

**Answers**

*Answers will vary.*

1. [Es lógico que] nosotros nos sentemos en el sofá.
2. [Ojalá que] tú puedas bailar salsa.
3. [Es importante que] ellos piensen llegar a tiempo.
4. [Es malo que] nosotros perdamos las direcciones.
5. [Es bueno que] ustedes puedan cocinar.
6. [Ojalá que] yo quiera ir.
7. [Recomiendo que] mi hermana cuente chistes.
8. [Es importante que] mis amigos puedan llegar a tiempo.
9. [Es probable que] nosotros volvamos al supermercado.
10. [Es importante que] tú encuentres las llaves del coche.
11. [Es bueno que] él recuerde la fecha de la fiesta.
12. [Ojalá que] ustedes piensen acompañarnos.

**Objective:** Transitional practice
Listening comprehension

**Answers** (See script, p. 265B.)

1. corresponde
2. no corresponde
3. corresponde
4. no corresponde
5. corresponde
6. corresponde

## Juego

**Answers**

1. perdamos 2. cuesten 3. despierten 4. vuelvas
La palabra: luna

## Block Schedule

**Retention** Use the verb charts in the back of the textbook to compare the present subjunctive conjugations with present indicative conjugations of stem-changing verbs. (For additional activities, see **Block Scheduling Copymasters.**)

## Teaching All Students

**Extra Help** Ask students to conjugate the following stem-changing verbs in the subjunctive: **jugar, acostarse, entender,** and **sentarse.** They can write the verbs in their notebooks and you can review them on a transparency or on the board.

**Native Speakers** Have Spanish speakers describe what people typically do on free afternoons in their community. Where do people go? What do they do? Who do they spend time with?

**Multiple Intelligences**

**Visual** Ask students to write a short description of the photo in **Actividad 7**. Have students try to guess where the people are going.

**Interpersonal** Ask students to share what they want to see change in their neighborhood. They may begin their statement with **Quiero que/Ojalá que/Pienso que...**

## Teaching Resource Options

**Print** 

*Más práctica* Workbook PE, p. 102
*Cuaderno para hispanohablantes* PE, p. 100
Block Scheduling Copymasters
Unit 4 Resource Book
*Más práctica* Workbook TE, p. 57
*Cuaderno para hispanohablantes* TE, p. 63
Information Gap Activities, p. 68

**Audiovisual** 

OHT 124 (Quick Start)

**Technology** 

*Intrigas y aventuras* CD-ROM, Disc 2

## Quick Start Review

Stem-changing verbs

Use OHT 124 or write on board: Divide your paper into four columns. Label the columns **e→ie, e→i, u→ue,** and **o→ue.** List as many stem-changing verbs as you can in each category. Use the infinitive when you list the verb. When your lists are complete, write one sentence in the present tense with a verb of your choice.

*Answers will vary but charts may include:*
**e→ie:** cerrar, despertarse, divertirse, entender, empezar, pensar, perder, preferir, querer, sentarse, sentirse; **e→i:** competir, despedirse, pedir, repetir, seguir, servir; **u→ue:** jugar; **o→ue:** acostarse, contar, dormir, encontrar, poder, mostrar, mover, recordar, volver

## Teaching Suggestions

### Presenting Stem-Changing -ir Verbs in the Subjunctive

- A good way to practice the formation of the subjunctive form of verbs is to write out the complete conjugations. Have students write out the conjugations of **sentarse, seguir, servir,** etc.
- Have students write additional sentences for **Actividad 8** for classmates to change to the subjunctive.

## GRAMÁTICA: Stem-Changing -ir Verbs in the Subjunctive

**¿RECUERDAS?** *p. 274* You have learned how to form the subjunctive of stem-changing **-ar** and **-er** verbs. The stems of these verbs change in all persons except **nosotros** and **vosotros.**

Now you will learn how to form the subjunctive of stem-changing **-ir** verbs.

Verbs ending in **-ir** with a stem change in the present indicative of **e → i** undergo the same stem changes in the subjunctive, but in all persons.

**pedir** *to ask for*
**e → i**

| | |
|---|---|
| pida | pidamos |
| pidas | pidáis |
| pida | pidan |

Es necesario que Isabel le **pida** permiso al señor Zavala.
*It is necessary for Isabel **to ask** Señor Zavala for permission.*

The **e → ie** and **o → ue** stem-changing **-ir** verbs that you learned in the present indicative make the following changes in the subjunctive:

The **e** changes to **ie** or **i**.

**preferir** *to prefer*
**e → ie, i**

| | |
|---|---|
| prefiera | prefiramos |
| prefieras | prefiráis |
| prefiera | prefieran |

The **o** changes to **ue** or **u**.

**dormir** *to sleep*
**o → ue, u**

| | |
|---|---|
| duerma | durmamos |
| duermas | durmáis |
| duerma | duerman |

Ojalá que **prefieras** una habitación con baño.
*I hope that **you prefer** a room with a bathroom.*

Sugiero que **durmamos** antes de salir.
*I suggest that **we sleep** before going out.*

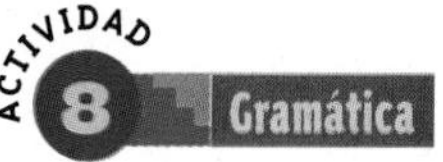

## ACTIVIDAD 8 Gramática

### ¿Qué quieres?

**Hablar/Escribir** ¿Qué quieres que hagan las siguientes personas? *(Hint: What should they do?)*

**modelo**

*El señor Zavala sugiere algunos lugares para visitar.*
*(No) quiero que el señor Zavala sugiera algunos lugares para visitar.*

1. Nosotros visitamos a Isabel en la pensión de los Zavala.
2. Nosotros dormimos en una habitación con aire acondicionado.
3. Andrea pide permiso para sentarse con Isabel.
4. Isabel se siente cansada.
5. Ustedes sonríen por la mañana.
6. Isabel regresa a México.
7. Tú repites la dirección de la pensión.
8. Andrea se divierte con sus amigas.
9. Nosotros nos reunimos con Isabel en la Plaza Mayor.
10. El mesero nos sirve la comida fría.

**MÁS PRÁCTICA** *cuaderno* p. 102
**PARA HISPANOHABLANTES** *cuaderno* p. 100



## Classroom Community

**Paired Activity** Ask students to review the vocabulary on p. 277 with a partner and give directions for getting to a place in their town/city, using at least 10 vocabulary words.

**TPR** **Prepare Ahead:** Write prepositional phrases on index cards, mix them up, and place them face down on the table. Have several objects available for students to use when illustrating each phrase, e.g., a box, a ball, a small doll, or car. Have students take turns choosing a card and demonstrating the phrase using gestures, props, or movements (e.g., **Está debajo de…, Está encima de…**).

## ¿Te perdiste?

**Hablar/Leer** Varias personas están en la Plaza de la Cibeles y te piden direcciones. ¿Qué les sugiere? *(Hint: What do you tell them?)*

**modelo**

**Compañero(a):** *Necesito ir a la Puerta de Alcalá.*

**Tú:** *Sugiero que siga por la Calle de Alcalá hacia el este.*

1. Con permiso, ¿cómo llego al Banco de España?
2. ¿Dónde queda la Calle Valenzuela?
3. Disculpe. Busco la Gran Vía. ¿Sabe usted dónde queda?
4. ¿Dónde está el Museo Nacional de Artes Decorativas?

## ¡Adivínalo!

**Hablar/Escribir** Piensa en un lugar en la escuela. Describe dónde queda en dos o tres oraciones sin mencionar el nombre. Tus compañeros(as) deben adivinar lo que es. *(Hint: Describe a location for others to guess.)*

**modelo**

**Tú:** *Está lejos de la biblioteca y detrás de las canchas de tenis. Está frente a la cafetería.*

**Compañeros(as):** *¿Es el gimnasio?*

**Tú:** *Sí, (No, no) es el gimnasio.*

la oficina de los maestros
la biblioteca
el auditorio
el estacionamiento

MÁS COMUNICACIÓN p. R12

## Vocabulario

### Para llegar a...

**bajar por** *to go down, to descend*
**el cruce** *crossing*
**desde allí** *from there*
**la distancia** *distance*
**el este** *east*
**girar** *to turn*
**hacia** *toward*
**hasta** *until, as far as*
**el norte** *north*
**el oeste** *west*
**parar** *to stop*
**seguir (e→i, i)** *to follow, to continue*
**subir por** *to go up, to climb*
**el sur** *south*

### Está...

**abajo** *down*
**alrededor (de)** *around*
**arriba** *above, up*
**debajo de** *underneath*
**delante de** *in front of*
**encima de** *on top of*
**frente a** *in front of, opposite*
**junto a** *next to*
**sobre** *on, about*

¿Qué palabras usas para describir dónde está tu libro de español?



## Teaching All Students

**Extra Help** Have students act out the following verbs as you say them in Spanish: **bajar por, girar, parar, subir por.**

**Native Speakers** Have Spanish speakers review the list of vocabulary on p. 277 and indicate if there are any other expressions they use for giving directions.

**Multiple Intelligences**

**Logical/Mathematical** Distribute a map of Spain that shows the distances between Spanish cities. Have students calculate the distances in miles and kilometers between the cities you give them.

**Kinesthetic** Have volunteers give the class (and you!) directions to locations in the school. (Remind students to be quiet in the halls!)

## Teaching Suggestions

When presenting the vocabulary for giving directions on p. 277, create visuals to best illustrate each expression (e.g., create a weathervane for **este, norte, oeste, sur**).

## Culture Highlights

- **LA PUERTA DE ALCALÁ** is a triumphal arch built by King Carlos III in 1778 to mark the city gates.
- **LA GRAN VÍA** is a wide avenue in Madrid known for its shopping and numerous outdoor cafés.

**Objective:** Controlled practice
Subjunctive of regular verbs and stem-changing **-ir** verbs

**Answers**

1. (No) quiero que nosotros visitemos a Isabel en la pensión de los Zavala.
2. (No) quiero que nosotros durmamos…
3. (No) quiero que Andrea pida permiso…
4. (No) quiero que Isabel se sienta…
5. (No) quiero que ustedes sonrían…
6. (No) quiero que Isabel regrese…
7. (No) quiero que tú repitas…
8. (No) quiero que Andrea se divierta…
9. (No) quiero que nosotros nos reunamos…
10. (No) quiero que el mesero nos sirva…

**Objective:** Transitional practice
Giving directions

**Answers**

*Answers will vary.*

1. Está frente a la plaza. Sugiero que cruce la calle y siga por la calle de Alcalá un poco hacia el oeste.

**Objective:** Open-ended practice
Describing location

*Answers will vary.*

## Block Schedule

**FunBreak** Scavenger Hunt: Ask half the class to close their eyes. Have the remaining students hide objects around the room, then have students pair up and try to find them. The "hider" must give directions to the "seeker" in order to find the object. (For additional activities, see **Block Scheduling Copymasters.**)

## Teaching Resource Options

**Print** 

*Más práctica* Workbook PE, pp. 103–104
*Cuaderno para hispanohablantes* PE, pp. 101–102
Block Scheduling Copymasters
Unit 4 Resource Book
*Más práctica* Workbook TE, pp. 58–59
*Cuaderno para hispanohablantes* TE, pp. 64–65
Audioscript, p. 81

**Audiovisual** 

OHT 125 (Quick Start)
Audio Program Cassette 11A / CD 11

**Technology** 

*Intrigas y aventuras* CD-ROM, Disc 2

## Quick Start Review

Hopes and wishes

Use OHT 125 or write on board: Match the first half of the sentence in column A to the second half in column B. Write out each sentence. There may be more than one way to complete each sentence.

| A | B |
|---|---|
| Prefiere que | vayas a la Plaza Mayor |
| Sugiero que | yo regrese a las diez |
| Ojalá que | mande un postal de México |
| Quiere que | visitemos el museo por la mañana |
| Insisten en que | haya una heladería cerca de aquí |

*Answers will vary.*

## Teaching Suggestions
### Presenting the Subjunctive and the Infinitive

Have students go back to **Actividades 3, 5, 6,** and **8** and change them from two-subject sentences to one-subject sentences.

## GRAMÁTICA: The Subjunctive and the Infinitive

**¿RECUERDAS?** *p. 252* When the **first verb** in the sentence expresses **a hope** or **a wish,** you often put the **second verb** in the **subjunctive.**

Isabel is stating a fact, that she wants Andrea to take her picture, so she uses the **indicative, quiero.**

Por favor, Andrea.
**Quiero** que me **saques** una foto.
*Please, Andrea.*
***I want** you **to take** a picture of me.*

She is not certain Andrea will take the picture, so she uses the **subjunctive, saques.**

Notice that the subject of the first verb is **different** from the subject of the second verb.

***different***
**yo quiero** — **tú saques**

When the subject of the first verb is **the same** as that of the second, don't change the second verb to the subjunctive. Leave it an **infinitive**.

***indicative*** ***infinitive***
**Quiero ver** más de la ciudad.
***I want to see** more of the city.*

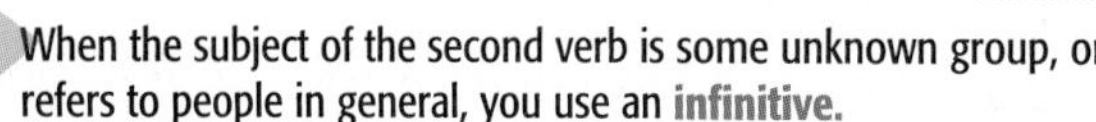

Here there is no change of subject. So the second verb, **ver**, remains an **infinitive**.

When the subject of the second verb is some unknown group, or refers to people in general, you use an **infinitive.**

**Es** bueno **caminar** con zapatos cómodos.
***It's** good **to walk** in comfortable shoes.*

## ACTIVIDAD 11 Gramática

### Un desacuerdo

**Hablar/Escribir** El señor Zavala e Isabel no están de acuerdo. Prepara la conversación. Luego, preséntasela a la clase.
*(Hint: Prepare and present the dialog.)*

**modelo**
*ir al museo*
**Isabel:** *No quiero ir al museo.*
**Señor Zavala:** *Quiero que vayas al museo.*

1. limpiar la habitación
2. cerrar con llave
3. bailar flamenco
4. ir al Palacio Real
5. comer en la pensión
6. escribirle una carta a la familia
7. visitar la juguetería en la esquina
8. ponerse zapatos cómodos
9. conocer a los otros huéspedes
10. llamar a sus padres inmediatamente

**MÁS PRÁCTICA** *cuaderno* pp. 103–104
**PARA HISPANOHABLANTES** *cuaderno* pp. 101–102



## Classroom Community

**Peer Review** Ask students to write 8–10 statements, leaving a blank in which either the subjunctive or the infinitive verb is missing. Collect the statements and read aloud. Have students fill in the blanks with the appropriate verb.

**Portfolios** Ask students to write a short paragraph expressing their wishes/desires about attending a concert or a movie of their choice.

**Rubric: Writing**

| Criteria | Scale |
|---|---|
| Accuracy | 1 2 3 4 5 |
| Logical organization | 1 2 3 4 5 |
| Vocabulary use | 1 2 3 4 5 |

A = 13–15 pts.
B = 10–12 pts.
C = 7–9 pts.
D = 4–6 pts.
F = < 4 pts.

## ¡No quiere hacer nada!

**Escribir** Andrea no quiere hacer ninguna de estas actividades y sugiere que otras personas las hagan. ¿Qué dice? *(Hint: Complete Andrea's thoughts.)*

**modelo**

*pedir la cuenta en el restaurante (mamá)*

*No quiero pedir la cuenta en el restaurante. Quiero que mamá la pida. (Quiero que mamá pida la cuenta.)*

1. manejar tu coche (tú)
2. llevar la ropa a la tintorería (mi hermano)
3. llamar al señor Zavala (usted)
4. visitar el palacio (nosotros)
5. comprar los boletos (tú)
6. seguir buscando la llave (mis hermanos)
7. revisar el mapa (Isabel)
8. obtener entradas al museo (ustedes)
9. poner la mesa (tú)
10. lavar los platos (nosotros)

## En mi vecindario

**Escuchar/Escribir** Andrea te dice cómo llegar a estos lugares desde su casa. Mira el mapa. ¿Son correctas sus direcciones? *(Hint: Are Andrea's directions correct?)*

1. el apartamento de mi mejor amiga
2. el parque
3. la parada de autobuses
4. la escuela
5. la tienda de rebajas

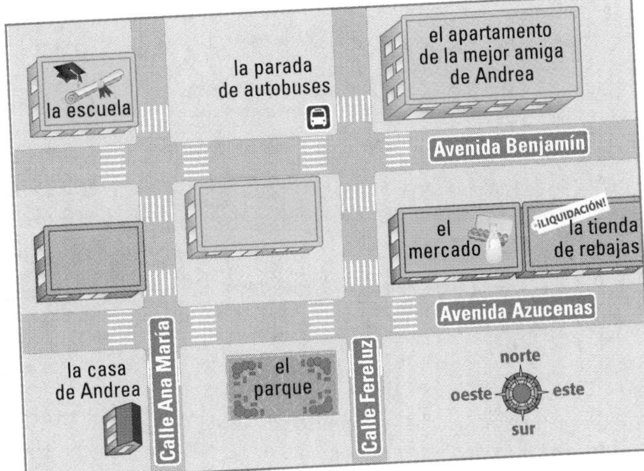


**TAMBIÉN SE DICE**

Ya conoces la palabra **cuadra,** que se usa en Sudamérica y América Central. Pero en España, es más común decir **la manzana** o **el bloque.** ¿Cuántas manzanas hay entre la Avenida Benjamín y la Avenida Azucenas?

## Teaching All Students

**Extra Help** Ask students to write 3 sentences expressing a wish/emotion followed by the subjunctive and 3 followed by an infinitive.

**Native Speakers** Ask Spanish speakers to discuss the information in **También se dice** and indicate which expression they would use to indicate city blocks. Have them give directions to their home or to a favorite location in their community using the expression.

**Multiple Intelligences**

**Verbal** Have students write out the directions to a place of their choice in the community. Then each student takes a turn reciting his/her directions to the place and the class has to guess the intended destination.

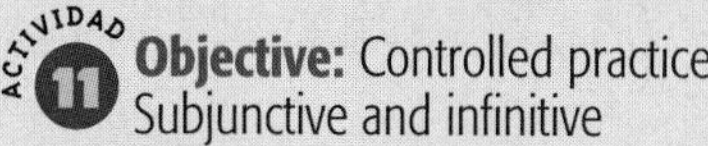

**Objective:** Controlled practice
Subjunctive and infinitive

**Answers**
1. No quiero limpiar la habitación. Quiero que limpies la habitación.
2. No quiero cerrar con llave. Quiero que cierres con llave.
3. No quiero bailar flamenco. Quiero que bailes flamenco.
4. No quiero ir al Palacio Real. Quiero que vayas al Palacio Real.
5. No quiero comer en la pensión. Quiero que comas en la pensión.
6. No quiero escribirle una carta a la familia. Quiero que le escribas una carta a la familia.
7. No quiero visitar la juguetería en la esquina. Quiero que visites la juguetería en la esquina.
8. No quiero ponerme zapatos cómodos. Quiero que te pongas zapatos cómodos.
9. No quiero conocer a los otros huéspedes. Quiero que conozcas a los otros huéspedes.
10. No quiero llamar a mis padres inmediatamente. Quiero que llames a tus padres inmediatamente.

**Objective:** Controlled practice
Subjunctive and infinitive
Direct object pronouns

**Answers**
1. No quiero manejar tu coche. Quiero que tú lo manejes.
2. No quiero llevar la ropa a la tintorería. Quiero que mi hermano la lleve.
3. No quiero llamar al señor Zavala. Quiero que usted lo llame.
4. No quiero visitar el palacio. Quiero que nosotros lo visitemos.
5. No quiero comprar los boletos. Quiero que tú los compres.
6. No quiero seguir buscando la llave. Quiero que mis hermanos la sigan buscando.
7. No quiero revisar el mapa. Quiero que Isabel lo revise.
8. No quiero obtener entradas al museo. Quiero que ustedes las obtengan.
9. No quiero poner la mesa. Quiero que tú la pongas.
10. No quiero lavar los platos. Quiero que nosotros los lavemos.

**Objective:** Transitional practice
Listening comprehension

**Answers** (See script, p. 265B.)
1. Sí
2. No
3. Sí
4. No
5. Sí

**Block Schedule**

**Change of Pace** Modify **Actividad 13** by putting a large city map up on the wall. Have students pick two locations and write directions for getting from one location to the other. Have them trade instructions and check each other's directions.

## Teaching Resource Options

**Print**

*Más práctica* Workbook PE, pp. 97–100
*Cuaderno para hispanohablantes* PE, pp. 97–98
Block Scheduling Copymasters
Unit 4 Resource Book
*Más práctica* Workbook TE, pp. 52–55
*Cuaderno para hispanohablantes* TE, pp. 60–61
Information Gap Activities, p. 69
Audioscript, pp. 81–83

**Audiovisual**

OHT 119, 119A, 125 (Quick Start)
Audio Program Cassette 11B / CD 11;
(*Para hispanohablantes* Cassette 11B / CD 11)

**Technology**

*Intrigas y aventuras* CD-ROM, Disc 2

## Quick Start Review

Irregular subjunctive

Use OHT 125 or write on board: Complete the sentences by conjugating the verb in the subjunctive.

1. es importante que nosotros / saber / como regresar al hotel
2. ojalá que el autobús / llegar / a tiempo
3. insisto en que ustedes / ir / al Parque del Retiro
4. prefiero que tú me / dar / los boletos
5. es malo que los conductores / ser / locos

**Answers**
1. sepamos, 2. llegue, 3. vayan, 4. des, 5. sean

## Teaching Suggestions

A suitable warm-up for **Actividad 15** is to have students give each other directions around the classroom first before giving directions around their community.

**Objective:** Open-ended practice Making/responding to suggestions
*Answers will vary.*

### Actividad 14 Quieren que yo lo haga

**Hablar/Escribir** Escribe una lista de cuatro cosas que otras personas (tus padres, amigos, profesores…) desean que hagas. Luego dile a un grupo de compañeros(as) si quieres hacerlas. *(Hint: Create a list of four things that others want you to do. Then tell your classmates whether you want to do them.)*

**modelo**

Mi mamá insiste en que yo regrese a casa antes de las diez.

Mis padres desean que yo no salga cuando estoy enferma.

Mi hermana menor quiere que yo la acompañe a la juguetería donde vio las muñecas.

Mi profesor de cálculo espera que yo haga la tarea.

**Tú:** *Mi mamá insiste en que yo regrese a casa antes de las diez, pero no quiero regresar antes de las diez los sábados.*

**Nota**

Sometimes question words, like **cuándo** and **dónde,** are used in the middle of a sentence as bridges or connectors. When not implying a question, they do not need accents.

**Fue una sorpresa enorme cuando me llamaron y me contaron quién ganó.** *It was a big surprise when they called me and told me who won.*

### Actividad 15 Ahora, en tu comunidad

**PARA CONVERSAR**
**STRATEGY: SPEAKING**
**Ask for and give directions** Locating an unfamiliar place requires clear directions. You can use compass points (**al norte, al este**) or state position relative to a landmark (**delante de, junto a**). Be clear about the starting point (**desde allí**), and use precise verbs (**sigue, para, gira, baja, sube**).

**Hablar** Pídele a un(a) compañero(a) direcciones para llegar a estos lugares desde tu escuela. Luego tu compañero(a) te puede pedir direcciones. *(Hint: Ask and give directions.)*

**modelo**

*el correo*

**Tú:** *¿Cómo llego al correo?*

**Compañero(a):** *Sigue dos manzanas por la calle Murillo y gira a la derecha. Desde allí, puedes ver el correo. Está junto al banco.*

1. el cine
2. tu casa
3. la discoteca
4. la heladería
5. la juguetería
6. un puente
7. tu restaurante favorito
8. la tintorería
9. un buzón
10. el banco
11. el parque
12. un quiosco



## Classroom Community

**Group Activity** Each group writes a letter for an advice column based on a given topic. Groups exchange letters and write responses. Students can use these letters and responses as a basis for **Actividad 17.**

**Cooperative Learning** Have the whole class contribute to the project described in **Actividad 16.** Divide the class into 3 groups and assign each group one of the tasks listed. You can have the class videotape the presentation and/or decorate a bulletin board with the final projects.

**Rubric: Class Project**

| Criteria | Scale |
|---|---|
| Vocabulary use | 1 2 3 4 5 |
| Correct verb use | 1 2 3 4 5 |
| Logical organization | 1 2 3 4 5 |
| Creativity | 1 2 3 4 5 |

A = 17–20 pts.
B = 13–16 pts.
C = 9–12 pts.
D = 5–8 pts.
F = < 5 pts.

## ¡Visita nuestro vecindario!

**Hablar/Escribir** En grupos, preparen una presentación y un folleto para atraer a otras personas a tu pueblo o ciudad. Sean creativos e incluyan los siguientes elementos. *(Hint: Create a presentation and brochure about your community.)*

Incluye:

- una descripción de tu comunidad
- unas fotos de las atracciones
- un mapa y instrucciones para llegar

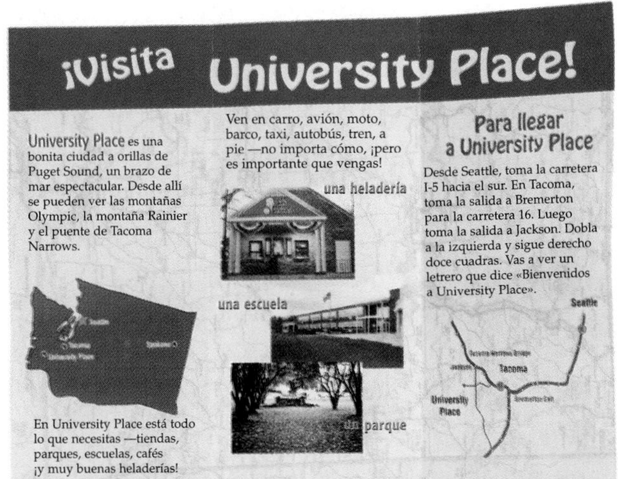

¡Visita University Place!
University Place es una bonita ciudad a orillas de Puget Sound, un brazo de mar espectacular. Desde allí se pueden ver las montañas Olympic, la montaña Rainier y el puente de Tacoma Narrows.
Ven en carro, avión, moto, barco, taxi, autobús, tren, a pie —no importa cómo, ¡pero es importante que vengas!
una heladería
una escuela
un parque
En University Place está todo lo que necesitas —tiendas, parques, escuelas, cafés ¡y muy buenas heladerías!
Para llegar a University Place
Desde Seattle, toma la carretera I-5 hacia el sur. En Tacoma, toma la salida a Bremerton para la carretera 16. Luego toma la salida a Jackson. Dobla a la izquierda y sigue derecho doce cuadras. Vas a ver un letrero que dice «Bienvenidos a University Place».
Seattle
Tacoma
University Place
¡Ojalá que te veamos pronto!


## Tu programa de radio

**Hablar** Tú eres el (la) locutor(a) en un programa de consejos en la radio. Recibes llamadas de tus amigos(as). Uno(a) tiene problemas con su maestro(a), otro(a) con su novio(a). ¿Qué les recomiendas? En pares, hagan una dramatización de estas situaciones. *(Hint: You are a radio announcer. Help solve your friends' problems.)*

**MÁS COMUNICACIÓN** p. R12

### Refrán

***Entra por aquí y sale por allá.***

¿Alguna vez creíste que alguien no te entendió o no te escuchó? En grupos, hagan una lista de ocasiones en que les pasó algo similar.



## Teaching All Students

**Extra Help** Ask students to write 5–6 sentences using **cuando** or **donde** as connectors. Use sentences they have already learned as models.

**Native Speakers** Have Spanish-speaking students give related Spanish **refranes** they may know and explain them to the class.

**Multiple Intelligences**

**Intrapersonal** Ask students to imagine their lives 10 years from now. Using expressions that take the subjunctive, have them write a short paragraph to describe what they want their friends or family to be doing in the future. **Yo quiero que...**

## Supplementary Vocabulary

Remind students of previous vocabulary for other places in a city/town:

**el museo**
**la biblioteca**
**el cine**
**el supermercado**
**el centro comercial**
**la farmacia**
**el correo**

**Objective:** Open-ended practice
Asking for/giving directions

*Answers will vary.*

**Rubric: Speaking**

| Criteria | Scale | |
|---|---|---|
| Vocabulary use | 1 2 3 4 5 | A = 17–20 pts. |
| Logical organization | 1 2 3 4 5 | B = 13–16 pts. |
| Fluency, intonation | 1 2 3 4 5 | C = 9–12 pts. |
| Accuracy | 1 2 3 4 5 | D = 5–8 pts. |
| | | F = < 5 pts. |

**Objective:** Open-ended practice
Making a presentation

*Answers will vary.*

**Objective:** Open-ended practice
Giving advice

*Answers will vary.*

### Quick Wrap-up

**Chain Activity** Give a command to the first student. For example: **Pon el libro debajo de la mesa.** S1 carries it out and then is responsible for handing the prop to S2 and giving that student a new command (e.g., **Pon el libro encima de la mesa**). S2 carries it out and gives a command to S3, etc.

## Interdisciplinary Connection

**Geography** Using a map of Spain and a list of ten major cities, have students use the compass points (**al norte, al este,** etc.) to relate the Spanish cities to each other, e.g., **Madrid está al oeste de Valencia.**

## Block Schedule

**Process Time** Set up a recording station in the corner of the room, facing away from the class. Place a cassette recorder and a copy of the textbook at that station. Set up several tasks similar to the tasks in **Actividad 16**. Have students take turns recording their answers to be evaluated by the teacher.

## Teaching Resource Options

**Print** 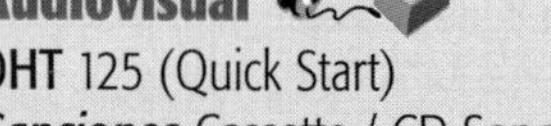

*Cuaderno para hispanohablantes* PE, pp. 103–104

Unit 4 Resource Book
*Cuaderno para hispanohablantes* TE, pp. 66–67

**Audiovisual**

OHT 125 (Quick Start)
*Canciones* Cassette / CD Song 2

## Quick Start Review

Expressing likes and dislikes, describing

Use OHT 125 or write on board: Answer the following questions with a complete sentence in Spanish.

1. ¿Qué tipo de música prefieres?
2. ¿Cuál es tu grupo favorito? ¿Cuántas personas hay en el grupo? ¿Cómo se llaman?
3. ¿Quién es tu cantante favorito?

Now write two more sentences on the same subject using the expressions **me encanta** and **me interesa**.

*Answers will vary.*

## Teaching Suggestions

- **Prereading** Have students review the **¿Comprendiste?** questions before starting their first pass through the reading.
- **Strategy: Identify characteristics of successful musical groups** Have students copy the chart in their notebooks and fill in the information in small groups. You may want to brainstorm a list of successful musical groups with the whole class before students start filling in the chart.

## Reading Strategy

Have students scan for nationalities. Ask them to list the countries associated with each nationality.

# En colores

## CULTURA Y COMPARACIONES

# Vamos a bailar —Gipsy Kings

### PARA CONOCERNOS

**STRATEGY: CONNECTING CULTURES**

**Identify characteristics of successful musical groups**

Among your favorite groups are there any that are "family"? What do you know about them? How do they compare to the Gipsy Kings?

| | Grupo 1 | Grupo 2 |
|---|---|---|
| nombre | | |
| lugar de origen | | |
| nombres de los cantantes | | |
| instrumentos que usan | | |
| tipo de música | | |
| canciones populares | | |

Los Gipsy Kings son un fenómeno internacional. La fama enorme de este conjunto[1] comenzó en 1987 con su primer éxito[2], «Bamboleo». La música de los Gipsy Kings es un nuevo tipo de música que tiene sus raíces[3] en el estilo flamenco tradicional de Andalucía, una región del sur de España.

Su música es difícil de clasificar. Tiene muchos nombres: rumba flamenca, rumba gitana, pop flamenco y flamenco moderno. Es una música que también demuestra influencias de salsa, jazz, música brasileña y nordafricana. Los Gipsy Kings cantan en gitano[4] y una mezcla de español y francés. Además de guitarras, usan teclados[5], percusión y contrabajo[6].

[1] group [2] hit [3] roots [4] Romany Gypsy dialect [5] musical keyboards [6] bass

### NOTA CULTURAL

**Los gitanos y el flamenco** No se sabe exactamente de dónde vienen los gitanos (*Gypsies*), pero los encontramos por todo el mundo. Se consideran los creadores del flamenco, un tipo de música y baile del sur de España. Este arte tan famoso mundialmente también tiene influencia de las canciones populares de Andalucía y de la cultura árabe que vivió en esa zona por más de setecientos años.



## Classroom Community

**Group Activity** Play the **Canciones** cassette or CD for the class and have students work in groups to describe the music they hear.

**Portfolio** Based on what they have learned about the Gipsy Kings musical group, have students write descriptions of their own favorite musical group in their journal.

**Rubric: Writing**

| Criteria | Scale |
|---|---|
| Accuracy | 1 2 3 4 5 |
| Logical organization | 1 2 3 4 5 |
| Vocabulary use | 1 2 3 4 5 |

A = 13–15 pts.
B = 10–12 pts.
C = 7–9 pts.
D = 4–6 pts.
F = < 4 pts.

¿Quiénes son estos músicos talentosos? Son los hermanos Reyes —Canut, François, Nicolas, Pablo y Patchai— y sus primos, los hermanos Baliardo —Diego, Paco y Tonino. Todos son gitanos catalanes que vienen de los barrios gitanos pobres del sur de Francia. Originalmente, sus familias eran de España.

Las estrellas del grupo son Tonino Baliardo, compositor[7] y guitarrista principal, y el cantante Nicolas Reyes. Reyes es el hijo de José Reyes, un cantante de flamenco que cantaba con el famoso guitarrista Manitas de Plata.

¿Cómo se explica la atracción universal de los Gipsy Kings? Su música es exótica, emocionante y divertida. Y para el público estadounidense es algo nuevo. Después de sus conciertos en Nueva York, Boston y San Francisco, los Gipsy Kings recibieron grandes aplausos y críticas muy entusiastas.

Los Gipsy Kings ya tienen quince álbumes de oro o de platino. ¡Todo esto en diez años!

[7] composer

## ¿Comprendiste?

1. ¿Quiénes son los Gipsy Kings? ¿Cuál es su origen?
2. ¿En qué lenguas cantan?
3. ¿Qué influencias tiene la música de los Gipsy Kings?
4. ¿Qué instrumentos tocan?
5. ¿Por qué a los estadounidenses les gustan los Gipsy Kings?

## ¿Qué piensas?

¿Conoces algunas canciones de los Gipsy Kings? ¿Te gustan? ¿Es importante entender todas las palabras? ¿Por qué sí o por qué no?

## Hazlo tú

Investiga el flamenco tradicional. ¿Qué es el flamenco? ¿Cuál es su origen? Descríbelo en una composición breve.



## Culture Highlights

- **LOS GIPSY KINGS** Some of the Gipsy Kings' albums include: *Gipsy Kings, Mosaique, Este Mundo, Love & Liberté, Tierra Gitana,* and *The Best of the Gipsy Kings*.
- **FLAMENCO** refers to both the music and the energetic, rhythmic dance that accompanies it. The music consists of guitar-playing, **palmadas** (handclapping), and soulful singing. The dance consists of foot-stomping and artistic movements.
- **GITANOS** Gypsies are considered a community of nomads who travel throughout Europe. They still live and travel in several regions of Spain.
- **MANITAS DE PLATA** was a famous gypsy guitarist who specialized in Flamenco music. **José Reyes** was a famous gypsy flamenco singer.

## Cross Cultural Connections

Ask students if they know of any other popular singers or musical groups in the U.S. that sing in other languages. Who are they? What languages do they sing in? Why are they popular?

## Community Connection

Have students research any Spanish-speaking musical groups or performers that may perform in their community.

## ¿Comprendiste?

### Answers

*Answers may vary.*

1. Los Gipsy Kings son un conjunto musical. Son gitanos de Francia. Sus familias eran de España.
2. Cantan en gitano y una mezcla de español y francés.
3. Tiene influencias de salsa, jazz, música brasileña y nordafricana.
4. Tocan guitarras, teclados, percusión y contrabajo.
5. Su música es exótica, emocionante y divertida, y es algo nuevo.

## Teaching All Students

**Extra Help** If you play samples of the Gipsy Kings' music, make a copy of the lyrics available to students to review.

**Native Speakers** Ask Spanish speakers if they can name musical groups from their cultural community that are popular in the U.S. Ask them to describe the music and the musicians and bring in sample music, if possible.

### Multiple Intelligences

**Musical/Rhythmic** Play some samples of music by the Gipsy Kings. Have students identify the musical instruments they hear. Ask students to compare the Gipsy Kings' music to the music of their favorite band.

## Block Schedule

**FunBreak** Play samples of the music mentioned in this reading: **rumba, flamenco, salsa, jazz, música brasileña, música nordafricana.**

## Teaching Resource Options

**Print** 

Block Scheduling Copymasters
Unit 4 Resource Book
Information Gap Activities, pp. 70–71
Family Involvement, pp. 72–73

**Audiovisual** 

OHT 120, 120A, 126 (Quick Start)

**Technology** 

Electronic Teacher Tools/Test Generator
*Intrigas y aventuras* CD-ROM, Disc 2

## Quick Start Review

Uses of the subjunctive

Use OHT 126 or write on board: Imagine you are a driving instructor. Complete the following guidelines to your student by using phrases to express hopes and wishes, such as **Insisto en que...** and **Sugiero que...** or impersonal expressions such as **Es bueno que... Es importante que...** Remember to use the subjunctive.

1. girar lentamente
2. tener cuidado cuando ves un semáforo
3. respetar a los peatones
4. no ir en las aceras

*Answers will vary.*

## Teaching Suggestions
### What Have Students Learned?

- Have students look at the "Now you can..." notes listed on the left side of pp. 284–285. Point out that if they feel they need to review material before doing the activities, they should consult the "To review" notes.
- Use the video to review vocabulary and structures.

*Now you can...*
- describe your city or town.
- ask for and give directions.

*To review*
- directions vocabulary, see p. 277.

# En uso
## REPASO Y MÁS COMUNICACIÓN

**OBJECTIVES**
- Describe your city or town
- Make suggestions
- Ask for and give directions

### En el pueblo

Imagínate que tú vives en este pueblo. Completa la descripción.
*(Hint: Describe the town.)*

**modelo**

*La taquilla está frente al (museo / aeropuerto).*
*La taquilla está frente al museo.*

1. Hay un (semáforo / buzón) entre el quiosco y la taquilla.
2. La parada de autobuses está delante de la (heladería / plaza).
3. Hay un (cruce / puente) de peatones delante del semáforo.
4. El estacionamiento está (junto al / debajo del) museo.
5. Hay una (juguetería / taquilla) delante del museo.
6. Para ir al aeropuerto, hay que (parar / subir) por la calle principal.
7. El quiosco está (frente a / encima de) la heladería.
8. La tintorería está (sobre / junto a) la plaza.
9. Un conductor espera (frente al / alrededor del) semáforo.
10. Hay un (puente / cruce) cerca de la heladería.
11. La juguetería está junto a un (buzón / estacionamiento).
12. Para ir al puente desde la plaza, hay que caminar hacia el (este / oeste).



## Classroom Community

**Paired Activity** Have students use the map on p. 284 to give each other directions to get from **el quiosco** to **la plaza**, from **la heladería** to **la tintorería**, and from **la juguetería** to **el museo**.

**Games** ¿Dónde está? Have the class create a giant, game board-sized representation of the map in **Actividad** 1. Tell them to add 5-10 additional places to the map. On slips of paper, write the name of each place. Place all papers in a box. Divide class into two teams. One student should act as the scorekeeper. A student from Team 1 draws a slip of paper and says to a student from Team 2 **¿Dónde está** (item on paper)**?** The student from Team 2 must look at the map and answer the sentence correctly using a preposition of location. If the student from Team 2 does not answer correctly, play returns to Team 1. If neither team is successful, the teacher gives the correct answer. Each correct answer earns 1 point. The team with the most points wins.

*Now you can...*
- make suggestions.

*To review*
- stem-changing verbs in the subjunctive, see pp. 274, 276.

## ACTIVIDAD 2 Ojalá que...

Tú y tus compañeros van a viajar a España. Usa las frases útiles para completar unos comentarios sobre el viaje. *(Hint: Talk about a trip, combining phrases from the list with the items below.)*

**No quiero que...** **Es bueno que...** **Sugiero que...**
**Ojalá que...** **Es ridículo que...** **Es importante que...**

**modelo**

*las tiendas: cerrar muy tarde*

*Ojalá que las tiendas (no) cierren muy tarde.*

1. el viaje: costar mucho dinero
2. nosotros: sentarse juntos en el avión
3. tú: perder los boletos de avión
4. nosotros: seguir las recomendaciones del agente de viajes
5. los estudiantes: encontrar la información sobre los hoteles
6. tú: preferir un asiento de ventanilla
7. yo: poder visitar muchos museos
8. nosotros: dormir mal en la pensión
9. el profesor: pedir habitaciones con baño
10. nosotros: entender a los españoles
11. los restaurantes: servir comida americana
12. ustedes: divertirse mucho

*Now you can...*
- make suggestions.

*To review*
- the subjunctive and the infinitive, see p. 278.

## ACTIVIDAD 3 ¡Hoy no trabajo!

Estás cansado(a) y no quieres ayudar con los quehaceres. ¿Qué dices? *(Hint: Persuade others.)*

**modelo**

*lavar los platos (papá)*

*No quiero lavar los platos hoy. Prefiero que papá los lave.*

1. hacer la limpieza (ustedes)
2. pasar la aspiradora (tú)
3. cortar el césped (papá)
4. quitar el polvo (ellos)
5. barrer el piso (mamá)
6. sacar la basura (tú)
7. tocar los muebles (él)
8. limpiar la bañera (ella)



### ACTIVIDAD 1 Answers

1. buzón
2. plaza
3. cruce
4. junto al
5. taquilla
6. subir
7. frente a
8. junto a
9. frente al
10. puente
11. estacionamiento
12. oeste

### ACTIVIDAD 2 Answers

*Answers will vary.*

1. [No quiero que] el viaje cueste mucho dinero.
2. [Ojalá que] nosotros nos sentemos juntos en el avión.
3. [No quiero que] tú pierdas los boletos de avión.
4. [Es importante que] nosotros sigamos las recomendaciones del agente de viajes.
5. [Sugiero que] los estudiantes encuentren la información sobre los hoteles.
6. [Es bueno que] tú prefieras un asiento de ventanilla.
7. [Ojalá que] yo pueda visitar muchos museos.
8. [No quiero que] nosotros durmamos mal en la pensión.
9. [Sugiero que] el profesor pida habitaciones con baño.
10. [Es bueno que] nosotros entendamos a los españoles.
11. [Es ridículo que] los restaurantes sirvan comida americana.
12. [Ojalá que] ustedes se diviertan mucho.

### ACTIVIDAD 3 Answers

1. No quiero hacer la limpieza hoy. Prefiero que ustedes la hagan.
2. No quiero pasar la aspiradora hoy. Prefiero que tú la pases.
3. No quiero cortar el césped hoy. Prefiero que papá lo corte.
4. No quiero quitar el polvo hoy. Prefiero que ellos lo quiten.
5. No quiero barrer el piso hoy. Prefiero que mamá lo barra.
6. No quiero sacar la basura hoy. Prefiero que tú la saques.
7. No quiero tocar los muebles hoy. Prefiero que él los toque.
8. No quiero limpiar la bañera hoy. Prefiero que ella la limpie.

## Teaching All Students

**Extra Help** Review each of the objectives listed at the top of p. 284 as a class. Then have students work in small groups to give examples and rules for each objective. Share the findings with the class.

**Multiple Intelligences**

**Visual/Verbal** Have students give 3 more descriptions based on the town map on p. 284. Then have them make up a name and location for the town.

**Musical/Rhythmic** Ask students to come up with a theme song that best represents their town/city. They can choose a song that already exists or they can make up lyrics to a melody that already exists.

## Block Schedule

**Retention** Have students go back to the **En colores** reading on pp. 282–283 and describe each of the pictures they see. How might these pictures and illustrations contribute to the comprehension of the reading? (For additional activities, see **Block Scheduling Copymasters**.)

UNIDAD 4 Etapa 2
**Review**

## Teaching Resource Options

**Print**

Unit 4 Resource Book
Cooperative Quizzes, pp. 84–85
Etapa Exam, Forms A and B, pp. 86–95
*Examen para hispanohablantes,* pp. 96–100
Portfolio Assessment, pp. 101–102
Multiple Choice Test Questions, pp. 173–175

**Audiovisual**

OHT 126 (Quick Start)
Audio Program Cassette 20A / CD 20;
(*Para hispanohablantes* Cassette 20A / CD 20)

**Technology**

Electronic Teacher Tools/Test Generator
www.mcdougallittell.com

## Quick Start Review

Talk about things in a city or town

Use OHT 126 or write on board: Imagine you have been hired to improve your town's image. You must create a promotion plan to attract tourism. Jot down three features of your area you would highlight. You might include events such as festivals, concerts, sporting events, natural resources, restaurants, museums, and places of historical interest.

*Answers will vary.*

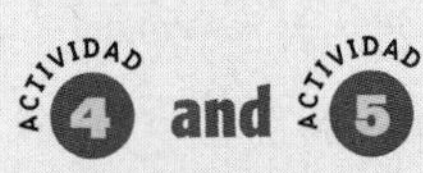


**Rubric: Speaking**

| Criteria | Scale | |
|---|---|---|
| Fluency | 1 2 3 4 5 | A = 13–15 pts. |
| Vocabulary use | 1 2 3 4 5 | B = 10–12 pts. |
| Pronunciation | 1 2 3 4 5 | C = 7–9 pts. |
| | | D = 4–6 pts. |
| | | F = < 4 pts. |

### En tu propia voz

**Rubric: Writing**

| Criteria | Scale | |
|---|---|---|
| Vocabulary use | 1 2 3 4 5 | A = 13–15 pts. |
| Accuracy | 1 2 3 4 5 | B = 10–12 pts. |
| Creativity | 1 2 3 4 5 | C = 7–9 pts. |
| | | D = 4–6 pts. |
| | | F = < 4 pts. |

## ¡Muchos preparativos!

**PARA CONVERSAR**
**STRATEGY: SPEAKING**
**Work cooperatively** Decisions require action: **hablar, buscar, comprar, hacer, obtener.** Discuss preferences (**quiero** o **no quiero obtener..., insisto en que tú hagas...**) Decide how to be fair in assigning responsibilities (**es necesario/lógico que...**) Finally, summarize who is doing what: **nosotros(as) juntos(as), tú, yo.**

Imagínate que tú y un(a) compañero(a) están planeando un viaje. Decidan cómo van a compartir las responsabilidades y completen la tabla. *(Hint: Decide who will do what.)*

hacer las reservas
comprar los boletos
buscar información sobre los museos
encontrar un buen hotel
ir a la agencia de viajes
obtener información turística

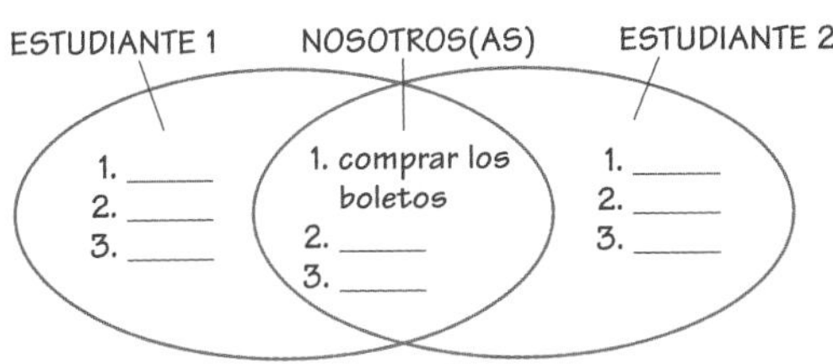

## Turistas

Prepara un dibujo de una sección de tu ciudad o pueblo. Incluye un mínimo de cinco edificios o lugares importantes. Entonces, usa el dibujo para darles un «tour» imaginario a unos turistas. Ellos te van a preguntar cómo llegar a otros lugares que no están en tu dibujo. Cambien de papel. *(Hint: Role-play a tour of a section of your city or town. Give directions.)*

**modelo**

**Tú:** *Estamos en la calle Main. Aquí vemos muchos edificios importantes. Al lado del correo hay un cine.*
**Turista 1:** *¿Hay otros cines en el pueblo?*
**Tú:** *Hay otro pero queda un poco lejos de aquí.*
**Turista 2:** *¿Cómo se va?*
**Tú:** *Suba por esta calle hasta llegar a la plaza. Gire a la derecha en la calle Oak. Entonces siga derecho...*

## En tu propia voz

**ESCRITURA** Imagínate que trabajas para una agencia de viajes. Prepara una descripción de tu ciudad o pueblo para darles a los turistas. *(Hint: Write a description of your city or town.)*

**modelo**

*Ojalá que usted nos visite pronto en Middletown. Nuestra ciudad tiene muchos lugares interesantes y hoteles excelentes. Por ejemplo,...*

**CONEXIONES**

**La tecnología** A la gente de tu comunidad le gustó mucho la presentación que hiciste en la Actividad 16 de la página 281. Quieren poner alguna información sobre tu pueblo en el website de la comunidad. Haz una página de web para presentarles.

## Classroom Community

**Game** Play "hangman" with vocabulary words. Describe a word and then ask students to guess by spelling the word.

**TPR** Have students take turns acting out the verbs and expressions in the *How to Get There* section of the vocabulary list for other students to guess.

**Portfolio** Ask students to give directions from their home to the school in their journal. Remind them to specify the most appropriate mode of transportation.

**Rubric: Writing**

| Criteria | Scale | |
|---|---|---|
| Vocabulary use | 1 2 3 4 5 | A = 13–15 pts. |
| Logical organization | 1 2 3 4 5 | B = 10–12 pts. |
| Grammar/spelling/accuracy | 1 2 3 4 5 | C = 7–9 pts. |
| | | D = 4–6 pts. |
| | | F = < 4 pts. |

# En resumen

## REPASO DE VOCABULARIO

### ASK FOR AND GIVE DIRECTIONS

**How to Get There**

| | |
|---|---|
| **bajar por** | *to go down, to descend* |
| **el cruce** | *crossing* |
| **desde allí** | *from there* |
| **la distancia** | *distance* |
| **girar** | *to turn* |
| **hacia** | *toward* |
| **hasta** | *until, as far as* |
| **parar** | *to stop* |
| **seguir (e→i, i)** | *to follow, to continue* |
| **subir por** | *to go up, to climb* |

**Directions**

| | |
|---|---|
| **el este** | *east* |
| **el norte** | *north* |
| **el oeste** | *west* |
| **el sur** | *south* |

**Specifics**

| | |
|---|---|
| **abajo** | *down* |
| **alrededor (de)** | *around* |
| **arriba** | *above, up* |
| **debajo de** | *underneath* |
| **delante de** | *in front of* |
| **encima de** | *on top of* |
| **frente a** | *in front of, opposite* |
| **junto a** | *next to* |
| **sobre** | *on, about* |

### DESCRIBE YOUR CITY OR TOWN

**City Streets**

| | |
|---|---|
| **la acera** | *sidewalk* |
| **el buzón** | *mailbox* |
| **el (la) conductor(a)** | *driver* |
| **el estacionamiento** | *parking space* |
| **la parada** | *stop, stand* |
| **el peatón** | *pedestrian* |
| **el puente** | *bridge* |
| **el semáforo** | *traffic light or signal* |
| **el vecindario** | *neighborhood* |

**Places of Business**

| | |
|---|---|
| **la heladería** | *ice-cream parlor* |
| **la juguetería** | *toy store* |
| **el quiosco** | *kiosk, newsstand* |
| **la taquilla** | *box office* |
| **la tintorería** | *dry cleaner* |

### MAKE SUGGESTIONS

**Ya sabes**

| | |
|---|---|
| **Es bueno que…** | *It's good that…* |
| **Es importante que…** | *It's important that…* |
| **Es lógico que…** | *It's logical that…* |
| **Es malo que…** | *It's bad that…* |
| **Es mejor que…** | *It's better that…* |
| **Es necesario que…** | *It's necessary that…* |
| **Es peligroso que…** | *It's dangerous that…* |
| **Es posible que…** | *It's possible that…* |
| **Es probable que…** | *It's probable that…* |
| **Es raro que…** | *It's rare (strange) that…* |
| **Es ridículo que…** | *It's ridiculous that…* |
| **Es triste que…** | *It's sad that…* |
| **Es una lástima que…** | *It's a pity that…* |
| **insistir (en)** | *to insist* |
| **ojalá que** | *I hope that, hopefully* |
| **sugerir (e→ie, i)** | *to suggest* |

### OTHER WORDS AND PHRASES

| | |
|---|---|
| **la ganga** | *bargain* |
| **ni** | *not even, neither, nor* |
| **obtener** | *to obtain, to get* |
| **olvidar** | *to forget* |
| **la rebaja** | *sale* |
| **regresar** | *to go back, to return* |
| **revisar** | *to review, to check* |

### Juego

Lo que busca Irene no está sobre la mesa. Tampoco está debajo del sillón. No está encima de los libros, pero sí está delante de la televisión. ¿Qué busca ella?

## Teaching All Students

**Extra Help** Ask students to review the words with a partner and write down any challenging/difficult words. Collect word lists and review with the entire class.

**Native Speakers** Ask Spanish speakers to read aloud the words in the vocabulary list for the class, paying special attention to pronunciation. Have the rest of the class repeat each word after the Spanish speaker.

**Multiple Intelligences**

**Verbal** Ask students to make up a short oral story using the vocabulary words. Encourage them to be creative. (You may wish to copy the vocabulary onto a transparency or on the board and cross out each word as it is used).

**Logical/Mathematical** Ask students to develop a crossword puzzle/word search or board game using words from the vocabulary list.

## Teaching Note: En tu propia voz

**Writing Strategy** Remind students to address the reader personally. Have them explain to the reader why they think he or she would like their town.

## Teaching Suggestion
### What Have Students Learned?

To prepare students for the **Conexiones** project, do a web search for community webpages. Have copies of this "community webpage" list ready for class distribution. Schedule a block of time with your school's library or computer department for groups of students to access the Internet. Instruct students to first investigate the webpages provided on the list before attempting to create their own pages. Some students may be proficient in HTML. If so, have these students assist others in creating their pages. If not, do a web search for sites that do HTML formatting for users who are planning to put up their own webpage.

## Project: Reviewing Etapa 2

Assign the following out-of-class activities:

- Interview a Spanish speaker about his or her favorite city or town.
- Bring in tourist information about shopping in Madrid.
- Find information about the Madrid metro and about other subway systems in the Spanish-speaking world.
- Find information on traveling by car in Spain.

**Extra Credit**

| | |
|---|---|
| Interview | 2 pts. |
| Tourist information | 2 pts. |
| Madrid metro | 2 pts. |
| Car travel | 2 pts. |

## Juego

**Answer**
el perro

## Block Schedule

**Retention** Using the vocabulary list, ask students to write a list of guidelines for walking around their city or town.

# Planning Guide CLASSROOM MANAGEMENT

## OBJECTIVES

**Communication**
- Talk about shopping for clothes *pp. 290–291, 292–293, 302*
- Ask for and give opinions *pp. 292–293, 299*
- Make comparisons *pp. 292, 296–297*
- Discuss ways to save and spend money *pp. 292–293, 300, 306–307*

**Grammar**
- Comparatives and superlatives *pp. 296–297*
- Use the subjunctive with expressions of doubt *pp. 298–299*
- Use the subjunctive with expressions of emotion *pp. 301–302*

**Culture**
- Use of **vosotros** *p. 294*
- Miguel de Cervantes *p. 295*
- **¿Qué talla usas?** *p. 300*
- **Nos vemos en Madrid** *pp. 304–305*
- **¿En qué te puedo atender?** *pp. 306–307*

**Recycling**
- Asking for and making suggestions
- Comparatives and superlatives
- Expressions of doubt
- Expressions of emotion

## STRATEGIES

**Listening Strategies**
- Listen and infer *p. 292*

**Speaking Strategies**
- Interpret the feelings or values of others *p. 302*
- Observe courtesies and exchange information *p. 310*

**Reading Strategies**
- Categorize details *p. 304*
- Analyze the title *TE p. 306*

**Writing Strategies**
- Support a general statement with informative details *Actividad 7, TE p. 311*
- Persuade your reader *pp. 312–313*

**Connecting Cultures Strategies**
- Analyze and draw conclusions about shopping as a cultural activity *p. 306*

## PROGRAM RESOURCES

### Print

- *Más práctica* Workbook PE *pp. 105–112*
- Block Scheduling Copymasters *pp. 97–104*
- Unit 4 Resource Book
  - *Más práctica* Workbook TE *pp. 103–110*
  - *Cuaderno para hispanohablantes* TE *pp. 111–118*
  - Information Gap Activities *pp. 119–122*
  - Family Involvement *pp. 123–124*
  - Video Activities *pp. 125–127*
  - Videoscript *pp. 128–129*
  - Audioscript *pp. 130–134*
  - Assessment Program, Unit 4 Etapa 3 *pp. 135–169; pp. 176–178*
  - Answer Keys *pp. 181–184*

### Audiovisual

- Audio Program Cassette 12A, 12B / CD 12
- *Canciones* Cassette/CD
- Video Program Videotape 4 / Videodisc 3B
- Overhead Transparencies M1, M5, GO 1–GO 5; 127–136

### Technology

- Electronic Teacher Tools/Test Generator
- *Intrigas y aventuras* CD-ROM, Disc 2
- www.mcdougallittell.com

### Assessment Program Options

- Cooperative Quizzes (Unit 4 Resource Book)
- Etapa Exam Forms A and B (Unit 4 Resource Book)
- *Examen para hispanohablantes* (Unit 4 Resource Book)
- Portfolio Assessment (Unit 4 Resource Book)
- Unit 4 Comprehensive Test (Unit 4 Resource Book)
- *Prueba comprensiva para hispanohablantes* Unit 4 (Unit 4 Resource Book)
- Multiple Choice Test Questions (Unit 4 Resource Book)
- Audio Program Cassette 20A / CD 20
- Electronic Teacher Tools/Test Generator

### Native Speakers

- *Cuaderno para hispanohablantes* PE, *pp. 105–112*
- *Cuaderno para hispanohablantes* TE (Unit 4 Resource Book)
- *Examen para hispanohablantes* (Unit 4 Resource Book)
- *Prueba comprensiva para hispanohablantes,* Unit 4 (Unit 4 Resource Book)
- Audio Program *(Para hispanohablantes)* Cassettes 12B, 20A / CD 12, CD 20
- Audioscript (Unit 4 Resource Book)

Dependienta

Andrea

Isabel

# Student Text Listening Activity Scripts

## Videoscript: Diálogo *pages 292–293*

• Videotape 4, 27:17 • Videodisc 3B
**Search Chapter 2, Play to 3. U4E3, En vivo (Dialog)**
• Use the videoscript with **Actividades 1, 2** *page 294*

**Isabel:** ¡Tienen ropa muy elegante en esta tienda! Debe ser muy cara, ¿no?
**Andrea:** Normalmente, sí. Pero las rebajas que tienen son bastante grandes. Mira. El precio original era muy alto. Pero rebajaron el precio el setenta porciento.
**Isabel:** ¡Qué ganga!
**Dependienta:** Buenas tardes. ¿En qué os puedo atender?
**Andrea:** Estamos mirando, nada más. Gracias.
**Dependienta:** Bueno. Si decidís hacer algo más que mirar, avisadme, por favor.
**Isabel:** ¡Uy! La dependienta está de mal humor, ¿no?
**Andrea:** Sí, ella espera que los clientes gasten mucho dinero, y ahora duda que tú y yo vayamos a comprar hoy. Me fastidia que los dependientes me traten así. Vamos, ¿le hacemos la vida un poquito difícil?
**Isabel:** ¿Cómo? Andrea, tengo miedo de que esto nos cause problemas.
**Andrea:** No te preocupes, Isabel. No voy a hacer nada terrible. Tú tranquila... ¿Te gusta este vestido, Isabel? Me parece ideal para el estreno en la galería de arte.
**Isabel:** No sé. Me parece un poco estrecho. ¿Qué talla usas?
**Andrea:** Uso la talla 36. A ver... ah, sí. Este vestido es la talla 34.
**Isabel:** Y además, no me gustan las rayas.
**Andrea:** Tienes toda la razón, Isabel. Las rayas son feísimas. A ver, ¿qué tal un traje?
**Isabel:** El traje es elegante, pero creo que debes vestirte con vestido. Cuando quieres arreglarte bien, un vestido sencillo es lo mejor.
**Andrea:** Sí, tienes razón. Supongo que debo escoger un par de zapatos y un sombrero también.
**Dependienta:** Tenemos varios vestidos elegantísimos por aquí.
**Andrea:** ¿Sí? Sabes, no creo que encuentre nada aquí. Necesito un vestido muy bonito para el estreno.
**Dependienta:** Estoy segura que te van a gustar estos vestidos. Son tan bonitos como los de los mejores grandes almacenes.
**Andrea:** ¿Ves? Ahora está de muy buen humor.
**Isabel:** Andrea, espero que sepas lo que haces.
**Dependienta:** Este vestido te queda muy bien.
**Andrea:** No sé, me parece un poco flojo. ¿Cómo me veo, Isabel?
**Isabel:** Te ves fenomenal. Me gusta mucho el color. Y no creo que te quede flojo, Andrea.
**Andrea:** Muy bien. Supongo que está bien. Me llevo éste.
**Dependienta:** Tenemos también unos zapatos buenísimos que hacen juego con el vestido. ¿Los quieres ver?
**Andrea:** Sí, gracias.
**Dependienta:** Ay, perdón. Tengo que contestar. Vuelvo en un momento.
**Isabel:** ¡Andrea! Esto no me gusta nada. No creo que sea buena idea.
**Andrea:** Ay, Isabel, lo siento. Estoy jugando contigo también.
**Isabel:** No te entiendo. ¿Qué quieres decir?
**Andrea:** No te lo dije, pero todo esto es verdad. El viernes voy a un estreno en una galería de arte. Y necesito un vestido y un par de zapatos de tacón.
**Isabel:** ¡No! ¿En serio? Pero, ¿cómo?
**Andrea:** Es muy sencillo. Mi padre es pintor y este viernes es el estreno de su nueva exposición. Va a ser en una galería de arte aquí en Madrid. ¡Estoy muy emocionada! Va a ser muy divertido.
**Isabel:** ¡Qué bueno! Pues, me alegro de que sea verdad. Me sentí un poco mal por la dependienta.
**Dependienta:** Perdón por la espera. A ver, ¿qué número de zapatos usas?
**Andrea:** El 35.
**Dependienta:** Ojalá que haya un par en tu número.
**Isabel:** ¡Qué buen precio en el vestido!
**Andrea:** Sí, y el precio de los zapatos fue buenísimo también. Apenas lo puedo creer. Quería comprarme un vestido pero no quería gastar mucho dinero.
**Isabel:** Me alegro que tengas un vestido nuevo.
**Andrea:** Mira, ésta es tu parada de metro. Y yo tengo que irme a casa. Pero Isabel, ¿por qué no nos reunimos mañana por la tarde? Podemos ir a un museo.
**Isabel:** ¡No! ¡No quiero ver ni un museo más!
**Andrea:** Je, je, je. Estoy bromeando. Bueno, quizás puedas venir a mi casa para conocer a mi familia. ¿Vale?
**Isabel:** Me encantaría. O mejor, ¡vale!
**Andrea:** ¡Ajá! Ahora hablas como española. Bueno, te llamo, entonces, a la pensión Zavala esta noche. ¿Vale?
**Isabel:** ¡Vale! Bueno, hasta luego.
**Andrea:** Hasta luego.

## Actividad 8 Catálogo de joyas *page 298*

*Isabel y Andrea hablan de varios artículos que ven en un catálogo. Escribe la letra que corresponde a lo que describen. Luego escribe tres descripciones originales.*

1. **Andrea:** Ay, los anillos son bellísimos. ¿Cuál te gusta más, Isabel?
   **Isabel:** Pues, tengo buen gusto. Mi favorito es el anillo más caro.
2. **Andrea:** ¿Qué piensas de las pulseras, Isabel?
   **Isabel:** A mí me gusta esta pulsera. Es la más grande y es muy elegante.
   **Andrea:** Sí, ¡es elegantísima!
3. **Andrea:** ¿Sabes qué le gustaría a mi madre?
   **Isabel:** Dime, ¿qué?
   **Andrea:** Los aretes verdes. Y éste es el mejor precio de la ciudad. Voy a hablar con mi padre porque el cumpleaños de mi madre es el próximo mes.
4. **Isabel:** ¿Vas a comprar algo?
   **Andrea:** Me gustaría comprar algo para el estreno en la galería de arte, pero no quiero que cueste mucho. Creo que voy a comprar la joya más barata de todas. Es bonita y hace juego con mi vestido nuevo.

## Actividad 11 ¿Cómo son con el dinero? *page 300*

*Varias personas están hablando del dinero. Escucha lo que dice cada persona. Luego escribe una oración para describir cómo usan estas personas el dinero.*

1. **Felipe:** En general, no voy mucho a las tiendas. No me gusta gastar mucho dinero en ropa. Los precios son altísimos. Yo prefiero vestirme de una manera sencilla, con jeans y una camiseta cómoda.
2. **Isabel:** A Andrea le gusta gastar dinero más que a mí. Creo que soy razonable con mi dinero. Compro algo de vez en cuando pero no voy a las tiendas todas las semanas. Claro que me encanta ir de compras, pero sé que también debo ahorrar dinero. Dudo que gaste tanto dinero como otras amigas mías.
3. **Andrea:** ¡Me encanta salir de compras! Para mí es como una aventura. A veces gasto demasiado y tengo que usar mis tarjetas de crédito pero creo que vale la pena. Tal vez yo no tenga dinero para viajar o para comprar otras cosas pero siempre estoy bien vestida.
4. **Sr. Zavala:** No comprendo a los jóvenes hoy en día. Siempre gastan su dinero en ropa que después a ellos no les gusta. Yo ahorro mi dinero para el futuro. Quiero vivir cómodamente cuando tenga setenta años. Compro lo mínimo y vivo modestamente. No creo que haya necesidad de muchos muebles o ropa.
5. **Angelina:** A mi esposo Felipe le molesta que yo gaste tanto dinero en ropa y decoraciones para la casa. Yo quiero tener ropa bonita y una casa elegante porque me encanta tener fiestas e invitar a nuestros amigos a visitarnos.

# Pacing Guide

## Sample Lesson Plan - 50 Minute Schedule

### DAY 1

**Etapa Opener**
- Quick Start Review (TE p. 288). 5 MIN.
- Anticipate/Activate prior knowledge: Have students look at *Etapa* Opener and answer questions. 10 MIN.

**En contexto: Vocabulario**
- Quick Start Review (TE p. 290). 5 MIN.
- Discuss pictures. Have students use context and pictures to learn *Etapa* vocabulary. Answer questions, p. 291. 10 MIN.

**En vivo: Diálogo**
- Quick Start Review (TE p. 292). 5 MIN.
- Review Listening Strategy, p. 292. Play audio or show video for the dialog shown on pp. 292–293. 8 MIN.
- Read aloud, students take on roles of characters. Ask Comprehension Questions (TE p. 293). 7 MIN.

**Homework Option**
- Video Activities, Unit 4 Resource Book, pp. 125–127.

### DAY 2

**En acción: Vocabulario y Gramática**
- Check homework. 5 MIN.
- Quick Start Review (TE p. 294). 2 MIN.
- Ask students for a summary of *En vivo* dialog to check recall. 3 MIN.
- Replay the *En vivo* dialog using the audiovisual resources and have students do *Actividades* 1 and 2 orally. 10 MIN.
- Have students complete *Actividades* 3 and 4 in pairs. 10 MIN.
- Present *Repaso:* Comparatives and Superlatives, p. 296. 10 MIN.
- Have students do *Actividades* 5 and 6 in writing. Check orally. 10 MIN.

**Homework Option**
- *Más práctica* Workbook, p. 109. *Cuaderno para hispanohablantes*, p. 107.

### DAY 3

**En acción (cont.)**
- Check homework. 5 MIN.
- Quick Start Review (TE p. 296). 5 MIN.
- Review Comparatives and Superlatives and have students complete *Actividad* 7. Expand with *Más comunicación,* p. R13. 12 MIN.
- Play audio and have students do *Actividad* 8. 10 MIN.
- Present *Gramática:* The Subjunctive with Expressions of Doubt, p. 298. 10 MIN.
- Have students do *Actividad* 9 in writing. 8 MIN.

**Homework Option**
- *Más práctica* Workbook, p. 110. *Cuaderno para hispanohablantes*, p. 108.

### DAY 4

**En acción (cont.)**
- Check homework. 5 MIN.
- Quick Start Review (TE p. 298). 5 MIN.
- Review the *Gramática,* p. 298, present vocabulary box on p. 299, and have students complete *Actividad* 10 in small groups. 10 MIN.
- Play audio and have students complete *Actividad* 11. 10 MIN.
- Present vocabulary box on p. 300 and have students complete *Actividad* 12 in pairs. 10 MIN.
- Present *Gramática:* The Subjunctive with Expressions of Emotion and *Vocabulario,* p. 301, and have students start *Actividad* 13 and complete the rest as homework. 10 MIN.

**Homework Option**
- Have students finish *Actividad* 13 as written homework. *Más práctica* Workbook, p. 111. *Cuaderno para hispanohablantes*, p. 109.

### DAY 5

**En acción (cont.)**
- Check homework. 5 MIN.
- Quick Start Review (TE p. 302). 5 MIN.
- Present Speaking Strategy, p. 302, and have students complete *Actividad* 14 in pairs. 10 MIN.
- Have students complete *Actividades* 15 and 16 in pairs. 15 MIN.
- Have students prepare dialogs in *Actividad* 17 and ask several volunteers to present them to the class. Expand with *Más comunicación,* p. R13. 15 MIN.

**Homework Option**
- *Más práctica* Workbook, p. 112. *Cuaderno para hispanohablantes*, p. 110.

### DAY 6

**En voces: Lectura**
- Check homework. 5 MIN.
- Quick Start Review (TE p. 304). 5 MIN.
- Review Reading Strategy, p. 304, and have students read *Nos vemos en Madrid* aloud taking turns. 10 MIN.
- Do *¿Comprendiste?* and *¿Qué piensas?* questions orally. 8 MIN.
- Quick Start Review (TE p. 306). 5 MIN.

**En colores: Cultura y comparaciones**
- Review Connecting Cultures Strategy, p. 306, and have students read the selection aloud. 10 MIN.
- Answer *¿Comprendiste?* and *¿Qué piensas?* questions orally. 7 MIN.

**Homework Option**
- Have students do *En uso Actividades* 1–4. *Cuaderno para hispanohablantes*, p. 106

### DAY 7

**En uso: Repaso y más comunicación**
- Check homework. 5 MIN.
- Review Speaking Strategy, p. 310. Then do *Actividad* 5 orally in pairs and *Actividad* 6 in groups. 15 MIN.

**En tu propia voz: Escritura**
- Have students complete *Actividad* 7. 5 MIN.

**En resumen: Repaso de vocabulario**
- Review grammar questions, etc. as necessary. 5 MIN.
- Complete *Etapa* 3 Exam. 20 MIN.

**Homework Option**
- Review for Unit 4 Comprehensive Test.

### DAY 8

**En resumen: Repaso de vocabulario**
- Check homework. 5 MIN.

**En tu propia voz: Escritura**
- Quick Start Review (TE, p. 312). 5 MIN.
- Start writing activity, pp. 312–313. 5 MIN.

**Unit 4 Comprehensive Test**
- Review grammar questions, etc. as necessary. 5 MIN.
- Complete Unit 4 Comprehensive Test. 30 MIN.

**Homework Option:**
- Have students complete the writing activity. Preview Unidad 5 opener, pp. 314-315.

# Sample Lesson Plan - Block Schedule (90 minutes)

## DAY 1

### *Etapa* Opener
- Quick Start Review (TE p. 288). 5 MIN.
- Anticipate/Activate prior knowledge: have students look at the *Etapa* Opener and answer questions. 10 MIN.

### En contexto: Vocabulario
- Quick Start Review (TE p. 290). 5 MIN.
- Discuss pictures. Have students use context and pictures to learn *Etapa* vocabulary. Answer questions p. 291. 10 MIN.

### En vivo: Diálogo
- Quick Start Review (TE p. 292). 5 MIN.
- Review Listening Strategy, p. 292. Play audio or show video for the dialog shown on pp. 292–293. 10 MIN.
- Read aloud, students taking roles of characters. Ask Comprehension Questions (TE p. 293). 10 MIN.
- Use Block Scheduling Copymasters for variety. 10 MIN.

### En acción: Vocabulario y Gramática
- Quick Start Review (TE p. 294). 5 MIN.
- Play the *En vivo* dialog using the audiovisual resources and have students do *Actividades* 1 and 2 orally. 10 MIN.
- Have students complete *Actividades* 3 and 4 in pairs. 10 MIN.

### Homework Option
- Video Activities, Unit 4 Resource Book, pp. 125–127.

## DAY 2

### En acción (cont.)
- Check homework. 5 MIN.
- Quick Start Review (TE p. 296). 5 MIN.
- Present *Repaso:* Comparatives and Superlatives, p. 296. 10 MIN.
- Have students do *Actividades* 5 and 6 in writing. 10 MIN.
- Have students complete *Actividad* 7 in pairs. Expand with *Más comunicación,* p. R13. 10 MIN.
- Play the audio and have students complete *Actividad* 8. 10 MIN.
- Quick Start Review (TE p. 298). 5 MIN.
- Present *Gramática:* The Subjunctive with Expressions of Doubt, p. 298. 10 MIN.
- Have students do *Actividad* 9 in writing. 10 MIN.
- Present vocabulary box on p. 299 and have students prepare *Actividad* 10 in small groups. 10 MIN.
- Play audio and have students complete *Actividad* 11. 5 MIN.

### Homework Option
- *Más práctica* Workbook, pp. 109–110. *Cuaderno para hispanohablantes*, pp. 107–108.

## DAY 3

### En acción (cont.)
- Check homework. 5 MIN.
- Quick Start Review (TE p. 300). 5 MIN.
- Present vocabulary box on p. 300 and have students complete *Actividad* 12 in pairs. 15 MIN.
- Present *Gramática:* The Subjunctive with Expressions of Emotion and *Vocabulario,* p. 301, and have students complete *Actividad* 13 orally. 15 MIN.
- Present Speaking Strategy, p. 302, and have students complete *Actividad* 14 in pairs. 10 MIN.
- Have students complete *Actividades* 15, 16, and 17 in pairs. Save time for students to present *Actividad* 17 dialogs to the class. 10 MIN.

### En voces: Lectura
- Quick Start Review (TE p. 304). 5 MIN.
- Review Reading Strategy, p. 304 and have students read *Nos vemos en Madrid* silently. 5 MIN.
- Have students read the *Lectura* aloud taking turns. 10 MIN.
- Call on volunteers to answer *¿Comprendiste?* and *¿Qué piensas?* questions. 10 MIN.

### Homework Option
- *Más práctica* Workbook, pp. 111–112. *Cuaderno para hispanohablantes*, pp. 109–110. Review for *Etapa* 3 Exam.

## DAY 4

### En colores: Cultura y comparaciones
- Check homework. 5 MIN.
- Quick Start Review (TE p. 306). 5 MIN.
- Review Connecting Cultures Strategy, p. 306, and have students read silently. 10 MIN.
- Read *¿En qué te puedo atender?* aloud with students. 10 MIN.
- Have students answer the *¿Comprendiste?* and *¿Qué piensas?* questions orally. 10 MIN.
- Divide students into small groups and have them work on the *Hazlo tú* activity. 10 MIN.

### En resumen: Repaso de vocabulario
- Review grammar questions, etc. as necessary. 10 MIN.
- Complete *Etapa* 3 Exam. 20 MIN.

### En tu propia voz: Escritura
- Have students complete *Actividad* 7. 10 MIN.

### Homework Option:
- Review for Unit 4 Comprehensive Test.

## DAY 5

### En uso: Repaso y más comunicación
- Quick Start Review (TE p. 308). 5 MIN.
- Do *Actividades* 1, 2, 3, and 4 orally. 10 MIN.
- Review Speaking Strategy, p. 310. Then do *Actividad* 5 orally in pairs and *Actividad* 6 in groups of four. 10 MIN.

### Unit 4 Comprehensive Test
- Review grammar questions, etc., as necessary. 10 MIN.
- Complete Unit 4 Comprehensive Test. 30 MIN.

### En tu propia voz: Escritura
- Quick Start Review (TE p. 312). 5 MIN.
- Start writing activity, pp. 312–313. 10 MIN.

### Ampliación
- Use a suggested project, game, or activity (TE pp. 243A–243B). 10 MIN.

### Homework Option
- Finish writing activity and preview Unit 5 Opener, pp. 314–315.

▼ Las nuevas amigas se despiden, pero van a reunirse mañana.

## Etapa Theme

**Talking about shopping, asking for and giving opinions, making comparisons, and discussing ways to save and spend money**

## Grammar Objectives

- Comparatives and superlatives
- The subjunctive with expressions of doubt and emotion

### Teaching Resource Options

**Print** 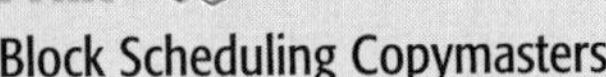

Block Scheduling Copymasters

**Audiovisual** 

OHT 106, 133 (Quick Start)
*Canciones* Cassette / CD Song 12

### Quick Start Review

Clothing

Use OHT 133 or write on board: How many items of clothing can you list in Spanish? Many of these words you may have learned before. List as many as you can.

**Answers**

*List might include:* la blusa, los calcetines, la camisa, la camiseta, la chaqueta, la falda, los jeans, los pantalones, el suéter, el vestido, los zapatos, el sombrero

### Teaching Suggestions
**Previewing the Etapa**

- Ask students to study the photo on pp. 288–289. Ask students to identify what they see in the photo—the people, the items, the clothes, the location.
- Use the **¿Qué ves?** questions to focus discussion.

UNIDAD 4

ETAPA
3

# Vamos de compras

- Talk about shopping for clothes
- Ask for and give opinions
- Make comparisons
- Discuss ways to save and spend money

### ¿Qué ves?

Mira la foto. ¿Qué ves?

1. ¿Conoces a algunas de las personas de la foto? ¿Cómo se llaman?
2. Describe lo que tiene cada chica en la mano.
3. ¿Qué es El Corte Inglés?

El Corte Inglés
TANTO QUE VER...
SO MUCH TO SEE...
El Corte Inglés
GRANDES ALMACENES
DEPARTMENT STORES
UN LUGAR PARA COMPRAR
UN LUGAR PARA SOÑAR
A PLACE TO SHOP A PLACE TO DREAM

288

### Classroom Management

**Planning Ahead** Prepare students to discuss clothes and shopping. Ask them to list their favorite clothing stores or shoe stores at the local shopping mall. Have students poll each other to see which are the most popular stores for young people.

**Peer Review** Have students work in pairs to create additional **¿Qué ves?** questions and write them on the board. Then have students answer the new questions in pairs. You can also have students move ahead to pp. 290–291 to write more **¿Qué ves?** questions.

### Critical Thinking

Have students try to guess what kind of store is shown in the photo on pp. 288–289. Ask them to guess who would shop there.

### Cross Cultural Connections

Have students name stores in their area that may look like the one in the photo. Or name a local store that students are familiar with and have them describe the differences and similarities.

### Culture Highlights

- **EL CORTE INGLÉS** is a chain of major department stores throughout Spain. They have departments that sell clothing, shoes, books and paper products, gifts, housewares, and even a supermarket. (See **En colores**, p. 306.)

## Teaching All Students

**Extra Help** Ask simple **Sí/No** questions about the picture. **¿Las chicas van de compras en un supermercado? ¿Buscan ropa elegante? ¿Venden zapatos en la tienda? ¿Venden vestidos?**

**Native Speakers** Ask Spanish speakers to describe the shopping scene in as much detail as possible. Have them mention the location, the people involved, and the items in the store.

**Multiple Intelligences**

**Logical/Mathematical** Ask students to assign a price (in U.S. dollars) to the clothing items in the picture. Then have them research the current exchange rate to determine the prices in Spanish **pesetas**.

**Musical/Rhythmic** Divide the class into groups and have them come up with short jingles in Spanish advertising **El Corte Inglés**.

### Block Schedule

**Variety** Have students create a shopping guide in Spanish for their local shopping mall. Have students make a list of the clothing stores at the shopping mall and identify who shops at each place. For example, **Las madres compran ropa en Tienda X.** (For additional activities, see **Block Scheduling Copymasters.**)

## Teaching Resource Options

**Print**

Unit 4 Resource Book
- Video Activities, p. 125
- Videoscript, p. 128
- Audioscript, p. 131

**Audiovisual** 

OHT 127, 128, 133 (Quick Start)
Audio Program Cassette 12A / CD 12
Video Program Videotape 4, 23:55 / Videodisc 3B

Search Chapter 1, Play to 2
U4E3, En contexto (Vocabulary)

**Technology** 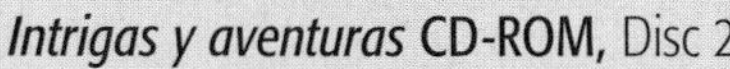

*Intrigas y aventuras* CD-ROM, Disc 2

## Quick Start Review

Giving directions

Use OHT 133 or write on board: Imagine a new student at your school wants to know the best place to buy clothes in your area. Tell him or her the name of the store and give directions on how to get there using the school as a starting point.

*Answers will vary.*

## Teaching Suggestions
### Introducing Vocabulary

- Have students look at pp. 290–291. Use OHT 127–128 and Audiocassette 12A/CD 12 to present the vocabulary.
- Write the Comprehension Questions on the board or copy and distribute them to the class. Have students work with a partner to answer them orally. S1 asks the question and S2 answers; then they switch roles.
- Introduce the characters and the setting: **¿Quién es Andrea? ¿Quién es Isabel? ¿Qué hacen en la ciudad?**

# En contexto
## VOCABULARIO

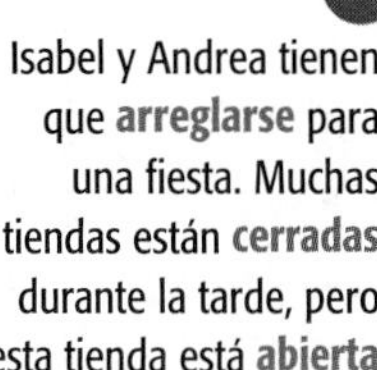

Isabel y Andrea van a ver qué tiene esta tienda de ropa.

**A** Isabel y Andrea tienen que **arreglarse** para una fiesta. Muchas tiendas están **cerradas** durante la tarde, pero esta tienda está **abierta** todo el día.

**B** Isabel quiere encontrar un vestido o unos pantalones. **Escoge** un vestido largo con **rayas** y otro que es más corto. Andrea quiere **vestirse** con **un traje. Usa la talla** 36, pero este traje es talla 38. Le queda un poco grande.

ConCaché
ESTILO 54656 TALLA 38

**C** Isabel se pone unos pantalones **sencillos** de color **oscuro,** pero le quedan **flojos.** Necesita una talla más pequeña. Andrea se pone unos pantalones blancos, pero son muy **estrechos.** Necesita unos más grandes.

## Classroom Community 

**Paired Activity** Ask students to work in pairs to interview each other using the **Preguntas personales** on p. 291.

**Game** Cut out models from a clothing store flyer and paste each one on a piece of cardboard. Hold up each card. The first student to raise his/her hand goes to the board and writes the description of one piece of the model's clothing. Continue until all the model's clothing is described, then go to the next picture.

**TPR** Have students stand up if they are wearing items of clothing that you describe, e.g., **ropa oscura, camisa de rayas, un chaleco, unos zapatos de tacón,** etc.

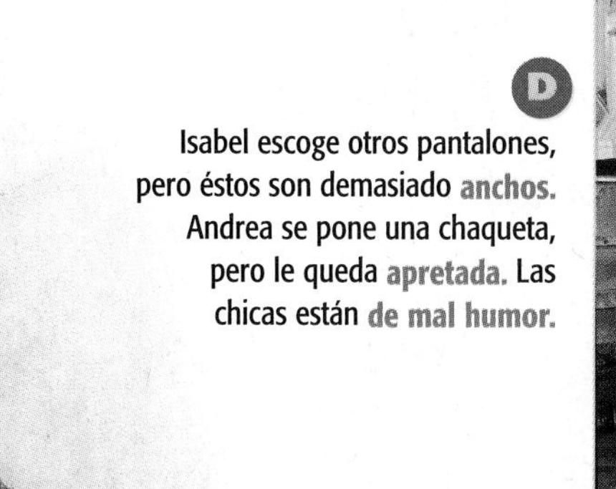

**D** Isabel escoge otros pantalones, pero éstos son demasiado **anchos.** Andrea se pone una chaqueta, pero le queda **apretada.** Las chicas están **de mal humor.**

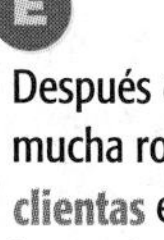

**E** Después de ponerse mucha ropa, **las clientas** encuentran lo que buscan. Ahora están contentas, y **la dependienta** está sonriendo. ¡Ella está **de buen humor** también!

el pañuelo

el chaleco

el zapato de tacón

**F** Están preparadas. **Apenas** son las siete y la fiesta empieza a las ocho. Andrea lleva una camisa que **hace juego con** los pantalones. Isabel lleva **un chaleco.** Las dos llevan **pañuelos** y **un par de zapatos de tacón** del **número** correcto. ¡Van a ser las más **elegantes** de todas las chicas de la fiesta!

### Preguntas personales

1. ¿Hay alguien en tu clase que lleve ropa oscura? ¿Ropa con rayas?
2. ¿Te gusta comprar ropa nueva cuando tienes que arreglarte?
3. ¿Tienes un traje? ¿Cuándo lo usas?
4. ¿Qué accesorios te gustan?
5. Si quieres unos zapatos, ¿qué le dices al (a la) dependiente(a)?



## Comprehension Questions

1. ¿Buscan ropa para una fiesta? **(Sí)**
2. ¿Están abiertas durante la tarde muchas tiendas? **(No)**
3. ¿Usa Andrea la talla 38? **(No)**
4. ¿Son anchos o estrechos los pantalones blancos? **(estrechos)**
5. ¿Le queda apretada o floja la chaqueta que se pone Andrea? **(apretada)**
6. ¿Están de buen humor o mal humor las chicas cuando buscan ropa? **(Están de mal humor.)**
7. ¿Por qué están de buen humor las chicas al final? **(porque encuentran la ropa que quieren)**
8. ¿Qué compra Isabel? **(un chaleco)**
9. ¿Qué compra Andrea? **(una camisa y pantalones)**
10. ¿Qué llevan las dos? **(un pañuelo y zapatos de tacón)**

## Culture Highlights

**SHOPPING HOURS** Shopping hours in Madrid are usually 10 A.M. to 1:30–2:00 P.M. and from 4:30–5:00 P.M. to 8:00 P.M. Some department stores, like the Corte Inglés, are open all day long. Nearly all stores are closed on Sunday.

## Teaching Suggestions

### Introducing Vocabulary

Have students explain how they would dress for the following situations: **para la escuela, para una fiesta, para ir al cine, para ir al trabajo, en casa,** etc. Then have students name additional situations and how they would dress.

## Language Note

Point out that some Spanish speakers use **estrecho** to mean *tight.*

## Block Schedule

**FunBreak** Gather fashion magazines in Spanish or cut out pictures from English fashion magazines and have students make a collage and label items in Spanish.

## Teaching All Students

**Extra Help** Review body parts with the class by bringing a large doll as a model. Call out a body part **(la pierna)** and have students come up to the doll and point to the appropriate part on the doll. Extend this activity to review articles of clothing by having a doll large enough to "wear" clothing. Call out an article of clothing **(la camisa)** and have a student come up to the doll and point to the appropriate clothing.

**Native Speakers** Have Spanish-speaking students describe a recent shopping trip for new clothes. Where did they shop? What did they try on? What did they buy?

### Multiple Intelligences

**Kinesthetic** Working in groups of three, ask students to associate articles of clothing with each of the parts of the body and act out putting on an article of clothing for other students to guess.

## Teaching Resource Options

**Print**

Block Scheduling Copymasters
Unit 4 Resource Book
Video Activities, pp. 126–127
Videoscript, pp. 128–129
Audioscript, p. 131

**Audiovisual**

OHT 131, 132, 133 (Quick Start)
Audio Program Cassette 12A / CD 12
Video Program Videotape 4, 27:17 / Videodisc 3B

Search Chapter 2, Play to 3
U4E3, En vivo (Dialog)

**Technology**

*Intrigas y aventuras* CD-ROM, Disc 2

## Quick Start Review

Persuading, suggesting

Use OHT 133 or write on board: Imagine you are a store clerk. Write three statements beginning with a phrase designed to persuade or suggest something to your customer. You might consider using words like: **sugiero que, recomiendo que / comprar, mirar, poner, considerar, llevar / blusa, chaqueta, falda, pantalones, suéter, vestido.** For example: **Sugiero que usted lleve zapatos negros con estos pantalones.**

*Answers will vary.*

## Teaching Suggestions
### Presenting the Dialog

After reviewing the Listening Strategy on p. 292, have students listen and infer to describe Isabel's personality with several adjectives.

# En vivo
## DIÁLOGO

Dependienta

Andrea

Isabel

**PARA ESCUCHAR • STRATEGY: LISTENING**

**Listen and infer** An inference is an opinion based on something implied but not directly said. Choose a word that describes Andrea's personality (**alegre, cómica, paciente, seria, inteligente,** or one of your own choice). Then tell which of Andrea's words or actions led you to make that choice.

### ¿Cómo me veo?

1 ► Dependienta: ¿En qué os puedo atender?
Andrea: Estamos mirando, gracias.
Dependienta: Bueno. Si decidís hacer algo más que mirar, avisadme, por favor.

5 ► Andrea: ¿Qué tal un traje?
Isabel: Debes vestirte con vestido. Cuando quieres arreglarte bien, un vestido sencillo es lo mejor.
Andrea: Tienes razón. Y debo escoger un par de zapatos.

6 ► Dependienta: Tenemos varios vestidos elegantísimos por aquí. Son tan bonitos como los de los mejores almacenes. Estoy segura que te van a gustar.
Andrea (a Isabel): ¿Ves? Ahora está de muy buen humor.

7 ► Dependienta: Te queda bien.
Andrea: Me parece un poco flojo.
Isabel: Te ves fenomenal. Me gusta mucho el color, y no creo que te quede flojo.
Andrea: Muy bien. Me llevo éste.

## Classroom Community

**TPR** Have students act out a fashion show, with you as the announcer. Describe what each student is "wearing" and how it looks. Include some "fashion don'ts."

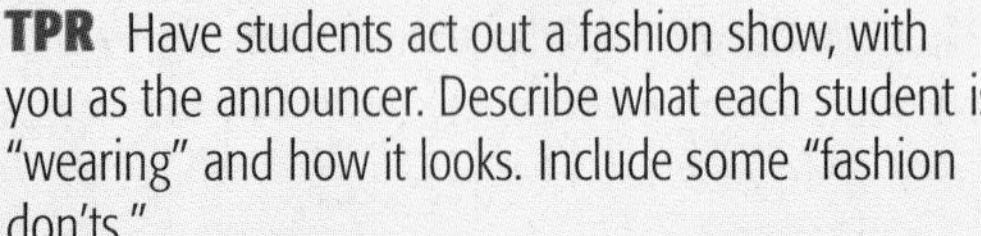

**Group Activity** Have students cover up the printed dialog under each frame on pp. 292–293. Assign each group several frames and have them create their own dialog to match the action in the photos. Then use the video, audiocassette, or CD to present the dialog and compare the actual dialog to the dialog they created themselves.

**Storytelling** Ask students to add three more scenes to the dialog. Imagine that Isabel also needs a new outfit for an upcoming party. Have students find her an outfit that fits and is appropriate for the event.

2▶ Isabel: ¡Uy! La dependienta está de mal humor.
Andrea: Ella espera que los clientes gasten mucho dinero, y duda que tú y yo vayamos a comprar hoy.

3▶ Andrea: Me fastidia que los dependientes me traten así. ¿Le hacemos la vida un poquito difícil?
Isabel: ¿Cómo? Tengo miedo.
Andrea: No te preocupes. No voy a hacer nada terrible. Tú tranquila.

4▶ Andrea: ¿Te gusta este vestido? Me parece ideal para el estreno en la galería de arte.
Isabel: No sé. Me parece estrecho. ¿Qué talla usas?
Andrea: Uso la talla 36.

8▶ Dependienta: Tenemos también unos zapatos buenísimos que hacen juego con el vestido. ¿Los quieres ver?
Andrea: Sí, gracias.

9▶ Isabel: ¡Andrea! Esto no me gusta nada.
Andrea: Lo siento. Estoy jugando contigo también. No te lo dije, pero todo esto es verdad. El viernes voy a un estreno en una galería de arte y necesito un vestido y un par de zapatos de tacón.

10▶ Isabel: ¡Qué buen precio en el vestido!
Andrea: Y el precio de los zapatos fue buenísimo también. Mira, ésta es tu parada de metro. ¿Por qué no nos reunimos mañana? ¿Vale?
Isabel: ¡Vale!



## Teaching All Students

**Extra Help** Ask students to write the names of the three characters on separate sheets of blank paper. Read aloud various lines from the dialog; students hold up the correct piece of paper to identify the character, e.g., **¿En qué os puedo atender? (Dependienta).**

**Native Speakers** Ask Spanish speakers to describe the types of stores, the store hours, and a particular shopping experience they have had in other countries.

### Multiple Intelligences

**Interpersonal** Notice how Andrea plans to wear a dress and high-heeled shoes to the opening night of an art gallery. Have pairs of students discuss what they might wear to such an occasion, to a friend's party, to a sporting event, or on a shopping trip.

## Video Synopsis

Andrea and Isabel go shopping for clothes in Madrid. For a complete transcript of the video dialog, see p. 287B.

## Comprehension Questions

1. ¿Va de compras Andrea con Isabel? **(Sí)**
2. ¿Está de buen humor la dependienta? **(No)**
3. ¿Le molesta a Andrea que la dependienta se porte mal? **(Sí)**
4. Andrea usa la talla 36. ¿Es la misma que la de Estados Unidos? **(No)**
5. ¿Busca Andrea un vestido para una fiesta o para un estreno? **(para un estreno)**
6. ¿Sugiere Isabel que Andrea compre un vestido o un traje? **(un vestido)**
7. ¿Le queda bien el vestido o es flojo? **(Le queda bien.)**
8. ¿Por qué está nerviosa Isabel? **(No le gusta el juego de Andrea.)**
9. ¿Qué decide comprar Andrea? **(un vestido y un par de zapatos)**
10. ¿Qué comentario hacen las chicas sobre los precios? **(Dicen que son buenos.)**

## Culture Highlights

● **SHOPPING IN MADRID** Students will read about shopping in Madrid in the **En colores** reading on pp. 306–307.

● **EUROPEAN SIZES** Refer to the **Nota cultural** on p. 300 for information on the sizes used in Spain.

## Gestures

Read lines from the dialog and have students mimic the corresponding gestures.

## Block Schedule

**Process Time** Before assigning the dialog reading for homework, have students stop for 2 minutes and make assumptions about the reading by looking at the pictures. This is a good lead-in to the Listening Strategy on p. 292. (For additional activities, see **Block Scheduling Copymasters**.)

## Teaching Resource Options

**Print** 

Unit 4 Resource Book
- Video Activities, pp. 126–127
- Videoscript, pp. 128–129
- Audioscript, p. 131

**Audiovisual** 

OHT 134 (Quick Start)
Audio Program Cassette 12A / CD 12
Video Program Videotape 4, 27:17 / Videodisc 3B

**Technology** 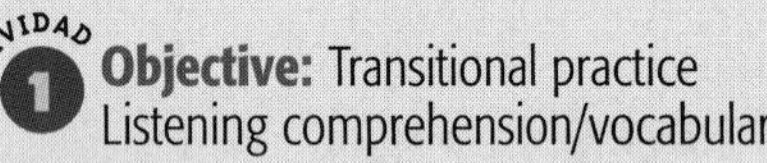

*Intrigas y aventuras* CD-ROM, Disc 2

## Quick Start Review

Using the subjunctive or the infinitive

Use OHT 134 or write on board: Choose the word that correctly completes each sentence.

1. Quiero ___ de compras. (ir / vaya)
2. Quiero que la dependienta nos ___. (ayudar / ayude)
3. Espero ___ un traje para el estreno. (comprar / compres)
4. Sugiero que tú ___ un vestido. (comprar / compres)
5. Prefiero ___ zapatos de tacón. (llevar / lleves)

**Answers**
1. ir; 2. ayude; 3. comprar; 4. compres; 5. llevar

Actividad 1 **Objective:** Transitional practice Listening comprehension/vocabulary

**Answers**

*Answers may vary.*
1. ¡Qué buen precio en el vestido!
2. Me parece estrecho.
3. ¿Le hacemos la vida un poquito difícil?
4. Tengo miedo.
5. El viernes voy a un estreno en una galería de arte y necesito un vestido y un par de zapatos de tacón.
6. ¿Por qué no nos reunimos mañana?

# En acción
## VOCABULARIO Y GRAMÁTICA

**OBJECTIVES**
- Talk about shopping for clothes
- Ask for and give opinions
- Make comparisons
- Discuss ways to save and spend money

Actividad 1 

### ¿Cómo lo sabes?

**Escuchar/Escribir** Todas las oraciones son ciertas. Escribe una línea del diálogo que confirme cada una. *(Hint: Write a line of dialog that supports each sentence.)*

1. Hay buenos precios en la tienda de ropa.
2. Isabel piensa que el primer vestido que escoge Andrea no es la talla correcta.
3. Andrea tiene un plan.
4. Isabel se preocupa un poco por el plan de Andrea.
5. Andrea realmente va a un estreno y necesita ropa nueva.
6. Andrea e Isabel se van a reunir al día siguiente.

**TAMBIÉN SE DICE**

En España, el plural de **tú** es **vosotros(as). Os** es el objeto directo e indirecto de **vosotros.** La dependienta usó las formas de los verbos que corresponden a **vosotros** cuando les habló a Isabel y Andrea.

Actividad 2 

### En orden

**Escuchar/Escribir** Pon las fotos en orden cronológico según el diálogo. Luego escribe una oración que describa cada foto. *(Hint: Put the photos in order. Then write a description.)*

a.

b.

c.

d.



## Classroom Management

**Streamlining** Have students reenact the story in the dialog by acting it out without the textbook. Ask for 3 volunteers to portray Isabel, Andrea, and the **dependienta** to act out the shopping scene. Then students can read the script from the book in groups of three.

**Peer Review/Peer Teaching** Have students work in pairs to do **Actividad 2**. Then extend the activity by having students work with their partner to write a new dialog that matches the series of photos.

- *Review: Use comparatives and superlatives*
- *Use the subjunctive with expressions of doubt and emotion*

## ¿Hacen juego?

**Hablar** Estás ayudando a un(a) amigo(a) que va de compras. Mira las fotos. ¿Hacen juego los artículos? *(Hint: Tell whether items match.)*

**modelo**

**Compañero(a):** *¿Crees que la bolsa y los zapatos hacen juego?*

**Tú:** *Sí, hacen juego.*

## ¿Qué me sugieres?

**Hablar** Pídele a un(a) compañero(a) sugerencias sobre las actividades de la lista. *(Hint: Ask a classmate for suggestions.)*

**modelo**

*qué (leer)*

**Tú:** *¿Qué sugieres que yo lea?*

**Compañero(a):** *Sugiero que leas* Don Quijote *porque es buenísimo.*

1. dónde (divertirse)
2. cómo (poder comprar boletos para un concierto)
3. cómo (vestirse para una fiesta)
4. qué (pedir en un buen restaurante)
5. dónde (encontrar gangas)
6. qué (servirles a mis amigos españoles para comer)

### NOTA CULTURAL

**Miguel de Cervantes** (1547–1616) nació en Madrid. Su novela *Don Quijote de la Mancha,* sobre las aventuras y fantasías de un hombre que quiere ser un héroe, es una de las obras más famosas de la literatura mundial.



## Teaching All Students

**Extra Help** Clothing vocabulary was first presented in Unit 3 of Level 1. Review with students the articles of clothing in the photos on pp. 294–295. Also demonstrate in class the different articles of clothing worn by students.

**Native Speakers** Ask Spanish speakers what they know about Cervantes and *Don Quijote de la Mancha* and have them share it with the class.

### Multiple Intelligences

**Logical/Mathematical** Have students work in small groups to create 3 statements that describe the current fashions for young people. For example, **Los muchachos se ponen pantalones anchos y flojos.** Each group will then survey other groups (or another Spanish class) using the statements and compile the results in a chart.

## Teaching Suggestions

- **Actividad 4** recycles vocabulary from the previous **Etapas**. Have students give additional suggestions for clothes shopping in their area.
- Have students find two examples where the **Dependienta** uses the **vosotros** form in the dialog on pp. 292–293. Then have them rewrite the **vosotros** form to the **ustedes** form.

**Objective:** Transitional practice
Listening comprehension/vocabulary

**Answers**

*Answers may vary.*

1. a. A Isabel no le gusta el vestido.
2. d. La dependienta ahora está de buen humor.
3. c. Andrea se lleva este vestido.
4. b. Andrea e Isabel se van a reunir mañana.

**Objective:** Transitional practice
**En contexto** vocabulary
Clothing

**Answers**

*Answers may vary.*

1. ¿Crees que el impermeable y el sombrero hacen juego? No, no hacen juego.
2. la camiseta y los shorts / Sí
3. el abrigo y la bufanda / Sí
4. la blusa y la falda / Sí
5. el chaleco y el traje / No, no
6. el vestido y las botas / No, no

## Language Note

A **pañuelo** is a dressy scarf. A **bufanda** is a warm scarf.

**Objective:** Open-ended practice
Asking for and making suggestions

**Answers**

*Answers will vary.*

1. me divierta / te diviertas
2. pueda /puedas
3. me vista / te vistas
4. pida / pidas
5. encuentre / encuentres
6. les sirva / les sirvas

## Cultural Highlight

**DON QUIJOTE** This rich novel reflected 17th century Spanish culture and the complexity of human nature. Don Quijote, the idealist, and his practical squire, Sancho Panza, travel together throughout Spain in search of adventures.

## Teaching Resource Options

**Print** 

*Más práctica* Workbook PE, pp. 109–110
*Cuaderno para hispanohablantes* PE, pp. 107–108
Block Scheduling Copymasters
Unit 4 Resource Book
*Más práctica* Workbook TE, pp. 107–108
*Cuaderno para hispanohablantes* TE, pp. 113–114
Information Gap Activities, p. 119

**Audiovisual**

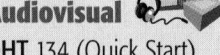

OHT 134 (Quick Start)

**Technology** 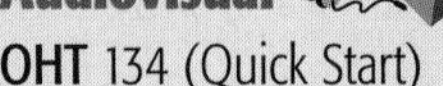

*Intrigas y aventuras* CD-ROM, Disc 2

## Quick Start Review

Adjective agreement

Use OHT 134 or write on board: Ana has made a list of clothes she wants to buy for school this year. Finish her list by changing the adjective ending to agree with the noun and write a complete sentence. For example: **2 faldas / oscuro Necesito dos faldas oscuras.**

1. 1 falda / estrecho
2. 3 suéteres / negro
3. 1 chaqueta / bonito
4. unas camisas / sencillo
5. pantalones / ancho
6. 1 blusa / rojo

**Answers**

1. una falda estrecha; 2. tres suéteres negros; 3. una chaqueta bonita; 4. unas camisas sencillas; 5. pantalones anchos; 6. una blusa roja

## Teaching Suggestions
### Reviewing Comparatives and Superlatives

Using some simple items (pencils, books, hats, etc.), demonstrate the meaning of comparisons of quantities: **más que/menos que**. Using family members, demonstrate the meaning of comparisons of age: **mayor que/menor que.** And using old or new clothing, demonstrate the meaning of comparisons of quality: **mejor que/peor que.** You can also demonstrate superlatives in a similar fashion.

## Comparatives and Superlatives

Spanish uses various structures when making unequal and equal **comparisons.**

Unequal **comparisons** are made in Spanish using más/menos… que.

más + **adjective, adverb,** or **noun** + que

menos + **adjective, adverb,** or **noun** + que

The thing or quality being compared is often between **más** or **menos** and **que.**

Isabel es más **alta** que Andrea.
*Isabel is **taller than** Andrea.*

Note other forms of unequal comparison in the vocabulary box.

Equal **comparisons** are made in Spanish with tan… como or tanto… como.

tan + **adjective** or **adverb** + como

tanto(a, os, as) + **noun** + como

The thing or quality being compared is often between **tan** or **tanto** and **como.**

La ropa de esta tienda es tan **buena** como la de los grandes almacenes.
*The clothes in this store are **as nice as** those in large department stores.*

No hay tantos **vestidos** como faldas.
*There aren't **as many dresses as** skirts.*

You have already learned that you can attach **-ísimo(a, os, as)** to an **adjective** for emphasis.

Nuestros trajes son **elegantísimos.**
*Our suits are **very (extremely) elegant.***

In English, **superlatives** are formed by saying *the most* or *the least* or by adding *-est* at the end of an **adjective.** In Spanish, you form **superlatives** like this:

el (la, los, las) + más/menos + **adjective** (+ **de**)

Nuestros trajes son los más **elegantes** (**de** Madrid).
*Our suits are **the most elegant** (**in** Madrid).*

Andrea es la más **alta** (**de** sus compañeros).
*Andrea is **the tallest** (**of** her classmates).*

### Vocabulario

**Unequal Comparisons**

 Ya sabes

**más que** *more than*
**mayor que** *older than*
**mejor que** *better than*
**menor que** *younger than*
**menos que** *less than*
**peor que** *worse than*

**Equal Comparisons**

 Ya sabes

**tan… como** *as… as*
**tanto(a, os, as)… como** *as… as*



## Classroom Community

**Group Activity** Ask small groups of students to look around the room and form 7–8 comparison statements about items or people in the room. Have students use the **Vocabulario** on p. 296.

**Paired Activity** Have students compare points of interest of their town or city using **Actividad 6** as a model. Have students work in pairs to create sentences that form an opinion using a comparison.

**Game** Prepare Ahead: Make a set of flashcards with the comparison vocabulary. Divide the class into 2 teams. Alternate showing a card to each team and asking students to form a complete sentence with the comparison word. Each team gets 1 point for each correct sentence. The team with the most points after 5 rounds is the winner.

## ¿Cómo es la ropa?

**Hablar/Escribir** Isabel y Andrea comparan la ropa que ven en una tienda. Combina las oraciones para hacer una sola. *(Hint: Combine the sentences.)*

**modelo**

*La camiseta es fea. La falda es más fea.*
*La falda es más fea que la camiseta. (La camiseta es menos fea que la falda.)*

1. La camisa es cara. Los jeans son más caros.
2. El suéter es viejo. El traje de baño es más viejo.
3. Los pantalones son elegantes. El vestido es más elegante.
4. El pañuelo es bonito. El collar es más bonito.
5. Los calcetines son baratos. Las gafas son más baratas.

**MÁS PRÁCTICA** *cuaderno* pp. 109–110
**PARA HISPANOHABLANTES** *cuaderno* pp. 107–108

## Las opiniones de Isabel

**Hablar/Escribir** Imagínate que eres Isabel y que estás expresando tus opiniones sobre Madrid. Completa las oraciones con **más... que, menos... que** o **tan... como.** *(Hint: Complete the sentences.)*

**modelo**

*el equipo Real Madrid / bueno / el equipo Real Zaragoza*
*El equipo Real Madrid es tan bueno como el equipo Real Zaragoza.*

1. el Museo del Prado / interesante / el Museo Nacional de Ciencias Naturales
2. la tortilla española / sabrosa / la paella
3. el Parque del Retiro / tranquilo / el Parque del Oeste
4. el teatro español / divertido / el cine
5. la Plaza Mayor / ocupada / la Ronda de Atocha

## ¡Cómo cambia la moda!

**Hablar/Escribir** Con un(a) compañero(a), miren los diferentes estilos de ropa. ¿Quién puede hacer más comparaciones? *(Hint: Make comparisons.)*

**MÁS COMUNICACIÓN** p. R13



## Teaching All Students

**Extra Help** Ask students to list 10 items (articles of clothing, items, or people in the classroom). Based on the list, ask students to work with a partner and form 5 comparative statements. For example, **Susan tiene más libros que John.**

**Native Speakers** Have Spanish speakers compare a town or city from their native country with the town or city they live in now. Have them write 3–5 sentences on the board to share with the class.

**Multiple Intelligences**

**Visual** Give students two pictures from a magazine. Ask them to form comparative statements based on what they see in the pictures.

**Intrapersonal** Ask students to write a short paragraph comparing the members of their family using the comparative expressions on p. 296.

## Teaching Suggestions

Extend **Actividad 7** by asking pairs of students to be models for class comparisons. Remind students that the adjective agrees with the first noun in the sentence.

**Objective:** Controlled practice
Comparisons

**Answers**

1. Los jeans son más caros que la camisa. (La camisa es menos cara que los jeans.)
2. El traje de baño es más viejo que el suéter. (El suéter es menos viejo que el traje de baño.)
3. El vestido es más elegante que los pantalones. (Los pantalones son menos elegantes que el vestido.)
4. El collar es más bonito que el pañuelo. (El pañuelo es menos bonito que el collar.)
5. Las gafas son más baratas que los calcetines. (Los calcetines son menos baratos que las gafas.)

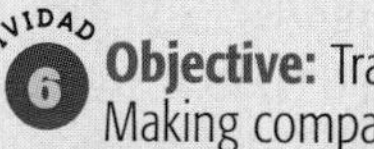

**Objective:** Transitional practice
Making comparisons

**Answers**

*Answers will vary.*

1. El Museo del Prado es [más/menos] interesante que el Museo Nacional de Ciencias Naturales.
2. La tortilla española es [más/menos] sabrosa que la paella.
3. El Parque del Retiro es tan tranquilo como el Parque del Oeste.
4. El teatro español es [más/menos] divertido que el cine.
5. La Plaza Mayor es [más/menos] ocupada que la Ronda de Atocha.

**Objective:** Open-ended practice
Comparing clothing and fashion

*Answers will vary.*

## Block Schedule

**FunBreak** Have students work in groups of 3–4 to develop survey questions for "The Best of (your town)." Each group should contribute 2 questions such as **¿Cuál es la mejor tienda de música? ¿...el cine más barato?** Have groups read their questions to the class while a student volunteer writes them on the board. Then do the survey orally in class. Solicit three nominations in each category and have the class vote with a show of hands. (For additional activities, see **Block Scheduling Copymasters.**)

## Teaching Resource Options

**Print**

*Más práctica* Workbook PE, p. 111
*Cuaderno para hispanohablantes* PE, p. 109
Block Scheduling Copymasters
Unit 4 Resource Book
*Más práctica* Workbook TE, p. 109
*Cuaderno para hispanohablantes* TE, p. 115
Audioscript, p. 132

**Audiovisual**

OHT 134 (Quick Start)
Audio Program Cassette 12A / CD 12

**Technology**

*Intrigas y aventuras* CD-ROM, Disc 2

## Quick Start Review

Uses of the subjunctive

Use OHT 134 or write on board: Conjugate the verbs in the following sentences to complete this fashion consultant's recommendations for this year's hottest styles.

1. es necesario que ustedes / comprar / pañuelos este año
2. recomiendo que las chicas / tener / un vestido de rayas
3. es importante que los chicos / llevar / chaquetas negras

Now write your own short fashion commentary using **sugiero que…**, **es bueno que…**, etc.

**Answers**
1. compren; 2. tengan; 3. lleven

## Teaching Suggestions
### Presenting the Subjunctive with Expressions of Doubt

Review the expressions of doubt on p. 299 before doing **Actividades 9** and **10**. Create sample sentences using the expressions that are meaningful for students. For example, **Dudamos que los estudiantes estudien toda la noche. No es seguro que terminen la tarea.**

ACTIVIDAD 8

### Catálogo de joyas

**Escuchar/Escribir** Isabel y Andrea hablan de varios artículos que ven en un catálogo. Escribe la letra que corresponde a lo que describen. Luego escribe tres descripciones originales. *(Hint: Identify what is being described. Then write three descriptions.)*

1. _____ 2. _____ 3. _____ 4. _____

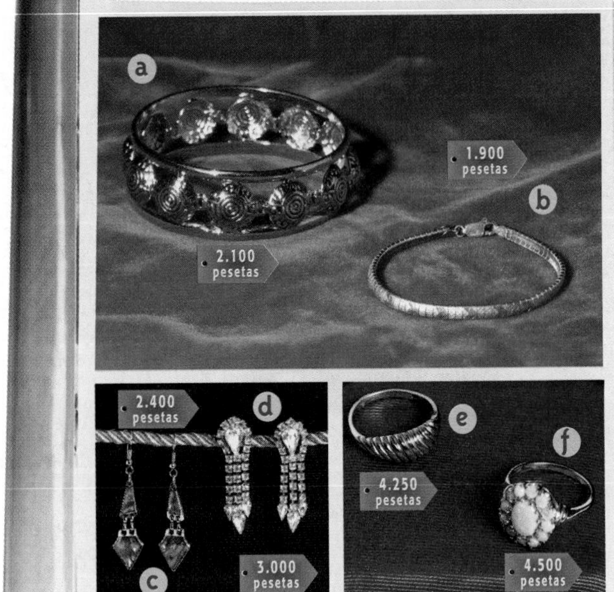


GRAMÁTICA

### The Subjunctive with Expressions of Doubt

**¿RECUERDAS?** *pp. 226, 252* You have already learned that the subjunctive is used after impersonal expressions and to express hopes and wishes.

The subjunctive is also used after verbs that imply **doubt.**

It is certain that the clerk is doubting, so Andrea uses the **indicative.**

But the clerk is uncertain they will buy anything (she is doubtful), so Andrea uses the subjunctive.

La dependienta **duda** que tú y yo **vayamos** a comprar hoy.
*The clerk **doubts** that you and I **are going** to buy anything today.*

In addition to expressing **doubt** with verbs like **dudar,** you can express doubt by saying that you don't think or believe something is going to happen.

Isabel is sure she likes the color, so she uses the **indicative.**

And she is sure of what she thinks, so she uses the **indicative.**

But the fit is a matter of doubt, so she uses the subjunctive.

Me **gusta** mucho el color, y **no creo** que te **quede** flojo.
***I like** the color a lot, and **I don't think it fits** loosely on you.*



## Classroom Community

**TPR** Divide the class into small groups. Each group role-plays the purchase of new clothes in a department store. One student acts as the salesclerk. Use the comparative expressions and the subjunctive with expressions of doubt as often as possible.

**Paired Activity** Have students work individually to write 4–6 sentences (some true, others false) about their community, school, class, etc. Then have them work in pairs to take turns reading their sentences while the student listening says **Creo que...** or **No creo que....**

## En la tienda de ropa

**Escribir** No estás de acuerdo con las opiniones de la dependienta. Sigue el modelo para responder a lo que dice, usando expresiones de duda. *(Hint: Respond to the clerk's comments.)*

**modelo**

*El traje es muy bonito.*

*No creo que el traje sea muy bonito.*

**Nota**

The subjunctive is used with expressions of doubt. Because they do not express doubt, **creer que, no dudar que,** and **estar seguro(a) que** are usually followed by the indicative. The same is true for **es cierto que, es seguro que,** and **es verdad que.**

**Creo que debes** vestirte con traje.
***I think that you should** wear a suit.*

**Estoy segura que** te **van** a gustar.
***I'm sure that** you **are going** to like them.*

1. La chaqueta roja de cuero es la más bonita.
2. Los chalecos con rayas son elegantes.
3. Las pulseras y los aretes se venden con frecuencia.
4. La ropa de las tallas pequeñas debe tener el mismo precio que la ropa de las tallas grandes.
5. Los suéteres son muy cómodos.
6. Sólo se deben usar zapatos de tacón los fines de semana.

**MÁS PRÁCTICA** *cuaderno* p. 111

**PARA HISPANOHABLANTES** *cuaderno* p. 109

## ¿Qué opinas?

**Hablar/Escribir** En grupos pequeños, expresen sus opiniones sobre las siguientes cosas. Usa el subjuntivo para expresar duda. *(Hint: Discuss your opinions with classmates.)*

**modelo**

*_____ es la mejor tienda de música de nuestra ciudad.*

**Tú:** *¿Creen que Musicworld es la mejor tienda de música de nuestra ciudad?*

**Compañero(a) 1:** *Sí, creo que Musicworld es la mejor tienda de música de nuestra ciudad.*

**Compañero(a) 2:** *No, dudo que Musicworld sea la mejor tienda de música de nuestra ciudad.*

1. _____ es la mejor tienda de ropa de nuestra ciudad.
2. _____ es la mejor marca de zapatos.
3. _____ son los jeans más populares.
4. Los estilos sencillos son los más elegantes.
5. Los pantalones anchos son más populares que los pantalones estrechos.
6. (Las chicas / Los chicos) compran mucha ropa.

### Vocabulario

**Expressions of Doubt**

**dudar que...** *to doubt that...*
**no es cierto que...** *it is not certain that...*
**no es seguro que...** *it is not certain that...*
**quizás** *perhaps*

**Ya sabes**

**no creer que...** *to not believe that...*
**no es verdad que...** *it is not true that...*
**tal vez** *maybe*

¿Qué expresiones significan lo mismo?

**Objective:** Open-ended practice
Listening comprehension/comparing jewelry

**Answers** (See script, p. 287B.)

1. f
2. a
3. c
4. b

*Descriptive answers will vary.*

**Objective:** Controlled practice
Subjunctive with expressions of doubt

**Answers**

*Answers will vary.*

1. No creo que la chaqueta roja de cuero sea la más bonita.
2. Dudo que los chalecos con rayas sean elegantes.
3. No es cierto que las pulseras y los aretes se vendan con frecuencia.
4. No es seguro que la ropa de las tallas pequeñas deba tener el mismo precio que la ropa de las tallas grandes.
5. Dudo que los suéteres sean muy cómodos.
6. No es verdad que sólo se deban usar zapatos de tacón los fines de semana.

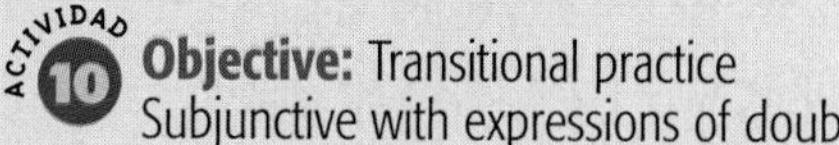

*Answers will vary.*

## Teaching All Students

**Extra Help** Have students go back to the Dialog on pp. 292–293 and pick out the uses of the subjunctive. Have them distinguish whether the subjunctive is used after an impersonal expression, to express hopes and wishes, or to express doubt.

**Multiple Intelligences**

**Verbal** Ask students to write at least 5 complete sentences using the vocabulary words in the box on p. 299. They should write about the current fashion in Spain, expressing doubts since they may not know much on the subject.

**Intrapersonal** Have students list situations in which they might express doubt and therefore need to use the subjunctive.

## Block Schedule

**Change of Pace** Prepare Ahead: Write each word of several subjunctive sentences on separate index cards, allowing one sentence per group. Give each group a set of cards and ask them to unscramble and form a complete sentence. (For additional activities, see **Block Scheduling Copymasters.**)

# UNIDAD 4 Etapa 3
## Vocabulary/Grammar

### Teaching Resource Options

**Print** 

*Más práctica* Workbook PE, p. 112
*Cuaderno para hispanohablantes* PE, p. 110
Block Scheduling Copymasters
Unit 4 Resource Book
*Más práctica* Workbook TE, p. 110
*Cuaderno para hispanohablantes* TE, p. 116
Audioscript, p. 132

**Audiovisual**

OHT 135 (Quick Start)
Audio Program Cassette 12A / CD 12

**Technology**

*Intrigas y aventuras* CD-ROM, Disc 2

### Quick Start Review

Subjunctive of stem-changing verbs

Use OHT 135 or write on board: Complete the following sentences with the correct form of the subjunctive.

1. No creo que nosotros / seguir / la calle correcta. Estamos perdidos.
2. Dudo que Alfonso / perderse. Conoce bien la ciudad.
3. Tal vez él / dormirse / todavía. Es muy temprano.

Now write a short dialog between a mother and her child using **no creo, dudo que,** and **tal vez**.

**Answers**
1. sigamos; 2. se pierda; 3. se duerma

**Objective:** Transitional practice Listening comprehension/talking about spending money

**Answers** (See script, p. 287B.)
*Answers will vary.*
1. Felipe tiene cuidado con su dinero.
2. Isabel es razonable con su dinero.
3. Andrea gasta mucho dinero.
4. El señor Zavala ahorra su dinero.
5. Angelina gasta demasiado dinero.

ACTIVIDAD 11

## ¿Cómo son con el dinero?

**Escuchar/Escribir** Varias personas están hablando del dinero. Escucha lo que dice cada persona. Luego escribe una oración para describir cómo usan estas personas el dinero. *(Hint: Write sentences describing how each person uses money.)*

1. Felipe
2. Isabel
3. Andrea
4. el señor Zavala
5. Angelina

### NOTA CULTURAL

**¿Qué talla usas?** Si estás en Madrid y quieres comprar ropa, vas a descubrir que las tallas de ropa en España son diferentes de las de Estados Unidos. Por ejemplo, si quieres comprar un vestido para tu madre y ella usa la talla 10, en Madrid debes comprarle una talla 42. Si los zapatos de tu hermano son el número 6, tienes que comprarle el número 39. Si tienes miedo de confundirte, es mejor que midas (*measure*) a todos antes de viajar, ¡en centímetros, por supuesto!

| | S | | M | | L | |
|---|---|---|---|---|---|---|
| Francia/España | 36 | 38 | 40 | 42 | 44 | 46 |
| E.E.U.U. | 2-4 | 6 | 8 | 10 | 12-14 | 16 |

ACTIVIDAD 12

## Los opuestos

**Hablar/Leer** Jaime y Lilia, los amigos de Andrea, tienen mucho en común, pero con el dinero son opuestos. Jaime es generosísimo pero irresponsable y Lilia es responsable pero tacaña. Con un(a) compañero(a), decidan quién (no) hace las siguientes actividades. *(Hint: Decide who does and doesn't do the following activities.)*

**modelo**

*ahorrar mucho dinero para el futuro*
*Es cierto que Lilia ahorra mucho dinero para el futuro.*
*Dudamos que Jaime ahorre mucho dinero para el futuro.*

1. darles préstamos a amigos frecuentemente
2. guardar dinero para las vacaciones
3. pagar la ropa nueva con tarjeta de crédito
4. depositar dinero regularmente en la cuenta de ahorros
5. preocuparse por los gastos
6. usar cheques de viajero cuando está de vacaciones
7. nunca prestarles dinero a sus parientes
8. sacar dinero del cajero automático frecuentemente

### Vocabulario

**En el banco**

**ahorrar** *to save*
**el cajero automático** *ATM*
**los cheques** *checks*
**los cheques de viajero** *traveler's checks*
**la cuenta de ahorros** *savings account*
**guardar** *to hold, to keep*
**el préstamo** *loan*
**prestar** *to lend*

**De compras**

**la caja registradora** *cash register*
**el (la) cajero(a)** *cashier*
**gastar** *to spend*
**los gastos** *expenses*
**suficiente** *enough*
**tacaño(a)** *stingy*
**valer** *to be worth*

¿Qué palabras usas cuando vas de compras?



### Classroom Community

**Learning Scenarios** Using the vocabulary words, have students explain to a foreign visitor how using the ATM machine (**el cajero automático**) is a common way to do banking today.

**Portfolios** Ask students to write about 3 things that they are glad about and 3 things that they hope happen regarding their financial situation. Remind them to use the subjunctive forms.

**Rubric: Writing**

| Criteria | Scale |
|---|---|
| Accuracy of information | 1 2 3 4 5 |
| Logical organization | 1 2 3 4 5 |
| Vocabulary use | 1 2 3 4 5 |

A = 13–15 pts.
B = 10–12 pts.
C = 7–9 pts.
D = 4–6 pts.
F = < 4 pts.

## The Subjunctive with Expressions of Emotion

 **¿RECUERDAS?** *pp. 226, 252, 298* You have already learned that the **subjunctive** is used with impersonal expressions, to express hopes and wishes, and with expressions of doubt.

The **subjunctive** is also used to convey **emotions,** such as frustration or happiness. When you express emotions, the event that you're expressing the emotion about is in the **subjunctive.**

*indicative* — *subjunctive*

Me **fastidia** que los dependientes me **traten** así.
*It **frustrates** me **to be treated** like this by clerks.*

Andrea is certain she is frustrated, so she uses the **indicative.** What she is frustrated about is the way the clerks treat her. Since she isn't describing the actual treatment (that would have been in the indicative, **me tratan**), but expressing her **emotion** about it, she uses the **subjunctive.**

Note that verbs ending in **-ger** change the **g** to **j** in the **subjunctive.**

Espero que **escojas** el vestido blanco.
*I hope that **you choose** the white dress.*

### Vocabulario

**Expressions of Emotion**

**alegrarse de que...** *to be glad that...*
**sentir (e→ie, i) que...** *to be sorry that...*

 **Ya sabes**

**esperar que...** *to hope that...*
**gustar** *to like*
**molestar** *to bother*
**sorprender** *to surprise*
**tener miedo** *to be afraid*

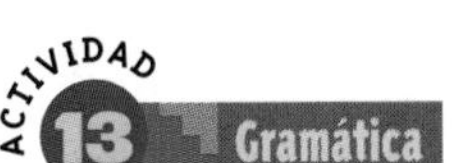

Actividad 13 Gramática

### ¿De qué tienes miedo?

**Hablar/Escribir** ¿Tienes miedo de que las siguientes cosas vayan a ocurrir? Empieza cada frase con **(no) tengo miedo de que.** *(Hint: What are you afraid of?)*

**modelo**

*Los monstruos existen.*
*No tengo miedo de que los monstruos existan.*

1. No hay vacaciones este año.
2. Mi bicicleta se va a romper.
3. Vienen los extraterrestres a la tierra.
4. Hay un temblor.
5. La clase de español es difícil.
6. Mis amigos(as) no me mandan cartas.

**MÁS PRÁCTICA** *cuaderno* p. 112
**PARA HISPANOHABLANTES** *cuaderno* p. 110



## Teaching Suggestions

### Presenting the Subjunctive with Expression of Emotion

Ask students to create new sentences using the list of expressions of emotion in the vocabulary box on p. 301. They can use the characters from the video/dialog in their sentences. For example, **Isabel espera que la dependienta la ayude en la tienda. Ella se siente contenta que la ropa le quede bien.**

Actividad 12 **Objective:** Open-ended practice
Discussing ways to spend and save money

**Answers**

*Answers will vary.*

1. Creemos que Jaime les da... Dudamos que Lilia les dé...
2. Es cierto que Lilia guarda... No es cierto que Jaime guarde...
3. Es seguro que Jaime paga... Dudamos que Lilia pague...
4. Es verdad que Lilia deposita... No es verdad que Jaime deposite...
5. Creemos que Lilia se preocupa.... No creemos que Jaime se preocupe...
6. Es seguro que Lilia usa... Dudamos que Jaime use...
7. Es cierto que Lilia nunca les presta... No es cierto que Jaime nunca les preste...
8. Creemos que Jaime saca... No creemos que Lilia saque...

Actividad 13 **Objective:** Controlled practice
Subjunctive with expressions of emotion

**Answers**

1. (No) Tengo miedo de que no haya vacaciones este año.
2. (No) Tengo miedo de que mi bicicleta se vaya a romper.
3. (No) Tengo miedo de que los extraterrestres vengan a la tierra.
4. (No) Tengo miedo de que haya un temblor.
5. (No) Tengo miedo de que la clase de español sea difícil.
6. (No) Tengo miedo de que mis amigos(as) no me manden cartas.

## Teaching All Students

**Extra Help** Form questions using the vocabulary words and ask students to answer orally, e.g., **¿Tienes una cuenta de ahorros? ¿Sacas dinero del cajero automático frecuentemente? ¿Escribes muchos cheques cada mes? ¿Guardas dinero para asistir a la universidad?** etc.

**Native Speakers** Ask Spanish-speaking students to provide additional examples of the subjunctive with expressions of emotion.

### Multiple Intelligences

**Verbal** As an expansion of **Actividad 13**, have students work in pairs to write a list of 3 things that scare them, 3 things that surprise them, and 3 things that bother them, using the expressions of emotion on p. 301.

## Block Schedule

**Retention** Have students share their fears by writing sentences on the board using **Tengo miedo de que....** Making the topic more real to them will help them absorb the subjunctive verbs as part of the "sound byte." (For additional activities, see **Block Scheduling Copymasters.**)

## Teaching Resource Options

**Print**

*Más práctica* Workbook PE, pp. 105–108
*Cuaderno para hispanohablantes* PE, p. 105
Block Scheduling Copymasters
Unit 4 Resource Book
*Más práctica* Workbook TE, pp. 103–106
*Cuaderno para hispanohablantes* TE, p. 111
Information Gap Activities, p. 120
Audioscript, pp. 133–134

**Audiovisual**

OHT 129, 129A, 135 (Quick Start)
Audio Program Cassette 12B / CD 12; (*Para hispanohablantes* Cassette 12B / CD 12)

**Technology**

*Intrigas y aventuras* CD-ROM, Disc 2

## Quick Start Review

Talking about money

Use OHT 135 or write on board: Complete the following sentences with the correct vocabulary word.

1. Si usted quiere ahorrar dinero, vaya al banco y ponga el dinero en una _____.
2. Si usted quiere comprar una casa, va a ser necesario pedir un _____.
3. Una persona que no es generosa es _____.
4. En el supermercado, antes de salir usted debe traer la comida a la _____ para pagarla.

**Answers**
1. cuenta de ahorros; 2. préstamo; 3. tacaña; 4. caja registradora

## Supplemental Vocabulary

| | |
|---|---|
| **¿En qué le puedo servir?** | How can I help you? |
| **Estar de moda** | To be in style |
| **Me llevo éste.** | I'll take this one. |
| **¿Me queda bien/mal?** | Does it look good/bad on me? |
| **¿Qué te parece?** | What do you think? |

## Reacciones

**PARA CONVERSAR**
**STRATEGY: SPEAKING**
**Interpret the feelings or values of others** Some topics, like money, are sensitive. Discussing them can cause hurt feelings. Evaluate the nature of your partner's response and choose an appropriate reaction. Use words that express gladness (**me alegro de que**), hope (**espero que**), or concern (**siento que**).

**Hablar** Hazle las siguientes preguntas a un(a) compañero(a) y responde con una expresión de emoción y el subjuntivo. *(Hint: Ask these questions.)*

Tengo miedo de que
Estoy furioso(a) que
Me molesta que
Siento que
Me alegro de que
Me encanta que
Me sorprende que

**modelo**

*¿Recibes dinero de tus parientes?*
**Tú:** *¿Recibes dinero de tus parientes?*
**Compañero(a):** *Sí, recibo dinero para mi cumpleaños.*
**Tú:** *Me alegro de que tus parientes sean generosos.*

1. ¿Tienes una cuenta de ahorros?
2. ¿Ahorras algún dinero?
3. ¿En qué gastas tu dinero?
4. ¿Tienes una cuenta de cheques?
5. ¿Dónde compras tu ropa?
6. ¿Regateas de vez en cuando? ¿Recibes buenos precios?
7. ¿Conoces a una persona tacaña?
8. ¿Conoces a una persona generosa?

## Diálogo incompleto

**Hablar/Escribir** Estás en una tienda de ropa. Completa el diálogo con oraciones lógicas. Luego, preséntalo con un(a) compañero(a). *(Hint: Complete the dialog.)*

**Cliente(a):** _____
**Dependiente(a):** Sí, para servirte.
**Cliente(a):** Necesito _____
**Dependiente(a):** _____
**Cliente(a):** Me parece un poco (flojo[a] / apretado[a]).
**Dependiente(a):** Busco una talla más (grande / pequeña).
*Luego…*
**Cliente(a):** _____
**Dependiente(a):** ¡Te queda bien!
**Cliente(a):** _____
**Dependiente(a):** (Me alegro de que / Espero que) _____
**Cliente(a):** _____

### Vocabulario

**Comprando ropa**

**¿Cómo me veo?** *How do I look?*
**¿Cómo te queda?** *How does it look on you?*
**¿Me puede atender?** *Can you help (wait on) me?*

¿Quién lo pregunta, el (la) cliente(a) o el (la) dependiente(a)?



## Classroom Community

**Learning Scenarios** Ask students to bring in specific clothes for a fashion show. Have some students "model" and others act as the "audience" by forming comparative/superlative expressions about the clothing, e.g., **La chaqueta roja es más bonita que... A mí me gusta la rosada porque es más elegante que...**

**Paired Activity** In pairs, have S1 be the vendor and S2 be the buyer. S1 should find a few things to sell (a backpack, a jacket, a book, etc.) and display them. S2 approaches S1 and offers to buy one or more of the objects. S2 should bargain for the best price. When a sale is made, students switch roles.

## ¡Qué vergüenza!

**Hablar/Escribir** Dos jóvenes fueron de compras. Cuenta lo que les pasó según los dibujos. *(Hint: Tell what happened based on the pictures.)*

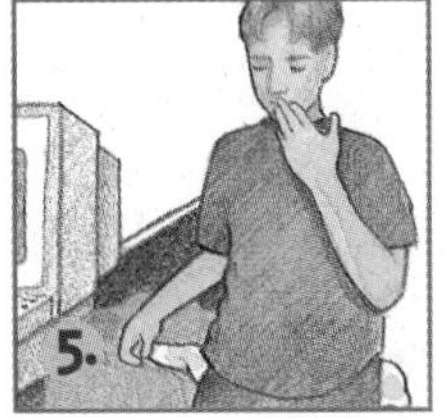

## A regatear en El Rastro

**Hablar** Imagínate que estás en El Rastro donde los clientes y los vendedores siempre regatean. Con un(a) compañero(a), hagan los papeles de vendedor(a) y de cliente(a), usando estas expresiones. *(Hint: Bargain.)*

**¿Me deja ver...?**
**¿Cuánto cuesta(n)?**
**¡Es demasiado!**
**Uuuf, ¡qué caro!**
**No puedo.**
**¿Me deja el (la)... en...?**
**Le puedo ofrecer...**

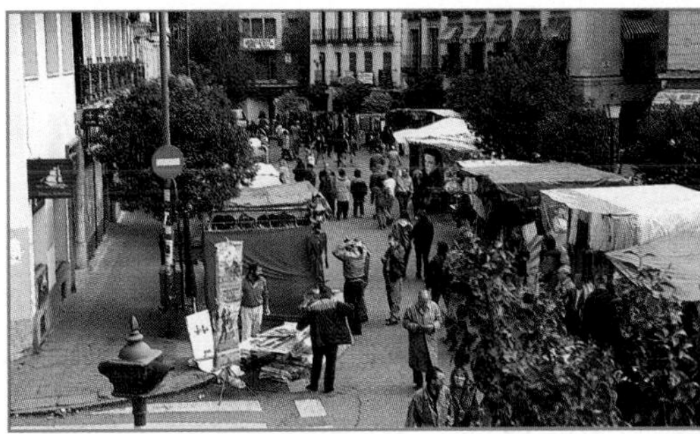

**MÁS COMUNICACIÓN** p. R13

### Refrán

**El traje no hace al hombre pero le da figura.**

¿Estás de acuerdo con este refrán? ¿Crees que la ropa que lleva una persona afecta la opinión de otras? ¿De qué manera?

**Objective:** Transitional practice
Talking about spending and saving money

*Answers will vary.*

**Objective:** Open-ended practice
Shopping for clothing

*Answers will vary.*

**Rubric: Speaking**

| Criteria | Scale | |
|---|---|---|
| Vocabulary use | 1 2 3 4 5 | A = 17–20 pts. |
| Logical organization | 1 2 3 4 5 | B = 13–16 pts. |
| Fluency, intonation | 1 2 3 4 5 | C = 9–12 pts. |
| Accuracy | 1 2 3 4 5 | D = 5–8 pts. |
| | | F = < 5 pts. |

**Objective:** Open-ended practice
Shopping for clothing

*Answers will vary.*

**Objective:** Open-ended practice
Bargaining in a market

*Answers will vary.*

## Cultural Highlights

**EL RASTRO** The Rastro flea market is open only on Sundays from 9:00 A.M. to about 3:00 P.M. It is the best and most popular handicraft showcase and offers many bargains for insightful shoppers. (See **En colores,** p. 307.)

## Community Connection

Have students discuss situations when they might bargain for a purchase here in the U.S. List the situations on the board (e.g., car shopping, at a yard sale or flea market, etc.). Then, using the vocabulary in **Actividad 17**, have students plan a dialog between a buyer and a seller in which they bargain for a deal.

## Teaching All Students

**Extra Help** Have students write out answers to the question in the **Vocabulario** box on p. 302.

**Native Speakers** Have Spanish-speaking students discuss any shopping situations in which they bargain for prices, either in the community or in their native country.

**Multiple Intelligences**

**Intrapersonal** Ask students to write a short paragraph using at least 5 of the expressions of emotion on p. 301. They can discuss their feelings about fashions at their school. Remind them to use the subjunctive when necessary.

## Block Schedule

**Refranes** Discuss the meaning of this **refrán** with the class. Then have the class take sides, agreeing or disagreeing with the **refrán** and supporting their opinions. (For additional activities, see **Block Scheduling Copymasters.**)

## Teaching Resource Options

**Print** 

Unit 4 Resource Book
Audioscript, p. 131

**Audiovisual**

OHT 135 (Quick Start)
Audio Program Cassette 12A / CD 12

## Quick Start Review

Talking about things to do in the city

Use OHT 135 or write on board: Imagine you are on vacation in a big city. Choose the city you would like to visit and write down two activities to do in the daytime and two activities to do in the evening. You may use the infinitive form of the verb in your answers.

*Answers will vary.*

*Possible answers:* dar una vuelta, ir a un museo, ir de compras, ir al cine, ver una obra de teatro, bailar, ir a un restaurante elegante

## Teaching Suggestions

- **Prereading** Ask students what they know about Madrid and what they might like to see while on a visit. Write their observations on the board. Then ask students to guess the topic of the reading, based on the photos and realia.
- **Reading** Have students make a list of the tourist attractions mentioned.
- **Strategy: Categorize details** Have students first make a list of all the places mentioned in the reading, then categorize them into **presente** and **pasado**.
- **Post-Reading** Based on the activities described in this reading, ask students to choose their favorite activity and explain why.

En voces

LECTURA

# Nos vemos en Madrid

### PARA LEER

**STRATEGY: READING**

**Categorize details** When visiting another country, it helps to participate in its contemporary life and get to know something of its past. **«Nos vemos en Madrid»** suggests places to visit. In which ones can you observe life in the present? Which ones tell you about the past? List them on the chart below.

| Una visita a Madrid | |
|---|---|
| El presente | El pasado |
| | |
| | |
| | |

Todo en Madrid llama la atención[1] —sus barrios, su arquitectura, sus museos, parques y diversiones. Para conocer esta gran ciudad, puedes ir a pie o en metro.

¿Por qué no empiezas con una visita al Museo del Prado? El Prado es uno de los museos más importantes del mundo. ¡Vas a necesitar un día entero solamente para ver las pinturas de Goya, Velázquez y El Greco!

Después de salir del museo, siéntate en el Parque del Retiro. Está a unas cuadras del Prado. En este parque hay un lago donde puedes alquilar un bote de remos[2], y artistas que pintan retratos de los visitantes. ¡Pero no hay tiempo para descansar!

Siempre hay gente en la Puerta del Sol.

Todos los madrileños conocen esta escultura de un oso (*bear*) y un madroño (*arbutus tree*).

Es esencial que vayas al Centro de Arte Reina Sofía. Este museo es famoso por sus obras del arte moderno. La

[1] catches your eye [2] rowboat



## Classroom Community

**Portfolio** Ask students to write a short description of one or two places in their town or city that best represents the local community or culture(s).

**Rubric: Writing**

| Criteria | Scale |
|---|---|
| Logical | 1 2 3 4 5 |
| Vocabulary use | 1 2 3 4 5 |
| Accuracy | 1 2 3 4 5 |

A = 13–15 pts.
B = 10–12 pts.
C = 7–9 pts.
D = 4–6 pts.
F = < 4 pts.

**Storytelling** Divide the class into groups. Have students tell a story about what they would do for a day (and night) in Madrid. The first student starts with getting up in the morning and adds a first activity for the day. Students continue until the day is complete.

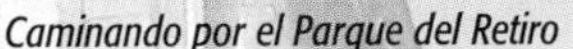

*Caminando por el Parque del Retiro*

*Saliendo de la Plaza Mayor*

*Divirtiéndose por la noche en un café*

pintura más conocida de su colección es *Guernica,* de Picasso, una representación de la Guerra Civil española.

¿Estás cansado? Ojalá que no, porque es importante que veas la Plaza Mayor. ¡Tiene tanto ambiente! Alrededor de la plaza hay calles pintorescas[3] y tiendas interesantes. ¿Tienes calor? ¡Toma un refresco en un café al aire libre!

[3] picturesque

***Mujer sentada acodada,** por Picasso*

Madrid tiene una vida nocturna también. El resto de España llama a los madrileños «los gatos» porque siempre están paseando por las calles. ¡Unos clubes de Madrid no abren hasta las tres de la mañana! Entonces, échate una siesta[4], y en la noche toma el metro a Bilbao. En la Plaza del Dos de Mayo vas a encontrar cafés llenos de jóvenes.

Hay mucho más que hacer, pero no hay tiempo. Debes regresar a Madrid. ¡A los madrileños les gustan los extranjeros!

[4] take a nap

## ¿Comprendiste?

1. ¿Qué es el Prado?
2. ¿Dónde está el Parque del Retiro?
3. ¿Qué es *Guernica*? ¿Dónde está?
4. ¿Qué hay alrededor de la Plaza Mayor?
5. ¿Qué hacen los madrileños por la noche?

## ¿Qué piensas?

Imagínate que estás de vacaciones en Madrid. ¿Qué vas a hacer durante el día? ¿Por la noche?



## Culture Highlights

- **EL CENTRO DE ARTE REINA SOFÍA,** Madrid's modern art museum, features art by Spanish artists such as Pablo Picasso, Salvador Dalí, and Joan Miró. It is named after the current queen of Spain. Picasso's *Guernica* is in the museum's main salon.
- **GUERNICA** is a huge black and white painting that Picasso created during the Spanish Civil War. It represents the horrors inflicted during the German bombing of Guernica, a small Basque town.
- **EL PARQUE DEL BUEN RETIRO** is a beautiful park in Madrid that has formal gardens, fountains, and a lake with rental rowboats. On weekends there may be strolling musicians and performers, and artisans.

## Interdisciplinary Connection

**Art** Find a reproduction of Picasso's *Guernica* and share it with the class. Ask students to study it and list the things and the action they see. Then have them give an opinion of the painting. What do they think is the meaning of the painting? Why did the artist paint it in black and white?

## ¿Comprendiste?

*Answers will vary.*

1. El Prado es uno de los museos más importantes del mundo.
2. El Parque del Retiro está a unas cuadras del Prado.
3. *Guernica* es una pintura de Picasso. Está en el Centro de Arte Reina Sofía.
4. Alrededor de la Plaza Mayor hay calles pintorescas y tiendas interesantes.
5. Por la noche, los madrileños siempre están paseando por las calles.

## Dictation

Dictate excerpts from the reading, leaving out place names. After the dictation, have students identify what is being described.

## Teaching All Students

**Extra Help** Have students study the pictures and try to match them with the following captions: **El Parque del Retiro, El Viejo Madrid, El Centro de Arte Reina Sofía, Madrid de noche, Madrid moderno, El símbolo de Madrid—el oso.**

**Multiple Intelligences**

**Naturalist** Have several students research the botanical gardens, the trees and the plant life found at **el Parque del Retiro** in Madrid.

**Logical/Mathematical** Have students research as many facts about the Prado as possible. For instance, the number of visitors, the size of the museum, the number of paintings it houses, etc., then organize the information in a chart and present it to the class.

## Block Schedule

**Internet** Have several students look up the sites mentioned in the article and present them to the class. Have other students locate the sites on a map of Madrid.

## Teaching Resource Options

**Print** 

*Cuaderno para hispanohablantes* PE, pp. 106, 111–112

Unit 4 Resource Book

*Cuaderno para hispanohablantes* TE, pp. 112, 117–118

Video Activities, p. 127

Videoscript, p. 130

**Audiovisual** 

OHT 136 (Quick Start)

Video Program Videotape 4, 34:08 / Videodisc 3B

Search Chapter 3, Play to end
U4E3, En colores (Culture), Spanish

Search Chapter 3, Play to end
U4E3, En colores (Culture), English

## Quick Start Review

Discussing preferences

Use OHT 136 or write on board: Imagine you are in Madrid and you are planning to buy yourself a few things to remember Spain. What will you buy? Choose two of the following items or use your own ideas and write a sentence explaining why you will buy that item.

**Voy a comprar...**
**joyas, un disco compacto, un artículo de cuero, ropa, una escultura, una pintura, libros**

*Answers will vary.*

*Sample answer:* Voy a comprar un disco compacto porque me encanta la música. Me interesa la guitarra clásica española.

## Cross Cultural Connections

Have students read the second paragraph of the reading about the **Corte Inglés** and compare it to a large department store that they frequent. Tell them to come up with 3 similarities and 3 differences.

# En colores

## CULTURA Y COMPARACIONES

### PARA CONOCERNOS

**STRATEGY: CONNECTING CULTURES**

**Analyze and draw conclusions about shopping as a cultural activity** Tour directors usually build in time for shopping in each city visited. They try to provide choices for those of different ages and different incomes. If you and your family visited Madrid, where would they shop? What would they look for? Jot down your ideas.

| | ¿Dónde? | ¿Qué cosas? |
|---|---|---|
| Tú | | |
| Tus hermanos(as) | | |
| Tus padres | | |
| Tus abuelos | | |

# ¿En qué te puedo atender?

¿Quieres ir de compras? Madrid tiene todo tipo de tiendas. ¿Por qué no vas primero a la Gran Vía? Esta calle principal en el centro de la capital es famosa por sus viejos negocios, almacenes modernos, librerías, joyerías y tiendas de cerámica tradicional.

Cerca de la Gran Vía está el almacén original de la cadena[1] El Corte Inglés. El más importante de los grandes almacenes españoles, El Corte Inglés tiene sucursales[2] en Madrid y por todo el país. Aquí puedes encontrar ropa, artículos de cuero, discos compactos, comida y mucho más. También puedes cortarte el pelo, revelar[3] las fotos y pagar todo con una tarjeta de crédito.

[1] chain [2] branches [3] develop

*Tiendas especializadas en la calle Serrano*

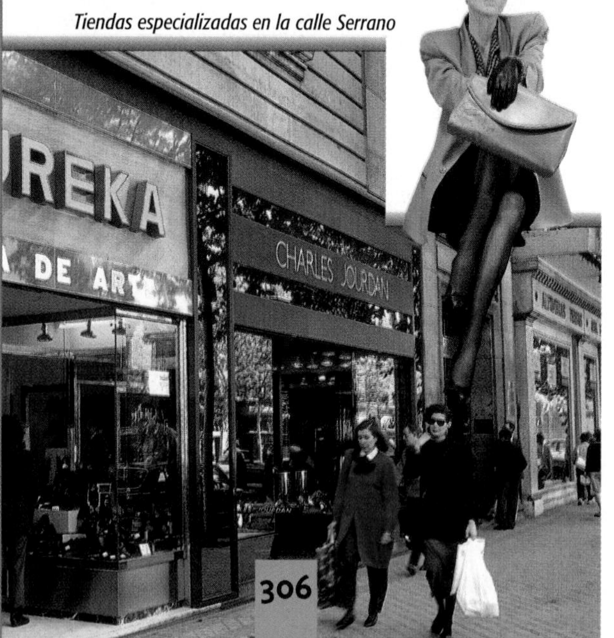


## Classroom Community

**Group Activity** Working in small groups, have students list the shopping options for visitors to their town or city. Have them make a list of some typical items that visitors might like to purchase.

**Portfolio** Based on what they have learned about shopping in Madrid, have students develop a paragraph describing where they would shop. Also have them include a shopping list.

**Rubric: Writing**

| Criteria | Scale |
|---|---|
| Accuracy of information | 1 2 3 4 5 |
| Logical organization | 1 2 3 4 5 |
| Vocabulary use | 1 2 3 4 5 |

A = 13–15 pts.
B = 10–12 pts.
C = 7–9 pts.
D = 4–6 pts.
F = < 4 pts.

El Corte Inglés tiene muchísimas cosas, pero si prefieres tiendas pequeñas, debes ir al barrio de Salamanca. Por sus calles Serrano, Ortega y Gasset, y Goya hay boutiques, joyerías, perfumerías y tiendas de decoración[4] conocidas por su calidad y elegancia. Si quieres ver algo en una de estas tiendas, habla con un dependiente. Él puede enseñarte las cosas que te interesan.

*El almacén que vende de todo*

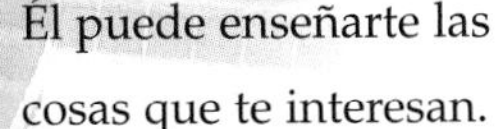

Para ver una galería[5] ultramoderna, visita La Vaguada, en el norte de la ciudad. Y si te gusta lo viejo, debes ir a El Rastro, un mercado popular de objetos de segunda mano[6]. Cerca de la Plaza Mayor, en el viejo Madrid, El Rastro se instala[7] en la Ribera de Curtidores y las calles próximas. Pero solamente puedes ir los domingos y los días festivos porque El Rastro no se instala los otros días. ¡Llega antes de las once para encontrar una ganga!

[4] interior decor
[5] mall
[6] used, secondhand
[7] is set up

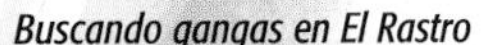
*Buscando gangas en El Rastro*

## ¿Comprendiste?

1. ¿Qué es la Gran Vía?
2. ¿Qué venden en El Corte Inglés?
3. ¿Cómo son las tiendas en el barrio de Salamanca?
4. Si quieres ver algo en una tienda de lujo, ¿qué haces?
5. ¿Qué es El Rastro? ¿Dónde queda?

## ¿Qué piensas?

1. ¿Adónde vas de compras en Madrid si quieres comprar unos regalos finos y caros? ¿Si quieres comprar cosas baratas?
2. ¿Qué cosas crees que puedes comprar en El Rastro?

## Hazlo tú

Vas a ir de compras en Madrid esta tarde. Haz una lista de los lugares donde vas a ir y de las cosas que vas a comprar.



## Teaching All Students

**Extra Help** Have students make a list of all the proper nouns in the reading. Then have them assign a category to each one, e.g., address, store name, street name, etc.

**Challenge** Have students brainstorm other shopping options that are available to them today (e.g., catalog shopping, shopping via the Internet, garage sales, auctions, outlet malls, etc.).

**Multiple Intelligences**

**Visual** Have students illustrate and label stores in their area that they associate with each of the store types mentioned in the reading: **almacén, librería, joyería, boutique, galería, mercado.**

## Teaching Suggestions
### Presenting En colores

- **Prereading** Have students study the photos that accompany the reading and try to name their locations. (Possible answers: **el centro comercial, tiendas pequeñas, el mercado al aire libre**)
- **Video** Use the video to expand and enrich the cultural information.
- **Strategy: Analyze and draw conclusions about shopping as a cultural activity** Have students first scan the reading and list all the options for shopping in Madrid. Then have them categorize these options according to where their family members would shop.

## Reading Strategy

Have students explain the meaning of the title, **¿En qué te puedo atender?** Who would say it? Where? What are some typical responses?

## Culture Highlights

**SHOPPING IN MADRID** In the Salamanca district of Madrid, shoppers will find boutiques and luxury shops that offer the most exclusive international brand names. Popular shopping centers include the successful **La Vaguada** and the **Multicentros: La Galería del Prado** and **El Jardín de Serrano.**

## ¿Comprendiste?

*Answers will vary.*

1. La Gran Vía es una calle principal en el centro de Madrid.
2. En el Corte Inglés venden de todo.
3. Las tiendas en el barrio de Salamanca son pequeñas y elegantes.
4. Si quieres ver algo en una tienda de lujo, habla con un dependiente.
5. El Rastro es un mercado popular de objetos de segunda mano. Queda cerca de la Plaza Mayor, en el viejo Madrid en la Ribera de Curtidores y las calles próximas.

## Block Schedule

**Change of Pace** Have students try to explain to a Spanish visitor what garage sales or yard sales are. Be sure they explain what items might be bought or sold at these sales.

## Teaching Resource Options

**Print** 

Block Scheduling Copymasters
Unit 4 Resource Book
Information Gap Activities, pp. 121–122
Family Involvement, pp. 123–124

**Audiovisual** 

OHT 130, 130A, 136 (Quick Start)

**Technology** 

Electronic Teacher Tools/Test Generator
*Intrigas y aventuras* CD-ROM, Disc 2

## Quick Start Review

Uses of the subjunctive

Use OHT 136 or write on board: Finish the following sentences.

Me alegro de que...
Dudo que...
No es verdad que...

*Answers will vary.*

## Teaching Suggestions
### What Have Students Learned?

Have students look at the "Now you can..." notes listed on the left side of pp. 308–309. To review material before doing the activities or taking the test, have them consult the "To review" notes.

### Actividad 1 Answers

1. Alberto es mayor que José.
2. Sara tiene tantos libros como Ana y José.
3. Alberto es el mayor.
4. Todos llevan tantos zapatos como Sara.
5. Sara es tan delgada como Alberto.
6. Alberto tiene menos libros que los otros.
7. Alberto es el más alto.
8. Ana es menor que Sara.

# En uso
## REPASO Y MÁS COMUNICACIÓN

**OBJECTIVES**
- Talk about shopping for clothes
- Ask for and give opinions
- Make comparisons
- Discuss ways to save and spend money

*Now you can...*
- make comparisons.

*To review*
- comparatives and superlatives, see p. 296.

### Actividad 1 Mis amigos

Describe a los amigos de Andrea.
*(Hint: Describe Andrea's friends.)*

**modelo**

*ser tan alto(a) como Sara*
*José es tan alto como Sara.*

1. ser mayor que José
2. tener tantos libros como Ana y José
3. ser el (la) mayor
4. llevar tantos zapatos como Sara
5. ser tan delgado(a) como Alberto
6. tener menos libros que los otros
7. ser el (la) más alto(a)
8. ser menor que Sara

Ana 13 años | José 15 años | Sara 15 años | Alberto 17 años

*Now you can...*
- ask for and give opinions.

*To review*
- the subjunctive with expressions of doubt, see p. 298.

### Actividad 2 ¡No es cierto!

No estás de acuerdo con las opiniones de tu amigo(a). ¿Qué le dices? *(Hint: Contradict your friend's statements.)*

**modelo**

*Creo que la ropa española es la más cara.*
*No creo que la ropa española sea la más cara.*

1. No es cierto que los jóvenes españoles caminen mucho.
2. Es verdad que las tiendas españolas están abiertas toda la noche.
3. Creo que pocos estudiantes quieren viajar a España.
4. Es cierto que los mejores futbolistas viven en España.
5. No creo que podamos usar cheques de viajero en España.
6. No es verdad que muchos españoles usen ropa elegante.

## Classroom Community

**Group Activity** As an extension of **Actividad 1**, have students write a list of comparisons that compare the students in the class (e.g., from tallest to shortest, from older to younger, etc.), members of a sports team, or a group of characters from a television show. Include visuals if possible.

**Paired Activity** Using **Actividad 1** as a model, have partners describe their own circle of friends by using structures of comparison. You could tell the students about this activity the day before and have them bring in photos of the friends they will be describing to their partners.

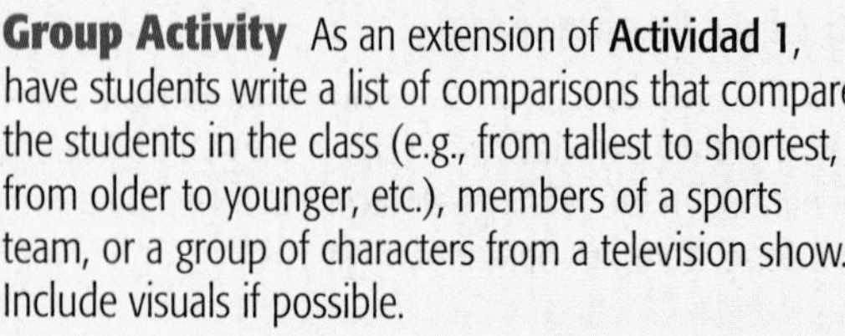

*Now you can...*
- talk about shopping for clothes.

*To review*
- the subjunctive with expressions of doubt, see p. 298.

## ACTIVIDAD 3 De compras

Isabel está comprando ropa en una tienda en Madrid. Completa los comentarios e identifica quién habla: ella o la dependienta.
*(Hint: Complete the comments and identify the speaker.)*

**modelo**

*creo / nuestra ropa / estar fenomenal*
*Creo que nuestra ropa está fenomenal. (dependienta)*

1. quizás / yo / poder ayudarte
2. creo / yo / necesitar un vestido más sencillo que éstos
3. tal vez / este vestido / quedarte bien
4. dudo / ustedes / tener el vestido en mi talla
5. creo / el vestido rojo / quedarme flojo
6. quizás / verte bien en el vestido con rayas
7. no es verdad / sus precios / ser bajos
8. es cierto / los zapatos / valer diez mil pesetas

*Now you can...*
- discuss ways to save and spend money.

*To review*
- the subjunctive with expressions of emotion, see p. 301.

## ACTIVIDAD 4 El dinero

Expresa tus opiniones sobre el dinero. *(Hint: Give your opinions.)*

**modelo**

*mi familia: guardar su dinero en el banco*
*Me gusta que mi familia guarde su dinero en el banco.*

**Me alegro de que...** **Me molesta que...** **Me sorprende que...** **Tengo miedo de que...** **Me gusta que...** **Siento que...**

1. el banco: no estar abierto los fines de semana
2. los bancos: darles préstamos a los estudiantes
3. el cajero automático: no funcionar
4. yo: tener mucho dinero en mi cuenta de ahorros
5. mis amigos: gastar mucho dinero en su ropa
6. los cajeros: no saber usar la caja registradora
7. yo: no ahorrar suficiente dinero para mis vacaciones
8. mis padres: prestarme dinero



## Teaching All Students

**Extra Help** Give students an expression and ask them to complete the sentence, e.g., **Dudo que..., Es necesario que..., Pido que..., Es raro que...**

**Challenge** Have students create a quiz on the subjunctive. They should have questions which use expressions of doubt and emotion, as well as questions which do not require the subjunctive. Students can administer the quiz.

**Multiple Intelligences**

**Verbal** Write a list of logical endings that could follow expressions with the subjunctive, then ask students to write a beginning for each ending, e.g., **... tenga paciencia. = Es raro que él no tenga paciencia. ... estudien mucho = Es dudoso que ellos estudien mucho.**

### ACTIVIDAD 2 Answers

1. Es cierto que los jóvenes españoles caminan mucho.
2. No es verdad que las tiendas españolas estén abiertas toda la noche.
3. No creo que pocos estudiantes quieran viajar a España.
4. No es cierto que los mejores futbolistas vivan en España.
5. Creo que podemos usar cheques de viajero en España.
6. Es verdad que muchos españoles usan ropa elegante.

### ACTIVIDAD 3 Answers

1. Quizás yo pueda ayudarte. (dependienta)
2. Creo que yo necesito un vestido más sencillo que éstos. (Isabel)
3. Tal vez este vestido te quede bien. (dependienta)
4. Dudo que ustedes tengan el vestido en mi talla. (Isabel)
5. Creo que el vestido rojo me queda flojo. (Isabel)
6. Quizás te veas bien en el vestido con rayas. (dependienta)
7. No es verdad que sus precios sean bajos. (Isabel)
8. Es cierto que los zapatos valen diez mil pesetas. (dependienta)

### ACTIVIDAD 4 Answers

*Answers will vary.*

1. [Me molesta que] el banco no esté abierto los fines de semana.
2. [Me alegro de que] los bancos les den préstamos a los estudiantes.
3. [Me molesta que] el cajero automático no funcione.
4. [Me sorprende que] (yo) tenga mucho dinero en mi cuenta de ahorros.
5. [Siento que] mis amigos gasten mucho dinero en su ropa.
6. [Me molesta que] los cajeros no sepan usar la caja registradora.
7. [Tengo miedo de que] yo no ahorre suficiente dinero para mis vacaciones.
8. [Me gusta que] mis padres me presten dinero.

## Block Schedule

**Process Time** Before assigning the **Repaso** for homework, give the class 5 minutes to read the instructions to each exercise. It will save precious time when you review these exercises beforehand. You won't have the students skipping sections because they didn't know what to do. (For additional activities, see **Block Scheduling Copymasters.**)

## Teaching Resource Options

### Print

Unit 4 Resource Book
- Audioscript, pp. 134–135
- Cooperative Quizzes, pp. 136–137
- Etapa Exam, Forms A and B, pp. 138–147
- *Examen para hispanohablantes,* pp. 148–152
- Portfolio Assessment, pp. 153–154
- Multiple Choice Test Questions, pp. 177–179
- Unit 4 Comprehensive Test, pp. 155–162
- *Prueba comprensiva para hispanohablantes,* Unit 4, pp. 163–170

### Audiovisual

OHT 136 (Quick Start)
Audio Program Cassette 20A / CD 20; (*Para hispanohablantes* Cassette 20A / CD 20)

### Technology

Electronic Teacher Tools/Test Generator
www.mcdougallittell.com

### Quick Start Review

Clothing

Use OHT 136 or write on board: Imagine your pen pal from Madrid wants to know the type of clothes you have in your closet. Name four items and describe them.

*Answers will vary.*
*Sample answer:* Tengo un chaleco negro. Tiene rayas y es mi favorito.

Actividad 5 and Actividad 6

**Rubric: Speaking**

| Criteria | Scale | |
|---|---|---|
| Fluency | 1 2 3 4 5 | A = 13–15 pts. |
| Vocabulary | 1 2 3 4 5 | B = 10–12 pts. |
| Pronunciation, rhythm | 1 2 3 4 5 | C = 7–9 pts. |
| | | D = 4–6 pts. |
| | | F = < 4 pts. |

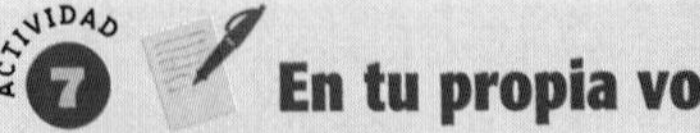

Actividad 7 En tu propia voz

**Rubric: Writing**

| Criteria | Scale | |
|---|---|---|
| Vocabulary use | 1 2 3 4 5 | A = 13–15 pts. |
| Accuracy | 1 2 3 4 5 | B = 10–12 pts. |
| Creativity, appearance | 1 2 3 4 5 | C = 7–9 pts. |
| | | D = 4–6 pts. |
| | | F = < 4 pts. |

## Actividad 5 En el almacén

**PARA CONVERSAR**
**STRATEGY: SPEAKING**
**Observe courtesies and exchange information** When shopping, you need to respond to certain questions: **¿En qué le puedo atender? ¿Qué talla/número usa? ¿Cómo prefiere pagar?** Be clear about your intentions: **Estoy mirando; Busco...** Give and ask for feedback: **¿Cómo me veo? Le queda ancho/apretado.** Compare items you might buy: **más elegante que..., un mejor precio que...** And remember that courtesy often insures good service!

Estás comprando ropa nueva para una fiesta elegante. Tu compañero(a) va a hacer el papel del (de la) dependiente(a). *(Hint: Shop for fancy clothes. Switch roles.)*

COMPRAR:
- un traje azul
- un chaleco con rayas
- una camisa blanca
- un par de zapatos número 10

## Actividad 6 Opiniones

Escribe cinco oraciones ciertas o falsas sobre el dinero, los bancos o las tiendas. Léelas. Tus amigos van a expresar sus opiniones. *(Hint: Express opinions about money, banks, or stores.)*

**modelo**

**Tú:** *Siempre uso cheques de viajero para comprar ropa.*
**Amigo(a) 1:** *Dudo que uses cheques de viajero para comprar ropa.*
**Amigo(a) 2:** *Me sorprende que uses cheques de viajero para comprar ropa.*
**Tú:** *No es verdad que use cheques de viajero para comprar ropa.*

## Actividad 7 *En tu propia voz*

**ESCRITURA** Quieres comprar ropa nueva para un evento especial, pero tus padres dicen que ya tienes algo apropiado. Haz un dibujo de la ropa que ya tienes y otro de la que quieres comprar. Entonces, escribe una comparación. *(Hint: Draw a picture of an outfit you already have and one that you want to buy. Compare the two.)*

**modelo**

*Mi vestido viejo es menos bonito que el vestido nuevo. El nuevo tiene rayas y es más flojo que el viejo porque es de una talla más grande. Yo me veo mejor en...*

### TÚ EN LA COMUNIDAD

**Graciela** tiene dieciséis años y es una estudiante de Florida. Usa el español para comunicarse con su madre y su abuela. También ayuda a algunos estudiantes de su escuela a aprender español. Graciela cuida a los niños de una familia hispanohablante de su vecindario. ¿Has hablado en español alguna vez con un niño?

## Classroom Community

**Games** This may be a good time to play one of the games described in the **Ampliación** section on p. 243B. Try the game called **¿Cuánto vale?** or **Voy de vacaciones y voy a llevar...**

**Paired Activity** Ask students to work with a partner and review the vocabulary list. Keep a list of the words that are more difficult to recall. As a class review the most "difficult" lists.

**Storytelling** Have students describe a recent shopping trip or trip to the bank using as many vocabulary words as they can from the list on p. 311. Students can work in small groups and tell each other their stories.

# En resumen
## REPASO DE VOCABULARIO

### MAKE COMPARISONS

**Unequal Comparisons**

**Ya sabes**

| | |
|---|---|
| **más que** | *more than* |
| **mayor que** | *older than* |
| **mejor que** | *better than* |
| **menor que** | *younger than* |
| **menos que** | *less than* |
| **peor que** | *worse than* |

**Equal Comparisons**

**Ya sabes**

| | |
|---|---|
| **tan… como** | *as… as* |
| **tanto(a, os, as)… como** | *as… as* |

### ASK FOR AND GIVE OPINIONS

**Expressions of Doubt**

| | |
|---|---|
| **dudar que…** | *to doubt that…* |
| **no es cierto que…** | *it is not certain that…* |
| **no es seguro que…** | *it is not certain that…* |
| **quizás** | *perhaps* |

**Expressions of Emotion**

| | |
|---|---|
| **alegrarse de que…** | *to be glad that…* |
| **sentir (e→ie, i) que…** | *to be sorry that…* |

**Ya sabes**

| | |
|---|---|
| **esperar que…** | *to hope that…* |
| **gustar** | *to like* |
| **molestar** | *to bother* |
| **no creer que…** | *to not believe that…* |
| **no es verdad que…** | *it is not true that…* |
| **sorprender** | *to surprise* |
| **tal vez** | *maybe* |
| **tener miedo** | *to be afraid* |

### TALK ABOUT SHOPPING

**At the Store**

| | |
|---|---|
| **abierto(a)** | *open* |
| **cerrado(a)** | *closed* |
| **el (la) cliente(a)** | *customer* |
| **el (la) dependiente(a)** | *salesperson* |
| **escoger** | *to choose* |
| **el número** | *shoe size* |
| **la talla** | *size (clothing)* |
| **un par de** | *a pair of* |
| **usar** | *to use, to wear, to take (a size)* |
| **vestirse (e→i, i)** | *to dress oneself* |
| **¿Cómo me veo?** | *How do I look?* |
| **¿Cómo te queda?** | *How does it look on you?* |
| **¿Me puede atender?** | *Can you help (wait on) me?* |

**Describing Clothing**

| | |
|---|---|
| **ancho(a)** | *wide* |
| **apretado(a)** | *tight* |
| **arreglarse** | *to get dressed up* |
| **el chaleco** | *vest* |
| **elegante** | *elegant* |
| **estrecho(a)** | *narrow* |
| **flojo(a)** | *loose* |
| **hacer juego con** | *to match with* |
| **oscuro(a)** | *dark* |
| **el pañuelo** | *scarf* |
| **las rayas** | *stripes* |
| **sencillo(a)** | *simple* |
| **el traje** | *suit* |
| **el zapato de tacón** | *high-heeled shoe* |

### DISCUSS SAVING AND SPENDING

**At the Bank**

| | |
|---|---|
| **el cajero automático** | *ATM* |
| **los cheques** | *checks* |
| **los cheques de viajero** | *traveler's checks* |
| **la cuenta de ahorros** | *savings account* |
| **el préstamo** | *loan* |
| **prestar** | *to lend* |

**Using Money**

| | |
|---|---|
| **ahorrar** | *to save* |
| **la caja registradora** | *cash register* |
| **el (la) cajero(a)** | *cashier* |
| **gastar** | *to spend* |
| **los gastos** | *expenses* |
| **guardar** | *to hold, to keep* |
| **suficiente** | *enough* |
| **tacaño(a)** | *stingy* |
| **valer** | *to be worth* |

### OTHER WORDS AND PHRASES

| | |
|---|---|
| **apenas** | *scarcely* |
| **de buen humor** | *in a good mood* |
| **de mal humor** | *in a bad mood* |

### Juego

¿Cómo le quedan a Arturo sus nuevos zapatos, pantalones y chaleco?

## Teaching Note: En tu propia voz

**Writing Strategy** Have students include informative details about both the old clothes and the clothes that they want to buy. The details must convince their parents that they should have the new outfit.

## Teaching Suggestions
### Reviewing Vocabulary

Have students take turns explaining in Spanish nouns and adjectives from the vocabulary list. Some students might like to create word puzzles to copy and share with the class.

## Juego
### Answer

Sus zapatos le quedan anchos, sus pantalones le quedan flojos y su chaleco le queda apretadísima y feísima.

## Project: Reviewing Etapa 3

Assign the following out-of-class activities:

- Interview a Spanish speaker about where he or she likes to shop.
- Bring in tourist information about shopping malls in Spain.
- Find out about the current exchange rate for Spanish **pesetas** (e.g., newspaper, Internet, etc.).
- Find more information on the largest banks in Spain.

**Extra Credit**

| | |
|---|---|
| Interview | 2 pts. |
| Information | 2 pts. |
| Exchange rate | 2 pts. |
| Banking | 2 pts. |

## Teaching All Students

**Extra Help** Ask students to study the vocabulary list. Close books. Read aloud a paragraph that incorporates numerous vocabulary words. Students listen and identify the words from the list.

**Challenge** Ask students to write a story comparing the clothing worn by students in the class (or two magazine photos) using as many vocabulary words as possible.

**Rubric: Writing**

| Criteria | Scale |
|---|---|
| Accuracy of information | 1 2 3 4 5 |
| Logical organization | 1 2 3 4 5 |
| Vocabulary use | 1 2 3 4 5 |

A = 13–15 pts.
B = 10–12 pts.
C = 7–9 pts.
D = 4–6 pts.
F = < 4 pts.

## Block Schedule

**Retention** Have students work in small groups to describe two objects or people using comparisons and superlatives without identifying them. Then have the groups present their descriptions to the class for them to identify the objects/people.

### Teaching Resource Options

**Print** 
Block Scheduling Copymasters

**Audiovisual**
**OHT** GO1–GO5, 136 (Quick Start)

**Technology**
www.mcdougallittell.com

### Quick Start Review

Comparisons

Use OHT 136 or write on the board: Write the name of your city/town, another city/town you know, and Madrid as column heads. Under each write words you associate with it. Use the information in your three columns to write comparisons.

*Answers will vary.*

### Teaching Strategy

**Prewriting**

- Have students gather brochures from several cities or towns to serve as models for their writing project. As a class they can brainstorm all the highlights of their city or town and organize them into categories in a chart.
- Point out the **PASS** list at the beginning of the page: **P**urpose, **A**udience, **S**ubject, **S**tructure. This will be their PASS key to a well-structured writing assignment.

**Post-Writing**

Have students exchange their drafts and practice their proofreading skills. Read their partner's draft aloud to hear as well as see any possible errors. Have them offer suggestions to improve the presentation of the town. Ask students to spend extra time on the introductory and closing remarks of the brochure.

UNIDAD 4

# En tu propia voz

**ESCRITURA**

## ¡Bienvenidos a nuestra ciudad!

Your local chamber of commerce needs brochures to attract Spanish-speaking tourists. Write a brochure to convince vacationers that your town is worth visiting.

**Purpose:** Provide information on local attractions
**Audience:** Potential Spanish-speaking vacationers
**Subject:** Your city or town
**Structure:** Tourist brochure

**PARA ESCRIBIR • STRATEGY: WRITING**

**Persuade your reader** A persuasive brochure offers simple, direct information in an intriguing format. Encourage the tourist to visit and explore. Give the reader strong images, both verbal and graphic, to make a lasting impression in his or her mind.

### Modelo del estudiante

The writer uses a catchy phrase to explain the purpose of the brochure.

**DENVER, Colorado**

¡Un lugar perfecto para visitar!

The author gives brief, concrete examples of attractions.

**Si te gusta la ciudad, ojalá que**

- te diviertas en Denver Zoo, uno de los parques zoológicos más grandes del país.
- visites el Museo de Historia Natural de Denver y el teatro IMAX.
- vayas al parque de diversiones Elitch Gardens, que tiene más de 40 atracciones, incluso la Torre de Desastre.

**Si te gusta el campo, sugerimos que**

The writer offers a wide variety of activities to appeal to all travelers.

- acampes en el Parque Nacional de Montañas Rocosas.
- navegues por rápidos.
- pasees en globo.

The author provides simple, straightforward directions to the city.

Estamos a media hora de Boulder hacia el sur por la carretera 36. ¡O puedes viajar en avión a nuestro nuevo aeropuerto internacional!



### Classroom Community 

**Paired Activity** Have students work with a partner to write an introduction to the brochure that attracts tourists' attention.

**Group Activity** Divide the class into 4 groups and have each group brainstorm a list of details for the guide. The 4 groups can be: **¿Por qué viene?, Actividades, Atracciones,** and **Direcciones**.

**Portfolio** Have students save this brochure for their portfolios. The work may also be submitted to the local chamber of commerce or kept on file at the local library. Students should be encouraged to use computers when possible for creating and "publishing" their pamphlets.

## Estrategias para escribir

### Antes de escribir...

An effective travel brochure provides important information travelers will need. Think about the highlights of your town and brainstorm the details for your brochure. Use a chart like this one to organize your ideas.

Columbus, Ohio

| Por qué viene | Actividades | Atracciones | Direcciones |
|---|---|---|---|
| • Es la ciudad capital. | • comer en restaurantes exquisitos | • la capital | • 171 hacia el norte de Cincinnati |
| • Hay mucho que hacer. | • bailar en las discotecas | • el barco Santa María | • 171 hacia el sur de Cleveland |
| • Es fácil de encontrar. | • remar en el río Scioto | • el museo de arte | • 170 hacia el este de Indianápolis |
| | | • COSI, el museo de ciencias | • 170 hacia el oeste de Pittsburgh |
| | | | |

### Revisiones

Share your draft with a partner. Then ask

- *How appealing is the presentation of my city or town?*
- *How well is the information organized? Are all the details appropriate?*
- *Is my explanation clear and easy to understand?*
- *What more would you like to know about my city?*

You may want to make revisions to your draft based on your partner's answers to the questions.

¡Ven a ¡visitar Columbus, Ohio!
¡Ojalá que vengas!
¿Quieres visitar una ciudad divertida? Sugerimos que escojas Columbus, porque ¡tenemos de todo! Es el capital de Ohio la y tiene muchas atracciones diferentes.
Qué ver:
Hay muchísimo que ver en la ciudad, así que es importante que decides qué vas a hacer antes de llegar. Hay dos museos, el museo de arte y museo de ciencias. el Puedes visitar también el edificio de la capital. Y si te gusta la historia, ¡

### La versión final

Before you create the final version of your brochure, look carefully for errors in grammar, spelling, punctuation, and usage. Mark them using the proofreading symbols (p. 97). Keep the following question in mind:

- *Did I use the subjunctive correctly?*

**Try this:** Underline verb phrases that express uncertainty, desire, doubt, or emotion. Be sure that the second verb is in the subjunctive, and that it is preceded by **que.**

Share your writing on www.mcdougallittell.com



### Supplementary Vocabulary

| | |
|---|---|
| **la carreterra** | highway |
| **en autobús (tren)** | by bus (train) |
| **el estadio** | stadium |

### Rubric: Writing

Let students know ahead of time which elements of their writing you will be evaluating. A global evaluation is more helpful to students than a correction of every mistake made. Consider the following in scoring compositions.

| | Sentences |
|---|---|
| 1 | Most not logical |
| 2 | In logical order |
| 3 | Flow purposefully |
| | **Details** |
| 1 | Few details |
| 2 | Sufficient basic details |
| 3 | Clear and vivid details |
| | **Organization** |
| 1 | Not well organized |
| 2 | Some organization |
| 3 | Strong organization |
| | **Accuracy** |
| 1 | Errors prevent comprehension |
| 2 | Some spelling and agreement errors throughout |
| 3 | Very few errors |

| Criteria | Scale | |
|---|---|---|
| Logical sentence order | 1 2 3 | A = 10–12 pts. |
| Clear and vivid detail | 1 2 3 | B = 7–9 pts. |
| Organization | 1 2 3 | C = 5–6 pts. |
| Accuracy | 1 2 3 | D = 4 pts. |
| | | F = < 4 pts. |

## Teaching All Students

**Extra Help** Review structures with students before writing:

- Use of **tú** commands
- Use of demonstrative adjectives and pronouns
- Use of the subjunctive in the right contexts

**Challenge** Have students research at least 5 reasons why Spanish speakers would want to visit their city or town. Have them find out about any cultural events, restaurants, publications, or places that might cater to Spanish speakers.

**Native Speakers** Have Spanish speakers develop a brochure about a city or town in their native country that would appeal to their classmates. They should follow the model outlined here.

## Block Schedule

**FunBreak** Have students illustrate their brochure with photos, drawings, or maps. They can post their finished projects on a bulletin board. (For additional activities, see **Block Scheduling Copymasters.**)

UNIDAD 5
# Cultural Opener

## Unit Theme
**Traveling in Costa Rica, talking about nature, ecology, and the environment, making predictions about the future.**

### Communication
- Describing geographic characteristics
- Making future plans and predictions
- Talking about nature and the environment
- Discussing outdoor activities
- Describing the weather
- Commenting on conservation, ecology, and the environment
- Talking about how you would solve problems

### Cultures
- Learning about the importance of conservation in Costa Rica
- Learning about wildlife, nature, and the environment in Costa Rica
- Learning about efforts to protect the environment in Central America

### Connections
- Connecting to Geography: Mapping and locating tropical forests
- Connecting to Social Studies: Developing a campaign to improve the environment

### Comparisons
- Comparing national parks and outdoor activities in Costa Rica and the U.S.
- Comparing geography and weather
- Comparing efforts to protect the environment

### Communities
- Using Spanish for personal enjoyment when traveling
- Using Spanish in volunteer work

## Teaching Resource Options
**Print**

Block Scheduling Copymasters

**Audiovisual** 

OHT 137–140

*Canciones* Cassette / CD

**Video Program** Videotape 5, 0:00 / Videodisc 3B

Search Chapter 4, Play to 5
U5 Cultural Introduction

UNIDAD 5

# SAN JOSÉ
## COSTA RICA
### LA NATURALEZA

**OBJECTIVES**

**ETAPA 1 — En el bosque tropical**
- Describe geographic characteristics
- Make future plans
- Talk about nature and the environment

**ETAPA 2 — Nuestro medio ambiente**
- Discuss outdoor activities
- Describe the weather
- Make predictions
- Talk about ecology

**ETAPA 3 — ¿Cómo será el futuro?**
- Comment on conservation and the environment
- Talk about how you would solve problems

**JOSÉ FIGUERES** En 1948 José Figueres, el presidente del país, eliminó el ejército (*army*). ¿Piensas que es bueno que un país no tenga ejército? Explica tu respuesta.

**GALLO PINTO** Este platillo nacional consiste en frijoles negros, arroz y cebolla. Frecuentemente se sirve con un desayuno que incluye huevos fritos y tortillas. ¿Tiene Estados Unidos un platillo nacional? ¿Cuál es?

314

## Classroom Community

**Group Activity** Ask small groups of students to make a Venn diagram. On one side, have them write the information about San José from the **Almanaque** and on the other side information from their town or city. Insert any similarities in the center.

**Paired Activity** Ask students to share three interesting facts about Costa Rica with a partner. Pairs should use a Venn diagram to compare their answers.

## ALMANAQUE

**Población:** 819.000
**Altura:** 1.150 metros (3.773 pies)
**Clima:** entre 23°C (73°F) y 27°C (81°F)
**Moneda:** el colón
**Comida típica:** coco, gallo pinto, chorreadas
**Gente famosa de Costa Rica:** José Figueres (político), Óscar Arias (político), Ana Istarú (actriz)

**¿Vas a San José?** ¡Habla con cuidado! No se usa la segunda persona **tú** sino **vos.** Pero ¡presta atención para no confundir las palabras **vos** y **voz**!

INTERNET Ve a www.mcdougallittell.com para más información sobre San José.

**FRANCISCO ZÚÑIGA** es uno de los artistas nacidos en Costa Rica de fama internacional. Él basa sus obras de arte en el cuerpo humano. Según este cuadro, ¿quiénes crees que son sus modelos?

**LA CERÁMICA DE NICOYA** El elemento indígena de Costa Rica se expresa en la cerámica de Nicoya. ¿Sabes qué grupos indígenas vivían en Centroamérica?

**EL QUETZAL** vive en el bosque nuboso de Monteverde. En peligro de extinción, hay aproximadamente mil quetzales en la reserva. Dicen que el quetzal es el pájaro más buscado de las Américas. ¿Por qué crees que dicen esto?

NICARAGUA
COSTA RICA
VOLCÁN POÁS
SAN JOSÉ
LIMÓN
MAR CARIBE
PUNTARENAS
CARTAGO
PANAMÁ
OCÉANO PACÍFICO
ISLA DEL COCO

**EL FÚTBOL** Como muchos países latinoamericanos, Costa Rica tiene un equipo nacional de fútbol. ¿Qué otros equipos nacionales de fútbol conoces tú?

315

## Teaching All Students

**Extra Help** Ask students to locate Costa Rica on a world map. Have them name the bordering countries.

**Native Speakers** Ask Spanish speakers what they know about Costa Rica. If any students have connections to Costa Rica, have them share with the class.

**Multiple Intelligences**

**Intrapersonal** Have students tell why they would or would not like to try **gallo pinto**. Would they eat it for breakfast? Is it like any other foods they usually eat?

**Musical/Rhythmic** Bring in a recording of rainforest sounds to share with the class. What moods does the music evoke?



## Teaching Suggestions
### Previewing the Unit

Tell students that this unit centers around Costa Rica and the environment. Ask students what they already know about Costa Rica or Central America. Use the video to preview the unit.

## Culture Highlights

- **JOSÉ FIGUERES,** known as "Don Pepe," was a central figure in Costa Rican politics from the 1940s–1970s. He eliminated the military and invested in education and public health. Costa Rica is known for its high literacy rate and low infant mortality rate.
- **GALLO PINTO** is one of Costa Rica's most common dishes. Costa Rica is also famous for its delicious coffee.
- **FRANCISCO ZÚÑIGA** (1912– ) is a successful sculptor, painter, and printmaker. The lithograph shown here is *Girls with Bread* (**Niñas con pan**).
- **NICOYA** is a peninsula on the northwestern Pacific coast of Costa Rica known for its beautiful beaches. Artists from this area have kept up the tradition of creating clay pottery in the manner of the pre-Columbian Chorotegan Indians.
- **EL QUETZAL** The world's largest population of the quetzal is found in the **Bosque Nuboso de Monteverde**. The quetzal is among the 450 species of birds found in this rain forest along with other rare wildlife. Its iridescent green tail feathers were used as adornments by Aztec and Mayan kings.
- **EL FÚTBOL** Soccer is Costa Rica's national sport and is played almost everywhere.

## Block Schedule

**Peer Teaching** Have students prepare the chapter by researching Costa Rica, San José, the tropics, and the environmental issues that are introduced. Each block, have a student do a 2–3 minute oral presentation on his/her topic. (For additional activities, see **Block Scheduling Copymasters.**)

# Ampliación

These activities may be used at various points in the Unit 5 sequence.

For Block Schedule, you may find that these projects will provide a welcome change of pace while reviewing and reinforcing the material presented in the unit. See the **Block Scheduling Copymasters**.

## PROJECTS

A LO MEJOR PIENSAN QUE UN POCO DE BASURA NO CAMBIARÁ NADA...

TAL VEZ ES LO QUE PIENSAN LOS DEMÁS.

La próxima vez... PIENSEN

Si ustedes nos ayudan, podremos preservar nuestras playas y ciudades. Si no, destruiremos nuestra tierra, la selva y toda la naturaleza. Será muy peligroso.

*Llamen a su representante legislativo. Esperamos su ayuda.*

**Create a recycling poster** in Spanish for your community. Include as many guidelines as possible for dealing with reuseable items.

PACING SUGGESTION: Upon completion of Etapa 3.

**Create a weather map** Create a weather map for Costa Rica. Divide the class into groups and assign each of them a city in Costa Rica. Have groups research the weather in their city, for both the rainy season (**invierno**) and the dry season (**verano**). Then have the class create two maps, illustrating the weather in all the cities in each season.

PACING SUGGESTION: Upon completion of Etapa 2.

## STORYTELLING

**En la tienda de campaña** After reviewing the vocabulary for camping and nature, model a mini-story (using puppets, student actors, or pictures from the text) that students will retell and revise:

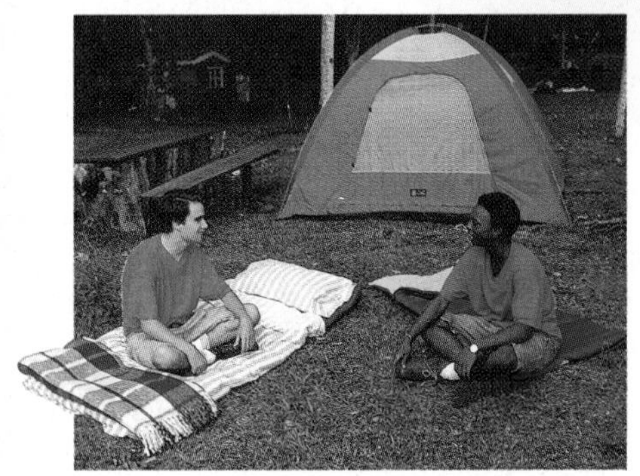

Este verano iremos a las montañas para las vacaciones. Espero que haga buen tiempo porque estaremos afuera todo el día y toda la noche. Durante el día vamos a pescar o escalar montañas. De noche nos sentaremos en frente de la fogata a comer. Dormiremos en la tienda de campaña con los sacos de dormir y sin almohada.

As you give your model, be sure to pause as the story is being told so that students may fill in words and act out gestures. Students should then write, narrate, and read aloud a longer main story. This new version should include vocabulary from **Unidad 5.**

**Cuando yo voy de vacaciones...**
Ask students to tell about some future plans they may have for vacationing or spending time outdoors. Have them use the future tense to discuss the adventure.

PACING SUGGESTION: Upon completion of Etapa 2.

## BULLETIN BOARDS / POSTERS

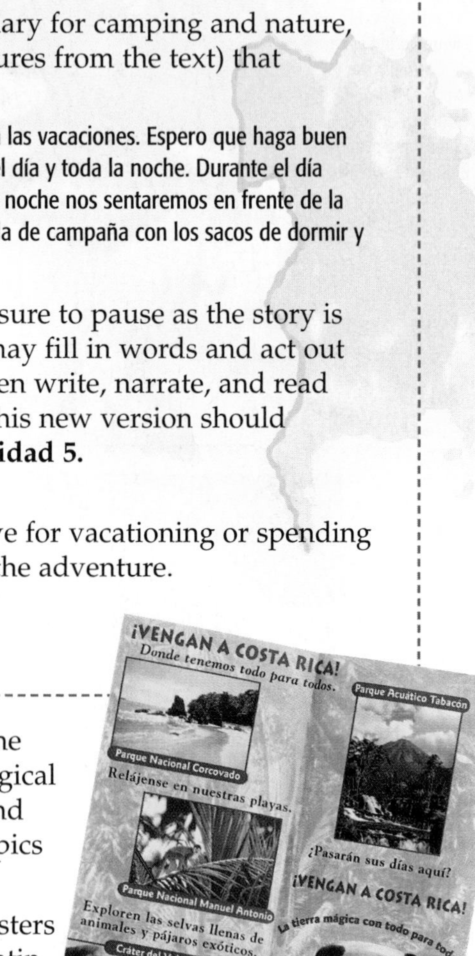

¡VENGAN A COSTA RICA!
Donde tenemos todo para todos.
Parque Acuático Tabacón
Parque Nacional Corcovado
Relájense en nuestras playas.
Parque Nacional Manuel Antonio
¿Pasarán sus días aquí?
¡VENGAN A COSTA RICA!
La tierra mágica con todo para todos.
Exploren las selvas llenas de animales y pájaros exóticos.
Cráter del Volcán Poás


**Bulletin Board** **Plan ahead:** Contact a travel agency or the Costa Rica Tourist Board for maps and brochures on ecological vacations to Costa Rica. Create a collage of places to see and things to do in Costa Rica that highlight environmental topics and conservation.

**Posters** Have students create • **Weather** maps • **Travel** posters for Costa Rica • **Advertisements** for outdoor vacations in Latin America • **Save-the-wildlife** posters for endangered plants or animals • **Community awareness** posters on recycling or preserving the environment

## GAMES

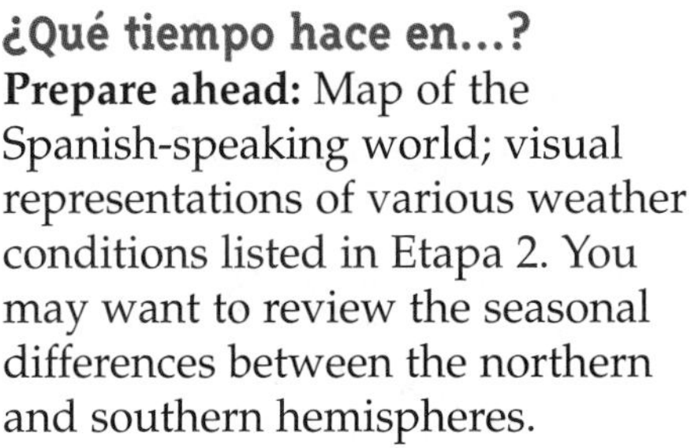

### ¿Cómo se llama este animal?

**Prepare ahead:** Gather pictures of different animals from the vocabulary list and put them facedown in a pile.

Divide the class in half. Tell students that a team member will choose a picture from the pile and try to act it out. The team member can imitate the actions and/or sounds of that animal. If the team guesses correctly, it gets a point. Each team will take turns, and the team with the most points wins. Give the class 10 minutes to play.

**PACING SUGGESTION:** Upon completion of Etapa 1.

### ¿Qué tiempo hace en...?

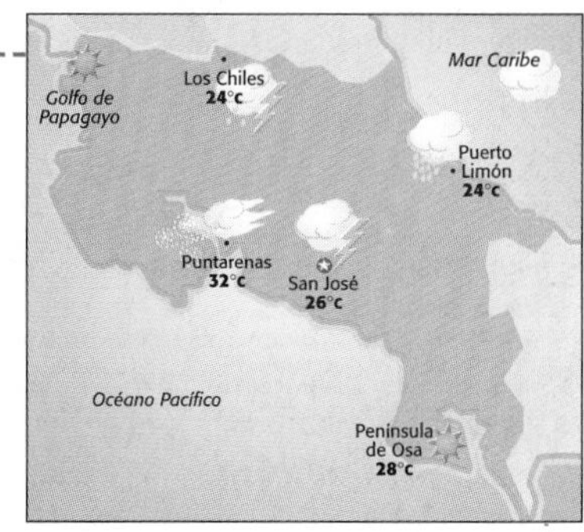


**Prepare ahead:** Map of the Spanish-speaking world; visual representations of various weather conditions listed in Etapa 2. You may want to review the seasonal differences between the northern and southern hemispheres.

Divide the class into two teams. Put the weather visuals faceup in the center of a table. One team member will point to a location on the map. The teacher will call out a month of the year. The rest of the teammates will pick out weather visuals that best describe the location's weather during that particular month. If the team guesses correctly, it gets a point. The team with the most points wins.

**PACING SUGGESTION:** Upon completion of Etapa 2.

## MUSIC

Much of Costa Rican music reflects African, pre-Columbian, and Spanish influences. The **marimba** (the xylophone, an instrument originally from Africa) and the drum are popular in some coastal Costa Rican music. The guitar is very popular; it is used in the **Punto Guanacaste**, the national folk dance of Costa Rica that consists of a heel-and-toe stomping dance for couples. Some pre-Columbian instruments used in folkloric music and dance include the **chirimia** (oboe) and the **quijongo** (a single-string bow on a gourd).

## HANDS-ON CRAFTS

More than 850 species of birds and hundreds of species of flowers have been identified in Costa Rica, including many orchids. Have students research some of the exotic birds or flowers found in the Costa Rican countryside and draw or paint them in color. You can decorate a bulletin board with the colorful spread.

## RECIPE

The typical diet in Costa Rica consists of tortillas, rice, beans, tropical fruit, and bread. Mangoes, papayas, and bananas are found fresh throughout the country. Try this mango and black bean salsa for an easy appetizer to serve your class with nacho chips.

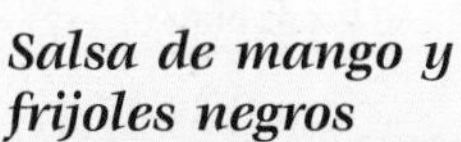

## Receta

***Salsa de mango y frijoles negros***

*1 lata de frijoles negros*
*1 lata de maíz*
*1 taza de mango, cortado en pedazos pequeños*
*1/3 taza de cilantro*
*1/3 taza de cebolla roja, picada*
*1/4 taza de jugo de limón verde*
*media taza de pimiento rojo, cortado en pedazos pequeños*

*Mezcle todos los ingredientes en una cacerola grande. Póngala en el refrigerador por lo menos una hora. Sirva la salsa con tortillas o con galletas. También se puede servir con pollo asado o con arroz.*

# Planning Guide CLASSROOM MANAGEMENT

## OBJECTIVES

| | |
|---|---|
| **Communication** | • Describe geographic characteristics *pp. 318–319, 320–321*<br>• Make future plans *pp. 324–325*<br>• Talk about nature and the environment *pp. 318–319, 320–321, 325* |
| **Grammar** | • The future tense *p. 324*<br>• Expressions with **por** *p. 326*<br>• Nosotros commands *p. 328* |
| **Culture** | • El voseo *p. 322*<br>• Cristobal Colón *p. 327*<br>• Los saludos *p. 330*<br>• El Parque Nacional del Volcán Poás *pp. 332–333* |
| **Recycling** | • The subjunctive and the indicative<br>• Adjective agreement<br>• Making plans |

## STRATEGIES

| | |
|---|---|
| **Listening Strategies** | • Organize and summarize environmental information *p. 320* |
| **Speaking Strategies** | • Share personal plans and feelings *p. 330*<br>• Anticipate future plans *p. 336* |
| **Reading Strategies** | • Confirm or deny hearsay with reliable information *p. 332* |
| **Writing Strategies** | • Use a story map to make predictions *Actividad 7, TE p. 336* |
| **Connecting Cultures Strategies** | • Recognize unique natural wonders *TE p. 332*<br>• Research the tropical rain forests throughout the world *p. 336* |

## PROGRAM RESOURCES

### Print

- *Más práctica* Workbook PE *pp. 113–120*
- Block Scheduling Copymasters *pp. 105–112*
- Unit 5 Resource Book
  *Más práctica* Workbook TE *pp. 1–8*
  *Cuaderno para hispanohablantes* TE *pp. 9–16*

Information Gap Activities *pp. 17–20*
Family Involvement *pp. 21–22*
Video Activities *pp. 23–25*
Videoscript *pp. 26–27*
Audioscript *pp. 28–32*
Assessment Program, Unit 5 Etapa 1 *pp. 33–51, 170–172*
Answer Keys *pp. 179–180, 184*

### Audiovisual

- Audio Program Cassette 13A, 13B / CD 13
- *Canciones* Cassette/CD
- Video Program Videotape 5 / Videodisc 3B
- Overhead Transparencies M1–M5; 137–150

### Technology

- Electronic Teacher Tools/Test Generator
- *Intrigas y aventuras* CD-ROM, Disc 2
-  www.mcdougallittell.com

### Assessment Program Options

- Cooperative Quizzes (Unit 5 Resource Book)
- Etapa Exam Forms A and B (Unit 5 Resource Book)
- *Examen para hispanohablantes* (Unit 5 Resource Book)
- Portfolio Assessment (Unit 5 Resource Book)
- Multiple Choice Test Questions (Unit 5 Resource Book)
- Audio Program Cassette 20A / CD 20
- Electronic Teacher Tools/Test Generator

### Native Speakers

- *Cuaderno para hispanohablantes* PE *pp. 113–120*
- *Cuaderno para hispanohablantes* TE (Unit 5 Resource Book)
- *Examen para hispanohablantes* (Unit 5 Resource Book)
- Audio Program *(Para hispanohablantes)* Cassettes 13B, 20A / CD 13, CD 20
- Audioscript (Unit 5 Resource Book)

# Student Text Listening Activity Scripts

##  Videoscript: Diálogo *pages 320–321*

• Videotape 5, 3:17 • Videodisc 3B

**Search Chapter 6, Play to end. U5E1, En vivo (Dialog)**

• Use the videoscript with **Actividades 1, 2** *page 322*

**Francisco:** ¡Qué bella es Costa Rica! Y este parque es fenomenal. Mi artículo sobre la conservación y el Volcán Poás será fantástico. Gracias por traerme aquí, Amalia.

**Amalia:** Con mucho gusto, Francisco. Como verás, conservar la naturaleza es muy importante para nosotros aquí en Costa Rica. Y mi hija Cecilia trabaja aquí este verano como guía. ¡Está perfecto! Bueno, esperemos a Cecilia aquí, ¿no?

**Francisco:** ¿Hay muchas diferencias de clima en Costa Rica?

**Amalia:** Pues sí, tenemos zonas húmedas, como ésta, en que crecen muchas plantas tropicales, y zonas áridas también. En el bosque tropical seco, llueve muy poco durante el año. Ah, aquí viene Cecilia.

**Cecilia:** Hola, mamá. Y vos debés ser Francisco García. Mi madre me dijo que venías hoy.

**Francisco:** Sí, soy Francisco. Es un placer, Cecilia.

**Cecilia:** Igualmente, Francisco.

**Amalia:** Cecilia te puede explicar mucho sobre el parque. Estudia biología en la universidad. Bueno, Ceci, comencemos con el tour, ¿no?

**Cecilia:** Sí, vamos. Ah, Francisco... ¿llevás botas? Las necesitarás. Vamos a caminar por tierra mojada.

**Francisco:** Sí, llevo botas.

**Cecilia:** Bueno, vamos.

**Francisco:** ¿A qué altura estamos?

**Cecilia:** Más o menos a 2.000 metros sobre el nivel del mar. ¿Por qué? ¿Estás cansado? Si querés, regresamos.

**Francisco:** No, no estoy cansado. Pero creo que la altura me afecta un poco.

**Amalia:** Pues, es natural que te afecte. Miami está al nivel del mar. Necesitás tiempo para acostumbrarte.

**Cecilia:** Bueno. Como decía, en este parque encontrarás diversos animales y plantas silvestres. Los animales son un poco tímidos. Pero si tenemos mucha suerte, verás tal vez una tortuga o una serpiente. Y hay muchas ranas y pájaros.

**Francisco:** ¿Hay loros o tucanes aquí?

**Cecilia:** No, los loros y tucanes prefieren un clima más cálido.

**Francisco:** ¿Hay animales feroces?

**Cecilia:** Sí, algunos son feroces. Hay jaguares en otras partes del parque.

**Francisco:** ¡Uy, me gustaría ver un jaguar!

**Amalia:** Pues, los únicos jaguares que verás hoy están en las tiendas de regalos.

**Francisco:** ¿Qué otros animales hay aquí? ¿Hay monos?

**Cecilia:** Sí, hay monos de diversos tipos.

**Cecilia:** Sabés, Francisco, la conservación de la tierra es muy importante en Costa Rica. Proporcionalmente, este país tiene más áreas silvestres protegidas que cualquier otro país.

**Francisco:** No lo sabía. Es un hecho interesante. Lo apuntaré en mi cuaderno.

**Cecilia:** Es por eso que es tan importante preservar nuestros recursos naturales. Si no preservamos los recursos, los turistas no nos visitarán. Y los turistas son importantes para la economía.

**Francisco:** ¡Es increíble! No lo puedo creer. Estoy mirando el cráter de un volcán. En Miami tenemos muchas cosas, pero no hay volcanes.

**Amalia:** Sí, debe ser muy diferente. No conozco Miami. Pero iré el año que viene. Y Cecilia me acompañará.

**Francisco:** Pues, espero que me vengan a visitar.

**Amalia:** Gracias, Francisco. Nos encantaría.

**Cecilia:** Mamá...

**Cecilia:** Francisco...

**Amalia:** ¿Te gustaría ir de camping con nosotros este fin de semana? Hace rato que no vamos, y Cecilia tiene el fin de semana libre.

**Cecilia:** ¿Porqué no le preguntamos a mi amigo Fernando si quiere venir?

**Amalia:** Me parece bien.

**Francisco:** ¡Estupendo! Me encanta ir de camping. ¡Qué buen viaje es éste! Estoy aquí en este lindo lugar, iré de camping, y ahora tengo nuevos amigos.

##  Actividad 9 ¿Qué harán los estudiantes? *page 326*

**Estudiante 1:** ¿Tú crees que vale la pena quedarnos en un hotel?

**Estudiante 2:** ¡Claro que no! Eso costará demasiado y, además, no encontrarás hoteles cerca del bosque.

**Estudiante 1:** Bueno, espero que lleves algo en que podamos dormir. Es posible que llueva durante la noche.

**Estudiante 2:** No te preocupes tanto. Yo soy un experto en ir de camping. Y otra cosa, nos darán agua para cocinar y bañarnos pero no traigas tu secador de pelo como la otra vez. No será posible usar la electricidad.

**Estudiante 1:** Está bien. No te olvides que esta vez sacaremos muchas fotos de los pájaros, especialmente de tucanes y loros.

**Estudiante 2:** Pues claro. Y tú no te olvides de los otros animales salvajes. Estudiaremos a todos los que encontremos para terminar nuestro proyecto.

## Actividad 12 Me encanta la naturaleza *page 328*

**Padre:** Bueno, Francisco, ¿qué harán hoy?

**Francisco:** Por la manaña iremos a la selva y después al parque zoológico. En la selva encontraremos unas plantas con hojas muy grandes. También veremos loros y tucanes volando por los árboles.

**Padre:** ¿Loros y tucanes? ¡Es increíble! ¿Y qué verán en el zoológico?

**Francisco:** Veremos otros animales salvajes. ¡A mí me fascinan los leones!

**Padre:** Y mañana, ¿adónde irán?

**Francisco:** Amalia me dice que nos llevará a ver el volcán. Caminaremos muchísimo. El sendero es largo porque el volcán es alto.

**Padre:** ¿Caminarán todo el día?

**Francisco:** Sí, cuatro horas, pero si me siento mal por la altura, descansaré un rato.

**Padre:** Pues, hijo. Espero que se diviertan mucho. Hablaremos mañana por la noche. Adiós.

# Pacing Guide

## Sample Lesson Plan - 50 Minute Schedule

### DAY 1

**Unit Opener**

- Present the *Almanaque* and the cultural notes on pp. 314–315. 5 MIN.

**Etapa Opener**

- Quick Start Review (TE p. 316). 5 MIN.
- Have students look at the *Etapa* Opener and answer questions. 5 MIN.

**En contexto: Vocabulario**

- Quick Start Review (TE p. 318). 3 MIN.
- Have students use context and pictures to learn *Etapa* vocabulary. Answer questions, p. 319. 10 MIN.

**En vivo: Diálogo**

- Quick Start Review (TE p. 320). 2 MIN.
- Review Listening Strategy, p. 320. Play audio or show video for the dialog on pp. 320–321. 10 MIN.
- Replay and have students take on roles of characters. 10 MIN.

**Homework Option**

- Video Activities, Unit 5 Resource Book, pp. 23–25.

### DAY 2

**En acción: Vocabulario y Gramática**

- Check homework. 5 MIN.
- Quick Start Review (TE p. 322). 5 MIN.
- Ask students for a summary of *En vivo* dialog to check recall. Then have students answer Comprehension Questions (TE p. 323). 10 MIN.
- Replay the *En vivo* dialog using the audiovisual resources and have students do *Actividades* 1 and 2 orally. 10 MIN.
- Have students complete *Actividades* 3 and 4 in pairs. 10 MIN.
- Present *Gramática:* The Future Tense, p. 324, and then have students complete *Actividades* 5 and 6 in writing. 10 MIN.

**Homework Option**

- *Más práctica* Workbook, pp. 113–116. *Cuaderno para hispanohablantes,* p. 113.

### DAY 3

**En acción (cont.)**

- Check homework. 5 MIN.
- Quick Start Review (TE p. 326). 5 MIN.
- Review the vocabulary in the box on p. 325, then have students complete *Actividad* 7 in writing and *Actividad* 9 in pairs. 10 MIN.
- Play the audio and have students complete *Actividad* 8. 10 MIN.
- Present *Gramática:* Expressions with por, p. 326. 10 MIN.
- Have students do *Actividad* 10 in writing. 10 MIN.

**Homework Option**

- *Más práctica* Workbook, pp. 117–118. *Cuaderno para hispanohablantes,* pp. 115–116.

### DAY 4

**En acción (cont.)**

- Check homework. 3 MIN.
- Quick Start Review (TE p. 328). 2 MIN.
- Have students complete *Actividad* 11 in writing. 10 MIN.
- Play audio and have students complete *Actividad* 12. 10 MIN.
- Present *Gramática:* Nosotros Commands, and have students complete *Actividad* 13 in pairs. 10 MIN.
- Present vocabulary box on p. 329 and have students complete *Actividad* 14 and/or *Actividad* 15 in small groups. 10 MIN.
- Present Speaking Strategy, p. 330, and have students do *Actividad* 16 in pairs. 5 MIN.

**Homework Option**

- *Más práctica* Workbook, p. 119. *Cuaderno para hispanohablantes,* p. 117.

### DAY 5

**En acción (cont.)**

- Check homework. 5 MIN.
- Quick Start Review (TE p. 330). 5 MIN.
- Have students complete *Actividad* 17 in writing. 10 MIN.
- Have students complete *Actividad* 18 in small groups. 15 MIN.

**En voces: Lectura**

- Review Reading Strategy, p. 332, and have students read silently. 5 MIN.
- Have students read *El Parque Nacional del Volcán Poás* aloud taking turns. 10 MIN.

**Homework Option**

- Have students answer the *¿Comprendiste?* and *¿Qué piensas?* questions as written homework. *Más práctica* Workbook, p. 120. *Cuaderno para hispanohablantes,* pp. 114, 118.

### DAY 6

**En uso: Repaso y más comunicación**

- Check homework. 5 MIN.
- Quick Start Review (TE p. 334). 5 MIN.
- Review the *¿Comprendiste?* and *¿Qué piensas?* questions as a class. 10 MIN.
- Do *Actividades* 1 and 2 orally. 10 MIN.
- Do *Actividades* 3 and 4 in writing. 10 MIN.
- Review Speaking Strategy, p. 336. Then do *Actividad* 5 orally in pairs. 10 MIN.

**Homework Option**

- *Cuaderno para hispanohablantes,* pp. 119–120.

### DAY 7

**En uso (cont.)**

- Check homework. 5 MIN.
- Quick Start Review (TE p. 338). 5 MIN.
- Have students do *Actividad* 6 in groups of four. 10 MIN.

**En tu propia voz: Escritura**

- Start writing activity. 10 MIN.

**Ampliación**

- Use a suggested project, game, or activity (TE pp. 315A–315B). 20 MIN.

**Homework Option**

- Complete writing activity. Review for *Etapa* 1 Exam.

### DAY 8

**En resumen: Repaso de vocabulario**

- Check homework. 5 MIN.

**Conexiones**

- Read and discuss. 5 MIN.
- Review grammar questions, etc., as necessary. 10 MIN.
- Complete *Etapa* 1 Exam. 20 MIN.

**Ampliación**

- Use a suggested project, game, or activity (TE pp. 315A–315B). 10 MIN.

**Homework Option**

- Preview next *Etapa* Opener, pp. 338–339.

# Sample Lesson Plan - Block Schedule (90 minutes)

## DAY 1

***Unit Opener***

- Anticipate/Activate prior knowledge: Present the *Almanaque* and the cultural notes on pp. 314–315. Use Map OHTs as needed. **10 MIN.**

***Etapa Opener***

- Quick Start Review (TE p. 316). **5 MIN.**
- Have students look at the *Etapa* Opener and answer questions. **10 MIN.**

***En contexto: Vocabulario***

- Quick Start Review (TE p. 318). **5 MIN.**
- Have students use context and pictures to learn *Etapa* vocabulary. Answer questions, p. 319. **10 MIN.**

***En vivo: Diálogo***

- Quick Start Review (TE p. 320). **5 MIN.**
- Review Listening Strategy, p. 320. Play audio or show video for the dialog on pp. 320–321. **10 MIN.**
- Replay and have students take on roles of characters. **10 MIN.**
- Ask Comprehension Questions (TE p. 321). **10 MIN.**

***En acción: Vocabulario y Gramática***

- Quick Start Review (TE p. 322). **5 MIN.**
- Have students do *Actividades* 1 and 2 orally. **10 MIN.**

***Homework Option***

- Have students prepare two true/false or yes/no questions about the dialog. *Más práctica* Workbook, pp. 113–116. *Cuaderno para hispanohablantes*, p. 113.

## DAY 2

***En acción (cont.)***

- Check homework. **10 MIN.**
- Quick Start Review (TE p. 324). **5 MIN.**
- Have students complete *Actividades* 3 and 4 in pairs. **10 MIN.**
- Have students complete *Actividad* 5 in small groups. **5 MIN.**
- Present *Gramática:* The Future Tense, p. 324, and then have students complete *Actividad* 6 in writing. **10 MIN.**
- Review the vocabulary in the box on p. 325, then have students complete *Actividad* 7 in writing and *Actividad* 9 in pairs. **15 MIN.**
- Play the audio and have students complete *Actividad* 8. **10 MIN.**
- Present *Gramática:* Expressions with por, p. 326. **10 MIN.**
- Have students do *Actividades* 10 and 11 in writing. **15 MIN.**
- Use Block Scheduling Copymasters for variety.

***Homework Option***

- *Más práctica* Workbook, pp. 117–118. *Cuaderno para hispanohablantes*, pp. 115–116.

## DAY 3

***En acción (cont.)***

- Check homework. **10 MIN.**
- Quick Start Review (TE p. 328). **5 MIN.**
- Play audio and have students complete *Actividad* 12. **10 MIN.**
- Present *Gramática:* Nosotros Commands, and have students complete *Actividad* 13 in pairs. **10 MIN.**
- Present vocabulary box on p. 329 and have students complete *Actividad* 14 and/or *Actividad* 15 in small groups. **10 MIN.**
- Present Speaking Strategy, p. 330, and have students do *Actividad* 16 in pairs. **10 MIN.**
- Have students complete *Actividad* 17 in writing. **10 MIN.**
- Have students complete *Actividad* 18, then have some volunteers share their predictions with the class. **10 MIN.**
- Use Block Scheduling Copymasters for a change of pace as needed. **15 MIN.**

***Homework Option***

- *Más práctica* Workbook, pp. 119–120. *Cuaderno para hispanohablantes*, pp. 117–118.

## DAY 4

***En voces: Lectura***

- Check homework. **10 MIN.**
- Quick Start Review (TE p. 332). **5 MIN.**
- Review Reading Strategy, p. 332. **5 MIN.**
- Have students read *El Parque Nacional del Volcán Poás*. **20 MIN.**
- Call on volunteers to answer *¿Comprendiste?* questions. Refer back to the reading if students give the incorrect answer. **10 MIN.**
- Have students do the *¿Qué piensas?* activity in writing, then discuss in class. **10 MIN.**
- Optional: Storytelling: Have students retell main points in their own words. **10 MIN.**

***Ampliación***

- Use a suggested project, game, or activity (TE pp. 315A–315B). **20 MIN.**

***Homework Option***

- Have students complete *¿Qué piensas?* as written homework. *Cuaderno para hispanohablantes*, pp. 114, 119–120.

## DAY 5

***En uso: Repaso y más comunicación***

- Check homework. **10 MIN.**
- Quick Start Review (TE p. 334). **5 MIN.**
- Do *Actividades* 1 and 2 orally, and *Actividades* 3 and 4 in writing. **15 MIN.**
- Review Speaking Strategy, p. 336. Then do *Actividad* 5 orally in pairs and *Actividad* 6 in groups of four. **15 MIN.**

***Conexiones***

- Read and discuss. **5 MIN.**
- Review grammar questions, etc., as necessary. **10 MIN.**
- Complete *Etapa* 1 Exam. **20 MIN.**

***En tu propia voz: Escritura***

- Start writing activity. **10 MIN.**

***Homework Option***

- Finish writing activity and preview next *Etapa* Opener, pp. 338–339.

▼ Francisco, Cecilia y Amalia observan al volcán.

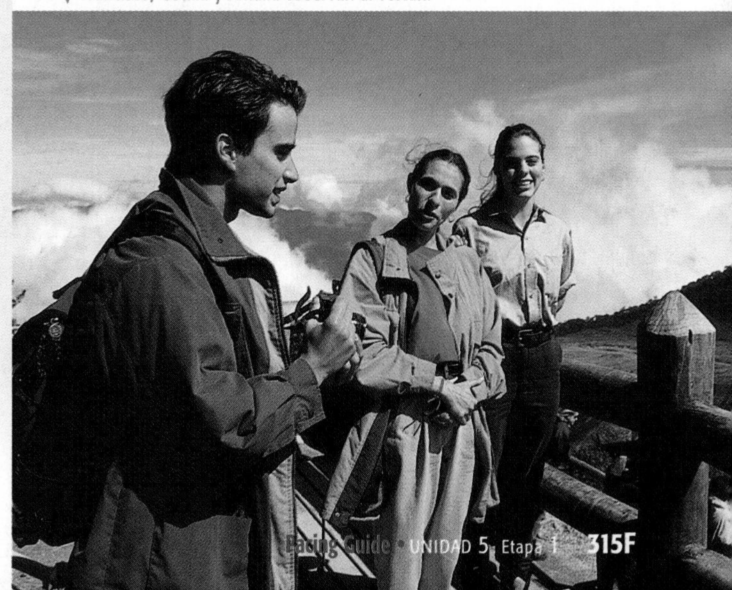

## Etapa Theme

**Describing geographic characteristics, making future plans, talking about nature and the environment**

## Grammar Objectives

- The future tense
- Expressions with **por**
- **Nosotros** commands

### Teaching Resource Options

**Print** 

Block Scheduling Copymasters

**Audiovisual** 

OHT 147 (Quick Start)

### Quick Start Review

Adjectives

Use OHT 147 or write on board: Write down three adjectives you might use to describe the location in the photo. The words could record physical characteristics such as size or color of certain features or they could express your impression of the scene, e.g., **bonito**. Choose one of the adjectives and write a sentence about the scene.

*Answers will vary.*

### Teaching Suggestions
**Previewing the Etapa**

- Ask students to study the photo on pp. 316–317 and identify where it was taken.
- Have students brainstorm about what activities the 3 people may be planning to do.
- Use the **¿Qué ves?** questions to start discussion.

### Cross Cultural Connections

Ask students to research the volcanoes in North America, Central America, and South America. Have them name the most recent volcanic eruptions in each region.

UNIDAD 5

# En el bosque tropical

- Describe geographic characteristics
- Make future plans
- Talk about nature and the environment

### ¿Qué ves?

Mira la foto y contesta las preguntas.

1. ¿Qué hacen las personas en esta foto?
2. ¿Qué tipo de ropa llevan?
3. ¿Qué actividad van a hacer?
4. Según el mapa, ¿dónde están estas personas?



### Classroom Management

**Planning Ahead** Prepare students to discuss any national parks they have visited. Have them collect any travel information on reservations or parks in their area. Discuss the activities one would do at these places.

**Peer Teaching** Have students work in pairs to create questions about visiting a national or state park near where they live. Then have them ask these questions of another pair of students.

## Culture Highlights

- **POÁS VOLCANO NATIONAL PARK** is the most visited park in Costa Rica. It is located only 37 miles north of San José, the capital. It is home to Poás Volcano, one of the world's largest volcanic craters that is still active. The volcano itself sits 2,700 meters (8,800 feet) high. There is also a sulfuric lake that bubbles and changes colors and, occasionally, shoots a large geyser of water.
- **VOLCANOES IN COSTA RICA** The highest volcano, Irazú, is also one of the most active. Irazú volcano has an elevation of 3,433 meters (or 11,260 feet).

## Supplementary Vocabulary

| | |
|---|---|
| **la cerca** | fence |
| **el cráter** | crater |
| **el humo** | smoke |
| **posar para la foto** | to pose for a photo |
| **la sombra** | shadow, shade |
| **el vapor** | steam |

## Teaching All Students

**Extra Help** Ask each student to share one sentence about the photo on pp. 316–317. Write the information on a transparency or on the board as a reference.

**Native Speakers** Ask Spanish speakers what they know about tropical rain forests. Have them list the animals or plants in Spanish that they might see upon visiting a tropical rain forest.

### Multiple Intelligences

**Visual** Ask students to compare the photo to another geologic formation, e.g., the Grand Canyon in the U.S. Have them describe each place in as much detail as they can.

**Naturalist** Discuss the phenomenon of a volcano and the effect it can have on the surrounding areas. Discuss active versus dormant volcanoes. If **Volcán Poás** erupted, what areas would it affect?

## Block Schedule

**Change of Pace** State various colors and ask the students to name animals or other things from the photos on pp. 316–317 of that color. (For additional activities, see **Block Scheduling Copymasters**.)

## Teaching Resource Options

**Print** 

Unit 5 Resource Book
- Video Activities, p. 23
- Videoscript, p. 26
- Audioscript, p. 28

**Audiovisual**

OHT 141, 142, 147 (Quick Start)
Audio Program Cassette 13A / CD 13
Video Program Videotape 5, 1:17 / Videodisc 3B

Search Chapter 5, Play to 6
U5E1, En contexto (Vocabulary)

**Technology**

*Intrigas y aventuras* CD-ROM, Disc 2

## Quick Start Review

Subjunctive with expressions of doubt

Use OHT 147 or write on board: Imagine your little brother is asking you questions about the rain forest. Answer all his questions with **Dudo que...** For example: **¿Hay arena en el bosque tropical? / Dudo que haya arena.**

1. ¿Hay piscinas en el bosque?
2. ¿Es pequeño el bosque tropical?
3. ¿Tienen supermercados allí?
4. ¿Nieva en el bosque?
5. ¿Se aburre la gente allí?

**Answers**
1. haya, 2. sea, 3. tengan, 4. nieve, 5. se aburra

## Language Note

Other words for *parrot* are **perico**, **cotorra**, and **papagayo**. Other words for *snake* are **víbora** and **culebra**.

# En contexto

## VOCABULARIO

Mira las fotos que Francisco sacó en el bosque tropical.

**¡Hola!** El bosque tropical es un lugar fascinante. Hay distintas plantas, animales **feroces** y animales amistosos. Acompáñame a ver qué hay…

la hoja

la mariposa

la planta silvestre

**A** **Las plantas silvestres** crecen entre **las piedras. Las mariposas** se esconden de otros animales entre **las hojas** de las plantas.

**B** **Las tortugas** y **las serpientes** andan por el agua y por **la tierra.**

la tortuga

la serpiente



## Classroom Community

**TPR** Ask students to take turns acting out the movements and sounds made by the animals on pp. 318–319. Have the class identify the animal.

**Storytelling** Have students take on the identity of animals presented on pp. 318–319. Have them "talk" to each other and tell a story of their lives. Encourage them to be creative!

D
Puedes ver monos, ranas o venados… animales amistosos.
el mono
el tucán
la rana
el loro
C
Y los tucanes y los loros vuelan por el aire.
el venado
E
¡Pero cuidado con los leones, los jaguares…
el jaguar
F
…y los lobos! ¡No estoy seguro de que sean tan amistosos!
el lobo
la leona

## Preguntas personales

1. ¿Recuerdas la última vez que visitaste un bosque o un zoológico? ¿Qué animales viste?
2. ¿Qué animales son amistosos con los seres humanos?
3. ¿Qué animales son feroces?
4. ¿Qué animal te gustaría tener como mascota (*pet*)? ¿Por qué?
5. Clasifica los animales según dónde viven: en el agua, en la tierra o en el aire. ¿Cuáles viven en más de un lugar? Si quieres, haz dibujos de tus clasificaciones.

## Teaching Suggestions
### Introducing Vocabulary

- Have students look at pp. 318–319. Use OHT 141–142 and Audiocassette 13A / CD 13 to present the vocabulary.
- Ask the Comprehension Questions in the margin of the Teacher's Edition on p. 319. You may write the questions on the board and have students work in small groups to answer them.
- Use the video vocabulary presentation for review and reinforcement.

## Comprehension Questions

1. ¿Hay una gran variedad de animales y plantas en el bosque tropical? **(Sí)**
2. ¿Son feroces todos los animales? **(No)**
3. ¿Es el árbol de bonsai una planta silvestre? **(No)**
4. ¿Vuelan las mariposas? **(Sí)**
5. ¿Anda rápidamente o lentamente la tortuga? **(lentamente)**
6. ¿Es exótico o común el tucán? **(exótico)**
7. ¿Cuál es un animal doméstico, el loro o el lobo? **(el loro)**
8. Cuando eras pequeño(a), ¿leías libros que contaba las aventuras de un mono? ¿Cómo se llamaba el mono? **(*Curious George*/Jorge el curioso)**
9. ¿Cómo es el león? ***(Answers will vary:* grande, feroz, fuerte)**
10. De los animales que ves en estas páginas, ¿cuáles te interesan más? ¿Por qué? ***(Answers will vary.)***

## Supplementary Vocabulary

| | |
|---|---|
| **la ardilla** | squirrel |
| **el cocodrilo** | crocodile |
| **el colibrí** | hummingbird |
| **el mapache** | raccoon |
| **el murciélago** | bat |
| **la oruga** | caterpillar |

(See p. R21 for additional animal words.)

## Teaching All Students

**Extra Help** Ask students simple **sí/no** questions, e.g., **¿Es el bosque tropical un lugar fascinante? (sí) ¿Se esconden los animales feroces de otros animales? (no) ¿Son simpáticos los monos? (sí) ¿Son amistosos los leones? (no)**

**Native Speakers** Ask Spanish speakers to name the animals or plants that are native to their country. Have them describe any national animal or tree.

**Challenge** Brainstorm a list of animals. Ask students to classify them according to category: **pájaro, insecto, mamífero, reptil** or **amfibio.**

### Multiple Intelligences

**Naturalist** Ask students what kinds of plants and animals are found in their area. Have them research what kinds of ferocious and friendly animals can be found in the wild.

## Block Schedule

**Retention** Encourage students to expand their vocabulary lists with animals that are of interest to them. Also, make a list of other items that may be needed in class discussions.

## Teaching Resource Options

**Print** 

Block Scheduling Copymasters
Unit 5 Resource Book
Video Activities, pp. 24–25
Videoscript, pp. 26–27
Audioscript, p. 28

**Audiovisual** 

OHT 145, 146, 147 (Quick Start)
Audio Program Cassette 13A / CD 13
Video Program Videotape 5, 3:17 / Videodisc 3B

Search Chapter 6, Play to end
U5E1, En vivo (Dialog)

**Technology**

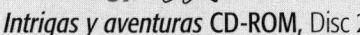

*Intrigas y aventuras* CD-ROM, Disc 2

## Quick Start Review

Clothing

Use OHT 147 or write on board: Look at the photos in the dialog and describe the clothing people are wearing. What are they carrying?

*Answers will vary but may include:*
chaqueta, pantalones, camisa, mochilas

## Teaching Suggestions
### Presenting the Dialog

- Prepare students for listening by focusing on the strategy in the **Para escuchar** box. You may want to review some of the new vocabulary, such as **el clima, la altura, animales silvestres, plantas silvestres, áreas protegidas**.
- Use the video, audiocassette, or CD to present the dialog. The video version offers expanded language opportunities.

# En vivo

**DIÁLOGO**

Francisco

Amalia

Cecilia

**PARA ESCUCHAR** • STRATEGY: LISTENING

**Organize and summarize environmental information** Cecilia gives information about the climate, plants, and animals of Costa Rica. Help Francisco organize this information in his notes:

1. **¿Cómo es el clima de Costa Rica?**
2. **¿Qué animales se pueden ver en el parque?**

Finally, find a statement in the dialog that summarizes Costa Rica's efforts to protect its environment.

## El Volcán Poás

1 ▶ Francisco: Este parque es fenomenal. Mi artículo sobre la conservación será fantástico.
Amalia: Mi hija Cecilia trabaja aquí este verano como guía. Bueno, esperemos a Cecilia aquí.

5 ▶ Francisco: ¿A qué altura estamos?
Cecilia: Más o menos a 2.000 metros sobre el nivel del mar.
Francisco: Creo que la altura me afecta un poco.
Amalia: Pues, es natural.

6 ▶ Cecilia: Como decía, encontrarás diversos animales y plantas silvestres. Si tenemos suerte, verás una tortuga o una serpiente. Y hay muchas ranas y pájaros.
Francisco: ¿Hay loros o tucanes?
Cecilia: No, prefieren un clima más cálido.

7 ▶ Francisco: ¿Hay animales feroces?
Cecilia: Sí, hay jaguares en otras partes del parque.
Francisco: ¿Hay monos?
Cecilia: Sí, hay monos de diversos tipos.



## Classroom Community 

**TPR** Play or read the dialog for the class. Divide the class into 3 groups. One group stands when they hear a description of an animal, another group stands when they hear a description of a plant, and the third group stands when there is a reference to climate.

**Group Activity** Divide the students into groups of three and let students take on the roles of the characters as they act out the dialog.

**Storytelling** Ask students to write 3 more captions, in which Francisco prepares for his camping trip, to continue the dialog. Students can include rough sketches to illustrate each new caption.

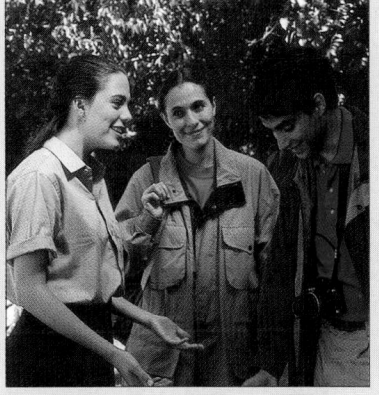

2 ▶ Francisco: ¿Hay muchas diferencias de clima en Costa Rica?
Amalia: Pues sí, tenemos zonas húmedas y zonas áridas. Ah, aquí viene Cecilia.

3 ▶ Cecilia: Vos debés ser Francisco García.
Francisco: Sí. Es un placer, Cecilia.
Cecilia: Igualmente, Francisco.
Amalia: Cecilia estudia biología en la universidad. Bueno, Ceci, comencemos con el tour, ¿no?

4 ▶ Cecilia: Sí, vamos. Francisco, ¿llevás botas? Las necesitarás. Vamos a caminar por tierra mojada.
Francisco: Sí, llevo botas.
Cecilia: Bueno, vamos.

8 ▶ Cecilia: Este país tiene más áreas silvestres protegidas que cualquier otro país.
Francisco: No lo sabía. Es un hecho interesante. Lo apuntaré en mi cuaderno.

9 ▶ Francisco: ¡Es increíble! No lo puedo creer. Estoy mirando el cráter de un volcán. En Miami no hay volcanes.
Amalia: Sí, debe ser muy diferente.
Francisco: Pues, espero que me vengan a visitar.

10 ▶ Amalia: ¿Te gustaría ir de camping con nosotros este fin de semana?
Francisco: ¡Estupendo! Me encanta ir de camping. ¡Qué buen viaje es éste!



## Video Synopsis

Francisco is writing an article on conservation in Costa Rica. He visits Amalia and her daughter, Cecilia, who works as a park ranger at Poás National Park and gives them a private tour. For a complete transcript of the video dialog, see p. 315D.

## Comprehension Questions

1. ¿Es Amalia la hermana de Cecilia? **(No)**
2. ¿Hay diferencias de clima en Costa Rica? **(Sí)**
3. ¿Estudia Cecilia biología? **(Sí)**
4. ¿Llevan botas o sandalias? **(botas)**
5. ¿Están en un lugar alto o bajo? **(alto)**
6. ¿Viven tucanes o tortugas en este parque? **(tortugas)**
7. ¿Tiene Costa Rica muchas áreas protegidas o muy pocas? **(muchas)**
8. ¿Qué cosa increíble miran? **(el cráter de un volcán)**
9. ¿Qué espera Francisco? **(que vengan a visitarlo en Miami)**
10. ¿Qué planean hacer el fin de semana? **(ir de camping)**

## Culture Highlights

● **PROTECTED PARKS** There are more than 32 national parks and refuges open to visitors in Costa Rica. Over 25% of the land in Costa Rica is protected. This is more than any other country in the world.

## Language Notes

The dialog uses the phrase **ir de camping**. **Acampar** is another acceptable term. Note that **Ceci** is a nickname for **Cecilia**.

## Gestures

Have students explain Francisco's gestures in frames 4 and 5.

## Teaching All Students

**Extra Help** Have students point out all the animals that are mentioned in the dialog.

**Native Speakers** Ask Spanish speakers about the **vos** form used by the Costa Ricans. See if they can give additional examples of its use in context. Then have Spanish speakers describe and give examples of any differences in their own Spanish dialect.

**Multiple Intelligences**

**Kinesthetic** Play the video again without sound and ask the students to role-play the dialog.

## Block Schedule

**Process Time** Have students ask each other simple **sí/no** questions. (Ex: **¿Lleva botas Francisco? (sí) ¿Está cansado Francisco? (sí) ¿Prefieren los loros y tucanes un clima frío? (no) ¿Hay monos en el bosque tropical? (sí)**

## Teaching Resource Options

**Print** 

Unit 5 Resource Book
Video Activities, pp. 24–25
Videoscript, pp. 26–27
Audioscript, p. 28

**Audiovisual**

OHT 148 (Quick Start)
Audio Program Cassette 13A / CD 13
Video Program Videotape 5, 3:17 / Videodisc 3B

**Technology** 

*Intrigas y aventuras* CD-ROM, Disc 2

## Quick Start Review

Leisure activities

Use OHT 148 or write on board: Which of the following activities would you do in Madrid and which would you do in Poás Volcano National Park? Are there some you could do in both places?

ir a una galería de arte
tomar fotos
mirar un partido de fútbol
dar un paseo
ir de camping

*Possible answers:*
Madrid: ir a una galería de arte, tomar fotos, mirar un partido de fútbol, dar un paseo. Poás Volcano National Park: tomar fotos, dar un paseo, ir de camping.

## Teaching Suggestions
### Comprehension Check

Have students write as many sentences as they can to describe the 3 characters in the dialog in as much detail as possible.

**Objective:** Controlled practice Listening comprehension/vocabulary

**Answers**

1. Cecilia
2. Cecilia
3. Francisco
4. Cecilia
5. Amalia
6. Francisco

# En acción
## VOCABULARIO Y GRAMÁTICA

**OBJECTIVES**
- Describe geographic characteristics
- Make future plans
- Talk about nature and the environment

ACTIVIDAD 1 

### ¿Quién habla?

**Escuchar** Según el diálogo, ¿quién habla: Francisco, Amalia o Cecilia?

Francisco

Amalia

Cecilia

1. «Vamos a caminar por tierra mojada.»
2. «Si tenemos suerte, verás una tortuga.»
3. «Creo que la altura me afecta un poco.»
4. «Este país tiene más áreas silvestres protegidas que cualquier otro país.»
5. «¿Te gustaría ir de camping con nosotros este fin de semana?»
6. «¡Qué buen viaje es éste!»

**TAMBIÉN SE DICE**

En el diálogo, en vez de usar la forma tradicional de **tú**, Cecilia conversa en una forma que es muy común en Costa Rica, la forma de **vos**: «Vos debés ser Francisco García.» Este dialecto tiene su origen en el lenguaje del castellano antiguo. Utiliza el pronombre **vos** y una variación del verbo. Repasa el diálogo para encontrar otros ejemplos de este dialecto.

ACTIVIDAD 2 

### ¿Qué sabes?

**Escuchar** Escoge las respuestas correctas, según el diálogo. ¡Ojo! Las oraciones tienen más de una respuesta correcta.

1. Cecilia…
   - a. es la hija de Amalia.
   - b. quiere ser periodista.
   - c. trabaja como guía en el parque.
   - d. invitó a Francisco a ir de camping.
2. Francisco…
   - a. va a escribir un artículo sobre las plantas silvestres.
   - b. está emocionado de ver el cráter del volcán.
   - c. siente los efectos de la altitud.
   - d. lleva sandalias porque hace calor.
3. Amalia…
   - a. observa un jaguar en el parque.
   - b. ayuda a Francisco a aprender sobre Costa Rica.
   - c. va a ir a Miami.
   - d. tiene una hija.
4. En Costa Rica…
   - a. no hay mucha variedad de clima.
   - b. conservar la tierra es muy importante.
   - c. hay loros y tucanes en el parque.
   - d. hay jaguares.



## Classroom Management

**Streamlining** Use the time for administrative tasks, such as taking attendance, for more than one purpose. With each name ask for a new word or phrase. Ask for questions from the homework or a piece of information about Costa Rica.

**Organizing Paired/Group Work** Actividad 3 can be done in pairs or threes to promote oral interaction. You may choose to have the group write the activity, but have them also say it out loud. If accountability is difficult with a particular group, have them record the exercise.

- *Use the future tense*
- *Use **por***
- *Use **nosotros** commands*

## Predicciones...

**Hablar** ¿Qué va a pasar cuando Francisco esté en Costa Rica? Tu compañero(a) te pregunta sobre las experiencias de Francisco y sus amigas. Contéstale usando las expresiones **creo que** y **dudo que.**

**modelo**

*¿Francisco va de camping con Amalia y Cecilia?*

**Compañero(a):** *¿Francisco va de camping con Amalia y Cecilia?*

**Tú:** *Sí, creo que va de camping con ellas. (Dudo que vaya de camping con ellas.)*

1. ¿Amalia encuentra un animal feroz en el bosque tropical?
2. ¿Francisco y Amalia observan las plantas silvestres?
3. ¿Llueve mucho?
4. ¿Se pierden los tres en el parque?
5. ¿Ven una serpiente en un árbol?
6. ¿Nadan en un río o un lago?
7. ¿Francisco y Cecilia caminan bajo las estrellas?
8. ¿Francisco y Cecilia se enamoran?

## ¿Cómo es?

**Hablar/Escribir** Francisco y Cecilia hablan de los animales que vieron en el parque zoológico, el bosque y la selva de Costa Rica. ¿Qué dicen? Usa las palabras de la lista.

bonito(a) · feroz · bello(a) · precioso(a) · feo(a) · tímido(a) · grande · pequeño(a)

**Objective:** Controlled practice
Listening comprehension/vocabulary

**Answers**

1. a, c
2. b, c
3. b, d
4. b, c, d

**Objective:** Transitional practice
Making predictions
Subjunctive and indicative

**Answers**

*Answers will vary.*

1. Sí, creo que encuentra un animal feroz. (No, dudo que encuentre…)
2. creo que las observan/dudo que las observen
3. creo que llueve/dudo que llueva
4. creo que se pierden/dudo que se pierdan
5. creo que ven/dudo que vean
6. creo que nadan/dudo que naden
7. creo que caminan/dudo que caminen
8. creo que se enamoran/dudo que se enamoren

**Objective:** Transitional practice
Talking about nature (animals)
Adjective agreement

**Answers**

*Answers will vary.*

1. El loro
2. La serpiente
3. El lobo
4. La tortuga
5. La mariposa
6. El venado

### Culture Highlights

- **COSTA RICANS** are referred to as **costarricenses** or sometimes as **ticos**. Review: **Guatemala, guatemaltecos(as); El Salvador, salvadoreños(as); Honduras, hondureños(as); Nicaragua, nicaragüenses;** and **Panamá, panameños(as).**

### Quick Wrap-up

Have students re-do **Actividad 3** using **Ojalá que** in each sentence. This will be a quick recycle of this use of the subjunctive. Ask students to come up with their own sentence using **Ojalá que**.

### Teaching All Students

**Extra Help** Ask students to list the geographic characteristics of Costa Rica and of their area. What are the similarities? Differences?

**Native Speakers** Ask Spanish speakers to respond to **Actividad 3** by relating the questions to the area their family comes from. For example, **Dudo que encuentre un animal feroz. Somos de una ciudad grande.**

**Multiple Intelligences**

**Visual Prepare Ahead:** Have students photocopy or cut out pictures of various areas from around the world–conceal the exact locations. Ask students to describe the geographical characteristics and to guess the locations. (Hint: National Geographic magazines from your library are a good source of material.)

### Block Schedule

**Peer Review** Have students work in pairs to do **Actividad 4**. Extend the activity by having students make a list of animals found in their local area. Have students describe these native animals using the same adjectives in the list.

## Teaching Resource Options

**Print** 

*Más práctica* Workbook PE, pp. 117–118
*Cuaderno para hispanohablantes* PE, pp. 115–116
Block Scheduling Copymasters
Unit 5 Resource Book
*Más práctica* Workbook TE, pp. 5–6
*Cuaderno para hispanohablantes* TE, pp. 11–12

**Audiovisual**

OHT 148 (Quick Start)

**Technology**

*Intrigas y aventuras* CD-ROM, Disc 2

## Quick Start Review

Making comparisons

Use OHT 148 or write on board: Imagine you and your family are trying to decide whether to get a dog or a cat for a pet. Write three sentences that compare the two. Use your own ideas or use some of the following adjectives. For example: **Un perro es más valiente que un gato.**

**inteligente / obediente / sucio / grande**

*Answers will vary.*

## Teaching Suggestions

- **Presenting the Future Tense** Use the verbs presented in the vocabulary of this chapter to model the conjugations of the future tense: **conservar, descubrir, preservar, valorar.**
- Have students review the dialog on pp. 320–321 to identify and list examples of the future tense.

**Objective:** Transitional practice **En contexto** vocabulary

### Answers

*Answers will vary.*

1. la rana
2. la tortuga
3. el mono
4. la piedra
5. la mariposa
6. el lobo

## ¡Juégalo!

**Hablar** Haz este juego de palabras con tus compañeros(as). Decide cuál de las palabras no pertenece al grupo y por qué.

**modelo**

*el jaguar, el venado, la selva, el león*

*La selva no pertenece porque no es animal.*

1. la rana, el árbol, la hoja, la planta
2. el venado, la tortuga, el león, el lobo
3. la serpiente, la rana, el mono, la tortuga
4. el bosque, la piedra, la montaña, el desierto
5. el lobo, la mariposa, el león, el jaguar
6. el lobo, el tucán, el loro, la mariposa

GRAMÁTICA

## The Future Tense

 **¿RECUERDAS?** You already know two ways to talk about something happening in the **future.** One way is by saying you are going to do something using

**ir a + infinitive**

Este fin de semana **vamos a acampar.**
*This weekend **we're going to** go camping.*

Another way to refer to the future is by using the **present tense.**

Me **voy** para Costa Rica el jueves por la mañana.
***I'm going** to Costa Rica on Thursday morning.*

**Llegan** al campamento mañana.
***They arrive** at the camp tomorrow.*

You can also use the **future tense** to talk about something that will happen in the future. The **future tense** in Spanish is the equivalent of the English construction *will* or *shall* plus a verb.

**Llegarán** al campamento mañana.
***They will arrive** at the camp tomorrow.*

To form the **future tense** of regular verbs, you:

| | future endings | |
|---|---|---|
| use the **infinitive** + | -é | -emos |
| | -ás | -éis |
| | -á | -án |

The **endings** for the future tense are the same for **-ar, -er,** and **-ir** verbs.

Cecilia says:

—No quiero ser periodista. **Estudiaré** para ser bióloga.
*I don't want to be a journalist. **I will study** to be a biologist.*

Amalia says:

—Después de tu visita a Costa Rica, **conocerás** bien el país.
*After your visit to Costa Rica, **you will know** the country well.*



## Classroom Community

**Learning Scenario** Divide the class into groups of 3. Tell them they need to present a list of environmental concerns and solutions (in the future tense) to the Spanish-speaking portion of their community. All students should contribute ideas for the list of concerns and solutions. S1 acts as the recorder, S2 acts as the proofreader and S3 acts as the presenter.

**Storytelling** Ask students to tell a short story describing the state of our environment ten years from now. They can describe the projected weather, the plant life, the animals, and/or the environmental concerns of that time. Encourage them to be creative!

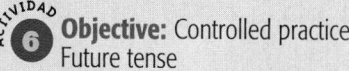

## Aventuras en Costa Rica

**Hablar/Escribir** Imagínate que tu clase está en Costa Rica con Francisco. Completa las oraciones explicando qué harán ustedes.

**modelo**

*Cecilia (trabajar) en el parque nacional todo el verano.*

*Cecilia trabajará en el parque nacional todo el verano.*

1. Yo (escribir) un artículo sobre la conservación.
2. Tú (acompañar) a Cecilia al cráter del volcán.
3. Nosotros (ir) a un campamento cerca de San José.
4. Amalia (sacar) fotos de las plantas silvestres.
5. Nosotros (ver) animales feroces en el parque zoológico.
6. Ustedes (observar) muchos monos y mariposas bonitas.
7. A todos les (gustar) ir de camping.
8. Yo (conocer) bien Costa Rica y su gente.

**MÁS PRÁCTICA** *cuaderno* pp. 117–118

**PARA HISPANOHABLANTES** *cuaderno* pp. 115–116

## La conservación

**Leer/Escribir** Estás de vacaciones en Costa Rica cuando ves este cartel. Escribe cinco metas (*goals*) para preservar el medio ambiente y evitar los problemas del desarrollo. Usa el vocabulario nuevo en tu respuesta.

**modelo**

*En Costa Rica, preservarán la selva en los parques nacionales.*

A LO MEJOR PIENSAN QUE UN POCO DE BASURA NO CAMBIARÁ NADA...
TAL VEZ ES LO QUE PIENSAN LOS DEMÁS.
La próxima vez... PIENSEN
Si ustedes nos ayudan, podremos preservar nuestras playas y ciudades. Si no, destruiremos nuestra tierra, la selva y toda la naturaleza. Será muy peligroso.
Llamen a su representante legislativo.
Esperamos su ayuda.


### Vocabulario

#### El medio ambiente

| | |
|---|---|
| **conservar** *to conserve* | **peligroso(a)** *dangerous* |
| **el desarrollo** *development* | **por todas partes** *everywhere* |
| **descubrir** *to discover* | **preservar** *to preserve* |
| **diverso(a)** *diverse* | **salvaje** *wild* |
| **el medio ambiente** *environment* | **la selva** *jungle* |
| **la naturaleza** *nature* | **valorar** *to appreciate* |

¿Qué piensas del medio ambiente?



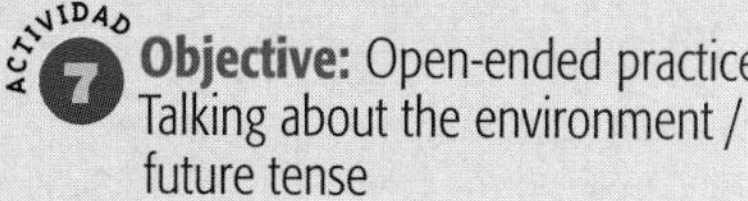

**Objective:** Controlled practice
Future tense

### Answers

1. Yo escribiré un artículo sobre la conservación.
2. Tú acompañarás a Cecilia al cráter del volcán.
3. Nosotros iremos a un campamento cerca de San José.
4. Amalia sacará fotos de las plantas silvestres.
5. Nosotros veremos animales feroces en el parque zoológico.
6. Ustedes observarán muchos monos y mariposas bonitas.
7. A todos les gustará ir de camping.
8. Yo conoceré bien Costa Rica y su gente.

**Actividad 7 Objective:** Open-ended practice
Talking about the environment / future tense

*Answers will vary.*

## Project

Have students create their own posters for protecting the environment. Have them use the vocabulary from the chapter and the future tense.

**Rubric: Writing**

| Criteria | Scale |
|---|---|
| Vocabulary use | 1 2 3 4 5 |
| Accuracy | 1 2 3 4 5 |
| Creativity, appearance | 1 2 3 4 5 |

A = 13–15 pts.
B = 10–12 pts.
C = 7–9 pts.
D = 4–6 pts.
F = < 4 pts.

## Block Schedule

**Change of Pace** For further practice of the future tense, form groups of 2–3 students. Have students imagine that they are camp counselors writing a daily schedule of activities to announce to the campers. They will conjugate the verbs in the future tense with **nosotros** as the subject. For example: **Jugaremos al fútbol a las nueve.** Possible verbs: **nadar, comer, observar, caminar, jugar, ir, cantar, acampar en las montañas.** (For additional activities, see **Block Scheduling Copymasters.**)

## Teaching All Students

**Extra Help** Ask students these simple **sí/no** questions using the future tense: **¿Estudiarás para el examen mañana? ¿Escribirás en español? ¿Hablará usted en francés o español? ¿Comerán ustedes a las cinco? ¿Escucharán ustedes el casete otra vez?**

**Native Speakers** Have Spanish speakers give sample sentences using the words in the vocabulary box on p. 325. Ask them to add other expressions they might use when discussing the environment.

### Multiple Intelligences

**Verbal** Ask students to write a sentence describing the environment of the following places using the vocabulary list: **en un bosque tropical, en las montañas, en la ciudad, en mi pueblo/ciudad.**

**Visual** Ask students to draw a picture of the globe in the year 2025, labeling as many elements as possible in Spanish.

## Teaching Resource Options

**Print** 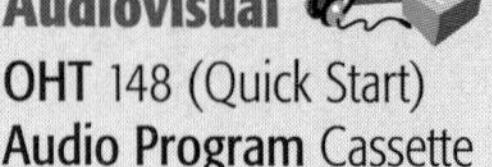

*Más práctica* Workbook PE, p. 119
*Cuaderno para hispanohablantes* PE, p. 117
Block Scheduling Copymasters
Unit 5 Resource Book
*Más práctica* Workbook TE, p. 7
*Cuaderno para hispanohablantes* TE, p. 13
Information Gap Activities, p. 17
Audioscript, p. 29

**Audiovisual**

OHT 148 (Quick Start)
Audio Program Cassette 13A / CD 13

**Technology**

*Intrigas y aventuras* CD-ROM, Disc 2

### Quick Start Review

Comparatives and superlatives

Use OHT 148 or write on board: Complete the following with a superlative.

For example: **Costa Rica es el país más interesante del mundo.**

1. El Everest es…
2. El bosque tropical es…
3. La mariposa es…
4. La tortuga es…

*Answers will vary.*

Actividad 8 **Objective:** Open-ended practice
Discussing future plans

**Answers**

*Answers will vary.*

1. ¿Trabajarás...? Sí, (No, no) trabajaré...
2. ¿Practicarás...? Sí, (No, no) practicaré...
3. ¿Viajarás...? Sí, (No, no) viajaré...
4. ¿Vivirás...? Sí, (No, no) viviré...
5. ¿Irás...? Sí, (No, no) iré...
6. ¿Buscarás...? Sí, (No, no) buscaré...

Actividad 9 **Objective:** Transitional practice
Listening comprehension

**Answers** (See script, TE p. 315D.)

1. a
2. b
3. a
4. a

Actividad 8 

## Los planes

**Hablar/Escribir** Habla con un(a) compañero(a) de sus planes para el futuro. Después escribe un resumen de la conversación.

*modelo*

**Tú:** *¿Tomarás una clase durante el verano?*
**Compañero(a):** *Sí, tomaré una clase de manejo.*

- tomar una clase de manejo
- practicar deportes
- trabajar en una oficina
- viajar a otro país
- buscar trabajo
- ir a la universidad
- vivir en otra ciudad o estado

**MÁS COMUNICACIÓN** p. R14

Actividad 9 

## ¿Qué harán los estudiantes?

**Escuchar** Estos estudiantes de la Universidad de San José conversan sobre sus planes. ¿Qué opción corresponde mejor?

1. a. Irán de camping.
   b. Se quedarán en un hotel.
2. a. Conservarán el agua.
   b. No usarán la electricidad.
3. a. Sacarán fotos de tucanes y loros.
   b. Estudiarán la tierra y las piedras.
4. a. Estudiarán los animales salvajes.
   b. Valorarán las plantas silvestres.

GRAMÁTICA

## Expressions with por

The preposition **por** has many different meanings. **Por** can be used to

- express **cause of** or **reason for** an action.

  **Por eso** *Onda Internacional* pidió un artículo sobre la conservación.
  ***That's why (for this reason)*** *Onda Internacional asked for an article on conservation.*

- express **periods of time.**

  Estuve en Costa Rica **por el mes de mayo.**
  *I was in Costa Rica* ***for (during) the month of May.***

  Saldremos del campamento el sábado **por la mañana.**
  *We'll leave the camp Saturday* ***in the morning.***

- express **means** of transportation or communication.

  Viajaremos **por tren.**
  *We will travel* ***by train.***

  Te llamaré **por teléfono** cuando regresemos de la selva.
  *I'll call you* ***by phone*** *when we return from the jungle.*

- express places to **move through.**

  **Caminaremos por** tierra mojada.
  ***We will walk through*** *wet ground.*

## Classroom Community

**Cooperative Learning** **Jigsaw:** Divide the class into 4 groups. Each group will skim one unit's **Diálogos** (2–3 students per **Etapa**) for uses of **por**. Students copy down the sentences, then as a group determine why **por** was used in each case. Then one student from each group reports the findings to the class.

**Paired Activity** Have students work in pairs to write as many sentences as they can using an expression with **por**. S1 starts a sentence that needs an expression with **por** and S2 completes the sentence using a logical expression with **por**. For example, S1: **Todos los días voy a la escuela....** S2: **por autobús.**

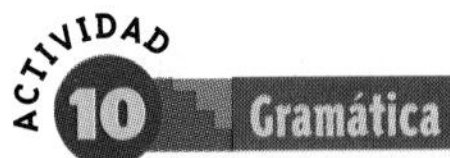

## En Costa Rica

**Escribir** Fernando, un amigo de Cecilia, es muy curioso y le hace muchas preguntas a Francisco. ¿Qué le dice Francisco?

**modelo**

*¿Cuánto tiempo estuviste en Los Ángeles? (una semana)*
*Estuve en Los Ángeles por una semana.*

1. ¿Cómo viajaste a Costa Rica? (avión)
2. ¿Por qué te cansaste? (la altura)
3. ¿Por dónde pasearon tú y Cecilia? (la selva)
4. ¿Por qué llevaste botas? (la tierra mojada)
5. ¿Cuánto tiempo estás aquí? (dos semanas)
6. ¿Cómo te comunicas con tu familia cuando estás aquí? (teléfono)
7. ¿Cuándo fuiste al parque? (la tarde)
8. ¿Por qué te duele el estómago? (comer tanto)

**MÁS PRÁCTICA** *cuaderno* p. 119
**PARA HISPANOHABLANTES** *cuaderno* p. 117

**NOTA CULTURAL**

**El 8 de septiembre de 1502** Cristóbal Colón llegó a lo que hoy es Puerto Limón y encontró a indígenas que usaban collares de oro y le contaron de minas de oro en el sur. Soñando con riquezas, Colón llamó a la tierra nueva «Costa Rica de Veragua». Los españoles nunca encontraron las riquezas minerales que imaginaba Colón, pero hoy Costa Rica ofrece una abundancia de naturaleza, animales y plantas que aprecia todo el mundo.

**ACTIVIDAD 11**

## Una carta a su prima

**Escribir** Francisco le escribió una carta especial a su prima. Escribe lo que quiere decir, cambiando los dibujos a expresiones con **por.**

Querida prima:

Yo viajé aquí __1__ (avión). Llegué __2__ (noche) y vi la misma luna que tú ves en Miami. Con mis nuevos amigos anduve __3__ (bosque) y saqué fotos de ranas y mariposas. ¡Qué divertido! Voy a estar aquí __4__ (calendario). Te mandaré otra carta __5__ (buzón) en unos días.

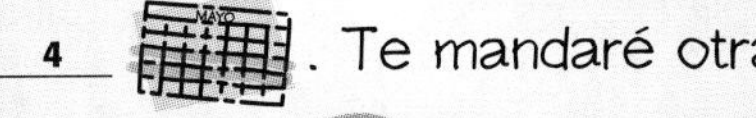

Un abrazo,
Francisco



### Teaching Suggestions
**Presenting Expressions with por**

Give several examples of each use of **por**. Reinforce them by prompting students to share information, e.g., **Yo voy a la escuela por autobús. ¿Y tú?**

### Supplementary Vocabulary

Other common expression with **por** include:

| | |
|---|---|
| **por otra parte** | on the other hand |
| **por completo** | completely |
| **por lo tanto** | therefore |
| **por supuesto** | of course |

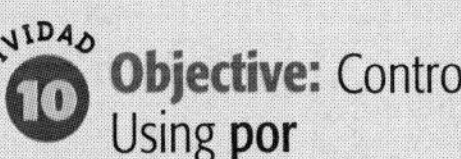

**Actividad 10 Objective:** Controlled practice
Using **por**

**Answers**
1. Viajé a Costa Rica por avión.
2. Me cansé por la altura.
3. Paseamos por la selva.
4. Caminaré por la tierra mojada.
5. Estoy aquí por dos semanas.
6. Me comunico con mi familia por teléfono.
7. Fui al parque por la tarde.
8. Me duele el estómago por comer tanto.

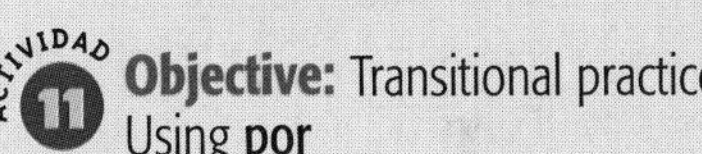

**Actividad 11 Objective:** Transitional practice
Using **por**

**Answers**
1. por avión
2. por la noche
3. por el bosque
4. por dos semanas
5. por correo

### Culture Highlights

● **HISTORY OF COSTA RICA** The first colony was called Cartago, located in the fertile central highlands. However, it took several decades for Spanish settlers to get used to the tropical climate and survive tropical diseases.

## Teaching All Students

**Extra Help** State sentences using **por** and ask students to give the reason for using it, e.g., **Iremos por avión** (when talking about transportation).

**Native Speakers** Have Spanish speakers point out any common expressions or uses of **por** that they might use regularly.

**Multiple Intelligences**

**Visual** Ask students to illustrate ways to use other expressions with **por**. (See **Actividad 11** for ideas.)

**Logical/Mathematical** Tell students that **por** is the way to say *times* when multiplying in Spanish. Have students write and demonstrate multiplication word problems in Spanish about nature and the environment.

### Block Schedule

**Change of Pace** Play a travel game with **por** expressions. The first person announces a trip, e.g., **Vamos a Costa Rica por un mes.** Another continues: **Viajaremos por avión.** Students take turns adding to the plans.

## Teaching Resource Options

**Print** 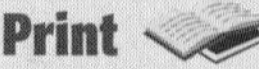

*Más práctica* Workbook PE, p. 120
*Cuaderno para hispanohablantes* PE, p. 118
Block Scheduling Copymasters
Unit 5 Resource Book
*Más práctica* Workbook TE, p. 8
*Cuaderno para hispanohablantes* TE, p. 14
Audioscript, p. 29

**Audiovisual**

OHT 149 (Quick Start)
Audio Program Cassette 13A / CD 13

**Technology**

*Intrigas y aventuras* CD-ROM, Disc 2

## Quick Start Review

Subjunctive with expressions of emotion

Use OHT 149 or write on board: Match one of the following phrases to each sentence below. Rewrite the sentence using that phrase and don't forget to use the subjunctive!

| | |
|---|---|
| Siento que | Me alegro de que |
| Tengo miedo que | Espero que |
| Me sorprende que | |

1. Ellos preservan la naturaleza.
2. Costa Rica tiene tantas áreas silvestres protegidas.
3. Nosotros podemos ver el cráter de un volcán.
4. Hay serpientes aquí.
5. No conservamos el medio ambiente.

**Answers**
*Sample answer:* 1. Me alegro de que preserven la naturaleza.

**Actividad 12 Objective:** Open-ended practice
Listening comprehension/nature

**Answers** (See script, TE p. 315D.)
Correct order: d, c, a, b

## Actividad 12 Me encanta la naturaleza

**Escuchar/Escribir** Francisco habla por teléfono con su padre de las actividades que hará en Costa Rica. Pon las fotos en orden según lo que escuchaste. Luego escribe una descripción original de cada foto.

a.

b.

c.

d.

## Gramática: Nosotros Commands

**¿RECUERDAS?** *p. 226* You have already learned to form the **subjunctive** of regular verbs. The nosotros command forms take the same endings.

When forming nosotros commands, use the same endings as you do with the **nosotros** form of the **subjunctive**.

- For -ar verbs: **infinitive** -ar ← -emos
- For -er and -ir verbs: **infinitive** -er or -ir ← -amos

¿Te interesa la naturaleza? **Escribamos** un artículo sobre los tucanes de Costa Rica.
*Are you interested in nature? **Let's write** an article about the toucans of Costa Rica.*

Remember that some verbs require spelling changes to keep pronunciation consistent.

**Comencemos** con el tour. ¡Vamos!
***Let's begin** the tour. **Let's go!***

The nosotros command form of the verb **ir** is **vamos**.

If the verb is used reflexively, the *let's do it* command ends in -nos.

***Remember to use an accent when you add -nos to the verb, so that the stress remains the same.***

***Also note that the -s of the verb ending is dropped.***

Estamos muy cansados; **sentémonos** a descansar.
*We're very tired; **let's sit** and rest.*



## Classroom Community

**Portfolios** Ask students to write a short paragraph entitled: **(No) Me gusta la naturaleza porque...**

**Rubric: Writing**

| Criteria | Scale |
|---|---|
| Vocabulary use | 1 2 3 4 5 |
| Accuracy | 1 2 3 4 5 |
| Creativity, appearance | 1 2 3 4 5 |

A = 13–15 pts.
B = 10–12 pts.
C = 7–9 pts.
D = 4–6 pts.
F = < 4 pts.

**Group Activity** Using the vocabulary list on p. 329, ask students to work in small groups and brainstorm words that can be associated with each item, e.g., **la altura: las montañas, los árboles, las rocas, las nubes...**, etc.

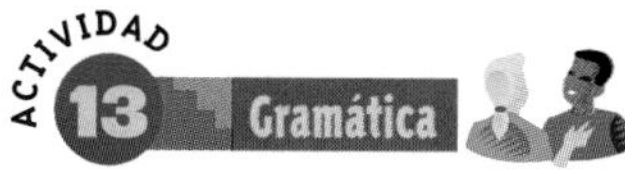

## Conversaciones por el sendero

**Hablar/Escribir** Amalia y su familia hablan mientras caminan por la selva. ¿Qué dicen? Completa sus comentarios según el modelo.

**modelo**

*Vamos a comer sobre esta piedra. (dejar la basura aquí después)*

**Compañero(a):** *Vamos a comer sobre esta piedra.*

**Tú:** *No dejemos la basura aquí después. (Dejemos la basura aquí después.)*

1. El valle es fenomenal. (sacar fotos)
2. La población valora la naturaleza. (preservar la belleza natural)
3. Las plantas son frágiles. (caminar fuera del sendero)
4. El clima es cálido aquí. (descansar en la sombra)
5. Estamos cansados. (subir la colina ahora)
6. La altura nos afecta. (sentarse en esta piedra)
7. Las flores silvestres son maravillosas. (cortarlas)
8. El medio ambiente es precioso. (conservar la naturaleza)

**MÁS PRÁCTICA** *cuaderno* p. 120

**PARA HISPANOHABLANTES** *cuaderno* p. 118

### Vocabulario

**La geografía**

- **la altura** *altitude, height*
- **la belleza** *beauty*
- **el clima** *climate*
- **la colina** *hill*
- **la isla** *island*
- **la población** *population*
- **el sendero** *path, trail*
- **la sombra** *shade, shadow*
- **el valle** *valley*

¿Puedes pensar en un símbolo o una acción para representar cada palabra?

## ¡Hagámoslo!

**Hablar/Escribir** Tú y tus amigos están de vacaciones en Costa Rica y hablan de sus planes. ¿Qué dicen?

**modelo**

*Levantarnos temprano para…*

*Levantémonos temprano para ver los animales nocturnos.*

1. Mirar…
2. Ponerse las botas para…
3. Observar las…
4. Ir a…
5. Sacar fotos de…
6. Sentarnos en…
7. Conservar…
8. Acampar…

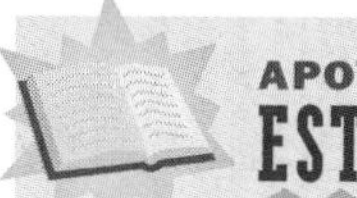

**APOYO PARA ESTUDIAR**

### Nosotros Commands

The **nosotros** commands and the subjunctive are formed the same way. For most verbs, the stem is from the **yo** form (**escrib**amos, **hag**amos). For stem-changing **-ar** and **-er** verbs, the stem is the infinitive, minus **-ar** or **-er** (**cerr**emos, **volv**amos). For stem-changing **-ir** verbs, there is a stem change from **e** to **i** (**sint**amos) or from **o** to **u** (**durm**amos).



### Teaching Suggestions
**Presenting Nosotros Commands**

- Point out to students that the **-s** is dropped from the verb before adding a reflexive pronoun: **sentémonos**. The **-s** is also dropped before the **se** pronoun is attached: **démoselo**.
- Remind students that an object pronoun of a negative command comes before the verb: **No lo miremos**.

**Objective:** Controlled practice **Nosotros** commands

**Answers**

1. Saquemos fotos.
2. Preservemos la belleza natural.
3. No caminemos fuera del sendero.
4. Descansemos en la sombra.
5. No subamos la colina ahora.
6. Sentémonos en esta piedra.
7. No las cortemos.
8. Conservemos la naturaleza.

**Objective:** Transitional practice **Nosotros** commands

**Answers**

*Answers will vary.*

1. Miremos…
2. Pongámonos las botas para…
3. Observemos las…
4. Vámos a…
5. Saquemos fotos de…
6. Sentémonos en…
7. Conservemos…
8. Acampemos…

### Teaching Note

Remind students that when forming the **nosotros** command for verbs ending in **-car**, **-gar**, or **-zar**, there is a spelling change in the stem.

| | |
|---|---|
| practicar | practiquemos |
| llegar | lleguemos |
| comenzar | comencemos |

### Block Schedule

**Process Time** Keep the routine of assigning journals as part of the block. For this unit, ask students to write in their journal about how they imagine their life will be in 5, 10, or 20 years (using the future).

### Teaching All Students

**Extra Help** Have students make flashcards of infinitive verbs and ask them to form **nosotros** commands.

**Native Speakers** Ask Spanish speakers to list the most common **nosotros** commands they hear in their community and explain the contexts in which they are used.

**Challenge** Ask students to design a travel brochure for a fictitious place based on the vocabulary on p. 329. Let them "sell" their trips to members of the class. (Hint: Look up travel brochures on the Internet for ideas.)

**Multiple Intelligences**

**Visual** Have the class decide on a visual symbol for each of the geography words. Ask students to draw/sketch the symbols and label each in Spanish.

## Teaching Resource Options

**Print** 

*Más práctica* Workbook PE, pp. 113–116
*Cuaderno para hispanohablantes* PE, pp. 113–114
Block Scheduling Copymasters
Unit 5 Resource Book
*Más práctica* Workbook TE, pp. 1–4
*Cuaderno para hispanohablantes* TE, pp. 9–10
Information Gap Activities, p. 18
Audioscript, pp. 30–31

**Audiovisual** 

OHT 143, 143A, 149 (Quick Start)
Audio Program Cassette 13B / CD 13;
(*Para hispanohablantes* Cassette 13B / CD 13)

**Technology**

*Intrigas y aventuras* CD-ROM, Disc 2

## Quick Start Review

Describing location

Use OHT 149 or write on board: Choose the phrase which best completes each sentence below.

1. Miremos la mariposa ___ las piedras. (debajo de / cerca de)
2. Saquemos una foto del tucán ___ del árbol. (dentro / encima)
3. Tomemos el sendero ___del lago. (alrededor / debajo)
4. Ponemos el almuerzo ____ la mochila. (dentro de / enfrente de)

**Answers**
1. cerca de, 2. encima, 3. alrededor, 4. dentro de

## Teaching Suggestions

Have students discuss the **Nota cultural** on p. 330. Have them discuss different ways of greeting friends, family, or people they don't know.

**Objective:** Open-ended practice
Making suggestions using **nosotros** commands

*Answers will vary but should include correct usage of **nosotros** commands.*

## ¡Vamos!

**Hablar/Escribir** Imagínate que estás en los siguientes lugares. ¿Qué (no) quieren hacer tú y tus amigos(as)? Haz dos sugerencias para cada lugar. Luego combina tu lista con las de unos(as) compañeros(as).

**modelo**

*la clase de español*
*¡Demos una fiesta!*
*No hagamos mucha tarea.*

1. el parque nacional
2. el desierto
3. una fiesta
4. las montañas
5. el centro comercial
6. la playa

**Los saludos** En todo el mundo, hay muchas maneras de saludar. En Estados Unidos frecuentemente la gente se saluda dándose la mano. En Japón se hacen una reverencia (*bow*). En Costa Rica, como en muchos otros países latinos, los hombres siempre se saludan dándose la mano. Las mujeres, por lo regular, no se dan la mano, sino que se besan en las mejillas (*cheeks*).

## ¡Viajemos a Costa Rica!

**PARA CONVERSAR • STRATEGY: SPEAKING**

**Share personal plans and feelings** All things are possible when planning a vacation from a brochure. Show variety in your actions (**dibujaré, treparé**) and anticipate how it will be (**será**). If you do not share the same ideas as your partner, say no. (**No iré al volcán. Será muy peligroso.**)

**Hablar/Leer** Estás planeando un viaje a Costa Rica. Mira este folleto turístico y dile a tu compañero(a) adónde irás y qué verás en tu viaje.

**modelo**

*Iré al Volcán Poás y veré el cráter. Será muy interesante…*

¡VENGAN A COSTA RICA!
Donde tenemos todo para todos.
Parque Acuático Tabacón
Parque Nacional Corcovado
Relájense en nuestras playas.
¿Pasarán sus días aquí?
¡VENGAN A COSTA RICA!
La tierra mágica con todo para todos.
Parque Nacional Manuel Antonio
Exploren las selvas llenas de animales y pájaros exóticos.
Cráter del Volcán Poás

## Classroom Community

**Portfolios** Ask students to write a short paragraph describing their favorite place from the list in **Actividad 15**.

**Rubric: Writing**

| Criteria | Scale |
|---|---|
| Vocabulary use | 1 2 3 4 5 |
| Accuracy | 1 2 3 4 5 |
| Creativity, appearance | 1 2 3 4 5 |

A = 13–15 pts.
B = 10–12 pts.
C = 7–9 pts.
D = 4–6 pts.
F = < 4 pts.

**TPR** Extend **Actividad 16** by having pairs act out one thing they plan to do on their trip.

## Una carta de Fernando

**Leer/Escribir** Fernando, un vecino de Amalia y Cecilia, te escribió una carta. Escríbele tú y contesta sus preguntas.

¡Hola!

¿Qué tal? Ojalá que estés muy bien. Te escribo porque estoy muy curioso. Ya sé un poco de Costa Rica, y quiero saber más de tu país y cultura. Deseo que me escribas y que contestes mis preguntas.

Primero, me interesa el medio ambiente donde vives. ¿Vives cerca de un bosque? ¿En una colina? ¿En el desierto? ¿Cómo es? ¿Hay animales diversos? ¿Cómo son las plantas? ¿Pasas mucho tiempo al aire libre? ¿Valora la gente de tu comunidad la naturaleza? ¿Hay programas para conservarla? ¿Qué haces para preservar el medio ambiente?

También me gustaría saber de los planes que tienen tú y tus amigos. ¿Dónde trabajarás tú? ¿Irán ustedes a la universidad? ¿Vivirán en la misma comunidad después de graduarse?

Bueno, espero recibir tu carta pronto. ¡Hasta entonces!

Fernando

## ¿Qué va a pasar?

**Hablar/Escribir** Con un grupo de compañeros(as), túrnense haciendo predicciones sobre el futuro. Luego hagan una lista de las predicciones que más les gusten.

**modelo**

*viajar a (Nueva York, Costa Rica, Madrid, ¿?)*

**Tú:** *Viajaré a Costa Rica para visitar los volcanes.*

**Compañero(a):** *Viajaré al sur de Francia para ir a la playa.*

1. vivir en (Nueva York, Fargo, Barcelona, ¿?)
2. manejar (un autobús, una moto, un carro deportivo, ¿?)
3. ser (periodista, presidente, deportista, ¿?)
4. comprar (una computadora, una casa grande, muchos discos compactos, ¿?)
5. escribir (una novela, una crítica, una carta a mi abuelita, ¿?)
6. dar (dinero a los pobres, regalos a mis amigos, una fiesta, ¿?)

**MÁS COMUNICACIÓN** p. R14

### Refrán

**Es el mismo gato, pero revuelto.**

Mira el dibujo y adivina el significado de «revuelto». A pesar de las características diferentes, ¿crees que el gato negro sea como el gato en el espejo? ¿En qué situación puedes usar este refrán? Piensa en tu día escolar o las relaciones con tus padres.

### Teaching All Students

**Extra Help** To help students to organize their thoughts for **Actividad 17**, have them make a list of answers to the questions first, then go back and incorporate them into a letter.

**Native Speakers** Have Spanish speakers explain the most common greetings in their native country between family members, friends, business associates, men, and women.

**Multiple Intelligences**

**Musical/Rhythmic** Ask students to choose musical selections which best describe each place listed in **Actividad 15**. Listen to some selections in class.

### Teaching Suggestions

In **Actividad 18**, have students write down a few ideas for themselves first, then have them share their predictions with others in their group.

### Culture Highlights

- **PARQUE NACIONAL CORCOVADO** is one of Costa Rica's wildest and most remote national parks with thick forests, deserted beaches, and swamps. It is located on the Osa Peninsula about 115 miles southeast of San José.
- **PARQUE NACIONAL MANUEL ANTONIO** (See **En colores** on pp. 354–355 and the note on TE p. 355 for more information on this park.)

**Objective:** Open-ended practice
Making future plans

*Answers will vary.*

**Rubric: Speaking**

| Criteria | Scale |
|---|---|
| Pronunciation | 1 2 3 4 5 |
| Accuracy | 1 2 3 4 5 |
| Intonation | 1 2 3 4 5 |

A = 13–15 pts.
B = 10–12 pts.
C = 7–9 pts.
D = 4–6 pts.
F = < 4 pts.

**Objective:** Open-ended practice
Talking about nature and the environment

*Answers will vary.*

**Objective:** Open-ended practice
Making future plans

**Answers**

*Answers will vary.*

1. Viviré en…
2. Manejaré…
3. Seré…
4. Compraré…
5. Escribiré…
6. Daré…

### Block Schedule

**Variation** Reinforce the **nosotros** command by having the class rewrite the agenda in **nosotros** commands before copying it down. For example, **practiquemos los verbos, repasemos la tarea y hagamos una actividad del libro.** (For additional activities, see **Block Scheduling Copymasters.**)

### Teaching Resource Options

**Print**

*Cuaderno para hispanohablantes* PE, pp. 119–120

Unit 5 Resource Book

*Cuaderno para hispanohablantes* TE, pp. 15–16

Audioscript, pp. 29–30

**Audiovisual**

OHT 149 (Quick Start)

Audio Program Cassette 13A / CD 13

### Quick Start Review

**Discussing nature and the environment**

Use OHT 149 or write on board: Complete the following sentences with the element of nature that matches each location.

el sistema solar
pirámides
el coquí, una rana especial
el cráter de un volcán
una vista del valle Yosemite

1. En El Yunque en Puerto Rico usted puede ver...
2. En el Observatorio de Arecibo en Puerto Rico usted puede ver...
3. En Teotihuacán, México usted puede ver...
4. Desde Glacier Point, Yosemite, California usted puede ver...
5. En el Parque Nacional del Volcán Poás usted puede ver...

**Answers**

1. el coquí, una rana especial, 2. el sistema solar, 3. pirámides, 4. una vista del valle Yosemite, 5. el cráter de un volcán

### Cross Cultural Connections

**Strategy: Recognize unique natural wonders.** Ask students if they have ever visited a volcano. If so, have them describe their visit and what they saw. Ask them to compare or contrast the volcano they visited with **Volcán Poás**, described here.

## En voces

**LECTURA**

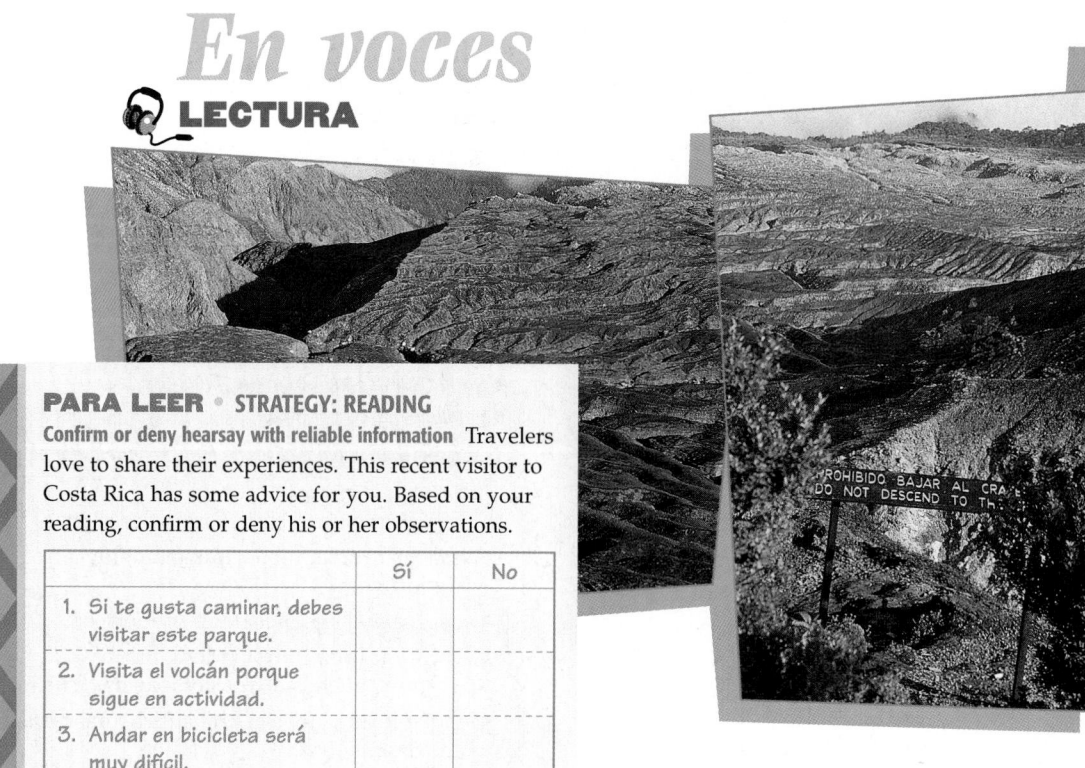

**PARA LEER • STRATEGY: READING**

**Confirm or deny hearsay with reliable information** Travelers love to share their experiences. This recent visitor to Costa Rica has some advice for you. Based on your reading, confirm or deny his or her observations.

| | Sí | No |
|---|---|---|
| 1. Si te gusta caminar, debes visitar este parque. | | |
| 2. Visita el volcán porque sigue en actividad. | | |
| 3. Andar en bicicleta será muy difícil. | | |

Do you think you should follow this person's advice? Why? Why not?

# El Parque Nacional del Volcán Poás

Para los amantes[1] de la naturaleza, no hay mejor lugar que Costa Rica. Este país centroamericano tiene un excelente sistema de parques nacionales. Uno de estos parques es el Parque Nacional del Volcán Poás que se encuentra al noroeste de San José. El parque tiene un volcán impresionante, un bosque nuboso[2] y un lago precioso de color verde-azul. Durante el viaje de San José a la cima[3] del volcán verán los panoramas bellos del valle Central.

[1] lovers [2] dwarf cloud forest [3] peak



### Classroom Community

**Paired Activity** Ask students to take turns reading aloud the first paragraph for pronunciation practice.

**Group Activity** Have students work in small groups to answer the **¿Qué piensas?** questions on p. 333.

¿A ti te gusta caminar? En el parque hay dos senderos. Uno te lleva a un gran lago dentro de un cráter extinto y otro te lleva a través del bosque nuboso.

El Volcán Poás tiene uno de los cráteres más grandes del mundo. La mayoría de las erupciones son del «tipo

géiser» y vienen del fondo de la laguna caliente. En este tipo de erupción, una columna de agua y ceniza[4] se levanta a diferentes alturas. En la erupción más grande (en 1910), la columna llegó a una altura de 8.000 metros sobre el nivel del cráter y llegó a caer a una distancia de 35 kilómetros. Todavía hoy echa humo[5].

[4] ash [5] emits smoke

## ¿Comprendiste?

1. ¿Dónde queda el Parque Nacional del Volcán Poás?
2. Además del volcán, ¿cuáles son otras atracciones en el Parque Nacional del Volcán Poás?
3. ¿Qué tiene de interés el Volcán Poás?

## ¿Qué piensas?

1. ¿Es el Parque Nacional del Volcán Poás un lugar donde podría ir toda la familia? ¿Por qué?
2. ¿Te gustaría ir al parque? ¿Por qué sí o no?



## Teaching All Students

**Extra Help** Have students pull out the main points of the article by reading the first and last sentences in each paragraph and making educated guesses about the content.

**Native Speakers** Have Spanish speakers comment on any geographical features that may be unique to their native country. Have them explain if these attractions are protected as part of a park.

**Challenge** Ask students to find out information about other national parks in Costa Rica (via the Internet or the library).

**Multiple Intelligences**

**Intrapersonal** Ask students to write a short paragraph on their plans to visit Costa Rica or another place of interest, e.g., **Yo viajaré a....**

## Teaching Suggestions

- **Prereading** Begin by asking students to scan the reading for cognates. Students should also review the chapter vocabulary lists and boxes on pp. 318–319, 325, and 329.
- **Strategy: Confirm or deny hearsay with reliable information** You can have students copy the travel writer's 3 suggestions in their notebook. Then have them identify the passage(s) from the reading that confirm or deny the suggestion.
- **Reading** Have students refer to a map of Costa Rica while reading this **Lectura**. Have them locate **San José, Volcán Poás,** and **el valle Central**.
- **Post-reading** Now have students go back and confirm or deny the 3 suggestions in the **Para leer** box. Then have them decide if they would take this visitor's advice and explain their answer.

## Culture Highlights

- **VOLCANOES IN COSTA RICA** Experts have found over 200 volcanic formations in Costa Rica.
- **BOSQUE NUBOSO** The area around Poás Volcano's crater is barren, but to the southeast visitors can hike through a dense, stunted forest in the clouds to Botos Lake, a cold-water lake.

## Interdisciplinary Connection

**Science** Have students research geysers in the U.S. to explore similarities with the geyser eruptions seen in **Volcán Poás**.

## ¿Comprendiste?

1. El Parque Nacional del Volcán Poás queda al noroeste de San José.
2. El parque tiene un bosque nuboso y un lago precioso de verde-azul.
3. El Volcán Poás tiene uno de los cráteres más grandes del mundo.

## Block Schedule

**Retention** Ask students to review the **Etapa** and make a list of the geographical characteristics they have learned about Costa Rica.

## Teaching Resource Options

**Print**  

Unit 5 Resource Book
Information Gap Activities, pp. 19–20
Family Involvement, pp. 21–22
Multiple Choice Test Questions, pp. 170–172

**Audiovisual** 

OHT 144, 144A, 150 (Quick Start)

**Technology** 

Electronic Teacher Tools/Test Generator
*Intrigas y aventuras* CD-ROM, Disc 2

### Quick Start Review

Talking about nature

Use OHT 150 or write on board: Imagine you are a photographer. Name five things you would take a picture of in the Costa Rican rain forest.

*Answers will vary.*

### Teaching Suggestions
**What Have Students Learned?**

- Have students look at the "Now you can..." notes listed on the left side of pp. 334–335. Point out that if they feel they need to review material before doing the activities, they should consult the "To review" notes.
- Use the video to review vocabulary and structures.

### Actividad 1 Answers

1. Nosotros descubriremos diversos animales y plantas.
2. Ustedes necesitarán botas para caminar por la tierra mojada.
3. Yo les mostraré un campamento cerca de San José.
4. Mi hermano encontrará lobos en el campamento.
5. La altura les afectará un poco.
6. Cecilia nos hablará del medio ambiente.

### Actividad 2 Answers

1. será
2. terminaré
3. volveré
4. esperarás
5. iremos
6. llevarán
7. veremos
8. escribiré



ETAPA 1

# En uso
## REPASO Y MÁS COMUNICACIÓN

**OBJECTIVES**

- Describe geographic characteristics
- Make future plans
- Talk about nature and the environment

*Now you can...*
- describe geographic characteristics.
- make future plans.
- talk about nature and the environment.

*To review*
- the future tense, see p. 324.

### Actividad 1 ¡Vamos a Costa Rica!

Imagínate que Francisco vuelve a Costa Rica con su familia. ¿Qué les dice?

**modelo**

*ustedes: ver el cráter del Volcán Poás*
*Ustedes verán el cráter del Volcán Poás.*

1. nosotros: descubrir diversos animales y plantas
2. ustedes: necesitar botas para caminar por la tierra mojada
3. yo: mostrarles un campamento cerca de San José
4. mi hermano: encontrar lobos en el campamento
5. la altura: afectarles un poco
6. Cecilia: hablarnos del medio ambiente

*Now you can...*
- make future plans.

*To review*
- the future tense, see p. 324.

### Actividad 2 Saludos de...

Francisco le escribe una carta a su amiga Alma. ¿Qué dice? Completa la carta con el futuro de los verbos.

Querida Alma:

Saludos de Costa Rica, un país bellísimo. Creo que mi artículo sobre la conservación __1__ (ser) fantástico. Yo lo __2__ (terminar) la próxima semana y __3__ (volver) a Miami el viernes. Tú me __4__ (esperar) en el aeropuerto, ¿no?

Este fin de semana Amalia, Cecilia y yo __5__ (ir) de camping. Ellos me __6__ (llevar) a un campamento cerca de San José. Allí nosotros __7__ (ver) más animales y plantas interesantes. Yo te __8__ (escribir) otra vez el lunes para contarte nuestras experiencias.

Con cariño, Francisco



### Classroom Community

**Learning Scenario** Divide students into pairs. Students should have already completed **Actividad 2** by completing the letter in the future tense. Tell them to now imagine that they are tutoring children in Spanish. (The children only know the present tense!) Using the letter from **Actividad 2**, pairs are to come up with an "answer sheet" of the verbs in the present tense for their tutees. S1 is the recorder and S2 is the presenter. Both students participate in generating answers. Have pairs then read their "answer sheets" to the class.

**Group Activity** Have students work in small groups to prioritize the measures to protect the environment listed in **Actividad 4** from the most important to the least important.

*Now you can...*
- make future plans.

*To review*
- **por,** see p. 326.

## ACTIVIDAD 3 Antes de la excursión

Cecilia habla con un grupo de turistas. Completa sus comentarios usando expresiones con **por.**

por correo   por tierra mojada

por teléfono  por la noche

por allí

**modelo**

*Todos caminaremos juntos _____.*
*Todos caminaremos juntos por allí.*

1. Ustedes necesitan llevar botas porque vamos a caminar _____.
2. También le mandaremos información _____.
3. Volveremos antes de las seis. No podemos estar en el parque _____.
4. Si usted quiere saber más sobre este parque o los otros, llámenos _____.

*Now you can...*
- talk about nature and the environment.

*To review*
- **nosotros** commands, see p. 328.

## ACTIVIDAD 4 El medio ambiente

¿Qué debemos hacer o no hacer para proteger el medio ambiente?

**modelo**

*cerrar los parques nacionales*
*¡No cerremos los parques nacionales!*

*proteger los animales salvajes*
*¡Protejamos los animales salvajes!*

1. valorar la belleza natural
2. preservar nuestros recursos naturales
3. cortar todos los árboles
4. ir de camping sin pensar en el medio ambiente
5. tener cuidado con la basura en los campamentos
6. dejar basura por todas partes
7. conservar las diversas plantas
8. estar informados sobre la conservación

### ACTIVIDAD 3 Answers

*Answers will vary.*
1. por tierra mojada
2. por correo
3. por la noche
4. por teléfono

### ACTIVIDAD 4 Answers

1. ¡Valoremos la belleza natural!
2. ¡Preservemos nuestros recursos naturales!
3. ¡No cortemos todos los árboles!
4. ¡No vayamos de camping sin pensar en el medio ambiente!
5. ¡Tengamos cuidado con la basura en los campamentos!
6. ¡No dejemos basura por todas partes!
7. ¡Conservemos las diversas plantas!
8. ¡Estemos informados sobre la conservación!

### Critical Thinking

Have students research and list other active and inactive volcanoes in Costa Rica. Have them list one interesting fact about each one and, if possible, have them determine when these volcanoes last erupted.

## Teaching All Students

**Extra Help** Have students go back to pp. 326–327 to review the expressions with **por**. Have them create sentences using at least 5 expressions with **por**.

**Native Speakers** Have Spanish speakers write at least 5 sentences using the future tense that will predict what people will do or see if they visit their native countries.

**Multiple Intelligences**

**Interpersonal** Divide the class into groups and have students debate/discuss from the point of view of industry and environmentalists. Then have students share their own views.

### Block Schedule

**Change of Pace** Remember to provide movement in each lesson. Have students do the **En uso** activities as pair work and ask them to pick a partner from across the room or behind them so they have to move around. At the end of each activity they must change partners to do the next one.

# UNIDAD 5 Etapa 1
# Review

## Teaching Resource Options

**Print**

Unit 5 Resource Book
- Audioscript, pp. 31–32
- Cooperative Quizzes, pp. 33–34
- Etapa Exam, Forms A and B, pp. 35–44
- *Examen para hispanohablantes,* pp. 45–49
- Portfolio Assessment, pp. 50–51
- Multiple Choice Test Questions, pp. 170–172

**Audiovisual**

OHT 141, 142, 150 (Quick Start)
Audio Program Cassette 20A / CD 20; (*Para hispanohablantes* Cassette 20A / CD 20)

**Technology**

Electronic Teacher Tools/Test Generator
www.mcdougallittell.com

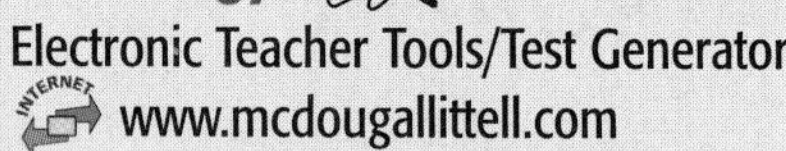

## Quick Start Review

Discussing leisure time, discussing the environment

Use OHT 150 or write on board: List three things people typically do on a camping trip. Use the infinitive in your responses.

*Answers will vary.*

**Actividad 5 and Actividad 6**

**Rubric: Speaking**

| Criteria | Scale | |
|---|---|---|
| Pronunciation | 1 2 3 4 5 | A = 13–15 pts. |
| Accuracy | 1 2 3 4 5 | B = 10–12 pts. |
| Intonation | 1 2 3 4 5 | C = 7–9 pts. |
| | | D = 4–6 pts. |
| | | F = < 4 pts. |

**Actividad 7 En tu propia voz**

**Rubric: Writing**

| Criteria | Scale | |
|---|---|---|
| Vocabulary use | 1 2 3 4 5 | A = 13–15 pts. |
| Accuracy | 1 2 3 4 5 | B = 10–12 pts. |
| Creativity, appearance | 1 2 3 4 5 | C = 7–9 pts. |
| | | D = 4–6 pts. |
| | | F = < 4 pts. |

## Teaching Note: En tu propia voz

**Writing Strategy** Have students create a story map (see p. 169), to set the scene and organize their predictions of the camping trip.

## Actividad 5 Actividades

**PARA CONVERSAR**

**STRATEGY: SPEAKING**

**Anticipate future plans** By looking ahead to summer vacation, you can plan for the real, the ideal, and the imaginary. Ask and answer questions that allow you and your partner to stretch your imaginations and set new goals:
- **¿(a)dónde ir / viajar / trabajar?**
- **¿qué hacer?**
- **¿cómo ganar... / ayudar... / mejorar...?**

Conversa con tu amigo(a) sobre sus planes para este verano y completa una tabla con sus respuestas.

**modelo**

**Tú:** *¿Estudiarás español?*
**Amigo(a):** *No, no estudiaré español.*
**Tú:** *Yo tampoco estudiaré español. ¿Viajarás?*
**Amigo(a):** *Sí, visitaré a mis primos en San Antonio. ¿Y tú?...*

| Sí | No |
|---|---|
| Viajará a San Antonio. | No estudiará español. |

## Actividad 6 ¡Hagamos un viaje!

Imagínate que viajarás a Costa Rica con tus compañeros de clase. Escribe cinco actividades que quieres que el grupo haga allí. Tus compañeros van a responder a tus sugerencias.

**modelo**

**Tú:** *Saquemos fotos de las diversas flores.*
**Estudiante 1:** *¡Sí! ¡Saquemos fotos de las flores!*
**Estudiante 2:** *¡Qué aburrido! No saquemos fotos de las flores. Saquemos fotos de los monos.*

## Actividad 7 En tu propia voz

**ESCRITURA** Francisco irá de camping con Amalia, Cecilia y Fernando. ¿Qué pasará? Escribe seis predicciones. ¡Usa tu imaginación y no mires la próxima etapa!

**modelo**

*Primero, Francisco llegará tarde a la casa de Amalia. Todos olvidarán muchas cosas importantes...*

## CONEXIONES

**La geografía** ¿Recuerdas dónde está el único bosque tropical en Norteamérica? Aparte de Costa Rica, ¿dónde hay otros bosques tropicales en Centroamérica y Sudamérica o en el resto del mundo? ¿Dónde hay parques nacionales? Haz un mapa del mundo e indícalos.

## Classroom Community

**Paired Activity** Have students make a list of items (clothing, equipment, etc.) they would take on a vacation to Costa Rica.

**Games** Have students write a description of the animals in the vocabulary list on separate pieces of paper, following the model in the **Juego** section. Have students divide into 2 teams and play a guessing game with the descriptions.

# En resumen

## REPASO DE VOCABULARIO

### TALK ABOUT NATURE AND THE ENVIRONMENT

**Plants**

| | |
|---|---|
| **la hoja** | *leaf* |
| **la planta silvestre** | *wild plant* |

**Animals and Other Living Beings**

| | |
|---|---|
| **el jaguar** | *jaguar* |
| **el león** | *lion* |
| **el lobo** | *wolf* |
| **el loro** | *parrot* |
| **la mariposa** | *butterfly* |
| **el mono** | *monkey* |
| **la rana** | *frog* |
| **la serpiente** | *snake* |
| **la tortuga** | *turtle* |
| **el tucán** | *toucan* |
| **el venado** | *deer* |

**The Environment**

| | |
|---|---|
| **la colina** | *hill* |
| **el desarrollo** | *development* |
| **la isla** | *island* |
| **el medio ambiente** | *environment* |
| **la naturaleza** | *nature* |
| **la piedra** | *stone* |
| **la selva** | *jungle* |
| **el sendero** | *path, trail* |
| **la tierra** | *land* |
| **el valle** | *valley* |

**Other Words**

| | |
|---|---|
| **la belleza** | *beauty* |
| **diverso(a)** | *diverse* |
| **feroz** | *ferocious* |
| **peligroso(a)** | *dangerous* |
| **salvaje** | *wild* |

### DESCRIBE GEOGRAPHIC CHARACTERISTICS

| | |
|---|---|
| **la altura** | *altitude, height* |
| **el clima** | *climate* |
| **la población** | *population* |
| **por todas partes** | *everywhere* |
| **la sombra** | *shade, shadow* |

### MAKE FUTURE PLANS

| | |
|---|---|
| **conservar** | *to conserve* |
| **descubrir** | *to discover* |
| **preservar** | *to preserve* |
| **valorar** | *to appreciate* |
| **volar (o→ue)** | *to fly* |

### Juego

Soy un animal feroz y salvaje.

Tengo manchas negras.

A causa de mi bella piel, estoy en peligro de extinción.

¿Quién soy?

## Teaching Suggestions

### Vocabulary Review

This is a good opportunity to have students do the **¿Cómo se llama este animal?** game as described in the **Ampliación** section on p. 315B.

## Interdisciplinary Connections

**Geography** Have students research the tropical rain forests in Central or South America via the Internet or at the library. Refer them to pp. 210–211 to review what they learned about **El Yunque** in Puerto Rico.

## Juego

**Answer**
un leopardo

## Project: Reviewing Etapa 1

Assign the following out-of-class activities:

- Interview a Spanish speaker about his/her opinions on preserving the environment.
- Bring in tourist information about what to do in Costa Rica.
- Find information on active volcanoes in Costa Rica via the Internet or the library.
- Find out about animals that are in danger of extinction in Costa Rica.

**Extra Credit**

| | |
|---|---|
| Interview | 2 pts. |
| Tourist information | 2 pts. |
| Volcanoes, Costa Rica | 2 pts. |
| Endangered animals | 2 pts. |

## Teaching All Students

**Extra Help** Ask students to create sentences using the vocabulary words in the list.

**Challenge** Ask students to imagine they are on their own for 24 hours in one of the national parks of Costa Rica. Using the **Etapa** vocabulary, students should write about what they would see, how they would spend their day, what problems might arise.

**Multiple Intelligences**

**Naturalist** Have students research the names of at least 3 wild plants found in the jungles of Costa Rica and post the new vocabulary for the class.

## Block Schedule

**FunBreak** Have students find photos or illustrations to match the vocabulary for the **Animals and Other Living Beings** section. They can make flashcards to help review vocabulary.

*pages 338–359*

# Planning Guide CLASSROOM MANAGEMENT

## OBJECTIVES

| | |
|---|---|
| **Communication** | • Discuss outdoor activities *pp. 340–341, 342–343*<br>• Describe the weather *pp. 348–349*<br>• Make predictions *pp. 345, 346–347, 353, 358*<br>• Talk about ecology *pp. 342–343, 352, 358* |
| **Grammar** | • The future tense: Irregular forms *pp. 346–347*<br>• Expressions with **para** *p. 350* |
| **Culture** | • Los parques nacionales de Costa Rica *p. 347*<br>• Navegar los rápidos *p. 352*<br>• Activities that appeal to ecotourists *pp. 354–355* |
| **Recycling** | • The regular future tense *p. 345*<br>• Weather expressions with **hacer** *pp. 348–349*<br>• Imperfect tense *p. 351* |

## STRATEGIES

| | |
|---|---|
| **Listening Strategies** | • Observe relationships between actions and motives *p. 342* |
| **Speaking Strategies** | • Describe it *p. 351*<br>• Make recommendations *p. 358* |
| **Reading Strategies** | • Skim and scan; use visuals to aid comprehension *TE p. 355* |
| **Writing Strategies** | • Tell who, what, where, when, why, and how *Actividad 6, TE p. 359* |
| **Connecting Cultures Strategies** | • Predict appeal to ecotourists *p. 354* |

## PROGRAM RESOURCES

### Print

- *Más práctica* Workbook PE *pp. 121–128*
- Block Scheduling Copymasters *pp. 113–120*
- Unit 5 Resource Book
  - *Más práctica* Workbook TE *pp. 52–59*
  - *Cuaderno para hispanohablantes* TE *pp. 60–67*
  - Information Gap Activities *pp. 68–71*
  - Family Involvement *pp. 72–73*
  - Video Activities *pp. 74–76*
  - Videoscript *pp. 77–78*
  - Audioscript *pp. 79–83*
  - Assessment Program, Unit 5 Etapa 2 *pp. 84–102, 173–175*
  - Answer Keys *pp. 180–181, 184*

### Audiovisual

- Audio Program Cassette 14A / CD 14
- Video Program Videotape 5 / Videodisc 4A
- Overhead Transparencies M1, M2; 151–160

### Technology

- Electronic Teacher Tools/Test Generator
- *Intrigas y aventuras* CD-ROM, Disc 2
-  www.mcdougallittell.com

### Assessment Program Options

- Cooperative Quizzes (Unit 5 Resource Book)
- Etapa Exam Forms A and B (Unit 5 Resource Book)
- *Examen para hispanohablantes* (Unit 5 Resource Book)
- Portfolio Assessment (Unit 5 Resource Book)
- Multiple Choice Test Questions (Unit 5 Resource Book)
- Audio Program Cassette 20A / CD 20
- Electronic Teacher Tools/Test Generator

### Native Speakers

- *Cuaderno para hispanohablantes* PE *pp. 121–128*
- *Cuaderno para hispanohablantes* TE (Unit 5 Resource Book)
- *Examen para hispanohablantes* (Unit 5 Resource Book)
- Audio Program *(Para hispanohablantes)* Cassettes 14B, 20A / CD 14, CD 20
- Audioscript (Unit 5 Resource Book)

# Student Text Listening Activity Scripts

## Videoscript: Diálogo *pages 342–343*

• Videotape 5, 11:59 • Videodisc 4A

Search Chapter 2, Play to 3. U5E2, En vivo (Dialog)

• Use the videoscript with **Actividades 1, 2** *page 344*

**Amalia:** Fernando, dejá esas cosas allí. A ver... ¿dónde pondremos las tiendas de campaña?

**Cecilia:** ¿Creés que las necesitamos? Me gusta dormir bajo las estrellas.

**Amalia:** Sí, las necesitamos. Ahora hace buen tiempo, pero es posible que llueva por la noche. No quiero que nos caiga un aguacero sin tienda de campaña. Vamos, ¿me ayudan?

**Amalia:** Francisco, siento no tener saco de dormir para vos. Espero que no haga mucho frío esta noche.

**Francisco:** Estaré bien con las mantas y las sábanas, muchas gracias.

**Fernando:** ¿Trajimos el abrelatas? No lo encuentro.

**Amalia:** Tendrás que buscar mejor. Sé que está en la mochila. .

**Fernando:** A ver... aquí están los fósforos... la linterna... la navaja... ¡Hay muchísimas cosas aquí!

**Amalia:** Pues, nunca se sabe, ¿verdad? Habrá un uso para todo. Ya verás.

**Cecilia:** ¿Ves, Francisco? Así es mi madre. Siempre trae más de lo que necesitamos. Vamos a Miami el año que viene... tendremos diez maletas.

**Francisco:** Ya está listo. Ahora, lo único que necesitamos es leña.

**Fernando:** ¡Ajá! Aquí está el abrelatas. Bueno, Francisco, ¿por qué no vamos vos y yo a buscar leña?

**Cecilia:** Yo los puedo acompañar.

**Amalia:** Buena idea. Pero no tarden mucho.

**Cecilia:** Ay, mamá... Mirá. Es un día soleado y todavía habrá muchas horas de luz. Apenas son las tres de la tarde.

**Francisco:** ¿Así que quieres ser bióloga, Cecilia?

**Cecilia:** Sí, me interesa muchísimo. Quiero dedicarme a salvar los animales en peligro de extinción. Es un asunto muy complicado; estoy a favor de desarrollar la economía de Costa Rica, pero estoy en contra de los proyectos que contaminan el medio ambiente. Ya verás... haré investigaciones para encontrar maneras de preservar los animales. ¡Seré famosa! Saldré en los periódicos: Cecilia Romero, ¡científica extraordinaria! ¡Ganaré un premio Nóbel!

**Francisco:** Así que en el futuro, yo podré decir que te conocía cuando no eras famosa todavía. Pero antes... tendremos que encontrar leña para esta noche. Si no, saldremos en los periódicos por otra razón...

**Cecilia:** ¿Cómo?

**Francisco:** El titular dirá... tres personas descubiertas muertas del frío en un sendero cerca de su campamento...

**Fernando:** ¿Dónde está tu mamá?

**Cecilia:** No sé.

**Francisco:** Tal vez está caminando un poco por el bosque.

**Cecilia:** Es muy extraño. No lo entiendo. Pronto va a atardecer y hace frío. ¿Dónde puede estar?

**Fernando:** No sé, Cecilia. Es extraño. ¿Querés ir a buscarla?

**Cecilia:** No, no sé, no lo sé... Espero que todo esté bien...

**Cecilia:** ¡Diay! ¡Mamá! ¿Dónde andabas? ¿Qué pasó? ¿Estás bien?

**Fernando:** Cuando regresamos con la leña, no estabas. ¡Y regresamos hace rato!

**Amalia:** Cálmense, claro que estoy bien. No me pasó nada. Me di cuenta que no tenía mi saco de dormir. El saco estaba en el carro. Así que regresé al carro. Desafortunadamente, se me cayeron las llaves en el sendero. Por suerte, las encontré, ¡pero después de una hora de buscar y buscar!

**Cecilia:** Mamá. Debés tener más cuidado con las llaves.

**Amalia:** Sí, hija, gracias por el consejo. Tendré más cuidado en el futuro.

**Amalia:** Vamos, ¿no quieren una fogata? Yo me muero de frío. Ceci, ¿por qué no preparás la fogata? Y muchachos, ayúdenme con la comida. ¿No tienen hambre?

## Actividad 12 El pronóstico del tiempo *page 350*

1. En el sur habrá una tormenta con truenos y relámpagos. También caerán fuertes aguaceros.
2. En la costa hará mucho viento. Hay peligro de un huracán y recomendamos que nadie salga de su casa esta noche.
3. Mañana será un día soleado y la temperatura estará entre veintinueve y treinta y un grados centígrados con humedad baja. Será un día hermoso.
4. El jueves empezará otra vez el frío. Habrá neblina por la mañana y la temperatura estará entre ocho y diez grados centígrados.

## Actividad 16 ¿Aventurera o cuidadosa? *page 352*

1. **Estela:** Este verano haré montañismo y escalaré montañas.
2. **Estela:** Cuando vaya de camping la próxima vez, dormiré bajo las estrellas sin una tienda de campaña.
3. **Cristina:** Yo dormiré en una tienda de campaña porque me molestan los mosquitos.
4. **Cristina:** Llevaré todo lo necesario para acampar... incluso las tijeras.
5. **Estela:** Saldré sin llevar mucha comida. Pescaré todos los días para comer.
6. **Cristina:** Siempre reciclo todo lo que puedo y nunca dejo basura en los campamentos.
7. **Cristina:** A mí me gustaría vivir en este pueblo para siempre. Tengo muchas amigas aquí.
8. **Estela:** En el futuro, viajaré por todas partes del mundo.

# Pacing Guide

## Sample Lesson Plan - 50 Minute Schedule

### DAY 1

**Etapa Opener**
- Quick Start Review (TE p. 338). 5 MIN.
- Anticipate/Activate prior knowledge: have students look at *Etapa* Opener and answer questions. 10 MIN.

**En contexto: Vocabulario**
- Quick Start Review (TE p. 340). 5 MIN.
- Have students use context and pictures to learn *Etapa* vocabulary. Answer questions, p. 341. 10 MIN.

**En vivo: Diálogo**
- Quick Start Review (TE p. 342). 5 MIN.
- Review Listening Strategy, p. 342. Play audio or show video for the dialog on pp. 342–343. 10 MIN.
- Read aloud, students taking on roles of characters. 5 MIN.

**Homework Option**
- Video Activities, Unit 5 Resource Book, pp. 74–76.

### DAY 2

**En acción: Vocabulario y Gramática**
- Check homework. 5 MIN.
- Quick Start Review (TE p. 344). 5 MIN.
- Ask students for a summary of *En vivo* dialog to check recall. Ask Comprehension Questions (TE p. 341). 10 MIN.
- Replay the *En vivo* dialog using the audiovisual resources and have students do *Actividades* 1 and 2 orally. 10 MIN.
- Have students complete *Actividades* 3 and 5 in pairs. 10 MIN.
- Have students do *Actividad* 4 in small groups or as a whole class divided into 2 teams. 10 MIN.

**Homework Option**
- *Más práctica* Workbook, pp. 121–124. *Cuaderno para hispanohablantes*, p. 121.

### DAY 3

**En acción (cont.)**
- Check homework. 5 MIN.
- Quick Start Review (TE p. 346). 5 MIN.
- Present *Gramática*: The Future Tense: Irregular Forms, p. 346, and then have students complete *Actividades* 6 and 7 first in writing, then review orally in pairs. 15 MIN.
- Have students complete *Actividades* 8 and 9 orally in pairs or small groups. Expand with *Más comunicación,* p. R15. 15 MIN.
- Present *Gramática*: Weather Expressions with **hacer** and vocabulary box, p. 348. Start *Actividad* 10 in writing. 10 MIN.

**Homework Option**
- Have students finish *Actividad* 10 in writing. *Más práctica* Workbook, pp. 125–126. *Cuaderno para hispanohablantes*, pp. 123–124.

### DAY 4

**En acción (cont.)**
- Check homework. 10 MIN.
- Quick Start Review (TE p. 348). 5 MIN.
- Review weather vocabulary on p. 348 and have students complete *Actividad* 11 in pairs. 10 MIN.
- Play audio and have students complete *Actividad* 12. 5 MIN.
- Present *Gramática:* Expressions with **para**, p. 350, and have students complete *Actividad* 13 in writing. 10 MIN.
- Present Speaking Strategy, p. 351, and have students complete *Actividad* 14 in pairs. 10 MIN.

**Homework Option**
- Preread advertisement in *Actividad* 15, p. 352. *Más práctica* Workbook, p. 127. *Cuaderno para hispanohablantes*, p. 125.

### DAY 5

**En acción (cont.)**
- Check homework. 5 MIN.
- Quick Start Review (TE p. 352). 5 MIN.
- Have students take turns reading the advertisement in *Actividad* 15 aloud and answer the questions in writing. Discuss answers with the whole class. 10 MIN.
- Play audio and have students complete *Actividad* 16. 5 MIN.
- Have students discuss questions in *Actividad* 17 in small groups and finish for homework. 10 MIN.
- Have students work in small groups to complete *Actividad* 18. Have students share their projects with the class. Expand with *Más comunicación*, p. R15. 15 MIN.

**Homework Option**
- Have students write out answers to *Actividad* 17. *Más práctica* Workbook, p. 128. *Cuaderno para hispanohablantes*, p. 126.

### DAY 6

**En colores: Cultura y comparaciones**
- Check homework. 5 MIN.
- Quick Start Review (TE p. 354). 5 MIN.
- Review Connecting Cultures Strategy, p. 354. 5 MIN.
- Read *Costa Rica, ¡la pura vida!* aloud with students. 10 MIN.
- Have students answer the *¿Comprendiste?* and *¿Qué piensas?* questions orally. 10 MIN.
- Divide the class into small groups and have them work on the *Hazlo tú* activity. 15 MIN.

**Homework Option**
- Have students finish the *¿Qué piensas?* questions in writing. p. 355. *Cuaderno para hispanohablantes*, p. 122.

### DAY 7

**En uso: Repaso y más comunicación**
- Check homework. 5 MIN.
- Quick Start Review (TE p. 356). 5 MIN.
- Do *Actividades* 1, 2, and 3 orally. 15 MIN.
- Review Speaking Strategy, p. 358. Then do *Actividad* 4 orally in pairs and *Actividad* 5 in groups. 15 MIN.

**En tu propia voz: Escritura**
- Start writing activity. 10 MIN.

**Homework Option**
- Finish writing activity. Review for *Etapa* 2 Exam. *Cuaderno para hispanohablantes*, pp. 127–128.

### DAY 8

**Tú en la comunidad**
- Check homework. 5 MIN.
- Read and discuss. 5 MIN.

**En resumen**
- Review grammar questions, etc., as necessary. 10 MIN.
- Complete *Etapa* 2 Exam. 20 MIN.

**Ampliación**
- Use a suggested project, game, or activity (TE pp. 315A–315B). 10 MIN.

**Homework Option**
- Preview next *Etapa* Opener, pp. 360–361.

# Sample Lesson Plan - Block Schedule (90 minutes)

## DAY 1

***Etapa* Opener**
- Quick Start Review (TE p. 338). 5 MIN.
- Anticipate/Activate prior knowledge: have students look at the *Etapa* Opener and answer questions. 10 MIN.

**En contexto: Vocabulario**
- Quick Start Review (TE p. 340). 5 MIN.
- Have students use context and pictures to learn *Etapa* vocabulary. Answer questions, p. 341. 10 MIN.

**En vivo: Diálogo**
- Quick Start Review (TE p. 342). 5 MIN.
- Review Listening Strategy, p. 342. Play audio or show video for the dialog on pp. 342–343. 10 MIN.
- Read aloud, students taking roles of characters. Ask Comprehension Questions on TE p. 343. 10 MIN.
- Students role-play in groups while looking at the photos in their texts. Encourage them to come up with logical dialog using familiar vocabulary. 10 MIN.

**En acción: Vocabulario y Gramática**
- Quick Start Review (TE p. 344). 5 MIN.
- Have students do *Actividades* 1 and 2 orally. 10 MIN.
- Have students complete *Actividades* 3 and 5 in pairs. 10 MIN.

**Homework Option**
- *Más práctica* Workbook, pp. 121–124. *Cuaderno para hispanohablantes*, p. 121. Video Activities, Unit 5 Resource Book, pp. 74–76.

## DAY 2

**En acción (cont.)**
- Check homework. 5 MIN.
- Have students do *Actividad* 4 in small groups or as a whole class divided into 2 teams. 10 MIN.
- Quick Start Review (TE p. 346). 5 MIN.
- Present *Gramática*: The Future Tense: Irregular Forms, p. 346, and then have students complete *Actividades* 6 and 7 first in writing, then review orally in pairs. 10 MIN.
- Have students complete *Actividades* 8 and 9 orally in pairs or small groups. Expand with *Más comunicación,* p. R15. 15 MIN.
- Present *Gramática*: Weather Expressions with *hacer* and vocabulary box, p. 348. 10 MIN.
- Have student complete *Actividades* 10 and 11 in pairs. 10 MIN.
- Play audio and have students complete *Actividad* 12. 10 MIN.
- Present *Gramática:* Expressions with *para,* p. 350, and have students complete *Actividad* 13 in writing. 10 MIN.
- Use Block Scheduling Copymasters for a change of pace. 5 MIN.

**Homework Option**
- Have students complete *Actividad* 10, p. 349, in writing. *Más práctica* Workbook, pp. 125–126. *Cuaderno para hispanohablantes*, pp. 123–124.

## DAY 3

**En acción (cont.)**
- Check homework. 5 MIN.
- Present Speaking Strategy, p. 351, and have students complete *Actividad* 14 in pairs. 10 MIN.
- Quick Start Review (TE p. 352). 5 MIN.
- Have students take turns reading the advertisement in *Actividad* 15 aloud and answer the questions in writing. Discuss answers with the whole class. 15 MIN.
- Play audio and have students complete *Actividad* 16. 10 MIN.
- Have students discuss questions in *Actividad* 17 in small groups and finish for homework. 10 MIN.
- Have students work in small groups to prepare *Actividad* 18. Save time for some students to present their projects to the class. Expand with *Más comunicación,* p. R15. 20 MIN.
- Use Block Scheduling Copymasters for variety.

**Ampliación**
- Use a suggested project, game, or activity (TE pp. 315A–315B). 15 MIN.

**Homework Option**
- Have students write out answers to *Actividad* 17. *Más práctica* Workbook, pp. 127–128. *Cuaderno para hispanohablantes*, pp. 125–126.

## DAY 4

**En colores: Cultura y comparaciones**
- Check homework. 10 MIN.
- Quick Start Review (TE p. 354). 5 MIN.
- Review Connecting Cultures Strategy, p. 354. 5 MIN.
- Read *Costa Rica, ¡la pura vida!* aloud with students. 10 MIN.
- Have students answer the *¿Comprendiste?* and *¿Qué piensas?* questions orally. 15 MIN.
- Divide the class into small groups and have them work on the *Hazlo tú* activity. 20 MIN.

**En uso: Repaso y más comunicación**
- Quick Start Review (TE p. 356). 5 MIN.
- Do *Actividades* 1, 2, and 3 orally. 20 MIN.

**Homework Option**
- *Cuaderno para hispanohablantes*, pp. 122, 127–128.
- Review for *Etapa* 2 Exam.

## DAY 5

**En uso: Repaso y más comunicación**
- Check homework. 5 MIN.
- Review Speaking Strategy, p. 358. Then do *Actividad* 4 orally in pairs and *Actividad* 5 in groups of four. 15 MIN.

**Tú en la comunidad**
- Read and discuss. 10 MIN.

**En resumen**
- Review grammar questions, etc., as necessary. 10 MIN.
- Complete *Etapa* 2 Exam. 20 MIN.

**En tu propia voz: Escritura**
- Start writing activity. 15 MIN.

**Ampliación**
- Use a suggested project, game, or activity (TE pp. 315A–315B) or assign a project from the Block Scheduling Copymasters. 15 MIN.

**Homework Option**
- Preview next *Etapa* Opener, pp. 360–361.

▼ Todos preparan el campamento.

# UNIDAD 5 Etapa 2
# Opener

## Etapa Theme

**Discussing outdoor activities, describing the weather, making predictions, and talking about ecology.**

## Grammar Objectives

- Irregular forms of the future tense
- Weather expressions with **hacer**
- Expressions with **para**

### Teaching Resource Options

**Print** 

Block Scheduling Copymasters

**Audiovisual** 

**OHT** 139, 157 (Quick Start)

### Quick Start Review

Giving opinions

Use OHT 157 or write on board: Complete the following sentences, using your imagination about the scene in the photo. Be creative and remember to use the subjunctive.

| Dudo que... | Quizás... |
|---|---|
| No creo que... | Me alegro de que... |

*Answers will vary.*

### Teaching Suggestions
**Previewing the Etapa**

Ask students to study the photo on pp. 338–339 and describe what they see. On the board, write a list of items that the students identify.

UNIDAD 5

ETAPA 2

# Nuestro medio ambiente

- Discuss outdoor activities
- Describe the weather
- Make predictions
- Talk about ecology

## ¿Qué ves?

Mira la foto de Francisco y sus nuevos amigos. ¿Qué ves?

1. ¿Dónde están Francisco y sus amigos?
2. ¿Qué van a hacer? ¿Dónde van a comer?
3. ¿Cuál es el tema del libro?

### Classroom Management

**Peer Review** **Brainstorming:** Prepare the **Etapa** by handing out butcher paper or flip chart paper and having groups of four write down all they know about outdoor activities, weather, ecology, and environment, etc. Students may look ahead in the chapter or use a dictionary.

**Planning Ahead** Keep a supply of manipulatives available to help students channel excess energy during seated or quiet activities.

## Cross Cultural Connections

Have students compare personal camping experiences with what they see in the photo. Have students discuss camping trips they may have taken in the past. Ask them to describe the items they took on their trip and the activities they did.

## Culture Highlights

- **CAMPING IN COSTA RICA** Many of the national parks in Costa Rica offer camping facilities. Camping on the beaches is also possible in many areas.
- **THE ECONOMY OF COSTA RICA** is based on the major industries of coffee, bananas, textiles, sugar, and tourism. Ecotourism has become especially popular in recent years.

## Critical Thinking

Have students speculate about the activities associated with camping and analyze and classify ecologically correct activities.

## Teaching All Students

**Extra Help** Ask students to list the pros and cons of staying in a hotel versus camping.

**Native Speakers** Have Spanish speakers describe any camping trips or hiking trips they may have taken in the past. They can describe the places they visited, the people they traveled with, and the activities they did.

**Multiple Intelligences**

**Kinesthetic** Ask students to study the photo for 2–3 minutes and then close their books. Describe the photo. If your statements are true, ask the students to stand up; if they are false, have them stay seated. Call on volunteers to correct the false statements.

**Verbal** Ask students to prepare a short dialog among the four characters in the picture.

## Block Schedule

**FunBreak** Ask students to bring in catalogs from sporting goods stores and use them to present and practice the camping vocabulary. Have students create a Spanish version of the catalog with labels and prices in Spanish. (For additional activities, see **Block Scheduling Copymasters**.)

## Teaching Resource Options

**Print** 

Unit 5 Resource Book
Video Activities, p. 74
Videoscript, p. 77
Audioscript, p. 79

**Audiovisual** 

**OHT** 151, 152, 157 (Quick Start)
**Audio Program** Cassette 14A / CD 14
**Video Program** Videotape 5, 9:30 / Videodisc 4A

Search Chapter 1, Play to 2
U5E2, En contexto (Vocabulary)

**Technology** 

*Intrigas y aventuras* **CD-ROM,** Disc 2

## Quick Start Review

Talking about nature

Use OHT 157 or write on board: Unscramble the words to discover the names of the following animals.

1. BOLO
2. ANAR
3. RUTAGOT
4. ONOM
5. PORIMASA
6. TENPIESER

**Answers**
1. lobo, 2. rana, 3. tortuga, 4. mono, 5. mariposa, 6. serpiente

## Teaching Suggestions
### Introducing Vocabulary

- Have students look at pp. 340–341. Use OHT 151–152 and Audiocassette 14A / CD 14 to present the vocabulary.
- Ask the Comprehension Questions in the margin of the Teacher's Edition on p. 341. You may write the questions on the board and have students work in small groups to answer them.
- Use the video vocabulary presentation for review and reinforcement.

# En contexto

## VOCABULARIO

Aquí Francisco va a acampar. Mira lo que trae.

**A** ¿Estás listo para **el campamento**? Francisco y sus amigos están listos para acampar. Tienen **una tienda de campaña** y **un saco de dormir.** También traen **una manta, sábanas** y **almohadas.**

**B** Para hacer **una fogata,** necesitan **leña** y **fósforos.** Para apagar **el fuego,** necesitan **un balde** con agua.

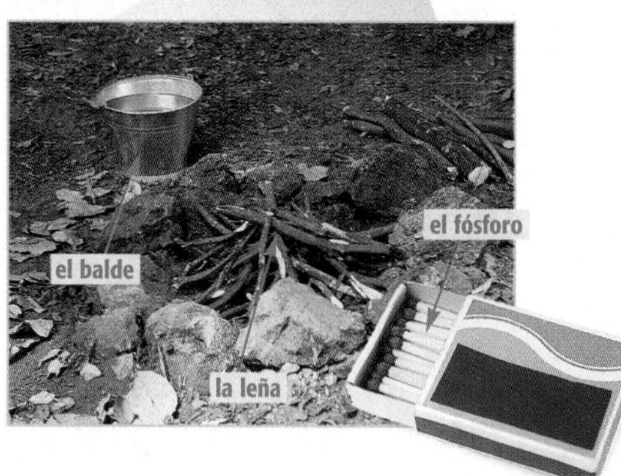




## Classroom Community 

**TPR** Have students act out the verbs as you say them in Spanish. (**remar, pescar, escalar montañas, acampar**)

**Cooperative Learning** Imagine that your class is going camping this weekend. Assign the following roles to student groups: Planners (seek campsite location, give weekend weather forecast and directions to site); Chefs (plan daily menus); Activity Coordinators (plan daily activities), First Aid Staff (discuss first-aid kit, safety rules); Accommodation Staff (list supplies needed, work with all groups to facilitate presentation). Each group should prepare an oral presentation and a poster showing what is needed for a successful trip. The Accommodation Staff oversees all groups.

**C** Para comer comida en lata, necesitan **un abrelatas. La navaja** y **las tijeras** son esenciales. Sin **la linterna**, no van a tener **luz.**

**D** ¡En el campamento se puede **escalar montañas** o hacer **montañismo**!

¡En el río se puede **remar**! ¡En el río se puede **pescar**!

### Preguntas personales

1. ¿Vas a acampar con tu familia o con tus amigos?
2. ¿Qué cosas son esenciales si vas a acampar?
3. ¿Qué necesitas para hacer una fogata?
4. ¿Qué actividades te gusta hacer en el campamento?
5. ¿Qué llevas cuando vas a un campamento? Haz una lista de las cosas que necesitas llevar contigo.





## Comprehension Questions

1. ¿Se hospedan los amigos en una pensión? **(No)**
2. ¿Traen una tienda de campaña? **(Sí)**
3. ¿Duermen en una cama? **(No)**
4. Cuando hace frío, ¿necesitas una manta? **(Sí)**
5. ¿Preparan la comida allí o van a un café? **(preparan la comida allí)**
6. ¿Traen una linterna o una lámpara? **(una linterna)**
7. Para hacer una fogata, ¿necesitas leche o leña? **(leña)**
8. ¿Qué necesitan para apagar el fuego? **(un balde con agua)**
9. ¿Qué actividades se puede hacer en el río? **(pescar, remar)**
10. ¿Es posible hacer montañismo cerca de tu casa? ¿Adónde va la gente cuando quiere escalar montañas? ***(Answers will vary.)***

## Teaching Suggestions

### Presenting the Vocabulary

Ask students to bring in examples of camping gear to help present the lesson's vocabulary. If possible, have students set up a campsite in the classroom, with tent, sleeping area, cooking area, and sporting equipment.

## Teaching All Students

**Extra Help** Ask students simple **sí/no** questions, e.g., ¿Van Francisco y sus amigos al hotel? (no) ¿Necesitan una tienda de campaña? (sí) ¿Tienen que traer sábanas y almohadas? (sí) ¿Necesitan una linterna? (sí) ¿Tienen que remar al campamento? (no)

**Native Speakers** Have Spanish speakers describe any rivers or mountains in their native countries and tell what kinds of outdoor activities are popular in those places.

**Multiple Intelligences**

**Intrapersonal** Ask students to write a list of the items they would take on a camping trip and a list of items they would take when staying in a hotel. Which accommodation would they prefer and why? You may want to suggest using a Venn diagram for this activity.

## Block Schedule

**FunBreak** Have students play a game to practice vocabulary. One defines a new word and another tries to guess it. They may work in teams to make up the definitions.

## Teaching Resource Options

**Print** 

Block Scheduling Copymasters
Unit 5 Resource Book
- **Video Activities,** pp. 75–76
- **Videoscript,** pp. 77–78
- **Audioscript,** p. 79

**Audiovisual**

**OHT** 155, 156, 157 (Quick Start)
**Audio Program** Cassette 14A / CD 14
**Video Program** Videotape 5, 11:59 / Videodisc 4A

Search Chapter 2, Play to 3
U5E2, En vivo (Dialog)

**Technology**

***Intrigas y aventuras* CD-ROM,** Disc 2

## Quick Start Review

**En contexto** vocabulary

Use OHT 157 or write on board: Look at the photos that accompany the dialog and make a list of all the camping equipment you see.

**Answers**

*Answers may include:* la tienda de campaña, el saco de dormir, las mantas, las sábanas, la almohada, la mochila, el balde

## Teaching Suggestions
### Presenting the Dialog

- Prepare students for listening by focusing on the dialog context using yes/no or either/or questions.
- Use the video, audiocassette, or CD to present the dialog. The video version offers expanded language opportunities.

# En vivo
## DIÁLOGO

Amalia

Cecilia

Francisco

Fernando

**PARA ESCUCHAR • STRATEGY: LISTENING**

**Observe relationships between actions and motives** Each person on this trip is looking for something. Tell what each is looking for and for what purpose.

Who would you prefer helping? Why?

| ¿Quién? | ¿Qué busca? | ¿Para qué? |
|---|---|---|
| Fernando | | |
| Francisco | | |
| Cecilia | | |
| Amalia | | |

## El campamento

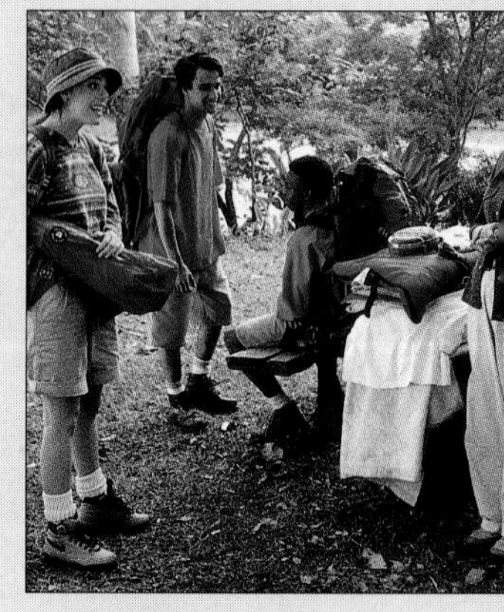

1 ▶ **Amalia:** A ver, ¿dónde pondremos las tiendas de campaña?
**Cecilia:** ¿Las necesitamos? Me gusta dormir bajo las estrellas.
**Amalia:** Sí, las necesitamos. Es posible que llueva.

5 ▶ **Francisco:** ¿Así que quieres ser bióloga?
**Cecilia:** Sí. Estoy a favor de desarrollar la economía, pero estoy en contra de los proyectos que contaminan el medio ambiente.

6 ▶ **Fernando:** ¿Dónde está tu mamá?
**Cecilia:** No sé.
**Francisco:** Tal vez está caminando un poco por el bosque.
**Cecilia:** Es muy extraño. No lo entiendo. Hace frío. ¿Dónde puede estar?

7 ▶ **Cecilia:** ¡Diay! ¡Mamá! ¿Qué pasó? ¿Estás bien?
**Fernando:** Cuando regresamos con la leña, no estabas.
**Amalia:** Cálmense. Claro que estoy bien. No me pasó nada.



## Classroom Community

**Portfolio** Ask students to write about losing something important and searching for it.

**Rubric: Writing**

| Criteria | Scale |
|---|---|
| Accuracy | 1 2 3 4 5 |
| Logical organization | 1 2 3 4 5 |
| Vocabulary use | 1 2 3 4 5 |

A = 13–15 pts.
B = 10–12 pts.
C = 7–9 pts.
D = 4–6 pts.
F = < 4 pts.

**TPR** Have students act out what they would do with each item of camping equipment (**el saco de dormir, la almohada, los fósforos, el abrelatas,** etc.). Have other students guess what they are using.

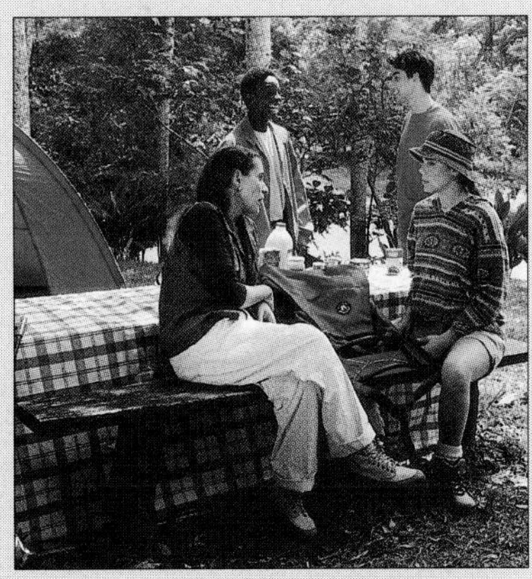

2 ▶ Amalia: Francisco, siento no tener saco de dormir para vos. Espero que no haga mucho frío esta noche.
Francisco: Estaré bien con las mantas y las sábanas, gracias.

3 ▶ Fernando: ¿Trajimos el abrelatas? No lo encuentro.
Amalia: Está en la mochila.
Fernando: A ver, aquí están los fósforos, la linterna, la navaja. ¡Hay muchísimas cosas!
Amalia: Habrá un uso para todo. Ya verás.

4 ▶ Fernando: Francisco, ¿por qué no vamos vos y yo a buscar leña?
Cecilia: Yo los puedo acompañar.
Amalia: No tarden mucho.
Cecilia: Ay, mamá, todavía habrá muchas horas de luz.

8 ▶ Amalia: No tenía mi saco de dormir. Así que regresé al carro. Se me cayeron las llaves en el sendero. Por suerte, las encontré, ¡pero después de una hora de buscar!

9 ▶ Cecilia: Mamá, debés tener más cuidado con las llaves.
Amalia: Sí, hija, gracias por el consejo. Tendré más cuidado en el futuro.

10 ▶ Amalia: Vamos, ¿no quieren una fogata? Yo me muero de frío. Ceci, ¿por qué no preparás la fogata? Y muchachos, ayúdenme con la comida. ¿No tienen hambre?



## Video Synopsis

Francisco accompanies Amalia, Cecilia, and Fernando on a camping trip. Each person has responsibilities to prepare the camping site. For a complete transcript of the video dialog, see p. 337B.

## Comprehension Questions

1. ¿Prefiere Cecilia dormir en la tienda de campaña? **(No)**
2. ¿Tienen un saco de dormir para Francisco? **(No)**
3. ¿Tiene Francisco una manta y sábana? **(Sí)**
4. ¿Trajeron muchas cosas al campamento? **(Sí)**
5. ¿Quiere Cecilia ser profesora o bióloga? **(bióloga)**
6. ¿Está Cecilia a favor o en contra de desarrollar la economía? **(a favor de)**
7. Cuando descubrieron que Amalia no estaba en el campamento, ¿estaba tranquila o nerviosa Cecilia? **(nerviosa)**
8. ¿Qué buscó Amalia por una hora? **(las llaves)**
9. ¿Quién va a preparar la fogata? **(Cecilia)**
10. ¿Quién va a ayudar con la comida? **(los muchachos)**

## Gestures

Have students identify any gestures they recognize in the photographs. Have them try to guess what is going on in frames 8–10 based on the facial expressions and gestures.

## Language Notes

Have students identify the uses of **vos** in the dialog. (Frame 2: Amalia says **para vos**; frame 4: Fernando says **vos y yo**; frame 9: Cecilia says **debés**; and in frame 10: Amalia says **preparás**.)

## Teaching All Students

**Extra Help** Ask students questions about each character. If the response is Francisco, students stand; Cecilia, raise right hand; Amalia, raise left hand; Fernando, remain sitting. **¿A quién le gusta dormir bajo las estrellas? (Cecilia); ¿Quién no tiene saco de dormir? (Francisco); ¿Quién busca el abrelatas? (Fernando); ¿Quién regresó al carro para el saco de dormir? (Amalia).**

**Challenge** Ask students to create a camping adventure for Francisco and his friends. They can write 2–3 more scenes about the camping trip and include illustrations to accompany the new dialog.

**Multiple Intelligences**

**Kinesthetic** Make copies of the dialog. Cut portions of the dialog into strips. Give each group of students a whole set of dialog strips and ask them to put them in the proper order.

## Block Schedule

**Process Time** Have students divide into groups of 4 and pick parts of the dialog to read out loud. Challenge them to memorize their parts for extra credit.

## Teaching Resource Options

**Print** 

Unit 5 Resource Book
- **Video Activities,** pp. 75–76
- **Videoscript,** pp. 77–78
- **Audioscript,** p. 79

**Audiovisual** 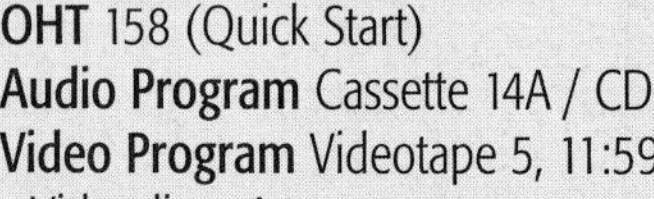

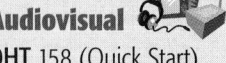

**OHT** 158 (Quick Start)
**Audio Program** Cassette 14A / CD 14
**Video Program** Videotape 5, 11:59 / Videodisc 4A

**Technology** 

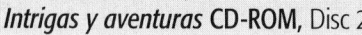

*Intrigas y aventuras* **CD-ROM,** Disc 2

## Quick Start Review

**Using por with periods of time**

Use OHT 158 or write on board: Imagine you are telling a friend what you did while camping. Your friend loves detail, so tell how long you did each activity. You decide the length of time for each activity, just be sure to use **por.** For example: **hicimos ejercicio / Hicimos ejercicio por treinta minutos.**

1. escalamos una montaña
2. relajamos cerca de un lago
3. pescamos
4. tomamos fotos de la naturaleza
5. bebimos refrescos y leímos revistas

*Answers will vary.*

**Actividad 1** **Objective:** Controlled practice
Listening comprehension/vocabulary

**Answers**
1. Falso. Ella quiere dormir bajo las estrellas.
2. Falso. Él tiene mantas y sábanas.
3. Cierto
4. Cierto
5. Cierto
6. Falso. Cecilia se preocupa mucho.
7. Cierto
8. Falso. Ella dice que tendrá más cuidado en el futuro.

**Actividad 2** **Objective:** Controlled practice
Listening comprehension/vocabulary

**Answers**
d, a, f, e, b, c

# En acción
## VOCABULARIO Y GRAMÁTICA

**OBJECTIVES**
- Discuss outdoor activities
- Describe the weather
- Make predictions
- Talk about ecology

ACTIVIDAD 1 

### ¿Es cierto?

**Escuchar/Escribir** Según el diálogo, ¿son **ciertas** o **falsas** las oraciones? Si son falsas, explica por qué.

1. A Cecilia no le gusta dormir bajo las estrellas.
2. Francisco tiene un saco de dormir.
3. El abrelatas está en la mochila.
4. Francisco, Fernando y Cecilia van a buscar leña.
5. Fernando no sabe dónde está su mamá.
6. Cecilia no se preocupa mucho de que Amalia no vuelva.
7. Amalia encontró las llaves después de una hora.
8. Amalia no tendrá más cuidado en el futuro.

ACTIVIDAD 2 

### ¿En qué orden?

**Escuchar** Pon las oraciones en orden según el diálogo.

a. Fernando buscó el abrelatas.
b. Fernando y Cecilia se pusieron nerviosos.
c. Amalia regresó con su saco de dormir.
d. Escogieron un lugar para las tiendas de campaña.
e. Los tres regresaron al campamento.
f. Cecilia, Francisco y Fernando fueron a buscar leña.

ACTIVIDAD 3 

### Cuando vas de camping...

**Hablar** ¿Qué llevas cuando vas de camping? Habla con un(a) compañero(a).

**modelo**

**Compañero(a):** *¿Llevas leña cuando vas de camping?*
**Tú:** *(No, no llevo leña.) Sí, llevo leña.*

1.

2.

3. 4.

5. 6.



## Classroom Management

**Streamlining** Ask for 4 volunteers to be Cecilia, Amalia, Francisco, and Fernando. Have them act out the scenes in the **Diálogo.** Then do **Actividades 1** and **2** while listening to the audio/video several times.

**Peer Review** Have students work in 2 teams to play "Piccionario" in **Actividad 4.** Then extend the activity by having students draw additional items from the previous **Etapa.** (Use the animal vocabulary from pp. 318–319.)

- *Use irregular forms of the future tense*
- *Review: Use weather expressions with **hacer***
- *Use **para***

## ¿Qué hay en el campamento?

**Hablar** Haz dibujos de estas cosas. Tus compañeros(as) adivinarán qué son.

la fogata
el saco de dormir
una linterna
la navaja
remar
escalar montañas
un balde de agua
la tienda de campaña
la leña
pescar

**TAMBIÉN SE DICE**

¡Diay!, la expresión que usa Cecilia en el diálogo, es una interjección muy popular entre los costarricenses. Puede indicar afirmación, interrogación o admiración. Una persona también puede usarla cuando quiere que otra deje de hablar. Es muy «tico» (*Costa Rican*), ¡y muy útil!

## ¿Qué vas a hacer este verano?

**Hablar** Pregúntale a tu compañero(a) si hará estas actividades durante el verano. Cuando te conteste, hazle otra pregunta relacionada con la primera.

**modelo**

*viajar*

**Tú:** *¿Viajarás durante el verano?*

**Compañero(a):** *Sí, viajaré un poco.*

**Tú:** *¿Adónde irás?*

**Compañero(a):** *Iré a la playa con mi familia.*

1. ir de camping
2. dormir bajo las estrellas
3. pescar en un río o un lago
4. andar en bicicleta
5. comer helado
6. dormir en un saco de dormir
7. caminar a las orillas del mar
8. escalar montañas
9. bajar un río en canoa
10. visitar a alguien que vive lejos



## Teaching All Students

**Extra Help** Ask students to conjugate the following verbs in the future tense: **escalar, pescar, remar, ir de camping, hacer montañismo.**

**Native Speakers** Have Spanish speakers discuss any expressions they might use for exclamations. Cecilia uses **¡Diay!** when her mother finally returns.

**Multiple Intelligences**

**Verbal** Ask students to write a short paragraph about sleeping in a tent vs. sleeping in a hotel room. Which do they prefer and why?

### Teaching Suggestions

As a warm-up for **Actividad 4**, write all the vocabulary words on the board and have students give an example of where the item could be used or the activity could be found in the community.

**Objective:** Transitional practice
Discussing outdoor activities

**Answers**

*Answers will vary.*

1. ¿Llevas helado cuando vas de camping?
2. ¿Llevas una linterna cuando vas de camping?
3. ¿Llevas sábanas cuando vas de camping?
4. ¿Llevas tijeras cuando vas de camping?
5. ¿Llevas una aspiradora cuando vas de camping?
6. ¿Llevas una tienda de campaña cuando vas de camping?

**Objective:** Open-ended practice
Discussing outdoor activities

*Answers will vary.*

**Objective:** Open-ended practice
Discussing outdoor activities

**Answers**

*Answers will vary.*

1. ¿Irás de camping durante el verano? Sí, (No, no) iré de camping.
2. ¿Dormirás bajo las estrellas durante el verano? / dormiré...
3. ¿Pescarás en un río o un lago durante el verano? / pescaré...
4. ¿Andarás en bicicleta durante el verano? / andaré...
5. ¿Comerás helado durante el verano? / comeré...
6. ¿Dormirás en un saco de dormir? / dormiré...
7. ¿Caminarás a las orillas del mar durante el verano? / caminaré...
8. ¿Escalarás montañas durante el verano? / escalaré...
9. ¿Bajarás un río en canoa durante el verano? / bajaré...
10. ¿Visitarás a alguien que vive lejos durante el verano? / visitaré...

### Block Schedule

**Variety** Divide the class into groups. Tell students that they will be preparing skits acting out the day before a camping weekend. (This activity should be prepared a day in advance, with the skits presented the following day. This will allow students to acquire props, etc.) Students should use as much camping vocabulary and verbs in the future tense as possible. Have them discuss what they will bring, what they will eat, and what they will do while on their camping weekend. All groups present their skits to the rest of the class.

## Teaching Resource Options

**Print** 

*Más práctica* Workbook PE, pp. 125–126
*Cuaderno para hispanohablantes* PE, pp. 123–124
Block Scheduling Copymasters
Unit 5 Resource Book
*Más práctica* Workbook TE, pp. 56–57
*Cuaderno para hispanohablantes* TE, pp. 62–63

**Audiovisual**
OHT 158 (Quick Start)

**Technology**
*Intrigas y aventuras* CD-ROM, Disc 2

## Quick Start Review

Future tense

Use OHT 158 or write on board: Choose a famous celebrity or your favorite band and imagine they are coming to your town. You are hired to plan the itinerary which will outline where they will stay and what they will do while in town. Use the future tense. For example: **Gloria Estefan se hospedará en el Hotel Valle.**

Some verbs to get you started: **hospedarse, comer, ir de compras, tomar fotos de..., divertirse en...**

*Answers will vary.*

## Teaching Suggestions
### Presenting the Future Tense: Irregular Forms

Have students write out the full conjugations of the irregular verbs in the future for extra practice.

**Objective:** Controlled practice
Irregular future tense

### Answers
*Answers may vary.*

1. Para tener un grupo muy grande, Paco y José vendrán con nosotros.
2. Tú tienes que asistir a clases hasta las siete, entonces saldrás para el campamento a las siete y media.
3. Ustedes van de camping frecuentemente; por eso sabrán qué debemos llevar.
4. Para dormir cómodo, nosotros pondremos las tiendas de campaña.
5. A Sofía le gusta la luz, por eso tendrá dos o tres linternas.
6. Voy a traer buena comida y haré la cena la primera noche.

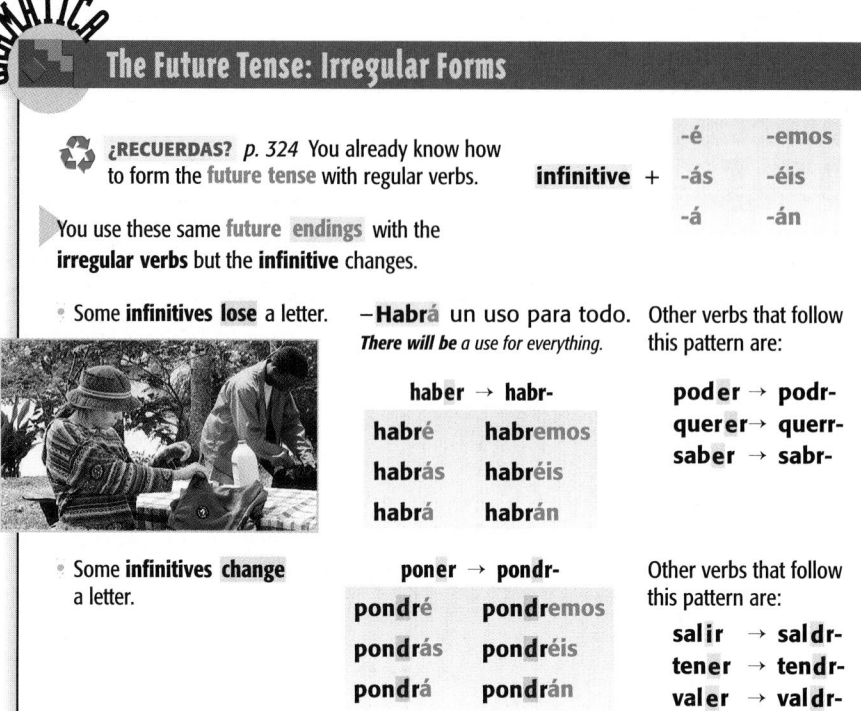

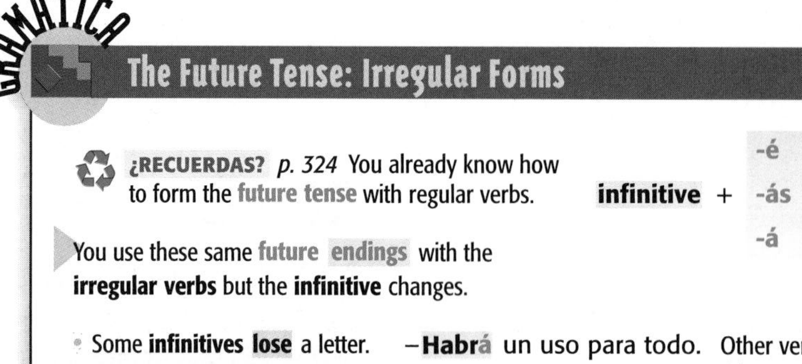

GRAMÁTICA

## The Future Tense: Irregular Forms

¿RECUERDAS? *p. 324* You already know how to form the **future tense** with regular verbs.

**infinitive** + -é, -ás, -á, -emos, -éis, -án

You use these same **future endings** with the **irregular verbs** but the **infinitive** changes.

- Some **infinitives lose** a letter.

—**Habrá** un uso para todo.
*There will be a use for everything.*

**haber** → **habr-**

| | |
|---|---|
| **habré** | **habremos** |
| **habrás** | **habréis** |
| **habrá** | **habrán** |

Other verbs that follow this pattern are:

**poder** → **podr-**
**querer** → **querr-**
**saber** → **sabr-**

- Some **infinitives change** a letter.

**poner** → **pondr-**

| | |
|---|---|
| **pondré** | **pondremos** |
| **pondrás** | **pondréis** |
| **pondrá** | **pondrán** |

Other verbs that follow this pattern are:

**salir** → **saldr-**
**tener** → **tendr-**
**valer** → **valdr-**
**venir** → **vendr-**

**Decir** and **hacer** do not follow either pattern. **decir** → **dir-** **hacer** → **har-**

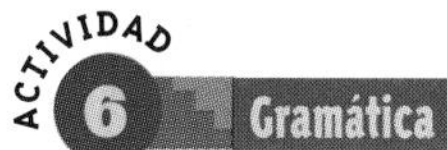

ACTIVIDAD 6 Gramática

## ¡Organicémonos!

**Escribir** Cecilia y sus primos van de camping y están organizándose. Combina elementos de las dos columnas para explicar lo que harán.

1. Para tener un grupo muy grande, Paco y José
2. Tú tienes que asistir a clases hasta las siete, entonces
3. Ustedes van de camping frecuentemente; por eso
4. Para dormir cómodo, nosotros
5. A Sofía le gusta la luz, por eso
6. Voy a traer buena comida y

a. (hacer) la cena la primera noche.
b. (poner) las tiendas de campaña.
c. (saber) qué debemos llevar.
d. (venir) con nosotros.
e. (tener) dos o tres linternas.
f. (salir) para el campamento a las siete y media.

## Classroom Community

**Portfolio** Have students write an itinerary for an upcoming trip to Costa Rica.

**Rubric: Writing**

| Criteria | Scale |
|---|---|
| Accuracy | 1 2 3 4 5 |
| Logical organization | 1 2 3 4 5 |
| Vocabulary use | 1 2 3 4 5 |

A = 13–15 pts.
B = 10–12 pts.
C = 7–9 pts.
D = 4–6 pts.
F = < 4 pts.

**Storytelling** Ask students to cut out a picture of the environment/nature/outdoors. In small groups, have them develop a short story based on the picture. Encourage them to be creative.

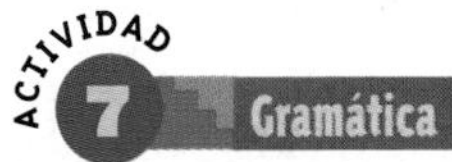

## ¿Qué harán?

**Hablar/Escribir** Cecilia habla de lo que ella y su familia harán en el Parque Tapantí. Completa sus descripciones según los dibujos.

modelo

*yo (saber montar a caballo)*
*Sabré montar a caballo.*

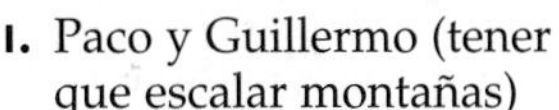

1. Paco y Guillermo (tener que escalar montañas)

2. tú (poder pescar)

3. José y yo (poner la tienda de campaña)

4. yo (hacer la fogata)

**MÁS PRÁCTICA** *cuaderno* pp. 125–126

**PARA HISPANOHABLANTES** *cuaderno* pp. 123–124

## Predicciones

**Hablar/Escribir** ¿Cómo será tu vida en diez años? Conversa con un(a) compañero(a).

modelo

*saber pilotear un avión*

**Tú:** *En diez años, yo no sabré pilotear un avión.*

**Compañero(a):** *Tampoco sabré pilotear un avión en diez años pero Marcos sabrá pilotearlo.*

1. tener (¿cuántos?) hijos
2. querer comprar el carro de tus sueños
3. saber hablar tres o más idiomas
4. casarse
5. hacer viajes por todas partes

NOTA CULTURAL

**Los parques nacionales** Hay muchos parques nacionales en Costa Rica donde se puede acampar y hacer montañismo. Uno de éstos es el Parque Nacional Braulio Carrillo. Tiene montañas, selvas, ríos y muchas cascadas (*waterfalls*).

## Teaching All Students

**Extra Help** Ask students questions in the future tense using the irregular forms, e.g., **¿Quién pondrá la mesa en tu casa? ¿Tendrás que trabajar por la tarde? ¿A qué hora saldrán ustedes? ¿Querrás ir al cine por la tarde? ¿Quién vendrá al campamento?** etc.

**Native Speakers** Have Spanish speakers give the future plans for their next vacation. Where will they go? What will they do there? Who will they spend time with?

**Multiple Intelligences**

**Visual** Ask students to design a mind map of irregular verbs in the future tense–include the present and subjunctive forms as well.

**Interpersonal** Have students work in pairs. Each student writes a list, in Spanish, of 5 places. Next, S1 asks, for example, **"¿Qué harás en el bosque?"** S2 answers the question in the future tense. Students then switch roles.

**Objective:** Controlled practice
Irregular future tense

### Answers

1. Paco y Guillermo tendrán que escalar montañas.
2. Tú podrás pescar.
3. José y yo pondremos la tienda de campaña.
4. Yo haré la fogata.

**Objective:** Transitional practice
Making predictions

### Answers

*Answers will vary but should reflect correct use of the future tense.*

1. En diez años, (no) tendré [dos] hijos.
2. ... (no) querré comprar el carro de mis sueños.
3. ... (no) sabré hablar tres o más idiomas.
4. ... (no) me casaré.
5. ... (no) haré viajes por todas partes.

## Cross Cultural Connections

Have students describe what they see in the pictures on p. 347. Have students discuss how camping in Costa Rica might be different from camping in their local area.

## Culture Highlights

- **PARQUE NACIONAL TAPANTÍ,** located 25 miles southeast of San José, is known for its beautiful cloud forest full of orchids, birds, and butterflies. The Orosi River has many scenic waterfalls.
- **PARQUE NACIONAL BRAULIO CARRILLO** is located to the north of San José. It is one of the larger parks, with many hiking trails. A dormant volcano, Barva Volcano, is located here. The Rain Forest Aerial Tram tours the northern part of the park.

## Block Schedule

**Variation** Have students work in small groups to write a typical day's announcements in Spanish with a focus on the future tense. **Haber** will most likely be the main verb used, but you may provide other examples to foster different ideas: **La reunión del club de español será en el cuarto número catorce a las tres. Los estudiantes del cuarto año irán a Washington el viernes. El autobús saldrá a las seis de la mañana.**

## Teaching Resource Options

**Print**

*Más práctica* Workbook PE, p. 127
*Cuaderno para hispanohablantes* PE, p. 125
Block Scheduling Copymasters
Unit 5 Resource Book
*Más práctica* Workbook TE, p. 58
*Cuaderno para hispanohablantes* TE, p. 64
Information Gap Activities, p. 68

**Audiovisual**

OHT 158 (Quick Start)

**Technology**

*Intrigas y aventuras* CD-ROM, Disc 2

## Quick Start Review

Using **por** when talking about transportation

Use OHT 158 or write on board: Complete the following sentences by adding a mode of transportation that makes sense in each case. Use **por** in each sentence. For example: **Fui a India... / Fui a India por avión.**

avión, tren, autobús, bicicleta, taxi

1. Vamos a la escuela...
2. Fui a la casa de mi amiga...
3. Viajarán a España...
4. Fueron al centro...
5. No me gustan los aviones. Voy a la casa de mis abuelos...

*Answers may vary.*
*Possible answers:* 1. por autobús, 2. por bicicleta, 3. por avión, 4. por taxi, 5. por tren

## Teaching Suggestions
### Presenting Weather Expressions with hacer

- Have students write a weather forecast for their local area using the vocabulary on p. 348.
- This might be a good opportunity for students to do one of the activities described in the **Ampliación** section of the book. See pp. 315A–315B for ideas.

ACTIVIDAD 9

## De camping

**Hablar/Escribir** Imagínate que vas de camping el próximo fin de semana. Conversa con tus compañeros(as) sobre el viaje.

modelo

*El próximo fin de semana mis amigos y yo iremos de camping. Iremos a un lugar no muy lejos de aquí donde hay un lago muy bonito. Traeré la tienda de campaña y mi amigo Raúl traerá la comida… ¿Y cómo será tu viaje?*

1. ¿Con quién(es) irás?
2. ¿Tendrás que ir muy lejos?
3. ¿Adónde irás?
4. ¿Habrá un río o un lago?
5. ¿Qué tipo de comidas harás?
6. ¿Harás una fogata?
7. ¿Tendrás una tienda de campaña?
8. ¿Qué actividades harás?

MÁS COMUNICACIÓN p. R15

## Weather Expressions with hacer

To talk about the weather, you usually use **hacer.**

**¿Qué tiempo hace?**
***What's it like out?***

En Puerto Rico **hace calor** todo el año.
*In Puerto Rico **it's hot** all year.*

**Hacía** 25 grados centígrados el día que salí para Costa Rica.
***It was** 25 degrees Celsius the day I left for Costa Rica.*

Remember, you don't use **hacer** to say it's **raining** or **snowing.** Instead, use the verbs **llover** (*to rain*) and **nevar** (*to snow*).

No me gusta el norte de España porque **llueve** mucho.
*I don't like the north of Spain because **it rains** a lot.*

If you want to describe a particular **kind** of day, you can say:

**Es un día soleado.**
***It's a sunny day.***

**Es un día caluroso.**
***It's a hot day.***

**Es un día frío.**
***It's a cold day.***

### Vocabulario

**El tiempo**

**el aguacero** *downpour*
**centígrado(a)** *centigrade*
**húmedo(a)** *humid*
**el huracán** *hurricane*
**la llovizna** *drizzle*
**la neblina** *mist, fog*
**la nube** *cloud*
**el pronóstico** *forecast*
**el rayo** *thunderbolt, flash of lightning*
**el relámpago** *lightning*
**soleado(a)** *sunny*
**el trueno** *thunder*
**violento(a)** *violent*

¿Qué tiempo hará mañana?



## Classroom Community

**Learning Scenarios** Give students copies of weather forecasts from newspapers. Ask them to present a weather update in Spanish for some exchange students who will be visiting the school.

**Storytelling** State a weather condition. Students share a story about what happened to them during the given weather, e.g., **Era un día frío. Oímos el trueno. Vimos muchos relámpagos...**

**TPR** Have students decide on a sound effect and action to represent the weather vocabulary on p. 348. Then when you say each word, students give the corresponding sound effect and action.

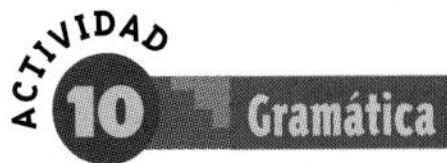

## ¿Qué se pondrán?

**Leer/Escribir** ¿Qué se pondrán estas personas después de escuchar el pronóstico?

**modelo**

*La llovizna pasará pronto y va a hacer sol pero hará frío. (yo)*

*Me pondré un sombrero y un abrigo.*

1. Es un día soleado hoy. Hace 30 grados centígrados. (nosotros)
2. Las nubes son oscuras y está húmedo. Habrá relámpagos. (tú)
3. Hace mucho viento hoy, pero no tan violento como un huracán. (ellas)
4. Ahora hay neblina pero hará sol por la tarde. (Francisco)


**MÁS PRÁCTICA** *cuaderno* p. 127

**PARA HISPANOHABLANTES** *cuaderno* p. 125

## ¿Qué tiempo hace?

**Hablar/Leer** Lee el mapa de Costa Rica y habla con un(a) compañero(a) sobre el tiempo en estos lugares.

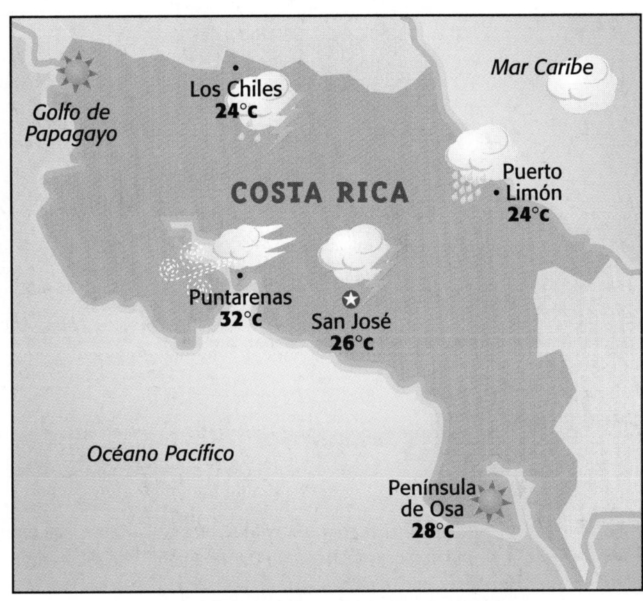


**modelo**

*Puntarenas*

**Compañero(a):** *¿Qué tiempo hace en Puntarenas?*

**Tú:** *Hace 32 grados centígrados. También hace viento y está nublado.*

1. San José
2. Puerto Limón
3. el golfo de Papagayo
4. el mar Caribe
5. Los Chiles
6. la península de Osa

**Objective** Open-ended practice
Irregular future/discussing outdoor activities

*Answers may vary.*

**Objective:** Controlled practice
Weather expressions

### Answers

*Answers may vary.*

1. Nos pondremos unas sandalias y un traje de baño.
2. Te pondrás unas botas.
3. Ellas se pondrán vestidos y chaquetas.
4. Francisco se pondrá unos pantalones y una camisa.

### Teaching Note

Have students refer to a detailed map of Costa Rica to locate the places listed in Actividad 11.

**Objective:** Transitional practice
Weather expressions

### Answers

*Answers may vary.*

1. En San José hace 26 grados centígrados. También está nublado y hay relámpagos.
2. En Puerto Limón hace 24 grados centígrados. También está lloviendo.
3. En el golfo del Papagayo hace sol.
4. En el mar Caribe está nublado.
5. En Los Chiles hace 24 grados centígrados. También hay llovizna y relámpagos.
6. En la península de Osa hace 28 grados centígrados. Hace sol.

### Supplementary Vocabulary

| | |
|---|---|
| **bajo cero** | below zero (degrees) |
| **caer aguanieve** | to sleet |
| **el ciclón** | cyclone |
| **granizar** | to hail |
| **la tormenta** | storm |

### Project

Have students research the Internet for actual weather reports for San José, Costa Rica; Madrid, Spain; San Juan, Puerto Rico; and Mexico City, Mexico.

## Teaching All Students

**Extra Help** Ask students to look up weather conditions in the newspaper and identify the local weather conditions in Spanish.

**Native Speakers** Have Spanish speakers review the list of vocabulary on p. 348 and predict the weather for the upcoming weekend using the future tense. You may also ask them to describe the weather conditions in their native countries.

**Multiple Intelligences**

**Visual** Ask students to illustrate a given weather condition and label it in Spanish. Hang the illustrations in the classroom.

### Block Schedule

**Peer Teaching** Have students take turns giving a weather forecast.The class can also recycle the preterite by telling what the weather was like yesterday.

## Teaching Resource Options

**Print**

*Más práctica* Workbook PE, p. 128
*Cuaderno para hispanohablantes* PE, p. 126
Block Scheduling Copymasters
Unit 5 Resource Book
*Más práctica* Workbook TE, p. 59
*Cuaderno para hispanohablantes* TE, p. 65
Audioscript, p. 80

**Audiovisual**

OHT 159 (Quick Start)
Audio Program Cassette 14A / CD 14

**Technology**

*Intrigas y aventuras* CD-ROM, Disc 2

## Quick Start Review

Using **nosotros** commands

Use OHT 159 or write on board: For each observation about the weather, suggest an appropriate activity using a **nosotros** command. For example:
Es un día frío. / Alquilemos un video.

1. Es un día soleado.
2. Llueve.
3. Hace frío.
4. Hace calor.

*Answers will vary.*

## Teaching Suggestions

- **Presenting Expressions with para** Hold an object and practice giving it away to different students around the classroom, for example, **este libro es para Juan, este lápiz es para María.**
- To present **para** with purposes, hold up several household objects and state their purposes, e.g., **un libro es para leer, una manzana es para comer, una taza es para beber,** etc.

## Supplementary Vocabulary

Remind students that they have already learned several expressions with **para**, such as: **¿para qué?** *(why?)*, **para siempre** *(forever)*, etc.

ACTIVIDAD 12

## El pronóstico del tiempo

**Escuchar** Escucha los pronósticos del tiempo y decide a qué foto corresponde.

a.

b.

c.

d.

GRAMÁTICA

## Expressions with para

Remember that one way to say *for* is with **por**. The preposition **para** can also mean *for,* as well as *in order to* and *to.* Use **para** when referring to

- **goals** to reach.
  Haré investigaciones **para encontrar maneras de preservar los animales.**
  *I will do research* ***to (in order to) find ways of saving animals.***
- **movement towards a place.**
  Salimos **para Costa Rica** mañana.
  *We leave* ***for Costa Rica*** *tomorrow.*
- **the recipient** of an action or object.
  Esta manta es **para Fernando.**
  *This blanket is* ***for Fernando.***
- **purposes** to fulfill.
  Necesitamos sacos de dormir **para ir de camping.**
  *We need sleeping bags* ***to (in order to) go camping.***
- **deadlines** to meet.
  Tendremos que encontrar leña **para esta noche.**
  *We will have to find firewood* ***for tonight.***
- **employment.**
  Francisco **trabaja para *Onda Internacional.***
  *Francisco* ***works for*** **Onda Internacional.**



## Classroom Community

**TPR** Have students take turns saying incomplete sentences with **para**, silently acting out the part of the sentence that follows **para**. For example, **Un lápiz es para...** (acts out writing). The class completes the sentence.

**Games** You can turn **Actividad 14** into a game. Divide the class into 2 teams and give each team half of the vocabulary words. Give each team 5 minutes to prepare short descriptions to give as clues. Then each team takes turns giving short descriptions for the other team to guess.

## Muy curioso

**Escribir** Francisco le muestra unas fotos de Costa Rica a un primo menor que hace muchas preguntas. ¿Cómo contesta Francisco?

modelo

*¿Para quién era?*

*El regalo era para Amalía.*

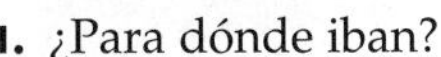

1. ¿Para dónde iban?

2. ¿Para qué necesitabas los fósforos?

3. ¿Para quién trabajaba?

4. ¿Para cuándo tenías que escribir el artículo?

**MÁS PRÁCTICA** *cuaderno* p. 128

**PARA HISPANOHABLANTES** *cuaderno* p. 126

## Actividad 14 ¿Para qué?

**PARA CONVERSAR**

**STRATEGY: SPEAKING**

**Find alternate ways to communicate** When you can't think of a word and you "talk your way around it," it's called circumlocution. Defining words gives you practice in circumlocution. Clues to meaning are uses (**para qué sirve**), the context of uses (**cuándo / dónde**), description (**pequeño**), or another word close in meaning (**una casita**). This skill helps you communicate even if you don't know the exact word.

**Hablar** ¿Para qué sirven estas cosas? Piensa en una de estas palabras y descríbesela a un(a) compañero(a). Él (Ella) tiene que adivinar qué palabra es. Cambien de papel.

modelo

*la tienda de campaña*

**Tú:** *Es para protegerte de los insectos y los aguaceros cuando acampas.*

**Compañero(a):** *Es una tienda de campaña.*

los fósforos · la leña · la selva · la conservación · el desarrollo · las tijeras · el sendero · la almohada · el campamento · la linterna · la manta · el abrelatas



## Teaching All Students

**Extra Help** Have students work with a partner to create a sample sentence using **para** for each of the six uses listed in the **Gramática** box on p. 350.

**Native Speakers** Ask Spanish speakers to give examples of other uses of **para**. You can also ask them to tell students how they determine when **por** or **para** should be used.

**Multiple Intelligences**

**Visual** Ask students to make a poster to describe the uses of **para**.

**Objective:** Transitional practice Listening comprehension/weather expressions

**Answers** (See script, TE p. 337B.)

1. b
2. c
3. d
4. a

**Objective:** Transitional practice Expressions with **para**

Imperfect tense

**Answers**

*Answers will vary.*

1. Iban para el cráter.
2. Los necesitaba para hacer una fogata.
3. Trabajaba para el parque.
4. Tenía que escribir el artículo para el viernes pasado.

**Objective:** Open-ended practice Expressions with **para**

*Answers will vary.*

## Speaking Strategy

**Rubric: Speaking**

| Criteria | Scale | |
|---|---|---|
| Vocabulary use | 1 2 3 4 5 | A = 17–20 pts. |
| Logical organization | 1 2 3 4 5 | B = 13–16 pts. |
| Fluency, intonation | 1 2 3 4 5 | C = 9–12 pts. |
| Accuracy | 1 2 3 4 5 | D = 5–8 pts. |
| | | F = < 5 pts. |

## Quick Wrap-Up

To continue the practice of **para**, have students imagine they must buy gifts for five people. They may choose family, friends, famous people, or well-known people in the school such as the principal. They may work alone, in pairs, or in a small group. Have them write a sentence telling what they will buy for each person—money is no object! For example: **Voy a comprar una pintura para mi madre.**

## Block Schedule

**FunBreak** The students have enough vocabulary and skills by now to create their very own newsletter. They can include stories about each other in the past, current events, a horoscope predicting the future, an advice column, and weather forecasts. They can distribute the newsletter to other Spanish classes for reading. (For additional activities, see **Block Scheduling Copymasters.**)

## Teaching Resource Options

**Print**

*Más práctica* Workbook PE, pp. 121–124
*Cuaderno para hispanohablantes* PE, pp. 121–122
Block Scheduling Copymasters
Unit 5 Resource Book
*Más práctica* Workbook TE, pp. 52–55
*Cuaderno para hispanohablantes* TE, pp. 60–61
Information Gap Activities, p. 69
Audioscript, pp. 80–82

**Audiovisual**

OHT 159 (Quick Start)
Audio Program Cassette 14A, 14B / CD 14; (*Para hispanohablantes* Cassette 14B / CD 14)

**Technology**

*Intrigas y aventuras* CD-ROM, Disc 2

## Quick Start Review

Talking about nature and the environment

Use OHT 159 or write on board: Fill in the blank with the correct word.
**conservar / población / senderos / peligroso / el medio ambiente / el desarrollo**

1. San José tiene una ___ de 819.000.
2. Es necesario controlar la contaminación del aire y del agua para preservar ___.
3. No me gusta ___ rápido de las ciudades. Necesitamos los parques y los árboles.
4. Es importante ___ la naturaleza.
5. Dar un paseo es popular en este parque. Hay muchos ___ excelentes.
6. Hay animales salvajes por todas partes. Es ___.

**Answers**
1. población, 2. el medio ambiente, 3. el desarrollo, 4. conservar, 5. senderos, 6. peligroso

## Culture Highlights

**RAFTING IN COSTA RICA** There are several popular rivers for rafting trips. They include the Reventazón, the Pacuare, and the Sarapiquí Rivers. Many tour groups offer the rafting trips as an excursion. There are white-water rivers for experienced rafters and gentler rivers for novice rafters and bird watchers.

## Nuestras obligaciones

**Leer/Escribir** Lee este anuncio y responde a las siguientes preguntas.

1. ¿Qué debemos hacer para proteger la naturaleza?
2. ¿Estás en contra del desarrollo de la selva? Explica tu respuesta.
3. ¿Estás a favor de poner límites a los visitantes de los parques nacionales? Explica.
4. ¿Por qué es complicado proteger el medio ambiente?

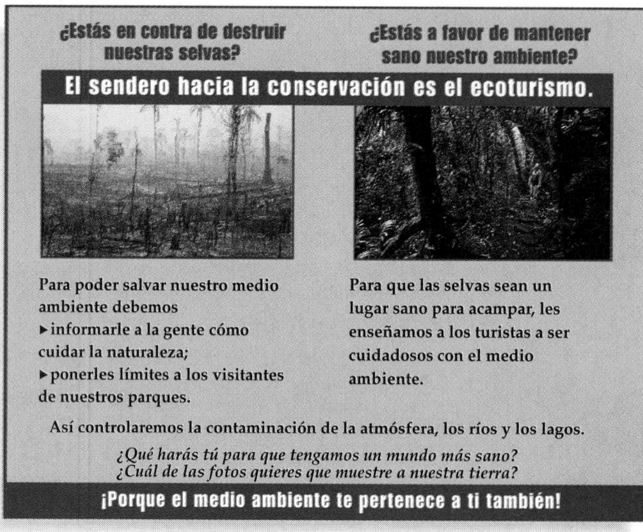

¿Estás en contra de destruir nuestras selvas?
¿Estás a favor de mantener sano nuestro ambiente?
El sendero hacia la conservación es el ecoturismo.
Para poder salvar nuestro medio ambiente debemos
▸informarle a la gente cómo cuidar la naturaleza;
▸ponerles límites a los visitantes de nuestros parques.
Para que las selvas sean un lugar sano para acampar, les enseñamos a los turistas a ser cuidadosos con el medio ambiente.
Así controlaremos la contaminación de la atmósfera, los ríos y los lagos.
¿Qué harás tú para que tengamos un mundo más sano?
¿Cuál de las fotos quieres que muestre a nuestra tierra?
¡Porque el medio ambiente te pertenece a ti también!


### Vocabulario

**Expresa tus opiniones**

**complicado(a)** *complicated*
**crear** *to create*
**estar a favor de** *to be in favor of*
**estar en contra de** *to be against*
**el permiso** *permission*
**permitir** *to permit*
**pertenecer** *to belong; to pertain*

¿Qué expresión es mejor para describir los problemas de la preservación?

## ¿Aventurera o cuidadosa?

**Escuchar/Escribir** Estela es muy aventurera y Cristina es más cuidadosa. Hablan de sus planes. ¿Quién dice cada oración: Estela o Cristina? Luego, explica si te pareces más a Estela o Cristina. ¿Por qué?

1. _____
2. _____
3. _____
4. _____
5. _____
6. _____
7. _____
8. _____

**NOTA CULTURAL**

**Navegar los rápidos** Costa Rica tiene muchos rápidos (*rapids*) donde se puede navegar. Aquí ves a algunos jóvenes en el río Sarapiquí.

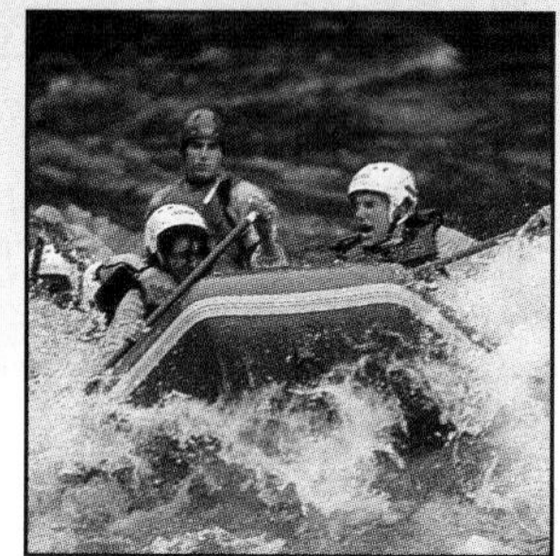



## Classroom Community

**Learning Scenarios** Divide the class into two groups for a simple debate regarding an environmental concern. G1 is "for" the chosen topic (**está a favor de**) while G2 is "against" (**está en contra de**). Each group should come up with at least 5 arguments that support its position. Allow time for each group to prepare a presentation.

**Cooperative Learning** You can turn **Actividad 17** into 5 class projects. Divide the class into 5 groups and assign a situation to each one. Have groups work together to give opinions and possible solutions to each situation. Assign a recorder to take notes and a presenter to present the findings to the rest of the class.

## ¿Qué harás tú?

**Hablar/Escribir** Habla con un grupo de compañeros(as) sobre sus opiniones e ideas para preservar el medio ambiente.

**modelo**

*En el futuro, ¿qué (decir) tus hijos del medio ambiente?*

**Tú:** *En el futuro, ¿qué dirán tus hijos del medio ambiente?*

**Compañero(a) 1:** *Dirán que valoran lo que hizo nuestra generación para protegerlo.*

**Compañero(a) 2:** *No estoy de acuerdo. En mi opinión, dirán que no hicimos lo suficiente.*

1. En 20 años, ¿(decir) tú que la generación de tus padres hizo lo suficiente para proteger el medio ambiente?
2. ¿(Haber) más o menos animales en peligro de extinción en 20 años? ¿Por qué?
3. ¿Qué (hacer) tú y tus amigos en el próximo año para conservar el medio ambiente? ¿(Reciclar) latas, papel y plástico? ¿(Usar) menos agua?
4. ¿(Andar) ustedes en bicicleta, a pie o por transportación pública? ¿Por qué?
5. ¿(Ayudar) tú a crear maneras nuevas de proteger el medio ambiente? Explica.

## En el año 2050...

**Hablar/Escribir** ¿Cómo será el mundo en el año 2050? En grupos, preparen una descripcíon para la clase, incluyendo ayudas visuales y comentarios sobre tres o más de las siguientes categorías.

**modelo**

*En el año 2050 habrá computadoras en todas las casas. Las computadoras ayudarán a la familia…*

¿Cómo será(n)…?

| | |
|---|---|
| las escuelas | las familias |
| la ropa | la televisión |
| el tiempo | las computadoras |
| la naturaleza | las tiendas |
| los pasatiempos | el cine |
| | ¿? |

MÁS COMUNICACIÓN p. R15

### Refrán

**Llueve a cántaros.**

Para adivinar este refrán mira el dibujo para saber qué es un cántaro. Ahora piensa en el agua cayendo de un cántaro. ¿Cae todo de una vez o poco a poco? ¿Qué imaginas que significa el refrán? Si todavía no lo entiendes, ¡piensa en un refrán del inglés: está lloviendo gatos y perros!

## Teaching All Students

**Extra Help** ¿Cómo debemos preservar el medio ambiente? ¿Por qué? List reasons on a transparency or on the board.

**Multiple Intelligences**

**Logical/Mathematical** Ask students to survey their classmates on their opinions on one of the following topics: **ir a la escuela por todo el año** (year-round schooling); **proteger el media ambiente; el campamento o el hotel de lujo,** etc. Have students quantify the results and share with the class.

**Objective:** Transitional practice
Talking about ecology

*Answers will vary.*

**Objective:** Transitional practice
Listening comprehension/discussing outdoor activities

**Answers** (See script, TE p. 337B.)

1. Estela
2. Estela
3. Cristina
4. Cristina
5. Estela
6. Cristina
7. Cristina
8. Estela

**Objective:** Open-ended practice
Talking about ecology

**Answers**

*Answers will vary.*

1. dirás / diré
2. Habrá
3. harán, Reciclarán, Usarán / Haremos, Reciclaremos, Usaremos
4. Andarán / Andaremos
5. Ayudarás / Ayudaré

### Actividad 17 Class Project

**Rubric: Speaking**

| Criteria | Scale |
|---|---|
| Vocabulary use | 1 2 3 4 5 |
| Correct verb use | 1 2 3 4 5 |
| Logical organization | 1 2 3 4 5 |
| Creativity | 1 2 3 4 5 |

A = 17–20 pts.
B = 13–16 pts.
C = 9–12 pts.
D = 5–8 pts.
F = < 5 pts.

**Objective:** Open-ended practice
Making predictions

*Answers will vary.*

### Interdisciplinary Connection

**Geography** Using a map of Costa Rica, have students locate the following:

Parque Nacional Braulio Carrillo
Parque Nacional Manuel Antonio
Parque Nacional Volcán Poás
Parque Nacional Tapanti

### Teaching Note

Divide the class into several small groups and have them each choose an area to predict into the future. Use same rubric as in **Actividad** 17.

### Block Schedule

**Change of Pace** Promote additional oral practice by expanding **Actividad 17.** Have students work in groups of 3 to debate the issues in **Actividad 17**.

### Teaching Resource Options

**Print** 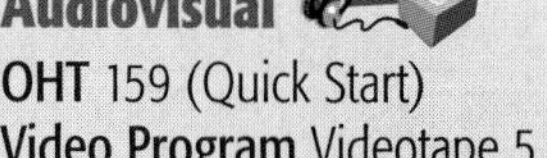

*Cuaderno para hispanohablantes* PE, pp. 127–128
Unit 5 Resource Book
*Cuaderno para hispanohablantes* TE, pp. 66–67
Video Activities, p. 76
Videoscript, p. 78

**Audiovisual**
OHT 159 (Quick Start)
Video Program Videotape 5, 17:36 / Videodisc 4A

Search Chapter 3, Play to 4
U5E2, En colores (Culture), Spanish

Search Chapter 3, Play to 4
U5E2, En colores (Culture), English

### Quick Start Review

Leisure activities

Use OHT 159 or write on board: Write down two activities you could do in each of these locations. Use the infinitive in your response. For example: **la playa / buscar caracoles, relajarse.**

1. la playa
2. el bosque tropical
3. el río

*Answers will vary.*

### Teaching Suggestions
#### Presenting En colores

- **Prereading** Have students review the **¿Comprendiste?** questions before starting their first pass through the reading.
- **Strategy: Predict appeal to ecotourists** Have students copy the chart in their notebooks and fill in the information in small groups. Add a third column for students to fill in the **Actividades** available at each location.
- **Post-reading** Have students use a map of Costa Rica to locate the places mentioned in the reading.

# En colores

## CULTURA Y COMPARACIONES

### PARA CONOCERNOS

**STRATEGY: CONNECTING CULTURES**

**Predict appeal to ecotourists** Ecotourism seeks to benefit both the environment and local economy by appealing to many people. For each tourist destination below, identify the major activities and check whether they would attract adults, young people, or both.

| Actividades | Adultos | Jóvenes |
|---|---|---|
| Teleférico del bosque lluvioso | | |
| Selva Verde | | |
| Río Sarapiquí | | |
| Parque Nacional de Diversiones | | |
| Parque Nacional Manuel Antonio | | |

Predict Costa Rica's desirability as an ecotourist destination for a broad range of people.

## Costa Rica, ¡la pura vida!

Ir de vacaciones a Costa Rica es combinar dos viajes en uno. Para aprender algo nuevo hay sitios históricos y parques ecológicos. Puedes relajarte en la playa o ir a un parque acuático. Hay actividades de interés para todas las edades.

Si te gusta la aventura, lleva a tu familia al río Sarapiquí para navegar los rápidos. La primera parte del río tiene corrientes fuertes, pero más abajo el agua pasa despacio y entras en la selva.

354

### Classroom Community

**Portfolio** Have students choose one of the attractions in Costa Rica described in the cultural reading. Ask them to expand on the information by researching additional facts about Costa Rica, then write up their future plans to visit it in their portfolio.

**Rubric: Writing**

| Criteria | Scale |
|---|---|
| Accuracy of information | 1 2 3 4 5 |
| Logical organization | 1 2 3 4 5 |
| Vocabulary use | 1 2 3 4 5 |

A = 13–15 pts.
B = 10–12 pts.
C = 7–9 pts.
D = 4–6 pts.
F = < 4 pts.

La Selva Verde, una reserva privada, ofrece cuartos construidos en la selva con el mínimo efecto negativo al medio ambiente. Allí sales de tu cuarto y estás arriba en los árboles. Camina por los senderos y observa las ranas venenosas fosforescentes[1] y pájaros exóticos.

Una atracción educativa y divertida es el Teleférico[2] del bosque lluvioso. El teleférico te lleva por la parte más alta del bosque donde puedes ver de cerca las orquídeas, los tucanes y las mariposas iridiscentes[3] de este ambiente húmedo.

Cuando te canses de la naturaleza, puedes ir al lugar favorito de los jóvenes, el Parque Nacional de Diversiones. Hay juegos mecánicos[4] y salen desfiles todas las noches.

Cuando toda la familia quiera relajarse en la playa, pueden ir al Parque Nacional Manuel Antonio, que está en la costa del océano Pacífico. Además de las playas, hay senderos donde puedes caminar y ver iguanas, loros y monos. En Costa Rica siempre es posible aprender algo sobre el medio ambiente mientras te relajas.

[1] neon-colored poison dart frogs
[2] aerial tram
[3] iridescent
[4] amusement rides

## ¿Comprendiste?

1. ¿Cuáles son las ventajas de la reserva Selva Verde?
2. ¿Qué transporte te lleva por el bosque lluvioso? ¿Qué puedes ver?
3. ¿Qué hay en el Parque Nacional de Diversiones?
4. Si tus padres quieren descansar en la playa y tú quieres explorar terrenos tropicales, ¿qué parque nacional deben visitar? ¿Por qué?

## ¿Qué piensas?

¿Crees que es posible que lleguen muchos turistas sin dañar *(hurting)* el medio ambiente de un lugar? Con el ecoturismo, ¿sería posible tener atracciones turísticas modernas?¿Cuáles imaginas que son las ventajas o las desventajas de los lugares mencionados en **«Costa Rica, ¡la pura vida!»**?

## Hazlo tú 

Con un(a) compañero(a), haz un folleto de viaje para Costa Rica. Mencionen algunos lugares de interés y dibujen algunos de estos lugares.



## Teaching All Students

**Extra Help** Write each glossed word, and any other difficult words from the reading, on index cards and quiz students after the reading is completed.

**Native Speakers** Ask Spanish speakers if they can name 3–5 attractions that might qualify as ecotourism in the area their family is from.

**Multiple Intelligences**

**Verbal** Have students define "ecotourism" in Spanish in their own words and give several examples based on what they have learned about Costa Rica.

**Naturalist** Have students make a list of the animals or plants mentioned in the reading. Then have students choose one to research further via the Internet or the library.

## Reading Strategy

Have students skim for the general idea, then scan for specific information. As students read about the tourist destinations in Costa Rica, have them identify the pictures on pp. 354–355 that match each destination.

## Culture Highlights

- **EL RÍO SARAPIQUÍ** is a popular river with class III rapids. It passes through rocky canyons, waterfalls, and forests.
- **EL TELEFÉRICO DEL BOSQUE LLUVIOSO** Cars that carry 6 passengers glide through the rain forest at a height of 120 feet above the ground. There is minimal disturbance to the forest and visitors can see a wide range of flowers, birds, and other wildlife.
- **PARQUE NACIONAL MANUEL ANTONIO** This park has nice beaches, well-marked trails, and an abundance of wildlife on the beaches and in the forests: birds, monkeys, lizards, etc.

## Cross Cultural Connections

Ask students if they know of any parks in the U.S. that might appeal to ecotourists. Where are they? What activities do they offer? What wildlife can be found there?

## ¿Comprendiste?

*Answers will vary.*

1. Ofrece cuartos construidos en la selva con el mínimo efecto negativo al medio ambiente.
2. El Teleférico te lleva por el bosque lluvioso. Puedes ver las orquídeas, los tucanes y las mariposas.
3. Hay juegos mecánicos y desfiles.
4. Debemos visitar el Parque Nacional Manuel Antonio. Hay playas y senderos por el bosque.

## Block Schedule

**Change of Pace** Have students take the information they gather from this reading and any other information throughout the **Etapa** and create travel brochures using the future tense and commands. For example: **No olviden de tomar el teleférico del bosque lluvioso. Verán aves magníficas.** (For additional activities, see **Block Scheduling Copymasters**.)

## Teaching Resource Options

**Print** 

Block Scheduling Copymasters
Unit 5 Resource Book
Information Gap Activities, pp. 70–71
Family Involvement, pp. 72–73

**Audiovisual**

OHT 160 (Quick Start)

**Technology**

Electronic Teacher Tools/Test Generator
*Intrigas y aventuras* CD-ROM, Disc 2

## Quick Start Review

Future tense

Use OHT 160 or write on board: Conjugate each of the following verbs in the future tense.

trabajar hacer salir
ir tener

**Answers**

trabajaré, trabajarás, trabajará, trabajaremos, trabajaréis, trabajarán
iré, irás, irá, iremos, iréis, irán
saldré, saldrás, saldrá, saldremos, saldréis, saldrán
haré, harás, hará, haremos, haréis, harán
tendré, tendrás, tendrá, tendremos, tendréis, tendrán

## Teaching Suggestions
### What Have Students Learned?

- Have students look at the "Now you can..." notes listed on the left side of pp. 356–357. Point out that if they feel they need to review material before doing the activities, they should consult the "To review" notes.
- Use the video to review vocabulary and structures.

# En uso
## REPASO Y MÁS COMUNICACIÓN

**OBJECTIVES**

- Discuss outdoor activities
- Describe the weather
- Make predictions
- Talk about ecology

*Now you can...*
- discuss outdoor activities.
- make predictions.

*To review*
- irregular forms of the future tense, see p. 346.

### ACTIVIDAD 1 ¡A las montañas!

Imagínate que Cecilia te invita a acampar. Para mejorar tu comprensión de la carta, cambia los verbos al futuro.

*Este fin de semana <u>hay</u> (1) una excursión a las montañas. Mi nuevo amigo, Francisco, <u>viene</u> (2) con nosotros. ¡Tú <u>tienes</u> (3) que venir también!*

*En las montañas <u>hacemos</u> (4) muchas cosas interesantes: escalar, remar, pescar... <u>Ponemos</u> (5) la tienda de campaña a orillas de un lago precioso. Francisco <u>quiere</u> (6) sacar fotos de los diversos animales y plantas que <u>podemos</u> (7) ver allí.*

*<u>Salimos</u> (8) el sábado temprano. Mañana <u>sé</u> (9) la hora exacta y te la <u>digo</u> (10).*

*Cecilia*

*Now you can...*
- describe the weather.
- make predictions.

*To review*
- weather expressions with **hacer,** see p. 348.

### ACTIVIDAD 2 ¿Va a llover?

Francisco escucha este pronóstico del tiempo en la televisión. Complétalo con las palabras de la lista.

centígrados neblina truenos soleado llovizna
aguacero calor nubes viento relámpagos

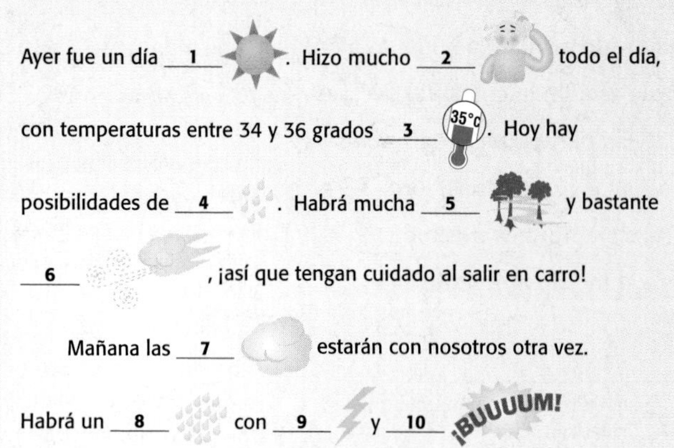

Ayer fue un día __1__. Hizo mucho __2__ todo el día, con temperaturas entre 34 y 36 grados __3__. Hoy hay posibilidades de __4__. Habrá mucha __5__ y bastante __6__, ¡así que tengan cuidado al salir en carro!
Mañana las __7__ estarán con nosotros otra vez.
Habrá un __8__ con __9__ y __10__ ¡BUUUUM!
35°C




## Classroom Community

**Portfolio** Ask students to write a weather report for the local region. Have them include short-range and long-range predictions. Add this weather report to their portfolio.

**Rubric: Writing**

| Criteria | Scale |
|---|---|
| Vocabulary use | 1 2 3 4 5 |
| Logical organization | 1 2 3 4 5 |
| Grammar/spelling/accuracy | 1 2 3 4 5 |

A = 13–15 pts.
B = 10–12 pts.
C = 7–9 pts.
D = 4–6 pts.
F = < 4 pts.

*Now you can...*
- talk about ecology.

*To review*
- **para,** see p. 350.

## ACTIVIDAD 3 ¡Llámanos hoy!

Lee este anuncio sobre una nueva organización y contesta las preguntas usando expresiones con **para.**

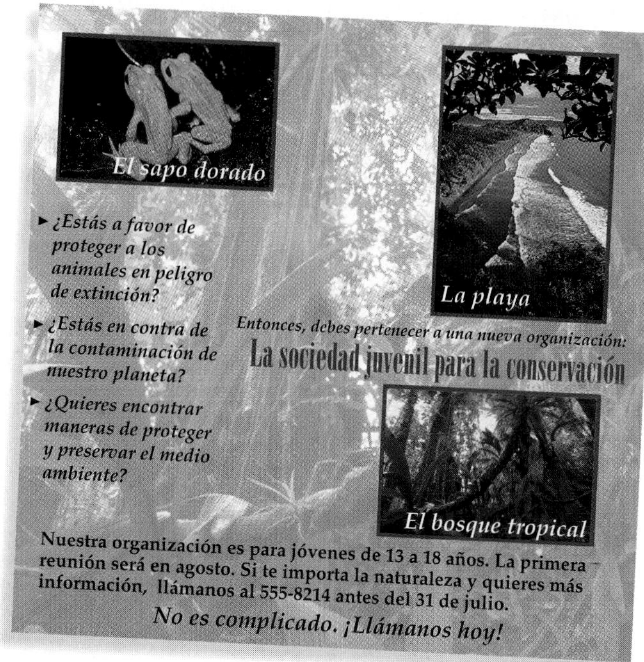
El sapo dorado
La playa
¿Estás a favor de proteger a los animales en peligro de extinción?
¿Estás en contra de la contaminación de nuestro planeta?
¿Quieres encontrar maneras de proteger y preservar el medio ambiente?
Entonces, debes pertenecer a una nueva organización:
La sociedad juvenil para la conservación
El bosque tropical
Nuestra organización es para jóvenes de 13 a 18 años. La primera reunión será en agosto. Si te importa la naturaleza y quieres más información, llámanos al 555-8214 antes del 31 de julio.
No es complicado. ¡Llámanos hoy!

**modelo**

*¿Para qué sirve este anuncio?*
*Sirve para informarnos sobre una nueva organización.*

1. ¿Para quiénes es la organización?
2. ¿A qué teléfono debes llamar para recibir más información?
3. ¿Para qué fecha hay que llamar?
4. ¿Quieren crear esta organización para preservar la historia o el medio ambiente?
5. ¿Estos jóvenes trabajarán para proteger a los animales o a los niños?
6. ¿Para ti es importante proteger el medio ambiente?

### ACTIVIDAD 1 Answers

1. habrá
2. vendrá
3. tendrás
4. haremos
5. Pondremos
6. querrá
7. podremos
8. Saldremos
9. sabré
10. diré

### ACTIVIDAD 2 Answers

1. soleado
2. calor
3. centígrados
4. llovizna
5. neblina
6. viento
7. nubes
8. aguacero
9. relámpagos
10. truenos

### ACTIVIDAD 3 Answers

*Answers will vary.*
1. La organización es para jóvenes de 13 a 18 años.
2. Debes llamar al 555–8214.
3. Hay que llamar antes del 31 de julio.
4. Quieren crear esta organización para preservar y proteger el medio ambiente.
5. Estos jóvenes trabajarán para proteger a los animales.
6. Para mí (no) es importante proteger el medio ambiente.

## Teaching All Students

**Extra Help** Have students answer the 3 questions in the **anuncio** in **Actividad 3**.

**Multiple Intelligences**

**Visual** Divide the class into four groups. Assign each group an objective from the list on p. 356. Have them make a poster to present an overview of the concept.

**Naturalist** Have students make a list of similar conservation groups (local or national) they know. Ask students to research the activities these groups promote.

## Block Schedule

**Process Time** Allow the class to work on the **Repaso** in class just before the bell. It will focus them on the vocabulary, they will see that others know certain items that they might not, and therefore it will encourage them to study for the assessment. Also, it gives them an opportunity to make sure they understand the instructions. (For additional activities, see **Block Scheduling Copymasters.**)

## Teaching Resource Options

### Print 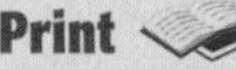

Unit 5 Resource Book
- Cooperative Quizzes, pp. 84–85
- Etapa Exam, Forms A and B, pp. 86–95
- *Examen para hispanohablantes,* pp. 96–100
- Portfolio Assessment, pp. 101–102
- Multiple Choice Test Questions, pp. 173–175

### Audiovisual 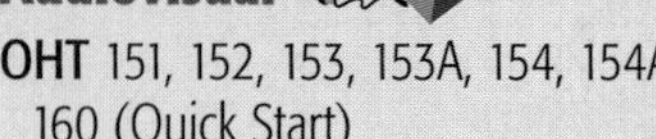

**OHT** 151, 152, 153, 153A, 154, 154A, 160 (Quick Start)

**Audio Program** Cassette 20A / CD 20; (*Para hispanohablantes* Cassette 20A / CD 20)

### Technology 

Electronic Teacher Tools/Test Generator

 www.mcdougallittell.com

## Quick Start Review

Talking about camping

Use OHT 160 or write on board: Make a list in Spanish of the items you would bring on a camping trip.

*Answers will vary but may include:*

**una almohada, la comida, los fósforos, una linterna, una manta, una navaja, una sábana, un saco de dormir, una tienda de campaña**

### Actividad 4 and Actividad 5

**Rubric: Speaking**

| Criteria | Scale |
|---|---|
| Fluency | 1 2 3 4 5 |
| Vocabulary use | 1 2 3 4 5 |
| Pronunciation | 1 2 3 4 5 |

A = 13–15 pts.
B = 10–12 pts.
C = 7–9 pts.
D = 4–6 pts.
F = < 4 pts.

### Actividad 6 En tu propia voz

**Rubric: Writing**

| Criteria | Scale |
|---|---|
| Vocabulary use | 1 2 3 4 5 |
| Accuracy | 1 2 3 4 5 |
| Creativity | 1 2 3 4 5 |

A = 13–15 pts.
B = 10–12 pts.
C = 7–9 pts.
D = 4–6 pts.
F = < 4 pts.

## Actividad 4 Recomendaciones

**PARA CONVERSAR**

**STRATEGY: SPEAKING**

**Make recommendations** Recommending action is the final step in problem-solving. Here the general problem is protecting and conserving the environment. Name specific aspects of the environment needing protection and possible actions. Why are some more important than others?

Haz una lista de cinco maneras de preservar y conservar el medio ambiente. Conversa con tu compañero(a) sobre sus ideas y seleccionen las tres acciones que tendrán más resultados.

**modelo**

1. Preservar diversas plantas
2. Proteger...
3.
4.
5.

**Tú:** *Estoy a favor de preservar las diversas plantas del mundo.*

**Compañero(a):** *¿Por qué es importante?*

**Tú:** *Porque las plantas limpian el aire.*

**Compañero(a):** *Sí, pero es más importante...*

## Actividad 5 Mañana habrá...

Imagínate que tú y tus amigos trabajan para un canal de televisión. Preparen y presenten el pronóstico del tiempo.

**modelo**

**Tú:** *Ayer hizo mucho frío, con temperaturas...*

**Estudiante 1:** *La temperatura va a subir hoy. Hace...*

**Estudiante 2:** *Mañana habrá un aguacero...*

## Actividad 6 En tu propia voz

**ESCRITURA** Imagínate que irás a acampar. Describe la experiencia ideal: cuándo, adónde y con quiénes irás, qué cosas llevarán, qué verán y harán allí, qué tiempo hará, etc.

**modelo**

*Yo iré de camping en el otoño con tres de mis amigos(as). El lugar ideal será un campamento muy lejos...*

## TÚ EN LA COMUNIDAD

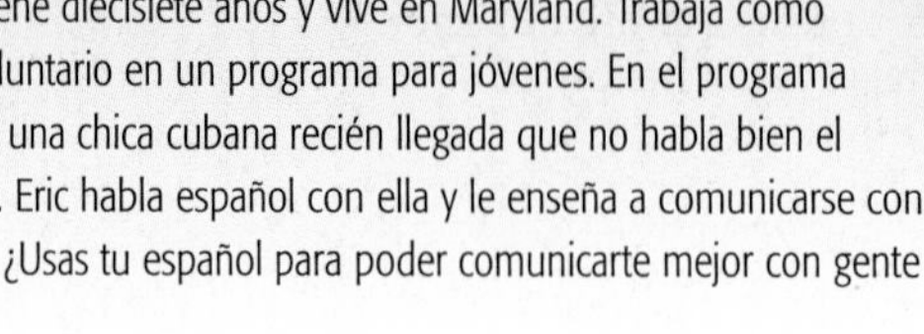

**Eric** lleva cinco años como estudiante del idioma español. Tiene diecisiete años y vive en Maryland. Trabaja como voluntario en un programa para jóvenes. En el programa hay una chica cubana recién llegada que no habla bien el inglés. Eric habla español con ella y le enseña a comunicarse con los otros jóvenes del grupo. ¿Usas tu español para poder comunicarte mejor con gente de otros lugares?



## Classroom Community

**Paired Activity** Have students work in pairs to review the Camping Necessities in the vocabulary list and state the purposes of each item using **para.** For example, **el abrelatas es para abrir latas; la almohada es para dormir,** etc.

**Game** Divide the class into teams. Give each team a set of scrambled sentences using **por/para**. Ask teams to unscramble the sentences and give a reason for the use of **por** versus **para**. The team that finishes all sentences and explanations correctly wins.

# En resumen
## REPASO DE VOCABULARIO

### TALK ABOUT ECOLOGY

| | |
|---|---|
| **complicado(a)** | *complicated* |
| **crear** | *to create* |
| **estar a favor de** | *to be in favor of* |
| **estar en contra de** | *to be against* |
| **el permiso** | *permission* |
| **permitir** | *to permit* |
| **pertenecer** | *to belong; to pertain* |

### DISCUSS OUTDOOR ACTIVITIES

**Outdoor Activities**

| | |
|---|---|
| **el campamento** | *camp* |
| **escalar montañas** | *to climb mountains* |
| **el montañismo** | *mountaineering* |
| **pescar** | *to fish* |
| **remar** | *to row* |

**Camping Necessities**

| | |
|---|---|
| **el abrelatas** | *can opener* |
| **la almohada** | *pillow* |
| **el balde** | *bucket* |
| **la fogata** | *campfire* |
| **el fósforo** | *match* |
| **el fuego** | *fire* |
| **la leña** | *firewood* |
| **la linterna** | *flashlight* |
| **la luz** | *light* |
| **la manta** | *blanket* |
| **la navaja** | *jackknife* |
| **la sábana** | *sheet* |
| **el saco de dormir** | *sleeping bag* |
| **la tienda de campaña** | *tent* |
| **las tijeras** | *scissors* |

### DESCRIBE THE WEATHER

| | |
|---|---|
| **el aguacero** | *downpour* |
| **caluroso(a)** | *hot* |
| **centígrado(a)** | *centigrade* |
| **húmedo(a)** | *humid* |
| **el huracán** | *hurricane* |
| **la llovizna** | *drizzle* |
| **la neblina** | *mist, fog* |
| **la nube** | *cloud* |
| **el pronóstico** | *forecast* |
| **el rayo** | *thunderbolt, flash of lightning* |
| **el relámpago** | *lightning* |
| **soleado(a)** | *sunny* |
| **el trueno** | *thunder* |
| **violento(a)** | *violent* |

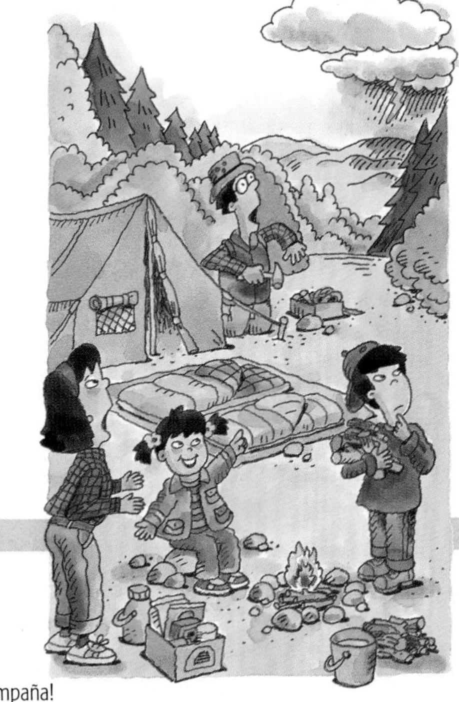

### Juego

**Cuando vas a acampar...**

Si quieres dormir sin frío, necesitas un ____ __ ______.

Si vas a cocinar, tienes que hacer una ______.

Y si hay un ________, ¡ojalá que tengas una buena tienda de campaña!



## Teaching All Students

**Extra Help** Have students write all the verbs they learned in this **Etapa** in their notebooks. They can conjugate each verb in the future tense for extra practice.

**Native Speakers** Ask Spanish speakers to read aloud the words in the vocabulary list for the class with special attention to pronunciation. Have the rest of the class repeat each word after the Spanish speaker.

**Multiple Intelligences**

**Logical/Mathematical** Have students locate a local or national weather map that lists the temperatures. Then have them calculate the temperatures in Celsius vs. Fahrenheit for 5 major cities. [Converting Celsius to Fahrenheit: C = 5/9 x (F - 32); Fahrenheit to Celsius: F = (9/5 x C) + 32]



### Teaching Note: En tu propia voz

**Writing Strategy** Ask students to make a list including as much information as possible before beginning to write. Have them answer the interrogatives Who? What? Where? When? Why? and How?

### Project: Reviewing Etapa 2

Assign the following out-of-class activities:

- Interview a Spanish speaker about his/her favorite outdoor activities.
- Make at least 3 predictions about the weather for the upcoming weekend.
- Find information about Costa Rica's ecotourism via the Internet or at the library.
- Find information on birds, wildlife, and plant life in Costa Rica.

**Extra Credit**

| | |
|---|---|
| Interview | 2 pts. |
| Weather predictions | 2 pts. |
| Ecotourism in Costa Rica | 2 pts. |
| Wildlife in Costa Rica | 2 pts. |

### Juego

**Answer**

saco de dormir, fogata, aguacero

### Community Connections

Have students prepare a community guidebook in Spanish to help visitors or newly arrived residents. Have students research local opportunities for helping others using their Spanish language skills.

### Block Schedule

**Brain-based Learning** For an activity like **Actividad 6**, have the class develop a rubric for assessing the writing exercise. It may have several components: task, message, grammar, or only one: use of the future tense. If the expectation is clear and the class has a vested interest in it, the writing will meet higher standards.

*pages 360–385*

# Planning Guide CLASSROOM MANAGEMENT

## OBJECTIVES

**Communication**
- Comment on conservation and the environment *pp. 362–363, 364–365, 371, 373*
- Talk about how you would solve problems *pp. 364–365, 367, 370–371, 373*

**Grammar**
- Choose between **por** and **para** *p. 368*
- The conditional tense *p. 370*

**Culture**
- Recycling in Costa Rica *pp. 364–365*
- Los campamentos *p. 369*
- La economía de Costa Rica *p. 374*
- La cascada de la novia *pp. 376–377*
- La Cumbre de la Ecología centroamericana *pp. 378–379*

**Recycling**
- The future tense *pp. 368, 369*
- Camping vocabulary *p. 369*

## STRATEGIES

**Listening Strategies**
- Propose solutions *p. 364*

**Speaking Strategies**
- Identify problems and your commitment to solving them *p. 367*
- Hypothesize about the future *p. 382*

**Reading Strategies**
- Recognize characteristics of legends *p. 376*
- Scan for cognates *TE p. 379*

**Writing Strategies**
- Support an opinion with facts and examples *Actividad 7, TE p. 382*
- Present a thorough and balanced review *p. 384*

**Connecting Cultures Strategies**
- Observe and generalize *TE p. 377*
- Prioritize *p. 378*

## PROGRAM RESOURCES

### Print

- *Más práctica* Workbook PE *pp. 129–136*
- Block Scheduling Copymasters *pp. 121–128*
- Unit 5 Resource Book
  - *Más práctica* Workbook TE *pp. 103–110*
  - *Cuaderno para hispanohablantes* TE *pp. 111–118*
  - Information Gap Activities *pp. 119–122*
  - Family Involvement *pp. 123–124*
  - Video Activities *pp. 125–127*
  - Videoscript *pp. 128–129*
  - Audioscript *pp. 130–134*
  - Assessment Program, Unit 5 Etapa 3 *pp. 135–169, 176–178*
  - Answer Keys *pp. 181–184*

### Audiovisual

- Audio Program Cassette 15A, 15B / CD 15
- Video Program Videotape 5 / Videodisc 4A
- Overhead Transparencies 161–170; M1, M2

### Technology

- Electronic Teacher Tools/Test Generator
- *Intrigas y aventuras* CD-ROM, Disc 2
- 

www.mcdougallittell.com

### Assessment Program Options

- Cooperative Quizzes (Unit 5 Resource Book)
- Etapa Exam Forms A and B (Unit 5 Resource Book)
- *Examen para hispanohablantes* (Unit 5 Resource Book)
- Portfolio Assessment (Unit 5 Resource Book)
- Unit 5 Comprehensive Test (Unit 5 Resource Book)
- *Prueba comprensiva para hispanohablantes* Unit 5 (Unit 5 Resource Book)
- Multiple Choice Test Questions (Unit 5 Resource Book)
- Audio Program Cassette 20A, 20B / CD 20
- Electronic Teacher Tools/Test Generator

### Native Speakers

- *Cuaderno para hispanohablantes* PE *pp. 129–136*
- *Cuaderno para hispanohablantes* TE (Unit 5 Resource Book)
- *Examen para hispanohablantes* (Unit 5 Resource Book)
- *Prueba comprensiva para hispanohablantes* Unit 5 (Unit 5 Resource Book)
- Audio Program *(Para hispanohablantes)* Cassette 15B, 20A / CD 15, CD 20
- Audioscript (Unit 5 Resource Book)

Francisco Fernando Amalia Cecilia

# Student Text Listening Activity Scripts

##  Videoscript: Diálogo *pages 364–365*

• Videotape 5, 21:40 • Videodisc 4A

Search Chapter 5, Play to 6. U5E3, En vivo (Dialog)

• Use the videoscript with **Actividades 1, 2** *page 366*

**Francisco:** Hoy en día, la protección del medio ambiente es un tema muy popular en los periódicos y las revistas. Todo el mundo tiene opiniones y puntos de vista al respecto. Todos saben que debemos conservar los recursos naturales de la Tierra. Y todos están a favor de reducir la contaminación.

Pero hablar del medio ambiente no es suficiente. Hay que actuar también. Muchas personas dirán "No soy más que una persona. ¿Qué puedo hacer yo para proteger el medio ambiente?" Pero hay mucho que podemos hacer. Y ustedes, los lectores de *Onda Internacional,* ¿qué pueden hacer?

Pueden comenzar en sus casas. ¡No lo echen todo al basurero! El reciclaje es fácil y ayuda a conservar nuestros recursos naturales. Si, por ejemplo, reciclamos las latas de aluminio, las botellas de vidrio y plástico, y el papel y el cartón, usaremos menos recursos. Así también mantienen limpio su pueblo o ciudad.

Muchos de ustedes dirán "Las industrias son otro problema grave."

Lo malo es que no son solamente las industrias las que son responsables por la contaminación. Cada ser humano comparte la responsabilidad. Los carros que manejamos queman gasolina, un combustible que produce contaminación. Si tú, Lector, pudieras manejar menos, habría menos contaminación del aire. Es nuestra responsabilidad también.

**Fernando:** ¡Hola, Francisco!

**Francisco:** ¡Fernando! ¿Cómo estás?

**Fernando:** Pura vida, ¿y vos?

**Francisco:** Bien, pero un poco triste. No quiero irme mañana. ¡Me encanta Costa Rica!

**Fernando:** Sí, es una pena. Pero sabés, si estudiás para ser periodista tal vez volvás un día. Bueno, ¿estás listo para ir a comer?

**Francisco:** Sí, un momento. Estoy terminando mi artículo para la revista..

**Fernando:** Ah, un artículo sobre el medio ambiente. Muy bien.

**Francisco:** Aunque la situación es difícil de resolver, si todos trabajamos juntos, podemos cambiar muchas cosas. Muchas personas están trabajando con grupos para la conservación y protección del medio ambiente. ¿Por qué no participas tú también?

**Francisco:** Bueno, ya está. Vamos.

**Francisco:** ¡Me encanta este lugar!

**Fernando:** Sí, es el lugar perfecto para tu fiesta de despedida.

**Francisco:** ¿Fiesta? ¿Qué fiesta?

**Todos:** ¡Buen viaje!

**Amalia:** Francisco, te deseamos todo lo mejor.

**Cecilia:** ¡Te vamos a visitar en Miami el año que viene! Vas a escribirnos, ¿verdad? ¡Espero recibir muchas cartas tuyas!

**Fernando:** Y yo te voy a mandar cartas por correo electrónico. ¡No te vayas sin darme tu dirección electrónica!

**Francisco:** Gracias... gracias a todos. No sé que decir.

**Amalia:** No digás nada, hijo. Sentáte, vamos a comer.

## Actividad 13 El noticiero *page 373*

1. En esta ciudad hay una situación difícil de resolver: la contaminación del lago. La situación es muy grave porque muchas personas van al lago a nadar y pescar.
2. Ayer los científicos de la reserva Santa Elena publicaron otro estudio sobre la destrucción de la capa de ozono. Dicen que la temperatura del planeta subirá si no se controla la contaminación.
3. La ciudad de San José anuncia que trabajará con los estudiantes para controlar la cantidad de basura en las escuelas.
4. Hoy hubo una conferencia internacional sobre el desarrollo de las selvas y el peligro para los animales.
5. Al terminar las noticias quiero leer una carta de un televidente. Dice: «Mucha gente tiene la actitud de que una persona sola no puede hacer nada para ayudar a mejorar el medio ambiente. ¿Qué le dirían ustedes a esa gente?»

## Actividad 16 Proyectos de limpieza *page 374*

**Voice 1:** ¿Qué podríamos hacer nosotros para proteger el medio ambiente?

**Voice 2:** Creo que sería muy fácil comenzar con proyectos simples. Por ejemplo, podríamos reciclar botellas y latas. También ganaríamos un poco de dinero haciendo eso.

**Voice 1:** ¡Qué bien! ¿Si pudieras, empezarías a limpiar el parque con otros compañeros?

**Voice 2:** ¡Claro! Yo podría llamar a todos nuestros amigos y así limpiaríamos el parque rápidamente.

**Voice 1:** Tengo otra idea. Viajar en autobús reduciría el nivel de smog en la ciudad. Todo el mundo debería hacer eso.

**Voice 2:** Tienes razón. ¿Cómo protegeríamos otros aspectos del medio ambiente, como la naturaleza y los animales en peligro de extinción?

**Voice 1:** Creo que el reciclaje del papel ayudaría a los bosques porque las industrias no tendrían que cortar tantos árboles. Eso protegería a los animales salvajes.

**Voice 2:** Estoy de acuerdo. Empecemos a llamar a nuestros amigos para convencerlos de que es muy fácil preservar el medio ambiente.

# Pacing Guide

## Sample Lesson Plan - 50 Minute Schedule

### DAY 1

**Etapa Opener**
- Quick Start Review (TE p. 360). 5 MIN.
- Anticipate/Activate prior knowledge: Have students look at *Etapa* Opener and answer questions. 10 MIN.

**En contexto: Vocabulario**
- Quick Start Review (TE p. 362). 5 MIN.
- Discuss pictures, have students use context and pictures to learn *Etapa* vocabulary. Answer questions, p. 363. 10 MIN.

**En vivo: Diálogo**
- Quick Start Review (TE p. 364). 5 MIN.
- Review Listening Strategy, p. 364. Play audio or show video for the dialog on pp. 364–365. 5 MIN.
- Replay twice. Read aloud, students take on roles of characters. Ask Comprehension Questions on TE p. 365. 10 MIN.

**Homework Option**
- Video Activities, Unit 5 Resource Book, pp. 125, 126.

### DAY 2

**En acción: Vocabulario y Gramática**
- Quick Start Review (TE p. 366). 5 MIN.
- Ask students for a summary of *En vivo* dialog to check recall. 5 MIN.
- Replay the *En vivo* dialog using the audiovisual resources, and have students do *Actividades* 1 and 2 orally. 10 MIN.
- Have students complete *Actividad* 3 in pairs. 10 MIN.
- Present Speaking Strategy, p. 367, and have students complete *Actividad* 4 in pairs. 10 MIN.
- Have students do *Actividad* 5 in writing then review orally. 10 MIN.

**Homework Option**
- *Más práctica* Workbook, pp. 129–132. *Cuaderno para hispanohablantes*, p. 129.

### DAY 3

**En acción (cont.)**
- Check homework. 5 MIN.
- Quick Start Review (TE p. 368). 5 MIN.
- Present *Gramática*: Choose Between *por* and *para,* p. 368. 10 MIN.
- Have students complete *Actividades* 6 and 7 in writing. 10 MIN.
- Have students do *Actividad* 8 in small groups. 10 MIN.
- Present *Gramática*: The Conditional Tense, p. 370, and have students do *Actividad* 9 in writing. 10 MIN.

**Homework Option**
- *Más práctica* Workbook, pp. 133–134. *Cuaderno para hispanohablantes*, pp. 131–132.

### DAY 4

**En acción (cont.)**
- Check homework. 5 MIN.
- Quick Start Review (TE p. 372). 5 MIN.
- Present *Vocabulario* box on p. 371 and have students complete *Actividad* 10 in pairs. 10 MIN.
- Have students complete *Actividad* 11 in writing. Present *Nota* and have students do *Actividad* 12 in small groups. Expand with *Más comunicación,* p. R16. 15 MIN.
- Play audio and have students complete *Actividad* 13. 5 MIN.
- Present *Vocabulario* box on p. 373 and have students start *Actividad* 14. 10 MIN.

**Homework Option**
- Have students finish Actividad 14 as homework. *Más práctica* Workbook, pp. 135–136. *Cuaderno para hispanohablantes*, pp. 133–134.

### DAY 5

**En acción (cont.)**
- Check homework. 5 MIN.
- Quick Start Review (TE p. 374). 5 MIN.
- Have students complete *Actividad* 15 in pairs. 5 MIN.
- Play audio and have students complete *Actividad* 16. 5 MIN.
- Have students play the game in *Actividad* 17 in small groups. 5 MIN.
- Have students work in small groups to discuss questions in *Actividad* 18. 5 MIN.

**En voces: Lectura**
- Quick Start Review (TE p. 376). 5 MIN.
- Review Reading Strategy, p. 376, and have students read silently. 5 MIN.
- Have students read *La cascada de la novia* aloud taking turns. 10 MIN.

**Homework Option**
- Write answers to *¿Comprendiste?* and *¿Qué piensas?* questions.

### DAY 6

**En colores: Cultura y comparaciones**
- Check homework. 5 MIN.
- Quick Start Review (TE p. 378). 5 MIN.
- Review Connecting Cultures Strategy, p. 378. 5 MIN.
- Read *La Cumbre de la Ecología Centroamericana* aloud with students. 10 MIN.
- Have students answer the *¿Comprendiste?* and *¿Qué piensas?* questions orally. 10 MIN.
- Divide students into small groups and have them work on the *Hazlo tú* activity. 15 MIN.

**Homework Option**
- Have students do *En uso, Actividades* 1–4.

### DAY 7

**En uso: Repaso y más comunicación**
- Check homework. 10 MIN.
- Review Speaking Strategy, p. 382. Then do *Actividad* 5 orally in pairs and *Actividad* 6 in groups. 15 MIN.

**En resumen: Repaso de vocabulario**
- Review grammar questions, etc., as necessary. 5 MIN.
- Complete *Etapa* 3 Exam. 20 MIN.

**Homework Option:**
- Review for Unit 5 Comprehensive Test. Have students write *Actividad* 7, p. 382.

### DAY 8

**En resumen: Repaso de vocabulario**
- Check homework. 5 MIN.
- Quick Start Review (TE, p. 384). 5 MIN.

**En tu propia voz: Escritura**
- Start writing activity, pp. 384–385. 5 MIN.

**Unit 5 Comprehensive Test**
- Review grammar questions, etc., as necessary. 5 MIN.
- Complete Unit 5 Comprehensive Test. 30 MIN.

**Homework Option:**
- Have students read *Conexiones,* p. 382, and prepare the 30 second announcement. Have students finish writing activity. Preview Unit 6 Opener, pp. 386-387.

# Sample Lesson Plan - Block Schedule (90 minutes)

## DAY 1

***Etapa* Opener**

- Quick Start Review (TE p. 360). 5 MIN.
- Anticipate/Activate prior knowledge: have students look at the *Etapa* Opener and answer questions. 10 MIN.

**En contexto: Vocabulario**

- Quick Start Review (TE p. 362). 5 MIN.
- Discuss pictures, have students use context and pictures to learn *Etapa* vocabulary. Answer questions, p. 363. 10 MIN.

**En vivo: Diálogo**

- Quick Start Review (TE p. 364). 5 MIN.
- Review Listening Strategy, p. 364. Play audio or show video for the dialog on pp. 364–365. 10 MIN.
- Read aloud, students taking roles of characters. Ask Comprehension Questions on TE p. 365. 10 MIN.
- Students role-play in groups while looking at the photos in their texts. Encourage them to come up with logical dialog using familiar vocabulary. 10 MIN.

**En acción: Vocabulario y Gramática**

- Quick Start Review (TE p. 366). 5 MIN.
- Have students do *Actividades* 1 and 2 orally. 10 MIN.
- Have students complete *Actividad* 3 in pairs. 10 MIN.

**Homework Option**

- *Más práctica* Workbook, pp. 129–132. *Cuaderno para hispanohablantes*, p. 129. Video Activities, Unit 5 Resource Book, pp. 125–126.

## DAY 2

**En acción (cont.)**

- Check homework. 5 MIN.
- Present Speaking Strategy, p. 367, and have students complete *Actividad* 4 in pairs. 10 MIN.
- Have students do *Actividad* 5 orally. 5 MIN.
- Quick Start Review (TE p. 368). 5 MIN.
- Present *Gramática*: Choose between *por* and *para,* p. 368. 10 MIN.
- Have students complete *Actividades* 6 and 7 in writing. Check orally. 10 MIN.
- Have students do *Actividad* 8 in small groups. 5 MIN.
- Present *Gramática*: The Conditional Tense, p. 370, and have students do *Actividad* 9 in writing. 10 MIN.
- Present *Vocabulario* box on p. 371 and have students complete *Actividad* 10 in pairs. 10 MIN.
- Have students complete *Actividad* 11 in writing. Present *Nota,* p. 372, then have students do *Actividad* 12 in small groups. 10 MIN.
- Play audio and have students complete *Actividad* 13. 10 MIN.

**Homework Option**

- *Más práctica* Workbook, pp. 133–134. *Cuaderno para hispanohablantes*, pp. 131–132.

## DAY 3

**En acción (cont.)**

- Check homework. 5 MIN.
- Quick Start Review (TE p. 372). 5 MIN.
- Present *Vocabulario* box on p. 373 and have students complete *Actividad* 14. 10 MIN.
- Have students complete *Actividad* 15 in pairs. 10 MIN.
- Play audio and have students complete *Actividad* 16. 10 MIN.
- Have students play the game in *Actividad* 17 in small groups and ask several volunteers to present their plans to the class. 10 MIN.
- Have students work in small groups to discuss the questions in *Actividad* 18. Assign paragraph as written homework. Expand with *Más comunicación,* p. R16. 15 MIN.

**En voces: Lectura**

- Quick Start Review (TE p. 376). 5 MIN.
- Review Reading Strategy, p. 376, and have students read silently. 5 MIN.
- Have students read *La cascada de la novia* aloud taking turns. 10 MIN.
- Call on volunteers to answer *¿Comprendiste?* and *¿Qué piensas?* questions. 5 MIN.

**Homework Option**

- *Más práctica* Workbook, pp. 135–136. *Cuaderno para hispanohablantes*, pp. 133–134.

## DAY 4

**En colores: Cultura y comparaciones**

- Check homework. 5 MIN.
- Quick Start Review (TE p. 378). 5 MIN.
- Review Connecting Cultures Strategy, p. 378, and have students read silently. 10 MIN.
- Read *La Cumbre de la Ecología Centroamericana* aloud with students. 10 MIN.
- Have students answer the *¿Comprendiste?* and *¿Qué piensas?* questions orally. 15 MIN.
- Divide students into small groups and have them work on the *Hazlo tú* activity. 15 MIN.

**En resumen: Repaso de vocabulario**

- Review grammar questions, etc., as necessary. 10 MIN.
- Complete *Etapa* 3 Examen. 20 MIN.

**Homework Option**

- Review for Unit 5 Comprehensive Test.

## DAY 5

**En uso: Repaso y más comunicación**

- Check homework. 5 MIN.
- Quick Start Review (TE p. 380). 5 MIN.
- Do *Actividades* 1, 2, 3, and 4 orally. 10 MIN.
- Review Speaking Strategy, p. 382. Then do *Actividad* 5 orally in pairs and *Actividad* 6 in groups of four. 10 MIN.

**En resumen: Repaso de vocabulario**

- Review grammar questions, etc., as necessary. 10 MIN.
- Complete Unit 5 Comprehensive Test. 30 MIN.

**En tu propia voz: Escritura**

- Start writing activity, pp. 384–385. 10 MIN.

**Ampliación**

- Use a suggested project, game, or activity (TE pp. 315A–315B). 10 MIN.

**Homework Option**

- Finish writing activity and preview Unit 6 Opener, pp. 384–385.

▼ Francisco se despide de sus amigos costarricenses.

## Etapa Theme

**Commenting on conservation and the environment, and talking about how you would solve problems.**

## Grammar Objectives

- **Por** or **para**
- The conditional tense

### Teaching Resource Options

**Print** 

Block Scheduling Copymasters

**Audiovisual**

OHT 140, 167 (Quick Start)

### Quick Start Review

Describing

Use OHT 167 or write on board: Imagine that the mural featured in this photo will be part of an upcoming art exhibition. You have been hired to write a description of this mural for the exhibition booklet. Use descriptive adjectives and comment on the theme of the mural, some of the images it contains, and the style of the art. Who do you think the artists are?

*Answers will vary.*

### Teaching Suggestions
**Previewing the Etapa**

- Ask students to study the picture on pp. 360–361. Use the **¿Qué ves?** questions to focus discussion.
- Have students take a closer look at the mural on the wall. Have them try to define **"Salvemos la tierra"** and explain how it might relate to the title. Then have students write a list of the items they see in the individual paintings. Based on this list, have them guess what the chapter is going to be about.

UNIDAD 5

ETAPA 3

# ¿Cómo será el futuro?

- Comment on conservation and the environment
- Talk about how you would solve problems

### ¿Qué ves?

Mira la foto y contesta las preguntas.

1. ¿Dónde están Francisco y Fernando?
2. ¿Cuál es el título del mural? ¿Quién lo pintó?
3. ¿Cuál de las pinturas te gusta? ¿Por qué?
4. ¿Qué crees que Francisco va a hacer con el papel?

360

### Classroom Management

**Planning Ahead** Prepare students to discuss pollution, conservation, and the environment. Have students write a list on the board of local problems concerning pollution. Then have them write a list of the measures or solutions that are being incorporated. You can also discuss recycling efforts at your school or in the community.

**Peer Review** Have students work in pairs to create additional **¿Qué ves?** questions and write them on the board. Then have students answer the new questions in pairs.

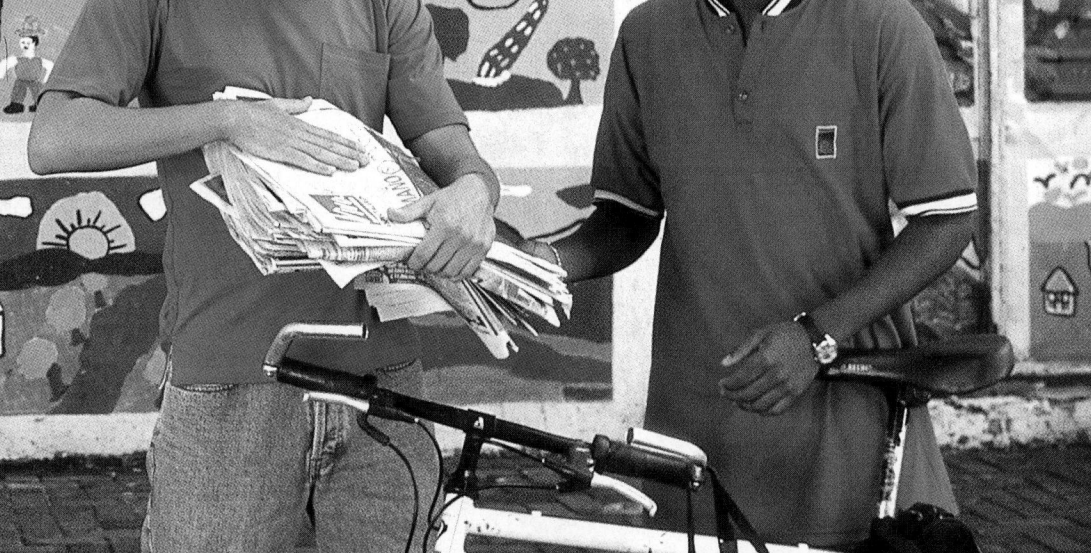

## Cross Cultural Connections

Based on what students have learned about Costa Rica in the last 2 **Etapas**, have students begin a list of the environmental concerns of Costa Rica (or Central America) compared to the environmental concerns of the U.S. Begin a list on the board and keep adding to it as you progress through this **Etapa**.

## Critical Thinking

Have students evaluate the mural, asking questions about how the mural would be similar and how it would be different if painted in your area. Have students begin an outline of environmental concerns.

## Teaching All Students

**Extra Help** Ask students **sí/no** questions about the photo on pp. 360–361. **¿Está Francisco en una escuela? (sí) ¿Está estudiando Francisco? (no) ¿Es Francisco el artista que pintó el mural? (no) ¿Es Fernando un amigo de Francisco? (sí)**

**Native Speakers** Have Spanish speakers give the names of schools (elementary or secondary) they attended in their native countries.

**Multiple Intelligences**

**Intrapersonal** Ask students to choose a frame from the mural and write a short paragraph about how it makes them feel.

## Block Schedule

**Variety** Have students create a class mural by illustrating their own squares like the ones in the photo. Tell students that the theme of the mural is the environment and conservation. Assemble the mural on a wall of the classroom, or in the school hall for other classes to see. Each student should do a short presentation in Spanish of his/her square for the class.

## Teaching Resource Options

**Print** 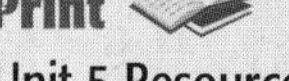

Unit 5 Resource Book
- Video Activities, p. 125
- Videoscript, p. 128
- Audioscript, p. 130

**Audiovisual** 

**OHT** 161, 162, 167 (Quick Start)
**Audio Program** Cassette 15A / CD 15
**Video Program** Videotape 5, 19:54 / Videodisc 4A

Search Chapter 4, Play to 5
U5E3, En contexto (Vocabulary)

**Technology** 

*Intrigas y aventuras* CD-ROM, Disc 2

## Quick Start Review

Talking about the weather

Use OHT 167 or write on board: Write a weather forecast for your region for today, tonight, and tomorrow.

Hoy...
Esta noche...
Mañana...

*Answers will vary.*

## Teaching Suggestions
### Introducing Vocabulary

- Have students look at pages 362–363. Use OHT 161–162 and Audiocassette 15A / CD 15 to present the vocabulary.
- Ask the Comprehension Questions in the margin of the Teacher's Edition on p. 363.
- Use the video for additional listening practice.
- Have students interview a partner using the **Preguntas personales** on p. 363.

# En contexto
## VOCABULARIO

Lee lo que piensa Francisco sobre la contaminación.

**A** La **contaminación** del aire es un problema serio. Muchas industrias lo **contaminan** porque queman **combustibles** y **químicos**.

la lata

la botella

el vidrio

SALVEMO

**B** ¡Qué lío! ¡**Latas** de **aluminio**, **botellas**, **cartón** y **vidrio** por todas partes!

el cartón

NO ESTIBE MAS DE 5 CAJAS

LIMPIADOR DESINFECTANTE Tronex



## Classroom Community

**TPR** In front of the class, set up recycling bins labeled **papel, aluminio, vidrio, cartón,** and **plástico**. Have the class bring in as many recyclable objects as possible and place them on a table at the back of the room. Begin to describe an object. The first student who raises his/her hand picks up the described object and places it in the correct recycling bin. Continue until all objects have been "recycled."

**Learning Scenario** Have students form pairs. S1 works for an environmental agency and needs to poll S2 to find if s/he recycles cans, bottles, plastics, newspapers, cardboard/paper, etc. After polls are taken, all S1s compile data and present it to the class, suggesting ways to improve recycling. S2s may ask questions of the environmental workers.

**C** Para conservar el medio ambiente, **echa** la basura al **basurero** o al cajón de **reciclaje.**

Si **reciclamos** y **mantenemos limpio** el medio ambiente, ¡podremos disfrutar de su belleza!

## Preguntas personales

1. ¿Conoces algún lugar de tu comunidad que tenga contaminación? Explica.
2. ¿Quién de tus amigos(as) o familiares ayuda a mantener limpio el medio ambiente? ¿Qué hace?
3. ¿Qué materiales reciclan tú y tus amigos(as)?
4. ¿Qué pueden hacer tú y tus amigos(as) para limpiar el aire?

### Comprehension Questions

1. ¿Es un problema nuevo la contaminación del aire? **(No)**
2. ¿A veces contamina el aire la industria? **(Sí)**
3. ¿Es posible contaminar el aire cuando se quema combustibles y químicos? **(Sí)**
4. ¿Hay industrias que contamina el agua también? **(Sí)**
5. ¿Se sirve la leche en una lata o en un cartón en la cafetería? **(en un cartón)**
6. ¿Bebes refrescos en botellas de vidrio o de plástico? **(muchas veces los bebo en botellas de plástico)**
7. ¿Tienes que traer tu cajón de reciclaje a un centro de reciclaje o lo pones en la calle enfrente de tu casa? ***(Both answers are possible.)***
8. ¿Qué haces cuando tienes basura y estás en el carro? ¿La traes a casa o la echas por la ventana? **(Traigo la basura a casa.)**
9. ¿Qué hacen ustedes para mantener limpia la escuela? ***(Answers will vary.)***
10. Es posible hacer productos nuevos con las cosas que reciclamos. ¿Cuáles son algunos de estos productos? **(cosas de plástico, papel, ropa—hay chaquetas hechas de plástico reciclado)**

### Language Notes

- Point out the relationship between the following nouns and verbs: **el reciclaje** (noun) and **reciclar** (verb); **la contaminación** (noun) and **contaminar** (verb); and **la conservación** (noun) and **conservar** (verb).
- Tell students that **mantener** is conjugated like **tener**.

## Teaching All Students

**Extra Help** Scramble words from **En contexto** on a transparency or on the board and ask students to guess what they are, then use them in a complete sentence.

**Native Speakers** If some of the Spanish speakers are familiar with recycling efforts in another country or another community, have them share their observations with the class.

**Multiple Intelligences**

**Visual** Ask students to design posters for recycling in Spanish. Put them up around your school.

**Verbal** Have students list the places in their community where they see recycling efforts taking place.

### Block Schedule

**Change of Pace** Have students research the needs of the community and design a clean-up or recycling program. Have them report to classmates what the situation was before they got involved and how things will be different with this program.

## Teaching Resource Options

**Print** 

Block Scheduling Copymasters
Unit 5 Resource Book
Video Activities, pp. 126–127
Videoscript, pp. 128–129
Audioscript, p. 130

**Audiovisual** 

OHT 165, 166, 167 (Quick Start)
Audio Program Cassette 15A / CD 15
Video Program Videotape 5, 21:40 / Videodisc 4A

Search Chapter 5, Play to 6
U5E3, En vivo (Dialog)

**Technology**

*Intrigas y aventuras* CD-ROM, Disc 2

## Quick Start Review

**Expressions with para**

Use OHT 167 or write on board: Give as many reasons as you can why we recycle.

Reciclamos para...

*Answers will vary. Possible answers:*
reducir la basura, conservar, preservar el medio ambiente

## Teaching Suggestions
### Presenting the Dialog

After reviewing the Listening Strategy on p. 364, have students try to list other action words related to conservation and preserving the environment.

# En vivo

 **DIÁLOGO**

Francisco

Fernando

Amalia

Cecilia

**PARA ESCUCHAR** • STRATEGY: LISTENING

**Propose solutions** A solution to a problem is a call for action. Listen for the key action word that best completes Francisco's ideas:

1. **Debemos _____ los recursos naturales.**
2. **Hablar no es suficiente. Hay que _____ también.**
3. **Si, por ejemplo, _____ ..., usaremos menos recursos.**
4. **Si todos _____ juntos, podemos cambiar muchas cosas.**

Do you participate in any of these actions? How? When?

## ¡Hay que actuar!

1 ▶ Francisco: Hoy en día, la protección del medio ambiente es un tema muy popular en los periódicos y las revistas. Debemos conservar los recursos naturales. Todos están a favor de reducir la contaminación.

5 ▶ Francisco: Los carros que manejamos queman gasolina, un combustible que produce contaminación. Si pudieras manejar menos, habría menos contaminación.

6 ▶ Francisco: ¡Fernando! ¿Cómo estás?
Fernando: Pura vida, ¿y vos?
Francisco: Bien, pero un poco triste. No quiero irme mañana. ¡Me encanta Costa Rica!

7 ▶ Fernando: Sí, es una pena. Pero sabés, si estudiás para ser periodista tal vez volvás un día. Bueno, ¿estás listo para ir a comer?
Francisco: Sí, un momento. Estoy terminando mi artículo.



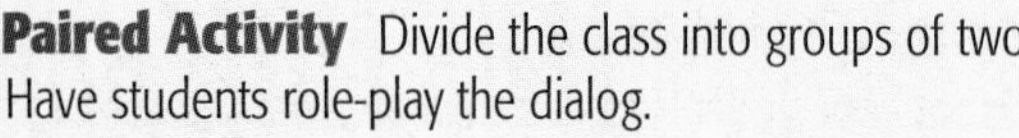

## Classroom Community

**Paired Activity** Divide the class into groups of two. Have students role-play the dialog.

**Learning Scenario** Have students try to identify and describe the pollution problems in frames 2–5. Assign each frame to a group of students and have them brainstorm possible solutions.

**Portfolio** Have students take on the role of Francisco and write a different conclusion to his article.

**Rubric: Writing**

| Criteria | Scale |
|---|---|
| Accuracy | 1 2 3 4 5 |
| Logical organization | 1 2 3 4 5 |
| Vocabulary use | 1 2 3 4 5 |

A = 13–15 pts.
B = 10–12 pts.
C = 7–9 pts.
D = 4–6 pts.
F = < 4 pts.

2 ▶ Francisco: Hablar no es suficiente. Hay que actuar también. Muchas personas dirán: «No soy más que una persona. ¿Qué puedo hacer yo?» Pero hay mucho.

3 ▶ Francisco: ¡No lo echen todo al basurero! El reciclaje es fácil. Si, por ejemplo, reciclamos las latas de aluminio, las botellas de vidrio y plástico, y el papel y el cartón, usaremos menos recursos.

4 ▶ Francisco: Lo malo es que no son solamente las industrias las que son responsables por la contaminación. Cada ser humano comparte la responsabilidad.

8 ▶ *(Escribiendo su artículo)*
Francisco: Aunque la situación es difícil de resolver, si todos trabajamos juntos, podemos cambiar muchas cosas. ¿Por qué no participas tú también?

9 ▶ *(En el restaurante)*
Todos: ¡Buen viaje!
Amalia: Francisco, te deseamos todo lo mejor.
Cecilia: ¡Te vamos a visitar en Miami el año que viene! Vas a escribirnos, ¿verdad?

10 ▶ Fernando: Y yo te voy a mandar cartas por correo electrónico.
Francisco: Gracias a todos. No sé qué decir.
Amalia: No digás nada, hijo. Sentate, vamos a comer.



## Video Synopsis

Francisco is finishing his article about conservation efforts in Costa Rica. On his last night he goes out to dinner with his Costa Rican friends. For a complete transcript of the video dialog, see p. 359B.

## Comprehension Questions

1. ¿Es un tema popular la protección del medio ambiente? **(Sí)**
2. ¿Hay mucha gente en contra de reducir la contaminación? **(No)**
3. ¿Es posible para un individuo contribuir a la conservación de los recursos naturales? **(Sí)**
4. ¿Sugiere Francisco que reciclemos? **(Sí)**
5. ¿Solamente contaminan las industrias o somos responsables también? **(Somos responsables también.)**
6. ¿Tiene tu familia un carro eléctrico o uno que quema gasolina? **(most will respond: un carro que quema gasolina)**
7. Para reducir la contaminación, ¿recomienda Francisco que manejemos más o menos? **(Recomienda que manejemos menos.)**
8. ¿Por qué está un poco triste Francisco? **(No quiere irse.)**
9. ¿Qué escribe Francisco? **(un artículo)**
10. ¿Cómo va a mandar cartas Fernando? **(por correo electrónico)**

## Language Note

Point out how Fernando uses the expression **Pura vida** in photo 6. Tell students that this is a very common response in Costa Rica when somebody asks *How are you?* **Pura vida** means *Doing well* or *Great.*

## Block Schedule

**Process Time** Continue the analysis of the dialog by having the students make a list of all they know about each of the speakers. Prompt them with questions. What is Francisco's opinion on the environment? What about Fernando? (For additional activities, see **Block Scheduling Copymasters.**)

## Teaching All Students

**Extra Help** Divide the class into pairs and have them work together to pick out the verbs in the future tense in the dialog.

**Native Speakers** Have Spanish speakers lead a discussion on ways to conserve gasoline and depend less on driving cars. Use the quote, **"Si pudieras manejar menos, habría menos contaminación"** as a point of departure for discussion.

### Multiple Intelligences

**Verbal** Ask students to brainstorm a list of important leaders in the Spanish-speaking community who might be influential in changing environmental conservation measures. Have them draft a letter to this person and list their concerns.

**Naturalist** Have students research the plants and animals from the local area that have experienced physical harm due to pollution.

### Teaching Resource Options

**Print** 

Unit 5 Resource Book
- Video Activities, pp. 126–127
- Videoscript, pp. 128–129
- Audioscript, p. 130

**Audiovisual** 

**OHT** 168 (Quick Start)
**Audio Program** Cassette 15A / CD 15
**Video Program** Videotape 5, 21:40 / Videodisc 4A

**Technology**

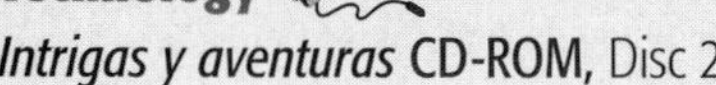

*Intrigas y aventuras* CD-ROM, Disc 2

### Quick Start Review

♻ Future tense: irregular verbs

Use OHT 168 or write on board: Conjugate the verbs in the future tense to complete the campaign promises of this candidate running for governor. Then write a campaign slogan of your own for the candidate.

Cuando sea gobernador...
1. (haber) más programas de reciclaje.
2. yo (decir) ¡No! a las industrias que contaminan.
3. yo (poner) más basureros en los parques.
4. nosotros (hacer) progreso porque es esencial para nuestro futuro.

**Answers**
1. habrá 2. diré 3. pondré 4. haremos.
*Slogans will vary.*

**Objective:** Controlled practice
Listening comprehension/vocabulary

**Answers**
*Answers will vary.*
1. Falso. Hay que actuar también.
2. Falso. Cada persona puede reciclar.
3. Cierto
4. Cierto
5. Falso. Francisco está un poco triste.
6. Falso. Fernando imagina que Francisco será un periodista.
7. Cierto
8. Cierto

# En acción
## VOCABULARIO Y GRAMÁTICA

**OBJECTIVES**
- Comment on conservation and the environment
- Talk about how you would solve problems

### Las soluciones

**Escuchar/Escribir** Indica si las oraciones son **ciertas** o **falsas** según el diálogo. Si son falsas, explica por qué.

1. Hablar del medio ambiente es suficiente.
2. Una persona sola no puede hacer nada para proteger el medio ambiente.
3. Francisco escribe que el reciclaje es fácil.
4. Los carros queman gasolina, un combustible que produce contaminación.
5. Francisco está emocionado porque se va de Costa Rica mañana.
6. Fernando imagina que Francisco será un gran ecólogo algún día.
7. Francisco escribe que podemos cambiar muchas cosas si todos trabajamos juntos.
8. Fernando le va a escribir a Francisco por correo electrónico.

### Corrígela

**Escuchar/Escribir** Cada oración sobre el diálogo tiene una palabra incorrecta. Corrígela con una de estas expresiones.

1. Todos están a favor de reducir la **llovizna.**
2. El **aluminio** es fácil y ayuda a conservar nuestros recursos naturales.
3. Para conservar, podemos **echar** el vidrio, el cartón y el plástico.
4. Un problema muy grande es la contaminación causada por las **linternas.**
5. A Francisco le **molesta** Costa Rica.
6. Francisco terminó su artículo sobre el **basurero.**
7. Los amigos costarricenses le hicieron una **lata** a Francisco.
8. Cecilia y su familia van a **caminar** a Francisco en Miami el próximo año.

**TAMBIÉN SE DICE**

Si un costarricense dice «palo de mango» o «palo de limón», ¿de qué habla? Habla de un árbol. En Costa Rica las palabras **palo** y **árbol** quieren decir lo mismo.



### Classroom Management

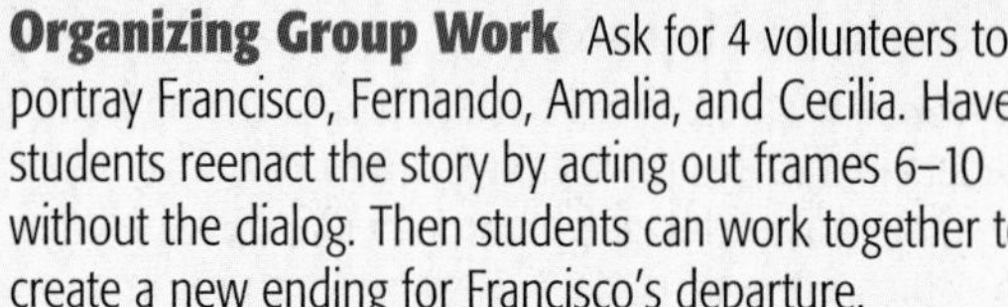

**Organizing Group Work** Ask for 4 volunteers to portray Francisco, Fernando, Amalia, and Cecilia. Have students reenact the story by acting out frames 6–10 without the dialog. Then students can work together to create a new ending for Francisco's departure.

**Peer Review/Peer Teaching** Have students work in pairs to do **Actividad** 3. Then extend the activity by having students work with their partner to comment on how the information in these headlines connects with the current recycling efforts in their school. Have students write up a list of recommendations for their school's future recycling efforts.

- *Use **por** or **para***
- *Use the conditional tense*

## En la escuela

**Hablar** Lee los titulares de este periódico escolar. ¿Están ayudando a mejorar el medio ambiente? ¿Ocurren estas situaciones en tu escuela? Habla con un(a) compañero(a) de clase.

**modelo**

Varios estudiantes están empezando un programa de limpieza en su escuela.

*Sí, creo que están ayudando el medio ambiente. No tenemos un programa de limpieza todavía.*

1. Dos estudiantes tiran basura en la tierra.
2. Una secretaria echa botellas de vidrio en el basurero.
3. Los niños reutilizan el cartón para crear su proyecto.
4. Todos los estudiantes van a la escuela en su propio carro.
5. Hay un programa nuevo para reciclar el papel.
6. El director de la escuela trata de mantener limpios los corredores y jardines de la escuela.
7. Todos reciclan latas de aluminio.
8. Para limpiar la escuela, a veces usan químicos que pueden contaminar.

## ¡Qué lío!

**PARA CONVERSAR**
**STRATEGY: SPEAKING**
**Identify problems and your commitment to solving them** Clearly state the environmental problems you see. Then state how you can help solve them. Indicate your level of commitment with these expressions: **Voy a..., Debo..., Es posible que..., Dudo..., No puedo...** Remember, if we are not part of the solution, we are part of the problem.

**Hablar/Escribir** ¿Qué cree la chica de la foto? ¿Estás de acuerdo? ¿Puedes sugerir soluciones?

No soy más que una persona. No puedo hacer nada.




## Teaching Suggestions

Bring in other magazine photos that represent environmental concerns (recycling stations, birds or animals nearing extinction, car pollution, deforestation, etc.) to extend **Actividad 4**. Divide the class into groups and have each choose a photo to describe and suggest possible solutions.

**Objective:** Controlled practice
Listening comprehension

### Answers

1. contaminación
2. reciclaje
3. reciclar
4. industrias
5. encanta
6. medio ambiente
7. fiesta
8. visitar

**Objective:** Transitional practice
Conservation and the environment

### Answers

*Answers will vary.*

1. No están ayudando…
2. No está ayudando…
3. Sí, están ayudando…
4. No están ayudando…
5. Sí, está ayudando…
6. Sí, está ayudando…
7. Sí, están ayudando…
8. No están ayudando…

**Objective:** Open-ended practice
Commenting on the environment

*Answers will vary.*

## Teaching All Students

**Extra Help** Have students form a collage of photos and headlines on the topic of recycling and label it with Spanish vocabulary words.

**Native Speakers** Have Spanish speakers bring in Spanish-language newspapers or magazines and distribute them to different groups. Have each group look for headlines or articles that deal with the issues of recycling or other environmental concerns.

**Multiple Intelligences**

**Verbal** Have students choose one of the environmental problems shown in **Actividad 4** and write a list of steps needed to implement a solution.

## Block Schedule

**Change of Pace** Extend **Actividades 3** and **4** by having students think of things they could do at your school to support the environment, improve environmental awareness, conserve energy, or maintain a cleaner building and grounds. Have them form groups of two or three and 1) identify two issues, 2) make a recommendation using the subjunctive **(Recomendamos que...)**. Each group reports its recommendations.

## Teaching Resource Options

**Print** 

*Más práctica* Workbook PE, pp. 133–134
*Cuaderno para hispanohablantes* PE, pp. 131–132
Block Scheduling Copymasters
Unit 5 Resource Book
*Más práctica* Workbook TE, pp. 107–108
*Cuaderno para hispanohablantes* TE, pp. 113–114

**Audiovisual**

OHT 168 (Quick Start)

**Technology**

*Intrigas y aventuras* CD-ROM, Disc 2

## Quick Start Review

Expressions with **para**

Use OHT 168 or write on board: This busy executive is constantly leaving for somewhere! Below you will find her destinations and the times she plans to leave. Write out her schedule and use any time that makes sense to you. For example: **a las nueve / aeropuerto.**

A las nueve sale para el aeropuerto.

a las seis de la mañana / a las seis de la tarde / a las ocho / a la una / a las cuatro

el restaurante Rivas
el club de ejercicio
la oficina
la reunión para la conservación
la fiesta de cumpleaños de su hija

*Answers will vary. Possible answers:*

1. A las seis de la mañana sale para el club de ejercicio. 2. A las ocho sale para la oficina. 3. A la una sale para el restaurante Rivas. 4. A las cuatro sale para la reunión para la conservación. 5. A las seis de la tarde sale para la fiesta de cumpleaños.

**Objective:** Open-ended practice
Making predictions

Future tense

### Answers

*Answers will vary.*

1. (No) Tendrá 15 años.
2. (No) Será de...
3. (No) Sabrá...
4. (No) Podrá...
5. (No) Querrá ir...
6. (No) Hará cosas divertidas como...
7. (No) Será...
8. (No) Dirá...
9. (No) Saldrá...
10. (No) Practicará...

## ¿Cómo será?

**Hablar/Escribir** Tu mejor amigo(a) te dice cómo será su novio(a) ideal. ¿Qué dice?

**modelo**

*ser (alto/a, bajo/a, ¿?)*
*Será muy alto/a.*
*(No será muy alto/a.)*

1. tener (¿cuántos?) años
2. ser de (aquí, otro estado o país, ¿?)
3. saber (esquiar, tocar la guitarra, ¿?)
4. poder (manejar, hablar español, ¿?)
5. querer ir (al cine, a los restaurantes, ¿?) mucho
6. hacer cosas divertidas como (bailar, escalar montañas, ¿?)
7. ser (chistoso/a, guapo/a, ¿?)
8. decir (la verdad, chistes, ¿?)
9. salir con tu amigo(a) (los sábados, todos los fines de semana, ¿?)
10. practicar (baloncesto, muchos deportes, ¿?)

## GRAMÁTICA: Choose Between por and para

¿RECUERDAS? *pp. 326, 350* You now know that to say *for* in Spanish, you can use the prepositions **por** or **para.** Remember that each word has specific uses.

You use **por** to indicate **causes** rather than purpose. Use **por** to indicate

- the cause of or reason for an action
- a means of transportation or communication
- places to move through
- periods of time

Think of **para** as **moving you toward** the word, or destination, that follows. You use **para** after **trabajar** to say *employed by*. You also use **para** to indicate

- purposes to fulfill
- goals to reach
- places to move towards
- deadlines to meet
- the recipient of an action or object

Referring to the guidelines above, compare the uses of **por** and **para** in the following sentences:

| Por | Para |
|---|---|
| Fui a Costa Rica por **curiosidad.**<br>*I went to Costa Rica **out of curiosity.*** | Fui a Costa Rica para **investigar la conservación.**<br>*I went to Costa Rica **to research conservation.*** |
| Voy a Miami por **avión.**<br>*I am going to Miami **by plane.*** | Muchas personas están trabajando para **la protección del medio ambiente.**<br>*Many people are working **for the protection of the environment.*** |
| Salimos por **Nueva York** mañana.<br>*We leave **by way of New York** tomorrow.* | Salimos para **Nueva York** mañana.<br>*We are leaving **for New York** tomorrow.* |
| Francisco está en Costa Rica por **una semana.**<br>*Francisco is in Costa Rica **for a week.*** | Tengo que terminar el artículo para **el viernes.**<br>*I have to finish the article **by (for) Friday.*** |



## Classroom Community

**Group Activity** Ask students to list adjectives that best describe how they picture themselves as adults (¿Cómo seré yo?), e.g., **honesto, trabajador, leal, divertido**. Write on a transparency or on the board. Students rank the characteristics from most important (10) to least important (1).

**TPR** Give students commands with **por** and **para** that they can act out. For example: **Ve para la escuela. Anda por el bosque.** Ask volunteers to take turns giving commands.

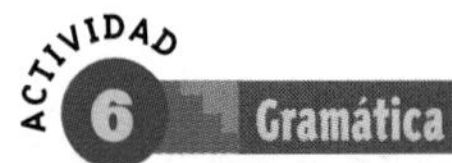

### ¿Por o para?

**Escribir** Cecilia describe su viaje de camping. Completa sus oraciones con **por** o **para.**

modelo

*Fuimos al campamento (dos días).*
*Fuimos al campamento por dos días.*

1. Trajimos leña (el fuego).
2. Caminé (la selva).
3. Tocamos la guitarra y cantamos (dos horas).
4. Pusieron la tienda de campaña (la tarde).
5. Llegamos al campamento (tren).
6. El sábado salimos (el volcán).
7. Un amigo trajo su canoa (remar).
8. Regresamos al campamento a las cuatro (la lluvia).

**MÁS PRÁCTICA** *cuaderno* pp. 133–134

**PARA HISPANOHABLANTES** *cuaderno* pp. 131–132

ACTIVIDAD 7

### Una carta

**Leer/Escribir** Francisco escribió todos los días sobre sus experiencias en Costa Rica. Completa su descripción con **por** o **para** para saber cómo pasó su último día en el país.

Sin título

Times 10

14 de julio

¿Cómo estoy aquí en Costa Rica? ¡Pura vida! Escribo esto __1__ la mañana y ya caminé en un aguacero. Me encanta el tiempo aquí. Estoy terminando mi artículo __2__ la revista. Tengo que terminarlo __3__ el viernes. Aquí la gente está trabajando __4__ la conservación. __5__ eso, mi artículo trata de la preservación del medio ambiente. Es __6__ todas las personas que quieran ayudar.

Ayer fui de compras y tengo regalos __7__ todos. También buscaba un recuerdo __8__ mí y compré una caja de madera __9__ un buen precio. Mañana vamos __10__ el aeropuerto. Me pondré triste al despedirme de Costa Rica y de mis nuevos amigos pero siempre tendré estos preciosos recuerdos.

NOTA CULTURAL

**Los campamentos** Un modo de ver la riqueza única de la belleza natural costarricense es ir a un campamento. Gracias al sistema de ecoturismo, todo se encuentra dentro de los parques nacionales donde se puede acampar.



## Teaching Suggestions

- Review the **En contexto** recycling vocabulary (pp. 362-363) before doing the Verbal Multiple Intelligences Activity.
- Write several sentences on the board, leaving blanks for **por** or **para**. Have students fill in blanks with the correct word and explain the reasoning for their choice to the class.

## Culture Highlights

**LOS PARQUES, RESERVAS Y REFUGIOS DE COSTA RICA** Besides the national parks, many of Costa Rica's reserves and wildlife refuges were created by individuals or groups who purchased the land to protect it from development. There are also numerous environmental groups which welcome international help in preserving Costa Rica's natural resources.

**Objective:** Controlled practice
Using **por** or **para**
Camping vocabulary

**Answers**

1. Trajimos leña para el fuego.
2. Caminé por la selva.
3. Tocamos la guitarra y cantamos por dos horas.
4. Pusieron la tienda de campaña por la tarde.
5. Llegamos al campamento por tren.
6. El sábado salimos para el volcán.
7. Un amigo trajo su canoa para remar.
8. Regresamos al campamento a las cuatro por la lluvia.

**Objective:** Controlled practice
Using **por** or **para**

**Answers**

1. por
2. para
3. para
4. para
5. Por
6. para
7. para
8. para
9. por
10. para

## Block Schedule

**Peer Teaching** Have students continue **Actividad 6** by making statements about things they did this weekend or on their last vacation. Give them two rules: 1. use the preterite, and 2. use **por** or **para**. Post these statements on flip chart paper around the classroom for peer editing. (For additional activities, see **Block Scheduling Copymasters**.)

## Teaching All Students

**Extra Help** Refer students back to **Etapas 1** and **2** for more complete explanations of the uses of **por** (p. 326) and **para** (p. 350). You can also have them review **En contexto**, pp. 362–363, and **En vivo**, pp. 364–365, to pick out the uses of **por** and **para**, and explain the reasons for each use.

### Multiple Intelligences

**Verbal** Have students compare recycling efforts in their town or city with the recycling efforts in another town or city. Have them write 3–5 sentences on the board to share with the class.

**Kinesthetic** Students should get in pairs/groups of three. On the board, compile a list of the adjectives students came up with in the Group Activity. Write each adjective on a piece of paper and distribute one to each pair/group. Students must come up with a silent skit which demonstrates their adjective while the rest of the class tries to guess the word.

## Teaching Resource Options

**Print**

*Más práctica* Workbook PE, pp. 135–136
*Cuaderno para hispanohablantes* PE, pp. 133–134
Block Scheduling Copymasters
Unit 5 Resource Book
*Más práctica* Workbook TE, pp. 109–110
*Cuaderno para hispanohablantes* TE, pp. 115–116

**Audiovisual**

OHT 168 (Quick Start)

**Technology**

*Intrigas y aventuras* CD-ROM, Disc 2

## Quick Start Review

Expressing opinions

Use OHT 168 or write on board: Choose two of the following themes and say whether you are for **(a favor de)** or against **(en contra de)** and why. For example: **Estoy a favor de carros eléctricos porque causan menos contaminación.**

El reciclaje
La destrucción de los bosques tropicales
El uso de combustibles y químicos
Cambiar la comida en la cafetería a un menú vegetariano

*Answers will vary.*

## Teaching Suggestions

### Presenting the Conditional Tense

Refer students back to p. 324 where they learned to conjugate the future tense. Also review the irregular forms of the future they learned on p. 346. Point out that the conditional uses the same irregular stems with conditional endings.

ACTIVIDAD 8

## ¿Qué foto?

**Hablar/Escribir** Con un(a) compañero(a) describe las fotos de Costa Rica. Usa estas expresiones con **por** y **para** en tu conversación.

**modelo**

*Compra gasolina por la tarde.*

- para el 30 de julio
- por escribir
- para cartón
- por tierra mojada
- para Francisco
- por eso
- para reciclar
- por la mañana
- para escribir

1.

2.

3.

4.

GRAMÁTICA

## The Conditional Tense

To talk about what you *should, could,* or *would do,* use the **conditional tense.**

Like the future tense, the **conditional tense** is formed by adding **endings** to the **infinitive** or the **irregular stem**.

**infinitive** + 

| | |
|---|---|
| -ía | -íamos |
| -ías | -íais |
| -ía | -ían |

**estudiar**

| | |
|---|---|
| **estudiar**ía | **estudiar**íamos |
| **estudiar**ías | **estudiar**íais |
| **estudiar**ía | **estudiar**ían |

The **endings** are the same for **-ar, -er,** and **-ir** verbs.

Verbs that have irregular stems in the future have the same **irregular stems** in the **conditional.**

| | |
|---|---|
| **decir** → | **dir-** |
| **haber** → | **habr-** |
| **hacer** → | **har-** |
| **poder** → | **podr-** |
| **poner** → | **pondr-** |
| **querer** → | **querr-** |
| **saber** → | **sabr-** |
| **salir** → | **saldr-** |
| **tener** → | **tendr-** |
| **valer** → | **valdr-** |
| **venir** → | **vendr-** |

In the **conditional** you can talk about what would happen under certain conditions and make polite requests.

¿Te **gustaría** proteger el medio ambiente?
***Would you like** to protect the environment?*

Te **pondrías** en contacto con tus representantes políticos.
***You would get** in touch with your political representatives.*

To be more polite, you could say:

**Deberías** ponerte en contacto con tus representantes políticos.
***You should get** in touch with your political representatives.*



## Classroom Community

**Learning Scenarios** Ask students to list professions. Write them on a transparency or on the board. Students choose a profession and interview each other about their choices. **¿Cómo podrías ayudar la comunidad?**, e.g., as a lawyer, teacher, social worker... For additional professions, see the **Vocabulario adicional** on p. R20 of the student text.

**Cooperative Learning** Divide the class into groups. Each group chooses one of the items from **Actividad 9**. S1 surveys the group members. S2 records the answers. S3 creates a graph to illustrate group responses. The whole group then produces a poster representing the group solution. Responses and posters are presented to the other groups.

## ¿Qué piensas?

**Leer/Escribir** Imagina las siguientes situaciones en tu ciudad. ¿Qué harías tú? ¿Qué harían tus amigos(as)?

1. Ves a un(a) amigo(a) echando basura en la calle. ¿Qué harías tú?
   a. Le diría algo a mi amigo(a).
   b. Pondría la basura en el basurero.
   c. No haría nada.
2. Una industria contamina un río con químicos tóxicos. ¿Qué harían tus amigos(as)?
   a. Le escribirían una carta al periódico.
   b. Llamarían a los representantes políticos.
   c. Protestarían enfrente de la industria.
3. Hay contaminación del aire en tu ciudad. ¿Qué harían tú y tus amigos?
   a. No saldría solo(a) en mi carro.
   b. Usaríamos transporte público.
   c. Andaríamos más a pie o en bicicleta.

**MÁS PRÁCTICA** *cuaderno* pp. 135–136

**PARA HISPANOHABLANTES** *cuaderno* pp. 133–134

ACTIVIDAD 10

## ¿Sería buena idea?

**Hablar/Escribir** Completa las siguientes oraciones sobre el medio ambiente. Luego habla con un(a) compañero(a). ¿Están de acuerdo?

**modelo**

*(Ser) inútil reciclar cartón.*

**Tú:** *(No) sería inútil reciclar cartón.*

**Compañero(a):** *Sí, (No, no) estoy de acuerdo. (No) sería inútil reciclarlo.*

1. Preservar la selva (proteger) las especies en peligro.
2. El reciclaje (reducir) la cantidad de basura.
3. Los nuevos programas de limpieza (contaminar) los ríos.
4. Reducir la pobreza (ayudar) a proteger los recursos naturales.
5. Quemar más combustibles (resolver) los problemas con la capa de ozono.
6. El planeta (ser) mejor sin la destrucción del medio ambiente de los animales.
7. No (ser) útil separar plástico y vidrio de la basura.
8. Reducir el uso de combustibles (ayudar) a resolver el problema del smog.

### Vocabulario

#### El medio ambiente

**la capa de ozono** *ozone layer*
**la destrucción** *destruction*
**increíble** *incredible*
**inútil** *useless*
**el planeta** *planet*
**la pobreza** *poverty*
**el problema** *problem*
**proteger las especies** *to protect the species*
**los recursos naturales** *natural resources*
**reducir** *to reduce*
**resolver (o→ue)** *to resolve*
**separar** *to separate*
**el smog** *smog*
**útil** *useful*

¿Qué dices del reciclaje?

**Objective:** Open-ended practice
Using **por** or **para**

**Answers**

*Answers will vary.*

1. Francisco y sus amigos caminan por tierra mojada.
2. Los carros contaminan el aire. Por eso prefiero caminar.
3. Es para reciclar cartón.
4. Francisco usa la computadora para escribir su artículo.

**Objective:** Controlled practice
Conditional tense

*Answers will vary.*

**Objective:** Transitional practice
Conditional / Conservation and the environment

**Answers**

*Answers will vary.*

1. protegería
2. reduciría
3. contaminarían
4. ayudaría
5. resolvería
6. sería
7. sería
8. ayudaría



## Teaching All Students

**Extra Help** Be sure to conjugate a few verbs in the conditional on the board for students, e.g., **reciclar, proteger, escribir, ir, ser, tener**, etc. Have students conjugate the following verbs in the conditional for extra practice: **contaminar, ayudar, separar, estar, hacer, poder, mantener, poner, resolver, reducir**, etc.

**Challenge** Have students form a word puzzle using the vocabulary.

**Native Speakers** Have Spanish speakers comment on the environmental issue of greatest concern to them using the vocabulary in the box on p. 371. Write the sentences on the board for all students to review and discuss.

### Multiple Intelligences

**Visual** Ask students to draw a visual hook (symbol) to represent the vocabulary words on p. 371.

## Block Schedule

**Retention** Have students write a journal entry on what they would do with a million dollars. **¿Qué harías tú con un millón de dolares?** They can discuss how they would change the world or what they would do to improve the environment. (For additional activities, see **Block Scheduling Copymasters**.)

## Teaching Resource Options

**Print** 

Block Scheduling Copymasters
Unit 5 Resource Book
Information Gap Activities, p. 119
Audioscript, pp. 130–131

**Audiovisual**

OHT 169 (Quick Start)
Audio Program Cassette 15A / CD 15

**Technology**

*Intrigas y aventuras* CD-ROM, Disc 2

## Quick Start Review

Conditional tense

Use OHT 169 or write on board: Say what you would do if you were camping in the following weather conditions. You may use the suggestions below or add some of your own. Use the conditional tense.

(volver) a casa
(hacer) una fogata
(ponerse) un sombrero
(nadar) en el lago

1. Comienza un aguacero.
2. Hace calor.
3. Hace frío por la noche.
4. Hay llovizna.

*Possible answers:*
1. Volvería a casa. 2. Nadaría en el lago. 3. Haría una fogata. 4. Me pondría un sombrero.

## Teaching Suggestions
### Presenting Nota (under Actividad 12)

Point out to students that this is a use of the conditional verb (**visitaría, ayudaría, habría**) and the **si** clause with a verb in the imperfect subjunctive (**estuviera, fuera, pudieras**).

## Si yo fuera profesor(a)...

**Hablar/Escribir** ¿Qué pasaría si tú fueras *(were)* profesor(a) de la clase de español? Haz oraciones afirmativas o negativas.

**modelo**

*los estudiantes / poder comer en clase*

*Los estudiantes podrían comer en clase. (Los estudiantes no podrían comer en clase.)*

1. todos los estudiantes / sacar buenas notas
2. nosotros / hacer comidas en clase frecuentemente
3. el día escolar / ser más corto
4. tú / tener que hablar con el (la) director(a)
5. yo / querer darles mucha tarea
6. los estudiantes / poder salir temprano los viernes
7. haber / menos exámenes
8. la clase / saber hablar español
9. yo / venir a la escuela todos los días
10. ¿?

## ¿Qué harías en Costa Rica?

**Hablar/Escribir** Si pudieras ir a Costa Rica, ¿qué harías? Usa los dibujos para darte ideas y habla con un grupo de compañeros(as).

**modelo**

*Si estuviera en la playa, caminaría a la orilla del mar con mis amigos(as).*

**Nota**

To say what would happen under certain circumstances, use the conditional with a **si** clause:

**Si estuviera** en Costa Rica, **visitaría** todos los parques nacionales.
***If I were** in Costa Rica, **I would visit** all the national parks.*

**Si** Francisco **fuera** político, **ayudaría** a proteger el medio ambiente.
*If Francisco **were** a politician, **he would help** protect the environment.*

**Si pudieras** manejar menos, **habría** menos contaminación del aire.
***If you could** drive less, **there would be** less air pollution.*

1.

2.

3.

4.

5.

6.

**MÁS COMUNICACIÓN** p. R16



## Classroom Community

**Learning Scenario** Divide class into groups of 3–4. On index cards, present a hypothetical environmental issue or crisis to each group. (For example, **Si pudiera ayudar al medio ambiente.**) Groups should create a poster on which they write the problem and all possible solutions using the **nosotros** form of the conditional. Each group presents their work to the class.

**Paired Activity** Have students work in pairs to create additional sentences using **Si pudiera..., Si estuviera...,** or **Si fuera...** with a verb in the conditional in the second part of the sentence. Write several sentences on the board and review them.

## El noticiero

**Escuchar** Escucha estas partes de un noticiero. ¿Qué opción escogerías?

1. **a.** Empezaría un programa de limpieza.
   **b.** Reduciría el smog.
2. **a.** Reduciría los químicos que echamos al aire.
   **b.** Protegería las especies en peligro.
3. **a.** Limpiaría el agua que sale de las industrias.
   **b.** Desarrollaría un programa de reciclaje.
4. **a.** Crearía un programa para proteger las selvas.
   **b.** Buscaría soluciones para la contaminación del aire.
5. **a.** Le sugeriría que todos podrían empezar en sus casas.
   **b.** Le diría que las industrias causan mucha contaminación.

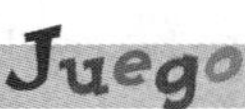

Te gusta esquiar y hablar español y vives en el norte de Estados Unidos. ¿Adónde irías en agosto para practicar las dos actividades?

**a.** Belice
**b.** Bolivia
**c.** Chile
**d.** China

## ¡A todos nos toca!

**Leer/Escribir** Lee este cartel e indica si las oraciones son **ciertas** o **falsas.** Luego haz un cartel para tu causa favorita.

**A todos nos toca...**

Nuestro país es precioso. Pero nuestros recursos naturales no son infinitos. El desarrollo de la economía puede tener efectos graves para el medio ambiente. Necesitamos los dos. ¿Qué puedes hacer tú para proteger el medio ambiente?

*Recicla aluminio, vidrio, plástico y cartón.*

*Ofrécete de voluntario para plantar árboles y revitalizar las selvas en peligro.*

*Contribuye con dinero para los programas de limpieza.*

*Habla con los representantes políticos cuando veas abusos cometidos por las industrias.*

**Cada ser humano puede ser parte de la solución.** **A todos nos toca...**

1. Es necesario balancear el desarrollo de la economía y la protección de los recursos naturales.
2. Las industrias tienen toda la responsabilidad.
3. Es importante estar en contra de los programas de reciclaje.
4. Cada ser humano debe cooperar.

### Vocabulario

**Para hablar del medio ambiente**

**A todos nos toca...** *It's up to all of us...*
**los efectos** *the effects*
**Lo malo es que...** *The trouble is that...*
**el ser humano** *human being*
**la situación** *situation*

¿Cuáles de estas expresiones puedes encontrar en el cartel?



### Teaching All Students

**Extra Help** Ask students to search a Spanish newspaper or one of the readings in their textbook for uses of the conditional tense.

**Native Speakers** Ask Spanish-speaking students to explain the expression **a todos nos toca...** and complete it with their opinions.

**Multiple Intelligences**

**Verbal Si fueras profesor(a) por un día, ¿qué harías?** Have students write a short paragraph about what they would do if they were the teacher for a day.

**Intrapersonal Si pudieras cambiar algo en tu vida, ¿qué harías/cambiarías?** If you could change some aspect of your life, what would you change? Ask students to answer in their journals.

**Objective:** Transitional practice
Conditional tense

**Answers**

*Answers will vary.*

1. Todos los estudiantes sacarían buenas notas.
2. Nosotros haríamos comidas en clase frecuentemente.
3. El día escolar sería más corto.
4. Tú no tendrías que hablar con la directora.
5. Yo no querría darles mucha tarea.
6. Los estudiantes podrían salir temprano los viernes.
7. Habría menos exámenes.
8. La clase sabría hablar español.
9. Yo vendría a la escuela todos los días.
10. *Answers will vary.*

**Objective:** Open-ended practice
Talking about what one would do

**Answers**

*Answers will vary.*

1. Si estuviera en un parque, caminaría por un sendero.
2. Si estuviera en la playa, practicaría el surfing.
3. Si estuviera en el supermercado, compraría comida.
4. Si estuviera en el bosque, iría de camping.
5. Si estuviera en el río, remaría.
6. Si estuviera en la sala, bailaría.

**Objective:** Transitional practice
Listening comprehension

**Answers** (See script, TE p. 359B.)

1. a
2. a
3. b
4. a
5. a

**Objective:** Transitional practice
Talking about solving problems

**Answers**

1. Cierto
2. Falso
3. Falso
4. Cierto

**Juego**

**Answer**

c. Chile

### Block Schedule

**FunBreak** Start the class by having a tape recorder ready and several strips of paper with situations on them. Hand out the situations one by one and give each student 2 minutes to prepare a "speech." Example situations could include: *You are traveling to Central America for 2 weeks. What would you take?* or *You have just found a wallet with a lot of money. What would you do?* Have them speak for 1 minute. (For additional activities, see **Block Scheduling Copymasters.**)

## Teaching Resource Options

**Print**

*Más práctica* Workbook PE, pp. 129–132
*Cuaderno para hispanohablantes* PE, pp. 129–130
Block Scheduling Copymasters
Unit 5 Resource Book
*Más práctica* Workbook TE, pp. 103–106
*Cuaderno para hispanohablantes* TE, pp. 111–112
Information Gap Activities, p. 120
Audioscript, pp. 131, 132–133

**Audiovisual**

OHT 169 (Quick Start)
Audio Program Cassette 15A, 15B / CD 15; (*Para hispanohablantes* Cassette 15B / CD 15)

**Technology**

*Intrigas y aventuras* CD-ROM, Disc 2

## Quick Start Review

Conditional tense

Use OHT 169 or write on board: Write three sentences about what you would do if you were Francisco. Use the conditional tense. For example: **Yo no regresaría a Miami.**

*Answers will vary.*

## Teaching Suggestions

Have students work in pairs to create the new sentences in **Actividad 15**. Write several on the board for all students to review. Remind them to conjugate the second verb in the conditional.

**Actividad 15 Objective:** Open-ended practice
Conditional tense

*Answers will vary.*

**Actividad 16 Objective:** Transitional practice
Listening comprehension

**Answers** (See script, TE p. 359B.)
b, d, c, a

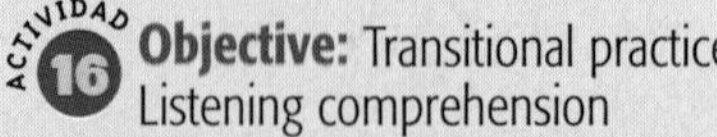

### Actividad 15 Si estuviera...

**Hablar/Escribir** ¿Qué harían tú y otras personas en las siguientes situaciones? Con un(a) compañero(a), haz oraciones originales. Escribe cinco de tus favoritas.

**modelo**

*Si estuviera enfermo(a), yo no iría a la escuela.*

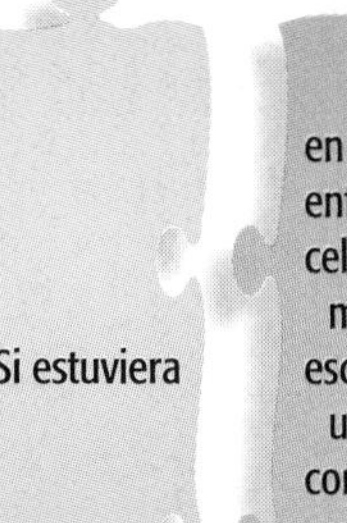

| Si estuviera | en Costa Rica<br>enfermo(a)<br>celebrando mi cumpleaños<br>escribiendo un libro<br>comprando un disco compacto<br>de vacaciones | yo<br>mi amigo (*nombre*)<br>usted<br>mi madre<br>mi padre<br>mi hermano(a) | ¿? |
|---|---|---|---|

### NOTA CULTURAL

**La economía** El turismo en Costa Rica contribuye a una economía que es básicamente agrícola. El país produce café, plátanos, caña de azúcar, arroz, frijoles y papas. El café y los plátanos son los dos productos de exportación más importantes.

### Actividad 16 Proyectos de limpieza

**Escuchar** Escucha a unas personas que están hablando de proyectos de limpieza. Pon las fotos en orden según las descripciones.

a.

b.

c.

d.



## Classroom Community

**Paired Activity** Ask students to share with a partner what they would do if they won the lottery. **¿Qué harías si ganaras la lotería?**

**Group Activity** Divide the class into small groups and assign each group one of the items in **Actividad 18**. Have each group present their answers to the class.

## Si yo fuera presidente...

**Hablar** En un grupo de cinco a ocho compañeros(as), completen la frase **«Si yo fuera presidente...»** Cada persona tiene que decir lo que haría y repetir lo que dicen las otras personas.

**modelo**

**Tú:** *Si yo fuera presidente, no habría pobreza.*

**Compañero(a) 1:** *Si yo fuera presidente, no habría pobreza y la universidad no costaría nada.*

**Compañero(a) 2:** *Si yo fuera presidente, no habría pobreza, la universidad no costaría nada y todos los niños tendrían...*

## ¿Qué harías?

**Hablar/Escribir** En grupos, contesten estas preguntas. Luego escoge la opción que más te gustaría y escribe un párrafo explicando tu respuesta.

1. Si pudieras gastar dos millones de dólares, ¿qué comprarías?
2. Si pudieras conocer a una persona nueva, ¿quién sería?
3. Si pudieras ir a tu universidad favorita, ¿adónde irías?
4. Si pudieras viajar a otro período de la historia, ¿a qué año viajarías?
5. Si pudieras vivir en otro lugar, ¿dónde vivirías?
6. Si pudieras cambiar una cosa en tu vida, ¿qué cambiarías?

**MÁS COMUNICACIÓN** p. R16

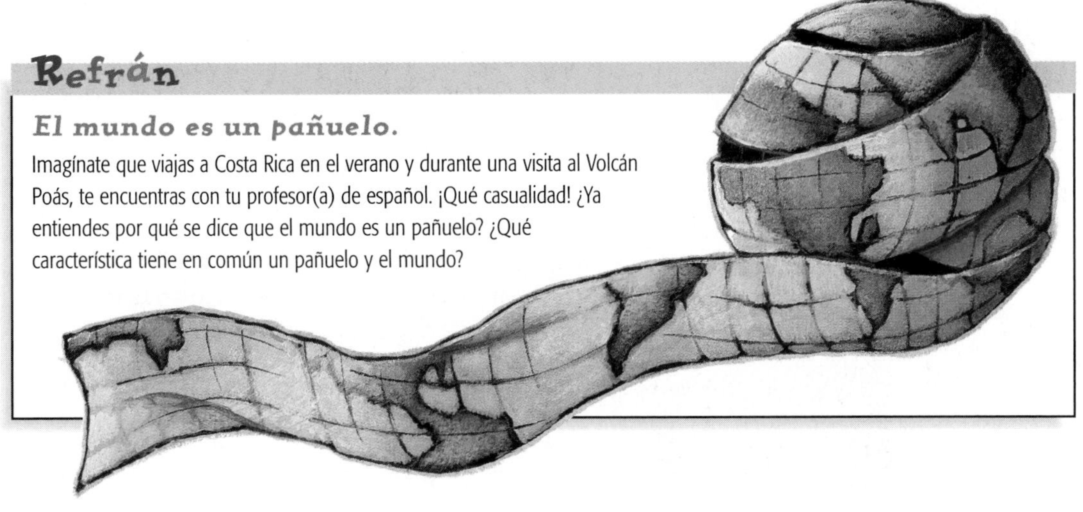

### Refrán

**El mundo es un pañuelo.**

Imagínate que viajas a Costa Rica en el verano y durante una visita al Volcán Poás, te encuentras con tu profesor(a) de español. ¡Qué casualidad! ¿Ya entiendes por qué se dice que el mundo es un pañuelo? ¿Qué característica tiene en común un pañuelo y el mundo?

**Objective:** Open-ended practice
Talking about solving problems

*Answers will vary.*

**Objective:** Open-ended practice
Hypothesizing about the future

*Answers will vary.*

### Community Connection

Have students do **Actividad 17** substituting their local government leader for the president and have them discuss changes they would make in their community. **Si yo fuera alcalde** (mayor), etc.

## Teaching All Students

**Extra Help** Have students write out complete answers to **Actividades 15, 17,** and **18** to provide lots of practice creating sentences with the conditional in the **si** clause.

**Native Speakers** Have Spanish-speaking students list 4–5 situations in which they would use the conditional tense.

**Multiple Intelligences**

**Intrapersonal** Have students cut out an article or picture from a newspaper/magazine. Then ask them how they would feel if they were in these headlines or in a magazine article. **¿Cómo te sentirías si estuvieras en este artículo?**

### Block Schedule

**Brain-based Learning** Create activities that include reading, writing, speaking and listening. For example, have each student pick a conditional question, poll his/her classmates, compile the data, make a visual aide with this information and present it to the class in a short oral presentation of 4 or 5 sentences. (For additional activities, see **Block Scheduling Copymasters**.)

### Teaching Resource Options

**Print**

*Cuaderno para hispanohablantes* PE, p. 130

Unit 5 Resource Book
*Cuaderno para hispanohablantes* TE, p. 112
Audioscript, p. 131

**Audiovisual**

OHT 169 (Quick Start)
Audio Program Cassette 15A / CD 15

### Quick Start Review

Talking about relationships

Use OHT 169 or write on board: Fill in the blank with the correct word.

de maravilla / se enamoraron / la novia / un beso

1. El novio se casa con ___.
2. Ellos ___ hace muchos años.
3. Fue una boda ___.
4. El novio le da ___ a la novia.

**Answers**

1. la novia, 2. se enamoraron, 3. de maravilla, 4. un beso

### Teaching Suggestions

- **Prereading** Begin by asking students what they know about legends. Have them list the names of legends they know from their own cultures. Write their observations on the board.
- **Reading** As students read the legend, have them paraphrase each paragraph to determine the main points of the story.
- **Strategy: Recognize characteristics of legends** Have students list other places they know that derived their names from a legend. (Remember the volcano, **Popocatépetl**, outside of Mexico City. See p. 99.)
- **Post-Reading** Have students write a different ending to this legend, either tragic or happy.

En voces

LECTURA

# La cascada de la novia

**PARA LEER**

**STRATEGY: READING**

**Recognize characteristics of legends** If you picked up "The Legend of Sleepy Hollow," what would you anticipate about the story? Do you think it takes place in the present or in the past? Is it based on written records or oral storytelling? Is it scientific or romantic? Is it happy or tragic? Which of these characteristics do you find in **«La cascada de la novia»**?

After reading this legend, try out your storytelling skills.

NOTA CULTURAL

**Las leyendas** forman parte de la tradición oral de un pueblo. A veces explican el origen de las cosas naturales, como los ríos, los volcanes, las plantas y los animales. Esta leyenda costarricense explica el origen de «la cascada (*waterfall*) de la novia» que se encuentra cerca del pueblo de Paraíso, a unas veinte millas de San José.

A pocos minutos de Paraíso se encuentra una cascada de seiscientos pies de altura que se llama «la cascada de la novia». Se cuenta que la cascada recibió ese nombre a principios del siglo, cuando según la leyenda, se hizo un paseo a ese lugar.

Para celebrar una boda, una popular pareja de novios organizó un paseo al Valle de Orosí. El grupo de amigos muy alegres salió de Cartago en caballo.

Por fin llegaron al maravilloso Valle de Orosí, un lugar de belleza espectacular. Hubo bailes, risas, algunos versos, sonrisas cariñosas, mucha alegría y algunos brindis[1]. El novio brindó por la novia, por su sonrisa, por su vestido elegante con su velo bordado a mano[2], por sus ojos grandes y su belleza singular.

[1] toasts [2] handmade veil



### Classroom Community

**Storytelling** Have students work together to create a legend about the following places or events in Costa Rica: **El Volcán Poás**, a thunder and lightning storm, or a rain forest. Students can write down their main ideas but should tell the story orally to the class, as most legends are passed on orally.

**TPR** Have students act out the actions and events during the party at **Valle de Orosí** (described in the third paragraph).

Como todo, lo bueno termina. El grupo tuvo que regresar. Todos montaron sus caballos y comenzaron la caminata de regreso a sus casas.

Al pasar cerca de la cascada, de repente el caballo de la novia, por una razón ya olvidada[3], se asustó de tal manera que se lanzó al abismo[4]. Se llevó con él a la novia buena de los grandes ojos.

Los detalles de la historia ya se han olvidado[5]. Solamente se acuerda la gente de cómo subió el velo blanco bordado a mano de la novia hermosa. Dicen que apareció como una cascada de agua —«la cascada de la novia».

[3] already forgotten
[4] hurled himself into the abyss
[5] have been forgotten

## ¿Comprendiste?

1. ¿De cuándo es la leyenda de «La cascada de la novia»?
2. ¿Por qué viajaron los novios y sus amigos al Valle de Orosí?
3. ¿Cómo viajaron?
4. Al llegar al valle, ¿qué hicieron?
5. ¿Qué le pasó a la novia?

## ¿Qué piensas?

1. ¿Cómo recibió su nombre «la cascada de la novia»?
2. La tragedia parece aún más fuerte porque la escena anterior es muy alegre. Explica.



## Culture Highlights

- **PARAÍSO** Near this town there are ruins of a small church from the colonial era, dating back to 1693.
- **VALLE DE OROSÍ** This area is known for its breathtaking views and lush landscapes of the rocky Orosí River and tropical rainforests.

## ¿Comprendiste?

*Answers will vary.*

1. La leyenda es de principios del siglo.
2. Viajaron para celebrar una boda.
3. Viajaron en caballo.
4. Al llegar al valle tuvieron una fiesta: hubo bailes, risas, versos, sonrisas y algunos brindis.
5. La novia se cayó al abismo con su caballo.

## Connecting Cultures

**Strategy: Observe and generalize.** Ask students to think about the details of the story, then generalize about how legends surrounding geographical features are created. What characteristics do they have in common?

## Teaching All Students

**Extra Help** Ask students to read the story aloud and summarize each paragraph.

**Multiple Intelligences**

**Visual** Ask students to analyze the artwork on pp. 376–377 to predict the topic of the legend they are about to read. Write the list of possibilities on the board.

**Logical/Mathematical** Have students locate San José, Paraíso, and Valle de Orosí on a map of Costa Rica and calculate the distances between each place.

## Block Schedule

**FunBreak** Find another short legend for the class to read and distribute copies to students *without the endings*. Have students work in small groups to create a logical ending. Then share the actual ending with the class and discuss.

## Teaching Resource Options

**Print**

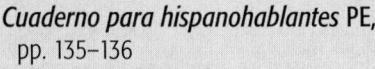

*Cuaderno para hispanohablantes* PE, pp. 135–136
Unit 5 Resource Book
*Cuaderno para hispanohablantes* TE, pp. 117–118

**Audiovisual**

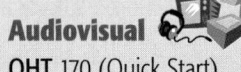

OHT 170 (Quick Start)

## Quick Start Review

Talking about the environment

Use OHT 170 or write on board: Based on the following list of environmental problems, choose the one you think is the most serious and write a sentence using a superlative. **En mi opinión ___ es el problema más serio de todos.** Then write a sentence explaining *why* it is the most serious.

animales en peligro de extinción
ríos contaminados
la contaminación del aire
la destrucción de bosques tropicales
la capa de ozono
el smog
la conservación de los recursos naturales

*Answers will vary on the most serious problem.*

## Teaching Suggestions
### Presenting En colores

- **Prereading** Have students describe any student conference or student organization meeting they have attended recently. Who attended? What was the purpose of the meeting? What did the students learn from the meeting?
- **Strategy: Prioritize** Have students make their own personal list of local priorities, then work as a class to determine a class list of priorities. You can also have them make a national list of priorities for the U.S.

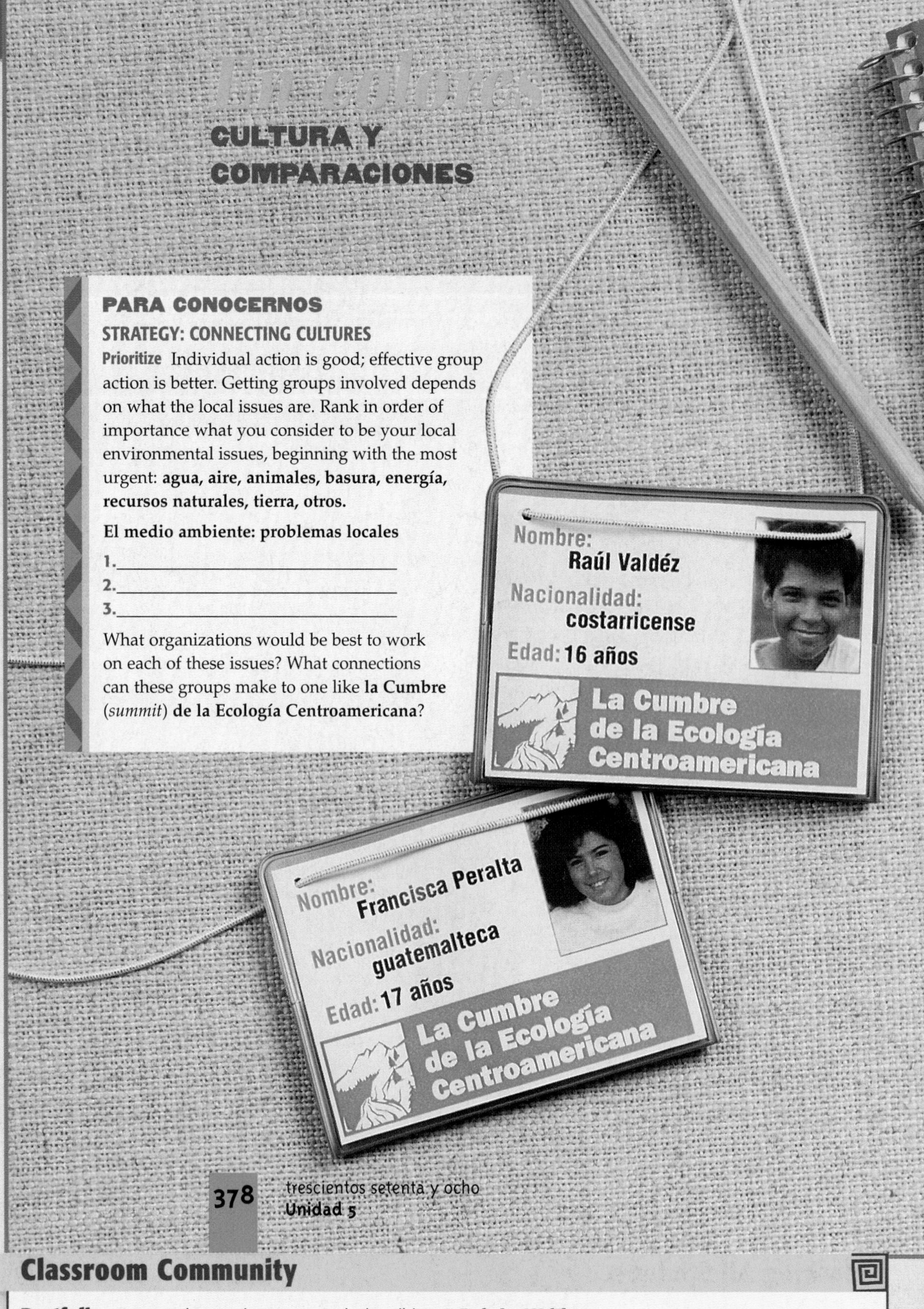


# En colores
## CULTURA Y COMPARACIONES

### PARA CONOCERNOS

**STRATEGY: CONNECTING CULTURES**

**Prioritize** Individual action is good; effective group action is better. Getting groups involved depends on what the local issues are. Rank in order of importance what you consider to be your local environmental issues, beginning with the most urgent: **agua, aire, animales, basura, energía, recursos naturales, tierra, otros.**

**El medio ambiente: problemas locales**

1. ______________________
2. ______________________
3. ______________________

What organizations would be best to work on each of these issues? What connections can these groups make to one like **la Cumbre** (*summit*) **de la Ecología Centroamericana?**



## Classroom Community

**Portfolio** Have students write a paragraph describing an environmental meeting's attendees, purpose, and conclusions or results.

**Rubric: Writing**

| Criteria | Scale |
|---|---|
| Accuracy of information | 1 2 3 4 5 |
| Logical organization | 1 2 3 4 5 |
| Vocabulary use | 1 2 3 4 5 |

A = 13–15 pts.
B = 10–12 pts.
C = 7–9 pts.
D = 4–6 pts.
F = < 4 pts.

# La Cumbre de la Ecología Centroamericana

## CUMBRE ECOLÓGICA CENTROAMERICANA: SE REÚNEN JÓVENES EN SAN JOSÉ

*Manuel Ocampo, San José*

En el auditorio principal de la Universidad de Costa Rica se reúnen algunos jóvenes centroamericanos para la Cumbre de la Ecología Centroamericana. Los participantes, estudiantes de la escuela secundaria, representan varios países centroamericanos —Costa Rica, Panamá, Nicaragua, Honduras, Guatemala y El Salvador. Los representantes de los seis países comenzaron la primera de tres reuniones ayer, hablando sobre el medio ambiente y la contaminación.

Estudiante Raúl Valdéz, el representante costarricense, habló sobre los ecosistemas de su país y la importancia de proteger nuestros bosques tropicales.

Francisca Peralta, la representante guatemalteca, habló de la necesidad de proteger ciertas especies de animales. Peralta explicó que el Centro de Estudios Conservacionistas de Guatemala está estableciendo áreas especiales para proteger animales silvestres, como el quetzal, el ave que es el emblema nacional de su país y da nombre a su moneda.

Hoy los estudiantes de El Salvador y Honduras van a hablar sobre el petróleo, los combustibles y los recursos naturales. Se terminará la cumbre mañana con un discurso[1] del representante de Panamá sobre el agua y otro discurso de un estudiante de Nicaragua sobre el reciclaje. Los representantes esperan firmar[2] una declaración de recomendaciones a los jóvenes centroamericanos para la protección del medio ambiente. El público está invitado a la sesión final de la cumbre.

[1] speech [2] to sign

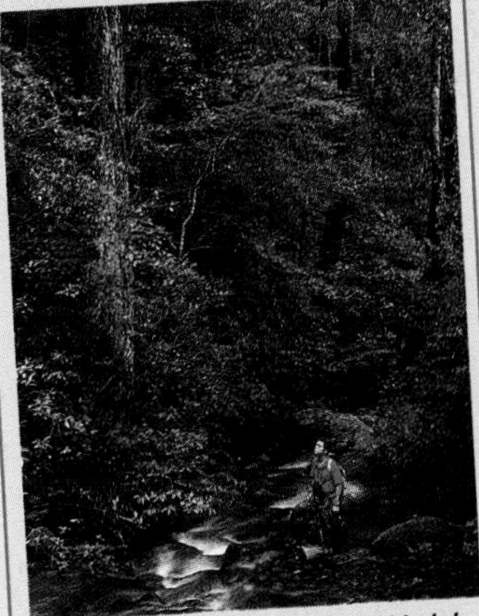

*Los jóvenes hablan de la necesidad de proteger el ambiente.*

### ¿Comprendiste?

1. ¿Quiénes participan en la Cumbre de la Ecología Centroamericana?
2. ¿Dónde tiene lugar la cumbre?
3. ¿Qué temas presentaron durante la primera sesión?
4. ¿De dónde son los representantes que pronuncian un discurso hoy?
5. ¿Cómo se terminará la cumbre?

### ¿Qué piensas?

1. En tu opinión, ¿cuáles son los temas más importantes de la cumbre?
2. ¿Crees que debe haber cumbres ecológicas de este tipo en Estados Unidos? ¿Por qué?

### Hazlo tú

Con un grupo de compañeros(as), escríbeles una declaración de recomendaciones a los jóvenes centroamericanos (o a los jóvenes de tu región) para la protección del medio ambiente.



### Reading Strategy

Have students scan for cognates. As students read the article, have them write a list of the cognates they recognize that will help them better comprehend the reading.

### Cross Cultural Connections

Have students summarize a list of the topics presented by the students from each country. Then have them determine what student representatives from the U.S. would have presented if they had attended this meeting.

### Cultural Highlight

**EDUCATION IN COSTA RICA**
Educational standards in Costa Rica are very high. Over 92% of the population over 15 years old is literate.

### Supplementary Vocabulary

| | |
|---|---|
| **la cumbre** | summit (meeting) |
| **el discurso** | speech |
| **la escuela secundaria** | high school |
| **los asuntos** | issues |

### ¿Comprendiste?

*Answers will vary.*

1. Participan estudiantes de escuela secundaria de Costa Rica, Panamá, Nicaragua, Honduras, Guatemala y El Salvador.
2. Tiene lugar en la Universidad de Costa Rica en San José.
3. Presentaron sobre la importancia de proteger los bosques tropicales y la necesidad de proteger ciertas especies de animales.
4. Son de El Salvador y Honduras.
5. Se terminará con un discurso del representante de Panamá sobre el agua y otro discurso de un estudiante de Nicaragua sobre el reciclaje.

### Teaching All Students

**Extra Help** Ask student to work with a partner to develop a new title and subtitle for the reading.

**Challenge** Plan a "Summit" to review *all* vocabulary learned thus far in all 3 **Etapas** of Unit 5. Students can work together to present the review through visuals, skits, songs, dialogs, etc.

**Multiple Intelligences**
**Verbal** Ask students to write true/false statements based on the reading. The class determines which ones are true, and corrects the false statements.

### Block Schedule

**Group Work** Divide the class into groups of 4 or 5 students. Have them do the **Hazlo tú** activity and prepare a presentation for the class. Make sure each group has a leader, a recorder, and a spokesperson.

## Teaching Resource Options

**Print** 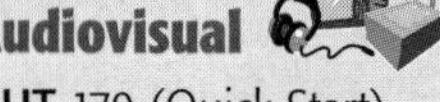

Block Scheduling Copymasters
Unit 5 Resource Book
Information Gap Activities, pp. 121–122
Family Involvement, pp. 123–124

**Audiovisual**

OHT 170 (Quick Start)

**Technology**

Electronic Teacher Tools/Test Generator
*Intrigas y aventuras* CD-ROM, Disc 2

## Quick Start Review

Conditional tense

Use OHT 170 or write on board: Conjugate the following verbs in the conditional.

| ser | hacer |
|---|---|
| tener | poner |

**Answers**

sería, serías, sería, seríamos, seríais, serían
tendría, tendrías, tendría, tendríamos, tendríais, tendrían
haría, harías, haría, haríamos, haríais, harían
pondría, pondrías, pondría, pondríamos, pondríais, pondrían

## Teaching Suggestions
### What Have Students Learned?

Have students look at the "Now you can..." notes listed on the left side of pp. 380–381. To review material before doing the activities or taking the test, have them consult the "To review" notes.

*Now you can...*
- comment on conservation and the environment.

*To review*
- the conditional tense, see p. 370.

*Now you can...*
- talk about how you would solve problems.

*To review*
- **por** or **para,** see p. 368.

# En uso
## REPASO Y MÁS COMUNICACIÓN

**OBJECTIVES**
- Comment on conservation and the environment
- Talk about how you would solve problems

### En el mundo ideal

Francisco le describe su mundo ideal a Cecilia. Cambia los verbos al condicional.

¿Cómo __es__ (1) mi mundo ideal? En primer lugar, los seres humanos __ayudan__ (2) a proteger el medio ambiente. Por ejemplo, nadie __echa__ (3) basura fuera de los basureros. Y no __hay__ (4) mucha basura porque __podemos__ (5) reciclar casi todos nuestros productos. Las industrias tampoco __contaminan__ (6) nuestro planeta. En fin, nosotros __vivimos__ (7) en un mundo bonito y limpio. ¡Y yo no __tengo__ (8) que escribir artículos sobre la conservación porque todos __trabajamos__ (9) juntos para preservar la Tierra!

Tú __estás__ (10) contenta viviendo en mi mundo ideal, ¿no?

### ¡A resolver los problemas!

Todos buscan maneras de resolver los problemas de su comunidad. ¿Qué opinas tú de estas ideas? Usa **por** y **para.**

**modelo**

*urgente / encontrar soluciones / todos los problemas*
*Es urgente encontrar soluciones para todos los problemas.*
*(No es urgente encontrar soluciones para todos los problemas.)*

1. lógico / escribirles a los representantes políticos / correo electrónico
2. necesario / resolver los problemas / el año 2050
3. ridículo / mandar muchas cartas / correo
4. útil / preparar información / las personas de la comunidad
5. esencial / expresar nuestras opiniones / cambiar la situación
6. inútil / trabajar / un futuro mejor



## Classroom Community

**Portfolio** As an extension of **Actividad 1**, have students write a paragraph about the ideal school. Remind them to use the conditional tense.

**Rubric: Writing**

| Criteria | Scale |
|---|---|
| Accuracy | 1 2 3 4 5 |
| Logical organization | 1 2 3 4 5 |
| Vocabulary use | 1 2 3 4 5 |

A = 13–15 pts.
B = 10–12 pts.
C = 7–9 pts.
D = 4–6 pts.
F = < 4 pts.

**Storytelling** Have the first student in the class begin by saying **Si yo fuera presidente (presidenta)**, and add an improvement s/he would make using the conditional. The next student repeats the sentence and adds his/her improvement. Continue around the class until all students have added an item. If a student can't remember the whole list, move on to the next student.

*Now you can...*

- comment on conservation and the environment.
- talk about how you would solve problems.

*To review*

- the conditional tense, see p. 370.

## Actividad 3 ¡Qué problemas!

Francisco está hablando con un grupo de jóvenes sobre los problemas ecológicos. ¿Cómo resolverían los problemas? ¿Estás de acuerdo con sus soluciones?

**modelo**

*Lucía: caminar más*

**Tú:** *Lucía caminaría más.*

**Compañero(a):** *Estoy de acuerdo. (No estoy de acuerdo.)*

1. los otros estudiantes: no hacer nada
2. tú: crear nuevos programas de limpieza
3. nosotros: trabajar juntos para reducir la contaminación
4. yo: escribir artículos sobre la conservación
5. Cecilia: buscar maneras de proteger las especies
6. mi familia y yo: reciclar muchos productos
7. ustedes: hablar con sus representantes políticos
8. ellos: no decirle nada a nadie

*Now you can...*

- comment on conservation and the environment.
- talk about how you would solve problems.

*To review*

- **por** or **para**, see p. 368.

## Actividad 4 Un mundo mejor

Francisco explica sus soluciones para los problemas ecológicos. ¿Qué dice? Completa el párrafo con **por** o **para.**

__1__ proteger el medio ambiente, hay que actuar. Todos podemos hacer algo __2__ conservar nuestros recursos, como participar en programas de reciclaje y limpieza. También podemos hablar __3__ teléfono con nuestros representantes políticos o mandarles cartas __4__ correo electrónico __5__ expresar nuestras opiniones. Ellos pueden trabajar __6__ reducir la contaminación causada __7__ las industrias. Todos los seres humanos somos responsables de los problemas ecológicos de nuestro planeta. __8__ eso, tenemos que trabajar juntos __9__ muchos años __10__ resolver estos problemas. Así podremos crear un mundo mejor __11__ nuestros hijos y nietos.



### Actividad 1 Answers

1. sería
2. ayudarían
3. echaría
4. habría
5. podríamos
6. contaminarían
7. viviríamos
8. tendría
9. trabajaríamos
10. estarías

### Actividad 2 Answers

1. (No) Es lógico escribirles a los representantes políticos por correo electrónico.
2. (No) Es necesario resolver los problemas para el año 2050.
3. (No) Es ridículo mandar muchas cartas por correo.
4. (No) Es útil preparar información para las personas de la comunidad.
5. (No) Es esencial expresar nuestras opiniones para cambiar la situación.
6. (No) Es inútil trabajar para un futuro mejor.

### Actividad 3 Answers

*Second part of response will vary.*

1. Los otros estudiantes no harían nada.
2. Tú crearías nuevos programas de limpieza.
3. Nosotros trabajaríamos juntos para reducir la contaminación.
4. Yo escribiría artículos sobre la conservación.
5. Cecilia buscaría maneras de proteger las especies.
6. Mi familia y yo reciclaríamos muchos productos.
7. Ustedes hablarían con sus representantes políticos.
8. Ellos no le dirían nada a nadie.

### Actividad 4 Answers

1. Para
2. para
3. por
4. por
5. para
6. para
7. por
8. Por
9. por
10. para
11. para

## Teaching All Students

**Extra Help** Have students follow up **Actividad** 4 by giving the reason they used **por** or **para** in each instance.

**Native Speakers** Have Spanish speakers list several environmental problems in their native country and give possible solutions to each one using the conditional.

**Multiple Intelligences**

**Verbal** Have students create a chart that summarizes the uses of **por** or **para** in their own words. They can include rules, visuals, and examples.

## Block Schedule

**Personalizing** Students choose a partner. Each student should pretend his/her partner is on a trip and write a postcard in which they correctly use **por** and **para** twice. Students read the postcards they have received in front of the class. The class should listen carefully and correct any incorrect usage of **por** and **para**.

## Teaching Resource Options

**Print**

Unit 5 Resource Book
- **Cooperative Quizzes,** pp. 135–136
- **Etapa Exam,** Forms A and B, pp. 137–146
- *Examen para hispanohablantes,* pp. 147–151
- **Portfolio Assessment,** pp. 152–153
- **Unit 5 Comprehensive Test,** pp. 154–161
- *Prueba comprensiva para hispanohablantes* **Unit 5,** pp. 162–169
- **Multiple Choice Test Questions,** pp. 176–178
- **Audioscript,** pp. 131–134

**Audiovisual**

**OHT** 161, 162, 163, 163A, 164, 164A, 170 (Quick Start)

**Audio Program** Cassette 20A / CD 20; (*Para hispanohablantes* Cassette 20A / CD 20)

**Technology**

**Electronic Teacher Tools/Test Generator**

www.mcdougallittell.com

## Quick Start Review

**Describing**

Use OHT 170 or write on board: Describe your ideal world. Start by completing the sentences below and then add a sentence of your own. You might talk about an event, an invention, or a technological advance you would envision taking place.

El mundo ideal ___. Habría ___.
Sería ___ y ___. No habría ___.

*Answers will vary.*

**Actividad 5 and Actividad 6**

**Rubric: Speaking**

| Criteria | Scale | |
|---|---|---|
| Fluency | 1 2 3 4 5 | A = 13–15 pts. |
| Vocabulary | 1 2 3 4 5 | B = 10–12 pts. |
| Pronunciation, rhythm | 1 2 3 4 5 | C = 7–9 pts. |
| | | D = 4–6 pts. |
| | | F = < 4 pts. |

## Actividad 5 Si pudieras...

**PARA CONVERSAR**

**STRATEGY: SPEAKING**

**Hypothesize about the future** Our goals reflect who we are and who we want to become. Get to know each other better by conjecturing about what you would do in the future (**¿qué harías?**) under certain conditions (**si pudieras / estuvieras / fueras...**).

Quieres conocer mejor a tu amigo(a). Hazle cinco preguntas sobre lo que haría o no haría en el futuro y por qué.

**modelo**

**Tú:** *Si tú pudieras viajar por todo el mundo, ¿lo harías?*

**Amigo(a):** *Sí, lo haría porque así podría conocer muchos países interesantes y no tendría que trabajar en una oficina. Me gustaría conocer…*

viajar por todo el mundo
Ser Presidente
Ser profesor(a) de español
Vivir en otro país
Escalar montañas altas
Conocer a una persona famosa
Escribir artículos para una revista


## Actividad 6 Si yo fuera...

Tú y tus amigos(as) quieren resolver los problemas ecológicos del mundo. ¿Qué harían en estas situaciones?

Si yo fuera... Haría...

**modelo**

**Tú:** *Si yo fuera periodista, escribiría muchos artículos sobre la conservación.*

**Estudiante 1:** *Es buena idea. Los artículos ayudarían a describir los problemas y explicar las soluciones.*

**Estudiante 2:** *Estoy de acuerdo, pero lo malo es que muchas personas no los leerían. Sería mejor producir programas de televisión.*

## Actividad 7 *En tu propia voz*

**ESCRITURA** ¿Cómo sería tu mundo ideal? Descríbelo en un mínimo de seis oraciones.

*(Hint: Describe your ideal world.)*

**modelo**

*En mi mundo ideal, no habría…*

## CONEXIONES

**Los estudios sociales** ¿Has visto anuncios en la televisión que apoyan el reciclaje? Los tienen en los países hispanos también. Haz tu propio anuncio de 30 segundos para apoyar el medio ambiente. Presenta tu anuncio enfrente de la clase y haz un eslogan para tu campaña (*campaign*).

## Classroom Community

**Games** This may be a good time to play one of the games described in the **Ampliación** section on p. 315B.

**Group Activity** Divide the class into 3 groups and have them do the activity described in the **Conexiones** box, but targeting a different age group. Have students develop 3 different ad campaigns for recycling that would target adults, high-school-age students, and young children.

# En resumen

## REPASO DE VOCABULARIO

### COMMENT ON CONSERVATION/THE ENVIRONMENT

#### Recycling and Conservation

| | |
|---|---|
| **el aluminio** | *aluminum* |
| **el basurero** | *trash can* |
| **la botella** | *bottle* |
| **el cartón** | *cardboard, cardboard box* |
| **el combustible** | *fuel* |
| **la lata** | *can* |
| **el químico** | *chemical* |
| **el vidrio** | *glass* |

#### Talk About the Environment

| | |
|---|---|
| **A todos nos toca…** | *It's up to all of us…* |
| **la capa de ozono** | *ozone layer* |
| **la contaminación** | *pollution* |
| **contaminar** | *to pollute* |
| **la destrucción** | *destruction* |
| **echar** | *to throw out* |
| **los efectos** | *effects* |
| **increíble** | *incredible* |
| **inútil** | *useless* |
| **mantener limpio(a)** | *to keep clean* |
| **el planeta** | *planet* |
| **la pobreza** | *poverty* |
| **el problema** | *problem* |
| **proteger las especies** | *to protect the species* |
| **¡Qué lío!** | *What a mess!* |
| **el reciclaje** | *recycling* |
| **reciclar** | *to recycle* |
| **los recursos naturales** | *natural resources* |
| **reducir** | *to reduce* |
| **separar** | *to separate* |
| **el ser humano** | *human being* |
| **el smog** | *smog* |
| **útil** | *useful* |

### TALK ABOUT HOW YOU WOULD SOLVE PROBLEMS

| | |
|---|---|
| **Lo malo es que…** | *The trouble is that…* |
| **resolver (o→ue)** | *to resolve* |
| **Si estuviera…** | *If I/you/he/she were…* |
| **Si fuera…** | *If I/you/he/she were…* |
| **Si pudieras…** | *If you could…* |
| **la situación…** | *situation* |

### Juego

Si reciclaras una lata de aluminio, podrías ahorrar suficiente electricidad para que tu televisor pudiera funcionar por ______.

**a.** 5 minutos
**b.** 30 minutos
**c.** 1 hora
**d.** 3 horas



## Teaching All Students

**Extra Help** Reinforce the vocabulary by having students make connections between words through definitions, synonyms and antonyms, and associated words. For example: **La lata se hace con aluminio.**

**Native Speakers** Have Spanish speakers add additional words they know that fall in the categories of recycling and conservation or talking about the environment.

### Multiple Intelligences

**Verbal** Scramble words from the vocabulary list on a transparency or on the board. Ask students to form complete sentences using them.

**Naturalist** Have students research the plants or animals in Costa Rica that might be in greatest danger due to the effects of pollution or other environmental problems.



### ACTIVIDAD 7 En tu propia voz

**Rubric: Writing**

| Criteria | Scale |
|---|---|
| Vocabulary use | 1 2 3 4 5 |
| Accuracy | 1 2 3 4 5 |
| Creativity, appearance | 1 2 3 4 5 |

A = 13–15 pts.
B = 10–12 pts.
C = 7–9 pts.
D = 4–6 pts.
F = < 4 pts.

### Teaching Note: En tu propia voz

**Writing Strategy** Encourage students to supply a brief summary of ideas before beginning to write. They should support their opinion with facts and examples.

### Juego

**Answer**
d. 3 horas

### Project: Reviewing Etapa 3

Assign the following out-of-class activities:

- Interview a Spanish speaker about his or her biggest concern for the environment.
- Bring in a newspaper article about an environmental issue and summarize it in Spanish.
- Find out about recycling efforts in Costa Rica or another Spanish-speaking country (e.g., newspaper, Internet, etc.).
- Find more information on local environmental agencies in the community.

**Extra Credit**

| | |
|---|---|
| Interview | 2 pts. |
| Newspaper article | 2 pt. |
| Recycling efforts | 2 pts. |
| Local agencies | 2 pts. |

### Interdisciplinary Connections

**Social Studies** Have students discuss why some people recycle and some do not. Have them poll the class, their families, and their neighbors in the community.

### Block Schedule

**Change of Pace** Have students plan a student conference on the environment. Have students work in groups to determine the issues for discussion, the invited guests or speakers, and a goal for the meeting. Use as many vocabulary words as possible to plan the conference.

## Teaching Resource Options

**Print**

Block Scheduling Copymasters

**Audiovisual**

OHT GO1–GO5, 170 (Quick Start)

**Technology**

*Intrigas y aventuras* CD-ROM, Disc 2

www.mcdougallittell.com

## Quick Start Review

Future tense

Use OHT 170 or write on board: Without looking at your book or your notes, try listing all the verbs that have an irregular stem in the future tense. List both the verb and the stem. Then choose one verb to conjugate fully. When you have finished, consult the book to check your answers, making any corrections or additions necessary.

**Answers**

caber: cabr-, decir: dir-, haber: habr-, hacer: har-, poder: podr-, poner: pondr-, querer: querr-, saber: sabr-, salir: saldr-, tener: tendr-, venir: vendr- , valer: valdr-

## Teaching Suggestions

### Prewriting

- Have students brainstorm a list of books or short stories they would like to review. Have them think of materials they are reading for other classes. They can brainstorm the list as a class or in small groups.
- Point out the **PASS** list at the beginning of the page: **P**urpose, **A**udience, **S**ubject, **S**tructure. This will be their PASS key to a well-structured writing assignment in every unit.

### Post-writing

- Have students exchange their drafts and practice their organizational skills. As they read their partner's draft, they should try to identify the positive and negative aspects on a chart like the one on p. 385. Have them offer suggestions to improve the organization of the review.

UNIDAD 5

# En tu propia voz

ESCRITURA

### ¿Qué te gusta leer?

Cuéntanos en español lo que te gusta leer. A ver si a los demás también le gusta.

*Buscamos reseñas de varios párrafos.*

*Tu biblioteca local, tel. 981-2647*

## Cuentos y más cuentos

Your local library is compiling book reviews for a catalog to be used by Spanish-speaking members of the community. Review a book or short story that you have read for inclusion in the teen section of the catalog.

| | | | |
|---|---|---|---|
| **Purpose:** | Review a book/short story | **Subject:** | A book or story |
| **Audience:** | Community | **Structure:** | Review |

**PARA ESCRIBIR • STRATEGY: WRITING**

**Present a thorough and balanced review** An informative review helps readers decide if material will be useful to them. Be sure to **summarize** the text and then **discuss** its **positive** and **negative** attributes.

## Modelo del estudiante

1

«La cascada de la novia»

The author states the **title** and tells the **main point** of the story.

«La cascada de la novia», una leyenda costarricense, explica el origen de la cascada de la novia, que queda cerca del pueblo de Paraíso, en el Valle de Orosí. Según la leyenda, para celebrar su boda, unos novios fueron de paseo al valle con sus amigos. Allá se divirtieron en una fiesta fenomenal. Pero cuando salieron, la novia sufrió una tragedia en el lugar donde ahora está la cascada.

A **summary** gives readers quick access to information, without using too many details or giving away the ending.

The writer gives a **personal perspective** on what was **enjoyable** about the story.

Me gustó leer esta leyenda. Cuando leí la descripción de la fiesta, me imaginé que estaba allí. Podía ver a la gente bailando y al novio admirando a la novia. Además, la explicación de la cascada es muy bonita.

2

The writer **balances** the review by reporting what was **bothersome.**

Pero me molestó que muchos detalles «se han olvidado». Me gustaría saber más sobre la historia de la cascada. ¿Qué causó la tragedia? ¿Cómo reaccionaron el novio y sus amigos? Para mí, la historia no está completa sin estos detalles.

In the **conclusion,** the writer explains what the reader will gain from reading the story, reviewing the positive and the negative.

Si lees esta leyenda, aprenderás un poco más sobre la naturaleza y las tradiciones de Costa Rica. Entenderás que una leyenda puede ser un cuento bonito. Desafortunadamente, también sabrás que las leyendas a veces no están completas.



## Classroom Community

**Paired Activity** Have students work with a partner to give their own personal opinions on the **cascada de la novia** legend and see how they differ or are similar to this book reviewer's opinion.

**Group Activity** Divide the class into 4 groups and have each group discuss other formats for writing a book review.

**Portfolio** Have students save this book review for their portfolios. Subsequent writing projects will show their progress in Spanish.

## Estrategias para escribir

### Antes de escribir...

Prepare to write your review by brainstorming the purpose of the story, its main events (¿?), the positive aspects (+), and the negative aspects (–). Be sure to write down the title and author. Before you begin to write, record your ideas on a chart like this one.

| ¿? | + | – |
|---|---|---|
| • hubo una boda | • hay un elemento dramático | • el novio es demasiado romántico |
| • los novios y los amigos fueron al Valle de Orosí | | |
| • | | |

### Revisiones

Share your draft with a partner. Then ask

- *How did you feel about the story?*
- *Would you like to read the story based on what I've written?*
- *What additional information would help you form a definite opinion about the story?*

You may want to make revisions based on your partner's responses to these questions.

### La versión final

Before you write the final draft, carefully mark errors in grammar, spelling, usage, and punctuation, using the proofreading symbols (p. 97). Look over your work with the following questions in mind:

- *Did I use **por** and **para** correctly?*

**Try this:** Underline each use of **por** and **para**. Refer to the grammar boxes to make sure the words are used appropriately.

- *Is the future tense used appropriately?*

**Try this:** Circle your uses of the future tense. Use irregular forms when necessary.

La cascada de la novia
Esta leyenda de Costa Rica explica cómo nació la cascada de la novia, que está cerca del pueblo de Paraíso. Hace muchos años, unos novios y sus amigos fueron al Valle de Orosí ~~por~~ para celebrar su boda. Todos participaron en una fiesta fantástica.

Si lees esta leyenda, tenerás -d- una experiencia positiva. Les gustarán los elementos dramáticos

 Share your writing on www.mcdougallittell.com



## Supplementary Vocabulary

| | |
|---|---|
| **el resumen** | summary |
| **la tragedia** | tragedy |
| **la comedia** | comedy |
| **(No) me gustó** | I (didn't) like |
| **lo positivo** | the positive part |
| **lo negativo** | the negative part |

## Rubric: Writing

Let students know ahead of time which elements of their writing you will be evaluating. A global evaluation is more helpful to students than a correction of every mistake made. Consider the following in scoring compositions.

| | |
|---|---|
| **Sentences** | |
| 1 | Most not logical |
| 2 | In logical order |
| 3 | Flow purposefully |
| **Details** | |
| 1 | Few details |
| 2 | Sufficient basic details |
| 3 | Clear and vivid details |
| **Organization** | |
| 1 | Not well organized |
| 2 | Some organization |
| 3 | Strong organization |
| **Accuracy** | |
| 1 | Errors prevent comprehension |
| 2 | Some spelling and agreement errors throughout |
| 3 | Very few errors |

| Criteria | Scale | |
|---|---|---|
| Logical sentence order | 1 2 3 | A = 10–12 pts. |
| Clear and vivid detail | 1 2 3 | B = 7–9 pts. |
| Organization | 1 2 3 | C = 5–6 pts. |
| Accuracy | 1 2 3 | D = 4 pts. |
| | | F = < 4 pts. |

## Teaching All Students

**Extra Help** Review structures with students before writing:
- Use of **por** and **para**
- Use of future tense verbs
- Use of preterite tense and imperfect tense verbs

**Challenge** Have students search the Internet to find other book reviews in Spanish from Spanish-language publications. They can share them with the class and discuss the book reviewer's techniques.

**Native Speakers** Have Spanish speakers write a review of a longer book, rather than a short story. If appropriate, challenge them to write a review of a Spanish book they have read.

## Block Schedule

**Variation** Have students write a review about a movie they have seen recently. Use the same technique of summarizing the movie, then discussing the positive and negative aspects. (For additional activities, see **Block Scheduling Copymasters**.)

## Unit Theme

**Discussing jobs and professions; conducting a job search and interview.**

**Communication**
- Discussing jobs and professions
- Describing people, places, and things
- Completing an application
- Preparing for a job interview
- Evaluating situations and people
- Talking on the phone
- Reporting about past, present, and future events

**Cultures**
- Learning about the professions in Spanish
- Learning about music from the Andes region
- Learning about the indigenous population in Ecuador

**Connections**
- Connecting to Geography: Researching countries located on the equator
- Connecting to Literature: Reading poetry in Spanish
- Connecting to Music: Learning about typical music from the Andes region

**Comparisons**
- Comparing a job search in Ecuador to a job search in the U.S.
- Comparing a job interview in English to a job interview in Spanish

**Communities**
- Using Spanish in a job interview and in the workplace
- Using Spanish for personal enjoyment in sports activities

## Teaching Resource Options

**Print**  
Block Scheduling Copymasters

**Audiovisual** 
OHT 171–174
*Canciones* Cassette / CD Song 5
**Video Program** Videotape 6, 0:00 / Videodisc 4A

Search Chapter 6, Play to 7
U6 Cultural Introduction

UNIDAD 6

# QUITO ECUADOR

## EL MUNDO DEL TRABAJO

**OBJECTIVES**

**ETAPA 1** Se busca trabajo
- Discuss jobs and professions
- Describe people, places, and things
- Complete an application

**ETAPA 2** La entrevista
- Prepare for an interview
- Interview for a job
- Evaluate situations and people

**ETAPA 3** ¡A trabajar!
- Talk on the telephone
- Report about past, present, and future events
- Describe duties, people, and surroundings

**LLAPINGACHOS** Este plato es típico de una región de los Andes que se llama la Sierra. Son papas cocidas (*cooked*) con queso y cebolla. Se fríen en aceite. ¿Qué platillos con papas comes tú?

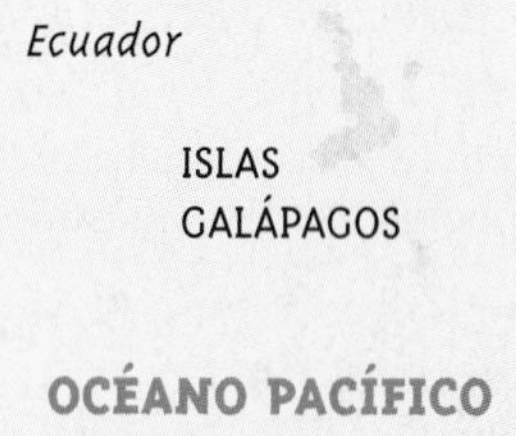

Ecuador

ISLAS GALÁPAGOS

OCÉANO PACÍFICO

**LAS ISLAS GALÁPAGOS,** de origen volcánico, forman un parque nacional. Este parque tiene especies de animales, pájaros, insectos y plantas que no se encuentran en otras partes del mundo. ¿Qué otros parques nacionales conoces?

## Classroom Community

**Paired Activity** Have students work with a partner to list what they know about Ecuador and about South America. Then have each pair join another pair and merge lists. Which group of 4 has the longest lists? Share lists with the class.

**Cooperative Learning** Assign groups of students a topic related to Ecuador, e.g., **la música, la gente, la geografía, la bandera, el clima, la historia, el gobierno, datos importantes, festivales,** etc. Have each group research their topic and briefly present their findings to the class.

## ALMANAQUE

**Población:** 1.500.000
**Altura:** 2.700 metros (8.775 pies)
**Clima:** 21°C (70°F) de día; 12°C (54°F) de noche
**Moneda:** el sucre
**Comida típica:** cebiche, lechón hornado, choclo (maíz) con queso, helado de paila, empanadas de verde (plátano) o morocho (maíz blanco)

**Gente famosa de Ecuador:** Jorge Carrera Andrade (poeta), Camilo Egas (pintor), Gilda Holst (escritora), Jefferson Pérez (campeón olímpico)

**¿Vas a Quito?** A 15 millas de Quito puedes poner un pie en el hemisferio norte y el otro en el hemisferio sur. Por allí pasa la línea ecuatorial que atraviesa todo el país y le da su nombre, Ecuador.

Ve a www.mcdougallittell.com para más información sobre Quito.

VENEZUELA

**LA MÚSICA ANDINA**
Conjuntos como Ñanda Mañachi y Siembra promueven la cultura indígena con sus melodías. Su música es popular a nivel internacional. ¿Qué crees que significa «música andina»?

**ANDAR EN BICICLETA DE MONTAÑA**
está de moda en Ecuador. Los ciclistas siguen los antiguos caminos que cruzan las montañas. ¿Sería fácil o difícil andar en bicicleta por los Andes? ¿Por qué?

OTAVALO
★ QUITO
ECUADOR
COLOMBIA
GUAYAQUIL
CUENCA
PERÚ

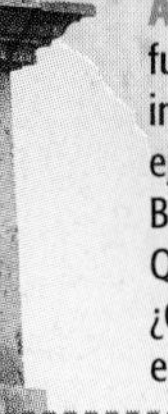

**ANTONIO JOSÉ DE SUCRE**
fue líder de las fuerzas de independencia contra el ejército español. Ganaron la Batalla de Pichincha, en Quito, en mayo de 1822. ¿Qué guerra parecida hubo en Estados Unidos?

**LA TOQUILLA**
Este sombrero recibió su nombre por su uso durante la construcción del canal de Panamá. La verdad es que los sombreros se hacen a mano en el sur de Ecuador. ¿Sabes el nombre famoso de este sombrero?

AL MARISCAL SUCRE EL ECUADOR

387

## Teaching Suggestions
### Previewing the Unit

- You may wish to use the video to preview the unit.
- Tell students that this unit centers around Ecuador and the world of work.
- Ask students what they might know about job searching in their areas of interest.

## Culture Highlights

- **LLAPINGACHOS** The **Ampliación** section on p. 387B contains a recipe for **llapingachos**. You can make them ahead of time and serve them to the class.
- **LAS ISLAS GALÁPAGOS** **Galápagos**, loosely translated, means "island of the tortoise." The islands are located about 600 miles west of Ecuador in the Pacific Ocean. There are 13 main islands and 6 smaller ones. The **Islas Galápagos** are famous for their unique bird and marine life.
- **LA MÚSICA ANDINA** Students will learn more about typical Andean music in the **En colores** reading on pp. 450–451.
- **ANDAR EN BICICLETA DE MONTAÑA** Mountain biking, hiking, and whitewater rafting are all popular sports in the mountains of Ecuador.
- **ANTONIO JOSÉ DE SUCRE** was a leader in Ecuador's war for independence. Ecuador became free from Spanish rule in 1822, yet was not truly independent until 1830, when it left a union with Venezuela and Colombia.
- **LA TOQUILLA** These **sombreros de paja toquilla** (straw hats), also known as "Panama hats," are made near the city of Cuenca in the southern part of Ecuador. **Toquilla** refers to the hat itself or to the straw used to make the hat.

## Teaching All Students

**Extra Help** Ask students to make a Venn diagram that compares facts about Quito from the **Almanaque** and facts about their city or town.

**Native Speakers** Ask Spanish speakers what they know about Ecuador. If any students have connections to Ecuador or other countries in South America, have them share with the class.

**Multiple Intelligences**

**Visual** Ask students to make a collage on Ecuador. Or refer to the **Ampliación** section on pp. 387A–387B for specific ideas for making posters or decorating a bulletin board.

**Intrapersonal** Ask students to generate 3–4 questions about Ecuador. By the end of the unit, refer back to their questions to make sure that they have been answered.

## Block Schedule

**Change of Pace** Have students refer to a larger, more detailed map of Ecuador and locate the following places: **Quito, Otavalo, Guayaquil, Cuenca, Las Islas Galápagos, los Andes, el Oriente, el río Amazonas,** and **la línea ecuatorial**. (For additional activities, see **Block Scheduling Copymasters**.)

# Ampliación

These activities may be used at various points in the Unit 6 sequence.

For Block Schedule, you may find that these projects will provide a welcome change of pace while reviewing and reinforcing the material presented in the unit. See the **Block Scheduling Copymasters**.

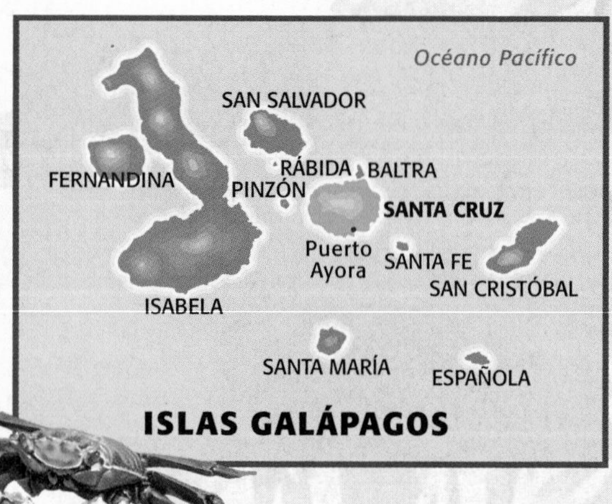


## PROJECTS

**Create a nature-lover's guide** to the Galápagos Islands, highlighting the wildlife that lives there. Have students work in pairs to research some of the bird and marine life, including penguins, turtles, iguanas, albatrosses, boobies, sea lions, whales, dolphins, and create a guidebook page. Put all the pages together to form a guidebook or display them on a bulletin board.

**Pacing Suggestion:** Upon completion of Etapa 1.

**Create job postings** for employment opportunities for Spanish speakers. Show students Spanish models of job postings. Then have students work in pairs to create a job posting for their "dream job" with Spanish language ability as a requirement. Put all the job postings together in a booklet or post them on a **"Oportunidades de empleo"** bulletin board.

**Pacing Suggestion:** Upon completion of Etapa 2.

## STORYTELLING

**La entrevista** After reviewing the vocabulary for professions and job interviews, model a mini-story (using puppets, student actors, or pictures from the text) that students will retell and revise:

> Cuando fui a entrevistarme para el nuevo trabajo, estaba muy nervioso(a). Sabía que era capacitado(a) para el trabajo porque tenía mucha experiencia, pero las entrevistas siempre son difíciles. Cuando llegué a la entrevista, conocí a la entrevistadora y le di mi currículum y me senté con ella. Cuando ella vio mi experiencia, sabía que todo saldría bien.

As you give your model, be sure to pause as the story is being told so that students may fill in words and act out gestures. Students should then write, narrate, and read aloud a longer main story. This new version should include vocabulary from **Unidad 6**.

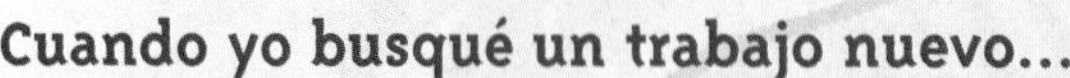

**Cuando yo busqué un trabajo nuevo...**
Ask students to tell about a job interview or other type of interview they have had. Have them use vocabulary from **Unidad 6** in their story.

**Pacing Suggestion:** Upon completion of Etapa 2.

## BULLETIN BOARDS / POSTERS

**Bulletin Board** **Plan ahead:** Contact a travel agency for maps and brochures on vacations to Ecuador. Create a collage of places to see and things to do in Ecuador.

**Posters** Have students create • **Advertisements** for hiking vacations in Ecuador • **Save-the-wildlife** posters for endangered plants or animals from the Galápagos Islands • **Travel** posters for Ecuador • **Job listings** for their "dream job"

## GAMES

### ¿Cuál es mi profesión?

**Prepare ahead:** Write the names of professions from the Unit 6 vocabulary list on index cards and place them facedown in a pile.

Divide the class into two teams. One team member will choose a card from the pile and try to describe it for their own team to guess. If the team guesses correctly, it gets a point. Each team will take turns, and the team with the most points at the end wins. Give the class 10 minutes to play. Variation: You can also have them act out the job or profession instead of describing them.

**PACING SUGGESTION:** Upon completion of Etapa 1.

### Hablar por teléfono

Have the class sit in a circle. One person whispers a message in Spanish of 10–12 words to the student seated immediately to his/her right. That student repeats the message to the student seated to the right. The message continues getting passed around the circle until the last person says the message out loud. Have the first student repeat the original message for comparison.

**PACING SUGGESTION:** Upon completion of Etapa 3.

## MUSIC

The **quena** is a wind instrument that is used in native Indian music found in the Andean mountains of Ecuador, Peru, and Bolivia. The **quena** looks like a series of flutes made from canes or reeds that are tied together in a row. It is said that these flute sounds are supposed to imitate the sounds of the wind in the high mountain altitudes. Other instruments used in native Indian music of Ecuador include drums, small guitars, and harps. After students listen to some Andean music, have them describe the sounds of the instruments. Play the *Canciones* Cassette/CD for the class to hear other music popular in South America.

## HANDS-ON CRAFTS

Wool from the llama, alpaca, and vicuña, animals native to Ecuador and the Andean region of South America, is used in weaving colorful sweaters, hats, blankets, and gloves or mittens. Work with the art department to expose students to the process of weaving from raw wool.

## RECIPE

**Llapingachos** are Ecuadorian potato pancakes. They can be prepared ahead of time and simply heated up for class time. They can be served alone with the tomato sauce or topped with fried eggs (**llapingachos montados**) for a more complete meal.

## Receta

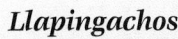

***Llapingachos***

*4 tazas de puré de papas*
*2 cucharadas de mantequilla*
*1 taza de queso blanco, rallado (se puede usar Monterey Jack o mozzarella)*
*1 huevo*
*sal y pimienta a su gusto*
*aceite para freír*
*una cebolla picada*
*una taza de tomates cocinados (o 1 lata de tomates cocinados)*
*(Opcional: huevos fritos)*

*Agregue la mantequilla, el huevo, la sal, la pimienta y el queso al puré. Mezcle bien para luego formar bolas. (Es más fácil formar las bolas si la masa está fría—póngala en el refrigerador por una hora.) Fría las bolas en aceite caliente hasta dorarlas. Sáquelas y póngalas sobre papel absorbente. En otro sartén, caliente un poco de aceite y cocine la cebolla hasta dorarla. Agregue los tomates. Sazone a su gusto con sal y pimienta y revuelva bien la mezcla hasta que la salsa se ponga más espesa. Para servir los llapingachos, sirva uno en cada plato con un poco de la salsa de tomate. También se puede poner un huevo frito encima. Estos se llaman "llapingachos montados."*

# Planning Guide CLASSROOM MANAGEMENT

## OBJECTIVES

**Communication**
- Discuss jobs and professions *pp. 390–391, 392–393, 397*
- Describe people, places, and things *pp. 392–393, 401, 403*
- Complete an application *pp. 400, 403*

**Grammar**
- Present and present progressive tenses *p. 396*
- The impersonal **se** *p. 399*
- Past participles used as adjectives *p. 401*

**Culture**
- Quito *p. 396*
- La ocarina *p. 398*
- La isla Santa Cruz *pp. 404–405*

**Recycling**
- The conditional tense *p. 396*
- Giving personal information *pp. 400, 403*

## STRATEGIES

**Listening Strategies**
- Evaluate a plan *p. 392*

**Speaking Strategies**
- Participate in an interview *p. 403*
- Check comprehension *p. 408*

**Reading Strategies**
- Use context to find meaning *p. 404*

**Writing Strategies**
- Visualize what you are describing *Actividad 7, TE p. 408*

**Connecting Cultures Strategies**
- Use computers to research employment opportunities *TE p. 391*
- Observe and generalize *TE p. 405*
- Research the other countries that border the equator *p. 408*

## PROGRAM RESOURCES

### Print
- *Más práctica* Workbook PE *pp. 137–144*
- Block Scheduling Copymasters *pp. 129–136*
- Unit 6 Resource Book
  - *Más práctica* Workbook TE *pp. 1–8*
  - *Cuaderno para hispanohablantes* TE *pp. 9–16*
  - Information Gap Activities *pp. 17–20*
  - Family Involvement *pp. 21–22*
  - Video Activities *pp. 23–25*
  - Videoscript *pp. 26–27*
  - Audioscript *pp. 28–32*
  - Assessment Program, Unit 6 Etapa 1 *pp. 33–51, 170–172*
  - Answer Keys *pp. 187–188*

### Audiovisual
- Audio Program Cassette 16A, 16B / CD 16
- *Canciones* Cassette/CD
- Video Program Videotape 6 / Videodisc 4A
- Overhead Transparencies M1–M5; 171–184

### Technology
- Electronic Teacher Tools/Test Generator
- *Intrigas y aventuras* CD-ROM, Disc 2
- 

  www.mcdougallittell.com

### Assessment Program Options
- Cooperative Quizzes (Unit 6 Resource Book)
- Etapa Exam Forms A and B (Unit 6 Resource Book)
- *Examen para hispanohablantes* (Unit 6 Resource Book)
- Portfolio Assessment (Unit 6 Resource Book)
- Multiple Choice Test Questions (Unit 6 Resource Book)
- Audio Program Cassette 20B / CD 20
- Electronic Teacher Tools/Test Generator

### Native Speakers
- *Cuaderno para hispanohablantes* PE *pp. 137–144*
- *Cuaderno para hispanohablantes* TE (Unit 6 Resource Book)
- *Examen para hispanohablantes* (Unit 6 Resource Book)
- Audio Program *(Para hispanohablantes)* Cassettes 16B, 20B / CD 16, CD 20
- Audioscript (Unit 6 Resource Book)

# Student Text Listening Activity Scripts

##  Videoscript: Diálogo *pages 392–393*

- Videotape 6, 3:28 • Videodisc 4A
  Search Chapter 8, Play to end. U6E1, En vivo (Dialog)
- Use the videoscript with **Actividades 1, 2** *page 394*

**Isabel:** No sé, no encuentro nada.
**Pablo:** No te preocupes, Isabel.
**Isabel:** Me parece muy buena idea escribir un artículo sobre las formas de encontrar trabajo. Es muy útil y ayudaría a los lectores, pero ¡no encuentro nada! No estoy capacitada para estos trabajos. Aquí necesitan un arquitecto o una arquitecta, y aquí necesitan un veterinario o una veterinaria. ¡No puedo solicitar esos trabajos!
**Pablo:** Ajá. Encontré algo. Ésta es una profesión en la que trabajas con la gente; el horario de trabajo es muy cómodo.
**Isabel:** ¿Sí? Léemelo.
**Pablo:** "Buscamos mecánico de carros."
**Isabel:** ¡Pablo! Ay, nunca vamos a encontrar nada.
**Pablo:** Espérate. Este puesto está perfecto.
**Isabel:** No te lo creo. ¿Qué es? ¿Cartero? ¿Bailarina?
**Pablo:** No, éste es un puesto perfecto. Escucha. "Buscamos periodista para trabajar en una revista de viajes. Preferimos experiencia en otra revista o periódico. Infórmese al cuatrocientoscincuenta y dos, ochocientos noventa."
**Isabel:** ¿En serio? ¿Buscan periodista? ¡Pero es un trabajo ideal! ¡Una revista de viajes!
**Pablo:** Sí. Ves, encontramos algo. Esta tarde los voy a llamar y les explico que estamos preparando un artículo sobre cómo se solicita un trabajo. Estoy seguro que nos ayudarán.
**Isabel:** Gracias, Pablo. A ver… ¿Qué ropa voy a ponerme para la entrevista?
Gracias. ¡Quieren muchos datos personales! A ver. Fecha de nacimiento. Ciudadanía. Estado civil. ¿Qué importancia tiene mi estado civil? Educación. Experiencia.
**Recepcionista:** Revista *Viajamundo,* buenas tardes… Hola, Sr. Montero… Sí, está aquí la señorita Palacios. Ya tiene una solicitud… Ah, muy bien… Claro… Hasta luego.
¿Señorita Palacios? Acaba de llamar el Sr. Montero. Va a llegar un poco tarde. Le pide que espere un poco más.
**Isabel:** Sí, está bien. No hay ningún problema.
**Sr. Montero:** ¿Así que Ud. trabaja con la revista *Onda Internacional*? Es muy buena revista.
**Isabel:** Sí, estoy trabajando como pasante. Me encanta. Y estamos preparando un artículo sobre cómo se solicita un trabajo. Nuestros lectores son jóvenes y van a comenzar a buscar trabajo. Tienen que saber qué se debe hacer y qué no se debe hacer. Por eso hacemos una entrevista simulada.
**Sr. Montero:** Me parece una excelente idea. Muchas veces, la gente llega a una entrevista sin saber qué hacer.
**Isabel:** ¿Me puede explicar un poco más?
**Sr. Montero:** Sí, claro, cómo no. Por ejemplo: ésta es su solicitud. Por lo que veo, está bien escrita. No hay errores. Aquí, donde se pone experiencia, Ud. no exageró. Explicó claramente y en pocas palabras la experiencia que tiene.
Sabe, es una lástima que Ud. no esté solicitando de verdad el trabajo. Sería una buena candidata. Bueno, empecemos nuestra entrevista simulada.
Señorita Palacios, ¿me puede contar un poco de usted? ¿Cómo se interesó en el periodismo? ¿De qué le gusta escribir? ¿Qué le gustaría hacer en el futuro?
**Isabel:** Sí, claro. Me interesé por el periodismo hace un año, más o menos. Supe del concurso en *Onda Internacional* y decidí escribir un artículo. Parece que el artículo les gustó; gané el concurso. Viajé a Madrid como pasante. Allí escribí un artículo con un tema turístico. Fue muy divertido escribirlo.

## Actividad 8 El proyecto *page 398*

1. **Isabel:** ¿Qué hace usted en su trabajo?
   **El taxista:** Todo el día trabajo en mi coche. Llevo a las personas a muchos lugares. A veces, recibo mensajes por radio para ir a buscar personas a hoteles o al aeropuerto.
2. **Isabel:** ¿Qué tipo de artesanías le gusta hacer?
   **El artesano:** Me gusta crear arte típico de mi país. En general, hago objetos de barro pero también trabajo con madera. Siempre uso colores muy brillantes, como se hacía tradicionalmente.
3. **Isabel:** ¿Me puede describir su trabajo?
   **La voluntaria:** En mi trabajo no recibo un sueldo. Ayudo a las personas en el hospital y hago muchas cosas diferentes. A veces, acompaño a los enfermos que están solos. Hoy estoy jugando con los niños que están en el hospital.
4. **Isabel:** ¿Dónde trabaja usted y qué hace allí?
   **El secretario:** Trabajo en una oficina y tengo que escribir reportes y cartas en la computadora. También tengo que contestar el teléfono y hacer fotocopias para mi jefe.
5. **Isabel:** ¿Qué debo estudiar para seguir su carrera y por qué debo estudiarlo?
   **La ingeniera:** Pues, las matemáticas y la computación, por supuesto. Yo uso las matemáticas en mi trabajo todos los días. Uso mi computadora para hacer muchos cálculos y también para preparar diagramas técnicos. Pero no siempre estoy sentada en mi oficina. De vez en cuando voy a diferentes lugares para supervisar proyectos.

## Actividad 13 La entrevista *page 400*

**Entrevistadora:** Bueno. Leí su solicitud y… dígame: ¿qué tipo de trabajo busca?
**Juan Manuel:** Quiero ser periodista pero sé que para empezar voy a tener que trabajar como asistente. Así que, realmente, busco un trabajo como asistente periodístico.
**Entrevistadora:** Muy bien. Siempre se puede empezar como asistente. ¿Qué tipo de periodismo le interesa?
**Juan Manuel:** Me gustaría trabajar en el área de política.
**Entrevistadora:** ¿Y qué experiencia tiene?
**Juan Manuel:** Trabajé tres veranos en la oficina de un senador. También escribí para el periódico del colegio. Me gustó escribir reportes sobre las elecciones locales.
**Entrevistadora:** ¿Trabajaste para un senador? ¿Qué aprendiste allí? Lo que yo busco es una persona que sepa dónde encontrar información sobre muchos temas diferentes. En este trabajo se usan las bibliotecas e Internet frecuentemente.
**Juan Manuel:** Pues, cuando yo escribí artículos, usé Internet y varios periódicos y revistas para encontrar información. También, cuando trabajé con el senador, tuve que ir a las bibliotecas para buscar estadísticas importantes. Creo que este trabajo es perfecto para mí ya que es exactamente lo que hice antes.
**Entrevistadora:** Me parece que sí. Muchas gracias por presentarse. Lo llamaremos por teléfono en un par de días para decirle nuestra decisión. Muy buenas tardes.
**Juan Manuel:** Gracias a usted y muy buenas tardes.

# UNIDAD 6 ETAPA 1 Pacing Guide

## Sample Lesson Plan - 50 Minute Schedule

### DAY 1

***Unit Opener***
- Anticipate/Activate prior knowledge: Present the *Almanaque* and the cultural notes on pp. 386–387. Use Map OHTs as needed. 5 MIN.

***Etapa Opener***
- Quick Start Review (TE p. 388). 5 MIN.
- Have students look at the *Etapa* Opener and answer questions. 5 MIN.

***En contexto: Vocabulario***
- Quick Start Review (TE p. 390). 5 MIN.
- Have students use context and pictures to learn *Etapa* vocabulary. Answer questions, p. 391. 10 MIN.

***En vivo: Diálogo***
- Quick Start Review (TE p. 392). 5 MIN.
- Review Listening Strategy, p. 392. Play audio or show video of the dialog. 8 MIN.
- Replay and have students take on roles of characters. 7 MIN.

***Homework Option:***
- Video Activities, Unit 6 Resource Book, pp. 23–25

### DAY 2

***En acción: Vocabulario y Gramática***
- Check homework. 5 MIN.
- Quick Start Review (TE p. 394). 4 MIN.
- Ask students for a summary of *En vivo* dialog to check recall. Then have students answer Comprehension Questions (TE p. 393). 8 MIN.
- Replay the *En vivo* dialog using the audiovisual resources and have students do *Actividades* 1 and 2 orally. 8 MIN.
- Have students complete *Actividad* 3 in writing, *Actividad* 4 in pairs, and *Actividad* 5 in groups. 15 MIN.
- Present *Repaso:* The Present and Present Progressive Tenses, p. 396, and then have students complete *Actividad* 6 in writing. 10 MIN.

***Homework Option***
- *Más práctica* Workbook, pp. 137–140. *Cuaderno para hispanohablantes*, p. 137.

### DAY 3

***En acción (cont.)***
- Check homework. 5 MIN.
- Quick Start Review (TE p. 396). 5 MIN.
- Review the vocabulary in the box on p. 397, then have students complete *Actividad* 7 in writing. 10 MIN.
- Play the audio and have students complete *Actividad* 8. 8 MIN.
- Have students work in small groups to complete *Actividad* 9. Expand with *Más comunicación,* p. R17. 12 MIN.
- Present *Gramática*: The Impersonal *se,* p. 399, and have students do *Actividad* 10 in writing. 10 MIN.

***Homework Option***
- *Más práctica* Workbook, p. 141. *Cuaderno para hispanohablantes*, p. 139.

### DAY 4

***En acción (cont.)***
- Check homework. 5 MIN.
- Quick Start Review (TE p. 400). 5 MIN.
- Present *Vocabulario* on p. 400, then have students complete *Actividades* 11 and 12 in writing. 10 MIN.
- Play the audio and have students complete *Actividad* 13. 10 MIN.
- Present *Gramática:* Past Participles used as Adjectives, p. 401, and have students complete *Actividad* 14 in pairs. 15 MIN.
- Have students complete *Actividad* 15 orally. 5 MIN.

***Homework Option***
- *Más práctica* Workbook, pp. 142–144. *Cuaderno para hispanohablantes*, pp. 140–142.

### DAY 5

***En acción (cont.)***
- Check homework. 5 MIN.
- Quick Start Review (TE p. 402). 5 MIN.
- Have students complete *Actividades* 16 and 17 in writing. 10 MIN.
- Present Speaking Strategy, p. 403, and have students do *Actividad* 18. Expand with *Más comunicación,* p. R17. 15 MIN.

***En voces: Lectura***
- Review Reading Strategy, p. 404, and have students read silently. 5 MIN.
- Have students take turns reading *Bienvenidos a la isla Santa Cruz* aloud. Call on volunteers to answer *¿Comprendiste?* questions. 10 MIN.

***Homework Option***
- Have students answer the *¿Comprendiste?* and *¿Qué piensas?* questions as written homework. *Cuaderno para hispanohablantes*, p. 138.

### DAY 6

***En uso: Repaso y más comunicación***
- Check homework. 5 MIN.
- Quick Start Review (TE p. 406). 5 MIN.
- Review the *¿Comprendiste?* and *¿Qué piensas?* questions as a class. 10 MIN.
- Do *Actividades* 1, 2, 3, and 4 in writing. Check orally. 20 MIN.
- Review Speaking Strategy, p. 408. Then do *Actividad* 5 orally in pairs. 10 MIN.

***Homework Option***
- Have students prepare 5 review questions. *Cuaderno para hispanohablantes*, pp. 143–144.

### DAY 7

***En uso (cont.)***
- Check homework. 5 MIN.
- Quick Start Review (TE p. 408). 5 MIN.
- Have students do *Actividad* 6 in groups. 10 MIN.

***En tu propia voz: Escritura***
- Do *Actividad* 7. 15 MIN.

***Ampliación***
- Use a suggested project, game, or activity (TE pp. 387A–387B). 15 MIN.

***Homework Option***
- Review for *Etapa* 1 Exam.

### DAY 8

***En resumen: Repaso de vocabulario***
- Review vocabulary. 5 MIN.

***Conexiones***
- Read and discuss. 5 MIN.
- Review grammar questions, etc., as necessary. 10 MIN.
- Complete *Etapa* 1 Exam. 20 MIN.

***Ampliación***
- Use a suggested project, game, or activity (TE pp. 387A–387B). 10 MIN.

***Homework Option***
- Preview next *Etapa* Opener, pp. 410–411.

# Sample Lesson Plan - Block Schedule (90 minutes)

## DAY 1

**Unit Opener**
- Anticipate/Activate prior knowledge: Present the *Almanaque* and the cultural notes on pp. 386–387. Use Map OHTs as needed. 10 MIN.

**Etapa Opener**
- Quick Start Review (TE p. 388). 5 MIN.
- Have students look at the *Etapa* Opener and answer questions. 10 MIN.

**En contexto: Vocabulario**
- Quick Start Review (TE p. 390). 5 MIN.
- Have students use context and pictures to learn *Etapa* vocabulary. Answer questions, p. 391. 10 MIN.

**En vivo: Diálogo**
- Quick Start Review (TE p. 392). 5 MIN.
- Review Listening Strategy, p. 392. Play audio or show video of the dialog shown on pp. 392–393. 10 MIN.
- Replay and have students take on roles of characters. 10 MIN.
- Ask Comprehension Questions (TE p. 393). 5 MIN.
- Use Block Scheduling Copymasters for variety. 5 MIN.

**En acción: Vocabulario y Gramática**
- Quick Start Review (TE p. 394). 5 MIN.
- Have students do *Actividades* 1 and 2 orally. 10 MIN.

**Homework Option**
- Video Activities, Unit 6 Resource Book, pp. 23–25. *Más práctica* Workbook, pp. 137–140. *Cuaderno para hispanohablantes*, p. 137.

## DAY 2

**En acción (cont.)**
- Check homework. 8 MIN.
- Quick Start Review (TE p. 396). 5 MIN.
- Have students complete *Actividad* 3 in writing, *Actividad* 4 in pairs, and *Actividad* 5 in groups. 15 MIN.
- Present *Repaso:* The Present and Present Progressive Tenses, p. 396, and then have students complete *Actividad* 6 in writing. 10 MIN.
- Review the vocabulary in the box on p. 397, then have students complete *Actividad* 7 in writing. 10 MIN.
- Play the audio and have students complete *Actividad* 8. 5 MIN.
- Have students work in small groups to complete *Actividad* 9. Expand with *Más comunicación,* p. R17. 15 MIN.
- Present *Gramática*: The Impersonal *se,* p. 399, and have students do *Actividad* 10 in writing. 12 MIN.
- Present *Vocabulario* on p. 400, then have students do *Actividades* 11 and 12 in writing. 10 MIN.

**Homework Option**
- *Más práctica* Workbook, pp. 141–142. *Cuaderno para hispanohablantes*, pp. 139–140.

## DAY 3

**En acción (cont.)**
- Check homework. 10 MIN.
- Quick Start Review (TE p. 400). 5 MIN.
- Play audio and have students complete *Actividad* 13. Replay the audio and discuss answers with class. 12 MIN.
- Present *Gramática:* Past Participles Used as Adjectives, p. 401, and have students complete *Actividad* 14. 15 MIN.
- Have students complete *Actividad* 15 orally. 8 MIN.
- Have students complete *Actividades* 16 and 17 in writing. 15 MIN.
- Present Speaking Strategy, p. 403, and have students do *Actividad* 18 in pairs. Expand with *Más comunicación,* p. R17. 15 MIN.
- Use Block Scheduling Copymasters for a change of pace as needed. 10 MIN.

**Homework Option**
- *Más práctica* Workbook, pp. 143–144. *Cuaderno para hispanohablantes*, pp. 141–142.

## DAY 4

**En voces: Lectura**
- Check homework. 10 MIN.
- Quick Start Review (TE p. 404). 5 MIN.
- Review Reading Strategy, p. 404. 5 MIN.
- Have students read *Bienvenidos a la isla Santa Cruz* silently. 10 MIN.
- Have students take turns reading the selection aloud. 10 MIN.
- Call on volunteers to answer *¿Comprendiste?* questions. 5 MIN.
- Have students do the *¿Qué piensas?* activity in writing, then discuss in class. 10 MIN.
- Optional: Storytelling: Have students retell main points in their own words. 10 MIN.

**Ampliación**
- Use a suggested project, game, or activity (TE pp. 387A–387B). 25 MIN.

**Homework Option**
- Review for *Etapa* 1 Exam. *Cuaderno para hispanohablantes*, pp. 138, 143–144.

## DAY 5

**En uso: Repaso y más comunicación**
- Check homework. 10 MIN.
- Quick Start Review (TE p. 406). 5 MIN.
- Do *Actividad* 1 orally, and *Actividades* 2, 3, and 4 in writing. 15 MIN.
- Review Speaking Strategy, p 408. Then do *Actividad* 5 orally in pairs and *Actividad* 6 in groups. 15 MIN.

**Conexiones**
- Read and discuss. 5 MIN.
- Review grammar questions, etc., as necessary. 10 MIN.
- Complete *Etapa* 1 Exam. 20 MIN.

**En tu propia voz: Escritura**
- Start writing activity. 10 MIN.

**Homework Option**
- Finish writing activity and preview next *Etapa* Opener, pp. 410–411.

▼ Isabel y Pablo leen los clasificados.

## Etapa Theme

**Discussing jobs and professions; describing people, places, and things; completing an application.**

## Grammar Objectives

- Review of the present and present progressive tenses
- The impersonal **se**
- Past participles used as adjectives

### Teaching Resource Options

**Print**

Block Scheduling Copymasters

**Audiovisual**

**OHT** 181 (Quick Start)

### Quick Start Review

Means of communication

Use OHT 181 or write on board: Circle the words that identify the people who work at a newspaper.

| | |
|---|---|
| maletero(a) | fotógrafo(a) |
| editor(a) | dependiente(a) |
| escritor(a) | periodista |
| enfermero(a) | reportero(a) |
| cantante | mesero(a) |

**Answers**

editor(a), escritor(a), fotógrafo(a), periodista, reportero(a)

### Teaching Suggestions
#### Previewing the Etapa

- Ask students to study the photo on pp. 388–389 and identify where the photo was taken.
- Have students brainstorm about what can be found in the **Clasificados** section of a newspaper. Bring in a copy, either in English or Spanish, for students to review.

UNIDAD 6

ETAPA 1

# Se busca trabajo

- Discuss jobs and professions
- Describe people, places, and things
- Complete an application

### ¿Qué ves?

Mira la foto. ¿Qué ves?

1. ¿Conoces a algunas personas de la foto? ¿Cómo se llaman?
2. ¿Dónde crees que están estas personas?
3. ¿Qué sección del periódico están leyendo?

388

### Classroom Management

**Planning Ahead** Prepare students to search for a job in a profession that interests them. Bring in job listings in Spanish from newspapers or from the Internet.

**Peer Review/Peer Teaching** Distribute the classified ads section of Spanish language newspapers to several small groups. Have students work together to identify the different types of classified advertisements. Ask students to list three jobs that interest them. Then write the qualifications needed for each job. Have each student locate 1 job description that interests them and share it with their partners.

## Cross Cultural Connections

- Ask students to discuss what they know about searching for a job in the U.S. Topics can include: how to contact potential employers, what to wear to an interview, how to prepare for an interview, etc.
- *El Nuevo Herald* (Miami), *El Mercurio* (Santiago, Chile), *La Nación* (Buenos Aires), and *El Tiempo* (Bogotá) all have web sites with classified sections.

## Culture Highlights

- **NEWSPAPERS IN ECUADOR** The major newspapers in Quito, the capital of Ecuador, are *El Comercio* and *El Telégrafo.*

## Teaching All Students

**Extra Help** Ask students simple **sí/no** questions based on the photo, e.g., **¿Hay dos personas que están leyendo el periódico? ¿Están leyendo la sección de clasificados?**, etc.

**Native Speakers** Ask Spanish speakers what they know about searching for a new job in other countries. If they have experiences working in another country, have them share with the class.

### Multiple Intelligences

**Verbal** Ask students to list 3–4 requirements for various professions: firefighters **(los bomberos)**, police officers **(los policías)**, teachers **(los profesores)**, lawyers **(los abogados)**.

**Logical/Mathematical** Have students review what they know about Isabel, then tell why they think she is reading the classifieds in Ecuador.

## Block Schedule

**FunBreak** Ask students to bring in three ads from the classified section of a local newspaper which require the knowledge of a second language. Design a bulletin board with ads. (For additional activities, see **Block Scheduling Copymasters.**)

## Teaching Resource Options

**Print** 

Unit 6 Resource Book
Video Activities, p. 23
Videoscript, p. 26
Audioscript, p. 28

**Audiovisual**

OHT 175, 176, 181 (Quick Start)
Audio Program Cassette 16A / CD 16
Video Program Videotape 6, 1:19 / Videodisc 4A

Search Chapter 7, Play to 8
U6E1, En contexto (Vocabulary)

**Technology**

*Intrigas y aventuras* CD-ROM, Disc 2

## Quick Start Review

Talking about health/describing what someone does

Use OHT 181 or write on board: List three things a doctor does.

*Answers will vary.*
*Possible answers:* Examina al paciente. Da una inyección. Da una receta.

## Teaching Suggestions
### Introducing Vocabulary

- Use OHT 175–176 and Audiocassette 16A / CD 16 to present the vocabulary on pp. 390–391.
- Ask the Comprehension Questions in the margin of the Teacher's Edition on p. 391. You may write the questions on the board and have students work in small groups to answer them.
- Use the video vocabulary presentation for review and reinforcement.

## Language Notes

Point out that the job titles **bombero** and **deportista** are used to refer to both males and females in those professions. Similar job titles are **el/la recepcionista, el/la modelo,** and **el/la periodista**.

# En contexto
## VOCABULARIO

Aquí Isabel busca información sobre unos trabajos en Internet.

**¡Hola!** Estoy buscando información por Internet sobre varios **empleos.** Como puedes ver, hay muchas maneras de **ganarse la vida.** Me interesa **una carrera** como periodista. ¿Hay **una profesión** aquí que a ti te interese?

Regresar | Adelantar | Inicio | Recargar | Im
Dirección: http://www.empleo.com
¿Novedades? | ¿Interesante? | Búsque

ENCONTRAR UNA PROFESIÓN
ENTREGAR TUS DATOS
SOLICITAR UN PUESTO

**A AGRICULTOR**

¿Quieres trabajar al aire libre cuidando las plantas y los animales? Tal vez quieras ser **agricultor** o **agricultora.**

**E CARTERA**

¿Te gustaría darles las cartas a las personas? Quizás quieras ser **cartero** o **cartera.**

**F DEPORTISTA**

¿Te gusta el fútbol? ¿Qué tal una carrera como **deportista**?

**J NIÑERA**

Si te gusta jugar con los niños, ¿qué tal **un puesto** como **niñero** o **niñera**?

**K PELUQUERO**

Para ser **peluquero** o **peluquera,** tienes que saber cortar el pelo. ¿Estás tú **capacitado(a)** para este trabajo?



## Classroom Community

**TPR** Ask students to act out a profession listed on pp. 390–391 and have other students guess the occupation, e.g., **músico(a), mecánico(a)**, etc.

**Portfolio** Ask students to write a short paragraph describing a career that is of interest to them. They can start with **En el futuro trabajaré como...**

**Rubric: Writing**

| Criteria | Scale |
|---|---|
| Accuracy | 1 2 3 4 5 |
| Logical organization | 1 2 3 4 5 |
| Vocabulary use | 1 2 3 4 5 |

A = 13–15 pts.
B = 10–12 pts.
C = 7–9 pts.
D = 4–6 pts.
F = < 4 pts.

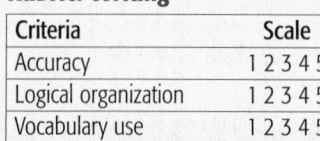

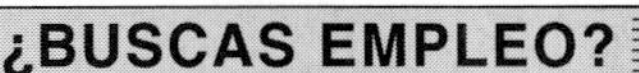

## ¿BUSCAS EMPLEO?

r | Imprimir | Buscar | Finalizar

ctorio | Software

¿Te gusta diseñar edificios? Podrías ser **arquitecto** o **arquitecta.**

Una persona que asiste a clases de baile y practica mucho puede ser **bailarín** o **bailarina.**

¿Te interesa apagar fuegos y rescatar gatos? Podrías ser **bombero.**

¿Te interesan el gobierno y la justicia? Tal vez quieras ser **juez** o **jueza.**

¿Sabes reparar carros? Podrías tener una carrera como **mecánico** o **mecánica.**

¿Sabes tocar un instrumento musical? Es posible que vayas a ser **músico** o **música.**

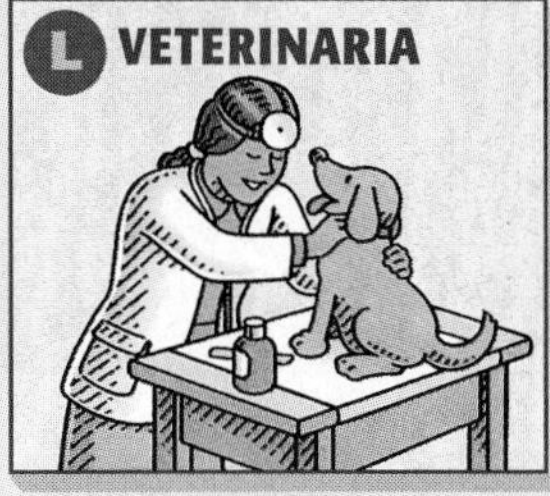


Si te gusta cuidar a los animales, quizás quieras ser **veterinario** o **veterinaria.**

### Preguntas personales

1. ¿Conoces a alguien que tenga una de estas profesiones? ¿Cuáles?
2. En tu opinión, ¿qué trabajo es más difícil, el de un(a) juez(a) o el de un(a) deportista?
3. ¿Preferirías trabajar o asistir a la escuela?
4. De las profesiones que están en esta página de Internet, ¿cuáles te interesan más? ¿Menos?
5. ¿Sabes qué quieres hacer después de graduarte de la escuela secundaria? ¿Qué es?





## Comprehension Questions

1. ¿Busca Isabel información en un libro? **(No)**
2. ¿Quiere Isabel informarse sobre varios empleos? **(Sí)**
3. ¿Le interesa una carrera como deportista? **(No)**
4. ¿Le recomendarías la profesión de agricultor(a) a una persona que no le gusta trabajar al aire libre? **(No)**
5. ¿Qué profesión le interesaría a una persona que baila bien, bailarín o juez? **(bailarín)**
6. Si tu carro no funciona, ¿buscas a un niñero o a un mecánico? **(un mecánico)**
7. ¿Quién necesita talento artístico, una arquitecta o un bombero? **(una arquitecta)**
8. ¿Quién les da las cartas a las personas? **(el/la cartero/a)**
9. ¿Qué hace una peluquera? **(Corta el pelo.)**
10. ¿Qué hace un veterinario? **(Cuida a los animales.)**

## Cross Cultural Connections

Ask students what kinds of job research they can do via the computer. What kind of jobs are advertised via the Internet? Which jobs might require the use of Spanish? Which jobs might involve travel to Spanish-speaking countries?

## Teaching All Students

**Extra Help** Ask students to write the 12 professions in one column, then in a corresponding column, write a short description about what each professional does on the job.

**Native Speakers** Ask Spanish speakers to expand the descriptions of the professions, perhaps by talking about professionals they know.

### Multiple Intelligences

**Logical/Mathematical** Have students rank the professions listed on pp. 390–391 in order of the most appealing to the least appealing. Have students share their answers with others in a small group.

**Intrapersonal** Ask students to write a short description on how one of the 12 professions has affected their lives, e.g., **un músico, una veterinaria...**

## Block Schedule

**Change of Pace** Have students make a list of other professions they know that are not listed here. Then have them research the Spanish equivalents for each profession on their list. (For additional activities, see **Block Scheduling Copymasters.**)

## Teaching Resource Options

**Print** 

Block Scheduling Copymasters
Unit 6 Resource Book
Video Activities, pp. 24–25
Videoscript, p. 26
Audioscript, p. 28

**Audiovisual**

**OHT** 179, 180, 181 (Quick Start)
**Audio Program** Cassette 16A / CD 16
**Video Program** Videotape 6, 3:28 / Videodisc 4A

Search Chapter 8, Play to end
U6E1, En vivo (Dialog)

**Technology**

*Intrigas y aventuras* **CD-ROM,** Disc 2

## Quick Start Review

Conditional tense

Use OHT 181 or write on board: Name three things you would do if you were a talented athlete. What sport would you play? On which team? How would you spend your free time? Use the conditional tense.

Si yo fuera deportista...

*Answers will vary.*

## Teaching Suggestions

### Presenting the Dialog

- Prepare students for listening by focusing on the strategy.
- Use the video, audiocassette, or CD to present the dialog.
- Point out that Isabel is not actually applying for the job with Señor Montero, but is interviewing him about the job application process.

# En vivo

## DIÁLOGO

Isabel

Pablo

Recepcionista

Señor Montero

**PARA ESCUCHAR** • **STRATEGY: LISTENING**

**Evaluate a plan** Isabel has a goal: to have an interview **(tener una entrevista).** Listen and identify the three main steps of her plan:

1. Leer _____
2. Presentarse para _____
3. Preparar o escribir _____

Name any important steps that have been omitted. What do you consider her chances for success?

## Se busca periodista

1 ▶ Isabel: No estoy capacitada para estos trabajos. Aquí necesitan un arquitecto o una arquitecta, y aquí necesitan un veterinario o una veterinaria. ¡No puedo solicitar esos trabajos!

5 ▶ Pablo: Los voy a llamar y les explico que estamos preparando un artículo sobre cómo se solicita un trabajo. Estoy seguro que nos ayudarán.
Isabel: Gracias, Pablo.

6 ▶ Isabel: ¡Quieren muchos datos personales! ¿Qué importancia tiene mi estado civil?
Recepcionista: ¿Señorita Palacios? Acaba de llamar el señor Montero. Va a llegar un poco tarde.
Isabel: Está bien. No hay ningún problema.

7 ▶ Señor Montero: ¿Así que usted trabaja con *Onda Internacional*?
Isabel: Sí, estoy trabajando como pasante. Me encanta. Estamos preparando un artículo sobre cómo se solicita un trabajo.

## Classroom Community

**TPR** Play the audio or have 4 students read the dialog aloud for the class. Have class members stand up each time they hear a profession or job title mentioned.

**Group Activity** Divide students into groups of four and have them role-play the dialog.

**Cooperative Learning** Ask students to use the Internet to find an ad for a job that requires a second language. Collect ads and divide the class into groups of three. Give one student in each group an ad, so that s/he can interview another student **(el/la candidato/a)** for the position. The third student takes notes during the interview and summarizes it for the entire class.

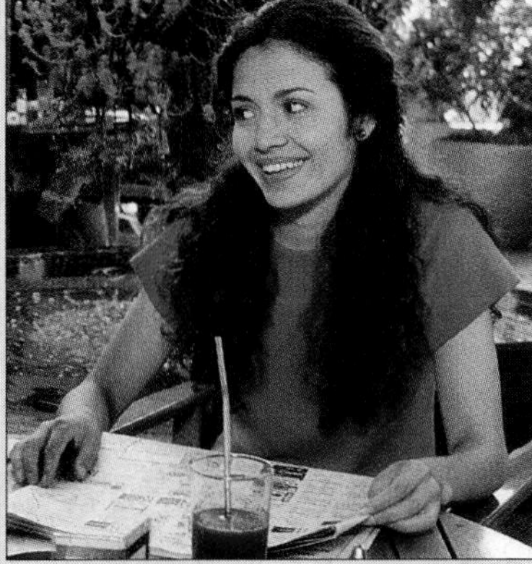

2► Pablo: ¡Ajá! Encontré algo. Ésta es una profesión en la que trabajas con la gente, el horario de trabajo es cómodo…
Isabel: ¿Sí? Léemelo.

3► Pablo: «Buscamos mecánico de carros.»
Isabel: ¡Pablo! Ay, nunca vamos a encontrar nada.
Pablo: Espérate. Este puesto está perfecto.
Isabel: No te lo creo. ¿Qué es? ¿Cartero?

4► Pablo: No, escucha. «Buscamos periodista para trabajar en una revista de viajes. Preferimos experiencia en otra revista o periódico. Infórmese al 452–890.»
Isabel: ¿En serio? ¡Es un trabajo ideal!

8► Señor Montero: Me parece una excelente idea. Muchas veces, la gente llega a una entrevista sin saber qué hacer.
Isabel: ¿Me puede explicar un poco más?

9► Señor Montero: Sí, cómo no. Por ejemplo, ésta es su solicitud. Por lo que veo, está bien escrita. Explicó claramente la experiencia que tiene. Sabe, es una lástima que usted no esté solicitando de verdad el trabajo. Sería una buena candidata.

10► Señor Montero: ¿Me puede contar un poco de usted? ¿Cómo se interesó en el periodismo? ¿De qué le gusta escribir?
Isabel: Sí, claro. Supe del concurso en *Onda Internacional* y decidí escribir un artículo…



## Teaching All Students

**Extra Help** Have students point out all the professions that are mentioned in the dialog. They include **arquitecto(a), veterinario(a), mecánico de carros, cartero, periodista**. Refer them to the chart on pp. 390–391.

**Native Speakers** Ask Spanish speakers to create the phone conversation that Pablo mentions in frame 5.

**Multiple Intelligences**

**Verbal** Ask students to describe what is going on in each of the pictures without reading the captions.

**Kinesthetic** Ask students to read a line from one of the scenes and have others guess which character said the line (**¿Quién lo dijo?**). Hold up 4 pictures–one for each character–and ask students to raise their hands for the appropriate character.

## Video Synopsis

Isabel and Pablo are searching the classified ads in search of a job interview prospect. They set up an interview with Señor Montero, who is looking for a reporter. For a complete transcript of the video dialog, see p. 387D.

## Comprehension Questions

1. ¿Está capacitada Isabel para todos los empleos que ven en el periódico? **(No)**
2. ¿Quiere solicitar el trabajo de mecánico de carros? **(No)**
3. ¿Le interesa el puesto de periodista? **(Sí)**
4. ¿Buscan periodistas para trabajar en una revista o un periódico? **(una revista)**
5. ¿Prepara Isabel un artículo sobre Ecuador o sobre cómo se solicita un trabajo? **(cómo se solicita un trabajo)**
6. ¿Va a trabajar Isabel en la oficina del señor Montero o va a entrevistarlo para el artículo? **(Va a entrevistar al señor Montero.)**
7. Según el señor Montero, ¿está bien preparada mucha gente para una entrevista o llega a la entrevista sin saber qué hacer? **(Llega sin saber qué hacer.)**
8. ¿Qué explica la solicitud de Isabel? **(su experiencia)**
9. ¿Qué opinión tiene el señor Montero de Isabel? **(Piensa que sería una buena candidata.)**
10. ¿Cómo se interesó Isabel en el periodismo? **(Supo del concurso y decidió escribir un artículo.)**

## Language Notes

Isabel is asked for her **estado civil**. It is illegal for U.S. employers to ask this.

## Gestures

Have students study frames 6–10 and comment on Isabel's body language in the interview. Does she look nervous or confident? Have students point out any gestures they recognize in the photos.

## Block Schedule

**Variety** Have students predict how Isabel's interview will continue and explain their reasoning.

# UNIDAD 6 Etapa 1
## Vocabulary/Grammar

### Teaching Resource Options

**Print** 

Block Scheduling Copymasters
Unit 6 Resource Book
Video Activities, pp. 24–25
Videoscript, p. 26
Audioscript, p. 28

**Audiovisual**

OHT 182 (Quick Start)
Audio Program Cassette 16A / CD 16
Video Program Videotape 6, 3:28 / Videodisc 4A

**Technology** 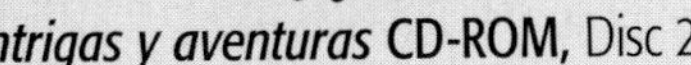

*Intrigas y aventuras* CD-ROM, Disc 2

### Quick Start Review

**Expressions with para**

Use OHT 182 or write on board: The newspaper that Pablo reads says: **Buscamos periodista para trabajar en una revista de viajes.** Complete these sentences using the newspaper ad as a model. Add your own details.

1. Buscamos mecánico(a) para...
2. Buscamos niñero(a) para...
3. Buscamos músico(a) para...

*Answers may include:*
1. reparar carros, 2. cuidar a los niños, 3. tocar la guitarra

**Objective:** Controlled practice
Listening comprehension

**Answers**
c, b, d, a

**Objective:** Transitional practice
Listening comprehension/vocabulary

**Answers**
*Answers may vary.*
1. Estamos preparando un artículo sobre cómo se solicita un trabajo.
2. Este puesto está perfecto.
3. ¡Quieren muchos datos personales!
4. Muchas veces, la gente llega a una entrevista sin saber qué hacer.
5. Sería una buena candidata.

# En acción
## VOCABULARIO Y GRAMÁTICA

**OBJECTIVES**
- Discuss jobs and professions
- Describe people, places, and things
- Complete an application

### En orden

**Escuchar/Escribir** Pon las fotos en orden según el diálogo. Luego escribe una oración que describa lo que pasa en cada foto.

a.

b.

c.

d.

### ¿Cómo lo sabes?

**Escuchar/Escribir** Todas estas oraciones son ciertas. Escribe una línea del diálogo que confirme cada una.

1. Isabel va a escribir un artículo sobre personas que quieren trabajar.
2. Pablo encontró un puesto que sería bueno para el artículo.
3. La solicitud requiere mucha información.
4. Hay muchas personas que no saben buscar trabajo.
5. Isabel está capacitada para el puesto.

**TAMBIÉN SE DICE**

Isabel y el señor Montero hablan del **artículo** que escribe Isabel para *Onda Internacional.* Otras palabras para describir la comunicación periodística son **reportaje, informe, editorial** y **crónica.** Como sus equivalentes en inglés, estos términos se usan también para referirse a la televisión y el ciberespacio.



### Classroom Management

**Paired Activity** Have students work in pairs to do **Actividad 4**. Extend the activity by having students ask about other professions.

**Time Saver** Have individual students write the answers to **Actividades 1–4** on the board. Check answers, then have the students correct their own work.

- *Review: Use present and present progressive tenses*
- *Use the impersonal **se***
- *Use past participles as adjectives*

## ¿Qué profesión?

**Leer/Escribir** Pablo lee las descripciones de varias profesiones. ¿Cuál es la profesión que corresponde a cada descripción?

**arquitecto(a)**
**cartero(a)**
**músico(a)**
**niñero(a)**
**veterinario(a)**
**agricultor(a)**
**bombero**
**peluquero(a)**

1. Tiene cartas y paquetes.
2. Lava y corta el pelo.
3. Diseña edificios y dibuja planos.
4. Cuida a los niños cuando los padres están trabajando.
5. Trabaja con animales enfermos.
6. Busca y controla fuegos peligrosos.
7. Toca un instrumento musical en la orquesta.
8. Cuida las plantas y los animales.

## ¿Qué quieres ser?

**Hablar** ¿Qué quieres ser? Habla con un(a) compañero(a) sobre estas profesiones.

**modelo**

**Tú:** *¿Quieres ser músico(a)?*

**Compañero(a):** *Sí, me gustaría tocar la guitarra en una banda. ¿Y tú?*

**Tú:** *No, no quiero ser músico(a). Quiero ser…*

**Objective:** Transitional practice
Discussing jobs and professions

**Answers**

1. cartero
2. peluquero(a)
3. arquitecto(a)
4. niñero(a)
5. veterinario(a)
6. bombero
7. músico
8. agricultor(a)

**Objective:** Open-ended practice
Discussing jobs and professions

**Answers**

*Answers will vary.*

1. ¿Quieres ser deportista? Sí, me gustaría jugar deportes profesionalmente. ¿Y tú? Sí, quiero ser deportista.
2. ¿Quieres ser bombero? Sí, me gustaría rescatar a la gente.
3. ¿Quieres ser juez? Sí, me gustaría trabajar en las cortes.
4. ¿Quieres ser agricultor(a)? Sí, me gustaría trabajar al aire libre con plantas y animales.
5. ¿Quieres ser bailarín(ina)? Sí, me gustaría bailar ballet.
6. ¿Quieres ser mecánico(a)? Sí, me gustaría reparar coches.

### Critical Thinking

Have students determine the training or education required for the professions listed in **Actividad 3** and represented by the photos in **Actividad 4**. Share the answers with the class on the board.

### Teaching All Students

**Extra Help** Ask students to give the name of the place where each job pictured in **Actividad 4** takes place. (Answers: **afuera, en una casa, en las cortes, en el campo, en un teatro, en un garaje**)

**Challenge** Ask students to comment on the role of technology in today's job market. Why is it important to know how to use a computer?

**Multiple Intelligences**

**Verbal** Ask students to design a Spanish job application for one of the positions in **Actividad 4**.

**Interpersonal** Have students work with a partner to interview each other for their chosen profession.

### Block Schedule

**Change of Pace** Have students answer the question **¿Me puede contar un poco de usted?** in the context of a job interview. They can work orally with another student. (For additional activities, see **Block Scheduling Copymasters**.)

## Teaching Resource Options

**Print**

*Más práctica* Workbook PE, p. 141
*Cuaderno para hispanohablantes* PE, p. 139
Block Scheduling Copymasters
Unit 6 Resource Book
*Más práctica* Workbook TE, p. 5
*Cuaderno para hispanohablantes* TE, p. 11

**Audiovisual**

OHT 182 (Quick Start)

**Technology**

*Intrigas y aventuras* CD-ROM, Disc 2

## Quick Start Review

Present tense: **estar**

Use OHT 182 or write on board: Fill in the blanks with the correct form of the verb **estar** in the present tense.

1. Yo ___ aquí en Ecuador.
2. Mis amigos y yo ___ cerca de la línea ecuatorial.
3. Mi amiga ecuatoriana ___ muy bien informada sobre la ecología.
4. ¿___ tú a favor de la conservación?

**Answers**

1. estoy, 2. estamos, 3. está, 4. Estás

## Teaching Suggestions

### Presenting Repaso: Present and Present Progressive Tenses

- Have students review the dialog on pp. 392–393 to identify examples of the present and present progressive tenses and write them in 2 lists.
- To review irregular verbs, refer students to pp. R33–R35.
- To review present participles of stem-changing verbs, refer students to p. R31.

**Objective:** Open-ended practice
Hypothesizing about the future
Conditional tense

*Answers will vary.*

ACTIVIDAD 5

### Una cápsula del tiempo

**Hablar/Escribir** ¿Qué pondrías en una cápsula del tiempo? Habla con un grupo de compañeros(as) de lo que pondrías y por qué. Luego hagan una presentación para la clase.

**modelo**

*Pondríamos esta revista de moda en la cápsula porque mostraría la ropa que llevábamos…*

Cápsula del tiempo

| Objeto | ¿Por qué? |
|---|---|
| 1. revista de moda | mostrar la ropa del año |
| 2. | |
| 3. | |

REPASO

## The Present and Present Progressive Tenses

**¿RECUERDAS?** *p. 17* To talk about things you do, use the present tense. Remember how to conjugate regular -ar, -er, and -ir verbs in the present tense?

| estudiar | | comer | | vivir | |
|---|---|---|---|---|---|
| estudio | estudiamos | como | comemos | vivo | vivimos |
| estudias | estudiáis | comes | coméis | vives | vivís |
| estudia | estudian | come | comen | vive | viven |

**¿RECUERDAS?** *p. 130* To describe an action that is actually going on at the time of the sentence, you use the present progressive tense. To form the present progressive, use:

the present tense of estar + **-ando**, **-iendo**/**-yendo** forms

*becomes*

**estudiar** → **estudiando**
**comer** → **comiendo**
**vivir** → **viviendo**

Los voy a llamar y les explico que **estamos preparando** un artículo sobre cómo se solicita un trabajo.

*I'm going to call them and explain to them that* ***we are preparing*** *an article on how to apply for a job.*

NOTA CULTURAL

**Quito,** fundada en 1534 sobre una ciudad inca, es un centro artístico y cultural de Ecuador, con tradiciones importantes de pintura, escultura y otras artes. La ciudad se conoce por sus edificios coloniales y sus numerosos museos.

## Classroom Community

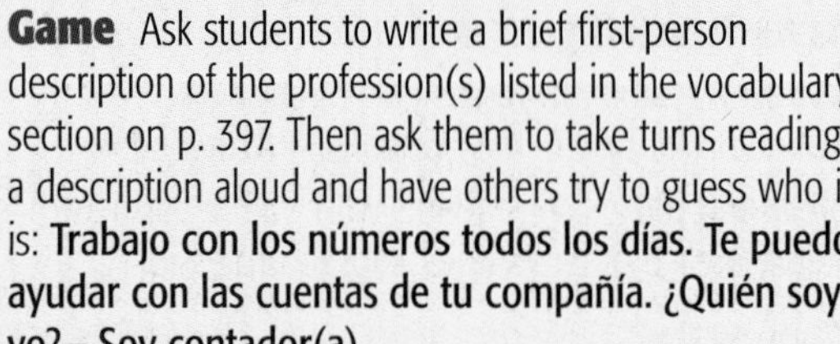

**Game** Ask students to write a brief first-person description of the profession(s) listed in the vocabulary section on p. 397. Then ask them to take turns reading a description aloud and have others try to guess who it is: **Trabajo con los números todos los días. Te puedo ayudar con las cuentas de tu compañía. ¿Quién soy yo?– Soy contador(a).**

**TPR** Ask students to act out the objects they chose for **Actividad 5** for the class to identify. For an extra challenge, have them act out their reasons for choosing the objects.

## Las profesiones

**Leer/Escribir** Unas personas hablaron con Isabel sobre sus profesiones. Completa sus oraciones con la forma correcta de los siguientes verbos. ¡Ojo! Algunos verbos no son regulares.

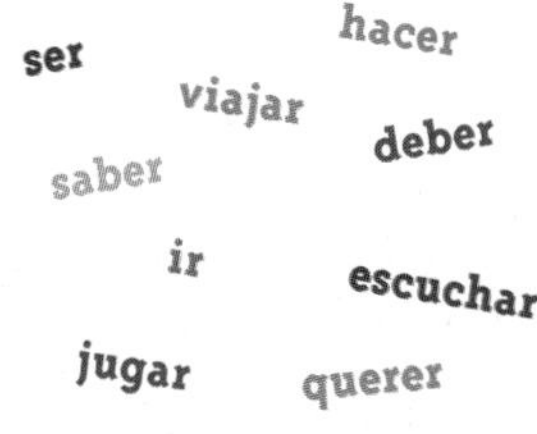


1. Me encanta ser periodista porque _____ por todas partes.
2. Los maestros _____ todo lo posible para ayudar a sus estudiantes.
3. Tú _____ que es muy divertido ser niñera… ¡y mucho trabajo!
4. Nosotros, los bomberos, _____ adonde haya emergencias.
5. En su profesión como juez, usted _____ escuchar bien.
6. Como deportistas, nosotros _____ en partidos frecuentemente.
7. Mi esposo y yo _____ doctores y _____ ayudar a los enfermos.
8. Soy música y _____ las diferencias del ritmo en una canción.

## Las carreras

**Hablar/Escribir** Todos hablan de su trabajo hoy. Completa las oraciones para saber cuáles son sus profesiones y qué están haciendo ahora. Sigue el modelo.

**modelo**

*La (dueña / operadora) ayudar / a los clientes con problemas de teléfono*

*La operadora está ayudando a los clientes con problemas de teléfono.*

1. La (técnica / secretaria) tomar / radiografías
2. Eres (ingeniero / voluntario) y por eso, no ganar / dinero hoy
3. El (taxista / contador) llevar / cuentas de un negocio
4. Somos (obreros / jefes) y hacer / trabajo manual
5. Aquí los (abogados / hombres de negocios) trabajar / en las cortes
6. Soy (gerente / asistente) y abrir / una tienda nueva
7. La (artesana / secretaria) crear / arte para vender

### Vocabulario

#### Más empleos

**el (la) abogado(a)** *lawyer*
**el (la) artesano(a)** *artisan*
**el (la) asistente** *assistant*
**el (la) contador(a)** *accountant*
**el (la) dueño(a)** *owner*
**el (la) gerente** *manager*
**el (la) hombre (mujer) de negocios** *businessman/businesswoman*
**el (la) ingeniero(a)** *engineer*
**el (la) jefe(a)** *boss*
**el (la) obrero(a)** *worker*
**el (la) operador(a)** *operator*
**el (la) secretario(a)** *secretary*
**el (la) taxista** *taxi driver*
**el (la) técnico(a)** *technician*
**el (la) voluntario(a)** *volunteer*

¿Qué te gustaría ser?

**MÁS PRÁCTICA** *cuaderno* p. 141

**PARA HISPANOHABLANTES** *cuaderno* p. 139



## Teaching All Students

**Extra Help** Ask students to choose 5 of the professions listed on p. 397 and describe them in Spanish. Have students share their descriptions with their classmates.

**Native Speakers** Have Spanish speakers add other job titles to the list on p. 397. Also have them review the list to see if they might use different titles for the same jobs.

**Multiple Intelligences**

**Verbal** Have students work in small groups to list the tasks and/or job titles they associate with volunteer workers (**voluntarios[as]**).

**Naturalist** Brainstorm a list of professions which deal directly with the environment, e.g., a park ranger or an environmentalist. Students can write a description of one of these professions.

**Objective:** Controlled practice
Present tense

**Answers**

1. viajo
2. hacen
3. sabes
4. vamos
5. debe
6. jugamos
7. somos, queremos
8. escucho

**Objective:** Controlled practice
Present progressive

**Answers**

1. La técnica está tomando radiografías.
2. Eres voluntario y por eso, no estás ganando dinero hoy.
3. El contador está llevando cuentas de un negocio.
4. Somos obreros y estamos haciendo trabajo manual.
5. Aquí los abogados están trabajando en las cortes.
6. Soy gerente y estoy abriendo una tienda nueva.
7. La artesana está creando arte para vender.

## Project

Have students create an advertisement for a training or educational program for one of the professions. Have them include a description of a program graduate's daily job activities.

## Block Schedule

**Retention** Continue **Actividad 7** with a related oral activity. Read the following "clues" and have students write down the profession each sentence suggests. Then go over the correct responses, having students volunteer answers.

1. Estoy diseñando un edificio nuevo.
2. Estoy contestando el teléfono en una oficina.
3. Estoy conduciendo a una persona al aeropuerto.
4. Estoy apagando un fuego.
5. Estoy cuidando mis plantas.

**Answers**

1. arquitecto(a), 2. secretario(a), 3. taxista, 4. bombero, 5. agricultor(a)

(For additional activities, see **Block Scheduling Copymasters**.)

## Teaching Resource Options

**Print**

Block Scheduling Copymasters
Unit 6 Resource Book
Information Gap Activities, p. 17
Audioscript, p. 29

**Audiovisual**

OHT 182 (Quick Start)
Audio Program Cassette 16A / CD 16

**Technology**

*Intrigas y aventuras* CD-ROM, Disc 2

## Quick Start Review

**Conditional tense**

Use OHT 182 or write on board: If you worked for an organization dedicated to protecting the environment, what types of tasks would you do? Change the verbs to the conditional tense.

Si yo fuera voluntario(a)...
(organizar) programas de reciclaje
(plantar) árboles
(escribir) a los representantes políticos
(informar) a la gente sobre los efectos de la contaminación
(pedir) contribuciones de dinero

**Answers**
organizaría, plantaría, escribiría, informaría, pediría

**Objective:** Open-ended practice
Listening comprehension/discussing jobs and professions

**Answers** (See script, TE p. 387D.)
*Answers will vary.*
1. Trabaja en su coche y lleva personas a varios lugares.
2. Hace objetos de barro y de madera.
3. Trabaja en un hospital y ayuda a los enfermos.
4. Escribe reportes y cartas en la computadora.
5. Usa las matemáticas y la computadora para hacer cálculos y preparar diagramas.

**Objective:** Open-ended practice
Describing daily activities

*Answers will vary.*

## El proyecto

**Escuchar/Escribir** Para su proyecto, Isabel les hace preguntas a varias personas. Escribe una oración que describa lo que hace cada persona según lo que escuchas.

1. el taxista
2. el artesano
3. la voluntaria
4. el secretario
5. la ingeniera

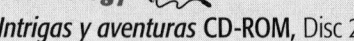

**NOTA CULTURAL**

**La ocarina** es un instrumento musical de cerámica hecho a mano. Es como la flauta y se toca soplando y tapando los huecos (*holes*). De origen precolombino, todavía se usan estos instrumentos en la música folklórica de Sudamérica.

## ¿Qué hacen ustedes?

**Hablar/Escribir** Habla con un grupo de compañeros(as) de lo que haces en estas situaciones. Usa las fotos para darte ideas.

por la tarde

**modelo**

*Por la tarde, juego al fútbol con el equipo de mi escuela. Corro y practico todos los días.*

1. por la mañana

2. durante el día

3. durante el almuerzo

4. después de las clases

5. con mi familia

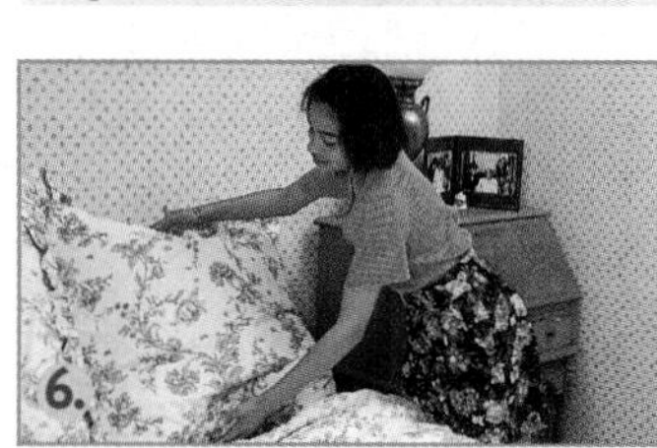
6. en mi casa

**MÁS COMUNICACIÓN** p. R17



## Classroom Community

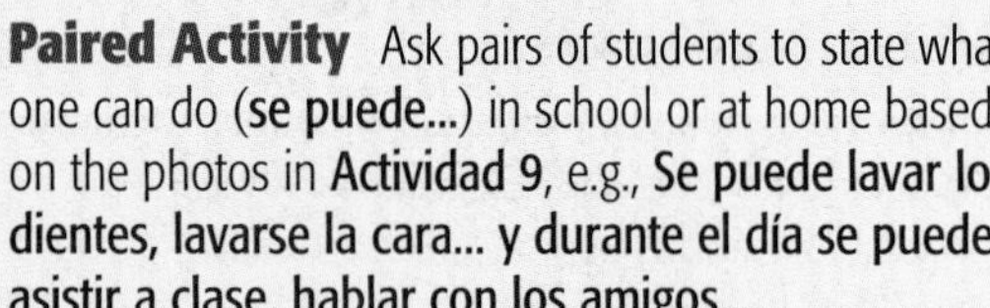

**Paired Activity** Ask pairs of students to state what one can do (**se puede...**) in school or at home based on the photos in **Actividad 9**, e.g., **Se puede lavar los dientes, lavarse la cara... y durante el día se puede asistir a clase, hablar con los amigos....**

**Storytelling** As a variation of **Actividad 9**, have those students who work tell a story about what they do while at their jobs. They could also tell a story about something interesting that happened to them while at work.

## GRAMÁTICA: The Impersonal se

¿RECUERDAS? p. 110 You already know that a reflexive pronoun is used with a **verb** when only the **subject** is involved in the action of the verb.

**Yo me escondo.**
*I hide (myself).*

**Tú te escondes.**
*You hide (yourself).*

**Carlos se esconde.**
*Carlos hides (himself).*

You can use the same se when the **subject** does not refer to any specific person. It's called the **impersonal se**.

Aquí **se habla** español.
*Spanish **is spoken** here.*

This phrase means someone speaks Spanish. It doesn't specify who speaks it.

Señor Montero might say:

—Aquí es donde **se escriben** los datos.
*Here's where **one writes down** the information.*

Señor Montero points out where in the application certain information is to be written.

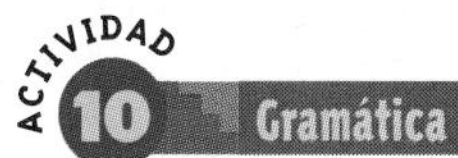

Since the noun is plural, the verb is also plural.

### ACTIVIDAD 10 Gramática

### En Ecuador

**Hablar/Escribir** Pablo le explica a Isabel lo que se hace en los siguientes lugares de Ecuador. ¿Qué dice? Escribe oraciones afirmativas o negativas según el mapa.

**modelo**

*Cuenca (hacer zapatos)*
*No se hacen zapatos en Cuenca.*

1. los Andes (escalar montañas)
2. las islas Galápagos (ver tortugas)
3. en el centro de Quito (cultivar plátanos)
4. en Guayaquil (escalar montañas)
5. en el Oriente (ver plantas silvestres)



### Teaching Suggestion
**Presenting Gramática: The Impersonal se**

Other examples of the impersonal **se** include:

**Se buscan periodistas buenas.**
Good journalists wanted.

**Se venden bicicletas nuevas.**
New bicycles for sale.

Explain that this usage is common in signs or advertisements. In these examples, the impersonal **se** could also mean "they," i.e., *They are looking for good journalists.*

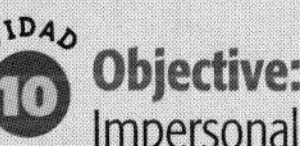

ACTIVIDAD 10 **Objective:** Controlled practice Impersonal **se**

**Answers**
1. En los Andes se escalan montañas.
2. En las islas Galápagos se ven tortugas.
3. En el centro de Quito no se cultivan plátanos.
4. En Guayaquil no se escalan montañas.
5. En el Oriente se ven plantas silvestres.

### Culture Highlights

- **CUENCA** is the third largest city in Ecuador, located in a valley of the Andes Mountains. It is known for its colorful markets and unspoiled colonial architecture.
- **QUITO** is the capital of Ecuador. It is located just 15 miles from the equator, but because of its high altitude, 9,350 ft., it has a mild climate all year long.
- **GUAYAQUIL** is a coastal city in the south of Ecuador. It serves as the main seaport and financial center of the country.
- **EL ORIENTE** refers to the vast rainforest between the Andes Mountains and the Amazon lowlands. El Oriente takes up about one-fourth of the land in Ecuador, but it is mostly undeveloped.

### Teaching All Students

**Extra Help** Ask students to work in small groups and list 10–12 activities that they do every day. Then ask them to rank the activities from most interesting (10) to least interesting (1).

**Native Speakers** Have Spanish speakers give additional examples of when one might use the impersonal **se**.

**Multiple Intelligences**

**Verbal** Ask students to choose a Spanish-speaking country (e.g., Mexico, Spain, Costa Rica, Puerto Rico, Ecuador) and write five activities that can occur there, e.g., **En España se ve la Torre de Oro en Sevilla; se comen mariscos y...**

**Musical/Rhythmic** Ask students to research the names of other musical instruments that are played in South America, via the Internet or the library.

### Block Schedule

**Variety** Have students list on the board any activities that can be done in their town/city. **Lo que se hace en mi pueblo/ciudad...** (For additional activities, see **Block Scheduling Copymasters.**)

## Teaching Resource Options

**Print**

*Más práctica* Workbook PE, pp. 142–144
*Cuaderno para hispanohablantes* PE, pp. 140–142
Block Scheduling Copymasters
Unit 6 Resource Book
*Más práctica* Workbook TE, pp. 6–8
*Cuaderno para hispanohablantes* TE, pp. 12–14
Audioscript, p. 29

**Audiovisual**

OHT 183 (Quick Start)
Audio Program Cassette 16A / CD 16

**Technology**

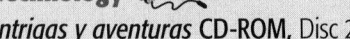

*Intrigas y aventuras* CD-ROM, Disc 2

## Quick Start Review

Talking about professions

Use OHT 183 or write on board: Imagine you are a guidance counselor. You need to suggest careers to the following people based on their interests. Follow the model.

Me interesa trabajar con niños.
Recomiendo que pienses en una carrera como niñera.

1. Me gustan los animales.
2. Me interesa el arte.
3. Me gusta estudiar las matemáticas.
4. Me interesa escribir artículos.

**Answers**

*Possible answers:* 1. veterinario(a), 2. pintor(a), 3. contador(a), 4. periodista

**Objective:** Controlled practice
Impersonal **se**/Completing an application

**Answers**

a. Se escribe el nombre en la línea uno.
b. Se escribe la fecha de nacimiento en la línea cinco.
c. Se escribe la dirección en la línea dos.
d. Se escribe la ciudadanía en la línea cuatro.
e. Se escribe la firma en la línea ocho.
f. Se escribe la fecha de la solicitud original en la línea seis.
g. Se escriben otros datos pertinentes en la línea siete.

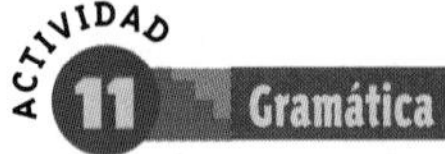

ACTIVIDAD 11 Gramática

## Datos personales

**Hablar/Escribir** Una empresa les pide a todos los empleados nuevos que completen esta tarjeta. ¿Dónde se escribe la información?

1. **Nombre y apellido** ____
2. **Dirección** ____
3. **Número de teléfono** ____
4. **Ciudadanía** ____
5. **Fecha de nacimiento** ____
6. **Fecha de la solicitud original** ____
7. **Otros datos pertinentes** ____
8. **Firma** ____

**modelo**

*dónde recibe llamadas telefónicas*
*Se escribe el número de teléfono en la línea tres.*

a. cómo se llama
b. el día en que nació
c. dónde vive
d. de dónde es
e. el nombre, en letra cursiva
f. cuándo solicitó el puesto
g. otra información importante

**MÁS PRÁCTICA** *cuaderno* p. 142
**PARA HISPANOHABLANTES** *cuaderno* p. 140

### Vocabulario

**La solicitud**

| | |
|---|---|
| **la ciudadanía** *citizenship* | **la firma** *signature* |
| **los datos** *facts, information* | **solicitar** *to request, to apply for* |
| **la fecha de nacimiento** *date of birth* | **la solicitud** *application* |

¿Qué información le importa más a un(a) jefe(a)?

ACTIVIDAD 12

## Se busca trabajo

**Hablar/Escribir** Con un(a) compañero(a), pongan en orden los pasos que se siguen para buscar trabajo. Exprésenlos usando expresiones con **se.**

a. buscar puestos en el periódico
b. escribir su firma
c. llenar una solicitud sin errores
d. escribir los datos personales
e. con buena suerte, aceptar la posición
f. hacer una entrevista
g. escoger el tipo de empleo
h. pedir una solicitud

ACTIVIDAD 13

## La entrevista

**Escuchar/Escribir** Juan Manuel acaba de graduarse de la universidad y está solicitando empleo. Escucha la entrevista. Luego escribe sobre la entrevista en tus propias palabras.

## Classroom Community

**Paired Activity** Have pairs ask each other questions using the words in the vocabulary box.

**Group Activity** Using the words in the vocabulary box as a guide, ask students to design a job application for a position at your school, e.g., **maestro(a), custodio, secretaria, entrenador(a), director(a), consejero(a),** etc.

**Learning Scenario** Tell students that they are supervisors who are hiring new employees. In groups of 3, they choose the job of their new employee and write 3 job-specific questions for the application.

## Past Participles Used as Adjectives

Some adjectives may be formed from verbs. The form you use is the **past participle**. Compare these **infinitives** with their form in the descriptions:

**cerrar** (to close) — La oficina está **cerrada.** *The office is **closed.***

**aburrir** (to bore) — Los empleados están **aburridos.** *The employees are **bored.***

When describing a noun using a past participle,

1. first form the **past participle** by dropping the **ending** from the **infinitive** and adding the appropriate **ending**:

for -ar verbs:

**hablar** ← **-ado** **hablado**

for -er and -ir verbs:

**comer** or **vivir** ← **-ido** **comido, vivido**

2. Then change the **past participle** to agree in number and gender with the noun being described the same as you would an adjective.

**Isabel** says: 1. 2.

—No estoy **capacitada** para estos trabajos.
*I am not **qualified** for these jobs.*

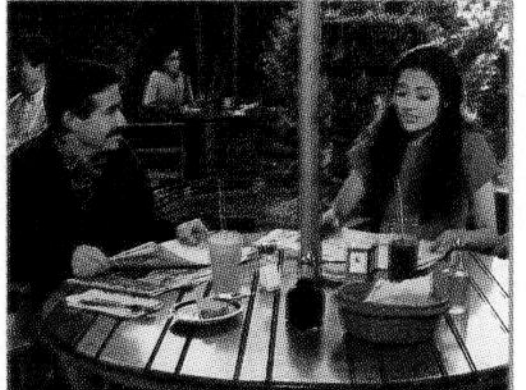

**Pablo** might have replied:

—Yo tampoco estoy **capacitado.**
*I am not **qualified** either.*

Many verbs have irregular **past participles**. Some are

| infinitive | past participle | infinitive | past participle |
|---|---|---|---|
| abrir | **abierto** | ir | **ido** |
| decir | **dicho** | poner | **puesto** |
| descubrir | **descubierto** | romper | **roto** |
| escribir | **escrito** | ver | **visto** |
| hacer | **hecho** | volver | **vuelto** |

Actividad 14 Gramática

### ¿Cómo están?

**Leer/Escribir** Pablo habla de su familia y amigos con Isabel. Completa las frases según el modelo.

**modelo**

*Mi hija tiene un examen mañana y estudia mucho. Creo que… (preparar)*

*Creo que está preparada.*

1. Isabel, ¡terminaste el artículo sobre cómo se busca un trabajo! Veo que… (cansar)
2. Nuestros amigos miran un partido de fútbol. Creo que… (aburrir)
3. Mi sobrina jugó todo el día en el parque. Mírala… (dormir)
4. Mis primos ven una película de aventuras en el cine. Estoy seguro de que… (interesar)
5. Mi amiga Ana tiene un novio. Es evidente que… (enamorar)
6. Mi esposa tomó el sol todo el día. ¿Ves que…? (quemar)

**MÁS PRÁCTICA** *cuaderno* pp. 143–144

**PARA HISPANOHABLANTES** *cuaderno* pp. 141–142



## Teaching Suggestions
### Presenting Past Participles Used as Adjectives

- Have students form the past participle for the following verbs: **firmar, solicitar, ganar, trabajar, escoger, pedir, ofrecer.**
- Have students look around the room and describe people and objects by using past participles as adjectives. For example, **Los estudiantes están sentados. Las ventanas están cerradas.**

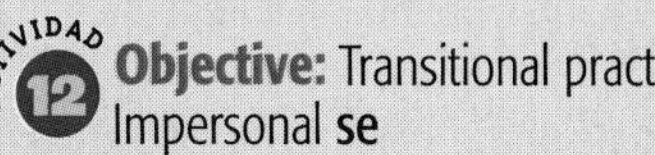

Actividad 12 **Objective:** Transitional practice Impersonal **se**

**Answers**
1. g. Se escoge el tipo de empleo.
2. a. Se buscan puestos en el periódico.
3. h. Se pide una solicitud.
4. c. Se llena una solicitud sin errores.
5. d. Se escriben los datos personales.
6. b. Se escribe su firma.
7. f. Se hace una entrevista.
8. e. Con buena suerte, se acepta la posición.

Actividad 13 **Objective:** Open-ended practice Listening comprehension

(See script, TE p. 387D.)
*Answers will vary.*

Actividad 14 **Objective:** Controlled practice Past participles as adjectives

**Answers**
1. Veo que estás cansada.
2. Creo que están aburridos.
3. Mírala. Está dormida.
4. Estoy seguro de que están interesados.
5. Es evidente que está enamorada.
6. ¿Ves que está quemada?

## Block Schedule

**FunBreak** Divide students into pairs and have them write instructions using the impersonal **se**. Depending on the level of your students, you may decide to limit the choices and give cues or ask for only 2–3 lines of instructions. Possible topics include: Setting up a campsite; fixing/building something; giving directions from school to another place. (For additional activities, see **Block Scheduling Copymasters.**)

## Teaching All Students

**Extra Help** Ask students to write 5 sentences using past participles as adjectives. For example, **La tienda está cerrada.**

**Native Speakers** Ask Spanish-speaking students to name the past participles they might use most often, e.g., **interesado, aburrido, cansado,** etc.

**Multiple Intelligences**

**Verbal** Have students describe themselves to a prospective employer, using past participles as adjectives.

**Musical/Rhythmic** Ask students to develop a chant to practice past participles used as adjectives. This can be a very creative activity. For example, **La puerta estaba abierta, los estudiantes estaban despiertos,** etc.

## Teaching Resource Options

**Print**

*Más práctica* Workbook PE, pp. 137–140
*Cuaderno para hispanohablantes* PE, pp. 137–138
Block Scheduling Copymasters
Unit 6 Resource Book
*Más práctica* Workbook TE, pp. 1–4
*Cuaderno para hispanohablantes* TE, pp. 9–10
Audioscript, pp. 31–32
Information Gap Activities, p. 18

**Audiovisual** 

OHT 177, 177A, 183 (Quick Start)
Audio Program Cassette 16B / CD 16; (*Para hispanohablantes* Cassette 16B / CD 16)

**Technology**

*Intrigas y aventuras* CD-ROM, Disc 2

### Quick Start Review

**Asking questions**

Use OHT 183 or write on board: You are the owner of a department store and you are looking for a new manager. Write three questions you would ask an applicant in an interview.

*Answers will vary.*

**Objective:** Transitional practice
Past participles as adjectives

**Answers**

1. El televisor está apagado.
2. Mis padres están ocupados...
3. Mi hermana está sentada... y no está aburrida.
4. Mi hermano está dormido... y está vestido...
5. Los periódicos están puestos...

**Objective:** Transitional practice
Past participles as adjectives

**Answers**

*Answers will vary.*

1. sentado(a)
2. vestidos(as)
3. abierta
4. casado(a)
5. ocupado(a)
6. puesta
7. escrito
8. hecha

## Me imagino que...

**Hablar/Escribir** Es sábado e Isabel imagina lo que pasa en su casa. Mira el dibujo y completa sus descripciones.

dormir aburrir sentar poner vestir cerrar ocupar apagar

**modelo**

*La ventana está _____.*
*La ventana está cerrada.*

1. El televisor está _____.
2. Mis padres están _____ pagando las cuentas.
3. Mi hermana está _____ en el sillón leyendo una buena novela y no está _____.
4. Mi hermano está _____ en el sofá y está _____ con pantalones cortos.
5. Los periódicos están _____ en el suelo.

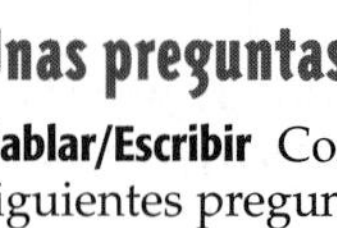

## Unas preguntas

**Hablar/Escribir** Completa las siguientes preguntas con el participio pasado. Luego házselas a un(a) compañero(a) de clase.

**modelo**

*¿La puerta está (cerrar)?*
**Tú:** *¿La puerta está cerrada?*
**Compañero(a):** *No, no está cerrada. (No, está abierta.)*

1. ¿Quién está (sentar) cerca de la puerta?
2. ¿Quiénes están (vestir) con jeans?
3. ¿La cafetería está (abrir) para los estudiantes ahora?
4. ¿Tienes un(a) hermano(a) (casar)?
5. ¿Estás (ocupar) después de las clases?
6. ¿Qué tipo de ropa llevas (poner)?
7. ¿Hay algo (escribir) en el pizarrón?
8. ¿Está (hacer) la comida?



## Classroom Community

**Group Activity** Ask students to bring in action pictures from magazines, newspapers, etc. Then let them describe the pictures in small groups using the verb **estar** + past participles. Post the pictures and the written descriptions on your bulletin board.

**Portfolio** Have students write a short paragraph in their journals about one important aspect they would like a prospective employer to know about them.

**Rubric: Writing**

| Criteria | Scale |
|---|---|
| Accuracy | 1 2 3 4 5 |
| Logical organization | 1 2 3 4 5 |
| Vocabulary use | 1 2 3 4 5 |

A = 13–15 pts.
B = 10–12 pts.
C = 7–9 pts.
D = 4–6 pts.
F = < 4 pts.

## La solicitud

**Escribir** Vas a solicitar un trabajo para este verano en un país de habla hispana. Escribe la información que se pide en esta solicitud.

**Solicitud para empleo**

**Información personal**

Nombre: ______ (apellido) (nombre)

Dirección: ______ (calle y número) (ciudad, estado, código postal)

Teléfono: ______

Edad (menor de 18): ______

Horas disponibles (número total de horas): ______

Horas cada día

| | dom | lun | mar | miér | jue | vier | sáb |
|---|---|---|---|---|---|---|---|
| de<br>a | | | | | | | |

**Educación**

Colegio ______

Promedio de notas ______ Último año completado ______

**Experiencia** Trabajos más recientes (pagados o voluntarios)

______

**Referencias** ______

**Actividades** ______

## Una entrevista

**PARA CONVERSAR**

**STRATEGY: SPEAKING**

**Participate in an interview** A job interview is important for providing valuable information about the job and the applicant. Both interviewer and interviewee share equal responsibilities to

- maintain a cordial atmosphere.
- ask for and give information about the job—duties, responsibilities, benefits, expectations.
- ask for and give information about the applicant—education, experience, qualifications, attitudes.

At the end of the interview both participants should make it clear what the next step is.

**Hablar** Ya llenaste la solicitud. Ahora ten una entrevista. Una persona será el (la) jefe(a) y la otra será la persona que busca trabajo. Luego cambien de papel. ¡Ojo! Debes usar la forma de **usted** en la entrevista.

Incluye:
- Una introducción (saludo, información sobre el puesto)
- Preguntas sobre la solicitud
- Preguntas sobre el trabajo
- Preguntas sobre los planes para el futuro

MÁS COMUNICACIÓN p. R17

### Refrán

*Lo que no se empieza, no se acaba.*

Cuando tienes un montón de trabajo, ¿siempre lo haces en seguida o buscas razones para evitarlo? Según el refrán, ¿cuál es el mejor consejo que puedes darle a la mujer del dibujo? En grupos pequeños, hagan una lista de cuatro proyectos que sean fáciles de completar y cuatro que sean difíciles. Luego comparen su lista con la de otro grupo.



### Teaching Suggestions

Call on several volunteers to act out their interview from **Actividad 18** for the class.

**Objective:** Open-ended practice
Completing an application

*Answers will vary.*

**Objective:** Open-ended practice
Jobs and professions

*Answers will vary.*

### Teaching All Students

**Extra Help** Ask students to list 10 positive characteristics that they would use to describe themselves in a job interview.

**Challenge** Ask students to describe 8–10 characteristics required for a given job, e.g., **profesor(a), abogado(a), dentista,** etc.

**Native Speakers** Have Spanish speakers model an interview situation with the teacher or another student before the whole class does **Actividad 18**.

**Multiple Intelligences**

**Interpersonal** Tape record the interviews from **Actividad 18** and play for the class. Ask students to list the candidates' strengths and weaknesses.

### Block Schedule

**Process Time** Have students swap information from their **solicitudes** from **Actividad 17** and take turns interviewing each other for a job. (For additional activities, see **Block Scheduling Copymasters**.)

## Teaching Resource Options

**Print**

*Cuaderno para hispanohablantes* PE, p. 144
Unit 6 Resource Book
*Cuaderno para hispanohablantes* TE, p. 16
Video Activities, p. 25
Videoscript, p. 27
Audioscript, p. 30

**Audiovisual**

OHT 183 (Quick Start)
Audio Program Cassette 16A / CD 16
Video Program Videotape 6, 10:13 / Videodisc 4B

Search Chapter 1, Play to 2
U6E1, En voces (Culture), Spanish

Search Chapter 1, Play to 2
U6E1, En voces (Culture), English

## Quick Start Review

Uses of **por** and **para**

Use OHT 183 or write on board: Fill in the blanks with either **por** or **para**.

1. Yo soy guía. Trabajo ___ el gobierno de Ecuador.
2. Hago los planes ___ las excursiones a Santa Cruz.
3. Vamos a la excursión ___ dos horas.
4. Es importante que hagamos cosas ___ proteger los especies en peligro.

**Answers**
1. para, 2. para, 3. por, 4. para

## Supplementary Vocabulary

| | |
|---|---|
| **el piquero patas azules** | blue-footed booby |
| **el pingüino** | penguin |
| **el león marino** | sea lion |
| **la tortuga** | tortoise |
| **los aves (pájaros)** | birds |

# En voces

**LECTURA**

**PARA LEER • STRATEGY: READING**

**Use context to find meaning** Find the words in the reading that fit these meanings:

a. **persona que acompaña a visitantes**
b. **el círculo máximo de la Tierra que separa el norte del sur**
c. **tranquilo o domesticado**
d. **sitio donde nadie vive**
e. **poner el pie sobre algo**
f. **el pie y la pierna de los animales**
g. **un animal del sexo masculino**

Jaime Carrillo Ochoa te va a dar una excursión por la isla Santa Cruz.

## Bienvenidos a la isla Santa Cruz

¡Buenos días! Me llamo Jaime Carrillo Ochoa y soy de Guayaquil, una ciudad en la costa del sur de Ecuador. Me gusta estudiar los animales silvestres. Trabajo de guía aquí en las Galápagos, donde hay muchos animales interesantes. Hoy voy a llevar a un grupo de turistas de excursión por la isla Santa Cruz. ¿Te gustaría acompañarnos? ¡Vámonos!

Santa Cruz es una de las islas más grandes de las Galápagos. Está muy lejos de Ecuador, a unas 600 millas al oeste del país en la línea ecuatorial. Los animales son mansos[1]; no tienen miedo porque

[1] tame



## Classroom Community

**Portfolio** Ask students to describe what it might be like to live on the **Islas Galápagos**. They should use the conditional tense.

**Rubric: Writing**

| Criteria | Scale |
|---|---|
| Accuracy | 1 2 3 4 5 |
| Logical organization | 1 2 3 4 5 |
| Vocabulary use | 1 2 3 4 5 |

A = 13–15 pts.
B = 10–12 pts.
C = 7–9 pts.
D = 4–6 pts.
F = < 4 pts.

**Cooperative Learning: Jigsaw** Distribute 4 different articles or brochures on the **Islas Galápagos** to groups of students to read and discuss. Reorganize the groups so that each new group's members read different articles. Each student tells the group about the article they read.

por muchos años estas islas estuvieron deshabitadas.

Comencemos, y por favor, tengan cuidado. Hay iguanas por todas partes y no debemos pisarlas[2].

En las Galápagos hay 58 tipos de aves. A la derecha pueden ver un ave que se llama el piquero patas azules. Como indica su nombre, estas aves tienen patas de color azul. Hay muchos pingüinos también. Ah, ¡miren! Hay un pingüino encima de esa piedra. A algunos turistas les gusta bucear con respiración[3] para mirar los pingüinos nadando debajo del agua. Los pingüinos no pueden volar pero pueden nadar rápidamente.

Otro animal famoso es el león marino. Pueden ver algunos allí en el agua. A los bebés les gusta jugar con los humanos, pero cuidado, ¡los machos no son tan simpáticos!

Ahora vamos a ir a la reserva de tortugas en Santa Cruz. Van a ver la especie más conocida por los turistas: la tortuga gigante. Una de estas tortugas puede pesar 550 libras. Estos animales son vegetarianos. No comen carne. Su dieta parece ser saludable porque las tortugas gigantes viven aproximadamente 150 años. Los animales y las plantas de las Galápagos son diferentes de los del continente por la falta de contacto con otras especies. Muchas especies se encuentran solamente aquí. ¡Espero que disfruten de sus observaciones!

[2] to step on them [3] snorkel

## ¿Comprendiste?

1. ¿Qué trabajo tiene Jaime Carrillo Ochoa?
2. ¿Dónde queda exactamente el lugar donde trabaja Jaime?
3. ¿Qué animales se ven en Santa Cruz?
4. ¿Cuál es el animal más conocido por los turistas?

## ¿Qué piensas?

1. ¿Crees que le gusta a Jaime trabajar en las Galápagos? ¿Por qué?
2. ¿Cómo se explican las diferencias entre los animales de las Galápagos y los del continente?

## Teaching All Students

**Extra Help** Ask simple **sí/no** questions based on the reading, e.g., **¿A Jaime le gusta estudiar los animales silvestres? (Sí) ¿Jaime asiste a la universidad para ser veterinario? (No) ¿Santa Cruz está cerca de Ecuador? (No–lejos),** etc.

**Challenge** Ask students to list names of other islands they know. Have them draw a Venn diagram to show similarities and differences between the Galápagos and one other island.

**Multiple Intelligences**

**Naturalist** Have students research and list other unique animals found on the Galápagos Islands.

**Visual** Ask students to draw a picture of the Galápagos Islands based on the reading.



## Teaching Suggestions

- **Prereading** Have students scan the reading and pick out the animals mentioned.
- **Strategy: Use context to find meaning** Divide the class into several groups and have each group work together to find the words that fit the meanings listed in the **Para leer** box.
- **Reading** Have students make a list of unfamiliar words on the board. Then review the contexts to determine meanings.
- **Post-reading** Have students research more about the Galápagos Islands via the Internet or at the library.

## Culture Highlights

- **ISLA SANTA CRUZ** is the largest of the Galápagos Islands. This is where many tours begin. The main city is Puerto Ayora.
- **ANIMALS OF LAS GALÁPAGOS** Many of the birds and animals found here are not found anywhere else. Since the islands are over 600 miles from the continent of South America, they have never had contact with other species.

## Cross Cultural Connections

**Strategy: Observe and generalize** Ask students if they have ever visited a zoo. If so, ask them to compare or contrast the animals they saw at the zoo with the animals found on the **Islas Galápagos**. Then ask students to generalize their observations about the animals of the **Galápagos**.

## ¿Comprendiste?

**Answers**

*Answers will vary.*

1. El es guía en las Galápagos.
2. Queda a 600 millas al oeste de Ecuador en la línea ecuatorial.
3. En Santa Cruz se ven iguanas, aves, pingüinos, leones marinos y tortugas.
4. El animal más conocido es la tortuga gigante.

## Block Schedule

**FunBreak** Have students create a nature lover's guide to the Galápagos Islands, as described in the first project in the **Ampliación** section on p. 387B.

UNIDAD 6 Etapa 1
**Review**

## Teaching Resource Options

**Print** 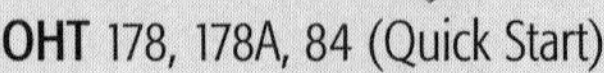

*Cuaderno para hispanohablantes* PE, p. 143
Block Scheduling Copymasters
Unit 6 Resource Book
*Cuaderno para hispanohablantes* TE, p. 15
Information Gap Activities, pp. 19–20
Family Involvement, pp. 21–22
Multiple Choice Test Questions, pp. 170–172

**Audiovisual**

OHT 178, 178A, 84 (Quick Start)

**Technology**

Electronic Teacher Tools/Test Generator
*Intrigas y aventuras* CD-ROM, Disc 2

## Quick Start Review

Past participles

Use OHT 184 or write on board: Write the past participles for the following verbs.

**beber, solicitar, escribir, decir, hacer, ver**

**Answers**

bebido, solicitado, escrito, dicho, hecho, visto

## Teaching Suggestions
### What Have Students Learned?

- Have students look at the "Now you can..." notes listed on the left side of pp. 406–407. Point out that if they feel they need to review material before doing the activities, they should consult the "To review" notes.
- Use the video to review vocabulary and structures.

# En uso
## REPASO Y MÁS COMUNICACIÓN

**OBJECTIVES**
- Discuss jobs and professions
- Describe people, places, and things
- Complete an application

*Now you can...*
- discuss jobs and professions.

*To review*
- present and present progressive tenses, see p. 396.

### ACTIVIDAD 1 ¡Es sábado!

Isabel habla con varias personas en el parque. ¿Cuáles son sus profesiones? ¿Qué están haciendo ahora?

**artesano(a)**
**cartero(a)**
**deportista**
**voluntario(a)**
**músico(a)**
**taxista**
**periodista**
**niñero(a)**

modelo

*mi hermana: cuidar a muchos niños (descansar)*
*Mi hermana es niñera. Cuida a muchos niños. Ahora está descansando.*

1. mis hijos: tener que llevar cartas a todas partes (escribir cartas)
2. ese señor: ir en carro a muchas partes de la ciudad (almorzar)
3. yo: escribir muchos artículos (hacer entrevistas en el parque)
4. tú: jugar al fútbol con el equipo nacional (pescar)
5. nosotras: hacer jarras de cerámica (comer unos tacos)
6. aquella señora: ayudar a muchas personas (comprar un helado)
7. mi hermano y yo: asistir a muchos conciertos (tocar la guitarra)

*Now you can...*
- discuss jobs and professions.

*To review...*
- the impersonal **se,** see p. 399.

### ACTIVIDAD 2 Buscando trabajo

Isabel y Pablo hablan de cómo se solicita trabajo. Completa sus ideas formando oraciones lógicas.

modelo

*(usar) ropa informal en las entrevistas*
*No se usa ropa informal en las entrevistas.*

1. (necesitar) experiencia para los puestos importantes
2. (llegar) tarde a la primera entrevista
3. (pedir) datos personales en la solicitud
4. (escribir) el nombre de los padres en la solicitud
5. (solicitar) puestos profesionales en el parque



## Classroom Community

**Cooperative Learning** Divide students into small groups and assign each group a "Now you can..." or "To review..." from the margin notes on pp. 406–407. Ask each group to review the concept and present an overview to the class using visuals and a written activity. One student should give an introduction, another should prepare and present the visuals, and another should present the written activity.

**Storytelling** Have small groups create chain stories about applying for a job. Have them include elements of a job application.

*Now you can...*
- describe people, places, and things.

*To review*
- past participles used as adjectives, see p. 401.

## Actividad 3 ¡A buscar trabajo!

Isabel habla con un amigo por teléfono. Completa lo que dicen usando el verbo **estar** y el participio pasado de cada verbo.

**modelo**

*Mi experiencia _____ (explicar) aquí.*
*Mi experiencia está explicada aquí.*

Isabel: Armando, la oficina de empleos __1__ (abrir). ¡Vamos! Tú y yo __2__ (capacitar) para muchos de los empleos que se ofrecen. Yo __3__ (preparar): todos mis datos personales __4__ (escribir) en mi cuaderno. Armando... ¿me oyes? ¿__5__ (dormir)?

Armando: Te oigo, Isabel, pero yo __6__ (cansar). No puedo acompañarte. Mis planes ya __7__ (hacer) para hoy. ¡Voy a descansar! Habla con mi hermana. Ella __8__ (aburrir).

*Now you can...*
- complete an application.

*To review*
- application vocabulary, see p. 400.

## Actividad 4 Una solicitud

Estás leyendo la solicitud de alguien que busca trabajo. Identifica los datos.

ciudadanía | educación | experiencia | fecha de nacimiento | firma | número de teléfono

**modelo**

*450-7225*
*número de teléfono*

1. Trabajé como cajero en un supermercado por dos años.
2. Estados Unidos
3. Me gradué del colegio en el año 2000.
4. Daniel Sánchez
5. 2 de febrero de 1983



### Actividad 1 Answers

1. Mis hijos son carteros. Tienen que llevar cartas a todas partes. Ahora están escribiendo cartas.
2. Ese señor es taxista. Va en carro a muchas partes de la ciudad. Ahora está almorzando.
3. Yo soy periodista. Escribo muchos artículos. Ahora estoy haciendo entrevistas en el parque.
4. Tú eres deportista. Juegas al fútbol con el equipo nacional. Ahora estás pescando.
5. Nosotras somos artesanas. Hacemos jarras de cerámica. Ahora estamos comiendo unos tacos.
6. Aquella señora es voluntaria. Ayuda a muchas personas. Ahora está comprando un helado.
7. Mi hermano y yo somos músicos. Asistimos a muchos conciertos. Ahora estamos tocando la guitarra.

### Actividad 2 Answers

1. Se necesita…
2. No se llega…
3. Se piden…
4. No se escribe…
5. No se solicitan…

### Actividad 3 Answers

1. está abierta
2. estamos capacitados
3. estoy preparada
4. están escritos
5. Estás dormido
6. estoy cansado
7. están hechos
8. está aburrida

### Actividad 4 Answers

1. experiencia
2. ciudadanía
3. educación
4. firma
5. fecha de nacimiento

## Teaching All Students

**Extra Help** Ask students to read aloud the conversation in **Actividad 3**. Have them add one more exchange to the scene using **estar** and the past participles of **cerrar**, **escribir**, and **interesar**.

**Native Speakers** Have Spanish speakers describe the ideal job: include information on the ideal coworkers, the ideal location, and the ideal boss.

**Multiple Intelligences**

**Kinesthetic** Ask students to act out the vocabulary in **Actividad 4**. Encourage them to be creative.

**Verbal** Ask students to list 5–6 characteristics of a good professional based on the list given in **Actividad 1**.

## Block Schedule

**FunBreak** Have students write a list of guidelines for their ideal job using the impersonal **se**. For example, **Se trabaja 3 horas por la tarde. Se puede llevar ropa cómoda.** (For additional activities, see **Block Scheduling Copymasters**.)

## Teaching Resource Options

**Print** 

Unit 6 Resource Book
- Audioscript, p. 32
- Cooperative Quizzes, pp. 33–34
- Etapa Exam, Forms A and B, pp. 35–44
- *Examen para hispanohablantes* pp. 45–49
- Portfolio Assessment, pp. 50–51
- Multiple Choice Test Questions, pp. 170–172

**Audiovisual** 

OHT 175, 176, 184 (Quick Start)
Audio Program Cassette 20B / CD 20; (*Para hispanohablantes* Cassette 20B / CD 20)

**Technology** 

Electronic Teacher Tools/Test Generator
 www.mcdougallittell.com

## Quick Start Review

Discussing preferences and professions

Use OHT 184 or write on board: Which profession do you prefer? Complete the following sentence with your own personal information.

**Me gustaría ser... porque me gusta (me interesa)...**

*Answers will vary.*

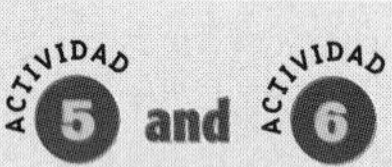

**Actividad 5 and 6**

**Rubric: Speaking**

| Criteria | Scale |
|---|---|
| Pronunciation | 1 2 3 4 5 |
| Accuracy | 1 2 3 4 5 |
| Intonation | 1 2 3 4 5 |

A = 13–15 pts.
B = 10–12 pts.
C = 7–9 pts.
D = 4–6 pts.
F = < 4 pts.

**Actividad 7 En tu propia voz**

**Rubric: Writing**

| Criteria | Scale |
|---|---|
| Vocabulary use | 1 2 3 4 5 |
| Accuracy | 1 2 3 4 5 |
| Creativity, appearance | 1 2 3 4 5 |

A = 13–15 pts.
B = 10–12 pts.
C = 7–9 pts.
D = 4–6 pts.
F = < 4 pts.

### Teaching Note: En tu propia voz

**Writing Strategy** Before writing their description, have students visualize their ideal job: What would they do? Where would they be?

## Actividad 5 ¡Alguien está dormido!

**PARA CONVERSAR**

**STRATEGY: SPEAKING**

**Check comprehension** If you want to see whether others are paying attention and understand what you are saying, make statements that are obviously true or false. *Obvious* means observing *who, what,* or *where.* (*When, why,* and *how* are less clear.) As you hear statements about people or things in the classroom, decide whether the observation is **cierto, falso** or whether it depends on interpretation **(no es cierto).** For example, can you tell the difference between a person who is **aburrido** and one who is **cansado**?

Mira a las personas y los objetos de tu clase y escribe cinco descripciones, usando participios pasados. Tu compañero(a) tiene que decir si son **ciertas** o **falsas.**

escritas, cansado, sentados, capacitados, dormida, ocupadas, perdido, preparados, hecho, emocionado, aburrida, puesto, preocupada, abierta

**modelo**

**Tú:** *La puerta está abierta.*
**Compañero(a):** *Falso. La puerta está cerrada.*

## Actividad 6 ¿Quién es?

Describe lo que está haciendo alguna persona profesional. Tus compañeros(as) tienen que hacerte preguntas para identificar la profesión.

**modelo**

**Tú:** *Está buscando información en muchos libros.*
**Estudiante 1:** *¿Es profesor o profesora?*
**Tú:** *No. También está hablando por teléfono con sus clientes.*
**Estudiante 2:** *¿Es abogado o abogada?*
**Tú:** *¡Sí!*

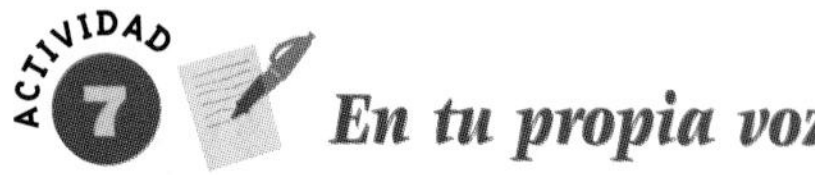

## Actividad 7 *En tu propia voz*

**ESCRITURA** Describe tu trabajo ideal. Incluye la información que se pide abajo.
- qué quieres ser y por qué
- cómo se solicita este trabajo
- por qué tú estás capacitado(a) para el trabajo

**modelo**

*Quiero ser… Para solicitar este trabajo, primero se lee el periódico…*

## CONEXIONES

**La geografía** En 1736, cerca de Quito, una expedición empezó a medir *(measure)* la línea ecuatorial. Mira un globo o mapa para saber qué países están en el ecuador. ¿Son estos países similares o diferentes? Haz una lista de los países e investígalos para comparar el terreno y el clima.

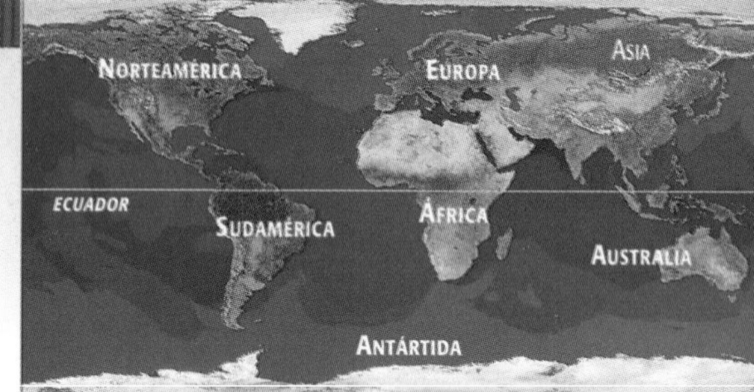




## Classroom Community

**Paired Activity** Ask students to review vocabulary words with a partner by asking each other the meanings.

**TPR** Ask students to act out the vocabulary and have others guess the word.

**Game** This is a good opportunity to have students play the game **¿Cuál es mi profesión?** as described in the **Ampliación** section on p. 387B.

# En resumen

## REPASO DE VOCABULARIO

### DISCUSS JOBS AND PROFESSIONS

**Jobs and Professions**

| | |
|---|---|
| **el (la) abogado(a)** | *lawyer* |
| **el (la) agricultor(a)** | *farmer* |
| **el (la) arquitecto(a)** | *architect* |
| **el (la) artesano(a)** | *artisan* |
| **el (la) asistente** | *assistant* |
| **el bailarín, la bailarina** | *dancer* |
| **el bombero** | *firefighter* |
| **el (la) cartero(a)** | *mail carrier* |
| **el (la) contador(a)** | *accountant* |
| **el (la) deportista** | *athlete* |
| **el (la) dueño(a)** | *owner* |
| **el (la) gerente** | *manager* |
| **el (la) hombre (mujer) de negocios** | *businessman/businesswoman* |
| **el (la) ingeniero(a)** | *engineer* |
| **el (la) jefe(a)** | *boss* |
| **el (la) juez(a)** | *judge* |
| **el (la) mecánico(a)** | *mechanic* |
| **el (la) músico(a)** | *musician* |
| **el (la) niñero(a)** | *child-care provider* |
| **el (la) obrero(a)** | *worker* |
| **el (la) operador(a)** | *operator* |
| **el (la) peluquero(a)** | *barber, hairstylist* |
| **el (la) secretario(a)** | *secretary* |
| **el (la) taxista** | *taxi driver* |
| **el (la) técnico(a)** | *technician* |
| **el (la) veterinario(a)** | *veterinarian* |
| **el (la) voluntario(a)** | *volunteer* |

**Aspects of Professional Life**

| | |
|---|---|
| **la carrera** | *career* |
| **el empleo** | *employment, job* |
| **ganarse la vida** | *to earn a living* |
| **la profesión** | *profession* |
| **el puesto** | *position* |

### DESCRIBE PEOPLE, PLACES, AND THINGS

| | |
|---|---|
| **capacitado(a)** | *qualified* |

### COMPLETE AN APPLICATION

| | |
|---|---|
| **la ciudadanía** | *citizenship* |
| **los datos** | *facts, information* |
| **la fecha de nacimiento** | *date of birth* |
| **la firma** | *signature* |
| **solicitar** | *to request, to apply for* |
| **la solicitud** | *application* |

### Juego

Un policía y un cartero almuerzan en un restaurante. Uno pide el menú del día. El otro quiere comer a la carta. ¿Quién crees que come a la carta?

## Teaching All Students

**Extra Help** Ask students to review the vocabulary for jobs and professions by grouping them into different categories. Categories may include: Office jobs, outdoor jobs, artistic jobs, technical jobs, jobs that require higher education, etc.

**Native Speakers** Ask students to form questions using the vocabulary and have others respond.

**Challenge** Ask students to prepare a short story using *all* of the vocabulary words. Read aloud and have students raise their hand when they hear a vocabulary word.

**Multiple Intelligences**

**Verbal** Have students copy the vocabulary list into their notebooks and add any additional professions that the class wanted to know about.

## Teaching Suggestions

- Review vocabulary words in **Actividad 5** to make sure students know what they mean. Also, students can add more words to the list before starting the activity. These can be written on the board.
- Go over the *Discuss Jobs and Professions* part of the vocabulary list before beginning **Actividad 6**.

## Community Connections

Take the class to the library and have students research and find job descriptions to match their interests. They should each find a job profile that interests them and a detailed job description.

## Project: Reviewing Etapa 1

Assign the following out-of-class activities:

- Interview a Spanish speaker about his or her profession.
- Bring in tourist information about what to do in Ecuador.
- Find information on the animals or marine life in the Galápagos Islands via the Internet or the library.
- Find out about job opportunities in your area that require knowledge of Spanish.

**Extra Credit**

| | |
|---|---|
| Interview | 2 pts. |
| Tourist information | 2 pts. |
| Animals/marine life | 2 pts. |
| Job opportunities | 2 pts. |

## Juego

**Answer**
el cartero

## Block Schedule

**FunBreak** Students can also create job listings for their ideal job, as described in the second project in the **Ampliación** section on p. 387B. You can post these job listings on a bulletin board and have students apply for them. (For additional activities, see **Block Scheduling Copymasters.**)

# *Planning Guide* CLASSROOM MANAGEMENT

## OBJECTIVES

**Communication**
- Prepare for an interview *pp. 412–413, 421, 425*
- Interview for a job *pp. 412–413, 414–415, 430*
- Evaluate situations and people *pp. 414–415*

**Grammar**
- The preterite and the imperfect *p. 418*
- The present perfect *p. 420*
- The present perfect with irregular verbs *p. 423*

**Culture**
- Los grupos indígenas *p. 422*
- Las empresas del mundo hispano *p. 424*
- Ciberespacio en Quito *pp. 426–427*

**Recycling**
- Past participles as adjectives *p. 417*
- The preterite and the imperfect *p. 418*
- The impersonal **se** *p. 425*
- Affirmative and negative **usted** commands *p. 425*

## STRATEGIES

**Listening Strategies**
- Evaluate behavior *p. 414*

**Speaking Strategies**
- Give advice *p. 425*
- Refine interview skills *p. 430*

**Reading Strategies**
- Recognize cognates *TE p. 427*

**Writing Strategies**
- Persuade your reader when describing your qualifications for a job *Actividad 7, TE p. 430*

**Connecting Cultures Strategies**
- Assess use of e-mail *p. 426*
- Compare musical styles and instruments of various groups *p. 430*

## PROGRAM RESOURCES

### Print

- *Más práctica* Workbook PE *pp. 145–152*
- Block Scheduling Copymasters *pp. 137–144*
- Unit 6 Resource Book
  - *Más práctica* Workbook TE *pp. 52–59*
  - *Cuaderno para hispanohablantes* TE *pp. 60–67*
  - Information Gap Activities *pp. 68–71*
  - Family Involvement *pp. 72–73*
  - Video Activities *pp. 74–76*
  - Videoscript *pp. 77–78*
  - Audioscript *pp. 79–83*
  - Assessment Program, Unit 6 Etapa 2 *pp. 84–102, 173–175*
  - Answer Keys *pp. 188–189*

### Audiovisual

- Audio Program Cassette 17A, 17B / CD 17
- *Canciones* Cassette/CD
- Video Program Videotape 6 / Videodisc 4B
- Overhead Transparencies M1–M5; 173, 185–194

### Technology

- Electronic Teacher Tools/Test Generator
- *Intrigas y aventuras* CD-ROM, Disc 2
-  www.mcdougallittell.com

### Assessment Program Options

- Cooperative Quizzes (Unit 6 Resource Book)
- Etapa Exam Forms A and B (Unit 6 Resource Book)
- *Examen para hispanohablantes* (Unit 6 Resource Book)
- Portfolio Assessment (Unit 6 Resource Book)
- Multiple Choice Test Questions (Unit 6 Resource Book)
- Audio Program Cassette 20B / CD 20
- Electronic Teacher Tools/Test Generator

### Native Speakers

- *Cuaderno para hispanohablantes* PE *pp. 145–152*
- *Cuaderno para hispanohablantes* TE (Unit 6 Resource Book)
- *Examen para hispanohablantes* (Unit 6 Resource Book)
- Audio Program *(Para hispanohablantes)* Cassettes 17B, 20B / CD 17, CD 20
- Audioscript (Unit 6 Resource Book)

# Student Text Listening Activity Scripts

##  Videoscript: Diálogo *pages 414–415*

- Videotape 6, 15:34 • Videodisc 4B

Search Chapter 2, Play to 3. U6E2, En vivo (Dialog)

- Use the videoscript with **Actividades 1, 2** *page 416*

**Sr. Montero:** Señorita Palacios, hábleme un poco sobre sus metas, por favor. ¿Qué es lo que Ud. quiere hacer en el futuro?

**Isabel:** Primero, voy a terminar mi educación. Después de graduarme del colegio, voy a asistir a la Universidad de México. Pienso estudiar periodismo. Me gustaría mucho trabajar para una revista en México, tal vez una revista de viajes como la suya.

**Sr. Montero:** ¿Ah, sí? ¿Le gusta viajar?

**Isabel:** Me encanta. Cuando era niña siempre les decía a mis padres que viajaría por todo el mundo. Ellos no me lo creían.

**Sr. Montero:** ¿Adónde ha ido? ¿Conoce Ud. otros países sudamericanos?

**Isabel:** Todavía no conozco otros países de Sudamérica, aunque me gustaría mucho. Mis padres y yo hemos viajado a Canadá y a Francia. Viajé sola a Madrid para *Onda Internacional* este año; estuve dos semanas allí.

**Sr. Montero:** Bueno, señorita Palacios, empecemos la entrevista. Tengo aquí su currículum. Ud. ha dicho exactamente cuáles son sus aptitudes y habilidades. Ud. ha puesto aquí que le gusta escribir sobre viajes. ¿Por qué le gusta?

**Isabel:** En mi opinión, viajar es una de las mejores maneras de entender a la gente de otros países y otras culturas. Y trabajar para una revista de viajes es una buena manera de hacer dos cosas que a mí me gustan: viajar y escribir.

**Sr. Montero:** Este trabajo tiene otros beneficios muy buenos. Por ejemplo, el contrato incluye seguro médico. Ud. debe escribir algo en su artículo sobre la importancia del seguro médico. Es una gran ventaja.

**Isabel:** Sí, ya lo he hecho. El seguro médico es muy importante.

**Sr. Montero:** El sueldo es de un millón quinientos mil sucres al mes. No es un sueldo muy alto, pero nuestra empresa es pequeña, y nuestra revista todavía tiene una circulación.

**Isabel:** No sólo me interesa el sueldo, Sr. Montero. La experiencia de trabajar para una revista como ésta vale mucho.

**Sr. Montero:** Me alegra que Ud. lo vea así. Aquí veo que Ud. tiene una recomendación del señor Pablo Barajas de *Onda Internacional.* Aquí dice que Ud. es una persona muy trabajadora, escribe bien y tiene mucho talento. También dice que Ud. es una persona muy puntual. Sabe, Señorita Palacios, la puntualidad es una cualidad importante en el mundo de los negocios.

**Isabel:** Para mí, es una cualidad personal muy importante. Siempre he sido una persona puntual.

**Sr. Montero:** Sabe, Isabel, es una lástima que Ud. no solicite de verdad este trabajo. Ud. me cae muy bien. Ud. sería una candidata muy buena para este puesto.

**Isabel:** Es Ud. muy amable en decírmelo, Sr. Montero. Creo que me gustaría mucho trabajar aquí. Y Ecuador me encanta.

**Sr. Montero:** Pues, señorita Palacios, nunca se sabe. Cuando Ud. termine sus estudios en la universidad, y si todavía quiere ser periodista y nosotros estamos aquí, ¿por qué no se pone en contacto conmigo? Si tenemos un puesto disponible, le daremos toda consideración.

**Isabel:** Muchas gracias, Sr. Montero. Me ha ayudado mucho con mi artículo para *Onda Internacional.*

**Sr. Montero:** Fue un placer. Adiós.

**Isabel:** Adiós y gracias.

**Isabel:** (V/O) Qué buena onda es el Señor Montero. Me cayó muy bien. Me gustaría pasar un rato aquí en Ecuador.

(V/O) Esta experiencia con *Onda Internacional* ha sido muy buena. He aprendido mucho y he visto partes del mundo que antes no conocía.

(V/O) Estoy muy triste. Mañana tengo que volver a México. Me ha gustado tanto Ecuador. Es un país mágico.

## Actividad 8 Buscando un trabajo *page 420*

**Roberto:** Cuando estaba buscando un trabajo por primera vez, empecé a leer los anuncios clasificados en los periódicos. Cuando me llamaron para una entrevista, revisé mi currículum y me vestí con mi mejor traje. Fui muy puntual y llegué a la compañía temprano. Esperaba en la sala de recepción cuando llegó una señora muy simpática. Ella me entrevistó. Me cayó muy bien.

## Actividad 12 ¿Ya? *page 422*

**Sra. Aguilera:** Hola. ¿Cómo estás? ¿Qué han hecho en casa hoy?

**Hija:** Hola, mamá. Hemos estado muy ocupados.

**Sra. Aguilera:** ¡Ah, qué bueno! Andrés ya ha cortado el césped.

**Hija:** Sí, ya ha terminado. También ha limpiado todo el patio.

**Sra. Aguilera:** Bien. ¿Y ustedes han lavado los platos y han limpiado la cocina?

**Hija:** No, todavía no hemos hecho eso.

**Sra. Aguilera:** No se olviden. Al menos han sacado la basura, ¿no?

**Hija:** No, tampoco.

**Sra. Aguilera:** ¿Pero qué pasa, hija mía? Yo he trabajado mucho hoy y no quiero llegar a casa y ver un desastre. ¿Oíste?

**Hija:** Sí, mamá, pero hemos tenido que estudiar muchísimo. Ya voy a decirles a los otros que empecemos a limpiar.

**Sra. Aguilera:** Está bien. Nos vemos pronto. Hasta luego.

**Hija:** Hasta luego.

# Pacing Guide

## Sample Lesson Plan - 50 Minute Schedule

### DAY 1

***Etapa* Opener**
- Quick Start Review (TE p. 410). **5 MIN.**
- Anticipate/Activate prior knowledge: Have students look at *Etapa* Opener and answer questions. **7 MIN.**

**En contexto: Vocabulario**
- Quick Start Review (TE p. 412). **5 MIN.**
- Have students use context and pictures to learn *Etapa* vocabulary. Answer questions, p. 413. **10 MIN.**

**En vivo: Diálogo**
- Quick Start Review (TE p. 414). **5 MIN.**
- Review Listening Strategy, p. 414. Play audio or show video for the dialog on pp. 414–415. **8 MIN.**
- Replay twice. Read aloud, students taking on roles of characters. **10 MIN.**

**Homework Option**
- Video Activities, Unit 6 Resource Book, pp. 74–76.

### DAY 2

**En acción: Vocabulario y Gramática**
- Check homework. **5 MIN.**
- Quick Start Review (TE p. 416). **5 MIN.**
- Ask students for a summary of *En vivo* dialog to check recall. Ask Comprehension Questions (TE p. 415). **10 MIN.**
- Replay the *En vivo* dialog using the audiovisual resources and have students do *Actividades* 1 and 2 orally. **15 MIN.**
- Have students complete *Actividades* 3 and 4 in pairs. **10 MIN.**
- Read and discuss *También se dice,* p. 416. **5 MIN.**

**Homework Option**
- *Más práctica* Workbook, pp. 145–148. *Cuaderno para hispanohablantes,* p. 145.

### DAY 3

**En acción (cont.)**
- Check homework. **5 MIN.**
- Quick Start Review (TE p. 418). **5 MIN.**
- Present *Repaso*: The Preterite and the Imperfect, p. 418, and have students complete *Actividad* 5 in writing, then *Actividad* 6 in pairs. **15 MIN.**
- Have students complete *Actividad* 7 in small groups. Expand with *Más comunicación,* p. R18. **20 MIN.**
- Play audio and have students complete *Actividad* 8. **5 MIN.**

**Homework Option**
- *Más práctica* Workbook, p. 149. *Cuaderno para hispanohablantes,* p. 147.

### DAY 4

**En acción (cont.)**
- Check homework. **5 MIN.**
- Quick Start Review (TE p. 420). **5 MIN.**
- Present *Gramática*: The Present Perfect, p. 420, and start *Actividad* 9 in writing. **10 MIN.**
- Present *Vocabulario* on p. 421 and have students complete *Actividades* 10 and 11 in small groups. **10 MIN.**
- Play audio and have students complete *Actividad* 12. **10 MIN.**
- Present *Gramática:* The Present Perfect with Irregular Verbs, p. 423, and have students begin *Actividad* 13 in writing. **10 MIN.**

**Homework Option**
- Finish *Actividades* 9 and 13. *Más práctica* Workbook, pp. 150–151. *Cuaderno para hispanohablantes,* pp. 148–149.

### DAY 5

**En acción (cont.)**
- Check homework. **5 MIN.**
- Quick Start Review (TE p. 424). **5 MIN.**
- Have students complete *Actividad* 14 in small groups. **10 MIN.**
- Have students read ads in *Actividad* 15 and assign the written portion of the activity as homework. **5 MIN.**
- Have students begin to create their resumes in *Actividad* 16. **10 MIN.**
- Present Speaking Strategy, p. 425, and have students complete *Actividad* 17. Expand with *Más comunicación,* p. R18. **15 MIN.**

**Homework Option**
- Finish *Actividades* 15 and 16 in writing. *Más práctica* Workbook, pp. 151–152. *Cuaderno para hispanohablantes,* pp. 149–150.

### DAY 6

**En colores: Cultura y comparaciones**
- Check homework. **5 MIN.**
- Quick Start Review (TE p. 426). **5 MIN.**
- Review Connecting Cultures Strategy, p. 426. **10 MIN.**
- Read *Ciberespacio en Quito* aloud with students. **10 MIN.**
- Have students answer the *¿Comprendiste?* and *¿Qué piensas?* questions orally. **10 MIN.**
- Divide the class into small groups and have them work on the *Hazlo tú* activity. **10 MIN.**

**Homework Option**
- Have students do the *¿Qué piensas?* questions in writing, p. 427. *Cuaderno para hispanohablantes*, p. 146.

### DAY 7

**En uso: Repaso y más comunicación**
- Check homework. **5 MIN.**
- Quick Start Review (TE p. 428). **5 MIN.**
- Do *Actividades* 1, 2, 3, and 4 orally. **15 MIN.**
- Review Speaking Strategy, p. 430. Then do *Actividad* 5 orally in pairs and *Actividad* 6 in groups. **15 MIN.**

**En tu propia voz: Escritura**
- Start writing activity. **10 MIN.**

**Homework Option**
- Finish writing activity. *Cuaderno para hispanohablantes*, pp. 151–152. Review for *Etapa* 2 Exam.

### DAY 8

**Conexiones**
- Check homework. **5 MIN.**
- Read and discuss. **5 MIN.**

**En resumen**
- Review grammar questions, etc., as necessary. **10 MIN.**
- Complete *Etapa* 2 Exam. **20 MIN.**

**Ampliación**
- Use a suggested project, game, or activity (TE pp. 387A–387B). **10 MIN.**

**Homework Option**
- Preview next *Etapa* Opener, pp. 432–433.

# Sample Lesson Plan - Block Schedule (90 minutes)

## DAY 1

***Etapa* Opener**
- Quick Start Review (TE p. 410). 5 MIN.
- Anticipate/Activate prior knowledge: Have students look at the *Etapa* Opener and answer questions. 10 MIN.

**En contexto: Vocabulario**
- Quick Start Review (TE p. 412). 5 MIN.
- Have students use context and pictures to learn *Etapa* vocabulary. Answer questions, p. 413. 10 MIN.

**En vivo: Diálogo**
- Quick Start Review (TE p. 414). 5 MIN.
- Review Listening Strategy, p. 414. Play audio or show video for the dialog on pp. 414–415. 10 MIN.
- Read aloud, students taking roles of characters. Ask Comprehension Questions (TE p. 415). 10 MIN.
- Students role-play in groups while looking at the photos in their texts. Encourage them to come up with logical dialog using familiar vocabulary. 10 MIN.

**En acción: Vocabulario y Gramática**
- Quick Start Review (TE p. 416). 5 MIN.
- Have students do *Actividades* 1 and 2 orally. 10 MIN.
- Have students complete *Actividades* 3 and 4 in pairs. 10 MIN.

**Homework Option**
- Video Activities, Unit 6 Resource Book, pp. 74–76. *Más práctica* Workbook, pp. 145–148. *Cuaderno para hispanohablantes*, p. 145.

## DAY 2

**En acción (cont.)**
- Check homework. 5 MIN.
- Quick Start Review (TE p. 418). 5 MIN.
- Present *Repaso*: The Preterite and the Imperfect, p. 418, and have students complete *Actividad* 5 in writing and *Actividad* 6 orally in pairs. 15 MIN.
- Have students complete *Actividad* 7 in groups. Expand with *Más comunicación,* p. R18. 15 MIN.
- Play audio and have students complete *Actividad* 8. 5 MIN.
- Quick Start Review (TE p. 420). 5 MIN.
- Present *Gramática*: The Present Perfect, p. 420, and start *Actividad* 9 in writing. 10 MIN.
- Review *Vocabulario* on p. 421 and have student complete *Actividades* 10 and 11 in small groups. 10 MIN.
- Play audio and have students complete *Actividad* 12. 10 MIN.
- Use Block Scheduling Copymasters, pp. 137–144, for a change of pace as needed. 10 MIN.

**Homework Option**
- Finish *Actividad* 9. *Más práctica* Workbook, pp. 149–151. *Cuaderno para hispanohablantes*, pp. 147–149.

## DAY 3

**En acción (cont.)**
- Check homework. 10 MIN.
- Quick Start Review (TE p. 424). 5 MIN.
- Present *Gramática:* Present Perfect with Irregular Verbs, p. 423, and have students complete *Actividad* 13 orally. 10 MIN.
- Have students complete *Actividad* 14 in small groups. 10 MIN.
- Have students read ads in *Actividad* 15 and do activity in writing. 15 MIN.
- Have students create their resumes in *Actividad* 16. 15 MIN.
- Present Speaking Strategy, p. 425, and have students complete *Actividad* 17. Expand with *Más comunicación,* p. R18. 15 MIN.

**Ampliación**
- Use a suggested project, game, or activity (TE pp. 387A–387B). 10 MIN.

**Homework Option**
- *Más práctica* Workbook, pp. 151–152. *Cuaderno para hispanohablantes*, pp. 149–150.

## DAY 4

**En colores: Cultura y comparaciones**
- Check homework. 10 MIN.
- Quick Start Review (TE p. 426). 5 MIN.
- Review Connecting Cultures Strategy, p. 426. 15 MIN.
- Read *Ciberespacio en Quito* aloud with students. 10 MIN.
- Have students answer the *¿Comprendiste?* questions orally. 10 MIN.
- Have students answer the *¿Qué piensas?* questions in writing. 10 MIN.
- Divide the class into small groups and have them work on the *Hazlo tú* activity. 10 MIN.

**En uso: Repaso y más comunicación**
- Quick Start Review (TE p. 428). 5 MIN.
- Do *Actividades* 1, 2, 3, and 4 orally. 15 MIN.

**Homework Option**
- Review for *Etapa* 2 Exam. *Cuaderno para hispanohablantes*, pp. 146, 151–152.

## DAY 5

**En uso: Repaso y más comunicación**
- Check homework. 10 MIN.
- Quick Start Review (TE p. 430). 5 MIN.
- Review Speaking Strategy, p. 430. Then do *Actividad* 5 orally in pairs and *Actividad* 6 in groups. 15 MIN.

**Conexiones**
- Read and discuss. 5 MIN.

**En resumen**
- Review grammar questions, etc., as necessary. 10 MIN.
- Complete *Etapa* 2 Exam. 20 MIN.

**En tu propia voz: Escritura**
- Do *Actividad* 7. 10 MIN.

**Ampliación**
- Use a suggested project, game, or activity (TE pp. 387A–387B), or assign a project from the Block Scheduling Copymasters, pp. 137–144. 15 MIN.

**Homework Option**
- Preview next *Etapa* Opener, pp. 432–433.

▼ Isabel y el señor Montero se despiden.

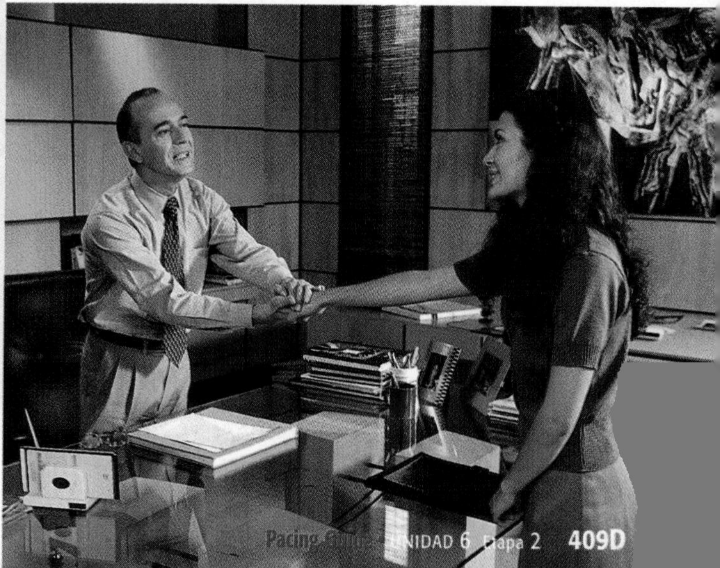

## Etapa Theme

**Preparing for an interview, interviewing for a job, and evaluating situations and people.**

## Grammar Objectives

- Review of the preterite and imperfect
- The present perfect
- The present perfect with irregular verbs

### Teaching Resource Options

**Print**

Block Scheduling Copymasters

**Audiovisual**

**OHT** 173, 191 (Quick Start)

### Quick Start Review

Clothing

Use OHT 191 or write on board: Note the clothing in the opening photo and complete the following sentence.

**Para una entrevista importante se lleva...**

*Answers will vary but may include:*
una falda con blusa, un vestido o un traje

### Teaching Suggestions
#### Previewing the Etapa

Ask students to study the photo on pp. 410–411 and describe what they see. On the board, write a list of people and items that the students identify. Have them try to guess why Isabel is in this office.

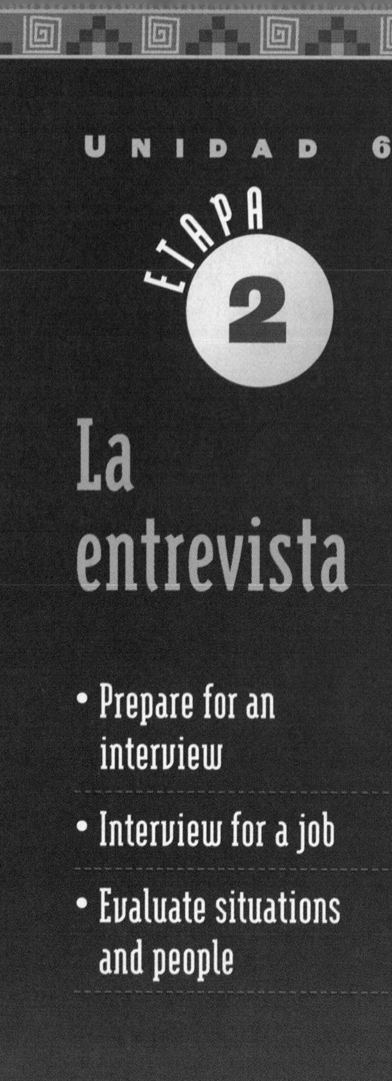

### ¿Qué ves?

Mira la página. ¿Qué ves?

1. ¿Quiénes son las personas principales de la foto?
2. ¿Qué hacen estas personas?
3. ¿Dónde crees que están?
4. ¿Qué es *Viajamundo*?

410

### Classroom Management

**Planning Ahead** Ask students to discuss and list with a partner how they would prepare for a job interview. Then have pairs share the lists with the whole class.

**Peer Review/Peer Teaching** Using the objectives, have students flip through the **Etapa** and make an outline of the main points, both content and grammar, that will be covered. At the end of the **Etapa**, students can fill in the outline with what they have learned.

## Cross Cultural Connections

Bring in samples of local business cards and have students compare the business card on p. 410 with these or others they may have seen before. What information is included? What is the same or different? Then have them create a business card for themselves or for someone they know.

## Culture Highlights

- **PHONE NUMBERS FOR CALLING ECUADOR** The phone and fax numbers on the business card on p. 410 include the country code for Ecuador (593), the city code for Quito (2), then a six-digit number. All international phone calls require a country code. Some need a city code as well.

## Teaching All Students

**Extra Help** Have students confirm or deny simple **sí/no** statements about the photo, e.g., **Una mujer está hablando por teléfono. (Sí) El hombre saluda al chico. (No),** etc.

**Native Speakers** Have Spanish speakers describe any work experience they may have had in an office setting. Others can list unfamiliar words as they listen.

### Multiple Intelligences

**Visual** Ask students to describe each of the characters' facial expressions and physical appearances.

**Interpersonal** Ask students to work together in small groups to list how they would prepare themselves for an interview.

## Block Schedule

**Variety** Have students write a list of interview questions on the board that they might expect to answer in a job interview. For example, **¿Me puede contar un poco de usted? ¿Cómo se interesó en...?** Then have them work in small groups to create answers to the questions. (For additional activities, see **Block Scheduling Copymasters.**)

### Teaching Resource Options

**Print**

Unit 6 Resource Book
Video Activities, p. 74
Videoscript, p. 77
Audioscript, p. 79

**Audiovisual**

OHT 185, 186, 191 (Quick Start)
Audio Program Cassette 17A / CD 17
Video Program Videotape 6, 12:56 / Videodisc 4B

Search Chapter 1, Play to 2
U6E2, En contexto (Vocabulary)

**Technology**

*Intrigas y aventuras* CD-ROM, Disc 2

### Quick Start Review

**Impersonal se**

Use OHT 191 or write on board: Imagine your friend from Ecuador asks you how one gets a job in the United States. Explain the necessary steps. Write at least three sentences and use the impersonal **se**.

*Answers will vary but may include:*

1. Se busca un puesto en el periódico.
2. Se solicita un puesto. 3. Se llena la solicitud.
4. Se hace una entrevista.

### Teaching Suggestions
**Introducing Vocabulary**

- Use OHT 185–186 and Audiocassette 17A / CD 17 to present the vocabulary on pp. 412–413.
- Ask the Comprehension Questions in the margin of the Teacher's Edition on p. 413. Or you can have students work in groups to create their own comprehension questions to ask each other.
- Use the video vocabulary presentation for review and reinforcement.

# En contexto

## VOCABULARIO

Isabel busca trabajo en una revista.

*Aquí* estoy en la oficina de la revista *Viajamundo*. Tengo mi **currículum** conmigo porque busco trabajo.

el currículum

**A**

Acabo de conocer al señor Montero, **el entrevistador**. Durante **la entrevista** él me hará preguntas sobre mis **metas** y planes para el futuro. También me dirá cosas sobre su **empresa**, la revista *Viajamundo*.

el entrevistador



### Classroom Community

**TPR** Read the captions A–D. Have students stand if the information is about Isabel, **la candidata**, or raise their hand if it is about Señor Montero, **el entrevistador**.

**Game** On the board, write the names of different professions. On strips of paper, write 4–5 one-line descriptions of things each professional does and put them in a hat. Each student chooses a slip of paper from the hat and places it under the correct profession. By the end, each profession should have a substantial resumé.

**Group Activity** Divide the class into 2 groups and have them debate the question, **¿Cuál sería mejor, tener un trabajo con un buen sueldo o tener un trabajo que te guste?**

**B** El puesto de periodista que estoy solicitando no es permanente. Como puedes ver, **el contrato** es por solamente seis meses. **El sueldo** es 1.500.000 sucres al mes, y **los beneficios** incluyen **el seguro** médico.

**C** El señor Montero asistió a **la Universidad** de Quito. Dice que tener una buena **educación** es una gran **ventaja.** La falta de educación es **una desventaja.** Sin suficiente educación, puede ser difícil que una persona encuentre un buen trabajo.

**D** La entrevista terminó y ahora me voy. ¡Qué amable fue el señor Montero! Él **me cayó bien.** Pienso que yo le caí bien también, porque me dijo que soy una buena candidata para el puesto.

## Preguntas personales

1. ¿Piensas que es una ventaja tener una educación universitaria?
2. ¿Preferirías un contrato de seis meses o un puesto permanente? ¿Por qué?
3. Para ti, ¿qué sería más importante, tener un trabajo con un buen sueldo o tener un trabajo que te guste? ¿Por qué?
4. En tu opinión, ¿cómo sería el trabajo perfecto?
5. ¿Tienes algunas metas, grandes o pequeñas, para el futuro? ¿Cuáles son?



## Comprehension Questions

1. ¿Tiene un currículum información sobre la educación y experiencia de una persona? **(Sí)**
2. ¿Es Isabel la entrevistadora? **(No)**
3. ¿Tendrá que hablar de sus metas durante la entrevista? **(Sí)**
4. ¿Le dará información a Isabel sobre la empresa el entrevistador? **(Sí)**
5. ¿Es el contrato por seis meses o un año? **(seis meses)**
6. ¿Es un trabajo voluntario o hay un sueldo? **(Hay un sueldo.)**
7. ¿Incluye beneficios el contrato o hay solamente un sueldo? **(Incluye beneficios.)**
8. ¿A qué universidad asistió el señor Montero? **(la Universidad de Quito)**
9. ¿Qué cosa menciona el señor Montero que sería una desventaja para un candidato? **(la falta de educación)**
10. El señor Montero hizo buena impresión a Isabel. ¿Por qué le cayó bien? **(Fue muy amable.)**

## Teaching All Students

**Extra Help** Ask students to read aloud in small groups. Have them summarize each paragraph in Spanish. Possible answers: **A. Isabel describe su entrevista. B. La descripción del puesto. C. Las ventajas de la educación. D. Las reacciones sobre la entrevista.**

**Native Speakers** Have Spanish speakers tell what information should be included in a resumé.

**Multiple Intelligences**

**Intrapersonal** Ask students to write a short paragraph describing their personal goals for the future.

**Interpersonal** Have students work with a partner to discuss their short-term goals and their long-term goals (**meta para este mes/año, meta para 5/10 años,** etc.).

## Block Schedule

**Variety** Write the new vocabulary words on the board. Read aloud the **En contexto** paragraphs and ask students to raise their hands whenever they hear the vocabulary words.

### Teaching Resource Options

**Print** 

Block Scheduling Copymasters
Unit 6 Resource Book
Video Activities, pp. 75–76
Videoscript, pp. 77–78
Audioscript, p. 79

**Audiovisual** 

OHT 189, 190, 191 (Quick Start)
Audio Program Cassette 17A / CD 17
Video Program Videotape 6, 12:56 / Videodisc 4B

Search Chapter 3, Play to 4
U6E2, En vivo (Dialog)

**Technology** 

*Intrigas y aventuras* CD-ROM, Disc 2

### Quick Start Review

Talking about professions

Use OHT 191 or write on board: For many professions, a good education is a clear advantage. Name at least four of these professions.

**Es una ventaja tener una buena educación si le interesa una carrera como...**

*Answers will vary.*

### Teaching Suggestions
#### Presenting the Dialog

- Prepare students for listening by focusing on the dialog context using yes/no or either/or questions.
- Use the video, audiocassette, or CD to present the dialog. The video version offers expanded language opportunities.

# En vivo

## DIÁLOGO

Señor Montero

Isabel

**PARA ESCUCHAR • STRATEGY: LISTENING**

**Evaluate behavior** Making a good impression depends on many factors. Assess Isabel's conduct in the interview. Would you rate Isabel **superior, regular,** or **no aceptable** in the following categories?

- **presentación**
- **manera de hablar**
- **metas**
- **lo que dice**
- **aptitudes**

## La entrevista

1 ▶ Señor Montero: Hábleme un poco sobre sus metas, por favor.
Isabel: Primero, voy a terminar mi educación. Pienso estudiar periodismo. Me gustaría trabajar para una revista de viajes.

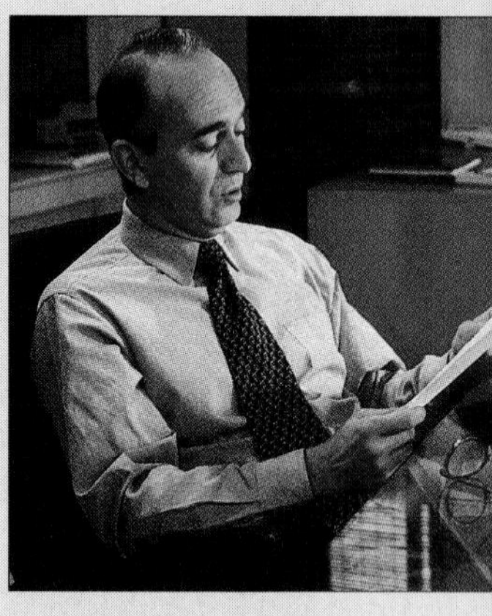

5 ▶ Señor Montero: Este trabajo tiene otros beneficios. Por ejemplo, el contrato incluye seguro médico. Debe escribir algo sobre la importancia del seguro médico. Es una gran ventaja.

6 ▶ Señor Montero: El sueldo es de 1.500.000 sucres al mes. No es un sueldo muy alto, pero nuestra empresa es pequeña.
Isabel: No sólo me interesa el sueldo, señor Montero. La experiencia de trabajar para una revista como ésta vale mucho.

7 ▶ Señor Montero: Me alegra que usted lo vea así. Veo que usted tiene una recomendación del señor Pablo Barajas. Dice que usted es una persona puntual. La puntualidad es una cualidad importante.



### Classroom Community 

**TPR** Have students act out a variety of personal goals for the class to identify.

**Paired Activity** Without reading the captions, ask students to work with a partner to describe what is going on in the scenes. Then have each pair of students meet with another pair to compare their stories.

**Cooperative Learning** In groups of four, S1 and S2 prepare interview questions for a mock job interview. S3 comes up with appropriate answers to the questions. S4 presents the mock interview to the class, explaining which job S3 is interviewing for, and the qualifications necessary, etc. S1 and S2 then interview S3 in front of the class.

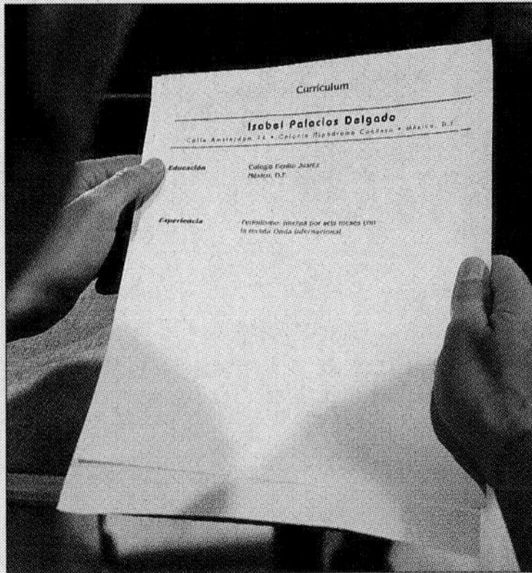


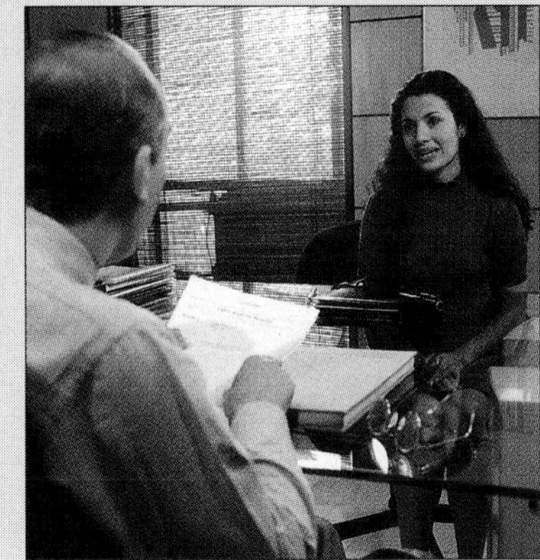

2 ▶ **Señor Montero:** ¿Le gusta viajar?
**Isabel:** Cuando era niña siempre les decía a mis padres que viajaría por todo el mundo. Viajé sola a Madrid este año…

3 ▶ **Señor Montero:** Bueno, tengo aquí su currículum. Usted ha dicho exactamente cuáles son sus aptitudes y habilidades. Usted ha puesto aquí que le gusta escribir sobre viajes. ¿Por qué le gusta?

4 ▶ **Isabel:** Viajar es una de las mejores maneras de entender a la gente de otras culturas. Y trabajar para una revista de viajes es una buena manera de hacer dos cosas que a mí me gustan —viajar y escribir.

8 ▶ **Señor Montero:** Es una lástima que no solicite de verdad este trabajo. Usted me cae bien.
**Isabel:** Es usted muy amable. Creo que me gustaría mucho trabajar aquí.

9 ▶ **Señor Montero:** Pues, cuando termine sus estudios, ¿por qué no se pone en contacto conmigo? Si tenemos un puesto disponible, le daremos toda consideración.
**Isabel:** Muchas gracias. Me ha ayudado mucho con mi artículo.

10 ▶ **Isabel:** Esta experiencia con *Onda Internacional* ha sido muy buena. He aprendido mucho y he visto partes del mundo que antes no conocía. Estoy triste. Mañana tengo que volver a México. ¡Me ha gustado tanto Ecuador!



## Teaching All Students

**Extra Help** Have students identify the interview terms that appear in the dialog.

**Native Speakers** Ask Spanish speakers to give excellent and average examples of **manera de hablar** in an interview situation.

**Multiple Intelligences**

**Verbal** Ask students to role-play the dialog as if Isabel were an actual candidate for the job. How would the dialog change? How would it end?

**Kinesthetic** Ask volunteers to demonstrate **la presentación** for an interview. The class can rate the examples as **superior, regular,** or **no aceptable.**

## Video Synopsis

Isabel has a mock interview for a job as a magazine reporter for *Viajamundo.* For a complete transcript of the video dialog, see p. 409B.

## Comprehension Questions

1. ¿Quiere el señor Montero que Isabel hable de sus metas? **(Sí)**
2. ¿Es su meta trabajar para una revista inmediatamente? **(No)**
3. ¿A Isabel le interesa viajar? **(Sí)**
4. ¿Tiene el señor Montero el currículum de Isabel? **(Sí)**
5. ¿Quiere Isabel viajar para divertirse o para entender a la gente de otras culturas? **(para entender a la gente)**
6. ¿Es seguro médico una ventaja o una desventaja? **(una ventaja)**
7. ¿A Isabel le interesa más el sueldo o la experiencia de trabajar para la revista? **(la experiencia)**
8. ¿Por qué dice el señor Montero que es una lástima que Isabel no solicite de verdad el trabajo? **(porque ella sería una buena candidata)**
9. ¿Qué sugiere el señor Montero que haga Isabel después de terminar sus estudios? **(Sugiere que se ponga en contacto con él.)**
10. ¿Por qué está triste Isabel? **(porque tiene que volver a México)**

## Critical Thinking

Ask students to analyze and evaluate the importance of a high school education, a college education, and job experience in applying for a new job.

## Gestures

Have students study Señor Montero's body language. How do his gestures reinforce or add to what he is saying?

## Language Notes

Point out to students that both Isabel and Señor Montero use the **usted** form. Explain that this form is used more commonly than the **tú** form in business settings in Central and South America.

## Block Schedule

**Process Time** Have students divide into groups of 4. Two students will read the dialog and two will listen and take notes. Then have the students switch roles.

## Teaching Resource Options

**Print**

Block Scheduling Copymasters
Unit 6 Resource Book
Video Activities, pp. 75–76
Videoscript, pp. 77–78
Audioscript, p. 79

**Audiovisual** 

OHT 192 (Quick Start)
Audio Program Cassette 17A / CD 17
Video Program Videotape 6, 12:56 / Videodisc 4B

**Technology**

*Intrigas y aventuras* CD-ROM, Disc 2

## Quick Start Review

Discussing professions, present tense

Use OHT 192 or write on board: Do you have a part-time job? Tell what you do at your job using the present tense. If you do not have a job, write about the job of someone in your family or someone else you know.

*Answers will vary.*

## Teaching Suggestions

Have students work together in small groups to change the ending of the dialog. Imagine that Isabel wants to pursue the job at *Viajamundo.*

**Objective:** Controlled practice
Listening comprehension/vocabulary

**Answers**

1. educación
2. Madrid
3. trabajar para una revista de viajes
4. el sueldo
5. la experiencia
6. puntual

**Actividad 2 Objective:** Transitional practice
Listening comprehension/vocabulary

**Answers**

1. e
2. c
3. a
4. f
5. g
6. h
7. b
8. d

# En acción
## VOCABULARIO Y GRAMÁTICA

**OBJECTIVES**
- Prepare for an interview
- Interview for a job
- Evaluate situations and people

Actividad 1 

### ¿Qué pasó?

**Escuchar/Escribir** Completa las oraciones según el diálogo.

1. Isabel va a seguir con su (viaje, trabajo, educación).
2. Ella le dijo al señor Montero que viajó sola a (Madrid, Buenos Aires, Bogotá).
3. Después de terminar los estudios, Isabel quiere (regresar a Ecuador, trabajar para una revista de viajes, asistir a la universidad).
4. El señor Montero le explicó que (el sueldo, el seguro, el contrato) no es alto.
5. A Isabel le importa también (la empresa, la recomendación, la experiencia).
6. Isabel y el señor Montero piensan que vale mucho ser (dependiente, rico, puntual).

Actividad 2 

### Frases revueltas

**Escuchar/Escribir** Combina elementos de las dos columnas de acuerdo con el diálogo.

1. En su currículum, Isabel
2. Según Isabel, si realiza su meta
3. El trabajo tiene
4. El sueldo es bajo porque
5. El señor Montero quiere que
6. El señor Montero ayudó a Isabel con
7. Al señor Montero, Isabel
8. A Isabel no le gusta que

a. buenos beneficios, incluyendo seguro médico.
b. le cayó muy bien.
c. podrá escribir y viajar en su empleo.
d. tenga que salir de Ecuador mañana.
e. escribió de sus aptitudes y habilidades.
f. la empresa es pequeña.
g. Isabel solicite el trabajo de verdad.
h. su artículo para *Onda Internacional.*

**TAMBIÉN SE DICE**

En español la palabra **carrera** significa **profesión,** como en inglés, pero también se refiere al programa de estudios necesario para prepararse para una profesión. Si un estudiante habla de **terminar la carrera,** quiere decir que termina los estudios universitarios y empieza su vida profesional. Otros verbos que se usan son **titularse** (recibir un título), **licenciarse** (recibir una licencia, generalmente equivalente a la maestría) y **egresar** (salir de la universidad).

IMPORTANTE EMPRESA DEL SECTOR AUTOMOTRIZ
NECESITA CONTRATAR
UN VENEDOR EXTERNO
Requisitos:
- Egresado o titulado en Administración de Empresas, Ingeniería comercial o carreras similares (no indispensable)
- Experiencia mínima de 3 años
- Buena predisposición para el trabajo
- Edad mínima 25 años

La empresa ofrece:
Sueldo, comisiones y beneficios de ley, estabilidad laboral, oportunidad de desarrollo profesional.
Personas interesadas enviar currículum a la casilla 17-03-4662- Quito.



## Classroom Management

**Streamlining** As students enter the room, stamp all complete homework and have a transparency of the assignment answers on the overhead. As students sit down, they start correcting their homework. If they didn't do it, they should write the answers down. Students get credit for doing the assignment completely and on time as well as for making corrections.

**Peer Review** Have students review the dialog, then have them work with partners to list the **ventajas** that will help a person's chances in a job interview and the **desventajas** that will hurt a person's chances. Review pp. 414–415 and 416–417.

- *Review: Use the preterite and the imperfect*
- *Use the present perfect*
- *Use irregular present perfect forms*

## ¿Qué está dibujado?

**Hablar/Escribir** Pablo lee las tiras cómicas y se las describe a Isabel. ¿Qué dice? Sigue el modelo. Usa estos verbos para formar los participios.

| | |
|---|---|
| esconder | cerrar |
| enamorar | cansar |
| abrir | enojar |
| ocupar | dormir |
| romper | |

**modelo**

*El joven no puede salir a jugar porque está ocupado.*

1.

2.

3.

4.

5.

6.

## ¿Ventaja o desventaja?

**Hablar/Leer** Unos gerentes están considerando a varios candidatos para unos puestos en una empresa. Lee las descripciones y con un(a) compañero(a) decide si cada situación sería una ventaja o desventaja para el (la) candidato(a).

1. Su currículum está bien escrito.
2. La candidata tiene metas muy claras.
3. Tiene más de la educación necesaria.
4. El entrevistador conoce al candidato.
5. Tiene un diploma del colegio pero no de la universidad.
6. Hay errores en su solicitud.
7. El candidato le cayó bien a la entrevistadora.
8. La candidata busca un sueldo alto y seguro médico.
9. Su currículum es demasiado largo.
10. El candidato es puntual.

**Objective:** Open-ended practice
Past participles as adjectives

### Answers

*Answers will vary.*

1. La ventana está abierta.
2. La mujer está enojada.
3. Los jóvenes están enamorados.
4. El restaurante está cerrado.
5. La chica está dormida.
6. Los niños están escondidos.

**Objective:** Open-ended practice
Interview vocabulary

### Answers

*Answers may vary.*

1. ventaja
2. ventaja
3. ventaja
4. ventaja
5. desventaja
6. desventaja
7. ventaja
8. desventaja
9. desventaja
10. ventaja

## Teaching All Students

**Extra Help** Ask students to describe three things, using past participles as adjectives. They may use the verbs in **Actividad 3**.

**Native Speakers** Have Spanish speakers discuss the words and expressions to describe the education and training necessary for a particular profession. Have them use the information in the **También se dice** box as a point of departure.

**Multiple Intelligences**

**Interpersonal** Ask students to bring in want ads from the newspaper. Students then choose classmates that seem to "fit" the personality type for a job and state their reasons for their selection.

**Musical/Rhythmic** After completing **Actividad 3**, have small groups create a song or chant about the drawing of their choice.

## Block Schedule

**Variety** Have students describe magazine pictures using past participles as adjectives. (For additional activities, see **Block Scheduling Copymasters**.)

## Teaching Resource Options

**Print**

*Más práctica* Workbook PE, p. 149
*Cuaderno para hispanohablantes* PE, p. 147
Block Scheduling Copymasters
Unit 6 Resource Book
*Más práctica* Workbook TE, p. 56
*Cuaderno para hispanohablantes* TE, p. 62
Information Gap Activities, p. 68

**Audiovisual**

OHT 192 (Quick Start)

**Technology**

*Intrigas y aventuras* CD-ROM, Disc 2

## Quick Start Review

Preterite tense

Use OHT 192 or write on board: Write the **yo** form of the following verbs in the preterite. Then choose one verb to conjugate completely.

| | | |
|---|---|---|
| solicitar | estar | saber |
| escribir | poder | tener |
| andar | poner | traer |
| decir | querer | venir |

**Answers**
solicité, escribí, anduve, dije, estuve, pude, puse, quise, supe, tuve, traje, vine

## Teaching Suggestions
### Presenting Repaso: The Preterite and the Imperfect

Remind students that it is important to discuss past experiences when interviewing for a job, so the past tenses are reviewed here. Students can refer back to pp. 134–135 for more information and practice.

**Objective:** Controlled practice
Preterite and imperfect

**Answers**

1. supe
2. gané
3. estaba
4. llamó
5. estaba
6. dijo
7. iba
8. conocí
9. fuimos
10. contó

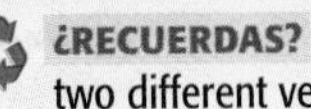

## The Preterite and the Imperfect

**¿RECUERDAS?** *p. 134* Remember that the **preterite** and the **imperfect** are two different verb forms for talking about the past.

- Use the **preterite** to describe a past action with a specific beginning and ending.
- Use the **imperfect** to tell about the past without reference to beginnings and endings.

Isabel says:

—Cuando **era** niña **me gustaba** tanto viajar que mis padres me **dieron** un mapa del mundo.

*When **I was** a little girl **I used to like** to travel so much that my parents **gave** me a map of the world.*

### La voz estudiantil

**Leer/Escribir** Isabel escribió un artículo para el periódico de su escuela sobre sus experiencias con *Onda Internacional*. Completa su artículo utilizando el pretérito o el imperfecto de cada verbo.

#### *Onda Internacional* —Un trabajo sensacional

Nunca olvidaré el día en que __1__ (saber) que __2__ (ganar) el concurso. Yo __3__ (estar) escribiendo una carta cuando una señora de la revista me __4__ (llamar) por teléfono. ¡Al oír las buenas noticias __5__ (estar) muy emocionada! Ella me __6__ (decir) que yo __7__ (ir) a escribir artículos en la Ciudad de México, Madrid y Ecuador. ¡Eso es la oportunidad más fenomenal!

En mis viajes, __8__ (conocer) a muchos nuevos amigos. En la Ciudad de México, Ricardo y yo __9__ (ir) un día a la casa de un hombre que me __10__ (contar) sobre un temblor...

**PARA HISPANOHABLANTES** *cuaderno* p. 147



## Classroom Community

**TPR** Have pairs of students act out sentences that combine the preterite and the imperfect. For example, **Mientras yo cenaba, me llamó mi amiga por teléfono.**

**Portfolio** Ask students to write a short paragraph describing their childhood activities. Use the imperfect/preterite tenses.

**Rubric: Writing**

| Criteria | Scale |
|---|---|
| Accuracy | 1 2 3 4 5 |
| Logical organization | 1 2 3 4 5 |
| Vocabulary use | 1 2 3 4 5 |

A = 13–15 pts.
B = 10–12 pts.
C = 7–9 pts.
D = 4–6 pts.
F = < 4 pts.

## Sí, recuerdo...

**Hablar** Todo el mundo tiene problemas cuando busca trabajo. Habla con un(a) compañero(a) sobre los problemas que pueden ocurrir.

**modelo**

*manejar a una entrevista*

**Tú:** *Una vez tuve un problema cuando manejaba a una entrevista.*

**Compañero(a):** *Sí, recuerdo que cuando manejabas a una entrevista tuviste un accidente.*

| Tú | Compañero(a) |
|---|---|
| manejar a una entrevista | perder un botón |
| vestirme con mi mejor traje | tener un accidente |
| irme a la oficina | olvidarte de la dirección |
| llenar la solicitud | darte cuenta de que no era suficiente |
| conocer a la jefa | contar mentiras |
| hablarme del sueldo | caerle mal |
| ofrecerme el trabajo | decirte que el contrato era solamente de seis meses |

## ¿Lo hacías? ¿Lo hiciste?

**Hablar/Escribir** Con un grupo de compañeros(as) habla de lo que hacías de niño(a) y compara aquellas actividades con las de la semana pasada. Luego escribe un resumen de siete oraciones o más.

**modelo**

**Tú:** *Cuando era niño(a), iba de compras con mi mamá. La semana pasada no fui de compras con ella.*

**Resumen:** *Antes, Teresa y yo íbamos de compras mucho con nuestras madres, pero la semana pasada no fuimos de compras con ellas...*

| Nombre | De niño(a)... | La semana pasada... |
|---|---|---|
| yo | iba de compras... | no fui de compras... |
| Teresa | ... | ... |
| ¿? | ¿? | ¿? |

**MÁS COMUNICACIÓN** p. R18



## Teaching All Students

**Extra Help** Ask students to conjugate any verbs they are unsure of in **Actividad 6** in the imperfect and the preterite tenses before doing the activity with a partner.

**Native Speakers** Have Spanish speakers discuss the activities they used to do (**hacían**) in their native country and the activities they did yesterday (**hicieron**). Then have students complete a chart like the one in **Actividad 7**.

**Multiple Intelligences**

**Visual** Have students illustrate one of the **compañero(a)** responses from **Actividad 6**. Then have the class say the correct sentence for each drawing.

**Verbal** Have students rewrite the paragraph in **Actividad 5** in the third person, i.e., **Isabel nunca olvidará el día....**

**Objective:** Transitional practice
Preterite and imperfect

**Answers**

*Answers may vary. In each sentence, the verb that follows **cuando** should be in the imperfect and the other verb should be in the preterite.*

Una vez tuve un problema cuando me vestía en mi mejor traje para una entrevista.
Sí, recuerdo que cuando te vestías para la entrevista perdiste un botón.
me iba / te ibas / te olvidaste
llenaba / llenabas / contaste
conocía / conocías / le caíste
me hablaba / te hablaba / te diste
me ofrecían / te ofrecían / te dijeron

**Objective:** Open-ended practice
Comparing childhood and recent activities

*Answers will vary.*

## Block Schedule

**FunBreak** Cut out the comics from your local newspaper. Ask students to form short stories using the imperfect/ preterite tenses. (For additional activities, see **Block Scheduling Copymasters**.)

## Teaching Resource Options

**Print** 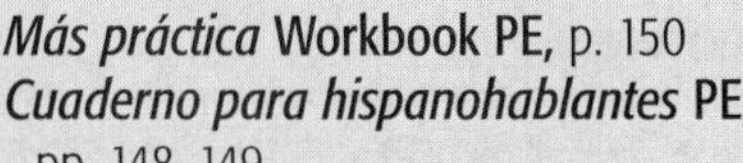

*Más práctica* Workbook PE, p. 150
*Cuaderno para hispanohablantes* PE, pp. 148–149
Block Scheduling Copymasters
Unit 6 Resource Book
*Más práctica* Workbook TE, p. 57
*Cuaderno para hispanohablantes* TE, pp. 63–64
Audioscript, p. 80

**Audiovisual** 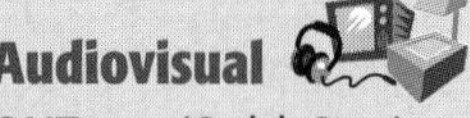

OHT 192 (Quick Start)
Audio Program Cassette 17A / CD 17

**Technology**

*Intrigas y aventuras* CD-ROM, Disc 2

## Quick Start Review

Past participles

Use OHT 192 or write on board: Imagine you are a secretary and at the end of the day you make a checklist of all the tasks that are complete. Follow the model and use a past participle in each response.

For example: **La reunión / planear**
**La reunión en Texas está planeada.**

1. las reservaciones / hacer
2. las cartas / escribir
3. mis papeles / organizar
4. todo / preparar

**Answers**
1. Las reservaciones están hechas. 2. Las cartas están escritas. 3. Mis papeles están organizados. 4. Todo está preparado.

## Teaching Suggestions
### Presenting the Present Perfect

Emphasize that if the past participle is used with **haber**, it does not agree in gender and number with a noun.

ACTIVIDAD 8

### Buscando un trabajo

**Escuchar** Roberto habla de la primera vez que buscó un trabajo. Pon los dibujos en orden, según su descripción.

a.

b.

c.

d.

GRAMÁTICA

## The Present Perfect

**¿RECUERDAS?** *p. 401* Remember the **past participle** form of the verb that is used as an adjective?

**habl**ar → **hablado**
**com**er → **comido**
**viv**ir → **vivido**

Past participles are also used with **haber** to form the present perfect tense. Just as in English, you use this tense to talk about things someone has done.

auxiliary verb haber

| | |
|---|---|
| he | hemos |
| has | habéis |
| ha | han |

\+ **past participle** of the main verb

Isabel says:

—He **aprendido** mucho.
***I have learned** a lot.*

The present perfect tense refers to actions **completed in the past** but that **relate to the present.**

—Esta experiencia con *Onda Internacional* ha **sido** muy buena.
*This experience with* Onda Internacional ***has been*** *very good.*

The **past participle** doesn't change to reflect **gender** or **number.** Only haber changes to agree with the subject.

When you use the **object pronouns** or **reflexive pronouns** with the present perfect, you put the pronoun **before** the conjugated form of haber.

Isabel says to Señor Montero:

—**Me** ha **ayudado** mucho con mi artículo.
***You have helped me** a lot with my article.*



## Classroom Community

**Paired Activity** Ask pairs of students to share 2–3 things that they have just done recently, e.g., **He terminado mi tarea. He comido el almuerzo.**

**TPR** Divide the class into several groups. Students take turns explaining the steps of a job search, acting out words and phrases as they speak.

## Bien preparados

**Escribir** Todos se han preparado para buscar un empleo. ¿Quién ha hecho bien y quién ha hecho mal?

**modelo**

*tú / investigar la empresa*

*Tú has investigado la empresa. ¡Qué bien!*

*Rosa / vestirse en ropa sucia*

*Rosa se ha vestido en ropa sucia. ¡Qué malo!*

1. yo / llegar tarde a la entrevista
2. nosotros / mirar los anuncios clasificados en el periódico
3. Pablo / molestarle al entrevistador
4. ellas / llenar la solicitud con cuidado
5. yo / llevar jeans y una camiseta a la entrevista
6. tú / llamar a las personas que conoces en la compañía
7. tus amigos / venir a la entrevista contigo
8. ustedes / llevar su currículum a la entrevista

**MÁS PRÁCTICA**
*cuaderno* pp. 149–150

**PARA HISPANOHABLANTES**
*cuaderno* pp. 148–149

ACTIVIDAD 10

## Tus experiencias

**Hablar/Escribir** ¿Ya has conseguido un trabajo o te has preparado para ir a la universidad? Di si ya has hecho lo siguiente.

**modelo**

*hablar con un(a) entrevistador(a) de mis habilidades*

*Ya he hablado con un(a) entrevistador(a) de mis habilidades. (No he hablado con un(a) entrevistador(a) de mis habilidades todavía.)*

1. ir a una entrevista
2. valorar la puntualidad
3. tomar un examen para un trabajo o para la universidad
4. buscar recomendaciones
5. identificar mis habilidades
6. participar en cursos de capacitación
7. solicitar un contrato de trabajo
8. conseguir un trabajo
9. preguntar sobre los beneficios
10. graduarme de la escuela

### Vocabulario

**En la entrevista**

**la capacitación** *training*
**conseguir (e→i, i)** *to get*
**las habilidades** *capabilities*
**la puntualidad** *punctuality*
**las recomendaciones** *recommendations*
**requerir (e→ie, i)** *to require*
**el requisito** *requirement*



### Teaching Suggestions

As a variation of **Actividad 9**, have students tell about a family member's experiences in a job search or application to the university.

**Objective:** Transitional practice
Listening comprehension/Interview vocabulary

**Answers** (See script, TE p. 409B.)
d, b, a, c

**Objective:** Controlled practice
Present perfect

**Answers**
1. Yo he llegado tarde a la entrevista. ¡Qué malo!
2. Nosotros hemos mirado los anuncios clasificados en el periódico. ¡Qué bien!
3. Pablo le ha molestado al entrevistador. ¡Qué malo!
4. Ellas han llenado la solicitud con cuidado. ¡Qué bien!
5. Yo he llevado jeans y una camiseta a la entrevista. ¡Qué malo!
6. Tú has llamado a las personas que conoces en la compañía. ¡Qué bien!
7. Tus amigos han venido a la entrevista contigo. ¡Qué malo!
8. Ustedes han llevado su currículum a la entrevista. ¡Qué bien!

**Objective:** Transitional practice
Present perfect

**Answers**
*Answers will vary.*
1. Ya he ido a una entrevista. (No he ido a una entrevista todavía.)
2. ... he valorado...
3. ... he tomado...
4. ... he buscado...
5. ... he identificado...
6. ... he participado...
7. ... he solicitado...
8. ... he conseguido...
9. ... he preguntado...
10. ... me he graduado...

### Teaching All Students

**Extra Help** Ask students to write sentences using the words in the vocabulary box on p. 421.

**Multiple Intelligences**

**Logical/Mathematical** Divide the class into groups of 4. Have students take turns predicting a result of each behavior in **Actividad 9**. For example, **Tú has investigado la empresa. Por eso sabes mucho de la compañía. El entrevistador lo notará.**

**Intrapersonal** If students have jobs, have them write in their journals about their first job hunt. If they don't work, have them write about what they think it will be like. Do this after **Actividad 8**.

**Naturalist** Have pairs of students role-play interviews for jobs in which plants or animals are cared for, e.g., **veterinario(a), agricultor(a), jardinero(a), florista**.

### Block Schedule

**Variety** Have students form pairs and write a short letter of recommendation for each other based on what they really know about their classmate and the profession he or she is interested in. Students can create details about their partner's education, work experience (**Ha trabajado...**), and personal qualities (**Es puntual...**).

## Teaching Resource Options

**Print** 

*Más práctica* Workbook PE, pp. 151–152
*Cuaderno para hispanohablantes* PE, p. 150
Block Scheduling Copymasters
Unit 6 Resource Book
*Más práctica* Workbook TE, pp. 58–59
*Cuaderno para hispanohablantes* TE, p. 65
Audioscript, p. 80

**Audiovisual**

OHT 193 (Quick Start)
Audio Program Cassette 17A / CD 17

**Technology**

*Intrigas y aventuras* CD-ROM, Disc 2

## Quick Start Review

Past participles

Use OHT 193 or write on board: Imagine you are applying for a job as an assistant in the office of a social service organization. Tell what experience you've had to convince them you are qualified for the job. Select items from each column to form logical sentences and use the present perfect.

| | | |
|---|---|---|
| He | estudiar | buenas notas |
| | sacar | a la gente en mi comunidad |
| | ayudar | con computadoras |
| | trabajar | español e inglés |

**Answers**

He estudiado español e inglés. He sacado buenas notas. He ayudado a la gente en mi comunidad. He trabajado con computadoras.

## ¿Qué han hecho?

**Hablar/Escribir** Habla con un grupo de compañeros(as) de lo que tú, tu familia y tus amigos(as) han hecho. Combina elementos de las dos columnas. Luego escribe seis oraciones basadas en su conversación.

mis padres
mis amigos(as) y yo
mi hermano(a)
yo
tú (*nombre*)
mi mejor amigo(a)
¿?

ganar dinero
viajar mucho
ir a una universidad
tener un(a) novio(a)
estar en el periódico
practicar un deporte en un equipo de la escuela
sacar (buenas / malas) notas
vivir en otro estado
¿?

## ¿Ya?

**Escuchar/Escribir** La señora Aguilera llama a casa a ver qué ha hecho su familia mientras ella estaba trabajando. Escucha el diálogo. Luego escribe lo que contesta su hija según los dibujos.

1.

2.

3.

4.

### NOTA CULTURAL

**Los grupos indígenas** En Ecuador viven unos diez grupos indígenas, cada uno con su propia lengua y cultura. La mayor parte de ellos hablan **quechua**, la lengua indígena más conocida del país. Hoy en día la mayoría de la población indígena es bilingüe, pero en las zonas más remotas del país todavía se encuentran comunidades donde solamente se oyen lenguas indígenas.

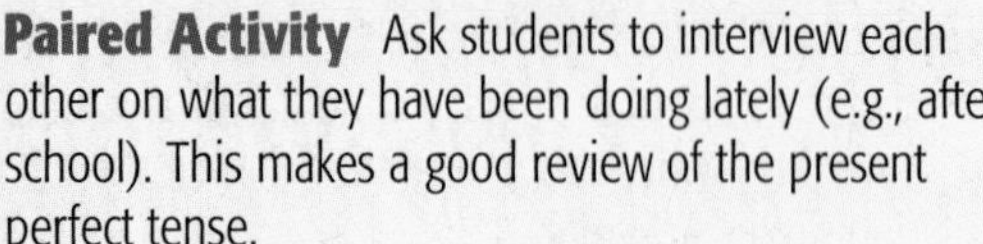

## Classroom Community

**Paired Activity** Ask students to interview each other on what they have been doing lately (e.g., after school). This makes a good review of the present perfect tense.

**Storytelling** Before listening to the audio with **Actividad 12**, have students work in pairs to tell their own story based on the photos.

## The Present Perfect with Irregular Verbs

**¿RECUERDAS?** *p. 401* Remember how to form regular **past participles**?

**-ar** verbs add **-ado**
**hablar** → **hablado**

**-er** and **-ir** verbs add **-ido**
**comer** → **comido**
**vivir** → **vivido**

There is a written accent in the past participle of **-er** and **-ir** verbs whose stems end in a vowel:

**caer** → **caído**
**leer** → **leído**
**oír** → **oído**

Some verbs have **irregular past participles** and do not follow this pattern. Use the chart below to review them.

| Infinitive | Past Participle |
|---|---|
| abrir | abierto |
| decir | dicho |
| descubrir | descubierto |
| escribir | escrito |
| hacer | hecho |
| ir | ido |
| poner | puesto |
| romper | roto |
| ver | visto |
| volver | vuelto |

These **irregular past participles** are also used with the verb haber to form the present perfect tense.

Señor Montero says to Isabel:

—Usted ha **puesto** aquí que le gusta escribir sobre viajes.
*You **have put** here that you like to write about travel.*

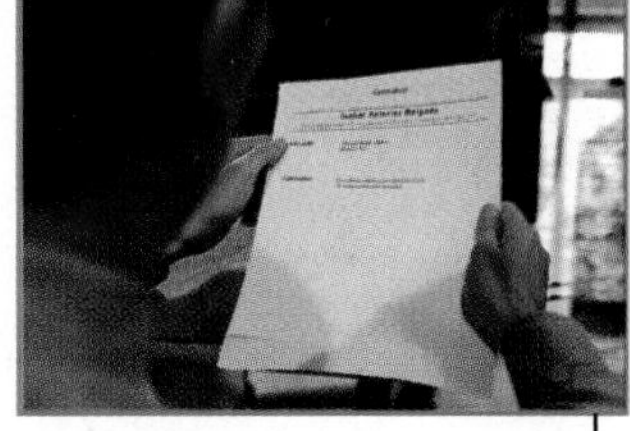

### Actividad 13 Gramática

## Recientemente

**Hablar/Escribir** ¿Qué han hecho recientemente tú y las personas que conoces? Contesta con oraciones afirmativas o negativas. Sigue el modelo.

**modelo**

*mis amigos y yo / volver / escuela primaria*

*Mis amigos y yo (no) hemos vuelto a nuestra escuela primaria recientemente.*

1. yo / decirles / mentira / padres
2. mis amigos / ver / estreno (*nombre*)
3. mi familia y yo / ir / parque juntos
4. mis amigos y yo / hacer / tarea
5. mi hermano(a) / poner / mesa
6. tú (*nombre*) / escribirme / carta
7. el (la) maestro(a) / abrir / ventana
8. un miembro de mi familia / romperse / brazo

**MÁS PRÁCTICA** *cuaderno* pp. 151–152

**PARA HISPANOHABLANTES** *cuaderno* p. 150



### Teaching Suggestions
**Presenting the Present Perfect with Irregular Verbs**

Have students write sentences using each irregular past participle form in the context of a job search.

**Objective:** Open-ended practice
Describing past activities

*Answers will vary.*

**Objective:** Open-ended practice
Listening comprehension/Present perfect

**Answers** (See script, TE p. 409B.)
*Answers may vary.*
1. Sí, ya ha terminado.
2. No, todavía no hemos hecho eso.
3. No, tampoco.
4. Sí, mamá, pero hemos tenido que estudiar muchísimo.

**Objective:** Controlled practice
Irregular present perfect

**Answers**
*Answers may vary.*
1. Yo (no) les he dicho una mentira a mis padres recientemente.
2. Mis amigos (no) han visto el estreno de *Zorro* recientemente.
3. Mi familia y yo (no) hemos ido al parque juntos.
4. Mis amigos y yo (no) hemos hecho la tarea todavía.
5. Mi hermana (no) ha puesto la mesa recientemente.
6. Tú, Carlos, (no) me has escrito una carta recientemente.
7. El (la) maestro(a) (no) ha abierto una ventana durante la clase.
8. Un miembro de mi familia (no) se ha roto el brazo recientemente.

### Block Schedule

**FunBreak** Have each student take a few minutes to write down something unusual he or she has done in the past or a similar statement that is believable. Call on students to share the statement and the rest of the class will guess whether it is **cierto** or **falso.** For example:

He ganado un premio en natación.
He rescatado un perro en peligro.
He visto...

(For additional activities, see Block Scheduling Copymasters.)

## Teaching All Students

**Extra Help** Ask students to write sentences using past participles in two ways, e.g., in the present perfect tense, **Él ha cerrado la puerta de la oficina,** and as an adjective, **La oficina está cerrada.**

**Challenge** Ask students to research on the Internet about the people of Ecuador and their customs, lifestyles, etc.

**Multiple Intelligences**

**Kinesthetic** Have students pantomime actions for the class. The class guesses what the student just did, using the present perfect.

## Teaching Resource Options

### Print

*Más práctica* Workbook PE, pp. 145–148
*Cuaderno para hispanohablantes* PE, pp. 145–146
Block Scheduling Copymasters
Unit 6 Resource Book
- *Más práctica* Workbook TE, pp. 52–55
- *Cuaderno para hispanohablantes* TE, pp. 60–61
- Audioscript, pp. 81–82
- Information Gap Activities, p. 69

### Audiovisual

OHT 187, 187A, 193 (Quick Start)
Audio Program Cassette 17B / CD 17; (*Para hispanohablantes* Cassette 17B / CD 17)

### Technology

*Intrigas y aventuras* CD-ROM, Disc 2

## Quick Start Review

Discussing professions, academic subjects

Use OHT 193 or write on board: Tell which subjects one might study if hoping to pursue the following professions.

Si quieres ser... veterinario(a)
contador(a)
periodista
ingeniero(a)
artesano(a)
es importante estudiar...

*Answers may vary.*
*Possible answers:* veterinario(a): biología; contador(a): matemáticas; periodista: inglés o ciencias sociales; ingeniero(a): computación; artesano(a): arte

ACTIVIDAD 14

## Una encuesta

**Hablar/Escribir** Tú y tus amigos buscan trabajo. Con un grupo de compañeros(as), pregúntense si han hecho las actividades de la lista. Luego haz una tabla para presentar los resultados.

**modelo**

*hacer capacitación para un empleo*
**Tú:** *¿Quién ha hecho capacitación para un empleo?*
**Compañero(a):** *Yo he hecho capacitación…*
**Luego:**

| | sí | no |
|---|---|---|
| hacer capacitación | IIII | II |
| ir a una exposición de carreras | II | I |
| decir la verdad en la solicitud | IIII | II |

1. escribir un currículum
2. ir a una exposición de carreras
3. decir la verdad en la solicitud
4. ver un contrato de empleo
5. tener miedo durante una entrevista
6. oír sobre puestos de amigos
7. romper una solicitud
8. leer los anuncios clasificados en el periódico

NOTA CULTURAL

**Las empresas del mundo hispano** Algunas de las normas empresariales del mundo hispano son diferentes de las de Estados Unidos. El respeto por el jefe es mucho más formal en varios países hispanos.

ACTIVIDAD 15

## Se solicita un puesto

**Leer/Escribir** Lee estos anuncios del periódico *El Comercio*. Escoge un puesto que te gustaría solicitar y explica por qué estás capacitado(a).

CHICAS-CHICOS
Estudiantes jóvenes, fin de semana, recreadores fiestas infantiles. Entrevistas: Amazonas 5532 y Tomás de Berlanga. Lunes 3 p.m.

INSTRUCTORES
pesas, aeróbicos requiere prestigioso gimnasio, 537040, 351593

CANTANTES
mujer y hombre necesito, grupo música mexicana, 1.200.000 mensuales. 548802, 573590

JÓVENES
Empresa de comida rapida requiere jóvenes con motocicleta propia, para trabajar en servicio a domicilio. Ofrecemos: gasolina, seguro personal, atractivo sueldo, etc.

MECÁNICO
Automotriz necesito urgente con experiencia en electricidad y mecánica general. Telf.473402

CHOFER PRIMERA
Dispuesto trabajar doce horas diarias, edad máxima 30 años, experiencia vehículos. Ulloa 1167 Mariana de Jesús.

PROFESORES
El centro Educativo Isaac Newton necesita contratar el siguiente personal:
a) profesor(a) de inglés
b) profesor(a) de grado para primaria
Interesados enviar currículum a dirección: Centro Educativo Experimental Issac Newton, Calle de los Guayable N50-120 y de Los Alamos, El Inca.

PASTELERÍA
Requiere personal responsable. Para mostrador. teléfono: 402663.

AGENTE VENDEDOR
con vehículo, distribución productos panadería, teléfonos: 648770, 603951.

VENDEDORES
se necesita contratar los mejores vendedores con experiencia y deseos de superación, excelente remuneración, presentarse con su carpeta al Iñaquito UNP, edificio UNP, oficina 301.

CONTADOR
medio tiempo con experiencia, empresa grande casilla 17079742

**modelo**

*Me gustaría solicitar el puesto de mecánico. No he tenido un trabajo todavía pero he hecho otras cosas para prepararme y tengo todos los requisitos. Soy…*

| | |
|---|---|
| tener experiencia | metas personales |
| educación | Soy… |
| valorar la puntualidad | los requisitos |
| capacitado(a) | llegar a tiempo |
| ayudar a… | participar |
| | ser voluntario(a) |



## Classroom Community

**Portfolio** Using the expressions in **Actividad 15**, ask students to write a short description of themselves to include in a cover letter to a prospective employer.

**Rubric: Writing**

| Criteria | Scale |
|---|---|
| Accuracy | 1 2 3 4 5 |
| Logical organization | 1 2 3 4 5 |
| Vocabulary use | 1 2 3 4 5 |

A = 13–15 pts.
B = 10–12 pts.
C = 7–9 pts.
D = 4–6 pts.
F = < 4 pts.

**Group Activity** Before doing **Actividad 16**, bring in several examples of a Spanish **currículum**. Have students work in small groups to comment on each one. Are they well organized? Are the objectives clearly stated? Are they easy to read?

## Tu currículum

**Escribir** Quieres trabajar en una oficina donde se habla español y tienes que mandar tu currículum. Usa una computadora si es posible para hacer tu currículum en español e incluye la siguiente información:

- tu nombre y apellido
- los datos personales
- tu objetivo (el trabajo que quieres conseguir)
- tu educación (las escuelas y fechas de estudio)
- las clases pertinentes al trabajo
- las habilidades que aprendiste en tus clases
- los trabajos y las experiencias como voluntario(a)
- las habilidades que aprendiste en otros trabajos
- tus metas para el futuro
- tus pasatiempos

## ACTIVIDAD 17 Para conseguir un trabajo...

**PARA CONVERSAR** • STRATEGY: SPEAKING

**Give advice** The best advice is brief and attention-getting. What verb form commands attention? Good advice can be made more dramatic by contrasting it with its opposite: **Llegue a tiempo a la entrevista. ¡Nunca llegue tarde!**

Help your classmates to experience your advice through seeing, hearing, and acting in addition to thinking.

**Hablar/Escribir** En grupos, hagan una lista de consejos para conseguir trabajo y escríbanla en un papel grande. Preséntenle cada regla a la clase. Consideren las siguientes preguntas:

1. ¿Dónde se buscan los puestos?
2. ¿Cómo se prepara para solicitarlos?
3. ¿Qué se escribe en un currículum?
4. ¿Cómo se llena la solicitud?
5. ¿Cómo se viste para una entrevista?
6. ¿Qué se debe hacer en el colegio para conseguir recomendaciones?
7. ¿Qué se debe hacer en la entrevista?
8. ¿Qué no se debe hacer?

**MÁS COMUNICACIÓN** p. R18

### Refrán

***Cortesía y bien hablar, cien puertas nos abrirán.***

¿Eres muy cortés con los demás? En grupos pequeños hagan una lista de situaciones en que la cortesía es una ventaja. ¿Cuál podrá ser el resultado en cada situación?

## Teaching Suggestions

**Actividad 16:** Have students work in small groups to create a **currículum** for Isabel. Share the results with the class and post as a model. Then have students create their own **currículum** in **Actividad 16** as homework.

**Objective:** Transitional practice
Irregular present perfect

### Answers

1. ¿Quién ha escrito un currículum? Yo (no) he escrito un currículum.
2. ¿Quién ha ido a una exposición de carreras? Yo (no) he ido...
3. ¿Quién ha dicho la verdad en la solicitud? Yo (no) he dicho...
4. ¿Quién ha visto un contrato de empleo? Yo (no) he visto...
5. ¿Quién ha tenido miedo durante una entrevista? Yo (no) he tenido...
6. ¿Quién ha oído sobre puestos de amigos? Yo (no) he oído...
7. ¿Quién ha roto una solicitud? Yo (no) he roto...
8. ¿Quién ha leído los anuncios clasificados en el periódico? Yo (no) he leído...

**Objective:** Open-ended practice
Applying for a job

*Answers will vary.*

**Objective:** Open-ended practice
Writing a résumé

*Answers will vary.*

**Objective:** Open-ended practice
Talking about job-hunting

**Impersonal se and usted commands**

*Answers will vary.*

### Rubric: Speaking

| Criteria | Scale |
|---|---|
| Fluency | 1 2 3 4 5 |
| Vocabulary use | 1 2 3 4 5 |
| Pronunciation | 1 2 3 4 5 |

A = 13–15 pts.
B = 10–12 pts.
C = 7–9 pts.
D = 4–6 pts.
F = < 4 pts.

## Block Schedule

**Change of Pace** Have students work with a partner to create a job listing in Spanish. They should include the job title, requirements, and a contact person. Compile all the job listings and create a *Clasificados* section of a newspaper. (For additional activities, see **Block Scheduling Copymasters**.)

## Teaching All Students

**Extra Help** In preparation for **Actividad 17**, have students review the affirmative and negative **usted** command forms on pp. 182–184.

**Challenge** Ask students to list common expressions, e.g., the early bird catches the worm, better late than never, a stitch in time saves nine, etc. In small groups ask students to explain (in Spanish) when they would use such expressions.

**Multiple Intelligences**

**Intrapersonal** Ask students to list their personal goals (**metas personales**), then share or write what they are currently doing that will help them reach their goals.

**Logical/Mathematical** Point out the cause and effect presented in the **refrán:** if you are courteous, you will have many opportunities in life. What work-related cause and effect connections can students make?

## Teaching Resource Options

**Print**

*Cuaderno para hispanohablantes* PE, p. 152
Block Scheduling Copymasters
Unit 6 Resource Book
*Cuaderno para hispanohablantes* TE, p. 67

**Audiovisual**

OHT 193 (Quick Start)

## Quick Start Review

Conditional tense

Use OHT 193 or write on board: If someone gave you a loan to start a new business, what would you do? Use the conditional in your response. For example: **Yo vendería computadoras. Compraría un restaurante.**

*Answers will vary.*

## Teaching Suggestions
### Presenting En colores

- **Prereading** Have students first review the Comprehension Questions before starting their first pass through the reading. Have students list the places in their school, home, or community where they can use a computer.
- **Strategy: Assess the use of e-mail** After students survey their classmates about their use of e-mail, have them survey at least 10 people outside of class. Compile the results on the board and discuss.
- **Post-reading** Have students discuss the question, **¿Qué influencia tiene la computadora en su vida y en la vida de sus padres?**

# En colores
## CULTURA Y COMPARACIONES

# Ciberespacio en Quito

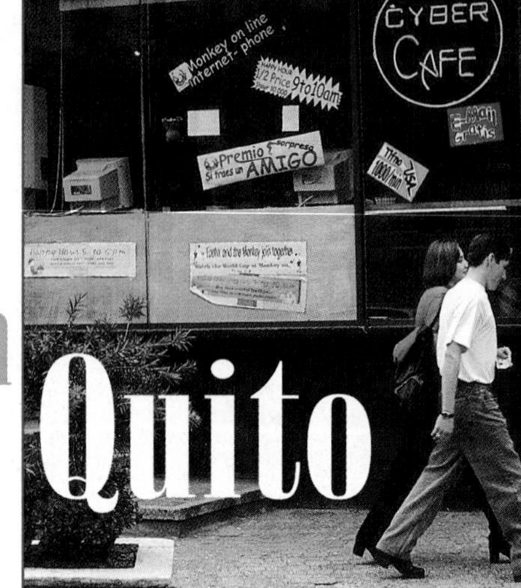


**PARA CONOCERNOS**

**STRATEGY: CONNECTING CULTURES**

**Assess use of e-mail** Are there places in your community where e-mail is available to the public? Would a café like the one in Quito be popular in your town? Survey your classmates to gather information.

1. **¿Usas correo electrónico?**
2. **Si lo usas, ¿dónde? ¿Qué cuota pagas?**
3. **Si no, ¿por qué? ¿Te gustaría usarlo?**

Imagina que estás en Quito y quieres mandarle un mensaje a tu amigo en Texas o quieres leer tu correo electrónico. ¿Qué haces? Vas al Café Net, al Cyber-C@fe o al C@féWeb.par. Pagas la cuota[1] y te sientas en una de las computadoras que dan acceso a Internet. Desde uno de estos cafés puedes ponerte en contacto con tu familia en Estados Unidos. También puedes hablar con muchos amigos.

Los cafés que ofrecen servicio de Internet son un concepto nuevo que une[2] el café tradicional con el ciberespacio. Estos cafés son diferentes porque aparte de servir comida, ofrecen más. Tienen acceso a Internet por medio de las computadoras que están en las mesas.

[1] fee [2] combines



## Classroom Community

**Group Activity** Ask students to read aloud in small groups. Students take turns summarizing each paragraph.

**Portfolio** Have students write a letter in Spanish via e-mail to another Spanish student, either within the school or globally. They may discuss future goals, weekend plans, or something that they have accomplished lately. Save a hard copy!

**Rubric: Writing**

| Criteria | Scale |
|---|---|
| Accuracy of information | 1 2 3 4 5 |
| Logical organization | 1 2 3 4 5 |
| Vocabulary use | 1 2 3 4 5 |

A = 13–15 pts.
B = 10–12 pts.
C = 7–9 pts.
D = 4–6 pts.
F = <4 pts.

¡WAOOOOOOOOOO
POR FIN EN QUITO
S/. 22.000/h
Internet
Café
NET
Y muy cerca de ti... el primer CYBERCAFE del Ecuador, podrás navegar en el Web, enviar e-mail con una de nuestras diez computadoras Pentium 166 MMX. Podrás hablar
Martes - Domingo
12h00 - 24h00
escuchado, música de Estados Unidos, Gran Bretaña, Ecuador, Argentina, México, Chile y otros países. Contarás con el apoyo de expertos para


Mientras mandas correo electrónico o haces tu tarea, puedes tomar un refresco y escuchar música de varios países: Estados Unidos, Inglaterra, Ecuador y más. ¡Te olvidas de que no estás en tu propia casa!

Ahora los cafés Internet son unos de los lugares más populares para los jóvenes de Quito. Allí se reúnen los amigos para conversar y usar las computadoras. ¿No te dan ganas de ir? ¡A teclear[3], pues!

[3] Let's key in

## ¿Comprendiste?

1. ¿Cómo es diferente el Café Net de los otros cafés en Quito?
2. ¿Qué acceso dan sus computadoras?
3. ¿Qué tiene que hacer uno para usar las computadoras de los cafés?
4. ¿Cuáles son las actividades posibles en el Café Net?

## ¿Qué piensas?

1. ¿Qué piensas del Café Net? ¿Es una buena idea? ¿Por qué?
2. ¿Usas Internet? ¿El correo electrónico? ¿Qué influencia tiene Internet en tu vida, en tus estudios y en la vida de tus compañeros?

## Hazlo tú 

En grupos, hagan un plan de un Café Internet para su colegio y luego preséntenselo a la clase. ¿Qué actividades se ofrecerán? ¿Cuántas computadoras habrá? ¿Qué buscarían los estudiantes en un «Café Net»?



## Reading Strategy

Many technical words or expressions are usually cognates of English. Have students identify the ones in the reading (e.g., **ciberespacio, electrónico, acceso,** etc.). Then have them list other technical cognates they might know in Spanish (e.g., **computadora, teléfono, técnico,** etc.).

## Cross Cultural Connections

Ask students if they know of any places similar to "Café Net" in their area. Where are they? What activities do they offer? What type of people go there? How is it different from the cafés in Quito described in the reading?

## ¿Comprendiste?

### Answers

*Answers will vary.*

1. El Café Net ofrece servicios de Internet por medio de las computadoras que están en las mesas.
2. Sus computadoras dan acceso a Internet.
3. Hay que pagar la cuota para usar las computadoras.
4. Puedes mandar correo electrónico, hacer la tarea, reunirse con amigos, tomar un refresco y escuchar música de varios países.

## Teaching All Students

**Extra Help** Have students work in pairs to answer the **¿Qué piensas?** questions on p. 427. Call on volunteers to share their answers with the class.

**Native Speakers** Ask Spanish speakers to share any computer terminology in Spanish they know with the rest of the class. Write the Spanish words on the board and have the rest of the class try to guess the English equivalents.

**Multiple Intelligences**

**Verbal** Ask students to list the pros and cons of having Internet access at their school. Make a T-chart showing their responses.

**Visual** Ask students to draw a picture that illustrates their interpretation of the inside of **Café Net**.

## Block Schedule

**Change of Pace** Have students write up a list of what there is to do at **Café Net**, e.g., **En el Café Net se puede usar las computadoras....** (For additional activities, see **Block Scheduling Copymasters**.)

## Teaching Resource Options

**Print**

*Cuaderno para hispanohablantes* PE, p. 151
Block Scheduling Copymasters
Unit 6 Resource Book
*Cuaderno para hispanohablantes* TE, p. 66
Information Gap Activities, pp. 70–71
Family Involvement, pp. 72–73
Multiple Choice Test Questions, pp. 173–175

**Audiovisual**

OHT 188, 188A, 194 (Quick Start)

**Technology**

Electronic Teacher Tools/Test Generator
*Intrigas y aventuras* CD-ROM, Disc 2

## Quick Start Review

Interviewing for a job

Use OHT 194 or write on board: Imagine Señor Montero is interviewing you. Write a response to **Hábleme un poco de sus metas, por favor.**

*Answers will vary.*

## Teaching Suggestions
### What Have Students Learned?

- Have students look at the "Now you can..." notes listed on the left side of pages 428–429. Point out that if they feel they need to review material before doing the activities, they should consult the "To review" notes.
- Use the video to review vocabulary and structures.

# En uso

## REPASO Y MÁS COMUNICACIÓN

**OBJECTIVES**

- Prepare for an interview
- Interview for a job
- Evaluate situations and people

*Now you can...*

- prepare for an interview.
- evaluate situations and people.

*To review*

- preterite and imperfect tenses, see p. 418.

### ACTIVIDAD 1 La entrevista de Pablo

Pablo describe su primera entrevista. ¿Qué dice? Cambia los verbos al pasado, usando el pretérito y el imperfecto. Luego di tu opinión sobre las situaciones.

**modelo**

*Tengo algunas recomendaciones, pero no las traigo.*
*Tenía algunas recomendaciones, pero no las traje. (Fue una desventaja.)*

1. Llego temprano porque me importa la puntualidad.
2. Cuando entro en la oficina, nadie está allí para recibirme.
3. El entrevistador está ocupado y no quiere pasar mucho tiempo conmigo.
4. Cuando el entrevistador me pregunta sobre mis habilidades, no sé qué decir y no digo nada.
5. El entrevistador me ofrece buenos beneficios.
6. Mientras hablo con el entrevistador, alguien llama por teléfono.
7. El entrevistador nunca me habla del sueldo.
8. Le caigo bien al entrevistador porque tengo metas claras.

*Now you can...*

- prepare for an interview.
- interview for a job.

*To review*

- preterite and imperfect tenses, see p. 418.

### ACTIVIDAD 2 La entrevista de Isabel

Isabel describe su entrevista con el señor Montero. Completa la descripción con el pretérito o el imperfecto de los verbos indicados.

Ayer yo __1__ (hacer) la entrevista con el señor Montero. __2__ (Estar) un poco nerviosa al principio, pero todo __3__ (salir) bien.

Yo __4__ (llegar) a la oficina temprano. __5__ (Ser) una oficina bastante lujosa. Primero, __6__ (tener) que llenar la solicitud. ¡Ellos __7__ (querer) muchos datos personales! Mientras yo __8__ (escribir), el señor Montero __9__ (llamar) por teléfono. Él le __10__ (explicar) a la secretaria que __11__ (ir) a llegar tarde.

Cuando el señor Montero __12__ (llegar), yo __13__ (estar) bien preparada para sus preguntas. Nosotros __14__ (hablar) por media hora. ¡ __15__ (Ser) una experiencia estupenda!



## Classroom Community

**Storytelling** Ask a student to state a sentence in the past tense. The next student makes a related statement in the past tense. The next student continues with the theme until everyone has added a sentence in the imperfect/preterite tenses to form a chain story.

**TPR** Read aloud a short story using the imperfect/preterite tenses. Each time an imperfect verb is mentioned students stand. For a preterite verb, the students raise their hands.

**Portfolio** Ask students to write a list of questions they would ask the interviewer in a job interview.

**Rubric: Writing**

| Criteria | Scale |
|---|---|
| Vocabulary use | 1 2 3 4 5 |
| Logical organization | 1 2 3 4 5 |
| Grammar/spelling/accuracy | 1 2 3 4 5 |

A = 13–15 pts.
B = 10–12 pts.
C = 7–9 pts.
D = 4–6 pts.
F = < 4 pts.

*Now you can...*
- prepare for an interview.

*To review*
- present perfect with regular verbs, see p. 420.

## 3 ¡A prepararnos!

¿Cómo se han preparado Isabel y sus amigos para su futuro trabajo? ¿Qué has hecho tú?

**modelo**

*Francisco: explicarles sus planes a sus padres*

*Francisco les ha explicado sus planes a sus padres. Yo (no) les he explicado mis planes a mis padres.*

1. Isabel: decidir asistir a la universidad
2. nosotros: preparar el currículum
3. tú: pedir una entrevista en una empresa
4. ustedes: terminar la escuela
5. ellos: conocer a personas importantes en la ciudad
6. Cristina: pensar en sus metas
7. él y yo: estudiar los requisitos para varios puestos
8. tú: conseguir el entrenamiento necesario para tu futuro empleo

*Now you can...*
- interview for a job.

*To review*
- present perfect with irregular verbs, see p. 423.

## 4 Las experiencias de Isabel

Piensa en las experiencias de Isabel en Ecuador. ¿Cuáles de estas cosas le han pasado?

**modelo**

*Isabel (ver) a Pablo en la oficina del señor Montero.*

*Isabel no ha visto a Pablo en la oficina del señor Montero.*

1. Isabel (poner) sus datos personales en la solicitud.
2. El señor Montero (decir) algo sobre sus planes para el futuro.
3. Pablo (escribir) el currículum de Isabel.
4. Isabel y Pablo (abrir) el periódico en la sección de empleos.
5. Isabel (hacer) capacitación para el puesto de periodista.
6. Pablo (ver) el contrato de empleo para la revista del señor Montero.
7. El entrevistador (romper) la solicitud de Isabel.
8. Isabel (volver) para una segunda entrevista.

### 1 Answers

1. Llegué temprano porque me importaba la puntualidad.
2. Cuando entré en la oficina, nadie estaba allí para recibirme.
3. El entrevistador estaba ocupado y no quiso pasar mucho tiempo conmigo.
4. Cuando el entrevistador me preguntó sobre mis habilidades, no sabía qué decir y no dije nada.
5. El entrevistador me ofreció buenos beneficios.
6. Mientras hablaba con el entrevistador, alguien llamó por teléfono.
7. El entrevistador nunca me habló del sueldo.
8. Le caí bien al entrevistador porque tenía metas claras.

### 2 Answers

1. hice
2. Estaba
3. salió
4. llegué
5. Era
6. tuve
7. querían
8. escribía
9. llamó
10. explicó
11. iba
12. llegó
13. estaba
14. hablamos
15. Fue

### 3 Answers

1. Isabel ha decidido asistir a la universidad. Yo (no) he decidido asistir a la universidad.
2. hemos preparado / he preparado
3. has pedido / he pedido
4. han terminado / he terminado
5. han conocido / he conocido
6. ha pensado / he pensado
7. hemos estudiado / he estudiado
8. has conseguido

### 4 Answers

1. Isabel ha puesto sus datos personales en la solicitud.
2. El señor Montero ha dicho algo sobre sus planes para el futuro.
3. Pablo no ha escrito el currículum de Isabel.
4. Isabel y Pablo han abierto el periódico en la sección de empleos.
5. Isabel ha hecho capacitación para el puesto de periodista.
6. Pablo no ha visto el contrato de empleo para la revista del señor Montero.
7. El entrevistador no ha roto la solicitud de Isabel.
8. Isabel no ha vuelto para una segunda entrevista.

## Teaching All Students

**Extra Help** Using **Actividad 2** as a model, tell a story in the past, stopping each time you come to a verb. Call out the infinitive and have the students give the preterite or imperfect form.

**Multiple Intelligences**

**Visual** Assign "Now you can..." and "To review" to groups. Each group designs and presents a visual aid for the class to review.

**Kinesthetic** Have students act out the preparations mentioned in **Actividad 3**. Then have them think of 5 more preparations to act out for the class to identify.

## Block Schedule

**Retention** Allow the class to work on the **Repaso** in class just before the bell. It will focus them on the vocabulary, help them see that others know certain items they might not, and therefore encourage them to study before the assessment. (For additional activities, see **Block Scheduling Copymasters**.)

## Teaching Resource Options

### Print 

Unit 6 Resource Book
- **Audioscript**, p. 83
- **Cooperative Quizzes**, pp. 84–85
- **Etapa Exam**, Forms A and B, pp. 86–95
- ***Examen para hispanohablantes***, pp. 96–100
- **Portfolio Assessment**, pp. 101–102
- **Multiple Choice Test Questions**, pp. 173–175

### Audiovisual

**OHT** 194 (Quick Start)
**Audio Program** Cassette 20B / CD 20; (***Para hispanohablantes*** Cassette 20B / CD 20)

### Technology 

**Electronic Teacher Tools/Test Generator**
www.mcdougallittell.com

## Quick Start Review

**Interviewing for a job**

Use OHT 194 or write on board: If you were to apply for a summer job, what job would it be? Write down a description of the job and some of the skills, education, and experience a person would need for that position.

*Answers will vary.*

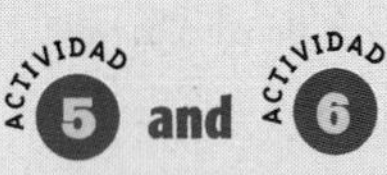

### Actividad 5 and Actividad 6

**Rubric: Speaking**

| Criteria | Scale |
|---|---|
| Fluency | 1 2 3 4 5 |
| Vocabulary use | 1 2 3 4 5 |
| Pronunciation | 1 2 3 4 5 |

A = 13–15 pts.
B = 10–12 pts.
C = 7–9 pts.
D = 4–6 pts.
F = < 4 pts.

### Actividad 7 En tu propia voz

**Rubric: Writing**

| Criteria | Scale |
|---|---|
| Vocabulary use | 1 2 3 4 5 |
| Accuracy | 1 2 3 4 5 |
| Creativity | 1 2 3 4 5 |

A = 13–15 pts.
B = 10–12 pts.
C = 7–9 pts.
D = 4–6 pts.
F = < 4 pts.

### Teaching Note: En tu propia voz

**Writing Strategy** To persuade a potential employer, students should use simple, direct language with clear examples.

## Actividad 5 ¡A entrevistar!

**PARA CONVERSAR**

**STRATEGY: SPEAKING**

**Refine interview skills** Both the interviewer and the candidate must be able to ask and answer clear, worthwhile questions and seek follow-up for more details. Good questions and answers reveal the nature of the job, employer expectations, and employee qualifications, such as education, experience, and personal qualities. Use the ideas listed in the table to guide you in forming questions and answers for your interview.

Entrevista a tu compañero(a) para un puesto en tu empresa. Después cambien de papel. El (La) entrevistador(a) y el (la) candidato(a) tienen que hacerse preguntas sobre las cosas en la tabla.

| Entrevistador(a) | Candidato(a) |
|---|---|
| • la puntualidad | • los requisitos |
| • el currículum | • las responsabilidades |
| • la educación | • la capacitación |
| • las recomendaciones | • el sueldo |
| • las habilidades | • los beneficios |

## Actividad 6 ¡Fue horrible!

Todos acaban de entrevistarse y tuvieron entrevistas malas. Compartan sus experiencias negativas y decidan quién tuvo la peor entrevista.

**modelo**

**Estudiante 1:** *Fue horrible. Llegué muy tarde, pero no había nadie en la oficina. Entonces…*

**Estudiante 2:** *Eso no es nada. Yo le caí muy mal a la entrevistadora porque…*

**Estudiante 3:** *Mi entrevista fue la peor. Mientras esperaba…*

## Actividad 7 En tu propia voz

**ESCRITURA** Imagínate que solicitas un trabajo de verano en una empresa donde se habla español. En una carta, explica cómo te has preparado para el puesto que se ofrece.

**modelo**

*Estimados señores:*

*Me interesa el puesto de… He estudiado español por dos años y…*

## CONEXIONES

**La música** La flauta de pan, o rondador, es una flauta de origen antiguo que es parte de la música andina de Ecuador hoy en día. Aparte de los grupos indígenas de Ecuador, ¿qué otros grupos tienen una música con su propio estilo e instrumentos? Usa Internet o tu biblioteca para encontrar la respuesta a esta pregunta y compártela con la clase. Si encuentras un casete de la música, ¡no te olvides de traerlo!



## Classroom Community

**Paired Activity** In preparation for **Actividad 7**, have partners discuss their preparation before writing.

**Group Activity** Have students work in small groups to rank in order of importance the items listed in **Actividad 5**. Which items would be most important to the **entrevistador(a)** and which would be most important to the **candidato(a)**?

# En resumen

## REPASO DE VOCABULARIO

### PREPARE FOR AN INTERVIEW

| | |
|---|---|
| **el currículum** | *resumé, curriculum vitae* |
| **la educación** | *education* |
| **la entrevista** | *interview* |
| **la meta** | *goal* |
| **la universidad** | *university* |

### EVALUATE SITUATIONS AND PEOPLE

| | |
|---|---|
| **caerle bien (mal) a alguien** | *to make a good (bad) impression on someone* |
| **la desventaja** | *disadvantage* |
| **la ventaja** | *advantage* |

### INTERVIEW FOR A JOB

| | |
|---|---|
| **los beneficios** | *benefits* |
| **la capacitación** | *training* |
| **conseguir (e→i, i)** | *to get* |
| **el contrato** | *contract* |
| **la empresa** | *business, company* |
| **el (la) entrevistador(a)** | *interviewer* |
| **las habilidades** | *capabilities* |
| **la puntualidad** | *punctuality* |
| **las recomendaciones** | *recommendations* |
| **requerir (e → ie, i)** | *to require* |
| **el requisito** | *requirement* |
| **el seguro** | *insurance* |
| **el sueldo** | *salary* |

### Juego

Haz este crucigrama, usando palabras de tu repaso de vocabulario.

**A través**

**2.** Muchos trabajos tienen _____ que incluyen el seguro médico.

**5.** Cuando un puesto no es permanente, un empleado tiene un _____ .

**6.** Isabel escribe muy bien. Es una de sus _____ .

**8.** Isabel va a la universidad para continuar su _____ .

**11.** Estudiar periodismo es una _____ importante de Isabel.

**Abajo**

**1.** Tener una buena educación es una _____ .

**3.** El _____ médico está incluido en un contrato.

**4.** La revista *Viajamundo* es la _____ del señor Montero.

**7.** Isabel no quiere mucho dinero o _____ si puede trabajar para una revista.

**9.** El señor Montero asistió a la _____ de Quito.

**10.** Al buscar un puesto es necesario tener un _____ .



## Teaching Suggestions

- Have students write a short job interview scene to review the **Etapa** vocabulary.
- Then divide the class into pairs and have them role play their interviews.
- Have students create their own word puzzles as homework to continue review.

## Project: Reviewing Etapa 2

Assign the following out-of-class activities:

- Interview a Spanish speaker about his or her job or profession.
- Make at least 3 suggestions to a friend who is preparing for an upcoming job interview.
- Find information about Net Cafés in your area and in Ecuador via the Internet.
- Find information on job opportunities in your chosen field. Try to find out if knowledge of Spanish would improve your chances of getting a job.

**Extra Credit**

| | |
|---|---|
| Interview | 2 pts. |
| Job interview preparation | 2 pts. |
| Information on Net Cafés | 2 pts. |
| Spanish job opportunities | 2 pts. |

## Juego

**Answers**

**A través:** 2. beneficios, 5. contrato, 6. habilidades, 8. educación, 11. meta

**Abajo:** 1. ventaja, 3. seguro, 4. empresa, 7. sueldo, 9. Universidad, 10. currículum

## Interdisciplinary Connections

**Music** Have students mimic the style of the music from Ecuador, using instruments available locally. Ask them to analyze the differences between the authentic music and their own recreation.

## Teaching All Students

**Extra Help** Ask students to write at least 5 questions they would ask in a job interview using the **Etapa** vocabulary.

**Challenge** Ask students to make their own crossword puzzle using some of the vocabulary words.

**Native Speakers** Ask Spanish speakers to read aloud the words in the vocabulary list for the class with special attention to pronunciation. Have the rest of the class repeat each word after the Spanish speaker.

**Multiple Intelligences**

**Verbal** ¿Qué soy yo? Ask students to describe a vocabulary word; the class determines the word based on the description.

**Musical/Rhythmic** Ask students to research other typical instruments heard in Andean music in Ecuador. Bring in a sample of music if possible.

## Block Schedule

**Variety** Have students write their own letter of recommendation to support their job application. Make sure they list their strengths and skills as well as their qualifications.

# Planning Guide CLASSROOM MANAGEMENT

## OBJECTIVES

**Communication**
- Talk on the telephone *pp. 436–437, 445–446*
- Report on past, present, and future events *pp. 434–435, 436–437*
- Describe duties, people, and surroundings *pp. 436–437*

**Grammar**
- The future tense *p. 440*
- The conditional tense *p. 442*
- Reported speech *pp. 444–445*

**Culture**
- Guayaquil *p. 441*
- Los festivales en Ecuador *p. 443*
- La música andina *pp. 450–451*
- Un poema ecuatoriano *pp. 448–449*

**Recycling**
- The present perfect tense *p. 439*
- The future tense *p. 440*
- The conditional tense *p. 442*
- Writing a thank-you letter *p. 446*
- Superlatives *p. 447*

## STRATEGIES

**Listening Strategies**
- Report what others said *p. 436*

**Speaking Strategies**
- Persuade or convince others *p. 447*
- Report on events *p. 454*

**Reading Strategies**
- Observe characteristics of poems *p. 448*
- Recognize cognates *TE p. 451*

**Writing Strategies**
- Brainstorm details before writing a letter *Actividad 7, TE p. 454*
- State your message using a positive tone *TE p. 456*

**Connecting Cultures Strategies**
- Reflect on music *p. 450*
- Make a historical timeline *TE p. 449*

## PROGRAM RESOURCES

### Print

- *Más práctica* Workbook PE *pp. 153–160*
- Block Scheduling Copymasters *pp. 145–152*
- Unit 6 Resource Book
  - *Más práctica* Workbook TE *pp. 103–110*
  - *Cuaderno para hispanohablantes* TE *pp. 111–118*
  - Information Gap Activities *pp. 119–122*
  - Family Involvement *pp. 123–124*
  - Video Activities *pp. 125–127*
  - Videoscript *pp. 128–129*
  - Audioscript *pp. 130–134*
  - Assessment Program, Unit 6 Etapa 3 *pp. 135–169, 176–186*
  - Answer Keys *pp. 189–191*

### Audiovisual

- Audio Program Cassette 18A, 18B / CD 18
- *Canciones* Cassette/CD
- Video Program Videotape 6 / Videodisc 4B
- Overhead Transparencies M1–M5; GO1–GO5; 174, 195–204

### Technology

- Electronic Teacher Tools/Test Generator
- *Intrigas y aventuras* CD-ROM, Disc 2
-  www.mcdougallittell.com

### Assessment Program Options

- Cooperative Quizzes (Unit 6 Resource Book)
- Etapa Exam Forms A and B (Unit 6 Resource Book)
- *Examen para hispanohablantes* (Unit 6 Resource Book)
- Portfolio Assessment (Unit 6 Resource Book)
- Unit 6 Comprehensive Test (Unit 6 Resource Book)
- *Prueba comprensiva para hispanohablantes* Unit 6 (Unit 6 Resource Book)
- Multiple Choice Test Questions (Unit 6 Resource Book)
- Final Exam (Unit 6 Resource Book)
- Audio Program Cassette 20B / CD 20
- Electronic Teacher Tools/Test Generator

### Native Speakers

- *Cuaderno para hispanohablantes* PE *pp. 153–160*
- *Cuaderno para hispanohablantes* TE (Unit 6 Resource Book)
- *Examen para hispanohablantes* (Unit 6 Resource Book)
- *Prueba comprensiva para hispanohablantes* Unit 6 (Unit 6 Resource Book)
- Audio Program *(Para hispanohablantes)* Cassettes 18B, 20B / CD 18, CD 20
- Audioscript (Unit 6 Resource Book)

Isabel Pablo Rosario Cristina

# Student Text Listening Activity Scripts

## Videoscript: Diálogo *pages 436–437*

• Videotape 6, 25:28 • Videodisc 4B

Search Chapter 5, Play to end. U6E3, En vivo (Dialog)

• Use the videoscript with **Actividades 1, 2** *page 438*

**Pablo:** ¿Aló?
**Isabel:** Hola, Pablo. Soy Isabel.
**Pablo:** ¡Isabel! ¿Cómo estuvo la entrevista?
**Isabel:** La entrevista estuvo muy bien.
**Pablo:** ¿Tienes la información para tu artículo?
**Isabel:** Tengo mucha información. ¡Qué buena onda es el Sr. Montero! Me cayó muy bien.
**Pablo:** Sí, fue muy amable en ayudarnos. ¿Y, qué dijo?
**Isabel:** Dijo que buscaban un periodista para un contrato de seis meses. Y dijo que necesitaban una persona con experiencia en otra revista. Sabes, Pablo, el puesto sería perfecto para mí. Podría trabajar aquí seis meses y luego regresar a México.
**Pablo:** Isabel, estás soñando. Tienes que graduarte del colegio primero.
**Isabel:** Sí, pero es una lástima. Y tengo que regresar a México mañana. ¡No quiero irme ya!
**Pablo:** Mira, Isa, ¿por qué no vuelves a casa ahora y hablamos? Tú sabes que es necesario tener una buena educación antes de comenzar a trabajar. Y sabes también que la entrevista con el Sr. Montero no fue una entrevista de verdad.
**Isabel:** Sí, pero él dijo que yo sería una candidata perfecta para el trabajo.
**Pablo:** Y no lo dudo, pero tienes que graduarte del colegio y luego de la universidad.
**Isabel:** Sí, lo sé. Pero...
**Pablo:** No hay peros. Ven, regresa a casa y podemos hablar de tu futuro. ¿Dónde estás ahora?
**Isabel:** Estoy en una cabina telefónica en la avenida Amazonas. Muy bien, voy para allá. Nos vemos pronto. Chao.
**Pablo:** Isabel está en la avenida Amazonas. Estará aquí muy pronto. ¡Vamos, tenemos prisa!
**Rosario:** Cristina, ¿me puedes hacer un favor? Ve a la cocina y trae el pastel. Lo pondremos aquí en la mesa.
**Cristina:** Cómo no. ¿Y quieres que traiga las cucharas también?
**Rosario:** No, ya las tengo aquí. Pero gracias.
**Pablo:** Muy bien. Isabel llegará en cualquier momento. Ustedes se quedarán aquí, muy quietos. Isabel entrará y todos le gritarán "¡Buen viaje!"
**Rosario:** Muy bien, capitán. ¿Y nos dirás qué hacer después?
**Pablo:** Lo siento. Es que quiero que todo salga bien. Isabel se siente un poco triste. ¡Chht! Es Isabel.
**Todos:** ¡Buen viaje!
**Rosario:** Isabel, ha sido un enorme placer llegar a conocerte. Y te deseamos todo lo mejor.
**Cristina:** Isabel, ¿puedo ir a México a visitarte algún día?
**Isabel:** Claro que sí, Cristina. Me encantaría.
**Pablo:** Isabel, sabes que siempre tendrás aquí en Ecuador amigos que te quieren. ¡Y espero que vuelvas pronto!
**Rosario:** Claro que va a volver. ¡Es una futura periodista que viajará por el mundo!
**Isabel:** Gracias, ay, gracias a todos. Los quiero muchísimo.
Quién sabe, tal vez trabajaré aquí algún día como periodista. ¡Después de terminar con mis estudios, claro! Pero estoy segura que regresaré a Ecuador.

## Actividad 8 ¿En qué orden? *page 442*

**Isabel:** Mañana regresaré a México, aunque me gusta mucho Ecuador. Mi familia estará muy alegre de verme. Descansaré un poco, tomaré el sol en la playa y empezaré el colegio en un mes. El verano que viene me graduaré del colegio y después viajaré a Texas por un mes para visitar a mis primos. En el otoño asistiré a la universidad y cuando termine mis estudios, buscaré un puesto de periodista en una revista de viajes. Si tengo suerte, volveré a Ecuador como periodista y visitaré a mis amigos especiales.

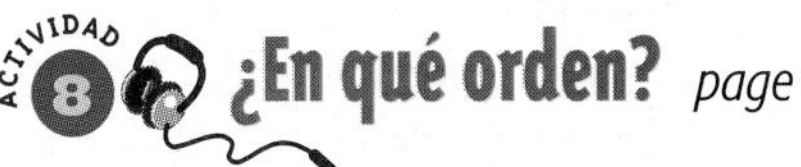

## Actividad 12 Llamadas por teléfono *page 445*

1. **Sr. Ramírez:** Diga.
**Verónica:** Buenas tardes. ¿Puedo hablar con Meche?
**Sr. Ramírez:** Lo siento, Meche no está. Va a volver a las cuatro y media.
**Verónica:** Pues, soy Verónica. Dígale que me llame, por favor, al 3-47-38.
**Sr. Ramírez:** Sí, como no.
2. *<Sound of dialing on a touch-tone phone, then a busy signal.>*
3. **Rosa:** Bueno.
**Paco:** Hola, soy Paco. ¿Está Meche?
**Rosa:** Sí, un momento, por favor. Meche, te habla una persona por teléfono. Dice que es Paco.
4. **Sra. Ramírez:** Bueno.
**Verónica:** Hola, soy Verónica llamando para Meche otra vez.
**Sra. Ramírez:** Lo siento, Verónica, todavía no está.
**Verónica:** Por favor, dígale que estaré en la casa de Juana.

# Pacing Guide

## Sample Lesson Plan - 50 Minute Schedule

### DAY 1

**Etapa Opener**
- Quick Start Review (TE p. 432). 5 MIN.
- Anticipate/Activate prior knowledge: Have students look at *Etapa* Opener and answer questions. 10 MIN.

**En contexto: Vocabulario**
- Quick Start Review (TE p. 434). 5 MIN.
- Discuss pictures; have students use context and pictures to learn *Etapa* vocabulary. Answer questions, p. 435. 10 MIN.

**En vivo: Diálogo**
- Quick Start Review (TE p. 436). 5 MIN.
- Review Listening Strategy, p. 437. Play audio or show video for the dialog on pp. 436–437. 8 MIN.
- Read aloud, students take on roles of characters. Ask Comprehension Questions (TE p. 437). 7 MIN.

**Homework Option**
- Video Activities, Unit 6 Resource Book, pp. 125–127.

### DAY 2

**En acción: Vocabulario y Gramática**
- Quick Start Review (TE p. 438). 5 MIN.
- Ask students for a summary of *En vivo* dialog to check recall. 5 MIN.
- Replay the *En vivo* dialog using the audiovisual resources and have students do *Actividades* 1 and 2 orally. 10 MIN.
- Have students complete *Actividades* 3 and 4 in small groups. 10 MIN.
- Present *Repaso*: The Future Tense, p. 440. 10 MIN.
- Have students complete *Actividad* 5 in writing. 10 MIN.

**Homework Option**
- *Más práctica* Workbook, pp. 153–156. *Cuaderno para hispanohablantes*, p. 153.

### DAY 3

**En acción (cont.)**
- Check homework. 5 MIN.
- Quick Start Review (TE p. 440). 5 MIN.
- Have students do *Actividades* 6 and 7 in pairs. 10 MIN.
- Play audio and have students complete *Actividad* 8. 10 MIN.
- Present *Repaso*: The Conditional Tense, p. 442, and have students do *Actividad* 9 in writing. 10 MIN.
- Have students complete *Actividad* 10 in pairs and *Actividad* 11 in small groups. 10 MIN.

**Homework Option**
- Have students complete *Actividad* 11 at home. *Más práctica* Workbook, p. 157. *Cuaderno para hispanohablantes*, p. 155.

### DAY 4

**En acción (cont.)**
- Check homework. 5 MIN.
- Quick Start Review (TE p. 444). 5 MIN.
- Present *Gramática:* Reported Speech, p. 444. 10 MIN.
- Play audio and have students complete *Actividad* 12. 10 MIN.
- Have students complete *Actividad* 13 in writing. 10 MIN.
- Have students complete *Actividad* 14 in small groups. 10 MIN.

**Homework Option**
- *Más práctica* Workbook, p. 158. *Cuaderno para hispanohablantes*, p. 156.

### DAY 5

**En acción (cont.)**
- Check homework. 5 MIN.
- Quick Start Review (TE p. 446). 5 MIN.
- Have students complete *Actividad* 15 in writing. 10 MIN.
- Present Speaking Strategy, p. 447, and have students complete *Actividad* 16 in small groups. 10 MIN.
- Have students prepare the presentations in *Actividad* 17 in small groups and ask several volunteers to present their "mensaje al mundo" to the class. 15 MIN.
- Quick Wrap-Up (TE p. 447). 5 MIN.

**Homework Option**
- *Más práctica* Workbook, pp. 159–160. *Cuaderno para hispanohablantes*, pp. 157–158.

### DAY 6

**En voces: Lectura**
- Check homework. 5 MIN.
- Quick Start Review (TE p. 448). 5 MIN.
- Review Reading Strategy, p. 448 and have students read *Pasajero del planeta* aloud, taking turns. 15 MIN.
- Have students answer the *¿Comprendiste?* questions orally. 5 MIN.

**En uso: Repaso y más comunicación**
- Do *Actividades* 1, 2, 3, and 4 orally. 10 MIN.
- Review Speaking Strategy, p. 454. Then do *Actividad* 5 orally in pairs and *Actividad* 6 in groups of four. 10 MIN.

**Homework Option**
- Have students complete the *¿Qué piensas?* questions in writing and do *Actividad* 7. *Cuaderno para hispanohablantes*, pp. 159–160. Review for *Etapa* 3 Exam.

### DAY 7

**En colores: Cultura y comparaciones**
- Check homework. 5 MIN.
- Quick Start Review (TE p. 450). 5 MIN.
- Review Connecting Cultures Strategy, p. 450. Then have students read the selection and answer questions. 15 MIN.

**En resumen: Repaso de vocabulario**
- Review grammar questions, etc. as necessary. 5 MIN.
- Complete *Etapa* 3 Exam. 20 MIN.

**Homework Option**
- Review for Unit 6 Comprehensive Test.

### DAY 8

**En resumen: Repaso de vocabulario**
- Quick Start Review (TE p. 456). 5 MIN.

**En tu propia voz: Escritura**
- Review strategy and start writing activity, pp. 456–457. 10 MIN.

**Unit 6 Comprehensive Test**
- Review grammar questions, etc. as necessary. 5 MIN.
- Complete Unit 6 Comprehensive Test. 30 MIN.

**Homework Option**
- Have students complete the writing activity.

# Sample Lesson Plan - Block Schedule (90 minutes)

## DAY 1

### Etapa Opener
- Quick Start Review (TE p. 432). 5 MIN.
- Anticipate/Activate prior knowledge: Have students look at the *Etapa* Opener and answer questions. 10 MIN.

### En contexto: Vocabulario
- Quick Start Review (TE p. 434). 5 MIN.
- Have students use context and pictures to learn *Etapa* vocabulary. Answer questions, p. 435. 10 MIN.

### En vivo: Diálogo
- Quick Start Review (TE p. 436). 5 MIN.
- Review Listening Strategy, p. 436. Play audio or show video for the dialog on pp. 436–437. 10 MIN.
- Read aloud, students taking roles of characters. Ask Comprehension Questions (TE p. 437). 10 MIN.
- Students role-play in groups while looking at the photos in their texts. Encourage them to come up with logical dialog using familiar vocabulary. 10 MIN.

### En acción: Vocabulario y Gramática
- Quick Start Review (TE p. 438). 5 MIN.
- Replay *En vivo* dialog. Have students do *Actividades* 1 and 2 orally. 10 MIN.
- Have students complete *Actividades* 3 and 4 in small groups. 10 MIN.

### Homework Option
- Video Activities, Unit 6 Resource Book, pp. 125–127. *Más práctica* Workbook, pp. 153–156. *Cuaderno para hispanohablantes*, p. 153.

## DAY 2

### En acción (cont.)
- Check homework. 5 MIN.
- Quick Start Review (TE p. 440). 5 MIN.
- Present *Repaso*: The Future Tense, p. 440. 5 MIN.
- Have students complete *Actividad* 5 in writing. 10 MIN.
- Have students do *Actividades* 6 and 7 in pairs. 10 MIN.
- Play audio and have students complete *Actividad* 8. 10 MIN.
- Quick Start Review (TE p. 442). 5 MIN.
- Present *Repaso:* The Conditional Tense, p. 442, and have students do *Actividad* 9 in writing. 10 MIN.
- Have students do *Actividad* 10 in pairs and *Actividad* 11 in small groups. 10 MIN.
- Present *Gramática:* Reported Speech, p. 444. 10 MIN.
- Play audio and have students complete *Actividad* 12. 10 MIN.

### Homework Option
- *Más práctica* Workbook, pp. 157–158. *Cuaderno para hispanohablantes*, pp. 155–156.

## DAY 3

### En acción (cont.)
- Check homework. 5 MIN.
- Quick Start Review (TE p. 444). 5 MIN.
- Have students complete *Actividad* 13 in writing. 10 MIN.
- Have students complete *Actividad* 14 in small groups. 10 MIN.
- Have students complete *Actividad* 15 in writing. 10 MIN.
- Present Speaking Strategy, p. 447, and have students complete *Actividad* 16 in small groups. 10 MIN.
- Have students prepare their presentations in *Actividad* 17 in small groups and ask volunteers to present their "mensaje al mundo" to the class. 10 MIN.

### En voces: Lectura
- Quick Start Review (TE p. 448). 5 MIN.
- Review Reading Strategy, p. 448, and have students read silently. 5 MIN.
- Have students read *Pasajero del planeta* aloud taking turns. 10 MIN.
- Call on volunteers to answer *¿Comprendiste?* questions. Start the *¿Qué piensas?* questions. 10 MIN.

### Homework Option
- Have students finish the *¿Qué piensas?* questions, p. 449, in writing. *Más práctica* Workbook, pp. 159–160. *Cuaderno para hispanohablantes*, pp. 157–158. Review for *Etapa* 3 Exam.

## DAY 4

### En uso: Repaso y más comunicación
- Check homework. 5 MIN.
- Quick Start Review (TE p. 452). 5 MIN.
- Do *Actividades* 1, 2, 3, and 4 orally. 15 MIN.
- Review Speaking Strategy, p. 454. Then do *Actividad* 5 orally in pairs and *Actividad* 6 in groups. 15 MIN.

### En resumen: Repaso de vocabulario
- Review grammar questions, etc., as necessary. 10 MIN.
- Complete *Etapa* 2 Exam. 20 MIN.

### Ampliación
- Use a suggested project, game, or activity (TE pp. 387A–387B). 20 MIN.

### Homework Option
- Have students do *Actividad* 7, p. 454. *Cuaderno para hispanohablantes*, pp. 159–160. Review for Unit 6 Comprehensive Test.

## DAY 5

### En colores: Cultura y comparaciones
- Check homework. 5 MIN.
- Quick Start Review (TE p. 450). 5 MIN.
- Review Connecting Cultures Strategy, p. 450, and have students read silently. 10 MIN.
- Read *Música de las montañas* aloud with students. 10 MIN.
- Have students answer the *¿Comprendiste?* questions orally. 5 MIN.
- Divide students into small groups and have them work on the *Hazlo tú* activity. 10 MIN.

### En resumen: Repaso de vocabulario
- Review grammar questions, etc., as necessary. 10 MIN.
- Complete Unit 6 Comprehensive Test. 30 MIN.

### En tu propia voz: Escritura
- Start writing activity. 5 MIN.

### Homework Option
- Have students complete the *¿Qué piensas?* questions in writing. Finish writing activity.

▼ Isabel habla con sus amigas ecuatorianas.

## Etapa Theme

**Talking on the telephone; reporting on past, present, and future events; describing duties, people, and surroundings.**

## Grammar Objectives

- Reviewing the future and conditional tenses
- Reported speech

### Teaching Resource Options

**Print** 
Block Scheduling Copymasters

**Audiovisual**
**OHT** 174, 201 (Quick Start)

### Quick Start Review

**The infinitive**

Use OHT 201 or write on board: Imagine the two women consulting the paper are discussing what to do that day in the city. Write a list of things they might do. Use the infinitive of the verb as you jot down your ideas.

*Answers will vary.*
***Possible answers:*** **ir al cine, ir a un concierto, ir a una obra de teatro, ir a un restaurante**

### Teaching Suggestions
**Previewing the Etapa**

Ask students to study the photo on pp. 432–433 and identify what they see in the photo—the people, the items, the location. Use the **¿Qué ves?** questions to focus discussion.

UNIDAD 6

# ¡A trabajar!

- Talk on the telephone
- Report on past, present, and future events
- Describe duties, people, and surroundings

### ¿Qué ves?

Mira la foto. ¿Qué ves?

1. ¿Dónde tiene lugar la foto?
2. ¿Reconoces el juego?
3. ¿Qué hace esta gente?
4. ¿Con quién crees que habla Isabel?

432

### Classroom Management

**Planning Ahead** Prepare students to practice talking on the telephone. Have them discuss appropriate greetings and other telephone etiquette. Bring a telephone to class to use in mock conversations. Toy telephones would also work.

**Peer Review** Have students begin a discussion summarizing what they have learned during the year. Review all the characters in the story line and the places they visited. How do they imagine the story will end?

## Supplementary Vocabulary

| | |
|---|---|
| **el teléfono público** | public phone |
| **la cabina telefónica** | phone booth |
| **la guía telefónica** | phone book |
| **la fuente** | fountain |

## Culture Highlight

● **PUBLIC TELEPHONES** To use a telephone in a phone booth in Ecuador, you need to have a token (**ficha**) or a phone card. However, it is more common to use a telephone in a store and pay a small fee.

## Critical Thinking

Have students expand their classifications from the Teaching Suggestions, p. 432, and predict the vocabulary items they will learn or review in this **Etapa**.

## Teaching All Students

**Extra Help** Ask students to write five questions about the photo. Review and use as an opener the next day.

**Native Speakers** Ask Spanish speakers to review telephone vocabulary with the class.

**Multiple Intelligences**

**Verbal** Ask students to choose two characters in the photo and create a dialog between them. Encourage them to be creative.

## Block Schedule

**Change of Pace** Ask students to form a chain story about the photo–one student begins to tell a story and the next adds to the plot. Students may include themselves in the story. (For additional activities, see **Block Scheduling Copymasters.**)

## Teaching Resource Options

**Print** 

Unit 6 Resource Book
Video Activities, p. 125
Videoscript, p. 128
Audioscript, p. 130

**Audiovisual** 

**OHT** 195, 196, 201 (Quick Start)
**Audio Program** Cassette 18A / CD 18
**Video Program** Videotape 6, 21:08 / Videodisc 4B

Search Chapter 4, Play to 5
U6E3, En contexto (Vocabulary)

**Technology**

*Intrigas y aventuras* CD-ROM, Disc 2

## Quick Start Review

Talking about the past, stating preferences

Use OHT 201 or write on board: Complete the following sentence.

**El personaje o el diálogo que me gustó más en este libro fue ___ porque ____.**

*Answers will vary.*

## Teaching Suggestions
### Introducing Vocabulary

- Use OHT 195–196 and Audiocassette 18A / CD 18 to present the vocabulary on pp. 434–435.
- Ask the Comprehension Questions in the margin of the Teacher's Edition on p. 435. You may write the questions on the board and have students work in small groups to answer them. Or have students work in groups to create their own Comprehension Questions and share them with the class.

# En contexto

## VOCABULARIO

Aprendiste mucho este año. ¿Recuerdas todo lo que ves aquí?

**¡Hola!** Este año ustedes aprendieron mucho español. ¿Se acuerdan de lo que han aprendido? Pues, vamos a ver un poco de todo.

CHICAGO
SAN JUAN
SAN JOSÉ
CIUDAD DE MÉXICO
QUITO

CHICAGO

**Talk about the past**

Pedro: Viniste directamente de Los Ángeles, ¿no?

Francisco: Sí, estuve con mi familia. Vi a mis abuelos y mis tíos, y salí con mi prima Verónica.

CIUDAD DE MÉXICO

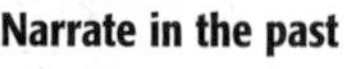

**Narrate in the past**

Don Miguel: Pero después ocurrió algo increíble, algo maravilloso. Todo el mundo respondió a la emergencia con acciones positivas. Todos ayudaban a sus vecinos.



## Classroom Community

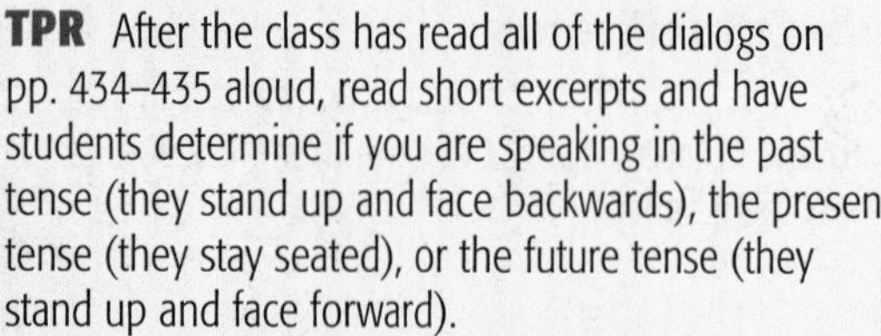

**TPR** After the class has read all of the dialogs on pp. 434–435 aloud, read short excerpts and have students determine if you are speaking in the past tense (they stand up and face backwards), the present tense (they stay seated), or the future tense (they stand up and face forward).

**Paired Activity** Ask students to tell a short story to a partner using *one* grammar point learned this year, e.g., talk about the past, give commands, etc. The partner draws a sketch of the story according to the description. Share the pictures with the entire class.

SAN JUAN

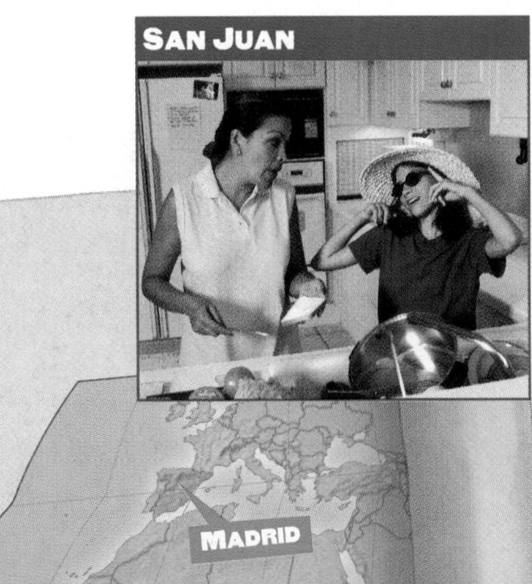


**Give commands**

**Tía Julia:** Susana, por favor, **no corras** por la casa. ¿Ya hiciste la cama?

**Susana:** No, no la hice.

**Tía Julia:** **Vete** y **haz** la cama inmediatamente. ¡Y **limpia** tu cuarto!

MADRID

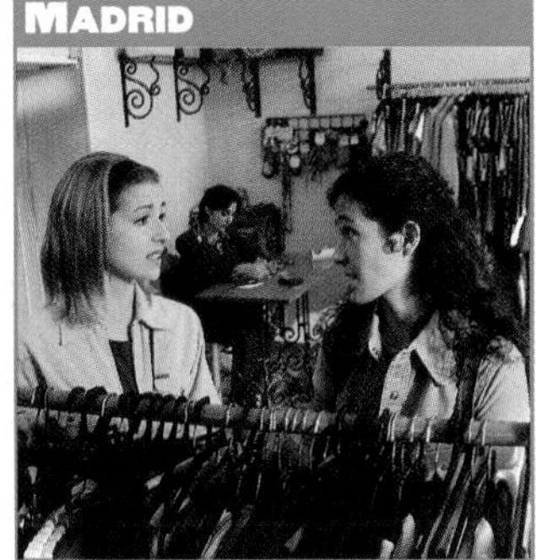

**Express wishes using the subjunctive**

**Isabel:** ¡Uy! La dependienta está de mal humor.

**Andrea:** Ella espera que los clientes **gasten** mucho dinero, y duda que tú y yo **vayamos** a comprar hoy.

SAN JOSÉ

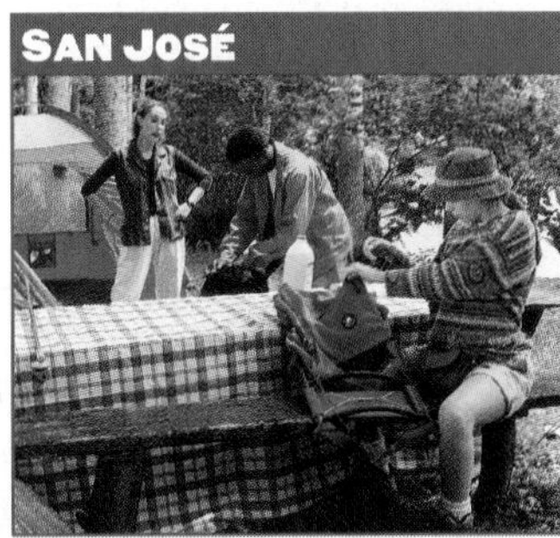

**Talk about the future**

**Fernando:** A ver, aquí están los fósforos, la linterna, la navaja. ¡Hay muchísimas cosas!

**Amalia:** **Habrá** un uso para todo. Ya **verás**.

QUITO

**Talk about what you have done**

**Isabel:** Esta experiencia con *Onda Internacional* **ha sido** muy buena. **He aprendido** mucho y **he visto** partes del mundo que antes no conocía. Estoy triste. Mañana tengo que volver a México. ¡Me **ha gustado** tanto Ecuador!

## Preguntas personales

1. ¿Qué hiciste la última vez que tuviste vacaciones escolares?
2. ¿Qué has hecho durante otras vacaciones?
3. ¿Qué harás cuando termine este año escolar?
4. ¿Qué te gustaría hacer en el futuro?



## Teaching Suggestions

Have students create a summary of the trips that Francisco and Isabel took throughout the textbook:

**Isabel: Ciudad de México, Madrid, Quito**

**Francisco: Chicago, Los Ángeles, San Juan, San José**

## Comprehension Questions

1. ¿Viajó Francisco directamente a Chicago? **(Sí)**
2. ¿Estuvo con amigos en Los Ángeles? **(No)**
3. ¿Habla Don Miguel de un temblor? **(Sí)**
4. ¿Ayudaba la gente a sus vecinos? **(Sí)**
5. ¿Prefiere Tía Julia que Susana corra o camine en la casa? **(Prefiere que camine.)**
6. ¿Quiere Tía Julia que Susana haga la cama o lave los platos? **(Quiere que haga la cama.)**
7. ¿Está de mal humor la dueña o la dependienta? **(la dependienta)**
8. ¿Qué espera la dependienta? **(Espera que los clientes gasten mucho dinero.)**
9. ¿Qué traerás la próxima vez que vas de camping? ***(Answers will vary.)***
10. ¿Por qué dice Isabel que su experiencia con *Onda Internacional* ha sido muy buena? ***(Porque ha aprendido y ha visto mucho.)***

## Language Notes

Point out the different language functions students have learned throughout the textbook. They can now talk about what they have done in the present, past, and future, and they can give commands and express wishes.

## Teaching All Students

**Extra Help** Ask students to refer back to Isabel's travels to Ciudad de México, Madrid, and Quito and write a short description about her experiences in each location.

**Native Speakers** Have Spanish-speaking students locate their native country and hometown on the map on pp. 434–435. You can also have them use a larger map for the entire class to see.

**Multiple Intelligences**

**Kinesthetic** Assign students to one of the six scenes. Ask students to expand the given dialog and role-play their scene. Allow each group to present to the entire class.

## Block Schedule

**Retention** After listening to the **En contexto**, have the students concentrate on the verbs being used in each paragraph. For more structured review, have them write the verbs on chart paper and compare the endings.

## Teaching Resource Options

**Print** 

Block Scheduling Copymasters
Unit 6 Resource Book
Video Activities, pp. 126–127
Videoscript, p. 128
Audioscript, p. 130

**Audiovisual**

OHT 199, 200, 201 (Quick Start)
Audio Program Cassette 18A / CD 18
Video Program Videotape 6, 25:28 / Videodisc 4B

Search Chapter 5, Play to end
U6E3, En vivo (Dialog)

**Technology**

*Intrigas y aventuras* CD-ROM, Disc 2

## Quick Start Review

Present perfect

Use OHT 201 or write on board: Name three things you have done this school year. You might consider using verbs such as: **aprender, ayudar, escribir, estudiar, leer.**

*Answers will vary.*

## Teaching Suggestions

### Presenting the Dialog

After reviewing the Listening Strategy on p. 436, have students discuss what Pablo reported to Cristina about his phone conversation with Isabel. What did Isabel say about her plans for the future?

# En vivo

## DIÁLOGO

Isabel

Pablo

Rosario

Cristina

**PARA ESCUCHAR** • **STRATEGY: LISTENING**

**Report what others said** Sometimes it is necessary to pass on to others what someone else said. Such a message usually starts with **dijo que.** Hearing accurately is important. What does Isabel report that Señor Montero said?

## ¡Buen viaje!

1 ► Isabel: Hola, Pablo. Soy Isabel.
Pablo: ¡Isabel! ¿Cómo estuvo la entrevista?
Isabel: Estuvo muy bien. Tengo mucha información. ¡Qué buena onda es el señor Montero!

5 ► Cristina: Cómo no. ¿Quieres que traiga también las cucharas?
Rosario: No, ya las tengo aquí. Pero gracias.

6 ► Pablo: Isabel llegará en cualquier momento. Ustedes se quedarán aquí, muy quietos. Isabel entrará, y todos le gritarán «¡Buen viaje!»
Rosario: Muy bien, capitán. ¿Y nos dirás qué hacer después?

7 ► Pablo: Lo siento. Es que quiero que todo salga bien. Isabel se siente un poco triste. ¡Chht! Es Isabel.
Todos: ¡Buen viaje!



## Classroom Community

**TPR** Have students act out Isabel's going-away party: the planning stage, Isabel's entrance, and the rest of the party.

**Paired Activity** Ask for 2 volunteers to portray Isabel and Pablo. Reenact their phone conversation and expand it to have Pablo ask more questions and Isabel give more information about her interview.

**Portfolio** Ask students to write a short description of Isabel's experiences in Ecuador. Ask them to explain why they would or would not like to travel there.

**Rubric: Writing**

| Criteria | Scale |
|---|---|
| Accuracy | 1 2 3 4 5 |
| Logical organization | 1 2 3 4 5 |
| Vocabulary use | 1 2 3 4 5 |

A = 13–15 pts.
B = 10–12 pts.
C = 7–9 pts.
D = 4–6 pts.
F = < 4 pts.

2 ▶ Isabel: Dijo que buscaban un periodista para un contrato de seis meses y que necesitaban una persona con experiencia en otra revista. Sabes, el puesto sería perfecto para mí.

3 ▶ Pablo: Isabel, tienes que graduarte del colegio primero. Regresa a casa y podemos hablar de tu futuro. ¿Dónde estás?
Isabel: Estoy en una cabina telefónica en la avenida Amazonas. Muy bien, voy para allá. Nos vemos pronto. Chao.

4 ▶ Pablo: Isabel está en la avenida Amazonas. Estará aquí muy pronto. ¡Vamos, tenemos prisa!
Rosario: Cristina, ¿me puedes hacer un favor? Ve a la cocina y trae el pastel. Lo pondremos aquí en la mesa.

8 ▶ Rosario: Isabel, ha sido un enorme placer llegar a conocerte. Te deseamos todo lo mejor.
Cristina: ¿Puedo ir a México a visitarte algún día?
Isabel: Me encantaría.

9 ▶ Pablo: Isabel, sabes que siempre tendrás aquí en Ecuador amigos que te quieren. ¡Espero que vuelvas pronto!
Rosario: Claro que va a volver. ¡Es una futura periodista que viajará por el mundo!

10 ▶ Isabel: Gracias… ay, gracias a todos. Los quiero muchísimo. Quién sabe, tal vez trabajaré aquí algún día como periodista. ¡Después de terminar con mis estudios, claro! Pero estoy segura de que regresaré a Ecuador.



## Teaching All Students

**Extra Help** Have students review the dialog and find examples of each of the following verb tenses: present, imperfect, preterite, future, conditional, present perfect, informal commands, and the present subjunctive.

**Native Speakers** Have Spanish speakers give examples of how they begin or end telephone conversations. Examples from this dialog include: **Hola, Pablo. Soy Isabel. Nos vemos pronto. Chao.**

### Multiple Intelligences

**Verbal** Ask students to predict Isabel's return home—who will meet her at the airport? Will she enroll in classes immediately? Will she begin working right away? How will her friends react to her arrival? etc.



### Video Synopsis

Isabel informs Pablo by telephone of the successful interview with Señor Montero. Meanwhile Pablo and his family are planning a surprise going-away party for Isabel. For a complete transcript of the video dialog, see p. 431B.

### Comprehension Questions

1. ¿Habla Isabel con su madre por teléfono? **(No)**
2. ¿Habla de la entrevista? **(Sí)**
3. ¿Piensa Pablo que sería buena idea aceptar el puesto ahora? **(No)**
4. ¿Está Isabel en la oficina del señor Montero o está en una cabina telefónica? **(en una cabina telefónica)**
5. ¿Sabe Isabel que van a hacer una fiesta o es una sorpresa para ella? **(Es una sorpresa.)**
6. ¿Llegará pronto Isabel o tardará mucho tiempo en llegar a la casa? **(Llegará pronto.)**
7. ¿Van a servir pastel o pasta? **(pastel)**
8. ¿Qué deben hacer todos cuando Isabel entra? **(Deben gritar «¡Buen viaje!»)**
9. ¿Qué quiere hacer Cristina? **(Quiere ir a México para visitar a Isabel.)**
10. ¿Qué va a terminar Isabel antes de trabajar como periodista? **(sus estudios)**

### Culture Highlights

- **AVENIDA AMAZONAS** in Quito is in the modern part of town. There are many sidewalk cafés and some of the best shopping in the city.

### Gestures

Ask students to pay particular attention to the gestures in frames 3, 6, 8, 9, and 10. Play the video without sound to see if the gestures "tell the story" without words. Play the audio version and see if students can add appropriate gestures.

### Block Schedule

**Retention** Have students make a list of all they know about each of the 4 speakers. Prompt them with questions: What is Isabel's report of Señor Montero? What is Pablo's response? (For additional activities, see **Block Scheduling Copymasters**.)

## Teaching Resource Options

**Print** 

Unit 6 Resource Book
Video Activities, pp. 126–127
Videoscript, p. 128
Audioscript, p. 130

**Audiovisual**

OHT 202 (Quick Start)
**Audio Program** Cassette 18A / CD 18
**Video Program** Videotape 6, 25:28 / Videodisc 4B

**Technology** 

*Intrigas y aventuras* **CD-ROM,** Disc 2

### Quick Start Review

Narrating in the past

Use OHT 202 or write on board: Have you ever had a surprise party? Describe what happened or use your imagination to write a 4–5 sentence story about a surprise party. You may organize your story in any way you wish or use the following questions as a starting point.

¿Quiénes asistieron?
¿Qué sirvieron?
¿Qué gritaron los invitados cuando entraste?
¿Te sorprendieron?

*Answers will vary.*

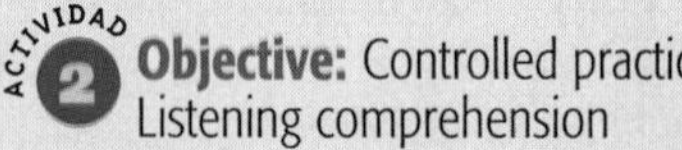

**Actividad 1 Objective:** Controlled practice
Listening comprehension/vocabulary

**Answers**

1. a, c
2. a, b
3. b, c
4. a, b

**Actividad 2 Objective:** Controlled practice
Listening comprehension

**Answers**

1. Isabel
2. Pablo
3. Isabel
4. Rosario, Cristina
5. Cristina
6. Rosario
7. Pablo
8. Isabel

# En acción
## VOCABULARIO Y GRAMÁTICA

**OBJECTIVES**
- Talk on the telephone
- Report on past, present, and future events
- Describe duties, people, and surroundings

### Actividad 1 ¿Lo comprendiste?

**Escuchar/Escribir** Escoge las respuestas correctas, según el diálogo. ¡Ojo! Algunas oraciones tienen más de una respuesta correcta.

1. Isabel…
   a. llamó a Pablo de la avenida Amazonas.
   b. dijo que el puesto sería perfecto para Pablo.
   c. regresará a Ecuador algún día.
2. Pablo…
   a. habló con Isabel por teléfono.
   b. planeó cómo sorprender a Isabel.
   c. dijo que Isabel llegaría a la casa en una hora.
3. Rosario…
   a. es la hija de Pablo.
   b. trajo las cucharas a la sala.
   c. dijo que Isabel viajaría por el mundo como periodista.
4. El señor Montero…
   a. le cayó bien a Isabel.
   b. hizo una entrevista con Isabel.
   c. buscaba un periodista para un contrato de nueve meses.

**TAMBIÉN SE DICE**

Después de la entrevista, Isabel regresa a la casa de Pablo. Aparte de **casa,** en Ecuador mucha gente usa la palabra **departamento** para referirse al **apartamento** o edificio donde vive. Otras palabras que puedes oír por el mundo de habla hispana incluyen **vivienda** y **piso.**

### Actividad 2 ¿Con quiénes hablaron?

**Escuchar** ¿Quiénes recibieron estos comentarios y preguntas: Isabel, Pablo, Rosario o Cristina? ¡Ojo! Puede ser más de una persona.

Isabel

Pablo

Rosario

Cristina

1. «¿Cómo estuvo la entrevista?»
2. «Sabes, el puesto sería perfecto para mí.»
3. «… tienes que graduarte del colegio primero.»
4. «¡Vamos, tenemos prisa!»
5. «Ve a la cocina y trae el pastel.»
6. «¿Quieres que traiga también las cucharas?»
7. «Muy bien, capitán.»
8. «¡Buen viaje!»



## Classroom Management

**Time-Savers** Provide the answers to **Actividades 1** and **2** for students to check their own work. Then have half the class work on **Actividad 3** and the other half work on **Actividad 4**. Have each group share their answers with the rest of the class.

**Peer Review/Peer Teaching** Have students work in groups of 3 to create and correct the sentences in **Actividad 4** in a round-robin format. S1 creates a sentence out loud; S2 writes it down; S3 corrects it and hands it back to S1 to confirm it. Then start again with another S1, S2, S3.

- *Review: Use the future tense*
- *Review: Use the conditional tense*
- *Report what someone said*

## ¿Nunca?

**Hablar/Escribir** Habla con un grupo de compañeros(as) sobre la frecuencia con que has hecho las siguientes actividades. Luego escribe un resumen.

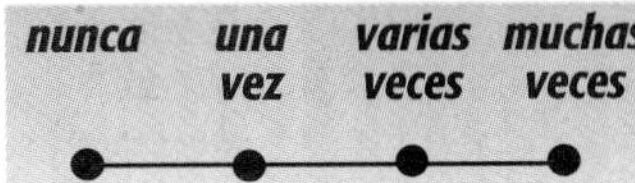


**modelo**

*esquiar en el agua*

**Tú:** *¿Han esquiado en el agua?*

**Compañero(a) 1:** *Sí, he esquiado en el agua una vez. ¿Y tú, Cristina?*

**Compañero(a) 2:** *No, nunca he esquiado...*

**Resumen:** *Andrew y yo hemos esquiado en el agua, pero Cristina todavía no ha esquiado en el agua.*

1. conocer a una persona famosa
2. escalar una montaña
3. ver una obra de teatro
4. manejar un carro
5. leer un buen libro
6. comprar un disco compacto en español
7. estudiar más de dos horas seguidas
8. ir a un partido de un equipo profesional

## ¿Quién lo ha hecho?

**Hablar/Escribir** Habla con un grupo de compañeros(as) para saber quiénes han hecho las siguientes actividades. Escribe los resultados, usando elementos de las cuatro columnas.

**modelo**

*Los padres de Emilia han visto la película* ***Casablanca.***

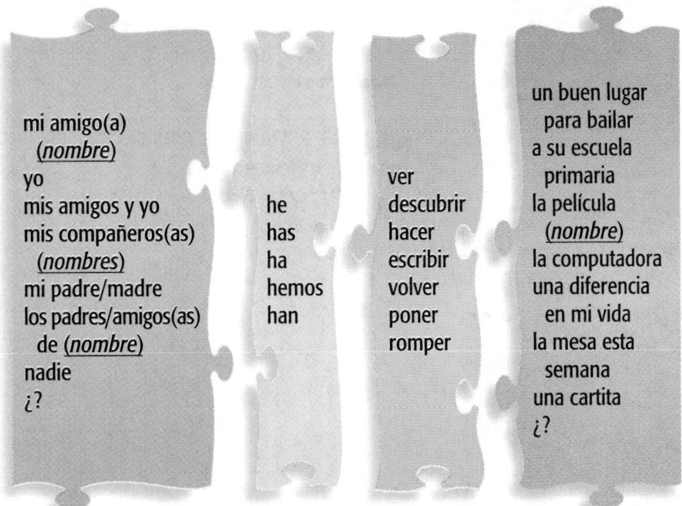

mi amigo(a) (nombre)
yo
mis amigos y yo
mis compañeros(as) (nombres)
mi padre/madre
los padres/amigos(as) de (nombre)
nadie
¿?
he
has
ha
hemos
han
ver
descubrir
hacer
escribir
volver
poner
romper
un buen lugar para bailar
a su escuela primaria
la película (nombre)
la computadora
una diferencia en mi vida
la mesa esta semana
una cartita
¿?






### Teaching Suggestions

Emphasize that **Actividad 2** asks to whom the quotes were directed, not who said them.

**Objective:** Transitional practice

Present perfect

### Answers

*Answers will vary.*

1. ¿Han conocido a una persona famosa? Sí, (No, nunca) he conocido a una persona famosa.
2. han escalado / he escalado
3. han visto / he visto
4. han manejado / he manejado
5. han leído / he leído
6. han comprado / he comprado
7. han estudiado / he estudiado
8. han ido / he ido

**Objective:** Transitional practice

Present perfect

*Answers will vary.*

## Teaching All Students

**Extra Help** Ask students to name things that they do and list them on the board or on an overhead transparency. Then have students rate how often they do the activities: 4 = **varias veces,** 3 = **muchas veces,** 2 = **una vez,** 1 = **nunca.** Discuss the results.

**Native Speakers** Expand on the **También se dice** note by having Spanish speakers discuss what they call a house, an apartment, or other living accommodation in Spanish.

**Multiple Intelligences**

**Visual** Give students a picture from a magazine, newspaper, etc., and ask them to describe the picture by using the present, past, or future tense.

## Block Schedule

**Variety** Survey the entire class to see who has done the activities in **Actividad 3**. Have students raise their hands if they have done each activity. Assign S1 to ask the question; S2 to count the raised hands; and S3 to state the results. Record the results on the board.

## Teaching Resource Options

**Print**
*Más práctica* Workbook PE, p. 157
*Cuaderno para hispanohablantes* PE, p. 155
Block Scheduling Copymasters
Unit 6 Resource Book
*Más práctica* Workbook TE, p. 107
*Cuaderno para hispanohablantes* TE, p. 113

**Audiovisual**
OHT 202 (Quick Start)

**Technology**
*Intrigas y aventuras* CD-ROM, Disc 2

## Quick Start Review

Present Perfect

Use OHT 202 or write on board: Complete the sentences to tell what the following people have accomplished this year. Use the present perfect.

1. Nuestro equipo ___ (ganar) el campeonato.
2. Carmen ___ (escribir) un cuento para niños.
3. Nosotros ___ (poner) un jardín en la entrada de la escuela.
4. Leo ___ (hacer) tres esculturas en la clase de arte.
5. Yo ___ (ver) los planetas con un telescopio.

**Answers**
1. ha ganado, 2. ha escrito, 3. hemos puesto, 4. ha hecho, 5. he visto.

ACTIVIDAD 5 **Objective:** Controlled practice Future tense

**Answers**
1. Ciro y José María serán obreros y no tendrán que ir a la universidad.
2. Yo seré veterinario(a) y tendré que ir a la universidad.
3. Tú serás taxista y no tendrás que ir a la universidad.
4. Andrés será cartero y no tendrá que ir a la universidad.

## The Future Tense

To talk about something that will happen in the future, you can use the **future tense.**

Remember that the endings you use are the same for **-ar**, **-er**, and **-ir** verbs.

| | | | |
|---|---|---|---|
| | | -é | -emos |
| **infinitive** | + | -ás | -éis |
| | | -á | -án |

—Estoy segura de que **regresaré** a Ecuador.
*I am sure that **I will return** to Ecuador.*

Rosario **traerá** los refrescos.
*Rosario **will bring** the soft drinks.*

Cristina **irá** a México algún día.
*Cristina **will go** to Mexico someday.*

Verbs that are irregular in the future all have some change to the **infinitive** before the **future endings** are added.

| Infinitive | Future Stem |
|---|---|
| decir | dir- |
| haber | habr- |
| hacer | har- |
| poder | podr- |
| poner | pondr- |
| querer | querr- |
| saber | sabr- |
| salir | saldr- |
| tener | tendr- |
| valer | valdr- |
| venir | vendr- |

—Isabel, sabes que siempre **tendrás** aquí en Ecuador amigos que te quieren.
*Isabel, you know that here in Ecuador **you will** always **have** friends who love you.*

—Muy bien, capitán. ¿Y nos **dirás** qué hacer después?
*Very good, captain. And **will you tell** us what to do after that?*

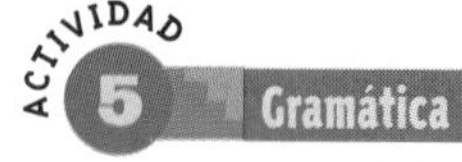

ACTIVIDAD 5 Gramática

### El futuro

**Escribir** Los amigos de Cristina están en la oficina de consejeros hablando de sus futuras profesiones. ¿Qué dicen? Di lo que serán según las fotos e indica si tendrán que ir a la universidad para serlo.

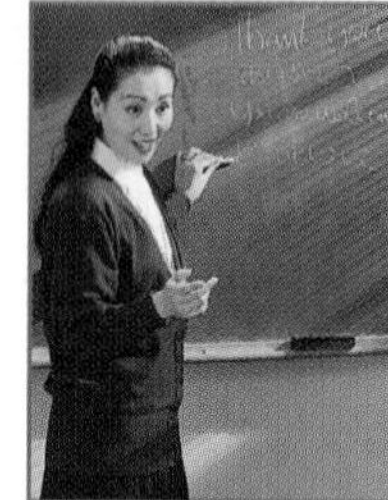
Carina

**modelo**
*Carina será profesora y tendrá que ir a la universidad.*

1. Ciro y José María

2. yo

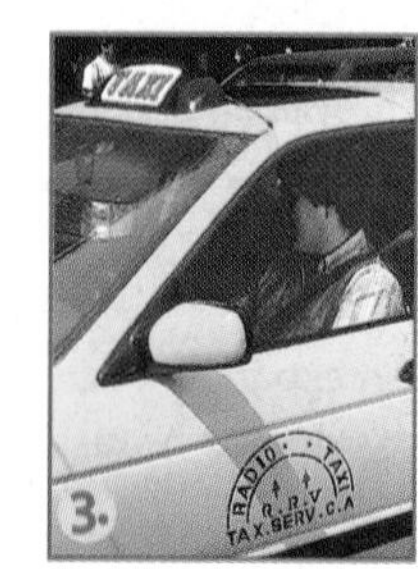

3. tú

4. Andrés



## Classroom Community

**Portfolio** Ask students to write about their plans for the weekend. Use the future tense.

**Rubric: Writing**

| Criteria | Scale |
|---|---|
| Accuracy | 1 2 3 4 5 |
| Logical organization | 1 2 3 4 5 |
| Vocabulary use | 1 2 3 4 5 |

A = 13–15 pts.
B = 10–12 pts.
C = 7–9 pts.
D = 4–6 pts.
F = < 4 pts.

**Paired Activity** Have students imagine they are attending their family reunion 20 years from now. Have them work in pairs to speculate about what members of their family will be doing then.

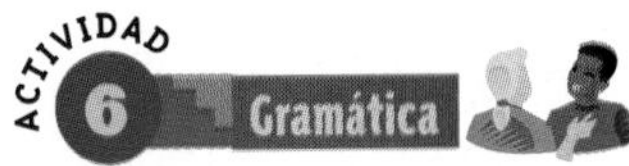


## La reunión

**Hablar/Escribir** Ya pasaron veinte años y estás en una reunión con tus compañeros(as) de la escuela secundaria. ¿Cómo será la vida de tus compañeros(as) y profesores(as) en ese tiempo? Compara tus respuestas con las de un(a) compañero(a).

modelo

*(nombre) y (nombre) (venir) de otro país para ir a la fiesta*

*Rebecca y Ryan vendrán de otro país para ir a la fiesta.*

1. (nombre) y (nombre) (ser) ricos
2. (nombre) (vivir) en una isla remota
3. (nombre) y (nombre) (estar) casados
4. (nombre) (tener) cinco o más hijos
5. (nombre) y (nombre) (contar) muchos chistes
6. (nombre de un/a profesor/a) (trabajar) en la escuela todavía
7. (nombre) (decir) mentiras sobre su vida
8. (nombre) (ser) político(a)
9. (nombre) (ser) estudiante de la universidad todavía
10. (nombre) (salir) en los periódicos

**MÁS PRÁCTICA** *cuaderno* p. 157

**PARA HISPANOHABLANTES** *cuaderno* p. 155

## ¿Qué harás durante el año que viene?

**Hablar** Haz una entrevista con un(a) compañero(a) de clase sobre sus planes para el año que viene. Luego preséntale sus planes a la clase.

modelo

**Tú:** *¿Serás voluntario(a) el año que viene?*

**Compañero(a):** *Sí, seré voluntario(a) para…*

### NOTA CULTURAL

**Guayaquil** tiene el puerto más grande y activo de la costa del Pacífico de Sudamérica y es el centro comercial del país. En los últimos años, por su proximidad a las playas ecuatorianas, se ha convertido también en un destino para los turistas.

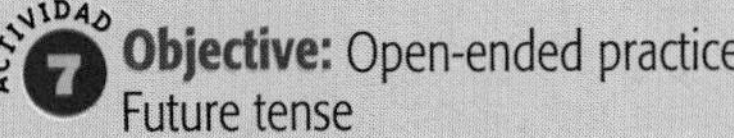


**Objective:** Controlled practice
Future tense

**Answers**
1. … serán ricos.
2. … vivirá en una isla remota.
3. … estarán casados.
4. … tendrá cinco o más hijos.
5. … contarán muchos chistes.
6. … trabajará en la escuela todavía.
7. … dirá mentiras sobre su vida.
8. … será político(a).
9. … será estudiante de la universidad todavía.
10. … saldrá en los periódicos.

ACTIVIDAD 7 **Objective:** Open-ended practice
Future tense

*Answers will vary.*

### Culture Highlights

● **GUAYAQUIL** is the largest city in Ecuador—even larger than Quito, the capital—with a population of over 2 million people. Guayaquil is a departure point to the Galapagos Islands. For more information, see p. 399.

### Teaching All Students

**Extra Help** Read the following sentences and have students change them to the future tense as they write them down. **Voy a solicitar el puesto. Tú vas a decir la verdad. Vamos a salir a las ocho. Ellos van a poner las llaves en la mesa. No va a haber tiempo suficiente.**

**Native Speakers** Have Spanish speakers interview another Spanish speaker and present his/her plans for the next year to the class.

**Multiple Intelligences**

**Visual** Ask students to draw a cartoon depicting themselves five years from now, with descriptive captions in Spanish.

**Logical/Mathematical** Ask students to create a timeline of the events that will occur over the next 15 years of their lives. Encourage them to be imaginative! Ask volunteers to share their timelines with the class.

### Block Schedule

**Variety** Ask students to write a paragraph about what they will be doing five years from now. Encourage them to be descriptive and creative. (For additional activities, see **Block Scheduling Copymasters**.)

## Teaching Resource Options

**Print** 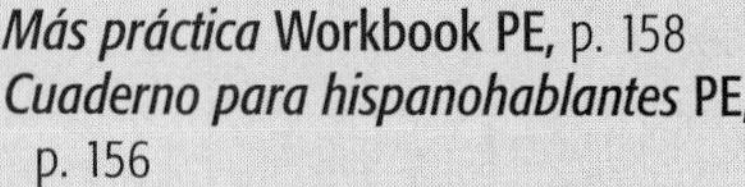

*Más práctica* Workbook PE, p. 158
*Cuaderno para hispanohablantes* PE, p. 156
Block Scheduling Copymasters
Unit 6 Resource Book
*Más práctica* Workbook TE, p. 108
*Cuaderno para hispanohablantes* TE, p. 114
Information Gap Activities, p. 119
Audioscript, p. 131

**Audiovisual**

OHT 202 (Quick Start)
Audio Program Cassette 18A / CD 18

**Technology**

*Intrigas y aventuras* CD-ROM, Disc 2

## Quick Start Review

Talking about professions

Use OHT 202 or write on board: Imagine you are a counselor preparing some charts to familiarize students with different professions. Fill in the chart with comments you will make to the students in each category.

ABOGADO(A)
educación:
capacitación:
habilidades:
sueldo:

*Answers will vary.*

## Teaching Suggestions
### Reviewing the Conditional Tense

- Refer students back to p. 370 where they learned to conjugate the conditional tense. Point out that the conditional uses the same irregular stems as the irregular future tense with the conditional endings.
- Be sure to conjugate a few verbs on the board for students, e.g., **escribir, ir, ser, tener,** etc.

ACTIVIDAD 8

## ¿En qué orden?

**Escuchar/Escribir** Isabel habla de sus planes para el futuro en la fiesta de despedida. Ponlos en orden y completa las oraciones.

**modelo**

*Primero, regresará a México.*

a. asistir a la universidad
b. volver a Ecuador
c. viajar a Texas
d. buscar un puesto de periodista
e. graduarse del colegio
f. regresar a México
g. tomar el sol en la playa

MÁS COMUNICACIÓN p. R19

## Juego

Cuando tú manejas hay algo que te dirá cuando debes detenerte y cuando tú continuarás.

¿Qué es?

## REPASO
### The Conditional Tense

You use the **conditional** to talk about what you *should, could,* or *would do,* and to describe what would happen under certain conditions.

To form the **conditional,** you add the **conditional endings** to the **infinitive**. The endings are the same for **-ar, -er,** and **-ir** verbs.

| | | | |
|---|---|---|---|
| | | -ía | -íamos |
| **infinitive** | + | -ías | -íais |
| | | -ía | -ían |

—Sabes, el puesto **sería** perfecto para mí.
*You know, the job **would be** perfect for me.*

Rosario dijo que Isabel **viajaría** por el mundo.
*Rosario said that Isabel **would travel** the world.*

The verbs that have **irregular stems** in the **future** have the same **irregular stems** in the **conditional.**

Algún día Isabel **podría** trabajar en Ecuador como periodista.
*Someday Isabel **could** work in Ecuador as a journalist.*

| Infinitive | Conditional Stem |
|---|---|
| **decir** | **dir-** |
| **haber** | **habr-** |
| **hacer** | **har-** |
| **poder** | **podr-** |
| **poner** | **pondr-** |
| **querer** | **querr-** |
| **saber** | **sabr-** |
| **salir** | **saldr-** |
| **tener** | **tendr-** |
| **valer** | **valdr-** |
| **venir** | **vendr-** |



## Classroom Community

**Paired Activitiy** Ask students to take turns changing the sentences in **Actividad 8** to the conditional tense, e.g., **Primero, regresaría a México.** Add more sentences as needed.

**Storytelling** Ask students to tell a chain story about what they would do on a class trip to Ecuador, using the conditional. Begin with **Si nosotros fuéramos a Ecuador…**

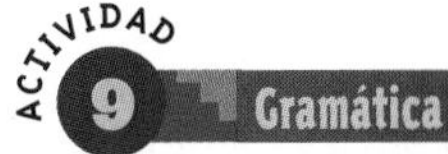

## Si vivieras en Ecuador...

**Escribir** Si vivieras en Ecuador, ¿cómo sería tu vida? Completa las oraciones con el condicional.

**modelo**

*nosotros: manejar (más / menos)*
*Nosotros manejaríamos menos.*

1. yo: tener (más / menos) clases
2. mis amigos: vivir (cerca / lejos) de mí
3. mi casa: ser (similar / muy diferente)
4. hacer (menos / más) calor
5. mis abuelos: (venir / no venir) con nosotros
6. mi madre: ir de compras en un (mercado / supermercado)
7. nosotros: esquiar (más / menos)
8. mi familia: hablar (español / inglés) todos los días

**MÁS PRÁCTICA** *cuaderno* pp. 157–158
**PARA HISPANOHABLANTES** *cuaderno* p. 156

## ¿Qué harías?

**Hablar** Pregúntales a tus compañeros(as) de clase si harían las siguientes cosas.

**modelo**

*ir a la Luna*
**Tú:** *¿Irías a la Luna?*
**Compañero(a) 1:** *Sí, (No, no) iría a la Luna.*
**Compañero(a) 2:** *Sí, (No, no)...*

1. comprar un carro de 30 mil dólares
2. darles dinero a los pobres
3. vivir en Australia
4. pintar tu cuarto de rojo
5. trabajar con animales feroces
6. comer caracoles *(snails)*
7. trabajar de maestro(a) en tu escuela
8. ser presidente de Estados Unidos

### NOTA CULTURAL

**Los festivales** La mayoría de los coloridos festivales que se celebran en Ecuador corresponden a los días festivos del calendario. En muchos de ellos se incorporan tradiciones indígenas relacionadas con la celebración del cambio de estaciones, cosechas *(harvests)* y otros eventos importantes del ciclo solar y de la vida en el campo.

**Objective:** Transitional practice
Listening comprehension/future tense

**Answers** (See script, TE p. 431B.)
*Answers will vary.*
Correct order: f, g, e, c, a, d, b

**Objective:** Controlled practice
Conditional tense

**Answers**
*Answers will vary.*
1. Yo tendría más/menos clases.
2. Mis amigos vivirían cerca/lejos de mí.
3. Mi casa sería similar/muy diferente.
4. Haría menos/más calor.
5. Mis abuelos (no) vendrían con nosotros.
6. Mi madre iría de compras en un mercado/supermercado.
7. Nosotros esquiaríamos más/menos.
8. Mi familia hablaría español/inglés todos los días.

**Objective:** Transitional practice
Conditional tense

**Answers**
1. ¿Comprarías un carro de 30 mil dólares?
2. ¿Les darías dinero a los pobres?
3. ¿Vivirías en Australia?
4. ¿Pintarías tu cuarto de rojo?
5. ¿Trabajarías con animales feroces?
6. ¿Comerías caracoles?
7. ¿Trabajarías de maestro(a) en tu escuela?
8. ¿Serías presidente de Estados Unidos?

## Cultural Highlight

**HOLIDAYS** Popular holidays in Ecuador include: All Soul's Day on November 2, Simón Bolívar's birthday on July 24, and Columbus Day on October 12. Corpus Christi in June is a traditional harvest festival in many highland towns. Most small towns and villages also have their own special festival days. Major festivals also occur during the week between Christmas and New Year's Day in Quito and Guayaquil.

## Juego

**Answer**
a. el semáforo

## Block Schedule

**Variety** As a variation of **Actividad 9**, use the locations from the other units of the textbook. **Si vivieras en San Juan (Madrid, Ciudad de México), ¿cómo sería tu vida?** (For additional activities, see **Block Scheduling Copymasters**.)

## Teaching All Students

**Extra Help** Have students write out the complete conjugations in the conditional tense of the verbs on p. 442. Have them keep these verb conjugations in their notebooks for reference and for future study.

**Native Speakers** Have Spanish speakers comment on the festivals or other local celebrations in their native country. What holidays are celebrated and how are they celebrated?

**Multiple Intelligences**
**Verbal** Ask students to complete the following: **Si pudiera viajar, yo...**
**Interpersonal** Extend **Actividad 10** by having students work in pairs to create additional things to ask their classmates. Encourage them to be daring and creative!

## Teaching Resource Options

**Print**

*Más práctica* Workbook PE, pp. 159–160
*Cuaderno para hispanohablantes* PE, pp. 157–158
Block Scheduling Copymasters
Unit 6 Resource Book
*Más práctica* Workbook TE, pp. 109–110
*Cuaderno para hispanohablantes* TE, pp. 115–116
Audioscript, p. 131

**Audiovisual**

OHT 203 (Quick Start)
Audio Program Cassette 18A / CD 18

**Technology**

*Intrigas y aventuras* CD-ROM, Disc 2

## Quick Start Review

Conditional, stating preferences

Use OHT 203 or write on board: If you could travel to any country featured in this book, which one would it be and why? You might consider using words like:

**Yo iría a... porque me gusta / me interesa / tengo ganas de...**

*Answers will vary.*

## Teaching Suggestions
### Presenting Reported Speech

Have students practice reporting speech by telling what their teacher said in their last class, or what their parents said to them before they left for school.

ACTIVIDAD 11 **Objective:** Open-ended practice Hypothesizing about the future

*Answers will vary.*

ACTIVIDAD 11

## Con tres deseos...

**Hablar/Escribir** Imagínate que tú, como Aladino, puedes pedir tres deseos. ¿Qué pedirías? Haz un cartel que explique lo que desearías y preséntaselo a un grupo de compañeros(as). (¡No puedes pedir más de tres deseos!)

- el medio ambiente
- personas famosas
- el bienestar
- la profesión perfecta
- los quehaceres
- soluciones a los problemas del mundo
- pasatiempos y viajes
- la salud
- ¿?

*modelo*

Con mi primer deseo... pediría un castillo. Sería muy grande y bonito. Habría una piscina y jardines elegantes. Los muebles serían cómodos y bonitos. El castillo sería mágico. Todos mis amigos y mi familia vivirían felices en mi castillo. Para mi segundo deseo...

GRAMÁTICA

## Reported Speech

In English when you "report" or summarize what someone has said or is saying, you say "He says that..." or "She said that..." In Spanish, to report what someone else has said, you use the verb **decir** followed by **que.**

When using the **present tense, dice que...,** the **second verb** tense is either the **present** or the **future**.

| | |
|---|---|
| Señor Montero says:<br>—Eres una candidata perfecta.<br>*You are a perfect candidate.* | Isabel **reports:**<br>—El señor Montero **dice que soy** una candidata perfecta.<br>*Señor Montero **says I am** a perfect candidate.* |
| Isabel says:<br>—Estaré allí muy pronto.<br>*I will be there very soon.* | Pablo **reports:**<br>—Isabel **dice que estará** aquí muy pronto.<br>*Isabel **says she will be** here very soon.* |

When using **dijo que...,** you use a **past tense** or the **conditional** for the information being reported.

| | |
|---|---|
| Isabel says:<br>—Estoy en la avenida Amazonas.<br>*I am on Amazonas Avenue.* | Pablo **reports:**<br>—**Dijo que estaba** en la avenida Amazonas.<br>***She said she was** on Amazonas Avenue.* |
| Isabel says:<br>—La entrevista estuvo muy bien.<br>*The interview went very well.* | Pablo **reports:**<br>—**Dijo que** la entrevista **estuvo** muy bien.<br>***She said** the interview **went** very well.* |
| Isabel says:<br>—Estaré allí muy pronto.<br>*I will be there very soon.* | Pablo **reports:**<br>—Isabel **dijo que estaría** aquí muy pronto.<br>*Isabel **said she would be** here very soon.* |

When you want to stress that the reported action is **still going on,** the second verb should be in the **present** tense:

**Dijo que buscan** periodistas.
*He said **they are looking for** reporters.*



## Classroom Community

**Game** Play the second game, **¿Hablar por teléfono?**, described in the **Ampliación** section on p. 387B.

**TPR** Have volunteers act out their wishes from **Actividad 11** for the class to identify.

**Group Activity** Test listening skills and practice reported speech with the following activity. Ask the class a question, such as **¿Cómo pasas el tiempo libre?** or **¿Qué hiciste este fin de semana?** Have another student report what was said. **Dice que...** or **Dijo que....** This could be done as a full-class activity or in small groups.

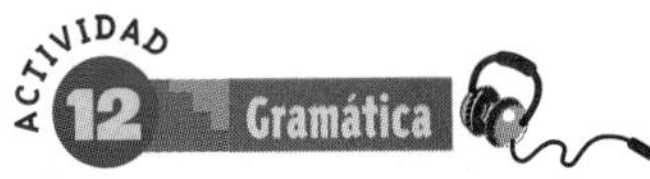

## Llamadas por teléfono

**Escuchar** Escucha estas llamadas de teléfono que se recibieron en la casa Ramírez. Luego escoge la letra que corresponde a cada llamada.

a.

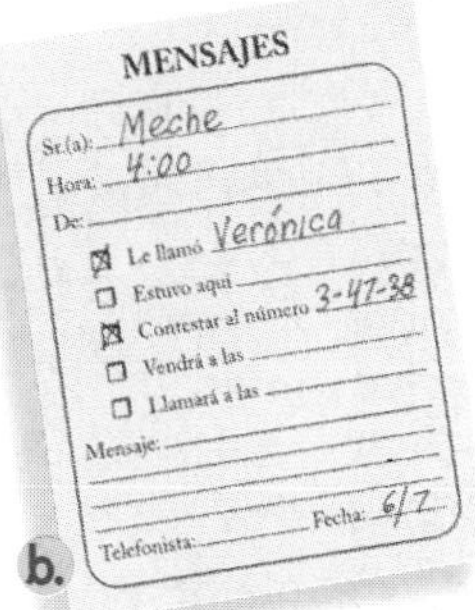
MENSAJES
Sr.(a): Meche
Hora: 4:00
De:
☒ Le llamó Verónica
☐ Estuvo aquí
☒ Contestar al número 3-47-38
☐ Vendrá a las
☐ Llamará a las
Mensaje:
Telefonista: Fecha: 6/7

b.

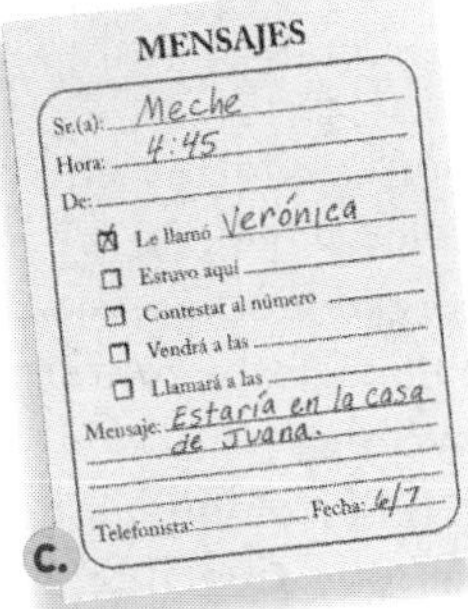
MENSAJES
Sr.(a): Meche
Hora: 4:45
De:
☒ Le llamó Verónica
☐ Estuvo aquí
☐ Contestar al número
☐ Vendrá a las
☐ Llamará a las
Mensaje: Estaría en la casa de Juana.
Telefonista: Fecha: 6/7

c.

d.

**MÁS PRÁCTICA** *cuaderno* pp. 159–160

**PARA HISPANOHABLANTES** *cuaderno* pp. 157–158

## La máquina contestadora

**Leer/Escribir** La señora Ramírez escucha los mensajes para su familia en la máquina contestadora. ¿Qué les dirá a todos?

**modelo**

*«Oye, soy Jaime. Quiero dejar un mensaje para Meche. Vamos a estudiar en la biblioteca a las tres.»*

*Meche, Jaime dijo que iban a estudiar en la biblioteca a las tres.*

1. «Muy buenas, habla José Calvo. Este mensaje es para el señor Antonio Ramírez. La reunión de mañana será a las dos.»
2. «Hola. Soy Chela. Quiero jugar con Juanita.»
3. «Oye, Meche. Habla Jaime otra vez. Cambiamos la hora de estudiar. Estudiaremos a las cuatro.»
4. «Soy Édgar Cruz y busco al señor Antonio Ramírez. Lo llamo más tarde.»
5. «Soy Mónica. Dígale a Meche que compré los boletos.»

**APOYO PARA ESTUDIAR**

### Reported speech

When you hear reported speech, you will often hear a shift of tenses in the second verb. Notice what happens:

**Isabel dice: «Estoy en la avenida Amazonas.»**
**Isabel dijo que estaba en la avenida Amazonas.**

**Pablo dice: «Isabel llegará en cualquier momento.»**
**Pablo dijo que Isabel llegaría en cualquier momento.**

What was reported may shift from present tense to imperfect, from future tense to conditional. Since reported speech in Spanish and English is similar, use the tense that best expresses your meaning.

### Teaching Suggestions

Record an answering machine message in Spanish and have students make a mock phone call to leave a message. Another student writes down the message and passes it along to the intended recipient.

**Objective:** Controlled practice
Listening comprehension/reported speech

**Answers** (See script, TE p. 431B.)

1. b
2. d
3. a
4. c

Actividad 13 **Objective:** Transitional practice
Reported speech

**Answers**

*Answers will vary.*

1. Antonio, José Calvo dijo que la reunión de mañana será a las dos.
2. Juanita, Chela dijo que quería jugar contigo.
3. Meche, Jaime dijo que cambiaron la hora de estudiar. Dijo que estudiarán a las cuatro.
4. Antonio, Édgar Cruz dijo que te llamaría más tarde.
5. Meche, Mónica dijo que compró los boletos.



## Teaching All Students

**Extra Help** Ask students to write 3–5 things that their parents usually tell them to do, e.g., **Mi mamá dice que yo necesito estudiar más.**

**Native Speakers** Ask Spanish speakers to create their own answering machine message in Spanish.

### Multiple Intelligences

**Verbal** Working in small groups, ask students to share how to prepare a favorite recipe using the expression **Dice que...**, e.g., How to make French toast: S1: **Se necesitan tres huevos, un poco de agua y por supuesto el pan.** S2: **Él/Ella dice que necesitamos...** Have them restate each step until the recipe is complete.

**Logical/Mathematical** Have students practice saying their own phone numbers or other important phone numbers in Spanish. Photocopy a telephone book page and distribute copies to the class and have them look up and recite the numbers for the names you give them.

## Block Schedule

**Variety** As a variation of **Actividad 11**, have students answer the question, **¿Dónde vivirías si pudieras tener la casa de tus sueños?** (For additional activities, see **Block Scheduling Copymasters.**)

## Teaching Resource Options

**Print** 

*Más práctica* Workbook PE, pp. 153–156
*Cuaderno para hispanohablantes* PE, pp. 153–154
Block Scheduling Copymasters
Unit 6 Resource Book
*Más práctica* Workbook TE, pp. 103–106
*Cuaderno para hispanohablantes* TE, pp. 111–112
Audioscript, pp. 132–133
Information Gap Activities, p. 120

**Audiovisual**

OHT 197, 197A, 203 (Quick Start)
Audio Program Cassette 18B / CD 18; (*Para hispanohablantes* Cassette 18B / CD 18)

**Technology** 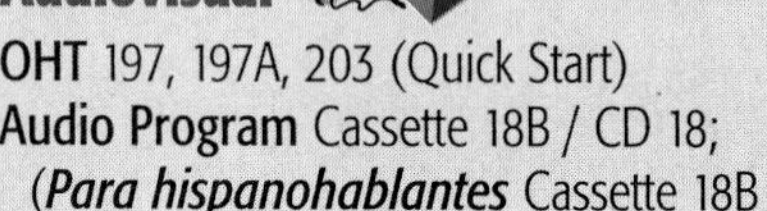

*Intrigas y aventuras* CD-ROM, Disc 2

## Quick Start Review

Talking about the future

Use OHT 203 or write on board: Answer the following question with 2–3 sentences in Spanish using the future tense. **¿Qué planes tienes para el futuro?**

*Answers will vary.*

## Teaching Suggestions

Have students take on the role of Isabel and write a thank-you note to Señor Montero for the interview.

Objective: Open-ended practice
Taking telephone messages

*Answers will vary.*

Objective: Open-ended practice
Review/Writing a thank-you note

*Answers will vary.*

## Los mensajes telefónicos

**Hablar/Escribir** Deja tres mensajes imaginarios en la máquina contestadora de un(a) compañero(a). Él (Ella) escribirá los mensajes. Luego combínense con otro grupo. Repite las llamadas para que ellos escojan el mensaje que corresponda a cada llamada. Cambien de papel.

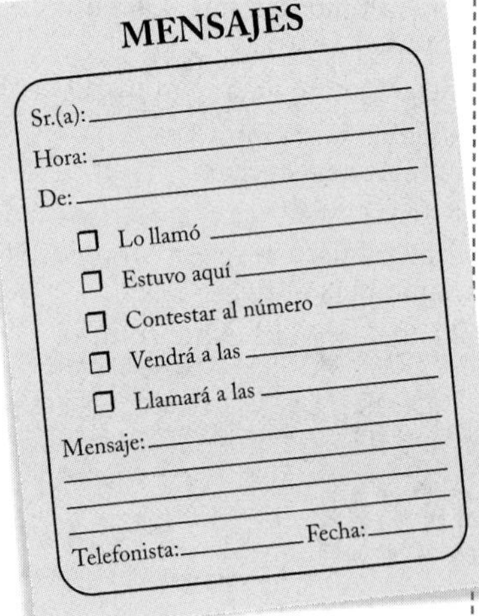
MENSAJES
Sr.(a): ____
Hora: ____
De: ____
☐ Lo llamó ____
☐ Estuvo aquí ____
☐ Contestar al número ____
☐ Vendrá a las ____
☐ Llamará a las ____
Mensaje: ____
Telefonista: ____ Fecha: ____

## Una cartita de agradecimiento

**Escribir** Escríbele una cartita de agradecimiento (*thanks*) a una persona de la clase de español o a otra persona que hable español. Puede ser estudiante o adulto… ¡hasta una persona famosa! Trata de usar todo lo que aprendiste este año. Describe lo que ha hecho esta persona que te haya ayudado o inspirado.

**Estimado(a) / Querido(a) (*nombre*):**

| | |
|---|---|
| **Gracias por…** | **Ojalá qué…** |
| **Es bueno que…** | **Tú has…** |
| **Eres…** | **Siempre…** |

**modelo**

Estimado David:

Gracias por ayudarme en la clase de español. Cuando no tenía papel, tú me lo dabas. Y cuando no comprendía la lección, me ayudabas. Siempre escuchabas cuando te contaba chistes malos… y te reías también.

Es bueno tener un amigo como tú en esta clase. Ha sido muy divertido. Eres muy paciente y simpático. Ojalá que tengas buena suerte el año que viene.

¡Hasta pronto!

Luis



## Classroom Community

**Portfolio** Have students write a thank-you note to Isabel or Francisco for helping them learn Spanish.

**Rubric: Writing**

| Criteria | Scale |
|---|---|
| Accuracy | 1 2 3 4 5 |
| Logical organization | 1 2 3 4 5 |
| Vocabulary use | 1 2 3 4 5 |

A = 13–15 pts.
B = 10–12 pts.
C = 7–9 pts.
D = 4–6 pts.
F = < 4 pts.

**Game** On separate pieces of paper, write short descriptions of famous people. On separate sheets list the names. Give some students the descriptions and others the names. Ask students to walk around the room, reading aloud their descriptions and names to find matches. Students who find their matches win.

## El salón de la fama

**PARA CONVERSAR**

**STRATEGY: SPEAKING**

**Persuade or convince others** It is not enough to assert that something is true. One must offer convincing proof. To justify your nominations to **«el salón de la fama»**, you can give reasons based on what they usually do, have done, or would do in certain circumstances. You can report what others have said or tell a story that illustrates your claim to their fame.

**Hablar/Escribir** Haz un «salón de la fama» para la clase de español. Escribe oraciones superlativas, escogiendo a un chico y a una chica para cada categoría. No uses el mismo nombre más de una vez. Luego forma un grupo de tres a cinco personas para votar y hacer una lista del grupo.

**modelo**

*alegre*

*Pablo y Marta son los estudiantes más alegres.*

1. sonrisa brillante
2. alto(a)
3. cómico(a)
4. pelo largo
5. pelo original
6. creativo(a)
7. trabajador(a)
8. divertido(a)
9. serio(a)
10. paciente
11. simpático(a)
12. ojos expresivos

## Ya se van

**Hablar/Escribir** Prepara una presentación de dos a cuatro minutos sobre tu vida y tus opiniones. Éste es tu «mensaje al mundo» antes de salir para las vacaciones. Practica tu presentación y finalmente, preséntasela a la clase. Expresa tu personalidad y diviértete.

Empieza con este formato y luego escoge las partes que te gusten más para incluir en tu presentación.

**A.** ¿Cómo eres?
1. Haz una descripción de tu personalidad.
2. Describe algo importante de tu niñez.

**B.** ¿Qué te importa?
1. Describe cómo pasas el tiempo.
2. Describe las cosas que te importan.
3. Describe lo que haces para ayudar a otros.

**C.** ¿Qué quieres para el futuro?
1. ¿Cuáles son tus metas personales?
2. ¿Qué planes tienes?
3. ¿Qué te gustaría hacer?

**D.** Un mensaje personal
1. ¿Qué quieres para los otros estudiantes?
2. ¿Qué vas a recordar siempre de tus experiencias en la escuela?

**MÁS COMUNICACIÓN** p. R19

### Refrán

**Querer es poder.**

En grupos pequeños hablen del significado del refrán. Luego identifiquen a unos personajes históricos que personifiquen este refrán. Hagan una lista de los esfuerzos que hizo cada persona para llegar a su meta. Léanle la lista a otro grupo para ver si ellos pueden identificar a los personajes.



**Actividad 16 Objective:** Open-ended practice
Review/Making superlative statements

*Answers will vary.*

**Actividad 17 Objective:** Open-ended practice
Review/Describing oneself

*Answers will vary.*

### Community Connection

Have students write a letter to students of the future. The letter will be placed in a time capsule for the next generation. They can answer the questions in **Actividad 17** and concentrate on how they want the next generation to remember this community.

### Quick Wrap-up

After the presentations for **Actividad 17**, have students form small groups and write a brief summary of what they have learned about their classmates. What are some of the things people have in common? Sample summary statements might be:

**Muchas personas van al cine en el tiempo libre.**

**La mayoría de los estudiantes quieren ir a la universidad.**

## Teaching All Students

**Extra Help** Have students first work in pairs to write out the answers to the questions in **Actividad 17**. Then have them choose only one question to answer in detail in their oral presentations.

**Native Speakers** Have Spanish-speaking students discuss the **refrán** on p. 447. What does it mean to them?

**Multiple Intelligences**

**Verbal** Ask students to pretend that they are running for the School Board in local elections next week. They should describe themselves in 2–3 sentences and propose *one* change they would implement in the school curriculum or facility.

### Block Schedule

**FunBreak** Have students create a **"salón de la fama"** for the teachers of the school. They may need to create a different list of adjectives and superlatives to describe them. (For additional activities, see **Block Scheduling Copymasters**.)

## Teaching Resource Options

**Print** 

*Cuaderno para hispanohablantes* PE, p. 154

Unit 6 Resource Book

*Cuaderno para hispanohablantes* TE, p. 112

Audioscript, p. 131

**Audiovisual**

OHT 203 (Quick Start)

Audio Program Cassette 18A / CD 18

## Quick Start Review

Talking about nature

Use OHT 203 or write on board: Name some of the images you see in the illustration on pages 448–449.

*Answers may include:*

un árbol, un pájaro, un pez, una piedra, un río

## Teaching Suggestions

- **Prereading** Begin by asking students what they know about poetry. Have them list the names of poets and poems they may already know in English on the board.
- **Reading** Have students take turns reading parts of the poem aloud. Then, as students read the poem again to themselves, have them pick out images and symbols that may have special meanings.
- **Strategy: Observe characteristics of poems** Have students find an example of each of the words listed: **verso, estrofa, imágenes, símbolo, ritmo, rima,** and **repetición**.
- **Post-Reading** Have students write a short paragraph on the title of the poem. Who is the **pasajero**? What is the **planeta**?

# En voces

## LECTURA

**PARA LEER**

**STRATEGY: READING**

**Observe characteristics of poems** A single line of poetry is called **un verso.** Several lines **(versos)** comprise a stanza **(una estrofa).** Words **(palabras)** form images **(imágenes)** that may also be symbols **(símbolos)** of other ideas. Like songs, poetry is meant to be performed aloud. So read it aloud and listen for rhythm **(ritmo),** rhyme **(rima),** and repetition **(repetición).**

## Sobre el autor

**Jorge Carrera Andrade** (1903–1978), poeta ecuatoriano, es considerado uno de los mejores poetas de lengua española del siglo XX. En sus poemas hay muchas imágenes inspiradas por la belleza natural de Ecuador.

Carrera Andrade viajó mucho durante su vida. Fue cónsul o embajador ecuatoriano en veinte países, entre ellos Estados Unidos, Francia y Japón. Escribió una autobiografía, *El volcán y el colibrí*[1], y varias antologías de poesía. También hizo traducciones de poesía francesa. En 1976 la Academia de la Lengua del Ecuador propuso su nombre para el Premio Nobel de Literatura. Ahora vas a leer unos versos de su poema «Hombre planetario».

[1] hummingbird



## Classroom Community

**Group Activity** Have students work together to write a list of the characteristics of a poem on the board.

**TPR** Ask students to act out the poem, using lots of expression and emotion. Choose one person for each stanza.

**Portfolio** Have students write a short paragraph about their personal reaction to the poem. How did it make them feel? What did they learn from reading it?

**Rubric: Writing**

| Criteria | Scale |
|---|---|
| Accuracy | 1 2 3 4 5 |
| Logical organization | 1 2 3 4 5 |
| Vocabulary use | 1 2 3 4 5 |

A = 13–15 pts.
B = 10–12 pts.
C = 7–9 pts.
D = 4–6 pts.
F = < 4 pts.

# «Pasajero del planeta»

*Eternidad, te busco en cada cosa:*
*en la piedra quemada por los siglos*
*en el árbol que muere y que renace,*
*en el río que corre*
*sin volver atrás nunca.*

............

*Eternidad, te busco en el minuto*
*disfrazado de[2] pájaro*
*pero que es gota[3] de agua*
*que cae y se renueva*
*sin extinguirse nunca.*
*Eternidad: tus signos me rodean[4]*
*mas yo soy transitorio,*
*un simple pasajero del planeta.*

............

*Soy hombre, mineral y planta a un tiempo,*
*relieve del planeta, pez del aire,*
*un ser terrestre en suma.*
*Árbol del Amazonas mis arterias,*
*mi frente de París, ojos del trópico,*
*mi lengua americana y española*

[2] disguised as [3] drop [4] surround

## ¿Comprendiste?

1. ¿Qué trabajos tuvo Jorge Carrera Andrade?
2. ¿De qué temas habla su poesía?
3. ¿Dónde busca el poeta la eternidad?
4. ¿Qué palabras indican que el poeta no es eterno?
5. ¿Cuáles son las cosas que son eternas, según el poeta?

## ¿Qué piensas?

1. ¿Cómo emplea el poeta las imágenes del cuerpo en los tres últimos versos? ¿Qué significan?
2. ¿Crees que esta poesía es optimista o pesimista? Explica.



## Culture Highlights

**ESCRITORES ECUATORIANOS** Other Ecuadorian writers include essayist Juan Montalvo (1832–1889) and novelists Juan León Mera (1832–1894), Jorge Icaza (1906–1978), and Adalberto Ortiz (1914– ).

## Critical Thinking

Ask students to study the poem excerpt for its structure. How many stanzas are there? Does it have rhythm, rhyme, or repetition?

## ¿Comprendiste?

### Answers

*Answers will vary.*

1. Fue poeta, consul y embajador.
2. Su poesía habla de la belleza natural de Ecuador.
3. Busca la eternidad en cada cosa.
4. Yo soy transitorio, un simple pasajero del planeta.
5. Piedras, árboles, ríos, pájaros, gota de agua, etc.

## Cross Cultural Connections

**Strategy** Make a brief historical timeline that covers the writing years of the author. Do any of the events seem to have influenced his poetry?

## Teaching All Students

**Extra Help** Ask students to locate 3 images they see in this poem. What do these images mean to them?

**Challenge** Ask students to search for other works by Jorge Carrera Andrade and share them with the class.

**Multiple Intelligences**

**Naturalist** Have students pick out the images from nature that are used in this poem. What message is the poet trying to give?

**Visual** Ask students to draw a picture of how they feel after reading the poem.

## Block Schedule

**Variety** In addition to reading this poem, the class might want to read other examples of poetry. Also, try giving the class the lyrics of a song to entice them to read the poetry of a song as well as listen to it.

## Teaching Resource Options

**Print**

*Cuaderno para hispanohablantes* PE, p. 160
Unit 6 Resource Book
*Cuaderno para hispanohablantes* TE, p. 118

**Audiovisual**

OHT 204 (Quick Start)
*Canciones* Cassette/CD

## Quick Start Review

Talking about professions

Use OHT 204 or write on board: **¿Cuáles son las ventajas y desventajas de ser músico?** Write a list of some of the advantages and disadvantages of being a musician.

**Ventajas** **Desventajas**

*Answers may include:*
Ventajas: Puedes ser muy creativo(a). No necesitas ir a una oficina cada día. Puedes viajar mucho. Conoces a muchas personas interesantes. Desventajas: Es posible que haya mucha competición. A veces es difícil encontrar trabajo y no tienes un sueldo regular.

## Teaching Suggestions
### Presenting En colores

- **Prereading** Have students brainstorm a list of traditional folk music from the U.S. (or different regions of the U.S.) What characteristics do these types of music have in common?
- **Strategy: Reflect on music** Have students listen to examples of Andean music and ask them to try to identify the instruments. If the record/CD/cassette label is available, have students read any explanations or list of musicians (and instruments).
- **Post-reading** Have students choose an instrument and write a brief description of it, based on the captions on p. 450.

# En colores
## CULTURA Y COMPARACIONES

### PARA CONOCERNOS

**STRATEGY: CONNECTING CULTURES**

**Reflect on music** How do you suppose the earliest musical instruments were made? How did they change over time? Identify groups that fuse old music and new instruments or vice versa. Present your thoughts in a time line, a mind-map, or a series of drawings. Show how a group like Ñanda Mañachi fits into your ideas and your visual.

La música andina tiene sus raíces[1] en la civilización de los incas y otras poblaciones indígenas que vivieron en los Andes hace más de mil años. Hoy este tipo de música es conocida en muchas partes del mundo. Hay grupos contemporáneos de Bolivia, Perú, Argentina, Chile y Ecuador que dan conciertos de música andina en Estados Unidos, Europa y Asia. La mayoría de estos grupos cantan en español, pero algunos también cantan en quechua, una lengua indígena de los Andes que todavía se habla en esa región. Y aunque usan guitarras eléctricas y equipo de sonido, los instrumentos originales son lo característico de su música.

[1] roots

**El instrumento de percusión que se usa más en la música andina es el bombo. El bombo tradicional se hace del tronco ahuecado (*hollowed out*) de un árbol y de la piel de llama.**

**La quena es uno de los instrumentos de viento más antiguos del mundo y una parte central de la música andina. Generalmente las quenas se hacen de caña.**

**La flauta de pan es otro instrumento de viento andino.**



## Classroom Community

**Portfolio** Have students write a paragraph in their journal describing their thoughts and opinions as they listen to samples of Andean music.

**Rubric: Writing**

| Criteria | Scale |
|---|---|
| Accuracy | 1 2 3 4 5 |
| Logical organization | 1 2 3 4 5 |
| Vocabulary use | 1 2 3 4 5 |

A = 13–15 pts.
B = 10–12 pts.
C = 7–9 pts.
D = 4–6 pts.
F = < 4 pts.

**Group Activity** Ask groups of students to make a list of musical instruments they know. Try to list them in English and in Spanish. Ask simple questions such as: **¿Cuántas personas tocan un instrumento musical? ¿A cuántas les gusta escuchar la música? ¿Cuál es el instrumento más popular?** etc.

# Música de las montañas

Se conoce el grupo musical Ñanda Mañachi por sus versiones modernas de la música andina. Aunque sus canciones se han pasado de una generación a otra, las palabras han cambiado. Y ahora estas palabras muestran los sentimientos de los músicos de hoy. Ésta es una de las razones principales por las que la música andina nunca se perdió.

## ¿Comprendiste?

1. ¿De qué países son los grupos de música andina?
2. ¿Cuáles son los nombres de algunos instrumentos andinos? ¿Son instrumentos de viento, de cuerda o de percusión?
3. ¿Puedes nombrar dos cosas sobre la música andina que muestren una influencia española?

## ¿Qué piensas?

1. ¿Cómo ha cambiado el uso de instrumentos en la música andina?
2. Se oye la música de los Andes en las calles y en los clubes de muchos países del mundo. ¿Por qué crees que ahora esta música es tan popular?

## Hazlo tú

Busca un casete o un disco compacto de música andina. Escoge una canción cantada en español que te guste y tócala para la clase. Con la clase, transcriban la letra de la canción.



## Reading Strategy

As students read the article, have them write a list of the cognates they recognize that will help them better comprehend the reading.

## Cross Cultural Connections

- Have students discuss any traditional folk music groups in the U.S. What instruments do they use? Are there any groups that fuse old music and new instruments or new music with old instruments? Who listens to this type of music? What kinds of messages do the songs have?
- Play a song from the *Canciones* Cassette/CD that is representative of another region of Central or South America and have students compare it to a recording of **música andina.**

## Cultural Highlight

**ÑANDA MAÑACHI** is a popular Andean music group. Others include: **Inca Son**, **Sukay**, **Inti Illimani**, and **Wayanay Inka**. Cassettes or CDs of these groups are available in the U.S.

## ¿Comprendiste?

### Answers

1. De Bolivia, Perú, Argentina, Chile y Ecuador.
2. La bomba, la quena, la flauta de pan y la guitarra. La bomba es de percusión; la quena y la flauta de pan son de viento; la guitarra es de cuerda.
3. Cantan en español y usan instrumentos de cuerda.

## Teaching All Students

**Extra Help** Bring music into class with copies of the accompanying lyrics. Play songs with very clear lyrics in Spanish so students can make connections with what they hear and what they read.

**Multiple Intelligences**

**Musical/Rhythmic** Play a short recording of **música andina**. Ask students to write about what they heard and identify the instruments being played.

## Block Schedule

**Change of Pace** Ask students to draw a Venn diagram comparing and contrasting **la música andina** and **la música rock**.

UNIDAD 6 Etapa 3
**Review**

### Teaching Resource Options

**Print**

*Cuaderno para hispanohablantes* PE, p. 159
Block Scheduling Copymasters
Unit 6 Resource Book
*Cuaderno para hispanohablantes* TE, p. 117
Information Gap Activities, pp. 121–122
Family Involvement, pp. 123–124
Multiple Choice Test Questions, pp. 176–178

**Audiovisual**

OHT 198, 198A, 204 (Quick Start)

**Technology**

Electronic Teacher Tools/Test Generator
*Intrigas y aventuras* CD-ROM, Disc 2

### Quick Start Review

Talking about the future

Use OHT 204 or write on board: **¿Qué harás durante el verano?** Using the future tense, write down some things that you will do this summer.

*Answers will vary.*

### Teaching Suggestions
**What Have Students Learned?**

Have students look at the "Now you can..." notes listed on the left side of pp. 452–453. To review material before doing the activities or taking the test, have them consult the "To review" notes.

# En uso
## REPASO Y MÁS COMUNICACIÓN

**OBJECTIVES**
- Talk on the telephone
- Report on past, present, and future events
- Describe duties, people, and surroundings

*Now you can...*
- talk on the telephone.

*To review*
- the future tense, see p. 440.

### ¿Qué pasará?

Isabel habla por teléfono con su madre sobre sus planes para el futuro. ¿Qué dice? ¿Lo crees tú?

**modelo**

*yo: volver a Ecuador en un año*
*Yo volveré a Ecuador en un año. (Lo creo. / No lo creo.)*

1. yo: asistir a la universidad en México
2. Pablo y yo: escribir otro artículo juntos
3. el señor Montero: ofrecerme un puesto en México
4. mis amigos mexicanos: invitarme a salir mucho
5. yo: trabajar para la empresa del señor Montero algún día
6. Cristina: venir a visitarme algún día
7. Pablo y su familia: mandarme cartas todas las semanas
8. tú: acompañarme a Ecuador la próxima vez
9. yo: ganar otro concurso
10. tú y yo: poder viajar por todo el mundo algún día

*Now you can...*
- describe duties, people, and surroundings.

*To review*
- the conditional tense, see p. 442.

### ¡Sería ideal!

Isabel habla por teléfono con su padre sobre el puesto con *Viajamundo*. Completa su descripción con el condicional de los verbos indicados.

El puesto con la revista *Viajamundo* __1__ (ser) perfecto para mí. Yo __2__ (tener) un contrato de seis meses con buenos beneficios. Así que __3__ (trabajar) aquí por seis meses y después __4__ (volver) a México. ¿Qué te parece?

Sí, sí... Yo sé que ustedes __5__ (estar) tristes, pero __6__ (poder) venir a visitarme, ¿no? Por favor, papá. En este puesto yo __7__ (ganar) 1.500.000 sucres al mes y __8__ (trabajar) en una oficina bonita con personas muy amables. Nosotros __9__ (escribir) artículos de viaje y __10__ (conocer) varios países de Sudamérica.



### Classroom Community

**Cooperative Learning** Assign students to the "Now you can..." and "To review" sections in the margins. Each group should prepare and present a short skit that reviews their objective, with each group member writing their own lines.

**Portfolio** As an extension of **Actividad 2**, have students write a paragraph in their journals about their ideal job. Remind them to use the conditional tense.

**Rubric: Writing**

| Criteria | Scale |
|---|---|
| Accuracy | 1 2 3 4 5 |
| Logical organization | 1 2 3 4 5 |
| Vocabulary use | 1 2 3 4 5 |

A = 13–15 pts.
B = 10–12 pts.
C = 7–9 pts.
D = 4–6 pts.
F = < 4 pts.

*Now you can...*
- report on past, present, and future events.

*To review*
- the conditional tense, see p. 442.
- reported speech, see p. 444.

## ACTIVIDAD 3 Alguien dijo...

Cristina habla por teléfono con una amiga sobre lo que le han dicho varias personas. ¿Qué dice?

**modelo**

*papá: él / ayudarme a buscar trabajo*

*Papá dijo que él me ayudaría a buscar trabajo.*

1. Isabel: ella / llamarme desde México el jueves
2. mamá: nosotras / hacer flan esta tarde
3. papá: él / venir a casa temprano hoy
4. la vecina: ella / enseñarme sus fotos de la fiesta
5. Diego: él y yo / ir al cine este fin de semana
6. mi prima: ellos / visitarnos en diciembre
7. Saúl: todos nuestros amigos / asistir al concierto el domingo
8. mamá: tú y yo / poder cocinar aquí mañana

*Now you can...*
- report on past, present, and future events.

*To review*
- reported speech, see p. 444.

## ACTIVIDAD 4 ¿Lo dijo Isabel?

Pablo habla con su familia sobre su conversación por teléfono con Isabel, pero no todo lo que dice es correcto. Di si la información es **cierta** o **falsa.** (Si te olvidas, lee otra vez el diálogo en las páginas 436 y 437.)

**modelo**

*«Estoy en una cabina telefónica en la avenida Amazonas.»*

*Isabel dijo que estaba en una cabina telefónica en la avenida Amazonas. (cierto)*

1. «La entrevista estuvo muy mala.»
2. «Tengo mucha información.»
3. «La compañía busca un periodista.»
4. «El contrato es de un año.»
5. «Ellos quieren una persona con experiencia.»
6. «Tendré que hacer otra entrevista mañana.»
7. «El señor Montero me cayó mal.»
8. «Estoy lista para volver a México.»
9. «La compañía me dará otro puesto en el futuro.»



### ACTIVIDAD 1 Answers

1. Yo asistiré a la universidad en México.
2. Pablo y yo escribiremos otro artículo juntos.
3. El señor Montero me ofrecerá un puesto en México.
4. Mis amigos mexicanos me invitarán a salir mucho.
5. Yo trabajaré para la empresa del señor Montero algún día.
6. Cristina vendrá a visitarme algún día.
7. Pablo y su familia me mandarán cartas todas las semanas.
8. Tú me acompañarás a Ecuador la próxima vez.
9. Yo ganaré otro concurso.
10. Tú y yo podremos viajar por todo el mundo algún día.

### ACTIVIDAD 2 Answers

1. sería
2. tendría
3. trabajaría
4. volvería
5. estarían
6. podrían
7. ganaría
8. trabajaría
9. escribiríamos
10. conoceríamos

### ACTIVIDAD 3 Answers

1. Isabel dijo que ella me llamaría desde México el jueves.
2. Mamá dijo que nosotras haríamos flan esta tarde.
3. Papá dijo que él vendría a casa temprano hoy.
4. La vecina dijo que ella me enseñaría sus fotos de la fiesta.
5. Diego dijo que él y yo iríamos al cine este fin de semana.
6. Mi prima dijo que ellos nos visitarían en diciembre.
7. Saúl dijo que todos nuestros amigos asistirían al concierto el domingo.
8. Mamá dijo que tú y yo podríamos cocinar aquí mañana.

### ACTIVIDAD 4 Answers

1. Isabel dijo que la entrevista estuvo muy mala. (falso)
2. ... tenía mucha información. (cierto)
3. ... la compañía buscaba un periodista. (cierto)
4. ... el contrato era de un año. (falso)
5. ... ellos querían una persona con experiencia. (cierto)
6. ... tendría que hacer otra entrevista mañana. (falso)
7. ... el señor Montero le cayó mal. (falso)
8. ... estaba lista para volver a México. (falso)
9. ... la compañía le daría otro puesto en el futuro. (falso)

## Teaching All Students

**Extra Help** Ask students to review one concept in the unit that they found more challenging or difficult.

**Native Speakers** Have Spanish speakers use the conditional to describe what their life would be like if they still lived in the country their family comes from. If they plan to live there someday, they should use the future tense.

**Multiple Intelligences**

**Interpersonal** Divide the class into three sections. Assign each group a tense—present, past, or future. Ask each group to prepare a dialog or skit about people and their community in the different verb tenses.

## Block Schedule

**Change of Pace** Ask students to write a list of responses to the question, **¿Cómo sería la escuela si todos hablaran español?** (For additional activities, see **Block Scheduling Copymasters.**)

## Teaching Resource Options

**Print**

Unit 6 Resource Book
- Audioscripts, pp. 133–134
- Cooperative Quizzes, pp. 135–136
- Etapa Exam, Forms A and B, pp. 137–146
- *Examen para hispanohablantes*, pp. 147–151
- Portfolio Assessment, pp. 152–153
- Unit 6 Comprehensive Test, pp. 154–161
- *Prueba comprensiva para hispanohablantes*, pp. 162–169
- Multiple Choice Test Questions, pp. 176–178
- Final Exam, pp. 179–186

**Audiovisual**

OHT 204 (Quick Start)
Audio Program Cassette 20B / CD 20;
(*Para hispanohablantes* Cassette 20B / CD 20)

**Technology**

Electronic Teacher Tools/Test Generator
www.mcdougallittell.com

## Quick Start Review

Describing people

Use OHT 204 or write on board: Imagine what your friend will be like in ten years. Write a short description in Spanish. You may use the following questions as a starting point.

¿Dónde vivirá? ¿Estará casado(a)? ¿Trabajará o estudiará? ¿Cómo pasará el tiempo? ¿Hará trabajo voluntario?

*Answers will vary.*

**Actividad 5 and Actividad 6**

**Rubric: Speaking**

| Criteria | Scale | |
|---|---|---|
| Fluency | 1 2 3 4 5 | A = 13–15 pts. |
| Vocabulary | 1 2 3 4 5 | B = 10–12 pts. |
| Pronunciation, rhythm | 1 2 3 4 5 | C = 7–9 pts. |
| | | D = 4–6 pts. |
| | | F = < 4 pts. |

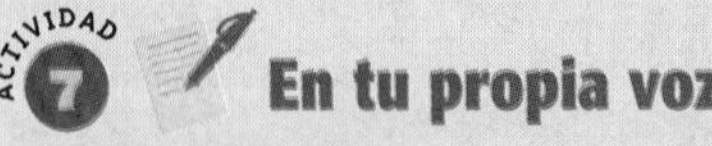

**Actividad 7 En tu propia voz**

**Rubric: Writing**

| Criteria | Scale | |
|---|---|---|
| Vocabulary use | 1 2 3 4 5 | A = 13–15 pts. |
| Accuracy | 1 2 3 4 5 | B = 10–12 pts. |
| Creativity, appearance | 1 2 3 4 5 | C = 7–9 pts. |
| | | D = 4–6 pts. |
| | | F = < 4 pts. |

## Actividad 5 Tu vida

**PARA CONVERSAR**

**STRATEGY: SPEAKING**

**Report on events** An important language skill is the ability to trace personal experiences across time. Think of ideas or events that took place in the past, that are happening now, or that may be part of your future. As you retell them, use expressions to place them in time (**hace dos años, en este momento, en cuatro años,** etc.), to sequence them (**antes, después, por fin,** etc.), and perhaps to contrast differences (**más / menos que...**)

Completa la tabla con tres eventos importantes de tu pasado, de tu presente y de tu futuro. Luego habla con un(a) compañero(a) sobre los eventos.

| El pasado | El presente | El futuro |
|---|---|---|
| 1. | 1. | 1. |
| 2. | 2. | 2. |
| 3. | 3. | 3. |

**modelo**

**Tú:** *¿Fuiste a la fiesta del club de español en septiembre?*

**Compañero(a):** *Sí, me encantó. Comí...*

## Actividad 6 ¿Quién llamó?

Imagínate que un personaje de este libro acaba de llamarte por teléfono. Explícales a tus compañeros(as) lo que dijo este personaje. Ellos(as) tienen que adivinar quién era.

**modelo**

**Tú:** *Dijo que ya no trabajaba como guía, pero que todavía le gustaba visitar los parques nacionales de su país.*

**Compañero(a) 1:** *¿Era Fernando?*

**Tú:** *No, no era Fernando.*

**Compañero(a) 2:** *¿Era Cecilia?*

**Tú:** *Sí, era Cecilia.*

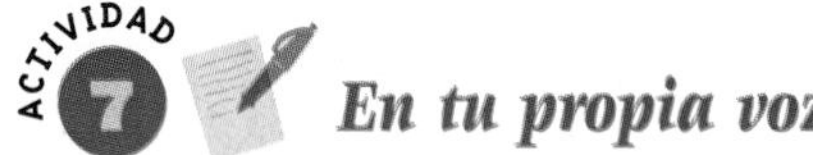

## Actividad 7 En tu propia voz

**ESCRITURA** Imagínate que han pasado diez años y que le escribes una carta a tu profesor(a) de español. ¿Qué le dices? Incluye la siguiente información.

- Preséntate y descríbete.
- Describe tu trabajo.
- Explica cómo te preparaste para tu trabajo.
- Describe tus planes para el futuro.
- Termina la carta con un mensaje personal.

## TÚ EN LA COMUNIDAD

**Judy** es una joven hispana que tiene diecisiete años y vive en Arkansas. Es estudiante del tercer año del colegio y es deportista. Le encanta jugar a todos los deportes, como el baloncesto, el golf y sobre todo el fútbol. Es la mejor jugadora de su equipo. Habla español en casa con su familia y cuando sale con sus amigos. Y claro, ¡le gusta hablar en español cuando juega al fútbol! ¿Cuándo y con quién te gusta hablar en español?



## Classroom Community

**Game** This may be a good time to play one of the games or do one of the projects described in the **Ampliación** section on p. 387B.

**Storytelling** Ask students to form a story based on the vocabulary by having each student add a sentence. You may even choose to write the story on a transparency for the visual learners.

**Learning Scenario** The Spanish 1 class wants to know what Spanish 2 is like. Have pairs summarize what they learned this year and tell what the highlights were for them. Ask volunteers to share their thoughts with a Spanish 1 class, if possible.

# En resumen

## YA SABES

### TALK ABOUT THE PRESENT

**The Simple Present Tense**

| | |
|---|---|
| Isabel, tienes que graduarte del colegio primero. | *Isabel, you have to graduate from high school first.* |
| Isabel está en la avenida Amazonas. | *Isabel is on Amazonas Avenue.* |

**Ir a + *infinitive***

| | |
|---|---|
| Claro que va a volver. | *Of course she is going to return.* |

### NARRATE IN THE PAST

**The Preterite Tense**

| | |
|---|---|
| ¿Cómo estuvo la entrevista? | *How was the interview?* |
| Estuvo muy bien. | *It went well.* |

**The Imperfect Tense**

| | |
|---|---|
| Dijo que buscaban un periodista para un contrato de seis meses y que necesitaban una persona con experiencia en otra revista. | *He said that they were looking for a journalist for a six-month contract and that they needed a person with experience on another magazine.* |

### GIVE COMMANDS

| | |
|---|---|
| Ve a la cocina y trae el pastel. | *Go to the kitchen and bring the cake.* |

### USE THE SUBJUNCTIVE

| | |
|---|---|
| ¿Quieres que traiga también las cucharas? | *Do you want me to bring the spoons, too?* |
| ¡Espero que vuelvas pronto! | *I hope you come back soon!* |

### TALK ABOUT THE FUTURE

**The Future Tense**

| | |
|---|---|
| Ustedes se quedarán aquí, muy quietos. | *You will stay here and be very quiet.* |
| Isabel, sabes que siempre tendrás aquí en Ecuador amigos que te quieren. | *Isabel, you know that here in Ecuador you will always have friends who love you.* |

**The Conditional Tense**

| | |
|---|---|
| Sabes, el puesto sería perfecto para mí. | *You know, the job would be perfect for me.* |
| Me encantaría. | *I would be delighted.* |

### TALK ABOUT WHAT YOU HAVE DONE

**The Present Perfect Tense**

| | |
|---|---|
| Isabel, ha sido un enorme placer llegar a conocerte. | *Isabel, it has been an enormous pleasure getting to know you.* |

### Juego

Lee y relee este trabalenguas en voz alta.

¿Cuántos cuentos cuentas?

Cuando cuentes cuentos,
cuenta cuántos cuentos cuentas,
porque si no cuentas
cuántos cuentos cuentas
nunca sabrás
cuántos cuentos sabes contar.

## Teaching All Students

**Extra Help** Have students review the earlier units to make a list of all the time expressions they have learned. Assign small groups to each of the 6 units and have them review the vocabulary lists at the end of each **Etapa.** Share the lists with the class.

**Native Speakers** Have Spanish speakers share additional tongue-twisters they may know. For example, **Pancha plancha con tres planchas. ¿Con cuántas planchas plancha Pancha?** Or repeat three times fast, **Un tigre, dos tigres, tres tigres.**

**Challenge** Ask students to write an idea for **Unidad 7** as a sequel to the text.

**Multiple Intelligences**

**Intrapersonal** Ask students to review past lessons and explain what they enjoyed most about learning Spanish this year.



### Teaching Note: En tu propia voz

**Writing Strategy** Before writing, have students read the questions in **Actividad 7** and brainstorm details of their life in ten years. Then they can organize their ideas in a letter.

### Teaching Suggestions
**Vocabulary Review**

Have students create their own sentences that fit in each category listed in the **En resumen** section.

### Juego

Have students give other tongue twisters they know in Spanish. Or have students create their own.

### Project: Reviewing Etapa 3

Assign the following out-of-class activities:

- Interview a Spanish speaker about his/her plans for the future.
- Research a festival celebration in Ecuador (via the Internet or the library).
- Find out about telephone etiquette in a Spanish-speaking country.
- Find more information on Andean music groups that might perform in the U.S.

**Extra Credit**

| | |
|---|---|
| Interview | 2 pts. |
| Festival in Ecuador | 2 pts. |
| Telephone etiquette | 2 pts. |
| Andean music | 2 pts. |

### Community Connections

Have students research local community and school teams to find out if there are Spanish-speaking players. Create a sports schedule in Spanish, including players' names and positions.

### Block Schedule

**Retention** Have students take the information on p. 455 and copy it into their notebooks in a format that they can understand and use. They should be encouraged to keep this page and constantly refer back to it in the future.

## Teaching Resource Options

**Print**

Block Scheduling Copymasters

**Audiovisual**

OHT GO1–GO5, 204 (Quick Start)

**Technology**

*Intrigas y aventuras* CD-ROM, Disc 2

www.mcdougallittell.com

## Quick Start Review

Talking about what you have done

Use OHT 204 or write on the board: Think of a job that you feel you might be qualified for and also suits your interests. Name the job and write down what makes you qualified for that job. Use the present perfect.

He estudiado...
He trabajado...

*Answers will vary.*

## Teaching Suggestions

### Prewriting

- Have students write a list of 10 positive attributes about themselves. Then prioritize the list into 3–5 things that would appeal to a potential employer. They should work on this independently first, then share their lists with a partner.
- Point out the **PASS** list at the beginning of the page: **P**urpose, **A**udience, **S**ubject, **S**tructure. This will be their PASS key to a well-structured writing assignment in every unit.

### Post-writing

- Have students exchange their letter drafts and offer suggestions to make their partner's letter as clear and concise as possible. Point out that cover letters should always be direct and concise.

UNIDAD 6

# En tu propia voz

ESCRITURA

## ¡A trabajar!

Your family is going to live in a Spanish-speaking country for a semester and you have the opportunity to work while you're there. Write a cover letter to the placement agency that offers positions to foreign students.

**Purpose:** Apply for a job
**Audience:** Potential employer
**Subject:** Employment
**Structure:** Cover letter

**PARA ESCRIBIR • STRATEGY: WRITING**

**State your message using a positive tone** Most formal letters are effective because the writer uses a positive, polite, and businesslike tone. Make your cover letter effective by beginning with a strong opening statement. Then provide details that make clear your value as an employee. Conclude by reemphasizing your enthusiasm.

## Modelo del estudiante

136 Berkeley Street
Boston, MA 02116
21 de abril

Sr. Ramón Unzueta, Director
Agencia de empleo Valdez
5 de Junio Nº 26
Quito, Ecuador

Estimado Sr. Unzueta:

Como mi familia y yo vamos a vivir en Quito entre septiembre y enero del año que viene, me interesa mucho solicitar empleo en la Escuela Primaria Bilingüe. Mi área de interés es la enseñanza de niños.

Me encanta mi trabajo en Boston como tutor de inglés para los niños recién llegados a Estados Unidos. Trabajo cinco horas a la semana en nuestro Centro de la Comunidad cerca de mi casa. Mis supervisores me han dicho que soy un maestro muy dedicado y que tengo un talento excepcional para enseñar.

Pienso estudiar la enseñanza en la universidad. La oportunidad de enseñarles inglés a los niños de Quito y prepararme para el futuro sería excelente. Además, podré entrenar a los estudiantes de mi ciudad para servir conmigo como tutores de inglés.

Atentamente,

Mark Benjamin
Mark Benjamin

The writer makes a **strong opening statement** about his interests.

The writer adds information about his **skills.**

Additional **examples** of employment qualifications are provided by the writer.

The final section shows the writer's enthusiasm and professional nature by **linking** the employment to his **future.**



## Classroom Community

**Paired Activity** Have students work with a partner to give each other advice on improving the opening and closing paragraph of their letters.

**Group Activity** Divide the class into 4 groups and have each group draft a cover letter from Isabel to Señor Montero in preparation for her interview.

**Portfolio** Have students save this cover letter for their portfolios. This letter may come to good use someday!

## Estrategias para escribir

### Antes de escribir...

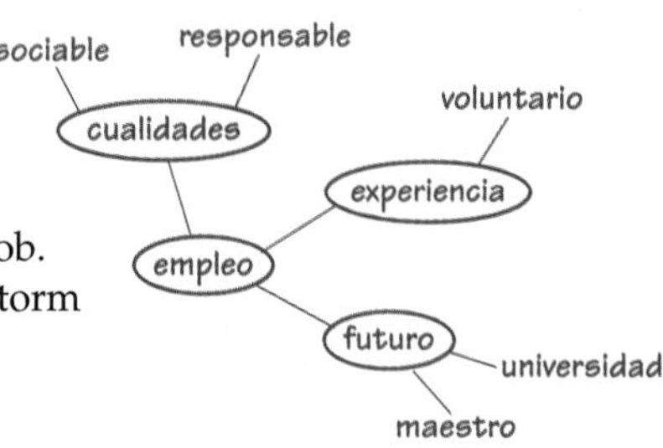


An impressive cover letter convinces your reader that you are an excellent, qualified candidate for a specific job. The letter gives clear examples of your suitability for the job. Before beginning the first draft of your cover letter, brainstorm the details using a word web like the one at the right.

### Revisiones

Share your draft with a partner. Then ask

- *Did I state my purpose simply and concisely?*
- *Did I provide necessary details about my background?*
- *Did I convey my message in a positive manner?*

You can revise your draft based on your partner's responses to these questions.

### La versión final

Before you write your final draft of your letter, carefully correct all errors using the proofreading symbols (p. 97). Look over your work with the following question in mind:

- *Did I remember special spellings of irregular past participles?*

**Try this:** Circle past participles used with *haber* and note if they are regular or irregular. Be sure you have used the correct forms.

Estimado Director:

Mi familia y yo vamos a vivir 6 meses en Caracas. seis
He leído mucho sobre los oportunidades que hay a allá. Me gustaría solicitar trabajo como ayudante en el Centro Bilingüe de Computación.

Tengo mucha experiencia con las computadoras. He usado muchos programas diferentes y he hacido hecho algunos websites. Estoy preparada para ayudar a los estudiantes del centro

 Share your writing on www.mcdougallittell.com



## Teaching All Students

**Extra Help** Review structures with students before writing:
- Use of future tense
- Use of conditional tense
- Use of preterite and imperfect tense
- Reported speech

**Native Speakers** Have Spanish speakers take on the role of the **Agencia de empleo** and respond to some of the students' cover letters.

### Multiple Intelligences

**Intrapersonal** Ask students to summarize those aspects of a given career that are important for success, e.g., **Para ser abogado tiene que conocer muchos casos históricos. Tiene que hablar bien y...**

## Supplementary Vocabulary

| | |
|---|---|
| **el saludo** | Letter greeting |
| **la despedida** | Closing of letter |
| **Sinceramente** | Sincerely, (formal closing in letter) |
| **Un saludo cordial** | (another formal letter closing) |

## Rubric: Writing

Let students know ahead of time which elements of their writing you will be evaluating. A global evaluation is more helpful to students than a correction of every mistake made. Consider the following in scoring compositions.

| | Sentences |
|---|---|
| 1 | Most not logical |
| 2 | Somewhat logical |
| 3 | In logical order |
| 4 | Logical with some flow |
| 5 | Flow purposefully |
| | **Details** |
| 1 | Few details |
| 2 | Some basic details |
| 3 | Sufficient basic details |
| 4 | Substantial details |
| 5 | Clear and vivid details |
| | **Organization** |
| 1 | Very little organization |
| 2 | Poorly organized |
| 3 | Some organization |
| 4 | Sufficiently organized |
| 5 | Strong organization |
| | **Accuracy** |
| 1 | Errors prevent comprehension |
| 2 | Comprehensible, yet many errors |
| 3 | Some spelling and agreement errors throughout |
| 4 | A few errors |
| 5 | Very few errors |

| Criteria | Scale | |
|---|---|---|
| Logical sentence order | 1 2 3 4 5 | A = 17–20 pts. |
| Clear and vivid detail | 1 2 3 4 5 | B = 13–16 pts. |
| Organization | 1 2 3 4 5 | C = 9–12 pts. |
| Accuracy | 1 2 3 4 5 | D = 5–8 pts. |
| | | F = < 5 pts. |

## Block Schedule

**Variation** Have students write up the job description for their ideal job in a Spanish-speaking country. Post these job descriptions and have students address their cover letters to the specific jobs. (For additional activities, see **Block Scheduling Copymasters.**)

# RECURSOS

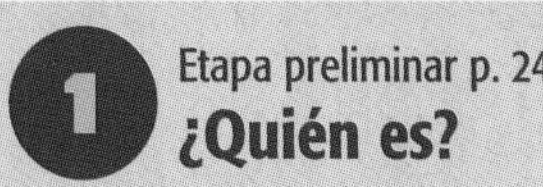

Etapa preliminar p. 24

## ¿Quién es?

**Estudiante A** Es necesario identificar a las personas de la foto para el periódico de la escuela. Si no sabes un nombre, describe a la persona. *(Hint: Describe the people to find out their names.)*

**modelo**

**Estudiante A:** *¿Quién es baja y tiene una camisa azul?*

**Estudiante B:** ...

**Estudiante B** Es necesario identificar a las personas de la foto para el periódico de la escuela. Si no sabes un nombre, describe a la persona. *(Hint: Describe the people to find out their names.)*

**modelo**

**Estudiante A:** *¿Quién es baja y tiene una camisa azul?*

**Estudiante B:** *Pilar es baja y tiene una camisa azul.*

**2** Etapa preliminar p. 24

## Información sobre estudiantes

**Estudiante A** Tu profesor(a) busca información sobre los estudiantes de la clase. Completa la tabla con tu compañero(a). *(Hint: Complete the chart.)*

**modelo**

**Estudiante A:** *¿A qué hora almuerza Meche?*

**Estudiante B:** *Ella almuerza a las...*

| nombre | edad | almuerzo | talento |
|---|---|---|---|
| Meche | 16 | | jugar al golf |
| Guillermo | | 11:15 | |
| tú | | | |
| tu compañero(a) | | | |

**Estudiante B** Tu profesor(a) busca información sobre los estudiantes de la clase. Completa la tabla con tu compañero(a). *(Hint: Complete the chart.)*

**modelo**

**Estudiante A:** *¿A qué hora almuerza Meche?*

**Estudiante B:** *Ella almuerza a las doce y diez.*

| nombre | edad | almuerzo | talento |
|---|---|---|---|
| Meche | | 12:10 | |
| Guillermo | 17 | | escribir |
| tú | | | |
| tu compañero(a) | | | |

MÁS COMUNICACIÓN



### 1 Answers

*Answers may vary. Suggested answers:*

A: María no es alta. Es morena y lleva gafas.
Jorge es guapo, alto, tiene pelo corto y es pelirrojo. Lleva una camisa roja.
Andrés es corto, un poco gordo y lleva gafas. Tiene un suéter verde y pantalones rojos.

B: Catalina es baja, bonita y castaña. Tiene pantalones amarillos.
Pilar es pequeña y bonita y tiene ojos negros. Lleva una camisa azul.
Alicia es alta, delgada y rubia. Tiene una camisa con rayas y pantalones morados.

### 2 Answers

A: ¿A qué hora almuerza Meche?
B: Almuerza a las doce y diez.
B: ¿Cuántos años tiene?
A: Tiene dieciséis años.
B: ¿Cuál es su talento?
A: Juega al golf.

A: ¿Cuántos años tiene Guillermo?
B: Tiene diecisiete años.
A: ¿Qué talento tiene?
A: Escribe.
B: ¿A qué hora almuerza Guillermo?
A: A las once y cuarto.

*Other answers will vary.*

## 3 Answers

A: ¿Almorzó Beatriz con amigos?
B: Sí, Beatriz almorzó con amigos.
A: ¿Jugó al ajedrez Beatriz?
B: Sí, Beatriz jugó al ajedrez.
A: ¿Tomó Beatriz un curso de natación?
B: Sí, Beatriz tomó un curso de natación.
A: ¿Bajó Beatriz un río en canoa?
B: Sí, Beatriz bajó un río en canoa.
A: ¿Tocó Beatriz el piano?
B: No, Beatriz no tocó el piano.

B: ¿Acampó Armando en las montañas?
A: Sí, Armando acampó en las montañas.
B: ¿Estudió Armando las artes marciales?
A: Sí, Armando estudió las artes marciales.
B: ¿Comió Armando en un restaurante?
A: Sí, Armando comió en un restaurante.
B: ¿Sacó fotos Armando?
A: Sí, Armando sacó fotos.
B: ¿Cantó Armando en el coro?
A: No, Armando no cantó en el coro.

## 4 Answers

*Answers may vary.*

1. A: ¿Fue Raquel al aeropuerto?
   B: Sí. Fue al aeropuerto.
2. A: ¿Fue Raquel a un café?
   B: No, no fue a un café.
3. A: ¿Fue Raquel a una piscina?
   B: No, no fue a una piscina.
4. A: ¿Fue Raquel a un campo de deportes?
   B: Sí. Fue a un campo de deportes.
5. A: ¿Fue Raquel al cine?
   B: Sí. Fue al cine.
6. A: ¿Fue Raquel a una clase de piano?
   B: Sí, fue a una clase de piano.
7. B: ¿Fue Juan a una agencia de viajes?
   A: Sí. Fue a una agencia de viajes.
8. B: ¿Fue Juan a las montañas?
   A: No, no fue a las montañas.
9. B: ¿Fue Juan a una fiesta?
   A: Sí. Fue a una fiesta.
10. B: ¿Fue Juan a otro país?
    A: Sí. Fue a otro país.
11. B: ¿Fue Juan a un río?
    A: No, no fue a un río.
12. B: ¿Fue Juan a la biblioteca?
    A: Sí. Fue a la biblioteca.

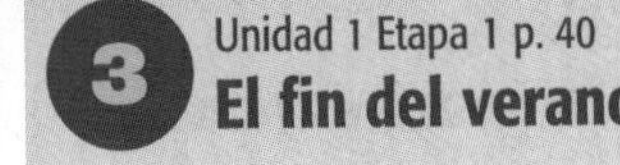

### 3 Unidad 1 Etapa 1 p. 40
## El fin del verano

**almorzar con amigos** **jugar al ajedrez**
**tocar el piano** **tomar un curso de natación**
**bajar un río en canoa**

**Estudiante A** Usa estas expresiones para preguntarle a tu compañero(a) qué hizo Beatriz. Luego usa los dibujos para contestar sus preguntas sobre las actividades de Armando. (*Hint: Ask what Beatriz did. Tell what Armando did.*)

**Estudiante B** Usa los dibujos para contestar las preguntas de tu compañero(a) sobre las actividades de Beatriz. Luego usa las expresiones para preguntarle a tu compañero(a) qué hizo Armando. (*Hint: Tell what Beatriz did. Ask what Armando did.*)

**acampar en las montañas** **cantar en el coro**
**sacar fotos** **estudiar las artes marciales**
**comer en un restaurante**

### 4 Unidad 1 Etapa 1 p. 43
## ¿Adónde?

**Estudiante A** Quieres saber adónde fue Raquel. Hazle preguntas a tu compañero(a) para saber adónde fue. Luego usa las pistas para contestar sus preguntas sobre las actividades de Juan. (*Hint: Ask if Raquel went to these places. Answer questions about Juan.*)

**modelo**

*el aeropuerto*
**Estudiante A:** *¿Fue Raquel al aeropuerto?*
**Estudiante B:** ...

**1.** el aeropuerto
**2.** un café
**3.** una piscina
**4.** un campo de deportes
**5.** el cine
**6.** una clase de piano

| Pistas sobre Juan | |
|---|---|
| Pasó por la aduana. | Buscó un libro. |
| Le dio información al agente. | Disfrutó con los amigos. |

**Estudiante B** Quieres saber adónde fue Juan, y tu compañero(a) quiere saber adónde fue Raquel. Usa las pistas para contestar sus preguntas, y hazle preguntas para saber adónde fue Juan. (*Hint: Answer questions about Raquel. Ask if Juan went to these places.*)

**modelo**

*el aeropuerto*
**Estudiante A:** *¿Fue Raquel al aeropuerto?*
**Estudiante B:** *Sí, fue al aeropuerto.*

| Pistas sobre Raquel | |
|---|---|
| Vio una película. | Jugó al fútbol. |
| Abordó un avión. | Tocó un instrumento musical. |

**7.** una agencia de viajes
**8.** las montañas
**9.** una fiesta
**10.** otro país
**11.** un río
**12.** la biblioteca



R2 RECURSOS Más comunicación

## 5 Unidad 1 Etapa 2 p. 60
## ¿Qué pide?

**Estudiante A** Tu compañero(a) sabe qué pide Sabrina cuando va al centro, y tú lo quieres saber. Hazle preguntas, usando las expresiones útiles, para aprender qué pide Sabrina. *(Hint: Ask about Sabrina.)*

| | |
|---|---|
| algo de beber | algo para leer |
| algo de comer | algo para manejar |
| algo para ponerse | algo para mirar |

**modelo**

**Estudiante A:** *¿Pide algo de beber?*

**Estudiante B:** ...

**Estudiante B** Tú sabes lo que pide Sabrina cuando va al centro, y tu compañero(a) lo quiere saber. Contesta las preguntas de tu compañero(a). *(Hint: Tell what Sabrina does.)*

**modelo**

**Estudiante A:** *¿Pide algo de beber?*

**Estudiante B:** *Sí, pide un refresco.*

| Lo que pide Sabrina | |
|---|---|
| unos zapatos | una hamburguesa |
| una novela | un refresco |
| una pintura | |

## 6 Unidad 1 Etapa 2 p. 65
## Una excursión

**Estudiante A** Sabes cuatro cosas que hicieron Iván y Linda ayer pero no sabes en qué orden las hicieron. En oraciones, dile a tu compañero(a) lo que sabes. Cambien de papel. Luego pongan en orden las ocho oraciones. Finalmente, completen la historia *(story)*. *(Hint: Make sentences and put them in order.)*

- (Venir) los padres de Linda a casa. (Ver) la vaca y…
- Linda (comprar) una escultura de una vaca.
- Ellos le (decir) a la vendedora: —Queremos una escultura.
- El sábado pasado, Linda (estar) sola en su casa, pensando en el arte.

**Estudiante B** Sabes cuatro cosas que hicieron Iván y Linda ayer pero no sabes en qué orden las hicieron. En oraciones, dile a tu compañero(a) lo que sabes. Cambien de papel. Luego pongan en orden las ocho oraciones. Finalmente, completen la historia *(story)*. *(Hint: Make sentences and put them in order.)*

- Ellos (llevar) la vaca a la casa de Linda.
- Iván y Linda (ir) a la tienda.
- (Llamar) a Iván por teléfono y lo (invitar) a ir de compras a la tienda de artesanía.
- De repente, (querer) comprar una escultura.



### 5 Answers

A: ¿Sabrina pide algo de beber?
B: Sí. Pide un refresco.
A: ¿Sabrina pide algo de comer?
B: Sí, pide una hamburguesa.
A: ¿Sabrina pide algo para ponerse?
B: Sí, pide zapatos.
A: ¿Sabrina pide algo para leer?
B: Sí, pide una novela.
A: ¿Sabrina pide algo para manejar?
B: No, no pide nada para manejar.
A: ¿Sabrina pide algo para mirar?
B: Sí, pide una pintura.

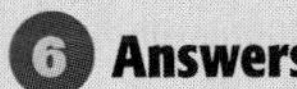

### 6 Answers

*Endings to story will vary.*

A:
- Vinieron los padres de Linda a casa. Vieron la vaca y … (8)
- Linda compró una escultura de una vaca. (6)
- Ellos le dijeron a la vendedora: –Queremos una escultura. (5)
- El sábado pasado, Linda estuvo sola en su casa, pensando en el arte. (1)

B:
- Ellos llevaron la vaca a la casa de Linda. (7)
- Iván y Linda fueron a la tienda. (3)
- Llamó a Iván por teléfono y lo invitó a ir de compras a la tienda de artesanía. (2)
- De repente, quisieron comprar una escultura. (4)

## 7 Answers

1. A: En Madrid, un señor capturó a un ladrón.
   B: El señor es español.
2. A: Unos pintores hicieron una exposición en Paris.
   B: Los pintores son franceses.
3. A: En Toronto, dos señoras rescataron a un niño.
   B: Las señoras son canadienses.
4. A: Todas las personas cantaron el himno nacional en Bogotá.
   B: Las personas son colombianas.
5. B: Unas escultoras mostraron sus obras en la galería de Boston.
   A: Las escultoras son estadounidenses.
6. B: Trajeron a las víctimas a un hospital de San Salvador.
   A: Las víctimas son salvadoreñas.
7. B: El actor empezó su carrera en Caracas.
   A: El actor es venezolano.
8. B: Susana de Silva abrió una tienda de arte en Buenos Aires.
   A: Susana es argentina.

## 8 Answers

1. A: Leí las noticias en el periódico.
   B: Prefiero leer las tiras cómicas.
2. A: Pedí un asiento de pasillo en el avión.
   B: Prefiero pedir un asiento de ventanilla.
3. A: Dormí en un hotel lujoso.
   B: Prefiero dormir en las montañas.
4. A: Competí en un juego de tenis.
   B: Prefiero ver un juego de tenis.
5. A: Comí la especialidad de la casa.
   B: Prefiero comer pollo asado.

MÁS COMUNICACIÓN

## 7 Unidad 1 Etapa 3 p. 81
## Unas nacionalidades

**Estudiante A** En voz alta, lee estas selecciones de las noticias. Tu compañero(a) va a decirte las nacionalidades de las personas mencionadas. *(Hint: Find out the nationalities of the people in the news.)*

salvadoreño(a) argentino(a) estadounidense venezolano(a)

**modelo**

**Estudiante A:** *Una princesa nació en Madrid.*

**Estudiante B:** *La princesa es…*

1. En Madrid, un señor capturó a un ladrón.
2. Unos pintores hicieron una exposición en París.
3. En Toronto, dos señoras rescataron a un niño.
4. Todas las personas cantaron el himno nacional en Bogotá.

**Estudiante B** Escucha las selecciones de las noticias y dile a tu compañero(a) las nacionalidades de las personas. Luego léele tus selecciones para que las adivine. *(Hint: Tell the nationalities of the people in the news.)*

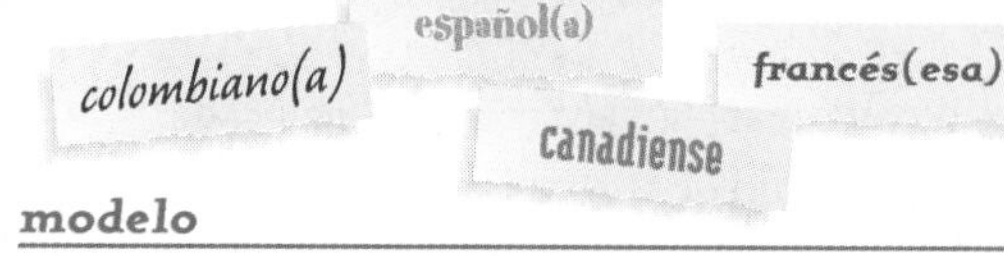


**modelo**

**Estudiante A:** *Una princesa nació en Madrid.*

**Estudiante B:** *La princesa es española.*

5. Unas escultoras mostraron sus obras en la galería de Boston.
6. Trajeron a las víctimas a un hospital de San Salvador.
7. El actor empezó su carrera en Caracas.
8. Susana de Silva abrió una tienda de arte en Buenos Aires.

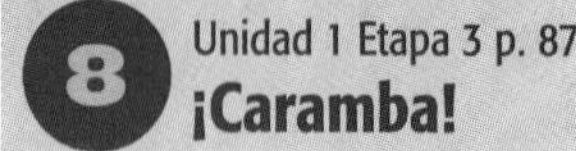

## 8 Unidad 1 Etapa 3 p. 87
## ¡Caramba!

**Estudiante A** Tú y tu compañero(a) hicieron actividades diferentes durante las vacaciones. Dile a tu compañero(a) qué hiciste. Tu compañero(a) va a decirte qué prefiere hacer. Cambien de papel. *(Hint: Tell what you did. Say what you like.)*

**modelo**

*leer las noticias en el periódico*

**Estudiante A:** *Leí las noticias en el periódico.*

**Estudiante B:** …

1. leer las noticias en el periódico
2. pedir un asiento de pasillo en el avión
3. dormir en un hotel lujoso
4. competir en un juego de tenis
5. comer la especialidad de la casa

**Estudiante B** Tú y tu compañero(a) hicieron actividades diferentes durante las vacaciones. Dile a tu compañero(a) qué hiciste. Tu compañero(a) va a decirte qué prefiere hacer. Cambien de papel. *(Hint: Tell what you did. Say what you like.)*

**modelo**

*leer las tiras cómicas*

**Estudiante A:** *Leí las noticias en el periódico.*

**Estudiante B:** *Prefiero leer las tiras cómicas.*

1. leer las tiras cómicas
2. pedir un asiento de ventanilla en el avión
3. dormir en las montañas
4. ver un juego de tenis
5. comer pollo asado

## 9 Unidad 2 Etapa 1 p. 112
## ¿Son tuyos o suyos?

**Estudiante A** Imagínate que unos objetos son tuyos y otros son de Jaime. Dale pistas a tu compañero(a) para que adivine de quiénes son. *(Hint: Give clues for your partner to guess to whom each object belongs.)*

**modelo**

**Estudiante A:** *A mí me gusta pelear.*

**Estudiante B:** *¿Los guantes son tuyos?*

**Estudiante A:** *Sí, son míos.*

| Los objetos de Jaime | Tus objetos |
|---|---|
| | |

**Estudiante B** Todos los objetos son de Jaime o de tu compañero(a). Adivina de quién son según las pistas de tu compañero(a). *(Hint: Guess who owns these objects according to your partner's clues.)*

**modelo**

**Estudiante A:** *A mí me gusta pelear.*

**Estudiante B:** *¿Los guantes son tuyos?*

**Estudiante A:** *...*

## 10 Unidad 2 Etapa 1 p. 115
## La niñez

**Estudiante A** Pregúntale a tu compañero(a) sobre la niñez de Nicolás utilizando los elementos de abajo. Luego contesta las preguntas de tu compañero(a). *(Hint: Take turns asking and answering questions.)*

**modelo**

*ser obediente*

**Estudiante A:** *¿Era obediente?*

**Estudiante B:** ...

1. ser obediente
2. saltar la cuerda
3. tener un muñeco de peluche preferido
4. portarse mal en clase

Ahora contesta las preguntas de tu compañero(a).

5. Era muy sociable.
6. No le gustaba estar en lugares altos.
7. Tenía miedo de los animales.
8. Era muy amable con su hermano.

**Estudiante B** Lee estas descripciones de la niñez de Nicolás y contesta las preguntas de tu compañero(a). Luego hazle tú otras preguntas. *(Hint: Take turns asking and answering questions.)*

**modelo**

*No hacía lo que decían sus padres.*

**Estudiante A:** *¿Era obediente?*

**Estudiante B:** *No, no era obediente. No hacía lo que decían sus padres.*

1. No hacía lo que decían sus padres.
2. Hacía actividades atléticas.
3. Siempre llevaba su gatito de peluche.
4. Escuchaba bien a sus maestros.

Ahora hazle otras preguntas a tu compañero(a).

5. ser tímido
6. trepar a los árboles
7. asustarse de los perros
8. pelearse con su hermano

MÁS COMUNICACIÓN



### 9 Answers

*Order of answers may vary.*

A: A mí me gusta dibujar.
B: ¿El dibujo es tuyo?
A: Sí, es mío.

A: A mí me gusta pelear.
B: ¿Los guantes son tuyos?
A: Sí, son míos.

A: A mí me gustan los juguetes.
B: ¿El muñeco de peluche es tuyo?
A: Sí, es mío.

A: A mí me gusta bajar un río en canoa.
B: ¿La canoa es tuya?
A: Sí, es mía.

A: A Jaime le gusta saltar la cuerda.
B: ¿La cuerda es suya?
A: Sí, es suya.

A: A Jaime le gusta correr.
B: ¿Los zapatos son suyos?
A: Sí, son suyos.

A: A Jaime le gusta sacar fotos.
B: ¿La cámara es suya?
A: Sí, es suya.

A: A Jaime le gusta leer.
B: ¿El libro es suyo?
A: Sí, es suyo.

### 10 Answers

1. A: ¿Era obediente?
   B: No, no era obediente. No hacía lo que decían sus padres.
2. A: ¿Saltaba la cuerda?
   B: Sí, saltaba la cuerda. Hacía actividades atléticas.
3. A: ¿Tenía un muñeco de peluche preferido?
   B: Sí, tenía un gatito de peluche. Siempre llevaba su gatito.
4. A: ¿Se portaba mal en clase?
   B: No, no se portaba mal en clase. Escuchaba bien a sus maestros.
5. B: ¿Era tímido?
   A: No, no era tímido. Era muy sociable.
6. B: ¿Trepaba a los árboles?
   A: No, no trepaba a los árboles. No le gustaba estar en lugares altos.
7. B: ¿Se asustaba de los perros?
   A: Sí, se asustaba de los perros. Tenía miedo de los animales.
8. B: ¿Se peleaba con su hermano?
   A: No, no se peleaba con su hermano. Era muy amable con su hermano.

## 11 Answers

*Order may vary.*

A: ¿Quién estaba rompiendo la piñata?
B: Carlota estaba rompiendo la piñata.
A: ¿Quienes estaban bailando?
B: Micaela y Jorge estaban bailando.
A: ¿Quienes estaban comiendo pizza?
B: Roberto y Bárbara estaban comiendo pizza.
A: ¿Quién estaba tocando la guitarra?
B: Diego estaba tocando la guitarra.
A: ¿Quién estaba cantando?
B: Dani estaba cantando.

## 12 Answers

1. A: ¿Qué hizo Roberto mientras Catalina jugaba al tenis?
   B: Mientras Catalina jugaba al tenis, Roberto ganó un premio.
2. A: ¿Qué hizo Roberto mientras Catalina buscaba información en Internet?
   B: Mientras Catalina buscaba información en Internet, Roberto tuvo un accidente.
3. A: ¿Qué hizo Roberto mientras Catalina hacía un experimento?
   B: Mientras Catalina hacía un experimento, Roberto vio el leopardo.
4. A: ¿Qué hizo Roberto mientras Catalina disfrutaba con las amigas?
   B: Mientras Catalina disfrutaba con las amigas, Roberto oyó música.
5. A: ¿Qué hizo Roberto mientras Catalina leía su libro?
   B: Mientras Catalina leía su libro, Roberto compró una limonada.



## 11 Unidad 2 Etapa 2 p. 132
## En la fiesta

**Estudiante A** Viste una foto de una fiesta y quieres saber qué estaban haciendo las personas. Pregúntale a tu compañero(a). *(**Hint:** Find out who was doing what.)*

**modelo**

**Estudiante A:** *¿Quién estaba tocando la guitarra?*

**Estudiante B:** …

**Estudiante B** Tu compañero(a) acaba de ver una foto de una fiesta tuya. Contesta las preguntas con los nombres de las personas. *(**Hint:** Identify who was doing each activity.)*

**modelo**

**Estudiante A:** *¿Quién estaba tocando la guitarra?*

**Estudiante B:** *Diego estaba tocando la guitarra.*

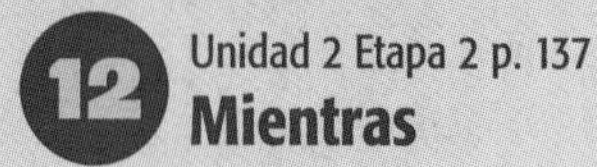

## 12 Unidad 2 Etapa 2 p. 137
## Mientras

**Estudiante A** Pregúntale a tu compañero(a) qué hizo Roberto mientras Catalina hacía otra cosa. *(**Hint:** Ask your partner what Roberto did.)*

**modelo**

*jugar al tenis*

**Estudiante A:** *¿Qué hizo Roberto mientras Catalina jugaba al tenis?*

**Estudiante B:** *Mientras Catalina jugaba al tenis, Roberto…*

1. jugar al tenis
2. buscar información en Internet
3. hacer un experimento
4. disfrutar con las amigas
5. leer su libro

**Estudiante B** Dile a tu compañero(a) qué hizo Roberto mientras Catalina hacía otra cosa. *(**Hint:** Tell your partner what Roberto did.)*

**modelo**

*ganar un premio*

**Estudiante A:** *¿Qué hizo Roberto mientras Catalina jugaba al tenis?*

**Estudiante B:** *Mientras Catalina jugaba al tenis, Roberto ganó un premio.*

1. ganar un premio
2. tener un accidente
3. ver el leopardo
4. oír música
5. comprar una limonada

## 13 Unidad 2 Etapa 3 p. 157
## ¿Lo hace?

**Estudiante A** Pregúntale a tu compañero(a) si a estas personas les gusta hacer las siguientes cosas. Luego haz una lista de sus respuestas. *(Hint: Ask your classmate about activities.)*

**modelo**

*Carlos / encantar / bailar*

**Estudiante A:** *¿A Carlos le encanta bailar?*

**Estudiante B:** …

1. Carlos / encantar / bailar
2. Ana / interesar / las noticias
3. Jorge / molestar / las matemáticas
4. Catalina / fascinar / los deportes
5. Juan / gustar / la carne

**Estudiante B** Tu compañero(a) te va a preguntar si a unas personas les gusta hacer varias cosas. Contesta las preguntas y responde con los verbos de abajo. Luego haz una lista de sus respuestas. *(Hint: Answer your classmate about activities.)*

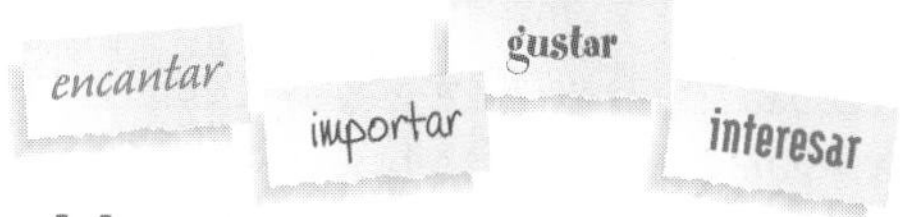


**modelo**

*Carlos va a la discoteca.*

**Estudiante A:** *¿A Carlos le encanta bailar?*

**Estudiante B:** *Sí, le encanta bailar. Le gusta ir a la discoteca.*

1. Carlos va a la discoteca.
2. Ana lee el periódico.
3. Jorge no estudia las matemáticas.
4. Catalina juega al fútbol.
5. Juan come muchas hamburguesas.

## 14 Unidad 2 Etapa 3 p. 159
## En tu restaurante preferido

**Estudiante A** Pregúntale a tu compañero(a) si le sirven estas comidas en el Restaurante Pirámide. *(Hint: Ask your partner if these foods are served.)*

**modelo**

**Estudiante A:** *¿Te sirven pollo asado en el restaurante?*

**Estudiante B:** …

| | sí | no |
|---|---|---|
| 1. pollo asado | | |
| 2. bistec | | |
| 3. pescado | | |
| 4. limonada | | |
| 5. leche | | |
| 6. plátanos | | |
| 7. papas fritas | | |
| 8. tacos | | |
| 9. pasta | | |
| 10. pan | | |

**Estudiante B** Dile a tu compañero(a) si te sirven varias comidas en el Restaurante Pirámide. *(Hint: Tell your partner if these foods are served.)*

**modelo**

**Estudiante A:** *¿Te sirven pollo asado en el restaurante?*

**Estudiante B:** *Sí, me lo sirven.*

### 13 Answers

*Answers may vary.*

1. A: ¿A Carlos le encanta bailar?
   B: Sí, le encanta bailar. Le gusta ir a la discoteca.
2. A: ¿A Ana le interesa las noticias?
   B: Sí, le interesa las noticias. Le encanta leer el periódico.
3. A: ¿A Jorge le molestan las matemáticas?
   B: Sí, le molestan las matemáticas. No le gusta estudiar las matemáticas.
4. A: ¿A Catalina le fascina los deportes?
   B: Sí, le fascina los deportes. Le interesa jugar al fútbol.
5. A: ¿A Juan le gusta la carne?
   B: Sí, le gusta la carne. Le encanta comer hamburguesas.

### 14 Answers

1. A: ¿Te sirven pollo asado en el restaurante?
   B: Sí, me lo sirven.
2. A: ¿Te sirven bistec en el restaurante?
   B: No, no me lo sirven.
3. A: ¿Te sirven pescado en el restaurante?
   B: Sí, me lo sirven.
4. A: ¿Te sirven limonada en el restaurante?
   B: No, no me la sirven.
5. A: ¿Te sirven leche en el restaurante?
   B: Sí, me la sirven.
6. A: ¿Te sirven plátanos en el restaurante?
   B: No, no me los sirven.
7. A: ¿Te sirven papas fritas en el restaurante?
   B: No, no me las sirven.
8. A: ¿Te sirven tacos en el restaurante?
   B: Sí, me los sirven.
9. A: ¿Te sirven pasta en el restaurante?
   B: Sí, me la sirven.
10. A: ¿Te sirven pan en el restaurante?
    B: Sí, me lo sirven.

## 15 Answers

1. A: ¿Se está maquillando María?
   B: No, necesita maquillarse.
2. A: ¿Se está arreglando María?
   B: No, necesita arreglarse.
3. A: ¿Se está lavando María?
   B: Sí, está lavandose.
4. A: ¿Se está secando el pelo María?
   B: No, necesita secarse el pelo.
5. A: ¿Se está mirando María?
   B: Sí, está mirandose.

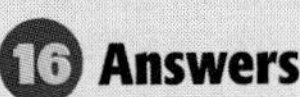

## 16 Answers

*Answers will vary.*

MÁS COMUNICACIÓN

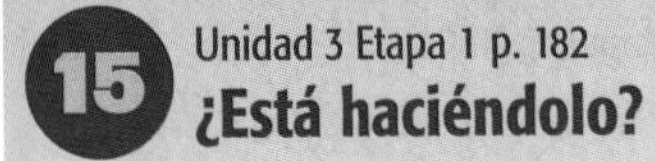

## 15 Unidad 3 Etapa 1 p. 182 ¿Está haciéndolo?

**Estudiante A** María se prepara para la escuela. Pregúntale a tu compañero(a) si ella necesita hacer las siguientes actividades o si ya está haciéndolas. *(Hint: Find out if María is doing or needs to do the following activities.)*

**modelo**

*maquillarse*

**Estudiante A:** *¿Se está maquillando María?*

**Estudiante B:** ...

1. maquillarse
2. arreglarse
3. lavarse
4. secarse el pelo
5. mirarse

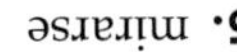

**Estudiante B** María se prepara para la escuela. Dile a tu compañero(a) si María necesita hacer las actividades mencionadas o si ya está haciéndolas. *(Hint: Tell your partner if María is doing or needs to do certain things.)*

**modelo**

*maquillarse*

**Estudiante A:** *¿Se está maquillando María?*

**Estudiante B:** *No. Necesita maquillarse.*

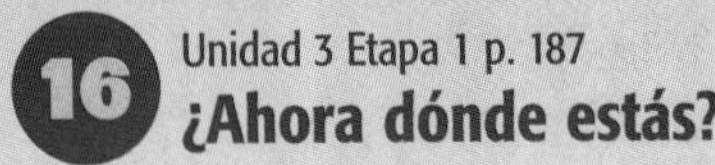

## 16 Unidad 3 Etapa 1 p. 187 ¿Ahora dónde estás?

**Estudiante A** Una persona famosa viene a tu escuela. Dale direcciones a las siguientes partes de la escuela. Tu compañero(a) (la persona famosa) va a adivinar el lugar. Cambien de papel. *(Hint: Use **usted** commands to give directions to the following places in your school. Identify places according to your partner's directions.)*

**modelo**

*la clase de arte*

**Estudiante A:** *Salga de la clase y doble a la izquierda. Camine hasta el auditorio, doble a la derecha y busque la próxima puerta.*

**Persona famosa:** *Es la clase de arte.*

1. el gimnasio
2. el auditorio
3. la biblioteca
4. el laboratorio de ciencias

**Estudiante B** Identifica los lugares de la lista de tu compañero(a) según sus direcciones. Luego cambien de papel y dale direcciones para ir a las siguientes partes de la escuela. *(Hint: Identify places in your school according to your partner's directions. Use **usted** commands to give directions to the places on your list.)*

**modelo**

*la clase de arte*

**Estudiante A:** *Salga de la clase y doble a la izquierda. Camine hasta el auditorio, doble a la derecha y busque la próxima puerta.*

**Persona famosa:** *Es la clase de arte.*

5. la cafetería
6. el estadio
7. la oficina
8. el salón de computadoras



R8 RECURSOS Más comunicación

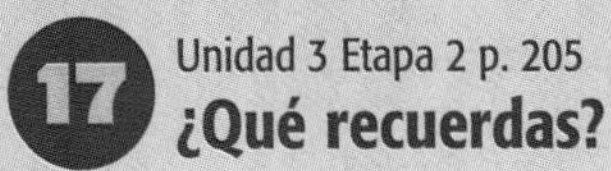

## 17 Unidad 3 Etapa 2 p. 205
## ¿Qué recuerdas?

**Estudiante A** Dile a tu compañero(a) que tiene que hacer las siguientes actividades. Él (Ella) te va a decir si es necesario hacerlas según el dibujo. *(Hint: Use tú commands to tell your partner to do these chores.)*

**modelo**

*barrer el piso*

**Estudiante A:** *Barre el piso.*

**Estudiante B:** …

1. barrer el piso
2. poner la mesa
3. sacar la basura
4. lavar los platos
5. quitar la mesa
6. pasar la aspiradora

**Estudiante B** Dile a tu compañero(a) si es necesario hacer las actividades mencionadas según el dibujo. *(Hint: Decide if the chores should be done.)*

**modelo**

**Estudiante A:** *Barre el piso.*

**Estudiante B:** *No es necesario.*

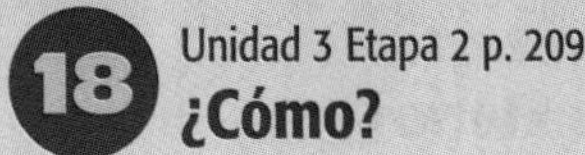

## 18 Unidad 3 Etapa 2 p. 209
## ¿Cómo?

**Estudiante A** ¿Cómo son estas personas en casa? Pregúntale a tu compañero(a) qué hacen, usando adverbios con **-mente.** *(Hint: Ask what people do.)*

**modelo**

*Juana / inmediatamente*

**Estudiante A:** *En casa, ¿qué hace Juana inmediatamente?*

**Estudiante B:** …

1. Juana / inmediatamente
2. Jorge / rápidamente
3. Catalina / tranquilamente
4. Andrés / normalmente
5. Alicia / lentamente
6. David / difícilmente

**Estudiante B** Contesta las preguntas de tu compañero(a). *(Hint: Tell your partner what people do.)*

**modelo**

*hacer la tarea*

**Estudiante A:** *En casa, ¿qué hace Juana inmediatamente?*

**Estudiante B:** *Hace la tarea inmediatamente.*

1. hacer la tarea
2. estirarse
3. hacer la cama
4. leer el periódico
5. lavar los platos
6. acostarse temprano

MÁS COMUNICACIÓN

### 17 Answers

1. A: Barre el piso.
   B: No es necesario. (Sí. Es necesario.)
2. A: Pon la mesa.
   B: Sí. Es necesario.
3. A: Saca la basura.
   B: No es necesario.
4. A: Lava los platos.
   B: Sí. Es necesario.
5. A: Quita la mesa.
   B: No es necesario.
6. A: Pasa la aspiradora.
   B: Sí. Es necesario. (No es necesario.)

### 18 Answers

1. A: En casa, ¿qué hace Juana inmediatamente?
   B: Hace la tarea inmediatamente.
2. A: En casa, ¿qué hace Jorge rápidamente?
   B: Se estira rápidamente.
3. A: En casa, ¿qué hace Catalina tranquilamente?
   B: Hace la cama tranquilamente.
4. A: En casa, ¿qué hace Andrés normalmente?
   B: Lee el periódico normalmente.
5. A: En casa, ¿qué hace Alicia lentamente?
   B: Lava los platos lentamente.
6. A: En casa, ¿qué hace David difícilmente?
   B: Se acuesta temprano difícilmente.

## 19 Answers

*Order may vary.*

A: ¿Cuánto tiempo hace que Andrés se lastimó?
B: Hace un año que se lastimó.
A: ¿Cuánto tiempo hace que Pedro está resfriado?
B: Hace seis días que está resfriado.
A: ¿Cuánto tiempo hace que Paco tiene tos?
B: Hace una semana que tiene tos.

B: ¿Cuánto tiempo hace que a María le duelen los dientes?
A: Hace dos meses que le duelen los dientes.
B: ¿Cuánto tiempo hace que Julia se cortó el dedo?
A: Hace tres horas que se cortó el dedo.
B: ¿Cuánto tiempo hace que Pepa lleva yeso?
A: Hace cinco semanas que lleva yeso.

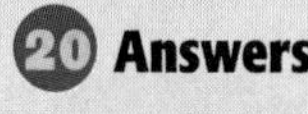

## Answers

*Answers will vary.*

MÁS COMUNICACIÓN

## 19 Unidad 3 Etapa 3 p. 227
## En el consultorio

**Estudiante A** Una enfermera escribió la información en la tabla de abajo. ¿Cuánto tiempo hace que les afectan las situaciones a las personas? Habla con tu compañero(a) para completar la tabla. *(Hint: Complete the chart.)*

**modelo**

**Estudiante A:** *¿Cuánto tiempo hace que Andrés se lastimó?*
**Estudiante B:** *Hace… que se lastimó.*

| | | |
|---|---|---|
| María | Le duelen los dientes. | 2 meses |
| Andrés | Se lastimó. | |
| Julia | Se cortó el dedo. | 3 horas |
| Pedro | Está resfriado. | |
| Pepa | Lleva yeso. | 5 semanas |
| Paco | Tiene tos. | |

**Estudiante B** Una enfermera escribió la información en la tabla de abajo. ¿Cuánto tiempo hace que les afectan las situaciones a las personas? Habla con tu compañero(a) para completar la tabla. *(Hint: Complete the chart.)*

**modelo**

**Estudiante A:** *¿Cuánto tiempo hace que Andrés se lastimó?*
**Estudiante B:** *Hace un año que se lastimó.*

| | | |
|---|---|---|
| María | Le duelen los dientes. | |
| Andrés | Se lastimó. | 1 año |
| Julia | Se cortó el dedo. | |
| Pedro | Está resfriado. | 6 días |
| Pepa | Lleva yeso. | |
| Paco | Tiene tos. | 1 semana |

## Unidad 3 Etapa 3 p. 231
## La telenovela

**Estudiante A** Imagínate que tu vida es como una telenovela y le vas a decir varias situaciones a tu compañero(a). Te va a responder con una expresión impersonal y su reacción. *(Hint: Tell your partner the following and listen for the response.)*

**modelo**

**Estudiante A:** *Mi hermana se cayó cuando se ponía los pantalones y está en la sala de emergencia.*
**Estudiante B:** ….

1. Mi hermana se cayó cuando se ponía los pantalones y está en la sala de emergencia.
2. Hubo un temblor y mi casa está destruida.
3. Mi profesor va a ser mi padrastro.
4. Acabo de darme cuenta de que tengo una gemela.
5. Hace mucho calor y no tengo desodorante.

**Estudiante B** Imagínate que la vida de tu compañero(a) es como una telenovela y te va a describir varias situaciones. Responde con una expresión impersonal y tu reacción. *(Hint: Listen to your partner's situations, and then react.)*

| | |
|---|---|
| Es triste que… | Es ridículo que… |
| Es probable que… | Es importante que… |
| Es bueno que… | Es una lástima que… |

**modelo**

**Estudiante A:** *Mi hermana se cayó cuando se ponía los pantalones y está en la sala de emergencia.*
**Estudiante B:** *Es importante que tu hermana tenga cuidado cuando se pone los pantalones.*

## 21 Unidad 4 Etapa 1 p. 257
## Quiero que vayamos a...

**Estudiante A** Contesta preguntas sobre tu hotel. Luego hazle estas preguntas a tu compañero(a). Trata de convencerle de hospedarse en tu hotel. *(Hint: Ask and answer questions about a hotel.)*

**modelo**

**Estudiante B:** *¿Tiene habitaciones hermosas?*
**Estudiante A:** *Sí.*
**Estudiante B:** *Ojalá que nos hospedemos…*

5. ¿Tiene cocinas en las habitaciones?
6. ¿Tiene televisor en las habitaciones?
7. ¿Tiene piscina?
8. ¿Tiene gimnasio?

Tu hotel tiene:
- baños grandes
- habitaciones hermosas
- comida maravillosa
- muebles antiguos
- una vista del mar

**Estudiante B** Pregúntale a tu compañero(a) sobre su hotel y contesta preguntas sobre el tuyo. Luego trata de convencerle de hospedarse en tu hotel. *(Hint: Ask and answer questions about a hotel.)*

**modelo**

**Estudiante B:** *¿Tiene habitaciones hermosas?*
**Estudiante A:** ….
**Estudiante B:** *Ojalá que nos hospedemos…*

1. ¿Tiene habitaciones hermosas?
2. ¿Tiene muebles antiguos o modernos?
3. ¿Tiene baños grandes?
4. ¿Tiene servicio excepcional?

Tu hotel tiene:
- una piscina grande
- aire acondicionado
- un gimnasio

habitaciones con…
- cocinas
- televisores

## 22 Unidad 4 Etapa 1 p. 259
## Siempre lo contrario

**Estudiante A** Tú y tu compañero(a) no están de acuerdo hoy. Cuando tú sugieres algo, él (ella) tiene otra idea. *(Hint: Suggest activities.)*

**modelo**

*preparar el almuerzo en el horno microondas*
**Estudiante A:** *Ojalá que preparemos el almuerzo en el horno microondas.*
**Estudiante B:** …

1. preparar el almuerzo en el horno microondas
2. poner la calefacción
3. dar una vuelta
4. ir a la librería
5. ir al centro comercial
6. lavar el perro en el lavabo
7. levantarse tarde
8. alquilar un video cómico

**Estudiante B** Tú y tu compañero(a) no están de acuerdo hoy. Cuando él (ella) sugiere algo, tú tienes otra idea. *(Hint: Suggest alternate activities.)*

**modelo**

*usar la estufa*
**Estudiante A:** *Ojalá que preparemos el almuerzo en el horno microondas.*
**Estudiante B:** *Prefiero que usemos la estufa.*

lavarlo en la bañera
ir a un mercado
usar un despertador
usar la estufa
sacar libros de la biblioteca
alquilar uno de horror
andar en bicicleta
poner el aire acondicionado



### 21 Answers

*Some answers may vary.*

1. B: ¿Tiene habitaciones hermosas?
   A: Sí, tiene habitaciones hermosas.
   B: Ojalá que nos hospedemos en...
2. B: ¿Tiene muebles antiguos o modernos?
   A: Tiene muebles antiguos.
   B: Ojalá que nos hospedemos en...
3. B: ¿Tiene baños grandes?
   A: Sí, tiene baños grandes.
   B: Ojalá que nos hospedemos en...
4. B: ¿Tiene servicio excepcional?
   A: No, pero tiene comida maravillosa.
   B: Ojalá que nos hospedemos en...
5. A: ¿Tiene cocinas en las habitaciones?
   B: Sí, tiene cocinas en cada habitación.
   A: Ojalá que nos hospedemos en...
6. A: ¿Tiene televisor en las habitaciones?
   B: Sí. Tiene televisor.
   A: Ojalá que nos hospedemos en...
7. A: ¿Tiene piscina?
   B: Sí, tiene una piscina grande.
   A: Ojalá que nos hospedemos en...
8. A: ¿Tiene gimnasio?
   B: Sí, tiene un gimnasio.
   A: Ojalá que nos hospedemos en...

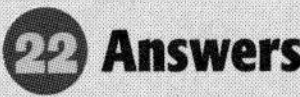

### 22 Answers

*Answers may vary.*

1. A: Ojalá que preparemos el almuerzo en el horno microondas.
   B: Prefiero que usemos la estufa.
2. A: Ojalá que pongamos la calefacción.
   B: Prefiero que pongamos el aire acondicionado.
3. A: Ojalá que demos una vuelta.
   B: Prefiero que andemos en bicicleta.
4. A: Ojalá que vayamos a la librería.
   B: Prefiero que saquemos libros de la biblioteca.
5. A: Ojalá que vayamos al centro comercial.
   B: Prefiero que vayamos a un mercado.
6. A: Ojalá que lavemos el perro en el lavabo.
   B: Prefiero que lo lavemos en la bañera.
7. A: Ojalá que nos levantemos tarde.
   B: Prefiero que usemos un despertador.
8. A: Ojalá que alquilemos un video cómico.
   B: Prefiero que alquilemos uno de horror.

## 23 Answers

*Answers may vary.*

1. A: ¿Cómo llego a la Puerta del Sol?
   B: Sugiero que sigas la Calle Mayor hasta la Puerta del Sol.
2. A: ¿Cómo llego al Teatro Español?
   B: Sugiero que sigas la Calle de Atocha hacia la Plaza J. Benavente. Desde allí caminas por la Calle del Prado al Teatro.
3. A: ¿Cómo llego al Banco de España?
   B: Sugiero que sigas la Calle Mayor hacia la Puerta del Sol. Desde allí sigue la Calle de Alcalá al Banco.
4. A: ¿Cómo llego a las Cortes Españolas?
   B: Sugiero que sigas la Calle Mayor hasta la Puerta del Sol. Cruza la plaza y sigue la Carrera de San Jerónimo hacia las Cortes.
5. A: ¿Cómo llego a la Catedral de San Isidro?
   B: Sugiero que camines hacia el sur a la Calle Colegiata.
6. A: ¿Cómo llego a la Academia de Bellas Artes?
   B: Sugiero que camines por la Calle Mayor. Cruza la Puerta del Sol y sigue por la Calle de Alcalá a la Academia.

## 24 Answers

1. A: ¿Te gustaría hacer la limpieza?
   B: No, sugiero que Juan lo haga.
2. A: ¿Te gustaría ver la película [nombre]?
   B: Sí, me gustaría ver la película.
3. A: ¿Te gustaría ir a un partido de béisbol?
   B: No, sugiero que María vaya.
4. A: ¿Te gustaría revisar la tarea?
   B: Sí me gustaría revisar la tarea.
5. B: ¿Te gustaría sacar la basura?
   A: No, sugiero que Catalina saque la basura.
6. B: ¿Te gustaría divertirte en una fiesta?
   A: Sí, me gustaría divertirme en una fiesta.
7. B: ¿Te gustaría jugar al baloncesto?
   A: Sí, me gustaría jugar al baloncesto.
8. B: ¿Te gustaría ir a la taquilla?
   A: No, sugiero que mi hermana vaya.



## 23 Unidad 4 Etapa 2 p. 277
## ¿Puedes ayudarme?

**Estudiante A** Estás en la Plaza Mayor y quieres ir a otros lugares de Madrid. Pregúntale a tu compañero(a) cómo llegar. *(Hint: Ask for directions.)*

**modelo**

**Estudiante A:** *¿Cómo llego a la Puerta del Sol?*

**Estudiante B:** *Sugiero que sigas...*

1. la Puerta del Sol
2. el Teatro Español
3. el Banco de España
4. las Cortes Españolas
5. la Catedral de San Isidro
6. la Academia de Bellas Artes

**Estudiante B** Estás en la Plaza Mayor y tu compañero(a) quiere ir a otros lugares de Madrid. Dale direcciones. *(Hint: Give directions to your partner.)*

**modelo**

**Estudiante A:** *¿Cómo llego a la Puerta del Sol?*

**Estudiante B:** *Sugiero que sigas esta calle hacia...*

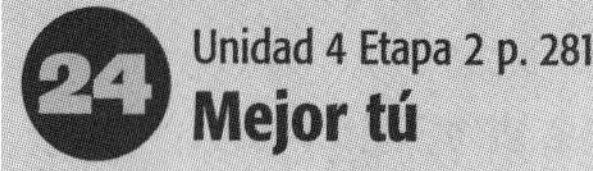

## 24 Unidad 4 Etapa 2 p. 281
## Mejor tú

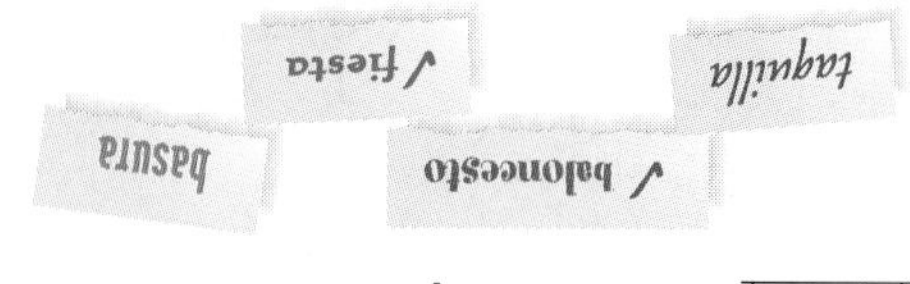


**Estudiante A** Pregúntale a tu compañero(a) si quiere hacer las siguientes actividades. Luego cambien de papel y responde según la lista. Una contraseña (*check mark*) indica que sí quieres hacerlo. Si no hay contraseña, sugiere que otra persona lo haga. *(Hint: Find out if your partner wants to do the following.)*

**modelo**

*hacer la limpieza*

**Estudiante A:** *¿Te gustaría hacer la limpieza?*

**Estudiante B:** ...

1. hacer la limpieza
2. ver la película (*nombre*)
3. ir a un partido de béisbol
4. revisar la tarea

**Estudiante B** Tu compañero(a) quiere saber si te gustaría hacer las siguientes actividades. Responde según la siguiente lista. Una contraseña (*check mark*) indica que sí quieres hacerlo. Si no hay contraseña, sugiere que otra persona lo haga. Luego cambien de papel. *(Hint: Say whether you want to do these activities or if you want someone else to.)*

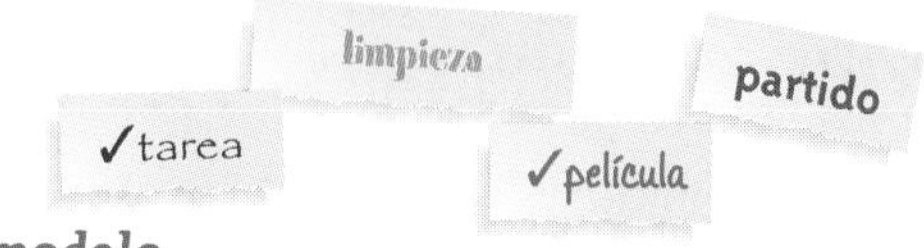


**modelo**

*hacer la limpieza*

**Estudiante A:** *¿Te gustaría hacer la limpieza?*

**Estudiante B:** *No, sugiero que mi hermana la haga.*

5. sacar la basura
6. divertirte en una fiesta
7. jugar al baloncesto
8. ir a la taquilla



R12 RECURSOS Más comunicación

## 25 Unidad 4 Etapa 3 p. 297
## ¿Qué compraste?

**Estudiante A** Imagínate que compraste las siguientes cosas. Compara lo que compraste con lo que compró tu compañero(a) para hacer oraciones utilizando las frases de abajo. *(Hint: Compare what you bought.)*

**modelo**

*suéter / talla*

**Estudiante A:** *Mi suéter es talla 14.*

**Estudiante B:** ...

**Estudiante A:** *Mi suéter es más...*

1. suéter / talla
2. chaleco / talla
3. traje / precio

| | | |
|---|---|---|
| **suéter** | talla 14 | $38 |
| **chaleco** | talla 10 | $35 |
| **traje** | talla 6 | $127 |

más grande — menos caro(a)
es tan grande como — **más pequeño(a)**
cuesta tanto como — más caro(a)

**Estudiante B** Imagínate que compraste las siguientes cosas. Compara lo que compraste con lo que compró tu compañero(a) para hacer oraciones utilizando las frases de abajo. *(Hint: Compare what you bought.)*

**modelo**

*suéter / talla*

**Estudiante A:** *Mi suéter es talla 14.*

**Estudiante B:** *Mi suéter es talla 16.*

**Estudiante A:** *Mi suéter es más pequeño.*

4. suéter / precio
5. chaleco / precio
6. traje / talla

| | | |
|---|---|---|
| **suéter** | talla 16 | $38 |
| **chaleco** | talla 12 | $20 |
| **traje** | talla 14 | $96 |

más grande — menos caro(a)
es tan grande como — **más pequeño(a)**
cuesta tanto como — **más caro(a)**

## 26 Unidad 4 Etapa 3 p. 303
## Comprando ropa

**Estudiante A** Imagínate que eres un(a) cliente(a) en una tienda de ropa y tu compañero(a) es el (la) dependiente(a). Usa las siguientes oraciones para hacer una conversación. ¡Ojo! No están en orden. Tú empiezas. *(Hint: Create a conversation.)*

- **a.** *(Te pones el chaleco.)* ¿Cómo me veo?
- **b.** Dudo que haya lo que quiero. Busco un chaleco.
- **c.** ¿Me puede atender?
- **d.** Quiero uno que haga juego con estos pantalones.
- **e.** Bueno, me lo llevo.
- **f.** Sí, el color oscuro es perfecto, pero no creo que me quede bien.

**Estudiante B** Imagínate que eres un(a) dependiente(a) en una tienda de ropa. Y tu compañero(a) es el (la) cliente(a). Usa las siguientes oraciones para hacer una conversación. ¡Ojo! No están en orden. Tu compañero(a) empieza. *(Hint: Create a conversation.)*

- **a.** Te ves fantástico(a).
- **b.** Me alegro de que tengamos varios estilos... con rayas, oscuros... ¿Qué prefieres?
- **c.** Sí, ¿en qué te puedo servir?
- **d.** Recomiendo que te lo pongas.
- **e.** Bueno, algo sencillo, entonces. ¿Te gusta éste?
- **f.** Excelente, espero que te guste.





### 25 Answers

1. A: Mi suéter es talla 14.
   B: Mi suéter es talla 16.
   A: Mi suéter es más pequeño.
2. A: Mi chaleco es talla 10.
   B: Mi chaleco es talla 12.
   A: Mi chaleco es más pequeño.
3. A: Mi traje cuesta 127 dólares.
   B: Mi traje cuesta 96 dólares.
   A: Mi traje es más caro.
4. B: Mi suéter cuesta 38 dólares.
   A: Mi suéter cuesta 38 dólares.
   B: Mi suéter cuesta tanto como tu suéter.
5. B: Mi chaleco cuesta 20 dólares.
   A: Mi chaleco cuesta 35 dólares.
   B: Mi chaleco es menos caro.
6. B: Mi traje es talla 14.
   A: Mi traje es talla 6.
   B: Mi traje es más grande.

### Answers

A: c. ¿Me puede atender?
B: c. Sí, ¿en qué te puedo servir?
A: b. Dudo que haya lo que quiero. Busco un chaleco.
B: b. Me alegro de que tengamos varios estilos... con rayas, oscuros... ¿Qué prefieres?
A: d. Quiero uno que haga juego con estos pantalones.
B: e. Bueno, algo sencillo, entonces. ¿Te gusta éste?
A: f. Sí, el color oscuro es perfecto, pero no creo que me quede bien.
B: d. Recomiendo que te lo pongas.
A: a. ¿Cómo me veo?
B: a. Te ves fantástico(a).
A: e. Bueno, me lo llevo.
B: f. Excelente, espero que te guste.

## 27 Answers

1. A: ¿Qué animal bailará sobre una hoja?
   B: La mariposa bailará sobre una hoja.
2. B: ¿Qué animal escuchará música rock?
   A: El lobo la escuchará. (El lobo escuchará música rock.)
3. A: ¿Qué animal se vestirá en ropa formal?
   B: La rana se vestirá en ropa formal.
4. B: ¿Qué animal se reirá mucho?
   A: El loro se reirá mucho.
5. A: ¿Qué animal beberá un refresco?
   B: El mono lo beberá. (El mono beberá un refresco.)
6. B: ¿Qué animal correrá lejos?
   A: La tortuga correrá lejos.
7. A: ¿Qué animal se dormirá bajo el sol?
   B: La serpiente se dormirá bajo el sol.
8. B: ¿Qué animal será feroz?
   A: El jaguar será feroz.

## Answers

1. A: Estoy cansado(a).
   B: ¡Durmamos una siesta!
2. A: Me gusta la naturaleza.
   B: ¡Vayamos al parque nacional!
3. A: Debemos ayudar al medio ambiente.
   B: ¡Trabajemos como voluntarios(as)!
4. A: Me molesta la altitud.
   B: ¡Bajemos por el sendero!
5. B: Estoy aburrido(a).
   A: ¡Hagamos algo divertido!
6. B: Va a llover.
   A: ¡Pongámonos impermeables!
7. B: Tengo calor.
   A: ¡Nademos!
8. B: Quiero fotos de los animales.
   A: ¡Saquemos unas fotos en el parque nacional!



## 27 Unidad 5 Etapa 1 p. 326
## Dibujos animados

1. bailar sobre una hoja
3. vestirse en ropa formal
5. beber un refresco
7. dormirse bajo el sol

modelo

comer una salchicha

**Estudiante A:** *¿Qué animal comerá una salchicha?*

**Estudiante B:** *El león la comerá. (El león comerá una salchicha.)*

**Estudiante A** Tu compañero(a) vio la propaganda (*preview*) de un programa de dibujos animados. Pregúntale qué animales harán las siguientes actividades. Cambien de papel.

**Estudiante B** Viste la propaganda (*preview*) de un programa de dibujos animados. Tu compañero(a) quiere saber qué animales harán las actividades mencionadas. Cambien de papel.

modelo

**Estudiante A:** *¿Qué animal comerá una salchicha?*

**Estudiante B:** *El león la comerá. (El león comerá una salchicha.)*

2. escuchar música rock
4. reírse mucho
6. correr lejos
8. ser feroz

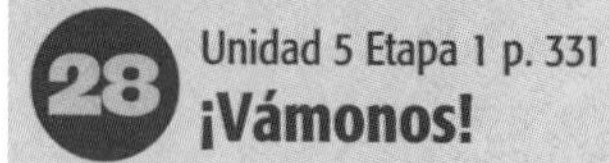

## 28 Unidad 5 Etapa 1 p. 331
## ¡Vámonos!

nadar

*sacar unas fotos en el parque nacional*

ponernos impermeables

hacer algo divertido

1. Estoy cansado(a).
2. Me gusta la naturaleza.
3. Debemos ayudar el medio ambiente.
4. Me molesta la altitud.

modelo

*Estoy cansado(a).*

**Estudiante A:** *Estoy cansado(a).*

**Estudiante B:** …

**Estudiante A** Dile las siguientes situaciones a tu compañero(a) quien va a recomendar que ustedes hagan ciertas actividades. Cambien de papel.

**Estudiante B** Tu compañero(a) te va a describir varias situaciones. Para cada situación, sugiere una actividad que ustedes puedan hacer. Cambien de papel.

bajar por el sendero

ir al parque nacional

*trabajar como voluntarios(as)*

dormir una siesta

modelo

*dormir una siesta*

**Estudiante A:** *Estoy cansado(a).*

**Estudiante B:** *¡Durmamos una siesta!*

5. Estoy aburrido(a).
6. Va a llover.
7. Tengo calor.
8. Quiero fotos de los animales.

## 29 Unidad 5 Etapa 2 p. 348
## Planes para diez años

**Estudiante A** Estas personas describieron sus planes para diez años en el futuro. Habla con tu compañero(a) para completar la tabla.

**modelo**

**Estudiante A:** *¿Qué será Margarita?*

**Estudiante B:** *Margarita...*

| nombre | profesión | edad | pasatiempo |
|---|---|---|---|
| Margarita | | 31 | |
| Andrés | profesor | | viajar |
| Amanda | | 27 | |
| Felipe | bombero | | escalar montañas |

**Estudiante B** Estas personas describieron sus planes para diez años en el futuro. Habla con tu compañero(a) para completar la tabla.

**modelo**

**Estudiante A:** *¿Qué será Margarita?*

**Estudiante B:** *Margarita será doctora.*

| nombre | profesión | edad | pasatiempo |
|---|---|---|---|
| Margarita | doctora | | pescar |
| Andrés | | 24 | |
| Amanda | escritora | | montar a caballo |
| Felipe | | 19 | |

## 30 Unidad 5 Etapa 2 p. 353
## ¿Hace buen tiempo?

**Estudiante A** Tú y tu compañero(a) tienen información sobre el tiempo de algunos días de la semana. Túrnense con preguntas sobre el tiempo que no sepan. ¡Ojo! Hay un día en que ustedes tienen información diferente.

**modelo**

*lunes*

**Estudiante A:** *¿Hace buen tiempo el lunes?*

**Estudiante B:** ...

| | |
|---|---|
| lunes | |
| martes | llovizna |
| miércoles | |
| jueves | húmedo |
| viernes | relámpago |
| sábado | |
| domingo | nubes |

**Estudiante B** Tú y tu compañero(a) tienen información sobre el tiempo de algunos días de la semana. Túrnense con preguntas sobre el tiempo que no sepan. ¡Ojo! Hay un día en que ustedes tienen información diferente.

**modelo**

*lunes*

**Estudiante A:** *¿Hace buen tiempo el lunes?*

**Estudiante B:** *Sí, es un día caluroso.*

| | |
|---|---|
| lunes | caluroso |
| martes | |
| miércoles | neblina |
| jueves | huracán |
| viernes | |
| sábado | aguacero |
| domingo | |



### 29 Answers

A: ¿Qué será Margarita?
B: Margarita será doctora.
B: ¿Cuántos años tendrá Margarita?
A: Tendrá 31 años.
A: ¿Cuál será el pasatiempo preferido de Margarita?
B: Le gustará pescar.

B: ¿Qué será Andrés?
A: Será profesor.
A: ¿Cuántos años tendrá Andrés?
B: Tendrá 24 años.
B: ¿Cuál será el pasatiempo preferido de Andrés?
A: Le gustará viajar.

A: ¿Qué será Amanda?
B: Amanda será escritora.
B: ¿Cuántos años tendrá Amanda?
A: Tendrá 27 años.
A: ¿Cuál será el pasatiempo preferido de Amanda?
B: Le gustará montar a caballo.

B: ¿Qué será Felipe?
A: Felipe será bombero.
A: ¿Cuántos años tendrá Felipe?
B: Tendrá 19 años.
B: ¿Cuál será el pasatiempo preferido de Felipe?
A: Le gustará escalar montañas.

### 30 Answers

A: ¿Hace buen tiempo el lunes?
B: Sí. Es caluroso.
B: ¿Hace buen tiempo el martes?
A: No. Hay llovizna.
A: ¿Hace buen tiempo el miércoles?
B: No. Hay neblina.
A: ¿Hace buen tiempo el jueves?
B: No. Hay un huracán.
B: ¿Hace buen tiempo el viernes?
A: No. Hay relámpagos.
A: ¿Hace buen tiempo el sábado?
B: No. Hay un aguacero.
B: ¿Hace buen tiempo el domingo?
A: Sí, pero hay nubes.

## 31 Answers

*Answers may vary.*

## 32 Answers

*Answers to guesses will vary.*

1. A: Si fueras director(a) de la escuela, ¿qué harías?
   B: Haría una fiesta cada viernes.
2. A: Si estuvieras escuchando música, ¿qué harías?
   B: Pondría música de los años setenta.
3. A: Si pudieras cambiar el color de tus ojos, ¿qué harías?
   B: Tendría ojos cafés.
4. B: Si estuvieras en un restaurante japonés, ¿qué harías?
   A: Comería «sushi».
5. B: Si estuvieras en una isla desierta, ¿qué harías?
   A: Nadaría todos los días.
6. B: Si estuvieras en las montañas, ¿qué harías?
   A: Esquiaría mucho.

MÁS COMUNICACIÓN

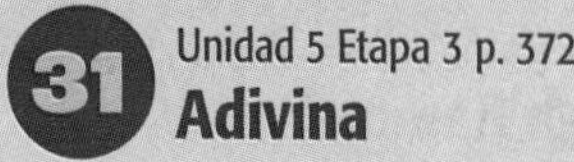

Unidad 5 Etapa 3 p. 372

## Adivina

**Estudiante A** Hazle a tu compañero(a) las siguientes preguntas. Tu compañero(a) va a dramatizar sus respuestas sin hablar. Adivina la actividad que preferiría hacer según sus acciones. Cambien de papel. Dramatiza lo que preferirías de las dos opciones.

**modelo**

*¿Qué harías en el parque?*

**Estudiante A:** *¿Qué harías en el parque?*

**Estudiante B:** *(Dramatiza la actividad.)*

**Estudiante A:** *(Adivina la actividad.)*

1. ¿Qué harías en el parque?
2. ¿Qué comprarías con veinte dólares?
3. ¿Qué animal preferirías tener?

**acampar / sacar fotos**
**volar / manejar**
**ajedrez / voleibol**

**Estudiante B** Cuando tu compañero(a) te pregunte, dramatiza lo que preferirías de las dos opciones. ¡Ojo! No puedes hablar. Tu compañero(a) va a adivinarlo usando el condicional. Cambien de papel.

**patinar / leer un libro**
**un disco compacto / una camiseta**
**un perro / un mono**

**modelo**

*patinar / leer un libro*

**Estudiante A:** *¿Qué harías en el parque?*

**Estudiante B:** *(Dramatiza la actividad.)*

**Estudiante A:** ...

4. ¿Qué harías en un bosque?
5. ¿Cómo irías a otro país?
6. ¿A qué jugarías con tus amigos?

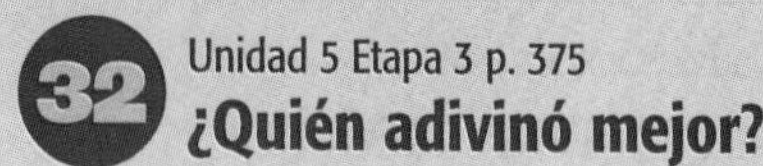

Unidad 5 Etapa 3 p. 375

## ¿Quién adivinó mejor?

**Estudiante A** Lee las siguientes preguntas y adivina cómo responderá tu compañero(a). Escribe tus respuestas. Luego túrnense para hacer y contestar preguntas. ¿Quién adivinó mejor?

**modelo**

*Si fueras director(a) de la escuela, ¿qué harías?*

**Estudiante A:** *Si fueras director(a) de la escuela, ¿qué harías?*

**Estudiante B:** ...

1. Si fueras director(a) de la escuela, ¿qué harías?
2. Si estuvieras escuchando música, ¿qué harías?
3. Si pudieras cambiar el color de tus ojos, ¿qué harías?

**comer «sushi»**
**esquiar mucho** **nadar todos los días**

**Estudiante B** Lee las siguientes preguntas y adivina cómo responderá tu compañero(a). Escribe tus respuestas. Luego túrnense para hacer y contestar preguntas. ¿Quién adivinó mejor?

**modelo**

*hacer una fiesta cada viernes*

**Estudiante A:** *Si fueras director(a) de la escuela, ¿qué harías?*

**Estudiante B:** *Haría una fiesta cada viernes.*

**poner música de los años setenta**
**tener ojos marrones**
**hacer una fiesta cada viernes**

4. Si estuvieras en un restaurante japonés, ¿qué harías?
5. Si estuvieras en una isla desierta, ¿qué harías?
6. Si estuvieras en las montañas, ¿qué harías?

## 33 Unidad 6 Etapa 1 p. 398
## En su tiempo libre

**Estudiante A** Quieres saber qué hacen tres de estas personas en su tiempo libre. Pregúntale a tu compañero(a). Luego cambien de papel.

**modelo**

*el operador*

**Estudiante A:** *¿Qué hace el operador en su tiempo libre?*

**Estudiante B:** ...

| | |
|---|---|
| el operador | |
| la artesana | jugar al fútbol |
| el cartero | |
| el bombero | |
| la mecánica | escribir cartas |
| el obrero | jugar al baloncesto |

**Estudiante B** Tu compañero(a) quiere saber qué hacen tres de estas personas en su tiempo libre. Contesta las preguntas. Luego cambien de papel.

**modelo**

*el operador*

**Estudiante A:** *¿Qué hace el operador en su tiempo libre?*

**Estudiante B:** *El operador lee.*

| | |
|---|---|
| el operador | leer |
| la artesana | |
| el cartero | nadar |
| el bombero | cocinar |
| la mecánica | |
| el obrero | |

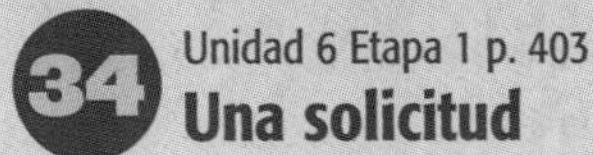

## 34 Unidad 6 Etapa 1 p. 403
## Una solicitud

**Estudiante A** Tienes una solicitud que no está completa. Pregúntale a tu compañero(a) si tiene la información. Luego cambien de papel.

**modelo**

**Estudiante A:** *¿Cuál es el nombre de esta persona?*

**Estudiante B:** ...

**Solicitud para empleo**

Nombre ______

Dirección ______

Teléfono 535-98-80

Fecha de nacimiento ______

Ciudadanía Ecuatoriana

Horas disponibles (número total por semana) 10

Actividades ______

Firma Carmen Julieta Vásquez

**Estudiante B** Tienes una solicitud que no está completa. Pregúntale a tu compañero(a) si tiene la información. Luego cambien de papel.

**modelo**

**Estudiante A:** *¿Cuál es el nombre de esta persona?*

**Estudiante B:** *Su nombre es…*

**Solicitud para empleo**

Nombre Carmen Julieta Vásquez

Dirección 4216 Contra Costa, Quito

Teléfono ______

Fecha de nacimiento 21 de marzo de 1984

Ciudadanía ______

Horas disponibles (número total por semana) ______

Actividades jugar al baloncesto, cantar en el coro

Firma ______



### 33 Answers

A: ¿Qué hace el operador en su tiempo libre?
B: El operador lee.
B: ¿Qué hace la artesana en su tiempo libre?
A: La artesana juega al fútbol.
A: ¿Qué hace el cartero en su tiempo libre?
B: El cartero nada.
A: ¿Qué hace el bombero en su tiempo libre?
B: El bombero cocina.
B: ¿Qué hace la mecánica en su tiempo libre?
A: La mecánica escribe cartas.
B: ¿Qué hace el obrero en su tiempo libre?
A: El obrero juega al baloncesto.

### 34 Answers

A: ¿Cuál es el nombre de esta persona?
B: Carmen Julieta Vásquez.
A: ¿Cuál es su dirección?
B: Su dirección es 4216 Contra Costa, Quito.
B: ¿Cuál es su teléfono?
A: Su teléfono es 535-98-80.
A: ¿Cuál es su fecha de nacimiento?
B: La fecha es el 21 de marzo de 1984.
B: ¿Cuál es su ciudadanía?
A: Ecuatoriana.
B: ¿Cuales son sus horas disponibles?
A: Diez por semana.
A: ¿Cuales son sus actividades?
B: Jugar al baloncesto, cantar en el coro.

## 35 Answers

1. A: Cuando era niño, Timoteo trepaba a los árboles. ¿Qué hizo ayer?
   B: Ayer Timoteo nadó en la piscina.
2. A: Cuando era niño, Timoteo saltaba la cuerda. ¿Qué hizo ayer?
   B: Ayer Timoteo jugó al baloncesto.
3. A: Cuando era niño, Timoteo construía con bloques. ¿Qué hizo ayer?
   B: Ayer Timoteo comió tacos.
4. A: Cuando era niño, Timoteo jugaba con sus primos. ¿Qué hizo ayer?
   B: Ayer Timoteo les contó cuentos a los niños.
5. A: Cuando era niño, Timoteo cantaba. ¿Qué hizo ayer?
   B: Ayer Timoteo cantó en el coro.

## 36 Answers

A: b. ha tenido
B: h. he trabajado
A: e. ha hecho
B: g. he trabajado, he servido
A: d. ha visto
B: f. he tenido
A: a. ha buscado
B: j. he querido, he demostrado
A: c. he visto
B: i. he visto

MÁS COMUNICACIÓN

## 35 Unidad 6 Etapa 2 p. 419 ¿Qué hizo?

**Estudiante A** Dile a tu compañero(a) lo que hacía Timoteo cuando era niño. Tu compañero(a) sabe lo que hizo ayer. Túrnense con preguntas.

**modelo**

*trepar a los árboles*

**Estudiante A:** *Cuando era niño, Timoteo trepaba a los árboles todos los días. ¿Qué hizo ayer?*

**Estudiante B:** ...

1. trepar a los árboles
2. saltar la cuerda
3. construir con bloques
4. jugar con sus primos
5. cantar

**Estudiante B** Tu compañero(a) sabe lo que hacía Timoteo cuando era niño. Dile qué hizo ayer. Túrnense con preguntas.

**modelo**

*nadar en la piscina*

**Estudiante A:** *Cuando era niño, Timoteo trepaba a los árboles todos los días. ¿Qué hizo ayer?*

**Estudiante B:** *Ayer Timoteo nadó en la piscina.*

1. nadar en la piscina
2. jugar al baloncesto
3. comer tacos
4. contarles cuentos a los niños
5. cantar en el coro

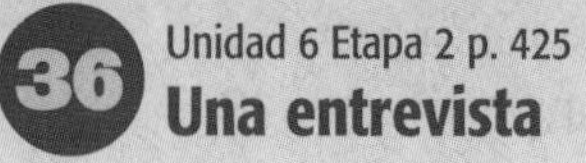

## 36 Unidad 6 Etapa 2 p. 425 Una entrevista

**Estudiante A** Eres el (la) entrevistador(a) y tu compañero(a) busca empleo. Hagan una conversación poniendo las oraciones en orden y conjugando los verbos en el presente perfecto. Tú empiezas.

a. Sí, la puntualidad es muy importante. ¿Por qué (buscar) un puesto con nuestra empresa?
b. Buenas tardes, señor (señorita) _____. ¿Ya (tener) otro empleo?
c. Bueno, yo (ver) su currículum y estoy de acuerdo. ¿Sabe que el contrato es para seis meses?
d. ¿(Ver) los requisitos para este puesto?
e. Muy bien. ¿Qué (hacer) en el restaurante?

**Estudiante B** Tu compañero(a) es el (la) entrevistador(a) y tú buscas empleo. Hagan una conversación poniendo las oraciones en orden y conjugando los verbos en el presente perfecto. Tu compañero(a) empieza.

f. Sí, (tener) mucha experiencia. Generalmente soy puntual.
g. Pues, (trabajar) con dinero y (servir) comida.
h. Sí, (trabajar) en un restaurante por dos años.
i. Sí, (ver) el contrato y es perfecto porque salgo para la universidad en seis meses.
j. (Querer) trabajar aquí por mucho tiempo y creo que (demostrar) las habilidades que usted busca.

## 37 Unidad 6 Etapa 3 p. 442
## ¿Quién lo dijo?

**Estudiante A** Tienes varios mensajes pero te falta información. Con tu compañero(a), completa los mensajes.

**modelo**

**Estudiante A:** *¿De quién es el primer mensaje? ¿Qué dijo?*

**Estudiante B:** *Es de... Dijo que necesitaría...*

**Estudiante B** Tienes varios mensajes pero te falta información. Con tu compañero(a), completa los mensajes.

**modelo**

**Estudiante A:** *¿De quién es el primer mensaje? ¿Qué dijo?*

**Estudiante B:** *Es de Carlitos. Dijo que necesitaría dinero.*

1.
Mensajes
A:
De: Carlitos Hora:
Mensaje: Necesitaré dinero mañana para comprar zapatos.
2.
Mensajes
A: Chalo
De: Hora: 10:15
Mensaje:
3.
Mensajes
A:
De: Hora: 1:00
Mensaje: Te invito a cenar con mi familia esta noche.
4.
Mensajes
A: Catalina
De: Ana Hora
Mensaje


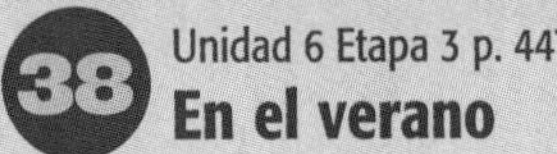

## 38 Unidad 6 Etapa 3 p. 447
## En el verano

**Estudiante A** Margarita ha planeado un horario para sus actividades este verano. Conversa con tu compañero(a) para completar el horario.

**modelo**

**Estudiante A:** *¿Qué hará el lunes?*

**Estudiante B:** ...

| | |
|---|---|
| 1. **lunes** | 5. **viernes** |
| 2. **martes** ser voluntaria | 6. **sábado** limpiar el cuarto |
| 3. **miércoles** ir de compras | 7. **domingo** |
| 4. **jueves** jugar al voleibol | |

**Estudiante B** Margarita ha planeado un horario para sus actividades este verano. Conversa con tu compañero(a) para completar el horario.

**modelo**

**Estudiante A:** *¿Qué hará el lunes?*

**Estudiante B:** *Practicará las artes marciales.*

| | |
|---|---|
| 1. **lunes** practicar las artes marciales | 5. **viernes** tomar un curso de computadoras |
| 2. **martes** | 6. **sábado** |
| 3. **miércoles** | 7. **domingo** bajar el río en canoa |
| 4. **jueves** | |



### 37 Answers

1. B: ¿Para quién es el primer mensaje? ¿Qué hora es?
   A: Es para Mamá. Son las tres y media.
   A: ¿De quién es el primer mensaje? ¿Qué dijo?
   B: Es de Carlitos. Dijo que necesitaría dinero mañana para comprar zapatos.
2. A: ¿Para quién es el segundo mensaje? ¿Qué hora es?
   B: Es para Chalo. Son las diez y cuarto.
   B: ¿De quién es el segundo mensaje? ¿Qué dijo?
   A: Es de Nacho. Dijo que iría a jugar al baloncesto a los 10:30 en el parque.
3. B: ¿Para quién es el tercer mensaje? ¿De quién es?
   A: Es para Irene. Es de Magdalena.
   A: ¿Qué hora es? ¿Qué dijo?
   B: Es la una. Dijo que te invita a cenar con la familia de Magdalena esta noche.
4. A: ¿Para quién es el cuarto mensaje? ¿De quién es?
   B: Es para Catalina. Es de Ana.
   B: ¿Qué hora es? ¿Qué dijo?
   A: Son las siete menos cuarto. Dijo que la fiesta sería a las ocho en la casa de Nadia.

### 38 Answers

1. A: ¿Qué hará el lunes?
   B: Practicará las artes marciales.
2. B: ¿Qué hará el martes?
   A: Será voluntaria.
3. B: ¿Qué hará el miércoles?
   A: Irá de compras.
4. B: ¿Qué hará el jueves?
   A: Jugará al voleibol.
5. A: ¿Qué hará el viernes?
   B: Tomará un curso de computadoras.
6. B: ¿Qué hará el sábado?
   A: Limpiará el cuarto.
7. A: ¿Qué hará el domingo?
   B: Bajará el río en canoa.

# Vocabulario adicional

Here is some additional vocabulary that you may want to use in conversation. If you do not find a word here, it may be listed in the glossaries.

## Más clases

| | |
|---|---|
| el alemán | *German* |
| la álgebra | *algebra* |
| el cálculo | *calculus* |
| la composición | *writing* |
| la contabilidad | *accounting* |
| la física | *physics* |
| la geografía | *geography* |
| la geometría | *geometry* |
| el latín | *Latin* |
| el ruso | *Russian* |
| la salud | *health* |
| la trigonometría | *trigonometry* |

## Otras expresiones

| | |
|---|---|
| ¿Cómo se dice… en español? | *How do you say… in Spanish?* |
| Con permiso. | *Excuse me.* |
| ¿Cuál es la fecha de hoy? | *What is today's date?* |
| ¿Cuál es la tarea para mañana? | *What is tomorrow's homework?* |
| ¿Puede(s) repetir, por favor? | *Would you please repeat that?* |
| ¿Qué hora es? | *What time is it?* |

## Más instrucciones

| | |
|---|---|
| Abran los libros. | *Open your books.* |
| Cierren los libros. | *Close your books.* |
| Escriban… | *Write…* |
| Escuchen… | *Listen (to)…* |
| Lean… | *Read…* |
| Levanten la mano. | *Raise your hand.* |
| Miren el pizarrón. | *Look at the chalkboard.* |
| Saquen un lápiz. | *Take out a pencil.* |
| Siéntense. | *Sit down.* |

## Objetos de clase

| | |
|---|---|
| el borrador | *eraser* |
| la calculadora | *calculator* |
| el cuaderno | *notebook* |
| el diccionario | *dictionary* |
| el escritorio | *desk* |
| el lápiz | *pencil* |
| el libro | *book* |
| la mochila | *backpack* |
| el papel | *paper* |
| el pizarrón | *chalkboard* |
| la pluma | *pen* |
| la tiza | *chalk* |

## La computadora

| | |
|---|---|
| la computadora | *computer* |
| la impresora | *printer* |
| la pantalla | *screen* |
| el ratón | *mouse* |
| el teclado | *keyboard* |

## Profesiones

| | |
|---|---|
| el (la) agente de bolsa | *stockbroker* |
| el (la) alcalde | *mayor* |
| el (la) asistente social | *social worker* |
| el (la) biógrafo(a) | *biographer* |
| el (la) ensayista | *essayist* |
| el (la) filósofo(a) | *philosopher* |
| el (la) funcionario(a) | *civil servant* |
| el (la) historiador(a) | *historian* |
| el (la) novelista | *novelist* |
| el (la) jefe(a) de producto | *product manager* |
| el (la) poeta | *poet* |
| el (la) representante | *sales representative* |
| el (la) vendedor(a) | *salesperson* |



R20 RECURSOS Vocabulario adicional

## Instrumentos musicales

| | |
|---|---|
| el acordeón | *accordion* |
| la armónica | *harmonica* |
| el arpa (fem.) | *harp* |
| el bajo | *bass* |
| la batería | *drum set* |
| el clarinete | *clarinet* |
| el corno francés | *French horn* |
| el corno inglés | *English horn* |
| la flauta | *flute* |
| la flauta dulce | *recorder* |
| el flautín | *piccolo* |
| la mandolina | *mandolin* |
| el oboe | *oboe* |
| el órgano | *organ* |
| la pandereta | *tambourine* |
| el saxofón | *saxophone* |
| el tambor | *drum* |
| el trombón | *trombone* |
| la trompeta | *trumpet* |
| la tuba | *tuba* |
| la viola | *viola* |
| el violín | *violin* |
| el violonchelo | *cello* |
| el xilófono | *xylophone* |

## Más animales

| | |
|---|---|
| el buey | *ox* |
| el burro | *donkey* |
| el conejillo de Indias | *guinea pig* |
| el conejo | *rabbit* |
| el elefante | *elephant* |
| el gerbo | *gerbil* |
| el hámster | *hamster* |
| el hurón | *ferret* |
| la jirafa | *giraffe* |
| la lechuza | *barn owl* |
| el leopardo | *leopard* |
| el (la) oso(a) | *bear* |
| la oveja | *sheep* |
| la paloma | *pigeon* |
| el puma | *American panther* |
| la rata | *rat* |
| el ratón | *mouse* |

## Los deportes

| | |
|---|---|
| el árbitro | *referee, umpire* |
| el arquero | *goalie* |
| el (la) bateador(a) | *batter* |
| el boxeo | *boxing* |
| el (la) campeón(ona) | *champion* |
| el campeonato | *championship* |
| la carrera | *race* |
| el cesto | *basket* |
| el (la) entrenador(a) | *trainer, coach* |
| el esquí | *ski* |
| la gimnasia | *gymnastics* |
| el golf | *golf* |
| los juegos olímpicos | *Olympics* |
| el (la) lanzador(a) | *pitcher* |
| el marcador | *scoreboard* |
| el palo | *stick, club* |
| el (la) parador(a) | *catcher* |
| la pista | *racetrack* |
| la red | *net* |
| la tabla hawaiana | *surfboard* |
| el trofeo | *trophy* |
| el uniforme | *uniform* |

## Más nacionalidades

| | |
|---|---|
| africano(a) | *African* |
| asiático(a) | *Asian* |
| australiano(a) | *Australian* |
| brasileño(a) | *Brazilian* |
| camboyano(a) | *Cambodian* |
| coreano(a) | *Korean* |
| danés(esa) | *Danish* |
| egipcio(a) | *Egyptian* |
| escocés(esa) | *Scottish* |
| europeo(a) | *European* |
| griego(a) | *Greek* |
| holandés(esa) | *Dutch* |
| indio(a) | *Indian* |
| irlandés(esa) | *Irish* |
| israelita | *Israeli* |
| portugués(esa) | *Portuguese* |
| ruso(a) | *Russian* |
| sudafricano(a) | *South African* |
| sueco(a) | *Swedish* |
| suizo(a) | *Swiss* |
| turco(a) | *Turkish* |
| vietnamita | *Vietnamese* |





RECURSOS
Vocabulario adicional R21

# Juegos-respuestas

## ETAPA PRELIMINAR

**En resumen,** p. 25: 9, 2, 2

## UNIDAD 1

**Etapa 1** **En uso,** p. 49: Pablo: acampar; Tania: ajedrez; Luis: coro; Josefa: artes marciales

**Etapa 2** **En uso,** p. 71: El pato pintó un retrato del gato.

**Etapa 3** **En acción,** p. 81: el inglés: pan francés; el francés: sándwich cubano; el mexicano: arroz mexicano; **En uso,** p. 95: una reportera

## UNIDAD 2

**Etapa 1** **En acción,** p. 112: 1. se sonríe 2. **m**e divierto; 3. se abu**r**ren; 4. t**e** caes; 5. se en**o**ja Respuesta: me río; **En uso,** p. 121: un muñeco de peluche

**Etapa 2** **En uso,** p. 143: el primero: Javier; el cuarto: Jorge; la tercera: Julia; el segundo: José

**Etapa 3** **En uso,** p. 167: una obra de teatro

## UNIDAD 3

**Etapa 1** **En acción,** p. 182: Es mi trompeta. **En uso,** p. 193: Marta: el secador de pelo; Antonio: el reloj; Beatriz: el jabón

**Etapa 2** **En uso,** p. 215: arena; protegernos; loción protectora

**Etapa 3** **En uso,** p. 239: la muñeca

## UNIDAD 4

**Etapa 1** **En uso,** p. 265: detrás del televisor

**Etapa 2** **En acción,** p. 274: 1. perd**a**mos 2. c**u**esten 3. despierte**n** 4. vue**l**vas; Respuesta: luna; **En uso,** p. 287: Busca su perro.

**Etapa 3** **En uso,** p. 311: Sus zapatos son demasiado grandes, sus pantalones son flojos y su chaleco le queda apretado.

## UNIDAD 5

**Etapa 1** **En uso,** p. 337: el jaguar

**Etapa 2** **En uso,** p. 359: saco de dormir; fogata; aguacero

**Etapa 3** **En acción,** p. 373: c. Chile; **En uso,** p. 383: d. 3 horas

## UNIDAD 6

**Etapa 1** **En uso,** p. 409: el cartero

**Etapa 2** **En uso,** p. 431: A través: 2. beneficios, 5. contrato, 6. habilidades, 8. educación, 11. meta; Abajo: 1. ventaja, 3. seguro, 4. empresa, 7. sueldo, 9. universidad, 10. currículum

**Etapa 3** **En acción,** p. 442: a. el semáforo

# Gramática—resumen

## Grammar Terms

**Adjective (pp. 7, 296, 401):** a word that describes a noun

**Adverb (p. 206):** a word that modifies a verb, an adjective, or another adverb

**Article (p. 7):** a word that identifies the class of a noun: masculine or feminine, singular or plural

**Command (pp. 182, 184, 202, 204, 328):** a verb form used to tell someone to do something

**Comparative (p. 296):** a phrase that compares two different things

**Conditional Tense (pp. 370, 442):** a verb form that indicates that the action in a sentence could happen at a future time

**Demonstrative (p. 82):** an adjective or a pronoun that points out someone or something

**Direct Object (pp. 152, 154, 157, 180, 184):** a noun or pronoun that receives the action of the main verb in a sentence

**Future Tense (pp. 324, 346, 440):** a verb form that indicates that the action in a sentence will happen in the future

**Gender (p. 7):** a term that categorizes a noun or pronoun as masculine or feminine

**Imperfect Tense (pp. 112, 134, 418):** a verb form that indicates that an action in a sentence happened over an extended period of time or repeatedly in the past

**Impersonal *se* (p. 399):** the pronoun **se** used when the subject's identity is not important

**Indirect Object (pp. 154, 157, 180, 184):** a noun or pronoun that tells to whom/what or for whom/what the action in a sentence is done

**Infinitive (pp. 5, 278):** the basic form of a verb, ending in **-ar**, **-er**, or **-ir**

**Interrogative (p. 13):** a word that asks a question

**Noun (p. 7):** a word that names a person, an animal, a place, or a thing

**Number (p. 7):** a term that categorizes a noun or pronoun as singular or plural

**Possessive (p. 108):** an adjective or a pronoun that tells to whom the noun it describes belongs

**Preposition (pp. 326, 350, 368):** a word that shows the relationship between its object and another word in the sentence

**Present Perfect Tense (pp. 420, 423):** a verb form that indicates that the action in a sentence has been done in the past

**Present Tense (p. 17):** a verb form that indicates that the action in a sentence is happening now

**Preterite Tense (pp. 36, 38, 40, 61, 84, 134, 418):** a verb form that indicates that the action in a sentence happened at a particular time in the past

**Progressive Tenses (p. 130):** compound present and past tenses that indicate action going on at the time of the sentence

**Pronoun (pp. 152, 154, 157, 180, 184):** a word that takes the place of a noun

**Reflexive Pronoun (p. 110):** a pronoun that is used with reflexive verbs





R24 RECURSOS Gramática—resumen

**Reflexive Verb (p. 110):** a verb of which the subject receives the action

**Subject (p. 10):** the noun, pronoun, or noun phrase in a sentence that tells whom or what the sentence is about

**Subjunctive Mood (pp. 226, 252, 255, 274, 276, 278, 298, 301):** a form that indicates that a sentence expresses an opinion, a hope or wish, doubt, or emotion

**Superlative (p. 296):** a phrase that describes which item has the most or least of a quality

**Verb (p. 9):** a word that expresses action or a state of being

# Nouns, Articles, and Pronouns

## Nouns

**Nouns** identify people, animals, places, or things. Spanish nouns are either **masculine** or **feminine.** They are also either **singular** (identifying one thing) or **plural** (identifying more than one thing). **Masculine nouns** usually end in **-o** and **feminine nouns** usually end in **-a**.

To make a noun **plural**, add **-s** to a word ending in a vowel and **-es** to a word ending in a consonant.

| Singular Nouns | |
|---|---|
| **Masculine** | **Feminine** |
| amigo | amiga |
| chico | chica |
| hombre | mujer |
| suéter | blusa |
| zapato | falda |

| Plural Nouns | |
|---|---|
| **Masculine** | **Feminine** |
| amigo**s** | amiga**s** |
| chico**s** | chica**s** |
| hombre**s** | mujer**es** |
| suéter**es** | blusa**s** |
| zapato**s** | falda**s** |

## Articles

**Articles** identify the class of a noun: masculine or feminine, singular or plural. **Definite articles** are the equivalent of the English word *the*. **Indefinite articles** are the equivalent of *a*, *an*, or *some*.

| Definite Articles | | |
|---|---|---|
| | **Masculine** | **Feminine** |
| *Singular* | **el** amigo | **la** amiga |
| *Plural* | **los** amigos | **las** amigas |

| Indefinite Articles | | |
|---|---|---|
| | **Masculine** | **Feminine** |
| *Singular* | **un** amigo | **una** amiga |
| *Plural* | **unos** amigos | **unas** amigas |

GRAMÁTICA–RESUMEN



RECURSOS
Gramática—resumen R25

# Nouns, Articles, and Pronouns cont.

## Pronouns

A **pronoun** takes the place of a noun. The choice of pronoun is determined by how it is used in the sentence.

| Subject Pronouns | |
|---|---|
| yo | nosotros(as) |
| tú | vosotros(as) |
| usted | ustedes |
| él, ella | ellos(as) |

| Pronouns Used After Prepositions | |
|---|---|
| de **mí** | de **nosotros(as)** |
| de **ti** | de **vosotros(as)** |
| de **usted** | de **ustedes** |
| de **él**, de **ella** | de **ellos(as)** |

| Direct Object Pronouns | |
|---|---|
| me | nos |
| te | os |
| lo, la | los, las |

| Indirect Object Pronouns | |
|---|---|
| me | nos |
| te | os |
| le | les |

| Reflexive Pronouns | |
|---|---|
| me | nos |
| te | os |
| se | se |

| Demonstrative Pronouns | |
|---|---|
| éste(a), esto | éstos(as) |
| ése(a), eso | ésos(as) |
| aquél(la), aquello | aquéllos(as) |

# Adjectives

**Adjectives** describe nouns. In Spanish, adjectives must match the **number** and **gender** of the nouns they describe. When an adjective describes a group containing both genders, the masculine form is used. To make an adjective plural, apply the same rules that are used for making a noun plural. Most adjectives are placed after the noun.

| Adjectives | | |
|---|---|---|
| | **Masculine** | **Feminine** |
| *Singular* | el chico **guapo** | la chica **guapa** |
| | el chico **paciente** | la chica **paciente** |
| | el chico **fenomenal** | la chica **fenomenal** |
| | el chico **trabajador** | la chica **trabajadora** |
| *Plural* | los chicos **guapos** | las chicas **guapas** |
| | los chicos **pacientes** | las chicas **pacientes** |
| | los chicos **fenomenales** | las chicas **fenomenales** |
| | los chicos **trabajadores** | las chicas **trabajadoras** |





R26 RECURSOS
Gramática—resumen

## Adjectives cont.

Sometimes adjectives are placed **before** the noun and **shortened**. **Grande** is shortened before any singular noun. Several others are shortened before a masculine singular noun.

| Shortened Forms | | | |
|---|---|---|---|
| alguno<br>bueno<br>malo<br>ninguno | **algún** chico<br>**buen** chico<br>**mal** chico<br>**ningún** chico | primero<br>tercero<br><br>grande | **primer** chico<br>**tercer** chico<br><br>**gran** chico(a) |

**Possessive adjectives** identify to whom something belongs. They agree in gender and number with the noun possessed, not with the person who possesses it.

| Possessive Adjectives | | | | |
|---|---|---|---|---|
| | **Masculine** | | **Feminine** | |
| *Singular* | **mi** amigo<br>**tu** amigo<br>**su** amigo | **nuestro** amigo<br>**vuestro** amigo<br>**su** amigo | **mi** amiga<br>**tu** amiga<br>**su** amiga | **nuestra** amiga<br>**vuestra** amiga<br>**su** amiga |
| *Plural* | **mis** amigos<br>**tus** amigos<br>**sus** amigos | **nuestros** amigos<br>**vuestros** amigos<br>**sus** amigos | **mis** amigas<br>**tus** amigas<br>**sus** amigas | **nuestras** amigas<br>**vuestras** amigas<br>**sus** amigas |

**Demonstrative adjectives** point out which noun is being referred to. Their English equivalents are *this*, *that*, *these*, and *those*.

| Demonstrative Adjectives | | |
|---|---|---|
| | **Masculine** | **Feminine** |
| *Singular* | **este** amigo<br>**ese** amigo<br>**aquel** amigo | **esta** amiga<br>**esa** amiga<br>**aquella** amiga |
| *Plural* | **estos** amigos<br>**esos** amigos<br>**aquellos** amigos | **estas** amigas<br>**esas** amigas<br>**aquellas** amigas |

## Interrogatives

**Interrogative** words are used to ask questions.

| Interrogatives | | |
|---|---|---|
| ¿Adónde?<br>¿Cómo?<br>¿Cuál(es)? | ¿Cuándo?<br>¿Cuánto(a)? ¿Cuántos(as)?<br>¿Dónde? | ¿Por qué?<br>¿Qué?<br>¿Quién(es)? |





RECURSOS
Gramática—resumen R27

# Comparatives and Superlatives

## Comparatives

**Comparatives** are used when comparing two different things.

| Comparatives | | |
|---|---|---|
| más (+)<br>**más** interesante **que...**<br>Me gusta correr **más que** nadar. | menos (−)<br>**menos** interesante **que...**<br>Me gusta nadar **menos que** correr. | tan(to) (=)<br>**tan** interesante **como...**<br>Me gusta leer **tanto como** escribir. |

There are a few irregular comparatives. When talking about people, use **mayor** and **menor.** When talking about quality, use **mejor** and **peor.**

| Age | Quality |
|---|---|
| mayor<br>menor | mejor<br>peor |

When talking about numbers, **de** is used instead of **que**.

**más de** cien...
**menos de** cien...

## Superlatives

**Superlatives** are used to distinguish one item from a group. They describe which item has the most or least of a quality.

The ending **-ísimo(a)** can be added to an adjective to form a superlative.

| Superlatives | | |
|---|---|---|
| | **Masculine** | **Feminine** |
| *Singular* | **el** chico **más** alto<br>**el** chico **menos** alto | **la** chica **más** alta<br>**la** chica **menos** alta |
| *Plural* | **los** chicos **más** altos<br>**los** chicos **menos** altos | **las** chicas **más** altas<br>**las** chicas **menos** altas |
| *Singular* | mole buen**ísimo** | pasta buen**ísima** |
| *Plural* | frijoles buen**ísimos** | enchiladas buen**ísimas** |

# Affirmative and Negative Words

**Affirmative** words are used to talk about something or someone, or to say that an event also or always happens. **Negative** words are used to refer to no one or nothing, or to say that events do not happen. Remember, to make a sentence negative, you must have **no** or another negative word before the verb.

| Affirmative | Negative |
|---|---|
| algo | nada |
| alguien | nadie |
| algún (alguna) | ningún (ninguna) |
| alguno(a) | ninguno(a) |
| siempre | nunca |
| también | tampoco |





R28 RECURSOS
Gramática—resumen

## Adverbs

**Adverbs** modify a verb, an adjective, or another adverb. Many adverbs in Spanish are made by changing an existing adjective.

| Adjective | → | Adverb |
|---|---|---|
| reciente | → | reciente**mente** |
| frecuente | → | frecuente**mente** |
| fácil | → | fácil**mente** |
| normal | → | normal**mente** |
| especial | → | especial**mente** |
| feliz | → | feliz**mente** |
| cuidadoso(a) | → | cuidadosa**mente** |
| rápido(a) | → | rápida**mente** |
| lento(a) | → | lenta**mente** |
| tranquilo(a) | → | tranquila**mente** |

## Verbs: Regular Verbs

### Simple Tenses

| | | Indicative | | | | | Subjunctive | |
|---|---|---|---|---|---|---|---|---|
| | | Present | Imperfect | Preterite | Future | Conditional | Present | Commands |
| *Infinitive*<br>*Present Participle*<br>*Past Participle* | habl**ar**<br>habl**ando**<br>habl**ado** | habl**o**<br>habl**as**<br>habl**a**<br>habl**amos**<br>habl**áis**<br>habl**an** | habl**aba**<br>habl**abas**<br>habl**aba**<br>habl**ábamos**<br>habl**abais**<br>habl**aban** | habl**é**<br>habl**aste**<br>habl**ó**<br>habl**amos**<br>habl**asteis**<br>habl**aron** | hablar**é**<br>hablar**ás**<br>hablar**á**<br>hablar**emos**<br>hablar**éis**<br>hablar**án** | hablar**ía**<br>hablar**ías**<br>hablar**ía**<br>hablar**íamos**<br>hablar**íais**<br>hablar**ían** | habl**e**<br>habl**es**<br>habl**e**<br>habl**emos**<br>habl**éis**<br>habl**en** | habl**a**<br>**no** habl**es**<br>habl**e**<br>habl**emos**<br>habl**en** |
| *Infinitive*<br>*Present Participle*<br>*Past Participle* | com**er**<br>com**iendo**<br>com**ido** | com**o**<br>com**es**<br>com**e**<br>com**emos**<br>com**éis**<br>com**en** | com**ía**<br>com**ías**<br>com**ía**<br>com**íamos**<br>com**íais**<br>com**ían** | com**í**<br>com**iste**<br>com**ió**<br>com**imos**<br>com**isteis**<br>com**ieron** | comer**é**<br>comer**ás**<br>comer**á**<br>comer**emos**<br>comer**éis**<br>comer**án** | comer**ía**<br>comer**ías**<br>comer**ía**<br>comer**íamos**<br>comer**íais**<br>comer**ían** | com**a**<br>com**as**<br>com**a**<br>com**amos**<br>com**áis**<br>com**an** | com**e**<br>**no** com**as**<br>com**a**<br>com**amos**<br>com**an** |
| *Infinitive*<br>*Present Participle*<br>*Past Participle* | viv**ir**<br>viv**iendo**<br>viv**ido** | viv**o**<br>viv**es**<br>viv**e**<br>viv**imos**<br>viv**ís**<br>viv**en** | viv**ía**<br>viv**ías**<br>viv**ía**<br>viv**íamos**<br>viv**íais**<br>viv**ían** | viv**í**<br>viv**iste**<br>viv**ió**<br>viv**imos**<br>viv**isteis**<br>viv**ieron** | vivir**é**<br>vivir**ás**<br>vivir**á**<br>vivir**emos**<br>vivir**éis**<br>vivir**án** | vivir**ía**<br>vivir**ías**<br>vivir**ía**<br>vivir**íamos**<br>vivir**íais**<br>vivir**ían** | viv**a**<br>viv**as**<br>viv**a**<br>viv**amos**<br>viv**áis**<br>viv**an** | viv**e**<br>**no** viv**as**<br>viv**a**<br>viv**amos**<br>viv**an** |

**Note:** The following regular verbs have irregular past participles:
abrir → abierto, descubrir → descubierto, escribir → escrito, romper → roto





RECURSOS
Gramática—resumen R29

# Verbs: Regular Verbs cont.

## Compound Tenses

| Present Perfect | | Present Progressive | | Past Progressive | |
|---|---|---|---|---|---|
| he<br>has<br>ha<br>hemos<br>habéis<br>han | hablado<br>comido<br>vivido | estoy<br>estás<br>está<br>estamos<br>estáis<br>están | hablando<br>comiendo<br>viviendo | estaba<br>estabas<br>estaba<br>estábamos<br>estabais<br>estaban | hablando<br>comiendo<br>viviendo |

# Stem-Changing Verbs

| Infinitive in -ar | Present Indicative | Present Subjunctive |
|---|---|---|
| cerrar **e→ie** | **cie**rro<br>**cie**rras<br>**cie**rra<br>cerramos<br>cerráis<br>**cie**rran | **cie**rre<br>**cie**rres<br>**cie**rre<br>cerremos<br>cerréis<br>**cie**rren |
| probar **o→ue** | pr**ue**bo<br>pr**ue**bas<br>pr**ue**ba<br>probamos<br>probáis<br>pr**ue**ban | pr**ue**be<br>pr**ue**bes<br>pr**ue**be<br>probemos<br>probéis<br>pr**ue**ben |
| jugar **u→ue** | j**ue**go<br>j**ue**gas<br>j**ue**ga<br>jugamos<br>jugáis<br>j**ue**gan | j**ue**gue<br>j**ue**gues<br>j**ue**gue<br>juguemos<br>juguéis<br>j**ue**guen |
| like **cerrar:** comenzar, despertarse, empezar, merendar, nevar, pensar, recomendar, sentarse<br>like **probar:** acostarse, almorzar, contar, costar, encontrar(se), mostrar, recordar, volar | | |





R30 RECURSOS Gramática—resumen

## Stem-Changing Verbs cont.

| Infinitive in -er | Present Indicative | Present Subjunctive |
|---|---|---|
| perder **e→ie** | **pier**do<br>**pier**des<br>**pier**de<br>perdemos<br>perdéis<br>**pier**den | **pier**da<br>**pier**das<br>**pier**da<br>perdamos<br>perdáis<br>**pier**dan |
| poder **o→ue** | **pue**do<br>**pue**des<br>**pue**de<br>podemos<br>podéis<br>**pue**den | **pue**da<br>**pue**das<br>**pue**da<br>podamos<br>podáis<br>**pue**dan |

like **perder:** atender, entender, querer
like **poder:** devolver (past participle: **devuelto**), doler, llover, mover, resolver (past participle: **resuelto**), volver (past participle: **vuelto**)

| Infinitive in -ir | Indicative | | Subjunctive |
|---|---|---|---|
| | **Present** | **Preterite** | **Present** |
| pedir **e→i, i**<br><br>present participle: **p**i**diendo** | **pi**do<br>**pi**des<br>**pi**de<br>pedimos<br>pedís<br>**pi**den | pedí<br>pediste<br>**pi**dió<br>pedimos<br>pedisteis<br>**pi**dieron | **pi**da<br>**pi**das<br>**pi**da<br>**pi**damos<br>**pi**dáis<br>**pi**dan |
| dormir **o→ue, u**<br><br>present participle: d**u**rmiendo | **due**rmo<br>**due**rmes<br>**due**rme<br>dormimos<br>dormís<br>**due**rmen | dormí<br>dormiste<br>d**u**rmió<br>dormimos<br>dormisteis<br>d**u**rmieron | **due**rma<br>**due**rmas<br>**due**rma<br>d**u**rmamos<br>d**u**rmáis<br>**due**rman |
| sentir **e→ie, i**<br><br>present participle: s**i**ntiendo | **sie**nto<br>**sie**ntes<br>**sie**nte<br>sentimos<br>sentís<br>**sie**nten | sentí<br>sentiste<br>s**i**ntió<br>sentimos<br>sentisteis<br>s**i**ntieron | **sie**nta<br>**sie**ntas<br>**sie**nta<br>s**i**ntamos<br>s**i**ntáis<br>**sie**ntan |

like **pedir:** competir, conseguir, despedirse, repetir, seguir, servir, vestirse
like **dormir:** morir (past participle: **muerto**)
like **sentir:** divertirse, preferir, requerir, sugerir





RECURSOS
Gramática—resumen R31

## Spell-Changing Verbs

### buscar

Preterite: bus**qu**é, buscaste, buscó, buscamos, buscasteis, buscaron
Present Subjunctive: bus**qu**e, bus**qu**es, bus**qu**e, bus**qu**emos, bus**qu**éis, bus**qu**en

like **buscar:** explicar, identificar, marcar, practicar, pescar, sacar, secar(se), tocar

### conducir

Present Indicative: condu**z**co, conduces, conduce, conducimos, conducís, conducen
Preterite: condu**j**e, condu**j**iste, condu**j**o, condu**j**imos, condu**j**isteis, condu**j**eron
Present Subjunctive: condu**z**ca, condu**z**cas, condu**z**ca, condu**z**camos, condu**z**cáis, condu**z**can

like **conducir:** producir, reducir, traducir

### conocer

Present Indicative: cono**z**co, conoces, conoce, conocemos, conocéis, conocen
Present Subjunctive: cono**z**ca, cono**z**cas, cono**z**ca, cono**z**camos, cono**z**cáis, cono**z**can

like **conocer:** crecer, nacer, ofrecer, pertenecer

### construir

Present Indicative: constru**y**o, constru**y**es, constru**y**e, construimos, construís, constru**y**en
Preterite: construí, construiste, constru**y**ó, construimos, construisteis, constru**y**eron
Present Subjunctive: constru**y**a, constru**y**as, constru**y**a, constru**y**amos, constru**y**áis, constru**y**an
Present Participle: constru**y**endo

### creer

Preterite: creí, creíste, cre**y**ó, creímos, creísteis, cre**y**eron
Present Participle: cre**y**endo
Past Participle: cre**í**do

like **creer:** leer

### cruzar

Preterite: cru**c**é, cruzaste, cruzó, cruzamos, cruzasteis, cruzaron
Present Subjunctive: cru**c**e, cru**c**es, cru**c**e, cru**c**emos, cru**c**éis, cru**c**en

like **cruzar:** almorzar (o→ue), comenzar (e→ie), empezar (e→ie)

### escoger

Present Indicative: esco**j**o, escoges, escoge, escogemos, escogéis, escogen
Present Subjunctive: esco**j**a, esco**j**as, esco**j**a, esco**j**amos, esco**j**áis, esco**j**an

like **escoger:** proteger

### esquiar

Present Indicative: esqu**í**o, esqu**í**as, esqu**í**a, esquiamos, esquiáis, esqu**í**an
Present Subjunctive: esqu**í**e, esqu**í**es, esqu**í**e, esquiemos, esquiéis, esqu**í**en

### llegar

Preterite: lleg**u**é, llegaste, llegó, llegamos, llegasteis, llegaron
Present Subjunctive: lleg**u**e, lleg**u**es, lleg**u**e, lleg**u**emos, lleg**u**éis, lleg**u**en

like **llegar:** apagar, jugar (u → ue), pagar

### reunir

Present Indicative: re**ú**no, re**ú**nes, re**ú**ne, reunimos, reunís, re**ú**nen
Present Subjunctive: re**ú**na, re**ú**nas, re**ú**na, reunamos, reunáis, re**ú**nan





R32 RECURSOS Gramática—resumen

# Irregular Verbs

### andar

Preterite: anduve, anduviste, anduvo, anduvimos, anduvisteis, anduvieron

### caer

Present Indicative: caigo, caes, cae, caemos, caéis, caen
Preterite: caí, caíste, cayó, caímos, caísteis, cayeron
Present Subjunctive: caiga, caigas, caiga, caigamos, caigáis, caigan
Present Participle: cayendo
Past Participle: caído

### dar

Present Indicative: doy, das, da, damos, dais, dan
Preterite: di, diste, dio, dimos, disteis, dieron
Present Subjunctive: dé, des, dé, demos, deis, den

### decir

Present Indicative: digo, dices, dice, decimos, decís, dicen
Preterite: dije, dijiste, dijo, dijimos, dijisteis, dijeron
Future: diré, dirás, etc.
Conditional: diría, dirías, etc.
Present Subjunctive: diga, digas, diga, digamos, digáis, digan
Commands: di (tú), no digas (neg. tú), diga (Ud.), digamos (nosotros), digan (Uds.)
Present Participle: diciendo
Past Participle: dicho

### estar

Present Indicative: estoy, estás, está, estamos, estáis, están
Preterite: estuve, estuviste, estuvo, estuvimos, estuvisteis, estuvieron
Present Subjunctive: esté, estés, esté, estemos, estéis, estén

### haber

Present Indicative: he, has, ha, hemos, habéis, han
Preterite: hube, hubiste, hubo, hubimos, hubisteis, hubieron
Future: habré, habrás, etc.
Conditional: habría, habrías, etc.
Present Subjunctive: haya, hayas, haya, hayamos, hayáis, hayan

### hacer

Present Indicative: hago, haces, hace, hacemos, hacéis, hacen
Preterite: hice, hiciste, hizo, hicimos, hicisteis, hicieron
Future: haré, harás, etc.
Conditional: haría, harías, etc.
Present Subjunctive: haga, hagas, haga, hagamos, hagáis, hagan
Commands: haz (tú), no hagas (neg. tú), haga (Ud.), hagamos (nosotros), hagan (Uds.)
Past Participle: hecho

### ir

Present Indicative: voy, vas, va, vamos, vais, van
Imperfect: iba, ibas, iba, íbamos, ibais, iban
Preterite: fui, fuiste, fue, fuimos, fuisteis, fueron
Present Subjunctive: vaya, vayas, vaya, vayamos, vayáis, vayan
Commands: ve (tú), no vayas (neg. tú), vaya (Ud.), vamos (nosotros), vayan (Uds.)
Present Participle: yendo
Past Participle: ido





RECURSOS
Gramática—resumen R33

# Irregular Verbs cont.

### oír

Present Indicative: oigo, oyes, oye, oímos, oís, oyen
Preterite: oí, oíste, oyó, oímos, oísteis, oyeron
Present Subjunctive: oiga, oigas, oiga, oigamos, oigáis, oigan
Present Participle: oyendo
Past Participle: oído

### poder

Present Indicative: puedo, puedes, puede, podemos, podéis, pueden
Preterite: pude, pudiste, pudo, pudimos, pudisteis, pudieron
Future: podré, podrás, etc.
Conditional: podría, podrías, etc.
Present Subjunctive: pueda, puedas, pueda, podamos, podáis, puedan
Present Participle: pudiendo

### poner

Present Indicative: pongo, pones, pone, ponemos, ponéis, ponen
Preterite: puse, pusiste, puso, pusimos, pusisteis, pusieron
Future: pondré, pondrás, etc.
Conditional: pondría, pondrías, etc.
Present Subjunctive: ponga, pongas, ponga, pongamos, pongáis, pongan
Commands: pon (tú), no pongas (neg. tú), ponga (Ud.), pongamos (nosotros), pongan (Uds.)
Past Participle: puesto

### querer

Present Indicative: quiero, quieres, quiere, queremos, queréis, quieren
Preterite: quise, quisiste, quiso, quisimos, quisisteis, quisieron
Future: querré, querrás, etc.
Conditional: querría, querrías, etc.
Present Subjunctive: quiera, quieras, quiera, queramos, queráis, quieran

### reír (e→i, i)

Present Indicative: río, ríes, ríe, reímos, reís, ríen
Imperfect: reía, reías, reía, reíamos, reíais, reían
Preterite: reí, reíste, rió, reímos, reísteis, rieron
Present Subjunctive: ría, rías, ría, riamos, riáis, rían
Present Participle: riendo
Past Participle: reído

like **reír:** sonreír

### saber

Present Indicative: sé, sabes, sabe, sabemos, sabéis, saben
Preterite: supe, supiste, supo, supimos, supisteis, supieron
Future: sabré, sabrás, etc.
Conditional: sabría, sabrías, etc.
Present Subjunctive: sepa, sepas, sepa, sepamos, sepáis, sepan

### salir

Present Indicative: salgo, sales, sale, salimos, salís, salen
Future: saldré, saldrás, etc.
Conditional: saldría, saldrías, etc.
Present Subjunctive: salga, salgas, salga, salgamos, salgáis, salgan
Commands: sal (tú), no salgas (neg. tú), salga (Ud.), salgamos (nosotros), salgan (Uds.)

### ser

Present Indicative: soy, eres, es, somos, sois, son
Imperfect: era, eras, era, éramos, erais, eran
Preterite: fui, fuiste, fue, fuimos, fuisteis, fueron
Present Subjunctive: sea, seas, sea, seamos, seáis, sean
Commands: sé (tú), no seas (neg. tú), sea (Ud.), seamos (nosotros), sean (Uds.)





R34 RECURSOS Gramática—resumen

# Irregular Verbs cont.

### tener

Present Indicative: tengo, tienes, tiene, tenemos, tenéis, tienen
Preterite: tuve, tuviste, tuvo, tuvimos, tuvisteis, tuvieron
Future: tendré, tendrás, etc.
Conditional: tendría, tendrías, etc.
Present Subjunctive: tenga, tengas, tenga, tengamos, tengáis, tengan
Commands: ten (tú), no tengas (neg. tú), tenga (Ud.), tengamos (nosotros), tengan (Uds.)

like **tener:** mantener(se), obtener

### traer

Present Indicative: traigo, traes, trae, traemos, traéis, traen
Preterite: traje, trajiste, trajo, trajimos, trajisteis, trajeron
Present Subjunctive: traiga, traigas, traiga, traigamos, traigáis, traigan
Present Participle: trayendo
Past Participle: traído

### valer

Present Indicative: valgo, vales, vale, valemos, valéis, valen
Future: valdré, valdrás, etc.
Conditional: valdría, valdrías, etc.
Present Subjunctive: valga, valgas, valga, valgamos, valgáis, valgan
Commands: val *or* vale (tú), no valgas (neg. tú), valga (Ud.), valgamos (nosotros), valgan (Uds.)

### venir

Present Indicative: vengo, vienes, viene, venimos, venís, vienen
Preterite: vine, viniste, vino, vinimos, vinisteis, vinieron
Future: vendré, vendrás, etc.
Conditional: vendría, vendrías, etc.
Present Subjunctive: venga, vengas, venga, vengamos, vengáis, vengan
Commands: ven (tú), no vengas (neg. tú), venga (Ud.), vengamos (nosotros), vengan (Uds.)
Present Participle: viniendo

### ver

Present Indicative: veo, ves, ve, vemos, veis, ven
Imperfect: veía, veías, veía, veíamos, veíais, veían
Preterite: vi, viste, vio, vimos, visteis, vieron
Present Subjunctive: vea, veas, vea, veamos, veáis, vean
Past Participle: visto





RECURSOS
Gramática—resumen R35

## GLOSARIO
# *español-inglés*

This Spanish-English glossary contains all of the active vocabulary words that appear in the text as well as passive vocabulary from readings, culture sections, and extra vocabulary lists. Most inactive cognates have been omitted. The active words are accompanied by the number of the unit and etapa in which they are presented. For example, **el campamento** can be found in **5.2** *(Unidad* **5**, *Etapa* **2**). **EP** refers to the *Etapa preliminar.* Roman numeral **I** refers to words or expressions taught in Level 1. For verbs, stem changes are indicated: **dormir (ue, u),** as are irregular **yo** forms: **hacer (hago).**

**a** to, at **I**
- **a continuación** next **2.2**
- **A la(s)...** At ... o'clock. **I**
- **a la derecha (de)** to the right (of) **I**
- **a la izquierda (de)** to the left (of) **I**
- **a pie** on foot **I**
- **¿A qué hora es...?** (At) What time is...? **I**
- **a tiempo** on time **4.2**
- **A todos nos toca...** It is up to all of us... **5.3**
- **a veces** sometimes **I, 2.1**

**abajo** down **I, 4.2**
**abierto(a)** open **I, 4.3**
**el (la) abogado(a)** lawyer **6.1**
**abordar** to board (a plane) **1.1**
**el abrazo** hug **2.2**
**el abrelatas** can opener **5.2**
**el abrigo** coat **I**
**abril** April **I**
**abrir** to open **I**
**la abuela** grandmother **I**
**el abuelo** grandfather **I**
**los abuelos** grandparents **I**
**aburrido(a)** boring **I**
**aburrir(se)** to be bored **2.1**
**acá** here **I**
**acabar de** to have just **I, 3.2**
**acampar en las montañas** to camp in the mountains **1.1**
**el aceite** oil **I, 2.3**
**las aceitunas** olives **I**
**la acera** sidewalk **4.2**
**aconsejar** to advise **3.1**
**acostarse (ue)** to lie down, to go to bed **I, 3.1**
**el actor** actor **2.3**
**la actriz** actress **2.3**
**la actuación** performance **2.3**
**actualmente** nowadays **I**
**Adiós.** Good-bye. **I**
**adivinar** to guess
**adónde** (to) where **I**
**los adornos** decorations **2.2**
**la aduana** customs **1.1**
**la aerolínea** airline **1.1**
**el aeropuerto** airport **I**
**afeitarse** to shave oneself **I, 3.1**
**el (la) agente de viajes** travel agent **1.1**
**agosto** August **I**
**agradecer (agradezco)** to thank
**el (la) agricultor(a)** farmer **6.1**
**el agua** (fem.) water **I**
**el agua de coco** coconut milk **3.2**
**el aguacero** downpour **5.2**
**ahora** now **I**
- **¡Ahora mismo!** Right now! **I**

**ahuecado(a)** hollowed out
**el aire acondicionado** air conditioning **4.1**
**el ajedrez**
- **jugar (ue) al ajedrez** to play chess **1.1**

**al** to the **I**
- **al aire libre** outdoors **I**
- **al contrario** on the contrary **2.2**
- **al lado (de)** beside, next to **I**

**alegrarse de que** to be happy that **4.3**
**alegre** happy **I**
**alemán(ana)** German **1.3**
**algo** something **I**
**alguien** someone **I**
- **conocer a alguien** to know, to be familiar with, or to meet someone **I, 1.3**

**alguno(a)** some **I**
**la alimentación** nourishment **3.1**

ESPAÑOL-INGLÉS



R36 RECURSOS
Glosario español–inglés

**el alimento** food **3.1**
**allá** there **I**
**allí** there **I**
**la almohada** pillow **5.2**
**almorzar (ue)** to eat lunch **I, 1.1**
**el almuerzo** lunch **I**
**alquilar** to rent **I**
  **alquilar un video**
    to rent a video **I**
**alrededor (de)** around **4.2**
**alto(a)** tall **I**
**la altura** altitude, height **5.1**
**el aluminio** aluminum **5.3**
**amable** nice **2.1**
**el (la) amante** lover
**amarillo(a)** yellow **I**
**el ambiente** atmosphere
**la ambulancia** ambulance **3.3**
**el (la) amigo(a)** friend **I**
**la amistad** acquaintance, friendship **2.1**
**el amor** love **2.2**
**anaranjado(a)** orange **I**
**ancho(a)** wide **I, 4.3**
**andar** to walk **1.2**
  **andar en bicicleta**
    to ride a bike **I**
  **andar en patineta**
    to skateboard **I**
**el anillo** ring **I**
**animado(a)** animated **2.1**
**el animal** animal **I**
**el aniversario** anniversary **2.2**
**anoche** last night **I, 2.2**
**anteayer**
  day before yesterday **I, 2.2**
**antes (de)** before **I**
**antiguo(a)** old **I, 1.2**
**el anuncio** commercial **1.3**

**el año** year **I**
  **el año escolar**
    the school year **EP**
  **el año pasado** last year **I**
  **¿Cuántos años tiene...?**
    How old is...? **I**
  **Tiene... años.**
    He/She is... years old. **I**
**apagar** to turn off **I**
  **apagar la luz**
    to turn off the light **I**
**el apartamento** apartment **I**
**aparte** separate **I**
  **Es aparte.** Separate checks. **I**
**el apellido**
  last name, surname **I**
**apenas** scarcely **4.3**
**el apoyo** support
**aprender** to learn **I**
**apretado(a)** tight **4.3**
**apuntar** to note
**los apuntes** notes
**aquel(la)** that (over there) **I**
**aquél(la)** that one (over there) **I**
**aquello** that (over there) **I**
**aquí** here **I**
**el árbol** tree **I**
  **trepar a un árbol**
    to climb a tree **2.1**
**la arena** sand **3.2**
**el arete** earring **I**
**argentino(a)** Argentine **1.3**
**el armario**
  closet, wardrobe **I, 4.1**
**el (la) arquitecto(a)**
  architect **I, 6.1**
**la arquitectura** architecture **I**
**el arrebato** rage
**arreglarse** to get ready **3.1**; to get dressed up **4.3**
**arriba** up, above **I, 4.2**
**el arroz** rice **I**

**el arroz con gandules**
  rice with peas
**el arte** art **I**
**la artesanía** handicraft **I**
**el (la) artesano(a)** artisan **I, 6.1**
**el artículo** article **1.3**
**los artículos de cuero**
  leather goods **I**
**el (la) artista** artist **1.2**
**el ascensor** elevator **4.1**
**el asiento** seat **1.1**
**así fue que**
  and so it was that **2.2**
**el (la) asistente** assistant **6.1**
**asistir (a)** to attend **EP**
**el asopao**
  chicken and tomato soup
**la aspiradora** vacuum cleaner **I**
  **pasar la aspiradora**
    to vacuum **I**
**la aspirina** aspirin **3.3**
**asustarse (de)**
  to be scared (of) **2.1**
**el atletismo** athletics **3.1**
**el atún** tuna **1.2**
**el auditorio** auditorium **I**
**aunque** even though **2.2**
**el autobús** bus **I**
**la autonomía**
  autonomy, freedom
**el (la) autor(a)** author **1.3**
**el (la) auxiliar de vuelo**
  flight attendant **1.1**
**la avenida** avenue **I**
**las aventuras** adventures **2.3**
**el avión** airplane **I**
**ayer** yesterday **I, 2.2**
**ayudar (a)** to help **I**
  **¿Me ayuda a pedir?** Could you help me order? **I**
**el azúcar** sugar **I**
**azul** blue **I**





RECURSOS
Glosario español–inglés R37

**bailar** to dance **I**
**el (la) bailarín/bailarina** dancer **6.1**
**bajar (por)** to go down, to descend **4.2**
**bajar un río en canoa** to go down a river by canoe **1.1**
**bajo(a)** short (height) **I**
**balanceado(a)** balanced **3.1**
**el balde** bucket **5.2**
**el baloncesto** basketball **I**
**el banco** bank **I**
**bañarse** to take a bath **I, 3.1**
**la bañera** bathtub **4.1**
**el baño** bathroom **I, 4.1**
**barato(a)** cheap, inexpensive **I**
**el barco** ship **I**
**barrer** to sweep **I**
**barrer el piso** to sweep the floor **3.2**
**bastante** enough **2.3**
**la basura** trash **I**
**sacar la basura** to take out the trash **I**
**el basurero** trash can **5.3**
**el bate** bat **I**
**el batido** milk shake **1.2**
**el bebé** baby **2.1**
**beber** to drink **I**
**¿Quieres beber…?** Do you want to drink…? **I**
**Quiero beber…** I want to drink… **I**
**la bebida** beverage, drink **I**
**el béisbol** baseball **I**
**las bellas artes** fine arts **1.2**
**la belleza** beauty **5.1**
**los beneficios** benefits **6.2**
**el beso** kiss **2.2**
**la biblioteca** library **I**
**la bicicleta** bike
**andar en bicicleta** to ride a bike **I**
**bien** well **I**
**(No muy) Bien, ¿y tú/usted?** (Not very) Well, and you? **I**
**el bienestar** well-being **3.1**
**bienvenido(a)** welcome **I**
**el (la) bisabuelo(a)** great grandfather/ great grandmother **2.1**
**el bistec** steak **I**
**blanco(a)** white **I**
**la blusa** blouse **I**
**la boca** mouth **I**
**la boda** wedding **2.2**
**la bola** ball **I**
**el boleto** ticket **1.1**
**boliviano(a)** Bolivian **1.3**
**la bolsa** bag, handbag **I**
**el bombero** firefighter **I, 6.1**
**bonito(a)** pretty **I**
**el borrador** eraser **I**
**el bosque** forest **I**
**el bosque nuboso** cloud forest
**las botas** boots **I**
**el bote** boat **3.2**
**el bote de remos** rowboat
**la botella** bottle **I, 5.3**
**el brazo** arm **I, 3.3**
**el brindis** toast
**el bronceador** suntan lotion **I**
**bucear** scuba diving
**bucear con respiración** to snorkel
**bueno(a)** good **I**
**Buenas noches.** Good evening. **I**
**Buenas tardes.** Good afternoon. **I, EP**
**Buenos días.** Good morning. **I, EP**
**Es bueno que…** It's good that… **3.3, 4.2**
**Hace buen tiempo.** It is nice outside. **I**
**la bufanda** scarf **I**
**buscar** to look for, to search **I, 1.1**
**el buzón** mailbox **4.2**

**el caballo** horse **I**
**la cabeza** head **I, 3.3**
**lavarse la cabeza** to wash one's hair **I**
**cada** each, every **I**
**la cadena** chain
**caer (caigo)** to fall **EP**
**Me cae bien (mal).** He/She makes a good (bad) impression on me. **6.2**
**caerse (me caigo)** to fall down **2.1**
**el café** café; coffee **I**
**la cafetería** cafeteria, coffee shop **I**
**la caja registradora** cash register **4.3**
**el (la) cajero(a)** cashier **4.3**
**el cajero automático** ATM **4.3**
**los calamares** squid **I**
**el calcetín** sock **I**
**la calculadora** calculator **I**
**la calefacción** heat, heating **4.1**
**la calidad** quality **I**
**caliente** hot, warm **I**
**¡Cállate!** Be quiet! **I**
**la calle** street **I**
**calor**
**Hace calor.** It is hot. **I**
**tener calor** to be hot **I**
**la caloría** calorie **3.1**
**la cama** bed **I, 4.1**
**hacer la cama** to make the bed **I**
**la cámara** camera **I, 1.3**
**el camarón** shrimp
**cambiar** to change, to exchange **I**
**el cambio** change, money exchange **I**
**caminar** to walk
**caminar con el perro** to walk the dog **I**
**el camino** road **I**
**la camisa** shirt **I**

ESPAÑOL–INGLÉS



R38 RECURSOS Glosario español–inglés

**la camiseta** T-shirt **I**
**el campamento** camp **5.2**
**el campeón** champion
**el campo**
field; countryside, country **I**
**canadiense** Canadian **1.3**
**el canal** channel **1.3**
**la cancha** court **I**
**la canoa** canoe
**cansado(a)** tired **I**
**cansarse** to get tired **2.1**
**el (la) cantante** singer **2.3**
**cantar** to sing **I**
**cantar en el coro**
to sing in the chorus **1.1**
**la capa de ozono**
ozone layer **5.3**
**capacitado(a)** qualified **6.1**
**la cara** face **I, 3.3**
**el caracol** shell **3.2**
**la carne** meat **I**
**la carne de res** beef **I, 2.3**
**la carnicería** butcher's shop **I**
**caro(a)** expensive **I**
**¡Es muy caro(a)!**
It's very expensive! **I**
**la carrera** career **6.1**
**el carro** car **I**
**la carta** letter **I**
**mandar una carta**
to send a letter **I**
**la cartera** wallet **I**
**el (la) cartero(a)**
mail carrier **I, 6.1**
**el cartón** cardboard,
cardboard box **5.3**
**la casa** house **I**
**casarse (con)** to get married
(to) **2.2**
**el casco** helmet **I**
**el casete** cassette **I**
**casi** almost **2.2**
**castaño(a)** brown (hair) **I**
**las cataratas** waterfalls
**catorce** fourteen **I**
**la causa** cause **1.3**
**el cebiche** raw fish marinated
in lemon juice
**la cebolla** onion **I, 2.3**
**el cedro** cedar
**celebrar** to celebrate **I**
**la cena** supper, dinner **I**
**cenar** to eat dinner **I, 2.3**
**la ceniza** ash
**centígrado(a)** centigrade **5.2**
**el centro** center, downtown **I**
**el centro comercial**
shopping center **I**
**cepillarse el pelo**
to brush one's hair **3.1**
**el cepillo** brush;
hairbrush **I, 3.1**
**el cepillo de dientes**
toothbrush **I, 3.1**
**la cerámica** ceramics **I**
**la cerca** fence **I**
**cerca (de)** near (to) **I**
**el cerdo** pig **I**
**el cereal** cereal **I, 1.2**
**la cereza** cherry **2.3**
**cero** zero **I**
**cerrado(a)** closed **I, 4.3**
**cerrar (ie)** to close **I**
**el chaleco** vest **4.3**
**el champú** shampoo **I, 3.1**
**Chao.** Good-bye. **EP**
**la chaqueta** jacket **I**
**charlar** to chat
**los cheques** checks **4.3**
**los cheques de viajero**
travelers' checks **4.3**
**chévere** awesome **I**
**¡Qué chévere!**
How awesome! **I**
**los chicharrones** pork rinds **I**
**comer chicharrones**
to eat pork rinds **I**
**el (la) chico(a)** boy/girl **I**
**chileno(a)** Chilean **1.3**
**los chiles rellenos** stuffed
chile peppers
**chino(a)** Chinese **1.3**
**el choclo con queso** corn on
the cob with cheese
**el chorizo** sausage **I**
**la chorreada** a sweet dish from
Costa Rica, made of corn and
served with sour cream
**los churros con chocolate**
sweet, fried dough served
with hot chocolate
**cien** one hundred **I**
**la ciencia ficción**
science fiction **2.3**
**las ciencias** science **I**
**cierto(a)** true
**la cima** peak
**cinco** five **I**
**cincuenta** fifty **I**
**el cine** movie theater **I**
**ir al cine**
to go to the movies **I**
**el cinturón** belt **I**
**la cita** appointment **I**
**la ciudad** city **I**
**la ciudadanía** citizenship **6.1**
**claro**
**¡Claro que sí!** Of course! **I**
**la clase** class, classroom **I**
**el (la) cliente** customer **4.3**
**el clima** climate **5.1**
**el cocido madrileño** a stew
commonly served in Spain
**la cocina** kitchen **I, 4.1;** cuisine
**cocinar** to cook **I**
**el coco** coconut
**el codo** elbow **3.3**
**el colibrí** hummingbird
**la colina** hill **5.1**
**el collar** necklace **I**
**colombiano(a)** Colombian **1.3**
**el color** color **I**
**¿De qué color...?**
What color...? **I**
**el combustible** fuel **5.3**
**el (la) comediante**
comedian/comedienne **2.3**
**el comedor** dining room **I, 4.1**
**comenzar (ie)** to start **1.1**
**comer** to eat **I, 1.1**
**comer chicharrones**
to eat pork rinds **I**
**darle(s) de comer** to feed **I**
**¿Quieres comer...?**
Do you want to eat...? **I**
**Quiero comer...**
I want to eat... **I**

ESPAÑOL–INGLÉS



RECURSOS
Glosario español–inglés R39

**cómico(a)** funny, comical **I**
**la comida** food, meal **I**
**como** like, as **I**
**cómo** how **I**
**¿Cómo es?** What is he/she like? **I**
**¿Cómo está usted?** How are you? (formal) **I**
**¿Cómo estás?** How are you? (familiar) **I**
**¿Cómo me veo?** How do I look? **4.3**
**¡Cómo no!** Of course! **I**
**¿Cómo se llama?** What is his/her name? **I**
**¿Cómo se va a...?** How do you get to...? **4.3**
**¿Cómo te llamas?** What is your name? **I**
**¿Cómo te queda?** How does it look on you? **4.3**
**Perdona(e), ¿cómo llego a...?** Pardon, how do I get to...? **I**
**cómodo(a)** comfortable **3.3**
**el (la) compañero(a)** companion, classmate **2.1**
**la compañía** company **I**
**competir (i, i)** to compete **1.2, 1.3**
**compartir** to share **I**
**compartir con los demás** sharing with others
**complicado(a)** complicated **5.2**
**el compositor** composer
**comprar** to buy **I**
**comprender** to understand **I**
**la computación** computer science **I**
**la computadora** computer **I**
**común** common **2.2**
**la comunidad** community **I**
**con** with **I**
**con rayas** striped **I**
**Con razón.** That's why. **I**
**el concierto** concert **I**
**el concurso** contest **I, EP**
**conducir (conduzco)** to drive **1.2**
**el (la) conductor(a)** driver **4.2**
**el congelador** freezer **I, 4.1**
**el conjunto** group (musical)
**conmigo** with me **I**
**conocer (conozco)** to know, to be familiar with, to meet **I, 1.3**
**conocer a alguien** to know, to be familiar with, to meet someone **I**
**conseguir (i, i) (consigo)** to obtain **6.2**
**el (los) consejo(s)** advice **3.1**
**conservar** to conserve **5.1**
**construir** to construct **2.1**
**la consulta** consultation **3.3**
**el consultorio** office (doctor's) **3.3**
**el (la) contador(a)** accountant **6.1**
**la contaminación** pollution **5.3**
**la contaminación del aire** air pollution **I**
**contaminar** to pollute **5.3**
**contar (ue)** to count, to tell or retell **I**
**contar chistes** to tell jokes **2.1**
**el contenido** table of contents
**contento(a)** content, happy, pleased **I**
**contestar** to answer **I**
**contigo** with you **I**
**el contrabajo** bass
**el contrato** contract **6.2**
**el corazón** heart **I**
**el corral** corral, pen **I**
**corregir (i, i) (corrijo)** to correct
**el correo** post office **I**
**correr** to run **I**
**cortar el césped** to cut the grass **3.2**
**cortarse** to cut oneself **3.3**
**corto(a)** short (length) **I**
**la cosa** thing **I**
**costar (ue)** to cost **I**
**¿Cuánto cuesta(n)...?** How much is (are)...? **I**
**costarricense** Costa Rican **1.3**
**crear** to create **5.2**
**crecer (crezco)** to grow **3.1**
**creer** to think, to believe **I, 1.3**
**Creo que sí/no.** I think/don't think so. **I**
**¿Tú crees?** Do you think so? **1.3**
**la crema** cream **I, 1.2**
**la crítica** criticism **1.3**
**el cruce** crossing **4.2**
**cruzar** to cross **I**
**el cuaderno** notebook **I**
**la cuadra** city block **I**
**cuadriculado(a)** square
**cuál(es)** which (ones), what **I**
**¿Cuál es la fecha?** What is the date? **I**
**¿Cuál es tu teléfono?** What is your phone number? **I, EP**
**cuando** when, whenever **I**
**cuando era niño(a)** when I/he/she was young **2.1**
**cuándo** when **I**
**cuánto** how much **I**
**¿A cuánto está(n)...?** How much is (are)...? **I**
**¿Cuánto cuesta(n)...?** How much is (are)...? **I**
**¿Cuánto es?** How much is it? **I**
**¿Cuánto le doy de propina?** How much do I tip? **I**
**¿Cuánto tiempo hace que...?** How long is it since...? **I**
**cuántos(as)** how many **I**
**¿Cuántos años tiene...?** How old is...? **I**
**cuarenta** forty **I**
**cuarto(a)** quarter, fourth **I, 2.2**
**y cuarto** quarter past **I**
**el cuarto** room **I**
**limpiar el cuarto** to clean the room **I**
**el cuatro** guitar
**un cuatro templado** a tuned guitar
**cuatro** four **I**
**cuatrocientos(as)** four hundred **I**


ESPAÑOL–INGLÉS
R40 RECURSOS Glosario español–inglés

**cubano(a)** Cuban **1.3**
**los cubiertos** utensils **2.3**
**la cuchara** spoon **I**
**el cuchillo** knife **I**
**el cuello** neck **3.3**
**la cuenta** bill, check **I, 2.3**
**la cuenta de ahorros** savings account **4.3**
**La cuenta, por favor.** The check, please. **I**
**la cuerda** rope
**saltar la cuerda** to jump rope **2.1**
**el cuero** leather **I**
**los artículos de cuero** leather goods **I**
**el cuerpo** body **I, 3.3**
**la cueva** cave
**cuidado**
**tener cuidado** to be careful **I**
**cuidadosamente** carefully **I**
**cuidadoso(a)** careful **I**
**cuidar** to take care of **I**
**la cumbre** summit (meeting)
**el cumpleaños** birthday **I**
**el (la) cuñado(a)** brother-in-law, sister-in-law **2.1**
**la cuota** fee
**el currículum** resumé, **6.2**

**dañar**
**dañarla** damaging it
**dar (doy)** to give **I**
**dar una vuelta** to take a walk, stroll, or ride **2.3**
**darle(s) de comer** to feed **I**
**darse cuenta de** to realize **2.1**
**los datos** facts; information **6.1**
**de** of, from **I**
**de buen humor** in a good mood **4.3**
**de cuadros** plaid, checked **I**
**de la mañana** in the morning **I**
**de la noche** at night **I**
**de la tarde** in the afternoon **I**
**de mal humor** in a bad mood **4.3**
**de maravilla** marvelous **2.2**
**De nada.** You're welcome. **I**
**de repente** suddenly
**¿De veras?** Really?
**de vez en cuando** once in a while **I**
**debajo de** underneath **I, 4.2**
**deber** should, ought to **I**
**decidir** to decide **I**
**la décima** ballad
**décimo(a)** tenth **I, 2.2**
**decir (digo)** to say, to tell **I, 1.2**
**la decoración** interior decor
**los dedos** fingers, toes **3.3**
**dejar** to leave (behind) **I**
**dejar la propina** to leave the tip **2.3**
**dejar un mensaje** to leave a message **I**
**Deje un mensaje después del tono.** Leave a message after the tone. **I**
**Le dejo… en…** I'll give… to you for… **I**
**Quiero dejar un mensaje para…** I want to leave a message for… **I**
**del** from the **I**
**delante de** in front of **I, 4.2**
**delgado(a)** thin **I**
**delicioso(a)** delicious **I**
**demasiado(a)** too much **I, 2.3**
**dentro de** inside **I**
**el (la) dependiente(a)** salesperson **4.3**
**el deporte** sport **I**
**practicar deportes** to play sports **I**
**el (la) deportista** sportsman/sportswoman **6.1**
**deprimido(a)** depressed **I**
**la derecha** right **I**
**a la derecha (de)** to the right (of) **I**
**derecho** straight ahead **I**
**desafortunadamente** unfortunately **3.2**
**desarrollar** to develop
**el desarrollo** development **5.1**
**desayunar** to have breakfast **I**
**el desayuno** breakfast **I**
**descansar** to rest **I**
**descubrir** to discover **5.1**
**desde** from **I**
**desde allí** from there **4.2**
**desear** to desire **1.2, 4.1**
**el desfile** parade **I**
**el desierto** desert **I**
**el desodorante** deodorant **3.1**
**despedirse (i, i)** to say good-bye **2.1**
**el despertador** alarm clock **I, 4.1**
**despertarse (ie)** to wake up **I, 3.1**
**después (de)** after, afterward **I**
**la destrucción** destruction **5.3**
**destruido(a)** destroyed
**la desventaja** disadvantage **6.2**
**el detalle** detail **1.3**
**detener** to detain
**detrás (de)** behind **I**
**devolver (ue)** to return (an item) **I**
**el día** day **I**
**Buenos días.** Good morning. **I**
**¿Qué día es hoy?** What day is today? **I**
**Tal vez otro día.** Maybe another day. **I**
**todos los días** every day **I**
**diario(a)** daily **2.2**
**dibujar** to draw **2.1**
**el diccionario** dictionary **I**
**diciembre** December **I**
**diecinueve** nineteen **I**
**dieciocho** eighteen **I**

ESPAÑOL–INGLÉS


RECURSOS
Glosario español–inglés R41

**dieciséis** sixteen **I**
**diecisiete** seventeen **I**
**el diente** tooth **I, 3.3**
**lavarse los dientes** to brush one's teeth **I**
**la dieta** diet **3.1**
**diez** ten **I**
**difícil** difficult, hard **I**
**el dinero** money **I**
**la dirección** address, direction **I**
**el disco compacto** compact disc **I**
**disculparse** to apologize **2.1**
**Discúlpeme.** Excuse me. **4.2**
**el discurso** speech
**disfrazar**
**disfrazado(a) de** disguised as
**disfrutar con los amigos** to enjoy time with friends **1.1**
**la distancia** distance **4.2**
**diverso(a)** diverse **5.1**
**divertido(a)** enjoyable, fun, entertaining **I, 2.1**
**divertirse (ie, i)** to enjoy (oneself) **2.1**
**doblar** to turn **I**
**doce** twelve **I**
**la docena** dozen **I**
**el (la) doctor(a)** doctor **1.1**
**el dólar** dollar **I**
**doler (ue)** to hurt **3.3**
**el dolor de cabeza** headache **3.3**
**domingo** Sunday **I**
**dominicano(a)** Dominican **1.3**
**el dominó** dominoes
**don/doña** Don/Doña (titles of respect) **EP, 2.1**
**dónde** where **I**
**¿De dónde eres?** Where are you from? **I**
**¿De dónde es?** Where is he/she from? **I**
**¿Dónde tiene lugar?** Where does it take place? **EP**
**dormir (ue, u)** to sleep **I, 1.3**
**dormirse (ue, u)** to fall asleep **I**
**dos** two **I**
**doscientos(as)** two hundred **I**
**ducharse** to take a shower **I, 3.1**
**dudar que…** to doubt that… **4.3**
**el (la) dueño(a)** owner **6.1**
**dulce** sweet **I**
**durante** during **I**
**duro(a)** hard, tough **I**

**echar** to throw out **5.3**
**echa humo** emits smoke
**Échate una siesta.** Take a nap.
**ecuatoriano(a)** Ecuadorian **1.3**
**la edad** age **I**
**la edición** edition **1.3**
**el edificio** building **I**
**el (la) editor(a)** editor **I, 1.3**
**la educación** education **6.2**
**la educación física** physical education **I**
**el efectivo** cash **I**
**los efectos** effects **5.3**
**el ejercicio** exercise **I**
**hacer ejercicio** to exercise **I**
**él** he, him **I**
**la electricidad** electricity **4.1**
**elegante** elegant **4.3**
**ella** she, her **I**
**ellos(as)** they **I**
**emocionado(a)** excited **I**
**la empanada** a stuffed pastry
**empezar (ie)** to begin **I, 1.1**
**el empleo** employment, job **6.1**
**la empresa** business, company **6.2**
**en** in **I**
**en cuanto a** as for
**en seguida** at once **2.2**
**en vez de** instead of **I**
**enamorarse (con)** to fall in love (with) **2.2**
**encantar** to delight **2.3**
**Encantado(a).** Delighted/Pleased to meet you. **I**
**la enchilada** enchilada **I**
**encima de** on top of **I, 4.2**
**encontrar (ue)** to find, to meet **I**
**el encuentro** meeting **I**
**la energía** energy **3.1**
**enero** January **I**
**la enfermedad** sickness **3.3**
**el (la) enfermero(a)** nurse **3.3**
**enfermo(a)** sick **I**
**enfrente (de)** facing **I**
**enojado(a)** angry **I**
**enojarse con** to get angry with **2.1**
**enorme** huge, enormous **I, 1.2**
**la ensalada** salad **I**
**enseñar** to teach **I**
**entender (ie)** to understand **I**
**entonces** then, so **I**
**entrar (a, en)** to enter **I**
**entre** between **I**
**el entrenamiento** training **6.2**
**entrenarse** to train **3.1**
**la entrevista** interview **I, 6.2**
**el (la) entrevistador(a)** interviewer **6.2**
**el equipaje** luggage **1.1**
**el equipo** team **I**
**el equipo de sonido** sound equipment
**escalar montañas** to climb mountains **5.2**
**la escalera** stairs **4.1**
**la escena** scene **2.3**
**escoger (escojo)** to choose **4.3**
**esconderse** to hide **2.1**
**escribir** to write **I, 1.1**
**fue escrita** was written
**el (la) escritor(a)** writer **I, 1.3**
**el escritorio** desk **I**
**la escritura** writing
**escuchar** to listen (to) **I**
**la escuela** school **I**
**el (la) escultor(a)** sculptor **1.2**
**la escultura** sculpture **1.2**

ESPAÑOL–INGLÉS



R42 RECURSOS
Glosario español–inglés

**ese(a)** that **I**
**ése(a)** that one **I**
**esencial**
**Es esencial que...**
It's essential that... **3.3**
**eso** that **I**
**el español** Spanish **I**
**español(a)** Spaniard **1.3**
**especial** special **I**
**la especialidad de la casa**
specialty of the house **1.2**
**especialmente** specially, especially **I, 3.2**
**el espejo** mirror **I, 4.1**
**esperar** to wait for, to expect, to hope **I, 4.1, 4.3**
**esperar que...**
to hope that... **4.3**
**la esposa** wife **I**
**el esposo** husband **I**
**esquiar** to ski **I**
**la esquina** corner **4.1**
**la estación de autobuses**
bus station **I**
**el estacionamiento**
parking space **4.2**
**las estaciones** seasons **I**
**la estadidad** statehood
**el estadio** stadium **I**
**estadounidense**
of the United States **1.3**
**estar** to be **I, EP, 1.2**
**¿A cuánto está(n)...?**
How much is (are)...? **I**
**¿Cómo está usted?**
How are you? (formal) **I**
**¿Cómo estás?**
How are you? (familiar) **I**
**¿Está incluido(a)...?**
Is... included? **I**
**estar a favor de**
to be in favor of **5.2**
**estar bien informado(a)**
to be well informed **1.3**
**estar de acuerdo**
to agree **I, 1.2**
**estar en contra de**
to be against **5.3**
**estar resfriado(a)**
to have a cold **3.3**
**la estatura** height **6.1**
**este(a)** this **I**
**éste(a)** this one **I**
**el este** east **4.2**
**estirarse** to stretch **3.1**
**esto** this **I**
**el estómago** stomach **I, 3.3**
**estrecho(a)** narrow **I, 4.3**
**la estrella** star **I**
**el estreno** new release **2.3**
**el estrés** stress **3.1**
**el (la) estudiante** student **I**
**estudiar** to study **I**
**estudiar las artes marciales**
to study martial arts **1.1**
**los estudios sociales**
social studies **I**
**la estufa** stove **I, 4.1**
**la etapa** step
**el examen** test **I**
**el exceso de equipaje**
excess luggage **1.1**
**exclamar** to exclaim **2.2**
**el éxito** hit
**explicar** to explain **1.1**
**la exposición** exhibit **1.2**
**el (la) extranjero(a)**
foreigner **4.1**

**fácil** easy **I**
**fácilmente** easily **I, 3.2**
**la falda** skirt **I**
**falso(a)** false
**faltar** to lack **2.3**
**la familia** family **I**
**la farmacia**
pharmacy, drugstore **I**
**fascinar** to fascinate **2.3**
**favorito(a)** favorite **I**
**febrero** February **I**
**la fecha** date **I**
**¿Cuál es la fecha?**
What is the date? **I**
**la fecha de nacimiento**
date of birth **6.1**
**la felicidad** happiness **2.2**
**felicidades** congratulations **I**
**feliz** happy **I**
**felizmente** happily **I**
**feo(a)** ugly **I**
**feroz** ferocious **5.1**
**la fiebre** fever **3.3**
**la fiesta** party **I, 2.2**
**el fin** end **I**
**el fin de semana** weekend **I**
**la firma** signature **6.1**
**firmar** to sign
**el flan** caramel custard **I**
**la flauta de pan** panpipe
**flojo(a)** loose **4.3**
**la flor** flower **I**
**la fogata** campfire **5.2**
**formal** formal **I, 1.2**
**el fósforo** match **5.2**
**la foto** photo, picture **I**
**sacar fotos**
to take photos, pictures **I**
**el (la) fotógrafo(a)**
photographer **I, 1.3**
**el francés** French
**francés(esa)** French **1.3**
**frecuente** frequent **I**
**frecuentemente** often, frequently **I, 3.2**
**la frente** forehead
**frente a** in front of, opposite **4.2**
**la fresa** strawberry **1.2**
**el frigorífico** refrigerator **I**
**los frijoles** beans **2.3**
**frío**
**Hace frío.** It is cold. **I**
**tener frío** to be cold **I**
**la fruta** fruit **I**
**fue cuando** it was when **2.2**
**el fuego** fire **I**
**fuera de** outside **I**
**fuerte** strong **I**

ESPAÑOL–INGLÉS



RECURSOS
Glosario español–inglés R43

**funcionar** to work, to run **4.1**
**el fútbol** soccer **I**
**el fútbol americano** football **I**

**las gafas de sol** sunglasses **I**
**la galería** gallery **1.2;** mall
**la galleta** cookie, cracker **I, 1.2**
**la gallina** hen **I**
**el gallo** rooster **I**
**el gallo pinto** a Costa Rican breakfast dish of beans, rice, and eggs
**el (la) ganadero(a)** farmer **I**
**el (la) ganador(a)** winner **I**
**ganar** to win **I**
  **ganarse la vida** to earn a living **6.1**
**la ganga** bargain **4.2**
**el garaje** garage **4.1**
**la garganta** throat **3.3**
**la gasolina** gasoline **5.3**
**gastar** to spend **4.3**
**los gastos** expenses **4.3**
**el (la) gato(a)** cat **I**
**los (las) gemelos(as)** twins **2.1**
**la gente** people **I**
**el (la) gerente** manager **I, 6.1**
**el gimnasio** gymnasium **I**
**girar** to turn **4.2**
**el (la) gitano(a)** gypsy
**el gitano** Romany Gypsy dialect
**los globos** balloons **2.2**
**el gobierno** government
**el gol** goal **I**
**el golf** golf
**gordo(a)** fat **I**
**la gorra** baseball cap **I**
**el gorro** cap **I**
**la gota** drop
**la grabadora** tape recorder **I**
**Gracias.** Thank you. **I, 1.1**
  **Gracias, pero no puedo.** Thanks, but I can't. **I**
**el grado** degree **I**
**el gramo** gram **I**
**grande** big, large; great **I**
**la granja** farm **I**
**la gripe** flu **3.3**
**gritar** to scream **3.3**
**el guante** glove **I**
**guapo(a)** good-looking **I**
**guardar** to hold, to keep **I, 4.3**
**guatemalteco(a)** Guatemalan **1.3**
**la guía telefónica** phone directory **I**
**la guitarra** guitar **I**
  **tocar la guitarra** to play the guitar **I**
**gustar** to like **I, EP, 4.3**
  **Le gusta...** He/She likes... **I**
  **¿Le gusta...?** Does he/she like...? **I**
  **Me gusta...** I like... **I**
  **Me gustaría...** I would like... **I**
  **Te gusta...** You like... **I**
  **¿Te gusta...?** Do you like...? **I**
  **¿Te gustaría...?** Would you like...? **I**
**el gusto** pleasure **I**
  **El gusto es mío.** The pleasure is mine. **I**
  **Mucho gusto.** Nice to meet you. **I**

**haber** to have
  **ha sido** has been
  **ha tenido** has had
**había** there was, there were **2.1**
**las habichuelas coloradas** red beans **1.2**
**las habilidades** capabilities **6.2**
**la habitación** bedroom, room **I, 4.1**
**hablar** to talk, to speak **I, 1.1**
  **¿Puedo hablar con...?** May I speak with...? **I**
**hacer (hago)** to make, to do **I, 1.1**
  **Hace buen tiempo.** It is nice outside. **I**
  **Hace calor.** It is hot. **I**
  **Hace fresco.** It is cool. **I**
  **Hace frío.** It is cold. **I**
  **Hace mal tiempo.** It is bad outside. **I**
  **¿Hace... que...?** How long has it been since...? **3.3**
  **Hace sol.** It is sunny. **I**
  **Hace viento.** It is windy. **I**
  **hacer ejercicio** to exercise **I**
  **hacer juego con...** to match with... **4.3**
  **hacer la cama** to make the bed **I**
  **hacer la limpieza** to do the cleaning **3.2**
  **hacer las maletas** to pack one's suitcases
  **¿Qué tiempo hace?** What is the weather like? **I**
**hacia** toward **4.2**
**la hamburguesa** hamburger **I**
**la harina** flour **I, 2.3**
**hasta** until, as far as **I, 4.2**
  **Hasta luego.** See you later. **I**
  **Hasta mañana.** See you tomorrow. **I**
**hay** there is, there are **I**
  **hay que** one has to, one must **I**
  **Hay sol.** It's sunny. **I**
  **Hay viento.** It's windy. **I**
**el hecho** fact **1.3**
**la heladería** ice-cream parlor **4.2**
**el helado** ice cream **I, 1.2**
**el helado de paila** ice cream made in a large copper pan
**el helecho** fern
**el (la) hermanastro(a)** stepbrother/stepsister **2.1**
**el (la) hermano(a)** brother/sister **I**
**los hermanos** brother(s) and sister(s) **I**

ESPAÑOL–INGLÉS



R44 RECURSOS Glosario español–inglés

**el héroe** hero **1.3**
**la heroína** heroine **1.3**
**el hielo** ice **I**
  **sobre hielo** on ice **I**
**la hija** daughter **I**
**el hijo** son **I**
**los hijos** son(s) and daughter(s), children **I**
**el hipermercado** superstore
**los hispanohablantes** speakers of Spanish
**la historia** history, story **I, 2.2**
**el hockey** hockey **I**
**la hoja** leaf **5.1**
**Hola.** Hello. **I**
**el hombre** man **I**
**el hombre de negocios** businessman **I, 6.1**
**el hombro** shoulder **3.3**
**hondureño(a)** Honduran **1.3**
**honrar** to honor
  **honra** (it) honors
**la hora** hour **I**
  **¿A qué hora es…?** (At) What time is…? **I**
  **¿Qué hora es?** What time is it? **I**
**el horario** schedule **I**
**la horchata** a sweet beverage commonly served in Spain
**la hormiga** ant
**el horno** oven **I, 4.1**
**el horno microondas** microwave oven **4.1**
**el horror** horror **2.3**
**hospedarse (en)** to stay (at) **4.1**
**el hotel** hotel **I**
**hoy** today **I**
  **Hoy es…** Today is… **I**
  **¿Qué día es hoy?** What day is it? **I**
**hubo** there was, there were **1.3**
**el (la) huésped(a)** guest **4.1**
**el huevo** egg **I, 1.2**
**húmedo(a)** humid **5.2**
**el huracán** hurricane **5.2**

**la ida y vuelta** round trip **4.2**
**la identificación** identification **1.1**
**la iglesia** church **I**
**Igualmente.** Same here. **I**
**el imán** magnet
**impaciente** impatient **2.1**
**el imperativo** imperative verb form
**el impermeable** raincoat **I**
**importante** important
  **Es importante que…** It's important that… **3.3, 4.2**
**importar** to be important **2.3**
**la impresora** printer **I**
**incluido(a)** included **I**
  **¿Está incluido(a)…?** Is… included? **I**
**increíble** incredible **5.3**
**la infección** infection **3.3**
**informal** informal **I**
**informar** to inform
  **estar bien informado(a)** to be well informed **1.3**
**el (la) ingeniero(a)** engineer **6.1**
**el inglés** English **I**
**inglés(esa)** English **1.3**
**inmediatamente** immediately **3.2**
**insistir (en)** to insist **4.1**
**instalarse**
  **se instala** is set up
**inteligente** intelligent **I**
**interesante** interesting **I**
**interesar** to interest **2.3**
**internacional** international **1.3**
**inútil** useless **5.3**
**el invierno** winter **I**
**la invitación** invitation **I, 2.2**
**invitar** to invite **I**
  **Te invito.** I'll treat you. I invite you. **I**
**la inyección** injection **3.3**
**ir** to go **I, EP, 1.1**
  **ir a…** to be going to… **I**
  **ir al cine** to go to the movies **I**
  **ir al supermercado** to go to the supermarket **I**
  **ir de compras** to go shopping **I**
  **Vamos a…** Let's… **I**
**iridiscente** iridescent
**irse** to leave, to go away **I**
**la isla** island **5.1**
**italiano(a)** Italian **1.3**
**la izquierda** left **I**
  **a la izquierda (de)** to the left (of) **I**

**el jabón** soap **I, 3.1**
**el jaguar** jaguar **5.1**
**el jamón** ham **I, 1.2**
**japonés(esa)** Japanese **1.3**
**el jardín** garden **I, 4.1**
**la jarra** pitcher **I**
**los jeans** jeans **I**
**el (la) jefe(a)** boss **I, 6.1**
**joven** young **I**
**el (la) joven** young person
**las joyas** jewelry **I**
**la joyería** jewelry store **I**
**el juego** game
  **los juegos mecánicos** amusement rides
**jueves** Thursday **I**
**el (la) juez(a)** judge **6.1**
**jugar (ue)** to play **I, 1.1, 1.2**
  **jugar al ajedrez** to play chess **1.1**
**el jugo** juice **1.2**
**el juguete** toy **I, 2.1**
**la juguetería** toy store **4.2**
**julio** July **I**
**junio** June **I**
**junto a** next to **4.2**
**juntos** together **I**





RECURSOS
Glosario español–inglés R45

**el kilo** kilogram **I**

**lacio** straight (hair) **3.1**
**el lado** side **I**
  **al lado (de)** beside, next to **I**
**el (la) ladrón(ona)** thief **1.3**
**el lago** lake **I**
**la laguna** lake
  **la laguna caliente** hot lake
**la lámpara** lamp **I, 4.1**
**la lana** wool **I**
**lanzar** to hurl
  **se lanzó al abismo** hurled himself into the abyss
**el lápiz** pencil **I**
**largo(a)** long **I**
**la lástima** shame **I**
  **Es una lástima que...** It's a shame that... **3.3, 4.2**
  **¡Qué lástima!** What a shame! **I**
**lastimarse** to hurt oneself **3.3**
**la lata** can **I, 5.3**
**el lavabo** bathroom sink **4.1**
**el lavaplatos** dishwasher **I, 4.1**
**lavar** to wash **I**
  **lavar los platos** to wash the dishes **I, 3.2**
**lavarse** to wash oneself **I, 3.1**
  **lavarse la cabeza** to wash one's hair **I**
  **lavarse los dientes** to brush one's teeth **I, 3.1**
**la lección** lesson **I**
**la leche** milk **I, 1.2**
**el lechón hornado** roasted pig
**la lechuga** lettuce **I**
**la lectura** reading
**leer** to read **I, 1.3**
**lejos (de)** far (from) **I**
  **¿Queda lejos?** Is it far? **I**
**la lengua** language **I**
**lentamente** slowly **I, 3.2**
**lento(a)** slow **I**
**la leña** firewood **5.2**
**el león** lion **5.1**
**el letrero** sign **1.1**
**levantar** to lift **I**
  **levantar pesas** to lift weights **I**
**levantarse** to get up **I, 3.1**
  **(sin) levantarte** (without) getting out
**libre** free **I**
  **el tiempo libre** free time **I**
**la librería** bookstore **I**
**el libro** book **I**
**ligero(a)** light
**la limonada** lemonade **I**
**limpiar** to clean **I**
  **limpiar el cuarto** to clean the room **I, 3.2**
**limpio(a)** clean **I, 3.2**
**la linterna** flashlight **5.2**
**listo(a)** ready **I**
**la literatura** literature **I**
**el litro** liter **I**
**la llama** llama **I**
**la llamada** call **I**
**llamar** to call **I**
  **Dile/Dígale que me llame.** Tell (familiar/formal) him or her to call me. **I**
  **llama la atención** catches your eye
  **Me llamo...** My name is... **I**
  **Se llama...** His/Her name is... **I**
**la llave** key **I, 4.1**
**la llegada** arrival **1.1**
**llegar** to arrive **I, 1.1**
**llenar** to fill up **2.3**
**lleno(a)** full **2.3**
**llevar** to wear, to carry; to take along **I**
**llevarse bien** to get along well **2.2**
**llorar** to cry **3.3**
**llover (ue)** to rain **I**
**la llovizna** drizzle **5.2**
**la lluvia** rain **I**
**Lo siento.** I'm sorry. **I**
**el lobo** wolf **5.1**
**local** local **1.3**
**la loción** after-shave lotion **3.1**
**la loción protectora** suntan lotion **3.2**
**loco(a)** crazy **I**
**lógico**
  **Es lógico que...** It's logical that... **3.3, 4.2**
**el loro** parrot **5.1**
**los demás** the rest of the people **2.2**
**luego** later **I**
  **Hasta luego.** See you later. **I**
**el lugar** place **I**
**lujoso(a)** luxurious **I, 1.2**
**lunes** Monday **I**
**la luz** light **I, 5.2**
  **apagar la luz** to turn off the light **I**

**la madrastra** stepmother **2.1**
**la madre** mother **I**
**los madrileños** people from Madrid
**el (la) maestro(a)** teacher **I**
**el maíz** corn
**la maleta** suitcase **1.1**
**el (la) maletero(a)** porter **4.1**
**malo(a)** bad **I**
  **Es malo que...** It's bad that... **3.3, 4.2**
  **Hace mal tiempo.** It is bad outside. **I**
  **Lo malo es que...** The trouble is that... **5.3**

ESPAÑOL–INGLÉS



RECURSOS
R46 Glosario español–inglés

**mañana** tomorrow **I**
**Hasta mañana.** See you tomorrow. **I**
**Mañana es...** Tomorrow is... **I**
**la mañana** morning **I**
**de la mañana** in the morning **I**
**por la mañana** during the morning **I**
**mandar** to send **I**
**mandar una carta** to send a letter **I**
**el mandato** command
**manejar** to drive **I**
**la mano** hand **I, 3.3**
**manso(a)** tame
**la manta** blanket **I, 5.2**
**el mantel** tablecloth **2.3**
**mantener**
**mantener limpio(a)** to keep clean **5.3**
**mantenerse sano(a)** to be healthy **3.1**
**la mantequilla** butter **I, 1.2**
**la mantequilla de cacahuate** peanut butter **1.2**
**la manzana** apple **2.3**
**el mapa** map **I**
**el maquillaje** makeup **3.1**
**maquillarse** to put on makeup **I, 3.1**
**la máquina contestadora** answering machine **I**
**el mar** sea **I**
**marcar** to dial **I**
**la marioneta** marionette **2.1**
**la mariposa** butterfly **5.1**
**marrón** brown **I**
**martes** Tuesday **I**
**marzo** March **I**
**mas** but
**más** more **I**
**más de** more than **I**
**más que** more than **I, 4.3**
**las matemáticas** mathematics **I**
**la materia** subject **I**
**mayo** May **I**
**mayor** older **I**
**mayor que** older than **4.3**
**la mayoría** majority **2.2**
**el (la) mecánico(a)** mechanic **6.1**
**la medianoche** midnight **I**
**la medicina** medicine **3.3**
**medio(a)** half **I**
**la media hermana** half-sister **I**
**el medio hermano** half-brother **I**
**el medio ambiente** environment **5.1**
**el mediodía** noon **I**
**mejor** better **I**
**Es mejor que...** It's better that... **3.3, 4.2, 4.3**
**el melón** melon **1.2**
**menor** younger **I**
**menor que** younger than **4.3**
**menos** to, before (time); less **I**
**menos de** less than **I**
**menos... que** less... than **I**
**el mensaje** message **I**
**dejar un mensaje** to leave a message **I**
**Deje un mensaje después del tono.** Leave a message after the tone. **I**
**Quiero dejar un mensaje para...** I want to leave a message for... **I**
**la mentira** lie **2.2**
**el menú** menu **I**
**el mercado** market **I**
**merendar (ie)** to have a snack **I**
**la merienda** snack **I**
**el mes** month **I**
**el mes pasado** last month **I**
**la mesa** table **I, 4.1**
**poner (pongo) la mesa** to set the table **I**
**quitar la mesa** to clear the table **I**
**el (la) mesero(a)** waiter (waitress) **I**
**la meta** goal **6.2**
**el metro** subway **I**
**mexicano(a)** Mexican **1.3**
**mi** my **I**
**el microondas** microwave **I**
**miedo** fear **I**
**tener miedo** to be afraid **I, 4.3**
**mientras** while **2.2**
**mientras que** while
**miércoles** Wednesday **I**
**mil** one thousand **I**
**un millón** one million **I**
**mirar** to watch, to look at **I**
**mismo(a)** same **I**
**la mochila** backpack **I**
**moderno(a)** modern **I, 1.2**
**mojado(a)** wet **2.3**
**molestar** to bother **2.3, 4.3**
**el momento** moment **I**
**Un momento.** One moment. **I**
**la moneda** currency
**el mono** monkey **5.1**
**la montaña** mountain **I**
**el montañismo** mountaineering **5.2**
**morado(a)** purple **I**
**moreno(a)** dark (hair and skin) **I**
**morir (ue, u)** to die **1.3**
**el mostrador** counter **1.1**
**mostrar (ue)** to show **1.2**
**la moto(cicleta)** motorcycle **I**
**mover (ue)** to move **I**
**mover los muebles** to move the furniture **I**
**la muchacha** girl **I**
**el muchacho** boy **I**
**mucho** often **I**
**mucho(a)** much, many **I**
**los muebles** furniture **I, 4.1**
**mover los muebles** to move the furniture **I**
**la mujer** woman **1.1**
**la mujer de negocios** businesswoman **I, 6.1**





RECURSOS
Glosario español–inglés R47

**el mundo** world **I**
**la muñeca** doll **2.1;** wrist **3.3**
**el muñeco de peluche** stuffed animal **2.1**
**el murciélago** bat
**el museo** museum **I**
**la música** music **I**
**el musical** musical **2.3**
**el (la) músico(a)** musician **6.1**
**muy** very **I**

**nacer** to be born
**nada** nothing **I**
  **De nada.** You're welcome. **1.1**
**nadar** to swim **I**
**nadie** no one **I**
**la nariz** nose **I, 3.3**
**las natillas** custard
**la naturaleza** nature **5.1**
**la navaja** jackknife **5.2**
**la neblina** mist, fog **5.2**
**necesario** necessary
  **Es necesario que...** It's necessary that... **3.3**
**necesitar** to need **I, 4.1**
**negociar** to negotiate
  **negoció** (he/she) negotiated
**negro(a)** black **I**
**nervioso(a)** nervous **I**
**nevar (ie)** to snow **I**
**la neverita** cooler **3.2**
**ni** nor, neither, not even **4.2**
**nicaragüense** Nicaraguan **1.3**
**la nieta** granddaughter **I**
**el nieto** grandson **I**
**la nieve** snow **I**
**ninguno(a)** none, not any **I**
**la niña** girl **I**
**el (la) niñero(a)** child-care provider **6.1**
**el niño** boy **I**
**no** no, not **I**
  **¡No digas eso!** Don't say that!
  **No es cierto que...** It is not certain that... **I**
  **¡No me digas!** Don't tell me!
  **no sólo** not only
  **¡No te preocupes!** Don't worry! **I**
**la noche** night, evening **I**
  **Buenas noches.** Good evening. **I**
  **de la noche** at night **I**
  **por la noche** during the evening **I**
**el nombre** name, first name **I**
**normal** normal **I**
**normalmente** normally **I, 3.2**
**el norte** north **4.2**
**nosotros(as)** we **I**
**la nota** grade **I**
  **sacar una buena nota** to get a good grade **I**
**las noticias** news **1.3**
**el noticiero** news program **1.3**
**novecientos(as)** nine hundred **I**
**la novela** novel **I**
**noveno(a)** ninth **I, 2.2**
**noventa** ninety **I**
**noviembre** November **I**
**el (la) novio(a)** boyfriend/girlfriend; groom/bride **2.1**
**la nube** cloud **5.2**
**nublado** cloudy **I**
  **Está nublado.** It is cloudy. **I**
**nuestro(a)** our **I**
**nueve** nine **I**
**nuevo(a)** new **I**
**el número** number **I;** shoe size **4.3**
**nunca** never **I**
**nutritivo(a)** nutritious **3.1**

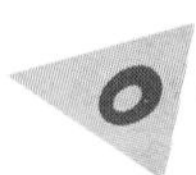

**o** or **I**
**obediente** obedient **2.1**
**la obra** work of art **1.2**
  **la obra de teatro** theatrical production **2.3**
**el (la) obrero(a)** worker **6.1**
**la obsidiana** hard, black volcanic rock
**obtener** to obtain, to get **4.2**
**el océano** ocean **3.2**
**ochenta** eighty **I**
**ocho** eight **I**
**ochocientos(as)** eight hundred **I**
**octavo(a)** eighth **I, 2.2**
**octubre** October **I**
**ocupado(a)** busy **I**
**ocurrir** to occur **2.2**
**el oeste** west **4.2**
**la oficina** office **I**
**ofrecer (ofrezco)** to offer **I, 2.3**
  **Le puedo ofrecer...** I can offer you... **I**
  **¿Se le(s) ofrece algo más?** Can I offer you anything more? **I**
**el oído** inner ear **3.3**
**oír (oigo)** to hear **I, 1.3**
**ojalá que** I hope that **4.1**
**el ojo** eye **I**
**la ola** wave **3.2**
**la olla** pot **I**
**olvidar** to forget **I**
  **ya olvidada** already forgotten
**once** eleven **I**
**el (la) operador(a)** operator **I, 6.1**
**la oración** sentence
**ordenar (las flores, los libros)** to arrange (flowers, books) **I**
**ordinario(a)** ordinary **I**
**la oreja** ear **I, 3.3**
**la orilla** edge, shore **3.2**
**el oro** gold **I**

ESPAÑOL–INGLÉS



R48 RECURSOS
Glosario español–inglés

**oscuro(a)** dark **4.3**
**el otoño** fall **I**
**otro(a)** other, another **I**

**paciente** patient **I**
**pacífico(a)** peaceful
**el padrastro** stepfather **2.1**
**el padre** father **I**
**los padres** parents **I**
**pagar** to pay **I, 1.1**
**el país** country **I**
**el paisaje** landscape
**el pájaro** bird **I**
**la palabra** word
**la palma** palm tree **3.2**
**el palmar** palm tree grove **3.2**
**el pan** bread **I, 2.3**
  **el pan dulce** sweet roll **I**
**la panadería** bread bakery **I**
**panameño(a)** Panamanian **1.3**
**la pantalla** screen **I**
**los pantalones** pants **I**
  **los pantalones cortos** shorts **I**
**el pañuelo** scarf **4.3**
**la papa** potato **I, 2.3**
  **las papas fritas** french fries **I**
**el papel** paper **I**; role **2.3**
**la papelería** stationery store **I**
**el paquete** package **I**
**para** for, in order to **I**
  **para empezar** to begin with **I**
**la parada** stop, stand **4.2**
**el paraguas** umbrella **I**
**paraguayo(a)** Paraguayan **1.3**
**parar** to stop **4.2**
**parecido(a)** similar
**la pared** wall **I, 4.1**
**el (la) pariente(a)** relative **2.1**
**el parque** park **I**
**el partido** game **I**
**los partidos** political parties
**el (la) pasajero(a)** passenger **1.1**
**el pasaporte** passport **1.1**
**pasar** to happen, to pass, to pass by **I**
  **pasar la aspiradora** to vacuum **I, 3.2**
  **pasar un rato con los amigos** to spend time with friends **I**
**el pasatiempo** hobby, pastime
**pasear** to go for a walk **I**
**el paseo** walkway **4.1**
**el pasillo** aisle **1.1**
**el paso** step
**la pasta** pasta **I, 2.3**
**la pasta de dientes** toothpaste **I, 3.1**
**la pasta de guayaba** guava paste
**el pastel** cake **I**; tamale-like mixture of plantain, yucca, and meat
**la pastelería** pastry shop **I**
**la pastilla** pill **3.3**
**el (la) pastor(a)** shepherd(ess) **I**
**la patata** potato **I**
**patinar** to skate **I**
**los patines** skates **I**
**la patineta** skateboard **I**
  **andar en patineta** to skateboard **I**
**el peatón** pedestrian **4.2**
**el pedazo** piece **I**
**pedir (i, i)** to ask for, to order **I, 1.2, 1.3**
  **¿Me ayuda a pedir?** Could you help me order? **I**
**peinarse** to comb one's hair **I, 3.1**
**el peine** comb **I, 3.1**
**pelearse** to fight **2.1**
**la película** movie **I**
**peligroso(a)** dangerous **I, 5.1**
  **Es peligroso que…** It's dangerous that… **3.3, 4.2**
**el (la) pelirrojo(a)** redhead **I**
**el pelo** hair **I**
**la pelota** baseball **I**
**el (la) peluquero(a)** barber, hairstylist **6.1**
**pensar (ie)** to think, to plan **I**
**la pensión** boarding house **4.1**
**peor** worse **I**
  **peor que** worse than **4.3**
**pequeño(a)** small **I**
**la pera** pear **2.3**
**perder (ie)** to lose **I**
**Perdona(e)…** Pardon… **I**
  **Perdona(e), ¿cómo llego a…?** Pardon, how do I get to…? **I**
**perezoso(a)** lazy **I**
**perfecto(a)** perfect **I**
**el perfume** perfume **3.1**
**el periódico** newspaper **I**
**el periodismo** journalism **1.3**
**el (la) periodista** journalist **1.3**
**el permiso** permission **5.2**
**permitir** to permit **5.2**
**el pernil** cut of pork
**pero** but **I**
**el (la) perro(a)** dog **I**
  **caminar con el perro** to walk the dog **I**
**pertenecer (pertenezco)** to belong, to pertain **5.2**
**peruano(a)** Peruvian **1.3**
**la pesa** weight **I**
  **levantar pesas** to lift weights **I**
**el pescado** fish **I, 2.3**
**el pescador** fisherman **3.2**
**pescar** to fish **5.2**
**el pez** fish **I**
**el piano** piano **I**
  **tocar el piano** to play the piano **I**
**picante** spicy **I**
**el pie** foot **I, 3.3**
  **a pie** on foot **I**
**la piedra** stone **5.1**
**la piel** skin **3.2**
**la pierna** leg **I, 3.3**
**el piloto** pilot **1.1**
**la pimienta** pepper **I, 2.3**
**pintar** to paint **I**
**el (la) pintor(a)** painter **1.2**
**pintoresco(a)** picturesque





RECURSOS
Glosario español–inglés R49

**la pintura** painting **1.2**
**pisar**
**pisarlas** to step on them
**la piscina** swimming pool **I**
**el piso** floor, story **4.1**
**el pizarrón** chalkboard **I**
**la pizza** pizza
**el placer** pleasure **I**
**Es un placer.** It's a pleasure. **I**
**el plan maestro** master plan
**planchar (la ropa)** to iron (the clothes) **I, 3.2**
**el planeta** planet **5.3**
**la planta** plant **I**
**la planta silvestre** wild plant **5.1**
**la planta baja** ground floor **4.1**
**la plata** silver **I**
**el plátano verde** plantain **1.2**
**el plato** plate **I**
**la playa** beach **I**
**la plaza** town square **I**
**la pluma** pen **I**
**la población** population **5.1**
**pobre** poor **2.1**
**la pobreza** poverty **5.3**
**poco** a little **I**
**poder (ue)** to be able, can **I, 1.2**
**Gracias, pero no puedo.** Thanks, but I can't. **I**
**Le puedo ofrecer...** I can offer you... **I**
**¿Me puede atender?** Can you help (wait on) me? **4.3**
**¿Puedes (Puede usted) decirme dónde queda...?** Could you tell me where... is? **I**
**¿Puedo hablar con...?** May I speak with...? **I**
**el poema** poem **I**
**la poesía** poetry **I**
**el (la) policía** police officer **1.1**
**el pollo** chicken **I**
**el pollo asado** barbecued chicken **1.2**
**el polvo** dust **I**
**quitar el polvo** to dust **I, 3.2**
**poner (pongo)** to put **I, EP, 1.2**
**poner la mesa** to set the table **I**
**ponerse la ropa** to get dressed **I, 3.1**
**por** for, by, around **I**
**por eso** that's why
**por favor** please **I**
**por fin** finally **I**
**por la mañana** during the morning **I**
**por la noche** during the evening **I**
**por la tarde** during the afternoon **I**
**¿por qué?** why? **I**
**por todas partes** all around **5.1**
**porque** because **I**
**portarse bien/mal** to behave well/badly **2.1**
**posible**
**Es posible que...** It's possible that... **3.3, 4.2**
**el postre** dessert **I**
**el pozole** corn and meat stew
**practicar** to play, to practice **I, 1.1**
**practicar deportes** to play sports **I**
**el precio** price **I**
**preferir (ie, i)** to prefer **I, 1.3, 4.1**
**la pregunta** question
**preguntar** to ask
**preocupado(a)** worried **I**
**preocuparse por** to be worried about **2.1**
**preparar** to prepare **I**
**presentar** to introduce **I**
**Te/Le presento a...** Let me introduce you (familiar/formal) to... **I**
**preservar** to preserve **5.1**
**el préstamo** loan **4.3**
**prestar** to lend **4.3**
**la primavera** spring **I**
**primero** first **I**
**el primero** first of the month **I**
**primero(a)** first **I, 2.2**
**el (la) primo(a)** cousin **I**
**prisa**
**tener prisa** to be in a hurry **I**
**probable**
**Es probable que...** It's probable that... **3.3, 4.2**
**el problema** problem **I, 5.3**
**producir (produzco)** to produce **1.2**
**la profesión** profession **I, 6.1**
**el programa** program **1.3**
**el pronóstico** report **5.2**
**pronto** soon **I**
**la propina** tip **I**
**¿Cuánto le doy de propina?** How much do I tip? **I**
**proteger (protejo)** to protect **3.2**
**proteger las especies** to protect the species **5.3**
**la prueba** quiz **I**
**el pueblo** town, village **I**
**el puente** bridge **4.2**
**el puerco** pork **I**
**la puerta** door **I, 4.1**
**puertorriqueño(a)** Puerto Rican **1.3**
**pues** well **I**
**el puesto** position **6.1**
**la pulsera** bracelet **I**
**la puntualidad** punctuality **6.2**
**¡Pura vida!** Doing great!
**¡Puro juego!** Real fun!

**qué** what? **I**
**¿A qué hora es...?** (At) What time is...? **I**
**¿Qué desea(n)?** What would you like? **I**
**¿Qué día es hoy?** What day is today? **I**





R50 RECURSOS Glosario español–inglés

**¡Qué (divertido)!** How (fun)! **I**
**¿Qué hora es?** What time is it? **I**
**¡Qué lástima!** What a shame! **I**
**¿Qué lío!** What a mess! **5.3**
**¿Qué lleva?** What is he/she wearing? **I**
**¿Qué me recomienda?** What do you recommend? **2.3**
**¿Qué pasa?** What's happening?
**¿Qué tal?** How is it going? How are you? **I, EP**
**¿Qué tiempo hace?** What is the weather like? **I**
**quedar (en)** to stay, to be (in a specific place); to agree on **I**
**¿Puedes (Puede usted) decirme dónde queda...?** Could you tell me where...is? **I**
**¿Queda lejos?** Is it far? **I**
**los quehaceres** chores **I, 3.2**
**quemado(a)** burned
**la quemadura** burn **3.2**
**quemar** to burn **3.2**
**la quena** cane, reed
**querer (ie)** to want **I, 1.2**
**¿Quieres beber...?** Do you want to drink...? **I**
**¿Quieres comer...?** Do you want to eat...? **I**
**Quiero beber...** I want to drink... **I**
**Quiero comer...** I want to eat... **I**
**Quiero dejar un mensaje para...** I want to leave a message for... **I**
**el queso** cheese **I**
**Quetzalcóatl** an Aztec god
**¿quién(es)?** who? **I**
**¿De quién es...?** Whose is...? **I**
**¿Quién es?** Who is it? **I**
**¿Quiénes son?** Who are they? **I**
**los químicos** chemicals **5.3**
**quince** fifteen **I**
**quinientos(as)** five hundred **I**
**quinto(a)** fifth **I, 2.2**
**el quiosco** kiosk **4.2**
**Quisiera...** I would like... **I**
**quitar**
**quitar el polvo** to dust **I, 3.2**
**quitar la mesa** to clear the table **I**
**quitarse la ropa** to take off one's clothes **3.1**
**quizás** maybe **4.3**

**el radio** radio **I**
**el radiocasete** radio-tape player **I**
**la radiografía** x-ray **3.3**
**la raíz**
**las raíces** roots
**la rana** frog **5.1**
**las ranas venenosas fosforescentes** neon-colored poison dart frogs
**rápidamente** quickly **I, 3.2**
**rápido(a)** fast, quick **I**
**la raqueta** racket **I**
**rara vez** rarely **I**
**raro(a)** rare, strange **1.2**
**Es raro que...** It's rare that... **3.3**
**las rayas** stripes **4.3**
**el rayo** thunderbolt, flash of lightning **5.2**
**la razón** reason **I**
**Con razón.** That's why. **I**
**tener razón** to be right **I**
**la rebaja** sale **4.2**
**la recepción** reception/front desk **4.1**
**el (la) recepcionista** receptionist **I**
**el receso** break **I**
**la receta** prescription **3.3**
**recibir** to receive **I**
**el reciclaje** recycling **5.3**
**reciclar** to recycle **5.3**
**reciente** recent **I**
**recientemente** lately, recently **I, 3.2**
**las recomendaciones** recommendations **6.2**
**recomendar (ie)** to recommend **1.2**
**recordar (ue)** to remember **I**
**recuperarse** to get better **3.3**
**el recurso** resource
**los recursos naturales** natural resources **5.3**
**reducir (reduzco)** to reduce **5.3**
**el refrán** saying
**el refresco** soft drink **I**
**el refrigerador** refrigerator **4.1**
**el refugio de aves** bird sanctuary
**el regalo** gift **I**
**regatear** to bargain **I**
**regresar** to return, to go back **I, 4.2**
**Regresa más tarde.** He/She will return later. **I**
**Regular.** So-so. **I**
**reírse (i, i)** to laugh **2.1**
**relajarse** to relax **3.1**
**el relámpago** lightning **5.2**
**el relieve** relief, projection
**el reloj** clock, watch **I**
**remar** to row **5.2**
**renovar**
**se renueva** is renewed
**el repaso** review
**repetir (i, i)** to repeat **1.2, 1.3**
**el reportaje** report **1.3**
**el (la) reportero(a)** reporter **1.3**
**requerir (ie, i)** to require **6.2**
**el requisito** requirement **6.2**
**el resbaladilla** waterslide
**rescatar** to rescue **1.3**
**el rescate** rescue **1.3**
**la reserva** reservation **4.1**
**resolver (ue)** to resolve **5.3**

ESPAÑOL–INGLÉS


RECURSOS
Glosario español–inglés R51

**respirar** to breathe **3.3**
**la respuesta** answer
**el restaurante** restaurant **I**
**el resumen** summary
**el retrato** portrait **1.2**
**la reunión** gathering **2.2**
**reunirse** to get together **2.1**
**revelar** to develop
**revisar** to review, to check **4.2**
**la revista** magazine **I**
**rico(a)** tasty **I**; rich **2.1**
**ridículo**
**Es ridículo que...**
It's ridiculous that... **3.3**
**el río** river **I**
**riquísimo(a)** very tasty **I**
**la risa** laugh, laughter **2.1**
**rizado** curly (hair) **3.1**
**robar** to steal **1.3**
**el robo** robbery **1.3**
**rodear**
**rodean** surround
**la rodilla** knee **3.3**
**rojo(a)** red **I**
**romántico(a)** romantic **2.3**
**romper**
**romper la piñata**
to break the piñata **2.2**
**la ropa** clothing **1.2**
**ponerse la ropa**
to get dressed **2.2**
**rosado(a)** pink **I**
**rubio(a)** blond **I**

**sábado** Saturday **I**
**la sábana** sheet **5.2**
**saber (sé)** to know **I, 1.2, 1.3**
**el sabio** sage, wise man
**el sabor** flavor, taste **1.2**
**sabroso(a)** tasty **I, 1.2**
**sacar** to take **I, 1.1**
**sacar fotos** to take
photos/pictures **I**
**sacar la basura**
to take out the trash **I, 3.2**
**sacar una buena nota**
to get a good grade **I**
**el saco de dormir**
sleeping bag **5.2**
**la sal** salt **I, 2.3**
**la sala** living room **I, 4.1**
**la sala de emergencia**
emergency room **3.3**
**la salchicha**
sausage **I**; hot dog **2.3**
**la salida** departure **1.1**
**salir (salgo)**
to go out, to leave **I**
**la salsa** salsa **I**
**saltar** to jump
**saltar la cuerda**
to jump rope **2.1**
**¡Salud!** Cheers! **2.3**
**saludable** healthy **3.1**
**saludar** to greet
**el saludo** greeting
**salvadoreño(a)** Salvadorian **1.3**
**salvaje** wild **5.1**
**las sandalias** sandals **3.2**
**la sangre** blood **3.3**
**el secador de pelo**
hair dryer **I, 3.1**
**secarse** to dry oneself **I, 3.1**
**seco(a)** dry **2.3**
**el (la) secretario(a)**
secretary **I, 6.1**
**seguir (i, i) (sigo)**
to follow, to continue **4.2**
**según** according to
**segundo(a)** second **I, 2.2**
**de segunda mano**
used, secondhand
**la seguridad** security **1.1**
**el seguro** insurance **6.2**
**seis** six **I**
**seiscientos(as)** six hundred **I**
**la selva** jungle **5.1**
**el semáforo**
traffic light/signal **4.2**
**la semana** week **I**
**la semana pasada**
last week **I**
**el semestre** semester **I**
**sencillo(a)** simple, plain **I, 4.3**
**el sendero** path, trail **5.1**
**sentar(se) (ie)** to sit down **2.1**
**el señor** Mr. **I**
**la señora** Mrs. **I**
**la señorita** Miss **I**
**separar** to separate **5.3**
**septiembre** September **I**
**séptimo(a)** seventh **I, 2.2**
**ser** to be **I, EP**
**Es la.../Son las...**
It is... o'clock. **I**
**ser de...** to be from... **I**
**el ser humano** human being **5.3**
**la serie** series **2.3**
**serio(a)** serious **I**
**la serpiente** snake **5.1**
**los servicios** bathrooms **4.1**
**la servilleta** napkin **2.3**
**servir (i, i)** to serve **I, 1.2, 1.3**
**sesenta** sixty **I**
**setecientos(as)** seven hundred **I**
**setenta** seventy **I**
**sexto(a)** sixth **I, 2.2**
**los shorts** shorts **I**
**si** if **I, 5.3**
**Si estuviera...**
If I/you/he/she were... **5.3**
**Si fuera...**
If I/you/he/she were... **5.3**
**Si pudieras...** If you could... **5.3**
**sí** yes **I**
**¡Claro que sí!** Of course! **I**
**Sí, me encantaría.**
Yes, I would love to. **I**
**siempre** always **I**
**siete** seven **I**
**el siglo** century
**del siglo III o IV**
third or fourth century
**siguiente** next **2.2**
**la silla** chair **I, 4.1**
**el sillón** armchair **I, 4.1**





R52 RECURSOS
Glosario español–inglés

**simpático(a)** nice **I**
**sin** without **I**
**sino también** but also
**la situación** situation **5.3**
**el smog** smog **5.3**
**sobre** on, about **4.2**
**sobre hielo** on ice **I**
**el (la) sobrino(a)** nephew/niece **2.1**
**sociable** sociable **2.1**
**¡Socorro!** Help! **3.3**
**el sofá** sofa, couch **I, 4.1**
**el sol** sun **I**
**las gafas de sol** sunglasses **I**
**Hace sol.** It's sunny. **I**
**Hay sol.** It's sunny. **I**
**tomar el sol** to sunbathe **I**
**soleado(a)** sunny **5.2**
**solicitar** to request, to apply for **6.1**
**la solicitud** application **6.1**
**sólo** only **I**
**solo(a)** alone **I**
**la sombra** darkness, shade, shadow **5.1**
**el sombrero** hat **I**
**la sombrilla de playa** beach umbrella **3.2**
**sonreírse (i, i)** to smile **2.1**
**la sopa** soup **I**
**sorprender** to surprise **I, 4.3**
**la sorpresa** surprise **I, 2.2**
**su** your (formal), his, her, its, their **I**
**subir**
**subir por** to go up, to climb **4.2**
**sucio(a)** dirty **I, 3.2**
**la sucursal**
**sucursales** branches
**sudar** to sweat **3.1**
**el sueldo** salary **6.2**
**el suelo** floor **I, 4.1**
**barrer el suelo** to sweep the floor **I**
**sueño** sleep; dream
**felices sueños** sweet dreams
**tener sueño** to be sleepy **I**
**suerte** luck **I**
**tener suerte** to be lucky **I**
**el suéter** sweater **I**
**suficiente** enough **4.3**
**la sugerencia** suggestion
**sugerir (ie, i)** to suggest **4.1**
**el supermercado** supermarket **I**
**ir al supermercado** to go to the supermarket **I**
**el sur** south **4.2**
**el surfing** surfing **I**

**tacaño(a)** stingy **4.3**
**el taco** taco **2.3**
**tal vez** maybe **I, 4.3**
**Tal vez otro día.** Maybe another day. **I**
**el talento** talent **1.2**
**la talla** size (clothing) **4.3**
**el taller** workshop **I**
**los tamales** cornmeal dough and filling wrapped in corn husks and steamed
**también** also, too **I**
**también se dice** you can also say
**tampoco** neither, either **I**
**tan** as **I**
**tan... como** as... as **I, 4.3**
**tanto** as much **I**
**tanto como** as much as **I, 4.3**
**las tapas** appetizers **I**
**la taquería** taco restaurant **2.3**
**la taquilla** box office **4.2**
**tarde** late **I**
**Regresa más tarde.** He/She will return later. **I**
**la tarde** afternoon **I**
**Buenas tardes.** Good afternoon. **I**
**de la tarde** in the afternoon **I**
**por la tarde** during the afternoon **I**
**la tarea** homework **I**
**la tarjeta de crédito** credit card **I**
**el taxi** taxi, cab **I**
**el (la) taxista** taxi driver **I, 6.1**
**la taza** cup **I**
**el té** tea **I**
**el teatro** theater **I**
**el teclado** keyboard **I**
**teclear**
**¡A teclear!** Let's key in!
**el (la) técnico(a)** technician **6.1**
**el teleférico** aerial tram
**el teléfono** telephone **I**
**¿Cuál es tu teléfono?** What is your phone number? **I, EP**
**la telenovela** soap opera **2.3**
**el (la) televidente** viewer **1.3**
**la televisión** television **I**
**ver la televisión** to watch television **I**
**el televisor** television set **I**
**el tema** theme **2.3**
**el temblor** earthquake
**la temperatura** temperature **3.3**
**temprano** early **I**
**el tenedor** fork **I**
**tener** to have **I, EP, 1.2**
**¿Cuántos años tiene...?** How old is...? **I**
**tener calor** to be hot **I**
**tener cuidado** to be careful **I, 2.1**
**tener envidia** to be envious **2.1**
**tener éxito** to be successful **2.1**
**tener frío** to be cold **I**
**tener ganas de...** to feel like... **I**
**tener hambre** to be hungry **I**
**tener miedo** to be afraid **I**
**tener prisa** to be in a hurry **I**
**tener que** to have to **I**
**tener razón** to be right **I**
**tener sed** to be thirsty **I**
**tener sueño** to be sleepy **I**
**tener suerte** to be lucky **I**

ESPAÑOL–INGLÉS


RECURSOS
Glosario español–inglés R53

**tener vergüenza** to be ashamed **2.1**
**Tiene... años.** He/She is... years old. **I**
**el tenis** tennis **I**
**tercero(a)** third **I, 2.2**
**terminar** to finish **I**
**la terraza** terrace
**terrible** terrible, awful **I**
**la tía** aunt **I**
**el tiempo** time; weather **I**
**Hace buen tiempo.** It is nice outside. **I**
**Hace mal tiempo.** It is bad outside. **I**
**¿Qué tiempo hace?** What is the weather like? **I**
**el tiempo libre** free time **I**
**la tienda** store **I**
**la tienda de deportes** sporting goods store **I**
**la tienda de música y videos** music and video store **I**
**la tienda de campaña** tent **5.2**
**la tierra** land, earth **5.1**
**las tijeras** scissors **I, 5.2**
**tímido(a)** shy **2.1**
**la tintorería** dry cleaner **4.2**
**el tío** uncle **I**
**los tíos** uncle(s) and aunt(s) **I**
**típicamente** typically **3.2**
**la tira cómica** comic strip **1.3**
**el titular** headline **1.3**
**la tiza** chalk **I**
**la toalla** towel **I, 3.2**
**el tobillo** ankle **3.3**
**tocar** to play (an instrument) **I, 1.1**
**tocar el piano** to play the piano **I**
**tocar la guitarra** to play the guitar **I**
**todavía** still, yet **I**
**todo(a)** all **I**
**todo el mundo** everyone **2.2**
**todos los días** every day **I**
**tomar** to take, to eat, to drink **I**
**tomar el sol** to sunbathe **I**
**tomar un curso de natación** to take a swimming class **1.1**
**el tomate** tomato **I, 2.3**
**la tormenta** storm **I**
**el toro** bull **I, 6.2**
**la torta** sandwich (sub) **I, 2.3**
**la tortilla española** potato omelet **I**
**la tortuga** turtle **5.1**
**la tos** cough **3.3**
**los tostones** fried plantains **1.2**
**trabajador(a)** hard-working **I**
**trabajar** to work **1.1**
**tradicional** traditional **I, 1.2**
**traducir (traduzco)** to translate **1.2**
**traer (traigo)** to bring **I, 1.2**
**¿Me trae...?** Could you bring me...?
**el tráfico** traffic **I**
**el traje** suit **4.3**
**el traje de baño** bathing suit **I**
**tranquilamente** calmly **I, 3.2**
**tranquilo(a)** calm **I**
**tratar** to treat **3.3**
**trece** thirteen **I**
**treinta** thirty **I**
**el tren** train **I**
**trepar**
**trepar a un árbol** to climb a tree **2.1**
**tres** three **I**
**trescientos(as)** three hundred **I**
**triste** sad **I**
**Es triste que...** It's sad that... **3.3, 4.2**
**la tristeza** sadness **2.2**
**el trueno** thunder **5.2**
**tu** your (familiar) **I**
**tú** you (familiar singular) **I**
**el tucán** toucan **5.1**
**el turismo** tourism **4.1**

**último(a)** last **I**
**un millón** one million **I**
**un par de** a pair of **4.3**
**la unidad** unit
**unir**
**une** combines
**unirse**
**se unen** unite
**la universidad** university **6.2**
**uno** one **I**
**uruguayo(a)** Uruguayan **1.3**
**usar** to use **I**; to wear, to take a size **4.3**
**el uso** use
**usted** you (formal singular) **I**
**ustedes** you (formal plural) **I**
**útil** useful **5.3**
**la uva** grape **1.2**

**la vaca** cow **I**
**vacío(a)** empty **2.3**
**valer (valgo)** to be worth **4.3**
**el valle** valley **5.1**
**valorar** to appreciate **5.1**
**el vaso** glass **I**
**el vaso de** glass of **I**
**el vecindario** neighborhood **4.2**
**el (la) vecino(a)** neighbor **I**
**vegetariano(a)** vegetarian **I**
**veinte** twenty **I**
**veintiuno** twenty-one **I**
**las velas** candles **2.2**
**el velo**
**el velo bordado a mano** handmade veil
**el venado** deer **5.1**
**vender** to sell **I**
**venezolano(a)** Venezuelan **1.3**

ESPAÑOL–INGLÉS


RECURSOS R54 Glosario español–inglés

**venir** to come **I, 1.2**
**la ventaja** advantage **6.2**
**la ventana** window **I, 4.1**
**la ventanilla** window **1.1**
**ver (veo)** to see **I, 1.1**
  **¿Me deja ver...?** May I see...? **I**
  **Nos vemos.** See you later. **I**
  **ver la televisión** to watch television **I**
**el verano** summer **I**
**la verdad** truth **I**
  **¿De veras?** Really? **1.3**
  **Es verdad.** It's true. **I**
  **No es verdad que...** It's not true that... **4.3**
**verde** green **I**
**la verdura** vegetable **I, 2.3**
**el vestido** dress **I**
**vestirse (i, i)** to dress oneself **4.3**
**el (la) veterinario(a)** veterinarian **6.1**
**viajar** to travel **I**
**el viaje** trip **I, 1.1**
**los viajeros** travelers
**la vida** life **I**
**el video** video **I**
  **alquilar un video** to rent a video **I**
**la videograbadora** VCR **I**
**el videojuego** video game **I**
**el vidrio** glass **5.3**
**viejo(a)** old **I**
**el viento** wind **I**
  **Hace viento.** It's windy. **I**
  **Hay viento.** It's windy. **I**
**viernes** Friday **I**
**violento(a)** violent **5.2**
**visitar** to visit **I**
**vivir** to live **I, 1.1**
  **Vive en...** He/She lives in... **I**
  **Vivo en...** I live in... **I**
**vivo(a)** alive
**volar (ue)** to fly **5.1**
**el voleibol** volleyball **I**
**el (la) voluntario(a)** volunteer **6.1**
**volver (ue)** to return, to come back **I**
**vosotros(as)** you (familiar plural) **I**
**la voz** voice
**el vuelo** flight **1.1**
**vuestro(a)** your (familiar plural) **I**

**y** and **I**
  **y cuarto** quarter past **I**
  **y media** half past **I**
**ya** already, now **3.2**
  **¡Ya lo sé!** I already know. **I**
  **ya no** no longer **I**
**el yeso** cast **3.3**
**yo** I **I**
**el yogur** yogurt **I, 1.2**

**la zanahoria** carrot **I, 2.3**
**la zapatería** shoe store **I**
**el zapato** shoe **I**
**el zapato de tacón** high-heeled shoe **4.3**
**el zumo** juice **I**

ESPAÑOL–INGLÉS


RECURSOS
Glosario español–inglés R55

**GLOSARIO**

# *inglés-español*

This English–Spanish glossary contains all of the active vocabulary words that appear in the text as well as passive vocabulary from readings, culture sections, and extra vocabulary lists.

**to be able** poder (ue) **I, 1.2**
**about** sobre **4.2**
**above** arriba **4.2**
**according to** según
**accountant**
el (la) contador(a) **I, 6.1**
**acquaintance** la amistad **2.1**
**actor** el actor **2.3**
**actress** la actriz **2.3**
**address** la dirección **I**
**adventures** las aventuras **2.3**
**advice** el (los) consejo(s) **3.1**
**to advise** aconsejar **3.1**
**aerial tram** el teleférico
**after** después (de) **I**
**afternoon** la tarde **I**
**during the afternoon**
por la tarde **I**
**Good afternoon.**
Buenas tardes. **I, EP**
**in the afternoon** de la tarde **I**
**after-shave lotion** la loción **3.1**
**afterward** después **I**
**against**
**to be against**
estar en contra de **5.2**
**age** la edad **I**
**to agree (on)** quedar (en) **I**;
estar de acuerdo **I, 1.2**
**air conditioning**
el aire acondicionado **4.1**
**airline** la aerolínea **1.1**
**airplane** el avión **I**
**airport** el aeropuerto **I**
**aisle** el pasillo **1.1**
**alarm clock** el despertador **4.1**
**alive** vivo(a)
**all** todo(a) **I**
**all around**
por todas partes **5.1**
**It is up to all of us…**
A todos nos toca… **5.3**
**almost** casi **2.2**
**alone** solo(a) **I**
**already** ya **3.2**
**also** también **I**
**altitude** la altura **5.1**
**aluminum** el aluminio **5.3**
**always** siempre **I**
**ambulance** la ambulancia **3.3**
**ancient** antiguo(a) **I**
**and** y **I**
**and so it was that**
así fue que **2.2**
**angry** enojado(a) **I**
**to get angry with**
enojarse con **2.1**
**animal** el animal **I**
**animated** animado(a) **2.1**
**ankle** el tobillo **3.3**
**anniversary** el aniversario **2.2**
**another** otro(a) **I**
**answer** la respuesta
**to answer** contestar **I**
**answering machine**
la máquina contestadora **I**
**ant** la hormiga
**apartment** el apartamento **I**
**to apologize** disculparse **2.1**
**appetizers** las tapas **I**
**apple** la manzana **2.3**
**application** la solicitud **6.1**
**to apply for** solicitar **6.1**
**appointment** la cita **I**
**to appreciate** valorar **5.1**
**April** abril **I**
**architect**
el (la) arquitecto(a) **I, 6.1**
**architecture** la arquitectura **I**
**Argentine** argentino(a) **1.3**
**arm** el brazo **I, 3.3**
**armchair** el sillón **I, 4.1**
**armoire** el armario **4.1**
**around** alrededor (de) **4.2;** por **I**
**to arrange (flowers, books)**
ordenar (las flores,
los libros) **I**
**arrival** la llegada **1.1**
**to arrive** llegar **I, 1.1**

INGLÉS–ESPAÑOL



R56 RECURSOS
Glosario inglés–español

**art** el arte **I**
**article** el artículo **1.3**
**artisan** el (la) artesano(a) **I**
**artist** el (la) artista **1.2**
**as** como **I**
**as… as** tan… como **I, 4.3**
**as far as** hasta **I**
**as for** en cuanto a
**as much as** tanto como **I, 4.3**
**ash** la ceniza
**to ask** preguntar
**to ask for** pedir (i, i) **I, 1.2, 1.3**
**aspirin** la aspirina **3.3**
**assistant** el (la) asistente **6.1**
**at** a **I**
**At… o'clock.** A la(s)… **I**
**at once** en seguida **2.2**
**athletics** el atletismo **3.1**
**ATM** el cajero automático **4.3**
**atmosphere** el ambiente
**to attend** asistir a
**auditorium** el auditorio **I**
**August** agosto **I**
**aunt** la tía **I**
**author** el (la) autor(a) **1.3**
**autonomy** la autonomía
**avenue** la avenida **I**
**awesome** chévere **I**
**How awesome!** ¡Qué chévere! **I**
**awful** terrible **I**
**Aztec**
**an Aztec god** Quetzalcóatl

## B

**baby** el bebé **2.1**
**backpack** la mochila **I**
**bad** malo(a) **I**
**It is bad (weather) outside.** Hace mal tiempo. **I**
**It's bad that…** Es malo que… **3.3, 4.2**
**bag** la bolsa **I**
**balanced** balanceado(a) **3.1**
**ball** la bola, la pelota **I**
**ballad** la décima
**balloons** los globos **2.2**
**bank** el banco **I**
**barbecued chicken** el pollo asado **1.2**
**barber** el (la) peluquero(a) **6.1**
**bargain** la ganga **4.2**
**to bargain** regatear **I**
**baseball (sport)** el béisbol **I**
**baseball cap** la gorra **I**
**basketball** el baloncesto **I**
**bass** el contrabajo
**bat** el bate **I;** el murciélago
**to bathe** bañarse **I, 3.1**
**bathing suit** el traje de baño **I**
**bathroom** el baño **I, 4.1**
**bathrooms** los servicios **4.1**
**bathtub** la bañera **4.1**
**to be** estar **I, EP, 1.2;** ser **I, EP, 1.1**
**to be worth** valer (valgo) **4.3**
**beach** la playa **I**
**beach umbrella** la sombrilla de playa **3.2**
**beans** los frijoles **2.3**
**beauty** la belleza **5.1**
**because** porque **I**
**bed** la cama **I, 4.1**
**to go to bed** acostarse (ue) **I**
**to make the bed** hacer la cama **I**
**bedroom** la habitación **I**
**beef** la carne de res **I, 2.3**
**before** antes (de) **I**
**to begin** empezar (ie) **I, 1.1**
**to behave well/badly** portarse bien/mal **2.1**
**behind** detrás (de) **I**
**to believe** creer **I, 1.3**
**to belong** pertenecer (pertenezco) **5.2**
**belt** el cinturón **I**
**benefits** los beneficios **6.2**
**beside** al lado (de) **I**
**better** mejor **I**
**It's better that…** Es mejor que… **3.3, 4.2**
**between** entre **I**
**beverage** la bebida **I**
**big** grande **I**
**bike** la bicicleta
**to ride a bike** andar en bicicleta **I**
**bill** la cuenta **I, 2.3**
**bird** el pájaro **I**
**bird sanctuary** el refugio de aves
**birthday** el cumpleaños **I**
**black** negro(a) **I**
**blanket** la manta **I, 5.2**
**blond** rubio(a) **I**
**blood** la sangre **3.3**
**blouse** la blusa **I**
**blue** azul **I**
**to board (a plane)** abordar **1.1**
**boarding house** la pensión **4.1**
**boat** el bote **3.2**
**rowboat** el bote de remos
**body** el cuerpo **I, 3.3**
**Bolivian** boliviano(a) **1.3**
**book** el libro **I**
**bookstore** la librería **I**
**boots** las botas **I**
**bored**
**to be bored** aburrirse **2.1**
**boring** aburrido(a) **I**
**born**
**to be born** nacer
**boss** el (la) jefe(a) **I, 6.1**
**to bother** molestar **2.3, 4.3**
**bottle** la botella **I, 5.3**
**box office** la taquilla **4.2**
**boy** el chico; el muchacho; el niño **I**
**boyfriend** el novio **2.1**
**bracelet** la pulsera **I**
**branch** la sucursal
**branches** las sucursales
**bread** el pan **I, 2.3**
**bread bakery** la panadería **I**
**break** el receso **I**

INGLÉS–ESPAÑOL



RECURSOS
Glosario inglés–español R57

**to break the piñata**
romper la piñata **2.2**
**breakfast** el desayuno **I**
**to have breakfast**
desayunar **I**
**to breathe** respirar **3.3**
**bride** la novia **2.1**
**bridge** el puente **4.2**
**to bring** traer (traigo) **I, 1.2**
**Could you bring me...?**
¿Me trae...? **I**
**brother** el hermano **I**
**brother(s) and sister(s)**
los hermanos **I**
**brother-in-law** el cuñado **2.1**
**brown** marrón **I**
**brown (hair)** castaño(a) **I**
**brush** el cepillo **I, 3.1**
**to brush one's teeth**
lavarse los dientes **I, 3.1**
**bucket** el balde **5.2**
**building** el edificio **I**
**bull** el toro **I**
**burn** la quemadura **3.2**
**to burn** quemar **3.2**
**bus** el autobús **I**
**bus station**
la estación de autobuses **I**
**business** la empresa **6.2**
**businessman**
el hombre de negocios **I, 6.1**
**businesswoman**
la mujer de negocios **I, 6.1**
**busy** ocupado(a) **I**
**but** pero **I;** mas
**but also** sino también
**butcher's shop** la carnicería **4.1**
**butter** la mantequilla **I, 1.2**
**butterfly** la mariposa **5.1**
**to buy** comprar **I**
**by** por **I**

## C

**cab** el taxi **I**
**café** el café **I**
**cafeteria** la cafetería **I**
**cake** el pastel **I**
**calculator** la calculadora **I**
**call** la llamada **I**
**to call** llamar **I**
**Tell him or her to call me.**
Dile/Dígale que me llame. **I**
**calm** tranquilo(a) **I**
**calmly** tranquilamente **I, 3.2**
**calorie** la caloría **3.1**
**camera** la cámara **I, 1.3**
**camp** el campamento **5.2**
**to camp in the mountains**
acampar en las montañas **1.1**
**campfire** la fogata **5.2**
**can** la lata **I, 5.3**
**can opener** el abrelatas **5.2**
**can** poder (ue) **I, 1.2**
**Can (May) I offer you anything more?** ¿Se les ofrece algo más? **2.3**
**Can you help (wait on) me?**
¿Me puede atender? **4.3**
**I can offer you...**
Le puedo ofrecer... **I**
**Thanks, but I can't.**
Gracias, pero no puedo. **I**
**Canadian** canadiense **1.3**
**candles** las velas **2.2**
**cane** el quena
**canoe** la canoa
**cap** el gorro **I**
**baseball cap** la gorra **I**
**capabilities** las habilidades **6.2**
**car** el carro **I**
**cardboard, cardboard box**
el cartón **5.3**
**career** la carrera **6.1**
**careful** cuidadoso(a) **I**
**to be careful** tener cuidado **I**
**carefully** cuidadosamente **I**
**carrot** la zanahoria **I, 2.3**
**to carry** llevar **I**
**carton** el cartón **5.3**
**cash** el efectivo **I**
**cash register**
la caja registradora **4.3**
**cashier** el (la) cajero(a) **4.3**
**cassette** el casete **I**
**cast** el yeso **3.3**
**cat** el (la) gato(a) **I**
**to catch**
**catches your eye**
llama la atención
**cause** la causa **1.3**
**cave** la cueva
**cedar** el cedro
**to celebrate** celebrar **I**
**center** el centro **I**
**shopping center**
el centro comercial **I**
**centigrade** centígrado(a) **5.2**
**century** el siglo
**third or fourth century**
del siglo III o IV
**ceramics** la cerámica **I**
**cereal** el cereal **I, 1.2**
**certain**
**It is not certain that...**
No es cierto que... **4.3**
**chain** la cadena
**chair** la silla **I, 4.1**
**chalk** la tiza **I**
**chalkboard** el pizarrón **I**
**champion** el campeón
**change** el cambio **I**
**to change** cambiar **I**
**has changed** se ha cambiado
**channel** el canal **1.3**
**character** el personaje
**to chat** charlar
**cheap** barato(a) **I**

INGLÉS–ESPAÑOL



R58 RECURSOS
Glosario inglés–español

**check** la cuenta **I**
**Separate checks.** Es aparte. **I**
**The check, please.**
La cuenta, por favor. **I**
**checked** de cuadros **I**
**checks** los cheques **4.3**
**Cheers!** ¡Salud! **2.3**
**cheese** el queso **I**
**chemicals** los químicos **5.3**
**chemistry** la química **I**
**cherry** la cereza **2.3**
**chess**
**to play chess**
jugar (ue) al ajedrez **1.1**
**chicken** el pollo **I**
**child-care provider**
el (la) niñero(a) **6.1**
**Chilean** chileno(a) **1.3**
**Chinese** chino(a) **1.3**
**to choose** escoger (escojo) **4.3**
**chores** los quehaceres **I, 3.2**
**church** la iglesia **I**
**citizenship** la ciudadanía **6.1**
**city** la ciudad **I**
**city block** la cuadra **I**
**class** la clase **I**
**classmate**
el (la) compañero(a) **2.1**
**classroom** la clase **I**
**clean** limpio(a) **I, 3.2**
**to clean** limpiar **I,** hacer la limpieza **3.2**
**to clean the room**
limpiar el cuarto **I, 3.2**
**climate** el clima **5.1**
**to climb** subir por **4.2**
**to climb a tree**
trepar a un árbol **2.1**
**to climb mountains**
escalar montañas **5.2**
**clock** el reloj **I**
**to close** cerrar (ie) **I**
**closed** cerrado(a) **I, 4.3**
**closet** el armario **I**
**clothing** la ropa **I**
**cloud** la nube **5.2**
**cloudy** nublado **I**
**It is cloudy**. Está nublado. **I**
**coat** el abrigo **I**
**coconut milk**
el agua de coco **3.2**
**coffee** el café **I**
**coffee shop** la cafetería **I**
**cold**
**to be cold** tener frío **I**
**It is cold.** Hace frío. **I**
**Colombian** colombiano(a) **1.3**
**color** el color **I**
**What color...?**
¿De qué color...? **I**
**comb** el peine **I, 3.1**
**to comb one's hair**
peinarse **I, 3.1**
**to combine** unir
**combines** une
**to come** venir (ie) **I, 1.2**
**to come back** volver (ue) **I**
**comedian, comedienne**
el (la) comediante **2.3**
**comfortable** cómodo(a) **3.3**
**comic strip** la tira cómica **1.3**
**comical** cómico(a) **I**
**command** el mandato
**commercial** el anuncio **1.3**
**common** común **2.2**
**community** la comunidad **I**
**compact disc**
el disco compacto **I**
**companion**
el (la) compañero(a) **2.1**
**company** la compañía **I**
**company (business)**
la empresa **6.2**
**to compete** competir (i, i) **1.2, 1.3**
**complicated** complicado(a) **5.2**
**composer** el compositor
**computer** la computadora **I**
**computer science**
la computación **I**
**concert** el concierto **I**
**congratulations** felicidades **I**
**to conserve** conservar **5.1**
**to construct** construir **2.1**
**consultation** la consulta **3.3**
**content** contento(a) **I**
**contest** el concurso **I**
**to continue**
seguir (i, i) (sigo) **4.2**
**contract** el contrato **6.2**
**contrary**
**on the contrary**
al contrario **2.2**
**to cook** cocinar **I**
**cookie** la galleta **I, 1.2**
**cool** fresco(a)
**It is cool.** Hace fresco. **I**
**cooler** la neverita **3.2**
**corn** el maíz
**corner** la esquina **4.1**
**corral** el corral **I**
**to correct** corregir (i, i) (corrijo)
**to cost** costar (ue) **I**
**Costa Rican** costarricense **1.3**
**couch** el sofá **I**
**cough** la tos **3.3**
**to count** contar (ue) **I**
**counter** el mostrador **1.1**
**country** el país; el campo **I**
**countryside** el campo **I**
**court** la cancha **I**
**cousin** el (la) primo(a) **I**
**cow** la vaca **I**
**cracker** la galleta **5.3**
**crazy** loco(a) **I**
**cream** la crema **I, 1.2**
**to create** crear **5.2**
**credit card**
la tarjeta de crédito **I**
**criticism** la crítica **1.3**
**to cross** cruzar **I**
**crossing** el cruce **4.2**
**to cry** llorar **3.3**




RECURSOS
Glosario inglés–español R59

**cuatro** guitar
**a tuned guitar**
un cuatro templado
**Cuban** cubano(a) **1.3**
**cuisine** la cocina
**cup** la taza **I**
**curly (hair)** rizado **3.1**
**currency** la moneda
**curriculum vitae**
el currículum **6.2**
**customer** el (la) cliente **4.3**
**customs** la aduana **1.1**
**to cut** cortar
**to cut oneself** cortarse **3.3**
**to cut the grass** cortar
el césped **3.2**

**daily** diario(a) **2.2**
**damage**
**damaging it** dañarla
**to dance** bailar **I**
**dancer**
el (la) bailarín/bailarina **6.1**
**danger** el peligro **I**
**dangerous** peligroso(a) **I, 5.1**
**It's dangerous that…**
Es peligroso que… **3.3, 4.2**
**dark** oscuro(a) **4.3**
**dark hair and skin**
moreno(a) **I**
**darkness** la sombra **5.1**
**date** la fecha **I**
**date of birth**
la fecha de nacimiento **6.1**
**What is the date?**
¿Cuál es la fecha? **I**
**daughter** la hija **I**
**day** el día **I**
**day before yesterday**
anteayer **I, 2.2**
**What day is today?**
¿Qué día es hoy? **I**

**December** diciembre **I**
**to decide** decidir **I**
**decor**
**interior decor** la decoración
**decorations** los adornos **2.2**
**deer** el venado **5.1**
**degree** el grado **I**
**delicious** delicioso(a) **I**
**to delight** encantar **2.3**
**Delighted to meet you.**
Encantado(a). **I**
**deodorant** el desodorante **3.1**
**departure** la salida **1.1**
**depressed** deprimido(a) **I**
**to descend** bajar (por) **4.2**
**desert** el desierto **I**
**to desire** desear **1.2, 4.1**
**desk** el escritorio **I**
**dessert** el postre **I**
**destroyed** destruido(a)
**destruction** la destrucción **5.3**
**detail** el detalle **1.3**
**to detain** detener
**to develop** desarrollar; revelar
**development** el desarrollo **5.1**
**to dial** marcar **I**
**dictionary** el diccionario **I**
**to die** morir (ue, u) **1.3**
**diet** la dieta **3.1**
**difficult** difícil **I**
**dining room** el comedor **I, 4.1**
**dinner** la cena **I**
**to have dinner** cenar **I**
**direction** la dirección **I**
**dirty** sucio(a) **I, 3.2**
**disadvantage** la desventaja **6.2**
**to discover** descubrir **5.1**
**disguised as** disfrazado(a) de
**dishwasher** el lavaplatos **I, 4.1**
**distance** la distancia **4.2**
**diverse** diverso(a) **5.1**
**to do** hacer (hago) **I, 1.1**
**doctor** el (la) doctor(a) **I**
**dog** el (la) perro(a) **I**
**to walk the dog**
caminar con el perro **I**

**doll** la muñeca **2.1**
**dollar** el dólar **I**
**Dominican** dominicano(a) **1.3**
**dominoes** el dominó
**door** la puerta **I, 4.1**
**to doubt** dudar **4.3**
**down** abajo **I, 4.2**
**downpour** el aguacero **5.2**
**downtown** el centro **I**
**dozen** la docena **I**
**to draw** dibujar **2.1**
**dream**
**sweet dreams** felices sueños
**dress** el vestido **I**
**to dress oneself** vestirse (i, i) **4.3**
**to get dressed**
ponerse la ropa **I**
**to get dressed up**
arreglarse **4.3**
**drink** la bebida **I**
**to drink** beber; tomar **I**
**Do you want to drink…?**
¿Quieres beber…? **I**
**I want to drink…**
Quiero beber… **I**
**to drive** conducir (conduzco)
**1.2;** manejar **I**
**driver** el (la) conductor(a) **4.2**
**drizzle** la llovizna **5.2**
**drop** la gota
**drugstore** la farmacia **I**
**dry** seco(a) **2.3**
**dry cleaner** la tintorería **4.2**
**to dry oneself** secarse **I, 3.1**
**during** durante **I**
**dust** el polvo **I**
**to dust** quitar el polvo **I, 3.2**

**each** cada **I**
**ear** la oreja **I, 3.3**
**early** temprano **I**
**to earn a living**
ganarse la vida **6.1**


R60 RECURSOS
Glosario inglés–español

**earring** el arete **I**
**earthquake** el temblor
**easily** fácilmente **I, 3.2**
**east** el este **4.2**
**easy** fácil **I**
**to eat** comer; tomar **I, 1.1**
**Do you want to eat...?** ¿Quieres comer...? **I**
**to eat breakfast** desayunar **I**
**to eat dinner** cenar **2.3**
**to eat lunch** almorzar (ue) **I, 1.1**
**I want to eat...** Quiero comer... **I**
**Ecuadorian** ecuatoriano(a) **1.3**
**edge** la orilla **3.2**
**edition** la edición **1.3**
**editor** el (la) editor(a) **I, 1.3**
**education** la educación **6.2**
**effects** los efectos **5.3**
**egg** el huevo **I, 1.2**
**eight** ocho **I**
**eight hundred** ochocientos(as) **I**
**eighteen** dieciocho **I**
**eighth** octavo(a) **I, 2.2**
**eighty** ochenta **I**
**elbow** el codo **3.3**
**electricity** la electricidad **4.1**
**elegant** elegante **4.3**
**elevator** el ascensor **4.1**
**eleven** once **I**
**emergency room** la sala de emergencia **3.3**
**to emit**
**emits smoke** echa humo
**employment** el empleo **6.1**
**empty** vacío(a) **2.3**
**enchilada** la enchilada **I**
**energy** la energía **3.1**
**engineer** el (la) ingeniero(a) **6.1**
**English** inglés(esa) **1.3;** el inglés **I**
**to enjoy**
**to enjoy oneself** divertirse (ie, i) **2.1**
**to enjoy time with friends** disfrutar con los amigos **1.1**
**enjoyable** divertido(a) **I, 2.1**
**enormous** enorme **I, 1.2**
**enough** bastante **2.3;** suficiente **4.3**
**to enter** entrar (a, en) **I**
**entertaining** divertido(a) **2.1**
**environment** el medio ambiente **5.1**
**equipment**
**sound equipment** el equipo de sonido
**eraser** el borrador **I**
**especially** especialmente **I, 3.2**
**essential**
**It's essential that...** Es esencial que... **3.3**
**even though** aunque **2.2**
**evening** la noche **I**
**during the evening** por la noche **I**
**Good evening.** Buenas noches. **I**
**every** cada **I**
**every day** todos los días **I**
**everyone** todo el mundo **2.2**
**excess luggage** el exceso de equipaje **1.1**
**to exchange** cambiar **I**
**excited** emocionado(a) **I**
**to exclaim** exclamar **2.2**
**Excuse me.** Discúlpeme. **4.2**
**to exercise** hacer ejercicio **I**
**exhibit** la exposición **1.2**
**to expect** esperar **I**
**expenses** los gastos **4.3**
**expensive** caro(a) **I**
**It's very expensive!** ¡Es muy caro(a)! **I**
**to explain** explicar **1.1**
**eye** el ojo **I**

**face** la cara **I, 3.3**
**facing** enfrente (de) **I**
**fact** el hecho **1.3**
**facts** los datos **6.1**
**fall** el otoño **I**
**to fall asleep** dormirse (ue, u) **I**
**to fall** caer (caigo) **EP**
**to fall down** caerse (me caigo) **2.1**
**to fall in love (with)** enamorarse (con) **2.2**
**false** falso(a)
**family** la familia **I**
**far (from)** lejos (de) **I**
**Is it far?** ¿Queda lejos? **I**
**farm** la granja **I**
**farmer** el (la) agricultor(a) **6.1**
**to fascinate** fascinar **2.3**
**fast** rápido(a) **I**
**fat** gordo(a) **I**
**father** el padre **I**
**favor**
**to be in favor of** estar a favor de **5.2**
**favorite** favorito(a) **I**
**February** febrero **I**
**fee** la cuota
**to feed** darle(s) de comer **I**
**to feel like** tener ganas de **I**
**fence** la cerca **I**
**fern** el helecho
**ferocious** feroz **5.1**
**fever** la fiebre **3.3**
**field** el campo **I**
**fifteen** quince **I**
**fifth** quinto(a) **I, 2.2**
**fifty** cincuenta **I**
**to fight** pelearse **2.1**
**to fill up** llenar **2.3**
**finally** por fin **I, 2.2**
**to find** encontrar (ue) **I**




RECURSOS
Glosario inglés–español R61

**fine arts** las bellas artes **1.2**
**fingers** los dedos **3.3**
**to finish** terminar **I**
**fire** el fuego **5.2**
**firefighter** el bombero **I**
**fireman** el bombero **6.1**
**firewood** la leña **5.2**
**first** primero(a) **I, 2.2**
**first name** el nombre **EP**
**fish** el pescado **I, 2.3;** el pez **I**
**to fish** pescar **5.2**
**fisherman** el pescador **3.2**
**five** cinco **I**
**five hundred** quinientos(as) **I**
**flash (of lightning)** el rayo **5.2**
**flashlight** la linterna **5.2**
**flavor** el sabor
**flight** el vuelo **1.1**
  **flight attendant** el (la) auxiliar de vuelo **1.1**
**floor** el suelo **1, 4.1;** el piso **4.1**
**flour** la harina **I, 2.3**
**flower** la flor **I**
**flu** la gripe **3.3**
**to fly** volar (ue) **5.1**
**fog** la neblina **5.2**
**to follow** seguir (i, i) (sigo) **4.2**
**food** el alimento **3.1;** la comida **I**
**foot** el pie **I, 3.3**
  **on foot** a pie **I**
**football** el fútbol americano **I**
**for** por; para **I**
**forehead** la frente
**foreigner** el (la) extranjero(a) **4.1**
**forest** el bosque **I**
  **cloud forest** el bosque nuboso
**to forget** olvidar **I**
  **already forgotten** ya olvidada
  **have been forgotten** se han olvidado
**fork** el tenedor **I**
**formal** formal **I, 1.2**
**forty** cuarenta **I**
**four** cuatro **I**
**four hundred** cuatrocientos(as) **I**
**fourteen** catorce **I**
**fourth** cuarto(a) **I, 2.2**
**free time** el tiempo libre **I**
**freedom** la autonomía
**freezer** el congelador **I, 4.1**
**French** francés(esa) **1.3;** el francés
**french fries** las papas fritas **I**
**frequent** frecuente **I**
**frequently** frecuentemente **I, 3.2**
**Friday** viernes **I**
**friend** el (la) amigo(a) **I**
  **to spend time with friends** pasar un rato con los amigos **I**
**friendship** la amistad **2.1**
**frog** la rana **5.1**
  **neon-colored poison dart frogs** las ranas venenosas fosforescentes
**from** de; desde **I**
  **from there** desde allí **4.2**
**fruit** la fruta **I**
**fuel** el combustible **5.3**
**full** lleno(a) **2.3**
**fun** divertido(a) **I, 2.1**
**funny** cómico(a) **I**
**furniture** los muebles **I, 4.1**

**gallery** la galería **1.2**
**game** el partido **I;** el juego
**garage** el garaje **4.1**
**garden** el jardín **I, 4.1**
**gasoline** la gasolina **5.3**
**gathering** la reunión **2.2**
**German** alemán(ana) **1.3**
**to get along well** llevarse bien **2.2**
**to get better** recuperarse **3.3**
**to get dressed** ponerse la ropa **3.1**
**to get hurt** lastimarse **3.3**
**to get out** levantarse
  **(without) getting out** (sin) levantarte
**to get up** levantarse **I, 3.1**
**gift** el regalo **I**
**girl** la chica; la muchacha; la niña **I**
**girlfriend** la novia **2.1**
**to give** dar **I, 1.1**
  **I'll give.... to you for...** Le dejo... en... **I**
**glass** el vaso **I;** el vidrio **5.3**
  **glass of** el vaso de **I**
**glove** el guante **I**
**go** ir **I, 1.1**
  **to be going to...** ir a... **I**
  **to go away** irse **I**
  **to go back** regresar **4.2**
  **to go down** bajar (por) **4.2**
  **to go down a river in a canoe** bajar un río en canoa **1.1**
  **to go for a walk** pasear **I**
  **to go out** salir (salgo) **I**
  **to go shopping** ir de compras **I**
  **to go to a movie theater** ir al cine **I**
  **to go to bed** acostarse (ue) **I, 3.1**
  **to go to the supermarket** ir al supermercado **I**
  **to go up** subir por **4.2**
**goal** el gol **I;** la meta **6.2**
**gold** el oro **I**
**golf** el golf
**good** bueno(a) **I**
  **Good afternoon.** Buenas tardes. **I, EP**
  **Good evening.** Buenas noches. **I**
  **Good morning.** Buenos días. **I, EP**

INGLÉS–ESPAÑOL


R62 RECURSOS Glosario inglés–español

**It's good that...** Es bueno que... **3.3, 4.2**
**Good-bye.** Adiós. **I**; Chao. **EP**
**good-looking** guapo(a) **I**
**government** el gobierno **I**
**grade** la nota **I**
**to get a good grade** sacar una buena nota **I**
**gram** el gramo **I**
**grandchildren** los nietos **I**
**granddaughter** la nieta **I**
**grandfather** el abuelo **I**
**great grandfather** el bisabuelo **2.1**
**grandmother** la abuela **I**
**great grandmother** la bisabuela **2.1**
**grandparents** los abuelos **I**
**grandson** el nieto **I**
**grape** la uva **1.2**
**gray** gris **I**
**great** grande **I**
**green** verde **I**
**to greet** saludar **I**
**greeting** el saludo
**groom** el novio **2.1**
**ground floor** la planta baja **4.1**
**group (musical)** el conjunto
**to grow** crecer (crezco) **3.1**
**Guatemalan** guatemalteco(a) **1.3**
**to guess** adivinar
**guest** el (la) huésped(a) **4.1**
**guitar** la guitarra **I**
**to play the guitar** tocar la guitarra **I,** el cuatro
**gymnasium** el gimnasio **I**
**gypsy** el (la) gitano(a)

**hair** el pelo **I**
**hair dryer** el secador de pelo **I, 3.1**
**hairbrush** el cepillo **I, 3.1**
**hairstylist** el (la) peluquero(a) **6.1**
**half** medio(a) **I**
**half past** y media **I**
**half-brother** el medio hermano **I**
**half-sister** la media hermana **I**
**ham** el jamón **I, 1.2**
**hamburger** la hamburguesa **I**
**hand** la mano **I, 3.3**
**handbag** la bolsa **I**
**handicraft** la artesanía **I**
**to happen** pasar **I**
**happily** felizmente **I**
**happiness** la felicidad **2.2**
**happy** alegre; contento(a); feliz **I**
**to be happy that** alegrarse de que **4.3**
**hard** difícil; duro(a) **I**
**hard-working** trabajador(a) **I**
**hat** el sombrero **I**
**to have** tener **I, EP, 1.2, 1.3**
**to have a cold** estar resfriado(a) **3.3**
**to have a snack** merendar (ie) **I**
**to have just...** acabar de... **I**
**to have to** tener que **I**
**one has to** hay que **I**
**to have** haber
**has had** ha tenido
**has been** ha sido
**he** él **I**
**head** la cabeza **I, 3.3**
**headache** el dolor de cabeza **3.3**
**headline** el titular **1.3**
**healthy** saludable **3.1**
**to be healthy** mantenerse sano(a) **3.1**
**to hear** oír **I, 1.3**
**heart** el corazón **I**
**heat** la calefacción **4.1**
**heating** la calefacción **4.1**
**height** la altura **5.1**; la estatura **6.1**
**Hello.** Hola. **I**
**helmet** el casco **I**
**to help** ayudar (a) **I**
**Could you help me order?** ¿Me ayuda a pedir? **I**
**Help!** ¡Socorro! **3.3**
**hen** la gallina **I**
**her** su **I**
**here** acá; aquí **I**
**hero** el héroe **1.3**
**heroine** la heroína **1.3**
**to hide** esconderse **2.1**
**hill** la colina **5.1**
**his** su **I**
**history** la historia **I**
**hit** el éxito
**hobby** el pasatiempo
**hockey** el hockey **I**
**hold** guardar **4.3**
**hollowed out** ahuecado(a)
**homework** la tarea **I**
**Honduran** hondureño(a) **1.3**
**to honor** honrar
**(it) honors** honra
**to hope** esperar **I, 4.1, 4.3**
**horror** el horror **2.3**
**horse** el caballo **I**
**hot** caliente **I**
**to be hot** tener calor **I**
**It is hot.** Hace calor. **I**
**hot dog** la salchicha **2.3**
**hotel** el hotel **I**
**house** la casa **I**
**how** cómo **I**
**How are you?** (familiar) ¿Cómo estás?; ¿Qué tal? **I**
**How are you?** (formal) ¿Cómo está usted? **I**
**How awesome!** ¡Qué chévere! **I**
**How do I look?** ¿Cómo me veo? **4.3**
**How do you get to...?** ¿Cómo se va a ...? **4.2**

INGLÉS–ESPAÑOL



RECURSOS
Glosario inglés–español R63

How does it look on you?
¿Cómo te queda? **4.3**
**How is it going?** ¿Qué tal? **I**
**How long has it been since…** ¿Hace… que…?; ¿Cuánto tiempo hace que…? **3.3**
**Pardon, how do I get to…?** Perdona(e), ¿cómo llego a…? **I**
**how much** cuánto **I**
**How much do I tip?** ¿Cuánto le doy de propina? **I**
**How much is (are)…?** ¿Cuánto cuesta(n)…?; ¿A cuánto está(n)…? **I**
**How old is…?** ¿Cuántos años tiene…? **I**
**hug** el abrazo **2.2**
**huge** enorme **I**
**human being** el ser humano **5.3**
**humid** húmedo(a) **5.2**
**hummingbird** el colibrí
**to be hungry** tener hambre **I**
**to hurl** lanzar
**hurled himself into the abyss** se lanzó al abismo
**hurricane** el huracán **5.2**
**hurry**
**to be in a hurry** tener prisa **I**
**to hurt** doler (ue) **3.3**
**to hurt oneself** lastimarse **3.3**
**husband** el esposo

**I** yo **I**
**ice** el hielo
**on ice** sobre hielo **I**
**ice cream** el helado **I, 1.2**
**ice-cream parlor** la heladería **4.2**
**identification** la identificación **1.1**
**if** si **I, 5.3**
**immediately** inmediatamente **3.2**
**impatient** impaciente **2.1**
**important** importante
**to be important** importar **2.3**
**It's important that…** Es importante que… **3.3, 4.2**
**impression**
**He/She makes a good (bad) impression on me** Me cae bien (mal). **6.2**
**in** en **I**
**in a bad mood** de mal humor **4.3**
**in a good mood** de buen humor **4.3**
**in front of** delante de **4.2;** frente a **I, 4.2**
**in order to** para **I**
**included** incluido(a)
**Is… included?** ¿Está incluido(a)…? **I**
**incredible** increíble **5.3**
**inexpensive** barato(a) **I**
**infection** la infección **3.3**
**to inform** informar
**to be well informed** estar bien informado(a) **1.3**
**informal** informal **I**
**information** los datos **6.1**
**injection** la inyección **3.3**
**inner ear** el oído **3.3**
**inside (of)** dentro de **I**
**to insist** insistir **4.1**
**insurance** el seguro **6.2**
**intelligent** inteligente **I**
**to interest** interesar **2.3**
**interesting** interesante **I**
**international** internacional **1.3**
**interview** la entrevista **I, 6.2**
**interviewer** el (la) entrevistador(a) **6.2**
**to introduce** presentar
**Let me introduce you (familiar/formal) to…** Te/Le presento a… **I**
**invitation** la invitación **I, 2.2**
**to invite** invitar
**I invite you.** Te invito. **I**
**iridescent** iridiscente
**to iron (the clothes)** planchar (la ropa) **I, 3.2**
**island** la isla **5.1**
**Italian** italiano(a) **1.3**
**its** su **I**

J

**jacket** la chaqueta **I**
**jackknife** la navaja **5.2**
**jaguar** el jaguar **5.1**
**January** enero **I**
**Japanese** japonés(esa) **1.3**
**jeans** los jeans **I**
**jewelry** las joyas **I**
**jewelry store** la joyería **I**
**job** el empleo **6.1**
**journalism** el periodismo **1.3**
**journalist** el (la) periodista **I, 1.3**
**judge** el (la) juez(a) **6.1**
**juice** el jugo **1.2;** el zumo **I**
**July** julio **I**
**to jump** saltar
**to jump rope** saltar la cuerda **2.1**
**June** junio **I**
**jungle** la selva **5.1**

**to keep** guardar **4.3**
**to keep clean** mantener limpio(a) **5.3**
**key** la llave **I, 4.1**
**keyboard** el teclado **I**

INGLÉS–ESPAÑOL



R64 RECURSOS Glosario inglés–español

**kilogram** el kilo **I**
**kiosk** el quiosco **4.2**
**kiss** el beso **2.2**
**kitchen** la cocina **I, 4.1**
**knee** la rodilla **3.3**
**knife** el cuchillo **I**
**to know**
conocer (conozco) **I, 1.3;**
saber (sé) **I, 1.2, 1.3**
**to know someone**
conocer a alguien **I**

**to lack** faltar **2.3**
**lake** el lago **I;** laguna
**hot lake** la laguna caliente
**lamp** la lámpara **I, 4.1**
**land** la tierra **5.1**
**landscape** el paisaje
**language** la lengua **I**
**large** grande **I**
**last** último(a) **I**
**last month** el mes pasado **I**
**last name** el apellido **I**
**last night** anoche **I, 2.2**
**last week** la semana pasada **I**
**last year** el año pasado **I, 2.2**
**late** tarde **I**
**lately** recientemente **I**
**later** luego **I**
**See you later.**
Hasta luego.; Nos vemos. **I**
**laugh** la risa **2.1**
**to laugh** reírse (i, i) **2.1**
**laughter** la risa **2.1**
**lawyer** el (la) abogado(a) **6.1**
**lazy** perezoso(a) **I**
**leaf** la hoja **5.1**
**to learn** aprender **I**
**leather goods**
los artículos de cuero **I**
**to leave** salir; irse **I**
**to leave behind** dejar **I**
**to leave a message**
dejar un mensaje **I**
**Leave a message after the tone.** Deje un mensaje después del tono. **I**
**to leave the tip**
dejar la propina **2.3**
**left** la izquierda **I**
**to the left (of)**
a la izquierda (de) **I**
**leg** la pierna **I, 3.3**
**lemonade** la limonada **I**
**to lend** prestar **4.3**
**less** menos **I**
**less than** menos de **I;**
menos que **I, 4.3**
**lesson** la lección **I**
**Let's...** Vamos a... **I**
**letter** la carta **I**
**to send a letter**
mandar una carta **I**
**lettuce** la lechuga **I**
**library** la biblioteca **I**
**lie** la mentira **2.2**
**to lie down** acostarse (ue) **3.1**
**life** la vida **I**
**to lift** levantar **I**
**to lift weights**
levantar pesas **I**
**light** la luz **5.2**
**light** ligero(a)
**lightning** el relámpago **5.2**
**like** como **I**
**to like** gustar **I, EP, 4.3**
**Do you like...?**
¿Te gusta...? **I**
**Does he/she like...?**
¿Le gusta...? **I**
**He/She likes...** Le gusta... **I**
**I like...** Me gusta... **I**
**I would like...**
Me gustaría... **I**
**Would you like...?**
¿Te gustaría...? **I**
**You like...** Te gusta... **I**
**lion** el león **5.1**
**to listen (to)** escuchar **I**
**liter** el litro **I**
**literature** la literatura **I**
**to live** vivir **I, 1.1**
**living room** la sala **I, 4.1**
**llama** la llama **I**
**loan** el préstamo **4.3**
**local** local **1.3**
**logical**
**It's logical that...**
Es lógico que... **3.3, 4.2**
**long** largo(a) **I**
**to look at** mirar **I, 1.1**
**to look for** buscar **I, 1.1**
**loose** flojo(a) **4.3**
**to lose** perder (ie) **I**
**love** el amor **2.2**
**to love** querer (ie) **I, 1.2**
**lover** el (la) amante
**lucky**
**to be lucky** tener suerte **I**
**luggage** el equipaje **1.1**
**lunch** el almuerzo **I**
**to eat lunch** almorzar (ue) **I**
**luxurious** lujoso(a) **I, 1.2**

**Madrid**
**people from Madrid**
los madrileños
**magazine** la revista **I**
**magnet** el imán
**mail carrier**
el (la) cartero(a) **I, 6.1**
**mailbox** el buzón **4.2**
**majority** la mayoría **2.2**
**to make** hacer (hago) **I, 1.1**
**to make the bed**
hacer la cama **I**
**makeup** el maquillaje **3.1**
**to put on makeup**
maquillarse **I, 3.1**

INGLÉS–ESPAÑOL


RECURSOS
Glosario inglés–español R65

**mall** la galería
**man** el hombre **I**
**manager** el (la) gerente **I, 6.1**
**many** mucho(a) **I**
**map** el mapa **I**
**March** marzo **I**
**marionette** la marioneta **2.1**
**market** el mercado **I**
**to marry**
**to get married** casarse **2.2**
**marvelous** de maravilla **2.2**
**match** el fósforo **5.2**
**to match with**
hacer juego con **4.3**
**mathematics** las matemáticas **I**
**May** mayo **I**
**maybe** tal vez **I, 4.3;** quizás **4.3**
**Maybe another day.**
Tal vez otro día. **I**
**meal** la comida **I**
**meat** la carne **I**
**mechanic** el (la) mecánico(a) **6.1**
**medicine** la medicina **3.3**
**to meet** encontrar (ue) **I,** conocer (conozco) **1.3**
**meeting** el encuentro **I**
**melon** el melón **1.2**
**menu** el menú **I**
**message** el mensaje **I**
**I want to leave a message for…** Quiero dejar un mensaje para… **I**
**to leave a message**
dejar un mensaje **I**
**Leave a message after the tone.** Deje un mensaje después del tono. **I**
**Mexican** mexicano(a) **1.3**
**microwave** el microondas **I**
**microwave oven**
el horno microondas **4.1**
**midnight** la medianoche **I**
**milk** la leche **I, 1.2**
**milk shake** el batido **1.2**
**million** un millón **I**
**mirror** el espejo **I, 4.1**
**Miss** la señorita **I**
**mist** la neblina **5.2**
**modern** moderno(a) **I, 1.2**
**moment** el momento **I**
**One moment.**
Un momento. **I**
**Monday** lunes **I**
**money** el dinero **I**
**money exchange** el cambio **I**
**monkey** el mono **5.1**
**month** el mes **I**
**more** más **I**
**more than**
más de **I;** más que **I, 4.3**
**morning** la mañana **I**
**during the morning**
por la mañana **I**
**Good morning.**
Buenos días. **I**
**in the morning**
de la mañana **I**
**mother** la madre **I**
**motorcycle** la moto(cicleta) **I**
**mountain** la montaña **I**
**mountaineering**
el montañismo **5.2**
**mouth** la boca **I**
**to move** mover (ue) **I**
**to move the furniture**
mover los muebles **I**
**movie** la película **I**
**movie theater** el cine **I**
**to go to a movie theater**
ir al cine **I**
**Mr.** el señor **I;** don
**Mrs.** la señora **I;** doña
**much** mucho(a) **I**
**as much as** tanto como **I**
**museum** el museo **I**
**music** la música **I**
**music and video store** la tienda de música y videos **I**
**musical** el musical **2.3**
**musician** el (la) músico(a) **6.1**
**must**
**one must** hay que **I**

**name** el nombre **I, EP**
**His/Her name is…** Se llama… **I, EP**
**My name is…**
Me llamo… **I, EP**
**What is his/her name?**
¿Cómo se llama? **I, EP**
**What is your name?**
¿Cómo te llamas? **I, EP**
**nap**
**take a nap** échate una siesta
**napkin** la servilleta **2.3**
**narrow** estrecho(a) **I, 4.3**
**natural resources**
los recursos naturales **5.3**
**nature** la naturaleza **5.1**
**near (to)**
cerca (de) **I;** junto(a) **4.2**
**necessary**
**It's necessary that…**
Es necesario que… **3.3**
**neck** el cuello **3.3**
**necklace** el collar **I**
**to need** necesitar **I, 4.1**
**to negotiate** negociar
**(he/she) negotiated** negoció
**neighbor** el (la) vecino(a) **I**
**neighborhood** el vecindario **4.2**
**neither** tampoco **I;** ni **4.2**
**nephew** el sobrino **2.1**
**nervous** nervioso(a) **I**
**never** nunca **I**
**new** nuevo(a) **I**
**new release** el estreno **2.3**
**news** las noticias **1.3**
**news program** el noticiero **1.3**





RECURSOS
R66 Glosario inglés–español

**newspaper** el periódico **I**
**next to** al lado de **I;** junto(a) **4.2**
**Nicaraguan** nicaragüense **1.3**
**nice** amable **2.1;** simpático(a) **I**
  **It's nice outside.**
    Hace buen tiempo. **I**
  **Nice to meet you.**
    Mucho gusto. **I, EP**
**niece** la sobrina **2.1**
**night** la noche **I**
  **at night** de noche **I**
**nine** nueve **I**
**nine hundred** novecientos(as) **I**
**nineteen** diecinueve **I**
**ninety** noventa **I**
**ninth** noveno(a) **I, 2.2**
**no** no **I**
**no longer** ya no **I**
**no one** nadie **I**
**none** ninguno(a) **I**
**noon** el mediodía **I**
**nor** ni **4.2**
**normal** normal **I**
**normally** normalmente **I, 3.2**
**north** el norte **4.2**
**nose** la nariz **I, 3.3**
**not** no **I**
**not even** ni **4.2**
**not only** no sólo
**to note** apuntar
**notebook** el cuaderno **I**
**notes** los apuntes
**nothing** nada **I**
**nourishment**
  la alimentación **3.1**
**novel** la novela **I**
**November** noviembre **I**
**now** ahora **I;** ya **3.2**
  **Right now!** ¡Ahora mismo! **I**
**nowadays** actualmente **I**
**number** el número **I**
  **What is your phone number?**
    ¿Cuál es tu teléfono? **I, EP**
**nurse** el (la) enfermero(a) **3.3**
**nutritious** nutritivo(a) **3.1**

**obedient** obediente **2.1**
**obtain** conseguir (i, i) (consigo)
  **6.2;** obtener **4.2**
**to occur** ocurrir **2.2**
**ocean** el océano **3.2**
**October** octubre **I**
**of** de **I**
  **Of course!**
    ¡Claro que sí!; ¡Cómo no! **I**
**to offer** ofrecer (ofrezco) **I, 2.3**
**office** la oficina **I**
**office (doctor's)**
  el consultorio **3.3**
**often** mucho; frecuentemente **I**
**oil** el aceite **I, 2.3**
**old** antiguo(a) **I, 1.2;** viejo(a) **I**
  **How old is...?**
    ¿Cuántos años tiene...? **I**
**older** mayor **I**
  **older than** mayor que **4.3**
**olives** las aceitunas **I**
**on** sobre **I, 4.2**
  **on ice** sobre hielo **I**
  **on time** a tiempo **4.2**
  **on top of** encima de **I, 4.2**
**once in a while**
  de vez en cuando **I**
**one** uno **I**
**one hundred** cien **I**
**onion** la cebolla **I, 2.3**
**only** sólo **I**
**open** abierto(a) **I, 4.3**
**to open** abrir **I**
**operator**
  el (la) operador(a) **I, 6.1**
**opposite** frente a **4.2**
**or** o **I**
**orange** anaranjado(a) **I**
**to order** pedir (i, i) **I**
  **Could you help me order?**
    ¿Me ayuda a pedir? **I**
**ordinary** ordinario(a) **I**
**other** otro(a) **I**
**ought to** deber **I**
**our** nuestro(a) **I**
**outdoors** al aire libre **I**
**outside (prep.)** fuera **I**
**oven** el horno **I, 4.1**
**owner** el (la) dueño(a) **6.1**
**ozone layer**
  la capa de ozono **5.3**

**to pack one's suitcases**
  hacer las maletas
**package** el paquete **I**
**to paint** pintar **I**
**painter** el (la) pintor(a) **1.2**
**palm tree** la palma **3.2**
**palm tree grove** el palmar **3.2**
**Panamanian** panameño(a) **1.3**
**panpipe** la flauta de pan
**pants** los pantalones **I**
**paper** el papel **I**
**parade** el desfile **I**
**Paraguayan** paraguayo(a) **1.3**
**Pardon...** Perdona(e)... **I**
  **Pardon, how do I get to...?**
    Perdona(e), ¿cómo llego
    a...? **I**
**parents** los padres **I**
**park** el parque **I**
**parking space**
  el estacionamiento **4.2**
**parrot** el loro **5.1**
**party** la fiesta **I, 2.2**
**to pass (by)** pasar **I**
**passenger** el (la) pasajero(a) **1.1**
**passport** el pasaporte **1.1**
**pasta** la pasta **I, 2.3**
**pastime** el pasatiempo
**pastry shop** la pastelería **I**
**path** el sendero **5.1**





RECURSOS
Glosario inglés–español R67

**patient** paciente **I**
**to pay** pagar **I, 1.1**
**peaceful** pacífico(a)
**peak** la cima
**peanut butter** la mantequilla de cacahuate **1.2**
**pear** la pera **2.3**
**pedestrian** el peatón **4.2**
**pen** el corral **I;** la pluma **I**
**pencil** el lápiz **I**
**people** la gente **I**
**pepper** la pimienta **I, 2.3**
**perfect** perfecto(a) **I**
**performance** la actuación **2.3**
**perfume** el perfume **3.1**
**permission** el permiso **5.2**
**to permit** permitir **5.2**
**to pertain** pertenecer (pertenezco) **5.2**
**Peruvian** peruano(a) **1.3**
**pharmacy** la farmacia **I**
**phone directory** la guía telefónica **I**
**photo** la foto **I**
  **to take photos/pictures** sacar fotos **I**
**photographer** el (la) fotógrafo(a) **I, 1.3**
**physical education** la educación física **I**
**piano** el piano **I**
  **to play the piano** tocar el piano **I**
**picture** la foto **I;** la pintura **1.2**
**picturesque** pintoresco(a)
**piece** el pedazo **I**
**pig** el cerdo **I**
**pill** la pastilla **3.3**
**pillow** la almohada **5.2**
**pilot** el piloto **1.1**
**pink** rosado(a) **I**
**pitcher** la jarra **I**
**pizza** la pizza
**place** el lugar **I**
**plaid** de cuadros **I**
**plain** sencillo(a) **I**
**plan**
  **master plan** el plan maestro
**to plan** pensar (ie) **I**
**planet** el planeta **5.3**
**plant** la planta **I**
**plantain** el plátano verde **1.2**
  **fried plantains** los tostones **1.2**
**plate** el plato **I**
**to play** jugar (ue) **I, 1.1, 1.2;** practicar; **(an instrument)** tocar **I**
  **to play chess** jugar al ajedrez **1.1**
  **to play the guitar** tocar la guitarra **I**
  **to play the piano** tocar el piano **I**
  **to play sports** practicar deportes **I**
**please** por favor **I**
**pleased** contento(a) **I**
  **Pleased to meet you.** Encantado(a). **I**
**pleasure**
  **It's a pleasure.** Es un placer. **I**
  **The pleasure is mine.** El gusto es mío. **I**
**poem** el poema **I**
**poetry** la poesía **I**
**police officer** el (la) policía **I**
**political parties** los partidos
**to pollute** contaminar **5.3**
**pollution** la contaminación **5.3**
**poor** pobre **2.1**
**population** la población **5.1**
**pork** el puerco **I**
**pork rinds** los chicharrones **I**
  **to eat pork rinds** comer chicharrones **I**
**porter** el (la) maletero(a) **4.1**
**portrait** el retrato **1.2**
**position** el puesto **6.1**
**possible**
  **It's possible that...** Es posible que... **3.3, 4.2**
**post office** el correo **I**
**pot** la olla **I**
**potato** la patata **I;** la papa **2.3**
**poverty** la pobreza **5.3**
**to practice** practicar **I, 1.1**
**to prefer** preferir (ie, i) **I, 1.3, 4.1**
**to prepare** preparar **I**
**prescription** la receta **3.3**
**to preserve** preservar **5.1**
**pretty** bonito(a) **I**
**price** el precio **I**
**printer** la impresora **I**
**probable**
  **It's probable that...** Es probable que... **3.3, 4.2**
**problem** el problema **I, 5.3**
**to produce** producir (produzco) **1.2**
**profession** la profesión **I, 6.1**
**program** el programa **1.3**
**projection** el relieve
**to protect** proteger (protejo) **3.2**
  **to protect the species** proteger las especies **5.3**
**Puerto Rican** puertorriqueño(a) **1.3**
**punctuality** la puntualidad **6.2**
**purple** morado(a) **I**
**to put** poner (pongo) **I, EP, 1.2**
  **to put on (clothes)** ponerse **I, 3.1**
  **to put on makeup** maquillarse **I, 3.1**

**qualified** capacitado(a) **6.1**
**quality** la calidad **I**
**quarter** cuarto(a) **I**
  **quarter past** y cuarto **I**


R68 RECURSOS Glosario inglés–español

**question** la pregunta
**quick** rápido(a) **I**
**quickly** rápidamente **I, 3.2**
**quiet**
  **Be quiet.** ¡Cállate! **I**
**quiz** la prueba **I**

## R

**racket** la raqueta **I**
**radio** el radio **I**
**radio-tape player**
  el radiocasete **I**
**rage** el arrebato
**rain** la lluvia **I**
**to rain** llover (ue) **I**
**raincoat** el impermeable **I**
**rare** raro(a) **1.2**
  **It's rare that...** Es raro que... **3.3**
**rarely** rara vez **I**
**to read** leer **I, 1.3**
**reading** la lectura
**ready** listo(a) **I**
  **to get ready (dressed)**
    arreglarse **3.1**
**to realize** darse cuenta de **2.1**
**Really?** ¿De veras? **1.3**
**reason** la razón **I**
**to receive** recibir **I**
**recent** reciente **I**
**recently** recientemente **I, 3.2**
**reception desk** la recepción **4.1**
**receptionist**
  el (la) recepcionista **I**
**recipe** la receta **I**
**to recommend**
  recomendar (ie) **1.2**
**recommendations**
  las recomendaciones **6.2**
**to recycle** reciclar **5.3**
**recycling** el reciclaje **5.3**
**red** rojo(a) **I**
**red beans**
  las habichuelas coloradas **1.2**
**redhead** pelirrojo(a) **I**
**reduce** reducir (reduzco) **5.3**
**reed** la quena
**refrigerator** el frigorífico **I;** el refrigerador **4.1**
**relative** el (la) pariente(a) **2.1**
**to relax** relajarse **3.1**
**relief (map)** el relieve
**to remember** recordar (ue) **I**
**to rent** alquilar **I**
  **to rent a video**
    alquilar un video **I**
**to renew** renovarse (ue)
  **is renewed** se renueva
**to repeat** repetir (i, i) **1.2, 1.3**
**report** el reportaje **1.3;**
  el pronóstico **5.2**
**reporter** el (la) reportero(a) **1.3**
**to request** solicitar **6.1**
**to require** requerir (ie, i) **6.2**
**requirement** el requisito **6.2**
**rescue** el rescate **1.3**
**to rescue** rescatar **1.3**
**reservation** la reserva **4.1**
**to resolve** resolver (ue) **5.3**
**resource** el recurso
**to rest** descansar **I**
**rest of the people**
  los demás **2.2**
**restaurant** el restaurante **I**
**resumé** el currículum **6.2**
**to retell** contar (ue) **I**
**to return** regresar; volver (ue) **I**
  **to return (an item)**
    evolver (ue) **I**
  **He/She will return later.**
    Regresa más tarde. **I**
**review** el repaso
**to review** revisar **4.2**
**rice** el arroz **I**
**rich** rico(a) **2.1**
**ride**
  **amusement rides**
    los juegos mecánicos
**ridiculous**
  **It's ridiculous that...**
    Es ridículo que... **3.3**
**right**
  **to be right** tener razón **I**
  **to the right (of)**
    a la derecha (de) **I**
**ring** el anillo **I**
**river** el río **I**
**road** el camino **I**
**roasted** asado(a) **I**
**robbery** el robo **1.3**
**role** el papel **2.3**
**romantic** romántico(a) **2.3**
**Romany Gypsy dialect**
  el gitano
**room** el cuarto **I;**
  la habitación **4.1**
**rooster** el gallo **I**
**root** la raíz
  **roots** las raíces
**rope** la cuerda
  **to jump rope** saltar
    la cuerda **2.1**
**round trip** la ida y vuelta **4.2**
**to row** remar **5.2**
**to run** correr **I**

**sad** triste **I**
  **It's sad that...**
    Es triste que... **3.3, 4.2**
  **It's a pity that...** Es una lástima que... **3.3, 4.2**
**sadness** la tristeza **2.2**
**sage** el sabio
**salad** la ensalada **I**
**salary** el sueldo **6.2**
**sale** la rebaja **4.2**





RECURSOS
Glosario inglés–español R69

**salesperson**
el (la) dependiente(a) **4.3**
**salsa** la salsa **I**
**salt** la sal **I, 2.3**
**Salvadorian** salvadoreño(a) **1.3**
**same** mismo(a) **I**
**sand** la arena **3.2**
**sandals** las sandalias **3.2**
**sandwich (sub)** la torta **I, 2.3**
**Saturday** sábado **I**
**sausage**
el chorizo; la salchicha **I**
**to save** guardar **4.3**
**savings account**
la cuenta de ahorros **4.3**
**to say** decir (digo) **I, 1.2**
**Don't say that!**
¡No digas eso! **I**
**to say good-bye**
despedirse (i, i) **2.1**
**saying** el refrán
**scarcely** apenas **4.3**
**scared**
**to be scared** tener miedo **4.3**
**to be scared (of)**
asustarse (de) **2.1**
**scarf**
la bufanda **I;** el pañuelo **4.3**
**scene** la escena **2.3**
**schedule** el horario **I**
**school** la escuela **I**
**science** las ciencias **I**
**science fiction**
la ciencia ficción **2.3**
**scissors** las tijeras **I, 5.2**
**to scream** gritar **3.3**
**screen** la pantalla **I**
**to scuba-dive** bucear
**sculptor** el (la) escultor(a) **1.2**
**sculpture** la escultura **1.2**
**sea** el mar **I**
**to search** buscar **I, 1.1**
**seasons** las estaciones **I**
**seat** el asiento **1.1**
**second** segundo(a) **I, 2.2**
**secondhand** de segunda mano
**secretary**
el (la) secretario(a) **I, 6.1**
**security** la seguridad **1.1**
**to see** ver **I, 1.1**
**May I see...?**
¿Me deja ver...? **I**
**to sell** vender **I**
**semester** el semestre **I**
**to send** mandar **I**
**to send a letter**
mandar una carta **I**
**sentence** la oración
**to separate** separar **5.3**
**September** septiembre **I**
**series** la serie **2.3**
**serious** serio(a) **I**
**to serve** servir (i, i) **I, 1.2, 1.3**
**to set**
**to set the table**
poner la mesa **I**
**to set up** instalarse
**is set up** se instala
**seven** siete **I**
**seven hundred**
setecientos(as) **I**
**seventeen** diecisiete **I**
**seventh** séptimo(a) **I, 2.2**
**seventy** setenta **I**
**shade** la sombra **5.1**
**shadow** la sombra **5.1**
**shame** la lástima **I**
**What a shame!**
Qué lástima! **I**
**shampoo** el champú **I, 3.1**
**to share** compartir **I**
**sharing with others**
compartir con los demás
**to shave** afeitarse **I, 3.1**
**she** ella **I**
**sheet** la sábana **5.2**
**shell** el caracol **3.2**
**shepherd(ess)** el (la) pastor(a) **I**
**ship** el barco **I**
**shirt** la camisa **I**
**shoe** el zapato **I**
**high-heeled shoe**
el zapato de tacón **4.3**
**shoe size** el número **4.3**
**shoe store** la zapatería **I**
**shopping**
**to go shopping**
ir de compras **I**
**shopping center**
el centro comercial **I**
**shore** la orilla **3.2**
**short (height)** bajo(a);
**(length)** corto(a) **I**
**shorts** los shorts; los
pantalones cortos **I**
**should** deber **I**
**shoulder** el hombro **3.3**
**to show** mostrar (ue) **1.2**
**shower**
**to take a shower**
ducharse **I, 3.1**
**shy** tímido(a) **2.1**
**sick** enfermo(a) **I**
**sickness** la enfermedad **3.3**
**sidewalk** la acera **4.2**
**sign** el letrero **1.1**
**to sign** firmar
**signature** la firma **6.1**
**silver** la plata **I**
**similar** parecido(a)
**simple** sencillo(a) **I, 4.3**
**to sing** cantar **I**
**to sing in the chorus**
cantar en el coro **1.1**
**singer** el (la) cantante **2.3**
**sink (bathroom)** lavabo **4.1**
**sister** la hermana **I**
**sister-in-law** la cuñada **2.1**
**to sit down** sentarse (ie) **2.1**
**situation** la situación **5.3**
**six** seis **I**
**six hundred** seiscientos(as) **I**
**sixteen** dieciséis **I, EP**
**sixth** sexto(a) **I, 2.2**
**sixty** sesenta **I**

INGLÉS–ESPAÑOL



R70 RECURSOS
Glosario inglés–español

**size (clothing)** la talla **4.3**
**to skate** patinar **I**
**skateboard** la patineta **I**
**to skateboard**
andar en patineta **I**
**skates** los patines **I**
**to ski** esquiar **I**
**skin** la piel **3.2**
**skirt** la falda **I**
**to sleep** dormir (ue, u) **I, 1.3**
**sleeping bag**
el saco de dormir **5.2**
**sleepy**
**to be sleepy** tener sueño **I**
**slow** lento(a) **I**
**slowly** lentamente **I, 3.2**
**small** pequeño(a) **I**
**to smile** sonreírse (i, i) **2.1**
**smog** el smog **5.3**
**smoke**
**emits smoke** echa humo
**snack** la merienda **I**
**to snack** merendar (ie) **I**
**snake** la serpiente **5.1**
**to snorkel**
bucear con respiración
**snow** la nieve **I**
**to snow** nevar (ie) **I**
**so** entonces **I**
**So-so.** Regular. **I**
**soap** el jabón **I, 3.1**
**soap opera** la telenovela **2.3**
**soccer** el fútbol **I**
**sociable** sociable **2.1**
**social studies**
los estudios sociales **I**
**sock** el calcetín **I**
**sofa** el sofá **I**
**soft drink** el refresco **I**
**some** alguno(a) **I**
**someone** alguien **I**
**to know (be familiar with) someone** conocer a alguien **I**
**something** algo **I**
**sometimes** a veces **I, 2.1**
**son** el hijo **I**
**son(s) and daughter(s)**
los hijos **I**
**soon** pronto **I**
**sorry**
**I'm sorry.** Lo siento. **I**
**soup** la sopa **I**
**south** el sur **4.2**
**Spaniard** español(a) **1.3**
**Spanish** el español **I**
**speakers of Spanish**
los hispanohablantes
**to speak** hablar **I, 1.1**
**May I speak with...?**
¿Puedo hablar con...? **I**
**special** especial **I**
**specially** especialmente **I**
**specialty of the house**
la especialidad de la casa **1.2**
**speech** el discurso
**to spend** gastar **4.3**
**spicy** picante **I**
**spoon** la cuchara **I**
**sport** el deporte **I**
**to play sports**
practicar deportes **I**
**sporting goods store**
la tienda de deportes **I**
**sportsman, sportswoman**
el (la) deportista **6.1**
**spring** la primavera **I**
**square** cuadriculado(a)
**squid** los calamares **I**
**stadium** el estadio **I**
**stairs** la escalera **4.1**
**star** la estrella **I**
**to start** comenzar (ie) **1.1**
**statehood** la estadidad
**stationery store** la papelería **I**
**to stay (at)** hospedarse (en) **4.1;** quedar (en) **I**
**steak** el bistec **I**
**to steal** robar **1.3**
**step** el paso
**to step on them** pisarlas
**stepbrother**
el hermanastro **2.1**
**stepfather** el padrastro **2.1**
**stepmother** la madrastra **2.1**
**stepsister** la hermanastra **2.1**
**still** todavía **I**
**stingy** tacaño(a) **4.3**
**stomach** el estómago **I, 3.3**
**stone** la piedra **5.1**
**to stop** parar **4.2**
**store** la tienda **I**
**storm** la tormenta **I**
**story** la historia **2.2**
**stove** la estufa **I, 4.1**
**straight ahead** derecho **I**
**straight (hair)** lacio **3.1**
**strange** raro(a) **1.2**
**strawberry** la fresa **1.2**
**street** la calle **I**
**stress** el estrés **3.1**
**to stretch** estirarse **3.1**
**striped** con rayas **I**
**stripes** las rayas **4.3**
**strong** fuerte **I**
**student** el (la) estudiante **I**
**to study** estudiar **I**
**to study martial arts**
estudiar las artes marciales **1.1**
**stuffed animal**
el muñeco de peluche **2.1**
**subject** la materia **I**
**subway** el metro **I**
**suddenly** de repente **1.3**
**to suffer** doler (ue) **3.3**
**sugar** el azúcar **I**
**to suggest** sugerir (ie) **4.1**
**suggestion** la sugerencia
**suit** el traje **4.3**
**suitcase** la maleta **1.1**
**summary** el resumen
**summer** el verano **I**
**summit (meeting)** la cumbre
**sun** el sol **I**

INGLÉS–ESPAÑOL


RECURSOS
Glosario inglés–español R71

to **sunbathe** tomar el sol **I**
**Sunday** domingo **I**
**sunglasses** las gafas de sol **I**
**sunny** soleado **5.2**
**It is sunny.** Hace sol.; Hay sol. **I**
**suntan lotion** el bronceador **I;** la loción protectora **3.2**
**supermarket** el supermercado **I**
**to go to the supermarket** ir al supermercado **I**
**superstore** el hipermercado
**supper** la cena **I**
**to have supper** cenar **I**
**surfing** el surfing **I**
**surname** el apellido **I**
**surprise** la sorpresa **I, 2.2**
**to surprise** sorprender **I, 4.3**
**to surround** rodear
**(they) surround** rodean
**to sweat** sudar **3.1**
**sweater** el suéter **I**
**to sweep** barrer **I**
**to sweep the floor** barrer el piso **4.1**
**sweet** dulce **I**
**sweet roll** el pan dulce **I**
**to swim** nadar **I**
**swimming pool** la piscina **I**

**T-shirt** la camiseta **I**
**table** la mesa **I, 4.1**
**to clear the table** uitar la mesa **I**
**to set the table** poner la mesa **I**
**tablecloth** el mantel **2.3**
**taco** el taco **2.3**
**taco restaurant** la taquería **2.3**
**to take** tomar **I;** sacar **I, 1.1**
**to take along** llevar **I**
**to take a bath** bañarse **I, 3.1**
**to take care of** cuidar (a) **I**
**to take off one's clothes** quitarse la ropa **3.1**
**to take out the trash** sacar la basura **I, 3.2**
**to take photos/pictures** sacar fotos **I**
**to take a shower** ducharse **I, 3.1**
**to take a size** usar **4.3**
**to take a swimming class** tomar un curso de natación **1.1**
**to take a walk, stroll, or ride** dar una vuelta **2.3**
**talent** el talento **1.2**
**to talk** hablar **I**
**tall** alto(a) **I**
**tame** manso(a)
**tape recorder** la grabadora **I**
**taste** el sabor **1.2**
**tasty** rico(a), sabroso(a) **I**
**taxi** el taxi **I**
**taxi driver** el (la) taxista **I**
**tea** el té **I**
**to teach** enseñar **I**
**teacher** el (la) maestro(a) **I**
**team** el equipo **I**
**technician** el (la) técnico(a) **6.1**
**telephone** el teléfono **I**
**What is your phone number?** ¿Cuál es tu teléfono? **I**
**television** la televisión **I**
**to watch television** ver la televisión **I**
**television set** el televisor **I**
**to tell** decir (digo) **I, 1.2;** contar (ue) **I**
**Don't tell me!** ¡No me digas! **1.3**
**Tell him or her to call me.** Dile/Dígale que me llame. **I**
**to tell jokes** contar (ue) chistes **2.1**
**temperature** la temperatura **I**
**ten** diez **I**
**tennis** el tenis **I**
**tent** la tienda de campaña **5.2**
**tenth** décimo(a) **I, 2.2**
**terrace** la terraza
**terrible** terrible **I**
**test** el examen **I**
**to thank** agradecer (agradezco)
**Thank you.** Gracias. **I**
**that** ese(a), eso **I**
**that (over there)** aquel(la); aquello **I**
**that one** ése(a) **I**
**that one (over there)** aquél(la) **I**
**theater** el teatro **I**
**theatrical production** la obra de teatro **2.3**
**their** su **I**
**theme** el tema **2.3**
**then** entonces **I**
**there** allá/allí **I**
**there is/are** hay **I**
**there was/were** había **2.1;** hubo **1.3**
**they** ellos(as) **I**
**thief** el (la) ladrón(ona) **1.3**
**thin** delgado(a) **I**
**thing** la cosa **I**
**to think** pensar (ie); creer **I**
**Do you think so?** ¿Tú crees? **1.3**
**I think so. / I don't think so.** Creo que sí/no. **I**
**third** tercero(a) **I, 2.2**
**thirsty**
**to be thirsty** tener sed **I**
**thirteen** trece **I**
**thirty** treinta **I**
**this** este(a); esto **I**
**this one** éste(a) **I**
**thousand** mil **I**
**three** tres **I**
**three hundred** trescientos(as) **I**


R72 RECURSOS Glosario inglés–español

**throat** la garganta **3.3**
**to throw out** echar **5.3**
**thunder** el trueno **5.2**
**thunderbolt** el rayo **5.2**
**Thursday** jueves **I**
**ticket** el boleto **1.1**
**tight** apretado(a) **4.3**
**time** el tiempo
  **free time** el tiempo libre **I**
  **to spend time with friends** pasar un rato con los amigos **I**
  **(At) What time is…?** ¿A qué hora es…? **I**
  **What time is it?** ¿Qué hora es? **I**
**tip** la propina **I**
  **How much do I tip?** ¿Cuánto le doy de propina? **I**
**tired** cansado(a) **I**
  **to get tired** cansarse **2.1**
**to** a **I**
  **to the left (of)** a la izquierda (de) **I**
  **to the right (of)** a la derecha (de) **I**
**toast** el brindis
**today** hoy **I**
  **Today is…** Hoy es… **I**
  **What day is today?** ¿Qué día es hoy? **I**
**toes** los dedos **3.3**
**together** juntos **I**
  **to get together** reunirse **2.1**
**tomato** el tomate **I, 2.3**
**tomorrow** mañana **I**
  **See you tomorrow.** Hasta mañana. **I**
  **Tomorrow is…** Mañana es… **I**
**too** también **I**
**too much** demasiado(a) **I, 2.3**
**tooth** el diente **I, 3.3**
**toothbrush** el cepillo de dientes **I, 3.1**
**toothpaste** la pasta de dientes **I, 3.1**
**toucan** el tucán **5.1**
**to touch** tocar **1.1**
**tough** duro(a) **I**
**tourism** el turismo **4.1**
**toward** hacia **4.2**
**towel** la toalla **I, 3.2**
**town** el pueblo **I**
**town square** la plaza **I**
**toy** el juguete **2.1**
**toy store** la juguetería **4.2**
**traditional** tradicional **I, 6.1**
**traffic** el tráfico **I**
**traffic light/signal** el semáforo **4.2**
**trail** el sendero **5.1**
**train** el tren **I**
**to train** entrenarse **3.1**
**training** el entrenamiento **6.2**
**to translate** traducir (traduzco) **1.2**
**trash** la basura **I**
**trash can** el basurero **5.3**
**to travel** viajar **I**
**travel agent** el (la) agente de viajes **1.1**
**travelers' checks** los cheques de viajero **4.3**
**to treat** tratar **3.3**
  **I'll treat you.** Te invito. **I**
**treble guitar** el tiple
**tree** el árbol **I**
**trip** el viaje **I, 1.1**
**trouble**
  **The trouble is that…** Lo malo es que… **5.3**
**true** cierto(a)
**truth** la verdad **I**
  **It's not true that…** No es verdad que… **4.3**
  **It's true.** Es verdad. **I**
**Tuesday** martes **I**
**tuna** el atún **1.2**
**to turn** doblar **I**; girar **4.2**
**to turn off** apagar **I**
  **to turn off the light** apagar la luz **I**
**turtle** la tortuga **I, 5.1**
**twelve** doce **I**
**twenty** veinte **I**
**twenty-one** veintiuno **I**
**twins** los (las) gemelos(as) **2.1**
**two** dos **I**
**two hundred** doscientos(as) **I**
**typically** típicamente **3.2**

**U.S. citizen** estadounidense **1.3**
**ugly** feo(a) **I**
**umbrella** el paraguas **I**
  **beach umbrella** la sombrilla de playa **3.2**
**uncle** el tío **I**
**uncle(s) and aunt(s)** los tíos **I**
**under** debajo (de) **I**
**underneath** debajo (de) **I, 4.2**
**to understand** comprender; entender (ie) **I**
**unfortunately** desafortunadamente **3.2**
**to unite** unirse
  **(they) unite** se unen
**university** la universidad **6.2**
**until** hasta **I, 4.2**
**up** arriba **I**
**Uruguayan** uruguayo(a) **1.3**
**to use** usar **I, 4.3**
**used** de segunda mano
**useful** útil **5.3**
**useless** inútil **5.3**
**utensils** los cubiertos **2.3**




RECURSOS
Glosario inglés–español R73

**to vacuum**
pasar la aspiradora **I, 3.2**
**vacuum cleaner** la aspiradora **I**
**valley** el valle **5.1**
**to value (to be worth)**
valer (valgo) **4.3**
**VCR** la videograbadora **I**
**vegetable** la verdura **I, 2.3**
**vegetarian** vegetariano(a) **I**
**veil** el velo
**handmade veil**
el velo bordado a mano
**Venezuelan** venezolano(a) **1.3**
**very** muy **I**
**vest** el chaleco **4.3**
**veterinarian** el (la)
veterinario(a) **6.1**
**video** el video **I**
**to rent a video**
alquilar un video **I**
**video game** el videojuego **I**
**viewer** el (la) televidente **1.3**
**village** el pueblo **I**
**violent** violento(a) **5.2**
**to visit** visitar **I**
**volleyball** el voleibol **I**
**volunteer**
el (la) voluntario(a) **6.1**

**to wait for** esperar **I**
**waiter** el mesero **I**
**waitress** la mesera **I**
**to wake up**
despertarse (ie) **I, 3.1**
**to walk** andar **1.2**
**to walk the dog**
caminar con el perro **I**
**walkway** el paseo **4.1**
**wall** la pared **I, 4.1**
**wallet** la cartera **I**
**to want** querer (ie) **I, 1.2**
**Do you want to drink…?**
¿Quieres beber…? **I**
**Do you want to eat…?**
¿Quieres comer…? **I**
**I want to drink…**
Quiero beber… **I**
**I want to eat…**
Quiero comer… **I**
**I want to leave a message for…** Quiero dejar un mensaje para… **I**
**wardrobe** el armario **I, 4.1**
**warm** caliente **I**
**to wash** lavar **I**
**to wash the dishes**
lavar los platos **I, 3.2**
**to wash one's hair** lavarse la cabeza **I**
**to wash oneself** lavarse **I, 3.1**
**watch** el reloj **I**
**to watch** mirar **I**
**to watch television**
ver la televisión **I**
**water** el agua (fem.) **I**
**waterfalls** las cataratas
**waterslide** la resbaladilla
**wave** la ola **3.2**
**we** nosotros(as) **I**
**to wear** llevar **I;** usar **4.3**
**What is he/she wearing?**
¿Qué lleva? **I**
**weather** el tiempo **I**
**What is the weather like?**
¿Qué tiempo hace? **I**
**wedding** la boda **2.2**
**Wednesday** miércoles **I**
**week** la semana **I**
**weekend** el fin de semana **I**
**weights** las pesas **I**
**to lift weights**
levantar pesas **I**
**welcome** bienvenido(a) **I**
**You're welcome.** De nada. **I**
**well** bien; pues **I**
**well-being** el bienestar **3.1**
**west** el oeste **4.2**
**wet** mojado(a) **2.3**
**what** cuál(es); qué **I**
**What (fun)!**
¡Qué (divertido)! **I**
**What a mess!** ¡Qué lío! **5.3**
**What a shame!**
¡Qué lástima! **I**
**What day is today?**
¿Qué día es hoy? **I**
**What do you recommend?**
¿Qué me (nos) recomienda? **2.3**
**What is he/she like?**
¿Cómo es? **I**
**What is your phone number?**
¿Cuál es tu teléfono? **I, EP**
**What would you like?**
¿Qué desean? **2.3**
**when** cuando; cuándo **I**
**it was when** fue cuando **2.2**
**when I/he/she was young**
cuando era niño(a) **2.1**
**When will it take place?**
¿Cuándo tiene lugar? **EP**
**whenever** cuando **I**
**where** dónde; adónde **I**
**Could you tell me where…is?** ¿Puedes (Puede usted) decirme dónde queda…? **I**
**Where are you from?**
¿De dónde eres? **I, EP**
**Where is he/she from?**
¿De dónde es? **I**
**Where will it take place?**
¿Dónde tiene lugar? **EP**
**which (ones)** cuál(es) **I**
**while**
mientras **2.2;** mientras que
**white** blanco(a) **I**

INGLÉS–ESPAÑOL



RECURSOS R74 Glosario inglés–español

**who** quién(es) **I**
**Who are they?** ¿Quiénes son? **I**
**Who is it?** ¿Quién es? **I**
**Whose is...?** ¿De quién es...? **I**
**why** por qué **I**
**That's why.** Con razón. **I**
**wide** ancho(a) **I, 4.3**
**wife** la esposa
**wild** salvaje **5.1**
**wild plant** la planta silvestre **5.1**
**to win** ganar **I**
**wind** el viento **I**
**windy**
**It is windy.** Hace viento.; Hay viento. **I**
**window** la ventana **I, 4.1;** la ventanilla **1.1**
**winner** el (la) ganador(a) **I**
**winter** el invierno **I**
**wise man** el sabio
**with** con **I**
**with me** conmigo **I**
**with you** contigo **I**
**without** sin **I**
**wolf** el lobo **5.1**
**woman** la mujer **I**
**wool** la lana **I**
**word** la palabra
**to work** trabajar **1.1;** funcionar **4.1**
**work of art** la obra **1.2**
**worker** el (la) obrero(a) **6.1**
**workshop** el taller **I**
**world** el mundo **I**
**worried** preocupado(a) **I**
**to worry** preocuparse **2.1**
**Don't worry!** ¡No te preocupes! **I**
**worse** peor **I**
**worse than** peor que **4.3**
**wrist** la muñeca **3.3**
**to write** escribir **I**
**was written** fue escrita
**writer** el (la) escritor(a) **I, 1.3**
**writing** la escritura

**x-ray** la radiografía **3.3**

**year** el año **I**
**He/She is...years old.** Tiene... años. **I**
**school year** el año escolar **EP**
**yellow** amarillo(a) **I**
**yes** sí **I**
**Yes, I would love to.** Sí, me encantaría. **I**
**yesterday** ayer **I, 2.2**
**yet** todavía **I**
**yogurt** el yogur **I, 1.2**
**you** tú **(familiar singular),** usted **(formal singular),** ustedes **(formal plural),** vosotros(as) **(familiar plural) I**
**young** joven **I**
**young person** el (la) joven
**younger** menor **I**
**younger than** menor que **4.3**
**your** su **(formal),** tu **(familiar),** vuestro(a) **(plural familiar) I**

**zero** cero **I**

INGLÉS–ESPAÑOL


RECURSOS
Glosario inglés–español R75

# Índice



ÍNDICE



R76 RECURSOS Índice

ÍNDICE



RECURSOS
Índice R77

R78 RECURSOS Índice

RECURSOS
Índice R79

R80 RECURSOS Índice

RECURSOS Índice R81

# Créditos

## Acknowledgments

Excerpted material from page 6TV of *El Nuevo Herald* del Domingo 7 al Sábado 13 de Junio de 1998. Copyright © 1998. Used with the permission of *El Nuevo Herald,* Miami, FL.

The words *vamos a bailar* from *The Best of the Gipsy Kings.* Used with the permission of Nonesuch Records, a Warner Music Group Company, New York, NY.

Material from a brochure entitled "El Morro" used with the permission of the Puerto Rico Tourism Company, Old San Juan, Puerto Rico.

Material from a brochure entitled "Jardín Botánico" used with the permission of The University of Puerto Rico, San Juan, Puerto Rico.

Excerpts from an issue of *La Voz Mundial,* a student newspaper, used with the permission of Miami Springs High School, Miami Springs, FL.

## Photography

**i** RMIP/Richard Haynes (b); **iii** Steve Ogilvy/Picture It Corporation (l); PhotoDisc (tr); Jon Chomitz (br); **v** Tom Stack & Associates (t); Kactus Foto, Santiago, Chile/Superstock (br); **vi** Victor Ramos/Liaison Agency (b); **vii** School Division, Houghton Mifflin Company (r); **viii** Robert & Linda Mitchell Photography (b); **ix** Robert Frerck/Odyssey Productions/Chicago (t); **x** E. R. Degginger/Photo Researchers, Inc. (t); **xii** Ken O'Donoghue (t); Suzanne Murphy-Larronde (cl); Puerto Rico Industrial Development Company (bl); **xvii** Michael Fogden/Animals Animals (t); **xix** Nebinger/Sichov/Gromik/Sipa Press (t); David Fritts/Tony Stone Images/PNI (br); **xxiii** Superstock; **xxxiii** Nebinger/Sichov/Gromik/Sipa Press (cr); **xxxiv** PhotoDisc (inset); Steve Ogilvy/Picture It Corporation (+); **2** Steve Ogilvy/Picture It Corporation (t, b); **3** Jon Chomitz; **4** Steve Ogilvy/Picture It Corporation (+); **6** Steve Ogilvy/Picture It Corporation (+); **8** Jon Chomitz; **9** Steve Ogilvy/Picture It Corporation; **10** Steve Ogilvy/Picture It Corporation; **11** Alan Schein/The Stock Market (l); Steve Ogilvy/Picture It Corporation (r); **12** F. B. Grunzweia/Photo Researchers (+); Jon Chomitz (inset); **13** Jon Chomitz (inset); **14** Jon Chomitz; **16** Jon Chomitz (+); **19** Jon Chomitz (l); **20** Jon Chomitz (+); **22** Peter Gridley/FPG International (bl); Walter Bibikow/FPG International (bc); J. Dunn/Monkmeyer Press (br); **26** Peter Menzel/Stock Boston (t); Liaison Agency (br); **27** Tom Stack and Associates (t); Nebinger/Sichov/Gromik/Sipa Press (bl); Courtesy of Univision (br); **30** Dana White/PhotoEdit (br); **31** DeRichemond/The Image Works (t); John Neubauer/FPG International (bl); George Haling/Photo Researchers, Inc. (br); **37** Tommy Dodson/Unicorn Stock Photos; **38** Dario Perla/International Stock Photo (tr); Dave G. Houser (cr); **42** Robin J. Dunitz; **43** Bruce Fier/Liaison Agency (tl); Nik Wheeler (tr); Tom McHugh/Photo Researchers (bl); Tony Freeman/PhotoEdit (br); **44** Sylvain Grandadam/Tony Stone Images (tr); Dave G. Houser (bl); Michael Newman/PhotoEdit (br); Ken O'Donoghue (background (+); **45** David Young-Wolff/PhotoEdit (tl); Eric Sander/Liaison Agency (tc); Michael Newman/PhotoEdit (tr); Cesar Vera/Leo de Wys Inc. (c); **48** Bob Daemmrich Photography (r); **52** Kactus Foto, Santiago, Chile/Superstock (br); **53** School Division, Houghton Mifflin Company (cr); **60** School Division, Houghton Mifflin Company; **66** Courtesy Alejandro Romero (cr); Vic Bider/PhotoEdit (+); **68** School Division, Houghton Mifflin Company; **74** Ryan Williams/International Stock Photo (br); **75** Martin Venegad/Allsport (tr); Dusty Willison/International Stock Photo (bl); School Division, Houghton Mifflin Company (br); **81** Herve Donnezan/Photo Researchers, Inc. (bl); **88** Jeff Greengold/Unicorn Stock Photos (bl); **89** Jeff Greengold/Unicorn Stock Photos (l); **90** Victor Ramos/Liaison Agency (t); Mauro Petrini/ Liaison Agency (c); Tom Stack and Associates (b); **91** John Boykin/The Picture Cube, Inc. (tl); Tanya Braganti/Tom Keller & Associates (tc); Tom Stack and Associates (tr); Susan Watts/Retna Ltd. (b); **95** Tony Freeman/Photo Edit; **98** Bob Daemmrich Photography (tr); **99** Owen Franken/Stock Boston (tl); North Wind Picture Archives (bl); Timothy Greenfield-Sanders/Outline Press (c); San Francisco Museum of Modern Art/ Albert M. Bender Collection/ Gift of Albert M. Bender (br); **102** RMIP/Richard Haynes (+); **103** Robert Frerck/Odyssey Productions/Chicago (br); **106** Robert Frerck/Odyssey Productions/Chicago; **109** School Division, Houghton Mifflin Company (t, cl, br, b); **110** RMIP/Richard Haynes; **113** J. P. Courau/ DDB Stock Photo; **115** C. R. Sharp/DDB Stock Photo; **118** Bob Daemmrich/Stock Boston; **120** School Division, Houghton Mifflin Company; **121** School Division, Houghton Mifflin Company; **128** Robert Frerck/Odyssey Productions/Chicago; **138** Barbara Cerva/ DDB Stock Photo (+); **139** Robert Frerck/Odyssey Productions/Chicago (tr); Jack Novak/Photri, Inc. (r); **140** School Division, Houghton Mifflin Company; PhotoDisc (r); **141** Robert & Linda Mitchell Photography; **142** Nicolas Sapieha/Art Resource, NY; **147** DDB Stock Photo (bc); **151** Tony Freeman/PhotoEdit (b); **153** Ken O'Donoghue; **160** N. Frank/Viesti Associates, Inc.; **161** Robert & Linda Mitchell Photography (t); Robert Frerck/Odyssey Productions/Chicago (cr); **162** Patricia A. Eynon (bl); **163** Ken O'Donoghue; **164** Ken O'Donoghue; **166** Robert Frerck/Odyssey Productions/Chicago (br); **167** PhotoDisc; **170** David Parker/Science Photo Library/Photo Researchers (t);

**171** The Granger Collection (tl); Francisco Oller/Museo de Arte de Ponce (tr); Pam Francis/Liaison Agency (bl); E. R. Degginger/ hoto Researchers (br); **172** Uniphoto (inset); **174** School Division, Houghton Mifflin Company (c); **180** W. Lynn Seldon Jr. (b); **185** Ken O'Donoghue (b); **186** Ulrike Welsch; **188** John F. Mason/The Stock Market (+); **189** Tom Stack and Associates (r); **192** Richard Rowan/Photo Researchers, Inc.; **197** David Matherly/Visuals Unlimited (tr); **208** W. Gregory Brown/ Animals Animals; **210** Thomas R. Fletcher/Stock Boston (+); Wolfgang Kaehler (tc); **211** Mark Bacon (bl); Fran Hall/Photo Researchers (tr); **214** Van Bucher/Photo Researchers (br); **222** Courtesy The Miami Herald (bl); **223** David Young-Wolff/PhotoEdit (t); Tom Stewart (cr); **225** Suzanne Murphy-Larronde; **229** School Division, Houghton Mifflin Company (t); Michael Newman/PhotoEdit (b); **231** Robert Frerck/Odyssey Productions/Chicago (cl); Kate Raisz/Seattle Filmworks (b); **232** Courtesy of the Honorable Carlos Romero Barcelo (cr); AP/Wide World (bc); **233** Andrew Lichtenstein/Impact Visuals/PNI (b); **234** Suzanne Murphy-Larronde (tr, bl); Courtesy of Puerto Rico Industrial Development Company (tc); Antonio E. Amador (br); Tom Bean/DRK Photo (+); **242** Robert Frerck/Odyssey Productions/ Chicago (tc); P.G. Sclarandia/Black Star (bl); Superstock (br); **243** P. Villard-P. Aslan/SIPA Press (tr); Liaison Agency (br); El Greco/ Metropolitan Museum of Art, New York/Superstock (br); **254** RMIP/Richard Haynes (t); Ken O'Donoghue (c); Eric Roth/The Picture Cube, Inc. (b); **257** Ken Straiton/The Stock Market (tl); Robert Essel/The Stock Market (tr); Anthony Albarello/FPG International (bl); Tom Carroll/FPG International (br); **260** Deborah Davis/PhotoEdit (bl); Jeff Greenberg/ Visuals Unlimited (bc); **261** Daniel Aubry (tl); Paul Redman/Tony Stone Images (tr); Daniel Aubry (background); **263** RMIP/Richard Haynes; **264** Diego Rodriguez Velasquez/Museo del Prado, Madrid, Spain/Bridgeman Art Library, London/SuperStock; **272** Vladimir Pcholkin/FPG International (bl); **273** Michael P. Gadomski/Dembinsky Photo Association (tr); Tim Hunt/McDougal Littell, Houghton Mifflin Company (br); **279** A.G.E. FotoStock; **282** Jose L. Pelaez/The Stock Market (bl); Peter Langone/International Stock (+); **283** TJ Collection/Shooting Star (t); Fotex/Jens Meyer/Shooting Star (b); **286** Jon Chomitz; **295** Ken O' Donoghue (l); Stock Montage (br); **297** Stephen Simpson/ FPG International (tl); SuperStock (tr); Archive Photos (bl, br); **304** Robert Frerck/Odyssey Productions/Chicago (br); **305** Macduff Everton (tr); Courtesy of Museo Nacional Centro de Arte Reina Sofia (bl); **306** Jose Luis Banus/FPG International (tr); Daniel Aubry (cl); Robert Frerck/Woodfin Camp & Associates (bl); Jim Harrison/Stock Boston (+); **307** Daniel Aubry (cl); Jeff Greenberg/ International Stock Photo (bl); Ubero/The Image Works (cr); **310** C/B Productions/ The Stock Market (br); **314** UPI/Corbis-Bettmann (tr); **315** Courtesy of Prospect Place Fine Art (tc); Michael Fogden/Animals Animals (tr); Kent Gilbert/AP Photo (b); **318** Michael Fogden/Animals Animals (t,c); Michael Fogden/DRK Photo (cl); Stephen J. Kraseman/ DRK Photo (b); **319** James Beveridge/Visuals Unlimited (tl); Tom Boyden (t); Roy Fontaine/Photo Researchers, Inc. (tc); Gregory Dimijian/Photo Researchers, Inc. (tr); Ken Lucas/ Visuals Unlimited (c); Jay Ireland & Georgienne Bradley/Earth Images (b); **323** Peter Weiman/Animals Animals (t); Tom Boyden (tl); Stephen J. Kraseman/DRK Photo (tr); Ken Lucas/Visuals Unlimited (cl); Jay Ireland and Georgienne Bradley/Earth Images (cr); L. M. Crowhurst/Animals Animals (bl); Juan Rafael Renjifo/Animals Animals (br); **325** Jose Azel/Aurora and Quanta/PNI (tr); Kirk Condyles/Impact Visuals/PNI (c); **327** North Wind Picture Archives; **328** Jay Ireland & Georgienne Bradley/Earth Images (tl); James Beveridge/Visuals Unlimited (bl); **330** James Beveridge/Visuals Unlimited (br); **332** Patricia A. Eynon (+); **333** UPI/Corbis-Bettmann (b); **335** School Division, Houghton Mifflin Company (t); Marshall Prescott/Unicorn Stock Photos (tr); Rich Baker/Unicorn Stock Photos (l); Galen Rowell/Peter Arnold, Inc. (cr); Kevin Schafer (b); **341** School Division, Houghton Mifflin Company (t); SuperStock (cl); Greg Johnston/International Stock Photo (cr); Roy Morsch/The Stock Market (b); **344** School Division, Houghton Mifflin Company; **347** Jay Ireland & Georgienne Bradley/Earth Images (br); **350** Ulf Sjostedt/FPG International (l); Kent Wood/Photo Researchers, Inc. (cl); Jose L. Pelaez/The Stock Market (cr); Max & Bea Hunn/ Visuals Unlimited (r); **351** RMIP/Richard Haynes (br); **352** Carlos Humberto/Contact Press/PNI (l); Davis/Tony Stone Images/PNI (c); Robert Ginn/PhotoEdit (r); **354** Tom Boyden (l); Bill Bachmann/PhotoEdit (tr); Gregory G. Dimijian/Photo Researchers, Inc. (b); **355** Jay Ireland & Georgienne E. Bradley/Earth Images (c); **357** Michael Fogden/Bruce Coleman (tl); Kevin Shafer/Tony Stone Images/PNI (tr); **358** Bob Daemmrich/Stock Boston (br); **362** Wally Eberhart/Visuals Unlimited (cl); **363** Jay Ireland & Georgienne Bradley/Earth Images (b); **367** Steve McCutcheon/Visuals Unlimited (tl); Wally Eberhart/Visuals Unlimited (tr); RMIP/Richard Haynes (bl); Wally Eberhart/Visuals Unlimited (br); **369** Alan Cave/DDB Stock Photo; **370** Martin Bond/Science Photo Library/ Photo Researchers, Inc. (tr); **373** School Division, Houghton Mifflin Company (l); Peter Essick/Aurora & Quanta (r); **374** Peter Weiman/Animals Animals (t); Gary Conner/PhotoEdit (tr); Jan Butchofsky/Dave G. Houser (cr); Gabe Palmer/The Stock Market (br); **376** Tom Boyden; **378** Kevin Schafer (tr); **386** School Division, Houghton Mifflin Company (tr); Michio Hoshino/Minden Pictures (br); **387** Mark Richards/PhotoEdit (cl); Wolfgang Kaehler (br); **388** School Division, Houghton Mifflin Company (c); **395** Mark E. Gibson/Visuals Unlimited (tl); Robert Fried/Stock Boston (cl); Dennis MacDonald/Unicorn Stock Photos (cr); Ken Gallard/ International Stock (bl); Bonnie Kamin/PhotoEdit (bc); Richard Hutchings/ PhotoEdit (br); **398** George Dillon/Stock Boston (t); David Young-Wolff/PhotoEdit (tl); Jeff Greenberg/Unicorn Stock Photo (tr); Lawrence Migdale/Stock Boston (cl); Michelle Bridwell/PhotoEdit (cr); Martin R. Jones/Unicorn Stock Photo (bl); Mary Kate Denny/ PhotoEdit (br); **404** Barbara Cushman Rowell/PNI Ltd (+); **405** Castellazo/Latin Stock/DDB Stock Photo (t); Dotte Larson/Bruce Coleman, Inc. (tr); David Fritts/Tony Stone Images/PNI (c); **408** Tom Van Sant/The Geosphere Project/The Stock Market (b); **413** School Division, Houghton Mifflin Company (c); **422** Spencer Grant/PhotoEdit (t); Aneal Vohra/Unicorn Stock Photos (c); **430** School Division, Houghton Mifflin Company; **440** Jose L. Pelaez/The Stock Market (tl); Bob Daemmrich (cl); Gabe Palmer/The Stock Market (cr); David Young-Wolff/PhotoEdit (br); **441** Walt Anderson/Visuals Unlimited (b); **442** PhotoDisc, Inc.(b); **445** RMIP/Richard Haynes (t); **450** Carolina Biological Supply Company/Phototake NYC (+); **454** James H. Simon/The Picture Cube (br).

*All other photography: Martha Granger/EDGE Productions*



Créditos R83

## Illustration

Lisa Adams **46**, **143**

Gary Antonetti/Ortelius Design **xxvi - xxxi, 434–435**

Fian Arroyo **25**, **65** (b), **71**, **87**, **159**, **168**, **251**, **259**, **287**, **303** (b), **311**, **425**, **R14**

Susan M. Blubaugh **174**, **175**, **337**, **372**, **R2**

Neverne Covington **236**, **341**

Christine Czernota **444**

Jim Deigan **35, 390, 391**

Veronique Deiss **88**

Mike Dietz **274, 281**

Elissé Goldstein **52, 53**

Nenad Jakesevic **124** (+), **290** (+)

Catherine Leary **43**, **65** (t), **137**, **209**, **265**, **353**, **359**, **383**, **455**, **R1**, **R6**, **R8**, **R9**

Jared D. Lee **115**, **203**, **409**, **417**

John Lyttle **190**, **347**

Patrick O'Brien **318**, **319**, **376**, **377**

Gail Piazza **111**, **142**, **303**

Mathew Pippin **30** (+), **146** (+), **246** (+), **268** (+), **412** (+)

Rick Powell **57**, **107**, **133**, **201**, **382**, **402**, **420**

Donna Ruff **83**

School Division, Houghton Mifflin Company **181**, **R5**

Stacey Schuett **218** (+), **331**, **362** (+), **375**

Jim Trusillo **74** (+)

Fabricio Vanden Broeck **116–117**, **448**, **449**

Randy Verougstraete **187**, **231**, **239**, **308**, **403**, **447**

Wood Ronsaville Harlin, Inc. **196** (+)



R84 Créditos